THE CAMBRIDGE
History of the Book in Britain

*

VOLUME III
1400–1557

This volume of *The Cambridge History of the Book in Britain* is an overview of the century and a half between the death of Chaucer in 1400 and the printing of the *English Works* of Thomas More in 1557 – a year that also saw the incorporation of the Stationers' Company. The profound changes during that time in British social, political and religious conditions are paralleled and reflected in changing modes of the dissemination and reception of the written word. By the end of the period the comparatively restricted manuscript culture of Chaucer's day had been replaced by an ambience in which printed books were becoming the norm, resorted to much more widely and in ways much more familiar to the modern reader.

The emphasis in this collection of essays by 27 specialists is less on the materials of book production than on demand and use by readers in schools, universities and monasteries, by the secular clergy and by other professionals such as lawyers and doctors, by scholars, gentlemen and gentlewomen, by royalty, statesmen and politicians, for purposes public and private, regulatory, instructive, devotional, or simply pleasurable. Patterns of ownership are identified. Questions of supply are also addressed and patterns established of where, why and how books were written, printed, bound, acquired and passed from hand to hand. The book-trade receives special attention, with emphasis on the large part played by imports of manuscripts but especially of printed books from continental centres of culture and learning, and on links with printers in other countries, which were decisive for the development of printing and publishing in Britain.

LOTTE HELLINGA retired in 1995 as Deputy Keeper in the British Library, London, and is currently Secretary of the Consortium of European Research Libraries

J. B. TRAPP was Professor of the History of the Classical Tradition and Director of the Warburg Institute, University of London

THE CAMBRIDGE
History of the Book in Britain

The history of the book offers a distinctive form of access to the ways in which human beings have sought to give meaning to their own and others' lives. Our knowledge of the past derives mainly from texts. Landscape, architecture, sculpture, painting and the decorative arts have their stories to tell and may themselves be construed as texts; but oral tradition, manuscripts, printed books, and those other forms of inscription and incision such as maps, music and graphic images, have a power to report even more directly on human experience and the events and thoughts which shaped it.

In principle, any history of the book should help to explain how these particular texts were created, why they took the forms they did, their relations with other media, especially in the twentieth century, and what influence they had on the minds and actions of those who heard, read or viewed them. Its range, too – in time, place and the great diversity of the conditions of text production, including reception – challenges any attempt to define its limits and give an account adequate to its complexity. It addresses, whether by period, country, genre or technology, widely disparate fields of enquiry, each of which demands and attracts its own forms of scholarship.

The Cambridge History of the Book in Britain, planned in seven volumes, seeks to represent much of that variety, and to encourage new work, based on knowledge of the creation, material production, dissemination and reception of texts. Inevitably its emphases will differ from volume to volume, partly because the definitions of Britain vary significantly over the centuries, partly because of the varieties of evidence extant for each period, and partly because of the present uneven state of knowledge. Tentative in so many ways as the project necessarily is, it offers the first comprehensive account of the book in Britain over one and a half millennia.

D. F. McKenzie · D. J. McKitterick · I. R. Willison
General Editors

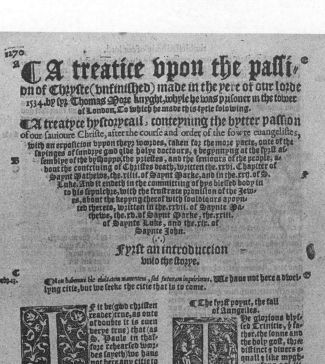

The opening of *A treatice vpon the passion* in *The Workes of Sir Thomas More*, London 1557, showing the use of black-letter, roman and italic typefaces, decorated and historiated woodcut initials and other variations in the aspect of the page.

THE CAMBRIDGE
History of the Book
in Britain

*

VOLUME III
1400–1557

*

Edited by
LOTTE HELLINGA
and
J. B. TRAPP

CAMBRIDGE
UNIVERSITY PRESS

PUBLISHED BY THE PRESS SYNDICATE OF THE UNIVERSITY OF CAMBRIDGE
The Pitt Building, Trumpington Street, Cambridge, United Kingdom

CAMBRIDGE UNIVERSITY PRESS
The Edinburgh Building, Cambridge CB2 2RU, UK   www.cup.cam.ac.uk
40 West 20th Street, New York, NY 10011-4211, USA   www.cup.org
10 Stamford Road, Oakleigh, Melbourne 3166, Australia

First published 1999

Printed in the United Kingdom at the University Press, Cambridge

Typeface TEFF Renard 9.5/13 pt.   *System* QuarkXPress® [SE]

A catalogue record for this book is available from the British Library

Library of Congress Cataloguing in Publication data
The Cambridge history of the book in Britain.
    p.   cm.
Includes bibliographical references and Index.
Contents: – vol. III. 1400–1557 / edited by Lotte Hellinga and J. B. Trapp
ISBN 0 521 57346 7 (vol. III)
1. Books – Great Britain – History.
I. Hellinga, Lotte.   II. Trapp, J. B. (Joseph Burney)
z8.G7C36   1999
002'.0941–dc21   98-4398 CIP

ISBN 0 521 57346 7 hardback

Contents

Contents

COLLECTIONS AND OWNERSHIP

READING AND USE OF BOOKS

I · BOOKS FOR SCHOLARS

——

II · PROFESSIONS

——

Contents

Contributors

J. J. G. ALEXANDER is Professor of Fine Arts at the Institute of Fine Arts, New York University.

E. J. ASHWORTH is Professor of Philosophy at the University of Waterloo, Ontario.

JANET BACKHOUSE recently retired as Curator of Illuminated Manuscripts at the British Library, London.

J. H. BAKER is Downing Professor of the Laws of England at the University of Cambridge.

DAVID N. BELL is Professor of Religious Studies at the Memorial University of Newfoundland, St John's.

JULIA BOFFEY is Reader in Medieval Studies in the School of English and Drama, Queen Mary and Westfield College, University of London.

JAMES P. CARLEY is Professor of English at York University, Toronto, and School of Graduate Studies, University of Toronto.

C. PAUL CHRISTIANSON is Professor of English (emeritus) at the College of Wooster, Ohio.

A. S. G. EDWARDS is Professor of English at the University of Victoria, British Columbia.

MARY C. ERLER is Professor of English at Fordham University, New York.

M. M. FOOT is Director of Collections and Preservation at the British Library, London.

MARGARET LANE FORD is an Associate Director of Christie's, London, and a specialist in the book department.

LOTTE HELLINGA retired in 1995 as Deputy Keeper in the British Library, London.

R. H. HELMHOLZ is Ruth Wyatt Rosenson Professor of Law in the University of Chicago.

KRISTIAN JENSEN is Curator in Special Collections at the Bodleian Library, Oxford.

PETER MURRAY JONES is Fellow and Librarian of King's College, Cambridge.

GEORGE R. KEISER is Professor of English at Kansas State University, Manhattan, Kansas.

JOHN N. KING is Professor of English at the Ohio State University, Columbus, Ohio.

ELISABETH LEEDHAM-GREEN is Deputy Keeper of the Cambridge University Archives and Fellow of Darwin College.

CAROL M. MEALE is Reader in Medieval Studies at the University of Bristol.

JOHN MILSOM is Christian A. Johnson Professor of the Arts at Middlebury College, Vermont.

PAUL NEEDHAM is Librarian, The Scheide Library, Princeton University.

PAMELA NEVILLE-SINGTON is Librarian, The Scheide Library, Princeton University.

NICHOLAS ORME is Professor of History at the University of Exeter.

JENNY STRATFORD is Research Fellow of the Institute of Historical Research, University of London.

J. B. TRAPP was Professor of the History of the Classical Tradition and Director of the Warburg Institute, University of London.

ALAIN WIJFFELS is Professor in the Law Faculties of the Universities of Leiden and Louvain-la-Neuve.

Illustrations

Frontispiece: *The workes of Sir Thomas More Knyght . . .*, London 1557, p. 1270.
The opening page of 'A treatice upon the Passion'.
Private collection.

Plates

Frontispiece to plates: Bartholomaeus Anglicus, *De proprietatibus rerum*.
[Cologne, Printer of Augustinus de Fide (i.e. William Caxton), *c*. 1472], f.1r.
Cambridge UL, Oates 590, Inc. 1.A.4.8 [507].

2.1 Book of prayers. 'St John the Evangelist', miniature signed by Herman
Scheerre.
London BL, Add. ms. 16998, f. 37r.

2.2 Epistolary of Cardinal Wolsey. 'The Feast of the Relics'.
Oxford, Christ Church, ms. 101, f. 34v.

2.3 Book of hours, Use of Sarum. Opening showing 'The Agony in the Garden'
and beginning of the Hours of the Virgin.
London BL, Harleian ms. 2985, fols. 41v–42r.

2.4 Book of hours, Use of Sarum. 'St George and the dragon'.
Swaffham Parish Church, Norfolk, ms. 1, f. 11r.

2.5 Book of hours, Use of Sarum. 'The Last Judgment'.
Cambridge, Fitzwilliam Museum, ms. 1055–1975, f. 57r.

2.6 Statutes of the Hospital of Sta Maria Nuova, Florence.
Oxford, Bodleian Library, ms. Bodley 488, f. 3r.

2.7 Book of hours of King James IV of Scotland, 'The donor, King James IV of
Scotland, in prayer'.
Vienna, Österreichische Nationalbibliothek, cod. 1897, f. 24v.

2.8 Book of hours of Queen Margaret of Scotland. 'St Anne teaching the Virgin
to read'.
Chatsworth, Trustees of the Devonshire Settlement, f. 35v.

2.9 Book of hours, Use of Sarum. 'King Henry VII kneeling before King David'.
New York, Pierpont Morgan Library, ms. M 815, f. 153v.

2.10 Cicero, *De officiis*, Mainz, Johann Fust and Peter Schoeffer, 1465. Initial 'Q'
showing Prince Arthur (?) receiving instruction and in the border the motto
'Ic dien'.
Cambridge, Emmanuel College, Inc. 5.3.11, f. [a]1r.

3.1 Bartholomaeus Anglicus, *De proprietatibus rerum.* [Cologne, Printer of
   Augustinus de Fide (i.e. William Caxton), *c.* 1472], f. 55r (detail).
   Cambridge UL, Oates 590, Inc. 1.A.4.8 [507].

3.2 Raoul Lefèvre, *The recuyell of the historyes of Troye* (translated from the French
   by William Caxton), [Bruges], William Caxton, [*c.* 1473]. f. [A]1r.
   Cambridge UL, Oates 3837, Inc. 3.F.3.2 [3307].

3.3 Raoul Lefèvre, *The history of Jason* (translated from the French by William
   Caxton), [Westminster, William Caxton, *c.* 1477], f. [a]2r.
   Vienna, Österreichische Nationalbibliothek, Ink. 2.D.30.

3.4 *Statuta Nova.* [London, William de Machlinia, *c.* 1484], f. k7r.
   Cambridge UL, Oates 4183, Inc. 3.J.3.4 [3608].

3.5 Rufinus, *Expositio Symboli Apostolorum.* Printer's copy. Written in Florence
   for Vespasiano da Bisticci and sold to Bishop John Goldwell.
   London BL, ms. Sloane 1579, f. 50v.

3.6 *Legenda ad usum Sarum.* Paris, G. Maynyal for William Caxton, 1488, f. C2v.
   London BL, IB.40010. Reproduced from *Library*, 5th ser., 12 (1957), Fig. 1.

3.7 Bessarion, *Epistole et Orationes.* (G. Fichet, editor.) [Paris, Ulrich Gering,
   Martin Crantz and Michael Friburger, *c.* 1471]. Frontispiece.
   Città del Vaticano, Biblioteca Apostolica Vaticana, lat. 3586.

3.8 Bartholomaeus Anglicus, *De proprietatibus rerum.*
   a English: Westminster, Wynkyn de Worde, [1495], f. m2r: 'The Ages of
   Man'.
   b English: Westminster, Wynkyn de Worde, [1495], f. K2r: 'Mining'.
   Cambridge UL, Oates 4144, Inc. 3.J.1.2 [3559].
   c Dutch: Haarlem, Jacob Bellaert, 1485, f. m7v: 'The Ages of Man'.
   Cambridge UL, Oates 3653, Inc. 3.1.11.1 [3125].
   d French: Lyons, Martin Huss, 1482, f. E2r: 'Mining'.
   London BL, IB.41688.

3.9 Galenus, *De temperamentis* (tr. T. Linacre). Cambridge, Johann Siberch, 1521,
   title-page.
   Cambridge UL, SSS. 23.17(2).

3.10 Hector Boece, *The hystory and croniklis of Scotland.* [Edinburgh,
   T. Davidson, *c.* 1540], title-page.
   Cambridge UL, SSS. 41.10.

4.1 Quintus Curtius Rufus, *De rebus gestis Alexandri Magni . . . opus.* Antwerp,
   1546. Binding: doublure of blind-tooled brown calf, probably taken from
   another binding.
   London BL, C.143.b.7.

4.2 Edmund Bonner, *A profitable and necessarye Doctryne.* London, in aedibus
   I. Cawodi, 1555. Bound by the King Edward and Queen Mary binder.
   London BL, C.27.e.13.

4.3 Lady Elizabeth Tyrwhit, *Morning and evening prayers.* London, H. Middleton
   for C. Barker, 1574. Gold binding with enamelled scenes made by Hans van
   Antwerpen, *c.* 1540–5 (*remboîtage*).
   London, British Museum, Department of Medieval and Later
   Antiquities.

Figures

Preface

Thanne was there a wighte, with two brode eyen,
Boke highte that beupere, a bold man of speche,
'By Godes body', quad this boke, 'I wil bere witnesse'.
[Then appeared a fellow with two wide eyes, a man of
authority, bold of speech, whose name was Book.
'By God's body', quoth Book, 'I will bear witness'.]

LANGLAND, *Piers Plowman*, B. XVIII, 228–30

A firm basis for a history of the book in Britain during the 150 years which saw the transition from manuscript to print is provided by a long-established and still flourishing British tradition of cataloguing and descriptive bibliography. Both manuscripts and earlier printed books have been thoroughly recorded within this tradition.

For manuscripts, a great debt is owed to M. R. James, Sir Roger Mynors, R. W. Hunt, N. R. Ker and their colleagues in previous generations and, in the present, A. I. Doyle, A. G. Watson and the editorial team of the *Corpus of British Medieval Library Catalogues*, with A. C. de la Mare – to mention no others and without forgetting the expert cataloguers in the great libraries of Britain, whose labours remain largely anonymous.

During our entire period, handwritten books were produced, imported, owned or used – often all four – by the members of every literate social category within the British Isles.[1] The context of the preservation of manuscripts, at that time in particular, was sometimes private and personal and sometimes institutional. Until the 1530s, at least, institutional preservation was chiefly monastic. What is not always clear from contemporary monastic lists, however, is which of the books in them were or had been in individual ownership.[2]

The record of manuscript production and dissemination in Britain

---

1. See especially the chapters below by Alexander, Backhouse, Baker, Bell, Boffey, Carley, Christianson, Edwards, Erler, Jones, Meale, Milsom, Stratford and Trapp.
2. Bell, below, pp. 229–54, esp. 233, 248; Doyle 1988.

during the late Middle Ages is fuller than for the reigns of Henry VII, Henry VIII, Edward VI and Mary. The varieties of script in which English vernacular books and documents were written have been thoroughly surveyed, as have Latin documentary hands; Latin book hands rather less fully, particularly for the sixteenth century.[3] Manuscripts illuminated in the British Isles during the Middle Ages have been described in a remarkable and comprehensive series of volumes.[4] The most recently published, Kathleen L. Scott's account of later Gothic manuscripts from 1390 to 1490, is the most important for us.[5] No similar survey yet exists for the sixteenth century.[6]

The means and processes by which the manuscripts were made get much attention in these catalogues and elsewhere, and will receive more in earlier volumes of this *History*. They have, moreover, recently been the subject of an invaluable collective volume, to which some of our collaborators contributed: *Book production and publishing in Britain 1375–1475*, edited by the late Jeremy Griffiths and D. A. Pearsall in 1989, which takes the story from late in the manuscript era to the advent of printing.[7] This is one reason why comparatively little space is given in our volume to the actual making of manuscripts in Britain. Another is that we attempt throughout to respond to the question 'In what respect is Britain in the period different from what prevailed elsewhere or in other times?' Manuscripts were not put together in our period in ways radically different from those in use either outside the British Isles or in the period before 1400, except for a much increased use of paper rather than parchment during the fifteenth century, and still more in the sixteenth. Our concern is chiefly with the dissemination – transmission, acquisition, circulation, reception, retention and use – of what had been transcribed. This is addressed in Griffiths and Pearsall with an emphasis on native British aspects.[8] We seek also to take into account practices in the rest of Europe, so as to give due weight to the role of production abroad for consumption at home (the reverse is so rare in our period as to call for incidental mention only).[9] The coverage by Griffiths and Pearsall ceases with

3. Denholm-Young 1952; C. E. Wright, 1960; Hector 1966; Parkes 1969, 1991. For punctuation, see Parkes 1992b.
4. J. J. G. Alexander (ed.), *A survey of manuscripts illuminated in the British Isles*, 6 vols., London 1975–96.
5. Scott 1996; see also, e. g., the relevant sections in Pächt and Alexander 1966–73; Alexander and Temple 1985.   6. Auerbach 1954 contains some material.
7. It is referred to below as *BPPB*.
8. See in *BPPB* the section on 'Patrons, buyers and owners', by Kate Harris, Carol Meale and R. J. Lyall.   9. Alexander, Needham, Ford, Trapp below.

the importation of printing into Britain. We have aimed throughout to bring manuscript and print closely together.[10]

For printed books also we have emphasized dissemination and use, bearing in mind that, if the distribution in the British Isles of such new-fangled productions to some extent took over the mechanisms existing for manuscript publication, printing itself was an import from abroad. Its early practitioners in Britain were predominantly not natives of the British Isles; indeed, soon after the first books were printed here, foreign book artificers of all kinds were encouraged by statute to take up residence; legislation favouring Englishmen was not passed until the sixteenth century was well advanced. Only a small portion of the books printed in Britain was in Latin, British books in that language being intended largely for particular occasions or purposes. Almost all were imported, whence the booksellers' and stationers' term 'Latin trade' for books from abroad.[11] Books printed in English left these shores comparatively seldom, and usually in special circumstances.

Of books printed in the British Isles there has existed since 1926, with a notable gain in fullness and accuracy in 1976-91, a full bibliographical record for the period from the beginning of printing to almost the mid seventeenth century. As in the case of manuscripts, all who study the period are indebted to generations of largely anonymous cataloguers in our great libraries. Particularly, however, they are indebted to the vision and the pioneering labours of A. W. Pollard and G. R. Redgrave, expanded and consolidated by their successors William A. Jackson, F. S. Ferguson and Katharine F. Pantzer.[12] For no other country is the coverage of our entire period so full.[13]

---

10. Cf. Bühler 1960; Härtel and Hellinga 1981; Trapp 1983; Nielsen, Borch and Sørensen 1986; *Bibliography and Civilization* 1987; Hindman 1991; Barker 1993.
11. Below, Ford, Hellinga, Trapp.
12. *A short-title catalogue of books printed in England, Scotland and Ireland, and of English books printed abroad, 1475-1640, first compiled by A. W. Pollard and G. R. Redgrave* [1926]. *Second Edition, revised and enlarged, begun by Wm. A. Jackson and F. S. Ferguson, completed by Katharine F. Pantzer*, 2 vols., London 1976-86; Vol. III: *A printers' and publishers' index, other indexes and appendices, cumulative addenda and corrigenda, by Katharine F. Pantzer; with a chronological index by Philip R. Rider*, London 1991. We refer to it as *STC*.
13. A few examples will highlight both the degree of coverage enjoyed by the British Isles and the length of time it has been available. European production of books printed before 1501 has long been well recorded; see Hellinga below, pp. 65-6. For the sixteenth century, Wouter Nijhoff and M. E. Kronenberg (NK) document Netherlandish printing from 1500 to 1540 and their work is continued for later years by the automated *Short-title catalogue of books printed in the Netherlands* (STCN; in progress); printing in Denmark to 1600 is recorded by Nielsen 1919 and 1931-3; sixteenth-century printing in the German-speaking lands in *VD16* (1983-95). The British (Museum) Library's short-title catalogues (1921-90), though limited to that institution's holdings, are indispensable. They are the model for a

Given that printed books have survived in vastly greater numbers than books written by hand, it is not surprising that we know proportionately less about ownership of them during our period. The record is nevertheless substantial, if biased towards identifiable names and towards men. Sears Jayne's impressive pioneer survey of library catalogues from the English Renaissance recorded almost 600 collections comprising 15 books or more.[14] From 1521, moreover, English law required that the property of any deceased person be recorded for probate. The inventories taken for this purpose in Cambridge, edited by Elisabeth Leedham-Green, are highly instructive.[15] So are the parallel Oxford inventories, in course of publication by Dr Leedham-Green, R. J. Fehrenbach and their collaborators.[16] Some 30 per cent of Jayne's and the Oxford lists and almost half the Cambridge lists relate to persons who died within our period. Two-thirds of Jayne's lists are from the university sector. Women figure infrequently in Jayne and not at all in Oxford and Cambridge.[17] Recently there have been valuable reconstructions of individual learned libraries, such as Andrew Perne's in Cambridge;[18] or Archbishop Cranmer's.[19] Recently, too, royal libraries have come under renewed scrutiny.[20] The data-base established by Margaret Lane Ford in connection with this volume is the first attempt to complement such archival evidence with the record of extant books for which a British provenance in our period is known or can be established.[21]

One earlier contribution to the history of the book in Britain is as relevant to us for the era of printing as was the volume of Griffiths and Pearsall for the manuscript age. H. S. Bennett's *English books and their readers 1475–1557* of 1952, taking up the story after the scribal period, deals with it primarily from the point of view of the circulation, reception and use in England of books printed in England. Bennett devotes only limited space to ownership and retention in libraries and does not consider the evidence of annotation by readers.[22]

Footnote 13 (*cont.*)

    similar catalogue of books in the National Library of Scotland (1970), as well as for H. M. Adams's catalogue of Cambridge holdings (1967). For printing in Paris in the early decades of the sixteenth century, the work of the late Brigitte Moreau is basic, as is that of Baudrier for Lyons. The Hand Press Book Database of the Consortium of European Research Libraries will provide an overview of books printed before 1830 in European libraries.

14. Jayne 1956–83.   15. Leedham-Green 1986.   16. *PLRE*.

17. See below, especially Bell, Erler, Ford, Meale and Boffey.

18. Collinson, McKitterick and Leedham-Green 1991.   19. Selwyn 1996.

20. See below, Backhouse, Carley and Stratford; Birrell 1987a.

21. Ford, below, pp. 179–201; see also Alston 1994, which covers a greater chronological span in less detail.   22. Cf. below, pp. 41–2; and Rosenthal 1997.

The book-trade's importance as mediator between author and owner or reader and so as an important indicator in intellectual history has long been recognized. Though the system of patronage survived long beyond our period, in the course of the fifteenth century production came to be comparatively less affected by it, and more speculative, anticipating and even creating demand. This was shown in a seminal study by A. I. Doyle and M. B. Parkes.[23] It indicates an increase in the reading public before the introduction of printing made books more readily available. The successive forms of organization and regulation of the trade reveal pressures and conflicts of interest between protectionism and professional control and the need for expansion in response to rising demand, and between censorship by Church or state on the one hand and the flow of communication on the other. A decisive change took place when, in 1403, a fraternity of London artisans was first granted ordinances of incorporation. From then on, the trade created an identity for itself among the many companies and other organizations in London. London was to dominate other centres in Britain for centuries to come. Early studies by E. Gordon Duff and Graham Pollard and more recent investigations by C. Paul Christianson charted these developments.[24] Pollard's work covered the entire period from 1400 to the incorporation of the Stationers' Company in 1557. Duff concentrated rather on the stationers and printers, and the foreign agents, from 1475. In more recent years their conception of the pivotal function of the trade has been somewhat obscured by concentration on book production. The business records of printers, stationers and booksellers from 1510 or thereabouts in London,[25] 1520 in Oxford,[26] and the 1520s, 1530s and early 1540s in Cambridge,[27] give much information about what could be and what was bought during that time. Correlation between the evidence of booksellers' lists and that of inventories, however, is less close than might be wished.[28]

It will be obvious that our approach owes much to the work of Lucien Febvre, Henri-Jean Martin and Roger Chartier.[29] Implicit in it is an insistence on the bibliographical record of book production, in manuscript

23. Doyle and Parkes 1978.
24. For example Duff 1905; G. Pollard, 1937; Christianson 1990 and below; and cf. G. J. Gray, 1904.   25. Plomer 1909; Duff 1907.   26. Madan and Bradshaw 1885–90.
27. Leedham-Green, Rhodes and Stubbings 1992; Leedham-Green 1986, no. 25 (Pilgrim).
28. For the book-trade, see especially the section on 'Technique and trade' below, pp. 47–201, but also Baker, Leedham-Green and Trapp.
29. Febvre and Martin 1958–76; H. J. Martin, Chartier and Vivet 1982; H. J. Martin 1987; Aquilon and Martin 1988; Bödeker 1995; Darnton 1980, 1986. Chaytor 1945 may still be read with profit.

and in print, particularly in the British Isles, as our most tangible evidence. In spite of its comprehensiveness as a record of what is extant, however, this can only be fragmentary in terms of what was actually produced. The rarity of many items implies that evidence for the existence of many manuscripts and printed editions has vanished. Printed materials, and especially printed materials as unspectacular as most English books of the period, seem not to have been highly valued in their day, but only when they became collectors' objects in the eighteenth century. They were particularly vulnerable to loss or defacement, whether from having been relegated to a remote corner of a library or, in an ordinary household, subject to the scribblings of children.

It is worth looking further at the nature of the record. Full though it is, it leaves a great many questions unconsidered, unanswered, or at least not answered with the scope, the fullness of detail or the definitiveness that one might wish. Book-trade archives, for example, revealing the mechanisms by which books came into the country, seldom specifically identify particular texts or editions. Inventories, giving a more or less complete and coherent account of books owned by an individual or an institution, usually specify both author and text, but seldom the precise edition, which would give a clue to place of writing, printing or acquisition. Individual copies in early British ownership give certainty as to the edition, though more often than not the copy itself has been separated from copies of other books once the property of an individual or even institutional owner. All these details must be painstakingly established before an analysis of the interaction of authorship, manufacture, trading, possession and use can produce patterns significant for intellectual and cultural history.

If we should therefore be cautious in coming to absolute conclusions from the record of production as it stands, the positive information to be derived from it remains valid: a text was chosen for reproduction, at a particular time, by a particular scribe or printer, and then became the property of an individual, a family or an institution, to be read or merely retained. To elaborate our knowledge of what happened to books, and as a result of them, after they left the scriptorium or printing house, we must turn to less direct and more elusive sources.

In spite of what has been said above, evidence for the traffic in books is relatively sparse. Its records provide less than the full picture for England. For Scotland, Wales and Ireland in our period it hardly exists, book ownership being there much more a matter of individual initiative.

Records for the trade in books actually printed in the British Isles are few and far between, but the surviving documents reflect the great numbers of books printed on the Continent and imported.[30] These records are invaluable, nevertheless, since they reveal the processes of the trade's operation: the relations of printers with wholesalers or retailers, whole-sale imports, stationers' shops, even advertisements.

For ownership, we have the inventories, individual and institutional. Discrepancy between them and what exists at the present day will again alert us to the fragmentary nature of survival, large as the heritage in book form may seem when compared to other artefacts. The inventories' evidence needs always to be supplemented from examination of what is still accessible, in early or in later collections. Only surviving copies give precise proof of identity. That is why a special effort has been made in connection with this volume to establish where individual books were located during the period we cover, as far as this may be inferred from the identification of owners.[31] For this a variety of evidence has been brought to bear: the names of identifiable or unidentifiable but unmistakably English or Scots owners, annotations, handwriting, styles of illumina-tion (most spectacularly, if rather infrequently, for copies of the Gutenberg Bible and other early Mainz printings).[32] Bindings, often to be connected with stationers in known locations, provide a convincing body of evidence for the presence of books in the British Isles, and may also indicate the kind of use to which they were put.[33]

We are aware that our attempt to treat the book in the British Isles as it reflects the intellectual and cultural life of England and, to a much lesser extent, of Scotland falls short of completeness. We hope, however, that the series of probes made by our contributors gives an indication of the state of the question on the most important matters, and that they will set other enquiries in train. Each contributor has made use of the wealth of information available to subject specialists of the period, whatever the particular area of their specialism. We owe them a great debt for having put their knowledge at the disposal of our readers and ourselves. We thank them for co-operation and for a patience in which they have been matched by our general editors, by the Leverhulme Trust as sponsors of the collaborative seven-volume *History of the Book in Britain*, and by the Cambridge University Press as publishers. Without the initiative of

30. Christianson, Needham, Ford below.   31. See especially Ford below, pp. 180–3.
32. E.g. König 1983; Alexander below, pp. 47–64; Hellinga below, p. 100.
33. Foot below.

the late Professor McKenzie, Dr McKitterick and Mr Willison, this project would never have been conceived; without the Leverhulme Trust's generous financial support, and that of the Pilgrim Trust, it could not have been begun, much less brought to its present state; and without the good will of the Cambridge University Press, it could not have been advanced to the point of publication.

More specifically, we thank our respective former institutions, the British Library and the Warburg Institute of the University of London, not least for allowing us to maintain, after retirement, a formal connection with them which ensured continued privileged access to their collections. We are also indebted to both our institutions for bearing, with the help of a conference grant from the British Academy, and the Bibliotheca Philosophica Hermetica of Amsterdam, and others from the Foundation for Intellectual History and the Wellcome Trust, the expense of the planning colloquium for our volume. To our colleagues we are grateful for assistance as needed and for forbearance. If we name only a very few, it is not from want of appreciation. We offer similar general but heartfelt thanks to librarians, colleagues and friends in other libraries and institutions on both sides of the Atlantic. It would be wrong, however, not to express thanks for particular help to M. J. Jannetta and Elizabeth McGrath.

This determined restraint in naming must not be allowed to apply to five persons, to whom we are especially indebted: Nicolas Barker read, and commented trenchantly and valuably on, the whole volume, as well as earlier acting as encourager and advocate; Kristian Jensen read and commented on a number of chapters; Kimberley Hart unflinchingly bore the labour of transferring the text, in many drafts, to floppy disk; and Caroline Bundy was our editor and Leigh Mueller our copy-editor at Cambridge University Press. We should have been lost without them.

Introduction

LOTTE HELLINGA and J. B. TRAPP

This volume begins with the manuscript book in Britain as it was when Geoffrey Chaucer died in 1400. It ends with the printed book as it was in 1557, the year in which the English book-trade was consolidated with the grant by Philip and Mary of a charter to the Stationers' Company of London. In this year also were published, in London, the *English Works* of Thomas More and, in Geneva, an important translation into English of the New Testament, the forerunner of the Geneva Bible.[1]

The first of these two books was printed and published, as its contents had been written before the Reformation, in the Catholic interest, then again briefly in the ascendant in England. It drew verbally on a vernacular poetic tradition in its echoes of Chaucer's phraseology, as well as spiritually on the authority of the Church, laying particular stress on the Church's role as arbiter of scriptural interpretation. The second book was the successor of several earlier reformed English Bible translations, of which one in particular had received the endorsement of Henry VIII. Taken together, these two volumes reflect changes and upheavals in British society during a century and a half. At the same time, they bear witness to continuities.

Continuities in change may be seen in all aspects of the book during our period, whether in the message of its text, the script or print in which that message was conveyed, or the modes of its dissemination, use and even suppression. On the social, political and religious conditions that they mirror, books may exert an influence both at home and abroad. As we shall see, books produced in the British Isles during our period had less authority and prestige outside Britain. Not being innovative in production technique and preferring to use English as an expressive medium, they are indicators of a historical process of nationalization and

---

1. *STC* 18076 and 2871.

1

secularization. The advance of this process, and the reversals, may be clearly seen in the rise of the vernacular and the growth of literacy in the British Isles. British vernacular literacy itself goes along with a constant, though fluctuating, presence of French, particularly at upper social levels and not merely in England during the Dual Monarchy. It goes along, too, with a gradual decline in the ascendancy of Latin, even in learned circles. This decline was accelerated on the one hand by anti-clerical sentiment, which also discerned a decline in clerical learning. It was slowed, on the other, by the introduction of Renaissance humanism from Italy, with France often the mediator. Secular humanism, however, did not achieve great strength in Britain, though translation flourished. Catholic Latin culture was virtually destroyed by the Reformation, and not long afterwards Protestant humanism also yielded to the vernacular.

At our beginning the professional author had not yet appeared, and even at our end is hardly to be seen. Chaucer's living came in large degree from his civil service appointments and throughout our period writers were sustained by patronage, religious and secular. Sometimes an author would receive support from both arms, as notably did John Lydgate, monk of Bury St Edmunds, whose work of translation, as well as his occasional verse and other poems, was materially supported by princely and noble benefactors as well as by his religious order. Scholars, too, found support from the same sources, but also from the universities, which were in some respects extensions of the monastic programme of study. Changes within these patterns of patronage become more apparent towards the end of the fifteenth century and the beginning of the sixteenth. Monastic patronage, supporting scholars working in Latin to a greater extent than writers in English, entirely disappeared with the dissolution of the monasteries; the royal, noble and ecclesiastical patronage, often exercised for political reasons, which then largely replaced it was much concerned with the vernacular. Study of Latin on the Italian humanist model, introduced into England in the early fifteenth century, received favour from such patrons as Humfrey, Duke of Gloucester, one of Henry V's brothers, whose support of humanism and attempts to create in England a humanist entourage on the Italian model were determined and sustained. His gifts of manuscripts were the founding collection of a university library in Oxford. A little later, the new methods of studying the classics, experienced in Italy and practised by churchmen such as Bishop William Gray and nobles such as John Tiptoft, Earl of Worcester, gained strength in the universities. Greek later came into favour on a par with Latin. The generation that was born and grew up under Henry VII – John Colet, Thomas More, Thomas Linacre and others – much influenced by Desiderius Erasmus, was largely responsible for the change of emphasis in the study of Latin and Greek towards the evangelical humanism that flourished under Henry VIII and Edward VI.

At the beginning of our period the professional scribe already existed, as well as the scribe who supplied from within a religious house the Latin works required for use in monastery and in church. There is evidence that authors who wrote in Latin, who were sometimes their own scribes for copies of varying degrees of luxury, also retained a scribe or a group of scribes. Copyists were also early in reacting to both Latin and vernacular commissions from owners and readers. The burgeoning London book-trade produced the scribal vernacular publisher: John Shirley, for example. If his productions and commissions are not to be compared in numbers, size or elegance with those of such scribes and booksellers as Vespasiano da Bisticci in Florence a little later, Shirley nevertheless played an important pivotal role, making more widely available not only the Chaucerian tradition but also other texts. As far as the history of the book is concerned, however, the most profound change during our period was the transformation of the comparatively restricted manu-script culture of the time of Chaucer and his successors into an ambience where printed books gradually became the norm. The process was all but complete by our terminal date of 1557. Manuscripts continued to be written throughout, however: printed books were sometimes copied in that way, and devotional works and English lyric poetry circulated in handwritten form.

The transformation wrought by the invention of printing and by its introduction into Britain twenty years later, by William Caxton in 1476, was far-reaching. It was, all the same, neither instantaneous nor, from some aspects, even radical. Caxton aimed to improve the quality of English life by translating into his mother tongue works embodying the lively and more widespread literary ambience he had come to know in Flanders. During his many years of residence in the Low Countries he had observed how a culture initially confined to the Burgundian court and its entourage had taken firm hold in a much wider social circle of civil servants, merchants and other citizens, within a flourishing urban context. Through his translations into English of works that had become popular in the social *milieu* with which he had become familiar, he blended a foreign culture with the continuing preoccupations of English and Scottish literary life. He made available in print the works of Chaucer, Lydgate, Gower and Thomas Malory in their original language, and he sought to enrich the expressive power of the vernacular at the same time as giving it a common and generally intelligible form. He also sought financial profit. To these purposes he brought an exceptional ability as a translator, as well as a sound commercial instinct, including how to find patronage. A short involuntary exile in Cologne, at a time when it was rapidly developing as a centre of printing, opened his eyes to the new technique for disseminating texts. Later he applied the new technique in an enterprise where, however, as stationer and book-seller, he continued an earlier tradition.[2]

The English book-trade in which Caxton was engaged had before his day been peopled largely, if not exclusively, by native artisans, who could supply both vernacular and Latin needs. Caxton, a native Englishman, was instrumental in introducing from the Low Countries and Cologne the skills, techniques and materials required for the new craft, and also men versed in them. English printing relied on these men for a long time. During Caxton's lifetime, legislation was passed to encourage book artisans to reside in England and for the next fifty years printing and publishing were predominantly in the hands of the non-native-born.[3] In the reign of Henry VIII encouragement began to be directed at the English-born, culminating in the Act of 1534, which asserted that printing was by now thoroughly naturalized and that Englishmen were able to take charge.[4] Foreigners continued their activity, however. Books in Latin were throughout the period imported rather than printed in Britain, but by now they were intended specifically for a smaller proportion of those who could read than before.[5] British printed output, chiefly in the vernacular, was directed at the much enlarged constituency who could read English.[6]

Such was the new-grown power of the printing press that suppression played almost as large a part as dissemination, especially in the rapid changes of Reformation and Counter Reformation.[7] The fortunes of Thomas More's writings are instructive, in this respect as well as others. *Utopia*, his most famous work, a humanist jest of which the Latin editions were printed abroad, seems to have circulated freely in this changing context. Ralphe Robynson's translation of 1551 is not, however, included in More's *English Works* of 1557, which comprises almost entirely works of unimpeachable Catholic orthodoxy, nine-tenths of them controversial

2. Hellinga, below, pp. 65–8, 73–5.   3. Appendix, p. 608.   4. Appendix, pp. 608–10.
5. Ford, Trapp, below.   6. Trapp, below, pp. 34–8.   7. Neville-Sington, King, below.

writings in defence of the Church and in support of its activities as censor and destroyer of heresy. These had been written and printed in the late 1520s and early 1530s, when More and his King still seemed united in defence of the faith, as they had previously been when writing in Latin against the German reformers. Proclamations were issued during 1529–30 in Henry's name against the import of Lutheran books in English. During the twenty years after More's execution in 1535 for his refusal to accept a secular ruler as head of the Church – an act of treachery according to Henry – these English works of his could not have been printed in England. They circulated only under risk there. In 1557, with Philip and Mary on the throne, More was openly a martyr. John Cawood, the Queen's Printer, bore part of the production costs.

In the first decade of the sixteenth century, the English clerical arm had moved against printed books. One of its chief concerns, since the beginning of the previous century, had been translations of Scripture into English, which had not been approved by Church authority. These had been the special object of condemnation in the Constitutions of Oxford of 1409. Copying and circulation in manuscript of Wycliffite New Testament translations and other works continued nevertheless, though their witness to the Word was not reinforced by diffusion other than in manuscript. By the time they came to be printed, they had long been superseded by other versions. In 1526, William Tyndale's New Testament had had to be printed abroad, and brought in clandestinely. The Henrician versions of the 1530s, at first printed abroad for different reasons, and later in England, were disseminated by royal command. The English version most widely used in the latter part of the sixteenth century had again to be produced abroad – in Geneva by a small group of Marian Protestant exiles – in 1560 and could not circulate freely in England until the time of Elizabeth I.

These examples are elaborated briefly in this introduction, and in detail and at length in the chapters that follow it.

*

Our period witnessed a vast increase in the sheer numbers of books that became available, first through scribal production, but largely as a result of the arrival in England of the new invention of printing and of a flourishing import trade in both manuscripts and printed books, in which supply – as ever – partly satisfied and partly created demand. The times witnessed great growth in vernacular literacy in the sense of ability to read, and a smaller but possibly proportional increase in ability to write. In the older-fashioned literacy, which defined the *literatus* as someone who could read Latin, the extension was less marked, despite the expansion of the universities, the growth in numbers of schools and the beginning and consolidation of humanism and the Renaissance movement. The increase in vernacular literacy was accompanied, from the second half of the fourteenth century onwards, by a concomitant and cumulative increase in what was written in English, both originally in the native language and translated. There was also a growing dissatisfaction with the Church and its practices, chief among grievances being the sense that the Christian message was being withheld from those whom it ought to benefit by clerical insistence on the privileges of the clergy and on retaining the Scriptures and the liturgy in Latin. Fifteenth-century Lollardy, with its anti-clericalism, levelling doctrines, vigorously proselytizing and laicizing character, was the first popular heresy to manifest itself on any scale in Britain. Many of its tenets, particularly its insistence on Scripture in English, reinforced by Lutheranism from the 1520s onwards, and by Henry VIII and the Reformation from the later 1530s, were the most powerful of factors. This did not mean that the English Church abandoned Latin for its offices, however, until the last years of Henry VIII and during the reign of Edward VI; and Latin was restored under Mary. In Scotland the Latin mass was not abolished until 1560.

A transformation took place also, about the middle of our period, in the ways in which words were recorded on the page, the material – parchment or paper – of which that page was made, the quantity of such pages made available, the ways in which the pages were disseminated by their producers and through the book-trade, as well as where and for whom these processes were set in motion, and what kind of book, in what language, was being made. Printing indeed wrought a dramatic change, not only in methods of book production, but also in the book-trade. This change in turn had an effect on communication and on intellectual life in general that was both profound and lasting. To characterize the production change in terms of binary opposites – bespoke to speculative – is clearly too stark. Nevertheless, there is truth in it. The transformation, moreover, was not wrought overnight; nor did it affect everyone in equal measure. Communication depends on language, and language is one indicator of the distinct social groupings affected by the word spoken, written and printed, and therefore by the production of books and, in particular, their movement from place to place at the behest of owners and readers.

During the years covered by this volume, at least half-a-dozen languages were current in the British Isles: English (in the variety of regional forms that moved Caxton to express his perplexity about which to choose), Latin, French, Law French – the peculiar legal idiom (quite distinct from the language current in France) that had developed in the Inns of Court of London – and Middle Scottish, as well as Gaelic in its Scots, Welsh and Irish forms. The Law French constituency was perhaps the smallest and most homogeneous: the lawyers of the Inns of Court. In no other context are writers and readers, production and trade, so narrowly defined and connected. Similarly, the Latin which was the exclusive vehicle for canon law kept readership within a field that was closely confined to the clerical, legal and administrative classes, those in short who were *literati* in the strict sense. Not until the common lawyers' attack on the ecclesiastical jurisdiction from the later 1520s onwards were matters of canon law aired in print in the vernacular. The current law of the realm, in the form of parliamentary statutes, on the other hand, was published in English from the time of Henry VII onwards. The body of earlier legislation was also issued in English in 1519 (John Rastell's *Abridgements*)[8] and 1533 (Robert Redman's *Great Booke*).[9] It seems clear that wider access was being encouraged.

It is hardly more difficult to characterize the public for books in Scots, Welsh and Irish than that for such books of professional concern to lawyers or the clergy,[10] nor for those in the French of France, though in all these cases actual readership is less narrowly confined. For 'French of Paris' there is evidence of female readership. The core constituency for French books is to be deduced from the books acquired by the monarch and by the royal entourage, under the immediate influence of the French and Burgundian courts. The collection of John, Duke of Bedford, once formed part of the French royal collection; Edward IV and his sister, Margaret of York, Duchess of Burgundy, commissioned their French-language manuscripts in Bruges, Ghent and Brussels; Henry VII received printed books in French from Antoine Vérard in Paris, and employed as his librarian the francophone Bruges scribe, Quentin Poulet.[11]

Reading French was not limited to the royal court and its members and the upper nobility. French nevertheless did not, as it did in many

---

8. *STC* 9515.5.   9. *STC* 9286.
10. The history of the book in Scotland, Ireland and Wales will have separate treatment: *Book Trade History Group Newsletter*, 27 March 1996, pp. 2–14 and now Jones and Rees 1998.
11. Stratford, Backhouse, Carley below.

continental countries, become the language of polite society. Translation from the French, on the other hand, was an important element in English culture throughout our period: John Lydgate's major translations, his *Troy Book*, *Siege of Thebes* and *Fall of Princes*, were all from French rather than directly from Latin; Margaret of York's well-known patronage of Caxton's first efforts as translator related to renderings from the French; and French influence remained profound. It is not too much to say that these versions had a dramatic effect on the extension of the English-reading public among the professional and merchant sectors. Caxton had witnessed the same extension in the cities of Brabant and Flanders, before his return to England.

Throughout the century and a half covered in this volume, the situations of English and Latin, the two chief book languages of the country, shifted in relation to one another.[12] If initially use of the two languages indicated two distinct circles of readership, those circles can be observed gradually drawing closer to each other, until finally they overlap. In spite of this overlap in readership and in intellectual impact, however, the two tongues present us with opposites in terms of the production of, and the trade in, books. Latin was written and read everywhere in the educated world of Europe; English in the British Isles only, and outside them only in the special circumstances and restricted circles of successive generations of expatriates. The production of and trade in Latin books knew no boundaries, though the administration of the British kingdoms could and did exploit geographical situation to control, rather more efficiently than other European states, the importation of books.

A flourishing local production of manuscripts, augmented by imports, in particular of illuminated manuscripts, from France and the Low Countries, was sufficient to supply demand. This changed when printed books began to appear on the market. For books printed in French and Latin, the British Isles came to rely almost entirely on what could be imported from the Continent. With few exceptions, the only Latin books produced in England during our period were those which could not more conveniently be obtained from elsewhere. Exceptions to this are all the more intriguing. The brief and unsuccessful attempt in the late 1470s and 1480s to establish a press in Oxford, and the later encouragement by Cambridge of the printing activities of John Siberch in the early

12. Mss. and modern editions of British Latin writers up to 1540 are listed by R. Sharpe 1997.

1520s, are understandable, since university demand accounted for a large part of the Latin market.[13] What, however, induced the merchant William Wilcok in 1481 to commission the printing of the *Expositiones super Psalterium* of Thomas Wallensis from the first printing press in the City of London?[14] This anomaly should not obscure the fact that early English printing in Latin was almost exclusively limited to liturgies and books of hours (some of which also were ordered from printers in Paris, Rouen or the Southern Netherlands), to school-books and to jobbing printing of texts that happened to include Latin, or to short texts in that language, such as indulgences.

On the Continent, certain printers, in Venice, Basel, Nuremberg, Lyons and elsewhere, quickly began to dominate in certain fields – law, Bibles, the Fathers, liturgy, for example – selling their books far and wide, so as to render competition from elsewhere hardly worthwhile. No other country with a lively book culture, however, confined its production so much to its own vernacular and was almost wholly reliant for its Latin books on what was produced elsewhere. In this respect, the British Isles are unique.

It follows that printers in England (and, from the early sixteenth century, in Scotland) printed what could not be obtained from outside Britain: books either in English or Scots, or books for use exclusively in the British Isles. The printers were responding to patronage, to political conditions, or to more widespread and general demand. The link between the provision of Latin and of English books is therefore an intimate one, in that it shows a constant interaction between production at home and importation from abroad. In both pre- and post-Reformation times, English poetry, as well as Scripture, heterodox sermons and devotional material in English, often circulated in manuscripts not produced by professional scribes. That circulation, however, was restricted by considerations of private taste or of public legality.[15] In the age of printing, the book-trade was the primary force in the provision of reading matter for the educated classes.

The pattern which was to remain characteristic for British printing over the whole period was set from the beginning by William Caxton in 1476, although in his activities a number of functions are found together

13. Roberts 1997; Ferdinand 1997.   14. *STC* 19627.
15. Croft 1973; Beal 1980; Marotti 1995; Woudhuysen 1996.

which, not much later, could be expected to be spread over a range of skilled occupations.[16] Caxton prepared texts as editor and translator. He introduced a significant section of contemporary literature in French into the English literary tradition, and in doing so made it accessible to readers to whom it had largely been unknown. He contributed substantially to the creation of a wider readership among the merchant and professional classes, mostly in London. The twenty or more years of his life spent in Flanders and Brabant in a similar metropolitan society may have encouraged him on this path. In the flourishing cities of these parts, burghers had become used to reading and owning books, as can be seen in surviving inventories. At the same time, Caxton played a considerable part in the diffusion of Burgundian chivalric ideas. He also commissioned the preparation of texts when he knew himself to be out of his depth, as with the secular Latin texts edited by Pietro Carmeliano or written by Lorenzo Guglielmo Traversagni.[17] The same is presumably true of publications such as the Psalter, the books of hours and the *Directorium sacerdotum* produced by his press.

Caxton organized a many-sided publishing business, which was thriving at the time of his death in 1492, and stable enough to be taken over successfully by Wynkyn de Worde. Initially wholly oriented towards the Netherlands and Cologne, Caxton imported not only his newly acquired knowledge of printing and publishing procedures, but also all materials required for printing: cast type, paper, presumably recipes for printing ink, and he engaged at least one skilled workman from the Netherlands. Less noticed is that he was probably also instrumental in importing books from overseas, as witness the extant volumes, printed in Basel, Lyons, Cologne, Nuremberg, Venice and Ghent, with bindings which can be related to him and his workshop.[18] Styles of book production changed drastically during his lifetime, and evolved into forms which became recognizably 'English', but he and his successors continued to rely on imported printing types, largely from Paris and Rouen. Although illustrations, invariably woodcuts, were usually produced by local craftsmen, printed books, whether printed in England and Scotland or imported, continued to show visible links with Western European countries throughout the first half of the sixteenth century.[19]

16. The most recent bibliography on Caxton is found in Blake 1985. See also Corsten and Fuchs 1988–93, pp. 662–84; and Hellinga, below.
17. Trapp below, p. 289.   18. Nixon 1976, pp. 94–6.
19. Hellinga, below, pp. 72–9, 97–108.

Very early in the development of the printing business in continental Europe, printers discovered the need to specialize in what they produced.[20] Since they were often booksellers too, they needed to complement their own production with what could be provided through the rapidly developing book-trade. Thus there were specialists in texts of a certain kind, such as classical Latin, Bibles, the Fathers, and canon law. There were also those who specialized in difficult typographical work, such as Erhard Ratdolt, who could produce mathematical figures and tables; the few printers, mainly in Venice, of music; and those who solved the related problems of printing Greek and Hebrew, Aldus Manutius being the most famous among them. Caxton, though his greatest achievements were with literary texts in English, might be termed a generalist. Until 1490, he held almost a monopoly on the press in England (with the exception of legal printing). Most other printers in England during the first century of printing showed signs of choosing areas of expertise, although the example of Caxton's enduring success with vernacular literary texts was not lost on them. The first attempt at specialization was the setting up of a learned press at Oxford in 1478. It was short-lived, as its products could not compete with the rather similar-looking books from Cologne and Louvain and other such centres, which were also offered for sale to the small academic world in England. Legal printing in London, on the other hand, was an area of specialism which continued through a succession of printers: William de Machlinia, Richard Pynson, Robert Redman and the two Rastells, John and William.[21] The title of King's Printer, first claimed by Pynson in 1506, went with a form of specialization and responsibility beyond that of the printing of Year-books and Statutes, though these works formed the bulk of production.[22] Thomas Berthelet, Richard Grafton and Reyner Wolfe succeeded Pynson in the title during the period covered by this volume. John Rastell is almost the only specialist printer of music.[23]

Meanwhile Wynkyn de Worde had continued over many years to cater mainly for the market opened by Caxton by producing illustrated books in English – devotional, spiritual and literary.[24] On his death in 1535, De Worde's establishment passed to John Byddell, and later to Edward Whitchurch.[25] By that time most of the texts favoured by De Worde had

---

20. See, for example, the conclusions drawn in L. Hellinga 1994.

21. See Baker, below, pp. 411–32.   22. See Neville-Sington, below, pp. 579–84.

23. See Milsom, below, pp. 551–2.

24. Bennett 1952, esp. pp. 182–93, 239–76; Hodnett; cf. Erler below, pp. 501–3.

25. Duff 1906, pp. 138–40; Plomer 1925, pp. 98–101; STC vol. III, pp. 187, 35.

become irrelevant. The business changed its character and became much more incidental, a sign that the modest printing industry in England was ready to respond to the changes which affected most of society in the British Isles. Not many years later these were paralleled in France and the Netherlands, by the profound disruption that the religious wars wrought on the book-trade.

*

We may now return to Thomas More's *English Works* of 1557.[26] Something has been suggested above about their significance within the religious context of the age, but they are also an important indicator of the linguistic situation, the extent to which English had conquered Latin.[27] In 1531, before the break with Rome, Sir Thomas Elyot had written his *Book named the Governor* in English, to make it more accessible to those he wished to influence;[28] in 1545 the Protestant Roger Ascham had used his native language for *Toxophilus*, his treatise on archery, because it was 'English matter, in the English tongue, for Englishmen'.[29] English was already the norm for technical, instructional treatises.[30] The English prayer-book and the English Bible had been in daily use before Mary succeeded to the throne. More's *English Works* of 1557 were an assertion, in the language accessible to everyone in England who could read, that England belonged again to Latin Catholic Christendom. At the same time, it should be added that a number of the works in the volume of 1557 had originally been written by More in, or translated from, the Latin in which he was as fluent as he was in the vernacular.

That this book is representative, as a piece of printing, of the level of technical competence attained in contemporary Britain is a fair assessment. It is equally true that this level was substantially below what had long before been reached in other countries for publications of this nature. That More's *English Works* had been printed in black-letter is indicative of the conservative religious character of most of its contents. That it had been printed in London is symptomatic of conditions that established and kept English printing's centre of gravity, for some centuries after its introduction, almost entirely in south-east England: London, as court, ecclesiastical and commercial centre, and the cities in which were situated the country's only two universities, Oxford and Cambridge. This is in contrast to much more considerable manuscript production in British provincial centres, monastic and secular. It is also

26. *STC* 18076; R. W. Gibson 1961, no. 73. 27. See, still, R. F. Jones 1953.
28. *STC* 7635. 29. *STC* 837; bk II, ch. 2. 30. Keiser below, pp. 470–94.

in pronounced contrast to the printing and publishing conditions prevailing in most continental countries, with their many more printing centres in seats of advanced learning and other cities.

*

From the beginning of our period there is perceptible interaction between 'native' and 'alien', whether in the movement of raw materials for books, of the books themselves or of people – wholesale merchants, stationers, scribes, printers and their journeymen and, not least, readers. Both the materials and those who transformed them into books were subject to administrative control. Throughout the period, constant shifts in, and changes of assessment for, taxation are also observable, culminating from time to time in changes in the law. Beneath that formal level, influences of a more subtle and less enforceable kind also operated.

Native scribal production of manuscript books was carried on throughout the country, with notable pockets of strength in certain provincial areas; books of an academic sort, whether written in the older native hand or, from about the mid fifteenth century, the new humanist script, were naturally transcribed and illuminated in university centres. The more opulent productions usually came from London workshops.[31] What proportion of the scribes and illuminators employed in the workshops were English-, Welsh- or Scottish-born is not easy to determine; certainly Frenchmen and Netherlanders were denizened in England from the 1430s onwards. A Dutchman who could write a good upright humanist hand was brought to Oxford via Italy in 1449, and died in England in 1478; another was employed there from 1503 to the time of his death in 1540. Italian professional copyists were already active in 1447. Greek visitors, long- and short-stay, wrote manuscripts in England in the second half of the fifteenth century.[32]

In exempting from control both the numbers and the activities of scribes, printers and bookbinders from outside Britain who could ply their trades here, the Act of 1484, regulating the numbers of aliens who might be denizened in Britain, recognized that such artificers were needed.[33] In particular, the new art of printing had so far attracted few native practitioners to follow Caxton: Thomas Hunt and possibly the St Albans printer seem to be the exceptions to the rule that printers active in the British Isles were French, Netherlandish or German by birth, until

31. Christianson 1989c, and below, pp. 128–48; Scott 1996, esp. pp. 25–30.
32. Trapp below, p. 302.   33. 1 Richard III, cap. 9. See Appendix.

Andrew Myllar began to print in Edinburgh and John Rastell in London, both in the first decade of the sixteenth century. An old estimate put production by aliens connected with the British book-trade, resident in Britain between 1476 and 1535, at two-thirds of the total.[34] By the second of these dates, inclusion of the book-trade in further legislation, partly consequent upon anti-alien riots, such as Evil May Day 1517, had given a legal if not necessarily a technical advantage to native sons. In 1515, for example, a double subsidy had been imposed on all denizens, while from 1523 alien printers could employ only English apprentices, and not more than two foreign journeymen. Six years later, in 1529, further aliens were prohibited from setting up to print in Britain, though those already active were permitted to continue. Finally, in 1534, the Act of 1484 was repealed, to be replaced by a further Act, of which the preamble announced that a 'marvellous number of printed books' had been made available during the preceding fifty years, and – more optimistically – that 'at this day there be within this Realme a greate nombre connyng and expert in the seid science or craft of pryntyng as abyll to exercyse the seid craft in all poyntes, as any Stranger in any other Realme or Countre'. Henceforth, aliens could sell only wholesale to a stationer or another printer who was English-born; and no books were to be imported already bound.[35]

Legislation of this kind was aimed at both encouraging the book-trade and protecting the rights of English craftsmen. It was reinforced, and given another, Reformation dimension, by royal proclamations against the import and sale of heretical works in English printed abroad.[36] Before these proclamations and before the later of the Acts, encouragement to law-abiding printers in both England and Scotland and protection of their commercial rights had also been offered through the adoption of the system of book privileges already in existence on the Continent.[37] This kind of proto-copyright first appears in Britain on 15 September 1507, with James IV of Scotland's grant of leave to Walter Chepman and Andrew Myllar to set up a press in Edinburgh, and prohibition of the import from elsewhere of texts they had printed.[38] Such privileges, generally prohibiting, during a given number of years, the printing by others of the text to which they were attached, were naturally valid only within the jurisdiction of the granter – prelate or king, prince

---

34. Duff 1905, p. 189; see also Worman 1906.   35. 25 Henry VIII, cap. 15. See Appendix.
36. Neville-Sington, below; for anti-Lollard moves, see below, pp. 26–7; see also Gleason 1982 for other evidence of ecclesiastical censorship.
37. E. Armstrong 1990; A. W. Pollard 1937.   38. E. Armstrong 1990, p. 9.

or nobleman, ecclesiastical or secular body. The earliest 'Cum privilegio' in England appears to have been granted by the University of Oxford to a book dated 15 May 1518, Johannes Dedicus's commentary on the *Ethics*, printed by John Scolar.[39] It was for seven years, and its scope was confined to the University of Oxford and its precincts. The first use of the phrase 'Cum privilegio regali' comes in Richard Pynson's edition of 13 November 1518 of Cuthbert Tunstal's *In laudem matrimonii oratio*: it was for two years only.[40] Later this formula, which gave rise to so much misunderstanding, was reinforced by the addition of the words 'Ad imprimendum solum'; its addition was enjoined by the proclamation of 16 November 1538, directed at 'wronge teachynge and naughtye printed bokes'.[41] Another of 8 July 1546 required that the printer of 'any maner of englishe boke, balet or playe' must put his name and the author's on it, give the date of printing and present the first copy to the mayor of his town, retaining the rest of the edition for two days.[42] Further steps in the regulation of the book-trade were taken by the proclamations of 28 April 1551 (Edward VI), and 18 August 1553, 13 June 1555 and 6 June 1558 (Mary).[43] As A. W. Pollard points out, the importance of Mary's reign for the story lies not in her proclamations but in the grant of a charter to the Stationers' Company in 1557, which is the concern of another volume of this *History*.

*

The evidence, unsurprisingly, suggests a growing reluctance during our period on the part of English men and, perhaps rather less in some categories of reader, English women to read and write works not in their own language. This is equalled, indeed surpassed, by the reluctance of readers of other nationalities to read works in English: it is rare in our period to find manuscripts produced in Britain passing out of the British Isles, except perhaps to receive illumination, in Ghent or Bruges, for example. Whether the perceptible decline in quality or quantity of native production was cause or consequence of imports, never easy to establish with certainty, can be suggested only in specific cases or situations. It is equally difficult to generalize about patronage, though it might be said that England of the time could boast no commissioner of manuscripts on the scale of Duke Federico of Urbino, the Medici, Cardinal Giovanni

39. *STC* 6458; Johnson and Gibson 1946, p. 2.
40. *STC* 24320; Neville-Sington below, pp. 585, 592; A. W. Pollard 1937, p. 3; E. Armstrong 1990, pp. 10–11.   41. *STC* 7790; *TRP* 186; Greg 1954.   42. *STC* 7809; *TRP* 272.
43. *STC* 7835, 7849, 7865, 7884; *TRP* 371, 390, 422, 443; A. W. Pollard 1937, pp. 5–9.

d'Aragona in Italy; Louis XII or Cardinal Georges d'Amboise in France; or Raphael de Marcatellis, abbot of St Bavo, or Louis de Gruythuse in the Low Countries. Among royalty, Edward IV and, to a lesser degree Henry VII, for whom some of Edward's manuscripts were made over, are the nearest approaches. Henry VIII received fine gifts, one of them – splendid though it was – more than half fabricated from something originally written for John Colet.[44] Cardinal Wolsey was the nearest approach to a continental prelate-Maecenas. This was part cause, part effect: scribes and illuminators in the required quantity and with the required skills were not available on the spot until the arrival of the Horenbouts in the second half of the 1520s and the permanent residence of Pieter Meghen, working for Wolsey by 1528 and appointed Writer of the King's Books in 1530.[45] These are few in number compared with Italy or France. English patrons seem to have been short of both the resources and the resolution to part with the sums required, and English officialdom to have been concerned not to allow money out of the country – if Erasmus's experience with the Dover customs officials in 1500, much lamented by him, is typical.[46]

At all events, though codices written in Britain in Latin and French occasionally circulated in Europe, manuscripts in English travelled only in special circumstances and/or in particular with Englishmen. It may well be that Peter Payne the Taborite, former Principal of St Edmund Hall, carried with him to Bohemia, when he fled there in 1411, manuscripts in English for his own use. What he wrote in exile, however, was in Latin. It was Wycliffe's own Latin writings and compendia of them that reached Prague, some as early as 1381, and it was his Latin works and those of his followers that were copied, glossed and used by Bohemian theologians, Hus included. Those of the 200 works of Wycliffite tendencies burned at Prague in 1410 which were not in Latin are likely to have been in Bohemian.[47] In England the Wycliffite Bible versions and the great Wycliffite sermon cycle had a circulation that was even more considerable than the large number of manuscripts would suggest, because they, or portions of them, were read aloud to willing audiences. Wycliffe's Latin works were never printed in Britain and, though both his writings and those of his opponents were available in editions in that language printed in Germany during the 1520s, those volumes seem not to have had much, if any, currency in his native country.[48]

44. Below, pp. 48, 313. 45. Below, p. 313. 46. Allen; *CE*, no. 199.
47. Keen 1986, esp. pp. 134–45.
48. In contrast to Wycliffite works in English; cf. below, pp. 25, 588.

A later example of a text in Latin by a British author, the European reputation of which was aided by special circumstances, but also – in contrast to Wycliffe – by its orthodoxy in the religious and social dimension, was Henry VIII's Latin *Assertio septem sacramentorum*. The presentation manuscript, written and decorated in London in 1521, is now in the Vatican Library. The London-decorated vellum and paper copies of the *Assertio*, published in London also in 1521 by the King's Printer, Richard Pynson, for despatch to the Vatican and to crowned heads in Europe, also benefited from special circumstances.[49] The book was reprinted the same year in Rome and Paris, and in Rome, Antwerp and Strasbourg in 1522, as well as being twice translated into German.[50] Copies of Thomas More's *Responsio ad Lutherum* of 1523, likewise printed by Pynson, are, on the other hand, rarely recorded outside the British Isles, and this counterblast to Luther's reply to Henry was not reprinted anywhere until it appeared, in Counter Reformation times, in the editions of More's Latin *Opera* of Louvain, 1565–6.[51] The printing of John Fisher's Latin works of religious controversy followed a rather different course. One work only, and that a translation from the English, was printed in Britain;[52] the rest, during our period, came out and were reprinted in Paris, Lyons, Cologne, Leipzig, Antwerp, Louvain, Alcalà and Venice; German translations came from Danzig, Dillingen, Dresden and Leipzig. Douai joined in later, in Latin, and there was a collected Latin edition from Würzburg in 1597.[53] This popularity reflects Fisher's skill, and a prestige that lasted into the Counter Reformation, as defender of the Church and opponent of Luther.

Some printing statistics may be useful here. Before 1501, in the incunabular period, some 402 items, 364 excluding broadsides, were printed in four English centres: Westminster, London, Oxford and St Albans, all but 20 or so in the two first named. Those in Latin (120) account for about 33%; in English (214) 59%; in Law French (30) 8%. This compares with an overall figure for European incunabula of something over 70% in Latin and under 30% in the various vernacular languages. The English situation is a reflection in part of market conditions, and in part of the fact that no work of prime importance was written in Latin in Britain during the fifteenth century.[54] It is tempting indeed to extend the generalization to

49. *STC* 13078; cf. 13079; Vian 1962; below p. 586.   50. Shaaber 1975, H140–51.
51. *STC* 18088.5–18089; R. W. Gibson 1961, nos. 74–7; CWM v; Shaaber 1975, M210–13.
52. *STC* 10898.   53. Shaaber 1975, F41–5, 47, 48, 50–2, 54–73, 76, 77, 79–87, 89–91, 94–101.
54. Sharpe 1997.

the mid sixteenth century, Thomas More's *Utopia* being the sole exception, his *jeu d'esprit* representing the summit of achievement and of European popularity. Naturally, during the incunabular period, in what might be called an official ecclesiastical context, there was a heavy predominance of Latin. This applied also to printed books in monastic libraries, though their holdings were largely manuscript: it has been calculated that, in the early sixteenth century, some 2 per cent of the books in the Syon library were in English, and in 1558 some 3.5 per cent of those in the Benedictine house of Monk Bretton.[55] Latin also prevails, if to a lesser extent, among the printed books used by the secular clergy. Of English printed production in Latin, about a fifth consisted of indulgences and bulls, and a large proportion ecclesiological, devotional and liturgical works – 8 clerical manuals, 13 Sarum *horae*, 8 office-books, besides psalters and expositions of the psalms, hymns and sequences. Printings of Lyndewood's *Provinciale* – a manual of canon law as applied to England – outnumbered printings of the secular statutes in Latin by 5 to 2. Learning good Latin and good morals, whether through old-fashioned or newer humanist-oriented books of instruction, also bulks large; a substantial number – some 15 per cent – were grammar books; and there were 7 printings of single plays by Terence.

Between the beginning of the sixteenth century and 1557, some further 4,000 items are recorded as printed in Britain. More than 150 indulgences survive, something over 250 Latin liturgical books of various kinds (including those printed abroad for the English market), and more than 200 Latin grammatical text-books, some of these also printed abroad. Britain continued to rely on supplying readily and profitably from elsewhere the demand for other works in the Latin *lingua franca* of learned and ecclesiastical Europe. The presence in the sixteenth-century picture of works whose publication was attended by special circumstances does not alter its general aspect. Henry VIII's and Thomas More's anti-Lutheran polemical works, Thomas Linacre's grammars and his translations of pseudo-Proclus and Galen, Lyndewood's *Provinciale* again, Robert Wakefield's contributions to Hebrew studies, together with short, sure sellers such as some Lucian in Latin, a little Cicero, Virgil's *Eclogues* and more than 20 printings of various highly popular works of Erasmus in the same language, with a little spurt of Latin–English dictionaries and of bilingual Gospels in the 1540s, were all,

55. Bell, below, p. 251–2.

it is true, printed in England.[56] By and large, however, the trade limited itself to the supply of local demand: what was easy to print and sure to sell. The legal printing that flourished during the first half of the six-teenth century in the hands of Pynson, and then of the Rastells, Redman and Berthelet, is an exception.[57] The number of editions, and the size of each, is ample testimony to the amount of capital tied up in legal printing, and to the printers' ability to cope, often in rivalry, with demand – and to their anticipation of quick returns. This was a demand which could not be supplied more quickly and more cheaply through the import trade.

The vast majority of books printed in Britain, being in English, enjoyed a continental circulation and influence as limited as those of manuscripts in the same language: copies of More's *English Works* of 1557, for example, are as rare in modern European libraries as copies of his Latin *Opera* of 1565, 1566 and 1689 are frequent. That some British Latin authors, first printed in London, fared better abroad was apparently because their work filled a gap in secular knowledge. Cuthbert Tunstal's arithmetic book, *De arte supputandi*, for example, was first issued, by Pynson in England, in 1522. Though never reprinted here, it won reputa-tion enough to be twice reprinted by Robert Estienne in Paris, in 1529 and 1538, and to be issued again in Strasbourg in 1543, 1544 and 1551.[58]

More frequently, Latin 'copy' was sent to France, the Low Countries, Germany or Basel for its first printing. More's Latin *Utopia*, earlier and less tendentious than his reply to Luther, carried off by Erasmus to Louvain for its first edition of 1516, and reprinted in Paris, Basel and Florence before 1520, was not printed in Britain until the second half of the seventeenth century, being superseded for English consumption by Ralphe Robynson's translation, first printed in 1551, with three further issues by the end of the century and two more before 1640.[59] Nor was the perhaps still more famous product of the intellectual affinity between More and Erasmus, the Latin *Encomium Moriae*, first published in Paris in 1511, printed in Britain before 1663.[60] Again, the English printing in Latin had been preceded by Sir Thomas Chaloner's English translation more than a century earlier, in 1549.[61] There is little or no evidence of the circulation outside Britain of British printings of Latin texts which

56. For Erasmus, see Jensen below, pp. 368–9, on the predominance of editions printed abroad, even of such works as *De copia*.   57. Baker below, pp. 423–32.
58. *STC* 24319; Shaaber 1975, T155–9; for this, and the counter-example of Thomas Linacre, see Trapp below, p. 310.
59. *STC* 18094–8; R. W. Gibson 1961, nos. 1–4, 81–2, 15, 25–9; below, pp. 308–10.
60. Wing E3206.   61. *STC* 10500.

already existed in continental editions, for example Pynson's printing of Celso Maffei's tract *Dissuasoria ne christiani principes ecclesiasticos usurpent census* of 1505.[62]

There is, on the other hand, much evidence of the production abroad of books sacred and secular, manuscript and printed, for the English market. During the incunabular period and as far as the second quarter of the sixteenth century this was in English as well as in Latin and French. Some books, both sacred and secular, were produced to supply an open demand, some chiefly a clandestine one. In the manuscript era, Latin Bibles, service books and books of devotion, books of hours especially, were more frequently written and decorated in France and the Low Countries than in Britain. It is significant that in 1506–9 John Colet's large, handsome and incomplete Latin New Testament manuscript – a late example – was copied by a Low Countries scribe, perhaps in the Low Countries and probably from a printed book. It may well have been illuminated there also, in the Ghent–Bruges manner.[63] This pattern continues in printed books: the Psalter and book of hours bound together that were Thomas More's companion in the Tower of London in 1534–5 (fig. 24.1) were both Paris-printed, though either or both may well have been bought in London.[64] From an early date, school-books adapted for an English market were imported from abroad.[65] Other printed books, containing more controversial matter and produced in the Rhineland and in Antwerp for a clandestine Reformed English market during the 1520s and 1530s might find themselves able to circulate more freely in the 1540s and early 1550s. They might be again forced underground in the second half of the 1550s, to re-emerge into legitimacy at the death of Mary.[66] The English proto-Protestant exiles William Tyndale, John Frith and Robert Barnes were all burned at the stake between 1533 and 1540. Their works, including the translations of the New Testament made without ecclesiastical approval, had been printed, some in Germany but most in Antwerp, in the 1520s and 1530s and smuggled into England. Tyndale's New Testament was not printed in England until 1536;[67] his works of controversy, along with those of Frith and Barnes, were later edited by John Foxe and issued in a substantial folio from Elizabethan London by John Day in 1572–3.[68]

These are all works specifically directed at and produced for the

62. *STC* 17181.5.
63. BL, Royal ms. 1.E.v; CUL, ms. Dd.7.3; see Brown 1984; Trapp 1991, 81–6; and Trapp below pp. 307, 313.   64. Martz and Sylvester 1969; Erler, below, p. 511.
65. Orme, Jensen below.   66. King below, pp. 164, 170–2.   67. *STC* 2838–9.
68. *STC* 24436.

English market. Printed books introduced from abroad for reasons of financial profit or intellectual or professional interest must have been many more in number.[69] Such imports look, not unnaturally, to have been markedly fewer in the manuscript era, though the activities of the great collectors, such as Humfrey Duke of Gloucester, in the first half of the fifteenth century, in the assemblage, as well as the writing in England, of learned texts meant that a great many codices were brought in, particularly from Italy. Some of these were copied in England. In the third quarter, the stately Flemish manuscripts written for or acquired by Edward IV reached his library. Many less affluent individuals acquired manuscripts, at both ends of the scale of richness of production, in smaller numbers, or even singly. At the end of the century, and on into the sixteenth, both Greek and Latin scribes from abroad, catering for the university and/or clerical sector of the market, could find a living in England: the Spartan George Hermonymos was in London in 1473-6, and John Serbopoulos, arriving in 1484, spent the dozen years from 1489 to 1500 in Reading Abbey.[70]

With the advent of printing, a more distinct pattern emerges: the largest number of surviving printed books imported into Britain in the incunabular period originated in Italy, in Venice in particular. Germany came next, then France and then the Low Countries. As to users, there is naturally some difficulty in making a clear-cut distinction between the university and the clerical constituency. In so far as the distinction can be made, university-humanist readers, apparently the largest group of owners of books printed abroad, got most of their books from Italy, especially from Venice; the clergy, regular or secular, tended to use books from the large German printing houses specializing in works of theology and canon law, though not necessarily by German-Latin authors, and obtained service and devotional books from France. The other professions – legal, medical and schoolmasterly – were supplied from a mixture of sources. Women may have read some of these books, but among the 50 women owners in a total of almost 2,000 recorded by Margaret Lane Ford, few were in possession of a printed book imported from the Continent. On the other hand, women are known frequently to have owned books, both manuscript and printed, in the vernacular; and manuscript books of hours and other devotional works were produced specifically for them.[71]

---

69. Ford below, pp. 179-201.
70. J. Harris 1995, pp. 135-49; cf. below, p. 310.
71. Ford, Erler, Meale and Boffey below.

Generalizations of this sort based on quantity need always to be controlled by scrutiny of particulars. Christopher Urswick (1448–1522),[72] and Richard Fox (c.1448–1528),[73] for instance, might equally well be placed in the university or the clerical constituency or in the upper-administrative / royal servant. The surviving manuscripts and printed books Urswick is known to have owned are all in Latin; most of the manuscripts were written in England in the first quarter of the sixteenth century, none of the other books were printed here.

Fox, like his contemporary Urswick, was an admirer of Erasmus's New Testament, and received the dedication of Erasmus's translation of one of Lucian's *Dialogues*. The printed books that he owned or that he presented to Corpus Christi College, Oxford, or to the collegiate church of Bishop Auckland, were almost exclusively Latin and printed by the main European printing houses.

Of the manuscripts owned by Urswick's and Fox's younger university-clerical contemporary, John Colet (1467–1519), only those written to his order, of his own works and of the Gospels and Epistles survive.[74] One of them at least, the fair copy of his Abstracts of the pseudo-Dionysian *Hierarchies*, is extant because it got into the hands of William Cecil, Lord Burghley (1520–98); and others because they were probably presented, in an augmented form, to Henry VIII (later, Burghley annexed the richest of these too). Of Colet's printed books one only is extant: a copiously annotated copy of Marsilio Ficino's *Epistolae*, published in Venice in 1495.[75] We can, on the other hand, be sure that he too owned works by Erasmus – the *De copia* of Paris (1512), for example, which is dedicated to him, as well as the *Praise of Folly*, also first published in Paris, in 1511, and the Basel Jerome and *Novum Instrumentum*, of 1516. He had briefly in his hands Johann Reuchlin's *De arte cabbalistica* (Hagenau 1517) which the little group of London Erasmians were that year passing round among themselves and of which he disapproved. Jacques Lefèvre d'Etaples's edition of Ambrogio Traversari's translation of the pseudo-Dionysian *Hierarchies*, in the edition of Paris 1498, was the edition on which he based his Abstracts of that work.[76] No domestically printed book from Colet's library is extant, though he surely must have possessed some.

---

72. Trapp 1990; and below, p. 304.
73. Bietenholz 1985–7, 11, pp. 46–9; and, particularly, *BRUO*, pp. 715–19; cf. Woolfson 1997; and below, pp. 305–6.   74. Trapp 1991, pp. 79–141.
75. *GW* 9873; All Souls College, Codrington Library; Trapp 1991, figs. 52, 53; Jayne 1963.
76. *GW* 8409; Trapp 1991, pp. 103–8.

To return yet again to Thomas More: little is known for certain about his library.[77] Surviving manuscripts, dedications of printed books, and the evidence provided by his own works all add to the picture, however – and show him not above using, in the heat of controversy, short-cuts to the main points of his opponent's doctrines – or above chiding his opponents for doing something similar. He made use of Johannes Cochlaeus's *Articuli CCC. Martini Lutheri . . .;*[78] and he made fun of Christopher St German for citing the confessors' manual *Summa Rosella*, instead of some more heavyweight work of canon law.[79] There is no evidence that More used the same easy means of access to Wycliffite tenets – the widely circulating *Floretum* and *Rosarium doctrine*, for example.[80] Temporarily, at least, he must have owned numbers of heretical works; and his knowledge of Livy and Sallust among classical authors, and of the Fathers, bespeaks careful reading and familiarity. Jean Gerson's *Monotessaron* he knew well and used extensively for the great Tower meditation, *De tristitia Christi*: it was in print from 1474 on. The *De tristitia* itself, not printed in More's lifetime, appeared first in his Latin *Opera* of 1565–6; the holograph manuscript found its way to Valencia about the time of Philip and Mary, in the hands of a Spanish Dominican who had visited England.[81]

Though this is a special case, there is evidence that works by English authors had some circulation in Spain from the reign of Henry VIII onwards, much of it in Counter Reformation times. The only work by Colet to be published in his lifetime – his Latin sermon to Convocation of 1512 – was printed in London.[82] A copy reached Spain in the sixteenth century. More's *Utopia*, his Lucian translations and his epigrams were known there at an early date; and so, later, were his works of Latin controversy.

These, as we have seen, form no part of the volume of More's *English Works* of 1557, to which reference has frequently been made above. The latter is interesting also from the point of view of production, having been set in type largely from editions printed in More's lifetime. That, at least, is the inference from a surviving copy of *The Supplication of Souls* (1529) at Yale University, which bears red chalk casting-off marks, and from modern editorial collation of the other works.[83] There was some contemporary editorial intervention, in part affecting sense in minor matters only, in part vindicating the author and at the same time enhanc-

---

77. Trapp 1991, pp. 39–78.   78. Printed Cologne 1525; *CWM* VI, pp. 544–5.
79. *CWM* IX 9, p. 146.   80. Hudson 1985, pp. 10–42.   81. *CWM* XIV.   82. *STC* 5545.
83. *STC* 18092; see *CWM* VII, esp. pp. 455–81.

ing the justness of his cause; William Rastell, who had at least a part in the publishing process, was More's nephew, and More was already seen as a martyr. No printing from More's lifetime existed of the *Dialogue of Comfort, The Four Last Things* and the letters of his last days. For the *Dialogue*, the long-posthumous first printing of December 1553, after Mary's accession, its veiled references to Henry under the name of 'the Grand Turk' now immune from retribution, was used, possibly in conjunction with a manuscript;[84] and papers surviving in family possession were used for the others. The result was exactly suited to an English-reading public of a well-defined constituency: English Catholics who could then read it with impunity at home. Copies both remained in England during the penal years that followed the death of Mary in 1559, and circulated outside it, making the book also a rare example from our period of a work in English which was current on the Continent. Within a year or so of its publication, it could be openly read only in exile outside Britain, in the expatriate community in the Low Countries and France. To this community its currency was, if not restricted, at least specially relevant. The growth and nature of that community and the provision made for it by Catholic presses, which lie outside our chronological limits, have been excellently surveyed and documented.[85]

Significantly, as has already been pointed out, the printer of More's *English Works* used – as the printers of his lifetime had done for his works in that language – black-letter for the bulk of the text (frontispiece). Roman type was employed hardly at all except for part of title-pages and in headings, and italic was reserved for the preface, the Latin prayers, epitaph and letters, and the Latin quotations embedded in the text. The use of black-letter is to some extent the result of a tradition beginning in the last decade of the fifteenth century, and for some seventy years it remained the style of type still most readily available in Britain. To some extent, too, its use in this volume was a recognition that almost all More's English works dealt with matters necessary to salvation. Works of a religious nature printed in Britain retained the use of black-letter type well into the seventeenth century. The Authorized Version of the Bible in 1611, for instance, still used it, where many printers of Bibles on the Continent had long abandoned it, at least in French-speaking parts. French vernacular Bibles were printed in roman from 1540 and, of English versions printed abroad, the Geneva Bible of 1560 on the

---

84. *CWM* xii, pp. xix–lvii.   85. Allison and Rogers; Coppens 1993.

Protestant side, and the Douai–Reims New Testament of 1582 on the Catholic, used roman. The authorized version in Dutch, however, known as the *Statenbijbel* and published in 1637, was printed in black-letter.

*

The complicated history of sixteenth-century printed editions of the Bible in Britain is also paradigmatic for printing, some 50 years and more after its introduction into Britain, as well as for the ecclesiastico-political and entrepreneurial background. Lollard English scriptural versions had been printed neither here nor abroad, nor had they circulated in manuscript out of England. That they had not been printed may indeed be attributed to what has been called the 'paralysing effect' of the Constitutions of Oxford, promulgated by Archbishop Arundel in 1409, which prohibited unauthorized Bible translation. The survival of some 200 manuscripts of the Wycliffite translations suggests that paralysis was not total. On the other hand, the copying and printing of the Latin Bible of the Church was not forbidden, and though manuscripts were made, some of them illuminated, they were few by comparison with those of the vernacular versions.

If English printers had been inhibited by the Constitutions of Oxford from printing the Wycliffite New Testament, they were under no such handicap as regards the Latin text as approved by the Church. They took no early advantage of their opportunity. This is attributable less to technical deficiencies than to commercial factors. Legal printing of some bulk and complexity, with a ready market, as we have seen, was executed by London printers. The demand for Latin Bibles on the other hand was readily supplied by continental houses who specialized in such production. Even copies of the first Bible ever printed, Johann Gutenberg's, were, soon after printing, in the hands of English owners.[86]

To this situation – along with, later, the progress of the English Reformation – is largely to be attributed the fact that no complete Latin Bible was printed in England until 1579–80.[87] The first English printing of the sacred text in Latin, Thomas Berthelet's of 1535, lacked the prophetic books;[88] and when Latin New Testaments were printed in 1538 by James Nicolson, probably a Dutchman resident in London, they were accompanied by an English translation.[89] The English Reformation is certainly a decisive factor in the decline in the production of Latin

86. König 1983.   87. *STC* 2056.   88. *STC* 2055.
89. *STC* 2816, 2816.5, 2816.7; DMH 37, 38.

liturgical books for England. No single Sarum missal, for instance, was printed between 1534 and the reign of Mary.[90]

By the end of the year in which Nicolson produced his bilingual New Testament, Thomas Cromwell's Injunctions of 5 September 1538 had required Scripture to be made available in English.[91] Nicolson had first used the English version of Miles Coverdale, which had already been in circulation for some years, and was to form the basis for the version finally approved. Coverdale was indebted to another version, also printed in Britain for the first time in 1538, by Robert Redman, again in tandem with a Latin version.[92] Redman's Latin and his English text were both a more radical challenge than Nicolson's to Catholic orthodoxy: in Redman, the Latin of Erasmus was accompanied by the English of William Tyndale, the writing of which pre-dates Coverdale's by almost ten years.

Tyndale's New Testament, against which much invective had been directed in Thomas More's polemical tracts, was the most famous and influential of sixteenth-century English versions. The translation itself showed a knowledge of the Greek text of Erasmus, first printed in 1516, as well as of Erasmus's new Latin translation. It was also much influenced by Luther's German version of 1522. Completed in Germany in or before 1525, Tyndale's version was put to the press in Cologne in that year. Printing having been interrupted by Church intervention, this edition now exists in a single fragment in the British Library.[93] In 1526, Tyndale's New Testament was issued entire, from Worms. One complete copy, one lacking the title-page but with its woodcut initials coloured and one much more defective copy now survive.[94] The book quickly began to circulate in England, and a little later in Scotland. Arundel's prohibition being still in force, copies were seized and burned, as well as being written and preached against. In the circumstances, it is not easy to establish the size of the edition or the scope of its circulation. Johannes Cochlaeus, who had denounced the first printing to the authorities in Cologne, speaks of 6,000; 3,000 has also been suggested. The gibe that the activities of the English authorities in buying up copies provided the money to reprint may or may not be bravado. At all events the book was

90. Duff 1905, p. xxiii.   91. LP Henry VIII, 2. 281.   92. STC 2815; DMH 36.
93. STC 2823; DMH 1; BL, G.12179; facsims. 1871, 1926.
94. STC 2824; DMH 2; the complete copy is in Stuttgart, Württembergische Landesbibliothek; the BL copy (G.12179; facsims. 1862, 1976), with coloured woodcuts, lacks the title-page; the fragmentary copy is in the library of St Paul's Cathedral, London. For the Stuttgart copy, see Jannetta 1997.

burned in 1526, and figured in the first royal proclamation against heretical books in 1529.[95] The bookseller Robert Necton's calculations under interrogation in 1530 are not confidence-inspiring: he admitted buying 20 or 30 books from Simon Fish, and selling 7 in Suffolk, 2 to James Bayfield, 15 or 16 to George Constantine, from whom he also bought; 18 from Geoffrey Lome, and to being offered 200 to 300 copies.[96] These may well have included Tyndale's Prologue to Romans of 1527;[97] his *Parable of the wicked Mammon;*[98] and other books also printed in Antwerp, as well as, possibly, pirated editions of Tyndale's New Testament, of which no copy now survives.[99] George Joye's revisions of Tyndale's translation and Tyndale's own revisions, all printed in Antwerp in 1534 and 1535, were to circulate later.[100] In 1534, after the petition of the Canterbury Convocation to the Crown for an English version, Tyndale's translation seems to have been parcelled out for correction among the bishops, at least one of whom refused to co-operate. The project came to nothing.[101] Editions printed in Antwerp and, probably, in France, continued to be brought into Britain.[102]

For reasons that are unclear, the first complete English Bible, Miles Coverdale's of 1535, was probably printed in Cologne;[103] sheets were bought and issued from London in 1535, and reprinted in 1537, by Nicolson.[104] 'Matthew's Bible', a composite version edited by John Rogers and issued from London in 1537 in an edition of 1,500 copies, had been printed in Antwerp.[105] Printing of the revised version known as the 'Great Bible' of 1539 had been begun in Paris in the shop of François Regnault; only when it was interrupted by the French Inquisitor-General were printers' copy, type, paper and workmen – after pressure upon François I – transferred to London and the job completed there; one twentieth-century estimate put the number of copies at 20,000.[106] The further editions of 1540–1 and later were London-printed.[107] A variety of factors are clearly involved, among them the initial caution of Henry VIII in authorizing a vernacular version; the realization by

---

95. STC 7772; TRP 122; cf. Neville-Sington below, p. 588.
96. A.W. Pollard 1911, no. 19, pp. 155–9.   97. STC 24438.   98. STC 24454.
99. Hume 1973.   100. STC 2825–30.5; DMH 12, 13, 17, 16, 15.
101. A. W. Pollard 1911, no. 29, pp. 196–8; cf. below, p. 35.
102. STC 2831–35.4; DMH 27, 19–22, 24, 23, 25.   103. STC 2063; DMH 18.
104. STC 2063.3–2065; DMH 32–3.   105. STC 2066; DMH 34.
106. STC 2068; DMH 46. The estimate is in Willoughby 1942, p. 8.
107. STC 2069–76; DMH 52–4, 60–3; for a remarkable decorated three-volume copy on vellum, now BL, C.18.d.10, see String 1996; for another such copy in St John's Coll., Cambridge, see MacCulloch 1996, p. 239; and there is another in NLW.

Antwerp printers that profit continued to be available in Britain; the Bible-printing experience of some workshops in the Rhineland and Paris; and the lack of it in London.

Setting up the English Bible in every parish church, as the royal proclamation of 6 May 1541 required, was perhaps calculated less to achieve uniformity of doctrine than to encourage the deference to learned authority in scriptural interpretation that the Injunctions of 1538 had required.[108] Reinforcement came from the *King's Book* of 1543, Henry VIII's formulation of the *Necessary doctrine and erudition for any Christian man*.[109] Under Edward VI, the Book of Common Prayer in English of 1549 and 1552 added its force. Edwardian legislation repealing Henry VIII's reactionary Act of the Six Articles of 1539 concerning Church belief and practice, and renewing the requirement to make the Scriptures in English generally available, was not repealed under Mary. The Catholic Church merely resumed its authority in the interpretation of the Scriptures, in Latin. No new Bibles were printed in England, in any language, and there was destruction of copies of English versions.

Once more, printing of the Bible in English moved abroad. In 1557, as we have seen, in the same year as More's *English Works* were issued in London, a group of Marian exiles in Geneva, led by John Knox, published there a new English version of the New Testament and the Psalms.[110] Its subsequent history is not our concern. Worth remark, nevertheless, is that an English Protestant book produced by a Calvinist exile community, and initially used by that community, began to be used in Elizabethan times in England and was popular enough to be preferred, for private reading at least, to the Bishops' Bible, translated in England and published in London in 1568–9. More than 140 editions, most of them English, attest its popularity and perhaps a feeling that it had achieved its aim of making available the purity of the Word and the right sense of the Holy Ghost, in the dominant language of the British Isles.

The subsequent history of the Bible in Britain will be told in later volumes in this *History*. During the time-span of these volumes the printing press was the chief, indeed virtually the sole, instrument of the widened diffusion of the written word – Scripture and liturgy included. Our period saw the invention of the new process and its rapid rise towards that position. Copying by hand of scribe or self, for limited or

108. *STC* 7793; *TRP*, 200; A. W. Pollard 1911, no. 43. 109. *STC* 5168–77.
110. *STC* 2871; DMH 106.

clandestine circulation, continued to be the recourse of seekers of patronage, of poets, or of the orthodox and the heterodox in religion, as well as, for no circulation at all, of those who merely wished to memorialize their thoughts. Manuscripts might be laid out and painted to produce effects that no mechanical process could achieve. At the beginning of the sixteenth century, however, printing had become so ubiquitous that only the rich would trouble to have substantial books written and decorated to their exclusive order.

The English Bible has been introduced here as our final example of the complex interaction of all the factors with which the historian of the book and of reading must be concerned. We have seen that British production of Latin manuscript Bibles in the fifteenth century was smaller than that of continental workshops, and that Latin Bibles, written and/or illustrated on the Continent, were imported. We have seen also that substantial numbers of printed Latin Bibles, and many more Latin liturgical books, were brought in. The tortuous history of the Bible in English reflects the changes wrought by a mechanical revolution on the one hand and a revolution in religious and national sentiment on the other. During the time of what has been called the premature Reformation, circulation of Scripture in English was at first limited by being in manuscript alone. The years 1525 to 1557 saw the beginning of the wider spread of the English Bible, in new translations. Printing was the vital element in accelerating its progress from limited and clandestine accessibility to availability not only in every church in the land, but eventually to many reformed households.

*

The biblical paradigm offers the historian of the book many insights, but may narrow unduly an investigation which seeks to encompass the use of books in general. The environment in which texts of any kind are produced and reproduced in manuscript or in print, and in which they have their effect, is an aggregate of the intellectual, religious, philosophical, scientific, literary and artistic, the individual, social and political. The book in Britain, throughout the century and a half with which we are concerned, reflects both the spread of literacy and the wavering balance between Latin and the vernacular. It also reflects the fortunes of the book-trade, the interaction of production at home and abroad. Related in terms only of those directly involved – authors, patrons, editors, translators, scribes and printers – this may seem to be the story of events that directly affect a few. Dissemination in manuscript, however, and much more dissemination in print, by definition means that the work of the few will affect the many. To be interpreted in terms of the history of the book, any single instance of patronage, writing, printing, embellishing and illustrating, purchase and collection needs to be placed in the widest possible context, not only of book-production, book-trade, use of books and their survival, but also within the greatest possible range of contemporary human activity.

1

Literacy, books and readers

J. B. TRAPP

Much close attention is given elsewhere in this volume to the details and the specific circumstances of the commissioning of books, both manuscript and printed, to how they were acquired and collected into libraries by individuals and institutions, and to their use, potential and actual. Something more general needs nevertheless to be said, in an introductory way, about literacy and reading.[1] It is difficult, even impossible, to be precise about so slippery a concept, hard to define and compute acceptably even today. An overall growth in the ability to read *and* write English during our period is certain enough. To what precise extent the same applies to Latin literacy is less clear.

Nevertheless, the quantity of what was progressively made available in manuscript and print propels us towards assumptions which the comparative absence of reliable statistics makes difficult to validate. The attempt may perhaps carry more conviction if generalization and inference are reduced to a minimum and the enquiry is conducted on the basis of the few specific contemporary statements that exist, and some examples. There is no reason to suppose that the statements in question are utterly to be relied upon; they are, for one thing, made in the heat of controversy, or at least *à parti pris*. The rest of the evidence, besides being largely random, requires much circumspection in interpretation.

That books large and small were composed is beyond dispute. That there was a reading public for them, varying in size from one person to many, from book to book and according to means, motive and opportunity, is therefore equally certain. Who composed that public, what gender, occupation, profession, social class and so on, and what proportion of their lives, private and public, individual and institutional, was

---

1. An up-to-date general survey of literacy, such as is available for an earlier time in Clanchy 1993, is lacking for our period; on the general question, see Goody 1968, and therein especially Schofield 1968.

occupied by writing and reading is largely imponderable. In any case, acquaintance with and comprehension of a text, in varying degree, whether Latin, French or vernacular, need not imply that it had been really read by those who knew it. In a society where learning by rote or by heart was common, how many attendances at mass or mattins would be necessary before the attender knew the Latin or the English words more or less by heart and in some sense at least understood their import; how many times would the participant in a Lollard conventicle need to hear the preacher convey to his hearers the words of the Sermon on the Mount or, for that matter, the message of the *Lantern of Light* or *Wiclif's Wicket*? We need to know far more of the social spread of Lollardy and of the attainments of those who taught it, as well as those who heard it. Conversely, how much, other than such texts, would Sir Thomas More's 'old cunnyng weuar', so apt in the corruption of others, have read or been able to comprehend?[2] How many of each gender were envisaged in the contemporary complaint that Wycliffe and his followers were making the Scriptures available to those lay persons, women included, who could read English but not Latin?[3] What of those Scots, Irish, weavers, ploughmen or even women whom Erasmus hoped would get the New Testament by heart?[4] To turn to a secular context, what readers are implied by the sixteenth-century practice of circulating poems in manuscript?[5] What poem or poems is 'Chaucer' reading to his cultured, court audience in the famous illustration which precedes a manuscript of his *Troilus and Criseyde* made in the first quarter of the fifteenth century, and what is implied by the representation?[6] The notion of oral/manuscript culture rapidly and comprehensively succeeded by print culture is impossibly crude. Such a succession is not yet complete and never will be. Was the audience for romances largely female, as is still often so widely assumed? What did the city merchant read, let alone his apprentices? Merchants wrote letters, especially the Celys, their wives and their friends, and so did some of their apprentices.[7] All wrote in English, and the masters recorded their formal deliberations and decisions in their native language also – the Brewers from 1422, the Mercers from 1453.[8] Such merchants' letters do not survive in the same numbers as those of the fifteenth-century gentry, the Pastons, Stonors and Plumptons in par-

---

2. *CWM* IX, p. 163.   3. Knighton 1995, pp. 242–5, cited from earlier edition by Adamson 1946, p. 40, and Aston 1984, p. 206.   4. *Paraclesis*; Olin 1987, p. 101.
5. Marotti 1995; Woudhuysen 1996.
6. Cambridge, Corpus Christi Coll., ms. 61, f. 1v; facsim. Cambridge 1978.
7. Adamson 1946, pp. 39–40; Hanham 1975.   8. E.g. Lyell 1936.

ticular, women and men both.[9] The 'English bills rhymed in part' posted by Walter Aslak in the 1420s on various gates and doors in Norwich, threatening murder to William Paston and others, imply a readership, or at least an audience,[10] as do the medical promises posted in 1558 by Thomas Luffkin.[11] How many more would have acquired the skill of reading in the intervening century and a half is not easy to establish. That royal proclamations were issued in printed form from 1504 may be relevant.[12] These are some of many questions, to which there are few answers. Whether one searches wills – where books are seldom mentioned, let alone particularized, unless they were especially prized or had some special association or were of some special kind (prayer-books are perhaps most frequent) – and legal instruments, probate inventories, letters, journals, surviving copies of books, library catalogues, or seeks to establish the sources used by an author, high or low, sacred or secular, precise documentation of the ability to read is scant. One is thrown back on inference, whether readers were professional, cultivated or pragmatic in their orientation.[13]

Three *ex cathedra* statements, and a comment or two, from the first half of the sixteenth century may therefore be a useful starting point; one is by a Dean of St Paul's and educationist, two by Chancellors of the realm under Catholic monarchs, one of whom was also a bishop. When the first of these, John Colet, framed in 1512 the statutes of the school he had re-founded and which was now ready for its first boy pupils in St Paul's Churchyard, he required that: 'The high Maister shall admytt thes Children as they shal be offeryde fro tyme to tyme, but fyrste see theye Can theyre Catechizon and also that he can rede and write Competentlye, elles lett hym not be admyttyde in no wyse.'[14] Clearly, this requirement was élitist; equally clearly, even in an élite social group, literacy was not the norm. What standard is represented by competence in reading and writing at the age of about seven years, and in what language, does not appear; nor what standard the 153 boys who made up the full complement of pupils at any one time can be judged, singly or as a group, to have attained. The list of distinguished scholarly Old Paulines is substantial, but surely represents only a small proportion of those who passed through the school. Multiply St Paul's by the number of grammar

9. Most, if not all, the surviving letters of the Paston women were written down by amanuenses.
10. N. Davis 1971–6, I, p. 8; II, p. 506; cited from earlier edition by Adamson 1946, p. 41.
11. Jones, p. 448 below.   12. Neville-Sington, p. 580 below.   13. Parkes 1973.
14. BL, Add. ms. 6274, f. 7v.

schools that existed by the time of Elizabeth in every large town, and some small ones, some of them survivors or re-foundations from an earlier era, and you might, making due allowance for the incompetent and unqualified keepers of schools that were already the subject in May 1446 of a Privy Seal writ, have some indication of extent. Precise numbers, however, cannot be attached to any element in the equation. There are many further complications. The entrance requirements of Winchester in 1400 and Eton in 1447 were that pupils should arrive knowing their Donatus, that is to say with some knowledge of Latin grammar; in 1446, the school at Newland, Glos., was less exigent.[15] What can hardly be doubted, however, is that the large increase in the number of schools in England during the fifteenth century must have led to an improved general level of literacy. Similarly, though there is debate about the precise effect of the Reformation, and particularly the Dissolution of the Monasteries and the Chantries Act of 1547, the first half of the six-teenth century must have witnessed a further increase. The Protestant ethic surely also played a part.[16]

Early in 1533, some twenty years later than his now-dead friend and mentor Colet, Sir Thomas More, repeating his case against scriptural translations not authorized by the Church, argues:

> For the people may haue every necessary trewth of scrypture, and euery thynge necessary for them to know, concernynge the saluacyon of theyr soules, trewly taught and preched vnto theym, though the corps and bodye of the scrypture be not translated vnto them in theyr mother tonge . . . Yf the hauynge of the scrypture in englyshe be a thyng so requysyte of precise necessyte that the peoples soules shulde nedes perysh but yf they haue it translated into theyre owne tonge, then muste there the most part perishe for all that, except the preacher make farther prouysyon besyde, that all the people shall be able to rede it when they haue yt, *of which people farre more then four partes of all the whole dyuyded into tenne, could neuer rede englysshe yet* [my italics].[17]

The exact meaning of 'rede' is far from clear: does it imply 'read' in our modern sense, or, at least in part, rather 'comprehend'? More's other statements are both more specific and less optimistic: in the same work he writes of a 'tynker or a tylar whyche could (for some there can) rede englysshe'.[18] More's brother-in-law John Rastell, writing from the other

---

15. Orme 1973, pp. 69–70.
16. Moran 1985, pp. 3–20; cf. Orme 1973, pp. 11–56; 1989, *passim*; M. G. A. Vale 1976; Cressy 1980.   17. *CWM* IX, p. 13.   18. *CWM* IX, p. 163.

side and almost contemporaneously, in 1534, to Thomas Cromwell, clearly had good expectations of the size of the reading public: he was anxious that 10,000 or 20,000 of the *Book of the Charge* should be printed and 'sparklyd abroad ... for lernyd men themselves but also the people to be instructed in the true lernyng and brought from ignorance to knowledge of the true fayth and to have no confidence in the Pope nor his laws'.[19]

Rather more than a decade on, Stephen Gardiner, Bishop of Winchester, writing on 3 May 1547 to Edward Vaughan, Captain of Portsmouth, about the destruction of religious images in that city, expresses his indignation:

> And if by reviling of stockes and stones, in which matter images be graven, the setting of the truth to be red in them of all men shal be contemned, how shal such writing continue in honor as is comprised in cloutes and pitch, wherof and wherupon our bokes be made, *such as few can skil of, and not the hundredth part of the realme? And if we, a few that can reade, because we can reade in one sorte of letters* [i.e. Latin]: so privileaged as they have manye reliefs, shall pull away the bookes of the reste, and woulde have our letters only in estimation and blind al them, shall not they have just cause to mistrust what is ment [my italics]?[20]

Whether Gardiner meant the truth to be read in English, or Latin, or both is left uncertain; probably – given his views on Scripture and the priesthood – he meant to indicate those who were *literati* in the old, strict sense. It is clear, at all events, that he was writing about reading at an advanced and sophisticated level, and that he had in mind Gregory the Great's dictum concerning images as the books of the illiterate.

H. S. Bennett's characterization of these last two examples as rhetorical flourishes, not to be taken seriously as evidence – especially, perhaps, the second – is true enough as far as it goes, though it removes the dimension of urgency deriving from the context of religious reform and its suppression: both More and Gardiner find the Church's authoritative interpretation of Scripture sufficient for every virtuous purpose.[21] Gardiner may be doing so rather more humanely in this instance than More. Others, such as John Stokesley, Bishop of London, refusing to take his share in New Testament translation in 1534, were more vehement in their denial of translations to the people.[22] Yet the primer had been avail-

19. Quoted in *CWM*, IX, pp. liii–liv.   20. Gardiner 1933, p. 274.   21. Bennett 1952, p. 28.
22. Adamson 1946, p. 45.

able in English since about 1400.[23] The problem became acute only when the heretical element had entered, and it was probably suspicion of heresy, rather than that they were reciting mattins aloud from an English primer, that caused an unspecified number of maidens to be turned out of the church of Langham, on the Essex–Suffolk borders, by a zealous sidesman on Ascension Day 1534.[24] By that time, both heretical Psalters and heretical primers in English, the work of Reformers such as George Joye, had been printed, first in Antwerp from 1530, and then in England, with Antwerp continuing.[25]

Lollard proposals to parliament in 1410 for an enlargement of the number of English universities from 2 to 15, at which 15,000 'priests and clerks' should be supported to study, may or may not be based on any sort of realistic estimate of available literates in various catchment areas. Inferences somewhat more reliable about literacy and a reading public of a specialized kind may, however, be drawn from fifteenth- and sixteenth-century Church proceedings and royal legislation against heresy, partial and indefinite though the indications these offer may be.[26] The writings of Wycliffe were already cited in Gregory XI's bull in 1377; from 1388 the dissemination of his doctrines in 'books, booklets, schedules and quires' which had been caused to be written in both English and Latin was the subject of Chancery documents; and already in 1388, 1397 and 1414 those under formal examination are specifically required to produce before their judges the heretical books they have written. The statute *De heretico comburendo* of 1401 mentions the making and writing of books apt to corrupt their readers, but cites none by name; the Constitutions of Archbishop Arundel, issued in 1409, are specific about Bible translation and about the dissemination of heresy by tract as well as by sermon and conventicle. On the face of it, like the fourteenth-century prohibitions and proceedings, with the exception of those of 1397, which specify books in English, all menace the *literatus* in the clerical sense; the man who could read Latin. This is an index of the way in which the Lollard movement in its first thirty or forty years kept its learned aspirations. The prohibitions were also, however, firmly directed against readers of

23. Littlehales 1895–7.   24. Adamson 1946, p. 44; cf. Collinson 1996, esp. pp. 80–1.
25. *STC* 2370ff., 13828.4; Hume 1973, nos. 12, 14; Butterworth 1953.
26. On the question in general, see Biller and Hudson 1994, and especially the essay by Hudson, 'Laicus litteratus', therein; and further on fifteenth-century England in particular, Hudson 1988, esp., in the excellent chapter on Lollard education, pp. 185–6, and cf. pp. 374, 511–12; and Aston 1984, pp. 196–218 ('Lollardy and literacy'). These fully documented studies are heavily drawn upon in the paragraphs which follow.

the vernacular, and this emphasis increases in the sixteenth century. Lollard tracts laid a duty on 'whoso can read books in his language and so knoweth the better God's law' to apply that advantage to the 'worship of God and the help of his even [i.e. fellow] Christians'. In Lollardy, the written English word, scriptural or other, became crucial. John Foxe records a story of how Robert Barnes sold new printed Testaments – Tyndale's or Joye's – to two merchants to replace their Lollard manuscripts, tattered from use.[27] Scripture had precedence, but the evidence of both length and format suggests that sermon texts were left by itinerant preachers for later reading and discussion by their audiences; and the trouble taken by some of those accused of heresy to deny that they could read, and by their accusers to establish that they could, is also telling. What none of this permits, unhappily, is a firm quantitative – or qualitative, for that matter – notion of literacy in either the clerical or the lay sense.

Nor do later Church constitutions or suppressions or royal proclamations against harmful and seditious books. The best one can say is that they recognize the danger of 'misorder and abusion' in Church and state implicit in the ability to read. The confiscations and bonfires of books under Wolsey and Cuthbert Tunstal, Bishop of London, in the 1520s, the warnings to booksellers, the processes against De Worde, Berthelet and others in the 1520s and 1530s (even though these were concerned with technicalities of licence to print), and the rest, all imply a readership, if of indeterminate size, at least with determination to read. So do known instances of the prosecution of known individual readers. The proclamations of 1529–30 were concerned to suppress the circulation of Lollard texts, such as John Purvey's *Compendious olde treatyse shewynge how that we ought to have the scripture in Englyshe* and *The examinacion of Master William Thorpe . . . [and] of . . . syr Ihonn Oldcastle* of 1530.[28] A more urgent concern was to hinder the importing into England of Lutheran heresy, 'pupil of the Wycliffite' in the words of Tunstal, licensing his friend More to retain and read heretical books for the purpose of refuting them.[29] Scripture in the vernacular, and the Lutheran–Tyndalean reduction of the sacraments to those two which were held to have their basis in Scripture itself, baptism and the Eucharist, excluding the doctrine of transubstantiation,

---

27. Cited in Collinson 1996, p. 81.
28. *STC* 7772, 7775; *TRP*, 122, 129; Hume 1973, nos. 16, 18. Others were inserted later; cf. *CWM* VI, p. 883; and cf., e.g., the *Lantern of Light* of about 1409–15, printed in London in about 1535 (*STC* 15225). 29. E. F. Rogers 1947, pp. 387–8.

the nature of the Church and of its priesthood, the veneration of the saints, the validity of works as well as faith, were all seen as dangers to spiritualty and temporalty alike.

Thomas Nix, Bishop of Norwich, is already complaining in 1530 that he cannot suppress such books and their readers, particularly since the readers invoke the support of the King: 'For divers saith openly in my diocese that the King's Grace would that they should have the said erroneous books and so maintaineth themselves of the King.' Nix's informants tell him that 'wheresoever they go, they hear say that the King's pleasure is the New Testament in English should go forth and men should have it and read it'. This, it has been convincingly suggested, is a misunderstanding of the phrase used on title-pages: 'cum privilegio regali'. Nix's impression is, however, that readership of such books is limited to merchants and those who lived near the coast: 'the gentlemen and the commonalty be not greatly infected'.[30] The proclamation of 1538 was intended to put an end to internal disputings in an already reformed context upon matters necessary to salvation, such as baptism and the Eucharist.[31] In the same year, Thomas Cromwell's injunctions directed all to the pure fount of doctrine, the Bible in English, of the largest size, in the copy to be provided by every parish priest in his church, placed where the 'parishioners may most commodiously resort to the same and read it' for themselves or have it read to them.[32] In that year, too, it is recorded that 'divers poor men in the town of Chelmsford in Essex' bought the New Testament in English, and sat on Sundays 'reading in the lower end of the church and many would flock about them to hear them reading'.[33] This need not imply illiteracy in all such hearers. Shortly before the time that Gardiner wrote, the Act 34–35 Henry VIII, c.1, of 1543, 'for the advancement of true religion and for the abolishment of the contrary', seems to indicate a mistrust of certain sections of an enlarged public, however. Women, artificers, apprentices, journeymen, servingmen of the rank of yeoman or under, husbandmen and labourers were forbidden to read the English Bible. Noblemen, gentlemen and merchants might read it in their own households; noblewomen and gentlewomen might read it privately, but not aloud to others.[34]

Whether as a result of powerful centralized control, made easier by the

30. Adamson 1946, pp. 43–4; cf. Bennett 1952, p. 36; A. W. Pollard 1911, no. 20, pp. 159–61; Christianson 1989c.   31. *STC* 7790; *TRP* 186.
32. A. W. Pollard 1911, no. 41, pp. 258–65; cf. *STC* 7793; *TRP* 200.
33. Adamson 1946, p. 44.   34. Adamson 1946, p. 146; cf. *TRP* 191.

confinement of printing to so few centres, or of English conservatism in matters of religion, especially in its royal manifestations, there is little or no sign until the late 1520s and 1530s of pamphlet warfare, certainly not on the scale and vehemence reached in Germany. England produced devotional woodcuts, many more than now survive, sometimes with a text, but nothing approximating to the Lutheran broadsheet (which was often equipped with a text of which the interpretation would have required substantial reading ability).[35] Diagrams figuring central doctrines of the Church, such as the Trinity, were readily available in books written or printed here and on the Continent, just as they were before the Reformation, more elaborately, in paintings on church walls.

It cannot be said that any of these sporadic testimonies disposes of our problem. Nor is a more precise index of the growth of ability to read provided by the evidence for the extended use, by those engaged in secular trades, of the simple test required to claim benefit of clergy that was available from the late fourteenth century onwards. From this time any man who could read was, whether in orders or not, for legal purposes a clerk and could plead his clergy. The privilege was extended to women under William and Mary. The Act 4 Henry VII, *c.* 13 of 1489, recognizing that, among the 'divers persons lettered emboldened' by the privilege, laymen had been figuring with increasing prominence, changed its nature by decreeing that laymen so pleading were henceforth, on a first conviction, to be branded and debarred from a second plea.[36]

Sir Thomas More's estimate, always quoted in discussions of literacy in Britain during our period, is almost always accompanied by a questioning rider, if not worse. Modern opinion tends to find it considerably too optimistic. It is, of course, generally conceded that lay literacy is likely to have been higher and more widespread by the 1550s than a century and a half earlier, partly because of a growing independence of education from the Church or of a growing middle class, or both.[37] Literacy, defined as the ability to write one's name, has been put at 10 per cent for men and 1 per cent for women at the beginning of the sixteenth century;[38] ability to read estimated at 30 per cent in the fifteenth century and 40 per cent in 1530, though many fewer could write; and 50 per cent of London laymen as literate by the 1470s.[39] A guess that, in the second

---

35. Scribner 1981.   36. Gabel 1928–9, pp. 64–87 (on *literatus*), 123–5.
37. Cressy 1977; Moran 1985; Hudson 1988, pp. 511–12; Aston 1984, pp. 193–217.
38. Cressy 1977.
39. Opinions quoted by Moran 1985, pp. 150–84 ('Literacy and laicization').

quarter of the sixteenth century, half the adult population of the country could, in some sense of the word, read English might not be wide of the mark. Thomas More was probably right. How far that proportion would be capable not only of reading but also of interpreting Scripture is another matter. Latin literacy is another matter again. Gardiner in 1547 may not have been so far wrong, though he gives no indication of how ability to read Latin was now a lay as well as a clerical accomplishment, and is silent on Greek.

Individual readers

Recent work on readers' marks and marginalia in surviving books has been concentrated on the lay, if learned, readership of the period rather later than that covered by the present volume.[40] Nevertheless the conclusions of Anthony Grafton, Lisa Jardine and William Sherman about the way in which the annotations of Gabriel Harvey and John Dee, for example, show them engaging with what they read have some relevance to an earlier time.[41] There is naturally in such notes a common element of the merely lexical, particularly for texts in Latin: any reader is at the mercy of his or her vocabulary. A similar common factor is the sententious, not solely in those books which are intended for serious instruction, but also in those which approach more nearly to the genre that is now called literature. There is also the overarching mnemonic function of such notes.

A pair of the few examples available from an earlier period, effectively the end of the fifteenth and the beginning of the sixteenth centuries, are worth a closer look. One is again Christopher Urswick, Henry VII's almoner (1448–1522). Several of his surviving books are annotated, some quite copiously, so as to evince an interest in history as *magistra vitae* or storehouse of profitable *exempla*, in the Augustinian view of the human condition, or in the religious politics and conditions of fifteenth-century Bohemia, presumably with reference to current Wycliffism in England. Several are manuscripts, some of them written specially for Urswick,

40. See Alston 1994 for a preliminary survey of annotated works in the British Library; for a curious, individual example, L. Hellinga 1988; and, for an extended set of examples, Rosenthal 1997.
41. Grafton and Jardine 1990; Sherman 1995; cf. G. K. Hunter 1951 and, in a larger context, Grafton 1981, 1985. Cf. also Grafton 1997a, b. For an insular account of the relation of reading to the reader's wit and will in a later period, see Kintgen 1996; and, for a broader consideration of how European reading and writing habits were formed and applied, Moss 1996.

seemingly to instruct the clergy in the obligations of priesthood, to combat contemporary anti-clericalism (one of these texts was printed, perhaps at Urswick's instigation, by Pynson in 1505), or to improve the moral condition in this world, or the purgatorial in the next, of the laymen to whom or to whose memory they were dedicated.[42]

The other instance is John Colet (1467–1519), Dean of St Paul's.[43] The manuscript volumes of his 'collected edition' of his own works all have copious author's annotations and second thoughts. There is, however, one extensive and highly revealing testimony to his consuming interest in contemporary Florentine Neo-Platonism in the shape of a copy of the *Epistolae* of Marsilio Ficino in the first printed edition, of Venice 1495. Colet probably bought his copy in either Italy or France rather than through the English 'Latin trade'. His copious marginal annotations of it reflect an eagerness to get at, and to convert to his own use, the exact message of Ficino's encapsulations of his doctrine, particularly as relating to St Paul.[44]

Like most of his contemporaries, Colet did not read for pleasure, but for edification, which could be transmitted to others.

The kings of our period, with exceptions, seem not to have been great readers. Though Henry V possessed a substantial library, there is no surviving evidence of his use of it. Of the more bookish sort, Henry VI has left no trace in the form of annotation. Edward IV was a collector, on a substantial scale, rather than a reader, it seems. Richard III, on the other hand, has recently been plausibly argued to have read or at least used all the eighteen texts in fourteen volumes that can be identified as his: a Wycliffite New Testament and books of devotion, history, romance chivalry and advice to rulers, all of them manuscripts.[45] Richard's conqueror, Henry VII seems, like Edward IV, to have been an accumulator, a converter of books-as-objects to his own use, as well as the first to appoint a royal librarian. His son Henry VIII left his mark on many surviving books and draft documents (fig. 13.1). He read and annotated assiduously, noting *sententiae* and the like which seemed to him especially relevant to his own situation and likely to be useful in improving it.[46] A case in point is his copy of the *Polyanthea* of the Ligurian protonotary apostolic, poet laureate, doctor of medicine and of canon law, Domenico Annio Mirabello (Dominicus Nannius Mirabellus, fl. *c.* 1500–20), archpriest of the cathedral in Savona. This collection of wise sayings and *exempla* was

---

42. Trapp 1990.   43. Above, p. 33.   44. Jayne 1963.
45. Sutton and Visser-Fuchs 1997.   46. Birrell 1987a, pp. 7–8.

printed at least half-a-dozen times in Italy and the German-speaking lands between 1503 and 1539, and re-issued in 1604; Henry's copy, the edition of Savona 1514, is now in the British Library.[47]

Henry's markings in this show him scanning the contents list for topics of interest and marking them, then, turning to the texts themselves, marking what seems to him relevant. The theological arsenal on which he drew for his *Assertio septem sacramentorum* in 1521 is not now reconstructible in copy-specific terms. It must have been considerable, whatever the labour of others such as Sir Thomas More, who characterized himself as a sorter-out and placer of the principal matters therein contained: Henry had, after all, been intended for a prelatical career until the death of Arthur made him heir apparent to the throne. Among the books he read later was Augustinus Triumphus of Ancona, *De potestate ecclesiastica*, in the edition of Cologne, 1475, where he could find and mark views on the papacy that suited his own concept of himself as head of the Church.[48] The surviving manuscript of the compilation *Collectanea satis curiosa*, justifying the royal supremacy and intended for government use, bears approving annotations by Henry.[49] It is impossible to determine precisely how much he contributed personally to it, any more than it is to characterize his part in *Gravissimae . . . totius Italiae, et Galliae Academiarum censurae; Determinations of the moste famous and mooste excellent vniuersities of Italy and Fraunce that it is so vnlefull for a man to marie his brothers wyfe / that the pope hath no power to dispence therwith.*[50] This was the work of a royal committee. Henry underlined and annotated passages in a dozen or so other printed books, almost all – in Professor Birrell's words – theological or devotional, including the Psalter, the Biblical Wisdom books and Erasmus's *Paraphrases* of the New Testament. Erasmus's *Paraphrase* of St Luke's Gospel was dedicated to Henry in 1523, as one of his Plutarch translations had been earlier. Henry owned and read a number of texts which are important in the history of the continental Reformation, and a good amount of Lutheran pastoral literature in French. Two printed books appropriated by him as a result of the Dissolution of the Monasteries survive.[51]

Royal ladies come off well. Elizabeth Woodville owned a copy of the first book printed by Caxton, the *Recuyell of the Historyes of Troye*.[52] From

47. Birrell 1987a, pp. 9–10.   48. GW 3051; Birrell 1987a, pp. 9–10.
49. MacCulloch 1996, pp. 54–5; Selwyn 1996.
50. *STC* 14286–7; Bedouelle and Le Gal 1987; Surtz and Murphy 1988.
51. Birrell 1987a, pp. 9–10.
52. *STC* 15375; Huntington. Cf. L. Hellinga 1991b.

Margaret of York to the grandmother of Henry VIII, Lady Margaret Beaufort, to Henry's first wife, Catherine of Aragon – for whom Joannes Ludovicus Vives was so influential – through his second, Anne Boleyn, to his last, Catherine Parr – whom he married in 1542, and whose influence on the religious settlement of Edward VI's reign is undoubted – the Tudor dynasty's women were readers. Among Catherine of Aragon's known books, works of Catholic theology and piety predominate; she also owned several works by Erasmus, Vives on women's education, and Petrarch, Dante and some Roman history in Spanish. Anne Boleyn's books show a strong reformist tendency, often mediated through France.[53] The court context during the 1540s of what has been characterized as an Erasmian, non-dogmatic, humanist pietism was very much Catherine Parr's creation. She wrote religious verse in French (she owned at least two New Testaments in that language); she encouraged her step-daughters in pious productions. An English translation was begun of one of Erasmus's *Paraphrases* of the New Testament, which were printed entire in 1548;[54] her own *Prayers and Meditations* were three times printed by Berthelet in 1545, and again in 1546(?), 1547 and as late as 1594;[55] and her *Lamentacion of a Sinner*, in 1547, 1548 and 1563.[56] Catherine sufficiently prized her copy of the Canzoniere and *Trionfi* of Petrarch, with Velutello's commentary (Venice 1544, now in the British Library), to have it bound in purple velvet embroidered in coloured silks and gold and silver thread; it bears no reader's notes.[57] Another book in Italian, an unidentified manuscript on vellum bound in silk or velvet, is recorded as having been in her possession at her demise.[58]

53. On royal ladies, see Foot below, pp. 122–3. On Lady Margaret, see Jones and Underwood 1992, Powell 1998, and Erler below, p. 521; on Catherine of Aragon, Dowling 1986, esp. pp. 219–45; on Anne, Ives 1986, Holman 1991, Dowling 1991, Carley 1998; and on Catherine Parr, McConica 1965, pp. 200–24, Bennett 1952, pp. 68, 232, and Erler below, p. 507. James Carley kindly provides a reference to a post-mortem list, in Society of Antiquaries ms. 129, of some twenty books which had belonged to Catherine Parr.
54. *STC* 2854.   55. *STC* 4818–26.7.   56. *STC* 4827–9.   57. BL, C.27.e.19.
58. Society of Antiquaries, ms. 129.

TECHNIQUE
AND
TRADE

2

Foreign illuminators
and illuminated manuscripts

J. J. G. ALEXANDER

No account of the history of the manuscript book in Britain in the fifteenth century would be complete without a discussion of the extent to which foreigners were involved in the native book trade, and, even more striking, of the very considerable numbers of manuscripts written and illuminated abroad which were imported at this time. This chapter confines itself to illuminators and deals only incidentally with scribes and binders. Even with this restriction, it can only be a brief and selective summary of a large and complex topic on which there is still much research to be done.

For the purposes of my discussion I want to distinguish five classes of production and/or importation. First, foreign illuminators may have themselves migrated to work in England. Secondly, manuscripts may have been made abroad and then imported and sold in England speculatively to buyers who had not specifically commissioned them. Thirdly, owners may have acquired manuscripts abroad and brought them back to England. Fourthly, manuscripts may have been sent from abroad as gifts. Fifthly, manuscripts may have been specially commissioned abroad by owners who remained in or returned to England.

*

Two well-known examples of immigrant artists from the beginning and end of the period respectively are Herman Scheerre and Gerard Horenbout. There are uncertainties as to the identification of the 'Hermann Scheerre' who signed a miniature in BL Add. ms. 16998 with individuals named 'Hermann' mentioned in documents as being in London at this time. It seems sure, however, that Scheerre – coming perhaps from Cologne or, as some think now, from the Netherlands – was actually present in London working in collaboration with native

47

artists in the first decade of the fifteenth century (fig. 2.1).[1] Horenbout was employed by King Henry VIII, entering his service at some time between September 1525 and February 1528.[2] His wife accompanied him, which suggests he intended a lengthy stay, though he retained property in his native Ghent. She died and was buried in London in November 1529, being commemorated by a brass with her coat-of-arms in All Saints, Fulham. Gerard died at some time between 1540 and 1541, though neither his age, which must have been considerable, nor the place of his death is known. His son, Lucas, is first mentioned in the royal accounts in 1525. His daughter, Susanna, from whom Dürer had bought an illuminated 'Platlein' in Antwerp in 1521, married John Parker, Yeoman of Henry VIII's Wardrobe of Robes and Keeper of the Palace of Westminster, at some time in the 1520s. Though a number of paintings, portrait miniatures and manuscript illuminations have been attributed to the three artist members of the family, a full study of the illumination which they executed in England and of their influence on and interconnections with native artists remains to be undertaken. Hugh Paget's claim that the Epistolary of Cardinal Wolsey, dated 1528 and now in Christ Church, Oxford, is signed 'Gherart' in the miniature of the Adoration of the Shepherds on f. 4v has, in my view, to be rejected.[3] The marks he claimed to read occur on the step above the right angel's mantle. Though they may possibly be letters, they are confused with other marks which may be part of the underdrawing. In any case they are not even decipherable, still less legible as 'Gherart'. The date, on the other hand, is written twice quite clearly in the border of f. 32.

The finest of the illuminations executed in England in the Horenbout style are the two miniatures of St Luke and St John in the New Testament which has the badges of Henry VIII and Catherine of Aragon in the borders and which was written in the late 1520s or early 1530s by Pieter Meghen.[4] The manuscript contains the Vulgate text and also Erasmus's translation from the Greek of the Acts of the Apostles and of the Apocalypse. The style of Cardinal Wolsey's Epistolary and Evangeliary,

1. Full references in Scott 1996; see also Rickert, esp. 1965, pp. 166–7, and the appendix to Rickert 1952. On Scheerre's origins, Hamburger 1991. Important articles by Meale 1989, and K. Harris 1989, set these imports in the wider context of manuscript production and readership in England at this date. See especially Meale, pp. 201–2, 205–6, for alien craftsmen, and K. Harris, pp. 180–3 for patrons and imports.
2. Campbell and Foister 1986, pp. 719–27, deal authoritatively with the documents.
3. Paget 1959, pp. 396–402, figs. 43, 45; cf. n. 5 below.
4. Hatfield House, Cecil Papers ms. 324; Trapp 1975, esp. p. 89; Trapp and Schulte Herbrüggen 1997, no. 38; Trapp 1981–2, fig. 6; Trapp 1991, pp. 90–3, fig. 35.

both manuscripts also written by Meghen, is at once less accomplished and more advanced. The former miniatures, therefore, are candidates for the work of the father and the latter, perhaps, of the son, Lucas, or the daughter, Susanna.[5] A miniature for the Feast of the Relics in the Epistolary, now in the library at Christ Church, Oxford, has a certain historical poignancy. Executed in 1528 on the eve of the Reformation it shows an altar covered with precious reliquaries (fig. 2.2). Above it, a note directing the deacon where to find the reading for the Feast of the Translation of St Thomas Becket has had the saint's name erased according to Henry VIII's direction of 1538.

A third foreign artist, to whom a number of manuscripts made in England have been attributed, is the anonymous 'Master of Sir John Fastolf', named after a copy of Christine de Pisan's *Epître d'Othée* dated 1450 and written by an English scribe for Sir John Fastolf.[6] This illuminator appears to have begun work in Paris in association with the Boucicaut Master and the Bedford Master and then to have followed the English fortunes in the last stages of the Hundred Years' War, moving first to Rouen and finally to England. A number of books of hours illuminated by him are of the Use of Sarum, though that does not, of course, guarantee they were written in England. An Hours in the Morgan Library with miniatures by the Fastolf Master has borders not in his usual French style, but executed by a different hand in English style. It must have been made in England, therefore. As with Scheerre and the Horenbouts, native artists were influenced by the Fastolf Master, for example William Abell, who copied the illustrations of the *Epître d'Othée*.[7]

The question is whether these cases are rather exceptional or not. We can assume a constant effort to keep out foreign competition on the part of the native craftsmen through their guilds. If the fifteenth-century

5. The Epistolary was Trapp and Schulte Herbrüggen 1977, no. 43; Trapp 1975, no. 15. The Gospel Lectionary is Oxford, Magdalen Coll., ms. Lat. 223; Trapp 1975, no. 14. For both manuscripts, see Alexander and Temple 1985, nos. 827–8, pl. LVII. I now think we were unwise to ascribe these manuscripts to Gerard. Pächt 1953–4, no. 624, more cautiously wrote of 'a member of the Horenbouts family'. The New Testament, Oxford, Corpus Christi Coll., ms. 13–14, also containing the Vulgate New Testament and Erasmus's translation from the Greek, has miniatures of very fine quality, by yet another illuminator, apparently (Alexander and Temple 1985, no. 825, pl. LVI; Trapp 1975, no. 8; Trapp 1991, p. 92, fig. 37).

6. Oxford, Bodleian, ms. Laud Misc. 570; Pächt and Alexander 1966–73, I, no. 695. For a preliminary list of works, see Alexander 1971, pp. 248–51. These include Bodleian, ms. Auct. D. inf. 2.11, Hours, which may have belonged to Henry VII and/or Henry VIII; Pächt and Alexander 1966–73, I, no. 670. The artist is also discussed by Farquhar 1976, pp. 82–8; by Plummer in Plummer and Clark 1982, nos. 1, 21–3 (the Glazier Hours, PML ms. G.9, is no. 23), and by Reynolds 1994, pp. 306–9.   7. Alexander 1972, pp. 166–70.

records of the Stationers' Guild in London, which was founded in 1403, survived, we might be able to tell how many foreigners managed nevertheless to insert themselves into the London book-trade.[8] Such documentary evidence as there is does not suggest that foreign artists domiciled here were ever very numerous.[9] As study of manuscripts illuminated in England in the fifteenth century progresses, however, it may be possible to recognize the work of other foreign, though anonymous, illuminators working alongside native artists.[10] One such, to whom a group of manuscripts have been attributed in this way, is the so-called Caesar Master, active *c.* 1450.[11] In the early sixteenth century, a member of the group known as the Masters of the Dark Eyes from the Northern Netherlands is thought to have been working in London.[12] A manuscript with illumination in this style is London BL, Royal ms. 2.B.XII–XIII, a Lectionary given to St Mary Aldermanbury by Alderman Stephen Jenyns and his wife, Margaret, during his term of office as Lord Mayor in 1508.[13]

It is not easy to be sure in particular cases whether a manuscript produced abroad was then completed or added to in England, or whether foreign and native artists are collaborating on a particular manuscript in England, or whether native artists have become proficient at copying foreign styles. Works by or associated with Hermann Scheerre are a case in point. In the Nevill Hours he appears to collaborate with native artists operating in styles close to his.[14] In the Scrope Hours, however, he may be completing the illumination of an imported manuscript produced in the Southern Netherlands, with the original miniatures executed in the style associated with the so-called Master of the Beaufort Saints.[15] As various hands are separated out, for example within the production which has been at various times associated with this Master of the Beaufort Saints, and as careful codicological, palaeographical and textual analysis of such manuscripts progresses, some of these questions of origin and geographical location may be resolved.

Aliens in England, even those with letters of denization, were subject to various regulations and also heavy taxes. They could avoid these only by becoming naturalized by Act of Parliament.[16] There were complaints

8. G. Pollard 1937a, pp. 1–38; Blagden 1960.   9. Duff 1905; Christianson 1990.
10. Scott 1996; this work reached me too late for full account to be taken of its conclusions.
11. Scott 1968; 1980a, ch. 8; 1989; 1996.   12. Marrow 1990, p. 286.
13. Warner and Gilson 1921, pp. 48–9.
14. Nevill Hours, Berkeley Castle, Gloucestershire; Spriggs 1974; Scott 1996, v. 2, cat. 23.
15. Scrope Hours, Oxford, Bodleian, ms. Lat. liturg. f.2; Rogers 1992, p. 125; Scott 1996, v. 2, cat. 22.   16. Duff 1905, p. xv.

of undenizened aliens who worked in Liberties and could not be touched, however. Regulations also stipulated that foreign merchants must reside with London merchants who were responsible for them during their presence in England.[17] In 1484, legislation was passed which aimed further to regulate and restrict the conditions under which foreigners carried on business or trade in England. This, however, specifically stated that the restrictions were not to apply to any

> Artificer or merchaunt straungier of what Nacion or Countrey he be or shalbe of, for bryngyng into this Realme, or sellyng by retaill or otherwise, of any manners bokes wrytten or imprynted, or for the inhabitynge within the said Realme for the same intent, or to any writer lympner bynder or imprynter of such bokes, as he hath or shall have to sell by wey of merchaundise, or for their abode in the same Realme for the exercisyng of the said occupacions.

(The statute is in Law French and the terms used are 'escrivener', 'alluminour', 'liour' and 'enpressour'.)[18] The 1484 Act, in specifically freeing foreign members of the book-trade, also implies that they had earlier been penalized. Plant's comment in relation to the Act that 'there was as yet nothing to protect [such members, unlike e.g. the woollen cloth trade]' can apply only to printing and not to manuscript production.[19] Though the Act refers to 'books written or printed', presumably the primary object was to encourage foreign craftsmen to bring knowledge of the new technology of printing to England, just as Henry VI had earlier tried to encourage the immigration of stained-glass artists from the Continent by inviting John Utynam from Flanders in 1449 to execute the stained glass for Eton and King's Colleges.[20]

In the later Middle Ages, perhaps not before the fourteenth century, certain major patrons attached illuminators to themselves as household servants, the Duke de Berry being a well-known example. Sometimes, as with the Limburg brothers, these illuminators were not native, but came from elsewhere. It may be that one of the advantages for the illuminator, offsetting the disadvantage that his ability to work for other patrons was now restricted, was precisely in avoiding guild and other regulations.[21] Like Horenbout, who had earlier been illuminator to Margaret of Austria, other illuminators who came over from abroad may have come at the invitation of, or with some promise of protection from, a specific

---

17. Thielemanns 1966. 18. Duff 1905, pp. xi–xii; Appendix, p. 608. 19. Plant 1965, p. 27.
20. Thielemanns 1966, p. 300. 21. Alexander 1992, pp. 27, 29.

patron. Scheerre, for example, is documented earlier working in Dijon for the Duke of Burgundy and later in Paris working for the Queen, Isabeau de Bavière. Some of his works may have been done for King Henry IV and either a direct invitation or, at the least, the prospect of court patronage can be assumed to have been the incentive for him to come to London. Two historiated initials in the Great Cowcher Book of the Duchy of Lancaster made for the King in 1402–7, now in the Public Record Office in London, have been thought to be by Scheerre.[22] Henry IV would also be the obvious patron for the Great Bible on which Scheerre worked with other artists.[23] Similarly, the Fastolf Master probably came to England at the invitation either of Sir John Fastolf himself, or with the prospect of working for others, like him, who had acquired the taste for such work as a result of the English occupation of parts of France.[24]

It is difficult to say what proportion of surviving foreign manuscripts were imported for sale speculatively, my second class of production. Books of hours form a special category here. There still survive considerable numbers of manuscript books of hours which were made abroad, particularly in Flanders, for use in England. In most cases their texts, specifically the Use of Sarum or York and the presence of suffrages and calendar entries for saints especially venerated in England, provide clear evidence for their destination. This evidence is sometimes corroborated by inscriptions of ownership or by coats-of-arms.

The Netherlandish examples have been studied by Nicholas Rogers, who earlier catalogued a total of 170 examples from the 1390s to the first decade of the sixteenth century.[25] Given that these are the sort of manuscripts which are still privately owned and thus pass regularly through the sale rooms, and also that at the Reformation they were liable to be scattered abroad, Rogers's list is undoubtedly susceptible of considerable amplification. More recently he has referred to 'some two hundred' examples known to him.[26] Rate of survival is always a difficult problem to gauge in view of Puritan destruction, but Kathleen Scott's volume on manuscripts illuminated in the British Isles in the same period includes 27 native-made books of hours in her total of 140 entries.[27] Though these

22. Alexander 1983, p. 149. S. A. Wright (1992) considers the Cowcher Master a separate artist.
23. BL, Royal ms. 1 E.ix; S. A. Wright 1986.
24. K. B. McFarlane 1957. For English patrons in Normandy, see Reynolds 1994.
25. Rogers 1982, ch. 11, includes a valuable discussion of what can be deduced about the production and marketing of these books of hours from such little evidence as is known. See also Colledge 1978; Arnould 1993, pp. 113–31.
26. Rogers 1992, p. 125; for examples discovered in Padua, see Limentani Virdis 1989, pp. 107–20. 27. Scott 1996.

are obviously only a selection from those known to Dr Scott, who elsewhere refers to a total of 102 'Books of Hours, manuals, prayerbooks'
from a total of 845 illustrated texts, these are nevertheless striking figures
in their imbalance to the foreign production.[28]

One piece of evidence that Hours were made for speculative buyers
rather than on commission is in manuscripts where blank spaces were
left in illuminated borders for coats-of-arms to be filled in when the manuscript found a buyer. Rogers quotes examples now in the British
Library (fig. 2.3a–b) and in Melbourne.[29] In the later fifteenth century,
very large quantities of printed Primers were being imported, as H. R.
Plomer showed from his examination of the London Customs Rolls.[30]
For example, in 1490–1 John Rey brought in 200 printed primers and, in
1502, 6 named individuals imported a total of 1,336 primers. If we
extrapolate from this a continuation from an earlier trade, it seems likely
that a considerable proportion of the 200 books of hours referred to by
Rogers were imported for sale speculatively. Rogers observes a falling in
numbers proportionally as the century progresses, which is surely
explained by the advent of cheaper printed copies. Books of hours were,
of course, not the only text imported, whether printed or manuscript,
but perhaps they were always in the majority. Presumably it was the
English merchants who provided the finance for their import. The
majority of these manuscripts are at the lower end of the market in terms
of the quality of the illumination. They use various techniques to hasten
mass production and the miniatures are often inserted on single leaves. A
typical example still in East Anglia is the early fifteenth-century Hours in
the parish church library in Swaffham, Norfolk (fig. 2.4), with 21 integral
miniatures by 2 illuminators, one close to the Master of Nicholas
Brouwer.[31] A more richly illuminated example is in the Fitzwilliam
Museum, Cambridge (fig. 2.5).[32]

My third class, books acquired abroad which returned with their
owners to England, are in my terms relatively unproblematic. John,
Duke of Bedford, for example, had exceptional opportunities for patron-
izing Parisian illuminators for himself and, as is well known, he also

28. Scott 1989, p. 32.
29. London, BL, ms. Harley 2985, Hours, Use of Sarum; Melbourne, State Library of Victoria,
    *f096/R66Hb, Hours, Use of York. For the latter, see Manion and Vines 1984, no. 56, fig.
    121.
30. Plomer 1923–4; 1928–9. Plomer gives figures for 1479–80, 1490/1, 1502/3, etc. Further, on
    the import of printed books, Armstrong 1979; and L. Hellinga 1991a, pp. 205–24.
31. Swaffham, ms. 1; Rogers 1982, Index of mss.; Ker 1969–92, IV, pp. 485–7. Photographs are
    in the Conway Library, Courtauld Institute of Art, University of London.
32. Ms. 1055–1975; Arnould 1993, no. 36.

brought back to England from Paris part of the French royal library.[33] Owners such as William Gray, Robert Flemmyng or John Tiptoft have been extensively studied in connection with the reception and spread of humanism in England and are discussed elsewhere in this volume.[34] Gray's manuscripts are preserved in Balliol College, Oxford; many of Flemmyng's are in Lincoln College, Oxford; and a small but lavishly illuminated group of manuscripts apparently made for Tiptoft in Padua, are in the Bodleian Library. Gray is interesting for the purchases he made in Cologne, since, apart from his books, there is, so far as I know, little other evidence for imports of manuscripts made on the lower Rhine, let alone further east in Europe, whether by purchase or gift.[35]

The scholars and patrons interested in humanism wanted a variety of specific texts, not just standard devotional books, and these were mostly texts which they could not have obtained in England for lack of exemplars, and which, therefore, could be obtained only in Italy. This situation changed in the course of the century as exemplars became available in England. Moreover, whereas initially such patrons turned to foreign scribes like Theodoricus Werken, who worked for Gray, or Milo de Carraria from Padua, who signed manuscripts in Cologne in 1444, in Bruges in 1445 and then in London in 1447, soon a number of native scribes learnt to write the new humanist script. Similarly, native illuminators began to decorate initials and borders in their own, often idiosyncratic, forms of Italian *bianchi girari* (white-vine). There is an unnoticed example of this type of English white-vine in a Psalter now in Modena, the English origin of which is confirmed by the presence of English saints, including St Frideswide, in the litany.[36]

The import of manuscripts by gift, my fourth class, is also relatively unproblematic in my context. In the fifteenth and early sixteenth centuries notable gifts of manuscripts produced abroad were received by the royal Dukes, both John, Duke of Bedford, and Humfrey, Duke of Gloucester, as well as by the Kings of England, Henry V, Henry VI, Edward IV, Henry VII and Henry VIII, sometimes from native, sometimes from foreign, donors.[37] Humanists dedicated texts to Humfrey of

33. Stratford below, p. 266.   34. De la Mare and Hunt 1970; Trapp below, pp. 293–6.
35. Alexander and Temple 1985, nos. 845, 847–67.
36. Modena, Biblioteca Estense, ms. α. Q.b.6.15; Fava and Salmi 1950–73, II, no. 114, pl. XII.
37. For John, Duke of Bedford, and Humfrey, Duke of Gloucester, nn. 33–4 above; for royal ownership of manuscripts in the fifteenth century, Alexander 1983; for Edward IV, see especially Backhouse 1987; McKendrick 1990; McKendrick 1992, pp. 153–4; 1994; for Henry VII and Henry VIII, Trapp 1991; for Henry VIII, Starkey 1991, *passim*; and Backhouse 1998, pp. 88–93. See, further, Stratford and Backhouse below, pp. 255–73.

Gloucester, some of which survive in presentation copies; he received French illuminated manuscripts from his brother Bedford, and other French manuscripts came as booty from the Hundred Years' War, for example those captured by Henry V at Caen and at Meaux.[38] Henry VI's queen, Margaret of Anjou, was given the large, lavishly illuminated manuscript of Alexander Romance material still in the Royal Library by John Talbot, Earl of Shrewsbury, probably as a marriage gift in 1445. The illumination is by a French artist, working perhaps at Rouen, perhaps further north, who also executed two books of hours for Talbot himself.[39] A copy of the Statutes of the Hospital of Sta Maria Nuova in Florence with illumination attributable to Attavante degli Attavanti, one of the leading illuminators in Florence, was sent as a gift from Francesco Portinari to Henry VII in connection with his plans to found a similar hospital in London (fig. 2.6).[40] A second manuscript,[41] also illuminated but by a different Florentine hand, and with the Portinari arms, is perhaps a copy retained by the donor. Another Italian manuscript illuminated by Attavante was presented to Henry VIII: the Lucian and Collenuccio written by Lodovico Arrighi between 1509 and 1517.[42] An Isocrates written by Pierantonio Sallando was presented by Giovanni Boerio to Henry before his accession, probably in 1507 (fig. 14.5).[43]

It is, however, uncertain whether other examples of foreign, luxury illuminated manuscripts in English or Scottish ownership came by gift or by purchase and, if the latter, what sort of purchase. For example, Pamela Tudor-Craig has suggested that the two books of hours owned by William, Lord Hastings, who was executed by Richard III in 1483, were a gift made by Margaret of York, wife of Charles the Bold, Duke of Burgundy, to her niece and nephew, the Princess Elizabeth and the Prince Edward, when she visited England in 1480.[44] She argues that Lord Hastings and/or his descendants obtained them only later. This attractive hypothesis does not ultimately convince, however, because it would mean that, in the Madrid Hours, the Hastings arms were added in England. On the contrary, I believe that the arms are part of the original

38. De la Mare and Hunt 1970, section 1; Alexander 1983, pp. 150, 158–9.
39. BL, Royal ms. 15. E.vi, f. 3; Alexander 1983, 151, pl. 12; for this artist see Plummer and Clark 1982, no. 24; and Reynolds 1993 and 1994, 304–7.
40. Oxford, Bodleian, ms. Bodley 488; Pächt and Alexander 1966–73, 2, no. 334.
41. BL, Add. ms. 40077.
42. BL, Royal ms. 12. C.viii; Trapp 1991, fig. 17; Starkey 1991, ii.15, col. plate; below, p. 313.
43. BL, Add. ms. 19553. I thank Professor A.C. de la Mare for drawing it to my attention.
44. BL, Add. ms. 54782 (D. H. Turner 1983; Backhouse 1996); and Madrid, Lazzaro Galdiano Collection; Tudor-Craig 1987.

illumination by the Master of Mary of Burgundy, and were therefore inserted in Ghent, and consequently that Lord Hastings himself commissioned both Hours in Ghent, even though it is quite possible that one was originally intended as a gift for the young Prince Edward.[45] Janet Backhouse has suggested that Sir John Donne and, possibly, other English patrons, who were active in diplomacy or posted to commands at Calais, may have employed scribes there and then had the manuscripts sent to Bruges or Ghent for illumination.[46] The second Hastings Hours was illuminated by the Flemish illuminator associated with the Master of Mary of Burgundy and known as the Master of Maximilian. Another Sarum Hours illuminated by the Master of Maximilian contains an ownership inscription of Katherine Bray (d.1507), wife of Sir Reginald Bray, an important member of Henry VII's court.[47] Though there are no arms in it and it cannot be certain that Katherine was the first owner, again it seems unlikely that such a fine-quality manuscript was produced for speculative sale.

One instance where it seems reasonably certain that an owner himself commissioned a manuscript abroad – my fifth category – is the Hours of James IV of Scotland.[48] James Wilkie notes that there is no identifiable reference to payment for King James's Hours in the State Treasurer's accounts and deduces that it is therefore possible that the King paid for it personally and not out of public funds. James IV, who was born in 1472, was betrothed to Henry VII's daughter, Margaret Tudor, and a marriage contract was signed on 24 January 1502. The couple were married a little over eighteen months later on 8 August 1503. If, as seems most likely, the manuscript was made for the marriage, then a commission would have to have been placed and the manuscript made within that eighteen-month period. The Hours contains a donor figure of the King in prayer on folio 24v (fig. 2.7) and a full-page miniature of the arms of Scotland with James's motto 'In my defens', with the arms of Scotland and England dimidiated in the border. The identification of the main illuminator, formerly known as the Master of James IV of Scotland, with the already-mentioned Gerard Horenbout, at this period working in Ghent, has been very generally accepted. The manuscript was later given by Margaret to her sister, Mary Tudor, who married Louis XII of France in 1514 (he died within the year and she returned to England). A note on folio 188 reads:

45. Alexander 1989b, p. 312 and n. 245.   46. Backhouse 1994.
47. Alexander 1989b.
48. Vienna, ÖNB., Cod. 1897; Unterkircher and Wilkie 1987; L. J. MacFarlane 1960.

'Madame I pray your grace remember on me when ye loke upon this boke. Your lofing suster Margaret'. Another similar example is Dean Brown's Hours, probably commissioned during his stay in Flanders in 1498.[49]

Unfortunately, with other manuscripts it is much harder, and in the end may prove impossible, to establish with certainty whether they were commissioned abroad, whether they were received as gifts, or whether the artist came himself to England or Scotland. Another book of hours with Flemish illumination, now at Chatsworth, bears an inscription of gift from Henry VII to his same daughter Margaret: 'Remember your kind and loving father in your good prayers' (fig. 2.8).[50] Two illuminators can be distinguished in the Chatsworth Hours, one of whom has been identified as the so-called Master of the Prayerbooks. The latter, however, is like the Master of the Beaufort Saints, an appellation conceal-ing an omnium gatherum of different illuminators working in a generic style. It is not inconceivable that further study might show that either or both illuminators involved in the Chatsworth Hours came to England. However, the manuscript has a fine blind-stamped leather binding which is likely to be Bruges work, and this would suggest that, like the Hours of James IV, it was commissioned in the Netherlands.

The same choices confront us with the Luton Guild Book which is datable 1475 and has a frontispiece showing the English royal family: Edward IV with his Queen and children in prayer. It is clearly by a major artist, in my opinion the Master of Mary of Burgundy.[51] When later entrants to the Guild were recorded, borders were added by a variety of artists and in a variety of styles, but all apparently by native illuminators, even if copying Flemish styles. The implication seems to be that the fron-tispiece, with the related border round the text on the recto opposite, was executed in Flanders, for it is surely highly unlikely that the Master of Mary of Burgundy who, as observed earlier, worked for both Margaret of York and for her step-daughter, Mary of Burgundy, left Ghent to come to England. This was the period during which Margaret's brother, Edward IV, was acquiring his collection of Flemish manuscripts, which were to form the core of the Royal Library and remain the most consider-

49. NLS, ms. 10270; McRoberts 1968; see also 1959.
50. Exhibited, Whitworth Art Gallery 1976, no. 55; reproduction, Chatsworth House 1991, pp. 190–1. Meale 1989, p. 205, contributes a list of other works for English patrons by this artist. See also De Kesel 1992.
51. Sold from the Bute Collection Sotheby's, 13 June 1983, lot 19; now in Luton Museum and Art Gallery; Scott 1996, v. 2, 330, 343, 344.

able surviving example of luxury manuscripts imported by a single owner in the period.

Whereas Edward IV's foreign purchases seem to have been made in a relatively short space of time and all in Flanders, Henry VII's acquisitions extend over a longer span and include manuscripts illuminated in France.[52] A book of hours of the Use of Sarum with a portrait of him kneeling before King David, is clearly French in script and illumination, the latter in the style of the Associate of Maître François (fig. 2.9). Though it might theoretically have been acquired by Henry in exile in France, it seems certain, in view of the royal arms and emblems in the borders, which cannot be later additions, to have been another foreign commission.[53] Imports from France do not appear ever to have been as numerous as from the Netherlands, though manuscripts were illuminated in Rouen for export, an example being the Playfair Hours in the Victoria and Albert Museum.[54] Though the original owner is not known, and the Hours may not in fact have left France until much later, the use is of Sarum and the calendar contains a number of Scottish saints. Further study of other imports from France is needed, both to provide a basic listing and then to attempt to decide whether they were produced for speculative sale or on commission.[55]

By the late fifteenth century, it is evident that an international trade in illuminated manuscripts, particularly those of the greatest luxury, had developed in Europe. This was a new phenomenon. Earlier manuscript production at all levels and throughout Europe had been mainly native, and consumption and marketing were within politically controlled and often even quite narrowly defined geographical areas. While it is certainly true that manuscripts written and illuminated in the university centres, above all Paris and Bologna, circulated very widely throughout Europe in the thirteenth and fourteenth centuries, it seems that prospective owners had to go themselves to Paris or Bologna to buy them.

But how did patrons order work from illuminators, especially when they were widely separated geographically? First, it should be pointed

52. Backhouse 1995; Scott 1996.
53. New York, PML, ms. M. 815; for the artist, Plummer and Clark 1982, nos. 89–93. I thank Kathleen Scott for originally drawing this to my attention. See also Meale 1989, pp. 205, 225 n. 29.
54. L. 475–1918; R. Watson 1984, who also cites two other Hours made in Rouen for Scottish patrons (pp. 35–6), and discusses the organization of the manuscript and printing trade in Rouen in the fifteenth century (ch. 4).
55. For French Hours of Sarum Use in the Walters Art Gallery, see Randall 1993, nos. 104 (ms. W. 234), 105 (ms. W. 248), 148 (ms. W. 283).

out that this did not happen everywhere, but rather occurs mainly in two specific geographical contexts, in Florence, and in Bruges and Ghent, and even there mainly in connection with a limited number of illuminators who evidently had an international reputation.[56] It cannot, therefore, be accidental that in these cities a flourishing book-trade developed in the context of a thriving entrepreneurial mercantile economy. In France, Jean Bourdichon, working at Tours, perhaps also received international commissions, if the dismembered leaves illuminated by him did indeed come from a book of hours belonging to Henry VII. This is very doubtful, however.[57]

Three factors came together to make this new development possible. These were good communications, the ability to transfer payment easily, and the appearance of a type of entrepreneur who stood between producer and patron. This latter could be a merchant dealing in a variety of goods, of which manuscripts might be one, such as Jacques Raponde (Rapondi) from Lucca in early fifteenth-century Paris;[58] or it might also be a professional of the book-trade, like Vespasiano da Bisticci in fifteenth-century Florence – a *cartolaio*, who one might say was a merchant specializing only in books, taking on the organization of their making and their selling and, in the process, putting capital at risk.[59] Occasionally, perhaps, it could be a very successful illuminator such as Simon Bening in Bruges, or Attavante degli Attavanti in Florence, who would himself have taken on the entrepreneurial role. More study of the scripts of such manuscripts is an essential task, still largely to be undertaken, as also of the vernacular components of the texts, including prayers in Italian, Spanish and other languages.[60]

It seems clear that in many instances an intermediary was appointed by the patron. For example, in the commissioning of the Genealogical Roll of Don Fernando of Portugal in 1530, this was the diplomat Damião de Goís, and in that of the Hours of Cardinal Albrecht of Brandenburg, Hans Schenitz.[61] Another documented example is the Bible for which there is a surviving contract between Attavante degli Attavanti and Clemens Cipriani Sernigi 'civis et mercator' of Florence, drawn up on 23

---

56. De Hamel 1983.   57. Voelkle and Wieck 1992, nos. 8–11.
58. Buettner 1988.   59. De la Mare 1985b, ch. 2.
60. De Hamel, 1983, emphasizes the priority of the scribe, who, he points out, was often a foreigner, and the stationer. He also emphasizes the need to study vernacular components. For Attavante, see n. 62.
61. BL, Add. ms. 12531; Kren 1983, no. 9. For the Hours of Albrecht of Brandenburg, formerly in the Astor Collection, see [de Hamel] 1988, lot 65, and Arnould 1993, no. 31.

April 1494.[62] Attavante was to decorate a complete Bible text, to which the Postillae of Nicholas of Lyra were added, the whole filling seven large, thick volumes, for Prince Manuel of Portugal, who succeeded as King in 1495, during the period of illumination. In this case the patron's intermediary and the artist agreed a model, they agreed a timetable as the scribes proceeded in their work, and payment was in stages as the illumination was completed. Another major patron purchasing manuscripts in Florence from outside Italy, in this period, was Matthias Corvinus, King of Hungary (d. 1490), whose library was built up mainly but not exclusively in Italy.[63]

It seems likely that this was the way in which Edward IV of England made his acquisitions in Flanders, c. 1475–80. Janet Backhouse has drawn attention to an account roll document of 14 February 1478 which records a payment to: 'Philip Maisertuell merchant stranger in partie of paiement of £240 for certaine bokes by the said Philip to be provided to the kyng's [Edward IV's] use in the parties beyond the see as in an endentur made betwene the kyngs highnes and the said Philip more plainly it may appier.'[64] The indenture was presumably similar to the Attavante contract, with Maisertuell acting as the intermediary.[65]

These various international patrons have in common a strong sense of what they wanted in terms of specific texts and of quality of production, together with a realization that it was not available to them at home. They therefore went to centres capable of absorbing a large demand for luxury books to be produced within a short space of time.[66] Such manuscripts, however, are at the very topmost echelon of the luxury market. The needs of less wealthy customers were increasingly fulfilled by printed books, the books of hours being now increasingly illustrated with lavish woodcuts, which could on occasion be hand-coloured to simulate illumination.

In conclusion, we can ask why there was such a contrast between the native production of illuminated manuscripts in England in the fourteenth century and that in the fifteenth. If we think of illuminated manuscripts of such major importance, in a European context, as the Queen Mary Psalter, the De Lisle Psalter, and the Tickhill Psalter of the early

62. Milanesi 1885, pp. 164–6; Alexander 1993, pp. 53, 181–2.
63. Balogh 1975.   64. Backhouse 1987, p. 27.   65. Backhouse below, p. 269.
66. Examples are New York, PML, ms. M.52, Breviary for Eleanor of Portugal, c. 1500, illuminated by Sanders Bening and Gerard Horenbout; Cleveland Museum of Art, ms. 63. 256, Hours of Isabella of Castile; and BL, Add. ms. 18851, Breviary of Isabella of Castile. For the latter two manuscripts, see De Winter 1981, and Backhouse 1993.

fourteenth century or, later in the century, of the Bohun manuscripts, there are no illuminated manuscripts surviving, from England in the fifteenth century, to equal them in quality or scale of illumination. Even the English Hours of John, Duke of Bedford, and the Hours of Elizabeth the Queen, both of the early fifteenth century, cannot be considered exceptions to this judgement.[67]

In particular, the question arises as to whether the numerous imports were a cause or a consequence of a decline of manuscript illumination in England. The answer is likely to be a mixture of both. Political instability and particularly the dynastic struggles between the houses of Lancaster and of York will have played a part. Money was available, however, for other artistic purposes, for architecture, for example, and for stained glass. There was no patronage of scribes and illuminators in England to come anywhere near equalling that of the Dukes of Burgundy and the Kings of France and the members of their court circles, or of the Renaissance princes in Italy. Nor did any Queen of England collect illuminated manuscripts on the scale of Margaret of York, after she became the wife of Charles the Bold of Burgundy, or, later, of Margaret of Austria as Regent of the Netherlands. The sums of money spent by these patrons served to underpin an enormous book-trade. In addition to providing guaranteed employment for very considerable numbers of artisans, this led to the development of much more sophisticated methods of book production. It seems likely, though it might prove hard to quantify it scientifically, that streamlined design methods (using the term 'design' to include all aspects of function as well as appearance) led to price effectiveness such that the imports from Flanders succeeded because they were economically so competitive. Codicological studies reveal both the complexity and the discipline involved, in terms of organization and design of these Netherlandish manuscripts.[68] The industry was certainly very self-conscious in terms of self-representation and, among the many examples of portraits of scribes at work, showing in detail their surroundings and their tools, two occur in manuscripts belonging to Edward IV.[69]

There are, of course, other important factors. Texts, it goes without

67. BL, Add. mss. 42131 and 50001; for the fourteenth-century manuscripts, see Sandler 1986 and Alexander and Binski 1987.
68. See, for example, the studies of the library of Raphael de Mercatellis, by Derolez 1979, and Arnould 1992.
69. BL, Royal ms. 14 E. 1, Vincent of Beauvais, vol. I, f. 3; Backhouse 1987, pl. 3; and Royal ms. 18 E.III, Valerius Maximus, f. 24, dated 1479.

saying, are crucial and the necessity of importing humanist texts from Italy has already been referred to. In one area, vernacular texts, English artisans were in a stronger position and it was harder for foreigners to compete. That, significantly, was the market on which early native printers, Caxton and his successors, also concentrated.

The question of quality and skill on the part of the illuminators arises here too, both in general and in relation to these secular texts. Though it is true that, throughout the history of manuscript illumination, liturgical or devotional manuscripts tend to be qualitatively of a higher standard than secular texts, there were more exceptions to this rule at the end of the Middle Ages than earlier, as part of a more general shift in patronage towards secular ownership. The grandest surviving native productions of the fifteenth century, especially later in the century, tend to be manuscripts such as the copy of Lydgate's *Troy Book* of *c.* 1460, now in the John Rylands University Library, Manchester.[70]

Another question, raised by Kathleen Scott, is whether Wycliffite criticism of religious imagery had a continuing effect in the fifteenth century in England.[71] English border work continues to be of a high standard of professionalism and it could be claimed that those responsible for it, whom Dr Scott shows to be likely to have been different individuals from those responsible for the miniatures, in many if not most cases, were able to produce consistently better-quality work than their colleagues. The decoration of Wycliffe Bibles of the late fourteenth to early fifteenth century, though always non-figurative, is frequently of a very high standard, too.

A last observation concerns the imitation of styles. This may not have been all one way. Some borders in fifteenth-century books of hours illuminated in Utrecht are in English style, for example an Hours of Sarum Use in the Bodleian Library, which had belonged to Queen Mary, according to Richard Connock, its owner in 1615.[72] Nicholas Rogers has argued that either an English craftsman went to Utrecht to work on this manuscript, or that, more likely, a Dutch artist had learnt to imitate English work.[73]

It is also clear that native craftsmen copied foreign styles, especially at the end of the fifteenth century and into the sixteenth. At this period, the *trompe l'oeil* borders of flowers, fruits and insects introduced by

70. Ms. English 1; Lawton 1983, pp. 41–69; Scott 1996, v. 2, cat. 93.
71. Scott 1996, v. 1, 43–7.
72. Oxford, Bodleian Library, ms. Auct. D. inf. 2.13; Pächt and Alexander 1966–73, I, no. 221.
73. Rogers 1984, ch. 11.

Ghent/Bruges illuminators from the 1480s onwards are widely adopted. Several manuscripts written for Christopher Urswick by a foreign scribe, Pieter Meghen, were apparently decorated by native artisans in England in this style.[74]

Another example is a copy of Cicero, *De officiis*, printed on vellum by Fust and Schoeffer in Mainz in 1465, now in Emmanuel College, Cambridge. This was later decorated with borders in this style and with the English royal arms and Prince of Wales's feathers. It has an historiated initial of a teaching scene: a young person richly dressed and a seated figure with doctor's cap (fig. 2.10). The young person must be either Prince Arthur – the traditional identification in the College – who died in 1502, or the future Henry VIII prior to his accession in 1509.[75] The work is expert, related to the Dark Eyes style, and there are additional initials and borders to books II and III and to *Paradoxa*. It is uncertain whether it is by a foreign or native illuminator. Another example of the same *trompe l'oeil* border style is in the presentation manuscript copy of Henry VIII's *Assertio septem sacramentorum adversus Martin. Lutherum*, sent to Pope Leo X by the King in 1521.[76] The style was by now so widespread that it was also copied by illuminators in France. Aspects of the decoration in the *Assertio* suggest a French, rather than a Flemish, version of the style.

If the ultimate purpose of the 1484 Statute was – as with other craft-related legislation, most notably regarding cloth finishing – to encourage a native production by making it possible for foreigners to come in to teach the necessary skills, we must conclude that it was, as with so many such well-intentioned governmental measures, too little and too late. The Statute was repealed in 1534, possibly in response to pressure from the native book-trade. That trade was in any case now mainly in the

---

74. Wells Cathedral, mss. Book 5 (Trapp 1991, fig. 4), and Oxford, Bodleian, ms. Rawl. A. 431 (Trapp 1991, fig. 7). Also Oxford, Bodleian, mss. Barlow 14 and Douce 110 (Pächt and Alexander 1966–73, 3, nos. 1170, 1173; Trapp 1975, nos. 20–1). Other relevant examples are the copies of the Quardipartite indenture of Westminster Abbey of 1504: Oxford, Bodleian, mss. Barlow 28, Rawl. C. 370 (Pächt and Alexander 1966, nos. 1171–2, pl. CVIII). The change is clearly apparent in the Luton Guild Book mentioned earlier, n. 51, and in the St Albans Benefactors' Book, BL, Cotton ms. Nero D vii (Sandler 1986, cat. no. 158). See also Scott 1989. Trapp 1991, p. 83, quotes Skelton's description of Wolsey's book 'enpicturid with gressoppis and waspis / with butterflys . . . and slymy snaylis' (Skelton 1983, p. 345)!

75. *GW* 6921. Cambridge, Emmanuel Coll., ms. 5.3.11, f. 1. Noticed in 1600 by the German traveller, Baron Waldstein: 'a copy of Cicero's de Officiis printed almost as soon as the printing press was invented'; see Waldstein 1981, 105, pl. IV. I am grateful to Dr F. H. Stubbings for the reference.

76. BAV, ms. Vat. lat. 3731; Trapp and Schulte Herbrüggen 1997, no. 117; Morello 1985–6, no. 127, colour pl.

hands of the printers, and the production of hand-written or hand-illuminated manuscripts was only a tiny fraction of what it had once been. When something special was needed, however, it seems it still had to be either commissioned abroad, or given to a resident foreigner such as Gerard Horenbout.

3
Printing

LOTTE HELLINGA

Early printers and the book-trade

In 1471, during his exile in Cologne, the art of printing first attracted the attention of William Caxton, at that time Merchant Adventurer and former Governor to the English Nation in Bruges. The technique was then still something of a novelty, though it was no longer new. In the city of Cologne a printing press had flourished since 1465, and since 1470 several other printers had set up shop. Ulrich Zell, Cologne's first printer, had been previously associated with the earliest ventures in printing in Mainz, and remained connected with the still-expanding business of Peter Schoeffer in that city. Zell became a specialist in the production of small scholastic texts, geared to use in universities, but printed in a style much influenced by the manuscript tradition of the local monastic houses. Schoeffer, by contrast, mainly published very large folio editions of legal and patristic texts, and several editions of the Latin Bible, all intended for a market much larger than local.

Zell's move down the Rhine was by no means the first migration of the new technique. Following its invention by Gutenberg, working in Strasbourg in the 1440s, and his first successful production of a major printed book, the famous Bible, in Mainz in the 1450s, printers leaving that city had set up presses in Bamberg and in Strasbourg. Soon after, in 1465, two other printers, clerics from the Mainz area, began printing in the monastery of Santa Scolastica in Subiaco, whence two years later they transferred themselves to Rome. Venice, as well as cities in the German-speaking countries – Augsburg, Basel, Nuremberg, Beromünster and Konstanz – introduced printing in the late 1460s. In this period there was also a venture by members of Gutenberg's family in Eltville, close to Mainz but on the other bank of the Rhine. In 1470, printing was introduced at the Sorbonne in Paris. In all these places, the first printers had in all likelihood some connection, even if tenuous, with Mainz and the first Mainz enterprises. By the 1470s, however, the exclusiveness of the circle of those initiated in the art had begun to break. Among the printers Caxton would have encountered in Cologne, only Ulrich Zell had direct links with Mainz.

Thus Caxton was introduced into a world which not only had recently acquired an innovatory technique, but also was adapting to the imperative of finding the means to expand communication: printing had forced the book-trade rapidly to develop channels by which to market the merchandise that could now be produced on a scale unimaginable only a few years before. Printers had already learned that it was necessary to strike a balance between production and sale, and discovered that the market for books in Latin had no limits (in the world of their time), provided one was in a location favourable to transport and long-distance communication, and could make use of organizations and mechanisms already in existence for goods of a more traditional nature. The early printers in Rome had had some hard lessons to learn, but Peter Schoeffer in Mainz soon traded with regular contacts in Venice, Basel, Strasbourg and Paris. The printers in Cologne were situated in a city that held a key position in commerce on the Rhine, as well as in the east–west overland route. There can be little doubt that these factors did not escape Caxton. They must have had an immediate appeal to the Merchant Adventurer, long-experienced in mediating between London and the main centres of commerce in Flanders.[1]

Although Caxton's name does not appear in any book printed in Cologne, and we therefore do not know the precise nature of his involvement in their production, he can now confidently be identified as being responsible for part of the books traditionally known as the work of the 'Printer of S. Augustinus de Fide', in 1471 and 1472. These are the years during which Caxton is documented as residing in Cologne.[2] Typographical analysis as well as documentary evidence have corroborated what his successor, Wynkyn de Worde, printed more than twenty years later, in his edition in English of Bartholomaeus Anglicus, *De proprietatibus rerum*: that Caxton had printed the same text in Cologne, in Latin.[3] Caxton may have led a small consortium consisting of Johann

1. General: *BMC* introductions to vols. I–VIII; Hirsch 1967, although now out of date for detail. For Caxton: Painter 1976; Blake 1996; Blake 1985 for a bibliography of literature on Caxton.   2. Needham 1986b; cf. Corsten 1999.
3. Introductory verse in De Worde's edition of Trevisa's translation of Bartholomaeus Anglicus, *STC* 1536.

Veldener, the punchcutter who was responsible for several of the types with which he began his career in printing, and Johann Schilling, a somewhat peripatetic printer who later worked in Basel and in Vienne in the Dauphiné. Three books can be ascribed to this enterprise, all in Latin, among which the Bartholomaeus Anglicus is largest and most ambitious (see frontispiece to pls. and fig. 3.1). Two are by English authors – Bartholomaeus, known as De Glanvilla, and Walter Burley; the third, the *Gesta Romanorum*, is a text with English associations.[4] Although Caxton may show a patriotic bias in his choice of publications, there is no sign that these books were intended for the English market. At all events, there is no record of early English owners for them. Although larger than other books produced in Cologne at the time, they conform entirely to the typographical style characteristic of that city – a style which we shall also encounter in the earliest printing in Oxford – and to the expectations of readers in the western part of the German-speaking lands. It is as if Caxton wished to bring the best of English writing to this part of the world, in the language in which it was accessible there.

If this may have been his policy in Cologne, he must have reversed it completely when he returned to Bruges a year later, in 1473.[5] In Bruges he turned towards publishing in the English language and for the English market, receiving encouragement to pursue this course from Margaret of York, Duchess of Burgundy, who at the time moved her court between the cities of Flanders and Brabant. Margaret of York was then, following Burgundian court traditions, collecting fine manuscripts, through purchase and by commission from the best scribes and artists working in Ghent and Brussels at that time. Her patronage of Caxton is in line with the interest she was showing in the world of books, although the text concerned, *The Recuyell of the Historyes of Troye*, mythically linked though it was with the history of the House of Burgundy, has nothing in common with the other works associated with her, which are all devotional.[6]

Late in 1475 or early in 1476, Caxton moved to Westminster, and began to concentrate on the market in England.[7] Having perceived the wide-ranging potential of the trade in Latin books, from then on he published only what could not be procured from elsewhere through the

4. *GW* 3403, 5784 and 10881.
5. *BMC* IX, pp. l–li, 129–31; *HPT*, pp. 21–4; Painter 1976, pp. 59–71.
6. *STC* 15375. Margaret of York's manuscripts are listed by Dogaer 1975, M. J. Hughes 1984 and L. Hellinga 1991b. Cf. N. Morgan 1992.   7. L. Hellinga 1982, pp. 80–3.

trade: books in the English language and, occasionally, Latin works exclusively for use in England, such as Books of Hours of Sarum Use, or Clement Maydestone's *Directorium Sacerdotum*. Some of this work was commissioned by others, for example the indulgences he printed. In adopting this strategy for his publishing venture, he set the pattern for the printed book in Britain for several centuries. It is a pattern with more than one inherent paradox. The character of book production in the British Isles had a strong national identity, long before the kingdoms became united. This was due to language, since there was a much higher percentage of vernacular texts, or texts with a specific English use – for example books of the common law – than was the average in other language areas. Production, however, was almost entirely dependent on materials, techniques and skills brought in from overseas, and it was a long time before English-born printers and book-sellers outnumbered their colleagues who had come from abroad. Not until 1534 did legislation end the supremacy of foreigners in the book-trade.[8] Similarly, most academics and professionals could avail themselves of more books printed abroad than of books produced in the British Isles. Their standards and expectations were set by those books, whose standards were not matched by the books produced in Britain until well into the seventeenth century. Yet this Englishness, imposed as a pronounced limitation in the selection of titles published by Caxton and his contemporaries, turned, centuries later into a great strength with the ascendancy of the English language in the world at large, and in learning in the British Isles. By the late seventeenth century, this was matched by much improved quality and sometimes even superiority in the techniques of book production. The basis of this subsequent superiority in publishing was laid, however, at the very beginning by concentration on printing in the English language; but by the end of the period covered in this volume the time when British books might be used as models of style was still far off.

Typography

Before considering in more detail the development of printing in the British Isles, it is necessary to survey briefly the technique adopted by Caxton and his successors at a time when it was no longer experimental. Almost everything that can be said about the technical aspects of the work of the early printers is based on assumption, either by applying to

8. See Appendix, pp. 608–10.

the earlier times the facts which are known with certainty about the techniques of the later period, or by interpreting what can be observed in the books they printed.

Technically, Gutenberg's invention was an advanced achievement in metallurgy, made possible by the rapid progressive development of the metal industry in southern Germany in the early fifteenth century. The production of type was an ingenious process.[9] For each character, a punch was cut in steel, the hardest available metal. The steel punch was used to stamp the character in a copper matrix of fixed dimensions. The matrix was carefully adjusted to fit exactly into a mould, an instrument – in itself a sophisticated invention – which in turn could be adjusted to the varying sizes of the matrices.[10] When closed, the mould was filled with hot liquid metal with a low melting point, an alloy of lead, tin and traces of other metals. A piece of type, a small bar of metal with a letter at its end, would be the result. The mould would dictate the dimensions of each piece, the height of the type to paper, which had to be uniform, and the body of the type, which would vary per fount, depending on the size of the impression the type was required to make. A complete set of letters and other symbols, of uniform body-size and designed to match, cast in the required quantities, is called a fount of type. Since type had always to be fitted with other type of the same fount, and since increasingly more than one style was to be combined to fit together on the page, standardization of body-sizes did not take long to develop. The number of individual pieces of type required for a fount would vary with each character: most languages need many e's and n's but very few z's. With a complete fount of type compositors could build up tightly fitting lines of text into metal pages, filled up and made firm where necessary with spacing material that was not to be printed on the page. The pages thus formed were tightly held together with string. The now solid typeset pages were then put together in frames, or 'chases', firmly secured with wooden quoins and wedges, in combinations called 'formes', allowing the printing of one side of a sheet. 'Imposition', as this process is called, required different patterns for the combination of pages in the chases, according to the number of times the printed sheet was to be folded to be part of a quire – once for an edition in-folio, twice for a quarto, and so on.[11] Each forme was then placed on the press. After the required number of copies

9. For a much more detailed description of typefounding after *c.* 1500, see Gaskell 1972.
10. For illustrations of the typefounder's mould, matrices and type, see Carter 1969, figs. 2–11; Gaskell 1972, fig. 2; Parker 1974.
11. For imposition schemes, see Gaskell 1972, pp. 78–117.

had been printed – on paper, or, less frequently, on vellum – the pages of type would be taken off the press. Once they had been cleaned, loosened and disassembled, the type was distributed by putting each piece back into the appropriate box in the type-cases, ready to be used again for forming new words. Preparation, in investment, organization and technical skill, was enormous in comparison with what was required for producing books in manuscript. The capacity, however, to produce quantities of books, the economies eventually made by this form of production, and the possibility of producing virtually uniform texts combined with potential profit, were incentive enough to offset the disadvantages of the initially slower production process.

Long before the fifteenth century, conventions had grown in medieval western scripts of linking small linguistic units together, contracting single words into larger linguistic units, and abbreviating long words, or even combinations of words which the reader would immediately recognize and absorb in their entirety. This was in the interests of economy in materials, relieving the writing hand, and reducing the time and repetitive effort required for copying out texts. Letter forms would vary according to their position in the word or even in the sentence. The much more complicated process of producing texts in type brought about a change in these conventions. The production of each type in metal, especially if the quality was to be high, was a lengthy and costly process compared with writing individual letters. The first typographers – Gutenberg himself and the makers of type who worked under his direct influence – attempted to match the standards of manuscripts of their day by reproducing the scribal conventions which were familiar to their readers' eyes. They went to great lengths to design a large number of separate units that represented current scribal ligatures, contractions and variant forms for the same grapheme. For Gutenberg's Bible type, and other types used as late as the 1480s, as many as 280 distinct typographical units, or 'sorts', have been counted, although logically a type-case should contain hardly more than 70 sorts for representing individual letters as capitals and minuscules ('upper case' and 'lower case'), for numerals, symbols and punctuation. Such large numbers made it clear to early typographers that it was in their interest to reduce the number of different characters represented in a fount, especially since, before long, most printers began to work with more than one fount in order to distinguish titles, chapter headings, commentary, marginalia and the like, by varying the design and the size of the typeface. The gradations of emphasis in presenting a text and the extraneous matter that might accompany it were effects that could easily be achieved by scribes, but in a printing house required considerable investment.

In the course of the first two or three decades of printing, a distinction developed between founts of type with very extensive type-cases representing all these graphic variations, but with short lives, and types that remained in use for a very long time, in which the number of characters is significantly lower. Behind this we may infer technical differences, a long-lived fount of type being the end-product of punches and matrices which had required greater skills to manufacture, and entailing a greater investment for the printer who purchased it. In due course, after some twenty to thirty years, the production of long-lived type, carefully designed but with a smaller number of sorts, became the prevailing practice. This meant that a simplification in the presentation of graphic forms had to be accepted. Typographers and printers had to decide what was relevant to convey their message, and what variant forms could be dispensed with. A continuous selection process can be observed in the further development of typographical form. The history of type-design is one of experiment and steady evolution, but the technique of typefounding remained based on Gutenberg's invention until late in the nineteenth century. From the beginning, the production of type was a specialism in the hands of a small number of experts, whose skills were in great demand. There is very little direct evidence for the trade in type in the early period, and none in the British Isles. It is doubtful that type was designed, cut and produced here on any significant scale, but in the early years some production of type may have been undertaken in Oxford and St Albans. Procuring suitable type was a priority for every printer, and there is much evidence that, for printers in Britain in the period covered in this volume, it was usually obtained from abroad through well-established relations with punchcutters and typefounders in France, Germany and the Low Countries, and, where necessary, was adapted for printing the English language.

Style and purpose

A set of conventions regarding styles of type developed early and was based on distinctions made in scribal traditions. This complicates what might at first appear to be a straightforward story of simplification, of reduction in the number of ligatures and contractions by a gradual departure from scribal conventions.

Long before the fifteenth century, a variety of styles of script had developed in manuscript books, which related to the purpose for which they were to be used and to the place of writing. Script style communicated to the contemporary reader a great deal about what to expect from the text: was it learned, professional, in the vernacular, for information or for entertainment? The script-forms used for writing Latin, the universal vehicle for learned expression and communication, had more features in common, throughout the whole ecclesiastical and academically educated community, than the forms of script used for the vernacular. In vernacular texts written in the Middle Ages (and much later) one can immediately perceive script-features linked to the use of a particular language, which express its identity, in graphic form, almost as strongly as the language itself.

In the literate world, scribes might move from place to place, and they adapted – up to a point – their hands to the requirements of location and purpose. With the introduction of mechanically produced letter- and word-forms, the need to adapt took on a different dimension: books could move far from the place where they were produced, and so could printing types. Ultimately it was the readers who had to adapt rather than the typographers and the printers who now had to judge what the market would bear. For printing in Latin, enough common ground was found to bridge any regional differences. Latin works of traditional learning were predominantly printed in a style now commonly named 'a rotunda', and sometimes by its contemporaries 'venetica' (because, although its use was ubiquitous, they were still aware that it had developed in Venice, the greatest centre for producing theological and legal texts; compare fig. 22.3, for a Venetian type with adaptations for English language). For texts of 'modern' learning and classical texts, influenced by the humanist scholars, printers in Venice and Rome had in the 1470s introduced the 'roman' typeface, based on the script developed by humanists in the fifteenth century. Liturgical works form a category on their own, with their own styles, often with a somewhat more regional character. For vernacular languages, however, the provision of adequate type expressing the identity of the language required variation in styles, even in places where no punchcutters were available. Nowhere can this be better demonstrated than for the earliest printing in English.

Printing types in England

In the period up to 1557 (and long after), printers in England and Scotland were almost fully dependent on the printing types that could be obtained from suppliers on the Continent. Although there may have been some experimentation in producing type by some of the printing houses outside the two capitals, the main printers all worked with types of foreign origin. The large-scale importation of books from the same continental centres of book production from where types were bought would have created an expectation of what a printed book should look like. It is useful to discuss first the mainstream of book production, before a more cursory look at the exceptions.[12]

As so often, Caxton's initiatives determined the course of events until well after his death in 1492, and his typography is reviewed here in some detail.[13] Caxton and Johann Veldener left Cologne at approximately the same time, at the end of 1472 or early in 1473, Caxton returning to Bruges and Veldener settling not far away in Louvain. It was at precisely this time that presses began to work elsewhere in the Netherlands, in Alost in Flanders and in Utrecht, and both Caxton and Veldener are among the earliest printers in the Low Countries.[14] It has to be assumed that neither of them lost any time in pursuing their new-found interests. Veldener continued to adapt and develop the family of typefaces he had started in Cologne, and to use it for his own publications, as well as producing a version for the Brethren of the Common Life in Brussels. Caxton began preparations for printing the *Recuyell of the Histories of Troye*.[15] At that point he must have decided that the typeface used in his publications in Cologne was not suited to a text in English, or for a book that was to be presented to readers in England as fit for the entourage of the Duchess of Burgundy. It cannot be a coincidence that the typeface in which the *Recuyell* is printed seems to be modelled on the hand of the scribe David Aubert, who at about the same time wrote, in Ghent, several of the splendid manuscripts commissioned by Margaret of York (cf. fig. 12.1).[16] There is no way of knowing for certain whether Johann Veldener created this typeface. Stylistically it stands on its own, and there are no material links with other typefaces. It is not related to any English hands, but English scribal conventions (terminal flourishes, looped ascenders)

12. *STC* vol. III surveys all printers in the British Isles active before 1640. For the fifteenth century: Duff 1917; *BMC* XI, forthcoming, including a detailed analysis and reproductions of all types used in England in the fifteenth century. For types used in the sixteenth century: Isaac 1930-2, 1936. See also below pp. 75-9.   13. Blades 1861-3, vol. II; Barker 1976.
14. *HPT* pp. 10-24.   15. *STC* 15375.
16. Guy de Thurno, *La vision de l'âme*, with date 1 February 1474, and *Les visions du Chevalier Tundale*, with date March 1474, both at the J. P. Getty Museum, Los Angeles CA; *Traités moraux et religieux*, with date March 1475, Oxford Bodl, ms. Douce 365; Frère Laurent, *Somme le Roi*, with date 1475; *Bible moralisée*, without date, Brussels RL ms. 9106 and ms. 9030-7; Boethius, *De consolatione philosophiae*, with date 1476, Jena UB ms. El.F.85. Cf. p. 67, note 6. For David Aubert, see Straub 1995.

are faithfully reproduced, making for a complicated and extensive type-case (see fig. 3.2).[17] It bears the hallmarks of a one-off experiment. When Caxton left Bruges for Westminster, he left his first English type behind, but took with him two new types (one of them already used in Bruges) which without any doubt were made by Veldener. One of them (Type 3) was also sold to a number of printers in the Netherlands; of the other, which for years to come was to be Caxton's main text type in bastarda style (Type 2), Veldener used a few lines in one of his own publications, when it was still in an experimental phase. It was a remarkably elegant typeface of generous size, clearly inspired by the scribal traditions of the ample, luxury manuscripts produced for the court of Burgundy (see fig. 3.3).[18] Its direct model is reputedly the hand of Colard Mansion, scribe and printer in Bruges, with whom Caxton must have entered some form of partnership before his departure for Westminster. In spite of some alien features, its rounded forms will have just, perhaps only just, made it acceptable to readers in England. They must soon have got used to it. The first edition of the *Canterbury Tales*, printed in the year after Caxton's arrival in Westminster,[19] would have won over even those unaccustomed to such graphic grace.

For many books printed in England, Caxton's bastarda type set a pattern which lasted for over ten years. In 1480, a scaled-down version made its appearance in his work (Type 4; see fig. 25.2).[20] It is again impossible to decide whether this was the work of Veldener, or of a punchcutter instructed to follow Veldener's example as closely as he could. The quality of Type 4 was high, as its durability testifies, and it may well have been the work of this very experienced punchcutter. Its smaller size made it much more economical than the large-size bastarda (Type 2), and it must have been an investment made when planning the editions of lengthy texts which were produced in the following years: a second edition of the *Canterbury Tales*, Thomas Malory's *Morte Darthur*, Gower's *Confessio Amantis*, and the *Golden Legend*, to name the largest.[21] By then the 'Burgundian' forms had clearly become acceptable. They were not only continued by Caxton himself, but echoes of them – if not derived directly

17. The composition of the typecase (lithograph): Blades 1861–3, pl. 11, rpt. Barker 1976; also Blades 1861–3, pls. 5, 6, 12; Duff 1917 pl. 1; *BMC* IX, pl. 1B (Type 120 B); *HPT* pls. 21–2.
18. The composition of the typecase (lithograph): Blades 1863, pl. 13, rpt. Barker 1976; also Blades 1863, pls. 7, 14–15; Duff 1917, pl. 2; *BMC* IX, pl. 1B (Type 135 B); *HPT* pls. 35, 37–8. Jeudwine 1979 helpfully surveys types and styles over the whole period.   19. *STC* 5082.
20. The composition of the typecase illustrated (lithograph): Blades 1861–3, pl. 18, rpt. Barker 1976; also Blades 1863, pls. 19–20; Duff 1917, pls. 5, 6.
21. *STC* 5083, 801, 12142, 24873.

from the same matrices, copied from Caxton's books – can be found in the work of other printers in the 1480s: the Schoolmaster Printer in St Albans, the London printers John Lettou and William de Machlinia and the anonymous printer of *The Siege of Rhodes* who was related to them.[22]

The heavy and rather decorative textura which Caxton had brought to England, and which had been obtained from Veldener (Caxton Type 3), was used by him for contrast, as a heading type, or to substitute for red printing as in his Boethius and in John Tiptoft's translation of Cicero.[23] He and his successor, Wynkyn de Worde, used it also occasionally for Latin books intended mainly for ecclesiastical use, for example an *Ordinale Sarum*.[24] Some of Caxton's contemporaries (the St Albans printer and William de Machlinia) also obtained the use of this type and adapted it for combining with lighter typefaces (see fig. 3.4).[25] Caxton himself commissioned, in 1486, two typefaces which were virtually copies of the earlier types (Types 5 and 6) and a much smaller type only rarely used (Type 7).[26] These three types may also have been obtained from Veldener.

In his last purchase of type, however, Caxton once again changed direction, and once again set a pattern which even more printers were to follow over a long period of time: in 1490 or 1491 he purchased a high-quality fount from Paris, where several expert typefounders were active. The type (Type 8) is in a textura style, adopted by many printers in Paris and Rouen, and obviously enjoying considerable popularity (scc fig. 3.6).[27] Although the bastarda types continued to be used for a while in England, the Parisian style became the style of choice; after it was adopted in the 1490s by Wynkyn de Worde and Richard Pynson, it developed during the sixteenth century into the 'black-letter' style. In England and Scotland, or, to be more precise, in London and in Edinburgh, the black-letter remained in general use for all vernacular printing long after the pre-black-letter textura was superseded in its country of origin by roman style for printing in French (cf. figs. 24.1, 26.2, 26.3, 28.1).[28] A bastarda style made only an occasional late appearance. Sometimes a specific intent

---

22. Reproduced in Duff 1917, pls. 44; 23, 24; 29. St Albans also in Barker 1979, pp. 260–1.
23. Composition of the type-case illustrated (lithograph): Blades 1861–3, pl. 16, rpt. Barker 1976; also Blades 1861–3, pl. 17; Duff 1917, pl. 4; *HPT* pls. 61–4; L. Hellinga 1982, pp. 69–76.   24. *STC* 16228. Cf. Duff 1917, pl. 16.
25. Duff 1917, pls. 23, 44; Partridge 1983.
26. Composition of the type-cases of Types 6 and 7 illustrated (lithograph): Blades 1861–3, pls. 21, 23, rpt. Barker 1976; also Blades 1861–3, pls. 22, 24; Duff 1917, pls. 7–9.
27. Not distinguished by Blades. See Barker 1976 for an analysis of the origin of the French types; Duff 1917, pl. 10.   28. Carter 1969, pp. 79–88.

can be surmised, as in the edition of Chaucer's works, printed by Thomas Godfray in 1532,[29] where the bastarda may have indicated the antiquity of the text. Robert Wyer used it for some English printing, perhaps more by chance than by design.[30] In legal printing by John Rastell it may have continued a tradition associating the style with Norman-French (see figs. 20.2a–b and 20.1),[31] whereas his son William used it for texts with a historical flavour, a translation of Caesar's *Commentaries* (1530),[32] and a small one as a contrasting type in his edition of Robert Fabyan's *Chronicle* (1533).[33] By Thomas Berthelet it could simply be used as a contrasting type, either for English or Latin.[34]

The sense of style in vernacular printing may well primarily have its roots in awareness of linguistic identity, after the Reformation mainly following the lines of the religious divide. The romance-language countries – the first among them being Italy in the 1490s, followed by France from the 1520s – adopted roman type for general use, whether Latin or vernacular. The countries with roots in the Germanic languages adopted either variations on the black-letter for their vernacular printing, or went down the route of the 'schwabacher' styles, as in the German-speaking countries. Here the influence of the great printing houses in south-west Germany, Anton Koberger in Nuremberg the first among them, had dominated the style. English and Scottish printers continued to work with black-letter and some bastarda types mainly obtained from France, later adding roman and italic types from Cologne, Basel and Antwerp. By using an abundance of ornamental material – fleurons, borders, initials – however, they often gave their work a character of its own. Adaptation to English-language use by expanding the type-case with tall or ornamental 'w', 'thorn' and 'yogh', and sometimes by adding looped ascenders, ligatures, contractions and terminal flourishes, would contribute to an English aspect of the page.[35]

Still belonging to the mainstream of book production are the gradual additions, in the course of the sixteenth century, of other styles to the repertoire. Pynson, in 1509, was the first to introduce a roman fount in Pietro Griffo, *Oratio* . . . and Savonarola, *Sermo* . . . , texts with obvious Italian associations.[36] He used, in 1519, a smaller roman type for printing English sentences in William Horman, *Vulgaria*,[37] a significant event in

29. *STC* 5068; Isaac 1930–2, fig. 77; 1936, pl. 30. 30. Isaac 1930–2, figs. 68–70; 1936, pl. 29.
31. Isaac 1936, pl. 13. 32. *STC* 4337, Isaac 1930–2, fig. 74; 1936, pl. 15.
33. *STC* 10660, Isaac 1930–2, fig. 75; 1936, pl. 14. 34. Isaac 1930–2, fig. 63; 1936, pl. 24.
35. Jeudwine 1979, p. 272. 36. *STC* 12413, 21800. 37. *STC* 13811. Isaac 1930–2, fig. 21.

education, for this was the first time in English printing that roman type was deemed suitable for children's reading matter. (For the roman type, see fig. 14.3.) From then on, roman types can be found for printing Latin, and sporadically in English-language books for providing contrast. John Siberch used a good roman type during his few years in Cambridge (1521–3/4), where he printed books in Latin, and combined it with Greek type.[38] Thomas Berthelet, one of the most distinguished and prolific of the London printers, used it very successfully, in layouts which seem to be modelled on books printed in Basel.[39]

It is not until the very end of the period discussed here that a major work in English heralds a change in the presentation of printed books. It is Robert Record, *The castle of knowledge*,[40] printed by Reyner Wolfe in 1556. Wolfe was an exceptional printer. Born in Gelderland he had been known as a book-seller in England from 1530, and became in 1536, after denization, a freeman of the Company of Stationers. While frequently visiting the Frankfurt fair and maintaining contact with the main printing houses in Basel and Cologne, he began printing in London in 1542, albeit on a modest scale. In 1547 he was appointed King's Printer in Latin, Greek and Hebrew, in what must have been a weak echo of the ambitions of the Imprimerie Royale in Paris and perhaps also of the Collegium Trilingue in Louvain. He fulfilled few of the aspirations to print in exotic types, and never even had a Hebrew fount, but that he was widely respected is evident from the fact that he was Master of the Stationers' Company in 1560, 1564, 1567 and 1572. He died in 1573.[41] *The castle of knowledge* shows that Wolfe was capable of producing work that could equal high-quality books of the period printed, for example, in Basel, a centre which seems to have influenced him most. There is an excellent balance of a combination of contrasting types, as well as good illustrative material and woodcut initials to lighten the effect. A lightening effect is also due to the judicious use of italic, which he had used earlier on, in the first edition of Robert Record, *The pathway to knowledge, containing the first principles of geometrie*,[42] adapted for English printing from its Basel origins by an extravagantly flourished w. Italic, with its flavour of high fashion, was first developed in Venice in the first decade of the sixteenth century, and its first appearance in England had been its use

38. Goldschmidt 1953, *passim* and esp. fig. 2; Isaac 1930–2, fig. 49; 1936, pl. 16.
39. Isaac 1930–2, fig. 66; Jeudwine 1979, p. 275.
40. *STC* 20796; Jeudwine 1979, p. 275; Isaac 1936, pl. 45.
41. Duff 1905, pp. 171–2; *STC* vol. III, p. 186.
42. *STC* 20812; Isaac, 1936, pl. 44; Jeudwine 1979, p. 276.

by Wynkyn de Worde in his editions, both of 1528, of Lucian,[43] and of Robert Wakefield's *Oratio de laudibus trium linguarum*.[44] In the latter book, a few words in Greek, Arabic and Hebrew scripts made an isolated appearance. They were inserted as small woodcut blocks in the text – the Hebrew, inappropriately, representing vocalized cursive script. Four years later, Thomas Berthelet used a good italic, obtained from Cologne, for the minutes of the hearing in the Roman Curia of Henry VIII's suit for divorce.[45] Italic remained in use for Latin only until Wolfe's disregard for the linguistic barrier.

There are a few exceptions to this general 'mainstream' pattern. The most notable is printing in Oxford. The anonymous printer of the first three books printed in Oxford, in 1478 and 1479, worked with a type obtained from Cologne and identifiable as used by Cologne printers, resulting in books which are indistinguishable in general aspect from the massive production of quarto editions in that city.[46] The type disappeared without trace, together with the printer. Although his successor, Theodoric Rood, hailed from Cologne, it is more difficult to determine the origin of the six types he used, sometimes in association with Thomas Hunt . They would all have felt at home in the Rhineland, and although the last type, a large textura, was mainly used for printing, in 1486, John Mirk's *Liber festivalis* in English,[47] it is not a type with an English character. Rood's types must have been either imported, or cut in Oxford by a punchcutter who came from the Cologne area. There was no further printing in Oxford for almost exactly a century, except for the short-lived venture of John Scolar, who produced eight books in the years 1517 and 1518. His stock of type seems to indicate that he had a connection with Wynkyn de Worde.[48]

Similarly, some types in London, of not fully determined origin, were probably obtained by alien printers through connections in their native countries. Whereas William de Machlinia used two rotunda types of unknown origin (Types 2 and 3), one of his bastarda types can be connected with printing in Bruges,[49] and perhaps with Johann Veldener, and another (Type 1) either with Veldener or with Caxton (see fig. 3.4).[50] Wynkyn de Worde probably obtained through his relations in Holland a

43. *STC* 16891; Isaac 1930–2, fig. 10b; 1936, pl. 2.
44. *STC* 24944; Isaac 1930–2, 12. Wakefield 1989. I am grateful to Dr A. K.Offenberg for his observations on the Hebrew forms.   45. *STC* 21310; Isaac 1930–2, fig. 65a; 1936, pl. 23a.
46. De la Mare and Hellinga 1978, pp. 196–7.   47. *STC* 17958; Duff 1917, pl. 42.
48. Isaac 1930–2, fig. 46; Barker 1978, pp. 4–5.   49. *HPT* pl. 86.
50. Duff 1917, pls. 23, 24; Partridge 1983.

square Dutch text-type, used for the *Book of Hawking* in 1496, perhaps with the intention of giving a familiar look to an old text (see fig. 23.1, p. 471).[51] Conversely, the type used in London by John Lettou, whose origins remain a mystery, may reveal at least part of his biography, for it is connected with printing in Rome, where he may have been active in 1478 and 1479 under the name John Bulle.[52] The only press, apart from Theodoric Rood's in Oxford, that may have been entirely independent of supply from abroad is that of the St Albans Schoolmaster Printer. It has been argued that three of the four types used at St Albans between 1479 and 1486 were cut locally by two different typecutters.[53] The first cut two types of very good quality and, so the surmise goes, must have learned the trade abroad, and then passed on his skills to a successor. The types, however, are not original in design. One is copied from a Caxton type, which in its turn came from Johann Veldener; the other shows similarity to a type cut by Guillaume le Talleur in Rouen, in 1490, for printing Law-French for the English market (see fig. 20.1). Whatever its origin, the second type is certainly an attempt to represent the English court hand. The second punchcutter would have copied and adapted Caxton's smaller Type 4. A large textura type was the same as Caxton's Type 3 and must have been obtained from him. These instances, rare as they are, of the manufacture of type in England in this period show that English printing can be understood only in the context of trade with the Continent.

The press

The printing press was a less sensational invention than that of movable type, and developed over the first decades of printing.[54] It began with a simple adaptation of the press which had been familiar over many centuries for pressing wine and oil. A flat plate, the platen, lowered by a screw, pressed a frame containing a sheet of paper inserted beneath it. This press was capable of printing one side of half a sheet of paper or vellum, corresponding with one folio page (or two quarto pages). This was brought into contact with a typeset area slightly smaller than the size of the platen. In the early 1470s a mechanical improvement to the press was

51. *STC* 3309; *HPT* pl. 182; L. Hellinga 1995, pp. 349–50.   52. *BMC* IV, p. 78.
53. Barker 1979.
54. For an extensive and illustrated description of the press after *c.* 1500, see Gaskell 1972, pp. 118–41. For the development in the fifteenth century, L. Hellinga 1997b.

introduced, first in Rome, and spread in the course of that decade to northern Europe. This was a movable carriage which enabled the printer to place a larger forme on the press, corresponding to the size of a whole sheet (of standard sizes of paper or vellum), and to print it in two pulls of the press. By the middle of the 1480s this new procedure had become generally available. In England the transition can be observed in Caxton's printing house in 1480, and in Oxford it took place in 1479 during the printing of Aristotle's *Nicomachean Ethics* in Leonardo Bruni's Latin translation.[55] This technical improvement, which speeded up the process of printing, had a profound effect on the production of texts. To understand this, we have to take a closer look at the manufacturing process.

Manuscript and printed books as we know them were all produced in codex form: sheets of paper or vellum were folded together to form quires, which were combined and bound together to form volumes. This had been the traditional form of book in the western world since it had gradually replaced the rolls of Antiquity during the second to fourth centuries. The size and bibliographical format of the book was determined by the size of the full sheet and by the number of times it was folded. As we have already seen, the smaller the format, the larger the number of times the sheet was folded; the larger the number of pages that must be combined on the same sheet, the more intricate the pattern of combination of pages.[56] This was probably not unknown in the production of manuscripts,[57] but with the introduction of the printing press, first the half-sheet, as printed on the fixed press, then the full sheet, as printed on the press with moving carriage, had to be the standard unit of production. Pages had therefore to be combined in 'formes' corresponding to the size of what the press could print in one operation. Since printers (until well into the seventeenth century in England) normally worked with a fairly limited supply of type, it was necessary to set and prepare pages in the combination required for the formes to be put on the press, but not in the order in which the text was to be read, which would have required the completion of many more pages before a forme could be put together. The printer – or whoever was delegated to carry out this task – would calculate on the exemplar (or printers' copy, i.e. the material form of the text chosen to be the basis for his edition, which could be manu-

55. L. Hellinga 1997b, pp. 1–23.   56. For imposition of pages, see Gaskell 1972, pp. 78–110.
57. G.Pollard 1941, pp. 105–8, with reference to examples of 'imposition' of manuscripts of the eighth and twelfth centuries in R. A. B.Mynors, *Durham Cathedral manuscripts*, Durham, 1939, pp. 19, 57. An example of imposition in a fourteenth-century manuscript: W. Gs Hellinga 1962, pls. 1–2, pp. 163–4. Vezin 1990 sums up earlier work published in France.

script or an earlier printed edition) the total size of the book and also its structure in pages, sheets and quires. When working with the early form of the press, typesetting and printing took place a page at a time for editions in folio, and sometimes even for quarto editions, if printed on a press with a very small platen (as was, for example, the case with the first book printed in Oxford, of which the exemplar has been identified; see fig. 3.5).[58] For books printed in this way, a great deal of adjustment to the original calculation and marking was possible. One has to bear in mind that typesetting and printing did not usually take place in the order in which the book was to be read.

When the press with moving carriage (or 'two-pull press') was introduced, the forecast had to be more precise and had to indicate with a degree of precision where in the text each page had to begin (and the previous page had to end), because typesetting and printing were likely to be executed in an order deviating from reading order. Usually, for about half of the pages in each quire, the following page (in reading order) had already been set and printed, and the transition between the two pages was meant to be invisible to the reader. Whether for half-sheet or for full-sheet printing, the forecast of the contents of each page was usually made on the exemplar by counting lines and marking the future pages, a process which is called 'casting-off'. Although the marks left on the exemplar look very similar, the function was different in full-sheet printing in that it imposed strict restraints on the space in which the compositor had to fit his text. However, the division of text in this way rapidly became an established routine. Mistakes were made, but compositors had become adept in coping with them and in making text fit in the space allocated by the casting off, using variations in spelling, abbreviation and contraction, or even introducing variations in the text. Manuscripts used for casting off survive from the early 1470s (and the practice must have been introduced with the earliest printing whenever text was divided among compositors and presses). England is particularly rich in examples of manuscripts used in this way in the printing houses, probably because they were mostly English texts of literary importance, and their use in printing-houses was recognized as they were intensely studied.[59] It is difficult to estimate a date for the discontinuation of the practice of

58. De la Mare and Hellinga 1978, pp. 198–209. Cf. L. Hellinga 1987, pp. 196–8.
59. Printers' copy for mostly English-language texts printed in the fifteenth century summarized in Blake 1989; Moore 1992, pp. 11–18. See also De la Mare and Hellinga 1978; Meale 1982; L. Hellinga 1983, p. 10 n. 3.

setting a text in an order different from that in which it was to be read. In England we can be certain that setting by formes still existed in the early seventeenth century, when it was used, in 1623, for Shakespeare's First Folio,[60] but in 1683–4 Joseph Moxon wrote in his *Mechanick Exercises* (1683–4) that 'no wise Compositer, except he work on Printed Copy that runs Sheet for Sheet, will be willing to Compose more Sheets to a Quire than he shall have a Fount of Letter large enough to set out, unless he will take upon him the trouble of Counting off his Copy: because he cannot Impose till he has Set to the last Page of that Quire; all the other Sheets being Quired within the first Sheet, and the last Page of the Quire comes in the first Sheet'.[61] These words show that the practice, although not entirely forgotten, had by that time become unusual. We can therefore be confident that it was prevalent in England during the whole period covered in this volume, although in the course of the sixteenth century the practice ended in some of the large scholarly enterprises on the Continent. By the 1560s the large printing houses in Lyons, Paris and Antwerp had sufficiently invested in type-supplies to abolish the traditional practice, with its complicated manoeuvring through the text and attendant risk to textual accuracy. It is important to realize that, until discontinuation of the practice of setting by formes, a text can be assumed to have been perceived during the whole production process, by master, compositors, correctors and printers, as a construction (the building site of a book) in which intellectual content and even the internal divisions of the text had no more than secondary significance.

Procedure and practice could vary considerably between different countries, towns and individual printing houses, whereas the basic technical equipment remained relatively stable until the end of the 'hand-press period' early in the nineteenth century.

The text in the printing house

The effects of printing-house procedures in the hand-press period on the transmission of texts has now, for several generations, been a subject of intense study. Textual bibliography, as it has become known, primarily in the English-speaking world, is partly a continuation of the development of textual criticism spanning many centuries. This field of study was extended when, early in the twentieth century, a group of English schol-

---

60. Hinman 1963; Bond 1948, for English printers in the period 1561–95.
61. Moxon 1962, pp. 210–11.

ars began to investigate printing-house procedures in relation to literary texts which had survived only in printed form. In a number of influential studies, each a classic in its own right, they concentrated on texts of the Elizabethan and Jacobean periods, thus initiating an entirely new evaluation of the significance of printers for the great English literary texts transmitted in print.[62]

The influence of these scholars on the study of printed texts goes far beyond their preferred terrain. Principles, first formulated on the basis of their experience, which was limited, have been generalized and amended for much wider application by successive generations of scholars in an ever-growing discipline. The principles have also been successfully applied to other areas of printing and other European vernacular literature,[63] but the dominantly Anglophone character of textual bibliography remains generally recognized. In the bibliographical discipline that developed round it, we may therefore find another unique characteristic attached to printing in England.[64]

Although the discipline has much expanded and the general literature on the subject is vast, application to earlier printing has been slow to follow, mainly because direct information or documentation leading to an understanding of printing-house practice in the early period is very scarce. It remains feasible, nevertheless, to discuss briefly some aspects of the transmission of texts in the early printing houses of the British Isles. Since their output had such a high proportion of important vernacular literary texts, some rewarding explorations have already been made.[65]

The direct influence of the printing house ranges from procuring and combining texts (in manuscript or in a previously printed version), often through patronage or commission, editing in preparation for printing, the technical procedures carried out by compositors and press-men, preceded by casting off the exemplar, to proof-reading, and sometimes, finally, reprinting with revisions. Usually these procedures were not recorded, and must be elaborately reconstructed. English printing is in an exceptional position, however, in that it has at its disposal the com-

---

62. The history of this phase in the discipline is well recorded in *Studies in retrospect* 1945, in particular the contributions by W. W. Greg and F. P. Wilson. Cf. P. Davison's modern assessment in introduction to Davison 1992; Roberts 1988. Fundamental in stating the principles and with lasting influence: McKerrow 1927.
63. See surveys by D. Shaw, J. L. Flood, C. Fahy, W. Kirsop and A. Yamada in Davison 1992. Also, W. Gs Hellinga 1962; Trovato 1991.
64. For surveys of the developments during the half-century 1942–92, see Davison 1992.
65. For example, Bühler 1940, 1950–1, 1953; Rhodes 1956b; Painter 1963; Meale 1982; Mukai 1997; studies undertaken in preparation of *BMC* xi (forthcoming).

ments William Caxton added to some thirty of his publications, in the form of personal prologues and epilogues.[66] Caxton's reflections on his work, where present, may form a useful basis for distinguishing the areas of responsibility for the quality of a text of which early printers may have been aware.

Caxton wrote either as translator or as editor; although there are frequent statements to the effect that 'I have endevourd me to enprinte', he was invariably silent on the technical procedures required to achieve this. As translator, from the French or, on one occasion, from the Dutch, he would give his reasons for translating the work, might mention how he obtained his source, and would name the patron who had either proffered a manuscript source or requested the publication in print of a particular text. As editor, Caxton would in addition specify his editorial work – dividing the text into chapters and compiling a table of contents accordingly, for example, or, as in the second edition of the *Canterbury Tales*, revising the first edition on the basis of a new manuscript source.

For vernacular printing of the period, this information is unparalleled. It should not be overlooked, however, that copious as it may seem, Caxton provided such extensive information in only 30 of his some 110 publications: 16 of his own translations and 14 editions for which he received manuscripts from others, because they were originally written in English or because they existed already in translation. Some material of this kind may have been lost.[67] In any case, however, the majority of Caxton's publications were issued without such personal additions. Since his statements are to be interpreted not merely as commendations of his efforts to the buyers and readers of his books, but also as an awareness of his accountability for the state in which the texts were issued, it should be noted that, more commonly, he would withhold this information. This silence may have been induced by a particular relation to an unnamed patron (as was probably the case with Latin material commissioned by ecclesiastics), or it may be an indication that a lower value in a scale of appreciation was attached to a text. It must be repeated that the information so copiously provided by Caxton is exceptional in the period. Generally, sources or editors would not be named in vernacular printing, and, where he did not name them, Caxton would be following

66. Blades 1861–3; Crotch 1928; Blake 1973.
67. For example, Caxton's texts accompanying his *Four sons of Aymon*, STC 1007, are known only through a later edition printed by W. Copland in 1554, STC 1010–11.5; Blake 1973, pp. 83–4, 159.

the pattern of his time. Nevertheless, his prologues and epilogues have permitted us to form a realistic image of Caxton the publisher operating in a network of overlapping circles, at the court, among the merchants of the city and in the Church, varying according to the rapidly changing political structures of his time.[68] His active role or influence may be open to speculation;[69] what is certain is that he depended on patronage from a variety of quarters for the first *conditio sine qua non* of a publishing house: the procurement of the best texts available.

There are sufficient indications that Caxton's successor, Wynkyn de Worde, continued on the same lines. Although his statements to this effect are intermittent, we can infer regular patronage from Margaret Beaufort, from the mercer Roger Thorney, and, perhaps most important of all, from religious houses.[70] Robert Copland, who was probably instrumental in finding literary manuscripts for De Worde, provides a contemporary vignette in a fictional dialogue with a potential patron:

> haue ye any copy
> That is a man myght enprynt it thereby
> And whan I se it, than I wyll you tell,
> If that the matter be ordred yll or well.[71]

Richard Pynson, on the other hand, who had started out in the 1490s with legal printing and some straightforward reprints, was probably somewhat slower to build up connections, until he became King's Printer.[72] Both De Worde and Pynson, however, are all too silent on the subject of procedures for revising and editing, or who carried out these procedures in the printing house.

Editing texts, whatever the value of the notion of 'editing', was a regular activity of the printing house. The first century of printing witnessed a shift from anonymous work, invisible to the later user of the book and unaccounted for, to the named editor held responsible for the final result. Towards the end of the fifteenth century, men of letters were known to play an important role in many of the learned printing houses on the Continent, as correctors to the press or as advisers to the printers. There are indications that such arrangements existed from the beginning

68. Painter 1976, *passim*.   69. Lowry 1987, 1988.
70. Croft 1958a, b; Edwards and Meale 1993; Jones and Underwood 1992; Powell 1996.
71. Robert Copland, Prologue to *The seuen sorowes*, STC 5734, written *c.* 1526, printed *c.* 1565; Copland 1993, p. 87, cf. P. Simpson, 1935, p. 225.
72. See Neville 1990 and Neville-Sington below, pp. 579–84.

of printing, although the identity of these early editors can at best be inferred only indirectly. The naming of editors would apply only to texts of major importance. Readers in the fifteenth or sixteenth century, whether using texts in manuscript or in print, would not be surprised to encounter a statement about editor or commentator in the major theological texts, Bibles, patristic texts, or scholastic works, although even here they were not invariably present. Major legal works, with an explicit responsibility to the community to which they applied, are more consistent in naming authors and commentators, and thus accounting for their authority. Similarly, canonical medical works tended to state the authority on which they were based, in contrast to popular medicine. The tradition of a particular text might lead to the expectation that certain information would be provided. To this, the printer might add his own statement, thus confirming the authoritative value of the publication.

In this scale of values, the preponderantly vernacular books produced in the British Isles rate fairly low, and, apart from Caxton, printers gave very little direct information about the editing of the texts they printed. Even for the publishing of texts of the common law, the active involvement of members of the Inns of Court, although undoubtedly intense, manifests itself only intermittently.[73] The printers John Rastell and his son, William, were respectively a barrister and a judge, and by producing their own compilations and editions contributed much to establishing legal printing in England as a specialist domain, which subsequently became a monopoly.[74] For literary texts, Robert Copland, working in conjunction with Wynkyn de Worde, seems to have used much more sophisticated methods than Caxton's, in that he may have compared various sources and constructed his versions of texts by what may be termed eclectic editing.[75] This has come to light in particular for his versions of Chaucer, at the pinnacle of the scale of values for vernacular literature.

The influence of the printing house was not limited to editing in preparation for printing, whether anonymous or by a named editor. Caxton's edition of Thomas Malory's *Morte Darthur*, published in 1485, may serve as an example.[76] Caxton states in his prologue that he improved the structure of the text by adding chapter headings.[77] Current opinion is that, although Caxton probably worked with only one available source

73. See Baker below, pp. 429–30.   74. See Baker below, pp. 425, 428–9.
75. See below, p. 90.   76. *STC* 801.
77. F. *3 verso, lines 16–20, ee6 recto l.19; Blake 1973, p. 109, lines 135–6, p. 111, lines 8–9.

supported by one additional manuscript for a section of the work, he also slightly revised the text when putting it into print, in spelling as well as substantively.[78] He himself, however, is silent on this point. Recent discussions concerning Caxton's edition of the *Morte Darthur* have highlighted the need to consider the influences, other than those of a named editor, which contributed to the form a text was given in the printing house. Caxton's silence is an indication of what could be taken for granted in publishing a text in print, and may help in perceiving a distinction between the responsibilities of a named editor, and what the printing house would undertake as a matter of course, assuming a responsibility beyond that of an individual.

A printing house, however small, is invariably an organization with a division of work and of responsibilities, and with a sense of hierarchy which in all likelihood grew stronger over the centuries. This may be the reason why modern text historians easily underrate the effect of those actually producing the books, in early printing houses, on the text they were re-creating. If press-men made a lasting impact on texts it was likely to be by an accident in imposing pages, but compositors had far more independence than they are generally given credit for. This is clear from instances of the resetting and reprinting of sheets following an error in imposition of pages (and the accidental preservation of the mis-imposed first setting) in Caxton's second editions of the *Mirror of the World* and Nicholas Love's translation of the *Meditationes vitae Christi*.[79] These show that compositors used individual systems of spelling, even when following very carefully a model set by a different compositor. The nine successive printed editions of Love's translation show that compositors could introduce their own notions of appropriate vocabulary, even when there were no constraints on space to force them to adapt the text.[80] This resulted in a gradual transformation of the text as it was printed between 1484 and 1530. A further direct example is the copy of the St Albans *Book of Hawking* prepared by an editor for Wynkyn de Worde's edition of 1496, with annotations amending the spelling, subsequently extended by De Worde's compositor who had his own way of improving on the St Albans version.[81] This is a far cry from Joseph Moxon's statement of 1683 that 'by the Laws of Printing, a Compositor is strictly to follow his Copy', to which even at this time was added 'a task and duty incumbent

78. L. Hellinga 1981b; Tieken-Boon van Ostade 1995; Meale 1996; Takamiya 1996; Kindrick 1997.   79. *STC* 24763 and 3260; see *BMC* xi (forthcoming).   80. L. Hellinga 1997a.
81. L. Hellinga 1981a; *BMC* xi (forthcoming).

on the Compositer, viz. to discern and amend the bad Spelling and Pointing of his copy, if it be English', and later: 'yet it is necessary the Compositers Judgment should know where the Author has been deficient, that so his care may not suffer such Work to go out of his Hand as may bring Scandal upon himself, and Scandal and prejudice upon the Master Printer'.[82] The responsibility of the compositor in the fifteenth and sixteenth century was even greater. Unlike the compositors of later periods, he was in a position to give the text on which he worked the stamp of his individual preferences or habits. The responsibility for making the text accessible to the anticipated readers fell in the first place to him, often weighing heavier than producing an accurate copy of the exemplar in front of him. Naturally, this is more perceptible in vernacular texts, but even in Latin this level of amendment – constant or intermittent – should not be ruled out. The role of the compositor was therefore interpretative, a function in direct continuation of the traditional responsibility of a scribe.

Before the work of the compositor was forwarded to the press to be printed, a phase of proof-reading may have taken place, carried out either by a corrector at the press or by an author or editor. In English printing there is hardly any evidence for proof-reading in the early years,[83] but such scant evidence as there is, for both continental and English printing, suggests that in-house proof-reading was a regular routine, albeit of varying quality (see fig. 3.6). The exigencies of keeping presses – and press-men – employed in a regular cycle limited the scope for proof-reading outside the printing house. Percy Simpson quoted a contract agreed in 1523 between Richard Pynson and John Palsgrave stipulating an output of one sheet per day.[84] This conforms to regulations formulated in the Plantin printing house some forty years later.[85] Among the many notable examples of intervention by editors or correctors quoted by Simpson for the hand-press era up to c. 1800, only a few are relevant to the period before 1557. This in itself is indicative of a continuous adjustment to the sense of editorial reponsibility in the printing houses. Simpson quotes two examples of correctors who undertook the correc-

---

82. Moxon 1962, pp. 192, 212.
83. A page (C2 verso) marked up with corrections survives in the unique copy of the *Legenda ad usum Sarum* printed for Caxton by G. Maynyal, Paris, 1488, *STC* 16136, BL, IB.40010; P. Morgan and Painter 1957, with illustration. Other examples from the first decades of the sixteenth century: P. Simpson 1935, pp. 63–5, pl. II; Moore 1992, pp. 72, 78–9.
84. P. Simpson 1935, p. 46.
85. Sabbe 1935; translation into English in L. Hellinga and W. Hellinga 1974.

tion of specialist material. In one case the author of *Lesclarcissement de la langue francoyse*, John Palsgrave, blamed 'my correctours handes' for a mistake that had been overlooked.[86] Here the responsibility for accuracy was left by the printer, Pynson, to the author who engaged a corrector. Simpson's other example is the *Abbreviamentum statutorum* of 1499, which was to be corrected by three gentlemen of the Middle Temple, '*after the pryntyng of the seid bokes*', in an edition of over 400 copies, as we learn from a petition by Pynson in which he complains that they failed to carry out what had been agreed.[87] In both examples it is to be noted that if the procedures had taken place as planned, we should never have known about them. It has also to be noted that the printing house apparently accepted that correction would take place after printing the whole edition. What frequently happened, however, is that, after the first sheets were printed, errors might be detected, either in the printing house or possibly by an author, and printing would be briefly interrupted in order to correct the errors, while the typeset page was on the press.

Authors' correction took place after the event, unless the author was installed in the printing house, as Guillaume Fichet once was at the Sorbonne press, or as was Erasmus in various printing houses where his work was obviously integrated in what, even then, was a controlled production cycle. There are no such striking examples in England or Scotland at this time. The author in the British Isles, confronted with the imperfections of the printing house, would compile a list of errata to be added to the book, and we may therefore infer that in some cases he saw printed sheets as they had come off the press or very shortly after. 'Fawtes escaped in the pryntynge', no fewer than 252 of them, were added to some copies of the first edition of Thomas More's *Dyaloge* of 1529, and were probably compiled by him, although apparently he managed to correct the last 3 leaves before they went to press. Most of the corrections were incorporated in the second edition published in the following year 'newly oversene by the sayd syr Thomas More', but in spite of this it was necessary to attach a list of 91 newly found errata to this version, to which More had made substantial additions.[88]

Contemporary texts, however, were in the minority during the first century of printing, and the direct influence of an author on the prepara-

86. P. Simpson 1935, p. 110.   87. *STC* 9515; P. Simpson 1935, p. 111; Baker below, p. 430.
88. *STC* 18084–5; *CWM* vi, esp. p. 575; cf. *CMW* ix, p. xc and, generally for the editing of the works of religious controversy, the textual introductions to *CWM* vi–xi; P. Simpson 1935, pp. 3–4.

tion of a text for a following edition is exceptional indeed. Much more common is the phenomenon of printing houses and their editors working with texts recognized as 'of earlier times', and addressing the often conflicting requirements of presenting them: conveying a sense of immediacy, or at least making them comprehensible to contemporary readers, remaining faithful to the ancient authors, and being adequate to the available sources. Caxton, in his prologues and epilogues, revealed the dilemmas of which he was aware, but his awareness should not be equated with the antiquarian sensitivity that began to develop in later decades. Caxton's term 'according to my copy', so often used by him, was a hallmark of authenticity as well as a disclaimer, the singular clearly indicating his limitations.

The problems expressed by Caxton were in principle no different from those faced by an editor a century later. Changes in methods began to manifest themselves, however, as a variety of sources, manuscript as well as early print, were accumulated in preparation for the publication of texts regarded as most important. In the first instance, this was in response to a need to verify authenticity and establishing textual completeness. Disposing over a variety of sources might then lead to attempts at establishing a *recensio*, as can be perceived, for example, in the editing of some of Chaucer's texts by Robert Copland and William Thynne.[89]

The accumulation of texts in the printing house, with a view to editing and publishing could have a lasting effect on their dissemination in yet another way. In the economics of publishing it was advantageous to market texts, more or less loosely related by themes, in new combinations which might tempt buyers. Caxton's early quarto editions of Chaucer and Lydgate, originally found together in substantial volumes, are a good example, out of many.[90] Such combinations sometimes became permanent features of those texts. To take only one example, John Mirk's *Liber festivalis* was first produced by Caxton in 1483; paper evidence indicates that it was preceded by a text now generally known as *Quattuor Sermones*.[91] Caxton must have found that the two texts sold well in combination, and some time later printed another edition of the *Quattuor Sermones*, presumably in order to match the larger number of copies printed of the *Liber festivalis*.[92] The *Liber festivalis* was also printed

89. Mukai 1996, 1997; Erler 1993, pp. 139–40; Blodgett 1979.
90. Needham 1986a, p. 70, 'Tract vol. 3' (CUL), also 'Tract vols. 1 and 2'.
91. *STC* 17957; paper evidence assembled by P. Needham in preparation for *BMC* XI (forthcoming). Cf. Needham 1986a, p. 87, Cx 54.
92. Webb 1970; Needham 1986a, p. 89, Cx 85.

in 1486 at Oxford by Rood and Hunt, on its own and from an independent source.[93] Caxton used this version some four years later, *c.* 1490, when he published the text a second time, now immediately followed by the *Quattuor Sermones*.[94] The combination – invented by Caxton, since there is no sign of it in the manuscript tradition of the two texts – was taken over in the many subsequent reprintings by Wynkyn de Worde, Richard Pynson and Julian Notary, as well as by printers in Paris and Rouen.[95]

Comparing manuscript sources with a printed version could lead to expanding the text, or to a re-arrangement, as happened, for example, with the *Canterbury Tales*.[96] As texts became more widely available through the medium of print, a remarkable phenomenon began to develop, in direct contradiction to what must have appeared initially to be the major advantage of the printing process: the standardization of texts by multiplication in large numbers. Once a text was issued in print, it could indeed be accepted as standard and copied in subsequent editions without being subjected to further critical assessment. However, first publication in print could also be the beginning of a process of comparison and improvement. Successive editions of Chaucer's *Parliament of Fowls*, for example, indicate a development in which the beginning of an awareness of authorial intent can be perceived. Caxton, Rastell, Pynson, Robert Copland for De Worde, and William Thynne for Godfrey each used independent sources, in manuscript and in print, the latter three emending the text on the basis of more than one source.[97] This development in English publishing is beginning to be studied much more closely than in other language areas. Many of these texts belong to a literary tradition for which interest has never been lost, as has happened for so many other texts – covering diverse subjects – produced in the first century of printing.

Printers' ink, vellum and paper

Vellum had been a traditional material for making books, rolls or codices since the days of Pergamon, but printing ink and paper, although not based on as recent an invention as movable type, were relative newcomers in western Europe.

---

93. *STC* 17958. 94. *STC* 17959, incorrectly stated to be a reprint of *STC* 17957.
95. *STC* 17960–75; the textual relation of the editions before 1501 was examined by Mrs Lucy Lewis in preparation for BMC xi (forthcoming). 96. L. Hellinga 1983.
97. Mukai 1997; Blodgett 1979.

Printing ink was directly related to the oil-based paints first used in Flemish painting early in the fifteenth century and was an adaptation of this invention.[98] Water-based inks, as used traditionally for writing, could not adhere to metal types, and the weight of the printing press would cause them to be absorbed by the paper. They were used in block-books, for which the text had been cut in wood, but these were not produced in England. Printers' ink was made up from oil, soot, adhesives, and albumen, and traces of metal have been found in ink used by some printers. It is likely that, in the workshops, small quantities were made up at a time, following a recipe owned by the firm. Lately, attempts have been made to determine by spectrum analysis whether inks can help in identifying the work of individual printing houses, thus introducing a new line of evidence into problematic identifications.[99] Recent research shows its merits as well as its limitations.

For inking the type, the press-men used ink-balls (large leather balls stuffed with a mixture of horse-hair and wool, with a wooden handle), one in each hand, dabbing them on the ink which was spread out on an ink-stone, and firmly transferring the ink onto the typeset pages waiting in their forme on the press.[100] Sometimes type would be loosened by this treatment, which then led to hasty and not always correct or invisible repairs, even leading to permanent consequences for the text. Because oil-based ink was used, it did not penetrate the paper to any great extent; the paper had to be dampened to melt the size if the ink was to make any mark at all. Both sides of the sheet could therefore be printed. The process of inking had of course to be repeated each time a forme was printed.

Ink could be used to introduce colour as a distinctive feature. The first book printed in English, Caxton's *Recuyell*, opens with a spectacular page entirely in red, containing his dedication to his patroness, Margaret of York. When colour was combined with printing in black ink on the same page, the printing procedures were complicated. Inking had to be very carefully carried out: either more than one colour had to be dabbed on the typeset page, or the page had to pass under the press more than once. In Bruges, where the *Recuyell* was printed, Johann Veldener may have guided Caxton's workshop through the intricacies of the technique. Caxton did not use colour printing in Westminster, but chose rather to employ a contrasting typeface.[101] Red, was, however, a necessity in litur-

98. Bloy 1967.   99. Schwab *et al.* 1983; Rosenberg *et al.* 1998.
100. Illustrated [by Jost Amman] in H. Sachs, *Eygentliche Beschreibung . . . mit kunstreichen figuren*, Frankfurt am Main, 1568, often reproduced.   101. See above, p. 75.

gical printing. It occurs frequently in the work of later printers of liturgical works, and in Scotland the extensive red printing in one of the first books printed in Edinburgh, the *Breviarium Aberdonense* of 1509 is very striking.[102] Here it is evident that the sheets passed twice through the press. English printing has a very rare example of early printing in several colours, the edition of the *Book of Hawking*, including treatises on *Hunting* and *The blasing of arms*, printed at St Albans in 1486, reprinted by Wynkyn de Worde in 1496.[103] In the St Albans edition, the blasons are printed using red, blue and yellow. In Wynkyn de Worde's reprinting, the colour was corrected in many instances, but here only red and blue were produced in print, and the yellow was applied by hand.

*

Vellum (or parchment) had been the only material used for medieval codices until paper offered a cheaper and often more manageable alternative. Vellum (made from soft animal skin) remained in use for manuscript codices as the more durable and more luxurious material; for printing, it was also extensively used in the first decade, especially in Mainz, but gradually paper became the normal material, and vellum was used only for luxury items, or where the books had to be especially hard-wearing, as with much-used liturgical books, primers and elementary schoolbooks. Indulgences, especially in the early years, were also usually printed on vellum. Once past its useful life, material printed on vellum might be valued for its sturdiness, ending up in binders' shops for covers, or cut into strips which were sewn into the middle of quires to protect the paper from the string, or used as paste-downs on the inside of boards, or even to repair a torn leaf, as in the manuscript of the *Morte Darthur*.[104] The unexpected confrontation of manuscript or printed materials from very different sources is often revealing for the history of book production, and vellum fragments play a considerable part in bibliographical investigations.[105]

Printing on vellum required extra care, for vellum is less absorbent than paper, and printed vellum had therefore to be dried longer than paper sheets. The impression of the type on the page is sharper than on paper, and shows to better advantage. Nevertheless, printers in England used it only sparingly, and, as E. Gordon Duff remarked in his survey of the subject,[106] the vellum they used was often 'of abominable quality,

102. *STC* 15791.   103. *STC* 3308–9.   104. L. Hellinga 1981b, pp. 133–4.
105. Ker 1954; Needham 1986a.   106. Duff 1902, p. 3.

coarse in grain and colour, and very variable in thickness'. Even when of
good quality, a soft surface may be a distinctive feature of English vellum.
Poor quality did not matter for school-books, nor for indulgences,
neither of which were to serve as objects of aesthetic appeal. Fragments
survive of only one school-book printed by Caxton on vellum. Since this
is a Donatus edition, a text not commonly used in English schools, but
produced on vellum in large quantities by the earliest presses on the
Continent, the material used here may be a further indication of a continental influence, as surmised by Orme.[107] Pynson's printing of a few
Donatus editions on vellum[108] is a further indication of such influence.
Liturgical works had to be hard-wearing too; the sequence of missals,
processionals, manuals, and breviaries, all of Sarum Use and splendidly
produced by Richard Pynson between 1500 and 1520, were printed on
vellum, and together probably represent the largest quantity of vellum
printing in England of the period.[109] Richard Pynson seems to have been
the specialist in vellum printing, but he was not the only printer to use it.
Books of hours of Sarum Use were printed on vellum by Caxton, William
de Machlinia, Wynkyn de Worde and Julian Notary, as well as by Pynson,
partly in competition with one another and with the Parisian printers,
and all clearly attempting to attract a discerning clientele. Here vellum
was to add a touch of luxury as well as longevity to the books.

Most revealing for understanding the value that was put on a publication is the use of vellum for particular copies. Where the early printers on
the Continent often produced part of their editions of major books on
vellum, apparently confident of finding buyers, printers in England and
later in Scotland seem to have printed special copies only when certain of
their destination, copies commissioned by clients either for their own
use or for dedication, where vellum was *de rigueur* for presentation to
those at the pinnacle of power. An outstanding example is Henry VIII's
Assertio, printed by Pynson in 1521, of which at least four copies were
printed on vellum, two of them presented to Pope Leo X.[110] There are
many earlier examples, however, and each marks the book in question as
out of the ordinary. The three major books printed by Theodoric Rood in
Oxford all survive with at least one copy printed on vellum.[111] Apart from
a book of hours and a Donatus, both in a category where printing on
vellum was to be expected, Caxton is known to have singled out only two

107. STC 7013. See below, p. 457.   108. STC 7014, 7017.   109. Duff 1902, pp. 7–11.
110. STC 13078; Vian 1962; illustrated in Grafton 1993, pl. 62.
111. STC 314 (Oxford, Brasenose; Rhodes 1982, 55b); STC 15297 (Oxford, All Souls, Balliol;
    Rhodes 1982, 1080a, b; Bodleian (fragments); BL (fragm.); Westminster Abbey, Vatican,
    BAV); STC 17102 (Paris, BNF, CBN L-306).

of his books in this way, the *Doctrinal of Sapience* and the *Myrrour of the Life of Christ*.[112] For this last text, of which many manuscripts on vellum are still extant, it is possible that issuing at least one copy on vellum may have been in response to a wish to conform to that tradition, even to strike an archaic note, which would agree with the archaic use of language still evident in that edition.[113] A deliberate archaizing element, conforming to a tradition for a particular text, may also be surmised in the three surviving vellum copies of Wynkyn de Worde's *Book of Hawking*, printed in 1496.[114] Even much later, the vellum copies of the B-text of *Piers Plowman*, printed in London in 1550 by Richard Grafton for Robert Crowley, may indicate that this was a text of earlier times, albeit with contemporary application.[115]

The conclusion should not be drawn, however, that vellum invariably indicates archaism. It could be used for editions of the *Statutes*,[116] for classical texts by John Siberch in Cambridge,[117] in Edinburgh for Boece's *Chronicles of Scotland* printed in 1540 by Thomas Davidson,[118] and for special copies of devotional texts. Its indication of a singular destination or use of books has been recognized by bibliographers from an early age on to the present day, and has led to a number of separate listings.[119]

*

By the time of the invention of printing, paper had been in use in manuscript production for about a century and a half. Over a period of about 600 years it had made a slow progress from China to the Muslim world, and, via Spain, had reached some Italian centres where paper was made from the thirteenth century on. From there the paper industry moved north of the Alps to locations in France, the foothills of the Alps south of Basel, and other places where there were the requisite supplies of fast-flowing water. Paper was manufactured from rags, mainly linen, in mills where they were soaked in water and reduced to the pulp from which the sheets were made. A further necessity was the proximity of a commercial centre for trading in the product.[120] Paper, like so much other merchandise, was sold in bulk and through retail along well-established trade

112. *STC* 21431 (Windsor Castle, including an extra chapter 'of the necligences happyng in the masse' not intended for lay readers); *STC* 3260, BL, IB.55119.
113. J. J. Smith 1997, pp. 138–9; L. Hellinga 1997a, p. 161.
114. *STC* 3309 (BL, JRUL, and the former Pembroke copy).   115. *STC* 19906 (BL, JRUL).
116. *STC* 9354 (Wynkyn de Worde, 1496, BL).
117. *STC* 11536 (Oxford, Bodleian, All Souls); *STC* 11719 (Duff 1902 records Chatsworth copy).
118. *STC* 3203 (Edinburgh UL; BL; Duff 1902 records Ham House copy).
119. Van Praet 1822, 1824–8; Duff 1902; Alston 1996.
120. Clapperton 1934; D. Hunter 1978.

routes. The main sources for paper supply for English printers can be traced to Normandy, the Champagne area and, in Italy, the area round Genoa and Piedmont.[121] There is no evidence that any difficulties in supply were experienced by printers in Britain, except when they wished to print on paper sizes larger than the standard Chancery.[122]

During the period we are dealing with, paper was made in England only for a short time in a mill named the Sele Mill near Hertford, which was owned by John Tate, son of a Mayor of London who belonged to a family of London Mercers.[123] The products of John Tate's mill survive mainly in works printed by Wynkyn de Worde, the earliest on record being a single-sheet papal Bull of the year 1494,[124] followed by more such documents,[125] but also by six very sizeable books ranging in date from 1495 to 1510, when some remnants were finally used up.[126] The most famous among them, the English translation of Bartholomaeus Anglicus, *De proprietatibus rerum* of 1495, ends with an epilogue in strophic verse in which the printer not only informs the reader that Caxton had printed the Latin version in Cologne, but also includes three lines on John Tate:

> And John Tate the yonger, Joye mote he broke
> Whiche late hathe in England doo make this paper thynne
> That now in our Englysh this boke is prynted inne.

In all these books an unusual paper size called 'Bastard' was used, somewhat larger than the standard Chancery. It is likely that the wish to use this format, not conveniently obtained from abroad, was one of the incentives for the paper-making enterprise. The paper historian Allan Stevenson observed a similarity to Genoese paper which led him to surmise that Tate brought in one or more experienced paper makers from Genoa, one of the sources of paper for the English printers.[127] The quality of the paper could bear comparison with that of imported paper. After John Tate died in 1507, what remained of his paper was presumably sold off by his heirs, and a few sheets are seen for the last time in *The jus-*

---

121. A. Stevenson 1967, pp. 23, 25; 1968, pp. *26–*27, *34–5.
122. A sheet of Chancery paper measured approximately 310 x 450 mm. Limited supplies of large paper – e.g. Royal, measuring *c*. 430 × 620 mm – may explain the partial reprinting of Caxton's *Golden Legend*, *STC* 24873–4, and of the Oxford Lyndewood, *STC* 17102.
123. A. Stevenson 1967; Hills 1992.   124. *STC* 14097; A. Stevenson 1967, p. 19.
125. *STC* 14098, 14098.5, dated by A. W. Pollard as printed early in 1499. Cf. A. Stevenson 1967, p. 19.
126. Bartholomaeus Anglicus (1495), *STC* 1536; *Golden Legend* (1498), *STC* 24876; *Canterbury Tales* (1498), *STC* 5085; Lydgate, *The assembly of the gods* (1498), *STC* 17005; *Thordinary of crysten men* (1506) *STC* 5199; *The justyces of peas* (1510), *STC* 14864.
127. A. Stevenson 1967, pp. 20, 25.

tyces of peas printed by De Worde in 1510.[128] After this episode, English printers continued to depend on paper imports, apart from two short-lived ventures in the 1550s at Fen Ditton near Cambridge and Bemerton near Salisbury, until John Spilman started a more enduring enterprise in about 1585.[129] As with printed books, production in the British Isles could not compete with the convenience of imports. This was clearly stated in the answer reportedly made by Sir Thomas Smith, written in 1549 but apparently referring to John Tate:

> Once a Booke Seller made mee when I asked him why, we had not white and browne paper made within the Realm as well as they had made beyonde Sea; then hee aunswered mee that there was paper made a while within the realm: at the last the man perceived that made it that he could not aforde his paper as good cheape as it came from beyond the sea, and so he was forced to lay downe making of paper; and no blame in the man, for men will geve never themore for his paper because it was made heere. But I would eyther have the paper stayed from comming in, or so burdened with custome, that by that time it came hether, our men myghte aforde theyr paper better cheape, then straungers myght do theirs, the customes considered.[130]

Illustration

Illustration and decoration, either by hand or as part of the printing process, will be discussed here only as part of the production of printed books. For treatment as subjects in their own right, the reader is referred, for woodcuts in England until 1535, to Hodnett, especially its introduction; for the period after 1535, to Luborsky and Ingram, forthcoming at the time of writing; and for engraving, to Hind's classic work on engraving in England. Jeudwine's surveying work is also helpful, if not widely available. Several studies by Martha Driver go into considerable detail.[131]

In the earliest printed books of the fifteenth century, decoration and, sometimes, illustration were painted by hand in direct continuation of the tradition of manuscript production. There were degrees of elaboration, from simple red initials, for which spaces were left open, paragraph marks and possibly headings of chapters written in by a rubricator, sometimes alternating with blue, to colourful painted initials and borders,

128. *STC* 14864.   129. Shorter 1957.

130. *STC* 23133–3a edited (?) by W[illiam] S[tafford], with the date 1581 (written in 1549).

131. Hodnett; Luborsky and Ingram 1998; Hind 1952; Jeudwine 1979; Driver 1987, 1989, 1995, 1996, 1997.

and, at the top of the scale, miniatures illustrating the text. In the first decades of printing it is not unusual to find, within one edition, representatives of each of these degrees of luxury, which determined the price the first buyer paid for the book. When this form of decoration was gradually replaced by woodcut blocks which could be integrated into the printing process, the product became more uniform, and the buyer had less choice. Woodblock illustration for printed books, the first step in the standardization of production, was first used in south-west Germany in the 1460s, where in cities such as Bamberg, Augsburg and Ulm, the technique soon reached a high level of aesthetic quality. In the Netherlands and later in the Rhineland, a sequence of blockbooks were produced, also probably beginning in the 1460s, combining text and images in one woodblock cut for each whole page. They were forerunners of a flourishing tradition of woodcut illustration in this area. Other centres of printing followed, each with a style characteristic for its place of origin.[132] Woodcut illustration, most often found in books in vernacular languages, contributes therefore significantly to establishing a recognizably national character for early printed books. In the early days, metal engravings are found only very rarely in printed books, their use confined to some exceptional volumes printed in Mainz, Florence and Bruges, and some decades later in Cologne and Milan. Not until the middle decades of the sixteenth century did copper engraving become a popular medium for book illustration.[133]

When Caxton acquainted himself, in Cologne, with the art of printing, the printers in that city had not made a link with any local traditions of manuscript illumination, as had happened, for example, in Mainz. In Bruges, however, Caxton was in the very centre of the great tradition of Flemish book illumination and illustration. This tradition is prominently present in the printed work of Colard Mansion, himself a scribe, who is likely to have been Caxton's partner in his Bruges venture. On Caxton himself, however, it seems to have had little effect.

The well-known dedication engraving in a copy of Caxton's *Recuyell of the Histories of Troye* appears to be the exception. This may not have been commissioned on Caxton's initiative. It is a very early example of a copper engraving, to a design attributed to the anonymous Master of Mary of Burgundy, also identified as one of the miniaturists of manu-

132. Hind 1935.
133. Early engravings in Bruges, Florence, Mainz and Cologne illustrated in Schäfer 1987, nos. 11, 13, 14, 17, 33.

scripts commissioned by Margaret of York.[134] It is undoubtedly through
the connection with Caxton's patroness that the engraving came into
being, and it was possibly even commissioned by her. The copy was destined for presentation to Margaret's sister-in-law Elizabeth Woodville,
Queen of Edward IV, and the engraving (which may have been printed a
few years later than the book) certainly succeeded in lifting it to something above the ordinary.[135]

It might have been what was expected if, in laying out the *Recuyell*,
Caxton had left spaces in the text for illustrations to be painted in, as
was done in other books printed by some of his contemporaries in
Flanders.[136] Some manuscripts of Raoul le Fèvre's *Recueil* and his complementary *Histoire de Jason* are illuminated with outstanding sequences
of miniatures, which in the 1480s were the inspiration for equally
remarkable sets of woodcuts, marking the beginning of sections of the
printed text, produced in Haarlem for Jacob Bellaert.[137]

There is only one important exception to Caxton's apparent
indifference to embellishing his books with painting. This is the large
presentation manuscript of his translation into English of the *Ovide
moralisée*, completed in 1480, of which no printed version survives. The
two-volume manuscript was written by professional scribes and provided with an unfinished series of equally professional grisaille miniatures with touches of colour by a Dutch artist.[138]

As it is, only some modest painting can be associated with Caxton's
printed books, whether printed in Bruges or in Westminster. It was as
likely to have been commissioned by their first owners as by the printer.
The substantial vellum fragment of the Sarum Hours[139] was given a
border in the style of Bruges, the city where it was probably printed. A
copy of the first edition of the *Canterbury Tales* has rich borders incorpo-

134. Peartree 1905; A. W. Pollard 1905; reproduced Painter 1976, pl.1; L. Hellinga 1982, fig. 6,
and many times elsewhere. Pächt 1948.   135. L. Hellinga 1991b.
136. For example Colard Mansion and the Printer(s) of Flavius Josephus and Valerius Maximus,
BMC ix, pp. 208–9.
137. *Recueil*: Brussels BR mss. 9261, 9262, 9263; London BL, Royal ms. 17. E.II; Paris BNF mss.
fr. 59, 697, 22552; Vienna ÖNB ms. 2586; see, further, Aeschbach 1989. *Histoire de Jason*:
Paris BNF ms. fr.331; cf. Pinkernell 1973; Baurmeister and Laffitte 1992, no. 49, with
illustration; Paris BNF ms. fr.12570, and Paris, Arsenal mss. 5067, 5068. For the
complicated relation of the illustrations in the Dutch-language *Jason* ms (BL, Add. ms.
10290) to the woodcuts printed by Bellaert, see, e.g., Nieuwstraten 1994.
138. Cambridge, Magdalene Coll., ms. f1. 34 (Scott 1976; 1980a; 1996, 1.75 n. 59, 11.353, 350).
Facsimile: Ovid 1968.
139. *STC* 15867 (New York, PML, Goff H-420). Illustrated in *William Caxton* 1976, p. 25. I am
grateful to Dr K. L. Scott for giving her opinion on this border, as well as on those
documented in the two following notes.

rating emblems of the Company of Haberdashers, and, although it is executed in a predominantly Flemish style, may have some English features.[140] A border in a copy of Caxton's *History of Jason* may well be English (see fig. 3.3).[141] Most copies of Caxton's early publications have simple initials in red, undoubtedly the work of limners in London, but with hardly any individual features to distinguish them. In 1484, Caxton began to introduce characteristic sets of decorated woodcut initials, and the work of limners disappeared from his books from that time on. The same initials also dominate the work of his successor, Wynkyn de Worde, whereas Richard Pynson obtained rather more refined material from France. Both of these printers tended, in the later decades of their activity, to overload their books with decorative material, borders, small ornaments and initials, creating an effect of overcrowding, especially in the small-format books. This fashion was followed by their near-contemporary, John Scot, working in Edinburgh and Aberdeen.

The only English printing to which limners made a significant contribution is found in books printed by John Lettou and William de Machlinia in London. A number of copies of their Littleton *Tenores Novelli* and of De Machlinia's *Statuta Nova* have very simple but distinctive initials in red and blue with penwork flourishes, uniformly executed (fig. 3.4).[142]

There is also very little evidence for English and Scottish limners and flourishers working on imported printed books. Two copies of Gutenberg's 42-line Bible have been shown to have arrived in England not long after they were printed because their generously painted decorations can be identified as the work of an artist active in London around 1460.[143] To these Bibles can be added another book printed in Mainz, a copy of the *Epistolare* of St Jerome, published in 1470 in Mainz by Peter Schoeffer, and now in Aberdeen University Library,[144] as well as the Mainz Cicero of 1465 (see fig. 2.10). Boccaccio's *De genealogia deorum*, printed in Venice in 1472, with marks of ownership of Cardinal John Morton, has an English painted initial (see fig. 9.3).

A few instances exist where painting was commissioned in books destined for the English kings. A vellum copy of Cardinal Bessarion's

---

140. *STC* 5082; Oxford, Merton Coll.; Rhodes 1982, 537b.
141. *STC* 15383, Vienna ÖNB Inc. 2.D.30; Pächt and Thoss 1977, p. 189, pl. 416.
142. *STC* 15719, 9347, e.g. BL IB.55413, C.12.i.9, G.2190(1), and IB.55443, C.11.c.13.
143. König 1983.
144. Hain *8553, Mitchell 1. Margaret Lane Ford encountered only a few such examples when surveying for her database (see below, pp. 179–201).

Orationes et epistolae ad Christianos principes (Paris 1471), was dedicated by its publisher, Guillaume Fichet, to Edward IV, and provided with a dedication miniature which was executed in Paris (see fig. 3.7).[145] Later, at least one copy – and probably more – of books printed by the Parisian printer, Antoine Vérard, with dedications to the French king Charles VIII, were adapted for presentation to Henry VII.[146] They are painted in vivid colours, the thick paint often obliterating the woodcut illustrations, and sometimes even the text underneath (see fig. 12.4). It is likely that this work was commissioned by the printer in Paris, but there is no documentary evidence.

*

Until about 1535, the year Wynkyn de Worde died, English printers relied almost entirely on woodcuts for their illustrations. Woodcuts were carved in relief on blocks of carefully planed plank wood.[147] The blocks with the cuts were fitted into the pages of metal type. The dimensions of the blocks had therefore to agree with the type area of the page, and be made to fit the height of the type. Woodblock illustrations were often cut as sets with the same dimensions, sometimes amounting to dozens for a single text. Commissioning them was therefore a considerable investment, and, as with type, their possession a valuable asset, sometimes providing a virtual monopoly on the production of a text for which the blocks were custom-made. Ownership of blocks might change through purchase or inheritance, and sometimes temporarily through loan. Blocks are therefore known certainly to have moved from place to place, but never on a scale that can be compared with the migration of printing types. For these, unlike woodblocks, punches would generate a progeny in the form of matrices and cast type which could change hands in either phase. Few continental woodblocks ever crossed the North Sea or English Channel in their original form.[148] Instead, many were copied by a succession of woodcutters commissioned to work for Caxton, Wynkyn de Worde and Richard Pynson. Without exception, they delivered work of a quality that could not match that of the original blocks they copied or other models from which they worked. Their low quality, often remarked upon, is difficult to explain. When, *c.* 1480, Caxton first introduced woodcuts in his books, the technique for combining them with letterpress was well established. Nevertheless, in Edward Hodnett's

---

145. GW 4184, Vatican, BAV Vat. lat.3586. Illustrated: Grafton 1993, pl. 57.
146. Winn 1983, 1997; *BMC* VIII, pp. XXVI n. 2, 84, 213, as well as other copies from the Old
   Royal Library.   147. Griffiths 1996, pp. 13–16.   148. L. Hellinga 1995, pp. 350–3.

words, 'England stumbles on to the book-illustration stage with some of the poorest cuts ever inserted between covers.'[149] If he referred to the sets illustrating the first edition of the *Mirror of the World* and, especially, the second edition of Caxton's translation of Jacobus de Cessolis, *The Game of Chess*,[150] his judgement is fully justified. When, occasionally, woodcuts of better quality appeared, as was the case in Caxton's edition of Nicholas Love's translation of pseudo-Bonaventura *Meditationes de vita Christi*,[151] it is assumed, possibly unfairly, that they were obtained from Flanders or France, although the source has not been established. On a theme as universal as the life of Christ, sets of woodcuts might be found, ready-made, while for uniquely English texts there was no alternative to commissioning sets. The existence of an iconographic tradition in manuscripts of an English text must have been a strong argument for including woodcut illustration in the printed version. Nicholas Love's translation, however, was only exceptionally accompanied by miniatures in the many manuscripts of this text still extant.[152]

Wynkyn de Worde and Pynson seem to have made up by quantity what they lacked in quality. Hodnett recorded in all over 2,500 woodcuts for the period 1480–1535, after which date he showed that woodcut illustration became much less important. Of the total, 381 had appeared in books printed by Caxton; Wynkyn de Worde acquired these when taking over Caxton's workshop, and during the more than 40 years of his further activity added over 1,000 cuts, of which a few were obtained from the Netherlands.[153] Most were of very average quality, but some, possibly commissioned by the Abbey of Syon, may be singled out – such as the fold-out woodcuts in William Bonde, *Pilgrimage of perfeccyon*.[154] Hodnett listed over 700 cuts for Richard Pynson, who did not have De Worde's advantage of inheriting a considerable stock and was confined to copying woodcuts when he reprinted Caxton's texts. He did not succeed in commissioning work of high quality.

Out of such a mass of material only a few examples can be examined, assessing their role in the presentation of the text rather than taking an aesthetic point of view. Roughly, they can be divided into those guiding the reader through the text by emphasizing its structure, and those which are explanatory. Even when the two functions overlap, as happens frequently, it is usually still possible to determine which of the two pre-

149. Hodnett, p. 1.   150. *STC* 24762, 4921, Hodnett 1–27.
151. *STC* 3259, Hodnett 309–33.   152. Scott 1996, p. 63.   153. See above, note 148.
154. *STC* 3277.

dominates. When cuts are repeated and serve to illustrate different objects or persons, their use as factotum clearly indicates that their primary function is structural. For example, probably the most famous set of woodcuts used by Caxton illustrates his second edition of the *Canterbury Tales*.[155] This set, consisting of twenty-three cuts, was used to relate the beginning of each section of the General Prologue to the tales of the individual pilgrims, and thus had a mnemonic function, emphasizing the structure of the text as well as giving faces to the persons speaking. The illustration of the individual pilgrims was not carried out consistently, since three of the cuts were used to indicate six different pilgrims;[156] nor would Caxton's readers have needed an illustration to enlighten them about the appearance of a knight, for instance. Caxton's decision to enhance the second printed version with illustrations may be associated with the manuscript tradition of the text on which, as Carlson has shown, his woodcuts were largely modelled. In his own prologue, Caxton refers to the 'beauteuous volumes' of Chaucer's works, and the desire expressed by him to be true to its author may well have been a factor in his decision. Its wisdom is evident from the success of the illustrations, which were repeated and copied as late as 1561,[157] and largely determined the image of the text for much longer, in spite of their imperfections. However, the success of the progress of pilgrims throughout the volume should not obscure the fact that they were inserted by the printer primarily to offer a guide to the reader.

In another illustrated Caxton edition, the function is purely explanatory. The set of woodcuts in his two editions of the *Mirror of the World*[158] clarifies the subject matter of the text, for example the relation of the earth to the sun and the moon, and includes other diagrams and world maps. These illustrations, too, belong to the manuscript tradition of the text, of which one or even two representatives were Caxton's direct source.[159]

Outside London, illustrations were rarely used. The last book printed by Rood and Hunt in Oxford, the John Mirk *Liber festivalis*, 1486,[160] includes a sequence of woodcuts of the life of Christ and of saints, which may originally have been intended for an edition of the *Golden Legend* which did not materialize. They are a departure from the manuscript tra-

---

155. *STC* 5083; Hodnett 214–36.   156. Carlson 1997.   157. Carlson 1997, appendix 2.
158. *STC* 24762–3.
159. The sources for the woodcuts are discussed in *BMC* XI (forthcoming).
160. *STC* 17958; Hodnett 2343–58.

dition of this text and are primarily a guide for the reader. Explanatory, and even indispensable for using the book, is the series of illustrations of coats of arms in *The Book of St Albans* printed by the St Albans Schoolmaster Printer,[161] whose ambition seems to have been to encompass every technique: typecutting, and typesetting, woodcut illustration and even colour printing. When Wynkyn de Worde reprinted the book in 1496,[162] he copied the woodcuts but reduced the number of colours to two. He inserted a *Treatise of fishing*, preceded by a well-known and delightful woodcut of an angler;[163] by this time the convention of beginning the text with an important woodcut had firmly taken root in the work of the Westminster and London printers, heralding the formal title-page which was to develop in the early decades of the sixteenth century.

By multiplying the stock of woodcuts, De Worde showed the importance he attached to illustration. One example has to suffice. De Worde's edition of John Trevisa's translation of Bartholomaeus Anglicus, *De proprietatibus rerum*, printed in 1495,[164] is one of his most handsome productions. More than one source for its contents and form can be identified. The printers' copy for all but one book of the text is the Plimpton manuscript,[165] its printing-house markings clearly indicating direct derivation. This manuscript is not illustrated, but iconographical traditions had developed in printed vernacular versions of the text, in French, Dutch and Spanish. In all these traditions, the beginnings of the nineteen books into which the text is divided were marked with appropriate illustrations referring to the subject matter. Primarily their function is to offer a visual guide through the text. Wynkyn de Worde chose to have two different models for the woodcuts. Seven are copied from an edition of the Dutch translation, printed in Haarlem in 1486 which had a series of magnificent woodcuts, but illustrated only eleven books;[166] for the others he took as model one of the editions printed in Lyons, with cruder but sometimes amusing and anecdotal illustrations (see fig. 3.8a–d). Practical considerations, such as the division of models over more than one woodcutter, may have influenced this procedure, which nevertheless testifies to a great deal of care over the visual presentation of the book.[167]

In the same book, Wynkyn de Worde displayed a large title printed

161. *STC* 3308.   162. *STC* 3309.   163. Hodnett 897.   164. *STC* 1536.
165. New York, Columbia University, Low Memorial Library, ms. Plimpton 263; De Ricci 263. Mitchner 1951.   166. *GW* 3423; Conway 1884, sect.11.8.
167. *GW* 3415–21; Driver 1986, pp. 13–26. *BMC* XI (forthcoming).

from a metal stencil plate, a technique he also used for the title of his posthumous publication of Caxton's translation of the *Vitas Patrum* printed in the same year.[168] Although the technique was different (and unusual), the effect is close to that achieved a few years earlier by the Antwerp printer Gheraert Leeu, who used a very large display type for the titles of some of his English publications. A more lasting form of title-page is found in books printed a few years later. Four-piece woodcut borders with flowers, cherubs or animals, and most often pillars, pilasters and ornaments, were for many decades to become an almost architectural gesture announcing the opening of the book (see fig. 3.9). The designs were often copied from French and German examples.[169] Occasionally a title-page border would incorporate an allusion to the author of the book. For example, the title-page border of Henry VIII's *Assertio septem sacramentorum adversus M. Lutherum*, printed by Pynson in 1521, displays a scene of a royal encampment (see fig. 28.2).[170] In addition to its borders and ornaments, a title-page could indicate with an image the main theme of the book it announced, sometimes in combination with a large woodcut title (see figs. 9.2, 22.1). Martha Driver reproduces, as striking examples of this style, *The crafte to lyve well and to dye well* (1505), *Thordinary of Crysten men* (1506) and *The boke named Royall* (1507), all printed by Wynkyn de Worde, and probably all the work of the same craftsman.[171]

As the century progressed, greater elaboration became the norm. A large woodcut title is seen on the final form of the title-page for Peter Treveris's edition of the *Polycronicon* of 1527,[172] whereas a version with a smaller title was apparently rejected. On both versions a Knight of St George, in full armour and brandishing his sword, sets the tone for the book. This was a step towards the title-pages designed to herald and celebrate truly great books. When they began to appear in the mid 1530s, the London printing houses did not take precedence. Hans Holbein the Younger designed an elaborate woodcut title-page border for the Coverdale Bible, printed in Cologne in 1535.[173] A very striking, if somewhat crudely executed, title-page was given by the Edinburgh printer Thomas Davidson to Hector Boece's *The hystory and croniklis of Scotland* (1540; see fig. 3.10).[174] Probably the most spectacular woodcut title-page of the period in the British Isles belongs to the Great Bible, or

168. *STC* 14507. Driver 1996, p. 354, fig. 3.   169. Jeudwine 1979, p. 278.
170. McK and F, 8.   171. *STC* 792, 5199, Driver 1996, figs. 8, 5; *STC* 21430, Driver 1989, pl.18.
172. *STC* 13440; P. Simpson 1935, pls. 3, 4; McK and F, 13.
173. *STC* 2063, McK and F, 31; Hind 1952, pl. 5.   174. *STC* 3203.

Cranmer Bible, authorized by Henry VIII.[175] The title-page (assigned by Hind to 'school of Holbein') was designed to convey a political as well as a spiritual message, depicting the King in his new role as Supreme Head of the English Church disseminating the Word of God to his people. In successive issues, the political topicality of the image was adjusted to changes in political fortune. In the original state of the title-page, Thomas Cromwell, identified by his coat of arms, is seen as an intermediary between King and people. In a reworking of the cut, used as title-page for further issues and reprints at a time after Cromwell's execution in 1540, his identity was obliterated by removing his coat of arms from the design.[176] A vellum copy of the first edition of Cranmer's Bible was prepared by the merchant Anthony Marler for presentation to the King.[177] It was given a unique character by having all woodcuts, including the other title-pages, small illustrations and ornamental initials, over-painted in bright colours. A title-page to the New Testament, with painted miniatures, was added. On the main title-page the themes were slightly altered to put the King in an even more flattering light.[178]

With this achievement, the woodcut title-page had reached its apogee. Regret has often been expressed that Hans Holbein the Younger did not illustrate more books during the period of his activity in England in the service of Henry VIII (1532–43). Hind lists a few woodcuts which are ascribed to him, included in books published by Reyner Wolfe and thus, perhaps, adding further evidence to Wolfe's connections with Basel.[179] None, however, can stand comparison with Holbein's major illustrative work accomplished in Basel and published in Lyons.

*

In the meantime, engraving in metal was becoming a more commonly used form of illustration. Unlike woodcuts, metal engravings, at this time executed in copper, were an intaglio process and required separate printing, with pressure much greater than that used on a letterpress. For this reason, engravings were in this period usually bound in as inserted sheets rather than integrated in the pages with letterpress printing.[180] Later on, a sophisticated method for combining text and engraving was

175. STC 2070; McK and F, 45; Hind 1952, pl. 6; String 1996, fig.114.
176. String 1996, p. 323, fig.116.
177. BL, C.18.d.10; String 1996, p. 315; see also Neville-Sington below, p. 592.
178. String 1996, p. 323, figs. 113, 115, 117.   179. Hind 1952, p. 5, pl. 7.
180. Griffiths 1996, pp. 31–9.

developed by passing sheets twice through the different presses. In the early sixteenth century, small engravings were sometimes inserted or even glued in appropriate places in a book, for example the engraved roundels found in the unique copy of Caxton's Psalter, in which they were affixed well after the date of printing.[181] Metal engraving would, on average, produce a more detailed and accurate image than woodcuts – except when the latter were the work of outstanding artists such as Holbein – and became the preferred medium for exact representation. It is therefore not surprising that copper engraving was first used in England for anatomical works. The first was a translation, with four plates, of Eucharius Roesslin, *The byrth of mankynde*, which was published in London by T. Raynald in 1540.[182] The next work, much more important, was an abridgement of Andreas Vesalius, *De humani corporis fabrica*, and his *Epitome*. Vesalius's works, both first published in Basel in 1543, were provided with spectacular anatomical woodcuts by Hans Stephan van Calcar, who was one of the exceptionally gifted woodcut illustrators of the period. Only two years after the original publication, in 1545, a new and virtually pirated edition was published in London, with copper engravings copied from Van Calcar's woodcuts by Thomas Geminus.[183] Geminus was an instrument maker who hailed from the region of Liège. He seems to have had a particular interest in medical works; the illustrations in the Roesslin translation are also ascribed to him, and he produced an illustrated table for bloodletting, probably published in 1546.[184] Finally, an English version of the pirated Vesalius was printed in 1553, with the same plates and the text translated by N. Udall.[185] Engraving, not medical science, was, however, Geminus's special skill. He used it also for a pattern book, *Morysse and damashin renewed and encreased . . . for goldsmythes and embroiderars*, published in 1548;[186] he produced a map of Spain, dated 1555;[187] and issued in the same year a revised map of the British Isles which had first been published in Rome in 1546.[188]

*

Towards the end of the years covered in this volume, the organization of the book-trade may not have changed as dramatically as the salient event, the incorporation of the Stationers' Company, would suggest. The

181. *STC* 16253, BL, IA.55038 (Erler 1992, pp. 188–91, fig. 2).
182. *STC* 21153; Hind 1952, p. 9, pl. 24.   183. *STC* 11714; Hind 1952, pp. 9, 39–58, pls. 19–23.
184. *STC* 11718.9.   185. *STC* 11715.5.   186. *STC* 11718.4; Hind 1952, pls. 25–7.
187. *STC* 11718.7; Hind 1952, pl. 28.   188. *STC* 11713.5.

technique of book production did not undergo any changes at all at this time. Books, however, began to take on a different aspect, and books printed in the British Isles began to assume a much closer resemblance to books produced in some large centres of printing on the Continent than they ever had in the previous eighty years.[189]

189. I am grateful to Nicolas Barker, Mary Erler and David McKitterick for reading an earlier version of this chapter and for their suggestions.

4
Bookbinding 1400–1557

M. M. FOOT

Since the eighth century, when the codex was first sewn on supports, western European techniques of binding books by hand have not changed much. The folded sheets or gatherings are sewn, one after another, to the supports running perpendicular to the pile of gatherings. The needle or bodkin pierces the fold of the gathering, taking the sewing thread through its centre; it then emerges on the outside of the folded sheets, circles the first support, re-enters the fold and comes out at the next support which is again circled until the whole gathering is firmly anchored. The next gathering is linked to the previous one by a link-stitch or kettle stitch near the head and tail. The boards are attached to the supports and the whole is then covered, usually in leather. Within this very basic and general scheme, there are wide variations, temporal and geographical, in materials and methods.

Hardly any decorated leather bindings that may have been produced in England during the first fifty years of the fifteenth century survive and the plain leather bindings from this period that have survived are difficult to date and to locate. Their structural differences may point to different localities or even reflect personal or work-place habits. Binders, however, like other craftsmen, moved around, they continued past traditions, as well as adopting new practices. Without firm supporting archival evidence, structural or technical features by themselves cannot be used to attribute bindings to a specific place or to date them, except very roughly. Small decorative hand tools, whether used blind or impressed through gold leaf, can provide firmer evidence, as the tools themselves were engraved and are therefore identifiable. Great caution has to be exercised here as well, as tools were bought, sold and inherited, and only the regular occurrence of a combination or set of tools can be used to make attributions to a particular workshop.[1]

1. Foot 1992, pp. 99–101.

The more detailed consideration of bookbinding in Britain that follows attempts to give a general picture, drawing on surviving evidence, while also indicating some of the variations in practice that can be found. British binders did not work in isolation; they used materials similar to those used by their continental brothers-in-the-craft and, although they often employed them in different ways, the habits of immigrant binders have left their mark on native British products. Most bindings of the period under discussion were sewn on alum-tawed leather thongs split across the width of the spine, but we also find bindings sewn on split tanned thongs. Cords made of flax or hemp, as used in Carolingian bindings, were re-introduced during the fifteenth century, while thinner and single tawed and tanned thongs came into use during the sixteenth. Vellum or parchment sewing supports were also used. The number of sewing supports varies, according to the size of the text-block, but English binders appear to have had a penchant for five supports. The supports themselves would lie on top of the back of the sections and show as raised bands on the spine. Sewing round split thongs can be done in a variety of ways: in a herring-bone pattern, in a figure-of-eight, in a spiral, or wrapped round each part of the thong. When sewing on single thongs or cords, the thread would circle the thong or cord once or be wrapped round it. The sewing thread itself appears to have been made of thin cord, hemp, linen, cotton or (in fine bindings of the sixteenth century) of silk.

In western Europe, the materials most frequently used for end-leaves at this time were vellum or parchment and plain white paper. Vellum manuscripts almost always have vellum or parchment end-leaves, but when, late in the fifteenth century, paper became the usual material for books, parchment end-leaves were gradually replaced by paper which was often strengthened at the fold with a strip of vellum or parchment, frequently a piece of manuscript waste. The use of both manuscript and printed waste for end-leaves and paste-downs is not uncommon, both in Britain and elsewhere, and vellum manuscript paste-downs are found with especial frequency in Oxford bindings of the end of the fifteenth and the beginning of the sixteenth centuries.[2] A single leaf, folded, sewn through the fold and leaving a stub; a folded sheet sewn through the fold forming two end-leaves, one of which could be pasted down; and multiple folded sheets, are all found. Sometimes parchment and paper end-

2. Ker 1954.

leaves were used in combination. Leather board-linings or doublures are exceptional in Britain at this time, and the earliest-known English leather doublure, in an Oxford binding, dates from *c*. 1550 (see fig. 4.1).[3]

The shape of a binding and the way it was constructed depended to a large extent on its function and on the way the book was stored. When, from the mid fifteenth century, books were more usually stored upright on shelves, a more fixed and rigid structure was needed than when they were stored flat or on sloping shelves or lecterns. In bindings with stiff boards the shape of the spine is influenced by the shape of the boards, as well as by the thickness and nature of the text-block material and by the thickness or amount of sewing thread. The rounding of the spine is a result of the swelling caused by the sewing thread in the centre fold of the sections, while wooden boards, shaped or bevelled on the side nearest the text-block, press the backs of the sections into a gently rounded shape. During the sixteenth century, the shaping of the spine was assisted by knocking the backs of the sections over with a hammer, a shape that could be further consolidated by the use of glue and various lining materials. Parchment, thin leather, textile or paper were used to reinforce the spine and hold its shape. Spine linings would cover the whole of the spine or only the components between the bands, leaving the latter uncovered. They would be glued or pasted into place or, occasionally, stabbed through with a bodkin. Spine liners were on occasion used to reinforce the joints. The edges of the leaves were cut with a knife. The marks of a draw knife (a two-handled knife pulled along the edges) can often be found on paper edges. As a rule the edges of the leaves of fifteenth- and early sixteenth-century books are plain. Red or yellow stained edges have been found and occasionally traces of decorative painting occur.[4] Gilt edges are mainly found on fine bindings, and gilt and gauffered edges occur on presentation and collectors' bindings from the early 1520s onwards.

The boards of fifteenth-century bindings were usually made of wood (oak and beech were most common), although limp and semi-limp vellum or parchment bindings (often used for account-books) are also found, and limp structures were used as temporary bindings or for cheap retail bindings from the sixteenth century onwards. The thickness of the

3. BL, C.143.b.7: Quintus Curtius Rufus, *De rebus gestis Alexandri Magni . . . opus*, Antwerp, 1546.
4. 'Medieval painted book edges', in Foot 1993, pp. 439–54; for fifteenth-century English examples, see especially pp. 446–7, 450.

wooden boards depended on the size and weight of the book, and the boards could be shaped (cushioned, chamfered or bevelled) in a variety of ways. Sharply bevelled boards, commonly found in Germany and sometimes in the Netherlands, are unusual in England, where gently bevelled or square-cut boards are more common. However, the Lily binder, undoubtedly an immigrant or someone who had received his training in the Low Countries, as witness a number of his Germanic-Dutch habits, used sharp bevels. During the sixteenth century, pasteboards became more and more common. Couched laminated boards, made by pressing together sheets of paper straight from the paper-maker's vat, and pulp board, made of pulped paper or paper shavings, were also used. Early on, the boards were cut flush with the text-block, but during the fifteenth century we see slight squares (the part of the boards that protrudes beyond the text-block) emerging, now often only visible at the head and tail (because the boards have shrunk). Squares all round are found from the sixteenth century onwards.

Board attachments show minor variations. The thongs were laced into the wooden boards, lying in grooves on the inside of them, secured by square or round pegs, sometimes in a staggered pattern. The grooves are usually straight, at right angles to the spine, but I have seen a few cases where pairs of thongs have been laced in to form a 'V'-shape, alternating with single thongs. Sometimes there are traces of a white-ish clay-like substance covering the exposed thongs, presumably used to make an even surface for the paste-downs. Single thongs or cords were laced in through holes punched or cut into pasteboards, often through two holes, either straight or at an angle.

Endbands draw the boards to the spine and prevent too much slackness between the book and the boards. They also hold the shape of the spine. Those that have survived from the period under discussion were frequently sewn in white or blue and white thread over alum-tawed, sometimes tanned, leather cores. The cores were either laced-in in tunnels on the inside of the wooden boards and pegged, or were brought over the outside of the boards, disappearing into holes in the wood. When pasteboards were used the cores were laced through holes, usually at an angle. Quite frequently during the fifteenth century the spine leather was turned over the endbands and sewn through. During the sixteenth century, endbands gradually lost their structural function and became purely decorative. Plaited endbands, such as occur on bindings from Germany and the Netherlands, are unusual in England. The

Greyhound binder, who possibly worked in Oxford or London in the 1490s, occasionally used them, and pink plaited endbands are found on bindings by the Lily binder, who was active from the 1480s till at least 1504.

The most common covering material was tanned leather, usually calf, sometimes sheep, while tanned goatskin was occasionally used for fine bindings from the 1540s onwards, becoming more common later in the century. Perhaps the earliest surviving English goatskin binding was made by the Medallion binder (active from at least as early as 1544 until 1559) on a manuscript, an account of Richard Chancellor's Voyage to Muscovy,[5] presented by Clement Adams, schoolmaster to the King's pages and the author of the manuscript, to Philip II of Spain, here addressed as Queen Mary's spouse and 'Rex Angliae'. The King Edward & Queen Mary binder (active from *c.* 1545 until at least 1558) also used tanned goatskin on occasion, as well as tawed leather, possibly buckskin, while the Greenwich binder (active in the late 1530s and early 1540s) was partial to white tawed goat- or kidskin. In order to secure the leather to the covers and the spine, the binding was tied up with ropes or cords, in England usually at each spine band. Rope marks are frequently visible at either side of the bands. The edges of the leather were turned in, sometimes trimmed, sometimes left with a rough edge, and pasted down. A variety of methods of dealing with the accumulation of leather at the corners was employed.

Clasps, normally two, were commonly used and have leather thongs, almost invariably hinging on the upper cover. The Lily binder again proved an exception and occasionally hinged his clasps on the lower cover in Germanic fashion. He also put metal shoes on the edges of the boards, again a habit more common in Germany and the Low Countries than in England. Tanned leather ties were used to fasten small books during the sixteenth century. Metal bosses were occasionally used, and chains or chain marks occur from time to time, often at the bottom right-hand corner, but also in the centre of the top edge of the upper cover.

On the whole, during the fifteenth century, bindings were soundly constructed; they were sewn with thick thread, all along (every gathering being fastened to each of the sewing supports), and all supports were laced in, while the endbands formed part of the structure. By 1500, the binders were well used to handling paper and techniques changed to

5. Illustrated in Nixon 1984a, pl. 29, p. xxv (Cambridge, Magdalene Coll., Pepys ms. 1663).

accommodate the thinner and more pliable text-block material. Once the invention of printing had properly caught on and multiple copies of texts were produced more cheaply, more easily and in greater numbers, the increase in the number of books available led to an increased demand for the binder's skill. This in turn forced binders to speed up production and to cut costs. Towards the end of the fifteenth century, but especially during the first quarter of the sixteenth, cheaper structures and less time-consuming practices were developed to keep pace with this increase in book production. Thinner paper and smaller formats called for thinner thread, single supports and lighter boards, as well as for less complex sewing and lacing-in methods. From the beginning of the sixteenth century we can observe a change to cheaper materials: pasteboard replaced wood, cheaper covering materials became more prominent and we find limp vellum used for school-books and for classical texts, as well as tanned sheepskin, especially for the smaller formats. Ties replaced clasps, paper replaced vellum for end-leaves, we find single cords or thongs, circled round by sewing thread, instead of split thongs with complex sewing patterns, and simpler lacing-in methods. Not all thongs were laced in any more and, later, the practice of sewing more than one section at a time also speeded up the process. Endbands are no longer tied down, their cores are cut off and not laced in and they are often lacking altogether. These cheaply produced bindings occur most frequently on educational, religious and legal texts in small formats. They look like mass productions for the impecunious scholar who nevertheless wanted his much-read texts to be protected from wear and tear. Indeed that is what they are. We find classical and religious texts, often heavily annotated in a contemporary hand and simply bound with a cheap structure, using cheap materials and with the covers either left plain or decorated with a few blind lines.

The more elaborately gold-tooled bindings of the sixteenth century were normally well constructed. Every section was sewn, all supports were laced in and they have proper endbands. Tanned calf over pasteboards was the norm, although tanned and tawed goatskins were used occasionally. Other lavish bindings of this period and earlier were made of embroidered textile, often velvet. It may well be the case that the dearth of decorative leather bindings dating from before 1450 was due to the fact that the grandest medieval bindings were made of rare fabrics or precious metals. Practically no English silver or silver-gilt bindings have survived, the majority having been melted down during the

Reformation, or having fallen into the rapacious hands of Henry VIII and his supporters, their components being used to adorn palace and person, house and armour of those that took them, while most of the fabric bindings of this period have suffered from the ravages caused by time and moths.

Nevertheless, there is a certain amount of evidence for the one-time existence of medieval treasure bindings, as well as for textile bindings made during the fifteenth and early sixteenth centuries. That most of the English cathedrals and abbeys possessed bindings of this kind is clear from various surviving inventories describing the plate, vestments and service books with covers of precious metal. *Textus* books, elaborately bound and decorated volumes from which the Epistles and Gospels were read during mass, are described as having silver or silver-gilt covers ornamented with precious stones, or with representations of the Crucifixion, usually with the Virgin and St John, the image of the Trinity, Christ in majesty, God the Father, the assumption or the coronation of the Virgin, angels, and the four Evangelists or their symbols. Important parish churches would also have had such elaborately decorated service books.[6] Hardly any examples of this type of binding made in England have survived. Most fabric-covered English bindings of the late Middle Ages were either of patterned silk, cloth of gold, or velvet, often provided with bosses and finely decorated clasps of precious metal. These bindings figure in wills and church inventories and usually cover benedictionals, pontificals, mass books, breviaries, psalters and primers.[7]

A few velvet bindings made in pre-Reformation England have survived, in particular two splendid copies of the Indentures between Henry VII and John Islip, Abbot of Westminster, concerning the foundation of Henry VII's Chapel, dated 16 July 1504. The King's copy is in the Public Record Office, the Abbot's copy, presented to the Harleian library by Sir Thomas Hoby, Bt., of Bisham, is now in the British Library.[8] The only surviving English medieval embroidered binding, that of *c.* 1300–30, covering the fourteenth-century Felbrigge Psalter, lies outside the period under consideration.[9]

During the fifteenth century, and at the beginning of the sixteenth, the book-trade in England was much influenced by imports and immigrants

6. For examples and quotations from inventories, see Nixon and Foot 1992, pp. 20–2.
7. See, for example, the will of Cecily, widow of Richard, Duke of York, proved in 1495, printed in Plomer 1904, pp. 99–121, especially 109–10.
8. Illustrated in Nixon and Foot 1992, fig. 18.   9. BL, Sloane ms. 2400.

from the Continent. The binding trade also owed much both to immigrant binders and to the importation of binding designs, tool designs and decorative panels, especially from the Low Countries, while influences on binding techniques are also discernible. Printed books were imported into England already in the 1460s, and these imports increased during the following three decades. Consignments from Germany, the Low Countries, Italy and France are mentioned in the customs rolls of the Port of London and initially both the importation of books and the immigration of foreign stationers were encouraged.[10] It seems that, as a rule, books were imported in sheets (in chests, boxes, baskets, tuns and barrels), and the existence of a substantial number of books with foreign imprints in early English bindings suggests that these books sold sufficiently well to be bound, and to be bound fairly soon after their arrival.

Decorative binding designs familiar on the Continent were also used in England; large decorative blocks or panels showing saints, religious scenes, animals in foliage, heads in medallions, and heraldic or allegorical motifs, are found on both sides of the Channel, while some rolls (engraved wheels used to form decorative borders or strips) also show similarities in design. There is a remarkably close connection in the design of many of the small hand tools used in the Netherlands and in England.[11] Many of the motifs, such as dragons, fighting cocks, double-headed eagles, various kinds of monster, pelicans, lambs-and-flags, roses, fleurs-de-lis and pine-cones are found in abundance in both countries. In England a revival of the production of tooled leather bookbinding took place shortly after 1450. These bindings were produced in monasteries in Canterbury, Jervaulx, Tavistock, at Osney Abbey, near Oxford, in Winchester, Durham, and possibly in Salisbury. However, the main centres of bookbinding during the second half of the fifteenth century were London, Oxford and Cambridge.[12] Two workshops, one in Oxford, the other in London, used tools with imitation Romanesque designs, the London shop at least as late as 1502, but many more shops produced bindings decorated with contemporary designs. A number of scholars, from J. B. Oldham onwards, have discussed the history of blind-tooled bindings in England,[13] using the evidence provided by the decorative tools to postulate groups of bindings and to identify workshops. Some

10. For further details and documentation, see Foot 1993, pp. 146–63. Cf. Needham, below pp. 148–63.   11. Foot 1993, pp. 146–63.   12. Foot 1993, pp. 98–120.
13. Oldham 1952, 1958. See also Nixon and Foot 1992, pp. 7–24 (with further literature).

valuable work has also been done in local archives, identifying binders by name and establishing where they lived and worked.[14] Nevertheless, there is still plenty of room for more precise identification of the work of the known and named workshops; work must continue to link, separate or confirm – on the basis of further evidence – workshops that have hitherto been proposed, and there is a great need to associate the surviving products with the names of binders found in archival sources. This can only very occasionally be done with any confidence. It is rare to find an inventory or a bill where the books listed can be identified as individual copies or to find an inscription naming the binder of a specific book. The evidence provided by the binding tools is also scarce. Some rolls and panels cut for use in blind have names or initials that can be linked to known binders or at least to known stationers. The only medieval British binder who signed his bindings with his full name was Patrick Lowes, a Scot, who bound and signed a manuscript translation of three French treatises into Scots by 'Gilbert of the Haye, knycht', dated 1456.[15] The binding, which is probably about thirty years later than the manuscript, is decorated with individual hand tools, showing roses, animals and saints, and word stamps, proclaiming: 'patricius lowes me ligavit'.

The technique of decorating leather bindings with gold leaf reached England relatively late. The earliest efforts, dating from c. 1519 and the early 1520s, are all of an experimental nature, using blocks, panels, rolls and tools that were clearly neither designed nor cut for the purpose. Tools used in gold are cut so that the pattern stands out in relief, while tools for use in blind have their pattern cut into the brass surface, in intaglio. From about 1530 tools influenced by Italian and French designs and cut to be impressed into the leather through gold leaf, showing a pattern in intaglio, emerge and increase in number and complexity. Especially fine work was produced for the successive monarchs from Henry VIII onwards.[16] Hardly any English gold-tooled bindings of the sixteenth century are signed and hardly any can be attributed to named binders on any other grounds.

The attribution of bindings or groups of bindings to individual workshops is based largely – often entirely – on the identification and combination of the engraved brass stamps or rolls that were used to decorate

14. Especially by G. Pollard 1970, and more recently by Christianson 1985, pp. 41–54; 1989c, pp. 81–91; 1990; 1993.   15. On deposit in NLS.
16. Nixon and Foot 1992, pp. 25–34 (with further literature). For early gold-tooled bindings, see Nixon 1964.

them. It is generally assumed that for the period under discussion, the binding trade, at least in England, was not divided into finishers and forwarders. In France the situation is different and there are indications that – at least by the 1550s and possibly earlier – the forwarder and the finisher were not necessarily the same person. It is by no means sure either that the person responsible for the binding (that is to say the person who was paid for it) actually bound the book: he could have masterminded the operation, possibly chosen the design, and farmed the work out to different forwarders and finishers, so that the evidence supplied by the tools alone becomes less conclusive. This evidence still serves to indicate the work of a particular finisher, but it becomes dangerous to identify him with the man who is paid for the overall job.

Similarly in England, the person who is mentioned in the accounts as receiving payment for binding is not necessarily the binder. Cyril Davenport's mistaken identification of Thomas Berthelet as Henry VIII's binder rests on a bill for the supply of bindings to this King in 1541–3.[17] It is clear that at least five different binderies were responsible for Henry VIII's bindings and even presentation copies of books printed by Berthelet appear to have been bound in at least three different workshops; King Henry's bindery, the Greenwich bindery and the King Edward and Queen Mary bindery (the latter, its nickname notwithstanding, was already active from about 1545). It is not possible to identify any of these shops as Berthelet's own, and it seems likely that he did not own a bindery at all. Decorated royal library bindings made between c. 1530 and 1558 show a considerable variety of tools, including a number of similar tools of the same basic design (inspired by French models), which fall into easily recognizable groups.

Although it may be assumed that, in England, forwarding and finishing were carried out in the same workshop, it is possible that tools were borrowed or that – on occasion – they belonged to a publisher or bookseller, possibly even to the owner of the books, and that they were supplied with the books to a number of different binderies. The ownership of some signed hand stamps can be traced back to specific monasteries where any number of monks or nuns could and would have used them (German examples from this period abound). It is still far from certain whether the signature or initials found on so many rolls and panels identify the binder or the publisher/book-seller who ordered copies either to

17. Davenport 1901.

be bound, on request from specific customers, or, in the case of popular, well-selling works, to be held ready-bound in stock. The fact that almost all rolls listed by Oldham have been found in varying combinations with other rolls and stamps, coupled with the enormous output of shops such as that of John Reynes, suggests that the latter may well have been the case.[18] Where the initials found on rolls or panels have been identified, such as those of Garrett Godfrey, John Siberch, Nicholas Spierinck, Martin Dature or John Reynes, the available evidence suggests that these men were stationers, book-sellers, sometimes publishers, even if they were binders or owners of binders' shops as well.

Tools were certainly inherited and sold. They could move from binder to binder. Their life-span would have been dependent on how frequently they were used and how carefully they were treated. It is not exceptional to find the same tool occurring over a period of thirty to fifty years, sometimes in combination with different sets of other tools. Groups of tools are slightly more reliable indicators, at least for the period under discussion, and if these turn up in the same combination over a sustained period, while the provenance of the books they decorate points to the same place of origin, we can be reasonably confident in attributing them to datable and locatable workshops, even if we can give these no more than nicknames (based on an owner, a place or a notable tool).

Decorating a binding with individual hand tools was a laborious business and the increase in book production during the second half of the fifteenth century brought in its wake attempts by binders to speed up the processes of forwarding and finishing. The shift towards cheaper materials and speedier working practices went hand in hand with the search for quicker ways to decorate the covers. The use of rolls and panels, by which whole areas (such as borders), or even whole covers, could be decorated in one operation, constituted a fairly cheap and quick way of embellishing a leather binding, and we find edition bindings, bindings on religious texts, on works by humanists, and on popular classical and educational texts frequently decorated in this way. The use of panels in particular (certainly in England during the first years after their introduction) is, however, not limited to the cheaper edition-bindings. Some 270 late fifteenth- and early sixteenth-century English panels are known, about half of which appear to have been imported from the Continent. The earliest use of a panel in London dates from about 1494. It occurs on a

18. Oldham 1952.

vellum copy of a Sarum book of hours at Lambeth Palace,[19] likely to have been produced with an important owner in view and to have been bound as soon as it was printed. Its ownership has been assigned to Lady Margaret Beaufort. The four panels impressed into the brown calves' leather, showing animals in foliage, were later used by Caxton's binder.

Although hand-engraved brass tools and rolls are recognizable and identifiable as individual objects, panels cannot be relied upon in the same way. Until recent years it had been assumed that panels too were hand-engraved and therefore individually identifiable. Recent research has thrown doubts on this long-standing view and has led to the conclusion that panels may have been cast, instead of engraved.[20] If the panel was indeed introduced as a cheap, labour-saving device, it must have been economic to produce, as well as easy to use. Casting multiple copies from one mould and applying these singly, in pairs, or four at a time, to decorate one cover in one operation, lining them up side-by-side before putting book and panels in a press, would have been comparatively cheap, quick and simple. The apparent longevity of some panels, the distance they seem to have travelled, the varying position and shape of nail-marks on otherwise identical panels, and the existence of identical panels with blank shields and with shields with different initials, all support the casting theory, although some panels, such as that used with gold leaf on Robert Whittinton's *Epigrams*, c. 1519, were probably engraved.[21]

We can but rarely link the products of the binders' shops that were at work in England at this time with actual named binders, men (or women) with their own working practices, but we can say a little more about some of the owners of these bindings. They fall roughly into four categories. Most scholars bought books and manuscripts mainly for the text and purchased these texts ready-bound, or had them bound, either through the publisher/book-seller or by a bindery whose work they liked and could afford. Some commissioned fine bindings, perhaps as much for the love of the artefact as to protect a favourite text. Others commissioned bindings in order to present them, with or without ulterior motives, to a friend or a patron, while some received bindings as gifts.

We know least about the first category of owners. They probably possessed the simpler bindings, either plain or decorated with a few hand tools, fillets, rolls or panels. The literate clergy, lawyers, other scholars, students and teachers belonged to this group and they kept the binderies

19. Illustrated in Nixon and Foot 1992, fig. 11 (left).   20. Fogelmark 1990.
21. Nixon and Foot 1992, p. 25, fig. 19.

in the metropolis and in the Cathedral and University towns busy. The vast quantity of blind-tooled bindings produced in Oxford and Cambridge during the late fifteenth, and the first half of the sixteenth, centuries bears witness to a clientele of dons and students. These bindings frequently contain classical texts, religious texts, the works of humanist scholars, and law books, as well as history books and grammars. The large majority of these are in Latin. Some binders worked for the book-sellers and publishers, but many bound for individual clients, and the number of identified binders and binders' shops in both towns and the surviving evidence of their considerable output suggest a thriving scholarly community that wanted its texts suitably protected. The work of these shops has been discussed in considerable detail elsewhere.[22]

The London binders also bound for the publishers and book-sellers whose initials can be found on rolls and panels, as well as for individual scholars. The Inns of Court produced custom for the binders. Law books, books of Statutes, legally binding deeds, and other legal documents frequently occur in bindings of note. The only English binder to use cut-leather work as part of the decoration, the Scales binder (active from the 1450s until after 1481), bound for several persons connected with the Inns of Court.[23]

The famous indenture between Henry VII and John Islip, Abbot of Westminster, in its lavish red velvet binding, is an extreme example. It is lined with pink damask and surmounted on both covers with gold and silver enamelled bosses showing portcullises in the corners and the royal arms in the centre, with five examples of the Great Seal in gilt metal boxes. The importance attached to the document is clearly shown in the lavishness of its binding. In a much lower key, the indentures made between Henry VII and Richard Chetham, Prior of Leeds, sealed on 20 April 1505, and between the King and Thomas Silkesteade, Prior of Winchester, sealed on 12 June 1503, both bound by the Crucifer binder (active from c. 1499 till at least 1507),[24] show also that sufficient care was taken to bind and decorate documents to which personal importance was attached.

Although the majority of bindings for scholars and students were fairly simple, either plain or decorated in blind, at least in England, some

22. Foot 1993, pp. 98-120 (with further literature).
23. Barker 1972; Nixon and Foot 1992, pp. 8-9; Foot 1993, pp. 121-4.
24. Foot 1993, pp. 128-30; the indentures are now respectively in BL (Henry Davis Gift M67) and the Royal Library, Windsor Castle.

of these learned men when they reached more exalted positions, became less modest in their taste and had their books decorated with gold tooling. William Bill can be taken as an example. He studied physics and divinity at St John's College, Cambridge, where he took his BA in 1532-3 and his MA in 1536. The College elected him a Fellow in 1535 and later he became Master of St John's (1546), a lecturer in physics, and Vice-Chancellor of the University. As a student, Bill owned two bindings, one by Garrett Godfrey, the other by Nicholas Spierinck, decorated in blind, on books which he may have bought ready-bound. Later, when he had become one of the chaplains to Edward VI, he patronized the King Edward and Queen Mary binder, and several finely gold-tooled bindings made for him in this shop are known.[25]

The study of religion, classics, history, or literature was not a male pre-rogative. Women are known to have owned such books in fine bindings. The pious and studious Mary Tudor owned a number of devotional books, often bound in sombre black with either the letter 'M' or the name 'Mary' tooled on the cover. All these books are scuffed at the corners and give the impression of having been much and regularly used. Mary's personal choice of devotional books is in the mainstream of devout humanism. A few of her more elaborately decorated bindings are in gold-tooled white leather and a number, perhaps of a less personal nature, were produced by the King Edward and Queen Mary binder in gold-tooled brown calf. These include presentation copies of works by English churchmen, such as Edmund Bonner's *Profitable and necessarye Doctryne* (London 1555; see fig. 4.2).[26]

The evidence for women scholars having studied their chosen texts in fine bindings is not extensive, however. Anne Bacon, the mother of Francis Bacon and the second wife of Sir Nicholas Bacon, Lord Keeper of the Great Seal, for example, was a highly educated woman, said to have been able to read Latin, Greek, Italian and French. She translated Bishop Jewel's *Apologia Ecclesiae Anglicanae* into English (1564). In 1553, her husband gave her a nicely bound copy of the 1551 Basel edition of St Basil's *Opera Graeca*, tooled in gold with her initials on the covers.[27] Another learned and pious lady, a strong follower of the Protestant faith, was Anne Seymour, Duchess of Somerset, wife of the Lord Protector. In 1550, Walter Lynne dedicated to her William Roye's translation of a popular Lutheran catechism for children, which he published under the

25. Foot 1978, pp. 20-2.   26. *STC* 3281.5; BL, C.27.e.13.   27. Nixon 1971, no. 28.

title *The True Beliefe in Christ and his Sacramentes*, twenty-three years after the suppression of the original edition. The dedication copy, bound in gold- and blind-tooled white leather with Anne's initials, was in turn presented by her to Edward VI, presumably to remind the King of her by then imprisoned husband's Protestant orthodoxy.[28]

Embroidered bindings are often associated with women owners, up and down the social scale. They were not limited to women. A very fine binding of reddish-brown velvet, embroidered with gold and silver thread, covering a folio Bible in Latin (1543) was made for Henry VIII. The King's initials are in the centre and the painted edges show the royal arms and the Tudor rose.[29] Another embroidered binding for Henry, also a folio, this time in red satin, has 'Rex in aeternum vive' painted in gold on the edges of the leaves. It covers six tracts dated between 1526 and 1536. The inscription on the edges links this binding with the Greenwich bindery. It is possible that this book was sewn and forwarded there before receiving its embroidered binding.[30] Queen Catherine Parr owned several embroidered bindings, one of which, a 1544 Venice Petrarch, is bound in purple velvet embroidered with coloured silks and gold and silver thread, showing her crowned arms prominently on both covers.[31] Embroidered bindings usually occur on prayer books and Bibles and they may have been used more for showing off in church, than for study or devotion. Another type of binding that was certainly meant for personal adornment consisted of jewelled or enamelled covers containing a small, usually devotional, book, worn as a jewel either at the girdle or round the neck. 'Bookes of golde' are mentioned in lists of jewels surviving from the reigns of Henry VIII and Edward VI. At the time they were very fashionable and every lady at court would have one. Renaissance portraits bear witness to how they were worn. A beautiful example, now in the British Museum, was made in London *c*. 1540, by the goldsmith Hans van Antwerpen (see fig. 4.3a–b).[32]

With embroidered bindings and 'bookes of golde' we have moved rather a long way from books for scholars and strayed into the fields of collecting and presentation, closer to the second category of owner, those who commissioned or ordered bindings because they clearly valued the

28. *STC* 24223.5; BL, C.46.a.7. See also Birrell 1987a, p. 17.

29. *Biblia Sacrosancta testamenti veteris et novi*, Zurich 1543 (illuminated title-page with English royal arms); BL, C.23.e.11; iIllustrated in Davenport 1899, pl. 16.

30. BL, C.21.f.14. Illustrated in Davenport 1899, pl. 34.

31. *Il Petrarcha con l'espositione di Alessandro Vellutello*, Venice, 1544; BL, C.27.e.19; illustrated in Davenport 1896, fig. 5; and in 1899, pl. 17.   32. Tait 1985, pp. 29–58.

artefact – or because they considered it suited their status. During the period under consideration, such owners are more numerous on the Continent, especially in France and Italy, than in England. For by far the majority of collectors who amassed books and had them put in fine bindings, there is no evidence, either direct or indirect, of whether or not they had any say in the choice of materials in which their books were bound or in the designs and tools used to decorate them. Many collectors had their coat of arms, their crest, their insignia, or their name or initials tooled on their bindings and they must at least have specified that to their binders, probably even providing them with a suitable stamp. Thomas Wotton, the son of Sir Edward Wotton, whose bindings frequently, but not always, display his ownership inscription or his arms, preferred to have his books bound in Paris. He was 'excellently educated, and studious in all the *Liberall Arts*, in the knowledge whereof he attained unto a great perfection'.[33] Wotton was a staunch Protestant and consequently in and out of favour at court. Mary Tudor had him imprisoned in 1554, but her sister released him on her accession and made him Sheriff of Kent. Elizabeth also invited him to her court, offering him a knighthood. However, Wotton refused, preferring the relative obscurity and peace and quiet of his country house in Kent. Edward Dering and Thomas Becon dedicated books to him, praising his steadfastness in religion and his godly way of life. With all his lack of taste for courtly splendour, Wotton had a taste for fine bindings, most of which he acquired in three batches during his visits to France in December 1547, in 1549 or soon thereafter, and in 1551 and/or 1552, where he patronized three different Parisian ateliers.[34] The bindings he ordered in England after his release from prison are decorated with his coat of arms showing nine quarterings, but are otherwise left fairly plain. Other lay owners of decorated bindings include Henry Fitzalan, 12th Earl of Arundel (*c.* 1511–80) – who is known to have patronized the Medallion binder *c.* 1555, specifying the use of his armorial stamp,[35] and later (beyond our chronological limit) the Dudley binder – and the Lord Protector Somerset, who owned a fifteenth-century manuscript of the *Decameron*, probably bound for him, also in the Medallion binder's shop (see fig. 4.4).

Most fine bindings of this period were made either for dignitaries of

33. Izaak Walton, 'The Life of Sir Henry Wotton', in *Reliquiae Wottonianae*, London 1651, fol. b2r.   34. Foot 1978, pp. 139–55.

35. Aristotle, *De natura animalium libri ix* [and other works], Venice, 1513: BL, C.54.k.1. Another binding for Arundel by the Medallion binder is Publius Ovidius Naso, [*Opera*], Venice, 1515, 1516: BL, C.65.f.9.

the Church or for members of the Royal family, whether they ordered them for themselves or received them as presents. Gilbert Keymer, physician to Humfrey, Duke of Gloucester, twice Chancellor of the University of Oxford, and treasurer, later Dean, of Salisbury Cathedral, owned two manuscripts written for him by Herman Zurke and bound (*c.* 1460–3), possibly in Salisbury or in Oxford, in blind-tooled brown calf, decorated with a set of word stamps and pictorial tools.[36] The same shop also worked for William Witham, Dean of the Arches and Canon of Wells. The Churchwardens of St Andrew's, Canterbury used the binder John Kemsyn in the 1480s and 1490s. Richard Chetham and Thomas Silkesteade have been mentioned already, while Richard Foxe, Bishop of Winchester and of Durham, founder of Corpus Christi College, Oxford, patronized the Greyhound binder, who was active in the 1490s.[37] Cardinal Wolsey owned the first English gold-tooled binding to have survived (*c.* 1519),[38] and Cardinal Reginald Pole presented New College, Oxford, with four Greek manuscripts bound for him by King Henry's binder.[39] Thomas Goodrich, Bishop of Ely, was the dedicatee of a French translation by François Philippe of Cranmer on the Eucharist (London 1552), bound for him by the King Edward and Queen Mary binder in gold-tooled calf with his initials and motto in the centre.[40] Cuthbert Tunstal, Master of the Rolls and Bishop, successively, of London and of Durham, whom Cardinal Pole considered the greatest of English scholars, acquired at least two of his bindings in France, a country which he visited on a number of occasions in the late 1520s, as well as in 1546. They are decorated with painted medallions. One, a 1528 Paris Bible, is now in the Bodleian Library, Oxford; the other, in the Walters Art Gallery, Baltimore,[41] covers a copy of the second edition of Tunstal's own *De arte supputandi*, printed in Paris in 1529, with his name, as Bishop of London, painted on the edges of the leaves.

The third category of owner, those who commissioned bindings for presentation, could do so either as an act of friendship, indicating the esteem in which the recipient was held, or in expectation that the noble recipient would oblige and grant the donor preferment in return. Sir Nicholas Bacon, who gave his wife Anne the finely bound works of St Basil, belongs to the first category, while some courtiers may well have

36. Oxford, Merton Coll., ms. 268 (illustrated in Hobson 1929, pl. 34), and Bodleian, ms. Laud, misc. 558.   37. G. Pollard 1970, p. 213.
38. Illustrated in Nixon and Foot 1992, fig. 19.
39. Oxford, New Coll., mss. 41, 146–7, 247; Hobson 1929, pl. xxii, nos. i–iv.
40. *STC* 6003.5; Foot 1993, pp. 332–5.   41. Nixon 1956, no. 22; D. E. Miner 1957, no. 344.

had the second aim in view. Thomas Linacre, physician to Henry VIII, gave his royal master a copy of Paulus de Middelburgo, *De recta Paschae celebratione* (Fossombrone 1513), which he had bound by John Reynes and decorated with a gilt panel showing the royal arms, at a time when gold-tooled bindings were still a novelty in England. The idea of using a panel, designed and cut for use in blind, with gold leaf was no doubt Linacre's. He had already had some gold-tooled bindings made for Henry VIII in Paris.[42] Clement Adams, whose presentation binding to Philip II has already been mentioned, may have intended to flatter Henry VIII with a lengthy inscription in Latin tooled on the binding of Martin Luther's *Enarratio Psalmorum LI & CXXX* (Strasbourg 1538), which reads (in translation): 'The wealthy, Sire, give their friends golden gifts, but this book contains something better than gold. Your Adam, who is your devoted servant, hopes that you will be as pleased to receive this as he is to give it.' The lavishly gold-tooled brown calf binding by the suitably named Flamboyant binder may also well be called a 'golden gift'.[43] The same binder produced, on the instruction of Wouter Deleen, a Dutch Protestant pastor resident in London, two finely decorated New Year's gifts for Henry VIII. One binding is on Deleen's own manuscript *Libellus de tribus hierarchiis*, the other on Hermann, Archbishop of Cologne, *Ein Christliche in dem Wort Gottes gegrünte Reformation* (Bonn 1543). Both bindings have the royal arms and the latter has the date 1545, together with a long presentation inscription, as well as a lengthy letter by Deleen to his King.[44] Two New Year's gifts for Edward VI from Deleen were bound in a hitherto unidentified shop. They contain two closely related manuscripts by the donor. Both are courses of lectures in Latin on the first four chapters of Genesis, and were possibly presented in 1552 and in 1553.[45] It was not at all uncommon for authors and editors to have copies of their work finely bound for presentation to a suitable patron. Robert Whittinton dedicated the manuscript of his *Epigrams* to Cardinal Wolsey and presented it to him in a brown calf binding decorated in gold with two large blocks, used sideways to fit the shape of the book, showing St George killing the dragon, and Tudor emblems.[46]

Royal recipients frequently fall into the fourth category of collectors: those who received bindings as gifts. Several of those have already been

---

42. Nixon 1978, no. 5.   43. Nixon 1978, no. 11.
44. Illustrated respectively in Davenport 1901, pl. v and in Philip 1951, pl. v.
45. Nixon 1978, no. 14; Holmes 1893, pl. 8.
46. Illustrated in Nixon and Foot 1992, fig. 19.

mentioned and more examples can be found in the literature.[47] All English monarchs of this period received finely bound books as New Year's gifts. Wouter Deleen's gifts to Henry VIII and Edward VI have been mentioned above. Apart from presentation bindings, the royal library contained texts chosen for, or even possibly by, the monarch[48] for their contents rather than for their exterior. Those that have survived in their original bindings suggest that we may possibly already talk of a standard royal library style (so much more obvious during later reigns). A number of folios from Edward VI's library appear to have been bound by the Medallion binder in brown calf, decorated with blind lines and tooled in gold to a similar design, showing a border composed of single tools, corner tools inside the panel, a large diamond formed by a roll, surrounding the arms and initials of Edward VI in the centre. The King Edward and Queen Mary binder produced a number of bindings with similar designs of circles, rectangles and lozenges formed by interlacing ribbons, often painted black, with solid gold fleuron tools around the royal arms, with or without initials. The gold-tooled white leather bindings produced by the Greenwich binder for Henry VIII, and decorated with delicately cut solid tools inspired by French models, frequently have 'Rex in aeternum vive' painted on the edges of the leaves.

It is not easy at this time to distinguish between library bindings and privately owned bindings, perhaps with the exception of chained bindings that were surely produced for use in a library. Those original plain or blind-tooled bindings that remain in Oxford and Cambridge college libraries may have been ordered for the library, although many were also presented. As bound books were expensive, it is more than likely that a useful text had several owners, and multiple, near-contemporary ownership inscriptions bear this out. That books and manuscripts, especially those in fine bindings, were considered desirable and precious is clear, both from wills where individual books, sometimes closely described, are bequeathed to named legatees, and from the many presentation bindings still in existence. That not all of these were read or used for study is apparent from the excellent condition in which several of the finest bindings from this period have survived.

47. E.g. Nixon and Foot 1992, pp. 25–33 (with further literature).   48. Birrell 1987a.

5

The rise of London's book-trade

C. PAUL CHRISTIANSON

Any study of the late medieval history of the book in Britain must eventually turn to London where, from the fifteenth century onwards, the enterprise of various people involved with making, importing or selling books made the City dominant in national book commerce. The years covered by the present volume take in a remarkable period in London's trade history, beginning in 1403, with civic ordinances of incorporation granted to a common fraternity of London book artisans (regularly known by the 1440s as the Mistery of Stationers), and ending in 1557, with the royal charter creating the Company of Stationers. Each of these formal organizations was itself the result of a separate major trade development: first, the rise of retail commerce in manuscript books, both newly commissioned and used, as a full-time occupation for book artisans and entrepreneurs drawn to London by its offer of economic opportunity; and second, the subsequent rise of broad-scale commerce in printed books, initially by foreign, but eventually by native, publishers and printers working to create a wholesale trade. Aspects of these two forms of book commerce constitute the basis of this chapter.

The early stages of London's book-trade history have long been a matter for speculation, largely because little evidence bearing on book commerce survives. In City of London archives, we find the first mention of the trade in 1403, when various book craftsmen sought to form a common fraternity, uniting older guilds of manuscript artists and of text-writers, whose trade interests were now also to be joined with those of other Londoners who bound and sold books.[1] The formation of a single-craft guild carries with it certain implications. It suggests that, by the turn of the century, the trade was already sufficiently developed and competitive to make its regulation desirable, if not essential. It also suggests

---

1. R. R. Sharpe 1889–1912, I, p. 25.

that the community of book artisans and sellers had grown to a critical size. As attested by a variety of property records, including rental lists for shops and tenements and those showing parish membership or residence, the area immediately surrounding old St Paul's Cathedral had already, by the 1390s, emerged as a book-craft neighbourhood, drawing artisans from various parts of the country and from abroad. Between 1404 and 1410, names of sixteen artisans appear in rental records as tenants in shops owned by London Bridge in Paternoster Row, the small lane to the north of the Cathedral Churchyard. Three were stationers, three text-writers, three bookbinders, and seven limners, i.e., decorative artists. Eight of these sixteen bookmen served as early wardens of the new trade fraternity.

Migration to Paternoster Row or to streets and lanes nearby continued steadily throughout the fifteenth century; as many as 136 stationers and book artisans, at various times, established business premises and residence in the environs of St Paul's. At least 125 other London bookmen may be identified during this period. In all, records attest more than 260 Londoners who made their living as makers and sellers of books before 1500, with the strongest concentration in the vicinity of the Cathedral.[2] The community was drawn to this area by its proximity to important markets for books: the City's educational and scholarly institutions were all located nearby, in the grammar schools at St Martin-le-Grand and St Mary-le-Bow, in St Paul's own educational establishments, and in the study centres of the London convents of Greyfriars, Whitefriars and Blackfriars. Only slightly more distant were other potential customers: the numerous London lawyers as well as Chancery masters and scribes located in the vicinity of Holborn and Chancery Lane. These literate communities were served also by the stationers' competitors for writing jobs, the legal scriveners, who as early as 1373 had founded their own Mistery of Writers of Court Letter, and who frequently took up residence near St Paul's.[3]

The evidence of an established community for book commerce has several implications. One can argue that the economy of book manufacture and sale was essentially altered by the existence of such a trade area. No longer were artisans the mobile element in book production, as had been the case when monasteries began to employ itinerant artists or binders or even copyists. Instead, it was easier and more profitable to

2. Christianson 1990.   3. Christianson 1989b, pp. 82–112.

move the books themselves or their component parts among the neigh-bouring shops of a book-craft community. The pattern of fixed locations for artisans had already become well established in university settings, such as Oxford and Paris, and it was on the university model of a super-vising stationer that London's own commercial model was based, but with book artisans themselves frequently taking on the role of stationer to oversee others' work.[4] Codicological and circumstantial evidence sug-gests that, throughout the fifteenth century, a book made for the com-mercial trade in London was typically the joint product of work done in many different places, with each step in a book's creation perhaps occur-ring in a different artisan's shop. The arrangement may now seem impractical, and yet the proximity of London shops, sometimes only a few feet or a flight of stairs away, shows that collaboration could easily work. A trade quarter made possible informal arrangements for common, albeit divided, labour on a book commission, even as it increased chances for regular employment.[5]

The rise of an <u>urban trade</u> did not mean an immediate end to older pat-terns of employment. On the contrary, itinerant artisans continued, through the fifteenth century, to work freelance, independently from any craft guild, sometimes in London, but often elsewhere in the country.[6] The Mistery of Stationers was powerless to regulate such trade, and no evidence survives to suggest that it had any interest in doing so. The Mistery seemed content to remain a minor City craft-guild. Despite such competition, however, London's book-trade community accurately fore-shadowed the future of book commerce in the country. Not least, the promise of steady employment continued to attract book craftsmen and apprentices, drawn by the City's trade opportunities.

Let us consider how book commerce operated in a manuscript culture. What, for example, were the costs of doing business? It would appear, from surviving property and rental records, that many, if not most, London bookmen worked out of very small shops, one room of which also served as living quarters. Rents were not high for these accommoda-tions. In Paternoster Row, the smallest shop units rented by the wardens of London Bridge cost 26s 8d per year, a charge that remained fixed from 1395, the year of earliest record, to 1554 and beyond. Frequently, bookmen held long tenure in their shops.[7] Other costs of business fluctu-

4. Christianson 1990, p. 24 and n.10.
5. Scott 1980a; 1968; De Hamel 1986, pp. 172–85; Doyle and Parkes 1978; Christianson 1989a.   6. Doyle 1957; Parkes 1961; G. Pollard 1970; Mynors 1950.
7. Christianson 1987b, pp. 48–53.

ated, dependent on current prices of the materials expended in making a book and on the frequency of commissions. Parchment, vellum and, eventually, paper represented major recurring expenditures, and other large costs involved certain binding materials used in more elaborate book commissions – deer and goat skins, silk tissues and knots, clasps and bosses – as well as gold used in decoration.[8] During the time of a book's production, a number of these costs had to be borne by the stationer co-ordinating the work of others, a service that required both entrepreneurial skills and an adequate line of credit or capital. Payment for labour in particular could not always wait until the book bill was settled by a patron. In the largely cashless society of fifteenth-century London, lines of credit could be extended by making a symbolic pledge of goods and chattels. Such debt transactions were entered into by various trade members on over eighty occasions recorded between 1431 and 1488, some of which would have represented specific instances of financing book-trade activities.[9] At times, a stationer might 'pay' for sub-contracted work by finding additional work for the craftsman involved. Such financial arrangements may be illustrated by an instance in which they failed: c. 1487, the stationer Philip Wrenne, who owed the limner Thomas Greneherst 5 marks, presumably for labour and materials on a book commission, brought as partial payment 'vnto the self Thomas asmoch werk in lymnyng as amounteth to the summe of xs yet the seid Thomas wil not alowe the seid x[s] . . . but intendeth to condempne your seid suppliaunt in the hole summe of v marcs'.[10]

As security for a book order or for craft services provided to a customer, some form of *agrement* or *acorde* was required by a stationer or by an artisan directly engaged by the customer. Such work orders have not survived, although there are a few references to them. In 1452, the London stationer, John Pye, who served as one of the executors for Richard Brown, the Archdeacon of Rochester, shared the responsibility for paying 'Johannes Bokebyndere' of Oxford for the illumination and binding of a 'Catholicum, prout in indenturis inter me et ipsum factis plenius continetur' – 'a *Catholicon* as in the contract made between me and him is more fully set forth'.[11] Bills were rendered once work was completed, as is sometimes cited in account records. In 1490, for example, the wardens of London Bridge noted payment of 40s to the stationer and binder William Barell, for binding and repairing books and for writing and noting masses, 'As by his bille therof made the parcellis

---

8. Lyall 1989; Christianson 1987b, pp. 10–25. 9. Christianson 1989c, p. 91.
10. Christianson 1987a. 11. Salter 1932, I, pp. 305–6, cited also in G. Pollard, 1978a, p. 10.

particulor remembring'.[12] Because the writing, decorating and binding of a new book involved separate steps in production, one finds a record of the total cost of a book broken down to its labour and material charges. Often, however, accounts record payment to individual artisans for specific work done. For decorating and binding a new missal for Westminster Abbey in 1386–7, the stationer and limner Thomas Rolf was paid 70s 11d, clearly a substantial commission. In 1423, the stationer John Robert was paid an even larger amount, £12 8s, for his work in writing out twelve books on hunting for the use of King Henry V. Few commissions were this costly, however, and not all jobs involved book production. In 1423, the binder Roger Dunce was paid 5s 6d for rebinding a gradual and a missal and for cleaning the backs of the same. In 1456, the stationer Robert Burton was paid 20s by the churchwardens at St Michael Cornhill 'for engrosyng & writyng of this accompt'. In 1447–78, the limner William Abell was paid £1 6s 8d for work in decorating a single sheet, the foundation charter of Eton.[13]

The price of a book commissioned or of a book service provided thus depended on a number of factors, not least of which were labour costs. What determined the charges book artisans could expect to levy, however, is by no means clear. Presumably competition led William Ebesham in 1468–9 to charge John Paston no more than '2d a leaff' for straight copying of a variety of texts, or led an unnamed copyist in 1395 to charge no more than 3s or '2s 6d per quaternion' for writing out two antiphoners commissioned for the chapel on London Bridge. Similarly, the 20s paid for labour in binding these same antiphoners in 1397 was a competitive price, even as was the 16s 10d paid more than a century later, in 1510, to the binder, Thomas Symondes, for similar work in 'byndyng gluyng and coueryng of two antyphoners wtyn the sayd chapell [on the Bridge] fyndeng to the same stuf and workmanship'.[14] Yet the competitive play of labour costs may also have been in part controlled by the Mistery of Stationers itself, insofar as it took on regulatory functions. Another factor affecting such costs may have been market pressure from older books available as retail items. It is important to note that the modern distinction between new and used books does not apply in the same way to the London book-trade in the fifteenth century. Books already a century or more old were still considered authoritative and directly useful, and one can argue that the notion of an out-of-date book

12. Christianson 1990, p. 64.   13. Christianson 1990, pp. 153, 152, 100, 77, 59.
14. N. Davis 1971–6, II, nos. 751, 755; Christianson 1987b, pp. 14–16.

would have been considered novel, if not extravagant.[15] A worn book in need of repair or refurbishment remained a prized possession. What seems clear – however interpreted – is that there was a market for older books of the sort which certain stationers, such as John Pye, Peter Bylton, Thomas Marleburgh or William Brereton, held as private stock but also as items for sale. Steady sellers included 'bokes of dyvynyte, matter in scole, or in lawe' – service books, grammar and school texts, legal writings – the stock Peter Bylton directed his executors to sell in his will in 1454.[16]

How large a portion of the book market the sale of older manuscripts represented remains unclear, but it cannot have been insignificant. The appraisal and pricing of such stock would have depended on dealers' judgement, both in London and elsewhere in the country, especially at trade fairs where older books were sold upon occasion. In the preamble to an Act of Parliament in 1487 repealing a City of London ordinance forbidding City freemen from selling at fairs outside the City, the following is noted:

> There be meny feyers for the comen Welle of your seid lege people as at Salusbury, Brystowe, Oxenforth, Cambrigge, Notyngham, Ely, Coventre, and at many other places, where lordes spirituall and temporall, abbotes, Prioures, Knyghtes, Squerys, Gentilmen, and your seid Comens of every Countrey, hath their comen resorte to by and purvey many thinges that be gode and profytable, as ornamentes of holy Church, Chalies, bokes, Vestementes, and other ornaments . . . and also for howsold, . . . as Lynen Cloth, wolen Cloth, brasse, pewter, bedding, osmonde, Iren, Flax and Wax, and many other necessary thinges.[17]

Certain stationers became known for their appraisals, as was the case with William Barough (fl. 1430–52) and William Barwe (fl. 1460–77), perhaps Barough's son or relative. Both men were frequently called on to evaluate market prices for books named in actions of debt in the courts.[18] The stationer John Pye, because he was one of those who 'ben connyng and have undirstonding in such matiers', served, in 1447, on a commission to locate, evaluate and secure books in great numbers for the libraries of the King's new foundations, Eton and King's Colleges.[19] The price of books, both new and old, apparently, was thus determined to a great extent by the London stationers, considered expert in these matters,

15. K. Harris 1989, p. 173 and *passim*.   16. Christianson 1990, pp. 81–2.
17. *S Realm*, II, p. 518, cited in G. J. Gray 1904, p. 15. See also Christianson 1990, p. 40.
18. Christianson 1990, pp. 66–8.   19. Christianson 1990, pp. 147–8.

especially those elected wardens of the Mistery. Such a calling was in many respects a continuation of a university stationer's role in evaluating pledge books and in selling those that were unredeemed.[20]

Perhaps the most difficult topic to explore in London's early book-trade history is the effect of time itself as cumulative events helped create continuity and lines of influence within the community. Long tenure within the same shop or parish suggests a certain tenacity, if not striking success for numerous bookmen, as does the continuity of many family names within a neighbourhood. Family ties must have fostered a sense of professional craftsmanship or even a certain shop style built up over time and shared as a matter of pride in achievement. Such habits of the hand, whether of binding, writing or decorating, would also have been taught to shop apprentices. While such influence is nearly impossible to docu-ment, one can cite probable cases, such as that of the limner, William Abell. On the basis of stylistic similarities, eighteen manuscripts have been identified by J. J. G. Alexander as Abell's work, with other work that may have influenced him also being noted.[21] In 1450, the man who had trained Abell as an apprentice, the limner, Thomas Fysshe, named him as executor of his will, leaving him the unexpired portion of indenture of two apprentices, Robert ffitz John and William Buttler, and asking him to continue their training. Fysshe's presumed influence on Abell and the subsequent presumed influence of both on the two apprentices seem to indicate a plausible channel of stylistic continuity over the course of years in a London shop. Other lines of influence must have come through fre-quent contact with fellow craftsmen in the close-knit community of the trade. Such connections show up most clearly in testamentary evidence, where virtually all surviving wills of stationers and other artisans name fellow bookmen in the guild as witnesses and overseers.

Eventually, from such continuity and contact, trends developed towards the repetition of certain patterns of craft work that had proved successful – whether in a book's format, its decoration, or its organiza-tion – as in the case of genealogical rolls or books of statutes.[22] For one genre, the books of hours, additional stimulus towards design repetition probably came from the influx of such books produced for the English market in the Low Countries, especially from shops in Bruges. Such

20. Christianson 1990, pp. 24–5 and n. 10.   21. Alexander 1972.
22. For discussion of a border artist who regularly worked on copies of *Nova Statuta* manu-scripts during the 1470s as part of a team of artisans working to produce these books, see Scott 1980a, pp. 56–8, 66–8. See also Meale 1989, especially p. 220.

foreign-made *Horae* survive in great numbers.[23] Comparable books from London shops stand very much second in terms both of quantities made and of their quality of execution and design. Yet there was interest among London craftsmen in supplying part of this market. Perhaps a typical example of a *Horae* designed for the domestic market is the small book of hours now in the College of Wooster (Ohio).[24] On the basis of its border design and figure drawing, the book can be located and dated as London shop-work of *c.* 1450–60, if not slightly later (see figs. 5.1 and 5.2).[25] A London connection is further indicated by the book's first owner, William Gurney, a friend of John and Margery Paston, whose obit is recorded in the Calendar on 21 August 1479; Gurney may have commissioned the volume while he was a resident at Lincoln's Inn.[26] The *Horae*, measuring only 11.5 x 7.6 cm, may represent what was a specialty line, that of small-size books of hours, offered by a certain London stationer and those artisans he frequently employed for such work. Both the border design and figure drawing resemble, for example, their counterparts in another miniature *Horae*, completed in London in 1474 and signed by the text-writer Roger Pynchcbck.[27] Such comparable work appears to show the effect of repeat business on design and presentation.

The fragmentary evidence here summarized attests to a small but growing market for books in London and a craft community ready to serve that market demand, even from the beginning of the fifteenth century. Providing services of repair and refurbishment as well as new and used manuscripts, London stationers and artisans were able to generate and sustain broad public interest in a book culture while at the same time realizing their own craft ambitions. When printing came, however, these ways of conducting business were to change, as was the role of London stationers.

The fifteen years following Caxton's return to England in 1476 became a time of unusual activity in London book commerce, of which Caxton's publishing venture in Westminster formed only one part. For more than a decade, printed books had been reaching England, albeit in small numbers and mostly from purchases abroad, with an early London sale recorded in 1477.[28] The novelty of such books soon became a matter of

---

23. K. Harris 1989, pp. 181–2; De Hamel 1986, p. 169.
24. Wooster, Ohio, Coll. of Wooster, Andrews Library ms. *Horae*.
25. I am indebted to Kathleen L. Scott for this identification and dating, in a letter of 10 February 1984.   26. Richmond 1981, pp. 253–4, n. 369.
27. Now BL, Add. ms. 58280; fols. 10v–11 are reproduced actual size in De Hamel 1986, p. 172. For Pynchebek, see Christianson 1990, p. 148.   28. E. Armstrong 1979, especially p. 272.

notice, at least among serious book collectors such as Robert Rowse, chaplain at St Stephen Walbrook. In his will of 1479, he interrupts a long line of book bequests to note: 'I wolle that Water Ayleworth shalle haue his iij prynted Bookes that I haue in kepyng'.[29] London stationers themselves must have welcomed such imports insofar as they provided additional business, including rubrication and decoration of books, as appears to have happened with two Gutenberg Bibles sent to London shops for illumination shortly after they were printed.[30] Less costly Bibles were soon to arrive and found a ready market. In 1486 Thomas Wyteacres, priest at St Michael Cornhill, noted in his will: 'I bequeth to Sir Thomas Mendepace my Bible inprynted.'[31]

Caxton was not alone in seeing England as now ready for its own printing enterprise. Caxton's arrival in Westminster was almost immediately followed by others from abroad. Some of these aliens looked outside London: the printer Theodore Rood, in Oxford, and the unidentified St Albans Schoolmaster Printer, in 1479, associated with the Abbey. Most, however, chose the City as a place to locate their business interests. These men are all well known to modern bibliographical historians, and yet it is instructive to review briefly their entry into the London book market, which soon was to be dominated by foreigners and by books printed abroad. By 10 May 1482, the alien book-seller, Henry Frankenbergh, with his trading partner Bernard van Stondo from Utrecht, had secured a lease on a tenement in the City's Langbourne Ward (near present-day Lombard Street), in St Mark's Alley, off St Clement's Lane, with their residence in the ward again noted twice the following year in lists of aliens to be taxed. Each man was identified as 'bokeprynter' and as a 'doche' (German or Netherlander) householder ('Theotonicus hospicium tenens') with a group of five named servants.[32] Despite the designation 'bokeprynter', no evidence survives that Frankenbergh and Van Stondo printed anything. A much stronger case can be made, based on Petty Custom Rolls of the Port of London, that the two men were in the City to manage the sale of books they were importing from abroad. Already by 1478, in the first surviving custom roll recording duty paid on books, Frankenbergh's name appears, on 10 January, as an importer, along with

29. Christianson 1990, p. 103.   30. König 1983; 1991, p. 145.
31. London, Guildhall Library ms. 9171/7, f. 72r. For early acquisition of printed books, see Doyle 1988.
32. The rent paid was a large amount, £3 13s 4d per year; see PRO *Ancient deeds* C146/1058. The Return of Aliens is PRO E179/144/75A m.1F and E179/242/25 m.1D. Frankenbergh and Van Stondo were assessed at 6s 8d each, their servants – Stephen Ree, Herman Groce, Dediricus and Adrian Derykson, and a woman named Katerina – at 2s each. For the designation 'printer', see King, below, p. 167.

his fellow 'docheman', John de Aken, i.e., of Aachen, the family name of John de Westfalia.[33] Frankenbergh's name, as an importer, continues through 1485, with books valued at more than £100. The relatively large number of servants employed by him and Van Stondo suggests that their work lay in transport and sale of books outside London, as pedlars or as agents at fairs. The appearance of the name of John de Aken (Johannes de Westfalia) on custom rolls between 1478 and 1491 (in the latter instance, in the name of Elizabeth van Acon, presumably his wife) points to a related model of foreign venture into an English market, in his case that of a foreign printer who chose for a time to direct marketing of his own books in England. In addition, De Westfalia for a time joined forces with the Savoyard, Peter Actors, supplying books for the Oxford market and visiting the University Stationer, Thomas Hunt, in 1483.

Peter Actors most clearly exemplifies the success possible in direct marketing of imported books during Caxton's lifetime. His is the most frequently occurring name on the custom rolls of this period: between 1478 and 1491 he imported more than 1,300 books valued in excess of £140. His aggressive marketing may have influenced the decision of the King's Council, under the guidance of the bibliophile John Russell,[34] to exempt foreign suppliers of books from the parliamentary Act of 1484 restricting actions among foreign merchants in England. By proviso to the Act, the book-trade was not to be affected, and free traffic in books was allowed. No barriers, other than the levy of import duties, would apply to any 'Artificer or merchaunt straungier of what Nacion or Countrey he be . . . for bryngyng into this Realme, or sellyng by retaill or otherwise, of any manners bokes wrytten or imprynted, or for the inhabitynge within the said Realme for the same intent'.[35] Actors would appear to have been one of the chief beneficiaries of this legislation, for a year later he had managed to get an appointment as Stationer to the King 'with license to import, so often as he likes, from parts beyond the sea, books printed and not printed anywhere in the kingdom and to dispose of the same by sale or otherwise, without paying customs, etc. theron and without rendering any accompt thereof'.[36] Custom rolls show at least seven other traders who enjoyed the government's encouragement of imports during the period 1485 to 1491, one of whom, John Rue, had a

33. PRO Exchequer K.R.: Custom Rolls E122 194/22 and 23, mems. 1D and 2F. The date on both rolls is 10 January 1478, not 30 December 1477, as reported by Kerling 1955, p. 191. On both rolls, De Aken's name appears as 'de Aker', paying duty on books valued at £6 13s 4d. See Juchhoff 1954. For discussion of these custom rolls, see Needham, below, pp. 148–63.
34. E. Armstrong 1979, p. 276.   35. *S Realm*, see Appendix, p. 608.   36. Duff 1905, p. 1.

shop in the Churchyard at St Paul's, which he must have opened at least by 1481, when his brother Andrew, with whom he was in business, also imported books.[37]

Two foreigners involved with the London trade during Caxton's printing career are more familiar to modern history than the book-sellers and importers, chiefly because they were printers and some of their work survives. The partnership of the printers John Lettou and William de Machlinia (1481–2), continued by De Machlinia alone to 1486, is often cited as a venture set up for too small a market, centred on books of English common law that no foreign printing shop was attempting to supply. Lettou had arrived in London and set up a printing shop by 1480 at the latest, supported by commissions given him by the draper, William Wilcock.[38] The shop was located in Dowgate Ward, as indicated in the Return of Aliens in 1483, near the churches of All Hallows the Less and the Great, by the river (in the area of present-day Cannon Street Station). Wilcock was resident nearby in Candlewick Street Ward (with his wife, an alien whose name also appears on the Return of 1483 – 'Johanna uxor Willi Wilcokkys draper, Theotonicus') and he may have been Lettou's sponsor.[39] In the Return, Lettou is identified as 'bokeprynter' and 'Theotonicus', along with his wife, Elizabeth, and his non-householder associate, William Ravenswalde, and four named servants: Peter Martynson, George van Hawyn, Bernard van Dentour and Joste de Fuller.[40] Lettou's establishment, it should be noted, was not far from that of Henry Frankenbergh, who was in Langbourne Ward, as was another 'doche bokeprynter', John Hawkes. Situated between these different establishments, in Walbrook Ward (perhaps near the Stocks Market), was the shop of John Richardson, identified as 'Stacyoner' and as 'doche' householder. Richardson appears to have been the bookbinder of that name, still active in London as late as 1520.[41] His early arrival in London would suggest that alien printers and book-sellers alike had encouraged the migration to London of trained bookbinders.

As Anne Sutton has recently argued, Lettou's associate in the Dowgate Ward establishment, William Ravenswalde, was the same William de Machlinia (i.e., Mechelen), who, by the end of 1483, moved the press he shared with Lettou to a shop near Fleet Bridge and subsequently to another shop in Holborn. Lettou may have died shortly before the move,

---

37. John's death occurred in 1492, Andrew's (b. 1450) in 1517.   38. *STC* 581 and 19627.
39. Plomer 1925, p. 157. See PRO E179/242/25 m.10D.   40. PRO E179/242/25 m.8D.
41. PRO E 179/242/25 m.9F & D; Duff 1905, p. 137.

for De Machlinia appears to have married Lettou's widow, Elizabeth – the same Elizabeth North, 'dochewoman', who at about this time (1483–5) brought a suit to Chancery over sixty-five copies of the *Newe Statutez* over which she had responsibility.[42] If this surmise proves correct, then De Machlinia's move from Dowgate, westward to Fleet Bridge and Holborn, illustrates not hostility encountered from London stationers, but instead a model of commerce based on book sales directed to a specific market, in this instance the lawyers in the Inns of Court. While enjoying a measure of success for a time, De Machlinia was finally not able to continue this trade model. What was needed was a broader sales strategy based on a much wider distribution of books.

Arguably, no such notions of large markets were yet occurring to London stationers and artisans, accustomed to manuscript-book sales in a retail and bespoke trade. Little attention has been paid to the traditional market for books during the fifteen-year period of Caxton's activities in Westminster, but surviving evidence indicates that not that much had changed in the volume of trade. Bookmen were still prospering, among them most of the eighteen stationers and binders who can be identified as shopkeepers in the Cathedral area, many of them in Paternoster Row.[43] Names of at least two dozen additional stationers and trade members elsewhere in the City or of unknown location are also recorded, as are the names of the wardens of the guild in 1491 (Stephen Baker and John Roulande) and in 1492 (Robert Burton and John Hebson). Activities of trade members thus identified indicate that business as usual was still very much the rule, despite the arrival of foreign traders in printed books. Yet the trade centre was not to hold, and inevitably the market was going to change in both demand and outlook. The complaint in a Chancery petition made in the 1480s by the stationer, Philip Wrenne, that 'the occupation ys almost destroyed by prynters of bokes' was premature and smacked of the rhetoric of special pleading in a lawsuit, but it was also prophetic.[44]

Caxton's death, probably in the early spring or late winter of 1492,[45] conveniently marks the beginning of a new phase in London's developing market for printed books, a period coinciding with the career of Caxton's successor Wynkyn de Worde (d.1535).[46] One way to describe the changes occurring is to note the gradual shift away from direct marketing of books by printers – such as De Machlinia, De Westfalia and

---

42. Sutton 1992. See also Duff 1907b, pp. 413–14.   43. Christianson 1987b, pp. 51–2.
44. Christianson 1987a, p. 260.   45. Nixon 1976, pp. 312–13.   46. M. C. Erler 1988.

Caxton himself – and by book-sellers – such as Frankenbergh, the Rue brothers and Actors – to a broader marketing scheme using a network of agents and factors, with wholesale distribution. The period saw the influx too of many more people into the English book market, and yet their presence has been overshadowed by the market dominance of De Worde and his chief rival, the Norman printer, Richard Pynson (d.1529). Among other printers turning now to London as a place for their enterprise were William and Richard Faques, Julian Notary and Jean Barbier. Yet the output of London's presses combined, including the near monopoly of power of De Worde and Pynson, could meet book demand only partially, in terms of both aggregate number and titles or types of book. The London (and English) market depended on what was rapidly becoming a large-scale importation of books printed on the Continent, especially of popular lines, such as books of hours and liturgical texts, but also of Latin texts used by educated and professional readers. In this undertaking, aliens continued to dominate; during the period from 1492 to 1535, the names of 98 aliens appear on custom rolls, paying duty on imported books. Most of these names appear only once or twice, which suggests the broad appeal of the English market, even for small-time operators. Other names show up frequently, suggesting book sales as a large operation for them. Not surprisingly, De Worde heads the list, with 29 shipments of books between 1503 and 1531, at a total value of £147 10s. In contrast, the name of Richard Pynson does not appear on the rolls.

Sharing dominance in the import trade with De Worde was Franz Birckman, a native of Cologne, who sold books there as well as in Antwerp and London, and whose name appears 29 times on the custom rolls between 1503 and 1521 (as well as 48 times in *STC* entries between 1504 and 1528). Birckman died *c.* 1530, but his family's involvement with importing into England continued unabated, with the name of his son, also called 'Franz', frequently occurring in the rolls from 1531 until at least 1557, and that of his nephew, John, on rolls from 1545 to 1554. The heavy involvement of the Birckman family in London sales may also have allowed them to play a major role in defining the market economy in books, determining the wholesale price as informed by their expertise and connections with markets in Antwerp and Cologne. Early on, the family's business interests became located in St Paul's Churchyard, in the shop of their factor, the bookseller Henry Harmon.

At various times, other foreign book-sellers were also in England overseeing books being shipped in their name, among them the Dutchman Frederick Egmont, whose books were also sold in St Paul's Churchyard by his factor, the book-seller Joyce Pelgrim. The Parisian dealer, Michael Morin, received shipments in Winchelsea in 1498 and 1500 and then again in London in 1503 and 1506, perhaps in connection with another Parisian book-seller, John de Coblencz, whose name appears on the custom rolls on seven occasions between 1502 and 1508.[47] That such imports could lead to a life-time career in London is indicated by Arnold Harrison, whose name appears frequently on the custom rolls and who became a permanent City resident, although never denizened, as indicated in his will of 1541, where he is identified as book-seller, not stationer. He requested burial in St Paul's Churchyard, where presumably he kept a shop. One of his witnesses was the denizened bookbinder and prominent stationer, John Reynes, which suggests a trade association. Part of Harrison's business, like that of Reynes, presumably lay with the wholesale book-trade, which, as an alien, he was allowed to follow. Two other witnesses to the will, one Mychell, 'bokebinder', and one Morus, 'claspe maker', may have worked for Harrison, binding unbound imports.[48]

The pricing of imported books required familiarity with domestic and foreign markets alike. Because of their extensive involvement in such overseas commerce, Egmont, De Worde, the Birckmans, Reynes and Harrison must have taken the lead in setting the price of books at each stage of their movement in England, from London custom shed to storehouse to shop – and perhaps beyond, to country dealers or agents. Importation also required at least a portion of venture capital or, more likely, a secure line of commercial credit. For those with such resources, the prospect of ready return on investments in book imports became increasingly brighter from the 1490s onwards, as is attested by the numerous foreign importers already mentioned and also now by increasing numbers of London merchants. Caxton himself imported foreign books in 1488, the same year that the London merchant Richard Brent imported five chests of books from Venice through Southampton.[49] In 1494 and 1495, miscellaneous shipments of goods, including books, were received by six other London citizens: the haberdasher (and Sheriff of London) Henry Somer, Thomas Coke, William Hethe, Bartholomew

---

47. For Winchelsea imports, see PRO E122/35/11(A) mems. 4D, 6F and E122/35/14 m.10F.
48. Harrison's will is found in London, Guildhall Library ms. 25626/1, *St Paul's Reg. of Wills A 1535–60*, f. 18.   49. E. Armstrong 1979, p. 275; Ruddock 1941, p. 75.

Monger, the skinner William Danyell, and William Michell, who again imported books in 1500 and 1502, this time at Southampton.[50] Comparable names continue to appear on surviving custom rolls during the next decades: in 1520, for example, showing imports by the following *indigenae*: Daniel Hicman, Thomas Marbury, John Sturgeon, Henry King, Nicholas Wethers, Robert Soper, Thomas Thorne and the bookbinder John Gough. In a number of instances, these importers were probably selling books as incidental items in a range of merchandise. As the London mercer (and bibliophile) John Coleyns noted in 1520, trade for him involved the 'Sellyng of Prynted bokes and other small tryffylles'.[51] In contrast, the Grocer and Merchant of the Staple, William Bretton, between 1506 and 1510, paid for the publication of six liturgical and religious books, printed in Paris and sold for him in St Paul's Churchyard by the book-sellers, Joyce Pelgrim and Henry Jacobi.[52]

In the light of an expanding market, based on international trade, on wholesale marketing and on foreign expertise, both in printing and in sales, a question frequently discussed has been that of the place left for London's traditional book commerce. Caxton, after all, was a mercer turned printer, not a stationer or a scribe, and there is no evidence to suggest that the art of printing was taken up in London by a text-writer, as had been the case in Bruges with Caxton's associate, Colard Mansion.[53] There is no good evidence that London limners or text-writers learned the new technology by gaining employment as assistants in a printer's shop.[54] Yet it would be incorrect to ignore the on-going presence and activities of numerous City stationers. During the first half of the sixteenth century, the Mistery of Stationers continued to sustain itself much as it had throughout the fifteenth, as a minor craft guild. In 1505, it ranked 59th of 64 guilds listed in City records; in 1520, 61st of 64; in 1549, 55th of 60.[55] Between Caxton's death and that of De Worde, one can find the names of at least 65 stationers, all identified as such in surviving records and therefore presumably members of the Mistery. Although evidence about these men does not document their involvement with the sale of printed books, a good case can be made that, beginning in the

50. For Michell's Southampton imports, see PRO E122/209/2(A–B) m. 3F and E122/209/2(C) m.12D.   51. Lyell 1936, p. 509. See also Meale 1992, pp. 290–1; 1983.
52. Duff 1905, p. 18. For Bretton's will, dated 1517, see Phelps 1979, pp. 49–50.
53. Edmunds 1991, pp. 36–7.
54. Caxton's employment of a ms. artist for decorating texts is discussed in Scott 1980a, pp. 54–5 and *passim*.
55. CLRO, mss. *Letter-Book Q, 1540–49*, fols. 263v–264r; *Journal of the Court of Common Council 11, 1505–18*, fols. 1v–2r and *12, 1518–26*, fols. 75v–76r.

1490s, a growing number of guild members, particularly bookbinders, were making a successful transition from trade in manuscript books to the sale, in multiple copies, of printed books drawn from a large stock in hand.

To illustrate this point, one can cite the career of the prosperous book-binder and stationer, John Taverner, whose worth, in 1523, was estimated in the Lay Subsidy Rolls to be £307. The amount is exceptional; in the same assessment, De Worde was valued at £201 11s 1d, Pynson at £60.[56] Taverner, from Brodoke, Essex, was established in London by 1500 at the latest, renting a shop in Paternoster Row from 1501 until his death in 1531; the business continued in his wife's name until her death in 1537, at which time the establishment was taken over by Taverner's son-in-law, the stationer and haberdasher, William Bull, who continued to rent the shop until 1570.[57] Taverner's wealth was probably based on a large stock of books he owned as an investment. Of the traditional book-making crafts, binding was the single art essential to the new technology of printing. Since many books were not bound until sold, bookbinders were in a highly favourable position to control the costs of this process and to exploit the retail sale of books in their own shops. While a number of binders were only that, in the employ of printers like De Worde or Pynson, more enterprising binders like Taverner could achieve eminence and wealth by combining book services and sales. In light of his high assessment, Taverner would seem to illustrate perfectly the comment made by the printer and book-seller Christopher Barker in 1582, looking back at past trade achievements: 'In the tyme of King Henry the eighte, there were . . . Stationers, which have, and partly to this day do use to buy their bookes in grosse of the . . . printers, to bynde them up, and sell them in their shops, whereby they well mayntayned their families.'[58] Taverner's own skills as a binder, or those of binders employed by him, must have been an important factor as well in his success, as attested by the record of a royal commission in 1521, for which he was paid £6 to bind, cover and clasp forty-one books for the King's Chapel at Windsor.

During his long tenure in Paternoster Row, Taverner would have had daily contact with a number of other London stationers. In nearby shops

56. Duff 1908, pp. 260–1.
57. Christianson 1987b, p. 52; Bull's tenancy in Paternoster Row is indicated in the annual rent lists in CLRO, mss. *Bridge House Rents 6, 1525–41; 7, 1541–54; 8, 1554–68; 9, 1568–83.*
58. Christianson 1989c, p. 354 and n. 4.

in the Row were located William Casse, Thomas Lawe, William Lawnde, Thomas Layton, William Taverner (perhaps a relative), and his former apprentices, the binders John Tornour and Thomas Symonds, all fellow members of the Mistery of Stationers.[59] At the end of Paternoster Row, by Paul's Gate into the Churchyard, stood the large tenement, the Mermaid, occupied by Taverner's most famous neighbour, John Rastell. At various times during his tenure, Taverner would also have known the shops inside the Churchyard, those of Richard Faques, Julian Notary, Henry Jacobi and Joyce Pelgrim, Franz Birckman and Henry Harman, John Reynes, François Regnault, Arnold Harrison and other prominent members of the group of alien traders, as well as the shop of the printer Henry Pepwell, originally from Birmingham, who in 1518 took over what had been Jacobi's premises. In addition, Taverner would have been acquainted with England's first native printer after Caxton, Robert Copland, working in Fleet Street, even as he would have known Copland's former master, De Worde. Because of his proximity to so many dealers, importers and printers, both alien and indigenous, Taverner would have had available to him ready sources for sundry books in stock. One can in fact make a good case that Taverner was the likely supplier of the eighty books purchased in June 1522 by the son of Christopher Columbus, the bibliophile Don Fernando Colon of Seville, on his visit to London. Half of the books sold to him were printed before 1501, the oldest being a bound copy of Albertus de Padua's *Expositio Euangeliorum*, printed in Venice in 1476 and now on sale in London for 4s 5d. For the entire lot of books, Don Fernando paid £3 7s 11d.[60]

While few others could match Taverner's apparent financial success, his career as a binder and book-seller may nonetheless prove exemplary. Yet the important issue is not so much how or when London stationers found new ways to follow the 'occupacion' of book-selling (which they had never abandoned), as it is the gradual redefinition of the English market for books as a domestic enterprise and not simply as an extension of international trade and of foreign interests. The rapid growth of the book market in England in the generation after Caxton made such a redefinition inevitable. In order for that change to occur, a merger of foreign and native trade participants was necessary, but with neither group attempting to swallow up the other. Graham Pollard argued that

59. Christianson 1987b, pp. 52–3.   60. Rhodes 1958; L. Hellinga 1991a, pp. 220–1.

such combining of interests did not occur until after *c.* 1500, when alien printers and sellers were able to join the Mistery of Stationers.[61] While it is true that it was necessary to become a member of a City guild in order to sell at retail within the City, and that membership in a guild was zealously guarded – one could become a London citizen only by apprenticeship, patrimony or sponsorship in a trade guild – it is also true that the proviso to the parliamentary Act of 1484, cited earlier, restricting activities of foreign merchants in England, made an exception for any 'Artificer or merchaunt straungier' who wished to import books, 'wrytten or imprynted', and to sell them 'by retaill or otherwise' while in residence. Such *carte blanche* presumably had the power to override City trade barriers. Certainly, one finds the use of the craft name 'stacioner' in various documents referring to foreign bookmen in London. Among early examples, one can cite the Norman printer John Rowse, who, *c.* 1492 was identified as 'stacioner' when serving as 'mainpernor' for another stationer, Richard Fulowsele; additional 'mainpernors' in the case were the stationers Nicholas Laterbourne and John Broke. Rowse was still a book-seller in London in 1526, and in 1544, at the age of seventy, he took out letters of denization, noting he was born in Normandy and had been in England fifty-two years.[62] Even earlier, the alien bookbinder John Richardson (cited above) was identified as 'stacioner' in 1483, and he continued to work in London until his death, *c.* 1520. In 1512, four bookbinders, Peter Baker, John Gerard, George John and Michael de Page, along with Michael Morin (cited above), now identified as 'stacioner', and the draper, John Hutton (later an associate of the printer Thomas Petyt), served as sureties in a bond of debt of £20 involving Richard Fawkes (i.e., Faques), who also was listed as 'stacioner'.[63] The question of acceptance of aliens into the Mistery of Stationers does not appear to have been the problem in the merging of trade interests.

Arguably, the greatest impetus towards alliance with foreign bookmen on a more nearly equal footing occurred when Londoners, starting with Copland and Pepwell, began to learn to print. As the preamble to the *Acte for Prynters and Bynders of Bokes* made clear in 1534, the situation of the market had changed considerably in the fifty years since the government's provision in 1484 granted privileges to foreign printers:

---

61. G. Pollard, 1978a, p. 18; 1937a, b.
62. CLRO, ms. *Journal of the Court of Common Council 9, 1482–92*, f. 330r; Worman 1906, p. 37.
63. CLRO, ms. *Journal of the Court of Common Council 11, 1505–18*, f. 152r.

[S]ithen the makyng of the seid provysion many of this Realme, being the Kynges naturall subjectes, have geven theyme soo dylygently to lerne and exercyse the seid craft of pryntyng that at this day there be within this Realme a greate nombre connyng and expert in the seid science or craft of pryntyng as abyll to exercyse the seid craft in all poyntes as any Stranger in any other Realme or Countre.[64]

Such a claim of equity in expertise with foreign printers was more rhetorical than real in describing the situation in 1534, and yet much had altered. Even so, before a national London-based trade in printed books could be achieved, London printers and stationers needed protection from new incursions of foreign printers and printed books, and this the government supplied, through a series of Acts, in 1512, 1515, 1523, 1528 and, finally, 1534, as here cited, each measure affecting aliens, both denizened and otherwise. E. Gordon Duff, in summarizing the effect of these government actions, saw them as burdensome restriction:

> The alien printer, stationer, or binder, when denizened, was in this position. He paid double subsidies and taxes, he could have none but English-born apprentices and only two foreign workmen. He was under the rule of the Warden of the Craft [of Stationers]. He could not deal in foreign bound books, nor buy books from foreigners except by engross. The alien not denizened had the further restrictions that unless he had been a householder before February 1528, he could not keep any house or shop in which to exercise any handicraft, nor could he sell any foreign printed books by retail.[65]

Seen from another perspective, these government measures, while affecting negatively the foreign bookmen already in London, also encouraged their identification with the City and its rightful power to generate trade in books, in opposition to new foreign competition. What appears to be a form of xenophobia in these trade developments was almost certainly the product of the religious controversies at play in the 1520s and 1530s.[66] Yet, taken in the broader context of an inevitable movement in the London trade towards autonomy, the government's attempts at censorship and control tended to help rather than hinder trade independence. The growth towards that independence is what finally draws attention. As Graham Pollard noted: 'the development of the book-trade, like the development of motor-cars, may be more com-

---

64. Duff 1906, p. 237; full text in Appendix, pp. 608–10.   65. Duff 1906.
66. Reed 1920; Winger 1956.

pletely understood by studying the mechanism of the engine rather than the brake'.[67] The formation of the force driving the trade in its development, it should be noted, depended foremost on the successful merging of commercial interests on the part of London stationers and of foreign bookmen already in residence. By 1534, that merger was already well in place.

The subsequent movement of the Mistery of Stationers towards a royal charter between 1534 and 1557 has been traced in detail by Graham Pollard[68] and lies outside the purview of the present chapter. It is important to note here, however, that the reemergence of the London trade, serving as an independent urban and national market, took place within a small but talented craft community, much of it located, as it had been for more than a century, in the environs of St Paul's.

67. G. Pollard 1937a, p. 35.   68. G. Pollard 1937b; see also Christianson 1993.

6

The customs rolls as documents for the printed-book trade in England

PAUL NEEDHAM

> Records, like the little children of long ago, only speak
> when they are spoken to, and they will not talk to
> strangers.[1]

The earliest examples of European printing, the primitive Mainz editions of the *Ars minor* of Donatus – all fragmentary in their survival – may well have been produced for sale more or less within the region; the localizations and provenances of the bindings in which they were preserved as waste material suggests that this was the case. The Gutenberg Bible of 1454–5, however, was sold much more widely – to or through Erfurt, Leipzig and Brixen; Cologne, Bruges, London and Lübeck; and into Alsace, Baden-Württemberg, Bavaria, Austria and Sweden.[2] The names of Cologne, Bruges and Lübeck suggest that even in these primordial years of the new bookmaking technology, long-established Hanseatic trading routes played a significant role in the distribution of copies. Such long-distance distributions became a characteristic feature of European printing, and the development of major printing towns – Venice, Paris, Strasbourg, Nuremberg, Cologne and others – was closely connected with their existing and growing dominant positions within the network of European trade.

England's participation in this great movement was for long neglected. Only in relatively recent years has it become clear to a number of historians that the importation of early printed books into England was not an interesting sideline, but a primary factor in the history of the English book-trade.[3] No quantitative estimates have as yet been made, but through the end of the fifteenth century, and well beyond, a printed

---

1. Cheney 1973, p. 8.
2. Illuminations: König 1979; English illumination: König 1983; early provenance inscriptions: Schwenke 1923, pp. 7–22, Hubay 1979.
3. E. Armstrong 1979; Barker 1985; Hellinga 1991a; Roberts 1997; see also Christianson, above, and Ford below, pp. 179–201.

book purchased in Britain would just as easily bear a continental imprint as a domestic one. The scale of printed-book importation is difficult to gauge. The richest single resource for assessing the scale is the series of customs accounts, both national and local, of London and other ports. Despite considerable losses, these provide a more detailed record of imported commodities, over a longer range of time, than is available for any other European country. Following two sketchy surveys made by the antiquary H. R. Plomer, the Dutch economic historian Nelly Kerling published in 1955 a fascinating introductory article on the early importation of printed books into England, as revealed by the London customs rolls.[4] The studies of Plomer and Kerling are not, however, comprehensive for any period, nor do they even provide a complete account of the book imports as contained on any particular roll. The chief addendum to this suggestive pioneer work has been an exemplary publication of London's Petty Customs Rolls for the year 1480–1, where some eighteen book importations are recorded.[5] The following survey of the evidence for book importation residing in England's – and, dominantly, London's – customs records through 1557, is based on original readings of the relevant rolls made by the present writer and by C. Paul Christianson.

It is necessary to review the documentary matrix of the English customs rolls, particularly as they relate to book importation. Awareness of the context of customs-house and Exchequer practice within which the rolls were written helps one to use their evidence accurately and fruitfully, with a lively cautionary awareness of its complications, limitations and ambiguities. No documentary study can be successful, failing a source criticism considering such questions as: for what original purpose were the records kept? How does that purpose limit or touch the accuracy and fullness of the information given? How were the documents stored, and where did they move? Students of the customs rolls with particular interests, such as book importation, are greatly indebted to the expert archival orientations into the workings of the early customs system that have been provided, in various articles, by Jarvis and Cobb.[6]

From the later thirteenth century through the sixteenth, the various customs duties levied on goods imported to or exported from England supplied one of the two chief regular sources of royal revenue – the other being rents and fees from crown lands. Duties were collected on exports and imports according to a detailed (which is not to say, fully efficient)

4. Plomer 1924, 1929; Kerling 1955.   5. Cobb 1990.
6. Jarvis 1959, 1977; Cobb 1959, 1971, 1990.

system of accounting. Various coastal towns were designated as ports; and there only, at appointed quays, could ships be loaded and unloaded for overseas trade. Insofar as these towns were ports under the royal prerogative (under the view that, in Blackstone's phrase, 'the king is lord of the whole shore'), they were to that extent removed from shire jurisdiction. Surveyors, collectors and searchers were appointed to these ports by royal letters patent. The records kept by these men give us an angle of approach into book importation which may be equated with the point of view of those merchants whose goods were unshipped at the ports, reviewed item by item by the collectors and their clerks, and assessed for duty.

It should be kept in mind that the records are financial ones: accounts of the payments made to the Exchequer. The information contained on the customs rolls is there because it aided toward justifying and rectifying the monies that the collectors rendered annually (or sometimes more frequently) to the clerks of the Exchequer at Westminster, according to the Exchequer's Michaelmas-to-Michaelmas year. The customs rolls are, in fact, part of the Exchequer's archive – specifically of the King's Remembrancer's archive – and not of that of the customs-houses of the individual ports. Following a characteristic practice of medieval English financial administration, an independent check upon receipts was provided by the appointment of a comptroller – literally, the keeper of a *contrarotulus*, or counter-roll of gathered accounts. The seal of the port, known as the cocket, was in two halves, one retained by the collector and one by the comptroller, in a further attempt to ensure that all official acts of the customs-house should be known to both sides. The comptroller's roll was compiled from the same ship-by-ship records as the surveyor's roll, but the comptroller was not involved in the collection of duty. The periodic auditing of customs receipts at the Exchequer included a collation of the surveyor's roll against the comptroller's, with any discrepancies noted. Both the surveyor's and the comptroller's rolls are, it may be noted, secondary, although official, records of ship activities. They were engrossed, as the day of accounting in the Exchequer drew near, from gatherings of shorter draft slips, which were the working records of the various customs-house clerks. A few such drafts have survived, apparently by accident, in the Exchequer archive.[7]

7. The Petty Custom roll for 21 August–17 September 1485, PRO E122/78/3, apparently contains, as membrane 7, a draft for membrane 8, which is a partial record of the Subsidy for this period.

The customs accounts were typical Exchequer rolls: they were written on both sides, face and dorse, of long narrow strips of parchment, which were stitched together at their head; the membranes of imports were typically placed before those of exports. The various dutiable cargoes of incoming ships were entered chronologically, ship by ship, under the names of the importers. The given date for each ship is apparently that on which it was cleared or began to be cleared by the customs men, not necessarily the date it arrived in port. In general, clearances could be made on any day except Sunday. As regards printed books, two characteristic entries from early rolls may be quoted:[8]

> De navi Dyryke de Meir eodem die [i.e. 10 January 1478, Sat.] . . . [5th cargo:] De Johanne Aker alieno pro una pipa & unum [*sic*] ffardell cum xxj libris diversarum istoriarum, precium: [£6 13s 4d], custuma [20d]

and:

> De navi lubert van boke vocata Mary de Styleyerd secundo die Octobris [1480, Mon.]
> [1st cargo:] De Petro Auctore alieno pro i Cista cum xxxij voluminibus diversarum historiarum, xij peciis lawen cours, iij peciis cotton, ij mantellis menyver: precium: [£20]

Thus, on 10 January 1478, it is recorded that 'John Aker' (the Louvain printer, Johannes de Westfalia), an alien, declared his import, on the ship of Dyryk de Meir, of a pipe and a fardel, containing '21 books of diverse histories'; their value was assessed as £6 13s 4d, and he paid on this the petty-custom duty of 3d in the £, or 20d total. On 2 October 1480, Peter Actors, alien, declared his import, on the *Mary de Styleyerd* – skipper, Lubert van Boke – of a chest containing 32 volumes of diverse histories, 12 pieces of coarse lawn, 3 pieces of cotton and 2 mantles of miniver, their value being assessed at £20. The duty, though not recorded, would have been 5s. The contents of the chest being various, one cannot be certain of the value placed specifically on the 32 books.

The early customs rolls of the various ports have many family resemblances, but in aggregate are a less formal and stereotyped record than are, for instance, the Exchequer's own digested totals of customs revenues, which were added up from the ports' rolls in annual reckoning. The personnel of the royal appointments in the ports, and their deputies

---

8. PRO E122/194/22, m.2; E122/194/25 m.1 (Cobb 1990, no. 1).

and clerks, all changed fairly rapidly; and with these changes came often rather conspicuous, if generally minor, changes: of hand, of layout, of fullness of detail, and of language. As the examples just reviewed indicate the language of the customs rolls is a bastard of English and Latin, with many variations from one record-keeper to another, and even one entry to another. On the Controlment of Petty Customs for 1480-1, entries lying close together within June and July 1481 are recorded respectively as 'v prentyd bokes', 'i fardel cum libris', and 'xcvj volumina diversarum istoriarum'.9 The abbreviation system of the rolls is so makeshift that in transcription one must impose some artificial regularization upon them. In particular, a final suspension mark (') is used so frequently with Latin words, English words, and English words that could in principle be Latinized, that any system of expansion must be, to a large degree, arbitrary. There is a vernacular tendency, as one moves into the sixteenth century, for the proportion of English to Latin words to increase.

The London rolls do not record the points of origin of the ships entered. It is apparent, however, from the many clusters of entries under particular dates, that ships commonly travelled in convoys. From the combined evidence of shipmasters' and merchants' names (and sometimes ships' names), and from the overall nature of the cargoes, one can often make a reasonable, but unprovable, guess at whether the respective convoys sailed either – to mention the two commonest cases for book imports – from the ports serving Bruges and later Antwerp, or from those serving Rouen. These were generally small ships. The record quoted above from 2 October 1480 is that of only 1 cargo out of 40 – divided between 7 ships entered that day – which comprised the wares brought in by over 30 alien and Hansard merchants. The imports ranged in size, value and weight from 3,000 ells of Osnabrück linen, or 12 hundredweight of wax, to such small quantities of manufactory as a half-dozen 'standyng' knives, a dozen and a half pouch rings, or 30 dozen pins. Peter Actors's chest, containing 32 printed books along with cloth and furs, was stowed on the *Mary de Stylyerd*. This was the ship owned by the Hansards in London, whose factory was located in the Steelyard, fronting on the Thames, just west of All Hallows the Great. The other ships of the convoy had home ports in London, Colchester, Rotherhithe and Rouen.

9. PRO E122/194/25, m.6d, 7d, 8d (Cobb 1990, nos. 144, 156, 174).

It is at least a fair guess that most of these cargoes were collected at Antwerp's Bamismart, which was held for 6 weeks from the end of August.[10] The less frequent Italian galleys stand out conspicuously on the rolls, for their tonnages could easily equal that of a whole convoy of northern ships, and the tally of their cargoes could occupy both sides of a long membrane, or more.

Kerling stated that she had examined all the relevant London rolls from the 1460s to 1492, and from these collected the names of 10 merchants who imported 29 distinct cargoes of, or including, printed books. Her survey, however, must have been quite cursory. Independent reading of the same rolls increases the record to 23 merchants, and 58 book cargoes, besides a cargo including nine dozen 'kalenders', and two more including, in all, 13 dozen 'passion bokes'. The total count of the surviving customs rolls of London and of such outports as Hull, Yarmouth, Winchelsea, Southampton and others, through the end of Queen Mary's reign, produces the names of more than 150 merchants entered as bringing in printed books, in about 600 distinct cargoes. Even these figures, though, as will be discussed presently, can hardly be treated as useful statistics without further scrutiny and qualification. Their sum shows that there is an extensive body of relevant data which can contribute significantly to our picture of England's printed-book trade during its first generations. To see the data in their appropriate context, however, several background topics must be considered: (1) the dutiable distinctions between natives of England, general aliens, and Hansards; (2) the survival rate of the rolls; (3) the quantification of books on the rolls; and (4) the duty on books.

Natives, Aliens, and Hansards

For various imports and exports, the duties to be paid varied according to whether one were a native of England, an alien or a privileged alien – a Hansard.[11] As concerns books and most other items of import, this especially affects the distinction between two separate forms of duty: the Petty Custom, an *ad valorem* tax of 3d in the £ ($1^{1}/_{4}$ per cent); and the special royal Subsidy, voted by Parliament, known as poundage, a tax of

10. Kerling 1958, p. 131.
11. The special privileges accorded to members of the Hanse (and, at times, only to members of the Cologne Hanse) were complex and contested; for a general orientation, see Postan 1933.

1s in the £ (5 per cent). By the later fifteenth century, the Subsidy was voted for the term of the incoming monarch, and so became in essence a steady rather than an exceptional tax. All classes of merchant were obliged to pay the Subsidy; but English natives were not liable to the Petty Custom, which fell only on aliens. In London, the two duties were collected by separate officials, and recorded on separate rolls. Thus, in a given year, from London, both a Petty Custom roll (and its controlment) and a Subsidy roll (and its controlment) would have been rendered to the Exchequer (besides other special rolls for the duties on wool exports). Because English natives were not liable to the Petty Custom on imports, however, their cargoes were never entered on the Petty Custom rolls. Book imports by natives can only appear on the Subsidy rolls.

In the period surveyed by Kerling, the 1470s through 1491, only one London Subsidy roll survives, that for the Michaelmas year 1487–8. On this roll we find the name of that very familiar Englishman, William Caxton, who appears as both an importer and (very unusually) an exporter of printed books. On 10 December 1487, Caxton exported a chest of 140 books printed in French, valued at £6; on 25 February 1488, he imported a fardel of 112 books, valued at £13; and on 25 April 1488, he imported 1,049 ('M xlix', but *recte* C xlix?) books valued at £17 5s, and a chest of books, uncounted, valued at £10 16s 8d (see fig. 6.1).[12] Kerling drew a misleading conclusion from this. Within these decades, she stated, 'The import [of books] into London was in the hands of several foreigners and of one Englishman', viz. Caxton.[13] This is not right. One should say, rather, that the surviving rolls in this period, representing – except for 1487–8 – only the accounts of the Petty Custom, can only, this one year apart, tell us about book importation by aliens and Hansards.

This is exemplified by the Petty Custom roll's entries for imports of 2 October 1480, including the abovementioned 32 'volumes of diverse histories' brought in by Peter Actors, and 44 more by Henry Frankenbergh. The cargoes of 7 ships were entered under that date, and all 33 merchants with listed cargo are qualified as being aliens or Hansards. The cargoes on the Hansards' London ship, *Mary de Stylyerd*, belonged to 21 merchants, and were valued at almost £400. By contrast, the only declared cargo on the *Mary* of Rotherhithe was 200 ells of Ghentish linen brought in by James Warre, alien, rated at £2 10s. We are not to suppose that the *Mary* of Rotherhithe came wobbling across the water with a near-empty hold,

12. PRO E122/78/7 m.8d, 3, 4d: Kerling 1955, p. 197, wrongly gives 10 December 1488 as the date of the export.   13. Kerling 1955, p. 191.

but rather that she carried, besides this linen cloth, the cargoes of many English merchants. Their goods, however, not being liable for the Petty Custom, were of course not listed on the Petty Custom rolls.

Kerling's silent merging of incompatible evidence from two classes of document, accounts of Petty Custom and of Subsidy of (Tunnage and) Poundage, in fact obscures the most curious and striking feature of the Subsidy roll of Michaelmas 1487–8. Within this year, Caxton was not merely an importer of books, he was the only importer of books, whether native, alien or Hansard. This contrasts both with the immediately preceding Petty Custom roll of August–September 1485 (covering only the remaining few weeks of the Michaelmas year, following Henry VII's seizure of the crown), when 5 aliens are listed as book importers; and with the immediately succeeding Petty Custom roll of Michaelmas 1490–1, when 7 aliens are listed as book importers. We may plausibly suspect that this year of Caxton's effective monopoly is related to the still-unexplained hiatus of English printing during 1486 to 1488. During these years, the English printing shops contemporary with Caxton's, in London, Oxford and St Albans, all ceased operation, and Caxton's shop was nearly inactive. There may, indeed, be a hint of royal favour in this circumstance. When Caxton exported books printed in French (probably still-unsold copies of his French-language Bruges editions of 1474–5), the only other cargoes on the ship were large quantities of lead, pitch and candles, exported by Henry VII's influential councillor, Sir Reginald Bray. Among his many positions, Bray was responsible for the receipts of the royal chamber, to which, at this time, the customs duties were directed.

The survival of the rolls

The preceding paragraphs have already indicated that the customs rolls of London, and of the smaller outports, by no means survive in unbroken series. Until the gaps in the record are taken actively into account, nothing quantitatively useful can be said about the evidence in the rolls. In principle, for studying the records of book importation, one would like to have for London, for each Michaelmas year, the collectors' (or surveyor's) roll and the comptroller's roll for the Petty Custom, and the same for the Subsidy of (Tunnage and) Poundage. Within our period, however, there is no year for which both a Petty Custom and a Subsidy roll survive; and there are many years for which neither survives. Once the rolls had been audited at Westminster Palace, once the collectors had been given quittance, and their figures transferred to the permanent Enrolled Customs Accounts, these Particular Accounts no longer needed consultation. They were not intentionally disposed of, but they rapidly became unconsulted records of that office, and so were soon warehoused. Like other parts of the Exchequer archive, they came to be stored in various makeshift locations in the precincts of Westminster, for many generations, until after the opening of the Public Record Office in 1858. It is clear from what survives that water, fire and rodents, besides general neglect, took a considerable toll.[14] For the 80 Exchequer years between 1475 and 1554, London customs rolls – sometimes the Petty Custom roll, sometimes the Subsidy roll – survive for only about 23 of the years, that is, just under 30 per cent. A good many of the survivors are concentrated in the reign of Edward VI, for which we have virtually complete records. If we consider only the years to the end of Henry VIII's reign, the preservation rate is for distinctly less than a quarter of the years. The gaps can be large ones – for instance, no London records survive between 1495 and 1502, and none between 1522 and 1531. If we count the gaps by months rather than Exchequer years, the rate of loss becomes even higher, for a significant number of the years are represented only partially. A similar rate of loss is found for the rolls of the other ports. Naturally, this presents major obstacles to various kinds of generalization. It is potentially misleading, for instance, to say that 'imports of printed books begin to show up' (or 'began to feature') in London's customs rolls in late 1477.[15] The situation is rather that no such book imports appear in the Petty Custom rolls for Michaelmas 1472–3, and that there is then a 4-year gap until the next surviving Petty Custom rolls of 1477–8. There is no way to know whether book imports were declared during the 4 intervening years.

Quantification and valuation of books

The way books are quantified on the rolls deserves careful consideration, for there are many subtle changes over the period. The earliest record of 1478, quoted above, specifies a particular number: 21 books; but most of the other records of 1478 refer only, unspecifically, to containers holding

14. See, generally, Wernham 1956; Hallam and Roper 1978.
15. E. Armstrong 1979, p. 279; Barker 1985, p. 255 (the references to 1477, derived from Kerling 1955, should be changed to January 1478).

books: a chest, vat or hogshead containing '(diversi) libri diversarum historiarum'. The theoretical basis of the valuation of the books would have
been, as for all articles paying *ad valorem* duty, the price paid for them
overseas, what 'they cost at the first buying or achate, by the oaths of the
same merchants ... or of their servants ... or by their letters, the which
the same merchants have of such buying from their factors': such was the
standard wording of the long series of parliamentary grants of the
Subsidy of Poundage.[16] Books were inherently more variable in their
costs than pouch-rings, wool-cards, knives, pack-thread, brushes and all
the other more traditional commodities, and so a statement of number of
books would not in any case lead directly to their value. Yet, by 1480-1, it
seems to have been felt in the London customs-house that the number of
volumes should always be detailed, as a sign of responsible prising;
through the 1480s that is what one generally finds. Obviously, books
were not yet assigned standard values per quantity, in the way of most
small imported manufactures. Of the dozen book importations of the
Exchequer year 1480-1 whose precise valuations can be determined, the
rated value per volume varied, from cargo to cargo, from about 1s to 6s
10d. This is one of the years when both the Surveyor's roll and the
Comptroller's roll survive for the London Petty Custom, and so their
texts can be collated. There is a considerable disagreement between them
as to one book importation, that of Andrew Rewe, on 21 July 1481:
according to the Comptroller's roll, Rewe brought in 77 books, according to the Surveyor's, 177.[17] Because of the wide variation in per-volume
ratings of books in this year, one cannot say definitively which figure is
correct: 77 (with a false 'C' added to the Surveyor's roll), at a per-volume
rating of 2.2s, or 177 (with a 'C' omitted from the Comptroller's roll,
perhaps the easier error to make), at a per-volume rating of nearly 1s. On
the other hand, the range of per-book valuations in the rolls of 1480-1,
April–July 1483 and August–September 1485 suggests that there may be
an error in the count of volumes for Caxton's importation of 25 April
1488: the roll's given count of 1,049 ('M xlix') volumes yields a per-book
value of only 4d, far below any other book rating of this decade.

In the 1490s and after, there seem to have been further conscious
changes in the treatment of printed books on the London customs rolls.
The exact counts of books were for the most part dropped. On the Petty
Custom roll of Michaelmas 1490-1, 3 cargoes of books were entered with

16. Cobb 1971, p. 2.   17. PRO E122/194/25 m.9; E122 194/24 m.9; Cobb 1990, no. 184.

exact counts (33 'libri'; 130 'libri'; 1,100 'libri'), but 6 others were defined only by their packing: a barrel, a basket, a chest, or a fardel 'cum diuersis libris impressis'.[18] The exact distinction between these packing or container names is no longer evident to us, but one may presume that by the shippers, merchants, and customs-house officials, each could be told at a glance. Imported books are found to have been packed also into coffers, doles, hogsheads, maunds, pipes, poncheons, trusses and vats. To modern ears, many of the names – hogshead, pipe, poncheon and vat – imply vessels for liquids. But one finds these container names were used on the rolls in reference not only to wine and oil imports, but also to a wide variety of dry goods. Occasionally, vats are specially qualified as dry vats. On the subsidy roll of Michaelmas 1494–5, one finds only references to the packings: 'vnum poncheon continens diuersos libros impressos' – 'iiij ffattes bokes impressati' – 'i cista prented bokes', etc. The exception is when books were one part only of a highly mixed cargo, requiring complex sub-valuations, e.g., Bartholomew Monger's import, on 27 February 1495, of, *inter alia*, 2 vats containing '20 bands latten wire, 3 gross bells, 24 dozen [packs of] thread, 3 dozen baskets, 10 pounds ivory, 10 dozen locks, [and] 98 *bokes prynted* [author's italics]'.[19] With the next surviving London roll, Petty Custom for Michaelmas 1502–3, the count of volumes entirely ceases, except occasionally in similarly mixed cargoes.

These changes in the treatment of books correlate with a larger movement within the national customs administration, in the early sixteenth century, to regularize the *ad valorem* duties by fixing the rated values of the many dozens of imported commodities. In 1507, a Book of Rates was prepared for the port of London, which is preserved in a manuscript copy of the slightly modified form in which it was reissued in 1532.[20] For the commodities listed thereon, the valuations would substitute for the merchant's oath or statement of his overseas cost-price. In standard Tudor histories, the introduction of a fixed book of rates is generally seen as a conscious attempt by the central administration to raise customs revenues, but comparisons with the rates of many commodities listed on preceding Petty Custom and Subsidy rolls show that, in large measure, the 1507 Book of Rates simply codified the traditional valuations.

18. PRO E122/78/9, Controlment of Petty Custom, m.2d, 3d, 4, 4d.
19. PRO E122/79/5 m.17, 18d, 21d, 10.
20. Printed in Gras 1918, 694–706; see Cobb 1971 (with important corrections to Gras's transcription); Jarvis 1977, pp. 515–18.

Whether intentionally or by omission, printed books are not included among the commodities listed in the 1507/1532 Book of Rates. One particular class of printed book, however, was included: 'Prynted prymers the dossen [rated value:] xx d'. This separate treatment of printed books of hours ('prymers'; 'libri matutinales') on the customs rolls is one of their most interesting features. Primers are not recorded on the Petty Customs roll of Michaelmas 1490–1, but they appear among three cargoes in the Subsidy roll of Michaelmas 1494–5. Thereafter, in the London rolls that survive, they are common through 1537. There is then a gap in the surviving record until the Subsidy roll for Easter–Michaelmas 1545. Primers disappeared as an item of import during that lost interval, and they do not reappear on any customs roll through 1557. The evidence of the customs rolls is in obvious correlation with, in the 1490s, the dramatic rise of the Paris-printed illustrated book of hours as a best-selling genre over a wide distribution area; and, in the 1530s, the break of England's church from the confession of Rome.

The valuation of primers by the dozen (and gross) is characteristic of many small manufactured goods that may be thought of as chapman's-ware: balances, beads, dog-chains, knives, playing cards and spectacles are among other commodities rated by the dozen or gross on the 1507/1532 Book of Rates. These units of measure serve to emphasize that the distribution of primers lay for the most part outside the standard channels of the book-trade. Printed primers are especially common in the rolls of the provincial ports. They are often qualified as being already-bound, and they were manifestly imported, for the most part, by chapmen or suppliers of chapmen. They are characteristically listed as part of the content of very mixed and inexpensive cargoes, packed with such rural goods as brushes, shears, combs, woolcards and what was often abridged to, simply, 'other haberdash ware'.

Although absent from the 1507/1532 Book of Rates, printed books appear as a commodity in the earliest surviving printed Book of Rates, *The Rate of the Custome House bothe Inwarde and Outwarde* of 1545, where they are entered as:

> Bokes vnbounde the basket or mande [£4]
> Bokes vnbunde the halfe mande. [40 sh][21]

These fixed valuations have their roots in the customs-house traditions of a good generation earlier. On the customs rolls of Michaelmas 1502–3 and

21. *STC* 7687 (8°), fol. a5ʳ.

1506–7, the rated value of the basket, maund or vat (etc.) of books was still highly variable between £1 and £5, and occasionally more; and must have depended on the importer's statement of cost. On the Customs roll of Michaelmas 1508–9, it becomes common, though not invariable, for the basket of books to be valued at £4. On the rolls of Michaelmas 1512–13 and after, the rating of a basket of books at £4 becomes commoner still; and by the time of the Michaelmas 1536–7 roll, it seems to have become standard. Over the first six decades of the sixteenth century, concurrently with the gradual fixing of the value of a basket of books at £4, the nomenclature for the packings or containers simplifies steadily. On the Michaelmas 1506–7 roll, books were imported variously in baskets, cases, chests, coffers, fardels, hogsheads, maunds, pipes, trusses and vats. On succeeding rolls, to the mid 1540s, there is an evident simplification, by which the basket and maund (as in the 1545 *Rate of the Custome House*) and the vat become the commonest packing units for books, all rated equally. These were accompanied by the truss, rated equal with the half-maund and half-basket at £2. For reasons unknown, from 1551 to 1557, the term 'basket' becomes much less common.

The exact meaning of all these packing units is difficult to ascertain, but it is worth keeping in mind that what to our ears sounds modest, the 'basket', must have been substantial in size. This emerges most clearly, perhaps, from the assigned valuation of printed books in the 1582 edition of the *Rates of the Custom House*: 'Books unbound the whole maund xl' [? but *recte* 24] remes: [£4].[22] The rated value appears to be identical to that of the 1545 edition. Therefore, if its specification of 24 reams of printed sheets per maund or vat can be applied backward to the packing sizes of earlier decades, we may visualize the typical size of a basket, maund or vat of books imported in the early Tudor age: it might contain some 12,000 printed sheets. Let us suppose that our mythical basket contained multiple copies of a single octavo edition of 80 leaves or 160 pages. If so, the basket could contain 1,200 copies, and the rated value of £4 would come to less than a penny per copy. The alien importer would pay a duty (combining the Petty Custom and the Subsidy of Poundage) of 6$\frac{1}{4}$ per cent on that penny per copy. We cannot know to certainty that this extrapolation holds, but there is good reason to suppose that the development of a fixed value on book imports effectively lowered their duty considerably.

22. *STC* 7689 (8°); Willan 1962, p. 9. In correspondence with the author, Peter Blayney convincingly argues that the '40 reams' specified in the 1582 and 1590 editions of the *Book of Rates* is a corruption, and that the true quantity should be 24 reams.

Close acquaintance with the language and diplomatic of the customs rolls leads one to question the view, often stated, that the Merchant Adventurers, the English company of overseas traders, played a particularly active role in the importation of books into England.[23] This view depends entirely on a document of the Mercers' Company which appears to contain a textual corruption. In September 1479, the Adventurers' Court met in London to regularize, in response to a complaint from Edward IV, the manner in which they made up their bills of custom, listing incoming cargoes. As part of their defence to the royal accusation that the king had been cheated in times past in the collection of Subsidy, they drew up a model bill of custom, to establish the proper form of the document to be supplied to the customs officials. This model bill was laid out as follows:

> First in the Caragon j pece, Item in the Trynyte Geffrey j pece, Item in the Gabryell of Corse a Maunde or a baskett, item in the Trynytte Bulle a fatt a barell &c.
> First in toill de IIcnaud g^t clx elles
> [2] Item in toill de brussell g^t cxl elles …
> [4] Item pece taffeta g^t xl elles
> [5] Item in toyle de Curtrik g^t lx elles …
> [7] Item in Cotton Kerchiffes iij dozen
> [8] Item xxv paper bokes
> [9] Item iiij pece Tuleis …
> [12] Item in toill de Satten g^t l elles
> [13] Item in toill de damaske xl elles
> [14] Item in toill de Flaundres g^t lxxx elles
> [15] Item xvj pece Fustian
> [16] Item Canvas to pak with[24]

The layout of this sample document is closely related to what appears on the London customs rolls of the time, for it was from such merchant's bills that the customs officials gathered the information that eventually ended up on their ship-by-ship accounts of imports. However, as one compares this model bill with the formulae of contemporary customs rolls, something is clearly amiss with the sample entry 'xxv paper bokes'. Except for this single entry, all the items on the bill are textiles, which provided the major share of the Merchant Adventurers' imports. There is

---

23. Blake 1969, p. 34; E. Armstrong 1979, p. 273; Barker 1985, p. 255: '"paper books" feature as a standard article of trade in the records of the Mercers' Company (to which Caxton belonged) from 1479–80'.   24. Lyell 1936, p. 118.

toile de Hainault, *toile de Cambray*, cotton kerchiefs, tulle, fustian, etc.; and each is measured by the ell, the piece, or the dozen pieces. These items, in fact, fit closely with the language of the customs rolls, which typically record, for each kind of cloth imported, not just the number of 'pieces', but the total number of ells of cloth. However, when we compare the wording '25 paper books' with the printed-book itemizations on the customs rolls, there is a disparity. The rolls of Michaelmas 1477–8 and 1480–1, of April–July 1483 and of August–September 1485 nowhere refer to 'paper books': book imports are, rather, 'libri diversarum historiarum', or 'volumina diversarum historiarum', with 'libri ligati' once, and 'prentyd bokes' once.

It is relevant to note that the Mercers' Acts of Court for this period do not survive in their original form, but in a transcript made from scattered archivalia by the Company's clerk, William Newbold, *c.* 1524 and after, and that this transcript has already been shown to embody a number of errors.[25] It is fair to suggest that several copying errors seem to have intruded on Newbold's transcript of this bill of custom. First, the rather mysterious abbreviation 'gᵗ' should be interpreted as 'cont', i.e. 'containing'. With this change, the model bill fits precisely with the formula of the customs rolls in listing imports of cloth: so many lengths of cloth of a particular region and type, containing so many ells. Second, the 'xxv paper bokes' should be interpreted as '25 papers [of] bokᵗ' or buckram. With such an emendation, the model bill of custom again falls into harmony at this point with what the customs rolls show us. All the sample entries on this bill are of cloth; there is no interpolation of 'paper books' into the midst of an itemization of different cloths. The phrase 'papers of buckram/bokram' shows up widely on the customs rolls, for the 'paper' was the standard packing term for this cloth. When the books of rates were compiled, the paper of buckram became a standard; thus, in the 1507/1532 *Book of Rates*, we find 'Buckroms in papers every paper i with another fyne that ys to saye iii peces in every papers [6s 8d]'.[26] In the 1545 *Rates of the Custome House*, the language is improved but the basis is the same: 'Bokeram the paper vz. iii. peces to one paper [6s 8d]'.[27]

Such a reinterpretation of the Mercers' Company transcript fits well not only with the language of the customs rolls and the Books of Rates, but also with what the customs rolls tell us, however incompletely, of the Merchant Adventurers as book importers. William Caxton was, of

25. Sutton and Hammond 1978.   26. Gras 1918, p. 695.   27. a3ʳ.

course, a Merchant Adventurer, and we know that he imported books in 1488. One man, however, does not make a tradition. Caxton aside, the native book importers recorded on the Subsidy rolls include only a few known Merchant Adventurers, and their imports of books are decidedly sporadic and relatively small. In 1494 and 1495, Henry Somer declared, in 2 miscellaneous cargoes, 5 dozen printed books, 300 printed books, and 12 dozen printed primers.[28] In 1513, Stephen Hudson imported a chapman's miscellany including $6^{1}/_{2}$ dozen primers; and in 1520, Robert Soper imported, *inter alia*, 2 gross of primers.[29] In general, the Merchant Adventurers trained their ambitions on larger quarry than books, and in fact, at another time in the Mercers' Acts, dealing in printed books was taken as symbolic of the small-time merchant. In September 1520, the Mercer John Colleyns applied for permission to take an apprentice, with payment according to the ordinance of the vestment makers rather than that of the Mercers. The Mercers' Court agreed to this 'in consideracion that the said John Colleyns doth nor occupieth no feat of Secrettes of the mercery but in Sellyng of Prynted bokes and other small tryffles'.[30] Such are the proud words of one of the great London Companies.

However trifling their value compared with fine cloths, wine and other great commodities, the register of printed books and primers on the Particular Accounts of England's ports enables us to form a picture of the international market in this cheap, but peculiarly influential, and even dangerous, commodity. Despite heavy losses of the rolls, their combined information provides an overview that cannot be elicited from any other surviving class of record.

28. PRO E122/79/5, m.2d, 12. Somer was a substantial figure, elected Sheriff of London later that year.   29. PRO E122/82/3 m.1; E122/81/8 m.36.   30. Lyell 1936, p. 509.

7

The book-trade under Edward VI and Mary I

JOHN N. KING

In memoriam Jennifer Loach

The reigns of Edward VI (1547–53) and Mary I (1553–8) exemplify sharply contrasting responses to the use of the book-trade as an ideological and political instrument and to the dissemination of religious propaganda.[1] Although these rulers shared little more than one decade of government between the long reigns of Henry VIII and Elizabeth I, Edward and Mary are remembered as the monarchs who endorsed vehement efforts, respectively, to impose the Protestant Reformation and to restore Catholic orthodoxy. During Edward's reign as a minor, Protestant propaganda flooded London book stalls and provincial markets. In contrast to Parliament's relaxation of prior restraints upon publication and extension of relative freedom of discussion to the Protestant reformers at the outset of Edward's reign, his government effectively silenced the Catholic opposition by denying it access to the press. Although Mary's government does not deserve its reputation for failing to understand the power of the press to influence public opinion, it chose to address itself to a continental audience instead of mounting a propaganda attack against Protestants in England. Furthermore, it proved incapable of preventing the importation and sale of reformist books that had been printed surreptitiously on the Continent.[2]

The accession of Edward VI was marked by a renunciation of prior censorship and licensing regulations that had been imposed during the reign of Henry VIII. After the Privy Council appointed the King's uncle, Edward Seymour, as Protector of the Realm during the royal minority,

1. This study was completed with the assistance of a grant-in-aid from the College of Humanities at The Ohio State University. David Frantz, Michael Riley, Christian Zacher and Marvin Zahniser supported this project. I would also like to acknowledge the valuable assistance with research that was rendered by Bryan Davis, who prepared the appendix, and by Robin Smith. Quotations incorporate the modern use of i/j, u/v, and vv.

Unless otherwise noted, evidence is drawn from imprints, colophons and STC entries.
2. Loach 1986, pp. 139–41.

the Royal Injunctions of 31 July 1547 led the way when they 'auctorised and licensed' all individuals to read and interpret the Bible and related writings.3 Parliament then repealed all treason and heresy statutes legislated since the reign of Edward I, including the prohibition against expression of unauthorized religious opinion that had been enforced by the notorious Act of Six Articles (1539).4 That law had been designed to suppress Protestant publication in England. Protector Somerset did not originate all features of the repeal act, because the Protestant faction that controlled both Houses of Parliament introduced more radical modifications into legislation that the government had originally proposed.5 Nevertheless, Somerset's identification with the relaxation of restraints may be noted in the idealized testimony of Protestant reformers like John Foxe, who declared: 'Through the endeavour and industry of this man, first that monstrous hydra with six heads (the Six Articles, I mean), which devoured up so many men before, was abolished and taken away.'6 The sole proviso remaining in place enabled the government to silence religious opposition under the authority of the King's headship of the Church of England.

The deposition of Somerset by John Dudley, Earl of Warwick (later Duke of Northumberland), and the outbreak of rebellion in 1549 led to the reimposition of prior censorship by the Privy Council. Nevertheless, for a brief interval at the outset of Edward's reign, the Protestant faction enjoyed a degree of press freedom that would not be exceeded until the Long Parliament's relaxation of censorship in 1640. General prior censorship did not cease until the lapse of the Licensing Act in 1695.7

A massive amount of publication appeared during the early part of Edward VI's reign, when English printers produced books at a higher rate than at any point since Caxton's establishment of the first English printing press.8 The London press had an average annual output of 171 books under Edward VI, in contrast to an annual average of 92.5 during Henry VIII's last decade and an average of 132 books *per annum* during the reign of Mary I. The Edwardian crests came in 1548, when 268 books were printed in London, and in 1550, when the total was 249. The output of those two years exceeded the totals for every five-year period between

---

3. *Injunccions* 1547, f. b1 recto. Created the Duke of Somerset at the outset of Edward's reign, Seymour is referred to in this essay as Protector Somerset.

4. *S Realm*, I Edward VI, c. 12.   5. Bush 1975, pp. 145–6.   6. Foxe, v, p. 703.

7. For detailed documentation, here and below, see J. N. King 1976a; 1982, pp. 76–113. See also Loades 1991, pp. 114–15.

8. Figure 1 in Bell and Barnard 1992 graphically demonstrates this spike in printing and publication.

1475 and 1544. Not until 1579 did London printers exceed the output of these peak years.[9]

Protestant propaganda comprised the great bulk of the flood of Edwardian publication. Much of this writing was produced by repatriated Protestant authors who had gone into exile under Henry VIII. Previously banned works by the following reformers were openly published: John Bale, Robert Barnes, Thomas Becon, Heinrich Bullinger, John Frith, John Hooper, Martin Luther, William Tyndale, William Turner and John Wycliffe. Of extant editions printed under Edward VI, 53 per cent dealt with religion in general, in contrast to 39 per cent under Mary I. A peak of 72 per cent was attained in 1548. Protestant propaganda is found in 16 per cent of extant editions printed under Edward VI; a peak of 25 per cent was attained in 1548. A very great number of those editions attacked the mass and agitated in favour of a Protestant communion service in the vernacular. The spate of anti-mass tracts that appeared in 1548 supported liturgical reforms introduced under the auspices of Archbishop Thomas Cranmer.[10] Because those publications were not inspired by government commission,[11] the enthusiasm of English authors, printers, stationers and readers provided the impetus for this activity. Protector Somerset also extended patronage to Protestant polemicists, albeit on a smaller scale than that of the master patrons, Thomas Cromwell and William Cecil.[12]

Works of that kind inundated the Catholic opposition, whose views informed only six extant pamphlets printed in England.[13] The government silenced Richard Smith, Regius Professor of Divinity at Oxford, and Miles Hogarde, the artisan poet, for writing those works. Smith was forced to recant at Paul's Cross for defending traditional doctrine in *A brief treatyse settynge forth divers truthes* (1547).[14] Because hiding or exile on the Continent were the recourse of those who would not remain silent, Smith's flight to Louvain in 1549 typified the beginning of the recusant movement. Robert Caly, a book-seller, exported forbidden Catholic books back to England during his French exile.[15]

9. These averages are based upon Bell and Barnard 1992, table 1. See also notes in Appendix, below.
10. See Appendix, below pp. 178–9, for statistics based upon a manual analysis of *STC* entries. Averages and percentages cited in the body of this chapter omit publication data for 1553 and 1558 because of the cautions cited in the notes to the Appendix.
11. Loach 1986, p. 143.   12. J. N. King 1982, p. 108; see Loach 1986, p. 142.
13. For the mistaken claim that 'Somerset's experiment opened the way for both Protestants and Roman Catholics to engage in a full-scale public debate', see Baskerville 1979, p. 4.
14. *STC* 22818.
15. Duff 1905, p. 21; Loades 1991, pp. 115–16. On Caly's unique status as an emigrant Catholic printer, see J. W. Martin 1981a, p. 237.

The bibliographical record indicates that, in accordance with the relaxation of restraints upon publication, Protestant printers, publishers and book-sellers thrived during Edward VI's reign. Under the protection of copyright afforded by their patents royal, Richard Grafton, the King's Printer, and Edward Whitchurch operated highly successful presses whose output often supported the government's programme of religious reform. Whitchurch issued the massive two-volume translation of Erasmus's *Paraphrases upon the New Testament* (1548–9) under government orders that permitted him to commandeer the workmen and equipment of other printers.[16] Under the auspices of the Archbishop of Canterbury, Walter Lynne issued his own Protestant translations and propagandistic pamphlets. Despite his title as Printer to the Archbishop of Canterbury, this Dutch immigrant functioned not as a printer but as the publisher and retailer of books produced on his behalf by various printers. At this time, 'printer' could designate any of the functions of printer, publisher or book-seller.[17]

Protestant noblemen patronized Protestant printers and book-sellers, whose number included John Day and his partner, William Seres.[18] Arguably the most successful English printer of the latter part of the sixteenth century, Day appears to have received the valuable monopoly on printing *ABCs* that he retained for the rest of his career through the good offices of William Cecil. Anthony Scoloker, John Oswen, Robert Crowley and John Bale received support from a variety of figures, including Mary Fitzroy, Duchess of Richmond; Catherine Brandon, dowager Duchess of Suffolk; and Elizabeth, Lady Fane, wife of a close associate of Protector Somerset.

Crowley and Bale furnish paradigmatic examples of the careers of Edwardian propaganda publishers. They engaged in the common enterprise of producing a small library of Protestant polemics and medieval literature with reputed Wycliffite associations, during the 1540s and early 1550s. After Crowley established a book shop specializing in the sale of popular octavo chap-books, he published nineteen texts under his own imprint between 1549 and 1551. His most notable offerings were two of his own works: the first English metrical psalter and the first printing of *Piers Plowman*, a text that he augmented with a doctrinally Protestant introduction and glosses.[19] It is important to note that the King's Printer, Richard Grafton, actually printed most of these editions without sharing the imprint with Crowley. This link, and the patronage that he

16. *STC* 2854; Devereux 1969.   17. Greg 1956, pp. 83–4.
18. King 1982, pp. 102–13, and *passim*.   19. *STC* 2725, 19906–7a.

received from Lady Fane suggest that Crowley's shop served as a conduit for controversial works favouring the Protestant regime.

After his return from exile on the Continent in 1547, Bale began to issue books under his own imprint including his own polemical writings. Those books were printed on his behalf by Stephen Mierdman, a Dutch immigrant to London, for sale by Bale himself at the book shop that he opened at the sign of St John the Baptist in the vicinity of St Paul's Cathedral, or by John Day or Richard Foster. Mierdman also printed for his fellow countryman, Walter Lynne. The collaboration between Bale and Mierdman exemplifies the leniency of Edwardian policy towards Protestant propaganda, compared with the attitude of Henry VIII, under whom Bale was effectively silenced in England. Bale had first sought out the services of Mierdman, a printer then resident in Antwerp who catered exclusively to the export trade, after the English propagandist fled from England following the fall of his patron, Thomas Cromwell. At considerable risk to his personal safety, Mierdman had surreptitiously printed the first edition of Bale's *Actes of the Englysh votaryes* (1546) for secret export into England. It seems likely that Mierdman used the imprint of Wesel as a false place of publication in order to protect himself from punishment.

Bale fled from Antwerp in 1546 when mounting imperial pressure culminated in prior censorship, book burnings and a ban on the printing of English books. He then found a safe haven in Wesel, a Rhineland port in the County of Cleves, a territory that lay on the border of the Holy Roman Empire and immediately beyond the jurisdiction of the Habsburg authorities. That site was an ideal location for the exportation of books forbidden in England because, of two continental cities with an open trade in Protestant books, it was the one that lay closest to London and nearby ports; the East Frisian port of Emden was the other haven. At Wesel, Bale entered into collaboration with Derick van der Straten (Theodoricus Plateanus), who specialized in the printing of German and Latin texts by German Protestants. After the accession of Edward VI, Van der Straten printed Bale's *Illustrium maioris Britanniae scriptorum . . . summarium* (1548),[20] the earliest known bibliography and history of English literature. Because this edition was designed for export into England, the imprint contains no reference to the book's overseas origin. The colophon states that the book was published by John Overton in Ipswich on

---

20. *STC* 1295.

31 July 1548 ('Excusumque fuit Gippeswici in Anglia per Ioannem Overton, anno a Christi incarnatione, 1548, pridie calendas Augusti').[21]

Provincial printing was a distinctive feature of the Edwardian book-trade. In contrast to the dearth of such activity during Henry VIII's last decade (average 1.3 books per year) and during Mary I's reign (1.75 per year), such printing averaged a rate of 8.67 books per year under Edward VI, but the average figure is misleading because 20 books were printed at outlying locations in 1548 and 10 books in 1549.[22] The relaxation of censorship, as of religious orthodoxy, is reflected in the rise of provincial printing; the charter granted to the Stationers' Company in 1557 reintroduced the ban on printing outside London.

Proximity to monastic libraries did not account for the flourishing state of printing and publication at Ipswich, Worcester and Dublin under Edward VI. The importance of Ipswich as a centre of printing and publication may be explained by the presence of a large literate population and the proximity of that port to the Continent. Ipswich was a Hanseatic port and, after London itself, the entrepôt with the most advantageous site for importation of books shipped from Wesel and other continental printing centres. The Ipswich imprint of Bale's *Summarium* may have been designed to circumvent restrictions on the importation of books printed abroad. Immediately after the relaxation of censorship, Anthony Scoloker and John Oswen printed a surprisingly large number of Protestant books at Ipswich during the single year of 1548. Those printers catered to lay readers interested in works ranging from translations of continental reformers to humble religious verse. After a brief burst of intense activity, Scoloker and Oswen relocated their presses in the same year. Oswen set up shop in Worcester as King's Printer for Wales. Scoloker went into partnership in London with William Seres, who also co-published with John Day. At about this time, the Privy Council commissioned Humphrey Powell to move from London to Dublin, where he set up shop as King's Printer for Ireland. The government presumably wished to sponsor the publication of Protestant propaganda for dissemination in Wales and Ireland, each of which had Catholic populations hostile to the central government.

Government sponsorship of activities of that kind disappeared at the

---

21. A variant issue (*STC* 1296) bears the imprint: 'Excudebatur praesens opus Wesaliae per Theodoricum Plateanum.' Although the new title-leaf states 1549 as the date of publication, the text and colophon are otherwise unchanged.
22. See Bell and Barnard 1992, table 1.

accession of Mary I. In line with her refusal to accept the Protestant elevation of the role of the literate laity in the religious life of the nation, her government devoted little attention to the generation of religious propaganda in the vernacular. It is inappropriate, however, to conclude that the Catholic Queen and her counsellors ignored the press and failed to comprehend its potential for generating effective propaganda.[23] Instead, her regime embraced a different policy with regard to the press. Ecclesiastical authorities showed little concern for 'lay self-education', but they did emphasize the publication of sermons, primers (see Appendix) and catechisms for 'the instruction of the laity by the clergy'. Although the Marian government devoted little attention to producing vernacular literature for consumption in England, it did gear itself to the printing of books on the Continent for a broad international readership.[24] Publication of *The saying of John late duke of Northumberlande uppon the scaffolde* (1553) by the Queen's Printer, John Cawood, represents a case in point.[25] If one considers this recantation by the recently executed leader of the Edwardian government in the context of the domestic book-trade, it appears to be a rare example of an effective counter-attack against the previous Protestant regime. In actual fact, Mary's apologists dedicated their energy to publishing translations into Latin, French, Italian, Spanish and Dutch, which were produced by continental printers and 'had a considerable impact on the English exile community and on continental Protestants'.[26]

Although Mary's coronation heralded defeat for the Protestant reformers in England, the 'flood of print' that greeted her accession, like that which appeared at the outset of Edward's reign, 'appears to have been spontaneous'. A sequence of proclamations, injunctions and other measures forbade the printing and sale of works of religious controversy. Parliament also revived the medieval statutes against heresy. Although one may not declare unequivocally that Church officials, notably those under the influence of Cardinal Pole, were 'unsympathetic' to the vernacular Bible,[27] the total absence of vernacular Bibles printed in England indicates that the 'cautious' views of Stephen Gardiner held sway until the Queen's death. In contrast, fifty-four editions of the English Bible were printed in England during Edward's reign.[28]

23. For opposed arguments, see Baskerville 1979, p. 13; J. W. Martin 1981a, pp. 231–47; and Loades 1991, pp. 141–2.
24. Loach 1986, p. 139, and see pp. 137, 140–1, 144–5. See also Loach 1975.
25. *STC* 7283. 26. Loach 1986, p. 144. 27. Loach 1986 pp. 138–9, 142.
28. See Appendix; and J. W. Martin 1981a, p. 239.

Despite the reimposition of traditional control measures, this government was no more successful than its predecessors at controlling the book-trade. It succeeded, however, at shutting off almost all domestic publication of Protestant propaganda. Government measures encouraged the flight of Protestant apologists, printers and book-sellers like Bale, Turner, Crowley, Whitchurch, Becon, Foxe and Coverdale, who chose to go into exile on the Continent. Even though the Protestants worked from various sites of exile, they published more religious propaganda than their opponents, who worked from a more advantageous base within England.[29] Furthermore, two extant leaves from the ledgers of a Marian printer demonstrate that the purchase and sale of forbidden books proceeded unchecked during the Queen's first year on the throne; this fragmentary account book, preserved at the British Library, suggests that practical business considerations presumably led to the sale of both Protestant and Catholic tracts at the shop of this stationer.[30] The Marian exiles produced three political treatises of enduring worth, which concern the limitation upon obedience to unjust sovereigns, the permissibility of female government, and the justification for tyrannicide: Christopher Goodman, *How superior powers oght to be obeyd of their Subjects: and wherin they may lawfully be disobeyed* (Geneva 1558); John Knox, *The first blast of the trumpet against the monstruous regiment of women* (Geneva 1558); and John Ponet, *A shorte treatise of politike power, and of the true obedience* (Strasbourg? 1556).[31]

The book-trade now underwent a general contraction. In contrast to the 81 stationers who were engaged in the domestic trade under the old regime, 41 remained in Marian England. The average annual production of 132 books by London printers fell far below the Edwardian average.[32] Miles Hogarde, the artisan poet, provides the sole example of a layman who duplicated the activity of Protestant pamphleteers by articulating opinions on ecclesiastical questions.[33] His works were published by Robert Caly, a printer who returned from exile in France because of the hospitable policies of the Marian regime. Other than Caly, the most active printer on the official, Catholic side was John Cawood, the Queen's Printer.[34]

29. Baskerville 1979, pp. 6–7.   30. BL, Egerton ms. 2974, fols. 67–8. See J. N. King, 1987.
31. *STC* 12020, 15070, 20178; Baskerville 1979, pp. 16, 20–30.
32. Bell and Barnard 1992, table 1; Took 1977, p. 245. Attributing the disparity in publication rates to commercial considerations, Loach 1986, p. 137, notes that the contraction may also have been due to the departure of continental printers.   33. J. W. Martin 1981b.
34. Baskerville 1979, pp. 7–8.

Under Mary, reformist printers and publishers reverted to the Henrician practice of relying upon surreptitious publication in order to confuse authorities and mock them with sardonic imprints. Book burnings destroyed many of those texts. A secret press produced a set of 10 extant Protestant polemics during the year after Queen Mary's accession. Their imprints falsely claim that the series originated at the press of 'Michael Wood' in 'Rouen'. Typographical evidence links them to John Day, who appears to have produced these pamphlets at an underground press within London itself. In addition to writings by the Protestant luminaries, Lady Jane Grey and John Hooper, the 'Michael Wood' pamphlets included the first and second editions of John Bale's translation of *De vera obediencia*, a treatise in defence of the royal supremacy by Stephen Gardiner, Bishop of Winchester, a one-time supporter of the Henrician Reformation.[35] Republication of this text with a preface, conclusion and satirical marginalia added by Bale could only serve to embarrass its author, now Mary's Lord Chancellor.[36]

Surreptitious importation of books printed on the Continent compensated for the cessation of overt Protestant book production in England. Wesel and Emden dominated the overseas trade, but English books were also produced at Strasbourg and Geneva.[37] Stephen Mierdman and Egidius van der Erve printed English books at Emden. As we have seen, Mierdman's association with the printing of Protestant propaganda went back to his Antwerp trade under Henry VIII, where he printed work by John Bale among others, and his residence in London during Edward VI's reign, when he printed work on behalf of Bale, Walter Lynne and other stationers. Like Mierdman and Lynne, Van der Erve had belonged to the Dutch Church in London under Edward VI. He attributed pamphlets by John Scory, John Olde and Rudolph Walther to the press of 'Christopher Truthal' at 'Southwark'. His editions of tracts by John Knox, John Olde, William Turner and Ulrich Zwingli appeared with the false imprints 'Kalykow', 'Waterford', 'Rome' and 'Geneva'.[38] Books by Thomas Cranmer, John Olde, and Nicholas Ridley also bear false imprints.[39]

John Bale was at the centre of surreptitious and satirical activity of this kind. Having fled from Ireland in 1553, where he had served unsuccess-

35. STC 11585.
36. Fairfield 1972. On other 'Michael Wood' imprints by Bale or possibly attributed to him, see Baskerville 1979, p. 53; and STC 10383.
37. Loades 1991, p. 116; Loach 1975, p. 34; Baskerville 1979, pp. 7–8. 38. Isaac 1931.
39. STC 5999, 18797–8, 21046, 21047.3.

fully as an Edwardian missionary bishop, Bale seems to have made his way to Wesel, where he had once found haven under Henry VIII. Foxe's 'Book of Martyrs' describes that city as 'a free town . . . under the said duke of Cleve's dominion, and one of the Hansa towns, privileged with the Steelyard in London, whither divers Walloons were fled for religion'.[40] Not the least of its attractions was the ease with which books could be transported by Hanseatic merchants who enjoyed trading privileges in England. At least we know on one occasion during his first exile, Hanseatic merchants sympathetic to Lutheranism had supplied Bale with a manuscript for publication: Anne Askew's *Examinations*, printed at Wesel by Derick van der Straten in 1546–7, to which Bale added a commentary.[41]

Wesel is the most likely place of publication for the autobiographical account of his Irish service, which Bale issued in December 1553: *The vocacyon of Johan Bale to the bishoprick of Ossorie in Irelande his persecucions in the same / & finall delyveraunce*. Despite a satirical colophon that claims that the work was 'Imprinted in Rome / before the castell of S. Angell / at the signe of S. Peter', it seems likely that Joos Lambrecht printed it in Wesel on behalf of Hugh Singleton, a printer who appears to have left London at some point after Edward VI's death. Even the date of publication may be false.[42] Lambrecht also appears to have printed the third edition of Bale's translation of Gardiner's *De vera obediencia* (November 1553) on behalf of Singleton, again with Castel Sant'Angelo in Rome as the stated place of publication.[43] Among books possibly produced by Lambrecht or Singleton at Wesel are tracts in English by Thomas Becon, John Bradford, John Knox, Wolfgang Musculus and Otto Werdmueller.[44]

The common use of anonymity, pseudonyms and satirical imprints was surely designed to protect printers and book-sellers from harassment by hostile authorities or attack by secret agents.[45] Although subterfuges were characteristically directed against the Pope, they also nettled English authorities. Thus, the colophon of Thomas Becon's *A confortable epistle, too Goddes faythfull people in Englande* (Wesel?, Lambrecht? 1554)

40. Foxe, VIII, p. 573.   41. *STC* 848, 850.   42. *STC* 1307; Bale 1990, p. 17.
43. *STC* 11587. For other examples of this false place of publication, see *STC* 4392, 15059.5, 19891.
44. *STC* 1716, 3480.5, 13457, 15059.5, 17821–2, 18312, 24219, 25251, 25256.
45. Loach 1975, p. 34, indicates that imprints were probably informed by 'a wish to inform the prospective reader what kind of book it was'. See also Baskerville 1979, p. 7. On the antecedents of those practices, see Kronenberg 1947.

describes publication at 'Strasburgh in Elsas, at the signe of the golden Bibel'.[46] The anonymous *Supplicacyon to the quenes majestie* (Strasbourg: W. Rihel, 1555) is attributed falsely to the Queen's Printer, John Cawood.[47] William Turner's *A new booke of spirituall physik for dyverse diseases of the nobilite and gentlemen of Englande* (Emden: Van der Erve, 1555)[48] alleges that it was 'Imprented at Rome by the vaticane churche, by Marcus Antonius Constantius. Otherwyse called, thraso miles gloriosus.' Although the Pope is obviously the object of satirical attack in this colophon, Stephen Gardiner is also ridiculed, both as Marcus Antonius Constantius, which he had employed as a pen name, and as Thraso, the braggart soldier of Terence's *Eunuchus*. Luther's *A faythfull admonycion of a certen trewe pastor* (Strasbourg: W. Rihel, 1554) bristles with false claims designed to annoy the Marian establishment.[49] They range from attribution of the translation to the forefather of Christian martyrology ('Eusebius Pamphilus'), and of the editing to the reformer Melanchthon, to a transparently allegorical printer ('Conrade Freeman'), a place of publication adjacent to a favoured royal palace ('Grenewych') and authority for publication 'with the most gracios licence and privilege of god almighty / kyng of heaven and erth'. Edmund Bonner, Bishop of London, comes under attack in the anonymous *Commyssion sent to the bloudy butcher byshop of London, and to al covents [sic] of frers, by the high and mighty prince, lord, Sathanas the devill of Hell* (John Day? 1557?),[50] whose colophon locates its composition 'in our brighte and burnyng chayre, from oure infernal kingdon'.

The reigns of Edward VI and Mary I represent a period of unprecedented turbulence in the history of English publishing. For a brief interval under Protector Somerset, the government allowed unheard-of liberty to Protestant authors, printers, publishers and book-sellers. The reimposition of restraints under the Duke of Northumberland and Queen Mary, and the flight from England of prominent Protestant authors and members of the book-trade during her regime, did little to stem the flourishing trade in Protestant propaganda. Under the Marian regime, publishers concentrated upon authorized publication of sermons, catechisms and primers. At the same time that Protestant books in the vernacular poured into England from the Continent, treatises in foreign languages for a continental readership were produced in England in defence of England's Catholic regime.

46. *STC* 1716.   47. *STC* 17562.   48. *STC* 24361.   49. *STC* 16980.   50. *STC* 3286.

The unruliness of the book-trade would not diminish until after the incorporation of the Stationers' Company on 4 May 1557. The granting of its charter improved the Crown's powers to control heretical and seditious publication effectively, for it vested in the freemen of the Company the power of policing fellow members in return for a monopoly on printing. Only the universities at Oxford and Cambridge were exempt from Company control, but neither possessed a printing press at that time.[51] Incorporation of the Company contributed to the existence of a much more tightly controlled book-trade under Elizabeth I and her successors.

Appendix
STC statistical breakdown for the years 1547–1558

The years that marked the transitions between the reigns of Edward VI and Mary I (1553), and between Mary I and Elizabeth I (1558) have been listed separately. An effort has been made to determine which books could definitely be assigned to the reign of one monarch or another and which books could not be assigned with any reasonable certainty. Assignments have been made on the basis of information in titles and colophons or examination of the contents of books. Because only one book (Smith's *Defence of the Masse, STC* 22821) printed in 1547 can be assigned definitely to the reign of Henry VIII, who died on 28 January, that year has not been classed as transitional. The totals in part 1 of the table include books listed in *STC* as being printed within 2 or 3 years of the date assigned ('?') and those listed as being within 5 years of the date assigned ('*c.*'). It is important to be aware that the '*c.*' titles cluster mostly around 1550 and 1555, thereby skewing the numbers somewhat for those years. For further cautions, see Bell and Barnard 1992, pp. 48–61. Percentages listed are approximate.

51. Greg 1956, pp. 1–5; Blagden 1960, pp. 19, 21, 30, 33.

STATISTICAL BREAKDOWN OF BOOK PRODUCTION

Part 1a: *Excluding transitional years*

	1547		1548		1549		1550		1551		1552		1554		1555		1556		1557	
1. General religious books (per cent total)	55	(39%)	163	(61%)	60	(35%)	110	(44%)	44	(34%)	28	(18%)	48	(34%)	57	(22%)	43	(22.5%)	16	(15%)
2. *Protestant propaganda* (% total)	26	(18%)	30	(17.5%)	30	(17%)	32	(13%)	14	(10.5%)	5	(3.2%)	9	(6.4%)	10	(5%)	12	(6.2%)	3	(2.9%)
3. *Catholic propaganda* (% total)	1	(0.7%)	1	(0.4%)	0	(0%)	3	(1.2%)	1	(0.7%)	1	(0.6%)	13	(10.1%)	4	(2%)	9	(4.7%)	3	(2.9%)
4. Total Bibles (% total)	11	(8%)	18	(7%)	30	(17%)	26	(10%)	22	(17%)	7	(4.5%)	1	(0.7%)	3	(1.5%)	4	(2%)	2	(1.9%)
5. *English Bibles* (% of Bibles)	2	(19%)	10	(56%)	12	(40%)	15	(58%)	11	(50%)	4	(58%)	0	(0%)	0	(0%)	0	(0%)	0	(0%)
6. Church of England documents (% total)	14	(10%)	3	(1.2%)	1	(0.5%)	1	(0.4%)	0	(0%)	1	(0.6%)	2	(1.4%)	1	(0.5%)	1	(0.5%)	0	(0%)
7. Liturgies (% total)	2	(1.4%)	9	(3%)	20	(12%)	5	(2%)	9	(7%)	23	(15%)	14	(10%)	36	(17%)	16	(8.3%)	10	(9%)
8. *Latin liturgies* (% of liturgies)	2	(100%)	3	(33%)	5	(25%)	3	(60%)	4	(45%)	1	(4.3%)	11	(79%)	36	(100%)	13	(82%)	9	(90%)
9. Total religious books (% total)	82	(58%)	193	(72%)	111	(65%)	142	(57%)	75	(56%)	59	(38%)	65	(46%)	97	(47%)	64	(34%)	28	(26%)
10. Total books	141		268		170		249		133		153		141		208		191		109	

Notes: Mary I became Queen following Edward VI's death on 6 July 1553 and John Dudley's unsuccessful effort to place Lady Jane Grey on the throne (10–21 July).

The figures in this part of the appendix are based on Bell and Barnard 1992, Table 1, who base themselves in turn on individual entries in *STC* and the 'Chronological index' to it by Philip R. Rider. There is substantial agreement between the broad trend revealed by these statistics and the findings of three studies published before revision of the *STC* was complete: J. N. King 1976a, pp. 1–2; Took 1977, p. 245 and appendix; and J. W. Martin 1981a, pp. 231–2. Loach 1986, p. 136, warns that the calibration of *STC* entries is a shaky method of assessing book production, since it depends to a large extent on the physical survival of a copy of a particular edition'.

Part 1b: *Transitional years:*

1553	Unassigned	Edward VI	Mary I	Total
1.	38 (26%)	4 (67%)	12 (70%)	54 (32%)
2.	5 (3.5%)	1 (17%)	2 (12%)	8 (4.7%)
3.	4 (2.8%)	2 (33%)	3 (18%)	9 (5.3%)
4.	0 (0%)	0 (0%)	0 (0%)	0 (0%)
5.	0 (0%)	0 (0%)	0 (0%)	0 (0%)
6.	0 (0%)	0 (0%)	0 (0%)	0 (0%)
7.	0 (0%)	0 (0%)	0 (0%)	0 (0%)
8.	0 (0%)	0 (0%)	0 (0%)	0 (0%)
9.	38 (26%)	4 (67%)	12 (70%)	63 (37%)
10.	145	6	17	168

1558	Unassigned	Mary I	Elizabeth I	Total
1.	13 (13.7%)	5 (36%)	0 (0%)	18 (16.2%)
2.	7 (7.4%)	0 (0%)	0 (0%)	7 (6.2%)
3.	0 (0%)	1 (7%)	0 (0%)	1 (0.9%)
4.	0 (0%)	0 (0%)	0 (0%)	0 (0%)
5.	0 (0%)	0 (0%)	0 (0%)	0 (0%)
6.	1 (1.1%)	0 (0%)	0 (0%)	1 (0.9%)
7.	11 (11.4%)	0 (0%)	0 (0%)	11 (10%)
8.	8 (8.4%)	0 (0%)	0 (0%)	8 (7.2%)
9.	25 (26%)	5 (36%)	0 (0%)	30 (27%)
10.	95	14	3	112

Part 2: *Overall Survey of book production 1547–1558*

	1547	1548	1549	1550	1551	1552	1553	1554	1555	1556	1557	1558
1.	35 (40%)	87 (55%)	39 (23%)	79 (57%)	32 (30%)	15 (15%)	48 (39%)	42 (37%)	40 (28%)	28 (19%)	13 (15%)	17 (20%)
2.	11 (12.5%)	28 (17%)	17 (10%)	23 (17%)	10 (9%)	0 (0%)	6 (5%)	7 (6.2%)	8 (5.6%)	9 (6%)	2 (2.2%)	6 (7%)
3.	1 (1.1%)	0 (0%)	0 (0%)	3 (2.2%)	0 (0%)	1 (1%)	8 (6.5%)	13 (12%)	4 (2.8%)	7 (4.8%)	3 (3.3%)	1 (1.1%)
4.	6 (6.7%)	15 (9%)	22 (13%)	20 (14%)	21 (19%)	7 (7%)	18 (15%)	1 (0.9%)	1 (0.7%)	1 (0.7%)	2 (2.2%)	0 (0%)
5.	2 (2.2%)	10 (6%)	12 (7%)	13 (10%)	10 (9%)	4 (4%)	5 (4.1%)	0 (0%)	0 (0%)	0 (0%)	1 (1.1%)	0 (0%)
6.	9 (10%)	3 (1.8%)	1 (0.6%)	1 (0.7%)	0 (0%)	1 (1%)	2 (1.6%)	2 (1.8%)	1 (0.7%)	1 (0.7%)	0 (0%)	1 (1.1%)
7.	2 (2.2%)	7 (4.2%)	17 (10%)	2 (1.4%)	8 (7.2%)	22 (22%)	4 (3.2%)	13 (12%)	33 (23%)	14 (10%)	7 (7.7%)	10 (11%)
8.	2 (100%)	1 (14%)	3 (18%)	0 (0%)	4 (50%)	1 (5%)	0 (0%)	11 (85%)	33 (100%)	11 (79%)	7 (100%)	7 (70%)
9.	52 (59%)	113 (70%)	79 (46%)	102 (75%)	61 (58%)	45 (45%)	72 (58%)	58 (51%)	75 (52%)	44 (30%)	22 (25%)	28 (32%)
10.	88	157	171	138	107	101	127	113	143	145	88	87

Note: the totals listed in part 2 include *only* those books for which we may assign a firm date. Because books from the transitional years that can be assigned to one reign or another have firm dates, those transitional years have not been listed separately as in part 1. The large divergence between the totals in this section and those in part 1 for the years 1550 and 1555 reflects the exclusion of 'c.' listings from the totals in part 2.

8

Importation of printed books into England and Scotland

MARGARET LANE FORD

The printed book may be seen as the natural outgrowth of several factors which were beginning to influence the manuscript book by the fifteenth century: specialization, standardization and speculation. All three contributed to the rapidly expanding market in books, which importation sought to satisfy. Manuscript books of hours produced in the Netherlands for an English market show evidence of standardization in the decoration programme, and of speculation in the shields left blank, to be filled in with the coats-of-arms of prospective owners.[1] Rouen also supported a specialist book-trade in, among other texts, books of hours, which seems to have supplied Scotland as well as England.[2] On native ground, there was routine production of Chaucer, Lydgate and Hoccleve texts in the fifteenth century which observed a scribal economy in a standardization of format for those texts. A centre in Suffolk 'seems to have specialized in issuing Lydgate's poems in copies ranging from the luxurious to the more routine'.[3] Thus specialization and standardization in some sorts of manuscript text already led to a speculative market before the introduction of printing.

Unlike manuscripts, which were produced in England and Scotland as well as on the Continent, no printed books were produced on native soil before Caxton set up his shop in Westminster in 1476, more than twenty years after the introduction of printing in Mainz. It was not until the sixteenth century that books were printed in Scotland. Thus any demand for printed books from the 1450s to 1476 – which, as we shall see, was considerable – had to be met from abroad. The importation of printed books continued and increased after the introduction of printing in England and Scotland.

The results of bibliographical analysis have put us in the fortunate

1. Rogers 1982; and J. J. G. Alexander above, pp. 52–3; fig. 2.3.
2. R. Watson 1984.   3. Meale 1989, pp. 218, 209.

position of being able to place and date with reasonable accuracy most printed books in this period. This enables us to record when, and from where, such books were being imported much more specifically than for manuscript books. The present analysis is based primarily on a systematic search for printed books with marks of English and Scottish ownership. It also draws on published catalogues and other publications which contain copy-specific information.[4] Personal examination revealed further features identifying early ownership in Britain. Because the place and date of printing are necessary to this analysis of importation, it comprises surviving books only. Wills and inventories have been of limited use, since the books listed there are often difficult to identify with actual editions. Similarly, Customs rolls provide invaluable information on the quantity of books being imported, but they do not detail what the books are and so could not contribute to this study. What is offered is a sample of printed books of which surviving copies bear evidence that they existed in England and Scotland up to the 1550s. Since it includes data on over 4,300 books it is the largest and most comprehensive such sample to date. It permits a preliminary analysis of where books were coming from, and when, as well as what books were circulating, and it indicates general trends which illuminate the intellectual climate as much as it comments on the book-trade.

There remain, however, a number of factors limiting any study of importation, and it would be as well to spell out the caveats and biases of the present study more clearly before embarking on an interpretation of the data. Survival is influenced by a number of factors: among them size, use, stability of a collection, political and religious turmoil among them. Big books are more likely to survive than small ones, and university and college libraries were more stable environments than religious institutions during this period. There is a bias in the sample towards books

4. The data are drawn from a systematic examination of libraries throughout Britain, including those of Westminster Abbey, Middle Temple, Gray's Inn, Lambeth Palace, University College London, York Minster, Ushaw College; the National Libraries of Wales and Scotland; and university libraries of Durham, Leeds, Edinburgh, Glasgow, St Andrews, and Aberdeen. I am grateful to the curators of these libraries for their help and interest. Published sources included Oates 1954; Rhodes 1982; *BRUC*; *BRUO*; *BRUO* 1540; Ker 1964–87; and Durkan and Ross 1961, 1978, 1982, 1985. Unpublished sources include Sheppard's record of the incunabula in the Bodleian Library and David Pearson's catalogue slips of incunabula at Durham Cathedral Library. Published and unpublished sources were further supplemented by personal examination of some of the books listed there. The method of compiling the data results in figures for England being considerably stronger before 1500 than after. On the other hand, the figures for Scotland before 1560 are as nearly comprehensive as survival permits.

owned by university-educated men, and thus towards books in Latin, but since these men comprised the biggest sector of the book-owning population, those needing books for their studies, this bias is not necessarily unrepresentative. Nor does a deposit in a college library guarantee survival, as is illustrated by Wayneflete's benefaction to Magdalen College, Oxford, of which not one book is now known to exist. Another bias in the sample is towards incunabula. This is due in part to the preferential treatment they have enjoyed in modern times. They are usually kept separately in libraries and thus are readily accessible. Also, catalogues of them, but rarely of later books, often contain much copy-specific information. Efforts have been made to rectify the imbalance, and as it stands, the survey comprises about equal numbers of books from pre- and post-1500. These same limitations (survival, access, lack of published catalogues) affect most adversely the number of books printed in England after 1500 (those printed in Scotland are almost non-existent, primarily for reasons of survival) in the survey, so that books printed on native soil are under-represented.

England and Scotland will here be treated separately in the discussion of the importation of books. They were separate countries, had different foreign alliances, different trade routes and looked to different intellectual centres. The books themselves will underline these differences.

Much work has been carried out previously on the English book-trade in general or on ownership of individual books.[5] The work of four scholars in particular bears especially on the present chapter. Graham Pollard significantly broadened our knowledge of the book-trade. His work on bindings helps greatly in localizing books in England, if not in actually assigning them to a binder or shop, and thus provides important evidence for book ownership. He has also concisely outlined the distribution networks of the book-trade, documented its mechanisms and found importations of printed books into England as early as July 1466.[6] Pollard was the first to look at individual acquisition of books by Englishmen abroad, citing John Russell's purchase, in Bruges in 1467, of a Cicero printed at Mainz by Fust and Schoeffer in 1466 (and the purchase of a second copy on vellum just a month later) as an example of the wide availability of printed texts on the Continent at an early date.

Elizabeth Armstrong's observations on the book-trade to 1526 echo

5. See, for instance Duff 1905; Plomer 1923–4, 1928–9; Kronenberg 1929; *BRUC, BRUO, BRUO 1540*; Ker 1964–87; Ker 1954.   6. Pollard and Ehrman 1965.

strongly those of Pollard: that the earliest printed books in England were primarily those acquired abroad singly, by individuals, but that in the (late, according to Armstrong) 1470s the trade in printed books began in earnest.[7] While the instances she cites of the first books printed in Italy, France and Germany to be found in England can be modified, some of her quantitative observations remain true, notably that Germany, the Netherlands and Italy at first dominated the trade in books to England, but were surpassed by France and Basel in the early sixteenth century. She credits Basel's rise to its prominent role in intellectual printing.[8] Julian Roberts has further suggested that the rise of Basel, or German-speaking centres in general, and France in the sixteenth century was due to the importance of the Birckman family in importing books to England, their business connections in France and Germany, and the rising importance of the Frankfurt book fair in the middle of that century.[9]

The present survey has grown out of a pilot study by Lotte Hellinga on the importation of printed books into Britain. In that study, she analysed 1,000 incunables with British ownership up to about 1530.[10] The pattern of importation she found for books printed between 1465 and 1500 was of an overall dominance by Italy with 40 per cent of the total, followed by the German-speaking countries with 31 per cent, then France with about 16 per cent and finally the Netherlands with about 11 per cent. Breaking these numbers down by decade, the 1480s saw a marked increase in imports which continued into the 1490s, led at first by the German-speaking countries and supplanted by Italy by the latter decade. French imports increased dramatically by the turn of the century, replacing German as the second most important. Hellinga then separated the books now at Oxford from the rest of the sample and found a striking dominance of Italy in general and Venice in particular in these university-related imports, whereas the percentage of Italian books in the remaining sample dropped to 29 per cent. She also found that only a few centres of printing supplied the great majority of all imports, namely Venice, Cologne and Paris in the 1480s, and Venice, Paris and Lyons in the 1490s.

The present survey elucidates and refines these conclusions by extending Hellinga's study by several decades, quadrupling the amount of data, and taking into account subject categories and the size of a book by calcu-

7. Needham, above, pp. 148–63, for a greatly refined interpretation of custom rolls detailing book importations.   8. E. Armstrong 1979.   9. Roberts 1989, and cf. Roberts 1997.
10. That study has since been published: L. Hellinga 1991a.

lating 'masterformes' on the basis of the number of sheets used to print each copy of an edition.[11] The results modify, rather than significantly alter, earlier findings. Now German-speaking countries, rather than Italy, dominate overall with 33 per cent of the whole. This no doubt reflects the relatively low number of books originating in Italy in the sixteenth century, which offsets its peak in the 1480s and 1490s, coupled with the increasingly significant presence of books printed at Basel from about 1520. Italy then follows Germany with 25 per cent of the whole, France with 24 per cent, and the Netherlands with 8 per cent; the remaining 10 per cent are accounted for by books from England.

Looking at sources of books by country or linguistic unity glosses over cultural, economic and political factors at work in individual cities, which affected trade. If we examine individual centres of printing for patterns of importation to England we find Venice as the leading supplier of books with 19 per cent of the total, followed by Paris (16 per cent), Basel (12 per cent), Cologne (8 per cent), Lyons (7 per cent), Strasbourg (5 per cent) and Nuremberg (4 per cent). Four per cent of the books in the survey were printed in Westminster or London. So far these percentages reflect the number of copies of books printed in each centre. This equates a thin tract with a complete Bible. A useful way to rectify this imbalance is to calculate the number of masterformes. This calculation is a simple one, made merely by dividing the number of leaves by the format of the book (in a folio, two leaves equal one sheet; in a quarto, four leaves equal one sheet, etc.), and it provides a basic unit for measuring and comparing the amount of work required to print a book. Since size would affect price, with a large Bible representing a greater capital outlay than a thin quarto, it can also affect our assessment of ownership. On the basis of masterformes, a slightly different picture emerges. Basel – with its production of multi-volume editions of St Augustine and large Bibles – and Venice stand equal, each with 18 per cent of the overall total, and Lyons increases its standing twofold, from 7 per cent of the number of copies to 14 per cent of the number of masterformes. Nuremberg too increases its percentage of the whole, rising to 7 per cent, whereas Strasbourg remains stable at 5 per cent. Cologne has the only decrease of significance in its percentage of the whole, falling from 8 per cent to 6 per cent. This is not surprising when one thinks of the thin quarto tracts in which early Cologne printers specialized. Indeed, 30 per cent of Cologne-printed

11. Chrisman adopted this method in her study of book production at Strasbourg (Chrisman 1982).

books supplied to England were quartos, as opposed to only 10 per cent and 18 per cent from Venice and Basel.

What is most striking is that, although a large number of printing centres is represented in the survey, only a few account for the majority of the books. Of the 88 places of printing represented, just 8 cities, those listed above, supplied 85 per cent of the total. Although which cities constitute the dominant few changes from decade to decade, these proportions are constant. Some decades show an even more marked dominance by just a few centres. In the 1480s supply is fairly evenly distributed among several centres of printing, but in most other decades one or two centres make up a significant percentage of the whole. For instance, in the first decade of the sixteenth century, Venice, Paris and Lyons combine to account for 67 per cent of the total, and in the next decade, the 1510s, Paris alone accounts for 45 per cent, the highest percentage for any single city in our period. Even Venice, at its peak in the 1490s providing 32 per cent of all books, does not stand out so dramatically from the other major suppliers.

Looking at centres of supply by decade (see fig. 8.1), the most obvious feature is the pattern for Venice. There is a sharp increase from the early 1480s and a huge jump in the 1490s. Venice as a centre of printing, once it recovered from the glut of printers and printed books of the early 1470s, was extraordinarily active to the end of the century, owing to its position as a main centre of trade throughout Europe, its wealth and its intellectual climate. Scholderer suggested that about 2,500 editions were printed there on the more than 100 presses operating between 1481 and 1501, whereas a recent count (1999) of editions recorded in the Incunabula Short-Title Catalogue (ISTC) gives close to 3,000.[12] After 1500, Venice is overtaken considerably by Paris as the main supplier of books to England in the survey, and its decline continues to the end of our period. This reflects the decline in Venetian book production as a consequence of foreign invasion and a more general economic decline in the first half of the sixteenth century.

Paris and Lyons were undoubtedly the major producers of books in France at this time, and hence are the only major suppliers of books to England from that country. Books from Rouen certainly made their way to England as well, but they never constitute more than 3 per cent of the

12. Scholderer 1966, p. 74. The second figure is derived from ISTC and, although that catalogue is not yet complete, the figure is based on the most comprehensive information to date.

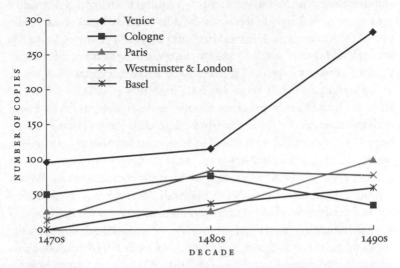

8.1 England: imports from main centres of printing 1470–1500. Westminster and London are included to show the comparative situation between imports and home production of books with marks of ownership in England.

total in the survey. The two peaks in books from Paris and Lyons are in the 1490s and 1510s. This pattern provides an interesting contrast to a table in the *Histoire de l'édition française* illustrating Parisian and Lyonese book production in the sixteenth century.[13] It shows an increase during the 1510s in books from both centres, a dip in the first half of the next decade, and the beginning of a steady increase over fifteen years to a high point of production around 1540 which is sustained in general over the rest of the century with only a slight decrease in Lyonese books in the 1560s. Thus the figures of importation into England reflect only in part (coincidentally?) the production rates for Paris and Lyons. One may speculate as to what extent the decline in imports from most foreign centres as the sixteenth century progresses is due to the supply of books being met by English printers, or to the effect of the protectionist act of 1534 which restricted the involvement of aliens in the book-trade.

Of the German-speaking centres, Cologne is recorded as having supplied the highest number of books to England in the 1480s, although, in general, Cologne, Nuremberg, Strasbourg and, sometimes, Basel are

13. H.-J. Martin 1982, p. 442.

about equal. In contrast to the declining imports from other centres after 1510, Basel rises sharply in the 1520s and dominates all other centres from the 1520s to the 1540s. The fact that Basel became a centre of humanist printing and thus was able to supply the texts in demand at this time in England certainly explains this trend. The Erasmian connection is also an important factor in these figures. Erasmus's presence in the city attracted humanists from across Europe to Basel, and his involvement with the printers there, particularly with Johann Froben, in publishing both his own work and texts edited by him, must have been a worthy recommendation for the products of the Basel presses.[14] The impetus given to Basel book production through the Erasmus connection was felt not just on the Continent but also in England. The reader is referred elsewhere for a discussion of Erasmus and his connection with England and English humanists, but the connection can begin to be quantified by the books in the survey.[15] Through Erasmus, works by his friend and fellow humanist, Sir Thomas More, were also printed there by Johann Froben, and copies of Basel editions of *Utopia* and *Epigrammata* are found in the sample. Erasmus, like More, had had works published elsewhere first, in Louvain, Antwerp and Paris, but the survey indicates that it was largely in Basel editions that Erasmus's works were most widely read in England. Aside from the circle of humanists connected with him, Erasmus would have been known to the public at large by the late 1540s when his *Paraphrases* on the New Testament were required to be placed in every church in England. The books in the survey bear out an Erasmian influence on the importation of books from Basel into England: books either by Erasmus or edited by him constitute 27 per cent of all Basel imports after 1515, the date of the first publication there of a text by Erasmus.

Turning to the Netherlands, only Louvain and Antwerp make their presence felt in the survey as centres of supply to England. Louvain's peak occurs in the 1480s, which surely is a direct consequence of business contacts between Johannes de Westfalia, Peter Actors and the Oxford book-seller, Thomas Hunt. Their association is concretely witnessed by the visit of De Westfalia and Actors to Oxford in about 1483 to supply books to Hunt.[16] In that decade, this survey suggests that Louvain supplied 9 per cent of all books coming to England but this drops to a negligible level in the 1490s. Netherlandish printing resurfaces in the 1510s to

14. Bietenholz 1971, pp. 37ff.   15. Trapp 1991; cf. Trapp below, pp. 306–7.
16. Madan and Bradshaw 1885–90.

reach another modest peak in the 1530s, this time with Antwerp contributing 5 per cent of all books supplied. Printing in the Low Countries, particularly at Antwerp, of books destined for the English market has been examined by M. E. Kronenberg and Frederick C. Avis and it will be informative to compare their findings with the pattern of Netherlandish importations which emerges in the survey.[17] Kronenberg noted, in the Low Countries, an ebb in book production aimed at an English market at the death of Gheraert Leeu in December 1492, with a resurgence again about 1504 with books printed by Jan van Doesborch, and the production of prohibited books for England beginning about 1528.[18] Although the number of copies in the survey is very small, those copies support this pattern to some extent. Netherlandish printing in the 1490s accounts for 3.5 per cent of all books of that decade in the survey. Two-thirds of that percentage (22 of 31 copies) were printed before Leeu's death, including 10 of the 12 books printed at Antwerp. On the other hand, only 3 of these Netherlandish books of the 1490s are in English (they were printed at Antwerp by Leeu) and thus are the only ones which concerned Kronenberg. What is more important to observe from the pattern in the survey is that books coming from the Netherlands remained predominantly Latin, so that while printers like Leeu may have produced books aimed specifically at Britain, they also took advantage of good trade connections in plying Latin books as well.

Turning to books printed in the Netherlands for English consumption, it is noteworthy that none of the liturgical books of Sarum Use occurs in the survey. Naturally, at the same time, none of the prohibited books, which surely constituted much of the Netherlandish market destined for England in the 1520s and 1530s, is to be found. Failure to survive explains much of this absence. Of Leeu's edition of a book of hours of Sarum Use printed in about 1492 (*STC* 1583), only a fragment has been recorded.[19] The only piece of Netherlandish printing dealing with the religious controversy is by the anti-Protestant Johannes Eck.[20] It is not surprising that Netherlandish books deemed heretical by the English authorities are so little represented in the survey. Although printed in large numbers and certainly exported to England, they were actively suppressed and burned, and their authors, printers and distributors persecuted. A case in point is the pirated text by George Joye of Tyndale's New Testament, no copy of which is in the survey. It was printed in Antwerp

17. Kronenberg 1929; Avis 1973.   18. Kronenberg 1929, p. 141.
19. At Brasenose College, Oxford: *STC* 1583 (now missing).   20. *STC* 7481.4.

in 1534 by the widow of Christoffel van Ruremund.[21] That edition of the New Testament in English is but one example of printing at Antwerp destined for the English market in these decades, and shows to what extent failure to survive may explain the paucity of such books in the survey and the resulting skewed pattern it shows of Netherlandish printing. Religious books, both Catholic and Protestant, were suppressed in these decades. Liturgical books printed at Antwerp in the 1520s had a short lifetime indeed in England before being rendered obsolete by the break with Rome, and proscribed books such as Tyndale's and Joye's were at risk even before they left the printing house.

Some reasons for peaks and valleys in patterns of importation have been posited above. Ideally, these patterns ought to be compared with production statistics for the major centres supplying books to England in order to distinguish mechanisms of the book-trade from sheer volume of production. While a comprehensive study of production levels is lacking, it is possible to gauge roughly the output of printing centres by a count of editions in the *ISTC*.[22] Even to look at the decades beginning in 1480 and 1490 will suggest that factors other than output determined importations to England.

The tables below show the 'top ten' producers of printed books in those two decades (a comparison with Scotland is included here).

For England, in each decade, only five or six centres are found common to both sets of figures. Rome and Lyons, the second and fourth most productive printing centres in the 1480s, have a negligible presence in the survey in the same period. In the 1490s, the third, fifth, sixth and eighth most important printing centres (Leipzig, Rome, Florence, Milan) sold very few books to England. Venice was the largest producer of books in the 1480s, just as it was the primary source of books for England. Venetian imports continue their marked rise in the 1490s, but rank just about even with Paris for number of editions produced. Basel, which accounted for 6 per cent and 7 per cent of imports in the 1480s and 1490s, respectively, was responsible for only 2.9 per cent and 2 per cent of all editions printed. Louvain produced 9 per cent of all books coming to England in the 1480s but was responsible for only 1.7 per cent of total production in that decade. It is to be expected that native printing accounts for a greater percentage of books owned in England since, theo-

21. *STC* 2825; Kronenberg 1929, p. 150; Hume 1973, p. 1086.
22. I am grateful to John Goldfinch (BL, *ISTC*) for providing me with these figures in 1994; they are intended to serve only as a guide to levels of production.

	ISTC (editions) (%)	Survey England (copies) (%)	Survey Scotland (copies) (%)
1480s			
Venice	12.5	18	23
Rome	7.1		
Cologne	5.4	12	11
Lyons	5.4		
Paris	5.1	4	2
Strasbourg	4.6	5	15
Milan	4.5		
Augsburg	4.2		
Nuremberg	3.9	6	6
Basel	2.9	6	10
1490s			
Venice	14.3	32	24
Paris	14.2	11	22
Leipzig	6.5		
Lyons	5.4	10	10
Rome	4.5		
Florence	4		
Cologne	3.9	4	7
Milan	3.7		
Nuremberg	3.3	6	5
Deventer	3.2		

retically, the entire output of English presses (certainly books in English) was geared for the home market. Westminster and London produced only 1.1 per cent of all books printed in the 1480s yet account for 12 per cent in the survey.

The comparison between importation and production levels for Scotland in these decades also reveals that one is not a simple reflection of the other. Venice dominates in both importation and production in the 1480s, but in the 1490s is almost on a par with Paris. Thus, although there is some correlation between overall production levels and books imported to England and Scotland, it is also clear that volume of production was only one of many factors determining the importation of printed books into Britain.

One of these factors, as mentioned in connection with Basel and its humanist editions, is the preference for certain texts at certain times, and so it may be revealing to look at what texts originated from which centres of printing and when. The books in the survey fall largely into ten categories: general theology, patristics, Bibles, classics, law, natural philosophy (including medicine), philosophy (including political philosophy), imaginative literature, grammar and history. The 1490s, the decade with the highest number of books coming into England in the survey, are dominated by theology, law, and natural philosophy. The sharp rise in theological books from the 1460s to the 1490s closely mirrors that of Venetian imports at that time. One might conclude that Venice is therefore responsible for the majority of theology books in England in the 1480s, and especially in the 1490s, yet that is not the case here. If one looks more closely at the kinds of book each printing centre was supplying, it becomes evident that the supply of theological books is not dominated by one printing centre, but rather shared between Paris, supplying the greatest number, Nuremberg, London, Strasbourg, Venice and Basel. The overall dominance of Venice in the 1490s is based on its supplying canon and civil law, but, even more so, supplying natural philosophy and classics, followed by philosophy. It far surpasses all other printing centres in the supply of books on natural philosophy and classics, not only in sheer quantity (which would be natural since Venice was the leading supplier in this decade), but also in relation to other subjects. Natural philosophy and classics make up 20 per cent and 18 per cent of all Venetian books in England in the 1490s, with 17 per cent law. Legal books are proportionately more important among Lyonese books in general (41 per cent) but law books printed at Lyons still account for only 26 per cent of imports of legal books in this decade, while Venice was supplying 58 per cent and 60 per cent of the demand for natural philosophy and classics.

When calculated by masterformes, again the striking difference is in the sharp jump in quantity in the 1520s, which is undetectable when looking only at the number of copies. In comparing the number of copies with the number of masterformes for each subject category in the 1520s, it is apparent that this jump reflects an increase in the size and number of Bibles being supplied to England. Whereas, in numbers of copies, theology is the largest subject category with 27 per cent, followed by patristics with 13 per cent, in numbers of masterformes, Bibles now constitute the largest category with 49 per cent – far surpassing theology – followed by patristics at 24 per cent and theology at only 10 per cent. Just as printers in Lyons were responsible for the sharp jump in imports in the 1520s, so too are they responsible for the increase in Bible production in that decade. Bibles make up 30 per cent of the number of copies of Lyonese printing imported to England in the 1520s, yet they make up 94 per cent of the number of masterformes. No other centre of printing in this survey was so dominated by printing one kind of book as Lyons in the 1520s.

A significant, if not so dramatic, increase in the importation of patristic texts in the 1520s, already seen in the number of copies, is further substantiated in the number of masterformes. Indeed, patristics is the only other subject to increase sharply in the comparison. Here, Basel is almost exclusively responsible for supplying these patristic texts to England, a number of which were edited by Erasmus or a member of his humanist circle. Patristics make up 23 per cent of the number of copies which Basel supplied in the 1520s, but 69 per cent of its production in masterformes. The predominance of patristic texts at Basel and of Bibles at Lyons makes clear the correlation between subject categories and centres of printing. It is also interesting to note that Venice, while supplying only a very small quantity of books to England in this decade, is supplying almost solely books of natural philosophy. At the same time, Paris was supplying an almost equal number of natural philosophy books but these form only a small proportion of the books originating from Paris, whereas they are almost the only type of book from Venice. A demand for books on that subject had not died out since the 1490s, but Venice no longer controlled the market.

One final statistical examination to be made is in comparing the books in the survey in general with those owned by the university-educated in order to correct findings by others, which indicated a difference between the learned and the general market. Armstrong found that Venice was the leading supplier of learned books for the English market.[23] This was a conclusion also drawn by Hellinga, who found that the percentage of Venetian books doubled when looking solely at books in Oxford colleges when compared with that in her sample as a whole. My criteria for defining this group, for determining the learned or university market, are more specific than Armstrong's and more stringent than Hellinga's, and benefit from enhancing the data to include biographical details. Thus I may speak of books owned by the university-educated quite literally, having included in this group only books owned by men known to have

23. E. Armstrong 1979, p. 277.

been at university and therefore to be found in university registers. Some owners are not in university registers, but they tell us in their inscriptions that they are or have been at university. I have not included books for which the only evidence of early ownership is an Oxford or Cambridge binding. These cities were, along with London, the chief binding centres in England at the time and did not cater exclusively for the university market, and thus ownership by a member of the university cannot be assumed. Also, I have not included books which were clearly intended for the university market as far as their subject matter is concerned and yet cannot be placed there on the basis of any surviving evidence. I restrict myself simply to those books known to have been owned by university-educated men.

The patterns of supply from the major printing centres are remarkably similar to those for the survey as a whole (see fig. 8.1). Contrary to Hellinga's findings, Venice still dominates in the 1470s, 1480s, and 1490s by approximately the same degree as in the survey in general. In these decades, it provides 29 per cent, 25 per cent and 39 per cent of books owned by the university-educated, as opposed to 28 per cent, 18 per cent and 32 per cent for book owners as a whole in the survey. Books from Paris in the 1540s and 1550s are much better represented here than in the general survey, but Louvain has almost no presence at all after the 1470s and 1480s, whereas it supplied a small percentage of books in the survey during the 1510s, 1530s and 1550s. Of the Netherlandish books owned by the university-educated, Louvain dominates other centres, and certainly English scholars patronized presses there. Thomas More's *Utopia* was first published at Louvain by Dirk Martens, and a copy of it in the survey was given to Corpus Christi College, Oxford, by John Claymond. However, the numbers of books from Louvain owned by the university-educated in the survey are never more than a few for any decade.

The number of books supplied by Westminster and London drops significantly when one looks only at books owned by university men, as one might expect, so that in the 1480s when Westminster and London printing made up 12 per cent of all books in the survey for England, it makes up only 2 per cent of the books owned by the university-educated. This lends credence to the truism that early English printers, with a few exceptions, directed their publications not at the universities, but rather at an English-reading, principally non-Latinate, public. Conversely, the survey shows Basel, as a centre of intellectual printing, providing almost the same proportion of books for the non-university as for the university market, and its percentages remain little changed, including its great prevalence in the 1520s, 1530s, and 1540s, and, among the university-educated, also in the 1550s when it cornered 24 per cent of the market, up from 19 per cent. While some printing centres may have produced books aimed at an English market, there is little evidence of 'targeting' a specific university market. Rather, foreign importations met the demands of a Latin, and, in that sense, learned, market, which extended beyond the universities.

It is immediately clear how different the patterns of importation into Scotland are from those of England. There is no dramatic leap in the 1490s, but rather a sharp, then steady, rise in imports from France and Germany after 1500. To some extent this may reflect the sources of the data. I have stated above that the survey for England is biased towards incunabula; for Scotland that is not the case. Durkan and Ross's *Early Scottish Libraries* and its supplements record almost all surviving early books with Scottish ownership. The survey of books with English ownership cannot begin to match the Scottish for comprehensiveness, yet comparisons between the two countries based on the data as they now stand are still valuable. In the period to 1557, imports to Scotland from France, accounting for 52.5 per cent of all books, lead those from other countries, with Germany (30 per cent), Italy (11 per cent) and the Netherlands (5 per cent) following. This is in contrast to England where French imports accounted for only 24 per cent, and Italy for 25 per cent. Scotland also contrasts with England in the specific printing centres supplying the books. Paris, as expected for reasons outlined below, constitutes 40 per cent of the total for Scotland, Basel 15 per cent, Lyons 11 per cent, Venice 8.5 per cent, Cologne 8 per cent, and Strasbourg 5 per cent. The greatest differences from England in these percentages lie in Paris (only 16 per cent for England) and Venice (19 per cent for England). Lyons differs too, although not as dramatically, in a 4 per cent increase from England. Thus, in general, the two countries differ most in the supply of books from Paris (coupled with Lyons to an extent) and Venice.

After the initial impression of the sustained growth in French and German imports to Scotland, the next most remarkable feature is the relatively static pattern in pre-1500 importations, in contrast to the dramatic leaps in the 1480s and 1490s for England. For Scotland, imports before 1500 are small in number and no one centre stands out sharply from another. Although German imports lead other countries in supplying books to Scotland before 1500, when looking at individual printing

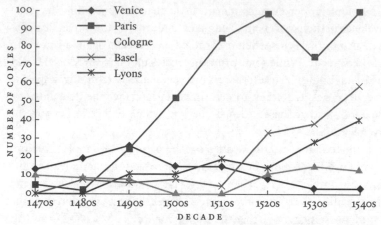

8.2 Scotland: imports from main centres of printing 1470–1550.

centres most books are still coming from Venice (see fig. 8.2). The percentages of Venetian imports for Scotland do not differ radically from those for England in the 1470s and 1480s (29 per cent and 23 per cent as opposed to 28 per cent and 18 per cent), but in the 1490s 24 per cent of books in Scotland were Venetian products, as compared with 32 per cent of those in England. The percentage of Venetian imports then drops off more significantly for Scotland than for England, mainly due to the growing dominance of Parisian books.

This dominance of Paris over other printing centres is to be expected. Scots were both students and teachers at the University of Paris, many had works printed there, and the university had served as a model for the establishment of St Andrews University; the Auld Alliance was still strong. It is revealing that the pattern of importation in the survey matches much more closely the production levels already outlined in *L'Histoire de l'édition française*, demonstrating that Scots obviously had access to, and availed themselves of, the whole range of books coming from Parisian, and Lyonese, presses.

The pattern of Netherlandish imports is similar for both England and Scotland, with a peak in the 1480s. Books from the Netherlands are proportionally greater for Scotland, where Louvain comprises 17 per cent of the whole in the 1480s and Antwerp 2 per cent. The peak in the 1480s in England has been explained in part by the active marketing of books through Thomas Hunt at Oxford by Johannes de Westfalia and Peter Actors; for Scotland, this peak results largely from the presence of individual Scots at Louvain in that period, and particularly from the purchases of William Schevez, Archbishop of St Andrews. None of the books printed by Gheraert Leeu for the English market are to be found in Scotland, emphasizing that it was specifically the *English* market he was catering for. Indeed, English-language books seem to have had no market in Scotland. Except for two English Bibles printed in 1551 and 1553, there are no books in English with Scottish ownership in the survey; the only books in the local vernacular are those in Scots printed at Edinburgh. Also, while books from Antwerp are found in the survey from the 1520s in addition to the 1480s and 1490s, they are not necessarily those printed specifically for the English market as described by Kronenberg. Perhaps, as for England, these reformist books, if they were in Scotland at the time, have perished owing to their controversial nature.

Imports from Germany are strong in the 1480s and 1490s, as they were for England, but show a marked rise from the 1520s. Looking at printing centres, it becomes clear that, before 1500, no one German city dominates others, but that in the 1520s and later, Basel is largely responsible for this sharp rise in imports from German-speaking areas. This may be attributed again to the position of Basel as a centre of humanist printing and intellectual circles, producing newly edited patristic tomes, Bibles and Erasmian works. While the connection between Erasmus and Scotland may not have been as strong as between him and England, Erasmus knew Hector Boece and other Scots in Paris, and he acted as tutor to the sons of James IV in Italy. Alexander Stewart invited Erasmus to Scotland, but his death at Flodden in 1513 broke any further close connection.[24] Erasmus evoked antipathy as well as sympathy, of course, and Scots such as John Major and George Lokert were involved in the examination of his works at Paris. Two copies of Erasmus's rebuttal of the Paris judgement are in the survey.

As already stated, there is a stronger correlation between production levels and levels of importation for French suppliers to Scotland than to England, but this correlation does not pertain to most other printing centres. As was the case for England, only five centres correspond between the top producers of books and the top suppliers to Scotland. Venice both printed and supplied the most books in the 1480s, but Rome and Lyons have, as with England, a negligible presence in the survey. Even Paris, which was the fifth leading producer of books in the 1480s,

---

24. Durkan 1953, pp. 6–7.

supplied only 2 per cent of books in the survey to Scotland. This changes in the 1490s when Paris and Venice are about equal, both in production and supply. German-speaking centres are proportionally more important in supplying books to Scotland than in producing them. Basel supplied 10 per cent of books to Scotland in the 1480s, as opposed to producing 2.9 per cent of the overall total, and Cologne supplied 7 per cent in the 1490s, whereas it produced only 3.9 per cent. Strong Scottish trade connections with the Netherlands, through whose ports many German, as well as Netherlandish, books were shipped, and intellectual ties to the universities at Cologne and Louvain thus contributed to keeping up levels of supply, even if production levels in those centres were falling in proportion to those in other centres of printing.

The correlation between printing centres and subject categories of books is again revealing. Overall, theology dominates and its rise mirrors that of the Parisian imports. The rise of patristic texts also follows that of books from Basel with Scottish ownership. In the 1490s, theology comprises 32 per cent of all books, Bibles 1 per cent, classics 14 per cent, grammar 5 per cent, history 8 per cent, law 5 per cent, literature 9 per cent, natural philosophy 5 per cent, patristics 9 per cent and philosophy 12 per cent. In that decade Paris and Venice were providing about equal numbers of books to Scotland. The Parisian imports are spread among many categories, but the Venetian are primarily of classics and law. Whereas Venice was the main provider of natural philosophy to England in the 1490s, it is Cologne which provides that category to Scotland. Most of these are commentaries on Aristotelian books of natural philosophy, suited to a university education. The proportion of natural philosophy books in Scotland is less than half that in England during this decade, again reflecting the lesser importance of Venice as a centre of supply. Law books are also substantially fewer in the 1490s in Scotland than in England, although Venice is still providing about the same proportion. Lyons, on the other hand, is providing no law books whatsoever to Scotland during this decade, which is rather surprising, given the number of law books printed there.

The 1520s are marked by the dominance of Parisian books and so Paris is the leading supplier of all types of book, except patristics where Basel leads already. History constitutes a larger proportion, 18 per cent, for Scotland than for England (12 per cent), and history also constitutes a larger proportion of Parisian imports than in England. That is a direct result of the publication at Paris of Boece's *Scotorum Historiae* and Major's

Historia Britanniae in 1527 and 1521, respectively. There are 9 copies of each of these works in the survey. Basel continues to be the chief supplier of patristic texts and now also of Bibles. Lyons, whose English market was so dominated by Bibles in the 1520s, was supplying to Scotland mostly general theology along with a small number of other works.

In looking at Scottish book ownership in detail, a direct correlation can often be established between an owner and his presence in the centre where his books were printed. William Schevez, Archbishop of St Andrews, is the most obvious example, with many of his 28 surviving books coming from the Netherlands – many surviving in contemporary Netherlandish bindings – following his matriculation at the University of Louvain in the 1470s, and repeated visits throughout his life. Not only could he have purchased them there himself, but he also certainly directed his agent, Andrew Halyburton, to purchase books there on his behalf to the value of 500 gold crowns in 1493.[25] This, and a number of other instances, raises the question of the nature of the book-trade in Scotland. Is it in fact accurate to speak of a book-trade in terms of organized importation before the middle of the sixteenth century, or were the majority of books actually purchased individually abroad?

It is generally agreed that the earliest printed books in England were purchases made by individuals on the Continent.[26] John Russell's purchase of two Ciceros in 1467 has been mentioned.[27] In 1465 in Hamburg, while on a diplomatic mission for Edward IV, James Goldwell bought a *Rationale divinorum officiorum*, printed at Mainz by Fust and Schoeffer.[28] These individual purchases were soon complemented by the importing of books into England in bulk. Pollard cites Gerhard von Wesel of Cologne, alderman of the German community in London, importing into London items including printed books between July 1466 and 1468. The evidence of a substantial printed book-trade in England is unequivocal.

Such evidence is lacking for Scotland, however. Owing in part to the depredations suffered at the hands of the English in the 16th century and later, customs rolls do not exist for Scotland as they do for England, depriving us of vital evidence of the volume of the book-trade. Perhaps because such evidence is lacking, so too is a sustained study of the fifteenth- and early sixteenth-century book-trade in Scotland. Such a study is beyond the scope of the present work, but it will be useful to

25. Halyburton 1867, p. 6.　　26. Pollard and Ehrman 1965, and E. Armstrong 1979.
27. *GW* 6922.　　28. *GW* 9101.

rehearse evidence of a Scottish book-trade in an attempt to judge whether it is accurate to speak of such a thing in Scotland at this time.

In his work on the cultural background of Scotland during this period, John Durkan cites the busy monastic scriptoria of the late fifteenth century; parchment-sellers; the binder Patrick Lowes; the involvement of Scotland's first printer, Andrew Myllar, with printing at Rouen in 1506; and the presence abroad of Scots, a few of whom worked in printing shops and other Scots who had works printed there.[29] Other references to books being sent to Scotland are included in the ledger of Andrew Halyburton where the scholars James Cumming and James Watson act as middlemen in sending books to Schevez, to the university rector (either Walter Drummond or Robert Keith) or to Richard Lawson. The Protocol Book of John Foular lists him doing business with Jean Richard, a Rouen merchant and printer. The accounts of the Lord High Treasurer of Scotland also contain several entries pertaining to books being supplied to James IV. On 28 April 1502, John Foular was paid for three printed mass books; on 16 July 1503, John Hervey was paid for books procured in Paris; and on 29 March 1503, Andrew Myllar supplied a number of books which are listed by title in the accounts. Myllar supplied books again in 1507. Further potential evidence of a prospering Scottish trade in books is the complaint of Chepman, Myllar's printing partner, in 1509–10, that Edinburgh merchants continued to sell Sarum books, contravening the prohibition set out in letters patent to protect the fledgeling printing enterprise of Chepman and Myllar. Chepman accuses a number of merchants of selling Sarum books: William Frost, Francis Frost, William Sym, Andrew Ross and others. Rather than indicating a flourishing book-trade, however, the complaint corroborates evidence that Sarum books were commonly sold by chapmen not otherwise engaged in the book-trade, and that the trade in primers was largely separate from the normal trade in books. Thus one cannot infer from Chepman's complaint an active book-trade in Scotland.[30]

It is clear that books could be bought in Scotland, but most of the evidence cited above supports the view that books were purchased abroad for individuals. The middlemen in Halyburton's ledger were acting for individuals and supplying requested material, so that to conclude that the ledger proves regular channels of trade is perhaps not quite accurate.[31] Similarly, the books supplied for James IV were also satisfying a

29. Durkan 1959, especially pp. 382–6.   30. See Needham above, especially p. 159.
31. Durkan and Ross 1961, p. 16.

specific request. If he was having his agent John Hervey procure books for him in Paris, it is a fair inference that they were not available at home. One clear witness to the acquisition of books on the Continent for an individual in Scotland is John Smyth, a monk at Kinloss. In his chronicle of the abbey he states that, in 1529, fine books were brought from France by Robert Reid at the request of Thomas Crystall.[32] The only evidence of books being provided in Scotland by merchants on speculation, then, is a statement by Giovanni Ferreri that, besides his many books bought at Paris, he had also 'bought not a few books at Edinburgh' while at court there from about 1528 to 1531.[33]

The books in the survey also point to individual purchase abroad. Very few specify where they were purchased, but those few name continental centres: Paris, Bruges, Louvain. Not one of the books states that it was purchased in Scotland. Durkan has indicated that the number of Scots students at the University of Paris is in part responsible for Parisian books being so well represented in early Scottish libraries.[34] A university student had a need of books and would tend to purchase them during his student years (and perhaps carry on doing so). Thus, many of those Parisian books (and probably books from elsewhere as well) purchased by men who were at the university of Paris would have been purchased in the city while they were there. This pertains to other centres as well. Gilbert Halden matriculated at the university at Louvain in 1491 and purchased there that same year Rolewinck's *Fasciculus temporum*, printed at Strasbourg in 1488.[35] Much later, David Henryson, a student at Paris, bought there a Lizetius printed in Lyons in 1552. Although not a student at the time, John Greenlaw took advantage of a trip to Paris in 1553 and bought a *Breviarium Romanum* there that year. A Scottish student at Cologne is also known to have left there the books he had presumably purchased for his studies.

These may be individual instances only in the face of many more which were purchased in Scotland but which remain silent about details of their acquisition. Another indication of individual purchase abroad, however, is the bindings which still cover a number of these books. Many of them are identifiably foreign. Many of the bindings covering Schevez's books are identifiably Louvain work, and others can be identified as German, Parisian or French. Binding was practised in Scotland, Patrick Lowes already being mentioned, and payments for binding books occur in the

32. Stuart 1872, p. 9.   33. Stuart 1872, p. xvi.   34. Durkan 1959, p. 386.
35. HC (Add) 6937*.

accounts of James IV. Some seal matrices were made in Scotland, so that the technology for producing binding tools was available, yet very few Scottish bindings from this period have been identified.[36] It is possible that this is a weakness in scholarship and that more bindings are Scottish but have simply not been recognized. Lacking such evidence, however, one must conclude that the bindings which look foreign are indeed foreign and that they thus join those which can be proved to be foreign work. It has hitherto been assumed that books were invariably shipped in bulk unbound and then bound either by the book-seller receiving the shipment or by the end purchaser. The large number of books in foreign bindings with Scottish ownership could perhaps indicate that the book-trade to Scotland did not observe this economic practicality and imported many books ready-bound. This would add substantially to the cost, since the book-seller would have to pay not only higher shipping costs owing to increased weight and bulk, but also the price for binding in advance of an assured sale. It seems more likely that the books were purchased individually abroad and bound there. These bindings may then be evidence of the role of the foreign book-seller in arranging binding for speculative retail, a role still emerging in the context of early printed books.

Much evidence has already been collected of book purchase abroad by Scots. Of the nine Venetian books owned by Scottish Blackfriars, seven can be associated with John Adamson or James Crichton who had visited Italy.[37] Cherry believed that Henry Sinclair acquired many of his books in France or the Netherlands; one had been given to Sinclair by Ferreri in Paris in 1557.[38] Many other books can be associated with their owners' travel abroad. Most of the armorial binding stamps used for Scottish owners date not from their rise to the position commemorated in the stamp, but rather from a trip abroad. The bindings which they adorn were thus probably executed abroad as well.[39]

The evidence of inscriptions, of bindings, of references to middlemen on the Continent acting for individuals, and the probability that Scots abroad acquired a wide range of books available there point to a book-trade in Scotland that was still nascent during this time. Books could be purchased there, as Chepman and Ferreri tell us, and university students would have had to be supplied by means other than personal visits to the Continent. It seems, however, that there was little bulk importation of

36. Mitchell 1955. See also Mitchell 1961.   37. Ross 1969, p. 15.   38. Cherry 1963, p. 14.
39. Mitchell 1955, pp. 27–30.

books by merchants for sale in Scotland on speculation. What the patterns of importation tell us is that Scots were well aware of what was available in print on the Continent and had the means to be supplied with it, whether through the extensive Scots networks abroad or through a book-trade at home. Particularly impressive is their participation in the trade in books printed in France in the first half of the sixteenth century. The slow start of printing in Scotland does not reflect on the intellectual life of the Scots; conversely, it indicates that the participation of Scots in the intellectual life on the Continent in this period obviated any need for a home-grown printing industry. As was the case with England, the demands of the Latin-reading public were met in Scotland by books printed abroad, and printing at home was not introduced until the demands of a lay, Scots-reading public made it a viable enterprise.

COLLECTIONS
AND
OWNERSHIP

9
Private ownership of printed books

MARGARET LANE FORD

The present discussion, like its predecessor on importation, is based on a sample of over 4,300 printed books which bear clear evidence of having been in private ownership in Britain before 1557. (For a sample of ownership inscriptions, see figs. 9.1–9.5, 21.1, 24.4, 25.1.) The same caveats as before apply in interpreting the data: the sample includes only surviving books (with factors such as size and subsequent custody influencing survival), and it is biased towards incunabula and perhaps towards books owned by the university-educated, and thus towards Latin books. Even with these limitations, however, the sample, as the largest so far assembled from individual instances, permits a broad view of book ownership among the literate population of the period. Concerned with private ownership of books, it excludes contemporary institutional libraries. Within these restrictions we can examine who owned books, what books they owned and what factors influenced that ownership.

Apart from availability, the primary factors influencing book ownership were need and means. Thus, the chief owners of books were university-educated and university educators, that is to say, the secular and regular clergy, including theologians, and other professionals such as lawyers and doctors. Merchants and gentry may not have had a need of books as easily defined as that of other groups, but they certainly had the means to acquire books, and they did. A number of these, and other, categories of reader are specifically examined elsewhere in this volume.

Within Britain, different conditions apply in different areas. In England, shortly after the invention of printing, printed books began to become available, with a substantial import trade quickly developing. This was supplemented after 1475 by English production of books. In Scotland, printing was not introduced until 1505, and it was sporadic until the mid sixteenth century. Trade in imported books also seems to have been scanty throughout our period, but books (in Latin) were sup-

9.4 A buyer noted that the price of this book, bought in the year 1497 'in nundinis Sterbreg' (i.e. at the Stourbridge Fair), was 13 shillings and 4 pence. The volume, bound by a Cambridge binder, contains several commentaries on civil law by Baldus de Ubaldis, all printed in Venice, c. 1495.

plied to Scottish readers through networks of Scots studying and travelling abroad.

Several features of book ownership overall, however, emerge from the sample, in Scotland as well as in England. On a basic level, people owned books which they needed: books were professional tools. This is most apparent in books owned by the university-educated but may also be found throughout the whole range of owners. For lay owners, such as the gentry and merchants, need is more difficult to define, and other factors, such as social networks, influenced their ownership of books. The personal networks which were suggested in discussing importation to Scotland continued to play a role there when this was no longer a significant factor in England, and we shall return at the end to examine more closely the nature of specifically Scottish ownership of books.

Wales merits special mention, if only to observe the paucity of examples of Welsh ownership in the sample. Among book-owners in Oxford and Cambridge, several Welshmen, such as Richard Griffith, Hugh Glynn, John Prise and Nicholas Robinson, can be identified by their names and recorded biographical details. Aside from these university men, however, Welsh owners of most of the other books in the sample remain entirely unidentified, and only their surnames reveal their origin. A systematic examination of the early collections at the National Library of Wales revealed two incunables with possible early sixteenth-century Welsh ownership. One is St Augustine, *Sermones*, printed at Paris c.1499,[1] with the names Gruffyth ap David and William ap Einan, among others. Its London binding and earlier non-Welsh ownership point to acquisition in England by the subsequent Welsh owners. The second book is Cicero, *Epistolae ad familiares*, printed at Venice in 1491,[2] bearing the names of William de la Pool and David ap Howell. More typical is a

---

1. *GW* 2921; NLW, I.F. Par 99.   2. *GW* 6845; NLW, I.E. Ven 91.

tract volume now in the Bodleian, containing five English-printed books from the 1530s and 1540s. The works are John Fitzherbert's *The boke of husbandry*, and *Surveying*, *A glasse for housholders*, *Xenophon's treatise of house holde* and *The maner of kepynge a courte baron*. It has a plain contemporary binding which may be British but otherwise cannot be localized, and it was first owned by Roger Lloyd, then by Foulk Lloyd. A Sarum missal dating from 1554 contains the obits of John ap Hugh and of the Ap Morris family.[3] None of these Welsh owners has been identified, so that we cannot know in what circumstances the books were in Wales. It is not even certain they were in Wales, rather than owned by men of Welsh ancestry living in England. Owing to this lack of evidence, it is impossible to judge the penetration of printed books into Wales in this period; this lack of evidence strongly leads to the conclusion, however, that there was almost none. The *History of the Book in Wales* will no doubt elucidate the early uses and ownership of books there, which have eluded the present investigation.

The university-educated, although a far from homogeneous group, may be the easiest to define. Their need for books is made explicit by university statutes prescribing set texts. Although the curriculum could be modified by individual tutors, the books in the sample show significant correlation between texts prescribed by statute and books owned by the university-educated. This correlation does not take into account the point at which a university man acquired his books – whether as a student in the arts or higher faculties, as a regent master, or even later in his career, but it shows a basic correspondence between need and ownership. As teachers of the curriculum, regent masters would have been influenced directly by university statute. When university men donated books, usually to their academic institutions, their choice would have been guided by the need for texts used in a university education. Thus, one may loosely, but not inaccurately, equate need and ownership in respect of prescribed texts and the university-educated.

One example of this correlation is the ownership of Aristotelian books in the sample. Aristotle dominated European university studies in the late Middle Ages, and English and Scottish universities were no exception. This dominance remained in place throughout our period, even surviving, at Oxford, the Edwardian statutes of 1549 and the Elizabethan *Nova Statuta* of 1564–5.[4] It is no surprise, then, that books by Aristotle

---

3. *STC* 10995.5, 11011, 11917, 26072, 7717; Bodleian 70.C.103. Missal: *STC* 16216; NLW, b55R8(1).   4. Fletcher 1986, p. 172.

dominate the collections of the university-educated. Aristotle is the most prevalent author owned by this group, and when books on Aristotelian philosophy are added to those by him, the number of copies triples. Mirroring this constant need, the editions of Aristotle found in the sample are also spread over all decades fairly evenly.

In addition to demonstrating by the sheer quantity of certain texts that need determines book ownership, the books by and on Aristotle in the sample highlight two other features of book ownership in England: they chart an evolution in intellectual attitudes with the introduction of new editions, commentaries and translations, while pointing to the concurrent longevity of older texts and editions. The change from scholastic to humanist commentaries on, and translations of, Aristotle was not a clear-cut or absolute one, as Charles Schmitt has made clear in speaking of a multiplicity of Aristotelianisms.[5] Commentaries by Thomas Aquinas and Duns Scotus underwent a revival at the same time that late Antique Greek commentaries of Simplicius, Philoponus and others were being discovered and embraced by humanists; new translations into Latin of Averroes's commentaries, based on his Hebrew intermediaries, were printed, notably in the monumental Giunta Aristotle–Averroes edition of 1550-2; thirteenth-century scholastic commentaries were printed together with fifteenth-century humanist translations to which they sometimes had little correspondence. Such multiplicity of Aristotelianisms is reflected in the present survey.

Among the earliest editions of Aristotle in the survey are indeed those with the scholastic commentary of Averroes. Thomas Rotherham gave copies of seven Aristotelian works with accompanying Averroes commentary, all printed at Padua by Laurentius Canozius in the early 1470s, to Cambridge University Library in 1484: *De anima*, the *Metaphysics*, *De caelo et mundo*, *De generatione et corruptione*, *Meteorologica*, *Parva naturalia* and *Physica*.[6] In contrast to these is another of the earliest printed books with documented English ownership: a copy of the humanist Donato Acciaiuoli's exposition of the *Ethics* (Florence 1478),[7] bought by John Shirwood in Rome in 1481. No one edition of, or commentary on, the works of Aristotle dominates the survey. The commentators most frequently found are the scholastics, Paul of Venice and Antonius Andreae, as well as the Greek commentators, Simplicius and Philoponus. Not sur-

5. Schmitt 1983a, b.   6. CUL, Oates 1954, 2542–8.
7. *GW* 140; Oxford, Magdalen Coll. B.III. 1.2, Rhodes 1982, no. 4.

prisingly, the most frequently recorded single edition is Alexander Bonini de Alexandria on *De anima*, printed at Oxford in 1481,[8] but even that is represented by only five copies in the survey: two were owned by known Oxford students, two by men whose education is undocumented (a vicar of East Dereham, Norfolk, and a monk at Butley Priory, Suffolk), and one owned rather later by Matthew Carew at Cambridge. Two copies of the 1479 Oxford edition of Aristotle's *Ethics*,[9] translated by the humanist, Leonardo Bruni, were owned by Oxford men, and two copies of Antonius Andreae's *Quaestiones super XII libros metaphysicae*, edited by Thomas Penketh and printed at London in 1480,[10] complete the home-grown editions with surviving records of early ownership.

By the end of our period virtually all copies of works by or on Aristotle are in some way touched by humanism. Editions of commentaries by Simplicius, Philoponus and Themistius are common, usually in Greek, but also in Latin translation, and commentaries by Agostino Nifo, Petrus Ramus and Coelio Secondo Curione accompany other Latin editions of Aristotle's works. Copies of Aristotle in Greek, edited by Erasmus, were owned by Thomas Cranmer,[11] Archbishop of Canterbury, and by George Acworth, a judge.

Even though the chronological sequence of editions may appear to indicate a changeover from old to new approaches to Aristotle, no matter how diverse those approaches may be, the extended lives of the earlier editions exemplify the multiplicity of Aristotelianisms coexistent through the middle of the sixteenth century. One volume now at Merton College, Oxford, containing commentaries by Duns Scotus and Antonius Andreae, was owned just after it was printed in Venice in the 1490s by William, a Carmelite friar at Newcastle, and then successively by at least five other owners in the sixteenth century before being given to Merton by Robert Barnes, a fellow.[12]

The books in the sample not only attest to the university-educated owning primarily books which they needed for their studies, either as students or as masters, but, conversely, that such texts were owned pri-

8. *STC* 314. CUL, Oates 1954, 4162; Bodleian Arch. G.d.37; Durham, Chapter Library, Inc. 61; Middle Temple; BL, 1B.55315.

9. *STC* 752; Bodleian S.Seld.e.2 and Chetham Mun. 7.B.6.19.

10. *STC* 581; CUL, Oates 1954, 4173; Oxford, Magdalen Coll. B.III.1.1; Rhodes 1982, no. 80.

11. Selwyn 1996.

12. Merton A 9/B 17 contains Duns Scotus, *Quaestiones in Universalia Porphyrii* ..., Venice: 1492/3 (*GW* 9090; Rhodes 1982, no. 715), and Antonius Andreae, *Scriptum in artem veterem Aristotelis*, Venice: 1496 (*GW* 1672; Rhodes 1982, no. 86).

marily by those who had attended university. Aristotelian texts may also be found in the hands of the regular clergy, some of whom may have received arts training within their houses.[13] Other Aristotelian texts in the survey, however, have anonymous but undoubtedly academic marks of ownership, and their ownership cannot be precisely defined, other than as being English. The recorded ownership of Aristotelian books is almost totally by the university-educated.

While Aristotelian texts are a convenient type of book with which to test ownership, other books prescribed by university statute present much the same picture, and this becomes even sharper when looking at the higher university faculties. Aside from texts required by statute, patristic and theological works, particularly pastoral theology and books of sermons, are frequently found to have been owned by the university-educated. Even when not prescribed by statute, such texts could in fact be necessary to follow lectures, as witnessed by a copy of St Augustine's *De civitate Dei*, now in the National Library of Scotland. It was sent to Oxford by William Wylom for use there by his fellow Durham monk, Roger Bell, a student at Oxford, who needed the text for lectures he was attending.[14] The *De civitate Dei* was not a text prescribed by statute, yet it was necessary to Bell's studies.

Students in the higher faculty of theology would have needed texts of systematic theology, but students of all levels needed more humble texts of pastoral theology. University study was 'by legal definition a clerical profession' and the Church provided an important source of funding for a university education.[15] Many students then followed a career in the Church, and so their ownership of books of theology, either contemporaneous with or subsequent to their student years, was informed by their university education.

Much the same picture emerges for other categories of book owner. The regular clergy, many of whom were provided with a university education or the equivalent, owned a range of books similar to that of the university-educated in general. They seem to have owned fewer works of the classics and of natural philosophy, and fewer books individually. This

---

13. In addition to elementary instruction conducted in claustral schools, advanced education could also be pursued within some orders at some houses. See, for instance, Richard and Mary Rouse, *CBMLC* ii, p. cxlii. The fact that members of the regular clergy were admitted directly to higher faculties at university also suggests that the equivalent of an arts education was available to some within their houses.   14. Doyle 1952.

15. Leader 1988, pp. 41, 43. F. J. Pegues estimated that about 900 of 1,200 students at Oxford around 1500 were supported by a benefice; see Trio 1984, p. 4.

is not surprising, when one thinks of their vow of poverty, of the monastic collections they could draw on,[16] or of the borrowing of books as between Durham monks William Wylom and Roger Bell, mentioned above. Such instances can be multiplied many times over. A correlation between means and ownership is still obvious. Many Benedictine houses were among the wealthiest in England, and it can be no mere coincidence that the ownership of printed books in the sample was also particularly prevalent within that order. Certainly other factors played a part in determining book ownership in the different orders, such as the attitude to education, individual versus communal ownership, and the vicissitudes of survival, but need and means remain primary determinants in book ownership among the regular clergy.

It will be useful to look briefly at the lower end of the social scale of book owners and then to look laterally, across the social scale, at other factors which influenced book ownership, such as personal association and social networks. If, in looking at book owners among the secular clergy, one leaves aside those who attended university, one is left with vicars, curates and rectors, most of whom, in the words of Margaret Bowker, are 'of obscure background'.[17] Only a few are represented in the survey. Undoubtedly some of the unidentified owners belong to this category, but the sheer lack of biographical information leaves their status in obscurity and makes it impossible to assess them as a category of owner. The lesser clergy had an obvious need of books such as pastoral aids, and, to some extent, they had the means derived from a benefice. While their books certainly reflect their clerical occupation, with books on moral, pastoral and devotional theology making up almost half the copies, the secular clergy also owned other types of book not strictly necessary to their occupation. It is these exceptions which warn against fixed assumptions regarding what types of book people *ought* to have owned. They also reflect the varied social make-up of this category of owner. Many such were indeed of obscure background, but others were sons of gentry, and so a wide range of influences determined their book ownership. Robert Yomanson owned the first edition of the *Book of Hawking, Hunting, and Blasing of arms*.[18] He is known only as vicar of Stretton-en-le-

16. See *CBMLC* for specific surviving library lists. Books need not have been in the library of a member's particular house in order for him to have access to them. For instance, the *Registrum Anglie*, compiled by the Oxford Franciscans, made it possible for 'a friar at any convent in the English Province [to] locate the nearest available copy' of a classical, patristic or moral theological text (*CBMLC* II, p. cxli).   17. Bowker 1968, p. 40.
18. *STC* 3308; CUL, Oates 1954, 4214.

Field, so that this gentlemen's book went beyond the strict boundaries of his need, and certainly beyond the boundaries of books as professional tools, although perhaps it hints at his undisclosed social status. Four books owned by Anthony Little, curate of Luton, survive, but only one, Lactantius *Opera*,[19] is primarily theological. The others point to wider interests: Breydenbach's *Peregrinatio in terram sanctam*, Diogenes Laertius's *Vitae et sententiae philosophorum*, and Seneca's *Opera*, edited by Erasmus.[20] As a description of a pilgrimage to the Holy Land, the Breydenbach may be seen as appropriate to Little's profession, but it was also a book read as a guide book and travel narrative. Other copies of his *Peregrinatio* are found owned as often by the gentry – such as James Horswell, MP for Plymouth, and John Prise – as by the clergy – such as William Smith, Bishop of Lincoln, or Ambrose Hilton, an Oxford Bachelor of Theology.[21]

Perhaps as surprising as the range of books owned by the lesser clergy is that they owned books at all. Bowker has calculated the average annual salaries in the Lincoln diocese in 1526 as ranging from a mere £5 3s 2d for a curate to £12 13s 8½d for a rector. With books, such as the *Chronicon* of St Antoninus, Archbishop of Florence,[22] costing its owner – Richard Skypp, rector of St George at Tambland – 4 shillings (although only volume II), that is a fair chunk of a meagre living. Patronage played a part in book ownership as well, with patrons giving books to clergy they were presenting. Ironically perhaps, such gifts seem to have been most prevalent among those who needed it least, the well-bred and well-connected clergymen whose connections were of material benefit. One among the non-university priests owed his book, as well as his living, to his patron, Humphrey Kervile. Kervile presented William Lacy to the living of Wiggenhall (St Mary the Virgin), Wigenhale, Norfolk, and, in commemoration of the event, presented him with a book by Petrus Bertrandi, *Libellus de iurisdictione ecclesiastica contra Petrum de Cugneriis*.[23] Cuthbert Sherbrooke, of the Sherbrooke family of Norfolk, is an example of a son of the gentry entering the clergy (he was rector of Rockland and of Thurton/Thurveton), and of the benefits his connections had for book ownership. Four of his books survive, three of them

---

19. Goff L-12; Durham UL, S.R.2.D.1.

20. *GW* 5076, *GW* 8382, Adams S-883, Lambeth Palace, 1490.3; Durham UL, S.R.2.D.1; Leeds UL, Ripon CL XVIII.H.21.

21. *GW* 5075, Oxford Bodleian, S.Seld.d.9; *GW* 5076, Hereford, Cathedral Library, *L.V.4., Brasenose Coll. UB/S.I.23, Rhodes 1982, no. 437; CUL, Oates 1123.

22. *GW* 2073, Leeds UL, Ripon CL XVIII.J.4.   23. *GW* 4179, CUL, Oates 1954, 3097.

gifts. One was from Thomas Cappe, doctor of canon law at Cambridge and official of the archdeaconry of Norwich under whose jurisdiction Sherbrooke came; another from Henry Woodhouse, rector of Newton Flotman, Norfolk; and a third from Edward Blundeville, gentleman, also of Newton Flotman. The books are entirely appropriate to the status of the benefactors, since Cappe gave a book on canon law, *Casus papales, episcopales et abbatiales*;[24] Sherbrooke's fellow rector, Henry Woodhouse, gave a work on the liturgy: Durandus's *Rationale divinorum officiorum*;[25] and Blundeville gave an educational aid, Ambrosius Calepinus's *Dictionarium*.[26]

The link between social networks and book ownership illustrated by Sherbrooke becomes even more evident, and indeed striking, when the view is broadened to look at ownership among the middle and upper classes, including the gentry, merchants, those attached to the royal court, and members of Parliament. What typifies their collections, and is unusual compared with the collections of other categories of owner, is the prevalence of books in English; about one-third of their books are in that language. A link among the upper classes is even more apparent when looking at the ownership in general of early English printed books, because they, specifically books printed by Caxton (and to some extent by De Worde and others), were owned almost exclusively within these groups. Furthermore, the links become stronger and more tangible when concentrating on specific examples of ownership of such early English printed books, since the connections may actually be charted. They show that many owners of Caxton's books were related or acquainted. Julia Boffey and Carol Meale have found a similar sort of network in which certain texts and women owners are linked.[27] For the present discussion the focus will be primarily on books printed by Caxton.

From the prologues and epilogues which Caxton frequently appended to books he printed, it is clear that his targeted audience was royalty, nobility, gentry, and his own peers among the merchant class. These groups and their common ground are made explicit, for instance, in the prologue to his edition of his translation of Cicero, *Of olde Age*, where he states that his book is for 'noble, wyse & grete lordes gentilmen & marchauntes' since they were alike 'occupyed in maters towchyng the publyque weal'.[28]

---

24. *GW* 6207, CUL, Oates 1954, 3990.   25. *GW* 9126, CUL, Oates 1954, 223.
26. Adams C-203, CUL, Rel.a.51.5.   27. See below, pp. 529-34.
28. Crotch 1928, p. 43; Blake 1973, p. 121.

If it is apparent that Caxton the translator, Caxton the author of these prologues, intended merchants, the gentry and nobility to be his readers, then the books themselves prove that Caxton the printer and business-man was a keen judge of his market, for it is precisely among these classes where one finds the majority of the owners of his books. Fully two-thirds of the Caxton books in the sample have that kind of owner. The remain-der have not yet been identified. Thus they are as likely to be among this class as not.

Caxton's royal associations are well known, and it is unnecessary here to discuss his relations with Margaret of York, Duchess of Burgundy, for whom he translated Raoul Lefèvre's *Recuyell of the Historyes of Troye*, or his relations with other royal patrons such as Margaret's brother, Edward IV, his Queen, Elizabeth, or her brother, Anthony Woodville, and the suc-ceeding house of Tudor. Instead, we shall concentrate on the network of overlapping social spheres surrounding these influential patrons, in which almost all of his owners may be placed, by virtue of either kinship or social association.

Patronage clearly put Caxton's books in the hands of royalty. A copy of the *Recuyell*[29] was owned by Edward's queen, Elizabeth. Henry VII may have owned Higden's *Polycronicon*,[30] and Lady Jane Grey owned Chaucer's *Troilus and Criseyde*.[31] An instance of royal patronage actually placing books in the hands of those associated with them concerns Caxton's successor, Wynkyn de Worde, rather than Caxton himself, for it is a copy of Hylton's *Scala Perfectionis*, printed by De Worde in 1494.[32] It bears the presentation inscription by Lady Margaret Beaufort and Queen Elizabeth addressed to Mary Roos, a lady of the Queen. Her intricate connections exemplify the kinds of network surrounding the ownership of books printed by the earliest English presses. In addition to Mary's own high status in the service of the Queen, her first husband, Hugh Denys, was also a trusted court attendant as Squire for the King's Body. When he died in 1511, Mary married Giles Capell, son of William Capell, a rich merchant and Lord Mayor of London. Giles himself had court con-nections, accompanying Henry VIII to France in 1513, and he was among those at the Field of the Cloth of Gold. His mother, Margaret Capell, is also known as a book owner, although, in this case, not an owner of a Caxton, or even an English book. She owned, or at least gave to Roger

29. *STC* 15375, Goff L-117 (Huntington).   30. *STC* 13438, BL, IB.550558.
31. *STC* 5094, BL, C.11.c.10.   32. *STC* 14042; Croft 1958a; Powell 1998.

Philpott, a copy of the Latin Bible printed at Naples in 1476.[33] Margaret Capell herself was related to the Queen Mother through Thomas Grey, whose marriage to Eleanor St John was arranged by Lady Margaret Beaufort. The St Johns also owned a Caxton book, *The dictes or sayengis of the philosophres*.[34]

To demonstrate most efficiently and succinctly the interconnectedness of early owners of Caxton books, it will be useful to take one owner and follow her lines of kinship, picking up along the way other Caxton owners to whom she is related. Elizabeth Englefield owned a book printed by Caxton, the *Royall Book*.[35] Elizabeth was the daughter of Robert Throckmorton, a Privy Councillor to Henry VII. Her brother George married Catherine, daughter of Nicholas Vaux, who had been raised in the household of Lady Margaret, whose patronage of early English printers has already been mentioned. Vaux's stepson was Thomas Parr, father of the future Queen Catherine. Through the Parrs there is a link with two other Caxton owners: the Treshams, Thomas, who married Anne Parr, owned a *Recuyell*,[36] and George Tresham, associated with Catherine Parr, owned Caxton's Bruges edition of *The play and game of chess*.[37] Returning to Elizabeth Englefield: Elizabeth married Thomas Englefield, son of the Speaker of the House of Commons; their fathers had been created knights of the Bath on the same day in 1501. Elizabeth and Thomas had a son, Francis, who married Catherine, daughter of Thomas Fetiplace.

The Fetiplace connection with the Englefields brings in two members of the family, Edmund and Eleanor Fetiplace, and in turn leads to the Elyots, to whom they were related through their mother's second marriage. Both families were owners of books, a few printed by Caxton, and some by other early English printers. Eleanor Fetiplace was a Brigittine nun at Syon, and her sister Susan entered as a vowess after 1514. Eleanor owned Richard Whitford's *The Pype or tonne of the Lyfe of Perfection*,[38] a book written by a Brigittine brother for his Syon sisters and printed by Robert Redman in 1532; she is also known to have owned a printed Sarum missal containing a memorial inscription to her sister Elizabeth who was a nun at the Benedictine house of Amesbury.[39] Her nephew Edmund Fetiplace owned the first edition of Littleton's *Tenores novelli*.[40]

33. *GW* 4220, Bodl. Auct.M.2.2.   34. *STC* 6828, BL, C.10.b.2.
35. *STC* 21429, BL, C.10.b.22.   36. *STC* 15375, Longleat (Christie's 23.6.1993 lot 51).
37. *STC* 4920, BL, IB.49432.   38. *STC* 25421, Bodl. 4° W2 Th. Seld.
39. *STC* 16217; Erler 1993, p. 14.   40. *STC* 15719, CUL, Oates 1954, 4176.

Edmund was probably a Middle Templar, and so this book was indeed a professional tool.

As already mentioned, the Fetiplaces were connected to the Elyots. Eleanor Fetiplace's mother, Elizabeth Bessels, married, as her second husband, Richard Elyot, King's Serjeant-at-law, who already had children by his first wife: Thomas, later Sir Thomas, author of the *Governour*, and Margery. The two families had been closely linked even before this marriage, with members of both serving jointly as justices of the peace for Oxfordshire and being fellow Middle Templars. In Richard Elyot's will, he provided for his step-children as well as his natural children, leaving, in a typical division,[41] his English books to his daughter Margery and his Latin and French books to Thomas. Thomas Elyot later dedicated his translation of a sermon by St Cyprian to his step-sister Susan Fetiplace, the Syon vowess.[42] One of Richard Elyot's few printed books to survive is a volume containing works by Paulus de Sancta Maria and Robertus Caracciolus.[43] As a Latin book, the volume clearly went to his son, and it bears Thomas's inscription as well. Thomas also owned Robert Wakefield's *Syntagma de hebreorum codicum incorruptione*,[44] printed by De Worde around 1530. The son of a gentleman, Thomas was educated at Oxford and the Middle Temple, although there is no evidence either that he was called to the bar or that he practised law. Elyot had strong humanist interests and inclinations, and the *Syntagma* represents these active pursuits.

One final link arising from the Englefield–Fetiplace–Elyot connection is through the *Tenores novelli* owned by Edmund Fetiplace. It was subsequently owned by Robert Broke, then at Strand Inn, and later also a Middle Templar, serjeant-at-law and Speaker of the House. In addition to this law book he also owned a copy of the *Vitas Patrum*,[45] translated into English by Caxton but published after Caxton's death by Wynkyn de Worde. That book was also owned by Martha Fabyan, Eleanor Verney and others. There begins again another line of connections through related families owning other English books, leading from the Fabyans and Verneys, to the Pastons and Tyrrells, the St Johns (and hence the Beauforts), the Poles, and the Treshams, cousins to the Verneys, and even back to the Parrs. Members of all these families

---

41. For division of books according to gender in wills at a slightly later period, see Pearson pp. 221–57, esp. 230–1. 42. *STC* 6157–8.
43. Goff P-205 and *GW* 6114, Bodl. Auct. 1Q.2.11. 44. *STC* 24946, Bodl. 4° W.1. Th.
45. *STC* 14507, Lambeth Palace, 1495.4.

owned English books, and their blood or social ties are reflected in the books they owned.

This example beginning with Elizabeth Englefield demonstrates the range of Caxton owners among the upper echelons of society. While still privileged and wealthy, not all owners of early English-printed books were connected with the royal household. Many more were gentlemen and merchants, and many of these were members of Parliament. Among these is John Pury, MP for Berkshire, who owned Caxton's edition of Boethius's *Consolation of Philosophy*,[46] printed about 1478. It was subsequently owned by a fellow MP, Thomas (also called Edmund) Hall of Greatford, Lincolnshire. William Warren, MP and Mayor of Dover in the 1490s, and master of the *Margaret*, owned Caxton's second edition of the ps-Bonaventura, *The myrroure of the blessyd lyf of Jhesu Cryste*, of about 1490.[47] James Horswell, MP for Plymouth, owned, in addition to the Breydenbach mentioned above, Christine de Pisan's *Fayttes of armes*, translated and printed by Caxton in 1489.[48] He was a sometime partner of the merchant William Hawkins, held a post in customs, thanks to Thomas Cromwell, and was associated with George Ferrers, owner of Lydgate's *The Horse, the Sheep and the Goose*, printed by Caxton about 1476–7.[49] Thomas Gibbon ('Guybon') was MP for Lynn and Sheriff of Norfolk and Suffolk; he owned Caxton's 1480 edition of Cicero, *Of olde Age*, in Tiptoft's translation.[50]

Aside from the merchants owning Caxton books already mentioned, Richard Story, fishmonger, owned a Boethius, *Consolation of Philosophy*,[51] and Robert Spensar, leatherseller of London (who later became a hermit), owned in 1525 a *Myrrour of the worlde* and the ps-Bonaventura *Myrrour* printed by Pynson in around 1506.[52] Richard Wright, draper of Chester, owned the first edition of Higden's *Polycronicon*.[53] He was admitted freeman in 1557–8 and apparently came from a long line of drapers there; a Robert Wright is listed as a freeman in 1492. This copy had previously been owned by John Lee, prior of St Werburg, Chester, and Thomas Clarke, abbot there at the Dissolution in 1540. This is the only Caxton book in the survey known to have been owned by a monk or friar,

46. *STC* 3199, Sion ARC L.40.4/1172.

46. *STC* 3199, Sion ARC L.40.4/1172.
47. *STC* 3260, NLW, IL W90; Scholderer 1940, no. 116.
48. *STC* 7269, Göttingen SUB, 2° Ars mil. 220/9.
49. *STC* 17018, CUL, Oates 1954, 4061.
50. *STC* 5293, CUL, Oates, 1954, 4075 (Oates read 'Enybon').
51. *STC* 3199; Bodl. Arch.G.d.13.
52. *STC* 24762, Göttingen SUB, 4° H. un. II, 42 Inc. Rara; *STC* 3263, see fig. 9.1.
53. *STC* 13438. NLW, IL W82; Scholderer 1940, no. 114.

although two others were owned by women religious. Here it is not surprising, since the translator of this edition was Johannes de Trevisa, himself once a monk at Chester. A copy of the first edition of the *Canterbury Tales* was elaborately decorated for the Haberdashers' Company of London.[54] It would be convenient to see a special association, if not patronage, between the Haberdashers and Caxton in this de luxe copy, since there is no other patron known for it, but no such association can be established. Roger Thorney, Mercer, is well known as a patron of De Worde. One volume he owned is a tract volume containing three books printed by Caxton – *Troilus and Criseyde*, the *Canterbury Tales* and *Quattuor Sermones* – and a manuscript of Lydgate's *Siege of Thebes*, which was used as printers' copy for De Worde's edition of about 1498.[55]

The owners mentioned above, and the lines of connection linking many of them, demonstrate clearly the network of owners of these early English-printed books among the merchant, gentry and noble classes, based, if not on actual blood-ties, then on professional and social associations, such as the Middle Temple, the House of Commons or mercantile endeavours. Prestigious patronage certainly influenced the ownership of these early English books, both directly through distribution of sponsored books, and indirectly through prestige placed on such ownership. Book ownership was an attribute of high social status, which Caxton not only understood but was able to exploit. From the evidence of surviving books, he was entirely successful at judging the market for his books. Unlike books owned by the university-educated, books owned by the gentry–merchant classes were not directly necessary to conducting their affairs, but, as devotional aids and works of edification as well as entertainment, Caxton's books were necessary to their life-styles. The social status of these classes provided the leisure to enjoy such books and the means to acquire them.

While many of the foregoing points on book ownership in England apply equally to Scotland, Scottish book ownership presents a picture different from English. Several factors which account in part for this difference affect the way the data in the sample can be interpreted. The main difficulty is not the identification of owners, since Durkan and Ross have provided basic identifications in their ground-breaking survey, but rather it is the categorization of owner.[56] It has been possible to speak of

54. *STC* 5082, Oxford, Merton Coll. Sacr. P.2.1; Rhodes 1982, no. 537, see above, pp. 99–100.
55. *STC* 5094, 5083, 17957 (11); St John's Coll., Oxford, Bone 1932.
56. Owing to Durkan and Ross (1961), attention has been paid to books in pre-Reformation

categories of owners for England: the university-educated, the religious, the clergy, gentry. There is certainly overlap between these spheres, but it has been possible to qualify the overlap and thus speak of secular or regular clergy who did not attend university versus those who did. The overlap for Scotland is both greater and more uncharted, and owners cannot be readily categorized. To some extent this is the result of bio-graphical information for Scots being less refined than for the English. Published university registers for England exist, and, for the fifteenth century (and, for Oxford, the beginning of the sixteenth century), the invaluable volumes of Emden include dates not only of matriculation and graduation, but also details of subsequent careers, and frequently sub-stantial lists of books.[57] For Scotland, published university registers exist for the three universities in the period, but they are simple transcriptions of the records, in which no further attempt has been made to identify the students or to follow their post-graduate careers. The problem is com-pounded when one tries to differentiate owners with the same name, a difficulty which seems to be encountered more often in Scotland. Until more work is done on the biographies of fifteenth- and sixteenth-century Scots, it is not possible to place all owners accurately within their proper social spheres.

Aside from a basic paucity of biographical information, the commen-datory system also makes categorization of owners difficult. The title of abbot could be bestowed on a commendator who could be a bishop, a court official or a cleric. The commendator reaped the revenues of the religious house and apportioned allowances to its members. The Scottish monarch retained the right of nomination, thereby contributing greatly to royal coffers. Although some of the appointees were conscientious and beneficial to the house and some took the religious habit of the order, there were also widespread abuses. Between 1534 and 1541, three of Scotland's greater monasteries were held by illegitimate sons of James V. The main impact of this on interpreting the data of book ownership is the blurring of boundaries between religious, clerical and lay. How can one speak accurately of books owned by religious when, at this highest level, their books could count equally towards books owned by nobility, or books owned by clergymen? With the substantial revenues some houses could produce, it is perhaps no surprise that some of the larger collec-

Scotland for almost forty years, resulting in a fairly comprehensive list of surviving books. This is in contrast to England, where years' more work would be needed before a compara-bly complete list could emerge.   57. *BRUC, BRUO, BRUO 1540*.

tions of surviving books were owned by those holding an abbey *in commendam*.

Given these and other influences in pre-Reformation Scotland, it is not possible to examine book ownership in the same way as for the English, i.e., by categories of owner. On the other hand, because there is a significantly smaller pool of books and owners to draw on, it is possible to paint a broad picture of ownership as a whole and look more closely at specific books and owners. This may be not only a more workable method of looking at the data, but also more appropriate for Scotland where physical movement was extensive. Thus, Franciscans moved from house to house, some university students and lecturers moved from one university to another, and, of course, many travelled abroad as well. This movement lent a continuity, regardless of regional differences.

Just as the initial impression of differences between England and Scotland may be found in the quantity of books coming from different continental centres, the overall picture also differs as to what those books are. A rough outline of the books most frequently owned by each nationality highlights this. The books in the sample most frequently owned by the English are, broadly speaking, dominated by texts required for university. They are, in order of prevalence, St Augustine, Aristotle, Cicero (particularly the philosophical works), Duns Scotus, Erasmus (largely the *Annotationes* and *Paraphrases* on the New Testament, but also the *Moriae encomium*), Bartolus de Saxoferrato, St Jerome, St Albertus Magnus, Jacobus de Voragine, Lyndewood, St Thomas Aquinas, St Antoninus, Virgil, Baldus de Ubaldis and Boethius (overwhelmingly *De consolatione philosophiae*). In contrast, the authors most frequently owned by Scots are Erasmus (particularly the *Annotationes* and parts of the Basel 1540 *Opera*), St Augustine, John Major (primarily on the *Sentences* or on the Gospels), Cicero, St Thomas Aquinas, Dionysius Carthusianus, Hector Boece, Aristotle, St Jerome, Origen, Duns Scotus, Marcus Antonius Sabellicus, Paolo Giovio, St John Chrysostom and Johannes Royardus. The fact that four of the authors in the English list are canon or civil lawyers surely reflects that the university law faculty, combining both civil and canon law, was the largest of the higher faculties. The requirement by this faculty that each student own his own texts probably also plays a role. Similarly, the paucity of law books in the Scottish list may reflect the meagre provisions for advanced legal education in Scotland for much of this period. It was a deficiency which William Elphinstone specifically set out to remedy with his foundation of a university at Aberdeen.

The relative importance of Aristotle in both lists is also noteworthy. Aristotle dominated the university arts course at Scottish universities just as much as in England, but books by Aristotle come only eighth in number of copies. When books on Aristotelian philosophy are added to those by Aristotle, the number triples, but even then comprises less than 3 per cent of all printed books recorded for Scotland. Aristotelian books in England account for double that proportion. This is particularly surprising. The logician John Major wrote commentaries on Aristotle, yet few copies are found in the survey. A glance at the provision of books at university may provide a partial explanation for this discrepancy. At St Andrews the arts curriculum consisted almost solely of Aristotle. After the first year of elementary logic, probably based on the work of Petrus Hispanus, students spent the next three years on Aristotle's logic, physics, natural philosophy and metaphysics.[58] St Andrews' students were required not only to have studied these set texts before obtaining a degree, but also to copy out the texts themselves. This statute was consistently flouted in the later fifteenth century, but the copying out of Aristotle texts would indeed have reduced the demand for printed editions. It would also have increased the number of manuscript copies, so that even when a student did not write out his own texts, he could presumably buy or borrow them from a former student. Any analysis of the influence of the manuscript trade on the printed-book trade must await a quantitative study of manuscripts in Scotland.

Just as an analysis of the centres of printing supplying books to Scotland suggested an awareness of what was available in print on the Continent, particularly in Paris, and thus a participation by Scots in intellectual life outside Scotland, a closer examination of the texts indicates similarly a participation in pressing debates of the time, particularly religious debates, and a concern for Scotland's position in them. It is immediately noticeable that among the most frequently owned authors listed above, five are contemporaries: Erasmus, Major, Boece, Giovio and Royardus. Looking more closely at which texts were most frequently owned, in addition to the works of Major (primarily his works on logic) and Boece, one finds Erasmus's *Annotationes* on the New Testament, Quiñones's *Breviarium S. Crucis*, the Canons of the Council of Cologne, Alphonsus de Castro on heresies, and Fisher's *Assertionis Lutheranae confutatio*. These show an active engagement with current religious issues.

58. Dunlop 1964, p. lxxxiv.

In the sample, Erasmus is the most frequently owned author in Scotland. This may not be surprising given his acquaintance with Scots in Paris, but, with the initial stifling of reformist views in the 1530s in Scotland, the prevalence is nonetheless striking. It is also perhaps ironic, since Erasmus condescendingly named the Scots (along with the Irish, Saracens and women) as among those who would benefit from reading the Scriptures directly. In 1528 Hector Boece was able to report to Erasmus that a Danish visitor to Aberdeen had been impressed to find Erasmus's Paraphrases in the hands of university students there.[59] There are three copies of the New Testament edited and translated by Erasmus (in 1522 and 1542 editions) in the sample, and six copies of Erasmus's Annotations on the New Testament (dating from 1522 to 1542), making that one of the most popular works in the survey. Erasmus's editions of patristic works are also particularly prevalent. When taken together, books written or edited by Erasmus account for almost 6 per cent of all books with Scottish ownership in the sample. Interestingly, among the most popular texts by Erasmus is his declaration against the censure of the university of Paris (1532). This had particular meaning for Scots, some of whom, such as John Major and George Lokert, had been involved in the examination of Erasmus's works at Paris. While many Scots remained sympathetic to Erasmus for other aspects of his thought, the virulence of the anti-reformists in Scotland in the 1530s and 1540s, fed in particular by the Franciscans, makes the preponderance of Erasmian books all the more significant, pointing to the widespread interest among Scots in the new thought on the Continent.

Other evidence of the Scots engaging broadly with the contemporary religious debate is the number of copies of the Quiñones breviary (1536 and 1546 editions). This is the single most popular liturgical book owned by Scots in the sample; there are five copies. While liturgical books of Sarum Use were commonly adapted for Scotland by the addition of feasts and saints, Elphinstone's call for the production of a specifically Scottish breviary was a motivating factor in the establishment of the printing press in Scotland. One edition was printed in 1510, but Chepman and Myllar ceased printing soon thereafter. The Quiñones breviary represents a revision more radical than Elphinstone's. It was composed largely of biblical texts, which were expanded to use virtually all of the New Testament and much of the Old, and it omitted almost all the communal elements of a breviary, such as the versicles and antiphons. Thus it was suited much

59. Durkan 1953, p. 10.

more to private recitation than earlier breviaries. Curiously for a book intended for private devotion, one copy seems to have enjoyed public use in Orkney as the breviary in the choir.[60] Four of the five copies are the 1546 Lyons edition. While that might point to a supply being imported into Scotland, one copy was purchased by John Greenlaw in Paris in 1553, one was owned by John Roul, who was in Paris in 1549 as bursar of the Scottish establishment, one was owned by James Stewart, who accompanied his half-sister Mary to France in 1548, and the Orkney copy was no doubt provided by the Bishop Robert Reid who regularly travelled to the Continent.[61] Thus the acquisition and ownership of the Quiñones breviary illustrates again that frequent travel to the Continent by Scots would have enabled them to avail themselves of a wide-ranging book-trade.

Another of the most popular authors owned by Scots in the sample is Johannes Royardus. A Franciscan, Royardus was sent to Scotland as Commissary in late 1535–6, presumably to repress any reformist views which might be surfacing among some Franciscans.[62] The Franciscans took their cue from the Dominicans who had just experienced upheaval with the espousal of unorthodox views by John Macalpine, John Macdowell and Alexander Seton, priors of Perth, Wigtown and St Andrews, and their subsequent flight to more tolerant climates abroad. Although his specific brief is unknown, the presence of Royardus in Scotland at this time strongly suggests a watchful eye from the Order. His presence, both physical and intellectual, in Scotland is made palpable by the books which survive. He is known to have been in Aberdeen, and six of the ten surviving copies of books by Royardus in Scotland were owned by men who may have met him during his visit in 1535–6: William Hay, Canon of Aberdeen, owned three works bound together (his work on the Passion of 1544, and the homilies of 1544 and 1548); John Watson, Canon of Aberdeen, owned the 1544 and 1548 homilies; and Andrew Abercromby, a Dominican, who had been at the Aberdeen house and was Prior there at the Reformation, owned the 1548 homilies.[63] John Duncanson and Henry Sinclair, Bishop of Ross, owned other copies of the same editions, while the Dominican house at Perth had a 1535 edition of the homilies.[64]

60. Adams L-876. Kirkwall Cathedral, Preshome, St Gregory's II; McRoberts 1952.
61. Preshome, St Gregory's (Greenlaw and Orkney copies); Aberdeen UL, Drummond 2510; St Andrews UL, PP.6.22.   62. Hill 1964, pp. 3–34.
63. All at Aberdeen UL. Durkan and Ross 1961, p. 115/9, 157/3, 66/4.
64. Dunblane, Leighton Library; Durkan and Ross 1961, p. 175/4; Edinburgh UL, Dd.2.7, Durkan and Ross, 1961, p. 59/93; St Andrews UL, Typ. NAn. B35CR.

The ownership of the Royardus books points to two phenomena in Scottish book ownership. First, as with the ownership of Erasmus and Quiñones, it illustrates the participation of the Scots in international concerns. Second, it suggests a personal link or association between authors and owners for many books in Scotland before the Reformation. I have suggested, in the previous chapter on the importation of printed books, that the Scottish book-trade's continued dependence on individual acquisition abroad is demonstrated in the linking of book acquisition and the presence abroad of the owner. So too does the link between author and owner demonstrate the personal networks which determined book ownership.

It is not surprising to find books by Scots, dedicated to Scots or on subjects of interest specifically to Scotland among the collections of Scottish owners, and two of the most popularly owned works are those by Hector Boece and John Major. Besides a general Scottish interest, however, a closer connection can sometimes be found, just as in the case of Royardus and the Aberdonians Watson, Hay and Abercromby. For instance, of the works by Boece in the sample, one, a copy of his *Scotorum historiae* printed in Paris in 1527, was a gift directly from Boece to Alexander Stevenson,[65] and at least three copies of that and his *Episcoporum Murthlacensium et Aberdonensium vitae* were owned by men closely associated with him, such as Alan Meldrum and William Hay.[66] Giovanni Ferreri, the Italian humanist who came to teach at Kinloss and who knew Boece at Aberdeen, gave a copy of the translation into Scots of Boece's *History of Scotland* to Henry Sinclair in Paris in 1557.[67] In addition to his intimate connection with Scotland, Ferreri dedicated most of his own books to Scottish prelates. Those in the sample are all owned by Kinloss monks. Personal connection can also be found in the ownership of Robert Galbraith's *Opus quadrupartitum in oppositiones* printed in Paris in 1516 and owned by John Forman, one of Galbraith's fellow students at Paris.[68] Archibald Hay presented to his brother, John, a copy of his panegyric on Cardinal Beaton.[69] Showing that personal association played a role in determining book ownership in Scotland does not prove that books by Scots printed in Paris were destined only for the Scottish market. Durkan has found books by Galbraith and Lokert in Louvain; by John Major in

65. Adams B-2308; NLS, RB.m.227.
66. Edinburgh UL, De.3.87; Durkan and Ross 1961, p. 113/9; Meldrum: Adams B-2308, Ann Arbor, Univ. of Michigan, DA. 775.B.67.   67. *STC* 3203, NLS, Blairs Coll.
68. Glasgow UL, Bh7.e3; Durkan and Ross 1961, p. 97/1.
69. NLS, Blairs Coll.; Durkan and Ross, 1961, p. 112.

Louvain, Seville and Nuremberg; by Lidell and Crab in Louvain and London; and by Cranston in Medina del Campo and Cologne.[70] Their books in Scotland, however, often illustrate personal association influencing ownership.

Books written by or dedicated to Scots account for 5 per cent of the books in the sample. If other books for which a link between owner and author exists were added to this number, it would increase significantly. Thomas de Vio, Cajetan, personally knew the Dominicans John Adamson, who was considered as a replacement for Cajetan when he was elevated to Cardinal in 1518, and James Crichton, who may have been Cajetan's pupil.[71] None of the surviving books by Cajetan was owned by Adamson or Crichton, but seven copies were owned by Dominicans and one by a Franciscan. Ross has further suggested a link between Adamson and Crichton and the purchase of books printed in Italy to be found with Dominican ownership in Scotland.[72]

Given the wide Scots network, innumerable books in the sample could be proved to have some personal link to Scotland. Symphorien Champier dedicated works to Robert Cockburn, Bishop of Ross. Lefèvre d'Etaples was associated with Ferreri, and Lefèvre's works featured on Ferreri's teaching programme at Kinloss.[73] These associations strengthen the view that the book-trade in Scotland was strongly influenced by a network of Scots, acting as conduits for both books and intellectual currents, between Scotland and the Continent.

Some of these factors influencing book ownership are not unique to Scotland, with personal association certainly playing a role in England as well, and no doubt in other countries. In Scotland, however, it does seem to account for a greater proportion of books with Scottish ownership. One example of personal association influencing acquisition for England concerns the ownership of the Aldine Aristotle edition of 1498. Eight copies of it have early English owners. Because Linacre is praised in the preface by Aldus as 'Thomas Anglicus homo et Graece et Latine peritissimus', was a close associate of Aldus, and sent his translation of ps-Proclus *De sphaera*, to be printed by Aldus in 1499, it has been presumed that Linacre was involved in the preparation of the Aldine Aristotle. What precisely his involvement was remains unclear, but Linacre was certainly connected with this edition, if only by close friendship with Aldus at the time of its preparation and printing.

70. Durkan 1959, p. 385.   71. Ross 1962.   72. Ross 1962, p. 196.
73. Durkan 1953, pp. 9, 15.

The ownership of this edition is striking first of all for the high number of copies in England at an early date. Schedel's Nuremberg Chronicle is the only book to be imported which exists with more (by two) copies with English ownership, but several of those were not in England until the mid sixteenth century. The Aldine Aristotle stands out not only for the number of copies, but also for the men who owned those copies: Linacre himself, John Claymond, Richard Foxe, Thomas Stanbridge, Thomas Lupset, John Foxe, Cuthbert Tunstal and Thomas Wendy. Most of these are known friends and associates of Linacre. Richard Foxe was his patient, and Linacre presented a copy of his translation of Galen's *De sanitate tuenda* (Paris 1517) to Foxe.[74] Linacre knew Lupset as his protégé, and it was Lupset who, in 1516, supervised the preparation for publication of Linacre's Galen, *De sanitate tuenda*. John Claymond was a fellow classicist who knew not only Linacre, as is proved by a letter to Claymond as president of Magdalen College,[75] but Thomas Lupset and William Grocyn as well. Linacre, Lupset and Claymond were all associated with the dispersal of Grocyn's renowned collection of Greek manuscripts and printed books. Linacre was an executor of Grocyn's estate, from which Claymond bought a large number of Grocyn's books, and Lupset wrote out a list of nine additional books of Grocyn's which were set aside as individual gifts. Claymond gave or bequeathed his acquisitions to Richard Foxe's foundation, Corpus Christi College, Oxford, of which Claymond was the first president. Cuthbert Tunstal was a close friend, a patient, and Linacre's executor. The connection between Linacre and Thomas Stanbridge, John Foxe and Thomas Wendy is less certain, but still probable. Stanbridge became master of Magdalen College School just as Claymond was moving from the presidency of Magdalen College to that of Corpus Christi, and could easily have come into contact with Linacre. John Foxe was very probably a relative of Richard Foxe,[76] and he is described as 'socius' of Corpus Christi College in 1523 during Claymond's presidency there. Thomas Wendy was perhaps too young to have known Linacre himself since he was just obtaining his MA when Linacre died, but Wendy was travelling in the same circles very soon after Linacre's death. He was physician to Henry VIII, as Linacre had formerly been, a fellow of the Royal College of Physicians, which Linacre had founded in 1518, and, as one of the great physicians of the mid sixteenth century, was treading in Linacre's footsteps.

74. Adams G-103–4. London, Royal College of Physicians, see Barber 1977, p. 297.
75. Weiss 1967, pp. 199.   76. Fowler 1893, p. 84n.

The ownership of the Aldine Aristotle, then, shows a network of personal associations, at work in England as well as Scotland, which could be responsible for the acquisition of a particular edition. Venetian books were certainly readily available in England through the trade, but at some level personal recommendation continued to play a role in the dissemination of books in England. While the example of the Aldine Aristotle may be a case of preaching to the converted, since these men either knew Aldus themselves or at least knew of his editions, it was another way into the English market, here at the most prestigious level.

One of the most important conclusions which can be drawn from a study of book ownership is that it is imperative to look beyond present-day national boundaries. Any study of intellectual history in Britain which relied primarily on the bibliography of books printed in England, exemplary as it is, would be based on only very partial evidence. Thus it is necessary to study the material in full awareness of existing communications in trade as well as in intellectual life. The previous chapter on the importation of books into Britain showed that large numbers of books were available in England from an early date, and that they dwarfed the number of editions being printed in England. One conclusion which can be drawn from an overall examination of book ownership in Britain is that those books ranged widely in subject matter, but that the Latin (i.c. imported) trade was aimed primarily at the universities, the religious and the clergy. In contrast, English printers (and continental ones printing for the English market) from the beginning set out to fill a gap by supplying books in English. Different in both subject and language from the books being imported, their readers were also different in comprising primarily the gentry and merchants. Lotte Hellinga has pointed to the significance of what may now be considered Caxton's first major book printed in England, the *Canterbury Tales*, an English work in English for an English public.77 Caxton could be assured of success, because he exercised a virtual monopoly on books in English and at the same time may have indulged an affection for English literature. We have seen that the initial demand for the works being printed by Caxton was among the gentry–merchant class, a class whose book interests were not being met by the Latin trade.

The short-lived Oxford presses serve to illustrate the relationship between foreign- and English-printed books. They produced several

77. L. Hellinga 1982, p. 101.

texts for the market at their very doorstep, the university; one example has already been mentioned above which corresponded with a university statute. Yet the first Oxford ventures ceased printing by 1486. That could not be due to the lack of demand, but rather because the demand was simply being met more effectively by continental imports. Successful early English presses, such as Caxton's, wisely produced what could not be obtained elsewhere.

This same maxim also applies in Scotland. William Elphinstone's aim to produce liturgical books specifically for Scottish use to supplant those of Sarum Use was a main motivating force in establishing the printing press in Scotland. Printing Elphinstone's breviary not only filled a gap in the market, but served nationalist aims as well. As was the case with the Oxford presses, however, the demand was not sufficient to sustain the first Scottish press, and we have seen in looking at the book-trade in Scotland that Sarum books continued to be widely available through Edinburgh merchants. The new Scottish breviary thus faced stiff competition, and its uniqueness to Scotland was not sufficient to dislodge other liturgical books from their primacy.

If, as I have portrayed it previously, the mechanism for acquiring books in Scotland depended to a greater extent than in England on tapping the market on the Continent, rather than importing on speculation large numbers and a wide range of printed books, then this too must also demonstrate that there was little demand for what could not be supplied through those networks of Scots on the Continent. It also shows again that Scots participated in the continental book-trade, which would be greater than a native one.

All these features of imported versus locally printed books changed over the course of the sixteenth century. With the rise of the vernacular and of native paper production, books printed in England, and later Scotland, could satisfy more and more of the native market. At least for our period, though, it is not a question of one supplanting the other, since the middle of the sixteenth century saw not only a rise in English printing but also increasing numbers of imported books, particularly due to the activity of the Birckman family. Any study of the way in which the imported and native trades complemented one another in later periods must await surveys similar to the present one. It is clear, however, that the early English market was indeed complementing the imported Latin trade by producing books not obtainable elsewhere and by tapping a public whose needs were not satisfied by that Latin trade.

10

Monastic libraries: 1400–1557

DAVID N. BELL

The century and a half from 1400 to the Dissolution of the Monasteries is one of the most interesting in the history of monastic libraries. It is dominated by the introduction of the New Learning and the invention of printing with movable type, but the period also witnessed the full impact of the universities, a growing dissatisfaction with the Church and a corresponding increase in private devotion, a dramatic improvement in vernacular literacy, and the dissemination of a great deal of religious literature in English. Indeed, it is perhaps an anomaly that the fifteenth century, which has been termed (not without some justice) 'a literary desert',[1] should also have been a period in which we see, as Derek Pearsall says, 'an increase in the demand for, availability and ownership of books of all kinds'.[2]

Let us begin our investigation with a glance at the source-materials at our disposal. N. R. Ker and A. G. Watson have drawn our attention to about forty-four records of books in monastic libraries for the period in which we are interested.[3] I exclude for the moment the lists compiled by John Leland. Most of these records are incomplete. Many are concerned only with donations or bequests; some list only the books in the church; some are no more than lists of volumes brought from or sent to one house from another; some list only alienations; some record only those volumes owned by, or acquired by or for, a particular prior or abbot; and one – St Mary of Graces in London – lists ten volumes which form part of an action for debt.

To these meagre relics – meagre when we consider that in England alone there were more than 850 monastic foundations, and double that

I am greatly indebted to Dr Richard Sharpe for taking the time to read the first draft of this chapter and for suggesting a multitude of improvements.
1. Knowles 1948–55, II, p. 273; but we must beware of over-exaggeration in this matter: see pp. 263–77, and Doyle 1989.　2. *BPPB*, p. 7.　3. Ker 1964–87.

number if we include alien priories, hospitals, and the houses of the Templars and Hospitallers[4] – may be added the lists compiled by John Leland in his *De rebus Britannicis collectanea*,[5] and the related, but anonymous, lists in BL, Royal Appendix 69, which were not, as Carley has demonstrated, written by Leland.[6] Between them they cover about 120 houses. Leland's lists date from the time of his antiquarian and bibliographical journeys from around 1536 to 1542, and those in the Royal manuscript were probably compiled around 1530.[7] The books they record, however, usually date from earlier times, and works by authors of the fifteenth and sixteenth centuries are rare. Despite the intrinsic interest of the lists, however, they tell us little of the monastic libraries to which they refer. Neither compiler was concerned with comprehensive cataloguing and the titles they record reflect their own interests and those of their royal master, Henry VIII. Theological works by English authors – especially uncommon theological works by lesser-known English authors – often caught their eye, as also did unusual texts and sources for English history. Leland and his anonymous compatriot were working on acquisitive rather than scientific principles, however, and although they reveal that monasteries could possess some curious volumes, it is rare that they tell us much more than that. One cannot posit the nature and extent of a forest from a handful of unusual twigs.

Apart from these fragmentary items, however, there are seven records which provide us with more complete accounts of the library holdings of a number of monastic houses from a variety of Orders. They are as follows:

1 York, St Mary's (Benedictine); a fifteenth-century index-catalogue of selected authors, identified only recently by Dr Richard Sharpe.[8] It is the only surviving example of a medieval index-catalogue (though the principle is anticipated in the 1389 catalogue of Dover), but it lists only about half the library. It confines itself to *theologica*, *biblica* and *legalia*, and the authors represented are restricted almost entirely to the twelfth and thirteenth centuries.[9]

---

4. I have counted those listed in Midmer 1979.
5. Leland 1774, ii. For a brief summary of Leland's bibliographical work, see Knowles 1948–55, iii, pp. 349–50; cf. Carley below, p. 275.
6. BL, Royal mss., Appendix 69; Liddell 1939; Carley 1989b, pp. 331–2. See also *CBMLC* iii, pp. xxiii–xxiv.
7. For Leland's journey, see Leland 1549; for the dates of the lists in the Royal manuscript, see Carley 1989b, pp. 332–3.   8. BL, Harl. ms. 2268, fols. 295r–304v.
9. Edited by Sharpe, in *CBMLC* iv, pp. 677–785.

2 Titchfield (Premonstratensian); a catalogue dated 29 September 1400.[10]

3 Hulne (Carmelite); an imperfect catalogue of 1443.[11]

4 Leicester (Augustinian); a catalogue of 1493–1502, compiled by the former Precentor and later Prior, William Charite.[12] As M. R. James remarked, 'the precentor . . . was in most monasteries the officer who had charge of the books',[13] though this was not always the case.

5 Canterbury, St Augustine's (Benedictine); a catalogue compiled shortly before 1497.[14]

6 Syon (Brigittine); a catalogue of the early sixteenth century.[15] We should note that the catalogue is that of the brothers' library at Syon, not the sisters'.

7 Monk Bretton (Benedictine; formerly Cluniac); an inventory dated 21 July 1558, compiled some two decades after the house had been surrendered, and listing volumes which had been saved from the library and preserved individually by a number of its former monks.[16] Monk Bretton began as a Cluniac priory but became Benedictine in around 1279. In 1291 it was officially removed from the Cluniac register.

We might also include in our list the inventory of the library of Meaux.[17] It was compiled by its quondam abbot, Thomas de Burton, in 1396, and provides us with a glimpse of a Cistercian book-collection just four years before the period of our concern. It must be remembered, however, that although these records (except the inventory for Meaux) all date from the fifteenth and sixteenth centuries, we cannot say the same of the books they list. The science of library cataloguing did not really develop until the fourteenth century,[18] and fifteenth-century catalogues obviously include books which monasteries acquired at much earlier dates. In some cases, in fact, the vast majority of the books listed predate the catalogues that list them by more than a century.

With this brief account of our sources, let us now move on to examine some of the developments in the fifteenth and sixteenth centuries which affected the nature and contents of monastic libraries. Most of these are

10. BL, Add. ms. 70507, edited by Bell in *CBMLC* III, pp. 180–254.
11. BL, Harl. ms. 3897, edited by Raine 1838, pp. 128–35.
12. Bodleian, ms. Laud misc. 623, edited by M. R. James 1936–41; and by T. Webber, in *CBMLC* v, pp. 104–399.
13. M. R. James 1936–41, 19, p. 122. Cf. Piper 1978, p. 217, notes 8–9.
14. Dublin, Trinity Coll. ms. D.1.19 (360), edited by M. R. James 1903, pp. 173–406.
15. Cambridge, Corpus Christi Coll., ms. 141, edited by Bateson 1898.
16. BL, Add. ms. 50755, fols. 4v–6r; edited by Sharpe in *CBMLC* IV, pp. 266–87.
17. BL, Cotton ms. Vitellius C.vi, edited by Bell in *CBMLC* III, pp. 34–82.
18. Wormald 1958, pp. 22–6, and (generally) Christ, Kern and Otto 1984, pp. 35–45.

considered in detail elsewhere in this volume and our discussion here need only be brief. Let us begin with some comments on the increase in vernacular literacy.

There is no doubt that, between the middle of the fourteenth and the early sixteenth century, the number of readers among the non-clerical population of England increased dramatically.[19] As we have already noted, however, this literacy was primarily vernacular literacy, and it is interesting to note that although about 73 per cent of all incunabula are written in Latin, 59 per cent of titles (excluding broadsides) printed in England were in English.[20]

This growth in English literacy coincided with a decrease in the use of French. At the beginning of the fifteenth century, French was still commonly used, but by the middle of the century it had been superseded by English;[21] and it is no coincidence that, whereas some 18 volumes, or about 8 per cent, of the books at Titchfield are in French (excluding a number of legal texts), the brothers' library at Syon could boast only 4 French volumes out of a total of more than 1,400: 0.3 per cent of the total.

Let us turn now to the immense impact of the universities on monastic libraries.[22] By the fifteenth century, monks regularly attended university. Often they were required to do so by the constitutions of their Orders. For the Dominicans, of course, academic studies were fundamental to their *raison d'être*, and, by the end of the thirteenth century, university teaching in theology and philosophy was dominated by Dominican and Franciscan professors. About 40 per cent of all incunabula titles were written by friars.[23] Even monks of the more conservative Orders were to be found pursuing higher education, however. The Benedictines, for example, were well established in Oxford at Gloucester Hall, Canterbury College and Durham College, and even the austere Cistercians had their own house of studies at Rewley Abbey.[24]

Monks who had studied at university naturally had an effect on the libraries of their mother-houses. It could hardly have been otherwise. Educated monks normally expected to occupy important positions in the monastic hierarchy,[25] and a university-trained abbot could have a pro-

19. Adamson 1946; Hirsch 1967, pp. 147–53; Parkes 1991.
20. Hirsch 1967, pp. 132, 134. Of the 25,368 pre-1501 editions recorded on the *ISTC* database in 1995, 72.9% are in Latin.   21. Suggett 1946.   22. Talbot 1958.
23. Hirsch 1967, p. 129, quoting Schulz 1924 and Lenhart 1935, whose classification systems he criticizes.   24. Sheehan 1984.
25. Sheehan 1984, pp. 217–18 and Talbot 1962, p. 203.

found influence on the intellectual atmosphere of his abbey. William Slade, Abbot of the Cistercian abbey of Buckfast at the beginning of the fifteenth century, was such a man. He himself had studied at Oxford and was the author of commentaries on Aristotle and Peter Lombard which testify far more to the world of academe than to the tradition of St Bernard. Leland saw other similar works when he visited the Buckfast library: a commentary on Seneca by Nicholas Trevet; *quaestiones* and *quodlibeta* by John Sutton, William Gainsborough and Gilbert Segrave; the *Universalia* on Aristotle's *Physica* by John Sharpe; and a commentary on Lombard's *Sententiae* by an obscure writer called Blaencot the Welshman. Slade, it seems, may have established a university tradition at Buckfast, and it is to be regretted that we have no catalogue of the abbey library. The *Registrum Anglie* lists titles of thirty-two works by patristic and medieval authors at Buckfast, but the compilers of the *Registrum* were just as selective as Leland in what they included.[26] An even more dramatic example of the impact of the universities may be seen in the huge library of the Brigittines of Syon. A number of the brethren – especially those who came to the abbey in the early sixteenth century – had been educated at university or were fellows of Cambridge colleges and, as we shall see in due course, they created one of the largest and most up-to-date monastic libraries of the time.

Sometimes, too, monks educated at university might leave their books to their monastery. Richard Guthrie, Abbot of the Benedictine abbey of Arbroath in the second half of the fifteenth century, had been educated at Cologne and St Andrews, and when he left Arbroath (or when he died: the circumstances are not quite clear), he left his collection of thirty-four volumes at the abbey. Apart from standard patristic authorities and common biblical commentaries, we also find Aristotle's *Ethica*, the ps-Aristotelian *Oeconomica*, part of the *Summa theologica* of Thomas Aquinas, a volume of *quodlibeta*, and seven commentaries attributed to Albert the Great. We should note, however, that, despite the late date of the list, all these works were written before 1300.[27]

The list of Guthrie's volumes also serves to remind us that, by the fifteenth century (and despite disapprobation by almost every Order), many monks and nuns owned their own books, although it is true that they may have possessed them only *ad terminum vitae*, and that after their deaths the volumes were to return to and remain in the convent.

26. D. N. Bell, *CBMLC* III, pp. 10–12 (and pp. lxxiii–lxxiv); *CBMLC* II, p. 282.
27. Durkan 1961a.

Inscriptions stating this are not uncommon in surviving manuscripts, but there can be no doubt that, during the period with which we are here concerned, personal possession – if not personal ownership – was not unusual;[28] nor were some monks averse to borrowing books from the monastery library and refusing to return them. When Alan Kyrketone, a Benedictine monk of Spalding, went to Oxford in the early 1430s, he took with him twelve books belonging to the priory library (seven of them were theological and five pertained to canon law) and in 1438, three years after he had left Oxford, they had still not been returned. We have no record, in fact, that they were ever returned.[29] William Alnwick, Bishop of Lincoln, was more honest when he borrowed a volume of Origen (in Latin) from the Cistercians of Garendon.[30] But then, as all librarians know, theft is one of the commonest of the many vices that student flesh is heir to.

University education also created a demand for up-to-date books and new approaches. The old, ruminative *lectio divina* of the earlier Benedictines and Cistercians had given way (not without protest) to the short, snappy *quaestio* and the clarity and precision of the scholastic method. We may see this reflected in the ubiquitous *distinctiones* that appear in all later catalogues. The staple spiritual food of an earlier age – the Bible and the gloss – had been swept away by the *summae*. Older volumes might now be dismembered and used to reinforce newer ones;[31] and when the community at Durham sent a collection of glossed books of the Bible to their confreres at Durham College in the early 1400s, it was not for the benefit of their academic education. The mother-house had kept them in the Spendement, a sort of genizah for old-fashioned and superseded volumes, and was probably quite happy to be rid of them.[32]

The nature and curricula of university education had profound effects not only on the contents of libraries, but on the books themselves and the provision of them. They needed, says Charles Talbot, to be 'immediately useful, practical, convenient for carrying around, relatively inexpensive and without frills and flourishes'.[33] On the other hand, many of them were also very long, for university education was based on the

---

28. Recorded lists make no distinction between books belonging to individuals and books belonging to libraries. This important point is not immediately evident in the repertoria of Ker 1964–87.
29. A. H. Thompson 1969, III, part 2, 1927; rpt 1969, p. 330. See also pp. 334, 336, 338, 341.
30. A. H. Thompson 1969, II, part 1, 1919; rpt 1969, pp. 112–13.
31. C. E. Wright 1958, pp. 148–9.   32. Piper 1978, pp. 220, 246.
33. Talbot 1958, p. 66.

commentary, and a commentary on Lombard's *Sententiae* or Aristotle's *Metaphysica* could be a monstrous tome, tedious and expensive to copy,[34] and by no means easy to use. To facilitate their use we see, from the twelfth century, the production of *tabulae* and *concordantiae*;[35] to facilitate their production, we witness the development of the *pecia* system, major changes in the size and style of handwriting, the appearance of dealers in both new and second-hand books and the burgeoning of the book-trade in England.[36] These developments produced a resurgence of monastic scribal activity in the second half of the fourteenth century, and at Norwich and St Albans new scriptoria were built to accommodate it.

Nevertheless, books remained expensive, even after the introduction of paper, a much cheaper alternative to parchment.[37] As Malcolm Parkes has said, 'Books were always a luxury in the Middle Ages, but the production of cheaper books meant that they could become a luxury for poorer people.'[38] Where, then, did the monasteries – especially the poorer monasteries – obtain their copies? There were three main sources.

First of all, books could be bought. The friars regularly bought books,[39] but so did members of other Orders. The Augustinians of Bolton have left us records of their purchases;[40] Abbot John Whethamstede of St Albans was a steady buyer of books between about 1420 and 1465,[41] and Prior More of Worcester was doing much the same thing in the second decade of the following century.[42] It seems, in fact, that the use of monetary gifts to purchase books was a common and widespread practice.[43]

Secondly, books could be copied in the scriptorium of the monastery, and those in charge of the libraries sometimes copied their own books: William Charite of Leicester, for example, provides us with a list of 'libri quos propria manu scripsit et compilavit'.[44] He also lists those he commissioned and bought.[45] By the fifteenth century, it is probable that a majority of male religious could write. The Carthusians had no choice in the matter, for their *Constitutiones* required each of them to have in his cell

34. Parkes 1969, p. xiii.   35. Rouse and Rouse 1982.
36. Destrez 1935; G. Pollard 1978b, and Bataillon *et al.* 1988; Ker 1949, and R. W. Hunt 1978, p. 263; *BPPB*. On the second-hand book-trade, Doyle and Parkes 1978, p. 197 n. 88.
37. On the cost of books, Schramm 1933, and H. E. Bell 1937. For the effects of the introduction of paper, Lyall 1989.   38. Parkes 1991, p. 287.
39. Wormald and Wright 1958, p. 74.   40. Wormald and Wright 1958, p. 29.
41. Ker 1964–87, p. 165, and Supplement, p. 59; further information in Howlett 1975.
42. Ker 1964–87, p. 205.   43. Doyle 1990, p. 1.
44. M. R. James 1936–41, 21, pp. 57–9; *CBMLC* v, pp. 394–6.
45. M. R. James 1936–41, 21, pp. 55–60; *CBMLC* v, p. 399.

the necessary implements for copying.[46] We should note, however, that scribes were sometimes lay-men living in the monastery. The monastic scribes seem to have had no hesitation in co-operating with their secular colleagues in the production of attractive volumes, and had been doing so since at least the end of the thirteenth century.[47] Whoever the scribe and whatever the Order, it now seems clear that there was more monastic book production in the fifteenth and early sixteenth centuries than has hitherto been supposed.[48] Nevertheless, the extent of this interest should not be exaggerated. The various houses might, at this time, have produced their own service-books, local hagiographical collections, cartularies and domestic histories, but voluminous writers like John Whethamstede of St Albans were very much the exception.[49] More general works in theology and philosophy were almost certainly acquired simply by purchase or by donation.

Donation was the third of the methods by which books might be acquired. As a major method of acquisition, as important as it was unregulated, it became more and more important from the thirteenth century. The catalogue of St Augustine's, for example, notes the names of donors as a matter of course, and the summary provided by M. R. James clearly indicates the size and significance of such donations. The catalogues of Leicester and Syon likewise note the names of donors.[50] The donations at St Augustine's range from a single volume to more than a hundred, and similar stories can be told of almost any other major house.[51] By the time we reach the brothers' library at Syon, about 86 per cent of its contents were the result of bequests and donations.[52]

The problem with donations, however, is that one rarely has any control over what is donated, and the contents of a donation may tell us more about the literary preferences of the donor than about the needs of the recipient. In 1306, for example, the Cistercian abbey of Bordesley received a donation of twenty-seven books in French from Guy de Beauchamp, Earl of Warwick. A few of these might have been useful for members of a monastic Order – there was a copy of the Gospels, some lives of saints, a psalter and an apocalypse – but the great majority are romances, and romances formed no part of the *lectio divina* of a Cistercian

---

46. Wormald and Wright 1958, p. 83, and Doyle 1990, p. 3; Guigues I 1984, pp. 222–5 (28, 1–4).   47. Doyle 1990, pp. 5, 15; *BPPB*, p. 3.   48. Doyle 1990, *passim*.
49. Doyle 1989, *passim*, and Knowles 1955, pp. 263–77.
50. M. R. James 1903, pp. lxxi–lxxvii. See also Emden 1968.
51. Knowles 1948–55, pp. 339–41.   52. De Hamel 1991, p. 80.

monk.[53] A Benedictine from St Augustine's appears to have enjoyed similar light reading and left to the library his copies of the romance of *Guy de Warwick*, *Ipomedon*, *Les quatre fils Aymon*, *Lancelot*, *L'Estoire del saint Graal*, *Perceval le Gallois*, the *Histoire de Guillaume le Maréchal* and other French books of a similar nature.[54] Another donor at the same house was particularly interested in science; another in canon law; another in medicine, and so on. 'The monastic library', wrote Dom David Knowles, 'even the greatest, had something of the appearance of a heap . . .; at the best, it was the sum of many collections, great and small, rather than a planned, articulated unit'.[55]

Let us now turn to a particular example of one of these 'heaps' and see how the general observations we have made above manifest themselves in practice. We shall begin with the library of Titchfield, whose catalogue dates from 1400, the very beginning of the period of our concern. The catalogue itself is a magnificent document, beautifully written, and it opens with a preface describing the Titchfield book-room and the arrangement of the books.[56] The catalogue proper then begins with a list of Bibles and glosses. This is a traditional arrangement which may be seen in all but one of the catalogues we shall be examining, and the sole exception – Syon – will be dealt with in due course. To what extent the glosses were used in the fifteenth century is unclear, but we may recall that the location of such volumes at Durham provides us with clear evidence for changing tastes. Mixed in with this biblical material we find the *Historia scholastica* of Peter Comestor and commentaries on the Psalter by Augustine and Peter Lombard. This, too, is common.

The biblical books then give way to patristic and medieval authorities. They begin, as usual, with Augustine, and move on to Jerome, Origen (in Latin), Ralph of Flaix, the ubiquitous Isidore, the *Sententiae* of Peter Lombard, and works by Innocent III and Gregory the Great. Just the same can be said for the catalogues of Meaux, Hulne, Leicester and St Augustine's. The order and number of the authors may differ, but the old familiar faces appear again and again.

Following the *auctoritates*, we find hagiographical texts and sermons, and then, at *distinctio* F, the catalogue proceeds to record a large collection of standard texts on canon law and an extensive selection of consti-

53. *CBMLC* III, pp. 4–10.   54. M. R. James 1903, pp. lxxiii–lxxiv.
55. Knowles 1948–55, p. 332.
56. *CBMLC* III, pp. 183–5 (an English translation may be found in Clark 1975, pp. 77–9, and elsewhere).

tutions. There are various decrees, the *Decretales* of Gregory IX, the *Liber sextus*, the *Liber Clementinus*, and standard works by Hugutio of Pisa, Innocent IV, William Durandus, Henry of Ostia, Goffredo di Trani and Raymond of Pennafort. Canon law is followed by civil law (primarily Justinian), and civil law gives way to a large collection of medical works.

There are 29 volumes of medical treatises, and they represent 13 per cent of the total of 224 volumes (excluding service-books) listed in the Titchfield catalogue. This is a higher proportion than appears in any of the other catalogues, from Meaux to Monk Bretton. The explanation for the anomaly, however, is simple: in all probability, the medical material at Titchfield was the result of a single large donation made towards the end of the thirteenth century. A similar, though smaller, donation of medical books was made to Christ Church, Canterbury, by a thirteenth-century prior.[57] Virtually all the treatises listed at Titchfield are standard and common authorities, and, from a medical point of view, all were out-of-date at the time the catalogue was compiled.

The medical books are then followed by *grammatica*. There is nothing here to surprise us. It is true that the collection is comprehensive, but the texts are standard, unexceptional and, for the most part, date from the late twelfth and early thirteenth centuries. The classical poets, however, are not well represented. We find Ovid, Horace, Virgil and Maximianus, but no Lucan, Statius, Persius or Juvenal.[58]

The section on *grammatica* is followed by a number of miscellaneous volumes which the librarian seems to have had difficulty in cataloguing. This, too, was not uncommon, and in the Leicester catalogue such volumes have their own classification: 'volumina de diversis materiis'.[59] In *distinctio* O, we come to the volumes on logic and philosophy, and what are immediately obvious are the consequences of the popularization of Aristotle by the universities. The section begins with the *Summulae logicales* of Peter of Spain, and then proceeds to list a comprehensive collection of Latin translations of works by and attributed to Aristotle. It is interesting, however, that the catalogue records no scholastic commentaries on these treatises (there is no Aquinas at all, an extraordinary situation), and after recording a pseudo-Aristotelian *Arithmetica*, proceeds to list a collection of English statutes, works on English law (in Latin and

57. Such is the argument of R. M. Wilson 1940, p. 151; M. R. James 1903, p. 122.
58. Cf. R. M. Wilson 1958, pp. 97–9.
59. M. R. James 1936–41, 19, pp. 428–33; *CBMLC* v, pp. 269–77.

French), and the registers, rentals and other *evidentiae* so important for Titchfield and every other abbey in a time of incessant litigation.

We are now almost at the end of the catalogue. The last *distinctio* comprises an unusually large and miscellaneous collection of volumes in French (we mentioned this earlier), where we find the *Livre des seintes medicines* of Henry of Lancaster, Wace's *Life of St Nicholas of Myra*, French translations of various biblical and apocryphal books, two copies of the romance of *Guy de Warwick*, instructions on the use of the astrolabe, the *Voyage d'outre mer* of John Mandeville, the romance of *Bueve de Hantone*, and a few items from the Cycle of Charlemagne. Only three works in English are recorded: a copy of *The Owl and the Nightingale*, a translation of the *Golden Legend*, and an English version of *The Fifteen Signs before Judgment*. The catalogue then concludes, as also do those of Leicester and St Augustine's, with a listing of common service-books.

Our examination of the Titchfield catalogue has been fairly detailed, but the same is not necessary for Meaux, Hulne, Leicester or St Augustine's. The five catalogues differ in degree rather than in kind, and a Premonstratensian monk from Titchfield would have found himself quite at home in the library of the Leicester Augustinians. Nevertheless, just as some Orders were more conservative than others, so the contents of their libraries reflected this conservatism, and our same monk may have been somewhat surprised to see what appear to be certain gaps in the holdings of the Cistercians of Meaux.

The Meaux inventory begins in the same way as that of Titchfield: we have Bibles and glosses followed by patristic and medieval authorities.[60] The selection of the latter is considerably wider than at Titchfield, and includes, as might be expected in a Cistercian house, a large amount of Bernard of Clairvaux. There are plenty of fourteenth-century *distinctiones*, the usual concordances and *tabulae*, and lots of *sermones*, a typical feature of later catalogues.[61]

On the other hand, there is no civil law and not very much canon law. The legal volumes in fact comprise less than 3 per cent of the total, as compared with 22 per cent at Titchfield. At Leicester the percentage is 17 per cent and at St Augustine's 12 per cent (canon law only).[62] Meaux, however, unlike Titchfield, was a Cistercian house, and the Cistercians did not approve of their monks either studying or having access to legal materials. Legal treatises, whether canon or civil, were not kept in the

---

60. I am excluding the service-books and beginning with *CBMLC* III, p. 39, item 29.
61. See n. 85 below.   62. See n. 64 below, however.

common *armarium*: 'Libri iuris civilis vel canonici in armario communi minime resideant.'[63] Texts on civil law are also absent from the catalogue of St Augustine's, and James could only conclude that the catalogue was unfinished.[64]

The situation with regard to the medical texts at Meaux is similar. Only three are recorded in the inventory – works by Platearius, Rhasis and Isaac Judaeus – and all three are old, standard authorities. It would be surprising, however, if this unimpressive list exhausted the medical material at Meaux. Every Cistercian abbey had at least one infirmary, and many of them had three: one for the monks, one for the lay-brothers and one for guests.[65] Rhasis, Isaac and Platearius would hardly have sufficed for a busy infirmarian, and it is quite possible that the medical volumes were kept either in the infirmarian's own chamber or in a safe place in the infirmary.

The *grammatica* collection is small, unexceptional and (like that of Titchfield) old-fashioned; but we must once again bear in mind that Meaux was a Cistercian house, and Cistercian monasteries did not operate as schools. The multiple copies of basic grammars such as we find at St Augustine's were therefore unnecessary. Nor is the variety of classical authors any more impressive than at Titchfield. Ovid, Lucan and Sallust all make an appearance, but there is no Horace or Virgil. Martial, however, is represented, though he is odd reading for a Cistercian monk, and Seneca and Cicero are here as they are everywhere.

Unlike Titchfield, however, Meaux possessed certain texts of scholastic philosophy – Aquinas, Bonaventure, Richard of Middleton and Henry of Ghent – but not only are they far from copious (they comprise only 2.5 per cent of the Meaux holdings), they are also, like so much else at Meaux, decidedly old. Richard of Middleton died around 1305, and he is the latest scholastic writer to be represented.

There is rather more in the way of history and chronicles (nearly 4 per cent of the total), but the English Cistercians had a marked interest in English history. Of the English language, however, there is no trace, and French is restricted to two volumes of sermons and Denis Piramus's *Vie de seint Edmund le Rei*.

The dominant feature of the Meaux library is theology: the theological holdings comprise more than 80 per cent of the total, and that is by far the highest percentage in any of the libraries with which we are here concerned. It is possible, however, that this high proportion reflects a deter-

---

63. Lucet 1977, p. 211 (*Dist.* 1, xi).   64. M. R. James 1903, p. lix.   65. D. N. Bell 1989b.

mined effort on the part of the Cistercians to limit the effects of academic scholasticism, to reduce the impact of the universities, and to retain the emphasis on *lectio* and spirituality which had been established by Bernard and the other great lights of the twelfth century.[66] In other words, although we may see the inventory of Meaux as a fifteenth-century record of what was essentially a thirteenth-century library, this could be the result not of lack of interest or funds, but of deliberate Cistercian policy. The only person cited by Thomas de Burton as a 'librorum maximus perquisitor' at Meaux was Abbot Alexander who died in 1210.[67] Orders differed in their interests, and nowhere is this more evident than if we compare the conservative catalogues of Meaux and Titchfield with the 1372 catalogue of the Austin Friars of York.[68]

We begin, as was traditional, with Bibles and commentaries; we find the usual concordances; we proceed, as usual, to Augustine and Gregory and Jerome and Hugh of Saint-Victor and Bernard. It is not long, however, before our eyes widen at copies of Caesar's *Gallic Wars*, the *Policraticus* of John of Salisbury, *summae* on Lombard's *Sententiae* by almost everyone, *repertoria* by little-known writers such as Peter of Ilkley and Thomas of Thornton, *quaestiones* and *quodlibeta* by the gross, Aristotle in abundance, a whole library of Latin classics, a variety of Arabic writers, and even works on magic, divination, and the Pentacle of Solomon. We are dealing here with Austin Friars, however, and, by the end of the fourteenth century, their life was centred on the world of learning.

When, however, we move on to the later catalogues of the Augustinians of Leicester and the Benedictines of St Augustine's, both compiled at the very end of the fifteenth century, we find ourselves once again in the conservative monastic world of the Premonstratensians and Cistercians. The libraries are larger, that is true (almost 1,000 volumes at Leicester; more than 1,800 at St Augustine's), but although this results in more copies of individual texts and a greater variety of authors, the authors themselves are, for the most part, well known, and few of them are any later than the first half of the fourteenth century. The same may well have been true of the library at St Mary's abbey in York. The index-catalogue (see n. 9) lists 653 titles, and Dr Richard Sharpe has estimated that in the fifteenth century the library probably contained about 1,500 volumes. At least half these holdings – the half we know – were much the same as those at Leicester and St Augustine's.

66. *CBMLC* III, pp. xviii–xix.   67. *CBMLC* III, p. 34.
68. In Dublin, Trinity Coll., D.1.17 (359), edited by Humphreys in *CBMLC* I.

It is inevitable, of course, that in such large collections we will come across less common volumes, and equally inevitable that a man like William Charite of Leicester – a bibliophile with a deep interest in astronomy – would leave his mark on his library. Charite's personal interests are reflected not only in the astronomical works recorded in the Leicester catalogue, but in the list, added at the end of the 'Astronomia' section, of his own astronomical instruments.[69] It is not surprising, therefore, to find at Leicester works of Wycliffe (including his sermons), and among the chronicles two copies of the uncommon *De institutione principum* of Gerald of Wales. Among the *summae* is a translation of the Qur'ān and, among the 'libri de diversis materiis', the *Philobiblon* of Richard of Bury (given to the library by Charite himself), and a work on arboriculture by Nicholas Bollard who flourished about 1500. Among the medical books are such rare works as Nicholas Ripon on the pulse, and the *Physica* of Alexander of Aileston, but, for the most part, the large medical collection comprises old and standard authorities. The legal volumes, as at Titchfield, include statutes and copies of the *Magna carta*, and the volumes in French are all common save one: the *Liber de Drian' et Madok*.

The same sort of analysis could also be done for St Augustine's, but there is no need. We would simply be repeating ourselves. The imperfect catalogue from the Carmelites of Hulne also merely reflects in miniature the essentially conservative nature of the larger collections.

Enough, I think, has been said to show that the fifteenth-century catalogues we have been discussing are not fundamentally dissimilar in either organization or content. What they give is an overwhelming impression of age. The collections they record are old collections, and there is little evidence of any interest in acquiring contemporary books by contemporary authors. In other words, they may be fifteenth-century catalogues, but they are not catalogues of fifteenth-century books. We should note, too, that despite the fact that the catalogues of both Leicester and St Augustine's post-date the invention of printing, neither seems to have been affected by what was, after all, the most revolutionary phenomenon to strike the west since the discovery of gunpowder. M. R. James drew attention to two works at Leicester which might have been printed books (the *Dialogus creaturarum* and the *Vita Aesopi fabulatoris*),[70] but, although other entries in the catalogues might possibly refer to incunab-

69. M. R. James 1936–41, 21, pp. 20–3; see also 19, pp. 123, 125; *CBMLC* v, pp. 324–5.
70. M. R. James 1936–41, 19, p. 123; *CBMLC* v, p. 399.

Monastic libraries: 1400-1557

ula, the advent of printing seems to have had no effect on the conservative nature of the collections. With but a few exceptions, both these libraries could easily be mistaken for collections dating not from the end of the fifteenth century, but from the middle of the fourteenth.

Further evidence for this general lack of interest in contemporary works by contemporary writers can be seen in the surviving volumes that are listed in the *repertoria* of Ker and Watson as belonging to particular houses or institutions. Dealing with these lists, however, requires the greatest care, for the number of books that survive from any particular house is often a matter of chance,[71] and the nature of the survivors may sometimes reflect more the interests of later collectors than those of the original owners. The anonymous compiler of the lists in BL, Royal Appendix 69, for example, was primarily interested in old and unusual manuscripts, and happily dismisses thirteen more recent collections as 'printed' and 'common'.[72] We know, too, that many of the sixteenth- and seventeenth-century antiquarians had a particular interest in preserving chronicles and similar historical materials, and the large number of *chronica* that survive, therefore, is not necessarily an accurate reflection of the place they once occupied in their original collections.

The only safe way to proceed, therefore, is to count every volume traced by Ker and Watson to a monastic institution, note the number of manuscripts classed as 's.xv' or 's.xvi', and calculate the percentage; alternatively, we might apply the same procedure to such large collections as Durham, Worcester, Christ Church, or St Augustine's, the first two of which, fortunately, have survived more or less intact. With this procedure we find rather lower percentages. If we proceed according to the first alternative (and it is a tedious task which I cannot recommend), we find that we are dealing with about 4,900 books, and, of those 4,900, 644 manuscripts – a fraction over 13 per cent – are of the fifteenth and sixteenth century. Since we are concerned only with monastic libraries, I have excluded the volumes from secular cathedrals, dioceses, parishes, parish churches, collegiate churches, hospitals, university colleges and secular institutions. The question of printed books will be considered below. If one prefers the second alternative, the percentages of fifteenth- and sixteenth-century volumes at Durham, Worcester, Christ Church and St Augustine's are, respectively, 8.9 per cent, 5.2 per cent, 12.3 per cent and 6.0 per cent. We might also note that the nature of these

71. Ker 1964–87, p. xi.   72. Liddell 1939, *passim*; cf. n. 88 below.

volumes is almost identical whichever procedure we adopt. The most common books are service-books and historical works; and after these – come various *tabulae*, fifteenth-century copies of older Latin writers from Ambrose in the fourth century to William Milverley in the fourteenth – and personal *collectanea*. Works in Latin which manifest a real spirit of creative scholarship are noticeable by their absence. The question of works in English is a matter we shall discuss in due course.

It seems, therefore, that most fifteenth-century monks were more interested in the past than the present, and that their reading habits tended to be somewhat old-fashioned. We may see corroboration for this in an interesting list of 93 items borrowed by 7 monks of St Albans between 1420 and 1437: despite the late date of the document, the majority of the volumes recorded contain twelfth- and early thirteenth-century theology.[73]

The only exception to this somewhat gloomy situation – apart from women's houses, which we shall consider in a moment – appears to have been the Carthusians, but, since their records are fragmentary, it is unwise to say too much too confidently. Nevertheless, it may be significant that out of about 120 volumes traced to 10 Carthusian houses (Axholme, Beauvale, Coventry, Hinton, Kingston-upon-Hull, the London Charterhouse, Mount Grace, Perth, Sheen and Witham), more than half (54.5 per cent) are manuscripts of the fifteenth and early sixteenth centuries and more than a quarter (26.5 per cent) are printed books. It is much to be regretted that we have no catalogue of a Carthusian library, but if their collections were anything like those of their European counterparts, they may indeed have been impressive.[74]

On the other hand, although the majority of monks seem to have had little interest in keeping abreast of the times, a great deal of work was still being done both on and in the monastic libraries. At Durham, for example, a brand new library was constructed between 1414 and 1418 and new press-marks and *ex libris* inscriptions were introduced to go with it.[75] Similar activities were taking place at Ely and Worcester. At Ely the commonest form of *ex libris* inscription was introduced in the fifteenth century,[76] and at Worcester, in about 1500, an unknown librarian pasted a label on the back cover of each volume listing its contents. We may compare the activities of Thomas Swalwell at Durham.[77] But – and it

73. R. W. Hunt 1978, pp. 254–7, 273–7 (edition). The other borrowers' lists cited by Hunt on p. 254, are either thirteenth- or early fourteenth-century.   74. Lehmann 1924.
75. Piper 1978, pp. 223–30.   76. Ker 1964–87, p. 77.
77. Ker 1964–87, p. 205; Piper 1978, pp. 228–30.

is an important but – the main concern of the fifteenth-century librarians lay not in purchasing new works by contemporary authors, but in recataloguing older volumes, and few of them seem to have evinced much interest in acquiring the printed products of the new presses.

We have seen already that the library catalogues of Leicester and St Augustine's list hardly any printed books, and, at first glance, the evidence of the surviving volumes would seem to confirm that the effect of the introduction of printing was minimal. Of 4,900 extant volumes which have been traced to monastic institutions, only about 320 (6.5 per cent) are printed books, and of the collections at Worcester, Christ Church and St Augustine's the percentage of printed volumes range from an abysmal 0.4 per cent to a meagre 1.5 per cent. There are 4 printed books (1 per cent) which have been traced to Worcester, 5 (1.5 per cent) to Christ Church, and 1 (0.4 per cent) to St Augustine's. We shall consider the case of Durham in a moment. In this case, however, the evidence of the surviving books is almost certainly misleading, and it is probable that many more printed books were to be found in monastic collections than have actually been traced to them. It is not difficult to suggest a reason. I suspect that the attitude of most early collectors and antiquarians was identical to that of the compiler of the lists in BL, Royal Appendix 69: printed books were neither of interest nor of value. A more accurate estimate of the situation may be derived from an examination of the library catalogues of the Brigittine brethren of Syon, and of the list of books which were saved from the Benedictine priory of Monk Bretton.

The library at Syon was dramatically different from that at Meaux, Titchfield, Leicester or St Augustine's; but we must remember that Syon was a fifteenth-century foundation, and that, unlike the other libraries we have been considering, it did not possess a historic collection. We must also remember that the Syon catalogue is a sixteenth-century catalogue, and that, as we shall see in a moment, is significant. Many of the titles recorded are new and unfamiliar, and even the arrangement of the books is unusual, possibly because, between 1504 and 1526 the library was reorganized.[78] We do not begin here with Bibles and glosses, but with grammar and poetry; and although the first author to meet our eye (Horace) is no one new, the volume in question was not a manuscript, but the printed edition of 1495. The second work listed leads us immediately into the world of the Renaissance: it is the printed *Grammatica* of

78. Bateson 1898, p. vi.

Giovanni Antonio Sulpizio, one of the most learned Latin grammarians of his generation.

Sulpizio is followed by 2 more printed books: the *De honesta disciplina* of Pietro Crinito of Florence (1475–1507), and the lengthy *Annotationes in quattuor et viginti Pandectarum libros* of the brilliant scholar, Guillaume Budé (1468–1540). After Budé, however, we come to a composite manuscript volume from an earlier age, and, apart from such rarities as the *Neutrale* of Adam Nizard and the *Deponentale* of Nicholas de Birkendalia, the names are once again familiar: Alexander of Hales, Serlo the Grammarian, Peter Helias, Donatus and Priscian. The next five volumes (one of which is a printed book) are likewise unexceptional.

We then come to more printed editions of up-to-date authors: the *Grammatica* of Niccolò Perotti (1429–80) and, a little later, his *Cornucopiae*, a colossal commentary on the first book of Martial. Perotti is followed by the printed *opera* of Marino Becichemo of Scutari (*c.* 1468–1526), but after Becichemo we are once again plunged back into the world of the Middle Ages with the *De institutione novitiorum* of Hugh of Saint-Victor; and so it continues. Contemporary authors give way to those from the Middle Ages, and those from the Middle Ages to those who were contemporary. The great strength of the Syon collection, wrote Mary Bateson,

> lay in the Latin translations of the Renaissance; for instance, Argyropoulos, Hermolaus Barbarus, Gaza, Marsilius Ficinus, G. Trapezuntios, and Erasmus are well represented as translators from the Greek. The monastery kept pace with the new learning in its Latin Renaissance literature; Coluccio, Leonardo Bruni, Poggio, Bessarion, Platina, Poliziano, Pico della Mirandola, are here, but there are no books in Italian . . . Reuchlin represents the German humanists, but there are no books in German. From the English Renaissance, Colet's sermon to the clergy of St Paul's is here, and Linacre's translation of Proclus. More is represented by the translations of Lucian . . . which he wrote with Erasmus.

Almost all of these works are in Latin or in Latin translation. The desultory study of Greek and Hebrew by isolated individuals had no significant effect on the content of monastic libraries, either before or after the invention of printing. A printed Hebrew concordance at Syon[79] or a printed Greek Aristophanes at Abingdon[80] are no more than curiosities,

---

79. Oxford, Merton Coll., 76.b.11.
80. Charlecote Park, Sir E. Cameron-Fairfax-Lucy.

and, although they may intrigue us, they do not warrant extended discussion.[81]

It is understandable that most of these contemporary works were to be found in printed editions, and the total number of printed books at Syon far exceeded the trifling 6.5 per cent revealed by an analysis of surviving volumes. Of the 1,421 volumes recorded in the catalogue, at least 400, or 28 per cent, were printed books, and the new edition at present being prepared by Drs A. I. Doyle and Vincent Gillespie may well increase this proportion. Whether the 23 pairs of spectacles in use at Syon in 1536–7 should be directly related to the presence of printed books in the library must remain a matter for speculation.[82]

That we are now in a new world can hardly be more evident, but the more dramatic aspects of the Syon catalogue must not be overemphasized. *Distinctio* D leads us back into the realm of the *Sententiae* and the usual commentaries, and the names are familiar: Aquinas, Bonaventure, Richard of Middleton, Duns Scotus and so on. In *distinctio* E we find copies of the Bible with its commentaries and concordances, the old, standard *Moralia* of Gregory the Great, and a large collection of the common *postillae* of Nicholas of Lyra and Hugh of Saint-Cher. Just the same sort of material continues through *distinctiones* F, G, H and I. In other words, although the library at Syon bears eloquent testimony to the impact of printing and the New Learning, it still remains a monastic library, solidly anchored in its patristic and medieval past.

The printed books bought by the last monks of Durham tell a similar story. A considerable number have been traced to the house – about 104, or just over 17 per cent – but despite the appearance of Johann Dietenberger's tract against Luther, or Pope Adrian VI on the *Sententiae*, many of the volumes reflect older traditional studies, and Augustine, Ambrose, Peter Comestor, Peter Lombard and Nicholas of Lyra are all represented.[83] On the other hand, the monk who is studying Ambrose now knows some Greek, and that would have been unusual in an earlier age.[84]

The nature of the printed books at Syon and Durham reflects the wider world of printing in general. The clergy remained the chief users of books, especially in Latin, and patristic literature remained of major

81. Bateson 1898, p. viii. For further examples, see Ker 1964–87, pp. 23, 33, 38, 40, 56, 85, 138, 142, 155, 157 and 186, but nearly all these volumes predate the fifteenth century. See also M. R. James 1903, pp. lxxxiv–lxxxvii, and Hirsch 1967, pp. 138–9.
82. Blunt 1873, p. xxvii; Dreyfus 1988.   83. Doyle 1988, p. 213.   84. Doyle 1988, p. 211.

importance. About 200 editions of Augustinian and ps-Augustinian works published before the end of the fifteenth century, about 160 of Jerome, 56 of Gregory the Great, and then fewer for Lactantius (20), who is uncommon in manuscripts, Ambrose (15) and Cyprian (7), are recorded on the *ISTC* database. Volumes of sermons were produced in substantial numbers. On the basis of *ISTC*, an estimate of some 1,000 editions of sermons printed before 1501 (or less than 4 per cent of total production) seems generous. An earlier estimate of 'about 5,000 volumes of sermon literature', representing about one-eighth of the total number of incunabula, is erroneous.[85] Sermon collections occur everywhere, nevertheless, in later monastic catalogues. Printers who wished to make a living had to respond to demand, and the contents of Latin incunabula reflect both the conservative tastes of the readers and the conservative nature of university education.

It may be objected, however, that Syon cannot be taken as representative of later monastic collections. It was, after all, both large and rich, and its library was composed primarily of books which had been donated by learned and generous donors with close university connections. Let us turn, therefore, to a list from a house that was neither large, rich, nor closely associated with any university: the Benedictine priory of Monk Bretton in Yorkshire. The document itself is extraordinary. It is dated 21 July 1558 and post-dates the suppression of the house by some two decades. It is therefore of the greatest importance in revealing to us something of the way in which monastic collections could be preserved rather than destroyed, sold or otherwise scattered.[86] It must be remembered, however, that the inventory is not a catalogue of the priory library, but a list of books saved from the collection by the former prior and two other monks. How much they were unable to save is unknown. Of the books listed, 114 were bought and/or owned by the three individuals concerned, and the other 28 comprise a single donation of volumes bought by a former sub-prior. We must also bear in mind that 'some of the books in this list may have been the spoils of other libraries, collected between 1534, when the house was dissolved, and 1558, when the catalogue was made'.[87]

The inventory begins, traditionally, with a copy of the Bible and six volumes of *postillae* by Hugh of Saint-Cher – but we are not dealing with

85. Hirsch 1967, p. 130, quoting E. Schulz.
86. Wormald and Wright 1958, pp. 160–1 (Wright).
87. J. Hunter 1831, p. viii; cf. *CBMLC* IV, pp. 266–8.

manuscripts here: the six volumes are the printed edition of 1504. We then find the popular *Vita Iesu Christi* written by Ludolf of Saxony, and a printed edition of Bede. After Bede, however, we again enter the world of the Renaissance. There are numerous volumes of homilies, but the authors are not the old, traditional authorities such as we find at Leicester or St Augustine's. At Monk Bretton, we are firmly in the fourteenth and fifteenth centuries with Diego Perez of Valencia, Peter de Palude, Johannes Nider, Vincent Ferrer, Conrad of Brudelsheim, Pelbart of Temesvar, Alexander Carpenter, Oliver Maillard, Leonard of Udine, Michael of Hungary and Antony of Bitonto. Every one of these is a printed book; many of them were also to be found at Syon. Also, although we find examples of the older patristic and medieval authorities such as Ambrose, Augustine, Aquinas and the rest, mixed in with them are two works by Erasmus, Gregor Reisch's *Margarita philosophica*, the dictionary of Ambrogio Calepino, and the letters of Marsilio Ficino, Angelo Poliziano and Pico della Mirandola.

Nearly all these volumes are printed books, and the inventory of Monk Bretton indicates dramatically – perhaps even more dramatically than the much larger catalogue of Syon – the differences between the contents of some later libraries and the more traditional, conservative holdings such as we find at Leicester or St Augustine's. Nor were Syon and Monk Bretton alone in their interest in acquiring printed volumes: the lists in BL, Royal Appendix 69, show clearly that in Lincolnshire alone, six houses of Augustinians, three of Gilbertines, and one each of Premonstratensians, Cistercians, Franciscans and Carmelites all alike had up-to-date libraries with printed books. It is to be regretted that the compiler of the lists, who was interested only in manuscripts, provides us with no record of their titles.[88]

I would suggest, therefore, that many monasteries might have acquired more printed books than is suggested by an analysis of the surviving volumes. I would also suggest, however, that, in the British Isles at least, such volumes did not find their way into the libraries in any quantity until the early sixteenth century. It must be admitted that, if this be the case, the monasteries in the British Isles differed markedly from many on the Continent situated near great centres of printing. We have already seen that the catalogues of Leicester and St Augustine's, both of which date from the very end of the fifteenth century, record hardly any printed

88. Liddell 1939, pp. 91–5.

books, whereas the sixteenth-century lists from Syon and Monk Bretton record large numbers. This is not difficult to explain. First of all, with regard to purchases of such books, it takes time for any new invention, however revolutionary, to become accepted, particularly by a group of people who, in general, were of conservative tastes and had behind them a century of intellectual stagnation. Secondly, with regard to bequests, if a rich merchant were buying printed books in the 1470s and lived his three score years and ten, he would not have died until the early years of the following century, and until that time his books would have remained in his own possession. I am confident, however, that after his death there would have been many religious eager to acquire them. What might have happened to the monastic libraries had Prince Arthur not died in his teens we do not know, but it is quite possible that the introduction of printing heralded a renaissance in the intellectual life of many monasteries which was, regrettably, cut short all too soon by their suppression. Some monastic houses continued to acquire books until the very last moment. Printed books dating from the 1530s were to be found at Abingdon (1532, 1537), Burton-on-Trent (1534), Durham (1530, 1532, 1534), Evesham (1537), Merton (1532), Sheen (1531) and Syon (1532, 1534–5).[89]

Our discussion so far has been restricted to the libraries of male religious. The reason for this is simple: we have no catalogue from any nunnery in the British Isles, and, apart from the volumes listed in Ker and Watson, the only other records that have survived are a note of donation to Swine and a few meagre lists that appear in wills, episcopal visitations and inventories taken at the time of the Dissolution.[90] Nevertheless, an analysis of the surviving manuscripts provides us with a certain amount of information and enables us to make some observations, albeit tentative, about the contents of the nuns' libraries.[91]

Excluding printed books and the donation to Swine, there are 144 manuscripts that have been traced to English nunneries,[92] but two-thirds of these – a remarkable number – date from the fifteenth and early sixteenth centuries. We may contrast this with the approximately 13 per cent which come from men's houses. Of all these 144 volumes, slightly more than half (53 per cent) are liturgical and the others primarily devo-

89. Ker 1964–87, pp. 2, 16, 131, 178, 185–6, and *Supplement*, pp. 1, 33–4, 64 (this list is not intended to be complete).   90. All are listed in part II of D. N. Bell 1995.

91. D.N. Bell 1995, part I.

92. All are listed and described in D. N. Bell 1995, part II (including a small number of manuscripts not recorded in Ker or Watson).

tional and theological. Of the non-liturgical manuscripts, however, it is significant that 23 per cent are in Latin, 10 per cent in French, and no less than 67 per cent in English.

It is well known that the standard of education among female religious was lower than that among clerical males.[93] There was, of course, the odd exception (especially at Syon), but for the great majority of nuns, their Latin was confined to the liturgy, and, by the fourteenth century, most of them needed their institutes, instructions and the like made available in the vernacular. In the fourteenth century, the vernacular might have been English or French, but by the fifteenth century, as we have seen, French had been superseded by English, and there is no doubt that during the period which is our concern in this chapter, all but a very few nuns thought and talked in English.

This, however, was no disadvantage. We observed at the beginning of this study that the spread of literacy in the fifteenth century was essentially a spread in vernacular literacy, and the researches of H. S. Bennett in 1946–7[94] and of Vincent Gillespie forty years later,[95] have clearly demonstrated the tremendous expansion in the distribution of vernacular religious literature during that period. Gillespie speaks of 'the new-found respectability' of English in religious contexts and observes that 'the evidence of the surviving manuscripts points to extensive ownership of vernacular religious books by religious houses and the clergy'. It appears, however, that it was primarily the nuns who evinced the greatest interest in what, for the time, was the modern movement, and, among the men's houses (*pace* Gillespie), only the Carthusians seem to have paid any significant attention to vernacular texts. Of 66 fifteenth- and sixteenth-century manuscripts traced to Carthusian libraries, 15 (23 per cent) are in English. We might also note that in a list of two dozen volumes taken from London to the Hull Charterhouse in the late fourteenth or early fifteenth century, half are in English.[96] There is little in English recorded at any of the other libraries we have discussed above, and of the printed books known to be owned by the last monks at Durham, only one – Trevisa's translation of the *Polychronicon* of Ranulph Higden – is in English.[97] The brothers' library at Syon contained 26 volumes in English out of a total of 1,421 (less than 2 per cent of the

93. The matter is considered in some detail in D. N. Bell 1995, part 1, chapter 3.
94. Bennett 1946–7.   95. Gillespie 1989.
96. Knowles 1948–55, p. 343; E. M. Thompson 1930, pp. 324–6, where the list is reproduced.
97. Doyle 1988, p. 213.

total), and the contrast with the sisters' collection is startling, but, by the early sixteenth century, the brothers and the sisters had developed quite different interests.[98] Of the 142 volumes saved from Monk Bretton, only 5 (3.5 per cent) were in the mother tongue. These small percentages are echoed in the trifling proportion – about 2.6 per cent (approximately 130 volumes) – of fifteenth- and sixteenth-century books in English among the surviving volumes listed by Ker and Watson, and they stand in marked contrast to the almost 30 per cent (48 out of a total of 161 manuscripts and printed books) that have been traced to the nunneries. It seems, therefore, that the nuns' ignorance of Latin forced them to concentrate on the riches of English religious literature, and, as a consequence, their devotional life may have been richer, fuller and more up-to-date than that of their brethren, who, for the most part, were still enmeshed in the consequences of a conservative and traditional education.[99]

So what are the main conclusions we may derive from this brief investigation? Whatever we say, we must be cautious, for it must always be remembered that we have only a limited number of lists and catalogues, and evidence from the surviving books can too easily be misinterpreted.

First of all, there can be little doubt that the fifteenth century was, in general, a period of intellectual stagnation in most men's houses. The Carthusians, and possibly the Friars, may have been exceptions, but their records are too fragmentary to permit us to state this with any certainty. This is not to say, of course, that the acquisition and production of books had entirely ceased – we have seen that it did not – but they were certainly being acquired and produced in smaller quantities than had been the case in earlier centuries. The catalogues of Meaux, Titchfield, Leicester and St Augustine's reveal large libraries, but they were essentially old libraries, and the main bulk of their collections dated from well before the fifteenth century.

On the other hand (and this is the second point), the fifteenth century also saw the building of new libraries and a renewal of activity on the part of librarians. Charles Kingsford called the period 'the age of libraries'.[100] In the early fifteenth century, monasteries, friaries, cathedrals and colleges were all alike interested in the construction of new book-rooms and new facilities. Sometimes, however the new book-rooms were the result

---

98. Lovatt 1992, p. 226.
99. A detailed account of nuns' interest in vernacular literature will be found in part 1, chapter 3, of D. N. Bell 1995; cf. below, pp. 520–5, 534.   100. Kingsford 1925, p. 42.

of generous donations, and may reflect more the piety of the donor (or his need for publicity) than the needs of the monastery.[101] Likewise, we find librarians recataloguing their collections, and, although the collections might have comprised primarily older books, the catalogues that record them are impressive examples of scientific librarianship. According to John Whytefeld, who compiled the catalogue of Dover Priory in 1389, the purpose of a library catalogue was to provide the librarian with an accurate record of the number of books owned by the house, to stir up studious brethren to read them, and to provide those interested with a speedy and effective way of finding the volume they needed.[102] The catalogues of Leicester and St Augustine's admirably fulfilled at least the first and the third of these principles.

Thirdly, I would suggest that a major change in both acquisition and intellectual activity comes with the introduction of printing. It may well have taken some time for monasteries in England to respond to the new medium – I doubt that significant additions were made before the early years of the sixteenth century – but the evidence from surviving books almost certainly provides an inaccurate picture of the impact of the printing revolution. The rich and educated brethren of Syon certainly possessed a library replete with printed editions, but the Benedictines of Monk Bretton and a number of different Orders in Lincolnshire, though very much poorer, may not have been far behind.

Lastly, the increase in vernacular literacy in the fifteenth century and the production of large numbers of devotional works in English appear to have had more impact on women's houses than on men's. The Carthusians *may* have shown a similar interest in English material, but, as we have seen, their records are incomplete and the evidence inconclusive. It was the nuns, not the monks, who seem to have been interested in acquiring fifteenth-century books, and it was the nuns, not the monks (again with the possible exception of the Carthusians), who stood at the forefront of the English vernacular devotional movement. Nuns' libraries, in fact, may not always have been the small and inconsequential collections many scholars have assumed. For example, fifteenth-century press-marks on two volumes from the Augustinian nunnery of Campsey read 'D.D.141' and 'O.E.94',[103] and if these reflect the usual *distinc-*

---

101. Knowles 1948–55, pp. 352–3.
102. M. R. James 1903, pp. 407, 410. We may compare the comments of the compiler of the Titchfield catalogue: *CBMLC* III, p. 185.
103. See BL, Add. ms. 40675, f. 35r, and CUL, Add. ms. 7220, f. 8r.

tio/gradus classification common at the time we may have a glimpse of a very large library.[104] It is time for a judicious reevaluation of the intellectual life of women religious in the later Middle Ages.

What might have happened to monastic libraries and monastic learning had there been no Dissolution of the Monasteries is an intriguing but unanswerable question. There is, I think, evidence for a reawakening of interest in books (not merely in recataloguing them), consequent upon the invention of printing, but it was a reawakening that was to last less than forty years. On the other hand, the contents of the books that were being printed and the subjects of academic study were rapidly changing, and whether the monasteries would or could have adapted to such changes remains open to question.

104. For a full discussion, see part I, chapter 2, of D.N. Bell 1995.

11

The early royal collections and the Royal Library to 1461

JENNY STRATFORD

> The Old Royal Collection is of respectable though not
> extreme antiquity. Its real founder was King Edward IV.[1]

Edward IV (1461–83) is usually considered to be the 'founder' of the English royal library as it is known today. As the first King to leave a coherent collection of books – the large and expensive illuminated histories and chronicles in French, made for him and imported from Flanders – Edward IV has good claims to this title. Documentary evidence, however, suggests that the royal library in England had considerably earlier origins, although not a continuous existence. This chapter focuses on the Lancastrian period, the reigns of Henry IV (1399–1413), Henry V (1413–22) and Henry VI (1422–61), but to make sense of what took place after the deposition of Richard II in 1399, there needs to be a context. Accordingly some reference is made to earlier reigns. Much research remains to be undertaken, and caution is needed in interpreting the fragmentary evidence known to date. Sufficient materials have already come to light to draw some provisional conclusions about the royal library as a collection and about the places where it was kept.

The English documentary sources are notoriously difficult to assemble and to interpret. There are two main reasons. First, there are no formal inventories in England before the Tudor period,[2] that is, there is no source comparable with the French and Burgundian inventories which allow us to know so much about the books, jewels, plate, textiles and other movables of the Valois kings and princes. A similar contrast could be drawn with the inventories of the Visconti, the Medici and the Aragonese kings of Naples.[3] The French inventories include the 1380

---

1. Gilson in Warner and Gilson 1921, I, p. xi.   2. Collins 1955, pp. 231–56.
3. Delisle 1868–81, I, *passim*; Pellegrin 1955; *Biblioteca Medicea* 1981; Fryde 1983; De Marinis 1947–69.

general inventory of the goods of Charles V, which describes books dispersed among the various royal residences.[4] Separate inventories were also made of the great Louvre library of Charles V and Charles VI in 1373, 1380, 1411, 1413 and in 1424, when the books were bought by John, Duke of Bedford, as Regent of France; after 1429 they were brought via Rouen to the Duke's wardrobe in London.[5] The Louvre inventories, made in France, not in England, are explicit enough to identify books which have survived. The 1411 Louvre inventory is especially valuable in that the books were listed by the opening words of the second leaf (*secundo folio*), and by the final words. This is usually enough for the provenance of a surviving book to be established, whether or not there is internal evidence. Over 100 Louvre books are known today, and additions to the list are still occasionally made, by no means all of them illuminated books. Estimates of how many extant books can be associated with English Kings and Queens from Edward I to Henry VI vary slightly. Even the most optimistic calculation, however, scarcely exceeds two dozen. The earliest known inventory of the books of an English monarch is the brief list of 143 manuscript and printed works seen by an anonymous French visitor to Richmond Palace in 1535.[6]

A second difficulty is that, in spite of the much greater loss overall of medieval records in France than in England, much more is known about the personal expenditure of the French kings in the fourteenth and fifteenth centuries than about that of English kings during the same period. This is largely because in England, by the second half of the fourteenth century, the Chamber, the department which after 1318 had come increasingly to deal with the personal expenditure of the Crown, was accountable only to the King, and was exempted from accounting at the Exchequer.[7] Some evidence about books can be found in other types of Crown record, notably those of the Wardrobe and the Exchequer. Well before 1300, and throughout the reign of Edward I, books were stored in the treasury of the Wardrobe. By the end of the reign of Edward II, books were also kept with charters and other documents in the Treasury of the Exchequer. Some dated back to the time of Henry III.[8] Other short lists of books crop up in administrative documents throughout the four-

4. Labarte 1879. Many of the published Valois inventories are listed in Paris 1981, pp. 436–7.
5. Delisle 1868–81, I, pp. 20–56, III, pp. 114–70, 328–36; Delisle 1907, *passim* (both with bibliography); Stratford 1987, pp. 339–41.   6. Omont 1891.
7. Tout 1920–33, IV, pp. 227–348; Given-Wilson 1986, pp. 85–92; Green 1980, esp. pp. 4–8.
8. BL, Add. ms. 7965, fols. 145–7v; *Liber quotidianus*, pp. 347–9, 351; Prestwich 1988, pp. 118, 123; *CCR, Edward II, 1313–18*, p. 10; Palgrave 1836, I, pp. 104–6, 116.

teenth and fifteenth centuries, but on the whole this evidence does not concern the personal books (except for some service-books) in use in the Chamber by the King himself.

Some years ago, Jonathan Alexander published a survey of the surviving illuminated manuscripts which can be connected with royal patrons from Edward III to Henry VII, and of some of the documents which concern them.[9] Subsequently, one of the manuscripts, the Hours of Catherine of Valois, has been acquired by the British Library,[10] and a few new pieces of documentary information (not necessarily all concerning illuminated books) have come to light. The account of John de Flete, Keeper of the Privy Wardrobe in the Tower from 1324 to 1341, is a survivor so exceptional that it must be mentioned, although it considerably predates the Lancastrian period. Flete was charged with the Privy Wardrobe under Edward II (1307–27) and Edward III (1327–77). From 1338, Flete also served as deputy of the Receiver of the Chamber; in 1341, he accounted to the auditors of the Chamber for both these offices. His account roll (now cut up and rebound as an exceptionally inconvenient tall manuscript) belongs to the last years of unconcealed Chamber accounting, and is precious evidence of what may have been in existence (although undocumented in the public records) at a later date. On the basis of this document, Juliet Vale concluded that 'there was in effect a royal library within the privy wardrobe in the Tower'. This hypothesis can be accepted with some important reservations.[11]

The receipt section of Flete's account shows that at the end of the reign of Edward II some 340 books and unbound quires were stored in the Tower. The books charged to Flete included 160 'libri diversi', 67 liturgical books, a Bible, 51 unbound quires and 59 books and pieces of 'romances' (meaning both romances in the modern sense and chronicles or other vernacular works). Some titles in Latin and French are recorded, a good deal about binding, some scraps about illumination, but almost nothing about the contents. Not quite all the books were in stock at one and the same time. The issue (*liberacio*), soon after Flete took office in 1324, of 14 'romances' and a French psalter to William de Langley, Clerk of Edward II's Chamber, and of a few more secular and liturgical books to other household and Chamber clerks, suggests that some of them could

9. Alexander 1983; cf. Cavanaugh 1980.
10. BL, Add. ms. 65100; Christie's, 2 December 1987, lot 34.
11. BL, Add. ms. 60584, Account of John de Flete, clerk, Keeper of the Wardrobe in the Tower of London; J. Vale 1982, pp. 49–50, and appendix 9.

have been in use in the King's household, although not necessarily by Edward himself. The *summa* of the receipt of books lists: 'De libris diversis, clx', 67 liturgical books (13 missals, 8 breviaries, 12 graduals, 2 ordinals, 3 primers, a legendary, 2 manuals, 7 psalters, 6 antiphoners, 4 graduals with tropers, 4 other tropers, 2 epistolaries, 2 collectars, an illuminated canon of the mass bound separately for display on an altar, from the goods of Humphrey de Bohun, Earl of Hereford), a Bible, 'De quaternis diversis, lj', and 'De libris et peciis de romancie, lix', and a few other specified items. Books specified in other sections of the receipt include 11 books of canon and civil law received from John [?Stratford], Bishop of Winchester, on 27 November 1326.[12]

Some books seem to have had a royal provenance and may even have been inherited from Edward I, before being passed on through Edward II to Edward III. A 'book of interludes of St Margaret which the king ordered, covered in red leather', describes a royal commission, although which king is meant is uncertain. The 66 'libri diversi' and other quires sealed in a canvas sack and stored in a chest, and quantities of other secular and liturgical books, all received in the Tower at one and the same time and stored in several other chests, may have been sent to the Privy Wardrobe from the Chamber or the Great Wardrobe. The seal of Thomas Ouseflete was affixed to the sack; he was clerk and Controller of the King's Chamber from 1319 to 1323, and Keeper of the Great Wardrobe from 1323 to 1326.[13]

On the other hand, comparison of the entries on the receipt and expenses sections of the roll demonstrates unequivocally that many of the books in the Tower had been confiscated with other movables from great magnates and bishops implicated in the political troubles of the end of Edward II's reign. Some were sent out within a few months of Edward III's accession to the leaders of the dominant court party: Isabella, the Queen Mother, and her lover, Mortimer. Others were returned to the heirs, widows and executors of the original owners. To this category belong 3 books 'de surgere', and a missal and 4 books of 'romances' delivered to Elizabeth de Burgh, Lady of Clare (whose third husband, Roger Damory, was executed in 1322). So do 4 'romances' and 6 or 7 liturgical books sent to her sister, Margaret, Countess of Cornwall (widow of Piers

12. BL, Add. ms. 60584, fols. 10v–12v and 8v. The expenses begin on f. 13v. For the books issued to Langley, f. 24v; other clerks, fols. 24v–26v; cf. J. Vale 1982, p. 49.
13. BL, Add. ms. 60584, f. 6v: 'j libro de interlud' de sancta Margar' quem dominus rex facere [*sic*] fecit, cooperato de coreo rubeo'; fols. 15, 16; and for Ouseflete, Tout 1920–33, II, 345; IV, 398–9.

Gaveston, murdered in 1312, and wife of Hugh Audley, who was implicated in the 1322 rebellion), 3 'romances' and a bestiary sent to the
executors of Thomas, Earl of Lancaster (executed in 1322), as well as
books returned to Isabella de Clare, Lady of Berkeley, and Margaret
de Umfreville, Lady of Badlesmere. Two dozen books taken from
Humphrey de Bohun, Earl of Hereford, were recovered by his heir, John
Bohun; another 32 secular and ecclesiastical books, a roll of polyphonic
music and other assorted quires were restored to Alexander Bicknor,
Archbishop of Dublin. They were packed up and issued from the Tower
in 'job lots' with other confiscated property from chambers and chapels:
secular and liturgical plate, vestments of cloth of gold, secular textiles,
clothing and horse-trappers. It is unlikely that any of the books returned
to magnates remained in royal ownership, or that, as has been suggested,
they constituted a lending library.[14]

Many books left the Privy Wardrobe during the early years of Edward
III's reign: among them the Arthurian and other romances sent to Queen
Isabella, and two service-books and a 'Flores beatae virginis' to Queen
Philippa. It seems, however, that 4 rolls of *mappae mundi* with 'portrai-
tures' (perhaps figures like those on the Hereford world map), issued in
1338, were the only items for Edward III's use (*opus*). This may not be significant; Edward had other sources for his books. Many of the remaining
books went to clerks and officers of the new Chamber and Household,
perhaps as rewards to men who had joined the new King's party. Some
were outright gifts (the term is *donacio*). For example, in 1328, Richard de
Bury, author of the *Philobiblon*, obtained 9 'libri diversi' and 5 liturgical
books, and, in 1329, another well-known clerk, Mr John Walwayn the
younger, obtained the 'romancia de Achilles' and the 'propheciae Sibille
Sapientis'. By 1337, only 23 books in various bindings and 26 unbound
quires were still in stock. After a further 6 Latin works had been delivered
to yet another chamber clerk in 1340, only 18 books remained. It can be
seen, therefore, not only that many of the books were in the Tower as the
result of forfeitures, but also that most had been dispersed by 1341.[15]
Nevertheless, the existence of a large collection of books stored in the
Tower at the beginning of the reign of Edward III is firmly established.
Some of the books in the French royal collections in the fourteenth

14. BL, Add. ms. 60584, fols. 13v–16v, 27v; for the Bohun books, fols. 19, 16v; T. H. Turner
1845; for Bicknor's books, fols. 6v, 7v, 15v; Wathey 1992.
15. BL, Add. ms. 60584, fols. 27v (Isabella), 18v and 27v (Philippa, 1328 and 1338), 22v (Edward
III), 17v and 18v (Bury and Walwayn), 17v, 18v, 19v, 21v, 23v, 27v (other clerks); stock after
1337, fols. 51v, 53v. For Edward's other books, n. 8 above.

century, such as the Belleville Breviary (and the lost Belleville Missal), came into the King's possession through confiscations, and other books were alienated when they were given or lent out by the King.[16]

The known documents for the reign of Richard II have been investigated by Richard Firth Green and others. Little evidence for the existence of a royal library in Richard's reign has so far come to light.[17] It is worth recalling, though, the history of one of the books securely connected with Richard, the *Epistre au roi Richart*, the letter to King Richard II of Philippe of Mézières, a presentation manuscript written and illuminated in Paris for Richard and sent to him by Charles VI of France at the time of the negotiations in 1395 for Richard's marriage to Isabella. This is a rare example of a codex which beyond question belonged to an English king before Edward IV; it was recorded in the reign of Henry VIII among the royal books at Richmond in 1535, and is still in the royal collections at the British Library.[18]

Something is known about at least one of the places where royal books were kept in the Lancastrian period. The payments in 1401–2 for works at Eltham Palace, which was rebuilt for Henry IV and was one of his favourite residences, describe a new study ('novum studium'), one of the rooms attached to the King's new chamber.[19] It was warmed by a brick fireplace with a chimney, and lit by seven large and expensive stained-glass windows. The windows required a total of 78 square feet 4 inches of glass, ordered from the London glazier, William Burgh, who also supplied glass for Westminster Hall. The cost of the Eltham glass was high at 3s 4d per square foot, amounting to a total of £13. It was sent down to Eltham carefully packed in straw. The windows were ornamented with birds and beasts and with figures of St John the Baptist, St Thomas, St George, the Annunciation (two windows), the Trinity and St John the Evangelist, probably with French inscriptions as suggested by the wording in French: 'la salutacion saincte Marie', 'la Trinité', inserted in the Latin account; in an earlier entry, 'coronez et florez cum soveignez vous de moy', French inscriptions are certainly meant.[20] The ceiling was

16. For the alienations, Delisle 1907, *passim*. For the Belleville missal, Labarte 1879, p. 339, no. 3300, and for the breviary (BNF, mss. lat. 10483–4), p. 338, no. 3294; Delisle 1907, I, pp. 182–5; Paris 1981, no. 240, with bibliography. Both were in the King's study at Vincennes in 1380.

17. Green 1976; Scattergood 1968; Cavanaugh 1980, II, pp. 725–33; Scattergood 1983.

18. BL, Royal ms. 20. B.VI; see Mézières 1975; Palmer 1972 (both with bibliography); Omont 1891, p. 10, no. 89.

19. PRO E101/502/23, mm. 3–4; Brown and Colvin 1963, p. 935.

20. The entries relating to the glass and ironwork are printed in translation by Salzman 1929–30, pp. 26–7, no. 59; for Burgh, and the context, see Marks 1993, pp. 48, 94–5.

of wood ('waynescotbord'), perhaps panelled, just possibly decorated like other parts of the new work with carved wooden bosses of archangels, angels and shields. One of two wooden screens ('spera'), may have been for the study. The study was furnished with two desks, listed among the 'necessaria': 'Et in uno magno deske facto de ij stagez pro libris intus custodiendis cum ij formulis emptis de Rogero Joynour pro studio regis, xxs. Et in uno alio deske minore empto de Johanne Deken pro dicto studio regis, xiijs. iiijd'.

Aspects of these payments at Eltham (in particular for the glass) have received much attention, but the purpose of the payments, to build and furnish a luxurious study for Henry IV's books, deserves much more emphasis than it has hitherto received. There may well have been similar studies and desks for books in other English royal palaces. There are many points of comparison with the 'estude' or private study of Charles V at Vincennes. The payments made by Charles V for the newly installed Louvre Library in 1367 and 1368, for panelling, protective wire trellis over windows, and reading desks differ, however, in being for a library on three floors detached from the King's private apartments.[21]

The recently discovered records of a suit brought in the King's Bench in 1419 against the London stationer, Thomas Marleburgh, have added to our knowledge of the books Henry IV owned – although not of what he did with them.[22] Also named in the accusation, which concerns books missing since 1413, is a keeper of Henry IV's books, Ralph Bradfield, gentleman, who seems to have been a yeoman of the Chamber by 1405–6.[23] The nine missing royal books were in English and in Latin: a *Polychronicon*, worth 10 marks; a *Catholicon*, worth £10; a small *Chronicles*, worth £5; a Bible in Latin, worth 10 marks; a Bible in English worth £5; Gregory, *Moralia in Job*, worth 10 marks; a Gower worth £5; and two psalters, one glossed, worth 20 marks – a total value of £58 6s 8d. The relatively high values mean that they are likely to have been illuminated. Two points need to be made. First, the co-operation of a great many people is needed to uncover the scattered records about royal or other books

21. Labarte 1879, 'estude', pp. 317–19, nos. 3045–66; chamber, pp. 336–41, nos. 3279–309; Berty 1885; Delisle 1907, I, 7–9.

22. PRO KB 9/212/2, m.1 (indictment), Hilary Term; PRO, KB 27/632 Rex, m. 4 (suit), Easter Term; cf. Meale 1989, pp. 203, 223, n. 14; K. Harris 1989. For Marleburgh, see Doyle and Parkes 1978, p. 198 and n. 91; cf. Christianson 1990. I thank Dr Henry Summerson for his help.

23. Ralph Bradfelde de Bradfelde, Berkshire, 'gentilman, custos librorum' of Henry IV (PRO KB 27/632, m. 4); yeoman of the King's Chamber (BL, Harley ms. 319, f. 46v; *CPR, 1405–8*, p. 464; *CPR, 1408–1413*, p. 470).

which happen to turn up at widely separated and unpredictable chronological intervals in large and uncalendared classes of records of this kind.
Secondly, biographical studies, which have not yet been undertaken, of
minor Crown officials such as Bradfield and the other named Keepers of
the Books after 1400, will probably prove revealing about their status
and that of the library.

The rediscovery at Eton in 1978 of a copy of Henry V's last will of 10
June 1421 and its codicils of 1422 has added valuable information about
Henry's books and his intentions for them.[24] There can be little doubt
that by 1421, and before he obtained the books from the Market of
Meaux in 1422,[25] Henry possessed a considerable learned library. He left
books to different religious houses, especially to his two new foundations, the double house of Brigittines at Syon and the Charterhouse at
Sheen. A glossed Bible in three volumes was to go to the monastic library
at Syon, the works of Gregory the Great (which had once belonged to
Archbishop Arundel), to Christ Church, Canterbury. Apart from these
few named bequests, the library at Syon was to have 'the whole residue'
of Henry's books of sermons useful for preaching, and Syon and the
Charterhouse to share his books for meditation. The 'common library' of
the University of Oxford was to have all his legal and scholastic books.[26]
The nuns of Syon were to keep all Henry's books currently in their possession, except his father's Great Bible, which was to be returned for the
unborn child. This Bible was of particular significance to Henry V when
he was compiling his will; he named it twice.[27]

It may be a reflection on the number of Henry V's books that in a
codicil he specified that neither Syon nor Sheen was to have any duplicates. In both the will and a codicil the King emphasized that his child
was to have the residue of his books, requiring, in a significant phrase in
1422, that they should be kept 'pro libraria sua'. Both in 1421 and 1422,
the context of the clauses suggests that Henry V was thinking of books
for the household and chamber. The 1421 clause is in a section with three
provisions, preceded by armour, and followed by the hangings and beds
called 'le stuff' at Windsor, Westminster and the Tower, all left to the
unborn child; the 1422 clause places the books and library third after
goods of the household chapel, and after arrangements for the tutelage

24. Strong and Strong 1981.   25. Harriss 1972.
26. Strong and Strong 1981, p. 93, clauses xix, xxij; p. 94, clause xxx; p. 100, clause [9]. For
    Gregory the Great, Rymer, 1739–45 IV pt 4, p. 105; for Oxford, Anstey (ed.), 1898, I, pp.
    151–3.   27. Strong and Strong 1981, pp. 93–4, clauses xxiij, xxvj, xxvij.

and guardianship of the child. These arrangements end with the Chamberlain and Steward, officers within the Chamber and household. The wording of the codicil of 1422 is: 'volumus quod omnes libri nostri, cuiuscumque fuerint facultatis aut materie, in nostro testamento aut codicillis non legati, filio nostro remaneant pro libraria sua'.[28]

Bequests of liturgical books were also made in Henry V's will, some substantially repeated in 1421 from his first will of 1415: his father's breviary in two volumes, said to be written by John, not Richard, Frampton, was left to his uncle, Cardinal Beaufort; his breviary and missal 'written in the same hand', given by his Bohun grandmother, the Countess of Hereford, were left to Thomas Langley, bishop of Durham. While these books do not belong to the library, they seem to be personal service-books, such as Charles V kept in his Chamber and study at Vincennes. Reserved for Queen Catherine were a missal for the altar in Henry's closet or private oratory, and the service-books needed for the use of the twenty chaplains of the household chapel. In 1421, the almoner and three named chaplains each were to receive a missal and a breviary worth £10. This did not exhaust the supply of liturgical books, since the residue of books and other valuables belonging to the household chapel were allotted to Henry's son in the codicil of 1422.[29]

The Bible which had belonged to Henry IV, and which was on loan to the nuns at Syon, is twice referred to by size as the Great Bible: 'magna Biblia'. Should it be identified with a surviving manuscript,[30] a giant illuminated lectern Bible, entirely suitable for the use of well-born nuns? A plausible case can be made out for this suggestion. The Bible has been dated on stylistic grounds to the reign of Henry IV; it was decorated in London by Herman Scheerre and by other artists associated with the Great Cowcher Books of the Duchy of Lancaster. These artists were responsible for a number of important commissions for secular and ecclesiastical patrons in the reigns of Henry IV and Henry V. Several Bibles are listed in English, French and Latin in the Richmond list of 1535. Only one is termed the 'magna Biblia'.[31]

A large number of Latin books, over 140 at least, were kept in the

28. Strong and Strong 1981, pp. 96, 99–100, clauses xxxvij, [3], [9]; K. Harris 1989, p. 195.
29. Rymer, 1739–45, IV, pt 2, pp. 138–9; Strong and Strong 1981, pp. 94–5, clauses xxxiij–xxxv; p. 99, clauses [1], [3]. For Richard Frampton and payments for a two-volume breviary for Henry IV, see Somerville 1936, pp. 599–600. Doyle 1982, pp. 93–4; cf. Christianson 1990, pp. 106–7.   30. BL, Royal ms. 1 E.IX.
31. Strong and Strong 1981, pp. 93–4, clauses xxiij, xxvj. For Herman Scheerre, see Alexander above, pp. 47–8; 1983, pp. 148–50, with bibliography; see also S. A. Wright 1986.

Treasury during the minority of Henry VI, to 1440 or later. Most, if not all, derived from the succession of Henry V and they seem to have been kept safely by the council for Henry VI during his minority, in accordance with the provisions of Henry V's will. All those known are summarily described at different dates and in several different documents by title and by *secundo folio*, but without other description of contents, binding or value. The largest group consists of the 110 books taken by Henry V after the capture of Meaux on 10 May 1422. Many must have been written in France. Of the Meaux books, 77 were given in perpetuity to King's Hall, Cambridge, in 1440. The second largest group consists of 27 books which went to All Souls in 1440.[32] Three of the All Souls manuscripts and one of the King's Hall manuscripts are known to survive.[33] The All Souls group contained at least one text (in Latin) by an English fifteenth-century writer, Edmund Lacy, Bishop of Hereford in 1417–20, Bishop of Exeter in 1420–55; this work is otherwise unknown.[34] Lists of a few other small groups of Latin books can be found among the Exchequer records. These documents indicate that, between at least 1434 and 1442, learned books charged to the Treasurer were kept in the Receipt of the Exchequer at Westminster. A warrant of 18 May 1440, to the Treasurer and Chamberlains, discharges them for a book called 'Armachan sinons', in Latin, 'that was nowe late put into oure receyte at Westmoustier with oother bookes of ours to be kept'.[35] There is evidence, moreover, that even after the dispersal of substantial numbers of books to King's Hall in 1435 and 1440, and to All Souls in 1440, other books were still left in the Exchequer and were circulating among men closely associated with the royal household. On 21 January 1441, 4 books (including the *Compendium Morale* of Roger of Waltham, and a corpus of civil law), which had earlier been lent to William Alnwick, Bishop of Lincoln, formerly Keeper of the Privy Seal, were now given to him;[36] on 23 March 1442, 4 works of canon law were lent to Fulk Bermingham, who was a king's clerk by 1436. Of the books lent to Bermingham, a two-volume set of the 'Lectura hostiensis', the commentary on the decretals by the Bishop of Ostia, had previously been in the keeping of the King's Secretary, Thomas Beckington; the other 3 works had earlier been charged to the Treasurer. These were: *Innocentius* (perhaps the commentary of Innocent IV on the decretals);

32. For the Meaux books, Harriss 1972, with references; for the All Souls books, Nicolas 1834–7, v, 117–19; Weiss 1942; Ker 1971, pp. 1–2.
33. Harriss 1972, no. 9; Weiss 1942, p. 104, n. 1; Ker 1971, pp. 1–2, nos. 14, 19, 20.
34. For Lacy, *BRUO*, ii, pp. 1081–3; Weiss 1942, pp. 104, 105; Ker 1971, no. 12.
35. PRO E404/56/320.   36. PRO E404/57/163.

Durandus, *Speculum iudiciale*; Guido de Baysio, *Rosarium in Decretum*.[37] Most, if not all, of these seem to have been duplicates of books sent to Oxford and Cambridge. They were being given or lent out to a narrow circle, the King's Confessor, a king's clerk, and secretaries and clerks of the Signet Office. This was recognizably a library in our modern sense of a lending library. Books which are known to have been lent, returned, and lent again to the same borrower are 2 from the Meaux group: Hegesippus, *Historia de bello Judaico*, and *Liber de observantiis Papae*. William Toly borrowed them in July 1434 for return in October, brought them back in January 1435, and borrowed them again in February 1435, this time for a year and a half. Toly had been a Signet clerk, was secretary to Cardinal Beaufort by 1429, and King's Secretary by 1443.[38] Perhaps the dispersal of a considerable proportion of Henry VI's books to Oxford and Cambridge should be seen as yet another example of his dangerous tendency towards excessive open-handedness after the end of his minority, as well as evidence of his patronage of learning.

The documents so far discovered among the Exchequer records of the reign of Henry VI record a handful of other books inherited from Henry V; further research will no doubt bring a few more to light. For example, the same 5 books are listed repeatedly in the Great Wardrobe accounts, among the *remanencia* or goods in stock, from the accession of Henry VI in 1422 to at least 1445 and perhaps later. These are a Priscian; a Bede, *De gestibus Anglie*; the *Sermones dominicales in Evangelia*; a glossed psalter; and a Bible. These 5 turn out to be a residue of the books confiscated from Henry Scrope after 1415, left for reasons which are not clear in the charge of the Keeper of the king's Great Wardrobe.[39] Payments for bindings are another potentially fruitful source, although these are likely to apply to liturgical books rather than library books. To take an example from 1444–5, the time of Henry VI's marriage: a pair of liturgical books, a primer and a breviary, in use in the King's closet – that is, his altar for private devotions within the chamber – were covered in fantastically expensive crimson and gold pile on pile velvet, the 'tissues' or straps and clasps lined with red satin.[40] Henry must have had many books of hours

37. PRO E404/58/127; for Bermingham, see *BRUO*, I, pp. 176–7.
38. Palgrave 1836, II, 152–3; Harriss 1972, nos. 28, 90. For Toly, see Otway-Ruthven 1939, pp. 14, 139, 154, 184; Stratford 1993, p. 425.
39. PRO, E101/407/13, f. 4v, 1–2 Henry VI; E 101/409/12, fols. 47v, 51v, 105v, 22–23 Henry VI, and all surviving particular accounts between 1422 and 1445 listed in Wardrobe Books; Kingsford 1918–20 (p. 83 for the books).
40. PRO E101/409/12, f. 55; cf., e.g., the payments by Charles V to Dino Rapondi, 22 April 1378, for precious silks to bind books of the Louvre Library, Delisle 1907, I, pp. 371–2.

and breviaries but these must have been something on the scale of the Bedford Hours, given to Henry by Anne, Duchess of Bedford, with her husband's consent, at Christmas 1431.

In conclusion, brief reference must be made to the books of the King's uncles, John, Duke of Bedford, who died in 1435, and Humfrey, Duke of Gloucester, who died in 1447. A few books from the great Louvre Library, which Bedford had acquired as Regent of France, were no doubt saved from dispersal after Bedford's death, since they remain in the Royal and Cotton collections. Other ex-Louvre books, with the same fifteenth-century English provenance, may in the future be identified in English, European and other manuscript collections.[41] A large number of Duke Humfrey's many books had been given to Oxford in his lifetime; those learned volumes still in his possession at his death were diverted to King's College, Cambridge, by 1452. On the other hand, Henry seems to have kept a few of Duke Humfrey's books, choosing the French illuminated manuscripts for himself.[42] A handful of books made for Henry himself are known, for example the presentation copy of Lydgate's *Life of St Edmund and St Fremund*, which is now among the Harley manuscripts. It does not seem to have been at Richmond in 1535, but to have been moved to Westminster by 1542.[43]

Given the dispersals which took place during the majority of Henry VI and at his own volition, it is, perhaps, rather Henry IV and Henry V who should be thought of as bibliophiles and founders of the royal library. They acquired their books by inheritance, by gift, by conquest and by forfeiture, as well as by purchase. There is good evidence for books made in England for both kings, as well as for luxury books imported by or for them. On the other hand, the new evidence which has come to light so far may turn out to need correction. Nothing new has yet turned up to add directly to the existing picture of what the Lancastrian kings actually read, or to determine what proportion of their books were imported. It seems possible, however, to say with some confidence that there was a royal library in England before the reign of Edward IV.

41. For Bedford's books and the Louvre Library, see Stratford 1987; Stratford 1993, pp. 91–6, and *passim*.   42. See Sammut 1980; De la Mare and Gillam 1988.
43. BL, Harl. ms. 2278; Carley 1989a, p. 21. I am very grateful to James Carley for his help.

12

The Royal Library from Edward IV to Henry VII

JANET BACKHOUSE

Despite constantly accumulating evidence of the ownership of books and of arrangements for their storage and care during earlier reigns, King Edward IV remains clearly identifiable as the founder of the old Royal Library which was eventually to be presented to the nation by George II in 1757. During the last few years of his reign he acquired a substantial collection of impressive secular manuscripts, many of them irrevocably associated with him by the inclusion of his arms and badges as a feature of their original decoration. The evidence provided by the surviving manuscripts is supported by a number of contemporary documentary references which suggest that something in the nature of a planned acquisitions policy was being carried out in the King's name towards the end of his second period on the throne.[1]

The bulk of Edward's manuscripts are large-scale copies of well-known and widely distributed library texts, all in French but frequently translated from Latin originals. Historical narratives are strongly represented, with copies of the chronicles of Froissart and of Wavrin (the latter dedicated to the King), of William of Tyre's *History of the Crusades*, and of several works on classical history of the type attractive to the noble society of the day.[2] The *Bible historiale* of Guyart de Moulins rubs shoulders with standard works of St Augustine, of Gregory the Great and of Vincent de Beauvais. Boccaccio contributes the *Decameron* as well as the more widely popular *Cas des nobles hommes et femmes malheureux*. Other late medieval writers include Christine de Pisan, Alain Chartier and Jean de Courcy. The manuscripts themselves, written and illuminated in the professional workshops of the Burgundian Netherlands, are extremely large and heavy and must have been designed to be read aloud from a lectern. Their lively and colourful decoration, designed to be an eye-

1. For a more detailed account, including a list of manuscripts, see Backhouse 1987.
2. McKendrick 1990, 1994.

catching and luxurious contribution to the rich room settings in which they would have been used, includes not far short of 600 individual miniatures. The best of these are excellent examples of the standard commercial workmanship of the day, the worst are clearly attributable to studio assistants. The quality of the miniatures in Edward's books has often been compared unfavourably with that to be seen in similar books from other major libraries of the time, notably that of the Dukes of Burgundy. It should however be borne in mind that the English king was entering the market comparatively late in the day, when major book painters who had worked on manuscripts commissioned for Duke Philip the Good (d. 1467) had already come to the end of their careers. The new generation of illuminators who appear with hindsight to be the leading figures of the 1470s and later are in fact more noted for their liturgical than for their secular books. A notable exception to this trend is Simon Marmion.[3] Furthermore, Edward was ordering from abroad through intermediaries and was not in the position of a patron such as his sister, Margaret, while she was Duchess of Burgundy, who would have had access to the artists of her personal choice.

It has long been held that the impetus behind Edward's book collecting came from his experiences in exile in Bruges in the winter of 1470-1, when he and his companions were the guests of Louis de Gruthuyse, one of the most famous bibliophiles of the late fifteenth century.[4] The Gruthuyse library which he then saw was, however, still some twenty years short of its zenith and many of its grandest manuscripts, including the major vernacular texts, had yet to be acquired. One of Gruthuyse's manuscripts did certainly come into Edward's hands. The Josephus now in the Soane Museum in London bears the English royal arms over the badges of Louis de Gruthuyse but the circumstances under which the volume changed hands are unrecorded. It is, however, clear that Edward's main book-collecting period did not begin until some eight years after his sojourn in Bruges. He must also have had some knowledge, albeit at second hand and perhaps through Duchess Margaret, of the superb library of the Burgundian dukes.

No inventory of Edward's books exists so there is no means of knowing what proportion of his library has survived. Fourteen volumes in the present-day Royal collection in the British Library bear his arms and badges together with those of one or both of his sons – Edward,

3. Avril and Reynaud 1993, pp. 80–9.   4. Martens 1992.

Prince of Wales (born 1470), and Richard, Duke of York (born 1473) – and several more display the royal arms accompanied by badges and devices indicating a Yorkist connection. Others of appropriate date contain the royal arms alone or have unfilled spaces into which arms should have been inserted. Of twenty volumes which were unquestionably made for Edward, five are dated 1479 and another 1480 (see fig. 12.1). This fits in exactly with a documentary reference, dated April 1479, which records the payment of £80 to 'Philip Maisertuell merchant stranger in partie of paiement of £240 for certaine bokes by the said Philip to be provided to the kyngs use in the parties beyond the see'. It has recently been suggested that 'Maisertuell' might have been the well-known illuminator, Phillippe de Mazerolles, who is known to have been a merchant for at least some part of his career.[5] The sum of money involved is substantial but is not inconsistent with the sums which Edward was spending at much the same time on other domestic equipment such as tapestries, and on building works which included the refurbishment of Eltham Palace.

A second documentary source for the library is the Great Wardrobe account for 1480, in which payments totalling more than £10 occur in respect of materials and labour involved in the complete binding of six books and the embellishment of two more.[6] The finished volumes would outwardly have made a brave show, with covers of crimson velvet and gilded clasps adorned with arms and devices. There are also payments for pinewood chests to contain them and for their carriage from the Wardrobe to Eltham Palace. This has given rise to the notion that Edward carried his books around with him from palace to palace and they do indeed seem to have been classed with the subsidiary furnishings, such as hangings and cushions, which were made available from the Wardrobe to adorn any residence about to be brought into use. It is, however, not unlikely that Eltham, where building work was approaching completion,[7] was the long-term destination of the manuscripts imported from the Low Countries.

Evidence of Edward's involvement with books other than this great series of Flemish tomes is not extensive. No liturgical manuscripts have been identified as his, though he must have had devotional books for both public and private use. One or two undistinguished reference books – medical treatises, legal formulae and a Latin copy of the *Secreta*

5. McKendrick 1992, pp. 153, 159 n. 91.   6. Nicolas 1830, pp. 125, 152, 237–8.
7. Brown and Colvin 1963, II, pp. 936–7.

secretorum – were owned by him personally before his accession to the throne in 1461.[8] A number of authors, including Hardyng, Capgrave, Carmeliano and Caxton, at various times dedicated works to him, in several instances in printed form. One of the grand Flemish manuscripts, the first volume of Wavrin's *Croniques dangleterre*,[9] is in fact a dedication volume, complete with presentation miniature and, although its decoration incorporates the arms and badges appropriate to Edward, the style is distinctly different from that of his other volumes of this type. Also worthy of special note is the manuscript copy of *Dicts and Sayings of the Philosophers*, translated by the Queen's brother, Anthony Wydeville, Earl Rivers, and published by Caxton in 1477. The manuscript,[10] reproducing Caxton's text, is dated 24 December 1477 and embellished with a presentation miniature which shows Rivers and a kneeling figure, perhaps his scribe, offering the book to Edward, who is accompanied by his wife and his heir, all in full royal robes. The existence of this volume implies that a printed book might not yet have been regarded as sufficiently distinguished for a formal gift of this kind.

Several members of Edward IV's immediate family are known to have owned books. His mother, Cecily, Duchess of York, his wife, Elizabeth Wydeville, and two of his daughters can all be identified as owners of specific volumes. It has also been suggested that Edward's Flemish purchases were made with the education of his two young sons in mind. Attention has been drawn to a passage in the instructions for the upbringing of the Prince of Wales where it is laid down that 'such noble stories as behooveth a prince to understand and know' should be read aloud to him at dinner. The contents of many of the manuscripts accord very well with this definition. However, when Edward embarked upon his main purchasing campaign, his elder son was well into his ninth year and had had his own household, based in Ludlow, since he was three. The second prince, Richard, three years younger and still at court, had been married for more than a year to the Norfolk heiress, Anne Mowbray. Edward's decision to include their arms alongside his own in the decoration of his manuscripts may merely have been intended to convey a sense of the solid position apparently achieved by the royal house of York and its optimistic prospects for the future.

Edward IV's elder son succeeded him as Edward V in April 1483. He reigned for only eleven weeks and thus made no direct impact on the

8. BL, Royal ms. 12. E.xv; Harl. ms. 3352.   9. Royal ms 15. E.IV.
10. Lambeth, ms. 265. For dating the edition (*STC* 6826), see L. Hellinga 1982, pp. 77–80.

development of the Royal Library. He was however credited with considerable learning and was, as we have seen, already associated with his
father's acquisitions through the inclusion of his arms in their decoration. At least two manuscripts and a printed edition can be linked to him
personally. Carmeliano had offered a Latin poem to him in 1482[11] and a
very elegant Flemish copy of the *Testament of Mohamet II*, inscribed with
the names of his sisters, Elizabeth and Cecily, bears his arms with the
ostrich-feather badge.[12] Caxton's translation of the *History of Jason*, a
legend central to the foundation of the Burgundian Order of the Golden
Fleece of which Edward IV was a member, was dedicated to him as Prince
of Wales on its initial publication in 1477 'to the end that he may begin to
read in English' (fig. 3.3).[13] Caxton's true target was however the King
himself, 'our said most redoubted liege lord which hath taken the said
Order', though he could 'doubt not his good grace hath it in French
which he well understandeth'.

The reign of Richard III was also too brief to allow him to make any
solid contribution to the development of the Royal Library, though he
was certainly a lover of books.[14] A dozen assorted volumes have been
identified as his property and have been subjected to an unusually intense
scrutiny for any clues which they may offer to his personal philosophies.
Only one of these books can be shown to have been made for him while
he was King. This is a Latin Vegetius, *De re militari*, containing his
crowned arms and the arms of his wife, Anne Neville.[15] The remainder –
which include historical materials in Latin and in French, a Wycliffite
New Testament, English romances and Mechtild of Hackeborn's *Booke of
Gostlye Grace*, a devotional treatise much favoured by his mother, Cecily
of York – are mainly modest utilitarian copies, often second-hand when
he acquired them. Even his own Book of Hours, which includes a long
and very personal added devotion, was not made especially for him but
dates back to the early years of the fifteenth century.[16] Richard's books
may in fact be regarded as the contents of a private bookshelf, in contrast
to his brother's formal collection of very grand manuscripts appropriate
to the furnishings of the public rooms in which they would have been
used and displayed.

The next major contributor to the English Royal Library was the first

11. BL, Royal ms. 12. A.xxix.   12. De Ricci 1937, vol. II, p. 2295.
13. *STC* 15383. On the dedication, see L. Hellinga 1982, pp. 95–8.
14. Sutton and Visser-Fuchs 1997.   15. BL, Royal ms. 18. A.xii.
16. Sutton and Visser-Fuchs 1990.

Tudor sovereign, Henry VII.[17] He was the first to appoint a named librarian, Quentin Poulet of Lille, who entered his service in 1492 and remained in the post well into the sixteenth century, at least until 1506. Poulet was a Fleming and he was also personally a craftsman. His apprenticeship as a pupil illuminator is recorded in Bruges in 1472-3 and he received several special payments from the King for his work as a scribe (see figs. 12.2 and 12.3). A beautiful copy of the *Imaginacion de la vraie noblesse*[18] was made by him for Henry in 1496 and is signed and dated at Sheen, afterwards Richmond, where he was apparently based.

In assessing Henry VII's contribution to the library, it must be remembered that he inherited Edward IV's collection of standard luxury library books along with the other furnishings and appurtenances of the royal palaces. His own acquisitions in this particular area were slight and seem to have been the result of gifts rather than purchases. Several of the many itinerant Italian scholars travelling in Europe in search of patronage offered him copies of their works during periods in England. Some of them produced manuscripts in the Italian style, others employed native craftsmen to prepare and decorate copies. A particularly grand gift was offered during the last year of the reign by the French ambassador, Claude de Seyssel, who presented a richly illuminated copy of a translation of a work by Xenophon from a Greek manuscript in the French royal library at Blois.[19] The original dedicatee of the translation had been Louis XII of France. Stylistically, this volume is closely similar to the one class of book that Henry does seem to have collected with what was apparently a consistent personal enthusiasm over a long period: the illuminated versions of the most popular library books printed in the Parisian workshops of Antoine Vérard. There are many references specifically to printed books among entries relating to the library in the royal accounts of the reign.[20] Much of the expenditure is relatively modest but purchases from Vérard are specifically mentioned and a substantial number of items issued from his press do survive among the Royal Library books in today's British Library. The best of these books, often embellished with dedication miniatures and printed on vellum, were never a poor man's substitute for illuminated manuscripts but major acquisitions in their own right (see fig. 12.4). Henry's taste for them reflects not so much a parsimonious approach to the purchase of books, nor even a deliberate

17. Backhouse 1995.   18. BL, Royal ms. 19. C.viii.
19. BL, Royal ms. 19 C.vi; Dionisotti 1995.
20. Plomer 1913; for Vérard, Winn 1997, pp. 138-53.

choice of the printed text in preference to that written out by hand, but rather a leaning towards current French fashion, in contrast to the taste for Flemish work shown by Edward IV. This was probably the natural outcome of the years which he had spent in exile in Brittany and in France during the 1470s and 1480s.

A number of manuscripts of earlier dates were apparently annexed by Henry and adapted by the addition of his arms or devices. He was also the owner of several richly decorated liturgical books. Though the very grand Book of Hours by Jean Bourdichon that traditionally bears his name[21] is perhaps more likely to have been the property of his son and successor, Henry VIII, he certainly received as a gift the splendid early fifteenth-century French Hours that had once belonged to René of Anjou, father-in-law of Henry VI.[22] Three further books of hours of French workmanship have been associated with him. A number of richly illuminated personal prayer books are also associated with the ladies of his family, and several of these were apparently heirlooms, though his mother, Lady Margaret Beaufort, owned at least one very grand contemporary Hours from a leading Parisian workshop.

Lady Margaret, celebrated for her piety and for her patronage of scholarship, not only owned a number of manuscripts, some of which are mentioned in her will, but also was a noteworthy patron of early printing in England. Caxton, Wynkyn de Worde and Richard Pynson all issued editions in her name or at her command, usually of devotional material and including continental works of which she was herself, on occasion, the translator.[23]

When Claude de Seyssel prefaced his eye-catching illuminated translation of Xenophon with suitably flattering remarks about the splendours of Henry VII's royal library, he must certainly have been exaggerating in the interest of attracting the favour of the English king. It is impossible to believe that it measured up to the undoubted magnificence of Louis XII's collection of illuminated books at Blois. Nonetheless, the assemblage of manuscripts and printed books brought together by Edward IV and Henry VII, as a feature of the trappings of the royal household rather than as a simple collection of books of personal choice, laid a firm foundation for the development of the Royal Library by their successors.

21. Backhouse 1973.   22. BL, Egerton ms. 1070.   23. Underwood 1987; Powell 1998.

13

The Royal Library under Henry VIII

JAMES P. CARLEY

At one time or another, Henry VIII owned more than fifty palaces, each presumably with its own collection of books. Books seem to have been moved from one library to another and it is not possible to divide the various collections rigidly by function. In the first decades of the sixteenth century, however, as earlier, the main collection was housed at Richmond, which had been rebuilt after Sheen was destroyed by fire in 1497. During the reign of Henry VII, Quentin Poulet had been granted an annual salary of 10 marks for keeping the King's Library, though Poulet would have been employed principally as scribe and illuminator (see figs. 12.2 and 12.3). In the first year of Henry VIII's reign, Giles Duwes was described as Keeper of the King's Library at Richmond, with an annuity of £10, and, in 1534, William Tyldesley was designated Keeper of the King's library 'in the manor of Richmond and elsewhere', also at £10 per year.[1] In February 1535, a French visitor, possibly Palamède Gontier, Treasurer of Brittany, drew up a list of 143 titles in the library at Richmond, almost all of which were in French, and many of which were large and elegant manuscripts of Burgundian-Netherlandish taste, prepared for Edward IV.[2] This list, which seems to cover the whole contents of the library, suggests that the Richmond collection was a personal one built up by successive monarchs, rather than an institutional repository. This is unlike the situation in France where 'from the sixteenth century onwards the *Bibliothèque du Roi* was always really a *Bibliothèque Nationale*, i.e. a fully-fledged organ of the state, claiming copyright deposit, with a powerful *maître* at its head, and pursuing from the outset an aggressive acquisitions policy for manuscripts and foreign printed books'.[3]

The most significant development in the history of the royal collection

1. *LP Henry VIII*, 1, 513; 7, 419.11.
2. Omont 1891. On Edward IV's books, see Backhouse 1987, and above, pp. 268–70.
3. Birrell 1987a, pp. 3–4.

during the sixteenth century was a direct consequence of the Dissolution of the Monasteries in the 1530s. When Henry VIII and his advisers started gathering together materials relating to the royal divorce, it was logical for them to turn to the monastic libraries, in the same manner as Henry's predecessors, most notably Edward I, had done in other circumstances. During the same period, John Leland, who was about to become Henry's chief agent in reconnoitring monastic collections, returned to England in about 1529. He had studied in Paris as King's Scholar and had there made the acquaintance of some of the great continental humanist scholar librarians, whose practices he hoped to emulate in England. By 1533, Leland received some sort of commission to examine monastic and collegial libraries, and he began a series of annual trips during which he compiled lists of what he considered to be the significant books at the various libraries he visited. In 1536, Leland wrote to Thomas Cromwell asking that his commission be extended, and it was probably at this point that he set about rescuing manuscripts in a concerted manner. He continued to gather manuscripts after the fall of the monasteries too:

> And where as Master Leylande at this prasente tyme cummith to Byri to see what bookes be lefte yn the library there, or translatid thens ynto any other corner of the late monastery, I shaul desier yow upon just consideration right redily to forder his cause, and to permitte hym to have the use of such as may forder hym yn setting forth such matiers as he writith for the King's Majeste.[4]

By the time he composed his New Year's Gift for Henry VIII in 1545 – the last work he completed before insanity overtook him in 1547 – Leland could look back with satisfaction at his endeavours and reflect that: 'I haue conserued many good authors, the whych otherwyse had ben lyke to haue peryshed, to no small incommodyte of good letters. Of the which parte remayne in the most magnificent libraryes of your royall palaces. Part also remayne in my custodie.'[5] Apart from its value as a testimony to Leland's assiduity as a preserver of manuscripts, this statement makes clear that there was more than one destination for the rescued materials. In fact, Leland's unpublished *Antiphilarchia* (written in the late 1530s), the presentation copy of which survives in Cambridge University Library,[6] lists three royal libraries established for this purpose – at Westminster (later renamed Whitehall), Hampton Court and Greenwich.

4. Undated letter; quoted in Toulmin Smith 1906–10, II, p. 148. The monastery at Bury St Edmunds was dissolved on 4 November 1539.   5. Leland 1549, f. C2r.
6. CUL, ms. Ee.v.14.

13.2 A press-mark of the Royal Library at Westminster *c.* 1548.

An inventory dated 23 April 1542 survives from Westminster, and this includes a list of 910 books contained in the Upper Library (for a press-mark corresponding to this inventory and its slightly later additions see fig. 13.2).[7] The list is divided into two sections: the first 573 items are headed 'Index librorum qui habentur in supradicta bibliotheca'; the remainder, 'Adhuc Index librorum qui habentur in prenominata biblio-theca, quorum quidam inculti, quidam ex antiqua impressione'. These two sections are arranged in independent alphabetical sequences. In both cases there is a mixture of manuscripts and printed books, but the former predominate in the second sequence.[8] The printed books include human-ist editions of works by the Fathers; many polemical texts relating to con-temporary theological issues; Froben editions, the prologue sometimes adapted for the English king; books printed by Thomas Berthelet; and elegant books on vellum provided by Antoine Vérard and others.[9] Vérard books, for the most part acquired by Henry VII or his buyers, were also found in other palace libraries and a number were at Richmond in 1535. As might be expected, among both the printed books and the manuscripts, there are a number of New Year's gifts to Henry and his predecessors, works by Bernard André presented to Henry VIII, theological tracts by Wouter Deleen, books by Claude de Seyssel, and verses by Leland and Nicholas Udall in celebration of the coronation of Anne Boleyn. As a result of sequestration, Wolsey's books came into the royal collection, and so did some of those of Thomas Cromwell a decade later. Books owned by Anne Boleyn and her brother, George Boleyn, Viscount Rochford, also turn up. There is a slight Spanish flavour, a result of Catherine of Aragon's influence: a copy of *De libero arbitrio aduersus Melanchthonem* dedicated to Catherine by her Spanish confessor, Alonso de Villa Sancta; translations of Erasmus into Spanish; and works by Juan Luis Vives.

Among the medieval manuscripts which can still be identified, a large

7. PRO, Augmentation Office, Misc. Books 160 [E 315/160], fols. 107v–120r.
8. The books themselves had an inventory number entered in the upper right corner of the first or second folio recto. Those beginning with 'a' in the first alphabetical sequence were numbered 1–41, those in the second, 42–85. The books beginning with 'b' in the first sequence started at 86, and the numeration continued in the same manner up to 910.
9. Winn 1997, pp. 138–53; Carley 1997b.

percentage represent recent arrivals from the monasteries. The chief source is Rochester, which can be linked with almost 100 of the identifiable survivors. St Albans supplied a large number of manuscripts, at least 11 of which carry a 'TC' monogram in a contemporary script, which occurs in several manuscripts from other locations as well. It is impossible, nevertheless, to determine the medieval provenance for many of the manuscripts and this can lead to distorted statistics. Lincolnshire, for example, appears to be a more important source than it really was because the royal agents gathering manuscripts from Lincolnshire in the late 1520s tended to enter in the manuscripts the name of the house from which they derived.

There seem to be different phases of acquisition from the monasteries. In the late 1520s, materials were being gathered to buttress the case for the King's divorce. By the early 1530s, texts relating to the powers of the pope and medieval councils, as well as some historical items, began to trickle in. Soon, however, this small stream turned into a veritable torrent as it became clear that the monasteries were going to fall. At this point, the collecting activity changed its focus and became more general: Leland and his compeers began to search out ancient and unusual texts simply to preserve them from destruction. They also turned their attention to materials by medieval British authors, as part of a scheme to glorify the British past and to produce a comprehensive record 'de viris illustribus' for their nation.

When Bartholomew Traheron was appointed Royal Librarian on 14 December 1549, and granted an annuity of 20 marks, he was specifically empowered to bring books from other royal libraries to Westminster, ostensibly because the King had 'determined to stock his library of Westminster with notable books'.[10] This process of consolidation, begun even before Traheron's appointment, explains why some 'Henrician' books surviving in the Old Royal Library and elsewhere have the remnants of two further alphabetical sequences carrying up to 1,450 and probably higher. Monastic books falling within the range 911–1450 in these sequences – some of which form matched sets with items in the lower sequences – must have been part of the collection amassed by Leland and others at Hampton Court and Greenwich and only subsequently brought to Westminster to be inventoried and amalgamated with books in the main library. Not all books left the other palaces after

10. *CPR Edward VI 1549–1551*, pp. 74–5.

Henry's death, however, and, in his description of a visit to Hampton
Court in 1602, Philip Julius, Duke of Stettin-Pomerania, referred to the
library: 'Here also was King Henricus octavus' library, where was a very
large Bible and some beautiful glasses, also the king's walking-staff, made
of [the horn of] a unicorn.' At Richmond, the Duke observed that:

> There were here manuscripta highly valued by Henricus octavus;
> among them were many curious things, amongst others a large Bible
> on parchment, its letters and margin being very neatly and splendidly
> painted with a pen; the genealogia of the kings of England, traced to
> our ancestors Adam and Eve; a round mirror in which the king was said
> to see everything, and it was almost believed he had a spiritum familia-
> rem sitting in it, for the mirror broke to pieces the moment after the
> king's death.[11]

Unlike the situation at Westminster, no inventory appears to have been
drawn up for either Hampton Court or Greenwich, and the post-mortem
inventory of Henry's palaces in 1547 is frustratingly imprecise.[12] For the
library at Hampton Court, the only reference is to 'a greate nombre of
bookes'.[13] Concerning the books found in the 'highest' library at
Greenwich there is a fuller description, although little precise information:

> First in one deske xxxi bookes couered with redde. / Item in an other
> deske xvi bookes couered with redde. / Item an other deske liii bookes
> couered with leather. / Item an other deske xii bookes. / Item an other
> deske xxv bookes. / Item an other deske xxx bookes. / Item an other
> deske xxxvii bookes. / Item under the table cvii bookes. / Item a booke
> wrytten in parchement of the processe betwene King Henry theight
> and the ladye Katheryne dowager. / Item the newe Testament glosed
> written unbounde. / Item undre the table xvi bookes. / Item in the
> iakeshouse a picture and certeyne cases. / Item in a long settell is cer-
> teyne olde papers and trasshe. / Item in a lyke settell is like olde
> papers.[14]

One of the eventual recipients of books from Hampton Court and
Greenwich was Sir Thomas Pope (?1507–59), who in 1546 had been made
fourth officer of the Court of Augmentations. Pope, who founded Trinity
College, Oxford, in 1555, made a bequest of ninety-nine volumes, including twenty-six manuscripts, to his new foundation. Among the printed

11. Von Bülow 1892, pp. 55–7. I owe this reference to Dr C. G. C. Tite.
12. BL, Harl. ms. 1419, and Society of Antiquaries, ms. 129; printed Starkey 1998.
13. BL, Harl. ms. 1419A, f. 245.   14. BL, Harl. ms. 1419A, f. 62v.

books, fifteen bear an erased inscription 'ex hampton court' and twenty-six are 'ex grenewych'. A presumed twenty-seventh book associated with Greenwich is an edition of Joannes Piscator, *Epitome omnium operum Augustini*.[15] It is cropped at the place on the title-page where the inscription would have occurred. Pope also gave a copy of Erasmus's edition of Jerome's *Opera* to Arthur Yeldard, who succeeded him as President of Trinity College.[16] It appears to have come from Greenwich but, because of mending, fragments only of the inscription are now visible. The printed books from Greenwich and Hampton Court consist almost entirely of theological works of the type found in many libraries of the period: there is a standard mix of up-to-date humanist editions of the Fathers, side by side with modern printings of older scholastic texts. A few works by contemporary theologians and philosophers appear and some historians of the ancient world. Three of the books are bound in white buckskin with gold tooling by the so-called Greenwich Binder. Another book, one of three in Greek given by Pope, and bound in brown calf is the work of the craftsman known as the 'King Edward and Queen Mary Binder'.[17]

Even though none of the twenty-six manuscripts given by Pope carry the 'ex hampton court' or 'ex grenewych' inscription, at least nine are from religious houses. Eight of the manuscripts contain a brief description in the top margin of the first folio in a sixteenth-century hand very similar to that of the main 'cataloguer' of the Westminster collection.[18] Many surviving books known to have been in Westminster Palace have a distinctive label under horn (with a brief title in the characteristic hand) attached by nails to the front cover: in four of the Trinity manuscripts, all rebound, this label can be found inserted at the bottom of the first folio.[19] Others of the manuscripts would almost certainly have had the label, but these four were the only ones where it was preserved at the time of rebinding. Apart from its occurrence in Henrician books now in Oxford and in the modern Royal Library, the same label is found in three books subsequently owned by Archbishop Matthew Parker: Ralph of Flaix on Leviticus; *Libellus de contrarietatibus sacre scripture* and other works; and another copy of Ralph of Flaix on Leviticus.[20] The same annotating hand

15. Cologne, 1539; Oxford, Trinity Coll., H.7.11.
16. Basel, 1524–6. Now University of Sussex, Travers College, 158.
17. Nixon 1978, p. 32; 1964, pp. 295–8; also Gameson and Coates 1988, pp. 50–1; Starkey 1991, pp. 158–9; Coates 1991, p. 476, n. 21, and the references cited therein; cf. Foot above, pp. 113, 122, 127.
18. Oxford, Trinity Coll., mss. 25, 26, 31, 50, 55, 58, 66, 70.   19. Mss. 50, 55, 66, 70.
20. Cambridge, Corpus Christi Coll., mss. 87 and 217; Cambridge, Trinity Coll., ms. B.iv.24.

and label also occur in a copy of Durandus's *Repertorium iuris* and other works.[21]

Six manuscripts were removed by Henry's agents from the collegiate church of the Holy Trinity at Tattershall in Lincolnshire in the late 1520s and three travelled to Westminster.[22] Two were brought into the Westminster collection from Hampton Court or Greenwich shortly after Henry's death.[23] The sixth manuscript, described as 'Distinctiones Willelmi de Montibus Lincolniensis cancellarii' in the Lincolnshire list,[24] survives in Oxford, but does not have any Westminster inventory number.[25] This is one of a group of eleven Henrician manuscripts (ten of which were bound in black or red velvet binding with brass clasps and fittings) given to Bodley by Charles Howard, Earl of Nottingham, in 1604. The same black velvet binding occurs on two Reading books that were removed to the Royal Library.[26] Nottingham's bequest included Zacharias of Besançon's *De concordantia evangelistarum*;[27] Bede's Commentary on Luke, bound in black velvet;[28] Ralph of Flaix's commentary on Leviticus;[29] Job, the General Epistles, and the Apocalypse with the *Glossa ordinaria*, bound in red velvet;[30] Peter Lombard's commentary on the Psalter;[31] William de Montibus's *Distinctiones*;[32] ps-Odo of Morimond on Genesis, Exodus and Leviticus;[33] the text of the Psalms with the commentary of Alexander Nequam;[34] Hugo Ripelinus's *Compendium veritatis theologicae* and various other theological texts;[35] saints' lives, bound by King Henry's Binder;[36] and the Psalms with the *Glossa ordinaria*.[37] Two of these have the 'TC' monogram, which may possibly be associated with Thomas Wolsey.[38] Seven also have the characteristic label under horn.[39] One has a poem in Leland's hand on the flyleaf.[40] The manuscripts come from a variety of locations. Some are important, including an early ninth-century book from Tours, which got to England by the first part of the eleventh century at the latest.[41] It was presumably rescued by Leland at the time of the Dissolution. Although some of the manuscripts duplicate materials in the Westminster list, this is not a

21. Lambeth, ms. 49.
22. BL, Royal mss. 8.G.vi [no. 217]; 11.A.xiii [no. 277]; 12.E.xxv [no. 730].
23. BL, Royal mss. 11.B.vi [no. 1018]; 8.G.ii [no. 1058].
24. BL, Royal ms., Appendix 69.   25. Bodleian, ms. Bodley 419.
26. Oxford, Queen's Coll., mss. 317 and 323; Liddell 1935, p. 51.
27. Bodleian, ms. Bodl. 209.   28. Ms. Bodl. 218.   29. Ms. Bodl. 245.
30. Ms. Auct. D.1.15.   31. Ms. Bodl. 411.   32. Ms. Bodl. 419.   33. Ms. Bodl. 331.
34. Ms. Bodl. 284.   35. Ms. Bodl. 458.   36. Ms. Bodl. 354; Nixon 1964, pp. 289–90.
37. Ms. Bodl. 862.   38. Mss. Bodl. 245, 458.
39. Mss. Bodl. 218, 245, 331, 411, 419, 458; Auct. D.1.15.   40. Ms. Bodl. 354.
41. Ms Bodl. 218.

characteristic feature and the Nottingham 'hoard' establishes that there cannot have been any coherent programme dictating what was to be kept in the royal library after Henry's death and what let go.

Nottingham also gave printed books to Bodley, a number of which have bindings by King Henry's Binder.[42] The label under horn also turns up in some of the printed books. The books include standard humanist editions of the works of the Fathers – Ambrose, Chrysostom, Gregory and Jerome – and are similar to texts obtained by Pope and others. Nottingham almost certainly inherited the Henrician books, printed and manuscript, from his father, William Howard, who, in turn, probably acquired them from Thomas Copley.[43]

N. R. Ker and C. E. Wright, two of the greatest modern experts on the dispersal of medieval libraries, have maintained that, in spite of his grandiose assertions, Leland did not really manage to make much of an impact at the time of the Dissolution. The evidence, if we include the Pope and Nottingham books and possibly others, can be interpreted in a different way, to suggest that the problem was one of post-Henrician dispersal rather than of lack of initial retrieval. A strong argument could be made that a significant number of those manuscripts which turn up in the libraries of later sixteenth- and seventeenth-century collectors such as Bale, Ussher, Cotton, Bancroft and Bodley, but whose slightly earlier provenance cannot be traced, may well have come first from the monasteries to the royal collection, only to be subsequently de-accessioned. Take, for example, the late ninth-century copy of the Acts of the Council of Constantinople, given by King Athelstan to Bath Abbey and rescued by Leland expressly for Henry's collection.[44] There are also manuscripts which Bale saw 'in bibliotheca regis', as his *Index Britanniae scriptorum* testifies, which are no longer in the Royal Library. What Henry's libraries provided, it seems, was a safe haven for a large number of monastic books during that brief period when their very existence was threatened, before a new generation of collectors and antiquaries emerged. John Bale's *cri de coeur* – 'to destroye all without consydcracyon, is and wyll be unto Englande for euer, a most horryble infamy' – may send shivers down one's spine, but without Westminster Palace, Hampton Court and Greenwich Palace the damage would have been considerably worse.

42. Hobson 1929, p. 66.   43. Carley 1997b.   44. BL, Cotton ms. Claudius B.v.

READING
AND
USE OF BOOKS

I

BOOKS FOR SCHOLARS

14

The humanist book

J. B. TRAPP

Introduction

The *(h)umanista* of the fifteenth-century Italian universities, where the name was coined, was a teacher of the *studia humanitatis*, who based his course of instruction on the grammar and rhetoric, the poetry and history, and the ethical writings of classical Antiquity. He characterized the education he offered as 'liberal', worthy of a free man, as opposed to the narrowly professional and personally deforming current university disciplines of medicine, law and theology.

The activities typical of the humanist in this strict sense were the editing and exposition of Latin and Greek texts, and the translation of Greek into Latin, with the aim of recovering and reviving ancient knowledge and ancient eloquence, ancient purity of diction and ancient techniques of argument. This involved him (female humanists of this kind were all but non-existent, or at least have left no legacy) in the search for texts of classical authors unknown or neglected in the Middle Ages, or for fuller and better texts of such authors than had been used by his medieval predecessors. Such Latin texts, or Greek texts newly translated into Latin, he transcribed and disseminated in a reformed, legible, upright script which he believed he was modelling on ancient Roman handwriting. The basis for the 'roman' type of the early Italian printers, it was in fact imitating twelfth-century letter forms.[1] The sloped, 'italic' letter, developed about the same time, entered printing a quarter-century later than the 'roman', being first used by Aldus Manutius for classical texts in 1501. The prevalence of both sets of letter-form, still today, in every sort of medium, is part of the western world's debt to Italy. The humanist

I owe thanks to Jonathan Woolfson for corrections and additions.

1. Ullman 1960; De la Mare 1973, 1977.

might apply his skills to teaching in university or school, to acting as tutor in a noble household, to serving as ambassador, secretary or member of the chancery of a prince of church or state – or indeed to all of these. His preoccupations were not known by the collective name of 'humanism' until the nineteenth century.

There is, as yet, no fully satisfactory account of humanists in England for the period covered by this volume, despite the pioneering labours of Roberto Weiss and Walter F. Schirmer.[2] The mass of detailed information about patrons, practitioners, scribes, illuminators, printers, booksellers, collections and libraries provided in their wake by A. C. de la Mare, R. W. Hunt, R. A. B. (Sir Roger) Mynors and N. R. Ker in particular for the earlier fifteenth century, and thrown up by P. S. Allen and others for the age of Erasmus, Colet, More and the later years of Henry VIII, as well as for the reigns of Edward VI and Mary, has yet to be digested into a coherent account. The special case of Scotland has been well served by John Durkan and Anthony Ross, in particular.[3]

Applied humanism, the use of classical material to enrich literature, art, thought and activity, flourished throughout our period, often through intermediaries such as France or the Burgundian Netherlands. In England during the fourteenth century, moreover, there already existed a kind of study often now called pre-humanist, many of its practitioners friars. Later, the Augustinian Osbern Bokenham was almost certainly responsible for the little manuscript of Claudian's *Consulship of Stilicho*, with facing English translation, made for Richard, Duke of York, in 1445.[4] Native Britons who can be called humanists in the Italian sense, however, are few enough during our whole period and fewer still in the first half of the fifteenth century.[5] Well before the mid fifteenth century, Italian humanist secretaries, book-hunters and teachers had made their presence felt in England, and Englishmen had begun to feel the touch of humanistic aspirations. Some – magnates, patrons and their clients – travelled to Italy to be instructed in *studia humanitatis*. Humanist manu-

2. Weiss 1967; Schirmer 1963; a useful up-to-date sketch in Carroll 1996; comprehensive listings of mss. and editions in R. Sharpe 1997.
3. Durkan 1953, 1959; Durkan and Ross 1961; Hillyard 1994; and see the list of Durkan's writings in MacDonald, Lynch and Cowan 1994, pp. 417–28, under 1963, 1977, 1978, 1980, 1981, 1982, 1985, especially.
4. Smalley 1960; see also Mynors 1957, and Bell above, pp. 245–6; Bokenham's ms. is now BL, Add. ms. 11814; see Sutton and Visser-Fuchs 1997, pp. 24–6.
5. In what follows I use 'Britain' and its derivatives to signify England, Scotland and Wales, using the names of the single countries where necessary to differentiate practice and conditions in them.

scripts began to be acquired by Englishmen, and to pass from hand to hand or from generation to generation by sale, gift or bequest.[6] In December 1464, John Shirwood, later Bishop of Durham (d.1494) bought in London a manuscript written in Florence a decade earlier;[7] while on 13 December 1491, the Italian Pietro Carmeliano acquired, also in London, a manuscript of Juvenal written in Padua.[8] Shortly after the mid-century, English professional scribes had learned to write competently and even elegantly, the new upright Italian humanist hand; by the century's end, an educated Englishman or Englishwoman would normally use humanist script to write Latin (or Italian), while retaining the gothic, 'secretary' style for English (fig. 14.1). By about the same time, Englishmen who could be called professional humanists had made their appearance.

At the accession of Henry VII in 1485, humanist studies had made much progress and continued to do so. In their more rapid development from about 1500 onwards, the example and the prompting of Desiderius Erasmus (1466–1536) was highly important. Medieval modes of thought and expression retained a strong hold even under the new King Henry VIII and his successors, however, as they did still more in Scotland under James V. In the inventories of rather more than 100 Oxford private libraries dating from 1507 to 1554 there is only a sprinkling of classical texts, including – as far as can be judged – few of those rediscovered at the Renaissance. Some 50 humanist works, including half-a-dozen in Greek, are listed. Almost 20 are by Erasmus, and there are 5 Lorenzo Vallas, with an occasional Francesco Filelfo, Jacques Lefèvre d'Etaples, Rudolphus Agricola and Melanchthon, and a large proportion of grammars and dictionaries, both Greek and Latin. Only in the inventories of the 1540s and 1550s do the humanists begin to predominate.

As Dr Leedham-Green points out, the evidence of the inventories does not square with that of such contemporary book-sellers' lists as we possess. The inventories of private libraries over some 50 years show some 20 copies of various works by Erasmus. This is to be set against a single Oxford book-seller's sale of 270 Erasmuses in the single year 1520. Whatever gap is postulated between private and learned professional interests, this is curious.[9] The lists from Cambridge begin later, in

6. Weiss 1967; De la Mare and Hunt 1970; De la Mare and Gillam 1988.
7. Oxford, Corpus Christi Coll., ms. 84; De la Mare and Hunt 1970, no. 101.
8. Bodleian, ms. Auct. F. 5. 4; De la Mare and Hunt 1970, no. 75.
9. Leedham-Green, below; *PLRE*; Madan and Bradshaw 1885–90.

1535–6, and they record the books of university men. Their humanist tinge is at once more pronounced and more diffuse than that of the private libraries. They record, for example, 24 copies of the *De elegantiis linguae latinae* of Lorenzo Valla (1407–57), the great humanist guide to Latin usage. There were 3 in the possession of a single owner.[10] There is no evidence from Scotland on a similar scale.[11]

Copying and printing

Between 1400 and 1557, neither classical texts nor humanist works were transcribed, edited or printed in any quantity by Englishmen or Scots, or in Britain at large – or at least in any quantity to challenge comparison with Italy, France or the German-speaking lands, or to dispute command of the market with the products of those countries.

The reformed formal humanist book script, developed in Florence at the end of the fourteenth century by Poggio Bracciolini and Niccolò Niccoli with the encouragement of Coluccio Salutati, was effectively not current in Britain until some fifty years later. No trace remains of any immediate influence that might have been exerted by Poggio himself during his four-year stay in England from 1418. In the 1440s, tentative experiments in the humanistic hand by Englishmen were supplanted by something more accomplished. The best native practitioners, such as Thomas Candour (d. 1477), learned the hand in Italy (fig. 14.2).[12] By the 1440s, Italians who could write it were resident in England, and Italian manuscripts were coming in. In that decade, Italian scribes were established in London. Somewhere about the mid-century, the first text written in humanist script by an Englishman in England was transcribed. A little later, the new hand was already being used for medieval Latin works, but in the older format with the text in double-column rather than extending across the whole page.[13] Even late in the century, texts in Latin were still sometimes transcribed in hands best described as chaotic. For manuscript transcription of printed books, the upright humanist hand was the norm.

The first Latin classic to be printed in Britain was a brief student text: Cicero, *Pro Milone*, which came, about 1483, from the press of the second printer to be active in Oxford, Theodoricus Rood, a German.[14] No Greek

---

10. Leedham-Green 1986; and below.
11. See, however, Durkan and Ross 1961; and cf. below.
12. De la Mare 1980, esp. no. 2; De la Mare and Hunt 1970, nos. 54–9.
13. De la Mare and Hunt 1970, esp. nos. 37, 87, 89–90.   14. *STC* 5312.

text was printed here until 1543: Sir John Cheke's edition of a pair of sermons by St John Chrysostom, and that was not only patristic, but even briefer. It was issued by another German, Reyner Wolf, working in London.[15] There was only one other piece of Greek printing in Britain before the great Eton Chrysostom of 1610–12:[16] Beza's Greek Testament, though licensed to Henry Bynneman in 1583, was issued in 1587 by Thomas Vautrollier, a French refugee.[17]

Caxton never printed a work in classical Latin, though he was responsible for a handful of humanist texts, including the first to be printed here: the *Margarita eloquentiae* or *Rhetorica nova* of the Italian Franciscan, Lorenzo Guglielmo Traversagni da Savona, in about 1478.[18] This he followed in 1480 with Traversagni's *Epitoma margaritae eloquentiae*;[19] a collection of half-a-dozen diplomatic letters in Latin in 1483, perhaps financed by the Venetians, employing an English printer in an attempt to influence English policy;[20] and Antonio Mancinelli's *Rudimenta grammatices*, a redaction of Donatus, in 1487.[21] The first humanist text to be printed at Oxford was Leonardo Bruni's Latin translation of Aristotle's *Ethics*, by Rood in 1479;[22] it was never reprinted in this country. Rood's productions, much fewer than Caxton's, also included the humanist Francesco Griffolini's *Epistles* of Phalaris, another student text with a prefatory poem by Griffolini's fellow-Italian Carmeliano, in 1485.[23]

Of almost 150 works printed before 1500 by Caxton, the St Albans Printer, and the aliens Lettou, De Machlinia and Rood (together with the first, anonymous, Oxford printer), it has been calculated that only 9 titles, most of them school texts, in 15 editions, could be called classical or humanist.[24] Nor, in spite of attempts at Cambridge to encourage such production by importing John Siberch in the 1520s and by securing a charter to appoint stationers and to print *ad lib.*, is there any substantial change during the first half of the sixteenth century.[25] When Wynkyn de Worde printed the oration delivered to Henry VII in 1506 by Louis XII's envoy, Claude de Seyssel, he botched the job so, according to Seyssel himself, that the text had to be handed over to Badius Ascensius in Paris to be reprinted in an acceptable form.[26]

15. *STC* 14634.   16. *STC* 14629.   17. *STC* 2793.
18. *STC* 24188.5, *STC* 24189; cf. *STC* 24190; below, p. 299.
19. *STC* 24190.3; below, p. 300.   20. *STC* 22588.   21. *STC* 7013; see Orme below, p. 457.
22. *STC* 752; De la Mare and Hunt 1970, p. 64; De la Mare and Gillam 1988, no. 116.
23. *STC* 19827.
24. Carlson 1993, p. 135; cf. Leedham-Green and Orme below, pp. 337–9, 457–9.
25. Leedham-Green below, pp. 343–4.
26. *STC* 22270.5; Dionisotti 1995, p. 77; cf. below, p. 304.

English humanists and Scots, moreover, published almost exclusively abroad.[27] Linacre's ps-Proclus and his Galen were printed earlier and more often in Italy, Germany, France, even in Poland than in London, though his grammatical works fared better at the hands of English printers (fig. 14.3).[28] The first five editions of More's *Utopia* came out in Louvain, Paris, Basel and Florence from 1516 to 1519; there was no printing of the Latin original in England until 1663 and Scotland until 1750; of More's Latin writings, only his *Epistola ad Brixium* in 1520,[29] and his *Responsio ad Lutherum* in 1523 (twice) issued from an English press.[30]

The first books to be printed in Britain in roman type were issued by Richard Pynson, a native of Normandy, in 1509: the Latin oration which the papal collector, Pietro Griffo, had intended to deliver before Henry VII, and a sermon by Savonarola.[31] Only a little later, italic was already being used to distinguish Latin quotations within a text in English. Black-letter remained common for vernacular texts.[32]

Imports

The most obvious and compelling reason why so few editions of the classics and humanist works were transcribed or printed in Britain during our period is that demand for them could be supplied more cheaply and easily from Europe, where the market for such books, created in Italy, was already well established. British patrons' and printers' capital need not be tied up in such a relatively small, difficult and unprofitable part of the market.

Classical and humanist texts owned and used in England therefore came in from Italy, Germany, France and the Low Countries. Before 1500, Venice was the dominant printing centre, from which books were imported sometimes direct and sometimes through a North European intermediary; in 1477, the papal collector Giovanni Gigli, recently arrived in London, bought there a copy of Poggio Bracciolini's Latin translation of Diodorus Siculus, the second edition, published at Venice on 31 January the same year.[33] John Skelton may have done something similar, though by about 1488, when he is thought to have finished his English translation of Diodorus from Poggio's Latin, there had been at

27. Shaaber 1975, *ss. vv.*   28. Barber 1977; Jensen below, pp. 366–7.
29. *STC* 18088; R. W. Gibson 1961, no. 60.
30. *STC* 18088.5, 18089; R. W. Gibson 1961, nos. 62–3.
31. *STC* 12413; Neville-Sington below, p. 585; *STC* 21800; Hellinga, above, p. 76.
32. Above, p. 24; Hellinga, above, pp. 76–7.   33. *GW* 8375; Weiss 1967, p. 198.

least one more Venetian printing.[34] From about 1490 to 1510, Paris began to take the lead, to be superseded in the 1520s and 1530s by Basel. Other lesser sources were Lyons, Cologne, Strasbourg and Louvain.[35]

The Scottish picture is more difficult to draw, even in outline. The libraries recorded by Durkan and Ross and a sample of surviving printed books with ascertainable provenances suggest no printing activity in Scotland that could be called humanist in the strict sense.[36] Most of the evidence for Scottish imports from continental Europe is sixteenth-century, and even here theology, law and philosophy, by which Scots meant especially logic, are still preponderant: the thin sprinkling of humanists are almost entirely represented by French printings. In imports overall, Italy does not figure large at perhaps 10 per cent, three-quarters of the percentage from Venice. The dominant country of origin is France, with Paris accounting for some 45 per cent and Lyons almost 15 per cent. Basel printers were responsible for rather more than 20 per cent and Cologne for rather more than 5 per cent. This is predictable, given the continuing dominance of Aristotle and the scholastic curriculum at home, and of Paris as the centre of Scottish university education away from it. In 1556, the Piedmontese humanist at the court of James V, Giovanni Ferrerio, was buying books in Paris for his patron, Archbishop James Beaton II, and the surviving books from his own library, including Filelfo, Poliziano and Pico della Mirandola, were probably Parisian editions. Even his Pietro Bembo came from Basel.[37] The printed books which survive from the late fifteenth-century library of the canonist, William Elphinstone the Younger (1431–1514), founder of Aberdeen University in 1495, were printed exclusively in continental Europe; the only humanist element in Elphinstone's extant books is a manuscript of Valla's *Elegantiae*, acquired by him, perhaps, in Paris or Orleans.[38] John Major (Mair; 1467–1550), the Greek scholar and philosopher, must have read his Marsilio Ficino and his Pico in Paris and probably in Paris editions; he combined the sympathetic interest in these philosophers which he shared with his English contemporary, John Colet, with a rejection of Valla's new humanist, rhetorical dialectic and of Valla's denunciation of

34. Skelton 1956–7.
35. These approximate conclusions are based on more detailed information kindly supplied by Margaret Lane Ford from her survey of printed books, owned by Britons during our period, which are preserved in a representative selection of modern British libraries. See also E. Armstrong 1979; Hellinga 1991a.
36. Unless *STC* 14435 – *Ad serenissimum Jacobum Quintum strena*, 1535?, four pages of elegiacs – is allowed.   37. Durkan and Kirk 1977, p. 404; Durkan 1981; below, p. 311.
38. Macfarlane 1994, pp. 68, 80; below, n. 94.

the Donation of Constantine.[39] Extant Scottish-owned copies of Italian humanist works, including Valla's *Elegantiae*, came almost entirely from Paris presses, though the new Aristotle and Flavio Biondo in Italian printings are also present.[40]

The first humanists in Britain

Though Manuel Chrysoloras, who had come from Constantinople to Florence in 1396 to teach Greek there, briefly visited England in 1408, the first humanist according to definition to be active in Britain was the Italian Poggio Bracciolini (1380–1459), who has a claim to be the initiator – or at least the promulgator – of the 'roman' hand.[41] Recruited at the Council of Constance by Cardinal Beaufort, who probably hoped thereby to introduce some of the polish of Roman curial style into his own chancery, Poggio reached Britain late in 1418. From the sessions of Constance he had made successful forays in search of manuscripts of ancient texts, and surely expected some sort of equivalent harvest from the unknown northern islands. His four years here yielded little; England was still sunk in the darkness of scholasticism, English libraries were not strong in the pagan classics, and he had to be content with finding late Antique authors such as Calpurnius Siculus, Cassiodorus and Nonius Marcellus; his most important discovery here was the *Cena Trimalchionis* of Petronius Arbiter. He turned his attention to reading the Fathers of the Church and to lamenting the poor quality of existing Latin translations of Aristotle.[42]

By Poggio's time, some of the Latin works of Petrarch (1304–74), the humanists' great exemplar – including his Letters, the *Africa* and the *De remediis utriusque fortunae* – were already available in England.[43] Most popular among them was the *De remediis*, a work both medieval and humanist in character which had already been transcribed, both complete and in abstract, at the end of the fourteenth century. Nicholas Bildestone (d. 1441), as Beaufort's Chancellor, became acquainted with Poggio during his visit, and was helped in his search for Petrarch's works by Poggio in Rome in 1424. A *De remediis*, probably written in Florence and owned by Bildestone, was given by him to Humfrey, Duke of

---

39. Durkan and Kirk 1977, pp. 156–8.
40. Ford, see n. 35; Durkan and Ross 1961, esp. pp. 15, 25–8, 31–4, 49–60, 77–8, 96–7, 155–6; below, p. 310.   41. Ullman 1960.   42. Weiss 1967, pp. 13–21; but see Rundle 1996.
43. Mann 1975b.

Gloucester (1390–1447), Beaufort's nephew and political rival.[44] The records of Duke Humfrey's gifts to Oxford University in 1439 and 1444 include several copies, as well as *Rerum memorandarum libri*, *Secretum*, *Epistolae* and *De vita solitaria*.[45] Almost all the 'Oxford humanists', from the early fifteenth century to the early sixteenth, owned works by Petrarch.[46]

Other papal officials and envoys brought with them humanist sympathies and humanist Latin along with, presumably, humanist books, and they found some desirable copies of ancient authors here, which they attempted to acquire. All this is difficult to quantify and it seems clear that even someone acquainted with these novel studies, such as John Whethamstede, Abbot of St Albans (d. 1465), was still strongly traditionalist in his own writings, which he presented to Duke Humfrey, together with Plato in Latin, Valerius Maximus and an unidentified text of Cato.[47] A later such visitor to London (briefly) and to Scotland in 1435, Aeneas Sylvius Piccolomini, secretary–diplomat, historiographer, poet laureate, Latin stylist of the stylists and later Pope Pius II, recorded his impressions of James I and his country.[48]

Humfrey, Duke of Gloucester

The history of the humanist book in Britain, however, may properly be said to begin with the patronage – and, perhaps, the reading – of Duke Humfrey, youngest brother of Henry V.[49] Humfrey seems to have conceived the idea of modelling his household on a contemporary Italian princely court. Why, and on whose advice, is not clear. In the 1420s and 1430s he was in contact with minor Italian humanists in Britain, and may have been informed by them or by Beaufort's friend, Zenone Castiglioni, Bishop successively of Lisieux and Bayeux from 1422 to 1459. About 1435, prompted by the new translation of the *Nicomachean Ethics* completed in 1417 by Leonardo Bruni Aretino (1370?–1444), he invited Bruni to enter his service. Bruni declined, but agreed to translate Aristotle's *Politics* for him: the translation arrived in 1438. A copy was part of Humfrey's first gift to Oxford University. Bruni's translations of the

44. BNF, ms. lat. 10,209; Pellegrin 1966, pp. 65–6; Mann 1975, p. 283; Sammut 1980, pp. 119–20. 45. Sammut 1980, pp. 60–84. 46. Mann 1975a-b.
47. Weiss 1967, pp. 30–8; Howlett 1975; Sammut 1980, pp. 115–16 – cf. pp. 78, 95, 106.
48. *Commentarii*, I. 6; Piccolomini 1984, I, pp. 22–5.
49. Weiss 1967, pp. 39–70; De la Mare and Hunt 1970; Sammut 1980, pp. 3–53, 146–230; De la Mare and Gillam 1988.

Ethics, the *Politics* and the ps-Aristotelian *Economics*, copied in an assured humanist hand by the scribe 'Jo. R.' (John Russell?) in 1452, are now in New College, Oxford.[50] The papal collector, Piero del Monte, in Britain in 1435–40, was one of Humfrey's resident advisers. In 1438, Piero asked Ambrogio Traversari (1386–1439) to send the Duke his works; he also suggested the appointment of Tito Livio Frulovisi of Ferrara (*c.* 1400 – after 1456) as 'poeta et orator' and of Antonio Beccaria of Verona (*c.* 1400–74), translator of Greek and Italian into Latin, as secretary. Frulovisi composed for Humfrey a *Vita Henrici V*, which included an encomium of the Duke: the dedication copy (to Henry VI) is now in Corpus Christi College, Cambridge,[51] and Humfrey's copy is in the College of Arms, London.[52] His Latin comedies, two of them written in England, were copied, perhaps by Frulovisi himself and certainly by the same humanist hand as wrote the two manuscripts of the *Vita*.[53] Humfrey's copies of Beccaria's Latin versions of Athanasius, transcribed in humanist script by the translator, survive in London and in Cambridge.[54] For Humfrey, Beccaria also translated Boccaccio's *Corbaccio* into Latin, the only extant manuscript being a later transcript by Robert Sherborn of New College in a gothic script, which was bound in Oxford about 1480.[55] Zenone gave Humfrey a Cicero *Epistolae*, written in a fine humanist hand, probably in Florence, in 1415;[56] and enlisted Lapo da Castiglionchio il Giovane, one of whose works – with one of Piero's, and several of Bruni's, translations from the Greek – was written in England by a probably non-English gothic hand.[57] The first professional Italian copyist in Britain of whom we have a record was, however, Milo da Carraria (b. 1393); he was active in London in 1447. In 1443, the Englishman Thomas Chaundler had already briefly attempted the humanist hand; he employed 'Jo. R.' and John Farley for later, more extended exercises.[58] In 1437, Gerardo Landriani suggested to the

50. Ms. 228; De la Mare and Hunt 1970, no. 37 – cf. no. 35; and De la Mare and Gillam 1988, no. 81.   51. Ms. 285/1; De la Mare and Hunt 1970, no. 4.
52. Ms. Arundel 12; De la Mare and Hunt 1970, no. 5.
53. Cambridge, St John's Coll., ms. C. 10; De la Mare and Hunt 1970, no. 6; Sammut 1980, p. 100.
54. BL, Royal ms. 5.F.II; King's Coll., ms. 27; De la Mare and Hunt 1970, nos. 7–8; Sammut 1980, pp. 105–6, 99–100; De la Mare and Gillam 1988, no. 32.
55. Bodleian, ms. Lat. misc. d.34; De la Mare and Hunt 1970, no. 23; De la Mare and Gillam 1988, no. 86.
56. BNF, ms. lat. 8537; De la Mare and Hunt 1970, no. 3; Sammut 1980, p. 119; De la Mare and Gillam 1988, no. 26.
57. Bodleian, ms. Auct. F. 5. 26; De la Mare and Hunt 1970, no. 20 – cf. no. 21; De la Mare and Gillam 1988, no. 78.
58. De la Mare and Hunt 1970, nos. 24–6, pl. XI; nos. 34, 36–9; De la Mare and Gillam 1988, no. 74.

Milanese Pier Candido Decembrio (1399–1477) that he offer Humfrey his translation of Plato's *Republic*: the autograph of the first five books, now in London, was written and decorated at Milan, and sent to Humfrey in 1438.[59] What is probably the presentation copy of the whole, also written and decorated in Milan and sent to Humfrey in 1440, is now in the Vatican.[60] Pier Candido remained Humfrey's client *in absentia*, and Humfrey did not grant his request for the wherewithal to buy Petrarch's house near Milan.

Between 1435 and 1444, Duke Humfrey gave some 274 books to Oxford. His intention to provide more was frustrated by death: King's College, Cambridge, secured the volumes which remained in his possession at that time.[61] The importance of Duke Humfrey's activities for humanist studies in Britain can scarcely be exaggerated. Though humanist texts are not numerically the largest component in his gifts, they do not figure at all in the libraries of his brothers, Henry V and John, Duke of Bedford.[62] Some of Humfrey's manuscripts later served as exemplars for copyists in England.[63]

In Duke Humfrey's first gift to Oxford medieval medical texts form the largest category, followed by astrological and theological works, followed by Bibles, encyclopaedias and dictamen. Among the authors of Antiquity, the old Aristotle is represented, and so are Bruni's new translations; Plato; Cicero the philosopher, and the rhetorician and letter-writer; Quintilian; the younger Seneca; the elder Pliny; Valerius Maximus, Aulus Gellius and works on Roman antiquities; Apuleius. Of French pre-humanists there is Nicolas de Clamanges, and of English, John Ridewall. There are three of Petrarch's Latin works, Boccaccio's *De genealogiis deorum* and one by Coluccio Salutati. The second gift is strong in St Augustine and includes Livy and Seneca. The third gift is approximately a fifth scholastic, an eighth canon or civil law, a tenth patristic. Its pre-humanist and humanist component is larger than before: the new Latin Plutarch's *Lives*, Vegetius, Aeschines, Cato and Palladius, Livy, Sallust and Julius Caesar, Symmachus, Ptolemy and Pomponius Mela, Vitruvius, Dioscorides, Boethius, Pliny, Varro, Claudian, Virgil, Terence, Nonius Marcellus. Ovid is represented only by Pierre Bersuire's *Ovidius*

59. BL, Harl. ms. 1705; De la Mare and Hunt 1970, no. 9.
60. BAV, ms. Vat. lat. 10669; De la Mare and Hunt 1970, nos. 9–10 - cf. nos. 11–12 and pl. I; Sammut 1980, pp. 124–5; De la Mare and Gillam 1988, no. 39.
61. Leedham-Green, below, pp. 317, 322; De la Mare and Gillam 1988, pp. 18–49.
62. Stratford, above, pp. 262–3, 266.
63. De la Mare and Gillam 1988, nos. 70–89.

moralizatus, and Nicolas de Clamanges is again present. So are the four chief Latin works of Boccaccio, and seven volumes of Petrarch's Latin. A sort of native humanist component is made up of three volumes by Whethamstede, some of whose gifts of classical authors to Humfrey may also be included in the list. Among Italian humanists are recorded Bruni, Pier Candido Decembrio (including his new translation of Plato's *Republic*), Piero del Monte and Lapo – and there are two manuscripts of Dante.

Humanist books: Oxford

With Duke Humfrey are connected, directly or indirectly, Thomas Bekynton, his chancellor in the 1420s and, from 1443 to 1465, Bishop of Bath and Wells; Andrew Holes, Fellow of New College from 1414 to 1420, student of canon law at Padua and King's Proctor at the papal Curia, one of three Englishmen to figure in the *Vite* of Vespasiano da Bisticci, who clearly thought well of him as an insatiable book collector; William Say, also Fellow of New College (1430–43); and Bekynton's client Thomas Chaundler of New College (1418?-90). To Bekynton, in about 1442–3, Flavio Biondo sent a manuscript of his *Decades III–IV*, now in Cambridge.[64] From Holes's library there survives – among others – a fine Florentine Cicero, *Orationes*;[65] and from Say's a Florentine Livy, and perhaps a Cicero, the new Lodi finds, which he may have acquired from Thomas Candour.[66]

The connection with Humfrey of a group associated with Balliol is, however, less close. Its chief member, William Gray, later Bishop of Ely, was already Chancellor of Oxford University and had ordered a number of books in a humanist script before he left England in 1442 to study, first in Cologne. His studious intentions on setting out seem to have been inclined rather to the traditional curriculum than to the new humanistic one, the books he acquired in Germany reflecting an interest that is philosophical and theological rather than humanist. At Cologne, the Dutch scribe Theodoricus (Diericx) Nicolaus Werken of Appenbroeck joined his entourage, travelling with him when he passed to Italy. There Werken began to write the roman hand; he seems to have been brought to England by Richard Bole, one of Gray's Balliol companions (the other

---

64. Cambridge, Corpus Christi Coll., ms. 205; De la Mare and Hunt 1970, no. 28.
65. Oxford, New Coll., ms. 249; De la Mare and Hunt 1970, no. 29.
66. Oxford, New Coll., mss. 277, 250; De la Mare and Hunt 1988, nos. 32–3.

was Nicholas Saxton), on his return in 1449. Bole himself, in 1446, wrote the first extant dated piece to be transcribed in humanist script by an Englishman.[67] On reaching Italy, Gray obtained books from Vespasiano da Bisticci in Florence, also ordering others direct from the scribes there (fig. 14.4). After receiving a D.D. from Padua in 1445, he passed on to Ferrara, where he enrolled with Guarino of Verona, as the first recorded Englishman so to be instructed directly in *studia humanitatis*. In Ferrara, he took the young Niccolò Perotti (1429–80) into his household. Perotti, whose *Cornucopia* was later in the century to be a dictionary much in use in Britain, and whose *Rudimenta grammatices* was to be a Latin grammar similarly much called upon, transcribed texts for Gray and accompanied him when he moved to Rome.[68] There Gray acquired more books, returning to England, apparently, in 1453. Gray's library, the largest collection of books ever formed by a medieval Englishman, Duke Humfrey apart, came to Balliol College after his death in 1478.[69] Among some 180 volumes still at Balliol are many humanist texts and humanist translations from the Greek; Gray seems, like Bekynton, to have known Flavio Biondo, whose *Italia illustrata* of 1454 he owned in manuscript; and he also came into possession of a manuscript of Valla's translation of Thucydides soon after it was completed in 1452.[70]

Gray patronized his fellow-countrymen as well as Italian humanists, fostering the studies of John Free (1430?–1465?) by sending him to Guarino in Ferrara in 1456. A couple of years later, Free moved to Padua, encountering there Tiptoft, who became his patron. Tiptoft had been at University College, Oxford, and was then newly returned from his Jerusalem pilgrimage; he had borne greetings from Henry VI to the new Pope Callistus III. Later, he was at Ferrara as Guarino's pupil, having visited Florence to hear Argyropoulos lecture, and acquired books from Vespasiano – a Sallust and a Catullus and Tibullus, for example. From 1459 to 1461, Tiptoft was at Padua, whence in 1460 he provided a list, now lost, of books to be sent to Oxford to improve that University's Latinity.[71] Most of his manuscripts were commissioned in Padua, including a Tacitus, *De oratoribus*, and Suetonius, *De grammaticis*, transcribed by

67. For Bole and Saxton, see Mynors 1963, pp. xlvi–xlix; De la Mare and Gillam, nos. 51, 73, 89, and p. 83.   68. For Perotti's grammatical works in Britain, see Jensen, below, pp. 359, 372.
69. Mynors 1963.
70. De la Mare and Hunt 1970, pp. 24–31, nos. 40–53, pls. v–viii; Mynors 1963, esp. pp. xxiv–xlv.
71. Tiptoft's letter, Cambridge, Corpus Christi Coll., ms. 423, fols. 65–65v; De la Mare and Gillam 1988, no. 53a.

Free. One of the scribes employed by them both seems also to have worked in England. Notable among Tiptoft's books are texts of the recently rediscovered authors, Lucretius, Manilius and Silius Italicus. Perhaps the most important in the whole group of classical and humanist texts, written and decorated in Padua, which is associated with Free and Tiptoft – some of them with Tiptoft's arms and some written or corrected by Free – is the Lucretius.[72] A copy of Basinio of Parma's *Astronomicon* was written for Tiptoft and bears his crest and arms.[73] Tiptoft's English translation from the Latin of Cicero's *De amicitia* was printed by Caxton in 1481, along with a version, from the French by another hand, of *De senectute*.[74] To Tiptoft, Free dedicated his translation from Greek into Latin of Synesius of Cyrene, *De laudibus calvitii*, completed by mid-1461. The only surviving manuscript of this bears the arms of Bekynton;[75] it was printed in editions of Erasmus, *Moriae encomium* published by Froben at Basel, in 1515–32. Free also translated Synesius, *De insomniis*, dedicating the result to Pope Paul II in 1464–5; it was never printed.[76] Free's notebook, later in the hands of John Gunthorpe (d. 1498), with its draft letters, texts on rhetoric and notes of lectures on classical authors, gives an illuminating picture of what Englishmen were making of *studia humanitatis*.[77] Free achieved some standing among the Italians. He used his Greek to annotate the manuscripts of Tiptoft and others.[78]

Lincoln College men, too, travelled to acquire humanist polish. Robert Flemmyng (*c.* 1415–83), nephew of the College's founder, followed Gray's example by matriculating at Cologne, in 1444; a couple of years later he was at Padua and, by 1446, could write a sort of humanist script; and he later moved to Ferrara to study with Guarino. At some point he learned Greek, and began a Greek–Latin dictionary. The rest of his life was passed in Oxford, Rome, Oxford again – Rome again, where he became friends with Platina, the papal librarian – and England again, for the last time, in 1478. In 1465, he had already made Lincoln College a fine gift of manuscripts, and he bequeathed further manuscripts and

72. Bodleian, ms. Auct. F. 1. 13; De la Mare and Hunt 1970, no. 72, and see pp. 41–51, pls. 16–20; De la Mare and Gillam 1988, no. 55, and see pp. 70–80.
73. Bodleian, ms. Bodl. 646; De la Mare and Hunt 1970, no. 73; De la Mare and Gillam 1988, no. 58.   74. STC 5293.
75. Bodleian, ms. Bodley 80; De la Mare and Hunt 1970, no. 83.
76. Presentation copy, BAV, ms. Vat. lat. 3713; De la Mare and Hunt 1970, no. 84.
77. Bodleian, ms. Bodley 587; De la Mare and Hunt 1970, no. 82; cf. Grafton and Jardine 1986, pp. 14–15 (disobliging); New DNB, s.v..
78. Bodleian, ms. Auct. F.3.25; De la Mare and Hunt 1970, no. 85.

printed books at his death. He too owned a copy of Valla's *Elegantiae*. In Rome, in 1473–7, he composed *Lucubratiunculae Tiburtinae* in celebration of Pope Sixtus IV, completing it in December 1477, according to the presentation manuscript for the Pope. It was the first work by an English humanist to be printed, and the printing seems to have been completed, at Rome, soon after the writing.[79]

Humanist books: Cambridge

The humanist book at Cambridge is even more difficult to characterize than at Oxford. Simon Aylward, Fellow of King's College, had learned to write the humanist hand by 1456, in which year he applied it to a thoroughly medieval text, the *De ludo scacchorum* of Jacobus de Cessolis. Aylward seems to have modelled his script on that of Pier Candido Decembrio.[80] The first serious Cambridge humanist, however, and certainly the first to have gone to school to Guarino, was Free's and Flemmyng's contemporary, Gunthorpe, who was in Ferrara in 1460 and back in England in 1465. Along with Free and Flemmyng, Tiptoft and Gray, he is named by Ludovico Carbone in his *Life* of Guarino. He wrote his own Seneca *Tragedies* in a humanist hand, annotating it from Guarino's lectures, and his own Horace; he was an assiduous annotator.[81] What remains suggests that he possessed a miscellaneous library of a humanist character, including classical and Renaissance texts, both printed and in manuscript, and he owned Free's notebook.

Gunthorpe's contemporary, John Doget (*c.* 1435–1501), Fellow and later Provost of King's, went to Italy in 1464, and studied at Padua and perhaps at Bologna. His commentary on Plato's *Phaedo*, still unpublished, is a rare example, perhaps the first, of a humanist work written in England: the sole surviving manuscript is in a proto-humanist hand.[82] Doget's successor as Provost of King's, the court physician John Argentine (1442–1508), may have visited Italy; the few manuscripts and printed books which have been identified as his include medical works and a humanist component.[83] Cambridge, too, can claim an early teacher, from 1476, of a sort of *studia humanitatis* in Traversagni, whose *Rhetorica*

79. Vienna, ÖNB, ms. 2403; De la Mare and Hunt 1970, nos. 65–6, cf. nos. 60–4, 67, pls. XII–XIV; *BMC*, IV, p. 77; Shaaber 1975, F127.
80. Oxford, Magdalen Coll., ms. Lat. 12; De la Mare and Hunt 1970, no. 90.
81. De la Mare and Hunt 1970, nos. 91–5; Rhodes 1982, no. 1359.
82. BL, Add. ms. 10344; De la Mare and Hunt 1970, no. 96; Weiss 1967, 164–7.
83. Rhodes 1967; Leader 1984.

nova or *Margarita eloquentiae*, and its *Epitoma*, were printed only in England.[84] There is, however, no evidence for the circulation here of Traversagni's *Modus conficiendi epistolas*, which had much success in manuscript in France and the German-speaking lands, and was printed there at least nine times in the incunabular period.[85]

Libraries: Oxford

A room intended for the University of Oxford's books had been constructed in the 1320s and 1330s through the bequest of Thomas Cobham, though it may not have been so used until 1412.[86] Henry V's will in 1418 bequeathed books of divinity to the common library of the University;[87] and Duke Humfrey had intended a building fit to hold his gifts. That purpose too was frustrated at his death and the first such library was not constructed until 1488.[88] What happened then is a mystery.[89] No gifts to the University Library are recorded after 1490. There was borrowing in the late 1520s; Leland found books there in the 1530s, and so did John Bale in the late 1540s; what Edward VI's commissioners saw in 1549–50 enhanced their anti-papal zeal. Then, if not before, the library stock was dispersed and a university library ceased to exist until it was reconstituted by Sir Thomas Bodley's enlightened enterprise at the end of the century.[90] Such fifteenth- and early sixteenth-century records of the College libraries of Oxford as exist do not include the bequests to Balliol and to Lincoln – for example – made by such men as Gray and Flemmyng. Contemporary evidence suggests that humanism had made no substantial gains in that milieu – though College libraries, then as now, are not always the best guides to what the young men are reading.[91] Corpus Christi in the early sixteenth century is an exception in its large humanist holdings;[92] the imperfect list of Merton's library in 1556 suggests that there was next to nothing of the sort there, and humanist works are not among the books borrowed by Fellows of Lincoln in 1543.[93] All Souls' library records give a more detailed picture. In a total, in 1502, of some

---

84. By Caxton; and the *Margarita eloquentiae* once by the St Albans Printer in 1480; *STC* 24188.5–24190.3; see above, p. 289; Traversagni 1971–86, 1978.

85. For Traversagni in general, *BRUC*, pp. 593–4; Ruysschaert 1953a, 1953b; Weiss 1967, pp. 162–3; Farris 1972; *New DNB, s.v.*

86. De la Mare and Gillam 1988, pp. 14–17; Parkes 1992a, pp. 470–3, pl. xvi; Leedham-Green below, pp. 316–17.   87. Stratford above, p. 262.

88. De la Mare and Gillam 1988; Parkes 1992a, pp. 473–7; Leedham-Green below, p. 317.

89. Ker 1986, pp. 465–6.   90. Macray 1890.   91. Ker 1986, pp. 445–65.

92. Below, pp. 305–6.   93. Parkes 1992a; Ker 1986, esp. pp. 479–97.

250 manuscripts and 100 printed books, All Souls could boast a manuscript copy of Valla's *Elegantiae*, acquired at Rome by James Goldwell in 1467, as well as other humanist works.[94] Goldwell also owned a copy of the *Elegantiae* in the edition printed at Rome in 1471.[95] Both are still at All Souls.[96]

Libraries: Cambridge

Traces have been detected of a university library at Cambridge in the fourteenth century, and such an institution certainly existed in the fifteenth, containing in the 1470s some 330 books.[97] There is no trace of humanism in its list of 1424, with additions to 1440, and little in the College library catalogues. King's was the exception, though even in its catalogue of 1452, which includes the books obtained from Duke Humfrey's estate, the humanist leaven is only a dozen in 175. Many of these are, indeed, the old classical standbys, with a work by Poggio and a couple of volumes of the new translations of Plato. The bulk is the Fathers, theology, medicine and law.[98] College library sizes varied: Clare had 111 books in 1440, Queens' 224 in 1472. Peterhouse's 380 in 1418 had risen to 439 in 1481; at Gonville, 350 survive from the fifteenth century.[99] In 1471, after the execution of the humanist Earl of Worcester, John Tiptoft, Cambridge laid claim, against Oxford, to his library; neither was successful.

Greek studies

The study of Greek in this country in the first three-quarters of the fifteenth century – with the exceptions noted above – yields little for the history of the book. The notebook of the Benedictine, Henry Cranebroke, monk of Christ Church and Fellow of Canterbury College, Oxford, in 1443–4, contains extracts from Italian humanist Latin translations from the Greek. The library of William Sellyng (*c.* 1430–94), also of Christ Church (later Prior) and Fellow of Canterbury College in

94. Ker 1959, 1971, 1986; Craster 1971, p. 33; Weiss 1967, pp. 176–7; cf. Macfarlane 1994, pp. 68, 80; and below, n. 101. The Valla is Oxford, All Souls Coll., ms. 93.
95. Oxford, All Souls Coll., S.R.14.E.1; De la Mare and Hunt 1970, no. 106.
96. For Goldwell and others, see *BRUO*, *s.vv.*; for such of their printed books as survive in various Oxford libraries, see Rhodes 1982, Index, *s.vv*; De la Mare and Hellinga 1978; and fig. 3.5.   97. Leedham-Green below, p. 318.   98. Sammut 1980, pp. 85–94.
99. Oates 1986, pp. 1–36.

1454–64, has perished.[100] Sellyng had heard the lectures on Latin rhetoric given at Oxford by the Milanese humanist, Stefano Surigone. He received a D.D. at Bologna, studied at Padua, and was later Royal Envoy to Rome. Leland says that he owned Greek manuscripts and – less plausibly – Cicero's *De republica*. Sellyng had a reputation as an orator, and some of his speeches survive.[101] There is a sample of his Greek hand in the notebook of William Worcestre;[102] and of his quality as a renderer of Greek into Latin in his translation of one of Chrysostom's sermons, made in 1488. This exists in two manuscripts, both written probably in the first years of the sixteenth century.[103]

Greek studies had been fostered at Oxford in the circle of George Neville (1433?-76), brother of the Kingmaker, Chancellor of the University, Bishop of Exeter and York and patron of Greeks in exile. To Neville, the Spartan George Hermonymos, who had come to England in 1475 or earlier, dedicated Latin translations from the Greek.[104] Neville may also have had in his household the Greek scribe Emanuel of Constantinople, who transcribed Greek manuscripts for him. Another Greek scribe, Joannes Serbopoulos, was here in 1484 and perhaps earlier; he was for some time resident in Reading Abbey. Both Hermonymos and Serbopoulos taught Greek as well as transcribing texts and grammars.

To John Shirwood, who had been a member of Neville's household, Hermonymos also dedicated Latin translations from the Greek. Shirwood collected an impressive humanist library in both ancient languages, including a good number of printed books bought chiefly in Italy.[105] Many of these later came into the possession of Shirwood's successor as Bishop of Durham, Richard Fox (*c.* 1448-1528), through whom they reached Corpus Christi College, Oxford. Wolsey's Cardinal College was less lucky, though its founder had made serious efforts to obtain copies of Greek texts in Venice and the Vatican.[106]

Grammars

A wish to improve one's Latin on humanist lines is reflected in the frequent occurrence in inventories of the newer grammars, including Valla's

---

100. Weiss 1967, pp. 153–9.   101. BL, Cotton ms. Cleopatra E. III.
102. BL, Cotton ms. Julius F. VII; De la Mare and Hunt 1970, no. 99.
103. BL, Add. mss. 15673, 47675; Trapp 1975, no. 17.
104. BL, ms. Harl. 3346; De la Mare and Hunt 1970, no. 100; Weiss 1967, pp. 142–8.
105. Oxford, Corpus Christi Coll., mss. 84, 60, c. 45; Bodleian, ms. Rawl. G.93; De la Mare and Hunt 1970, nos. 101–4; *BRUO*, pp. 1692–3; Weiss 1967, pp. 149–53; Rhodes 1982, pp. 422–3.   106. For Corpus Christi Coll., see below, pp. 305–6.

Elegantiae.[107] Greek was also in demand.[108] The need for less advanced aids was sufficient for Perotti's *Rudimenta grammatices* to be printed twice at Louvain in 1486, with English *vulgaria* replacing the original Italian;[109] Perotti was printed only once in England, by Wynkyn de Worde in 1512.[110] Giovanni Sulpizio da Veroli's grammar was printed three times by Pynson before 1500 and another dozen times, by Pynson, De Worde and others, before 1531.[111] In 1483, John Anwykyll's *Compendium totius grammaticae*, a compound of Valla and Perotti with the outmoded Alexander de Villa Dei, was printed at least twice at Oxford;[112] it was reprinted in Deventer (1489) and Cologne (*c.* 1493) for the English market. Surviving copies of both continental and British printings bear marks of Scottish and English ownership.[113]

Italian and French humanists in Britain

During the third quarter of the fifteenth century, Italian humanists of the second or third rank, and often professed religious, began to seek advantage in Britain, sometimes on their own initiative. Surigone was among the first; Traversagni another. Domenico Mancini (*c.* 1434–*c.* 1514), poet laureate and author of verse treatises *De quatuor virtutibus* and *De passione Domini*, as well as the prose *De usurpatione Ricardi III*, was here in 1482–3, apparently sent by his Italian physician–patron in France; no manuscript of his works was written in Britain, but his edifying verse was printed here by Pynson, *c.* 1518–20, in English versions.[114] The Lombard Poet Laureate, Johannes Michael Nagonius (*c.* 1430–*c.* 1510), was Papal Envoy to Henry VII in 1496, presenting him, as he had presented other monarchs and prelates, with a verse encomium in an elaborately illuminated autograph manuscript.[115] Pietro Carmeliano of Brescia (1451–1527) sought royal and noble patronage through illuminated autograph presentation copies of his Latin poems: *De vere* for Prince Edward in 1482;[116] a verse *Vita B. Katherinae* in copies for Richard III, for John Russell, Bishop of Lincoln, and for Sir Robert Brackenbury in 1483–5;[117] and the

107. See Jensen below, pp. 368, 370–1, however; and, for school grammars, Orme below, pp. 452–69.   108. For Greek grammars, see Jensen below, pp. 369–70.   109. *STC* 19767.7.
110. *STC* 19767.3.   111. *STC* 23425–9a.5.   112. *STC* 695–6.
113. Ford, database, see her contributions; see, further, Orme below, pp. 458–9; Jensen, pp. 359–62; Bell above, p. 246; Weiss 1967, pp. 169–71.
114. *STC* 17241–2; cf. 17239.3–40; Mancini 1969.   115. Gwynne 1990; Trapp 1991, pp. 33–5.
116. BL, Royal ms. 12.A.xxix.
117. Richard's copy does not survive; the other two are Cambridge, Gonville and Caius Coll., ms. 196/102, and Bodleian, ms. Laud Misc. 501.

Suasoria laeticiae to Henry VII on the birth of Prince Arthur in 1486.[118] Carmeliano was pensioned by the King the same year and made Latin Secretary in 1498. In the early 1480s, he did editorial work for Caxton and for Rood, and contributed prefatory verses to their books.[119] The Servite, Philippus Albericus of Mantua, sought the favour of Henry VII by similar means: a large-format, rather provincial, codex, illustrated by a French hand, of his verse version of the *Tabula Cebetis*, seems to have been a New Year's gift to the King in 1507.[120]

Italian humanist influence was very frequently mediated through France. The blind Augustinian from Toulouse, Bernard André (*c.* 1450–*c.* 1522), for example, enjoyed a long career in favour at the English court, with his congratulatory Latin verse and his prose *Vita Henrici Septimi*; he was tutor to Prince Arthur and presented manuscripts of edifying works to the young Henry VIII.[121] He did not achieve print in this country until the nineteenth century, though his *Hymni christiani* were printed in Paris in 1517. The Savoyard humanist, jurist, administrator and diplomat Claude de Seyssel, later Bishop of Marseilles and Archbishop of Turin, was here more briefly on behalf of Louis XII. For presentation to Henry VII, he commissioned an opulent manuscript of his translation of Xenophon's *Anabasis*, illustrated in the style of the School of Rouen.[122]

Early Tudor times

Two poles of early Tudor humanism are represented by two contemporaries, Christopher Urswick (*c.* 1448–1522) and William Grocyn (*c.* 1450–1519), both ecclesiastics, the first as innocent of Greek as the other was adept in it, alike in leaving almost no writings of their own behind them.

Urswick, Cambridge-educated, was one of those who helped establish the new dynasty on the throne and a person of some authority at court: his taste was for manuscripts – often in handsome copies made for him by Pieter Meghen (1466–1540) – of ecclesiological texts. His library included Cicero's *De officiis*, George of Trebizond's Latin version of Chrysostom on St Matthew, Leonardo Bruni Aretino and Aeneas Sylvius Piccolomini in manuscript, and, in print, Platina, the St Jerome and the *Novum Instrumentum* of Erasmus (1516), and others.[123]

118. BL, Add. ms. 33736.   119. Carlson 1993, chapter 2; Trapp 1991, pp. 31–2.
120. BL, Arundel ms. 317; Sider 1990; Carlson 1993, chapter 1.   121. Carlson 1993, chapter 3.
122. BL, Royal ms. 19.C.VI; Dionisotti 1995, pp. 90–5; cf. above pp. 272, 289.
123. Trapp 1991, pp. 13–29; for Meghen, see Bietenholz 1985–7, II, pp. 420–2.

Grocyn was an Oxford don, highly regarded by fellow scholars. Having probably begun Greek in Oxford, he left for Italy in 1488, where he studied in Florence under Poliziano and Chalcondyles, and met Aldus Manutius. From 1491 he taught Greek in Oxford and later undertook to distribute 100 copies of Erasmus's *Adagia* in the edition of 1500. To Grocyn's scholarly tastes and attainments, his remarkable library – listed after his death by Thomas Linacre, with help from Thomas Lupset – is our chief witness. It contained at least 17 manuscripts and 105 printed books, which are predominantly classical and patristic. Grocyn's collection of Greek books was the best in Britain, some of its manuscripts having been written for him here; some 30 manuscript and printed items from it are now in Corpus Christi College, Oxford, some having been bought by the College at the instance of John Claymond, its first President; and more, in 1537, by his bequest.[124] The Latin humanist element in Grocyn's library included Petrarch, George of Trebizond, Filelfo, Pomponio Leto, Perotti, Ficino, Aeneas Sylvius Piccolomini, Pietro Crinito, Valla (on the New Testament and the Psalms, and the *Elegantiae*), Erasmus and Robert Gaguin.[125]

Oxford: Corpus Christi College

Corpus Christi had been founded in 1517 by Urswick's and Grocyn's contemporary Richard Fox, then Bishop of Winchester and, like Urswick, a power at court, but in the reign of Henry VIII as well as that of Henry VII. He too left small literary remains, and his tastes and aspirations must be gauged from his letters, his library and his patronage, in particular for his new humanist College. Like many English ecclesiastics, Fox admired Erasmus and received dedications from him, as well as from Italians such as Giovanni Gigli and Philippus Albericus. Some ninety books have been identified in the Corpus library catalogue of 1589 as given or bequeathed by Fox to the College; twenty-seven of them had belonged to John Shirwood.[126] These were all Latin; Fox acquired his Greek books, including the Aldine editions, elsewhere. The greater proportion of the printed books are Greek or humanist, including Aeneas Sylvius Piccolomini, Poggio, Valla's *Elegantiae*, George of Trebizond, Leonardo Bruni Aretino,

---

124. Liddell 1937–8, p. 401.
125. For Grocyn, see Bietenholz 1985–7, II, pp. 135–6; *BRUO*, II, pp. 827–30, which lists his books; for his printed books, see also Rhodes 1982, p. 407; cf. Trapp 1996. For Claymond, see Bietenholz 1985–7, I, pp. 307–8; *BRUO*, I, pp. 428–30, where the books he left to Corpus Christi are named; for his printed books, cf. Rhodes 1982, p. 399; see also Woolfson 1997.   126. Liddell 1937–8, p. 400.

Domizio Calderini, Leon Battista Alberti, Pico, Cristoforo Landino, Ficino's *Epistolae* and his Latin Plato, as well as the Latin classics.[127]

Though Corpus Christi received seven Hebrew manuscripts by Claymond's bequest, it had never been the 'collegium trilingue' that Erasmus had called it.[128] Rather, it was aimed at increasing learned piety through the study of Latin and Greek, much like St John's and Christ's Colleges in Cambridge.[129] Fox provided for public lectures in Greek, humanity (Latin) and theology, the humanity reader being required to give instruction from Aulus Gellius, Valla's *Elegantiae* and Poliziano's *Miscellanea*.

Humanists Spanish (Juan Luis Vives), German (Nikolaus Kratzer) and English (Thomas Lupset and John Clement among others) were associated with Corpus Christi. No work by Lupset – except a single Latin letter and perhaps an English translation[130] – by Clement or by Kratzer was printed during its author's lifetime. Lupset and Clement assisted with the Aldine Greek Galen, a copy of which came to Corpus Christi from Claymond. Two short treatises by Kratzer were transcribed in England by Meghen. Vives was not printed in Latin in Britain until the early seventeenth century, but frequently at Antwerp, Louvain, Bruges, Paris and Basel in the sixteenth. Surviving copies indicate that these continental editions were available, even fashionable, here.

Erasmus and Christian humanists

On this generation of English humanists and the next, especially as regards their European reputation, the great influence was Erasmus. He built up, through dedications, a circle of English patrons from the time of his first visit to England in 1499, when he made the acquaintance of his two greatest English friends, John Colet (1467–1519) and Sir Thomas More (1478–1535), whose interests he tirelessly promoted. With Thomas Linacre (*c.* 1460–1524), his relations were always cordial, though he was less concerned with securing publication for Linacre.

Of Erasmus's own works, only the *Colloquia*, the *De contemptu mundi*,

---

127. Bietenholz 1985–7, II, pp. 46–9; *BRUO*, II, pp. 715–19; cf. Rhodes 1982, pp. 404–5; Jensen below, p. 376. For Cuthbert Tunstal's gift of Greek books to Cambridge in 1529, see Oates 1986, pp. 60–9.

128. Liddell 1938, pp. 389–90; McConica 1986, pp. 17–29.

129. Below, p. 315; for evangelical humanism in general, see below, pp. 311–12, and CHB, III; and for humanist books in a monastic context, especially in the libraries of Syon and Monk Bretton, during our period, see Bell above, pp. 245–9 and CBMLC IV.

130. Basel 1520; *STC* 5550; Shaaber 1975, M218.

the *De copia* and *De conscribendis epistolis* and the grammar books, together with the *Institutum christiani hominis*, prescribed by Colet for St Paul's School, and similar works were printed in England in their original language during our period.[131] Erasmus's connections with printers in Louvain, Paris and Basel in particular, as well as elsewhere, made it easy for him, for example, to see to the publication by Froben, at Basel in 1518, of the full account of his and Colet's disputation concerning the Agony in the Garden, just as he had guided More's *Utopia* through the press at Louvain, Paris and Basel, in 1516, 1517 and twice in 1518 respectively, adding More's Latin epigrams to the Basel printings. His own preference was always for the better production and distribution that such publication could command.

John Colet

The only extant work of Colet's to be printed in England in his lifetime was his Latin sermon to Convocation, by Pynson in 1512;[132] the first surviving copy of an edition of one of his grammatical works dates from 1527.[133] Colet himself read ps-Dionysius – in Ambrogio Traversari's translation, as edited by Lefèvre d'Etaples and printed in Paris in 1498 – his Ficino and his Pico della Mirandola carefully; his copy of Ficino's *Epistolae*, printed at Venice in 1495, is copiously annotated in his rapid, cursive italic.[134] So are the manuscripts of his own writings which he caused to be made by Pieter Meghen in his bold, upright, roman script, including the 'collected edition' of probably just after 1505. Besides these, Colet commissioned Meghen to copy the imposing New Testament codices of 1506–9. To these, Erasmus's new translation was added, and a final volume even more finely illuminated made for Henry VIII, by the same scribe after Colet's death. Meghen also wrote another handsome pair of New Testament manuscripts with the Vulgate and Erasmus on alternate lines, perhaps for Wolsey. These New Testaments, like most of Meghen's productions and those of a good many other contemporary scribes, were copied from printed books.[135] Some of Meghen's manuscripts were decorated by native British artists, some by artists from the Netherlands, sometimes working in England.[136]

---

131. Leedham-Green below, pp. 337–9; cf. Carlson 1993, pp. 135–41; for English translations, see Devereux 1968.   132. *STC* 5545.   133. *STC* 5542.
134. *GW* 8409, 9873; Jayne 1963.   135. Trapp 1991, pp. 79–141.
136. Alexander, above, p. 49.

Sir Thomas More

Like Erasmus, More can be numbered among Christian humanists, particularly for his defences of Erasmus as editor and translator of the New Testament.[137] Unlike Erasmus, he was not active only in contesting on paper views which differed fom his own. Much of his intellectual effort in the last ten years of his life was concentrated on denying his fellow-countrymen access to books written, and New Testaments translated, by those whose religious beliefs were contrary to those of the Catholic church. Against such writings and their authors he fiercely and unremittingly used his personal and official advantages.[138]

In considering the humanist book in Britain during our period, however, More's English translation of Giovanni Francesco Pico della Mirandola's life of his uncle, made in the first decade of the sixteenth century, must be set aside. A New Year's gift to the nun Joyeuce Leigh, it reduces the bold philosopher to a model of learned piety.[139] So must his *Historia Ricardi III* of perhaps ten years later, since it was not printed in Latin until 1565, and then at Louvain; no version of the Latin has ever been printed in Britain.[140] With these exceptions, More's humanist activity begins in two literary contests, continues in his masterpiece *Utopia* and ends in patriotic and metrical dispute.

The translations of some of Lucian's *Dialogues* from Greek into Latin which More undertook in competition with Erasmus engage with a favourite Greek satirical author of the Renaissance. They were published, by the agency of Erasmus, in Paris in 1506; by 1563 they had been printed in Venice, Basel, Florence, Frankfurt, Lyons, Leiden and Louvain.[141] They too have never been printed in Britain. The epigrams from the *Greek Anthology* which More also translated in competition, this time with William Lily (d. 1522), the first High Master of Colet's St Paul's School, are accomplished exercises. They and other Latin poetry by More were included in the editions of his *Epigrammata* published, along with *Utopia*, by Froben at Basel in 1518 and 1520; they were not printed in Britain until 1638.[142] Erasmus, who had written down his *Moriae encomium* (Paris 1511) in More's London house, was again the promoter. Among his services to More's works at large was the important humanist

137. *CWM* xv.   138. *CWM* vi–xiv.
139. *STC* 19897.7, 19898; *CWM* i, pp. 47–123.   140. *CWM* ii, xv.
141. *CWM*, iii.i; R. W. Gibson 1961, nos. 78–94.
142. R. W. Gibson 1961, nos. 3–4, 57–8; *CWM*, iii.ii.

one of securing prefatory commendations from the learned and the influential.

The one surviving contemporary manuscript of any of More's Latin poems is modest: the presentation copy of his epigrams to the newly crowned Henry VIII has English embellishment of no great quality.[143] Some of More's short Latin poems were printed elsewhere, as examples or prefatory pieces, in England in the 1510s. Another was contributed to the first printed arithmetic, the *De arte supputandi* of More's friend and bishop, the Paduan-educated Cuthbert Tunstal (1474–1559).[144] This was first published by Pynson in 1522,[145] and reprinted in Paris and Strasbourg, 1529–51.[146]

Like his works against the English reformers, More's Latin works against Luther and his followers, with one exception, first came out from English presses. The exception was his letter against Bugenhagen, printed at Louvain in 1568.[147] Henry VIII's *Assertio septem sacramentorum*, in which More had a hand, was twice printed by Pynson in 1521 (fig. 28.2);[148] copies bound in the London shop of John Reynes, with somewhat provincial illumination, and a presentation manuscript of rather better quality, were sent to the pope and to various European rulers.[149] More's own pseudonymous Latin *Responsio ad Lutherum* was printed in London, also by Pynson.[150]

The Latin theological and controversial works of John Fisher (1469–1535), on the other hand, were printed almost exclusively in continental Europe, at Antwerp, Louvain, Paris and Cologne during his lifetime, and after his death in Cologne and Würzburg. The one exception is the Latin version of a sermon, made by Richard Pace (d.1536) and printed at Cambridge by John Siberch in 1521.[151] Pace's own sole important piece of humanist writing, *De fructu qui ex doctrina percipitur* was printed once, at Basel in 1517, and his Latin Plutarch at Venice and Rome.[152]

The only work of More's, printed in Britain during our period, which

143. BL, Cotton ms. Titus D. IV; Trapp 1991, pp. 39–43; Carlson 1993, pp. 142–62.
144. *CWM* III, ii, pp. 68, 304–5. There is an excellent summary account of Tunstal's other publications, chiefly Latin, and dedications to him in Bietenholz 1985–7, III, pp. 349–54. See also n. 127 above, and Jensen below, p. 376. The library list in BL, Add. ms. 40676, is far from certainly his, in spite of the claim made by Herendeen and Bartlett 1991.
145. *STC* 24319.   146. Shaaber 1975, T155–9.
147. *CWM* VII; Gibson 1961, no. 61; Shaaber 1975, M217.
148. *STC* 13078–9; Neville-Sington below, p. 586.
149. BAV, ms. Vat. lat. 3731; Vian 1962; Trapp and Schulte Herbrüggen 1977, no. 117; Alexander above, p. 63; Neville-Sington below, p. 586.
150. *CWM* V; *STC* 18088.5, 18089; Neville-Sington below, p. 587; above, p. 290.
151. *STC* 10898; above, p. 17.   152. Shaaber 1975, P3–P7.

can strictly be called humanist is his brief, polemical *Epistola ad Germanum Brixium* of 1520.[153]

No copy of any of More's works, *Utopia* included, has been recorded as surviving from an early Scottish library.[154]

Thomas Linacre

In despite of this, Linacre, from whom More learned some of his Greek, may provide evidence for the view that English printers, from about 1518, were more ready to hazard their capital on humanist works. Certainly, they published the texts that flew back and forth in the 'Grammarians' War' of the early 1520s, though it must be said that these did not match, in quantity and quality of production, similar works printed in the chief European centres and available in Britain.[155] Linacre had studied in Florence and taken a medical degree in Padua. During 1497–9 he was occupied with Aldus's *editio princeps* of Aristotle in Greek, for which he was rewarded with a copy on vellum, the gift of the printer, now in New College, Oxford.[156] He wrote a very beautiful italic hand, and was adept at securing exalted patronage. The latter may have been one reason why his humanist works – Latin versions of ps-Proclus and Galen, as well as advanced Latin grammars – were printed in Britain as well as in Europe.

Scottish humanists

The English humanist pattern of publication abroad holds for Scotland also, though France occupies a more exclusively prominent place in it. The greatest of Scots Renaissance humanists, George Buchanan, much of whose life was spent in France, is too late for this volume. The Latin works of Erasmus's fellow-student in Paris, Hector Boece (*c.* 1465–1536), who was brought back by William Elphinstone in 1497 to introduce humanist studies in Aberdeen, for example, were published in Paris.[157] A little later, John Vaus followed the same pattern.[158] So too did John Major, like Boece both student and teacher at the Sorbonne, who came back to Glasgow and St Andrews.[159] Those of Florence Wilson

153. Printed by Pynson in 1520; *STC* 18088; *CWM* iii.ii, pp. 551–694.
154. Durkan and Ross 1961, p. 15.
155. Carlson 1993, chapters 5–6; Leedham-Green below, p. 337; Jensen below, pp. 366–9.
156. *GW* 2334; Rhodes 1982, 130 (*I*).
157. Durkan 1980; Macfarlane 1994, pp. 69–70; Shaaber 1975, B586–92; cf. p. 196 above.
158. Shaaber 1975, V2–6; Jensen below, pp. 360–2.
159. Shaaber 1975, M25–74; Durkan and Kirk 1977, pp. 155–65; cf. p. 196 above.

(Volusenus; *c.* 1505–*c.* 1551) came out from Lyons, though his Latin commentary on the *Somnium Scipionis* appeared in London, probably in 1535.[160] Gavin Douglas's Scots translation of the *Aeneid*, with its addition of the humanist thirteenth book by Maffeo Vegio, was printed in London, and not until 1553.[161] Giovanni Ferrerio published almost exclusively in Paris.[162]

John Colet, St Paul's School and school texts

It is instructive to compare what John Colet prescribed, by his statutes of 1512, for use in St Paul's School, and what we know to have been in use there, besides what he recommended in a more general way, with what would have been available from English presses, mostly in London but occasionally in the provinces (York, for example), up to, say, 1530.[163] Given contemporary methods of instruction, it is likely that only the High Master, the Surmaster and perhaps the Chaplain would have needed copies, and the Catechism would probably be dealt with orally. The grammar books named or suggested by Colet were available in English printings; and so were Erasmus's *Institutum christiani hominis* (from 1520);[164] and his *De copia* (but not until 1528).[165] The prescribed Fathers come off badly: of Lactantius, only a scrap from Pynson in 1522;[166] of Prudentius, the *Cathemerinon* only, from De Worde in 1523;[167] of Proba and Sedulius, nothing; of Juvencus, an Antwerp edition of 1534, available in Ipswich;[168] of Baptista Mantuanus, *Bucolica* - if that is the work that Colet means: it was certainly in use in the School later - two editions, by De Worde, of 1523 and 1526.[169] Of the classical and other patristic authors that Colet goes on more sweepingly to name, there is no Cicero and no Sallust; Virgil is represented by one *Opera* (Pynson *c.* 1515);[170] and four *Bucolica* (De Worde, 1512–29) - perhaps a good indicator of what the school-Virgil was;[171] three Terences (Pynson 1497; Badius, Paris 1504, obtainable from De Worde; and De Worde *c.* 1510);[172] plus seven Latin and English Vulgaria (Rood and Hunt 1483; De Machlinia *c.* 1485, 1486; Antwerp 1486; Faques *c.* 1505; De Worde *c.* 1510, 1529);[173] only ps-Jerome (Rufinus, *Expositio in symbolum apostolorum*, Oxford

160. *STC* 5317.5; Shaaber 1975, V153–61; Baker-Smith 1984.
161. *STC* 24797; Caldwell 1957–64.
162. Durkan and Kirk 1977, pp. 404–5; Durkan 1981; above, p. 291.
163. Cf. above, p. 303; Orme, below, pp. 462–7; Jensen below, p. 368; Trapp 1991, pp. 109–18.
164. *STC* 10450.2–10450.5.   165. *STC* 10471.4–10473.   166. *STC* 15118.
167. *STC* 20453.5   168. *STC* 14893.5.   169. *STC* 22978, 22979; Piepho 1993.
170. *STC* 24787.   171. *STC* 24813–5.   172. *STC* 23885–5.5.   173. *STC* 23904–8.

1478);[174] of St Ambrose nothing; of St Augustine, only the *Excitatio ad eleemosynam* (Rood and Hunt *c*. 1483);[175] the Rule (De Worde 1510, 1525, 1527);[176] and a supposititious work or two. Every author on Colet's list, on the other hand, existed in a continental edition or editions.

The schoolboy's seniors and teachers, and university men at large, were not limited by local stocks, whether printed in England or in Europe. They could also take advantage of periods abroad for study and other purposes. Some - such as Urswick, Fox and Colet - could hope to acquire desirable items in return for patronage: each received a copy of Erasmus's *Novum Instrumentum* (1516) by this means; and, in 1516 also, Erasmus distributed his edition of St Jerome in Britain with a lively sense of future favours. Urswick's now-lost printed Aeneas Sylvius Piccolomini, *Historia Bohemorum*, and Bruni, *De primo bello punico*, which he had copied by hand on receipt, were bought for him by Colet in Rome in 1493; Colet may have got his Ficino and his Pico in Italy, but his Latin ps-Dionysius may well have been acquired in Britain. It is not clear where More got his pre-Aldine Livy, or the text of the *Life* of Pico for translation, in the edition of Strasbourg, 1504.[177]

The schoolmaster wishing to publish could be obliged only so far by British printers: as we have seen, grammar books were, with exceptions, their limit.[178] The wandering pedagogue, Leonard Cox (fl.1514–49), published where he happened to be.[179] At Kraków, for example, he published the first humanist educational treatise written by a Welshman. After his return to Britain, he published almost exclusively in English and in England: translations of Erasmus's *Paraphrases* (1534, 1548–9),[180] and the first humanist rhetoric in the language (1532).[181] His edition of William Lily's *De constructione* came out in 1540.[182]

Presentation copies

The manuscripts presented by Carmeliano, Alberici, André and Seyssel to Henry VII were all written and decorated in north Europe. Handsome though some of them are, neither they nor the Italian product offered to Henry by Nagonio match in refinement and quality of decoration those written in Italy for, say, Federico d'Urbino or the Medici twenty years

174. *STC* 21443; De la Mare and Hellinga 1978.   175. *STC* 922.   176. *STC* 922.3–4.
177. Cf. E. Armstrong 1979; Hellinga 1991a; above, p. 308.
178. Cf. Orme below, pp. 461–8.
179. Bietenholz 1985–7, I, pp. 353–4; Breeze and Glomski 1991.   180. *STC* 10503, 2854.
181. *STC* 5947.   182. *STC* 15610.5.

or so earlier. Nor, indeed, are Colet's New Testament manuscripts of 1506–9, or the Psalter and Chrysostom written and decorated for Urswick in 1514 and 1517, the equal of some written and decorated for, or acquired by, Edward IV. The manuscript of Sir Thomas More's epigrams presented by him to Henry VIII on his accession in 1509 is written with some elegance, if decorated to a provincial standard.

Already, however, there were signs of a recognition that better was available. In 1507, the future Henry VIII was given a superb small manuscript with texts of Isocrates and Lucian written by Pierantonio Sallando (fig. 14.5);[183] and the king later received a Lucian and Collenuccio which was even finer, written by Lodovico Arrighi, and decorated by Attavante degli Attavanti at some time between 1509 and 1517.[184] These were imports. By the late 1520s, with Pieter Meghen still active in England and about to become Writer of the King's Books and the arrival here of the Horenbouts, something almost equally accomplished, but in the northern style, could be commanded. The final volume of the New Testament, with the Vulgate and Erasmus's Latin in parallel columns, written by Meghen and decorated by one of the Horenbouts for Henry in about 1530, and the New Testament volumes perhaps intended for Wolsey, of a few years earlier, both serve the evangelical humanist cause in exalted circles and are fine examples of what was by then available on the spot.[185]

Acquiring a manuscript from Italians in Italy or employing Meghen and the Horenbouts in England gave by then a clear advantage to those who could afford it. The means of a career humanist or an aspiring young courtier and man-of-affairs would not have stretched to seeking abroad what was not yet available at home. Royal resources were required for even the provincial decoration of presentation copies of the *Assertio septem sacramentorum*. The humanist could sometimes afford something a little more lavish, however, such as the copies of Linacre's Galen translations of 1517–19 that the translator presented to Henry VIII and Wolsey: decorated as well as printed in Paris, with coloured title- and other pages, and their Parisian bindings.[186] The presentation manuscript of about 1519, for Wolsey, of Robert Whittinton's *De difficultate iusticiae servandae* and other works, too, is encased in the earliest surviving English gold-

---

183. BL, Add. ms. 19553.
184. BL, Royal ms. 12 C.viii; Alexander above, p. 55; Trapp 1991, pp. 52–3; Starkey 1991, section II. no. 15.
185. Hatfield House, Cecil Papers, ms. 324; Oxford, Corpus Christi Coll., mss. 13–14; cf. Oxford, Christ Church, ms. 101; Magdalen Coll., ms. 223; Alexander above, pp. 48–9; Trapp 1991, pp. 79–94.   186. Above, p. 310; and cf. Trapp 1991, pp. 95–100.

tooled binding.[187] Kratzer, for his New Year's gift to Henry in 1528–9, employed Meghen as scribe and Holbein as decorator, and had the result bound in green velvet.[188]

Book-sellers, book-buyers and patterns of publication

Sporadic detailed information about purchases is available from various sources.[189] On a larger scale, some dozen stock and sales lists of Oxford and Cambridge book-sellers survive to give some idea of what was moving locally, and how. The two most significant record the transactions of 'Dutchmen'.

The Day-Book of John Dorne in Oxford, the fullest of them, lists his sales for the year 1520, in which the humanist component is strong: in just over 2,000 entries, Erasmus, with his 270 copies of 150 titles, outnumbers Aristotle.[190] Though a good many of these are grammatical and rhetorical, including 48 copies of the *Colloquia*, 31 of his and Lily's *De constructione* and 9 of the *Adagia*, a good proportion relate to *pietas litterata*. There are 15 copies of the *Enchiridion*, 7 New Testaments, and 11 copies of the *Apologia*. The new commentaries on Aristotle by Lefèvre d'Etaples were popular, and so were those curricular aids George of Trebizond, Theodore of Gaza's Greek grammar and Valla, chiefly the *Elegantiae*. There were also Lucian in Greek and in More's and Erasmus's Latin, some anti-papal literature and a couple of copies of the *Epistolae obscurorum virorum*.[191]

Less full at a little over 1,000 items sold to 820 customers, and about a decade later (*c.* 1527–1533), is the list of Garrett Godfrey, friend of Erasmus, in Cambridge, where the three leading contemporary stationers were all natives of the Low Countries.[192] Almost half Godfrey's list are elementary works, half of them grammars: text-books and standard classical teaching texts. Erasmus accounts for about 12 per cent, the specific works being much as in Dorne, though the overall proportion is much lower in Godfrey. Like Dorne, Godfrey sold Lefèvre d'Etaples, Lucian, Mantuan, Poliziano and Valla; most books in Godfrey's list but not in Dorne's are by those who had more recently come into fashion: Rudolphus (and Georg) Agricola, Cornelius Agrippa and Guillaume

187. Bodleian, ms. Bodl. 523; Nixon and Foot 1992, pl. 19; Carlson 1993, pp. 71–4, 110, 115.
188. Bodleian, ms. Bodl. 504; Trapp 1975, no. 25.   189. Above, pp. 287–8.
190. Madan and Bradshaw 1885–90; Leedham-Green below, p. 341.
191. See the excellent analysis in McConica 1965, pp. 88–90.
192. Leedham-Green, Rhodes and Stubbings 1992; cf. Leedham-Green, below, p. 340.

Budé, among them; and there was some Hebrew as against Dorne's single *Alphabetum Hebraicum*.

As to Hebrew studies, Robert Wakefield was teaching in Cambridge from 1524, and later in Oxford; some of his works were printed in England, among them being the first British book to use Hebrew type.[193] Most books necessary for Hebrew, however, had to be imported.[194]

Evidence from books for the progress of the Reformation is, perhaps surprisingly given Cambridge's Lutheran reputation, less strong in Godfrey than in Dorne.[195] At Cambridge also, in 1528, John Fisher's mentor William Melton owned, besides the scholastics and the Fathers, Valla, Erasmus, Pico and the New Testament in Greek; and Greek studies had flourished even more in Cambridge after Fisher had prevailed upon Erasmus to take up residence at Queens' (1511–14), and upon the Lady Margaret to establish the two colleges of Christ's and St John's in the first decade of the sixteenth century.[196]

Erasmus and others, however, continued to publish in Europe, especially in Basel and Paris: Richard Croke, the Greek scholar, for example, helped see the *Moria* through the press in Paris in 1511, publishing his own Ausonius, his *Tabulae graecae* and his translation of Theodore Gaza at Leipzig, and his *Orationes duae* in Paris. The pattern continued into Mary's reign (when other reasons than scholarly additionally applied) and into Elizabeth's: the controversy of 1542–3 between Sir John Cheke and Stephen Gardiner, Chancellor of Cambridge University, with Sir Thomas Smith intervening – concerning the 'reformed', Erasmian pronunciation of Greek – was published in Basel in 1555;[197] Smith's contribution, *De recta et emendata linguae Graecae pronuntiatione*, was issued later, from Paris, in 1568. Cheke, in exile, was taking advantage of facilities he could not have commanded in his native country; Smith, recently appointed, yet again, England's ambassador to France, was doing the same.[198]

193. *STC* 24943–6; Wakefield 1989; Rex 1990.   194. Lloyd Jones 1983, pp. 181–220, 274, 278.
195. Leedham-Green below, and 1986; *PLRE*.
196. Underwood 1989. On Fisher's own library, see Rex 1991, pp. 198–200; cf. Helmholz below,
    p. 395, n. 54.   197. Shaaber 1975, C243.
198. Shaaber 1975, S276–7; cf. Jensen below, p. 370.

15

University libraries and book-sellers

ELISABETH LEEDHAM-GREEN

In a modern context, nothing would seem more natural than for an account of the provision and use of books in universities to start with an assessment of their corporate libraries, both those of the university itself and those of the constituent colleges. These surely constitute the major repositories of learning, the essential resource of both students and teachers. In the fifteenth and sixteenth centuries, however, this was not always the case. An affluent scholar, at least in the sixteenth century, whether or not resident in a university for most of his career, might well, if he were so disposed, amass a collection of books larger than those that either his college or even his university could boast, and it is in the records of private rather than of public collections that shifts in academic fashion may first be detected. Nonetheless, it was in the institutional libraries that the standard texts, the embodiment of the received curricula, accumulated and it is against this background that the provision and use of books in the universities is best viewed.

While statutes for college libraries occur from the last quarter of the thirteenth century at Oxford, and Thomas Cobham had attempted to establish a common library there as early as 1320, in the event the University Library was not to open its doors until 1412. Similarly, Cambridge University was left a chest of books by Richard de Lyng, three times Chancellor, in 1355, but the first references to the 'common library' are not until 1416. The earliest evidence for books owned by the University of Oxford consists of a copy made in 1432 of an inventory of the university's property.[1] The lost original is datable to before 1350 and records two manuscripts: one a Bible divided into four parts so that, on deposit of a surety, scholars might borrow parts to correct their own copies, and the other an old copy of Exodus. Their original donor, Roger

---

1. CUL, ms. Dd.14.2.

de Holdernesse, or de Skeffling, Dean of York, had been a master in Oxford in the 1250s. It appears also, from a copy of a letter from the university surviving by chance in the letter formulary of Richard de Bury, Bishop of Durham, that Henry de Harkeley, Chancellor of the University, bequeathed books to it on his death in 1317. We do not know whether the university ever secured the bequest. In about 1320, however, Adam de Brome, Rector of the University Church, started to construct next to the church, at the expense of Thomas Cobham, a building that was to house a chained collection of his books. On Cobham's death in 1327, however, the building was not completed and his books were pawned to pay for his funeral. They were redeemed by De Brome, now Provost of Oriel, who kept them in his college until they were forcibly removed by 'a great multitude of members of the University' in 1338/9. In 1367, they were installed in the upper room next to the church, but the dispute between the college and the university was to continue until 1410, when it was settled by Archbishop Arundel paying Oriel 40 marks for the collection, out of his own pocket. The library formally opened in 1412, with a priest appointed as Chaplain/Librarian, to report annually to the university.

The first substantial donations to the library were those of Duke Humfrey of Gloucester, with perhaps 9 books in 1435, 120 in 1439, 17 in 1441 and 135 in 1444. The university was, however, to be frustrated by King's College, Cambridge, in its attempts to secure the Duke's remaining books confiscated on his death in 1447. The subjects of the books donated included biblical commentaries, patristics, scholastic theology, civil and canon law, medicine and, more significantly, rare philosophical texts, classical humanist texts and modern French and Italian humanist books. Duke Humfrey's books, with 80 or so others variously acquired, were transferred to the splendid construction erected for their reception above the divinity schools in 1488. It was perhaps at Duke Humfrey's prompting that a new arts course was established in 1431 in the seven liberal arts and the three philosophies, with more emphasis on rhetoric and classical literature. Certainly his books could have furthered the humanist cause in Oxford since not all of them were in fact to be confined to the library. Books relevant to the new arts course were to be kept in a special chest for loan to lecturers and, if not so required, to the principals of halls for the use of their pupils.

At Cambridge a modest collection of books was housed in chests, perhaps in the University Church, by the late fourteenth century, but major developments only became feasible with the piecemeal construction of university buildings on a central site in the course of the fifteenth century, with ranges devoted partly to library use being completed in about 1420, 1470 and 1475. The first catalogue, drawn up in 1424, with additions to 1440, lists 122 volumes, more than half of them theological. There were also strong holdings in canon law. By 1473 the library had moved into the newly completed south range of the building and a new catalogue was compiled listing 330 books in 17 desks. A large number of the books acquired since 1440 had come with the bequest of 93 volumes from Walter Crome, Fellow of Gonville Hall. With the completion of the east range between 1469 and 1475, built and furnished with books by the munificence of Thomas Rotherham, Archbishop of York, the library expanded to fill two rooms, one serving as the 'common library' of the university and the other, the 'new library' or 'library of our Lord the Chancellor', as a rare book room. By the time of Rotherham's death in 1500, the total holdings of the library came to about 600 volumes. The influence of the Renaissance, manifest in Duke Humfrey's books at Oxford, was not, however, to be seen in the Cambridge library until Cuthbert Tunstal's donation of its first Greek texts in 1529.

Meanwhile, in Scotland, the establishment of the university library of St Andrews had been triggered by Alan Cant's donation in 1456 of a *Magna Moralia* and John Dunning's further gift of texts by Aristotle and Aquinas. The University of Glasgow, thanks to donations from, among others, Duncan Bunch at some time after 1467, from Bishop John Laing in 1475, and from Principal John Brown in 1483, assembled a modest working library for use by lecturers, covering both the 'old' and the 'new logic'. The books of the first Dean of the faculty of arts, William Elphinstone, several of them copied by himself during his sojourn at the newly founded University of Louvain in the 1430s, may also have been available to his contemporaries at Glasgow. They were, however, to descend to his son, William Elphinstone and to his foundation of King's College, Aberdeen. To Aberdeen also, on and after its foundation in 1492, came the books of Hector Boece, the first Rector, and of John Vaus, both friends of the founder. Elphinstone the Younger, in his turn, donated not only his father's books but also his own, including acquisitions from his years in Paris and in Orleans. The experience of study overseas, for Scotland even more markedly than for England, distinguishes many of the notable early donors to university libraries.

College libraries

Until the last quarter of the fourteenth century, college libraries grew gradually, book by book, usually given or bequeathed by Fellows. The pattern had been established by the friars, whose books, when they died, reverted to their houses, either in the universities themselves or elsewhere, for loan to another generation of students.[2] Archbishop Kilwardby indeed, as Visitor of Merton, had enjoined on the Fellows, in 1276, the obligation to leave their books to the college either on their death, or on entering an Order, or else to make compensation for their failure so to do. Colleges did buy some books for their libraries: Exeter College, Oxford, for instance, commissioned a copy of Dumbleton's *Logic* in 1366, and other books were acquired when their owners had deposited them against loans of cash which they had been subsequently unable to repay. Bequests and gifts, however, easily outnumbered books from other sources, and it follows that the books found in college libraries were of precisely the same nature as those owned by individuals. Standard texts in theology and in law predominated, followed by medicine and natural philosophy with the arts, which were less dependent on substantial, indeed on presentable, volumes, lagging well behind. By the same token, the texts acquired were likely to embody traditional learning rather than any new departures.

In speaking of these early libraries, we summon up an image of large volumes chained to desks or lecterns in a room set aside specifically for that purpose. For this there is an early precedent, of about 1338, at Merton, and it was Merton's 'new library' (now the Old Library) of 1373–8, with its desks of chained books, which established the pattern which other colleges were to follow over the next 200 years or so.[3] The 1350 statutes of Trinity Hall, in Cambridge, clearly envisage a special room for the library, but New College, founded in 1379, was the first at either Oxford or Cambridge to incorporate provision for a separate library room in its original plan. In the absence of a special reading room, books were kept in chests. Dr Gaskell has calculated that one in use at Trinity College, Cambridge, in the early 1550s must have been 67 inches long, by 23 wide and 18 deep to house its listed contents of 100 volumes.[4]

2. For an account of the library of the monks of Durham at their cell, Durham College, at Oxford, and the movement of books between Oxford and the mother house, see Piper 1978, pp. 244ff.   3. At Lincoln College some of the books at least were still chained after 1739.
4. Gaskell 1983, p. 335.

In some colleges the passive accumulation of standard texts continued unrelieved well into the sixteenth century, but, by the end of the fourteenth century, certain privileged colleges had acquired collections of quite another character. In 1374, William Rede, Bishop of Chichester, donated to Merton some 99 volumes, with smaller bequests to the libraries of Exeter, Oriel and Queen's Colleges. On his death, 10 years later, he confirmed his gift to these colleges and left in his will 100 books to New College. His books were accompanied by cash for library use – specifically, in some cases, for chaining. Rede's collection has been assessed as 'one of the largest and most important in fourteenth-century England',[5] but others were not so very far behind. By 1376, Merton had also benefited from a substantial bequest from John Reynham. Meanwhile, between 1379 and 1386, William Wykeham presented his foundation of New College over several years, with some 246 volumes; Rede's bequest added another 60-odd. Later founders were to follow suit: Henry Chichele presented All Souls with some 370 books on its foundation in 1437, and William Wayneflete was reported to have endowed his foundation at Magdalen, some 22 years later, with no fewer than 800 volumes. No comparably spectacular donations seem to have come to Cambridge colleges at this time.

These large donations, in the half-century before the appearance of the printed book, attracted others in their wake, many of them substantial, although the lack of contemporary records of accession, whether in benefactors' books or in indentures acknowledging their receipt, often makes it impossible to do more than guess at the numbers involved. A well-stocked library obviously carried prestige. More than that, it was regarded as a vital resource. Few books, indeed, are recorded as purchased by, or copied at the expense of, colleges, between 1375 and about 1500, and it may be that, for lack of reliable records, we underestimate their number. What does seem clear, however, is that the books recorded as purchased were not, on the whole, rare or exotic texts but rather further exemplars of staple texts for which demand might outrun supply. It was recognized that few scholars could afford to own the legal and theological works essential to their studies, and multiple copies of the central texts were of more obvious use than the more recondite or more novel texts which might appeal to the *cognoscenti*.

Up to the last quarter of the fourteenth century, accordingly, the

5. Parkes 1992a, p. 460.

books which we find recorded in college libraries are limited in scope, consisting largely of biblical texts and glosses; the *Sentences* of Peter Lombard with their commentators; Scotus, Aquinas and Augustine for the theologians; Justinian, Gratian, Boniface and Bonaventura for the lawyers; with a selection of Aristotelian texts to represent philosophy. These works characterize the gifts of many an obscure donor and such texts are also to be found in the libraries of the collectors who now gave or bequeathed their books on a more lavish scale. The enthusiasm of these collectors, however, extended also to new texts: Rede's gift to Merton, for example, includes texts of the Latin classical authors, Horace, Lucan and Claudian; of Plato, in translation; of Martianus Capella in a splendid twelfth-century manuscript, still surviving;[6] and of Averroes and Avicenna. Theology and logic are there in quantity, but so also are history and mathematics beyond the requirements of the university course. These were the treasures of book-lovers intended for the like-minded. The extent to which they were appreciated, except by the few, remains doubtful.

It was not until the middle of the fifteenth century that substantial numbers of true humanist texts started to arrive in college libraries: William Gray, who entered Balliol College, Oxford, in 1431 had copies made, in 1442, of books from the library of Duke Humfrey – Valerius Maximus and a volume of Latin panegyrics which contained also works by Bruni and by Gianozzo Manetti – the first humanist texts, perhaps, to be copied in Oxford. Gray went on to take a doctorate at the University of Cologne and later travelled to Padua where he acquired a collection of books including further humanist texts. His library was left to Balliol in 1478. Similarly, the magnificent donation to Lincoln College by Robert Flemmyng, nephew of the founder, in 1465, consisted in part of manuscripts which he had acquired from Vespasiano da Bisticci's shop in Florence, including Cicero's letters and orations, Aulus Gellius, Aelius Donatus's commentary on Terence and Leonardo Bruni's translation of Aristotle's *Ethics*, as well as works by Sts Cyril and Cyprian and ps-Dionysius. There was also a single Greek manuscript: a tenth-century copy of the Acts of the Apostles. Briefly, Lincoln possessed what by our standards would be regarded as the finest of the Oxford college libraries.

Accounts of celebrated benefactions of fine volumes and of the arrival in the universities of the first texts representative of the renaissance of

6. Merton Coll. ms. 291.

classical learning on the Continent might be multiplied,[7] but they are revealing rather of the tastes and the travels of an élite than of the experience of the many and the expectations which they had of their institutional libraries. Those who sought the new learning sought it, if they possibly could, abroad, in Padua and in Ferrara; their careers were to lie beyond the confines of the university. The great majority of those who studied in Oxford and in Cambridge in the second half of the fifteenth century showed little interest in these new texts which stood or lay, long neglected, in their libraries.

The most fully recorded reader in mid fifteenth-century Oxford, Dr Thomas Gascoigne (1403/4–1457/8), is remarkable for the evidence he has left us, in the 5,000 or so citations in his *Liber de veritatibus* and his memorandum book, and in his annotations in surviving manuscripts, of his systematic use of a large number of libraries, including that of the Greyfriars where he consulted the manuscripts of Grosseteste. He, at least, clearly had no lack of access or of pertinent curiosity, and Duke Humfrey's manuscripts were among those he perused; but, as a proponent of practical theology and an opponent of Reginald Pecocke, his quarry took the form of patristic rather than classical texts.[8]

Similarly, at King's College in Cambridge, where Henry VI had envisaged a huge library room, 110 by 34 feet, not to be realized, a major scoop was achieved with the acquisition in the late 1440s of many of the books, rightly due to Oxford, of Duke Humfrey of Gloucester. Among these were what were almost certainly the only classical and neo-classical books to be found in Cambridge institutional libraries at that time. Use was made there of some of Duke Humfrey's texts: a manuscript of Jacobus de Cessolis's *De ludo scacchorum*, signed and dated by Simon Aylward in 1456, was probably based on the copy in the library at King's.[9] A catalogue drawn up in 1452, however, shows that, of the 16 *distinctiones* or classes made up of 175 books, 3 were devoted to philosophy, 2 to classical and general literature, 1 each to medicine, to astrology and mathematics, to canon law and to grammar, and no fewer than 7 to theology. Of books donated to the library between this time and 1500, only the Statius and the Horace given by William Warmystre in 1457 reflect humanist interests: the remainder consist of standard texts in

---

7. For an overview, see Weiss 1967 and the works cited in his bibliography.
8. For Thomas Gascoigne, see Pronger 1938–9; *BRUO*, II, pp. 745–8; Catto 1992, pp. 769–83. The publication of the study on 'Dr Gascoigne at work' by Dr R. M. Ball is eagerly awaited.
9. Now Oxford, Magdalen Coll. ms. 12; De la Mare and Hunt 1970, no. 90, pl. 21; cf. above, p. 299.

medicine, in canon law, in philosophy and in theology: the sort of books that were of immediate use to students in the higher faculties. The two earliest known Cambridge collectors of literary books were John Argentine, D.D., Provost of King's from 1501 to 1507/8, and Bryan Rowe, Vice-Provost, who died in 1521.[10] They may perhaps have been inspired by the presence of Duke Humfrey's books in their college.

The holdings of college libraries varied widely in size: a somewhat defective catalogue of King's College library in 1391 lists 101 volumes; Peterhouse in 1418 had 302, Queens' in 1472 had 224; and it appears that Gonville Hall by the early sixteenth century had over 300. The larger Oxford libraries put these in the shade, with more than 800 volumes at Magdalen by 1480. Merton had probably about 500 books as early as 1372 and continued to attract donations, to the number of about 40 by 1500. New College had over 650 books by the same date and All Souls about 400. Balliol, Oriel and Lincoln had significant stocks also, but the smaller Oxford collections were comparable with those at Cambridge.

Electiones

The chained library, as it evolved, never served as the sole repository of a college's books. The less valuable books were made available on loan to the Fellows, and sometimes the Scholars, in order of seniority, at *electiones*. The normal procedure was for the books to be returned, checked and redistributed annually; but some colleges, as their libraries increased, could afford to relax the system and lend books at irregular intervals and for longer periods, even for life, with predictably tiresome negotiations when and if they endeavoured to regain possession of them. A register covering the years 1440 to 1517 for loans from two sets of books donated to Corpus Christi College, Cambridge, illustrates the standard system of annual distributions. The books, their values ranging from £10 to 1s, consist of 'standard texts and commentaries with less formal books of pastoral instruction (e.g. *Pupilla oculi* of John de Burgo), and concordances, dictionaries and elementary works on grammar'.[11] They were normally returned annually, albeit often redistributed to the same Fellow

10. Rhodes 1956a; J. M. Fletcher 1961; Rhodes 1967; and Norton 1958.
11. *Electio* lists from Merton for 1372, 1375, *c.* 1410 and 1452 in Powicke 1931, pp. 60–3. The fourteenth-century lists are further discussed by Ker 1981. The King's Hall lists are described by Cobban 1969, pp. 249–50, and 1988, pp. 386–8; and the Corpus register by Cheney 1988; and, at greater length, in 1987. For an account of the conduct of *electiones*, see Garrod 1928.

for a further year, or years. In some cases, books appear to have been retained over a period of years without being formally 'checked in'. The most highly valued volume, a compilation described as *Magna moralia Aristotelis*, was probably borrowed every year from 1440 to 1517; but almost as popular was another volume, with contents unusually remote from academic demands, including Mandeville's *Travels*; an account of Prester John; the journeys of the Franciscan, Odorico da Pordenone, in Asia; Petrarch's story of the patient Griselda in Latin; and Sir John Grandisson's life of Thomas Becket, as well as a number of devotional works.[12] It was valued at 8s. The register also charts the falling-off of annual distributions in the years 1508 to 1515, with a sudden increase in 1516 to forty-six loans, all renewed in the following year, the last in which they were registered. Few of the manuscripts that were *in electione* at Corpus survive there now, and it seems possible that the apparent attempt at revival may in fact have been a general hand-out of books thought to have been rendered obsolete by newer, printed, texts. In general it would appear that the *electiones* were made in order of seniority, with priority given to the three *custodes* of the collections, so that in 1445, for instance, each of them had ten volumes and the Master and five Fellows took seven each.

It appears that at Corpus Christi, Cambridge, in the fifteenth century, each Fellow made a genuine *electio* or choice among the books available. At Merton, in the late fourteenth century, it seems, on the other hand, as if the distribution of 'philosophical' books was controlled according to a deliberate scheme designed to ensure that, insofar as was compatible with the claims of seniority, essential texts were allotted to meet the immediate academic needs of each Fellow before the allocation of 'extra' volumes. Here, too, the value of the books available for distribution ranged widely, from about £6 to 6d. Seniority also dictated the number of books that each Fellow might receive. In 1372, three Fellows received eight books each; ten received seven each; seven, five each; and two, four each.

Merton had many more books available for distribution than are shown in the Corpus register, and also many more Fellows to satisfy. So also at the King's Hall where, in 1386–7, with a similar number of claimants (twenty-three against twenty-two) the Warden and one Fellow each had eleven books; two Fellows had seven each; one had five; two

---

12. Now Corpus Christi Coll., Cambridge, ms. 275.

had four; three, three; nine, two; and four, only one. The Fellows of the King's Hall ranged from the very eminent to undergraduates – hence, perhaps, the large discrepancies in the number of books allotted to each.[13]

It need not, of course, be supposed that a Fellow read in his own room only those books which he had received at the annual *electio*. He was responsible for returning that book at the end of the year, but may well in the course of the year have exchanged books with his peers. Conversely, we do not know that he read his allocated texts at all: certain texts available for distribution were, in despite of many regulations to the contrary, deposited by their recipients in the university or college chests as sureties against loans, often year after year, their cash value having long since surpassed their academic usefulness.[14]

As we have seen, the register of *electiones* at Corpus Christi College, Cambridge, terminates abruptly in 1517, and a similar pattern is observed in all colleges except Lincoln College, Oxford, which seems to have been strangely old-fashioned in library matters, and where there is evidence for *electiones* as late as 1596.[15] The reasons for this cessation are nowhere stated explicitly, but the increased availability of less expensive, and often demonstrably better, texts following on the invention of printing must have some bearing on the case, as well as an increasing tendency for donors to specify that their books are to be kept chained or, at least, *in libraria*, rather than circulated among the Fellows. Nonetheless, if formal registers of annual distributions of books are not found after the early years of the sixteenth century, stray references in the books themselves, in bequests and in other records, indicate that the *electiones*, or some more casual arrangement for the circulation of texts among Fellows, continued in some colleges at least.

Dr John Moreman, D.D. of Exeter College, and appointed Chaplain to Queen Mary in 1554, the year of his death, left to the Rector of the College, 'the hole of S. Awsten in tenne greate volumys of frobenyes prent for his use as longe as he is or shalbe rector and so from one Rector unto another as long as the bookes may endure', on condition that any request from a Fellow studying theology to use one or other volume be granted by the Rector, 'of his courtesie'. There also survives at the Royal Library in Brussels, however, a much more modest volume, Erasmus's

13. The most useful account of the evolution of university and college library regulations, as well as of library furnishings, for this period, remains that of Clark, in Willis and Clark 1886, III, pp. 387–471.   14. See, in particular, Lovatt 1993.   15. Ker 1985 at p. 386.

Epistolae duae [*Contra quosdam qui se falso iactant evangelicos* and *Ad quosdam impudentissimos Græculos*], printed in octavo by Maerten de Keiser in Antwerp in 1530, inscribed 'Ex dono Johannis moreman sacre theologie professoris in usum scripture sancte studiosorum ea lege ut a scholare in scholarem transeat' ('. . . on condition that it pass from scholar to scholar').[16] Such a book would have been too small to find a place in most college libraries, where the desks or stalls were usually reserved for more impressive volumes in folio and, occasionally, quarto. We cannot tell how many other donors may have presented such slim, controversial or innovative texts for informal circulation in their colleges. As late as 1589, Dr Andrew Perne defined the books from his private library which were to go to Peterhouse as 'the best and largest sort of all my bookes of divinitie Lawe Phisicke or of any other Sciences . . . *in folio & in quarto . . .*'. The specification as to size limited his benefaction to some 800-odd books, about one-third of his total holdings. Perne also specified, vainly, that these books should be chained, further evidence of the different concepts which he entertained as to the proper character of college libraries as opposed to private ones.

Use of libraries

What traffic, meanwhile, did the closed libraries admit? In their furnishings they remained, until late in the sixteenth or early in the seventeenth century, much as they had been since their beginnings, with the books lying sideways, chained to a bar, on desks consisting of one pair of shelves rising to meet like a gable, with one or two flat shelves below, or occasionally above, to hold the books not currently in use. Such a desk, 5 or 6 feet in length, would probably hold some 40 books at the most, and it is small wonder, therefore, that even the larger college libraries tended to contain no more than about 500 volumes. There was no room for more. Merton is estimated to have had this number of books as early as 1375 and as late as 1541, but only 375, perhaps, in 1500. Trinity College, Cambridge, which had inherited the libraries of both Michaelhouse and the King's Hall in 1546, had only about 250 volumes by 1600, most of which had been there since the 1560s. King's had some 175 volumes in 1452 and had increased these to about 350 by 1500 and to 500 by 1530. By 1557, this number had been reduced, by neglect and, perhaps by religious

16. *Bibliotheca Erasmiana Bruxellensis* 1993, no. 226.

purges, to 113. In this context, it is particularly interesting to note the 2 octavo volumes of the 1526–7 edition of Erasmus's *Hyperaspistes* apparently purchased by New College, probably within two decades of their publication. They are anything but typical.

A similar pattern marks the history of the university libraries. At Oxford the library had entirely disappeared by 1556 and the library furniture was sold; Cambridge University Library had 122 books in 1427, 330 in 1473 and 500–600 in 1500. By 1556/7 this number had fallen to 175. That such a decline should have occurred at both Oxford and Cambridge prompts questions as to the use which had been made of these communal libraries. When the Oxford library opened in 1412 it was to be open to graduates, to monks and friars of eight years' standing, and to the sons of the nobility, for two hours in the morning and three in the afternoon. From the late 1440s dispensations are recorded allowing access to members of religious houses who were not graduates in arts, sometimes with the proviso that MAs were to have priority, or that contributions should be made to the cost of repairing, or even of purchasing, books. The rules were sufficiently flexible for permission to be granted in 1451 for an undergraduate to copy 'certain necessary matter' in the library, for the University Registrar. From this time, strenuous efforts were made to increase the library's stock and large benefactions were received from Cardinal Beaufort, Thomas Kempe, Bishop of London, and others. At Cambridge it appears that undergraduates were initially admitted to the library, since it was found necessary in 1471/2 to disbar them, unless accompanied by a graduate, because they had abused the contents. Four centuries were to pass before the ban was revoked. Non-resident graduates were to assume their academical dress before entering the library. As at Oxford, access was granted from time to time to individual friars. Among the colleges of Oxford and Cambridge only New College and the King's Hall admitted undergraduates to their libraries before 1500.

It would appear that, in the latter part of the fifteenth century, access to the communal libraries was a privilege of which many were glad to avail themselves. In order to guess at the reasons for their falling off after 1500, it may be helpful to consider a little more closely the sources of their holdings. As we have seen, the great majority of the books both in college and in the university libraries were acquired as gifts or bequests. Where did the donors acquire these books in the first place?

Many, if not most, of the great donations of the fourteenth century which we now admire for the rarity or beauty of their texts, or for their place in the early stirrings of Renaissance humanism in Britain, had been acquired by their owners in the course of studies at universities overseas, perhaps in Padua or Ferrara, or, as in the case of the Elphinstones, in the Low Countries and in France. Few of these books, however, formed part of the staple reading of the average scholar. The books which he needed were more often those that came in ones and twos from scholars of earlier generations who had been sufficiently industrious to copy texts for themselves or sufficiently affluent to buy copies from the local stationers. Until late in the fourteenth century, the modernity of a text was not at issue. There is plenty of evidence for manuscripts 200 or 300 years old circulating in *electiones*, as well as being pledged in chests. So far from being regarded as old-fashioned, these ancient manuscripts were held in high esteem. Nor was this unreasonable: the older a copy of a text, the less likely it might seem to have been corrupted in the process of copying.

What of new academic texts in the early years of the fifteenth century? The religious houses in the universities seem, at this time, rather to have collected than to have originated scholarly texts (and we remember Roger Bacon's much earlier complaints about the difficulties of getting new works safely into circulation). Production, if not consumption, of Lollard texts had moved away from Oxford, at least after the bonfire of 1410, and from about this date the composition of texts that were to have an international circulation declined there as the emphasis of the Oxford schools shifted away from logic and natural philosophy in the direction of practical theology. Few classical texts, as Poggio Bracciolini experienced, still lay undiscovered in monastic or collegiate libraries. New books lay beyond the seas and when they found their way to British universities it was seldom if ever in response to academic wants, institutionally perceived; rather it was in the luggage of students returning from Italy, from the Low Countries and from France and, in the second half of the century, of English diplomats returning from the papal Curia.

Provision of manuscript books

Susan Cavanaugh's census of books privately owned in England, between 1300 and 1450, reminds us that some senior academics managed to amass substantial private libraries: Henry Abingdon on his death in 1437 had out on loan to a single individual no fewer than fifteen of his own books. William Byconnell, who had left Oxford at least eight years before his death in 1448, still had in his custody a number of books which he had borrowed from All Souls College library, to which, he directs, they are to be restored, apparently when the immediate legatees no longer have a use for them. One of these survives to this day – in the Bodleian.[17] The manoeuvrings of King's College in 1447 in pursuit of Duke Humfrey's books, and John Pye's commission to acquire books for them and for Eton, might perhaps be taken as examples not only of breath-taking gall but of a perceived difficulty in equipping a library solely from local resources.

Evidence for the activity of stationers in the university towns before the sixteenth century is patchy, especially in Scotland, where the void seems largely to have been filled by enterprising notaries diversifying their professional skills. The Oxford stationers of the fifteenth century have left more copious traces, both in documents and in surviving manu-scripts, but even here it is unclear to what extent the university endea-voured to regulate their trade, still less how far it succeeded. A composition between the university and the Archdeacon of Oxford in 1346 refers to four official stationers, while a statute of 1373 restricts the value of books that were to be offered for sale by those not sworn as sta-tioners, so offering a measure of protection to those that were. The oath imposed on stationers, in addition to many clauses dealing with their responsibilities as appraisers of goods (not necessarily books) deposited in the loan chests, also requires that all books lent out for copying should be 'integra, completa, correcta ac fidelia'. Significantly, however, this is to apply not only to the sworn stationers but to anyone lending out *exem-plaria*. It is not certain that there ever prevailed at either Oxford or Cambridge a fully fledged system whereby collections of approved copies of texts were maintained by the universities for lending out in quires, or *peciae*, for copying.[18] Certainly the religious houses had *exemplaria* which were used in this way, and it is inconceivable that texts were not lent out by others in a piecemeal form in such a way that more than one copy could be made simultaneously. What is in doubt is the extent to which, if at all, the universities attempted to regulate the practice.

There is ample evidence for students copying texts both for themselves and for others for a fee. At the other end of the scale, the Oxford Chancellor, Gilbert Keymer, brought with him to the university in the 1440s the distinguished scribe, Hermann Zurke of Greifswald, who in

17. Ludolphus de Saxonia, *De vita Christi*, 2 vols., Bodleian, mss. Bodl. 741–2; both inscribed 'Liber Collegii Animarum Omnium fidelium defunctorum Oxonie ex dono magistri Willelmi Bygonell' post mortem magistri Byrkhed'.   18. Parkes 1992a, pp. 464ff.

due course followed his patron to Salisbury. Other professional scribes from the Low Countries and elsewhere are also known to have worked in both Oxford and Cambridge. In between, there were resident scribes who made at least part of their living from copying texts on commission – a characteristic script can be distinguished; but the surviving texts do not provide a secure basis upon which we can form any estimate as to the proportion of texts copied professionally to those copied by scholars on their own account. When the time for discarding manuscripts came, those professionally copied may have had slightly better chances of survival than the less attractive 'amateur' productions. Presumably, in all universities, the most junior scholars, whose needs before the early sixteenth century were only for the most minimal texts, were more likely to copy their own than were their seniors, who were more likely to have the means to commission copies of such standard texts as were not available on loan. The smaller the text, however, the less likely it is to survive. At some colleges, such as New College and All Souls in Oxford, the stocks of standard texts were sufficient for students of canon and of civil law, obliged by university statute to possess their 'own' copies, to retain those they had received at the *electiones* for the duration of the course, provided that they did not own personal copies. Lawyers at less well-equipped colleges were much burdened by the cost of procuring their texts.

The appearance of printed books in increasing numbers seems for a time to have thrown confusion on the perceived status of libraries. There was clearly no need to continue to amass manuscript copies of standard texts, many of which were in any case at last beginning to appear old-fashioned. On the other hand, the new printed versions of these texts lacked the precious exclusivity inherent in the manuscript. As to printed volumes of new texts, only time could tell which would acquire the canonical status which would earn them a place *in libraria*. The great Aldine editions of the classics earned places fairly fast, as did Erasmus's New Testament and *Paraphrases* later; but it is possible that, for two or three decades at least, donors may have been uncertain as to what now was a suitable book for presentation to an academic library. Furthermore, the newest texts were likely to find purchasers among younger men destined to enjoy their possession for some years before the time came to bequeath them to their colleges. Certain it is that the early years of the sixteenth century witnessed a quite dramatic diminution in accessions to libraries.[19]

19. Ker 1985, pp. 393–4.

The need for books

In 1400 the university student (as distinct from the master or doctor) had relatively little use for books, or, rather, for substantial texts. University and college statutes required him to hear, to repeat and, on a limited scale, to dispute. His essential booklessness is well illustrated by the fact that, unlike the schools of the senior faculties, the arts school in Oxford was furnished not with desks but with benches only. Here the student sat to hear his Regent Masters read and expound the prescribed texts, sentence by sentence. The manuscripts which he begged, borrowed, stole or transcribed to assist him in his studies might, indeed, include a small number of short texts, very probably annotated by a generation or more of previous users, but he had more use for compilations of *quaestiones* and of *tabulae*, synopses of the received wisdom of his teaching masters. He probably begged, borrowed, stole or bought the majority of them from his peers or from students barely senior to himself, either as individual items or as collections of booklets more or less roughly bound together. As he increased in seniority, the scholar's requirement for written texts grew: the bachelor still relied to a greater or lesser extent on compilations of *quaestiones* but the need for the basic texts themselves, as of Aristotle's natural philosophy, increased.

Similarly the Regent Master did not, perhaps, scorn to employ the lecture notes of his predecessors, but he could scarcely have proceeded satisfactorily with his studies without access to substantial texts. Thus, Richard Calne, an Augustinian canon of Llanthony Priory, as a student in Oxford, purchased there in 1413 a fourteenth-century manuscript containing twelve works by Walter Burley including his commentaries on Porphyry's *De praedicabilibus*, on Aristotle's *Perihermeneias*, *Praedicamenta*, *Posterior Analytics* and *Topica*; and William of Ockham's *Apparatus* on Aristotle's *Elenchi*.[20] In 1414, he bought a twelfth-century manuscript with commentaries on Aristotle's *De generatione et corruptione* and *De anima* by Aegidius Romanus, valued at 2s 6d, and, probably at about the same time, a manuscript with eleven other natural philosophy texts copied in 1390 and 1391.[21] In 1415, he spent 3s on a late thirteenth-century copy of Thomas Aquinas on Aristotle's *Metaphysics*, *De anima* and *De sensu et sensato*, and on ps-Aristotle, *De causis*.[22] Two other manuscripts from his years in the arts faculty, one containing Oxford *quaes-*

20. Lambeth, ms. no. 70.   21. Lambeth, mss. 111 and 74.   22. Lambeth, ms. 97.

tiones on logic texts and the other on natural philosophy texts, were copied partly by himself and partly at his direction.[23]

As he progressed up the academic ladder the student's dependence on texts increased. In 1418 Calne acquired a recent copy of an anonymous set of *quaestiones* on Peter Lombard's *Sententiae*, a text central to the studies of all theologians. Also dating from about this stage in his career must be his purchase of a collection of twenty-one theological texts, thirteen of them by St John Chrysostom, copied between the twelfth and the fifteenth centuries.[24] All these manuscripts duly came to rest in Llanthony Priory library for the use both of residents and, potentially, of any member of the house following in his footsteps.

In 1424 Richard Holme, Warden of the King's Hall – subsequently clerk and councillor of Richard II, Henry IV and Henry V and proctor for Walter Skirlaw, Bishop of Durham, at the Roman Curia – bequeathed to Cambridge University Library a dozen or so substantial volumes. They comprised a Bible in two volumes, Nicholas de Lyra in three volumes, Augustine's *De civitate Dei* and *Retractationes*, and, in canon law, the *Decreta*, the *Decretales* and the commentaries on them by Joannes Andreae and Innocentius, Boniface VIII's *Liber Sextus Decretalium* and a commentary upon it, Guido de Bayso's *Rosarium decretorum*, and the *Summa aurea* of Henricus de Segusio (Hostiensis). Had he left also a glossed text of Peter Lombard's *Sentences* the bequest would have neatly encapsulated all the texts which budding theologians and canon lawyers aspired to own and which he would certainly have hoped, if not expected, to have found in his college library. After these would have come a host of secondary *desiderata*, typified by the bequest of John Pelham (fl. 1430) to Clare College of glossed Epistles of St Paul, Holkot on Wisdom, Rabanus Maurus's *De naturis rerum*, Lyra (again) on the New Testament and a *Postilla super psalterium*, which was to be chained in the college chapel; or that in 1442 of Henry Osborne, *quondam* Fellow, to Gonville Hall, of Higden's *Polychronicon*, a commentary on the *Sentences*, and Aquinas, *De veritate theologica*, the last bound with other tracts including a *tabula* of the *Sentences*.[25]

Just as the canonist required before all else his *Decreta* and *Decretales*, so the civil lawyer required his Justinian. His staple diet, indeed, remained more constant than the canonist's who had to take cognizance of new

23. Lambeth, mss. 393 and 396.   24. Lambeth, mss. 370 and 145.
25. The fifteenth-century Higden and the thirteenth-century commentary on the *Sentences* survive as Gonville and Caius Coll. mss. 82 and 321, respectively.

enactments of canon law and of corresponding adjustments to the *corpus juris canonicae*. From the later years of the fifteenth century, however, new vistas opened before the theologian, and still more before the student in the faculty of arts.

The introduction of humanist texts and ideals

If the timetable for the transformation of the arts course and the mechanism whereby it was achieved cannot be precisely plotted, it is largely because there was neither timetable nor mechanism. It was not until after the transformation had been wrought that it was recognized in statute. Changes in syllabus, however dramatic, have seldom, until modern times, provided sufficient impetus for universities to undertake the onerous task of large-scale revision of statutes, and although the statutes of Oxford and Cambridge were revised more frequently in the sixteenth century than in any other, the revisions were imposed by external authorities impelled by religious and ideological considerations which in fact had remarkably little to do with the prescribing of approved texts. True it is that several of the codes of statutes did indeed make such prescription, and proscription too, but their enactments were always somewhat out of touch with reality, condemning the use of texts which had already been discarded, often long since, and commending others which, if they usually stood in some reasonable relationship to texts that were already in use, were not always actually adopted. The major transition – from a medieval syllabus to a 'humanist' one; from one based on dialectic and Aristotle to one emphasizing, rather, rhetoric and Erasmus; from one based on hearing to one based on reading – took place largely independently of any formal declaration that these things should be.

The developments which had been set in motion in Italy by Petrarch (1304–74), and which gradually spread through Europe in the course of the fifteenth century, arrived belatedly on British shores. The religious, moral, political and psychological impulses tending to these developments have been much discussed.[26] For our present purpose, it is sufficient to state simply that the scholars identified with the movement turned their attention more and more towards language, and towards the ancient classical authors in whose works they discovered a form of discourse both eloquent and morally relevant, which they endeavoured ini-

26. For a recent summary, see Rüegg 1992, pp. 42–52, and, for a corrective to the familiar Italo-centric accounts, Porter and Teich 1992.

tially to set not so much against the earlier academic concerns with speculative grammar, natural philosophy and 'scholastic' theology as alongside them. In their search for a 'purer' Latin style they turned to
Quintilian and his models and adopted from them the concept that the
aim of education was to produce an orator, a man of the world whose
leisure would be spent with the 'best authors', a man of culture who
could acquit himself well both at the courts of kings and in the law
courts. The gap between the scholar and the man of affairs was to be nar-
rowed. At this level, the new ideas were to have their primary impact on
the faculties of arts.[27] At the same time, the new enthusiasm for the word,
issuing in the search for neglected manuscripts and the cultivation of
Greek, was to have an impact on all areas of study. In theology, a new
brand of scholarship began to emerge, based not on the *Glossa Ordinaria*
and Nicholas de Lyra but on an investigation of the text of the Bible,
fortified by a knowledge not only of Greek but of Hebrew and, on the
Continent at least, of Syriac and Aramaic, and a study of a far wider range
of the early Fathers than had hitherto been cultivated.

The new developments in the arts courses required students no longer
just to listen, but to read and to write, and their need was met by the
availability of relatively cheap texts from the printing presses – texts,
moreover, which, might (but might not) be identical, one with another.
This, however, is to advance too fast. The need for multiple text-books
had first of all to be established, and the stages by which this was done are
not as clear as we might wish. William Gray and other English scholars
encountered humanism in the course of their European travels, studied
Greek abroad, and brought back with them notable examples of humanist texts. Duke Humfrey patronized Italian humanists, and even brought
them to Britain. These early pioneers, however, remained for long an
élite.

Gradually, however, as more and more scholars returned from their
continental travels, the new learning began to permeate the universities.
John Gunthorp, for example, after incepting as an MA in Cambridge in
1452, travelled to Italy, where he learned Greek and studied under
Guarino in Ferrara before returning in 1460 to the university, where he
became Warden of the King's Hall before, like many another Warden,
going on to higher things, as a diplomat, secretary and Chaplain to the
Queen and, ultimately, Keeper of the Privy Seal. We have no direct evi-

27. These developments are critically examined in Grafton and Jardine 1986.

dence that Gunthorp incorporated his new learning into his formal teaching, though it is possible.

Between 1472 and 1482, however, albeit not continuously, the Italian Franciscan, Lorenzo Traversagni, was lecturing in Cambridge on the *Rhetorica ad Herennium* attributed to Cicero, and on Aristotle's *Ethics*. Traversagni's *Margarita Eloquentiae* or *Nova Rhetorica* was printed by Caxton in *c.* 1478, and in 1480 by the St Albans Printer; and Caxton also printed the summary, *Epitome Margaritae eloquentiae*, in 1480.[28] The new interest in literature and in literary style had sufficient support in 1488 (while Rotherham was Chancellor of Cambridge) for a substantial alteration to be made to the requirements for the BA whereby the first two years were taken from logic and assigned rather to humane letters, leaving logic for the third year and philosophy for the fourth.

More such examples of travellers could be adduced, especially for Oxford, and some at least must have passed on what they had learned. When Thomas Linacre and William Grocyn left Oxford for Italy in or about 1488, they had already acquired the rudiments of Greek, possibly from Cornelio Vitelli, a pupil of Francesco Filelfo and perhaps of Niccolò Perotti, later his rival.[29] Indeed, Emanuel of Constantinople, whose chief employment was as a scribe to the Chancellor, George Neville, had been teaching some Greek in Oxford from 1462, and it is likely that John Serbopoulos, with whom Emanuel worked while in Oxford, also had some pupils in Greek. There seems, however, to have been no promise of continuity in official instruction in Greek in the university as such until Grocyn returned, in about 1490, from his studies with Chalcondylas and Politian and started lecturing in the schools. Private tuition within individual colleges, such as Magdalen, there probably was. The most impressive affirmation of faith in a humanist model for education, however, came with Richard Fox's foundation of Corpus Christi College, Oxford, in 1517, with provision for three 'praelectors' in Greek, Latin and theology and for two Scholars or Fellows to retain their emoluments, without graduating, so long as they devoted themselves to the study of Greek and Latin. Fox was also instrumental in attracting to the rhetoric lecture founded by Wolsey the great Spanish humanist and educationalist Juan Luis Vives, who taught in Oxford, if sporadically, from 1523 to 1528.

---

28. *STC* 24188.5 and 24189 (in two distinct states); *STC* 24190 (St Albans) and *STC* 24190.3 (*Epitome*). Cf. Trapp, above, pp. 289, 299–300.
29. For the problematic dates of Cornelio Vitelli's years in Oxford, and his status there, see Clough 1977, p. 10.

In Cambridge the establishment of Greek on a permanent footing probably dates from the arrival there of no less a mentor than Erasmus, unquestionably the most distinguished humanist scholar of his generation in northern Europe. Erasmus's first visit to England in 1499 had been prompted by three of his pupils at the Collège de Montaigu in Paris: Robert (kinsman of John) Fisher, Richard Whitford of Queens' College and William Blount, Lord Mountjoy. He first came to Cambridge in 1506, probably in the entourage of Henry VII and the Lady Margaret who were received by John Fisher, as Chancellor, and it was Fisher who persuaded Erasmus to teach in Cambridge from 1511. There he did the preparatory work for his new edition of the New Testament, the *Novum Instrumentum*, and occupied himself with his *Adages*, his editions of Jerome's letters and of Seneca, and his translations from Basil, Plutarch and Lucian, as well as with those of his pedagogic texts which were to saturate the market for decades to come: the *De copia verborum*, *De conscribendis epistolis* and *De ratione studii*, along with his edition of Cato's *Disticha*, a very elementary text but one that was bought in large quantities by teachers and students all over Europe.

In Cambridge, Erasmus's lectures in Greek were elementary, first on Chrysoloras's *Grammar*, which attracted a smaller audience than he had hoped for, and then on that of Theodore Gaza. His private lessons perhaps bore more fruit: we know that Thomas Lupset and others were paid in Greek lessons for their research assistance. Of the generation which came to prominence in the university between about 1515 and 1525, many had embraced humanism and many are known to have experienced Erasmus's teaching.[30]

The mantle of public instruction in Greek, however, was inherited by Richard Croke who had been away from Cambridge for the whole period of Erasmus's residence. After graduating BA from King's in 1509 he had pursued his studies in Paris, Louvain and Cologne before, at the age of twenty-six, becoming the professor of Greek at Leipzig, where he published an elementary Greek accidence and an edition of book IV of Gaza's grammar. He returned to Cambridge to take his MA in 1517 and was appointed lecturer in Greek in 1518. Typical of many of his generation, Croke made it clear in his inaugural lecture that he regarded the study of the classical languages, especially Greek, essentially as a handmaid to theology and was at pains to express his esteem also for Scotus and other scholastic theologians.

30. For Erasmus in Cambridge, see Thomson and Porter 1963; Twigge 1987; Brown 1984, pp. 351–80.

The teaching of Greek was not, of course, the only manifestation that the 'new learning' had arrived. Many embraced, or were inculcated with, a 'humanist' education without acquiring proficiency in the language, but provision for Greek teaching is a useful indication of a shift in priorities accepted by the authorities. No less significant for the introduction of new approaches, however, were Erasmus's Cambridge lectures on Jerome, perhaps as Lady Margaret Professor.

The provision of printed texts

We have said that the spread of these new studies must have been facilitated by the proliferation of printed texts, although, of course, the old texts also became more widely available in the new medium. Unfortunately, we have only scattered evidence about the stages by which printed texts became increasingly commonplace in the universities. This was not a regular progress. Neil Ker, for example, estimated that, in 1540, Merton library was still 'almost completely devoid of printed books'.[31]

It is not easy to tell whether the cheap student texts printed overseas which first became available in Oxford and Cambridge, were produced with the English market in mind. In the first instance, presumably, books produced, say, with the students of the Sorbonne in mind, were brought to England as a speculative venture. Their existence, with their potential for the introduction of new teaching texts and ones which could be made available almost at once to a substantial number of students, provided an opportunity for a new style of teaching. Students could now, to an extent previously unknown, own, however briefly, those texts which were their immediate objects of study; hearing began to give way to reading, the tutorial first to supplement and soon to replace, in succession, the cursory and the ordinary lecture. New authors became the object of routine study, and old authors the object of new commentaries. We cannot be sure, however, and perhaps it is a question scarcely worth asking, to what extent these phenomena were the results of the mere mechanics of cheap production, given that such developments coincide so neatly with the new pedagogical theories expounded in the books themselves. At any event, students now wanted books for reading pri-

31. Ker 1985, p. 395. The list of books, with their valuations, is printed on pp. 141 and 142 of Madan and Bradshaw 1885–90. The continuation on p. 143 is probably unconnected (see the note on p. 456 of *Collectanea*, 2nd ser.). For the identification of Johannes de Westfalia as bookseller at Oxford, see Juchhoff 1954.

vately, and not just for the lecture room; their tutors and their friends could and did recommend, far more freely than before, the reading of other texts or other commentaries for the purposes of comparison. Vacation tasks began to rear their ugly heads. Where did students actually get their books? To a large extent students got them, either new or second-hand, from their predecessors or their tutors, and their tutors got them from the local book-sellers. But where did the local book-sellers get them from?

With some few partial exceptions – such as Caxton's printing of Traversagni, the output of the St Albans Printer in the 1480s and of John Siberch, brought to Cambridge to print humanist texts in the early 1520s – few English printing houses up to the end of our period made a serious, let alone a sustained, attempt to meet the need for Latin texts; still less, Greek or Hebrew. The main exceptions are the Oxford houses of the Printer of Rufinus' *Expositio*, of Theodoric Rood, sometimes in partnership with Hunt, and of John Scolar. The anonymous printer, working with type obtained from Cologne, continued after Rufinus with Aegidius Romanus' *De peccato originali* and Bruni's translation of the *Nicomachean Ethics* in 1479.[32] In 1481 Rood, in a new enterprise, followed these with Alexander ab Alexandria's *Expositio super libros Aristotelis de anima* and, in 1482, with John Lathbury's *Liber moralium super trenis iheremie prophete*.[33] In 1483 he must have invested a substantial amount of capital to print a glossed text of Lyndewood's *Constitutiones provinciales*, a standard work for canon lawyers.[34] Slightly more adventurously, in 1485, he produced Francesco Griffolini's much-printed humanist text on the Epistles of Phalaris,[35] but most of his remaining output was of small volumes of grammar, dialectic or practical theology. The texts which John Scolar printed between 1517 and 1528 were all of this class, with a marked emphasis on school and elementary university text-books. These experiments were not sufficiently rewarding to inspire a succession.[36]

Pynson and De Worde in London were better equipped to supply the mass market for school grammars and the *Libelli sophistarum* for both universities, and the continental printers to furnish up-to-date university texts. When John Dorne decided to venture his capital on two small philosophical texts in and around 1527, it was Peter Treveris in Southwark

32. *STC* 21443 and *STC* 752. 33. *STC* 314 and *STC* 15297. 34. *STC* 17102.
35. *STC* 19827.
36. For Siberch's eclectic and markedly humanist output, see Goldschmidt 1955; Treptow 1970 and the sources cited in his bibliography; and McKitterick 1992, pp. 38–9. For a discussion of Rood's and Scolar's enterprises in Oxford, see Barker 1978, pp. 2–6.

who undertook the printing.[37] When, therefore, the University of Cambridge procured in 1534 a charter empowering them to appoint three stationers and to print, subject to the *imprimatur* of the Chancellor, 'omnimodos libros' ('all manner of books'), it was not inspired by the ambition immediately to establish a learned press but by a desire to circumvent the Act of 1534 which specifically withdrew from foreign stationers the exemptions from the legislation against alien craftsmen which were embodied in the Act of 1484, and which had already come under threat under the terms of the Acts of 1523 and 1529 obliging them to submit to the rules of the appropriate craft guild. The Act of 1534 made it an offence for alien stationers to sell books retail or to import books which had been bound abroad. The three major stationers in Cambridge at this time, Garrett Godfrey, Nicholas Spierinck and Segar Nicholson, were in fact all from the Low Countries, and they it was who not only prompted the university to procure its charter but also met the expenses of doing so. Their aim was to protect their livelihood as retailers, and it may even be that the clause granting the right to print was added by the King. The Act of 1534 reflected not only the increasing size and confidence of the indigenous book-trade, but also Henry's, and certainly Cromwell's, appreciation of its potential for propaganda, and in the propaganda battles stemming from the rift with Rome the University of Cambridge might well have seemed a promising ally.[38]

Evidence for book ownership

How does the available information on the availability and ownership of texts fill out the picture? Until the sixteenth century our knowledge of book-ownership is necessarily based very largely on surviving books and on records of bequests. Large books have a far better chance of survival than small books, because of both their physical structure and their value; and large books are, especially in the context of universities, likelier to be the objects of bequests, being perceived, as we have seen, as more suitable for housing in libraries. A list of books bequeathed can seldom be assumed to include all of the testator's books. In the absence of a continuation of Susan Cavanaugh's census of manuscripts up to the year 1500, the surviving evidence for the sale and for the ownership of books in Oxford and Cambridge is far more plentiful for the fifty years after 1500

37. *STC* 18833a and *STC* 15574.
38. See McKitterick 1992, pp. 22–37, for a detailed account of the charter and the background to it.

than for the preceding half-century.[39] It is provided chiefly by the Day
Book of the stationer John Dorne in Oxford, covering the period January
to December 1520 (excluding June and July when, significantly, he went
overseas);[40] the fragments of the account-book of Erasmus's friend, the
stationer Garrett Godfrey, in Cambridge, for around 1527 to 1533;[41] the
inventory of the stock of Godfrey's successor, Nicholas Pilgrim, drawn
up for probate in 1546;[42] and records of the books owned by individuals at
both universities, including those found among the records of the university courts.[43] Inventories on decease share some of the shortcomings of
wills: large books, typically in the ancient languages, are likelier to be
individually listed than small books, which more often included vernacular texts and which were frequently valued as a single item: 'other books,
bound and unbound' or some such catch-all phrase. Also likely to be
under-represented in the inventories are manuscript volumes, whose
titles were often harder to ascertain at a glance, and naughty books,
whether magical or heretical, which seem to have been discreetly passed
over by the appraisers. It is important to have these limitations always in
mind.

The evidence for sales and the evidence for ownership at the two
English universities would complement each other if we could be reasonably confident that the spread of the new texts proceeded *pari passu* at
both universities. In the absence of sure grounds for such confidence we
have rather an unfortunate mis-match. The Day Book of John Dorne tells
us with considerable precision what books he sold from day to day in the
course of a single year and, in many cases, their place of printing. It does
not reveal the extent of his stock or the identity of his customers.
Godfrey's accounts are far more fragmentary, and the great majority of
the entries can be only tentatively dated within the tolerably certain
span, 1527 to 1533. The extent of Godfrey's stock is likewise unknown.
As his accounts actually consist of a record of debts, however, his customers' names and addresses are preserved, except in the many cases
where Godfrey's own knife, or that of someone in his bindery, has
trimmed them off.[44] From Godfrey's accounts also, we often learn the
names of the students for whom their tutors purchased these texts as well

39. See Margaret Lane Ford above, pp. 207–10.   40. Madan and Bradshaw 1885–90.
41. Leedham-Green, Rhodes and Stubbings 1992.
42. Gray and Palmer 1915, pp. 10–30; re-edited in Leedham-Green 1986, I, pp. 61–70, and II,
    passim; and discussed by Bennett 1950.
43. *PLRE*, II for the Oxford lists; and the two volumes of Leedham-Green 1986.
44. Emmanuel Coll. ms. 401, removed from the binding, since reconstituted, of Emmanuel
    Coll. 310.5.6, Zacharias, Bishop of Chrysopolis, *In unum ex quatuor, sive de concordia evange-
    listarum* ([Cologne], Eucharius Cervicornus, 1535).

as the names of printers or cities of origin of the books and something of his business methods. We see him, for example, sending books to customers 'on approval' and buying in second-hand stock. Pilgrim's inventory appears to record his total stock but tells us nothing of his pattern of sales, except what can be deduced from the presence of multiple copies of popular text-books.

As for the owners, the records published as collections comprise, for Oxford, 62 inventories dated between 1507 and 1554: 32 of them between 1507 and 1514, 12 between 1527 and 1530, 10 between 1531 and 1539, and 8 between 1541 and 1554. The Cambridge lists start later, but we have 63 lists for private individuals between 1536 and 1553–4, with almost every year represented but with particularly numerous examples for 1545 (9), 1546 (10) and 1551 (10) (cf. fig. 21.3). The total number of titles listed in the Oxford sample is 1,097, in the Cambridge sample 4,108, an eloquent demonstration in itself of the boom in book-ownership in the first half of the century.

A simple test demonstrates the dangers of drawing conclusions from negative evidence presented by the statistically insignificant proportion of members of the university whose books were listed in most periods. The 32 Oxford lists falling in the period 1507–14 present not a single copy of any work or edition by Erasmus. The register covering the years 1515–26 is unfortunately lost, but in the period 1527–30 only 13 Erasmus works are recorded, all in the ownership of 2 individuals out of a possible 12; a single example appears among the 10 lists in the period 1531–9. From this evidence, it would seem that Erasmus was neglected in Oxford until after 1540: 8 owners recorded in the years 1541–54 boast between them 25 examples, making a less than grand total, for the years 1507–54, of 32. An almost identical number of Cambridge men, admittedly clustering far nearer the end of the chronological spectrum, had between them 323 Erasmian works or editions. Godfrey's accounts record the sale of some 100 specimens between 1527 and 1535, and Pilgrim's stock in 1546 included 69, 22 of them being copies of the compendious *De civilitate morum puerilium*. Conclusive evidence, this would seem, of a far greater enthusiasm for Erasmus in Cambridge than in Oxford. Yet in 1520 John Dorne sold in Oxford something like 270 copies of works by Erasmus.

It may just be that, in spite of Oxford's head start, and the humanist foundations there of Corpus Christi, Magdalen and Cardinal Colleges, the 'new learning' came to flourish more widely in Cambridge after the first years of the century. It is not, however, conceivable that the books sold by Dorne were destroyed as soon as read, and were not replaced. The great majority of the texts in question were theologically neutral and were welcomed as much by Catholic as by Protestant pedagogues in England at this time. We need not look for a bonfire. A likelier explanation is that the Oxford appraisers who drew up these inventories were simply more impatient than their Cambridge counterparts and even less inclined to take the trouble to list small books. Indeed, a tendency to impatience is clearly manifest in the messiness of many of the Oxford lists. Unfortunately, this suggested solution to the enigma is not susceptible of demonstration. Of the 1,440 Oxford books listed in inventories, the format of only 176 can be determined, either from the appraiser's statement or as a result of the text in question only having been issued in a single format. Of these 176, 63 are folio, 39 quarto and 5 sextodecimo; 69, however, must be octavo. Our impression that the Oxford books listed are predominantly such as more often appeared in large formats must remain an impression only, borne out only by such suggestive facts as that a typically small-format book, Terence, is listed more than twice as often at Cambridge as at Oxford in the first half of the century.

The evidence from marks of ownership in surviving books also needs to be handled with great care. The great majority of signed books known to us have, very predictably, been found in institutional libraries. A large proportion of them were donated to these libraries within a few years of their possession by their last user and, as we have seen, such books were far more likely to be large than small, and this remained true even after institutional libraries had consciously started to accommodate 'modern' texts. Fifteenth- and sixteenth-century libraries had no place for the everyday small-format text-books on which the undergraduates almost uniquely depended and which, passing from hand to hand, must have disintegrated in their thousands. Such little books are now far rarer than the imposing folios in which contemporary seniors buried themselves. The *Introductiones ad logicam* of Jacques Lefèvre d'Etaples, of which certainly nine, and perhaps eighteen, copies are recorded among Cambridge owners between 1546 and 1558, and of which Dorne sold between two and ten in 1520, is now an extremely scarce text. (The uncertainty of the numbers arises from the impossibility of determining which of several of Lefèvre's works is intended by an entry reading simply 'Introductiones fabri'.) Nor is size the only factor to increase a book's chances of survival. *Pietas* might dictate that a book presented by a particularly honoured donor be not discarded. Fine bindings would plead eloquently for retention. The value of Aldine texts of the classics was early and long recognized, and fine print and lavish illustration must also have had their influence. For these reasons, we should interpret with caution statistics based on surviving books and compiled with a view to determining the relative numbers of books imported from, say, Italy, a notable source of fine books, and France and the Low Countries, both convenient sources of cheap text-books.

It is clear that the evidence both from inventories and from surviving books, set about as it is with such pitfalls, must be handled with great care. It will come to bear with greater or lesser force according to the nature of the text under investigation; quantitative analyses, comparisons between universities, and arguments from absence must often be, if not rejected, then constructed with a degree of elaborate caution for which space can scarcely be found in a survey of this breadth. Thus it is easier to refute the supposition that Scotus and Lombard, almost always in folio, were indeed banished after 1540 than it is to chart with any accuracy the arrival and adoption in the British universities of the new texts, often, and most influentially, in small, affordable formats.

If no one of the different types of evidence can alone provide a sure guide to the circulation of texts, can we, by using them all together, arrive at a more accurate picture? A closer look at the case of evidence for the circulation of Erasmian texts may be instructive. If we examine the 270 or so Erasmian works sold by John Dorne in 1520, it is striking how many of them were of elementary texts: 41 copies of the *Colloquia* (including 9 of the editions issued with Lucian's *Dialogues* in Greek), 31 of his and William Lily's *De constructione octo partium orationis*, 17 of the *De duplici copia verborum ac rerum* and, in a slightly different line, 15 of the *Enchiridion militis christiani*. One of the copies of the *De copia* is attributed to Wynkyn de Worde, evidence either of an edition of which no copies survive or of a slip of the pen. Similarly, of Godfrey's 100 such sales, ten to fifteen years later, 32 were of the *Colloquia* (including one sale of 6 copies), 7 of the *De copia*, 7 of the *Enchiridion* and 6 of the *De immensa dei misericordia*. He also records sales of 10 copies of the *Adagia*, ranging in size and state from 6-shillings'-worth to 8d-worth, against Dorne's 9 (nearly all specified as 'parva' and sold for about 8d).

The two Oxford inventories recording Erasmus texts before 1530, those of Edmund Burton, MA, and William Woodruff, MA,[45] feature,

---

45. *PLRE*, II 43 and 47, respectively.

respectively, on the one hand a *Paraphrasis in epistolas Pauli*, a *Dialogus*, the *De immensa dei misericordia*, a New Testament in five volumes, the *Spongia*, and the *Adagia* (3s), and on the other, the *Paraphrasis in evangelium Matthaei*, and the *Colloquia* (8d), the *Parabolae* or *Similia*, a commentary on the Psalms, the *De conscribendis epistolis*, an unidentified *Apologia* (8d) and, again, the *Spongia*. Still at Oxford, the next Erasmus text inventoried was to be Dunstan Lacey's *Paraphrases in Novum Testamentum*,[46] presumably incomplete since it is valued at only 1s, and there is then nothing before 1550, with the notable exception of a mysterious Bisley in 1543,[47] with 3 copies each of the *De preparatione ad mortem* and the *De copia*, 2 copies of the *Parabolae* and 1 each of the *Adagia* (6d), the *Catalogus*, and the *Annotationes in Novum Testamentum*, along with something doubtfully designated 'Retho'.

In Cambridge inventories before 1551, the texts that reach double figures among the 46 private collections are: the *Adagia* (ranging from 1d to 6s), 23 copies; the *De copia*, 19 copies; the *Colloquia*, 14 copies; the *Enchiridion* and the *Encomium Moriae*, 13 copies each; the *De conscribendis epistolis*, 12 copies; and assorted *Paraphrases*, 39 copies (again ranging from 1d to 6s). Of these texts, we find Nicholas Pilgrim in 1546 stocking 3 copies of the *Adagia*, 9 of the *De copia*, 8 of the *Epitome Colloquiorum*, 6 of the *Enchiridion* and only one each of the others, the *Paraphrases* in two volumes. He also had in stock, however, 15 copies of Erasmus's edition of Cato's *Distichs* and no fewer than 22 of the *De civilitate morum puerilium*.

Surviving early editions of Erasmus, with ownership inscriptions associating them with the English universities, do not, as it happens, throw light on the years before 1520 since the date of purchase is seldom noted. In several cases the first, or only, owner cannot have acquired the book less than ten years or so after publication, and in most cases we cannot be sure that they did not buy a book already thirty years old. Sometimes the lapse of years is demonstrable; Nicholas Udall dates his purchase of the 1522 edition of the *Annotationes in Novum Testamentum*: it was in 1537. We have no way of guessing at its previous history. What is, perhaps, significant, is that, alongside the names of known humanists – John Claymond, Sir John Cheke, Nicholas Udall and Thomas Paynell – we find many names not so known to fame, suggesting a wide circulation. In Scotland, by contrast, the names of Henry Sinclair, Archibald Crawford, John Grierson and James Crichton recur with a frequency which suggests a far

46. *PLRE*, II 52:15.   47. *PLRE*, II 60.

smaller, élite readership. The dating of the Scottish purchases is again problematical. At least one of Henry Sinclair's purchases, of at least parts of the *Opera*, is dated 1550; and perhaps only James Crichton's 1514 *Adagia* can confidently be stated to have been acquired before 1530.

This highlights yet another likely distortion in the evidence from inventories: only 8 of the 62 pre-1555 Oxford lists are of undergraduates' goods, perhaps 6 of 64 at Cambridge. Students seldom retained their elementary texts once they had mastered them. Where such texts appear in the libraries of older men, it is usually because they were using them as teaching texts.

One source of information we have not tapped as yet. How did contemporaries see the changes? How reliable are their accounts? Richard Layton's triumphalist account of the visitation which he and his companions carried out at Oxford in 1535 is justly memorable: 'We have set Dunce in Bocardo, and have utterly banisshede hym Oxforde for ever, with all his blind glosses, and is now made a comon servant to evere man, faste nailede up upon postes in all common howses of easement. *Id, quod oculis meis vidi.*' He it was also who reported seeing 'one Mr Grenefelde a gentilman of Bukynghamshire' gathering the blowing leaves 'to make him sewells or blanswherrs to kepe the dere within the woode, thereby to have the better cry with his howndes'.[48] Others were to write of the destruction in this year and especially of Duke Humfrey's library in 1549, in other terms. The books destroyed in 1535 seem mostly to have been just pulled apart. Neil Ker has noted that scarcely a book was bound in Oxford from 1520 to 1570 that did not incorporate fragments of vellum manuscripts as pastedowns or endpapers.[49] The 1549 destruction is described by Edward Weston as a bonfire; and it may be that there is an element of truth in this. No book known to have been in Oxford's University Library, at that time, has as yet been detected as a pastedown.[50]

But to return to Richard Layton. Had the visitors indeed banished Scotus, and for ever? Out of 48 private individuals in Oxford whose books were inventoried by 1534, 19 owned copies of Scotus. None of the 14 listed from then until 1554 had one. It looks convincing. In Cambridge, on the other hand, 17 copies are to be found in the 68 lists surviving from 1537 to 1554-5. Cambridge was visited also of course, and it is recorded that books were burned there too, but it is recorded in a matter-of-fact

---

48. Strype 1822, I, p. 324.   49. Ker 1954, VII, p. 188.   50. Ker 1986, p. 466 n. 3.

kind of way. There were fewer books there to destroy, of course; but one has the impression that the proportion destroyed was also smaller and, perhaps, the impact on individual collections correspondingly less. Cargill-Thompson, indeed, pondering the possible reasons for the falling off of donations to college libraries after 1535, attributed by some to a general sense of insecurity as to the future of colleges, has concluded that 'more books probably disappeared from theft or neglect than as a result of the official purges of the government'.[51]

At the time of the visitation, Cambridge received injunctions forbidding the official teaching of canon law (since the laws of the Roman Church were to have no more force, and no further canon law was to be enacted as such in England). It is likely that the same injunctions were sent to Oxford, although they do not survive. Canon law continued to be *studied*, regardless, since it was still essential to the business of the Church Courts, and no very significant diminution in the ownership of canon law texts seems to have struck Cambridge, although the surviving Oxford lists, once more, would seem to suggest that 1535 was indeed some sort of watershed, were it not for the evidence of surviving books.[52]

The Cambridge injunctions had also forbidden the study of Scotus, and of his commentators: Walter Burley, Antonio Trombetta, Thomas Bricot and Stephanus Brulefer. All but the last of these four 'frivolous glossators' feature in Oxford lists prior to 1534, with only a single copy of Bricot between then and 1554. Cambridge also shows only a single work by Bricot in these years. There is, however, some reason to suppose that they were not widely in use in Cambridge before 1535. Not one of them occurs among books sold by Godfrey, whereas Dorne in 1520 sold 19 copies of Scotus, 13 of Burley, 2 of Bricot and 1 each of Trombetta and Brulefer. Scotus himself, however, remained a familiar and useful author: at least 8 copies of Scotus texts are recorded by Margaret Lane Ford as having been purchased by Oxford men in the years following 1535, and 11 occur in Cambridge inventories drawn up between 1535 and 1551.

Positive instructions were also received, prescribing the study of Aristotle, Rudolph Agricola, Melanchthon and George of Trebizond. Aristotle, of course, always had been studied, but there were now new texts and new editions of Aristotle and new uses for old texts. An examination of whether, how and when the old gave way to the new would

---

51. Cargill-Thompson 1954, p. 42.   52. See Helmholz below, pp. 395–7.

require more elaborate treatment than can be afforded here.[53] As to the other authors, so far as Cambridge was concerned the advice was otiose – Godfrey was already selling all three before 1535, and was selling them, moreover, to tutors for their pupils: 3 copies of George of Trebizond, 11 of Agricola and 39 of Melanchthon. The Oxford lists, by contrast, show only 1 of each before 1535, and 2 of each (all 6 in the possession of a single individual) before 1554; another instance, surely, of the discrepancy in the practices of the appraisers at the universities. We know that Anthony Frobysher was required to lecture on Melanchthon's dialectic at Oxford in 1527.[54]

Perhaps we are on safer ground confining ourselves to a single university and contemplating Roger Ascham's rosy account of Cambridge University and particularly of St John's College in 1542, as compared with its state twenty years earlier when his correspondent, John Brandesby, had graduated:

> Aristotle and Plato are now read in their own language by the boys – as indeed we have done for five years in our own college. Sophocles and Euripides are more familiar than Plautus was when you were here. Herodotus, Thucydides, Xenophon are more on the lips and in the hands than Titus Livius was then. Now you would hear of Demosthenes what once you did of Cicero. More copies of Isocrates are in the boys' hands than there were formerly of Terence.[55]

That there is an element of exaggeration here can scarcely be doubted; or, if not, then Nicholas Pilgrim did not know his trade. He had in stock no copies of Isocrates, but 9 of Terence, and 44 works of Cicero to 2 of Demosthenes. He did, however, have 3 texts of Sophocles, if none of Euripides, and 1 each of Plato and Xenophon. On the other hand, none of Ascham's 'new' authors is recorded as sold by Godfrey, but all occur, in Greek as well as in Latin editions, in at least two Cambridge inventories, each before 1546.

Supply of books to the trade

What facilities did the university book-sellers have, in the years when printed books first became plentiful, for selecting and procuring their stock from overseas? Already in the 1480s, Michel Morin and Jean

---

53. For an account of the new treatment of Aristotle's dialectic, see Jardine 1988.
54. Register of Congregation, 1518–35, f. 168.
55. Ascham, 1864–5 I, pt i, p. 26.

Anthoine were operating in England as salesmen for the editions of Jean Dupré.[56] English merchants trading regularly via continental ports not only carried books but began to commission editions, and, although London remained the chief centre for the distribution of continental printing, some foreign printers seem to have warehoused goods in Oxford. We have already mentioned the transaction between Thomas Hunt at Oxford and Peter Actors and John of Acon in 1483. From the earliest years of the sixteenth century, the Birckman family were establishing a presence in the English trade, which was to continue, dominating the competition, until as late as 1570. Members of the family were active in the English universities as well as in London, sometimes employing in the courts the mediation of their trading partners, if denizens, sometimes that of their more influential customers. There is evidence that, in 1540, a widow Birckman owned property in Cambridge where she was assessed at £20 for the relief of the poor,[57] but we have no evidence that she was trading there.

The Oxford stationers, then, from the early years of the century, presumably obtained most of their continental stock either from the Birckmans and their rivals, from the agents of continental presses who settled – usually in London – for a few years at a time, or, later, from the London stationers specializing in the Latin stock. In Cambridge there is room to entertain one more possibility. Although some, and perhaps most, of their stock came though the same channels as that of the London stationers, as witness the appearance of Nicholas Spierinck's name in the port books, the East Anglian ports also had a flourishing overseas trade from at least the fourteenth century. A cargo impounded by the searcher of Lynn for non-payment of dues in about 1430 contained besides 12 dozen lenses 'pro spectaculis', 4 bagpipes, 6 dozen harpstrings, lacing points (long and short), needles, ear picks, calendar cases, writing tables, inkhorns and a rich variety of other hardware, 6 sheets of paper – containing 1,500 pins – and, gloriously, 1 dozen 'lewde-calenders' valued at 6d.

Moreover, foreign traders at Stourbridge Fair conveyed their goods thither by water, and we know from annotations in the books themselves that books were sold there (see fig. 9.4, p. 206), albeit the surviving records of the University Court at the fair are obstinately silent as to stationers. There is evidence that, in 1609, a consignment of the books of Hendrick Niclaes, the familist, came by water to Ely (where the officials

56. Ryan 1963, p. 19, quoted in G. Pollard 1970, at p. 206.
57. Corpus Christi Coll., Cambridge, ms. 106, f. 167v.

failed, as those in Cambridge might not have done, to appreciate their pernicious nature). Unfortunately, the records for the Wash ports, of which Lynn was the most active, lack the detail which has made possible the study of the importation of books for the London trade. It would be odd if the only books coming to Cambridge and its neighbourhood by this route were naughty ones, even if a 'lewdecalender' was not that fifteenth-century prototype of the car mechanic's solace which one dreams of finding some day as an endpaper in a copy of Boccaccio, but rather a layman's astrological almanac.

Looking at the question from the standpoint of demand rather than of supply leads us back again to similar considerations. The earliest printed undergraduate texts finding their way to the English universities may or may not have been produced with that destination in mind. Once that market had been defined, however, both printer and importer could cater for it without taking any great entrepreneurial risks. To what extent was an unwillingness to take such risks responsible for the longevity of so many university texts? Did the greater ease of communication, trade and travel on the Continent accelerate the shifting of academic preoccupations? In England, at least, editions of Erasmus sold and sold and sold, far outstripping holy writ in the private ownership of junior members; Valla's *Elegantiae*, Lefèvre d'Etaples's *Introductiones in logicam*, and, later, certain Ramist texts all found, for many decades, enthusiastic purchasers in numbers which were not only substantial but relatively easy to predict, and it would be possible to name further examples such as Nicolaes Cleynaert's Greek grammar and the numerous text-books of Melanchthon, especially his dialectic. Much the same is true of the required Aristotelian texts of Bachelors. To these as his staple, the importer could add more speculative wares: new tracts and commentaries on academic topics, new editions of classical authors, the works of Machiavelli and other political theorists, courtesy books, a leaven of *belles lettres* – Mantuan, Boccaccio, and so on – and, above all, the latest blasts and counter-blasts of theological controversy. All of these found willing readers at the universities.

The quantity and variety of material emanating from the Continent might well baffle choice. How were the book-sellers to tell what there was, and how to get it? Printed publishers' catalogues from houses active in the academic market-place – Colines, Wechel, Estienne and others – survive from the 1540s,[58] and it may be that the gap separating these from

58. Coppens 1992, for examples.

the catalogues surviving from the 1470s and 1480s is merely the product of chance. On the other hand, the broadsheet catalogues may, as Hirsch surmises, have suffered at least a temporary eclipse as fixed shops took the place of itinerant book-sellers.[59] The university bookshops, however, can scarcely have had the space, nor their proprietors the capital, to accommodate a large stock of recondite texts bought 'on spec'. Such evidence as there is suggests that, then as now, customers requiring new specialist texts either had them specially ordered for them or made arrangements either directly with foreign book-sellers or through the mediation of their friends on the Continent.

The reforming party in the reign of Edward VI and the Marian exiles returning on Elizabeth's accession maintained contact with their continental mentors, and the correspondence known as the *Zürich Letters* teems with references to books recently published, books sent as gifts, books enquired after, and books to be acquired, usually by Froschauer, at Frankfurt and committed to the care of one or other of the English merchants trading in those parts.[60] It is impossible to estimate the probable extent of similar correspondence in the earlier years of the sixteenth century. A relatively high proportion of medical students studied abroad, but as a breed they were scarce; so did Scotsmen, but the average Oxbridge scholar of the early sixteenth century was usually content to study at home, at least until he began to be aware of the crackling of the flames. Until then, the university student travelling on the Continent probably did not expect thereafter to return to his roost, but rather to move on to more lucrative fields. Foreign students, similarly, were not at all common until driven here by persecution at home. It seems unlikely that, in the first quarter of the century, private correspondence flowed on any considerable scale between continental and English academics, except for a very few, noted already as controversialists.

Between May and August of 1520, John Dorne travelled overseas, very probably to his native Brunswick; the first book he sold on his return in August 1520 was Aristophanes' *Plutus*, the first of the several editions of that text occurring in his list which is specified as being Greek. Had someone ordered it, or was it a speculation? It is inconceivable that Dorne did not return from his travels with at least some new stock; almost as inconceivable that he had not compiled a list of recent editions which he had not the space, the capital or the confidence to buy for stock.

---

59. Hirsch 1967, p. 65.   60. *Epistolæ Tigurinæ* 1848; Robinson 1842–5.

Such lists were, presumably, compiled and carried about also by the Birckmans and their competitors, and perhaps left with their client book-sellers. We have no evidence, at this date, however, for any such practice.

Godfrey too seems to have returned from time to time to his native land: Erasmus met him in Antwerp in 1517. His accounts record from time to time not only the place of printing but, more frequently than Dorne's, the name of the printer. With the exception of De Worde and, once, of Pynson, the printers specified are not those printing in England. Kerver (that is, Yolande Bonhomme), Colines and Froben all feature prominently. This is not, of course, to say that the London houses are unrepresented, even if the printers are not specifically named. (Godfrey's accounts, limited as they are to sales to his 'credit customers', record scarcely any of those ballads and chap-books which Dorne sold in such quantities.) Rastell's books are clearly there, as are Berthelet's, and there are numerous texts, notably grammars and the like, which could have come from any of a number of London houses. It is possible, it is indeed probable, that where printers are specified this represents a mental note of no recoverable significance. Texts certainly from the houses of those printers who are on occasion named are often listed without any such note, while the printer's name *is* noted where there can have been no ambiguity; but there is one very faint hint that Godfrey *may* have dealt direct with continental printers, and that is an entry for 'unum portiforium pars hiemalis *pro* froben'. A breviary as present? A sample? We cannot tell. Certainly not a slip of the pen, as Froben was not in the business of printing breviaries of the Use of Sarum. Moreover, while the bulk of Godfrey's recorded sales are of standard, not to say elementary, texts, we find, suddenly, a rather spectacular purchase by a Mr (not yet Dr) Thixtell, of fourteen items simultaneously. Two of them were missals – annotated 'ignoro utensel' as though supplied 'on spec' – one, or perhaps more, are lost to the binder's knife, but, of the remaining eleven, ten are Hebrew and Syriac works printed by Froben. These were precisely the sort of goods which might have been acquired by special order.

At the other end of the scale we find Godfrey selling books in multiple copies, not just in twos and threes but, on seven occasions in these fragments, in dozens. The dozens, to be sure, consist of elementary grammars – a sizable, but not calculable, proportion of them to one Thomas Patenson, apparently a schoolmaster, who also took eleven copies of Mancinus's *De quatuor virtutibus*. Elementary schoolmasters were not the only teachers to take elementary grammars. Dr Buckmaster bought the *Distichs* and a selection of the works of Stanbridge and/or Whittinton in fours; but someone, alas unidentifiable, bought four copies of Mantuan, not further identified, although at 1s a piece they were more probably the *Eclogues* or *Bucolica* than the *Opera*. Godfrey did, however, stock the *Opera varia*.[61] Someone in King's bought no less than six copies of Henry VIII against Luther. These, and a few other, exceptions apart, we get a clear impression from the sale of multiple elementary grammars and texts to college tutors not only of the unromantically low attainments of at least some first-year students, but also of a standardization of pedagogy. Godfrey, incidentally, also sold, on a very considerable scale, quires of paper (2d a quire): a reminder of the increasing popularity of the 'commonplace book'.

The holding of substantial quantities of standard texts is even more vividly apparent in the probate inventory of Godfrey's heir, Nicholas Pilgrim, dying in 1545/6. The figures are not comparable, in that the inventory, of course, records Pilgrim's stock rather than individual sales, and indeed his holding of twenty copies of *Acolastus* (unbound) becomes less impressive in the light of the fact that, fifteen or so years earlier, Godfrey sold a batch of six of the same text to a single customer. A detailed comparison of the nature of the stock of the two shops (or perhaps of the same shop) over an interval of ten to eighteen years would extend this chapter far beyond its proper bounds, but it is interesting to note that Erasmus's *De civilitate morum puerilium*, of which Pilgrim held twenty-two copies (his most popular text), already occurs five times among Godfrey's sales although not published until some three years after the earliest dated entry, and that, although the popularity of particular Erasmian texts naturally varied between the earlier period and the later, their popularity *en bloc* remained fairly constant: Erasmian texts represent about 11 per cent of Pilgrim's stock and about 12 per cent of Godfrey's identifiable sales.

Texts of this kind must surely have been ordered, as well as stocked, in bulk, and it seems probable that in these cases the university book-sellers dealt directly with the printers. Of the text-books sold by Godfrey he tells us that 9 were printed by Simon de Colines in Paris. By inference, 9 more were almost certainly from the same house. In total, 174, almost a quarter of the books recorded, were titles that Colines printed and so

61. Neil Ker's notes, preserved variously in the Bodleian and in CUL (Add. ms. 8966), record the sale of a copy bound by Godfrey at Sotheby's on 31 July 1917 (lot no. 127).

could have come from his press, although nearly all were printed by at least one other house. It seems likely, though we cannot be certain, that there was sufficient business between the two to justify dispensing with any intermediary. It is certain, however, that any such arrangements between Cambridge stationers and continental printers were not on a scale to impinge seriously on the import business of the Birckman family which, until far later in the century, continued to dominate the traffic in academical books.

The English universities, after the decline of the Merton school early in the fifteenth century, could claim but little distinction in the advancement of learning or in the proliferation of biblical and classical studies which occupied the continental universities. With the abolition of the religious houses in the 1530s, the decline in Greek studies in the later 1540s and a concurrent drop in student numbers, they could claim little distinction among the universities of western Europe, save by virtue of their antiquity. It is, nevertheless, in a European context that their provision and use of books must be surveyed. As markets for English books, except possibly in the field of religious controversy, they were by the middle of the sixteenth century probably scarcely more significant than many another prosperous market town.

16

Text-books in the universities:
the evidence from the books

KRISTIAN JENSEN

Text-books may be defined as books, normally in small format, for use as teaching tools within an educational institution, organizing as well as summarizing standard material on a specific topic into a more or less systematic overview of a discipline, or a well-defined part of a discipline; this is in opposition to the large scholarly tomes on which they are based. Text-books are linked directly to the curricula of schools and universities and their history reflects the evolution of institutional teaching.

*

Surviving library lists from the late Middle Ages show that university and college libraries did not contain text-books. Chained collections – as a rule not accessible to undergraduates – comprised standard texts and commentaries on them, mainly large books in folio: it would have been wasteful of space to keep small books chained on lecterns. Nor did undergraduates have access to the books *in electione*: those books which were available for members of colleges to select for their use outside the library. These books in any case appear also to have been standard texts in large formats. Because evidence for text-books available to students in the late Middle Ages is not to be found in library lists, because institutional books tend to survive more easily than privately owned books,[1] and because large books tend to survive more easily than small ones, the temptation to rule out the ownership of books by individual undergraduate students should be resisted. Nevertheless, it seems plausible that text-books in the later Middle Ages tended to be owned by masters.[2] Medieval methods of instruction were oral. In cursory lectures for undergraduates, newly graduated Bachelors of Arts read out prescribed texts

---

1. Margaret Lane Ford's database of surviving printed books with early English and Scottish private owners has been most useful; cf. above, pp. 205–8.
2. Parkes 1992a, p. 407; J. M. Fletcher 1986, pp. 166–7; Ker 1986, p. 467.

and provided basic information on them in the form of a related word-by-word commentary. Masters of Arts, as Regent Masters, gave ordinary lectures for two years after they received their degree. For example, a copy, now in the Bodleian Library, of Aristotle's *Nicomachean Ethics* in the translation of Leonardus Brunus, contains copious contemporary notes to the text, and a list of pittances received from the Prior of Osney Abbey as clear evidence of its use in Oxford by someone who presumably was not a Fellow of a college, probably by a master as a text to read from, not by a student as a text-book in moral philosophy.[3] In these more advanced lectures, issues which arose from the texts were examined in greater detail. Student exercises took the form of disputations, most of which were among undergraduates, known as disputations *in paruiso*. In a fifteenth-century elementary school-text much used in Germany, *Es tu scholaris*, a pupil is asked what he reads at school.[4] Using classroom jargon, he answers cheekily, 'Non lego, sed audio' ('I do not read, but listen'). This joke relies on the distinction between the activity of teachers and students: the word for 'teaching' was 'legere' ('to read') and the word for 'being a student' was 'audire' ('to listen'). Students did not confine themselves to passive listening, however. They took notes from lecturers, who read slowly enough for their words to be copied down. Lecture notes could constitute a text-book. Ready-made text-books gained importance, however, as more books were produced in smaller formats and as prices began to fall. By the first decade of the sixteenth century, a student could hope to own books which he could use for his studies, possibly second-hand copies, in which there was a trade.[5] Richard Holyngbourne, the Warden of Canterbury College, Oxford, who died about 1508, had owned a number of books in small format, some of which contained new and rare texts. His successor suggested that Holyngbourne had bought these with his own money, and sought permission of the Prior at Canterbury Cathedral for the books to be distributed among the young scholars. The same suggestion was made for the small books owned by Anthony Wooton who died in the same year.[6] Such small books were not valuable enough to take up space in a college library, however important their texts might be, and were now cheap enough to hand on to students. The Day Book of the Oxford book-seller John Dorne, from 1520, shows how some elementary books sold for a few pence, although the comparison of late

3. Oxford, [Pr. of the *Expositio in symbolum apostolorum*], 1479, *STC* 752; Bodleian, S. Seld. e.2.
4. *GW* 9398–425; cf. Henkel 1988.   5. Godfrey 1992, p. xviii.
6. Pantin 1947–50, I, pp. 87–8; Ker 1986, pp. 464–5.

fifteenth-century prices with the prices of 1520 made by J. M. Fletcher is misleading, as it compares prices of library books in folio with prices of often pamphlet-sized booklets in octavo. Prices put on books by the Oxford and Cambridge probate courts during the sixteenth century point in the same direction as Dorne's Day Book, and further indicate how book prices continued to fall throughout the sixteenth century and how the sizes of private libraries grew, even among men of modest means.7

In 1522, John Vaus (*c.* 1490–*c.* 1538) published a commentary to Alexander de Villa Dei's metrical grammar of 1199, the *Doctrinale*. In his prefatory letter, the Aberdeen professor of humanities described the transition from local manuscript lecture-notes to imported printed textbooks. Vaus reflected on how errors had crept into the text when it was taken down from his dictation by students, untrained as scribes; a shortage of printed books had been a serious impediment to his work as a teacher, and that was why he had a grammar printed for the use of his students: *In primam Doctrinalis Alexandrini de nominum ac uerborum declinationibus atque formationibus partem ab Iodoco Badio Ascensio recognitam, magistri Ioannis Vaus natione Scoti et percelebris Abredonensium Academiæ grammatici commentarii ab eodem Ascensio ibidem recogniti atque impressi.*8 The provision of printed books was probably more inadequate in Aberdeen in the 1520s than in cities closer to centres of the European book-trade. In Nuremberg only a decade earlier, however, Johannes Cochlaeus, on becoming rector of the city school, found that the only grammar generally available there was that of Pylades, that is the commentary on the *Doctrinale* by the conservative Italian grammarian, Johannes Franciscus Buccardus. Cochlaeus was therefore constrained, he tells us, to produce something better for his pupils. It was printed in an edition of 1,000 copies in 1511.9 Already in 1489 an edition of John Anwykyll's *Compendium totius grammaticae*, printed in Deventer for use in England, was stated to be aimed at teachers and pupils alike.10 The printed text-book was becoming the expected norm.

Nonetheless, lecture-note text-books continued to exist. In the sixteenth century, student notes were often printed without the consent of

---

7. Madan and Bradshaw 1885–90, pp. 72–177; J. M. Fletcher 1986, p. 166; *PLRE*, II; Leedham-Green 1986.
8. Paris, J. Badius Ascensius, 1522, also editions from 1523 and 1524; later editions with glosses in Scottish were published in Paris 1531 (*STC* 24623.5) and 1553 (*STC* 24623.7) and in Edinburgh 1566 (*STC* 24623a). Prefatory material published by Delisle 1896, pp. 4–5.
9. Müller 1882, pp. 252–5.
10. Deventer, R. Paffraet, 1489 (*GW* 2264; *STC* 696.1); cf. Orme below, pp. 458–9, 461.

the lecturer/author. Thereby a type of material previously restricted to a fairly local area became accessible throughout Europe. This, in turn, weakened local traditions; as a result, in the course of the sixteenth century, teaching within each single institution became less standardized.[11] The 1579 Oxford statutes note that the books on which Bachelors lectured were not the ones which were prescribed.[12] This example, and other sixteenth-century complaints of excessive diversity in teaching materials, must be seen in the context of the ever more international provision of text-books, and the consequent wider choice. Wider ownership of elementary introductions to a range of topics must have been a decisive factor in the collapse during the first half of the sixteenth century of the system of teaching by Regent Masters of Arts.[13]

While the teaching within individual institutions became less uniform, European universities with similar religious attitudes became more alike, as the same, or similar, text-books became available throughout the Continent. The international nature of the sixteenth-century text-book was particularly important in England and Scotland where, with notable exceptions, local book production did not cater for scholars, and where the academic market therefore relied more heavily on imported books than where universities were in close contact with prolific presses. An important exception was Wynkyn de Worde, who kept up a significant production of educational books. In general the English and Scottish educational market was so sporadically served by resident printers that text-books specifically for use in England and Scotland were printed abroad, chiefly in the Low Countries and in France. As a result, English and Scottish institutions relied on books not made precisely for their requirements. This dependence can perhaps most easily be demonstrated by listing some standard classical authors who were very widely owned in England and Scotland, according to surviving book-lists. Only two editions of Cicero's *De officiis* printed in England and Scotland survive from before the 1570s – both bilingual and probably meant for teaching; no *De oratore* until 1573; no *Epistolae ad familiares* until 1571. Only one edition of Horace survives from before 1574 – a typical school edition from 1549 with the notes of Henri Estienne and also containing the *Satires* of Juvenal and Persius. Although printed in this country, the book claims to be Parisian: an English printer

---

11. See also Ashworth below, pp. 383–4 on the disappearance of the local Oxford tradition in the discipline of logic.   12. S. Gibson 1931, pp. 415–16.
13. J. M. Fletcher 1986, p. 187.

felt the need to pass off his product as French – a measure of the habit of acquiring classical texts from abroad. We know of no English or Scottish edition of Virgil's *Aeneid* from between around 1515 and 1570, and no six-teenth-century edition of the *Eclogues* survives from after 1529 when Wynkyn de Worde published it with a school commentary. Not until 1589 are editions known of either Livy or the tragedies of Seneca. No Latin Caesar survives from before 1585, and no Latin Tacitus, and no Lucretius, survive from the sixteenth century. Looking at text-books in England and Scotland in this period, it is natural to look at local book production, but it is essential to be aware of the extensive and diverse material which was imported.

Late Antiquity had seen the proliferation of works summing up the knowledge of the ancient world within the covers of slim volumes. Grammar, logic and rhetoric, the most basic disciplines, were most often compendiarized. Many such text-books were in use in the later Middle Ages, but many had lost their text-book function, themselves becoming the basis for extensive and advanced commentaries, removing them from the elementary sphere, and necessitating the creation of further summaries and compendia. This was true even of the most elementary and fundamental of all disciplines, that of grammar. While the medieval curriculum prescribed the late Antique grammarian Priscian – in Oxford this text is stipulated in the statutes of 1431 – a very abbreviated compendium of Priscian, the *Remigius*, formed the basic introduction to the discipline. Even the elementary late Antique grammar text-book by Donatus was further abbreviated to meet the needs of pupils who learned Latin as a foreign language. Preparing for the elementary logic course, more advanced teaching of grammar was conducted through text-books systematizing, organizing and commenting on material from Priscian. Priscian's own work was chained in libraries for consultation by senior members of the universities, while text-books based on Priscian were used for teaching students.

During the period which we consider here, the discipline of Latin grammar changed both its function in relation to the discipline of logic and the type of Latin which it aimed at teaching. These interrelated developments are expressed in the text-books examined. Universities, in theory, presupposed that, when admitted, students knew basic Latin grammar. However, even fairly elementary grammatical instruction was given. In 1409, the Oxford statutes required Bachelors of Arts to lecture on Donatus's *Barbarismus*, an appendix to his grammar, and graces granted seem to indicate that the requirement was expected normally to be fulfilled.[14] Thus, on 27 February 1449/50, Robert Bennet was granted permission to omit lecturing on the *Barbarismus* and some other named statutory texts because he had read on two books of Aristotle's *Physics*, a much more advanced text.[15] The late twelfth-century *Doctrinale* was also in use at university level in England and Scotland.

The position of the *Doctrinale* as a bridge between school and university curricula may be illustrated by three works which were once bound together, now separated, in a volume owned by a Walter Slugg. They are John Anwykyll's *Compendium totius grammaticae* and the *Vulgaria Terentii*, a collection of idiomatic Latin phrases derived from Terence – the two probably issued together – and a *Doctrinale* with the commentaries of Ludovicus de Guaschis.[16] John Anwykyll's grammar is elementary. With little justification, it proclaims itself a reworking of the Latin grammar of Niccolò Perotti, the Italian humanist, and hostile to barbaric, medieval Latin. The Deventer edition of the work says it is a 'compendium . . . totius barbarie destructorium', listing Lorenzo Valla, Perotti, as well as the late Antique grammarian Servius, as its sources. The Oxford edition from 1483, in a final verse, claims Perotti as the author. The *Doctrinale* is representative of the Latin which Anwykyll purportedly strove to replace. The commentary, ascribed to Ludovicus de Guaschis, was chiefly concerned with the correlation of grammar with logic, giving the *Doctrinale* an interface between the school and the university curricula.[17] The use in England of De Guaschis's commentary is further documented by Rood and Hunt's edition from Oxford around 1485[18] and by Pynson's printing of the *Doctrinale* in London in 1492 and 1498, and 1509.[19] Walter Slugg probably began his studies at Oxford in the first half of the 1490s, not long after the *Doctrinale* was printed in Deventer. He supplicated for the degree of Bachelor of Civil Law in 1508: the statutory course for an MA was seven years, plus two years of regency; he probably spent six years at the law faculty, and a year, or more, lecturing on the Digest and the Code before being allowed to supplicate for the BCL.[20]

While the other texts in the preceding example illustrated the links of

14. S. Gibson 1931, p. 200.   15. Boase 1885, p. 8.
16. Anwykyll, *Compendium totius grammaticae*, *Vulgaria Terentii* [Oxford, T. Rood, not after 1483] (*GW* 2263; *STC* 696 and *STC* 23904). The *Doctrinale* (Campbell-Kronenberg 113a) was printed in Antwerp by G. Leeu, between 12 October 1485 and 28 January 1486. The former item is now Bodleian (Inc. e. E.2.1483.1) and the latter in CUL (Oates 1954, 3920).
17. Heath 1971, pp. 9–64.   18. *GW* 991; *STC* 315; a fragment only survives.
19. *GW* 1020; *STC* 316; and *GW* 1027; *STC* 317.   20. *BRUO 1540*, p. 519.

the *Doctrinale* to the normative grammar of the schools, another English volume may illustrate the link of the *Doctrinale* upwards, from the school towards the curriculum of the arts course at university level. This volume, now in the Bibliothèque Nationale de France in Paris,[21] belonged to a John Bambrogh, who took his MA from Cambridge in 1493 and died in 1524.[22] It consists of a late fifteenth-century manuscript of the *Doctrinale* bound with a copy of Thomas of Erfurt's *De modis significandi* printed in St Albans in 1480,[23] and with Johannes de Sacro Bosco's *Sphaera*. Both are texts central to the arts course and the former in particular shows the link between the *Doctrinale* and philosophical grammar as taught at university.

John Vaus was the only author from England and Scotland to write a commentary on the *Doctrinale*. Having studied in Paris he returned to Scotland in 1515–16 to teach humanities at Aberdeen. He was a *humanista* in the fifteenth-century sense of the word: a teacher of Latin at a level higher than that of the most elementary grammatical instruction. His work at Aberdeen University was similar to that described in William of Waynflete's statutes for Magdalen College, Oxford, from 1480, where provisions were made for 'demies'. Possibly because they were poor students, it was recognized that they had insufficient knowledge of Latin to be admitted immediately to the study of logic – part of the regular curriculum of the arts faculty. They were required first to read grammar, and a few of them were to continue their study of grammar along with poetry and the other *artes humanitatis* so that they could instruct others.[24] At Cambridge, degrees in grammar were frequently awarded until 1539.[25] The function which Vaus performed in Aberdeen was thus characteristic of propaedeutic university teaching elsewhere in England and Scotland. Thirty-two of Vaus's books are still in Aberdeen, in the University Library, and a further two are in St Andrews.[26] They are preponderantly small text-books, mainly in octavo or in quarto, and provide a good point of departure for getting an impression of the books used in England and Scotland for teaching the humanities. Vaus and his collection of text-books will serve as an example providing a focus for much of the following discussion.

21. *CIBN* T-219.   22. *BRUC*, p. 34.
23. St Albans, [Schoolmaster Printer], 1480 (*STC* 268).
24. McConica 1986, pp. 4–5; see Bond 1853, II, pp. 6 and 16.
25. Venn 1910, p. xi; also Bartlett 1977, pp. 1–8.   26. Durkan and Ross 1961, p. 187.

Several of Vaus's books can be related to his work on the *Doctrinale*. Condemned in Italy by adherents of the new Latin style of the humanists, the *Doctrinale* was criticized also in northern Europe, but here attempts were made to modify it to suit new demands, partly because significant sections of Latin syntax, traditionally part of north European Latin teaching, were not covered by Italian humanist grammarians. Vaus explained that he had chosen to work on the *Doctrinale* because that was the text his students would expect to use. His commentary was normative and followed the pattern displayed by three commentaries on the *Doctrinale*, copies of which were in Vaus's possession: an edition with the commentary of Badius Ascensius, another edition with a commentary ascribed to Johannes Synthen,[27] and one with the commentary of Hermannus Torrentinus (d. *c.* 1520).[28] The title-page of Vaus's *Doctrinale* acknowledges the debt to Badius's version of the *Doctrinale*. His books also reflect his personal acquaintanceship with Badius. In England and Scotland as a whole, moreover, Paris, and Badius in particular, were of chief importance for the supply of modern text-books. With relatively few vestiges of the logical functions of grammar, both these commentaries stem from north-European, Rhenish, humanism, where Badius Ascensius with his Netherlandish background also had his place. Johannes Synthen was from the St Lebuinus School in Deventer;[29] however, Torrentinus, probably a reliable witness, claims in his introduction to his *Doctrinale* edition that the ascription of that commentary to Synthen is spurious. Torrentinus, himself another Netherlander, was close to the circle of Jacob Wimpheling (1450–1528) and other Alsatian humanists further up the Rhine. A moderate reviser of the *Doctrinale*, highly recommended by Wimpheling, Torrentinus mentions parental objections to change in the curriculum, even to his modifications of the *Doctrinale*. This recalls Vaus's reason for editing the *Doctrinale*, a text more likely to be accepted by his students. The *Doctrinale* was officially abandoned in Vienna in 1509 and in Ingolstadt in 1519, while the reason given for its abolition in Leipzig, in 1515, was that it was no longer in use in other universities or even in elementary schools in the region: 'In presentacione baccalaureandorum conclusum fuit per magistros de consilio facultatis arcium tunc congregatos ut alia legeretur ordinarie grammatica

---

27. Paris, J. Badius Ascensius and J. Petit, 25 August 1504.
28. *In primam (- secundam) partem Alexandri* (Leiden, J. Seversz, 1509; NK 85); see Durkan and Ross 1961, addenda, p. 187 no. 21.   29. Chomarat 1981, pp. 278–82.

cum Alexandrum Gallum scholastici prorsus abiicerent neque in aliis circumiacentibus gymnasiis nec in scholis quidem triuialibus profiterentur.'[30] At about the same time, in 1516, Pynson produced the last known edition in England of the *Doctrinale*. Vaus's use of Alexander, however, was not completely out of line with contemporary practice. In Paris, just before 1517, an unnamed master of the College of St Barbara declared that, despite the protestations of the moderns, students would benefit from reading the *Doctrinale*: it was well organized and the verses easy.[31] Thus Vaus's use of the *Doctrinale* reflected attitudes still current in Paris while he studied there, and his work was printed as late as 1566. We have evidence of the *Doctrinale* being in use much later. For instance an interleaved copy of the *Doctrinale*, books I-II with the commentary of De Guaschis, printed by Wynkyn de Worde about 1515,[32] contains copious manuscript notes referring to a grammar by Nicodemus Frischlin which must be either the *Strigilis grammatica* or the *Quaestionum grammaticarum libri viii*, both first published in Venice in 1584.

In Oxford and Cambridge, Fridays during Lent were set aside for grammatical disputations. They were not discussions of the nicer details of Latin usage, but of the kind of grammar for which logic-oriented commentaries on the *Doctrinale* prepared students. These disputations were based on a text identified as 'Albertus'. At least two different grammatical texts went under this name. One was the grammar of Thomas of Erfurt, also erroneously ascribed to Duns Scotus. The other was by an author as yet unidentified.[33] They were speculative grammars, which used grammar as a point of departure for uncovering logical structures that govern human thought and expression. Both pseudo-Albertus texts were modist grammars, thus called because of their attempt to correlate syntactic functions of the parts of speech – *modi significandi* – to metaphysical properties of the real world – *modi essendi*. This kind of grammar was part of the logic course and this link is demonstrated by a number of volumes containing such grammars bound with treatises on logic: one copy in

30. Kink 1854, II, p. 316; Von Prantl 1872, II, p. 160; G. Erler 1895–1902, p. 511. See also Seifert 1984, esp. p. 143.
31. Goulet 1965 p. 623: 'Heptadogma seu septem pro erigendo gymnasio documenta ad generosos prudentesque dominos et ciues eximios, litteratorum amicissimos super universitate nova vel veteri restauranda subitaria responsio'.
32. *STC* 24623a; Bodleian, 4° D 12.50 Linc.
33. London, J. Notary for J. Barbier and I H [*c.*1496] (*STC* 270); see Pinborg 1967, p. 309, no. A.1; J. M. Fletcher 1992, p. 328 assumes that 'Albertus' refers only to the work of Thomas of Erfurt.

Peterhouse, Cambridge, in 1418, was bound with Antonius Andreas on Aristotle's logic and Burley on the *Posterior Analytics*.[34] In 1452 Merton College in Oxford purchased a volume which contained two modist treatises bound with Duns Scotus's commentaries on two of Aristotle's works on logic.[35] A copy in Canterbury College, Oxford, in 1501, was bound with a commentary on Porphyry.[36] Thomas Colyer[37] of Michaelhouse in Cambridge, at his death in 1506, left to Christ's College a *De modis significandi* bound with Brunus's translation of Aristotle's *Ethics*, also part of the philosophy course.

While many surviving fifteenth-century manuscripts of modist grammarians are Italian or central European, the majority of surviving printed modist grammars are from towns which form part of the hinterland of the English Channel: Antwerp, Rouen, even Deventer, London and St Albans, and we have ample evidence for their use until the early 1520s. Probate inventories from Oxford show that William Thomson, MA (d. 1507), owned a 'Modus significandi', and John Rothley, BCL, (d. 1507), owned an 'exposicio modorum significandi'.[38] A copy, now in Norwich City Library, of Thomas of Erfurt's *Modi significandi*,[39] was owned by a Benedictine monk, William Edys (fl. 1514–44) who bought it in Oxford in 1514, the year in which he supplicated for his degree as Bachelor of Theology.[40] A copy of the *Quaestiones de modis significandi* from about 1496, survives in a binding which must be from 1513 or some time shortly after, with four other books. One of these items is another modist text, Johannes Josse de Marvilla's metrical grammar, the most elementary of surviving modist works, *Expositiones modorum significandi*.[41] In 1520, John Dorne sold nine modist works, quite a substantial number compared with, for instance, five sales of the grammar of Perotti. They were, however, only six separate sales: three *Quaestiones de modis significandi*,[42] five *De modis significandi*,[43] and one Johannes Josse, *Expositiones modorum significandi*.[44] One sale accounts for one copy of each, bound together and costing 1s 1d; another sale accounts for two items, one of

34. Leader 1988, pp. 113–14 n. 22.   35. Oxford, Merton Coll., ms. 60, fols. 2–25 and 34–61.
36. Pantin 1947–50, I, p. 25.   37. *BRUC*, p. 151.
38. *PLRE*, II: Thompson, no. 10.21 also p. 16; Rothley, no. 22.20 also p. 56.
39. London, W. de Worde, 1510 (*STC* 268.3).
40. *BRUO 1540*, p. 187; also Ker 1964–87, p. 232.
41. Rouen, [about 1507]; Bodleian, 4° C1 Art. Seld; with a commentary unrecorded by Pinborg 1967.   42. Madan and Bradshaw 1885–90, nos. 121, 201 and 639.
43. Madan and Bradshaw 1885–90, nos. 98, 122, 136, 617, 638.
44. Madan and Bradshaw 1885–90, no. 120.

the *Quaestiones* with a *De modis significandi*, for 2s. These were quite expensive books, compared with the cheapest items which were sold for 2d or 3d. Such texts cannot have been in general use much later than that. Oxford probate lists reveal three owners of the *Doctrinale*, who died in 1507, 1508 and 1513. The Cambridge probate lists do not begin until 1536 and they contain neither *Modi significandi* nor any sixteenth-century owner of the *Doctrinale*. The last printing of a modist grammar for educational use was by Wynkyn de Worde in London in 1515: the *Quaestiones de modi significandi*, a year before the last English edition of the *Doctrinale*. Philosophical grammar had now disappeared.

Apart from the two commentaries on the *Doctrinale*, Vaus owned the grammars by Franciscus Niger and by Giovanni Sulpizio Verulano, based on Badius Ascensius's revised edition.[45] These represent the Italian tradition of humanist normative grammar, which differed from its medieval predecessors both in reducing terminology imported from philosophical grammar and, just as importantly, in prescribing a more classical selection of words and constructions. Such lists of words, however, tended to be changed as grammars were reprinted and many north European grammars which travel under the names of Perotti, Sulpizio, Antonio Mancinelli or Franciscus Niger in fact prescribe usages which had been specifically condemned by their Italian authors. In particular, the name of Perotti became a mark of authority which could be attached to a wide variety of works. This status was confirmed by Erasmus (d. 1536) who found that Perotti's was marginally better than other humanist grammars.[46]

In a letter contained in Vaus's commentary on the *Doctrinale*, Robert Gray explained that Vaus had used the name of the *Doctrinale* to reassure his students with a semblance of familiarity. In reality, he claimed, Vaus was inspired by a canon of modern grammarians – Sulpizio, Perotti, Aldus and Torrentinus.[47] We have seen that Vaus owned works ascribed to at least two authors from this list. It becomes explicit that the title of the book is not so much a statement of authorship and contents, as an advertising opportunity.

The *c.* 1486 Louvain edition of Perotti's grammar, printed with glosses in English, is closer to the text produced by Perotti than many other

---

45. Franciscus Niger, *Grammatica* (Paris, G. Wolf and T. Kerver, for J. Petit, 1498; Goff N-228); Franciscus Niger, *Modus epistolandi* (Paris, P. Levet, [not before 1492]; Mitchell 187, Pell. ms 8570); Giovanni Sulpizio, *Grammatica Sulpitiana* (Caen, *c.* 1506).
46. In the second version of his *De ratione studii* published first 1512, of which Erasmus sent John Colet a manuscript copy in 1511; Margolin 1971, pp. 83-5.   47. Delisle 1896, p. 7.

north European versions.[48] On the other hand, we saw that Anwykyll's grammar was billed as a compendium of the work of Perotti. In a little text-book of declensions, *Declinationes nominum tam Latinorum quam Grecorum patronymiconem et barbarorum e Prisciano, Sipontino* [i.e. Perotti], *Sulpitio, et Ascensio amussatim collecte*, Robert Whittinton claimed the authority of Perotti and Sulpizio, on an equally slender basis.[49] Pynson's little Sulpizio from around 1498 and Wynkyn de Worde's from 1499 are, although much abbreviated, textually close to the printing by Jean Petit of Paris in 1495. Petit's text, in its turn, is a much altered compendium of Sulpizio, but selected passages bear a close resemblance to the original. On the other hand, Badius Ascensius's editions of Sulpizio are longer, admittedly, but more distant from their proclaimed Italian model: first printed in Paris in 1502, partly for a London-based publisher, they contain much material which is derived from the north European syntactic tradition, ultimately based on the structure of the *Doctrinale*. Badius's edition was later printed several times in Paris, sometimes for English use, and also in England itself. The pattern of transmission of text-books from various parts of Europe is less transparent than it might appear because of the instability of the detailed rules contained in texts which claim identical authorship.

In addition to the moderately reforming grammars which Vaus owned, he also possessed a copy of the *Graecismus* ascribed to Ebrardus Bethuniensis, another late medieval text-book frequently denounced by humanists.[50] However, he also owned an edition of the Latin grammar of Antonius de Lebrixa whose description of Latin was closer to a classical norm than that found in the works of several of the more widely read Italian grammarians.[51]

Although the grammatical texts owned by Vaus do not prescribe radical humanist Latin, they imply another evident change: they no longer teach grammar with the aim of providing students with elementary skills in logic. This created problems for the arts course where logic was taught as an extension of grammar. Although there was instruction in humanist Latin at university, normative grammar text-books were not suitable replacements for the advanced speculative grammar which humanists had expelled from the curriculum of the arts faculty. A weak-

48. *Rudimenta grammatices* ([Louvain], A. v. d. Heerstraten [*c.* 1486]; *STC* 19767.7).
49. London, W. de Worde, [1511?]; *STC* 25443.4.
50. Lyons, J. du Pré, 1492; *GW* 9222, Mitchell 207.
51. *Grammatica* ([Lyons], I. Maillet, 1514–15).

ening of the logic-based arts course of the universities was beginning to show.

In Cambridge in 1527, the grammatical disputations on Fridays in Lent were transformed into philosophical ones.[52] The traditional grammatico-logical nature of the disputations might lead to the assumption that they were replaced by disputations on logic, but this was probably not so. In Oxford, Fox's statutes for Corpus Christi of 1517 stipulated disputations on moral philosophy for Friday lectures during Lent, a suitably humanist alternative to the traditional speculative grammatical topics.[53]

The humanist version of logic, dialectic, aimed less at analysis of statements than at the convincing use of arguments. For elementary philosophy, the Henrician injunctions to the University of Cambridge of 1535, rejecting the use of commentaries and *quaestiones*, required lectures on Aristotle, Rudolphus Agricola, Philipp Melanchthon, Georgius Trapezuntius and such authors.[54] The requirement to read Aristotle himself now seems purely a formality. This development recalls that in Germany, where Uldaricus Zasius in 1523, wrote on the teaching of Aristotle in Freiburg, that the text itself was neither lectured on nor used for exercises. In Ingolstadt the verdict was brief: the text-book by Johannes Caesarius was read, but 'Aristoteles non legitur.' The humanist desire for a return to the classical texts was losing out to the desire for fast and systematic teaching from text-books.[55] Such manuals on dialectic are among the most widely owned books mentioned in the probate lists. The most difficult one was Agricola's, from 1479.[56] Much more basic was Philipp Melanchthon's from 1520.[57] The dialectic of Caesarius from about 1522 was also widely owned in this country.[58] As it was a Catholic counterpart to Melanchthon, it is not surprising that it did not get a mention in the Henrician injunctions as a suitable text-book.[59] The text-book on dialectic by Johannes Sturmius, from 1549, was widely owned in the last years of our period.[60]

In the Oxford statutes of 1563 and 1564-5,[61] Virgil, Horace or a part of Cicero's letters, and the Latin grammar of Thomas Linacre were proposed as topics for lectures as an alternative to Priscian's grammar.[62]

52. Leader 1988, p. 303.
53. On the lectures, see McConica 1986, p. 24, and Bond, II, pt 10, p. 56.
54. *Statuta Academiae Cantabrigiensis*, p. 137.
55. On the development in Germany, see Seifert 1984, p. 149.
56. Leedham-Green 1986, II, pp. 9–10.   57. Leedham-Green 1986, II, p. 539.
58. Leedham-Green 1986, II, pp. 168–9.   59. Seifert 1984, p. 143.
60. Leedham-Green 1986, II, p. 725.   61. J. M. Fletcher 1986, p. 172.
62. S. Gibson 1931, pp. 378, 389.

First printed in London in 1524,[63] but never again in England, Linacre's grammar was the most successful attempt in the sixteenth century to write a grammatical text-book which went beyond the elementary level. Probably because Philipp Melanchthon recommended it for use in all higher institutions of learning, Linacre's work was frequently issued in Protestant areas, but it was also in use in Catholic parts of Europe.[64] It would, however, seem that, although his grammar was added to the curriculum in Oxford in the 1560s, it was never widely used. We know of a copy of the 1524 edition, given around 1559 to St John's College, Oxford, by Henry Cole (c. 1500–80).[65] There was a copy in the extensive library of the Oxford scholar, Bisley, valued at 6d in his probate inventory from 1543.[66] Two copies are found in the Cambridge probate lists from before 1560. One was valued at 4d in an anonymous list from 1558; the other was valued at 12d in the probate list of W. Johnson from 1559.[67] The possibility of replacing a classical text with the study of an advanced grammar like Linacre's illustrates how the reading of texts was perceived as part of grammatical instruction. The reading of most classical literature had no obvious place in the curriculum: it added nothing to the philosophical basis which the arts faculty traditionally had sought to provide; nevertheless, classical texts were read. Fletcher cites four examples from the sixteenth century of Bachelors being required to lecture on classical texts – Sallust, Terence, Cicero and Virgil.[68] Terence's comedies were a school text of long standing, and Virgil – probably including some pseudo-Virgilian poems – had been a statutory requirement at Oxford since 1431, as had the pseudo-Ciceronian *Ad Herennium*. Cicero's *Topica* was a standard required text, but the evidence of surviving copies does not suggest that it was one of the most widely read, whereas the *De officiis*, not mentioned in the statutes, was one of the most widely owned books and probably used as part of the ethics curriculum.[69] Sallust was a new figure in the university, not printed in England and Scotland in our period. One of five Fellows elected to fellowships at Merton College in Oxford in 1538/9 was required to lecture on the *Catilina*.[70] In the first half of the sixteenth century, we know of lectures on Lucan and Quintilian also. Lucan

63. *De emendata structura Latini sermonis* (London, R. Pynson, 1524); *STC* 15634.
64. Barber 1977; Jensen 1986.
65. *BRUO 1540*, pp. 128 and 717, now Oxford, St John's Coll., 4.29.
66. *PLRE*, II, no. 60.37.   67. Leedham-Green 1986, I, p. 229, no. 15, and I, p. 202, no. 13.
68. J. M. Fletcher 1992, p. 343.
69. Amply documented by the lists of books owned by members of Oxford and Cambridge University published by Leedham-Green 1986 and in *PLRE*; see also Jardine 1975.
70. Ker 1956, p. 53; J. M. Fletcher 1974, p. 77: 25 March 1538/9.

was, at least in continental Europe, part of the advanced medieval school curriculum,[71] whereas Quintilian was a characteristic humanist addition to the body of studied texts.

Classical texts may not be what we would call text-books, but they were used in a way which makes the distinction less clear-cut: they were read for linguistic purposes, more or less as a collection of grammatical examples. The 'Commentum familiare' in Wynkyn de Worde's editions of Virgil's *Eclogues* is concerned mainly with linguistic problems. So was a substantial part of the commentary accompanying the *Silvae morales*, a reader compiled by Badius Ascensius: another example of the caution shown in abandoning traditional teaching practices. The *Silvae* consists mainly of passages which were also widely used as school-texts in the late Middle Ages: ps-Virgilian poems from the *Appendix Vergiliana*; excerpts from the *Satires* of Persius and Juvenal; *Satires*, *Letters* and *Odes* by Horace; the *Disticha Catonis*; and Alain of Lille's *Doctrinale minus*. Only Baptista Mantuanus's *Contra poetas impudice loquentes* and Sulpizio's didactic poem on table manners were modern additions to the traditional reading list. The Bodleian copy has an English binding from between 1526 and 1545.[72] The compilation into text-books of phrases from frequently read authors is only the logical consequence of using texts as collections of grammatical examples. Thus the *Vulgaria Terentii*, printed both in this country and in the Netherlands for use in England and Scotland, and Nicholas Udall's *Flouers for Latine Spekynge Selected and Gathered oute of Terence*[73] both performed this function. So did compendia of Valla's *Elegantiae*. Erasmus's *Familiarium colloquiorum formulae*[74] and his *De duplici copia rerum et verborum*[75] were both small collections of phrases. Prepared for St Paul's School in London and dedicated to John Colet, the latter work was particularly important in England. However, printed first by Badius in Paris, later in Strasbourg, Basel, Hagenau, Sélestat and Mainz, it was not printed in England until 1528; there was then only one more English edition before 1557, and even this may have been printed in Antwerp for an English publisher.[76] Although this indicates that these works of Erasmus were probably primarily aimed at preuniversity students, the *Colloquia* and the *De duplici copia rerum et*

---

71. Rizzo 1986, p. 396.   72. Lyons, J. Trechsel, 1492; *GW* 3154; Bodleian, S. Seld. d.16(2).
73. London, Berthelet, 1533; *STC* 23899.
74. Basel, J. Froben, 1518; on the development of the text, see Halkin, Bierlaire and Hoven 1972.
75. Paris, J. Badius, 1512; see Knott 1988.
76. *STC* 10471.1; [Antwerp for?] S. Roedius, London, 1556.

verborum were particularly frequently sold by Dorne in Oxford in 1520[77] and are also among the books most frequently encountered in the Cambridge probate lists. The accounts of Garret Godfrey also show that Erasmus was the most frequently sold author, but again chiefly for books used before university level.[78] While such books served much the same purpose as classical texts in teaching Latin grammar, we have no evidence that they were used as the basis for lectures at English universities.

J. M. Fletcher suggests that, while the university allowed lectures on classical authors, it was not prepared to give up its core curriculum of logic and philosophy, and that such lectures were usually given to students aiming at appointments as school teachers.[79] This would emphasize the grammatical function of such lectures. The study of the Christian alternative to Virgil, the poems of Baptista Spagnuolo Mantuanus, would on the other hand seem to have taken place largely at pre-university level. We know of Colet's interest in the author, which mirrors that of the pious humanist Wimpheling, who also recommended the Mantuan as a replacement for Virgil. Most of the surviving copies of Mantuan with early English ownership seem to have no university connection, but in Scotland the professor of humanities, Vaus, again forms a link between school and university level: he had a copy of Mantuan's much-studied poem on the Virgin[80] bound with other elementary school texts: Niger's grammar, the manual on letter-writing by Carolus Virulus or Karel Maneken (born *c.* 1413), the *Epistolae* of Barzizius and Fliscus's *Synonyma*.[81]

Greek was also studied at the two English universities in the sixteenth century, but no Greek text-book was printed in England in our period.[82] Greek fitted the traditional arts curriculum no better than the study of Latin authors, possibly even worse, and here we have evidence of the

---

77. Madan and Bradshaw 1885–90, pp. 72–177.
78. Leedham-Green, Rhodes and Stubbings 1992, p. xix, on the sale of multiple copies to schoolmasters.   79. J. M. Fletcher 1986, p. 179.   80. Piepho 1993.
81. Baptista S. Mantuanus, *Parthenice Mariana; Contra poetas impudice loquentes carmen* (Paris ?, n.d.; Mitchell 226), bound with Franciscus Niger, *Modus epistolandi* (Paris, Pierre Levet, [not before 1492]; Pell. ms. 8570); Gasparinus Barzizius, *Epistolae* (Paris, G. Marchant, 1498/9; *GW* 3688); Carolus Virulus, *Formulae epistolarum* ([Paris, A. Bocard for J. Petit], 1499; *CIBN* M-104); Dio Chrysostomus, *De Troia non capta* (Paris, A. Denidel for R. Gourmont, *c.* 1500; *GW* 8373); Stephanus Fliscus, *Libellus compositionis preceptorum commode elocutionis* (Paris, A. Chappiel, 1502); and other works printed in Paris around these dates. See Mitchell 186,187, 197, 203, 204, 205, 226.
82. On the teaching of Greek and on the authors who were read in the newly founded Corpus Christi Coll., see McConica 1986, p. 22. On the public professors of Greek in Oxford, certainly from 1543 but possibly already from 1541, see Duncan 1986, p. 354.

disruption which its introduction caused when Bishop Gardiner prohibited the use at Cambridge of the reformed pronunciation of Greek.[83]

In Oxford in 1537 one of five Fellows elected at Merton, William Browne, was to lecture on the Greek grammar of Ceporinus or, if he preferred, Clenardus. When he died in 1558, Browne had a substantial library containing several Greek grammars; one of them the grammar of Ceporinus.[84] Dominus Hickell was to lecture on two orations by Isocrates.[85] Evidence from probate inventories, from both Cambridge and Oxford, makes it clear that the grammars of Ceporinus and Clenardus were quite widely owned in the 1530s–50s. Present evidence does not provide us with numerous examples of surviving copies with contemporary English or Scottish ownership, although a copy is known, with an early English ownership, of the text-book on Greek grammar by Johannes Varennius.[86] On the other hand, we have an impressive number of more advanced Greek grammatical and rhetorical manuals, and lexica which belonged to men from the group of Cambridge reformers of Greek pronunciation, but these books are clearly instances of teachers' reference works rather than text-books.[87] Probably as a direct result of his contact with Badius in the early 1520s, John Vaus owned a copy of Theodorus Gaza's Greek grammar with a parallel Latin translation, published by Badius.[88] It is doubtful if this is evidence that Greek text-books were widely used in Aberdeen.

A strict distinction cannot be maintained between learning correct, idiomatic and elegant Latin and learning rhetorical structures: text-books on grammar, idiom, style and rhetoric form a continuum. On the level of learning idiomatic Latin, Valla's *Elegantiae*, published in its final version in 1444, was initially far too extensive and expensive to become a

---

83. John Cheke, *De pronuntiatione Graecae potissime linguae disputationes cum Stephano Wintoniensi* (Basel, 1555); Sir Thomas Smith, *De recta et emendata linguae Graecae pronuntiatione* (Paris, 1568); Gardiner 1933, pp. 100–120.
84. Probate Court list, Oxford University Archives; *PLRE*, III, no. 67, pp. 1–35.
85. J. M. Fletcher 1974, p. 77.
86. *Syntaxis linguae Graecae* (Basel, B. Lasius, 1539), now in BL, was the copy of one of the Cambridge reformers, John Ponet (*c.* 1514–56), and later belonged to Thomas Cranmer and John, Lord Lumley; Selwyn 1996, no. 541.
87. These include Hesychius, *Lexicon* (Hagenau, T. Anshelm, 1521), now in St John's Coll. in Cambridge, Adams 509, the copy of John Cheke (1514–57), Regius Professor of Greek 1540–51, which he later gave to Roger Ascham (1515–68), a pupil of Cheke, appointed Greek reader 1538. Hermogenes, *Ars rhetorica* (Paris, C. Wechelus, 1530), now in Shrewsbury School Library, was the copy of John Redman (1499–1551) – a pupil of Sir Thomas Smith – which also later belonged to Roger Ascham. Theodorus Gaza, *Grammatica introductiva* (Venice, A. Manutius, 1495; *GW* 10562): a copy now in CUL (Oates 1954 2166) belonged to Sir Thomas Smith (1513–77).
88. Theodorus Gaza, *Grammatica introductiva* (Paris, J. Badius Ascensius and J. Vatel, 1521).

text-book, but compendia brought rules and examples related to the observations of Valla to the level of students.[89] In the fifteenth century, another popular work which could stand in for a student's version of Valla was Augustinus Datus's *Elegantiolae*, excerpts from classical authors combined with advice on the writing of letters and orations. This work lost its importance in the first decades of the sixteenth century.[90] At the elementary level, the tradition of such compendia was continued by Erasmus's *Epitome* of Valla, and his *De copia verborum*. At a higher level, during the first three decades of the sixteenth century, Valla's *Elegantiae* themselves became available in smaller editions, in quarto and even fat octavos – for instance, the copy now in the Liverpool Athenaeum, which belonged first to an Alexander Hepburne who gave it to the Aberdeen Franciscan, Thomas Hutchinson, and later again was owned by John Scott, also an Aberdeen Franciscan, probably as a student there in 1531. He thereby probably acquired a group of texts which when new would have been beyond the reach of most undergraduates.[91]

Active use of language was taught primarily through the writing of letters. The manuals owned by John Vaus in Aberdeen may again be used as illustrations of how these text-books and their use developed. He owned a copy of a manual on letter writing by Carolus Virulus, teacher at the College of the Lily in Louvain.[92] Virulus betrays no trace of the new humanist Latin, and was sharply rejected by Heinrich Bebel (1472–1518) in his *Contra epistolas Caroli*.[93] Bebel went into great detail in his many polemical writings against contemporary text-books which proposed unclassical Latin. Later Erasmus attacked Virulus with even greater force

---

89. A copy of *Elegantiarum viginti præcepta* ('s-Hertogenbosch, [G. de Leempt, 1487]; *GW* 284), bound with Perotti, *Regulae grammaticales* ([Louvain], A. v. d. Heerstraten [1486]; Campbell 1380; Duff 346; Bodleian, Arch. G.e.6), is in a contemporary Oxford binding: see S. Gibson 1903, p. 26.
90. First edition probably Cologne, U. Zell, *c.* 1470, *GW* 8123; see *GW* 8032–138 for fifteenth-century editions. Copies listed in *PLRE*, II: Robert Bryan, DCnL., probate inventory 1508, 11.18, 4d; Edmund Burton, MA, probate inventory 1529, no 43.8, 4d; also the epitome by Guido Juvenalis. Aberdeen UL has *Interpretatio in Laurentii Vallae Elegantias Latinae linguae* (Paris, P. Levet, 1500; Mitchell 189), which belonged to at least seven Aberdeen students in the first half of the sixteenth century; a copy now in the BL of an edition from Paris, for J. Petit, 1500 (IA.39948), has copious notes in a sixteenth-century hand: 'By me Steven B. . .'. A copy of the edition with notes by Badius and other additions [Strasbourg, *c.* 1510], owned by Thomas Cranmer, is now in BL, 625.d.4; Selwyn 1996, no. 459.
91. *Elegantiae linguae Latinae* (Paris, S. Colinaeus, 1529), bound with Jerome de Hangest, *Liber proportionum* (Paris, 1518), a work on mathematics, here in-quarto, most often published in-folio.
92. [Paris, A. Bocard for J. Petit], 1499, Mitchell 197; Pell. ms 7601. On Virulus, see De Vocht 1951, pp. 90–8.
93. *Commentaria epistolarum conficiendarum* (Pforzheim, T. Anshelmi, 1509).

---

in his *De conscribendis epistolis*.[94] Copies of Virulus were owned by English scholars at the beginning of the century. A copy now in Cambridge University Library;[95] another copy of the same edition, now in the Royal College of Physicians;[96] and a copy of another edition of the text, now in Cambridge University Library;[97] all show signs of early English ownership. Richard Wood, MA, Oxford, 1505, owned a copy of 'Epistule Caroli' at his death in 1508, appraised at 2d;[98] but no copy is found in the Cambridge probate lists, which do not begin until 1535/6. Soon after the second decade of the sixteenth century, the work must have fallen out of use: in 1521, Erasmus observed that nobody any longer found its study worthwhile.

Vaus also owned a copy of Franciscus Niger's manual of epistolography.[99] If we compare this book with the one by Carolus Virulus, the difference is striking. Niger was an Italian humanist and his book on letter writing, first published in Venice in 1480, was popular for the rest of the fifteenth century. When Vaus taught in Aberdeen, Niger was no longer as fashionable as he had been: a book which in the 1480s had been perceived to advocate classical Latin no longer seemed to do so. In a letter written in Oxford in November 1499 to William Blount, Lord Mountjoy (d. 1534), Niger's text-book was roundly condemned by Erasmus as being not at all useful for the attainment of humanist Latin.[100] Much more modern was the epistolography by Perotti which was available widely, for this appendix to Perotti's grammar remained nearly unchanged in most editions which we know to have had connections with England and Scotland, although in several editions Badius Ascensius added notes containing much material which would not have been deemed relevant by an Italian humanist. Along with Augustinus Datus, this remained the most important aid to letter writing and composition in general until the publication in 1521 of Erasmus's *De conscribendis epistolis*, which then became a standard text-book for many years.[101]

Although it seems clear that before the advent of humanism, the

94. *ASD*, I, 2 (1971), pp. 230–1.
95. Louvain, J. de Westfalia, [1477–83] (Campbell 1204; Oates 1954, 3767).
96. London, Royal Coll. of Physicians, 83.d.
97. [Strasbourg, J. (Reinhard) Grüninger], 1486 (1118.5, not in Oates). Goff M17a? = *BMC* I 104?
98. *PLRE*, II, no. 16.10.   99. N. 45 above.   100. Allen, I, no. 117, p. 272; *CE*, 1, p. 234.
101. First, incomplete pirate edition (Cambridge, J. Siberch, 1521; *STC* 10496); first full edition, Basel, J. Froben, 1522; see Margolin 1971b, pp. 166–72. Leedham-Green 1986 knows of twenty-two owners between 1543 and 1560; *PLRE*, II lists only two owners, one of whom had two copies.

Trivium was already by far the most important part of the curriculum of the arts faculty, there is ample evidence for the basic works used for astronomy. Johannes de Sacro Bosco's *Sphaera astronomica* was required reading according to the statutes of 1409.[102] We know for instance that Dorne in 1520 sold four copies of the *Sphaera*, two with the commentary of 'Faber'.[103] This is unlikely to be an edition with the commentary of Jacques Lefèvre d'Etaples: they all appeared in folio, and the entry suggests a small format. It is more likely to be that of Wenceslaus Faber, as suggested by Madan in his index to Dorne, although the evidence of surviving books does not suggest that this book was widely owned in England and Scotland. At Merton, in 1535, a Dominus Hulet was required to lecture on Johannes de Sacro Bosco. Here again, however, we are told less than we might wish, for we do not know which edition and which additional text he might have used.[104] However, copies of the work are frequently found with English or Scottish ownership from the fifteenth and early sixteenth centuries. Many surviving copies belong to editions with the commentaries of Lefèvre d'Etaples, but as this is not a book for student use, it is not considered here. More relevant are examples of copies of editions in quarto. Conservative tendencies are indicated by a copy now in Glasgow University Library, with an ownership inscription dated 1553 by Henry Gibson:[105] it also contains the ps-Gerardus of Cremona's *Theorica planetarum*, a text required by the Oxford statutes in 1434,[106] whereas three copies with known early English ownership contain Georg Peurbach's *Nova theorica planetarum*, a text based on lectures given in Vienna in 1454. All these three English copies also contain a modern work by Johannes Regiomontanus, *Disputationes contra Cremonensia deliramenta*. Two of these volumes are known to have been in England in the late fifteenth century, one being owned by a John Baker who was somehow linked to St Frideswide in Oxford,[107] while the

102. S. Gibson 1931, p. 200. The requirement was repeated in 1563 (p. 378).

103. Madan and Bradshaw 1885–90, nos. 392, 1570, 1618, 1625.

104. J. M. Fletcher 1974, p. 66. See also *PLRE*, ii, no. 10.24; 2d in 1507; and Leedham-Green 1986, ii, p. 431.

105. Johannes de Sacro Bosco, *Sphaera mundi* with ps-Gerardus Cremonensis, *Theorica planetarum* (Venice, F. Renner, De Heilbronn, 1478; Goff J-402), bound with *inter alia* Dionysius Periegetes, *De situ orbis* (Venice, F. Renner, 1478; *GW* 8427); Pomponius Mela, *Cosmographia* (Venice, n. pr., 1477; Goff M-448); and *Compotus chirmentalis* ([Cologne, J. Koelhoff, *c.* 1480–5]; *GW* 7280): Glasgow UL, Bk.5.g.22.   106. S. Gibson 1931, p. 234.

107. Johannes de Sacro Bosco, *Sphaera mundi* with Georg Peurbach, *Theoricae novae planetarum*, and Regiomontanus, *Disputationes contra Cremonensia deliramenta* (Venice, J. L. Santritter and H. de Sanctis, 1488; Goff J-407); bound with *Mensa philosophica* (Louvain, J. de Westfalia, [about 1485]; Campbell 1241 (and *Suppl.* ii)) and *Auctoritates Aristotelis* (Deventer, R. Pafraet, 1499; Campbell 194, *GW* 2830): Bodleian, Auct. 2Q5.3.

binding of the other establishes its early English ownership.[108] The third volume was owned by a Thomas Sparke (fl. 1516–72).[109]

Such collections of texts indicate that in a strict sense Sacrobosco's *Sphaera* was no text-book, but that, together with others, it was part of a more or less standardized body of texts which constituted the astronomy course.[110] It is doubtful whether volumes such as these would have been owned by undergraduate students: it is more likely that they were volumes used by Regent Masters for their lectures. A Scottish volume which suggests such ownership also contained the *Perspectiva communis* of John Peckham, a standard text for lecturing, along with Jerome de Hangest's modern work on mathematics, *Liber proportionum*. This volume, now in Edinburgh University Library, belonged to David Melville, and was put together after he became Principal of Glasgow University in 1514.[111] A comprehensive text-book was provided by Gemma Frisius in 1530.[112]

Apart from logic, throughout the greater part of our period the philosophies were taught from standard texts with commentaries. At a higher level there were specialist studies, and at a lower level summaries and *quaestiones* can in some ways be said to be akin to text-books. The *Quaestiones naturales* of Adelard of Bath, for instance, widely used in the fifteenth century, gave access to some of the problems of the discipline of physics. For instance, a copy of Adelard of Bath, *Quaestiones naturales*, was bought in Oxford by a friar, John Grene, in 1483, with alms given by his friends. The fact that it is bound with the *Vulgaria* reaffirms its

---

108. *Sphaera* ([Paris], F. Baligault, [1494]; Goff J-412), bound with an edition of the *Sphaera mundi* published with Georg Peurbach, *Theoricae novae planetarum*, and Johannes Regiomontanus, *Disputationes contra Cremonensia deliramenta* (Venice, G. Anima Mia, Tridinensis, 14 January 1491; Goff J-410). The volume also contains Albumasar, *Flores astrologiae* (Augsburg, E. Ratdolt, 1488; *GW* 837); Petrus de Alliaco, *Concordantia astronomiae cum theologia* (Augsburg, E. Ratdolt, 2 January 1490; Goff A-471); Pomponius Mela, *Cosmographia, sive De situ orbis* (Venice, F. Renner, De Heilbronn, 1478; Goff M-450); Marcus Antonius Sabellicus, *De vetustate Aquileiensis patriae* ([Padua], A. de Avinione, [between 1481 and 1483]; Goff S-10): Bodleian Library, Ashm. 463.
109. Johannes de Sacro Bosco, *Sphaera mundi* with Georg Peurbach, *Theoricae novae planetarum*; and Regiomontanus, *Disputationes contra Cremonensia deliramenta* (Venice, E. Ratdolt, 1485; Goff J-406; Bodleian, Auct. N 5.7); bound with Al-Kabisi, *Libellus isagogicus* (Venice, E. Ratdolt, 1485; *GW* 844) and Hyginus, *Poeticon astronomicon* (Venice, E. Ratdolt, 1485; Goff H-561). 110. For this *Corpus astronomicum*, see North 1992, p. 119.
111. John Peckham, *Perspectiva communis* (Venice, 1504); Thomas Bradwardine, *Geometria speculativa* (Paris, 1517); Petrus Alliacus, *Spherae mundi commentum* (Paris, 1508); Jerome de Hangest, *Liber proportionum* (Paris, J. Petit, n. d.); Jacques Lefèvre d'Etaples, *Textus de sphera cum geometria Euclidis* (Paris, 1507): Edinburgh, UL, DS.c4.39; see Durkan and Ross 1961, pp. 129–30. 112. *De principiis astronomiae et cosmographiae* (Antwerp, 1530).

function as a book for student use.[113] Also, the *Mensa philosophica*, the *Auctoritates Aristotelis* and the ps-Aristotelian *Secreta secretorum* and *Problemata* serve this function. In 1541, Dominus Barnes, Dominus Wale and Dominus Carter were all required to lecture on parts of Aristotle's *Problemata* when they were made Fellows of Merton College in Oxford.[114] The *Problemata* are often found bound with other elementary texts related to the discipline of natural philosophy, part of a group of texts which constituted a physics course, but none of which was a text-book of physics. A copy in an early sixteenth-century English binding at Stonyhurst College, of Aristotle's *Problemata*[115] is bound with Albertus Magnus, *Liber aggregationis*,[116] and the *Quaestiones naturales antiquorum philosophorum*.[117] A volume now in Oxford, Bodleian Library,[118] contains, with an edition of the *Auctoritates Aristotelis*, also an edition of the *Mensa philosophica* and Johannes de Sacro Bosco, *Sphaera*. Another volume in an early English binding contains *Repertorium siue tabula generalis authoritatum Aristotelis et philosophorum per modum alphabeti*. The *Repertorium* is a medieval florilegium which compendiarized the study of logic, ethics and natural philosophy. This alphabetical edition contains commentaries on the dicta which are relevant to the study of physics.[119] The volume also contains 'Albertus magister', *Quaestiones de modis significandi*, and Johannes Josse,[120] and two further items relevant for the arts course: letters of Cicero and Pliny,[121] and Niger's manual on letter writing.[122] This was clearly a volume for the use of a Regent Master. Similarly, an edition now in Aberdeen University Library was for the use of the Dominican friar, William Gibson (fl. 1545–60), and therefore not an example of a text-book for the use of a student.[123]

113. [Louvain, J. de Westfalia, *c.* 1476–7]; *GW* 218. It is bound as third item with Terence, *Vulgaria* ([Oxford, T. Rood, not after 1483]); *STC* 23904, Petrus Paulus Vergerius, *De ingenuis moribus ac liberalibus studiis* ([Louvain], Johannes de Westfalia, [*c.* 1476–1477]); Campbell 1724: Bodleian, Arch. G e.5(3).
114. J. M. Fletcher 1974, p. 86, for the year 1541.
115. [Cologne, H. Quentell, *c.* 1493]; *GW* 2472.
116. London, W. de Machlinia, [*c.* 1483] (*STC* 258; *GW* 653).
117. [Cologne, C. de Zierikzee, *c.* 1500], Goff Q-9; the volume also contains Albertanus Causidicus Brixiensis, *De arte loquendi et tacendi* (Antwerp, G. Leeu, 1484; Campbell 60; *GW* 536); *Historia septem sapientium Romae* (Antwerp, G. Leeu, 1490; Campbell 950).
118. Auct. 2Q5.3. See note 107 above.
119. Paris, 1513; Bodleian, 4° C1 Art. Seld. Cf. Hamesse 1974, pp. 115–334.
120. Mentioned in note 41 above. 121. Deventer, J. de Breda, 1504 (NK 2648).
122. *Modus epistolandi* (Venice, H. Liechtenstein, 1488; Goff N-32).
123. Paris, J. Petit, 1506: Aberdeen UL, π888508a.

Although such elementary texts did not provide an overview or an introduction to a discipline, the late fifteenth and early sixteenth centuries saw a tendency towards teaching philosophy less from standard texts with commentaries, and more from compendia and summaries of the standard texts. Such summaries and compendia point towards the philosophy text-book as a work relatively independent of the standard text on which it was ultimately based. With the Reformation, this independent philosophy text-book became of paramount importance as a genre and therefore has an impact only on the last few years of the period with which we deal here.[124] The most important examples of the summaries of standard texts are the many works of Jacques Lefèvre d'Etaples. In 1538, Dominus Hughes, a newly elected Fellow at Merton, was required to lecture on Lefèvre's introduction to moral philosophy.[125] Lefèvre's paraphrases of Aristotle's natural philosophy also, first printed from 1492, were much used in England and Scotland. They were published in octavo from 1528. Lefèvre's text-books were highly important in modernizing the curriculum in English and Scottish universities, a process which was paralleled in the universities in Germany in the two first decades of the sixteenth century.[126] The importance of this work is given expression by the frequent entries in Dorne's Day Book, particularly for Lefèvre's works on logic and on metaphysics, and his edition of Boethius's *Arithmetica* – a text required by the Oxford statutes for arts students.[127] Cuthbert Tunstal, the only contributor to this genre from England and Scotland in our period, published a compendium of the *Ethics* in Paris in 1554, where he conformed to the pattern of providing summaries book by book. On the other hand, Jerome de Hangest's *Moralia* was a real text-book which presented the discipline systematically and not in the form of summaries of standard texts. It appeared first in folio, but was later also edited in octavo. A copy now in the Bodleian Library[128] was owned by a Philip Acton (fl. 1530–41),[129] but book-lists do not suggest that this was a widely read text in England and Scotland.

Although it is not always easy to distinguish between commentaries, summaries and text-books, in the course of the sixteenth century the dis-

124. An excellent survey is Schmitt 1988.
125. Probably the *Moralis in Ethicen introductio* with the commentary of Josse Clichtove, first published Paris, A. Caillaut, 1494 (*GW* 9640).   126. Seifert 1984, p. 140.
127. Also Leedham-Green 1986, II, pp. 333–4.
128. [Paris, F. Regnault, P. Gaudoul, N. de la Barre, J. Petit, 1526], Bodleian, 8° C 86(2) Th.
129. *BRUO 1540*, p. 71.

tinction became much clearer, as the commentary as a vehicle for teaching lost ground and the text-book gradually moved further away from the standard texts which had originally defined the disciplines with which they dealt. Melanchthon's *Philosophiae moralis epitome* from 1538, the *Ethicae doctrinae elementa* from 1550, and his *Initia doctrinae physicae* were all independent manuals and no longer summaries.[130]

The disciplines of grammar, letter writing, rhetoric and logic have always to a great extent depended on text-books. The same may be said to be true of mathematics. In Dorne's Day Book, Lefèvre's Boethius edition is found along with the common medieval mathematics text-book, the *Algoritmus*.[131] In the 1540s both the *Algoritmus* and Lefèvre were increasingly replaced by Gemma Frisius, *Arithmeticae practicae methodus facilis*. This was recognized by the statutes of Oxford in 1564/5, one of the few cases where the statutes were modified to take modern developments into account.[132] Jerome de Hangest's *Liber proportionum* was only published in folio and will not have had the function of a student text-book. Cuthbert Tunstal's *De arte supputandi* was first printed by Pynson in London in 1522, in a format which probably put it beyond the pocket of most students. This work shared the fate of Linacre's grammar: printed once only in England and Scotland, it was quite frequently printed abroad, in small formats, and in this more modest form was also often owned in this country.[133]

This study has focused on the disciplines of the arts faculty. The text-book as here defined was in most of our period much less important in the higher faculties. The faculty of medicine, apparently numerically the least important of the higher faculties, required its students to lecture on a number of standard texts, all of which are part of the *Articella*,[134] a collection consisting mainly of texts by Hippocrates and Galen and of commentaries on them.[135] This work constitutes a 'cursus medicus' containing the authoritative texts and commentaries on them, not a systematic presentation of the discipline. The folio format of most editions of the *Articella* also indicates that it is not a text-book in the normal

---

130. In 1527, an Anthony Frobysher was required to lecture on the logic of Melanchthon, presumably as a BA, for the benefit of junior students: see J. M. Fletcher 1986, p. 179. Leedham-Green 1986 shows that Melanchthon's text-books were frequently used in England.
131. *GW* 1269–78; Madan and Bradshaw 1885–90, nos. 473, 474, 554, 978, 987, 1239, 1286; no. 978 records a sale of three copies, 987 of two – again a tutor or teacher buying for his students.   132. S. Gibson 1931, p. 378.
133. Leedham-Green 1986, II, p. 760; North 1992, p. 139; Sturge 1938, pp. 71–8.
134. Getz 1992, pp. 383–4.   135. On the texts, see Kristeller 1986.

sense. An example of a copy of an edition which was probably in England not long after it was printed is that now in the Bodleian Library, of an edition in folio from Venice from 1483.[136] The copy was certainly in Oxford by 1605 and is in a sixteenth-century London binding.[137] The theological faculty depended on lecturing, first on the sentences of Petrus Lombardus and, later in the course, on the texts of the Bible, for both purposes using the extensive body of commentary developed on these texts. *Summae* and sentences were not text-books, but rather reference works guiding towards relevant passages of the standard texts. In theology also, the later sixteenth century saw developments towards the creation of systematic text-books, partly developed in parallel to text-books of philosophy, ethics, physics and metaphysics.[138] The faculty of law likewise depended chiefly on sets of standard texts. The requirement of students was the attendance at ordinary lectures on the texts of the laws themselves, of either the civil or the ecclesiastical law. The creation of a systematic and methodical introduction to Roman law became a central preoccupation of the later sixteenth century;[139] some such attempts at systematization of the law into text-books were used in England, notably Nicolaus Vigelius's *Methodus regularum utriusque iuris* from Basel (1584), but such attempts at a systematic reorganization of the law into compendious text-books all fall after our period.[140]

The greater importance of the text-book made the subtle interplay between tradition and renewal less easy to detect but made renewal easier to achieve. Text-books made it easier to modify the structure of the curriculum, often in a very informal way and, in modifying the way in which disciplines were divided from one another, to modify the way in which knowledge was structured. It is doubtful if one can claim this as a victory for humanist over medieval teaching methods. If humanists had begun their attempts to reform the arts faculty in their own mould, emphasizing a return to the original texts of Antiquity – models of clarity of thought and expression – the result was different from their aspirations. Summaries, compendia and finally text-books designed to avoid the intricacies of medieval doctrine evicted the ancient texts from the

136. Venice, H. Liechtenstein, 29 March 1483 (*GW* 2679).
137. T. James 1605, p. 199; Bodleian, Auct. O 3.29.
138. On some important theological text-books of the late sixteenth century, see Leinsle 1984.
139. On a number of such attempts at methodical presentations of the law in text-book form, see Jensen 1993.
140. Barton 1986, pp. 260–1, on the use in Oxford of one such methodic presentation of legal material.

curriculum. Much more than the medieval literature of commentaries and *quaestiones* and *summulae*, text-books allowed a development away from the texts themselves. The use of the text-book made it easier to adapt teaching to new requirements, whether they were imposed by political and religious considerations or by other intellectual or scientific trends. The production of text-books partly reflects the changing relationships of disciplines as the late medieval curriculum underwent serious modifications. Text-books were also partly aimed at ensuring control over the teaching of universities, and the production of approved text-books to be used in the schools and universities became part of a ruler's political control. In reality, however, the use of Latin as the language of teaching and the international nature of the trade in books for education made this control less easy to achieve. Particularly in the sixteenth century in England and Scotland, the absence of a consistent local production of text-books made such goals elusive. The effects of the replacement of the standard text with a commentary by the text-book, as a tool of teaching were therefore primarily to facilitate faster and less formal changes in the curriculum and to make teaching less dependent on local traditions, and on oral instruction through lectures.

17

Text-books: a case study – logic

E. J. ASHWORTH

This book covers the years 1400 to 1557. In such a long period, we would
expect great changes in the logic text-books used at Oxford and
Cambridge. Indeed, there were great changes, but their timing is somewhat unexpected. If one considers just books written by Englishmen and
copied or printed in England, then there is hardly any change at all
between 1400 and 1530, the year in which the last surviving edition of the
compilation text-book known as *Libellus Sophistarum* was printed. A
period of fifteen years follows in which no surviving logic text was either
written or printed, and then suddenly in 1545 we are confronted with the
Dialectica of John Seton, a work which was to go through fourteen editions by the end of the sixteenth century, and which represents a completely different type of logic.[1] In what follows, I shall focus on the *fortuna*
of just one type of logic text in use between 1400 and 1530, namely the
treatises devoted to *obligationes*, or the rules prescribing what one was
obliged to accept and reject in a certain kind of logical disputation.[2]

It is necessary first to consider the place of logic in the curriculum and
the type of instruction which was offered, then to say something about
fourteenth-century logicians and the *obligationes* texts used in the fifteenth century, and finally to examine the *Libelli Sophistarum* and other
early printed texts in relation to fifteenth-century manuscript collections.

The Curriculum

Until the sixteenth century, and even after, logic was the foundation of
the arts curriculum at both Oxford and Cambridge.[3] The study of logic

---

1. A useful chronological list of logic books printed in England before 1620 is in Schmitt
   1983b, pp. 225–9. For English logic during the sixteenth century: Ashworth 1985b, especially pp. xxiii–xxxii; 1991; Giard 1985; Jardine 1974. No attention should be paid to
   Howell 1956, whose account of developments in logic, particularly during the medieval
   period, is wildly inaccurate, and this vitiates his judgements about the texts described.
2. For more about these texts: Ashworth 1985a.
3. For Cambridge: Leader 1988. For Oxford: J. M. Fletcher 1962; and 1992.

dominated the first two years of the four-year course leading to a Bachelor's degree, and the type of logic taught was closely linked with the natural philosophy that dominated the two final years. Generally speaking, the statutory requirements focused on the reading of Aristotle's *Organon* and on Porphyry's *Isagoge*, but in fact a good deal of more modern logical material was studied. This material can be roughly divided into three groups. First, there are the *Summulae*, or general summaries of logic. The best-known *Summulae* today is a substantial text written in the thirteenth century by Peter of Spain, but he seems never to have been popular in England, and the *Summulae* which forms part of the Oxford and Cambridge logical tradition is a very brief work indeed. Second, there are works on supposition theory, often referred to as the *Parva Logicalia*, and on such topics as the proofs of terms, or the study of the way in which the truth-conditions of propositions are affected by the presence of logical operators, or modal and epistemic terms. Third, there are the so-called treatises of the moderns, dealing with consequences, that is, logical inferences; with insolubles, that is, semantic paradoxes; and with obligations. All these treatises are found, whether in manuscript collections or in their early printed form, in close conjunction with works on natural philosophy.[4]

In their written form, these texts have a feature which is closely related to their actual use in the curriculum, that is, they are full of *sophismata*.[5] A *sophisma* was typically a puzzling sentence for whose proof and disproof plausible arguments could be offered, and the point of the written discussion was to show how the rules of obligations, say, or the distinctions found in treatises on proofs of terms, could be used both to settle the truth-value of the *sophisma* in question, and to illustrate the weaknesses in some or all of the arguments that had been offered.

The relationship of *sophismata* to the curriculum becomes clear when we realize that a very important part of teaching took place through disputations. Many disputations were about particular substantive questions, but others, and particularly those involving undergraduates, were about *sophismata*. They provided a way of giving practice in using logical rules. At the same time, they prepared students for natural philosophy by training them to pursue the logical consequences of an arbitrary description of some logically possible situation. Such arbitrary descriptions or

---

4. For a list of manuscripts: J. M. Fletcher 1962, appendix 6, pp. 219–36; discussion of two manuscript collections: De Rijk 1975; and 1977; discussion of the printed texts: Ashworth 1979a, b; and 1978.
5. Discussion of sophismata and their relation to natural philosophy: Sylla 1982.

casus were the distinguishing feature of the kind of natural philosophy particularly associated with fourteenth-century Oxford, and popular through the fifteenth century. So far as I can tell, the *obligationes* treatises gave instructions specially directed to the holding of this kind of practice-disputation; but all the other types of logic text I have mentioned were relevant to such disputations as well, in that they provided the rules, definitions and distinctions which had to be used.

The changes in logic texts in the sixteenth century go hand in hand with changes in the curriculum which brought about a new emphasis on humanist studies, including Greek, classical poetry and history, and which tended to replace natural philosophy with ethics and politics. The kind of disputation described by *obligationes* treatises disappears altogether, along with the use of *sophismata* and of *casus*. Logic remains at the heart of the curriculum, at least in theory, but it is now the logic of Aristotle, neatly summarized, and supplemented by the work of such humanists as Rudolph Agricola. The intended application is not to natural philosophy, but to literature. John Seton's *Dialectica* is an excellent example of the new type of logic. He retained a little of the medieval supposition theory, but otherwise his work has nothing in common with the logic texts used in the previous century.

The fourteenth century and texts used in the fifteenth century

In the first half of the fourteenth century such men as William of Ockham, Walter Burley, Richard Swyneshead (the Calculator), Roger Swyneshead and William Heytesbury gained a European reputation for their sophisticated and innovative work in logic, as well as in philosophy and theology generally. They were read and commented on at European universities into the sixteenth century, and were frequently printed. In England, some attention continued to be paid to Roger Swyneshead and William Heytesbury during the fifteenth and early sixteenth centuries, and works by them appear in *Libelli Sophistarum*. Burley, however, was the only one of the early logicians to retain any kind of genuine popularity in his homeland. There are strong arguments for associating William Caxton with one of the Cologne editions of Burley's *De vita et moribus philosophorum*.[6] His commentary on Aristotle's *Posterior Analytics* was printed in England in 1517,[7] and in 1520 the Oxford book-seller John Dorne recorded the sale of ten volumes by Burley.[8] Even so, it would be

---

6. *GW* 5784. See Hellinga above, p. 67. 7. *STC* 4122.
8. Madan and Bradshaw 1885–90, pp. 78–139.

hard to argue that these great figures of the past had anything like the importance in England that they had elsewhere.

If we turn to the period 1350–1400, we find that Englishmen were still writing logic texts, but that their work, while good, was no longer innovative.[9] I shall mention just the *obligationes* texts. The longest and best was written in 1359–60 by Ralph Strode, Chaucer's friend, and a successful common lawyer after he had left Oxford for London. A short treatise was written a little earlier by another Mertonian, Richard Billingham, and other short texts were produced by John Wycliffe and Richard Brinkley as part of their comprehensive logic text-books. Richard Lavenham wrote a short text in the 1370s, and at the turn of the century we have another short but interesting text by John Tarteys, who may have been at Balliol. In addition, there are a few anonymous treatises, such as the Oxford *Obiectiones Obligationum*. From the fifteenth century itself, there is absolutely nothing new on *obligationes*. Nor is there much sign of new writing on any logical topic other than that of universals,[10] and even that seems to have ceased after about 1430.

Two questions now need to be asked: what were students reading to satisfy the demands of the curriculum, and what happened to the authors I have mentioned from the latter half of the fourteenth century? To begin with the second question: so far as Wycliffe, Brinkley and Lavenham are concerned, the answer, at least with respect to their works on *obligationes*, is that they did not survive. The same is true of John Tarteys. One English manuscript remains, but otherwise his *obligationes* is known only through two Prague manuscripts and one from Salamanca.[11] Ralph Strode is a more interesting case. Fourteen manuscripts of his *obligationes* survive, and there were at least six printed editions.[12] Of the manuscripts, three are in the Bodleian Library, but all three are Italian. One manuscript is in Seville. All the rest are in Italy, and seem to be of Italian origin.[13] Of

9. Ashworth and Spade 1992.
10. For discussion, see the editorial material in J. Sharpe 1990.
11. Oxford, New Coll. ms. E 289, fols. 204v–210v (incomplete); Praha, Knihovna Metropolitní Kapituly, ms. M.CXLV (1506), fols. 46v–59r; Praha, Statni Knihovna CSR, ms. VIII E II (1536), fols. 120r–132r; Salamanca, Biblioteca da la Universidad, ms. 2358, fols. 26v–33v. An edition of the text: Ashworth 1992.
12. Full details in the forthcoming edition of Strode's *Logica* by Maierù and Ashworth, the latter editor responsible for the *obligationes*.
13. Florence, Biblioteca Nazionale Centrale, ms. Conv. Soppr. J VIII 19 (115), fols. 54r–85ra; Mantua, Biblioteca Comunale, ms. A III 12, fols. 116r–133r; Naples, Biblioteca Nazionale, ms. Principale V.H.149, fols. 246v–254v (incomplete); Bodleian, mss. Canon.misc. 219, fols. 37ra–47ra, Canon.misc. 221, fols. 12r–22v, Canon.misc.506, fols. 462va–482va; Parma, Biblioteca Palatina, ms. misc.744, fols. 103ra–121vb; Ravenna, Biblioteca Classense ms. 32, fols. 81r–149v; Seville, Biblioteca Colombina ms. 5-1-14, fols. 1r–31r; BAV mss. Chigi E VI 193, fols. 22va–34va, Vat.lat. 3045, fols. 85va–126vb, Vat.lat. 3065, fols. 126rb–138vb, Vat.lat. 7125, fols. 73r–86r (incomplete); Viterbo, Biblioteca Capitolare ms. 56, fols. 2ra–14ra.

the printed editions, all but one are Italian. The exception is from *c.* 1512 when Olivier Senant in Paris printed a new *obligationes* treatise by the Scottish logician David Cranston, along with what he hailed as the first edition of Strode north of the Alps. I know of no evidence that anyone in England paid the slightest attention to Strode's *obligationes* during the fifteenth and early sixteenth centuries.

This leaves us with Richard Billingham; and indeed it seems to have been Billingham's *obligationes*, in some form or other that was read in Oxford and Cambridge in the fifteenth century, and that was printed in the various editions of the *Libelli Sophistarum*. I say 'seems', because only one manuscript actually attributes the work to Billingham;[14] and because all the texts that survive are somewhat different, one from another. On the other hand, Billingham is a very likely candidate for authorship, since he was a prolific and popular writer of simplified logic manuals.[15]

So much for the known authors of *obligationes* texts. Now I shall look more closely at the question of what students were reading to satisfy the demands of the curriculum, at least insofar as these related to non-Aristotelian logic. Unfortunately, any firm judgements about what went on at Oxford and Cambridge in the fifteenth century are rendered somewhat problematic by the low survival rate of manuscripts in England, as compared to the Continent.[16] Thus, if we consider Billingham's *obligationes* and its Oxford variants, of the fifteen complete manuscripts I know, only four are found in England, and one of these is of Italian origin.[17] Four are in Spain, copied by Spaniards, and the rest are in Italy, copied in most, if not all, cases by Italians. The copyists frequently tell us that we are dealing with an *obligationes* 'secundum usum Oxonie', but this alone is not enough to settle the question of the fifteenth-century curriculum. The manuscript evidence for the Cambridge *obligationes* text, also fairly closely related to that of Billingham, is even more sparse. Of the

14. The manuscript in question is Salamanca, Biblioteca de la Universidad, ms. 1735, fols. 89r–95v. The other manuscripts De Rijk attributes to Billingham are: Barcelona, Archivo de la Corona de Aragón, ms. Ripoll 166, fols. 49r–54r; Rome, Casanatense ms. 5445, fols. 119v–130v; Toledo, Biblioteca del Cabildo, mss. 94–27, f. 63r (opening lines only), 94–28, fols. 164r–168v. The Oxford variants are found in the following manuscripts: Barcelona, Archivo de la Corona de Aragón, ms. Ripoll 166, fols. 55r–59r; Cambridge, Corpus Christi Coll. mss. 244–5, fols. 13v–18v, 378, fols. 48r–57r; Bodleian, ms. lat.misc.e 79, fols. 18ra–24ra; Padua, Biblioteca Antoniana, ms. 407, fols. 34v–36r; Padua, Biblioteca Universitaria, ms. 1123, fols. 3vb–5va; Rome, Biblioteca Angelica, ms. 1053, fols. 36v–39v; BAV, mss. Urb.lat. 1419, fols. 62v–66v; Vat.lat. 3065, fols. 95vb–98vb, Vat.lat. 4269, fols. 192v–196r; Worcester, Cathedral Library, ms. F 118, fols. 8vb–10ra.
15. On Billingham: De Rijk 1976.   16. Courtenay 1987, p. 360.
17. Oxford, Bodleian, ms lat.misc. e 79.

two relevant manuscripts, one is in Wrocław, and the other, in Gonville and Caius College, Cambridge, is quite late. Some of the works in the collection were copied by Thomas Water, who received his MA in 1482.[18]

The *Libellus Sophistarum*

At this point, however, we can appeal to the early printed texts to support the hypothesis that the fifteenth-century curriculum at both Oxford and Cambridge involved the reading of a particular series of mainly anonymous fourteenth-century texts. Apart from two Aristotle commentaries by Antonius Andreas and Walter Burley, all but one of the logic text-books published in England up to 1530 were unadorned reprints of earlier English works. The single exception is the 1483 *Logica* published by Theodoricus Rood,[19] which was clearly put together by a single compiler, and which draws heavily on the Frenchman, Jean Buridan, and the Italian, Paul of Venice. Of the texts which reprinted English material, the most important are the two series of *Libelli Sophistarum*. The Cambridge series was printed four times between 1497 and 1524,[20] though the second in the series is somewhat different in content.[21] The Oxford series was published six times in England between 1499 and 1530,[22] as well as in France,[23] in Cologne,[24] and in Seville in 1503.[25] There is also a complete manuscript copy of much later date of one of the printed editions, which is to be found in the Bodleian Library.[26]

I shall illustrate my claim that the contents of the printed texts reveal what was taught during the fifteenth century by considering just the tracts on *obligationes*. The simplest case is that of the Oxford version of the *Libellus Sophistarum*, for each edition contains the same variant of the Oxford *obligationes* text which stems from Billingham, though, unlike Billingham's original, it lacks a section on imposition – that is, the process of endowing works and phrases with an arbitrarily chosen new meaning. The Cambridge version is more interesting, for it contains two

18. Leader 1988, p. 128. The manuscripts are Cambridge, Gonville and Caius Coll., ms. 182/215, pp. 42–7; Wrocław, Biblioteka Uniwersytecka, ms. IV Q 3, fols. 194v–197r.
19. *STC* 16693. 20. *STC* 15574.5–15576.4. 21. *STC* 15575.5.
22. *STC* 15576.6–15578.3, 15578.7. 23. See Ashworth 1979b. 24. *STC* 15578.5.
25. *Summa utilissima dialetice oxoniensis: que communiter sophisteria dicitur anglie . . . in civitate hispalensi*, 1503. (Not in *STC*.) Tracts 8, 9, 11, 12, 13, 14 and 15 of the Oxford text are omitted. I thank Professor Angel d'Ors, who kindly obtained a copy of the text for me.
26. Bodleian, ms. Rawl. D 1059, is bound with some of the sheets uncut and out of order. The hand may be seventeenth-century, and on the flyleaf is written 'Tho. Hearne Julii 23° 1709'.

texts. One is a very brief version of Billingham's *obligationes*, stripped of all *sophismata*, and with a quite different section on imposition. This is the version found in the two manuscripts mentioned above. The second text is the *Obiectiones Casuum*, a collection of *sophismata* to do with *obligationes*. This collection is found in the Gonville and Caius manuscript, though it lacks the first four pages of my typed transcription;[27] and it corresponds to the Oxford *Obiectiones Obligationum*, a collection of *sophismata* which is found in four manuscripts. Two of these are English, and a third, in Wrocław, also contains the Cambridge *obligationes* text.[28] The Oxford *Obiectiones*, however, orders the *sophismata* differently, and the discussion of each *sophisma* is somewhat different. Finally, we should look at the 1483 *Logica*. Much of the tract on *obligationes* is copied from Paul of Venice, but a number of additional *sophismata* are taken from the Oxford *obligationes*, and half the section on imposition comes directly from the Cambridge *obligationes*.

This seems to me good evidence that the surviving manuscripts represent what was used for teaching in fifteenth-century Oxford and Cambridge, and it is certainly very strong evidence that the logic curriculum did not change substantially in the first decades of the sixteenth century.

27. Cambridge, Gonville and Caius Coll., ms. 182/215, pp. 92–101.
28. *Obiectiones Obligationum secundum usum Oxonie*: Oxford, New Coll., ms. E 289, fols. 21r–23v; Padua, Biblioteca Universitaria, ms. 1123, fols. 16ra–18ra; Worcester, Cathedral Library, ms. F 118, fols. 38rb–41rb; Wrocław, Biblioteka Uniwersytecka, ms. IV Q 3, fols. 213r–218v.

II

PROFESSIONS

18

The canon law

R. H. HELMHOLZ

This chapter describes what is known about the existence and the use of canon law books in Britain. It may be admitted at the outset that segregation of the literature of the canon law from that of the civil law, covered in the chapter by Alain Wijffels, is somewhat artificial.[1] The two learned laws were combined for many purposes in the European *ius commune*.[2] Nonetheless, the canon law always maintained a distinct identity. Many books dealt primarily with canonical problems or texts, and the canon law was in a real sense the dominant partner in the *ius commune*. It is not inappropriate to treat it as a distinct entity.

The canon law's importance

Together with rules drawn from the Roman law, the canon law provided the principal source of the jurisprudence in the English ecclesiastical courts.[3] These courts, held by every bishop and archdeacon, as well as by many lesser clerics, played a wide and important role in the legal life of medieval England. Indeed, they held significant jurisdiction over the law of marriage, wills and probate, and part of the law of defamation, well into the nineteenth century. In addition, they long exercised a 'criminal' jurisdiction over both the clergy and the laity, extending from the sins of the flesh, such as adultery and fornication, to more properly religious offences such as absenting oneself from the parish church or doctrinal dissent.

The significance of the canon law, with the literature that accompanied it, went beyond the immediate needs of practice in the ecclesiastical courts. It was taught formally at the English universities until the canon law faculties were abolished in the 1530s. Probably it continued to be

---

1. Below, pp. 399–410.   2. See Schrage 1992; Helmholz 1990, pp. 151–4.
3. D. M. Owen 1990, pp. 1–16; Woodcock 1952.

studied informally afterwards.[4] It was a formal part of the curriculum at Scottish universities until a time well beyond the terminal date of this volume.[5] The canon law was also immediately relevant to parochial clergy, partly in their exercise of the cure of souls, partly in their role as functionaries for the ecclesiastical courts. It governed several aspects of the sacrament of penance in the 'internal forum', for example. It was also a source for religious, political and legal thought more generally.[6] Many issues of public and constitutional history were touched by the canon law.

A serious examination of canon law books must therefore cast a wide net. It must take account of the contents of the libraries that belonged to universities, monastic houses, diocesan courts, parish churches and individual men and women. Indeed, all of them provide useful information, for all can be shown to have contained canonical works. It is unfortunate that much of the information about their collections can only be described as fragmentary.[7] On the other hand, there *are* a great many fragments,[8] and what they suggest is consistent enough across Britain to inspire some confidence in generalizations based upon them.

Importation and production of canon law books

Englishmen and Scotsmen were importers rather than producers of books relating to the canon law. British scriptoria and printing presses never produced copies of canonical treatises, written in England or elsewhere, in anything like the numbers or regularity with which they were published on the Continent. This generalization is as true for the fifteenth century as for the sixteenth; the introduction of print caused little change. This relative paucity in production in fact mirrors the general state of canonical learning in England and Scotland. Although the canon law was taught and used throughout this period, and although there were many Englishmen one might legitimately describe as professional canonists, the country was never at the forefront of learning on the subject. The great canonists were Italian, French, German and Spanish.

4. Barton 1986, pp. 256–62; Mullinger 1873, p. 630.   5. D. B. Smith 1936, p. 191.
6. E.g., Tierney 1982.
7. For a promising source of future progress, see Osler 1988. Bennett 1952 unfortunately deals solely with legal literature of the common law.
8. Jayne 1983. I have tried to follow Jayne's approach (p. 9) of 'working the vein to the point of uneconomical returns' in what follows.

There had been a time – the twelfth century – when this was not so.[9] Then, Englishmen had been in the van, or at least among the forward troops. Those days had long since passed, however, by the fifteenth century, and what canonical book production there was within the confines of the British Isles concentrated on works designed for local practice and local conditions. When one examines English inventories of manuscripts and early printed books, including even the most celebrated of the medieval canonists – writers such as Hostiensis (d. 1271), Innocent IV (d. 1254) and Panormitanus (d. 1445 or 1453) – or seeks out the basic texts of the canon law collected in the *Corpus iuris canonici*, one finds that the places of production and publication were invariably cities across the English Channel.[10] English library catalogues leave the identical impression,[11] and that impression is not confined to books owned by ecclesiastical lawyers.[12] The *STC* itself demonstrates that England was not a centre of canonical book production.

Works produced in England

To this generalization, there was one exception, and it proves the rule. The *Manipulus curatorum*, written by the Spanish jurist Guido de Monte Rochen (fl. 1330), was not simply imported; it was printed in England seven times between 1498 and 1520.[13] This introductory handbook on the duties of parochial clergy met an obvious need. In 1513, for example, an Essex rector bequeathed a copy, together with a chain to hang it by, to his parish church. The Spaniard's book was sometimes even found in laymen's libraries.[14] The *Manipulus* has been described as 'scientifically worthless' by a German commentator,[15] and it is quite true that it is not a sophisticated work. This harsh judgement may be justified. However, the *Manipulus* was exactly suitable for parochial and immediate purposes. It was popular for that reason; hence its several English printings.

The combination of practical canon law and pastoral theology characteristic of the *Manipulus* also re-appears in the books designed for parochial needs, particularly those for the confessional, that were produced by English authors during the medieval period. William de Pagula's two works, *Oculus sacerdotis* and *Summa summarum*,[16] together with the

9. Duggan 1963; Kuttner and Rathbone 1951.   10. Von Schulte 1875–80, II, pp. 23, 31, 81.
11. E.g., Oates 1954. See also Wijffels 1992b; inventory of David Pole, in *BRUO 1540*, pp. 452, 730–3.   12. Ives 1969, p. 107.   13. *STC* 12470–5.
14. Darlington 1967, No. 84; of Richard Brereton (1558), in Piccope 1857, p. 174.
15. Von Schulte 1895, II, p. 430.   16. Surveys by Boyle 1955, and 1965.

manual of Ranulf Higden,[17] and John de Burgh's *Pupilla oculi*,[18] clearly fit this pattern: they, too, were written prior to the fifteenth century. All these are attested by enough surviving manuscripts (and the last in a 1510 printing), and they figured in enough clerical testamentary bequests,[19] for us to speak justly of their perceived utility.[20] Penitential literature like these English treatises always contained quite a bit of canon law.[21] The only one of these works to have achieved more than one English printing, however, is the *Exornatorium curatorum*, of which several editions were produced in the first decades of the sixteenth century; indeed a steady trade in this rudimentary but obviously popular clerical manual occurred at Oxford during these years.[22]

Local and practical needs also stand out in the more impressively learned work by William Lyndewood (d. 1446), Dean of the Court of Arches and later Bishop of St Davids. His *Provinciale (seu Constitutiones Angliae)* digested and commented upon the principal constitutions of the province of Canterbury, also relating them to the general law of the Church.[23] English parochial clergy, academics and professional ecclesiastical lawyers owned copies of this book.[24] This choice would have been natural, because the provincial constitutions were the basis for many of the local rules of legal practice. That no treatment of English constitutions was to be found in any of the imported treatises by continental authors would also help to explain Lyndewood's popularity and relatively frequent printing. There are at least fifty-five surviving medieval manuscripts, and seventeen editions appear in the *STC*.[25] Folio editions were in print by 1525, and there were nine Latin octavos by 1529 (the next in Mary's reign, 1557). Apart from this special case, however, the history of the local production of canonical books is unimpressive. It may well be that there was no perceived need and that, with the significant exception of Lyndewood's work, imported works sufficed.

17. I have relied in this instance on the manuscript copy found in the Library of the University of Illinois, Champaign-Urbana, ms. 251 H 53. Other copies are apparently found in Balliol Coll., Oxford, ms. 69, and CUL, ms. Mm.i.20.   18. *STC* 4115; Davis 1914.

19. For the *Pupilla oculi*, see will of John Burn (1479), in *Testamenta Eboracensia*, III, p. 199; will of Richard Goldthorp (1476), in *Visitations and memorials*, p. 100; will of Richard Stone (1509), *Archaeologia Cantiana* 43 (1931), p. 105; will of John Hurte (1476), in *Testamenta Eboracensia*, III, pp. 220–2; will of Robert Barker (1581), in Cross 1989.

20. Luxton 1977, p. 64.

21. A valuable introduction and survey by Broomfield in Chobham 1968, pp. xi–lxxxvii; Wenzel 1989.   22. Madan and Bradshaw 1885–90, pp. 79–138.

23. Ferme 1989, pp. 677–78.

24. E.g., will of Robert Barra (1526), in *Visitations and memorials*, p. 126; will of William Pope (1485), in Elvey 1975, no. 37; will of Henry Turton (1533), in Piccope 1857, p. 13. See also D. M. Owen 1985, and Leedham-Green 1986, II, pp. 513–14.

25. *STC* 17102–13; Cheney 1961, rpt pp. 178–84.

Imported treatises

When one turns to the imported canonical treatises, the situation looks quite different. Almost all the principal continental treatises were imported into England and Scotland,[26] and they were routinely used by English and Scottish ecclesiastical lawyers.[27] It appears that England may have lagged behind slightly in the acquisition of some of the newer and less traditional types of canonical literature (of which much more was written at the end of our period than at the beginning). *Consilia*, *Decisiones*, together with many works of *praxis*, did come into English libraries,[28] particularly towards the end of the sixteenth century.[29] But the standard texts and the better-known medieval commentators on them figured much more prominently in English collections than did these newer classes of books.[30]

A possible addition to the latter, notable by its ubiquity in England and therefore an exception to the generalization, is penitential literature, as, for instance, the *Summa angelica* by Angelus de Clavasio (d. 1494), the *Summa Rosella* by Baptista de Salis or Trovamala (d. after 1494), or the *Summa de penitencia* by Raymond de Peñaforte (d. 1275).[31] A good deal of it was imported into England, and it might be classed with the works that went beyond commentary on the texts. However, outside the 'internal forum', the works of the great decretalists held pride of place. When Archbishop Morton (d. 1500) needed to know the canon law about canonization of saints, for example, the information he received came exclusively from the principal commentators on the texts of the *Corpus iuris canonici*: Joannes Andreae, Hostiensis, Innocent IV, Panormitanus, Guido de Baysio, Joannes Monachus and Dominicus de Sancto Geminiano.[32] He, like many men of authority, was guided by the great commentators of the canon law rather than by specialized literature.

Among these commentaries, the comprehensive work on the Gregorian *Decretals* by Nicolaus de Tudeschis, commonly called Panormitanus, was particularly (and deservedly) popular before the turn of the sixteenth century. It maintained that place in the hundred years that followed. It is, for example, the only canon law book recorded as

---

26. E. Armstrong 1979.
27. Below, text accompanying footnotes 68–75. For Scotland, see Barry 1967, pp. xxiii–xxvii.
28. E.g., Ker 1985, p. 482; rpt 1985, p. 416; will of John Price (1554), in *BRUO 1540*, p. 734, recording his ownership of the *Practica* of Lanfrancus de Oriano.
29. E.g., Stein 1988, pp. 207–8.   30. Wijffels 1993a, p. 64.
31. E.g., Leedham-Green 1986, II, p. 225; will of Thomas Rotherham (1500), in Leach 1903, p. 163; *CWM*, IX, pp. 384–5.   32. Harper-Bill 1987–91, I, No. 181.

actually having been purchased (in 1508) for the library at Corpus Christi College, Cambridge, as indicated in an inventory of printed books owned before 1569;[33] and the will of James Goldwell (1499) contains a bequest of the commentary by Panormitanus to Norwich Cathedral, 'to be chained in the Library for use of . . . the consistory'.[34] Similarly, in a notation in a fifteenth-century formulary discussing the law of tithes, besides Panormitanus, only the texts and commentaries by Hostiensis, Henricus Bohic (d. *c.* 1350) and Innocent IV were mentioned.[35] Overall, the evidence suggests that, even though some obscure names figure among the canonical works in British hands – such as the copy of Franciscus Duarenus, *De sacris ecclesiae ministeriis ac beneficiis* (Paris 1551), in a library otherwise without canon law books[36] – the great names among the classical commentators on the *Corpus iuris canonici* held the predominant position among the imported works. This certainly is the impression given by reading John Dorne's Day Book of 1520.[37]

The establishment towards the end of the fifteenth century, of Doctors' Commons, the College of Advocates in London, must have made a positive difference in the importation of canon law books. It may have included specialized works of practice as well as the standard treatises. It is far from certain that there was a common library there, but a conditional bequest of 1469 at least suggests its probable existence from an early date.[38] Similar but smaller collections were also being put together at the sites of the various consistory courts throughout the country. However, most fit the pattern described above. A catalogue, still in manuscript, compiled at Canterbury just after the terminal date of this volume, for instance, lists most of the basic canonical works, but not a large number of civilian or canonical ephemera. It contains the *Corpus iuris canonici*, and works by Hostiensis, Panormitanus, Joannes Andreae, Lyndewood (two copies) and several other more minor works from the *ius commune*.[39] The early library lists at Oxford and Cambridge were also dominated by the basic works of canon law.[40] Because individual benefaction rather than systematic purchase was the source of most of these collections, there was more duplication of these basic works than would

---

33. J. M. Fletcher and McConica 1961, pp. 191, 196.
34. Jacob 1971, pp. 214–15, listing the copies of his works in Oxford libraries; Goldwell's will is noted in *BRUO*, p. 785.   35. Somerset Record Office, Taunton, ms. D/D/Ca, p. 248.
36. Liddell 1937–8, p. 415.   37. Madan and Bradshaw 1885–90, pp. 79–138.
38. Will of Thomas Kent; *BRUO*, p. 1038; Squibb 1977, pp. 88–97.
39. Canterbury Cathedral Library, ms. Z.3.25. See also the list of civil and canon law books (*c.* 1600) in BL, Harl. ms. 6048.   40. Bradshaw 1889, pp. 16–53.

now be thought desirable, and perhaps it was only natural that some of the works in the libraries came to be sold from time to time.

The contents of British libraries

It is possible to go beyond generalizations about the nature and strength of imported canonical works by looking more closely at particular kinds of collection. For some of these categories we know more than for others, although some uncertainties exist throughout. The categories are also not mutually exclusive, since there was movement between different types, as from private into monastic libraries and from monastic into both private and academic libraries. Broadly speaking, however, an examination of separate kinds of library confirms the patterns just described.

Monastic libraries

Most of the smaller medieval monastic libraries seem to have been quite poor in canonical works. They might own a volume or two, but not much more. The smaller houses were the objects of no more than occasional benefaction by ecclesiastical lawyers, and they seem to have purchased few such books on their own. For instance, the Carthusians of St Hugh's, Parkminster, possessed only 2 canon law manuscripts in an otherwise quite extensive collection: a copy of the *Decretum* and of the Clementines.[41] Flaxley Abbey in Gloucestershire held just 1 canonical book, the Gregorian Decretals, in a collection of 79 titles.[42] At the Dissolution, Monk Bretton in Yorkshire possessed only 3 canonical works; this in a library of almost 150 works.[43]

On the other hand, some of the older, larger and richer houses had extensive libraries that contained substantial numbers of canon law works. The libraries of St Augustine's, Canterbury, or Dover Priory, for instance, had quite good collections – all the basic texts and several of the medieval commentaries on them.[44] The library of Syon monastery in Isleworth contained 104 books on the canon law, taken from a total of 1,421 volumes.[45] If one were also to count the libraries in the several monastic cathedrals, where consistory courts were also held, the number

41. Ker 1969–92, VI, pp. 7–154.
42. *CBMLC*, III, p. 18; Williams 1908. See also D. N. Bell 1992; 1984; Durkan 1961a.
43. J. Hunter 1831, pp. 1–7; *CBMLC*, IV, pp. 266–87; Bell, above, p. 231.
44. M. R. James 1903, pp. 389–406, 424–8. Similarly see M. R. James 1909, pp. 62–4; and *CBMLC*, I, pp. 104–8.   45. Bateson 1898, p. vii.

of such large libraries with canonical manuscripts would of course be multiplied. Since the cathedrals were also home to the diocesan courts, however, it is by no means clear whether these libraries should be attributed to the monastery or to the officials of the courts.[46]

Parochial and private collections

Three observations can be made about parochial and private libraries. First, the great age of their creation occurred immediately after the period covered by this volume.[47] Second, even before that period of expansion, some parishes, or at least some parochial clergy, owned canon law books – mostly either texts from the *Corpus iuris canonici*, a commentary on them, or else works like the *Pupilla oculi* of John de Burgh or one of the *Summae confessorum*, works designed for immediate and penitential purposes.[48] Third, despite the great amount of work done in indexing and printing wills, except where we can connect an individual with a consistory court, we know less about the books of individuals than we do about any of the other sources mentioned.

Outside the universities, it very often appears that individual clerics who possessed canonical works owned only one or two such works, where they owned any at all: Robert Raulyn, Commissary General at Canterbury bequeathed a Bible and a copy of the Decretals; Robert Blakamor (d. 1482), a chantry priest, bequeathed a *Liber decretalium* and perhaps one other book on canon law; George Simon (d. 1532), Rector of Maidford, Northants, left 'my decretals' and one other book to named legatees.[49] A Scottish rector who died in 1552 was thus typical of many British clerics in having only a copy of Gratian's *Decretum* and one of the commentaries of Dominicus de Sancto Geminiano to bequeath.[50]

Even these indications of limited canon law book ownership may exaggerate the extent of canonical collecting by individuals. In several of the cases where the titles of the books are detailed in wills or inventories, those found in the hands of the parochial clergy included, and were perhaps limited to, copies of the provincial and synodal constitutions. Specific examples are William Pope, Rector of Loughton, Bucks.

---

46. E.g. Durham Cathedral, described in Ker and Watson 1964–87, *Supplement*, pp. 16–34. See also text below, accompanying notes 71–3.
47. See, generally, Church of England 1959, pp. 42–3.
48. E.g. Richard Cokerham (d. 1475), in *BRUC*, p. 147; the frequency of the *Pupilla* is noted also by Savage 1911, p. 132.   49. Woodcock 1952, p. 116; *BRUC*, p. 64; *BRUO 1540*, p. 701.
50. Alexander Galloway, in Drummond 1979, p. 299. See also William Boston (d. 1474), in Munby 1951, p. 285.

(d. 1485); William Hugham, Vicar of Northgate, Canterbury (d. 1417); and Adam Kinghorn, Rector of Newdosk (sixteenth century).[51] None possessed more than these basic pastoral works. The English clergy were required by the law to read these constitutions publicly during the parish services, in order to acquaint their flocks with the Church's laws.[52] Such immediate needs may explain contemporary clerical purchasing and collecting habits.

College libraries

We are better informed about the contents of college libraries than about any other sort, although the system of putting books out to long-term loan (called *electio sociorum*) that prevailed into the sixteenth century prevents us from recovering fuller information.[53] It is fair to say that canon law books were regarded as a normal, perhaps a necessary, part of all of them. This period witnessed the creation and organization of several of the great collegiate libraries. There was also considerable variation among them, both in extent and in coverage of canon law works. Some of the colleges were quite basic in both senses. The library at St John's, Cambridge, for example, contained ninety-two books in 1544. Of these only six were canon law books, and all but one of these was either a volume of the *Corpus iuris canonici* or a basic commentary on it. The one slightly unusual volume was Johannes Koelner de Vanckel, *Summarium textuale et conclusiones super Sexto [et] Clementinis*, first published in 1483.[54]

On the other hand, some colleges made law a speciality, and had assembled quite good collections by the start of Elizabeth's reign.[55] All Souls College, Oxford, right from the time of its foundation during the first years covered by this volume, provided an extensive choice for its scholars. Of course it held the several parts of the *Corpus iuris canonici*. It also possessed, however, commentaries by Hostiensis, Guillelmus Durandus (d. 1296), Raymond de Peñaforte, Joannes Andreae (d. 1348), Guido de Baysio (d. 1313), Antonius de Butrio (d. 1408), Franciscus Zabarella (d. 1417), Innocent IV, Geoffrey of Trani (d. 1254), Petrus de Salinis (fl. thir-

---

51. Elvey 1975, no. 37; Jacob and Johnson 1938–47, II, p. 103; Durkan and Ross 1961, p. 121.
52. Deposition of William Hayward, in *Woodthorp v. Bayly* (Diocese of Norwich 1500); Norfolk Record Office, DEP/1, fol. 16, shows this happened.   53. Ker 1978, pp. 294–6.
54. *GW* 9712; McKitterick 1978, pp. 144–53. For other examples of libraries similar to St John's, see Liddell 1937–8; J. M. Fletcher and McConica 1961; Searle 1864, pp. 179–80.
55. Cobban 1969, pp. 254–5 shows a preponderance of civilian works, however; Leach 1896, pp. 235–40; Wijffels 1992a; Malden 1902, pp. 270–1.

teenth century), Joannes de Lignano (d. 1383), Petrus de Ancharano (d. 1416) and Johannes Calderinus (d. 1365).[56] Others were added as time went on. The *Decisiones* of the Roman Rota, books of *praxis*, and various *repertoria* and *consilia*,[57] some of them quite difficult to identify today,[58] found their way into the All Souls College Library. This did not constitute a complete collection of the works of medieval and early modern canonists, but it was an extensive one by any standard. It went well beyond what would have been needed for practising ecclesiastical lawyers.

Although it seems an unlikely result at first sight, the abolition of the canon law faculties at the English universities in the 1530s had little negative impact on the accumulation of canon law books in college libraries.[59] If anything, the numbers grew. This expansion may be explained in part by the fact that the canon law was kept *in commendam* with the civil law, which continued to be taught at Oxford and Cambridge.[60] Continued collection of canonical materials may also be attributed partly to the continuity in enforcement of the *ius commune* in the courts of the Church.[61] It is even not beyond thinking that an increase in buying canonical works can be attributed partly to their utility in the many religious controversies of the Reformation period.[62] Canon law was used on both sides.

Perhaps there was even an intrinsic interest in the canon law among contemporary common lawyers and other scholars. The resources of the *ius commune* were drawn upon by lawyers and publicists of different persuasions. It is natural to account on this basis for purchases of canon law books by men whose careers and other purchases show no particular canonical proclivity.[63] Extinguishment of papal authority did not extinguish interest in the papal law books.

Whatever the full explanation may be for England, it is demonstrable that the same continuation of collection of canonical works occurred also in Scotland, where the canon law better maintained its formal place in academic life.[64] It was later said in Scotland that 'The canon law is in a

---

56. Ker 1971, pp. 10–11.
57. Will of Walter Stone (1519), in *BRUO*, pp. 1788–9; will of James Goldwell (1499), in *BRUO*, p. 785.   58. Ker 1971, p. 71: 'Quedam Summa cum aliis contentis'.
59. This is a theme of Helmholz 1990; see esp. pp. 152–4.
60. Fuller 1840, p. 225. For another, nearly contemporary statement of the same point, Duck (d. 1648) bk 1, cap. 10: Duck 1668, p. 109.   61. Helmholz 1990, p. 36.
62. Rex 1991, pp. 198–200, noting the presence of works by Angelus de Clavasio, Joannes Andreae and Panormitanus.
63. Leedham-Green, Rhodes and Stubbings 1992, pp. 14–15, 107.   64. Drummond 1979.

great measure the law of Scotland.'[65] Perhaps that was something of an exaggeration. It was not altogether false, however, either for Scotland or for England, and it helps to explain book-collecting habits even after the Reformation.

The libraries of ecclesiastical lawyers

It is often difficult to separate the libraries of English ecclesiastical lawyers from those of the diocesan courts. Often one cannot even know the exact contents of a lawyer's library, even though one knows from testamentary bequests of 'my law books' that testators owned law books of an unspecified sort.[66] There are some exceptions: Robert Alne, Examiner-General of the consistory court at York, for example. In his 1440 testament he bequeathed: the provincial constitutions with the gloss of John de Atho; Guido de Baysio on the *Decretum*; Innocent IV on the Decretals; and (surprisingly) a collection of *Decisiones* of the Roman Rota, perhaps the earliest collection, made in 1337; the *Extravagantes* of John XXIII; and several theological works.[67] John Lovelych, Registrar of the Commissary Court of Canterbury, who died two years before Alne, left only a copy of the *Liber sextus* and the *Clementines*, though he also left a copy of the Roman law Digest.[68] The overall picture is one of small collections containing the major texts and perhaps one or two other volumes.[69] This picture is confirmed by examination of the probate inventories of lawyers in Oxford.[70]

If one takes notice of the various formularies and memoranda books of ecclesiastical lawyers serving in the diocesan courts, making the assumption that the compilers had access to the books they cited, then much the same sort of evidence predominates. A fifteenth-century formulary now in the British Library contains references to the *Corpus iuris canonici* and to the treatise by Joannes Andreae.[71] A similar formulary at Canterbury includes the same basic canonical texts, adding only the treatise on them by Innocent IV.[72] A precedent book with documents from 1470 to 1492, now at Wells Cathedral, contains only one reference to a canonical book: the Clementines.[73] Although these examples do not prove that no other

---

65. *Maxwell* v. *Gordon* [1775]; Browne 1826, 624 at 626, per the Lord President.
66. E.g. will of John Brown (1479), in *Visitations and memorials*, p. 104.
67. *Testamenta Eboracensia*, II, pp. 78–9; see also will of John Underwood (1515), an advocate at York, in IV, p. 69.   68. Jacob and Johnson 1938–47 II, p. 560.
69. The pattern and exceptions to it are well set out in Allmand 1982.   70. *PLRE*, II–IV.
71. BL, Harl. ms. 862, fol. 239.   72. Canterbury Cathedral Library, ms. D.8, fols. 68, 73.
73. Wells Cathedral Library, fifteenth-century ms., 'The Precedent Book', f. 166v. For the Clementines, see Schrage 1992, p. 106.

books were then available to any of the consistory courts, they suggest a relative thinness of resources. Particularly is this so when they are compared with similar formularies written and compiled fifty years later. In these later documents, frequent references to a much broader variety of canonical treatises, some of them quite specialized in scope, became the norm.[74]

Conclusion

It seems fair to say in conclusion that books of the canon law were in regular use throughout Britain between 1440 and 1558. However, for the most part, the books available and actually in the hands of users were relatively limited in numbers and variety. There certainly were exceptions to this rule. William Lyndewood used a very wide variety of canonical treatises in compiling his *Provinciale* in the mid fifteenth century.[75] The same can be said of some ecclesiastical lawyers and also, though in a slightly lesser measure, of the Scottish theologian, William Hay (d. 1542), who wrote on the law of marriage.[76] A full range of imported canonical books was therefore certainly to be found in academic centres in Britain. If we look at the normal situation, however, the texts of the *Corpus iuris canonici* and the basic commentaries on them are what stand out. They were sufficient for most needs of practice. The relative paucity of prominent canonists in Britain thus seems to have run on a parallel track with most canonical book collections.

74. E.g., Helmholz 1992.
75. See the list of the commentaries cited at the beginning of the 1968 reprint of the 1679 edition: Lyndewood 1679.   76. Barry, 1967, pp. xxiii–xxvii.

19

The civil law

ALAIN WIJFFELS

The general development of civil law literature[1]

During the fifteenth century and the first half of the sixteenth, civil law underwent important changes which affected both the text of the collections encompassed in the *Corpus iuris civilis* and legal scholarship. Throughout the period, legal methods both *in scholis* and *in curiis* were dominated by the *mos italicus*, which ignored a general systematization of the law and emphasized the application to the present of rules derived from a scholastic analysis of the authoritative texts. This was strongly challenged, in particular from the 1520s onwards, by legal humanists and their sympathizers, who devoted themselves to the understanding of ancient law by the application of historical and philological method (*mos gallicus*).

The literature of the late medieval and sixteenth-century *mos italicus* has often been branded as characterizing a period of decline in legal science, although it is acknowledged to have contributed strongly to the so-called 'reception' of *ius commune* in Europe. It certainly enjoyed considerable success, to judge by the numerous sixteenth-century editions

---

1. The present chapter relies mostly on the (printed) lists mentioned in Savage 1911, Durkan and Ross 1961, Jayne 1983; including lists from Cambridge and Oxford probate inventories, published since then in Leedham-Green 1986 and *PLRE*, II–IV, Cavanaugh 1980, *BRUC*, *BRUO*, *BRUO* 1540; printed and unprinted material mentioned in Wijffels 1992a; and Margaret Lane Ford's database set up during the course of the preparations for *A History of the Book in Britain 1400–1557*. For a general survey of the civil law literature during the fifteenth and sixteenth centuries, including further information about the civilian authors and their work, the reader should consult Schrage 1992, Coing 1973 and 1977, Holthöfer 1977, Horn 1973, Söllner 1977 and Troje 1977. The organization of civil law studies at Oxford and Cambridge during the later Middle Ages and the sixteenth century has recently been outlined by Barton 1984, 1986 and 1992 (Oxford) and Leader 1988 (Cambridge); earlier developments are discussed in Zulueta and Stein 1990. For a general assessment of the role of Roman (i.e., civil) law in medieval and (to some extent) sixteenth-century England and Scotland, reliable scholarly surveys are offered by Allmand 1982 (England), Barton 1971 (England) and Stein 1988, pp. 269–359 (Scotland).

and reprints of the standard *mos italicus* works, often in multi-volume folios. At the beginning of the seventeenth century, *mos italicus* authors were still all-important at Oxford and Cambridge and provided the authorities most widely quoted by the practitioners of Doctors' Commons. The proliferation of *mos italicus* authorities also had an influence on some broader developments within itself. The texts of the *Corpus iuris civilis*, almost always accompanied by the standard Accursian gloss, remained the foundation of the whole civil law system. Especially from the fourteenth century onwards, generations of university teachers followed the collections' *ordo legalis* for their lectures and commentaries. The most successful and authoritative of the commentators were almost all Italians. The accumulation of their commentaries was not without influence on their method, since an important part of their legal reasoning, which often set a model for forensic argumentations, consisted in quoting scholarly literature; references to *auctoritates* were essential to buttress a particular point or to discuss the merits of a controversial argument. As a result, late medieval *mos italicus* works are characterized by increasingly complex references to authorities, even though a handful of commentators enjoyed a greater prominence: Bartolus de Saxoferrato, forerunner of the 'Bartolist' approach and his most eminent epigones, Baldus de Ubaldis, Paulus de Castro, Alexander de Imola (Tartagnus) and Jason Maynus. The works of each of these authors filled several folio volumes in the printed sixteenth-century editions, and a host of secondary authors were also more or less frequently quoted and, hence, copied or printed. By the end of the fifteenth century, an adequate reading of a civil law work, whether a scholarly text or an elaborate legal opinion, thus required an impressive library. Conversely, drafting a legal argument according to the late medieval *mos italicus* canon supposed the availability of both the *Corpus iuris civilis glossatum* and a large selection of scholarly works.

The extensive quotation of authorities according to a more or less esoteric *modus citandi* became a favourite target not only for satirists, but also for the supporters of legal humanism. Although its founding fathers were fifteenth-century authors such as Valla and Poliziano, whose works soon reached institutional and private English libraries, it was not until the sixteenth century that legal humanism started to undermine the supremacy of the *mos italicus* in European scholarship. Whether legal humanism ever appealed very much to practitioners remains doubtful, despite its authors' claim that their philological and historical criticism of legal sources necessarily had major practical implications. One of the most important contributions of the legal humanists was to change dramatically the appearance and, to some extent, the substance of the texts of the *Corpus iuris*. Throughout the sixteenth century, editions of the *Corpus iuris civilis* reflect these changes, as well as compromises between the *mos italicus* and legal humanism. In addition, legal humanism gave rise to new forms of legal scholarship, some of which aspired to replace the *mos italicus*. Although the old approach still prevailed in legal practice and often among academic lawyers too, its persistence cannot be explained by lawyers' conservatism alone. The Bartolist commentators are sometimes also characterized as 'consiliators', i.e. authors of legal opinions (*responsa*, *consilia*). The *consilia* of a jurist were often collected, and these sometimes vast collections were copied and eventually printed, adding to the bulk of *mos italicus* learning, but linking that learning directly to legal practice. At the same time, *mos italicus* developed further forms of legal literature, which, on the whole, met the needs and expectations of lawyers entrenched in practice more adequately than the publications of legal humanism.

The English market for civil law books

The quasi-monopoly of Italian authorities was only very gradually eroded by scholars from transalpine universities. During the sixteenth century, larger numbers of non-Italian authors following the *mos italicus* approach were published and used as authorities. Their reliance on the major fourteenth- and fifteenth-century authors contributed to ensure that the late medieval commentaries, collections of *consilia*, treatises and other works continued to circulate extensively throughout the western European market, England included. The presses of Venice and Lyons, by then the most important centres of legal printing, catered for this market, their publications obviously responding to a general demand at the same time as reinforcing that demand. Despite the success of legal studies at Oxford and Cambridge, the formation of a professional *esprit de corps* among academically trained legal practitioners and a prestigious past in contributing to legal scholarship, the British Isles did not, at the time, count any civil lawyers who contributed significantly to the corpus of (legist) *ius commune* literature.[2] During the fifteenth century, it seems

---

2. Works by late medieval English civil lawyers are discussed in Allmand 1982; for surveys of early modern English civilian literature: Coing 1975; Coquillette 1988.

that civil law students and scholars still relied largely on older manuscripts, or on imported material, which they often acquired during their
academic peregrinations on the Continent.[3] Later, although the
members of Doctors' Commons were the immediate neighbours of a
thriving centre of the book-trade,[4] their numbers appear to have been
too limited to encourage English printers to consider the production of
civil law imprints.[5] As a result, printed *ius commune* literature had to be
almost entirely imported;[6] yet although one of the first Englishmen to
bring printed books to England had studied law at Oxford, no legal work
was among his purchases.

The 'standard' civil law library

Civil law learning was specialized learning in so far as both the texts of
the *Corpus iuris* and civilian literature were largely absent from the
reading-list required for a general education, and remained virtually
unquoted in non-legal texts. One exception may have been Justinian's
Institutes, a small work which had been conceived as a primer for law students, but which could also be regarded as a readable, general and concise
introduction for a broader public. It seems to have enjoyed a wide circulation,[7] but the entries for it in less specific book-lists can easily be confused with other, non-legal works, and the extent of its potential
readership therefore remains uncertain.

The essential tools of the civil lawyer's trade consisted primarily of the
Corpus iuris civilis, including the gloss, and, in addition, the commentaries
from Bartolus onwards. The libraries, both private and institutional,
which reflect an attempt to build up a coherent collection of civil law
books show precisely this highly conventional pattern, even though
comparatively few succeeded in acquiring an adequate range of commentaries. The other forms of civilian literature remained scarce, except for
monographic literature on procedure or legal practice, which often inter-
twined with canonist methods and learning. The acquisition of standard
commentaries was a gradual process. It would seem that, during the fifteenth century, canonist commentaries gained earlier access to English
collections than the corresponding civilian works. At the beginning of

3. Senior 1931; K. Harris 1989 and below, p. 406.   4. Christianson 1989.
5. See Bennett 1952.   6. For early examples, cf. E. Armstrong 1979.
7. Leedham-Green 1986, II, pp. 471–2; cf. Madan and Bradshaw 1885–90.

the fifteenth century, authorities which would later largely be superseded by the commentaries of Bartolus and later generations of legists still appeared more frequently: Pilius, Placentinus, Odofredus and, above all, Azo. Azo's *Summa Codicis* was one of the few pre-Accursian works which enjoyed a lasting success, as evidenced by both the number of manuscripts and, later, the many printed editions of the book; this was a general European phenomenon, and its English manifestations do not necessarily imply a link with Bracton.

For a civilian, canon law was not relevant only to questions of procedural law. A *ius commune* collection was expected to include works *in utroque iure*. Our often fragmentary sources on legal book-holdings defy any attempts to quantify the ratio of legist to canonist works – even more so than the controversial efforts to number the evolution of canonists and legists at the universities of Oxford and Cambridge.[8] It seems clear nevertheless that English libraries contained on the whole substantially more canon law books than civilian literature. Both the collections of the *Corpus iuris canonici* and canonist commentaries outnumber (in the surviving evidence) their civilian counterparts. The well-known saw 'legista sine canonibus parum valet, canonista autem sine legibus nihil valet' is seemingly reversed in pre-Reformation English book-holdings. This can to some extent be explained by the importance of ecclesiastical administration and court practice for the career of university-trained lawyers, civil lawyers being admitted to practise also in Church courts.[9] On the other hand, canonist works often relied heavily on civil law authorities, even in areas of substantive law which correspond to the domains of ecclesiastical jurisdiction. Roman law was sometimes adapted in the practice of English Church courts.[10] Yet, in many cases, English legal collections contained canon law either exclusively or overwhelmingly, whereas the reverse, a preponderance of civil law books, seemingly occurred far less frequently.

The 'standard' civilian library, usually achieved only partly in specific collections, was the ideal for both private and institutional collections, and the growth of the latter seems to have been more often the result of individual benefactions of actual copies than the outcome of a policy of acquisition. Accordingly, the pattern of institutional and larger private collections is fundamentally the same. Moreover, since it is a conven-

8. For a *status quaestionis*, Evans 1992.   9. Cf. Helmholz 1974, p. 142; Lovatt 1993.
10. E.g. Helmholz 1987, pp. 211–45.

tional pattern, it is not surprising that it can be recognized in the main environments where civil law books can be traced: the collections of scholars and practitioners, and the ecclesiastical and monastic libraries.

The scholarly library

The provision of books in colleges and universities depended mainly on private benefactions. Purchases of law books by these institutions remained exceptional and the benefactions (mostly *mortis causa*) do not reveal that the particular selection of books donated had been suggested by the recipients. Colleges with a strong legal bias (New College and All Souls at Oxford; and Trinity Hall and the King's Hall at Cambridge) came closest to an acquisitions policy. As their founders and other benefactors ensured that their libraries contained an adequate legal collection, these 'specialist institutions attracted specialist bequests'.[11] The early history of All Souls College Library, well-documented, shows that a 'standard civil law library' was available soon after the foundation: the chained books included a *Corpus iuris civilis* and a fine selection of important authors, partly belonging to the *mos italicus* (where both older authors, such as Azo, Odofredus and Rofredus, and more recent prominent authors, including Cinus, Bartolus and Baldus, figure), partly also representing the four-teenth-century School of Orleans (Jacques de Révigny and Pierre de Belleperche). The list of books circulating among the Fellows contained fewer works of legal literature, possibly because it was more difficult, even for a college library, to provide duplicates. Though Bartolus's commentary on the New Digest appears here, there is an array of (at least) seven to ten copies of each of the five volumes of the *Corpus iuris*, and seven copies of the Institutes. By the beginning of the sixteenth century, the lists do not show any fundamental changes: the work of Baldus, by then well established as a major authority, was now perhaps completely available, several minor authors were also represented, and the collection included more practical works such as Giovanni Bertachin's repertory and a few procedural treatises. Other types of civil law literature (*consilia*, *singularia*, *tractatus*, *repetitiones*, etc.) had remained marginal. However, some major commentaries (e.g. Paulus de Castro, Jason Maynus) were either still only partly available, or completely absent. These omissions had been largely corrected by the middle of the century.[12]

11. Allmand 1982, p. 103.   12. Ker 1971, lists I–II, V–VI, XVIII–XXII.

The general orientation of All Souls' developing civil law collection is paradigmatic for contemporary scholars' libraries, whether at Oxford or Cambridge, though few other libraries could compete with its variety of legal literature. The accumulated total of civil law books in surviving pre-1558 probate inventories at Oxford provides a much more incomplete list, though the same general pattern emerges here again, allowing for some differences as to minor authors. The collection of a student – regarding his books, a very privileged one – in 1551 contained, besides canonistic works, two copies of the Institutes; two copies of the *Corpus iuris civilis* (the Codex possibly missing in both cases); most parts, if not all, of Bartolus's commentaries; and two smaller, but popular, civil law books: Angelus's commentary on the Institutes and Decius's *De regulis iuris*.[13] The pre-1558 Cambridge probate inventories yield similar results, though the harvest of civil law books is richer, mainly thanks to a handful of more abundant legal lists.[14] That of John Wyer, a Fellow of Trinity Hall who died in 1556, would have matched many collegiate collections: he owned two apparently complete sets of the *Corpus iuris*; two copies of the Institutes; a five-volume set of Bartolus; Baldus's commentaries on the Code, the Digest and feudal law; some minor yet useful commentaries, including some by sixteenth-century authors (Johannes Faber, Johannes de Platea, Lucas de Penna, Johannes de Ferrariis, Philippus Decius, Joachim Mynsinger, Ludovicus Maynus's *De actionibus*, etc.); further, several 'practical' works, of varying quality (Bertachin's repertory; Baldus's *Margarita*; *Practicae* by Johannes Petrus de Ferrariis and others; Bartholomaeus Caepolla's *Cautelae*; etc.); more or less commonly quoted monographic works (e.g. Nicolaus Everardus's *Loci legales*, Angelus Aretinus's *De maleficiis*, as well as a collection of *Tractatus diversorum doctorum*); even some *consilia*, *singularia* and *decisiones*; and finally several works by representatives of the humanistic school (Guillaume Budé, Andrea Alciati, Ulrich Zasius, Johan Oldendorp, Aymar du Rivail [Rivallius]). His collection of canonist books was equally impressive. From a traditional *mos italicus* perspective, this exceptionally rich collection lacked some important commentaries, whereas by legal-humanistic standards, it obviously did not include most of the major scholarly achievements published during Wyer's professional tenure.[15] The collections of Wyer's colleagues in Cambridge and Oxford were, however, far less adequate regarding legal scholarship, and it was not until

---

13. *PLRE*, II; and no. 61.   14. Leedham-Green 1986, I, lists 1–93.
15. Leedham-Green 1986, I.

Elizabethan times that the better-endowed institutional academic libraries would provide scholars with more comprehensive legal collections, at least for traditional *mos italicus* authorities.[16]

Most of the authors here referred to as minor authorities and found in the late medieval and early modern collections were still fairly popular by contemporary European standards. Less prominent jurists of the *ius commune* tradition occur only occasionally, and sometimes the presence of their work can be directly linked with the *curriculum vitae* of their owner. Probably one of the best-known examples of such a link is a series of lecture-notes from Louvain, shortly after the foundation of the university, which William Elphinstone (the Elder) brought back to Scotland.[17] The lecturers never became established authorities and the circulation of such manuscripts remained limited, though Henricus de Piro's commentary on the Institutes occasionally appears in British holdings.[18] Other law students from the British Isles acquired more conventional literature while abroad. Richard Rudhale, for instance, who later bequeathed at least nine law books to Hereford Cathedral Library, bought a few works second-hand, and could afford to have others made to order when he was in Padua; these were all standard texts and authorities.[19]

The presence of English and Scottish law students in continental universities raises the question of the extent to which they were exposed to continental *iura propria*, i.e., the municipal law of the different territories and cities, whether statutes or customary law. These laws were not formally taught in the faculties, though *ius commune* teaching explained how to deal with such legal sources. Gradually, however, monographs appeared which dealt with *ius proprium*, treated more or less extensively according to *ius commune* concepts. Collections of what is known as *decisiones*, and even to some degree *consilia*, also tended to include some substantive municipal law. These works became a feature of the general *ius commune* literature and circulated accordingly throughout Europe – *consilia* and *decisiones* naturally more readily than commentaries on a particular custom or legislation. Such works, although exercising a fundamental influence for the blending of *ius commune* and the emerging national laws, which is characteristic of the early modern development of Western European legal systems outside the sphere of English common law, remained vastly under-represented in English, and probably also

16. Wijffels 1992a, and 1993a, b.   17. MacFarlane 1957–8.
18. For an updated description of Elphinstone's manuscripts: Ker 1969–92, II, 12–14.
19. Mynors and Thomson 1993.

Scottish, collections. Similarly, academic legal collections in England took little notice of English legal publications, except for collections of statutes. Even by the middle of the sixteenth century, a small holding of books related to foreign *ius proprium* in a single collection remained exceptional. Such an exception is John Marjoribank's collection of around 1555, which included commentaries on specific French customary laws by Tiraquellus and Publitius, as well as a part of the collection by Boerius of *decisiones* from the Supreme Court in Bordeaux.[20]

The most surprising aspect of English sixteenth-century collections is the extremely limited appearance of legal-humanistic works. Admittedly, our main source-material at this stage makes it, in most cases, impossible to determine to what extent acquisition of the *Corpus iuris civilis* was following the pace of a continuous flow of new editions claiming to provide the latest stage of scholarship, in what has been described as the sixteenth-century printers' struggle for the legal book-market. The general impression is that neither individual scholars nor the college libraries systematically acquired the editions which stood out as milestones in the scholarly effort to publish the ancient Roman law according to new historical and philological standards. Editions of the rediscovered Greek texts or publications of pre-Justinian legal collections, for example, appear only exceptionally. Legal-humanistic scholarship, or *mos gallicus*, is also only sporadically and very incompletely represented in academic book-lists, except for 'first-generation' works by the 'triumvirate', Budé, Alciati and Zasius, which were apparently widely available among scholars. Later sixteenth-century book-lists and other evidence suggest that legal humanism was, apart from these early works, largely disregarded by English civil lawyers. It may be that in the 1530s and 1540s, some scholars at least showed a greater interest in *mos gallicus*, but that, because of the uncertainties which clouded the perspectives of the collegiate universities at the time, and the confusion which prevailed in most academic libraries, their interest did not materialize in major acquisitions of legal-humanistic works. Sir Thomas Smith's inception of the Regius Chair of civil law at Cambridge seemed to herald a determined legal-humanistic approach, which is partly reflected in his personal library. It did not establish a tradition, however, and perhaps aptly illustrates the passing regard for the new school among English civil lawyers.[21]

20. Durkan and Ross 1961, pp. 128–9.   21. Stein 1988, pp. 91–100, 186–96.

The practitioner's library

Both canonists and civilians were admitted to practise in the ecclesiastical courts. In London, the membership of Doctors' Commons evolved gradually during the sixteenth century from a society with a distinctly ecclesiastical character to a professional association of laymen. By the end of the fifteenth century, the civil lawyers' arguments were still steeped *in utroque iure*: canon law literature, including Catholic post-Reformation works, continued to be used in the ecclesiastical courts, though in the arguments before the High Court of Admiralty civilian authorities prevailed. The wider use of civilian works (apart from the *Corpus iuris civilis* and the most common standard works) probably developed during the second half of the sixteenth century, when such works became more widely available through printing.

Practitioners' libraries are scantily documented. In many cases, however, academics at Oxford and Cambridge were combining their educational or scholarly activities with a more or less intensive legal practice. Many clerics who are known to have owned law-books were also in some capacity involved in the practice of the Church courts. As they had usually studied law, their collections, though mostly less extensive, were no different in kind from those found in a university or college environment. In the libraries which are in some way connected with Church court practice, canon law (including canonist scholarship) is usually predominant, but texts of the civil law course and (usually the better-known) civilian authorities are also represented, though to a lesser degree. The books of John Underwood, practitioner in the Court of York, ob. 1515, offer a good example.[22]

Institutional libraries linked with legal practice call for a similar remark: ecclesiastical court officials and practitioners probably depended to some degree on the availability of legal books in the cathedral libraries. Although it has been disputed whether Doctors' Commons had its own library until after the Great Fire, one of the first indications that some form of professional association of practising academic lawyers was in existence during the second half of the fifteenth century, is precisely a bequest of books by Dr Thomas Kent in 1469.[23]

To judge by a few examples, common lawyers' libraries, during this period, seem to have eschewed civilian literature.[24]

22. *Testamenta Eboracensia*, v, pp. 68–70.   23. Squibb 1977, pp. 3 and 88–9.
24. E.g. Moreton 1991; cf. Baker below, pp. 411–32.

Ecclesiastical and monastic libraries

Different reasons have been offered for the presence of legal books in ecclesiastical and monastic collections. The accumulation of wealth and the defence of vested interests may only partly explain why legal works (but, apparently only few common law works, apart from collections of statutes) could have been useful to churchmen, even if one were to admit that 'monks were among the most litigious and quarrelsome people in the realm'.[25] The technical aspects of pastoral work and clerical discipline were occasionally invoked to justify and encourage the study of canon law books in the cathedral library.[26] The intellectual aspirations of many clerics trained in the universities, often combined with more temporal ambitions, would also have fostered some interest in civil law books. Books related to the learned feudal law (i.e., the *Libri Feudorum* or the commentaries thereon) would hardly have been of much practical use for litigation in England, yet they occur among other *ius commune* texts in ecclesiastical collections.

Moreover, the provenance of many legal manuscripts in ecclesiastical holdings had been academic. Clerical wills provide several examples of a bequest of one or more legal works to a fellow or younger cleric in order to facilitate his study of the law. Two are those of Thomas Felde, whose will was proved in 1419,[27] and of John of Upton in 1396.[28] Thus, a legal manuscript was often transferred from one generation to another in an academic environment, before it eventually reached an ecclesiastical library.[29] The motives for bequeathing civil law books to an ecclesiastical institution could be manifold, and are impossible to assess when one does not know whether a specific donation was meant to remedy a hiatus or not. In some cases, a testator left his civil law books to an ecclesiastical library, but his canon law books to a college. More often the canonist books seem to have been reserved for an ecclesiastical beneficiary, such as in the will of William of Waltham, proved in 1416.[30] In 1415, William Loryng, Canon of Salisbury, left his civil law books to the university library of Cambridge, but ordered his executors to sell the canon law books.[31] Richard Bruton, in 1417, made a like bequest.[32] When a will provides that specific law-books are bequeathed to a monastery, unless a certain private beneficiary expresses the wish to acquire them by

25. Haines 1928, p. 81.   26. Alexander 1980, pp. 151–2.
27. Jacob and Johnson 1938–47, II, pp. 163–4.   28. Weaver 1901–5.
29. Alexander 1980; Mynors and Thomson 1993.   30. *Testamenta Eboracensia*, III, p. 59.
31. Jacob and Johnson 1938–47, II, p. 81.   32. Weaver 1901–5.

payment of a fixed sum of money to the monastery, the testator's intention was apparently to facilitate the private person's studies, whereas the monastic library's interests could be secured through a pecuniary bequest.[33] The infamous example of early legal imprints taken in 1543 as booty, from Edinburgh to England, may further illustrate that even law books could be regarded as a prized possession among the less intellectually oriented classes of society.[34] In this particular case, they probably caught the attention of the looter more because of their bindings and appearance than for the learning they included, however relevant some of it may have been to military law.

The contents of ecclesiastical and monastic libraries do not differ significantly from the standard pattern, although the predominance of canonist works is here perhaps even more evident. Surprisingly, the *Corpus iuris civilis* is often not mentioned as a set, but only through some of its individual collections. Canonist scholarship is in general far better represented than civilian literature. Like the scholars' libraries, ecclesiastical libraries show vast discrepancies in the extent of their legal holdings. Major private collections could, here too, match some of the better-endowed institutional libraries. At the beginning of the fifteenth century, Bishop Trefnant's collection contained an unusual range of works in both civil and canon law, including several scholarly authorities which tended to be disregarded later.[35] Most ecclesiastical holdings, however, particularly in the later period, were more modest and conservative in outlook.

33. *CBMLC*, I, D5.   34. Duff 1907c, pp. 432–3.
35. Charles and Emanuel 1949–50; cf. also Durham 1838, p. 114.

20

The books of the common law

J. H. BAKER

Introductory

Although the common law of England was considered by academic lawyers as 'unwritten law', the upper branches of the English legal profession were necessarily learned in books. Chaucer's man of law may not have owned books of cases literally stretching back to the time of the Conquest, but the poetic exaggeration must have worked upon fact; a serjeant at law was expected to possess an impressive array of law books. The library of a common lawyer in Chaucer's day, or in 1557, would nevertheless have been unlike that of any other lawyer in the world. This was a result of the insularity of the English legal system, centred on the courts in Westminster Hall, which followed arcane procedures developed indigenously and was independent of Romanist terminology or method. Since the universities of Oxford and Cambridge disdained to notice a body of law that was not written in Latin and could not be expounded in *lecturae*, advanced instruction in the common law was provided by another university. The collegiate law school known as the Inns of Court probably dates from the 1340s, when it replaced a shadowy earlier *studium* for apprentices following the Common Bench. In addition to the four Inns of Court, there were a number of lesser colleges known as the Inns of Chancery, which provided lectures and exercises for less advanced students.[1]

Though the writs and records of the law were in a sort of Latin, law French was used for virtually all professional literature. Probably it was no longer used for argument in court, but it was still spoken at exercises in the Inns of Court and was the only language in which formal pleadings could be framed orally at the bar before the clerks engrossed them in Latin. By 1450, law French was a language more often written than spoken, with its own arcane abbreviations.[2] Though derived from the

1. Baker 1990a.   2. Fortescue 1942, p. 114 ('sepius scriptus quam locutus').

vernacular Anglo-Norman of the thirteenth century, it was as different from that of Stratford-atte-Bow as from that of Paris or Rouen. The words for trees and cows might be recognizably the same, but the lawyers had converted many ordinary words into a technical abstract vocabulary all their own.[3] Even the Latin of our common lawyers was far removed from that of ancient Rome. Well might Sir Thomas More confound a continental know-all with the question, 'utrum averia capta in withernamia sint irreplegibilia?'[4]

A medieval civil lawyer looking at the common law might have found even more striking the virtual absence of treatises or monographs. The most erudite of the common lawyers owned or knew the Latin treatises called Glanvill and Bracton, but those ancient books were of little practical use even in 1400 and copies had ceased to be made long before, although Glanvill was printed in about 1555,[5] and Bracton in 1569.[6] No one would attempt another comprehensive survey of the common law until long after our period. The only current legal treatise of any significance in the fifteenth century was Littleton – Sir Thomas Littleton's *New Tenures* (c. 1460) – first printed within a year or two of the author's death in 1481.[7] It soon superseded the much shorter *Old Tenures*, a title attached to several tracts, the latest seeming to date from Richard II's reign. Manuscripts of *Old Tenures* ceased to be produced in the fifteenth century, though the printing press gave the Ricardian version a brief revival.[8] *New Tenures* was an enormous success in the age of printing: there were more than sixty editions in the sixteenth century alone.[9] But it was very much a student primer. It stated the axioms of land law, with few doubts and no citations. The most basic requirements for a law student going to London were some bedding and a Littleton.

Almost as successful in the sixteenth century was *Doctor and Student* (1528–30), written by Christopher St German (d. 1540).[10] This was not a law book at all in the usual sense, but its elementary discussions of selected legal principles made it useful for the student. It was probably not aimed at lawyers, but was part of St German's intellectual campaign to justify the separation of canon law in England from papal authority.[11] Again, it contains no legal citations.

This absence of citations is another peculiarity of the English law book before the middle of the sixteenth century, and by no means confined to

3. Baker 1990b.   4. Ro: Ba: 1950, p. 112; Stapleton 1928, pp. 138–9.   5. *STC* 11905.
6. *STC* 3475.   7. *STC* 15719.   8. *STC* 23877.7–23884a.2.
9. *STC* 15722.5–15753 and, in English, *STC* 15759.5–15776.
10. *STC* 21559 (with the date 1528, in Latin); *STC* 21561 (1530? in English); followed before 1600 by nineteen editions in English, *STC* 21562– 76.   11. Baker 1988.

student books. It seems unlikely that books were much used in court; we find vague references to 'les livers' or 'nos livers', and sometimes a vague threat to produce a book if pressed ('jeo puis monstrer a vous un liver'), but not the reading of specific texts in the course of argument.[12] The courts themselves had no library, apart, perhaps, from precedent books kept in the offices. For example, a printed *Liber Intrationum* (1510) was given to the King's Bench office in the 1530s.[13] Neither the judges nor counsel had desks or lecterns in court. But it was not merely practical inconvenience which discouraged citation. There was a professional tradition that the law should be stated in a way which appealed to the right reasoning of a legally trained audience or readership; a proposition was therefore backed up not by strings of citations but by examples which showed its correctness. As late as the seventeenth century, the rules for mooting in the Inner Temple defiantly preserved this tradition out of pedagogic perversity: 'en arguing, les barristers ne doint cite le livers per nosme, 1 H.7 etc., mes doint dirre "en un ancient liver" ', though benchers were allowed to cite book and folio.[14] The body of received wisdom hidden in these mysterious old books, and displayed orally in argument, was known by the mid fifteenth century as *communis eruditio* (common learning).[15] No one could hope to share in this learning without belonging to the Inns of Court. There the resident student of our period would listen to readings, that is to say lectures on the statutes. There were two courses each year, one in the Lent vacation and the other in the Autumn vacation. He would also take part in moots, attend the courts in Westminster Hall, discuss law with senior and junior fellows, read books and copy manuscripts.

Law libraries

There were no common-law libraries comparable with those of the universities or large monasteries. The Inns of Court had nascent libraries around 1500, but few books in them, not all legal; security was weak and most of the early contents were lost long ago. By his will, Edmund Pykeryng (d.1488) left six chained books to the library of Gray's Inn; one was a statute-book of Edward III, but the others were not legal.[16] None remain in the Inn, which still has a small number of non-legal manu-

---

12. Baker 1977–8, p. *162*.   13. *STC* 14116; Baker 1977–8, p. *356*, n.6.
14. Baker 1990c, p. xcii.
15. Baker 1977–8, p. *161* ('nostre auncien erudition' mentioned in 1454, 'common erudition' in 1469); 1986, p. 100; 1990c, p. lxxii. For Fortescue's reference to 'eruditio' (*c.* 1470), see Ives 1973, pp. 67–9.   16. PCC 32 Milles. Information from Dr A. I. Doyle.

scripts, some of them of monastic origin and probably obtained soon after the Dissolution of the Monasteries.[17] BL, Add. ms. 34901 is a stray fifteenth-century register of writs formerly inscribed 'Iste liber pertinet societati de Greysynn'. The earliest recorded gift to have survived to the present in any of the inns is the Cholmeley bequest of 1563 in Lincoln's Inn. Nevertheless, Lincoln's Inn had had a library as early as 1475, and rebuilt it in 1505–9; in 1519, a judge bequeathed to it all his law books, and by 1550 it had a number of volumes of medieval reports and a Bracton. The gift of 1519 is in the will of Sir John Boteler: 'do et lego magistris et sociis de Lincoln' Inne omnes libros meos de lege quos habeo in domo mea in Silverstrete et Serjaunts Inne in venella Cancellarie'.[18] None can now be traced. Likewise all the books in the 'symple lybrary' of the Middle Temple were lost before 1540.[19] The Inner Temple had a library by 1506, but by the nineteenth century none of its pre-1550 acquisitions survived.[20]

Law libraries were mostly personal, and books changed hands frequently, usually within the walls of each inn, by gift or exchange, by loan, or by bequest. Changes of possession were often carefully recorded on flyleaves.[21] Moreover, legal manuscripts of the fifteenth and early sixteenth centuries frequently end with an 'Explicit ... quod John Style' (or whatever the name might be). There has been some controversy as to whether these names after the 'quod' were the names of scribes, as Ker supposed, or of owners.[22] No doubt frequently they were the same, since law students learned by copying. In fact, the names seem nearly always to belong to lawyers or law students, and the explicits were certainly treated as ownership inscriptions, substitutions being made by subsequent owners. We even find an early printed year book with a blank space provided in such an explicit for the owner's name to be inserted.[23] As late as 1549, Serjeant Fletewoode used an ownership inscription in the form

17. Ker 1969–92, I, p. 50.   18. PCC 22 Ayloffe; *ELM*, II, p. 1; Baker 1977–8, p. *131*.
19. Baker 1977–8, p. *132* n. 3.   20. Inderwick 1896–1919, I, p. 6.
21. Sometimes a gift was recorded: e.g. *ELMUSA*, pp. 18 ('Heydon ex dono Butery anno xvii° H. viii. vii die Julii' – both members of Lincoln's Inn), 30 ('Iste liber constat Willelmo Good de Furnyvals Ynne etc. muneris D.H.'), 32 ('Johannes Whittyngton est hujus libri possessor ex dono Thome Troute de Bodmyn in com. Cornubie', Troute being an attorney of the Common Pleas). For an example of lending, probably for copying, see p. 419, below, n. 54. John Watnow (d. 1484) of Gray's Inn left to Chief Justice Huse (formerly a fellow bencher) three or four quires of parchment 'the which I understood been parcellis of bokes which I suppose I had of hym': PCC 6 Milles.
22. A. W. B. Simpson 1957, p. 501; with the further note (referring to Ker) in A. W. B. Simpson 1971, p. 108.
23. Pynson's edition of 5 Hen. VII, fol. k6 (*STC* 995): see *ELM*, I, p. 64 (illustrated on p. 103).

' . . . quod Willelmus Fletewoode'.[24] Other inscriptions are in the common form 'Iste liber pertinet . . .', sometimes witnessed by fellows of the owner's Inn.[25]

Our first known Inns of Court book-list, scribbled down by John Eltonhede in the 1450s, reminds us that lawyers without public libraries needed to find out who owned what:[26]

Memorandum quod Johannes Eltonhede junior recepit de Thoma
Dunne xxiiij qua[tern]os de novis statutis incipiend' *Cum Hugo
Despenser* et finiend' *Devaunt cez heurez.*[27]
Item, Morton habet librum de xlii E. tercii, v^{ti} ix^o, v^{ti} quinto.[28]
Item, Catesby habet abregement de anno v^{ti} ix^o.[29]
Item, Fulbrok[30] habet *Natura Brevium.*
Item, Johannes Asplond senior habet *Old Termes* de Armeston.[31]

Although few detailed lists of law libraries exist from our period,[32] a good idea of their typical contents can be reconstructed from several different kinds of source.[33] We may take by way of illustration three members of the Inner Temple who became judges under Henry VI,

24. *ELMUSA*, p. 73.
25. For examples of such attestations, see, e.g. *ELM*, II, pp. 36 (Inner Templars), 51 (Lincoln's Inn men), 95 (Middle Templars), 143 ('teste meipso') and 195 (Gray's Inn men); *ELMUSA*, pp. 12, 21 (where one of the witnesses is the scribe), 27 ('. . . teste Edmundo S. cum multis aliis quos nunc perscribere mora est'), 36 ('. . . teste Simone Wormleo cum multis aliis quos nunc perscribere longum est'), 37 ('. . . teste Thoma Coke, Thoma Gaude et multis aliis', Inner Templars; '. . . teste meipsum [*sic*] et Magistro Fayreclow').
26. BL Lansdowne ms. 1176, fol. 188r. This could only be read completely by means of ultra-violet light and has not previously been noticed. On fol. 188v is: 'Iste liber pertinet constat [*sic*] Johanni Eltonhed de Throp Testibus Johanni Andrewe et Johanni Harewold.' This is probably the John Eltonhede MP admitted to Lincoln's Inn in 1445, and John Andrewe may be the one admitted there in 1443. Harewold was a Northants. attorney in 1445, not connected with Lincoln's Inn. Only one of the names on the list (Asplond) was a member of that Inn.
27. I.e., *Nova Statuta*, beginning with 1 Edward III and probably here ending with the Statute of York, 9 Edward III ('Come avant ces heures . . .').
28. I.e., Year Books 42 Edward III, 9 and 5 Henry V.
29. I.e., of 9 Henry V. The owner is probably John Catesby of the Inner Temple and Northants., later a judge. One 'Catesby' owned BL, Harl. ms. 3626 (Year Books 3–10 Edward III), and Hargrave ms. 297 (Year Books 38, 40, 42, 45, 46 Edward III).
30. John Fulbroke was an attorney in 1461.
31. The 'old termes' were probably a year book of Edward II. John Asplond was a bencher of Lincoln's Inn. A Richard Armeston, attorney in 1455, owned BL, Add. ms. 18600 (ms. register and tracts).
32. Jayne 1983, p. 46, did not even recognize lawyers as a book-owning class; but he was justifiably criticized for this omission by Schoeck and Ives (next note).
33. Only a few before 1557 have been noted in print: Jayne 1983, p. 93; Schoeck 1962; Ives 1969; 1983, pp. 445–7 (thirty-six volumes in Serjeant Kebell's library; only four were legal, but this was his home library and he would have had more in Serjeants' Inn); Moreton 1991 (over forty volumes belonging to Sir Roger Townshend (d. 1493), Justice of the Common Pleas, including sixteen law books).

Henry VII and Henry VIII: Sir Peter Arderne, Sir Thomas Frowyk and Sir John Port. Sir Peter Arderne (d.1467) provided a detailed list of books in his will.[34] They included a *Legenda Sanctorum*; a book of old statutes with a register (*Registrum Brevium*) and 'newe tales' (*Novae Narrationes*); new statutes and a 'boke of termes of parchemyn'; 'a good book compiled of lawe with a yalowe leddir coveryng'; 'a grete boke of lawe of termes of Second Edward in parchemyn'; 'my best registre of lawe'; 'my booke of assisez of lawe' (i.e. the *Liber Assisarum*, an unusual year book of Edward III, containing cases from assizes and King's Bench sessions away from Westminster); 'my owne grete compiled booke of lawe covered with reed leddir and a horn upon itt'; 'a boke of lawe of parchemyn compiled and bokeled'; and 'a boke of termes of lawe of paper anno xxxii[do] anno xxxxix and other yeris therin'. Books of terms were what later generations called year books: that is, anonymous law reports cited by regnal year and term.[35] They were sufficiently valued to be mentioned in several early wills.[36] The 'compiled' books were probably abridgments.[37]

The library of our second subject, Sir Thomas Frowyk (d.1505), can be partly reconstituted from surviving manuscripts. His three volumes of year books of Edward I, Edward II and Edward III are all in the British Library, as is his illuminated volume of *Statuta Nova* which had belonged to another judge, William Calow (d.1487).[38] This last is presumably the 'book of newe statuts' mentioned in Calow's will, made in 1483 when he was a serjeant. Calow bequeathed, in addition, a book of assizes, a Bracton and 'ii bookes of abriggements, oon of myne owen labour and thother of Lincolnesin labour'.[39] Frowyk also owned a 'great book of entries', which cannot be found. It was given, with an illuminated statute book, to the Inner Temple, under the will of Thomas Jakes (d. 1514), who married Lady Frowyk: 'my fayer boke of the newe statutes wryten and lymed and my greate boke of entres which were my singuler good Lord Frowekes'.[40] Frowyk would certainly have owned other less valuable books.

34. PCC 19 Godyn.   35. For this terminology, see Baker 1989b, p. 20 nn. 29–30.
36. An earlier example is the will of Richard Bankes (d. 1415), Baron of the Exchequer: Jacob and Johnson 1938–47, II, pp. 66–8 ('volo quod liber terminorum qui fuit Roberto de Plesyngton ac alii libri et quaterni pertinentes ad legem terre custodiantur ad usum filiorum et eorum alterius diutius viventis'). Still earlier (1393) is the will of Robert Peke of Gray's Inn (Lincs. Arch. Office, Reg. Beaufort, fol. 23v: 'illos libros meos de lege regni Anglie vocatos terminos' and 'omnes terminos meos antiquos'). This last was discovered by Dr N. L. Ramsay.   37. See below, p. 418.
38. BL, Add. ms. 37657 (Edward I); Add. ms. 37659 (Edward III); Hargrave ms. 210 (Edward II); Cotton ms. Nero C.1 (statutes, with Calow arms).   39. PCC 7 Milles.
40. PCC 2 Holder. This suggests that Jakes had only one such statute-book, and it may therefore be the Cotton manuscript. There is no record of either book having been in the Inner Temple.

Our third judge, Sir John Port (d.1540), was admitted to the Inner Temple in the 1490s and became a bencher in 1507. His library may be conjecturally reconstructed from the citations in his autograph notebook. It included year books of Edward I, Edward II and Edward III, the *Liber Assisarum*, year books from Henry IV to Edward IV, a *Natura Brevium*, Littleton, Statham's abridgment, and some readings. It is possible that some of these were borrowed; but the numerous scattered references suggest constant access.[41]

These collections are all very similar in kind. A good working library in 1450 or 1550 included year books from the earliest times (that is, Edward I rather than the Conqueror) down to the present, abridgments, statutes, precedents of writs and pleadings, and perhaps the occasional tract. Of these principal types of law book, a little more needs now to be said.

Cases

Long before 1400 there was a tradition of law reporting in the royal courts.[42] Nothing is known of its organization, if there was any; but by 1400 there seem to have been only a few reporters at any one time, and much of their work circulated throughout the profession. For the chosen or self-chosen few, reporting seems to have been a lifelong commitment. The earliest known reporter apparently had his career cut short and may be untypical.[43] Our known reporters after 1450 all began as students and continued through careers at the bar and on the bench. Roger Townshend (d. 1493) began reporting as a student of Lincoln's Inn in the 1450s and was still reporting as a judge in the 1480s;[44] John Caryll (d. 1523) began as a student of the Inner Temple in the 1480s and continued until near the time of his death as a king's serjeant; some of their work is found in the printed year books. Other reports did not circulate contemporaneously, though the reporters conform to the same pattern: John Port (d. 1540) began as a student of the Inner Temple in the 1490s and continued until he was a judge in the 1530s; John Spelman (d. 1546) began as a student of Gray's Inn around 1500 and continued while he was a judge until about 1540; James Dyer (d.1582) began as a student of the Middle Temple in the 1530s and continued throughout his career.[45] Port's notebook (now in the Huntington Library) is the only identifiable autograph to survive. Written on paper, in a vellum wrap-around cover, it is a vade mecum including an old year book, readings and alphabetically arranged notes.

41. Baker 1986, pp. xxix–xxxi.   42. Baker 1989b.   43. Baker 1989a.
44. Baker 1977–8, p. 165 n. 5; p. 424 n. 102, below.   45. For Caryll, Baker 1977–8, pp. 165–7.

The last reports printed as year books are from the year 1535. But nothing happened to law reporting in that year; it was simply that the canon was arbitrarily limited by the law printers. Lawyers went on reporting current cases in manuscript, and some collections reaching back into the 1530s and 1540s – notably Dyer's – were printed in later times.[46] The reports of William Dalison (d. 1559) and William Bendlowes (d.1584) were not printed until the Restoration period; the editors chose imperfect texts, and the reports printed as Dalison's seem to be at least partly by Richard Harpur (d.1577). The recovery of other individual series of early Tudor reports, so far as they can be distilled from the manuscripts, has only recently begun. It is unlikely that many of them were circulated in manuscript before 1557, though Spelman's notebook was being copied in the 1560s, and Dyer's unprinted notes in the 1580s.[47]

In order to gain access to these ever-growing chronological series, lawyers used 'abridgments': that is, digests of case-law under alphabetical titles.[48] These are not found until the time of Henry VI, but become quite common in the 1450s.[49] The earliest dated example was written in 1457 for Thomas Segden, Principal of Furnival's Inn, by John Luke of the same Inn.[50] A typical abridgment of the same period was printed in a specially cut Law French type at Rouen in about 1490, without title;[51] it has been known since the 1490s as 'Statham', after a bencher of Lincoln's Inn who is supposed to have compiled it (see fig. 20.1). Two much larger ('graunde') abridgments were compiled in Henry VIII's reign; one (by Anthony Fitzherbert) was printed in 1514–17,[52] the other (by Sir Robert Brooke) not till 1573.[53] Until well after our period, lawyers still made their own alphabetical commonplaces of material not in the printed abridgments.

Readings

The learning derived from readings in the Inns of Court and Chancery – and, to a lesser extent, from moots – was preserved through a purely man-

46. For Dyer, see STC 7388–93, with dates ranging from 1585 to 1621 (STC 7393 wrongly '1622'); cf. Wing 2926–7, with dates 1672–88.   47. Baker 1977–8, 1986, 1994.
48. Winfield 1923.
49. Thirteen fifteenth-century examples (all with cases up to the 1450s or 1460s) are BL, Harl. ms. 2051, Royal ms. 17 E.VI, Add. ms. 16168; Lincoln's Inn mss. Hale 149, 181; Guildhall Lib., London, ms. 208; CUL, mss. Kk.5.1 and Ll.3.1; Essex Record Office, ms. D/DP L34; Harvard Law School, mss. 41 and 186; Philadelphia Free Lib., mss. LC 14.34 and 35. BL, Sloane ms. 775 seems to be slightly earlier (up to the 1440s).
50. Guildhall, ms. 208; Barker 1972 at pp. 365, 374. For Serjeant Calow's abridgments, one of which was 'of Lincoln's Inn labour', suggesting co-operative work, see p. 416 above.
51. STC 23238. Cf. Barker 1979, pp. 262–9.   52. STC 10954–5; below, p. 425; Cowley 1932.
53. STC 3827. Brooke died in 1558.

uscript tradition. No readings were printed in our period, and very few thereafter. Many of the surviving manuscripts were student lecture notes; but prominent readings were copied over and over again and served virtually as text-books. Much-copied early examples are Thomas Marow on justices of the peace (Inner Temple, 1503), George Treherne on the forest law (Lincoln's Inn, 1520) and John Densell on fines (Lincoln's Inn, 1530). There is evidence of lending between members of Lincoln's Inn.[54] There were also books of moot-cases, the set problems used for routine pleading exercises.[55] Both genres have been largely ignored by historians. But the remaining corpus of unprinted lectures is quite large, and affords the nearest parallel to the doctrinal writings of Roman lawyers.

Precedent books and practice manuals

The first requirement for any common lawyer was a knowledge of the writs and forms of action whereby justice was distributed through the royal courts. The body of available forms of action ceased to develop before 1400 and most lawyers made do with old manuscripts containing precedents of writs, the most recent being the most valuable; a Chancery clerk in the 1460s might pay as much as 41s for one.[56] In the legal mind there was one notional 'register of writs' containing all the authorized formulae, in Latin. In practice, the contents of the manuscript books differ somewhat, and they have varying encrustations of notes and *regulae* emanating from the teaching of masters and clerks in Chancery up to the time of Edward IV. Once the *Registrum Omnium Brevium* was printed in 1531,[57] the fiction of a single common register became reality (see figs. 20.2 a–b). There was no need for a continuing manuscript tradition, as there was with law reports, since there was nothing to update. An introduction to the register was provided by the *Natura Brevium*, containing the most important writs with French commentary. The old *Natura Brevium*[58] was superseded in 1534 by Sir Anthony Fitzherbert's *Novel Natura Brevium*, which survived as the primer on the writ system until the nineteenth century.[59]

---

54. Harvard Law School, ms. 13, pp. 377 ('M. Ayloffe constat xxv leves wretyn in this quayer delyvered to Mr Parker'), and 464 ('Memorandum delyvered to Mr Lampton ii quayers of the redyng of Magna Carta . . . Memorandum delyvered this quayer to Mr Parker conteyning xviii leves wretyn'): *ELMUSA*, p. 17, no. 43.   55. Baker 1990c, pp. xxxiii–xlv.

56. *ELMUSA*, p. 33 ('Explicit registrum novum precium istius libri xli s. quod constat Baldewino Hyde clerico uni clericorum cancellarie domini regis Edwardi quarti'). Hyde was admitted to Lincoln's Inn in 1466. Cf. p. 53 ('Iste liber constat Johanni Chamberleyn uni sex clericorum cancellarie Regis Edwardi quarti et sunt contenti 37 quaterni a principio usque finem'; contents 1448–83). The register as printed contains no *regulae* later than the time of Edward IV.   57. *STC* 20836.   58. *STC* 18385–11.5.   59. *STC* 10958–93.9.

Precedents of conveyancing and pleading were made by lawyers for their own use, the former largely by lowly practitioners, the latter (in the form of Latin books of entries) by prothonotaries and clerks; but they were used more widely, and we have seen that Chief Justice Frowyk owned a 'great' book of entries. 'Entries' were entries on the plea rolls, in Latin, as opposed to oral pleadings in French; forms of oral pleading were to be found in books of earlier origin called *Novae narrationes*.[60] An early example of an identifiable book of entries is that compiled by Simon Elryngton (d. 1481–5), filazer of the Common Pleas from 1442 to 1475.[61] Substantial books of entries were printed in 1510 (*Intrationum Excellentissimus Liber*),[62] 1545 (a different anonymous compilation)[63] and 1566 (William Rastell's *Colleccion of Entrees*).[64] The first of these overlaps considerably with the great book of entries compiled by John Jenour (d. 1542), second prothonotary of the Common Pleas 1513–42. The book (now in the Library of Congress) was much revered by Chief Justice Dyer.[65] Rastell's book combined the entries of Edward Stubbe (d. 1533), chief prothonotary of the Common Pleas 1518–33, whose son married Rastell's niece,[66] Sir John More (d. 1530), the judge, and John Lucas (d. 1525), filazer and secondary of the King's Bench.[67]

By contrast, the printed precedents of conveyancing from our period were archaic and slight in content: the *Carta Feodi Simplicis*, first printed around 1505,[68] and translated into English by or for Rastell (1545?),[69] was probably of fourteenth-century origin. *A New Boke of Presidentes* (1543), with a preface by Thomas Phaer, was also, despite the promising title, decidedly out of date.[70]

Guides to the law and practice of inferior courts were less advanced than those relating to the courts in Westminster Hall, and, at the lowest level, practice was learned without the aid of books at all. But some local courts followed countrywide usages, and there was a growing practical literature by the end of the fifteenth century. The oldest genre was that of manuals of procedure in manorial courts, originally known as *La Court Baron* or *Curia Baronum*. A late redaction of this kind of manual,

---

60. *STC* 18361–3.   61. CUL, ms. Ee.1.3.   62. *STC* 14116.   63. *STC* 14117.
64. *STC* 20730.   65. Baker 1977–8, pp. 103, 377 n. 9; *ELMUSA*, p. 11, no. 29.
66. The original (or a copy of it) is BL, Add. ms. 24078. A partial collation of Rastell with the plea rolls shows that most of the Henry VII entries are from the rolls of William Mordaunt (Stubbe's predecessor, 1490–1518), and so it seems probable that Stubbe's collection was derived from Mordaunt. For Mordaunt's book of entries, see Baker 1977–8, p. 375 n. 10.
67. The original is in the Library of Congress: *ELMUSA*, p. 11, no. 30.   68. *STC* 15579.3.
69. *STC* 15587.5.   70. *STC* 3327.

which has an ancestry stretching back to the thirteenth century, was printed by Pynson around 1501 under the title *Modus tenendi Curiam Baronis*.[71] It was reprinted many times, and was joined by the *Modus tenendi unum Hundredum* (1521?),[72] the *Modus observandi Curiam cum Leta* (1525?),[73] the *Diversite de Courtz* (1526)[74] and *The Office of Sheryffes* (1538?).[75]

Justices of the peace were rather better served, since the active justices were Inns of Court lawyers, and questions arising at quarter sessions could be discussed centrally. The first coherent treatment of the authority of county magistrates is found in lecture form, most notably in Thomas Marow's reading of 1503 in the Inner Temple.[76] But there were also fifteenth-century collections of precedents for clerks of the peace, including indictments, warrants and other instruments. Some of these were unique compilations for use in a particular county;[77] but some from the 1490s have elements in common, such as *La Forme doffice dun Clerk de Pes*, a practical guide to sessions procedure of a type not represented in print until the 1660s.[78] In 1505 or thereabouts, Richard Pynson printed a simplified version of one of these collections as *The Boke of Justices of Peas*.[79] In 1538, a much larger and far superior work, *The New Boke of Justices of the Peas* by Sir Anthony Fitzherbert (d. May 1538), was printed by Robert Redman.[80] This was a translation, with some variations, of *Loffice et Auctoryte des Justyces de Peas*, printed earlier the same year.[81] These two 'books of justices' are hailed as the first printed treatises on English criminal law, and Fitzherbert's 'new' book remained in use (in revised editions) until it was overtaken by Dalton and Coke in the seventeenth century. Nevertheless, their treatment of substantive criminal law was less thorough than that found in the manuscript readings and in Sir William Staunford's *Les Plees del Coron* (1557),[82] which was heavily based on the crown cases in Fitzherbert's abridgment.

---

71. STC 7705.7. Cf. CUL ms. Add. 7558, fols. 51r–56v, copied for Richard Brynkley, a Lincoln attorney, c. 1505–45.   72. STC 7725.9.
73. STC 7713.7. Examples of manuscripts of around this date, with the same title, are in Derbs. Record Office, ms. D2440, and London/Oslo, the Schøyen Collection, ms. 1641 (bought in 1991: see *Journal of Legal History* 13 (1992), 180 n. 337).   74. STC 10946.
75. STC 10984.   76. Putnam 1924, pp. 286–414.
77. E.g., the Warwickshire collection from the 1420s printed in Putnam 1924, pp. 237–86.
78. A collection containing Suffolk precedents associated with Sir Robert Drury (d. 1535) is found in BL, Harl. ms 1777; London Guildhall, ms. 3035; Derbs. RO, ms. D2440; and Schøyen Collection, ms. 1641.
79. STC 14862. For the difference between the two versions, see the introduction by Glazebrook 1972.   80. STC 10969.   81. STC 10968.   82. STC 23219.

Statutes

Statutes have a somewhat different history from law books produced within the closed world of the Inns of Court and Chancery. In the first place, there are more signs here of an organized manuscript trade in the fifteenth century, especially in the series of illuminated books of *Statuta Nova*, the Acts of Parliament from 1 Edward III down to the present (usually Edward IV, Richard III or early Henry VII), emanating from the same workshops.[83] A beautifully executed group from the third quarter of the century has been described by Kathleen Scott.[84] The volumes frequently have coats of arms on the first page, apparently painted in for the original purchaser,[85] and many of these arms can be identified as belonging to prominent lawyers:[86] Adgore, Kebell, Pygot and Fitzwilliam were benchers of the Inner Temple in the 1480s and 1490s; Calow and Elyot were benchers of the Middle Temple, Molyneux of Gray's Inn; five of them became serjeants. But these were hardly working copies. They may be considered rather as status symbols, and were doubtless marketed as such.[87]

Secondly, the printing press here displaced manuscript production entirely in the time of Henry VII.[88] No manuscript statute-books were made after 1500. The printed texts were readily available, were much more reliable and there was no scope for private versions (as in the case of the other sources). Moreover, they were in English. Machlinia printed

83. There are also a few undecorated books apparently signed by a professional scribe: e.g. Library of Congress (Law Div.) ms. Phillipps 3114, sig. & iij^v ('Expliciunt statuta ... quod Fassetus Thomas Amen'); Harvard Law School, ms. 40 (Prestun); *ELMUSA*, pp. 10, 24.
84. Scott 1980a, pp. 45–60, 66–8; 1980b.
85. Lincoln's Inn, ms. Hale 183 has the escutcheons left blank for this purpose. Many of the arms (next note) have not previously been identified. A few remain unidentified: e.g. Harvard University, Houghton Lib., ms. Richardson 40 (*ELMUSA*, p. 39). BL, Hargrave ms. 274 has the arms of Gylle, but no contemporary lawyer of that name is known.
86. BL, Cotton ms. Nero C.1 (William Calow, Justice of the Common Pleas, d. 1487); Lincoln's Inn, ms. Hale 71 (Gregory Adgore, Serjeant at Law, d. 1504); Yale Law School ms. G. St.11.1 (Richard Elyot, Justice of the Common Pleas, d. 1522: *ELMUSA*, pp. 73–4); Philadelphia Free Library, ms. LC 14.9.5 (paternal arms of Robert and Thomas Molyneux, both of Gray's Inn: *ELMUSA*, pp. 59–60); BL, Lansdowne ms. 522 (arms, reversed mirrorwise, of Elryngton of Hackney: probably for John Elryngton, filazer of the Common Pleas); Bodl. Lib., ms. Hatton 10 (Thomas Pygot, Serjeant at Law, d. 1520); Dyson Perrins sale, Sotheby's, 9 December 1958, lot 21 (Sir Thomas Fitzwilliam, d. 1497). Serjeant Kebell's 'great boke of lawe wreten in velom and covered with blak velvet', with latten clasps, valued at 10 marks, was probably of the same type: cf. Ives 1983, p. 445 (Ives suggests Bracton, but the book apparently began with *c.* 1 of a statute in French).
87. Kebell's, if we have correctly identified it, was kept at his country home rather than in chambers.   88. For the printing history, see Elton 1978; Pantzer 1983.

the statutes of Richard III in French,[89] but thereafter – according to Rastell, at Henry VII's personal suggestion – English was used.[90]

If statutes are an exception to the general characterization of law books offered above, it is as well to remember that statutes circulated widely outside the legal profession, especially once they were promulgated in the vernacular, and that, even if a common lawyer of our period would have regarded them as only a subsidiary source of law, they were texts which no lawyer could afford to be without. It is noteworthy that the books left by Mr Justice Townshend (d.1493) included eleven volumes of statutes (some old, some more recent, and two printed), but only four or five year books.[91]

The law book trade and the press

In contrast with the statutes, the books of the common law, even in the second half of our period, were primarily hand-written. Many of them would have been written or copied out by the lawyer himself or his clerk, or a junior member of his Inn. Occasionally, down to the mid fifteenth century, we find illuminated law books, which must indicate professional production; apart from the well-known series of *Statuta Nova*, mentioned above, they include registers of writs[92] and even an occasional student primer.[93] But these are uncommon, and we do not find such things at all in 1500 or 1550; nor is there any known evidence from this period of a book-selling trade in law manuscripts. The vast majority of law books throughout our period were written on paper, without decoration, and many of them have an amateurish appearance.

There was, nevertheless, by the sixteenth century, a trade in printed law books, dominated by the law printers.[94] It had begun in 1481 or

89. *STC* 9347.
90. For the retrospective translation of the older statutes by George Ferrers (d. 1579), see Graham 1965.   91. Moreton 1991.
92. BL, Cotton ms. App. xv; Library of Congress (Law Div.) ms. 138 (with name of John Shirlond in first writ); Harvard Law School mss. 25 (with arms of Hastings in border) and 26; Maggs, *European Bulletin* 14 (1988), no. 3 (dated 1468).
93. Huntington ms. HM 47619 (*Old Tenures* and *Natura Brevium*).
94. The oeuvre of the law printers down to 1600 was investigated in some detail in Beale 1926, with *A Supplement to Beale's Bibliography* . . . by R. B. Anderson, Cambridge, MA, 1943, both reprinted together in 1966. However, the subject has been placed on a new footing by Dr K. F. Pantzer in the second edition of *STC*. The writer is grateful to Dr Pantzer and Dr Neville-Sington for helping him to avoid some errors; those which remain are of his own making.

thereabouts with the immigrants John Lettou and William de Machlinia, who had acquired a cast of Caxton's large display type.[95] Together they printed Littleton's *Tenures* and the year books of 33, 35 and 36 Henry VI;[96] Machlinia alone added 34 and 37 Henry VI.[97] These are now very rare books: the only complete set appears to be in the Cambridge University Library. The years were apparently chosen not because they were well-known texts, but because the printers had come by some unique reports which were quite different from the manuscript versions of those years already in circulation. Machlinia's largest undertaking was the first printing of the *Statuta Nova* in the time of Richard III (see fig. 3.4).[98]

The trade of law printing passed in the early 1490s to Richard Pynson (d.1530), a Norman by birth, who at the time was variously described as a glover, a pouchmaker and a bookbinder.[99] It is possible that he acquired Machlinia's goodwill and stock, since some of Machlinia's waste has been found in his earliest bindings.[100] As his first ventures, he had Littleton and Statham printed in Rouen,[101] but thereafter he seems to have used London presses. In around 1500 he moved from St Clement's parish to The George in Fleet Street, near St Dunstan's church and opposite the Temple. He printed numerous year books, beginning well before 1500 with a continuation of the Machlinia series into 1–9 Edward IV.[102] All the year books were issued singly, for a few pence each, to be made up into volumes by the purchaser. Beale listed 139 editions by Pynson, including 92 year books.[103] Pynson succeeded William Faques (d.1508) as King's Printer, and thereafter used the title 'regius impressor' on his books. Although this office apparently carried a modest stipend, it conferred no privilege in relation to law books generally, and from around 1513 and 1514 Pynson had competition, especially from the Rastells and Robert Redman.

95. Partridge 1983.   96. *STC* 15719, 9731, 9742 and 9749.   97. *STC* 9737, 9755.
98. *STC* 9264. Pantzer 1983, pp. 74–5; Neville-Sington below, pp. 577, 580.
99. Plomer 1923, p. 49. In an action of 1492 against him, he was described as 'bokebynder': PRO, KB 27/924, m.22d. In 1496, he was described as 'pouchemaker': PRO, CP 40/938, m.473.   100. Plomer 1925, pp. 112, 162.   101. *STC* 15721 and 23238.
102. The printing history of 1–9 Edward IV is complicated. About 1490, Pynson printed two issues of 1 Edw. IV (*STC* 9770 and 9771), and one of 9 Edw.IV (*STC* 9825); about six years later, *c.* 1496, he printed 3–8 Edw. IV (*STC* 9784, 9790, 9796, 9806, 9812, 9819); again some six years later, *c.* 1502, 3–8 Edw. IV were all reprinted (*STC* 9784.4, 9790.4, 9796.5, 9806.4, 9812.5, 9819.5); in 1510 (?), 1 and 2 Edw. IV were printed from a different manuscript with the explicit 'secundum Townsend' (*STC* 9771.5 and 9779; Beale 1926, pp. 78–9, nos. R225, R233); for Roger Townshend, see p. 417, above. In 1523–4, the years 3–8 Edw. IV were once again reprinted (*STC* 9784.7, 9790.7, 9797, 9806.7, 9813, 9820), and finally 9 Edw. IV was reprinted in an edition to which *STC* 9826 allocates the date 1525.
103. Beale 1926, pp. 188–90.

John Rastell (d.1536), a barrister of the Middle Temple, made an impressive contribution. He continued the printing of year books, and the first official prices occur in his colophons, reflecting a standard rate of 2d per five sheets.[104] He also printed the first edition of the *Liber Assisarum* (1514) and the first English translation of Littleton (1523–5),[105] the first part of *Doctor and Student* (1528),[106] and the first law dictionary, his own compilation called *Expositiones Terminorum* (1523–30),[107] which also served – by means of parallel texts – to introduce students to law French. This last work enjoyed a long life under the later title *Les Termes de la Ley*.[108] However, Rastell's principal achievement in the history of printing was his publication of Serjeant Fitzherbert's three-volume *Graunde Abridgement* (1514–17), the production of which is thought to have consumed a quarter of a million large sheets of paper.[109] It was so far superior to Statham that the latter was never reprinted.

An inventory of John Rastell's stock in 1538, two years after his death, reveals that he left 700 copies of his *Expositiones* (480 in English, 220 in French only),[110] 430 Littletons in English,[111] 124 *Old Tenures*,[112] 100 'Talis' (*Novae Narrationes*),[113] twelve acts of 21 Henry VIII,[114] and eight abridgments of statutes in English.[115] The *Narrationes* and the statutes were valued at 1d each, the abridgments at 4d each; the rest were not individually valued.[116] There is no mention of Fitzherbert or the year books, and the legal part of the stock seems to be confined to student books; but this was probably not the entire Rastell stock. John had given up printing in 1530, though since 1529 his son William (d.1565), a student of Lincoln's Inn and later a judge, had become a printer in his own right and had probably taken over some of his father's stock. William's principal contribution as a law printer was the first edition of the *Registrum*

---

104. Cf. the valuation of Kebell's pre-1500 printed year books: Ives 1983, p. 445.
105. *STC* 9599 and 15759.5.   106. *STC* 21559.
107. *STC* 20701. Reprinted three times by *c.* 1530 (*STC* 20702–3.3).
108. First used in 1624, *STC* 20716, and found as late as 1742 in England and 1819 in Philadelphia.
109. *STC* 10954–5; Graham 1954, p. 17; Graham and Heckel 1958; Boersma 1981. For Rastell, see also Reed 1926; Geritz and Laine 1983.
110. 'iiij^{c}lxxx expositions english cont. xx remys, ij^{c}xx exposition french cont. ij remys et di.' This divergence is at first sight surprising, since the French edition (1527) was about half the length of the 'English' (which had parallel texts). But the former was printed in sextodecimo, the latter in large folio. See *STC* 20701–3.3.   111. *STC* 15760 (Rastell, 1528–30).
112. *STC* 23880.3.   113. *STC* 18362.5.   114. *STC* 9363.6 and 9363.8.   115. *STC* 9521.
116. Roberts 1979. Roberts suggests a different (non-legal) identification of the 'Talis'; but cf. p. 416 above (Arderne's will), and note Beale 1926, p. 111, no. T1 (reference to 'the new talys' on a Rastell title-page of 1534). The valuation may be on the low side, since in 1554 Rastell's abridgment of statutes cost 2s 8d: *BLJ* 13 (1987), at p. 46.

Omnium Brevium in 1531 (see fig. 20.2 a–b); this is not mentioned in the inventory either.[117] He also produced in 1534 an omnibus handbook containing the *Natura Brevium*, the *Old* and *New Tenures*, the *Book for Justices*, *Novae Narrationes*, *Returna Brevium* and *Carta Feodi*.[118] However, William did not continue long in the business. Firmly opposed to the Reformation, he ceased printing in 1534, was called to the bar in 1539, and after a few years in practice fled to Louvain. He was appointed a judge by Mary I in 1558, and was reappointed by Elizabeth I a month later, but he resigned in 1562 and went into exile again.

Robert Redman (d. 1540) also provided stiff competition for Pynson in the 1520s, acquiring Pynson's old premises in St Clement Danes. The competition came close to passing-off, since Redman used not only Pynson's sign of The George but also an 'RR' monogram calculated to resemble Pynson's 'RP'. Pynson attacked Redman as incompetent, calling him 'Rudeman', and Redman retaliated. Unpublished editorial work on the year books suggests that Redman was in fact the better. His new edition of 40 Edward III in 1534[119] even shows unusual signs of thorough editing, with copious notes and cross-references throughout by an anonymous editor ('my frende'); there is an English preface criticizing Pynson and calling for the profession to support Redman's enterprise. Redman's innovations included a kind of supplement to Littleton called 'Perkins' *Profitable Book*' (1528), a best-seller which was still being reprinted in the nineteenth century.[120] Eventually he purchased Pynson's business, and may have taken over some of Rastell's type, including the legal abbreviations.[121] The office of King's Printer, however, went to Thomas Berthelet (d. 1555), who exercised it for the rest of Henry VIII's reign. The King's Printer by this time monopolized the production of statutes; Berthelet also printed a few year books, but after 1532 the King's Printers did not concern themselves at all with reports or the more advanced law books.

The George passed after Redman's death to William Middleton (d. 1547), who reprinted several law books. Middleton's widow married William Powell, who succeeded to the business and is best known as the

---

117. *STC* 20836–6.5. There were, however, 'ij old french bokes of the statutes and of the register'. Roberts read this literally as meaning some (non-legal) register in French, but it seems more likely that these were typical manuscript *Statuta Vetera*, in which most of the contents were French, though of course the register would have been Latin.   118. *STC* 18394–.5.
119. *STC* 9587.
120. *STC* 19629 (French). First published in English by R. Tottell in 1555: *STC* 19633.
121. Information on abbreviations from Dr K. F. Pantzer.

first printer of the Long Quinto,[122] a unique long year book of 5 Edward IV, similar in style to the long reports of late Henry VI printed by Machlinia, not to be confused with the Quinti Quinto, the popular name for 5 Henry V. Powell continued in business until 1567, but stopped printing law books in 1553.

A lawsuit against Powell in 1553 lists the contents of a London house, including the entire stock of a book-seller. Plomer suggested that the house might be identified as The Sun where De Worde's successor, Whitchurch, ceased printing in 1553. The stock certainly included many non-law books. But there may instead be a connection with Powell's financial difficulties and the loss of his law business.[123] Law is strongly represented, more so than might be expected of a general bookshop. There are over 1,500 year-book pamphlets, on average 50 copies of each year.[124] Some had dwindled to 3 or 4 copies, but there were over 100 copies of some years of Edward IV and 170 copies of 7 Edward III. Some of the titles are known today only in editions by Redman, Berthelet or Rastell. There were also 100 copies of *Britton* (printed by Redman in 1533),[125] 100 of *Diversite de Courtz*,[126] 50 *Old Tenures*, 50 *Natura Brevium* in French (and 40 of the English translation) and 50 Littletons (but only 16 of the English translation, which had obviously sold well). These figures, like those of Rastell's stock inventory of 1538, suggest print-runs well into three figures in respect of books which now survive only in a handful of copies. Pynson's abridgment of statutes (1499) ran to 409 copies.[127]

The underlying cause of the Powell litigation does not appear from the record, but 1553 was a critical year in the history of law printing. Berthelet was dismissed as King's Printer, for religious and political reasons; Powell ceased publishing common-law books, probably for financial reasons; and Richard Tottell became the sole law printer. The printing of common-law books thus became virtually a *de facto* monopoly. The reason was largely economic. Law printing was a specialized craft, requiring a facility with abbreviated French and some Latin, and it could not easily be carried on as a sideline. The bulk of the work lay not in printing new texts for immediate sale, but in maintaining permanent stocks of the traditional books of the law.[128] Lawyers collected, and probably bought, their year books in miscellaneous bundles of year pamph-

---

122. *STC* 9802.5.   123. Plomer 1915.
124. Details of the law books are taken from the original record: PRO, CP 40/1156, m.525.
125. *STC* 3803.   126. *STC* 10946-52.   127. Plomer 1909, p. 131; *STC* 9514-5.
128. For the economic factors, see Byrom 1927, p. 210.

lets; it is not uncommon to find volumes made up of a few Pynsons, a few Redmans, and perhaps the odd Berthelet or Middleton.[129] If a bookseller had a good stock of Pynson remainders, he would not have needed to order more copies of the same year from Redman. The printer therefore came to make his living by continuous reprinting of years already in circulation. This was the state of the business to which Tottell succeeded in 1553, and he did not greatly change it in nearly forty years of law printing.

Tottell had been an apprentice of Middleton, worked briefly for Elizabeth Middleton (who married Powell), and around 1553 took over the printing house and shop of Henry Smyth (d. 1550) near the Temple, which he called 'The Hand and Star', presumably in allusion to the familiar watermark. He must at the same time have acquired the law side of the Powell business. It is difficult not to think that there is some connection here with the lawsuit of 1553, but the precise way in which Tottell established his monopoly remains a mystery. It is possible that the judges had intervened to rescue law printing from disarray by securing the advancement of a prominent youngster. It was said in 1582 that 'Tottell, at sute of the judges, hath the comon law bokes', which suggests that the judges had been somehow involved in the grant of monopoly.[130] Certainly Tottell managed at this time to obtain a privileged position by patent. Previous law printers had obtained limited grants of copyright in respect of particular titles, such as that given to Rastell in 1531 for seven years in respect of the *Registrum Omnium Brevium*, according to the colophon.[131] Following various precedents from other fields in the 1540s, the patent granted to Tottell in 1553 gave him and his assigns the privilege of printing all common-law books for seven years, excepting those in which anyone else had a specific privilege – meaning those already in print *cum privilegio regali ad imprimendum solum* – and provided the books were licensed by a judge, two serjeants at law, or three apprentices of the law.[132] Tottell does not seem to have been under any restraint in reprinting law books first printed by others, doubtless because there was no competitor left in business. He did, however, have to negotiate with William Rastell over Rastell's own compilations.[133] The patent did not, in terms, grant a monopoly, but provided that, if anyone printed a book

129. There are good examples of such composite volumes in the British Library, Lincoln's Inn and Norwich Public Library.
130. Burghley papers, BL, Lansdowne ms. 48, fol. 186r; cf. Byrom 1927, p. 220.
131. *STC* 20836; Beale 1926, p. 148, no. T310.   132. Graham 1954, p. 15.
133. Pat. 7 Edward VI, pt 3, m. 29; *CPR Edward VI*, v, p. 47 (12 April 1553).

which Tottell had printed first, it would be forfeited; in other words, it was a grant of limited future copyright in all the books he chose to print, obviating the need for specific licences. A more extensive patent followed in 1555, which omitted the licensing requirement and also made him the sole printer of common-law books;[134] in 1559, this privilege was renewed for life.[135] These last two patents turned Tottell into a monopolist, prohibiting all other printers and book-sellers from printing common-law books, on pain of fine. For the next two and a half centuries, law printing would remain a monopoly, preserved despite protracted and bitter litigation with the disgruntled Stationers.

The law printers and the legal profession

The law printers must obviously have kept closely in touch with the needs of the profession they supplied. Their premises were conveniently situated close to the Inns of Court. Pynson's shop, The George, which was the principal outlet for common-law books throughout the reigns of Henry VIII and Edward VI, was on the corner of Chancery Lane, close to Clifford's Inn and Serjeants' Inn, facing the Temple. Tottell's shop, The Hand and Star, was just across the street, by the Middle Temple gateway. It has been identified as no. 7 Fleet Street, immediately east of the gatehouse, the shop occupied by the law publishers Messrs Butterworth until the end of the nineteenth century. Law books were probably also available in St Paul's Churchyard: the colophon to one issue of Rastell's *Registrum Omnium Brevium* (1531) says that it was to be sold in Rastell's own house, or in Paul's churchyard, or in Redman's house at Temple Bar (fig. 20.2b).[136] But no evidence has yet been discovered of sale in Westminster Hall.[137]

How far the printers worked on commission for members of the profession must be a matter of conjecture, though the fact that Pynson printed a *Natura Brevium* and *Old Tenures* in the 1490s 'at the instaunce of my maistres of the company of Stronde Inne with oute tempyll Barre'[138] suggests that orders for student books might sometimes have been placed by the Inns. Strand Inn (on the site now occupied by Somerset House) was one of the Inns of Chancery, where students went to learn by rote the

134. Pat. 2 & 3 Philip & Mary, pt 1, m. 28; *CPR, 1555–57*, p. 18 (5 May 1555).
135. Pat. 1 Elizabeth I, pt 4, m. 23; *CPR, 1558–60*, p. 62 (12 January 1559).
136. *STC* 20836, BL C.64.e.9; Beale 1926, p. 148, no. T309b.
137. Plomer 1905 (no evidence before 1640).
138. *STC* 18385, linked to *STC* 23877.7. Colophon in Beale 1926, p. 119, no. T69.

writs in the *Natura Brevium*. Some professional involvement in book-selling might also be inferred from the fact that an attorney in 1492 complained of the loss from his house (in 1485) of sixty copies of Littleton and two bales of paper; but his stock also included sixty copies of 'The Fox' – presumably Caxton's[139] – and it is possible that he was dealing in books, or taking them as surety for a loan, rather than selling.[140]

The work of editing law books for these printers is largely concealed from our sight, since it was rare for editors to be mentioned by name on title-pages or in explicits. Yet it is certain that members of the Inns of Court were employed as editors. John Rastell, who doubtless did his own editing, was of the Middle Temple. Most editors known to us were likewise members of the Middle Temple. Plomer's discovery of a dispute between Pynson and three Middle Temple editors showed that Christopher St German was one of them.[141] The suit concerned the printed abridgment of statutes, and it seems possible that editing was St German's principal occupation in the missing years between his quitting chambers and his becoming a successful writer in the late 1520s. Another member of the Inn heavily involved in editing was William Owen (admitted 1514). He was responsible for *Le Bregement de Toutes les Estatutes . . . par Guillaume Owen du Medile Temple* (Pynson, 1521),[142] and he is said to have acted as Fitzherbert's amanuensis in copying out the *Graunde Abridgement*. Owen was described as Fitzherbert's chamber-fellow; if that is true, he may have migrated to the Middle Temple from Gray's Inn. But his son says he was a 'fellow student and neere cozen' to Sir Thomas Elyot, who was admitted to the Middle Temple in 1510. According to Chief Justice Dyer, Owen was also an editor of *Natura Brevium*.[143]

Impact of the printing press on the law

The printed book certainly had an impact on the law, though it was not wholly beneficial. The most positive consequence of printing, no doubt,

139. *STC* 20919.
140. *Hugh Parsons v. Johnson* (1492), CP 40/919, m. 134d ('sexaginta libros de novis tenuris et sex-aginta libros vocatos Le Fox'; pleads 'not guilty').   141. Plomer 1909, p. 131.
142. *STC* 9516; G. Owen 1892, I, p. 237. (This was drawn to our notice by Mr D. E. C. Yale.)
143. Baker 1994, p. xxix n. 78. Pynson's edition (*STC* 18388; Beale 1926, p. 120, no. T 82) was said to be 'nunc (non parva solicitudine) emendata, castigataque a viro in legum multum solerti studio'. Some five years later, Pynson issued a new edition, *STC* 18389, which claimed to be revised by Robert Chidley of the Inner Temple 'ut ille nonmodo mille in locis castigasset, sed etiam addidisset tot annotationes'.

was the introduction of a single authoritative and carefully printed text of the current statutes. Even this, however, was offset by a more literal approach to the interpretation of legislation, which now left little room for textual manipulation.[144] In the context of case-law, it made possible specific folio-citations to reported cases, a practice which became commonplace during the sixteenth century, and thereby perhaps increased reliance on individual reported precedents. The change is noticeable in Fitzherbert's *New Natura Brevium* (1534),[145] and Staunford's *Les Plees del Coron* (1557),[146] both of which draw on Fitzherbert's *Graunde Abridgement*. Plowden's reports, unlike the year books, are crammed with citations.[147] It is a matter of taste whether the addiction to citations which has beset the English lawyer ever since represents an improvement in legal technique; but at least the profession now had common access to what was being cited. The most negative effect of printing, and more particularly of Tottell's monopoly, was that it served over time – more or less unconsciously – to reduce the canon of known or citable authorities, and to discourage recourse to manuscripts which might correct errors in the vulgate text.

The profession soon forgot how year-book printing had started. From the beginning in the 1480s, and throughout our period, reports were usually printed in pamphlets containing one year each. No doubt these printed pamphlets were originally intended merely to supplement those available in manuscript; indeed, in some early books we find the printed and manuscript years bound up together. But the printers began by choosing rare texts from previous generations rather than current material, perhaps because there was a greater demand for such rarities than for currently circulating material. The closest they ever came to printing recent cases was the unusual edition of 12–14 Henry VIII, printed about ten years after the event, though even this seems not to have been prepared for the press by the reporter.[148] This publishing policy had the odd consequence that texts which were originally rare or unique later became the vulgate reports, while the reports which had been the standard text in manuscript were never printed and passed out of use. Here the tyranny of the printing press had a harmful effect on legal literature, which has even damaged modern historical scholarship. Moreover, the printers mixed together the work of different hands, with little regard to historical accuracy or textual purity, making it almost

144. Baker 1994, pp. lix–lxi.   145. *STC* 10958.   146. *STC* 23219.
147. Henderson 1975, p. 293.   148. Baker 1977–8, pp. 168–9.

impossible now – the manuscript sources having largely disappeared – to disentangle the component texts. Indeed, the impression they set out to create, and did create, was that the year books were a single series backed by some single authority. Until Maitland demolished it in 1903, everyone accepted Plowden's statement in the preface to *Les Comentaries* (1571),[149] that they had been produced by four official reporters, paid by the Crown. But even Maitland was misled into thinking that when the year books stopped in 1535, something dreadful had happened to the common law.[150] In fact, as we have seen, reporting continued unabated; but the year books had always been printed in arrears, and at some point the printers made the decision not to continue the anonymous annual series further. The printers' decision was hardly a rational one, since they called a halt before any of Richard II had been printed, and they omitted many available years (including 11–19 Edward III, which exist in many manuscripts). And they excluded anonymous reports after 1535 from the year-book canon. Perhaps we should not be too hard on the printers themselves, who doubtless relied on professional advice both in selecting texts for publication and in editing and proof-reading. Moreover, the profession seems to have acquiesced in the prevailing balance between print and manuscript. Yet the result was an unintended narrowing of the canon of legal literature. A still more drastic narrowing of the canon resulted from the complete omission of readings. Perhaps it was right to encourage students to attend lectures or copy texts themselves. But the failure to print readings helped to exclude doctrinal literature completely from the later common-law mind. The common law of the future was to be case-law, and printed case-law at that.

149. *STC* 20040. For the demolition: Maitland 1903, pp. lxii–lxiii.
150. Maitland 1901, pp. 21–2 ('this ominous event').

21

Medicine and science

PETER MURRAY JONES

For much of the Middle Ages, philosophers differed over whether medicine could be counted as a true science, or a mere mechanical art. Some argued for the dignity of medical philosophy; others for the degrading character of the practice of medicine. Learned physicians themselves liked to characterize medicine as both science and art – and indeed argued that this duality distinguished medicine above other subjects, which could only pretend to be one or the other. Medicine could not just be left to the philosophers, and at the same time those who practised medicine without knowledge of the true principles were ignorant empirics. So, even as scholastic medicine achieved its zenith in the fourteenth century, and flourished in the European universities, there were always two sorts of medical literature, one reflecting the study of *theorica* and *practica* as a university subject, and another which provided the practitioner with guidance on diagnosis, preventive medicine, *materia medica* and therapeutics. Since many, if not most, of those who taught at universities also practised, they were authors as well as consumers of both sorts of literature.

Before about 1375 most medical books owned and used in Britain would have been in the first category, books to do with the university study of medicine. A great change then took place, however. In effect, medicine and science as transmitted at the universities leapt the walls and found a readership outside. We can register this change by looking at the numbers and kinds of texts written; by looking at the change in language use for medicine and science; and by looking at the selection and editorial processes involved in the creation of new manuscripts. Other branches of science followed the lead of medicine insofar as they had practical applications, like astrology and prognostication, or alchemy, that is to say insofar as they could be arts as well as sciences.

These developments may be regarded as an 'information revolution' in medicine and science.[1]

The most obvious measure of the explosion in interest in science with a practical orientation is the handlist of scientific manuscripts in the British Isles dating from before the sixteenth century, compiled by Dorothea Waley Singer.[2] This deals with an estimated 30,000 to 40,000 written texts found in library collections, and I have further estimated that the proportion of texts surviving from the fifteenth century to those from the fourteenth century is of the order of 6:1. Now, of course, more manuscripts from the fourteenth century than from the century after will have disappeared in the course of time – but against this we must weigh the higher attrition rate that will have operated on texts written for practical purposes rather than for scholastic use. The earlier manuscripts are more likely to have found safe haven in college, monastic or secular collections because of their more scholastic character. The vaster numbers of surviving fifteenth-century texts on medicine and science, set against a declining population (and stagnant figures for student numbers at Oxford and Cambridge overall), argue sufficiently strongly for dramatic developments in the way medical and scientific books were valued and used.

The survey of manuscript book production in England between 1375 and 1500 carried out by Linda Voigts consolidates the impression made by the Singer handlist, by providing evidence drawn from the physical make-up, and juxtaposition, of texts, use of illustration and diagrams, and language of writing, in a representative sample of these manuscripts. Linda Voigts's survey demonstrates conclusively the multi-lingual character of most medical and scientific books.[3] That is to say, Middle English and Anglo-Norman are to be found alongside the Latin of the scholastics. Most of these Middle English and Anglo-Norman texts were not composed in those languages but were adapted and translated from Latin. It is in fact safest to assume that every vernacular text of medicine and science, for which conclusive evidence to the contrary does not exist, was originally translated out of Latin. This great exercise in translation out of Latin developed overwhelming momentum after 1375, and must reflect

1. The idea is explored further in P. M. Jones 1994. The essays in Matheson 1994 provide an excellent introduction to the varieties of science in fifteenth-century England.
2. The cards are held in the manuscript collections in the British Library and (incompletely) at the Warburg Institute Library in London. Microfilm copies are held at Cornell University and the Library of Congress, and elsewhere. See also Singer 1919. The slips on which the handlist was compiled are filed as cards in subject order, and then date order within subjects.   3. Voigts 1989.

directly an interest in medical and scientific texts amongst those who preferred to read them in the vernaculars.

Some impressively academic materials were included amongst those translated out of Latin in the fifteenth century. Linda Voigts has pointed out that, alongside the Middle English phlebotomy (bloodletting) text she edited, there are a number of other texts, still in Middle English, of a much less obviously practical bent.[4] We find lists of the things natural, non-natural and contra-natural drawn from the basic university introduction to the theory of medicine, the *Isagoge* of Johannitius. Similar lists of elements, complexions, humours, members, virtues, senses or operations, spirits, and ages, refine the category of the naturals. The manuscript concludes with a lengthy compendium on medicine in Middle English, drawing on Latin originals for both the theory and practice of medicine, all of unimpeachably academic origin. This compendium, dating on lexical grounds from the first quarter of the fifteenth century, begins with a prologue which tells us that the compendium was translated in an era lacking wise physicians by someone named Austin, for Thomas Plawdon, citizen and barber of London. Thomas Plawdon would undoubtedly have practised, at the very least, bloodletting and minor surgery, but it is at first sight surprising that he should have taken such an interest in the theoretical basis of medicine. What he seems to have wanted, and his Latin-reading friend Austin to have provided, is a distillation of some of the theoretical and practical material which would have been covered in the six-year medical curriculum in a university medical faculty. Perhaps he wanted these materials in Middle English to reassure himself and his clientele that he was no mere unlearned empiric – but, in any case, ultimately the point of such distillation and translation was to take medicine beyond the bounds of the university, and to make it relevant to the business of the barber.

Most of the Latin writings adapted and translated for a new audience were of a more immediately practical relevance than those included for Thomas Plawdon. For every one excerpt from Galen in Middle English, there are a hundred rules for diagnosis from urine, or for bloodletting, or collections of recipes. Almost all were of Latin origin, but their parentage becomes hard to trace as the Middle English translator was a great adapter and editor of his source text. A popular Latin medical text, like that of the writings of the English surgeon, John of Arderne, might

---

4. Gonville and Caius, ms. 176/97; Voigts and McVaugh 1984, pp. 14–16, 24, 25.

generate as many as four separate translations that can be identified today. Each translation reflected the particular interests of the translator, or perhaps those of his client, and might accordingly be more or less free in character.[5] This applied not only to translators, however. Each scribe of a manuscript of a particular translation might become his own adapter. It is possible to watch the process of adaptation at work, and to speculate about its purpose, where a particular manuscript of a translation of a well-known work is examined closely. This is the case with the *Compendium medicinae* of Gilbertus Anglicus, composed in Latin in the thirteenth century. Faye Getz has edited the Middle English translation found in Wellcome ms. 537, which proves to differ from other versions of the same translation found in many manuscripts. One of the popular sections of the Gilbertus text was the part dealing with diseases of women; it circulated independently in Middle English translation. The Wellcome scribe chose to leave out of his version all the bits dealing with the diseases of women and children, perhaps because he was writing for a particular audience, a community of males only. Yet he also added to the Gilbertus text recipes drawn from elsewhere, presumably because he thought them useful additions to those given by Gilbertus.[6] The liberties which translators and scribes were willing to take with texts of medicine and science reflected the practical interests that they brought to them.

Similar motives impelled others to construct their own guides to practice, by excerpting from their reading and combining that reading with the fruits of personal experience. The fifteenth century is the first for which we have a number of commonplace books written by practitioners. One example is the *Practica* and surgery written by Thomas Fayreford, a medical practitioner in north Devon and Somerset in the first quarter of the century. He included these texts written on the commonplace book principle with others he copied out in his own hand in Harley ms. 2558, along with a list of the cures he claimed to have performed. The whole was obviously intended to be used by his heirs or apprentices, since he took the trouble to have the manuscript decorated and illuminated (including a fine cartouche with his own name inscribed within).

The commonplace book sections include extracts from various 'doctors' or 'authorities' as he calls them, which demonstrate a wide reading of medical authors possibly seen by Fayreford in Oxford (though

5. See the variations recorded in P. M. Jones 1989. The process of translation emerges in detail from P. M. Jones 1990.   6. See the introduction to Getz 1991.

he never took a degree there). It also includes recipes in Latin and Middle English, however, some of which Fayreford tells us he had by word of mouth from various people, including a cure for migraine from one of his patients, Lady Ponynges. Another cure for toothache is so effective, he tells us, that barbers would give him silver for it. He also entered remedies which he claims have the warrant of his own medical experience. This mixture of remedies from different sources was entered under the headings of particular ailments at various times, as can be seen from the colours of the ink and from the gaps that occur frequently when the page has not been filled. Such intensely practical book compilation may have been much more frequent than surviving examples might lead us to expect – such books must frequently have been used to destruction or discarded as they became less legible to later generations.[7]

Access to scientific books of the sort Fayreford required was probably only available at Oxford and Cambridge, where both institutional and private collections were built up with a deliberate bias towards medicine and science.[8] This development had already been foreshadowed in the second half of the fourteenth century when William Rede and Simon Bredon both acquired scientific books which they then donated to college libraries. In the fifteenth century, their equivalents were Gilbert Kymer in Oxford and Roger Marchall in Cambridge. Kymer, who served as Chancellor of the University, collected books himself, but also guided the collecting of medical and scientific books by Humfrey, Duke of Gloucester. Kymer commissioned the writing of manuscripts, chiefly on alchemy and medicine, from the scribe, Hermann Zurke, and others. He was also responsible for the successive donations by the Duke of Gloucester to the university library in Oxford, in which medicine and science played a prominent part. Kymer's interest in alchemy led him, along with other physicians, to petition Henry VI, to secure a licence to practice alchemy in 1456. Kymer's commissioning, collecting and donating of books seem to have been guided by the desire to provide a corpus of texts on alchemy and medicine which would secure the future of these studies in Oxford.[9]

7. P. M. Jones 1995a; T. Hunt 1987.
8. A good appreciation of the standing of medicine and science at Oxford in the fifteenth century can be gained from the relevant chapters by Getz 1992 and North 1992.
9. On Kymer and his scribe, Hermann Zurke, see the remarks in Voigts 1989, pp. 385–6; De la Mare and Gillam 1988, pp. 57–64. For the petition of 1456, Geoghegan 1957. Duke Humfrey's role as a collector of manuscripts is dealt with in Weiss 1967, ch. 4; De la Mare and Hunt 1970; and Sammut 1980.

Roger Marchall (MD 1453) of Cambridge was, if anything, still more devoted to these aims, though his interests were in astronomy or astrology and medicine, rather than alchemy. Linda Voigts has identified a corpus of forty-three manuscripts (and a dozen more not now traceable), not all of which were necessarily owned by Marchall himself, but on which Marchall left his stamp. 'Stamp' almost literally, for Marchall's manuscripts are characterized by his habits of providing a contents list for each and annotating many texts in them thoroughly in his own hand (see fig. 21.1). It is particularly striking that he chose only to identify those texts in his manuscripts which corresponded to his scientific and medical interests, ignoring the presence of devotional, historical or literary texts in the same volumes. His annotation evidently was meant to make it easier for others to use these manuscripts, as well as to make it easier for himself. This dedication to making his books a means for others to study medicine and astrology led Marchall to give manuscripts during his lifetime to those colleges in Cambridge where the study of these subjects was already established: Peterhouse, King's and, quite possibly, Gonville Hall, where the largest number of his manuscripts remain today.[10]

Marchall's commissioning, purchasing, annotating and disposing of books gives us an idea of how a fifteenth-century academic and medical practitioner might have used manuscripts. Marchall was evidently an exceptionally bookish person, and to get an idea of the sorts of scientific information wanted by others we need to look at more popular books. The scientific best-seller of the fifteenth and sixteenth centuries was undoubtedly the almanac. Of course, almanacs were almost infinitely variable in content, so it is safer to think of them as a genre – and one which deserves comparison with the ballad in terms of its popularity with every section of the literary market. The evolution of the almanac from the medieval *kalendarium* has not been studied for England as it has been for Germany, but the outlines of its development are reasonably clear. Well before the fifteenth century, the *kalendarium* was an essential tool for the literate cleric. The science of *computus*, as it was taught at European universities as part of astronomy in the Quadrivium had for its central aim the determination of the proper date of Easter and the other movable feasts. Tables which used astronomical data derived from the Greeks and Arabs enabled each day of the calendar year to be given its

10. Voigts 1995.

own appropriate dominical letter from 'a' to 'g', and each year too had its own letter, determined by the day of the week on which 1 January fell. The *Kalendarium* which included these dominical letters together with the golden number for the year within its Metonic or nineteen-year cycle (used to reconcile the solar and lunar calendars), as well as the calendar dates of the principal fixed church feasts and local saints' days, were familiar to laymen too, as they came to be included often at the beginning of books of hours.[11]

The fifteenth-century almanac, however, might include much more than this. In England, the most readily identifiable versions of a *kalendarium* which had turned into a book in itself in fact originated towards the end of the fourteenth century, as the work of the friars John Somer and Nicholas of Lynn. These were quite elaborate documents. That of Nicholas of Lynn, composed in 1386, included, within its month-by-month calendar, columns which record such detailed astronomical matter as shadow tables and the lengths of the artificial (measured from sunrise to sunset) and vulgar (including twilight) day. There were also tables of solar and lunar eclipses, including figures which illustrated them, ascendants and beginnings of celestial houses, the reign of each planet, tables of movable feasts, the motion of the sun and the dignities of the planets, which sign the moon is in each day, and finally the canons, which are a series of rules to explain all the tables and figures. The astrological significance of Nicholas's *kalendarium* is already clear, but the canons bring out the considerable importance of these tables to the physician too. If a patient is bled at a time when the moon is in an inauspicious phase, he will haemorrhage and die. In fact, Nicholas goes on to lay down rules not just of bloodletting but of the giving of medicines too.[12]

Both the *kalendarium* of Nicholas of Lynn and that of John Somer won considerable popularity in the fifteenth century, measured at least by the number of extant manuscripts. There were other calendars by English authors, and some copyists were happy to cut and paste from different calendars to make up their own. One particularly interesting adaptation of the document to a distinctive physical format was the folding calendar. Most of the surviving examples contain a great deal of medical information – on the use of the zodiac, the influence of the moon and the planets on the body, rules for diagnosis from urine colours, and instructions for bloodletting – and they have accordingly been categorized as physicians'

11. North 1988, pp. 87–109; 1969.   12. Eisner 1980; Mooney 1998.

calendars. They were designed to be worn suspended in a pouch worn at the belt, and consist of a number of vellum folios folded twice lengthways and once across, and sewn together through tabs at the top of each folio. Each folio typically contains a table or tables with the appropriate canons and illustrations alongside. Each separate section is identified on the dorse by a line of inscription meant to be read once the folio is folded inwards. They are usually quite elaborately illuminated, with fine pictures of a zodiac man, a bloodletting man, and urine glasses, and must have been favoured by comparatively rich medical practitioners. More than twenty English examples are still extant, all based on the Metonic cycle of nineteen years.[13]

If the folding calendar represents a version adapted particularly to medical use, there are many other fifteenth-century calendars which cater to prognosis and prophecy in a more general sense. These combine calendrical information with textual material whose origin is often impossible to trace. Prognostics for the coming year were very popular, forecasting with respect to crops and cattle, birth and death, the possibility of war and, most important of all, perhaps, the weather. Some calculate from the day of the week on which Christmas or New Year falls, or from the character of the weather in the twelve days after Christmas. That the weather prognostications were taken seriously, at least by some users of these prognostics, can be seen from the careful record of the weather in the days after Christmas made, possibly, for 1429.[14]

Most popular of all of the varieties of prognostication to be found with calendars, or circulating independently, were the lunar prognostics. These are perpetual prognostications of the lunar month arranged either according to the thirty days of the moon's cycle from one new moon to the next, or according to the moon's passage through the signs of the zodiac. Nearly a hundred manuscripts containing one or other, or both, of these types, dating from the fifteenth century, have so far been identified. Lunar prognostics predict the outcome of actions undertaken at a given point in time, advise people on medical matters, and prophesy the fate of children. Lunaries according to the days of the moon also deal with dreams, predict whether lost or stolen property will be regained, and tell whether a fugitive will be caught. Lunar prognostics, unlike the physician's folding calendars, were not restricted in use to a handful of wealthy professionals. The manuscripts in which they are found vary

13. Talbot 1961; P. M. Jones 1984, pp. 67–9, and figs. 27–8.
14. BL, Royal ms. 17 A.xvi; Robbins 1939b; Means 1984.

widely in quality of script and decoration. One example, on poor-quality paper and written in an unprofessional hand, includes marginal drawings of ploughs, winnowing fans, barns, hunting dogs and obscene caricatures. John Metham's prose prognostications were commissioned, on the other hand, by Sir Myles and Lady Stapleton of Norfolk, and accordingly he concentrates not on agriculture, theft and prison, but on birth, illness, hunting, hawking and merchandising. Other examples were owned by physicians like the 'Young Doctor Walker' of the sixteenth-century example in Ashmole ms. 6, or by the humbler John Crophill, Bailiff of Wix in Essex, whose manuscript also contains lists of his prescriptions for his patients. Pocket-size versions of these lunary manuscripts can be found, like Ashmole ms. 8, as is the case with prognostics in general.[15]

The coming of printing to England would seem at first sight to have neglected the almanac. Very few almanacs, calendars or prognostics were produced by English presses, almost none in the incunabular era (the first *STC* almanac dates from 1498). This is misleading in two respects, however. It ignores the appearance of calendrical, astrological and bloodletting information in books of hours, which, although far less sophisticated than in the manuscript almanacs, covered some of the ground. And, as Capp has pointed out, the English market for printed almanacs before the mid sixteenth century was dominated by imports printed, and often translated into English, on the Continent.[16]

The first printed almanac was produced by Gutenberg probably in about 1458; by the 1490s they were being produced in large numbers in Germany. Early printed almanacs, not surprisingly, resembled the upmarket manuscript versions; in fact the famous *Volkskalender* and its companions had circulated in manuscript early in the fifteenth century. These early German almanacs, both manuscript and printed, were close cousins of the English calendars for the Metonic cycle. Printers in Germany, however, rapidly took advantage of the relatively low cost of printing almanacs yearly, and also appreciated the potential market for much more condensed and cheaper versions of the almanac than the elaborate *Volkskalender* and its like. Many printed almanacs were produced, before the end of the fifteenth century, which compressed calendrical, medical and astrological information on to one sheet – the almanac broadside. Bloodletting almanacs seem to have had particular vogue.

15. Taavitsainen 1987, pp. 18–26; 1988; Means 1993.
16. Capp 1979, pp. 23–66. See also Mooney 1997.

Lunar prognostication and other divinatory material, including the *Practica*, which specialized in lurid and sensational predictions of floods, epidemics and disasters in the coming year, also took advantage of the simplest printed formats.[17]

Unfortunately our knowledge of the import of this material into England is extremely sketchy. We can be confident, however, that such importing did take place, and on a scale considerable enough to discourage English printers from competing. Almanacs and broadsides were not the kind of material which appears in such records of the import trade as survive. The Laet de Borchloen family of Antwerp, however, produced a series of almanacs and prognostications from 1469 onwards, which circulated widely in Flanders, and, in translation, in France and England too. The first printed prognostication in English, printed *circa* 1498, is one such translation,[18] but we may be sure that Latin printed versions circulated in England well before that date. Editions for the English market were at first translated abroad, printed in Antwerp and then shipped to England.[19] The first English printer to seek to exploit the market was Richard Pynson, who organized the translation of the Laet family prognostications.[20] Others imitated him, exploring all the forms from broadside – designed to be hung on a wall – to quarto, octavo (later to become the standard form of the combined almanac and prognostication) and the small pocket sextodecimo.[21] Naturally very few of the broadside versions have survived, and those that have are normally fragments identified in the paste-downs of later bindings (see fig. 21.2).[22]

At the luxury end of the market was the famous *Kalendar of Shepherdes*, first translated out of French into English in 1503 – and a true heir to the manuscript tradition.[23] However, English authors and printers were too wary of authority to venture too far into the more dangerous field of prognostics, which might expose them to prosecution for sorcery or treason – the first native product does not seem to have been published, anonymously, until 1539. The characteristic combination of almanac and prognostication printed together – but usually with separate title-pages and imprints – is first found in 1541, printed in London by John Redman, and was destined to become the dominant form in the market for the following century and a half. English prognostications stuck cautiously to weather and sickness in the coming year, eschewing the forecast of peace,

17. Brévart 1988; Simon 1988.   18. *STC* 385.3.   19. *STC* 470.2, 470.3, 471.
20. *STC* 470.5–470.6. Cf. 470.4 (in Latin).   21. *STC* 474, 474.5, 475, 476, 477, 477.5.
22. Capp 1979, ch. 2; *STC*, See under 'Almanac'; Bosanquet 1917.   23. Sommer 1892.

war, and the fortunes of rulers and of whole kingdoms to be found in continental versions (which, of course, circulated in England alongside the native books).

The medical bias of English almanacs and prognostications survived from the manuscript to the printed era, as most of the authors identified on the title-pages proclaimed themselves 'Doctors of Physick' (Andrew Boorde and Anthony Askham, for instance), but the same feature is observable in continental books. Members of the Laet family and William Parron, the continental authors of the earliest prognostics circulating in England, were also professed doctors of medicine. Even in the broadside almanacs, rules for bloodletting and the zodiac man are usually prominent. By contrast, the role of astronomers in the production of almanacs was insignificant, no doubt because precise astronomical data were not the reason for which almanacs were bought. Only in the *Ephemeris anni 1557*[24] do we find an attempt to take account of the theories of Copernicus in the tables drawn up by John Feild, a mathematical instructor in London. This work has a preface by John Dee, and was obviously intended for the advanced student, rather than the casual almanac purchaser.

The failure of such ephemeral items as almanacs and prognostications to survive to the present should not lead us into misunderstanding their currency or appeal. Our best indication of the popularity of almanacs and prognostications is the frequency with which they appear in the sales of a book-seller like John Dorne. Dorne's Day Book records his sales, day by day, for twelve months coinciding almost exactly with the year 1520. Under the heading 'cyclus' or 'ciclus', or sometimes 'ciclus vel almanack' we find 26 entries for the sale of almanacs, which always cost 1d when sold separately. There is in addition a 'ciclus pronosticon', also sold at 1d; an 'almanac de uno folio' (i.e., a broadside almanac, at 2d); 2 'almanac pro uno anno' (one of which sold at 2d), and 2 almanacs for 30 years (at 4s 8d each). That gives us 32 sales of almanacs, with sales of more than one at a time accounting for a further 5 copies. It is clear though that the 30-year almanacs belong really to a different category, and when bound were far more expensive items, equivalent to a luxury book like the *Kalendar of Shepherdes*.

Even the sales of almanacs, however, are overshadowed by those of prognostications, for which 61 separate sales were recorded by Dorne,

24. *STC* 443.9.

and a further 24 copies were sold in sales of more than one at a time. Only ballads outsold prognostications in Dorne's shop, and even the grammars, so useful to Oxford students, could not keep pace with these sales figures. The prognostications sold at prices varying from 1d to 3¹/₂d, and 49 copies sold were identified as being in English. Some of the others, recorded simply as prognostications, might have been in English, but most were probably Latin. Named examples include the prognostications of Gaspar Laet. As we have seen, both Latin and English prognostications were probably still predominantly continental imports. These cheap books were evidently a staple and vital part of the book-seller's stock, although, as might be expected, they sold in great numbers from January to April, and much more slowly in the rest of the year (for calendar purposes the year started in March). Very approximately 5 per cent of the sales that Dorne made were of almanacs and prognostications, and they made up a rather higher percentage of the copies of all books sold. Despite their cheapness, their value to the book-trade was nevertheless significant.[25]

When placed alongside almanacs and prognostications, the other medical and scientific works sold by Dorne make a very slight showing. The most popular named authors were Albertus Magnus and Pliny, whose *Historia naturalis* represents the most expensive scientific work which Dorne managed to sell. The Paris edition of 1511 or 1514 sold for 4s 8d or sometimes for 4s 4d, bound in leather, and for 2s 8d in sheets. Dorne sold 9 copies in all, bound but for 1 copy. Albertus, by contrast, is represented by a number of different works, on minerals, plants and (pseudonymously) on the secrets of women. These were all what we might call student editions, the most expensive of which cost 8d. In all, 8 copies were sold. In the same price bracket, we find that Dorne sold copies of works on the sphere (probably Sacrobosco), Euclid's *Geometria*, algorisms, and a work on manual *computus*, which would have formed part of the syllabus of the 'Quadrivium'. Books like the *Articella* or Gilles de Corbeil on urines played a similar role in the medical curriculum at Oxford.

The handful of copies of these books sold in 1520, is, however, roughly balanced by those oriented towards more practical than academic use. Books on cooking, carving, chiromancy, husbandry, the Salernitan *Regimen sanitatis* and books on equine medicine ('medicina vers hors') are

25. Madan and Bradshaw 1885–90.

listed by Dorne. There are also a variety of medical works on *Practica*, some of which are in a different price bracket (e.g. the *Practica* of Valesco de Taranta, bound at 3s), and were probably bought by Oxford physicians. Most of these scientific books, both academic and practical, would have been in Latin, though one or two of the latter may have been in English, to judge by Dorne's entries. Finally though, there are a select few sales which represent a new trend in scholarship. Thomas Linacre's new translations of the *Methodus medendi* of Galen (folio, published in Paris 1519), and of *De sanitate tuenda* (folio, Paris 1517), were sold together to a customer, apparently both in sheets, for 4s 4d. Together with the impressive sales of the Paris Pliny, which would have included the textual notes of Ermolao Barbaro, these represent the first effects of medical humanism on Oxford. In the context of the standard fare offered for sale by Dorne, however, they are but straws in the wind. In any case, as we shall see, medical and scientific humanism was destined to be very much a specialized minority interest, even at the English universities.[26]

The picture we get from Dorne's cash sales book is not the same as that we get from the contemporary accounts of a Cambridge stationer, Garrett Godfrey. Godfrey's fragmentary accounts of 1527–32, unlike those of Dorne, are the accounts of credit customers, and what those customers bought on account did not include the staple items of almanacs, prognostications and ballads, for which they would pay cash. Admittedly, there is one account for 4 books of ballads in 1½ quires (945), and two 5s sales of 30-year almanacs (665,671) – but these exceptions, involving larger sums, only serve to remind us that Godfrey, like Dorne, probably sold dozens of the more ephemeral items for cash, and they do not emerge from the credit accounts. This split between cash and credit accounts also serves to reveal a split in the market for medical and scientific printed books – even the elementary student text-books which made up 40 per cent of Godfrey's sales belonged to the more expensive end of the market and represented significant outlay for his customers (who were often the tutors of the students).[27]

The customers for the medical and scientific works of both sorts sold by Dorne and Godfrey emerge more clearly from the surviving probate inventories of books. Those for the University of Cambridge included lists of books not only of MAs, but also of other 'privileged persons' connected with the university, from undergraduates to stationers and

26. Durling 1977.   27. Leedham-Green, Rhodes and Stubbings 1992.

medical practitioners in the town (see fig. 21.3). Again almanacs and prognostications disappear from view, because of their ephemeral character and low cost. It is clear from the lists, however, that medical books in particular were of interest to a much wider readership than those engaged in teaching and learning in Cambridge. Of the 101 lists that survive from 1535 to 1558, most contain medical works belonging to owners who did not formally study or practise medicine. These books are evidence for a medical culture which extended well beyond the faculty, which was small in any case before the major expansion of the Elizabethan era. One example of a lay owner is Richard Gosynell, who died in 1552, a Fellow of Peterhouse but also an inn-keeper in St Edward's parish. He kept 5 medical books in his study according to the inventory of his possessions, including an *Articella* – until about this time, the staple of university medical teaching. Gosynell probably turned to his books not just for self-diagnosis and treatment, but as a source of advice to those who turned to him as the first line of health-care, among his family, wider household, neighbours, or even the customers at his inn. Only if his advice was not felt to be working would a sick person take him or herself to one of the professional Cambridge medical personnel.[28]

Medical books played a big part in the lives of medical practitioners in Cambridge, and the size of their libraries increased markedly as the sixteenth century went on. Two of the earliest inventories belong to surgeons, John Thomas and John Perman, who both died in 1545. Their libraries are surprisingly large and learned in character, for men whose only academic qualifications were licences to practise from the university. Most of their books are in Latin rather than in English, and show that they were willing to invest money in building up collections of printed books which would be of use to them in their practice of surgery and medicine. These surgeons were able to dispose of libraries of medical books which bear comparison with the number of manuscripts that an exceptional bibliophile like Roger Marchall had been able to build up, less than a hundred years earlier.[29]

What is conspicuously missing from the libraries of Oxford and Cambridge men, whether professional medical men or not, is much sign of the vernacular medical literature beginning to be produced in England before 1558. Even the lay book owners do not seem to have had many of

28. Leedham-Green 1986.
29. Leedham-Green 1986, I, pp. 44–7, 49–55. By the second half of the sixteenth century, the situation had changed drastically again. See P. M. Jones 1995b.

these texts, though they might be expected to be good customers for medical advice couched in simplified terms, and in English rather than Latin. As with almanacs and prognostications, there may well have been a tendency on the part of those making inventories to ignore these books or lump them into parcels (though they could not have been regarded as ephemera). Paul Slack's survey of vernacular medical literature begins around 1520, and shows a significantly rising trend of publication of such works, measured by new titles, up to 1550, when something of a plateau was reached, before a new surge in the 1560s. He shows that it would be a mistake, however, to regard this development of a medical literature in the vernacular as the creation of an original popular medicine, aimed at a new readership.[30]

Many of the most 'popular' books, measured by the frequency of editions, turn out to be printings of works that had been in circulation in the previous century. This is true of Thomas Moulton's *Mirror or Glass of Health*, which went through at least seventeen editions between 1530 and 1580, and yet which is not the work of a contemporary, but of a Dominican writing a century earlier. The same is true with the plague treatise traditionally attributed to 'Canutus',[31] Roesslin's *Byrth of man-kynde*,[32] Thomas Vicary's anatomy[33] (based on a work written in 1392 in Middle English), and probably many more than we can as yet identify. It is simply not the case that a new genre of medical advice book was being created in the sixteenth century to exploit the possibilities afforded by cheaper print. These are much the same kinds of books as had already circulated in manuscript, and for much the same purpose. In the prefaces to these writings, the claim is usually that the intention is to enlighten practitioners of medicine, who are in danger of practising unlearned medicine to the detriment of their patients – the same claim made by those who had been translating from Latin to the vernacular from 1375 onwards. What evidence we have for the readership of these books – almost entirely from later in the century – points in the direction of a social élite, members of the professions, gentlemen, some merchants and their wives, rather than those further down the social scale, who would not have been able to afford them.

If we ask what books on medicine and science were available to those lower down the social scale, to yeomen or to artisans, then we must return to the almanacs and prognostications, the works to be had for a

---

30. Slack 1979.　　31. *STC* 4589–93.5; cf. p. 487.　　32. *STC* 21153–64.　　33. *STC* 24707–13.

penny or two pence. Unfortunately there is no direct evidence to show that such works were owned by people who had no other books. A glimpse of the role of the single-sheet publication, which might be an almanac, or prognostication, or an advertisement, can be had from the writings of a surgeon from Maidstone in Kent, John Hall (1529?–1566?), in the preface to his translation (actually adapted from that of a fifteenth-century translator) of the medieval surgeon, Lanfranc of Milan. Hall tells us that:

> in the year of our Lord a thousand fyve hundred fyftie and eyght, there came to Maydstone one Thomas Lufkyn, by occupation a Fuller, and bucler of clothe, and had bene brought up (by reporte of divers honest men), at the fullyng mylles there besyde the towne, nevertheless he had ben longe absent from that contrie, in whiche tyme he had by roving abroade becomde a Physicien, a Chirurgien, an Astronomier, a palmis-ter, a physiognomier, a sothsayer, a fortune devyner, and I can not tell what. This deceaver was the beastliest beguiler by his sorcerys that ever I herd of, making Physicke the onely colour, to cover all his crafty thefte, and mischieves, for he set uppe a byll at his fyrste commynge, to publishe his beyng there, the tenour wherof was in effect as followeth: If anye manne, womanne, or childe, bee sicke, or would be let bloud, or bee diseased, with anye maner of inward or outwarde grefes, as al maner of agues, or fevers, plurises, cholyke, stone, strangulion, impos-tumes, fistulas, kanker, goutes, pocks, bone ache, and payne of the joynts, which commeth for lacke of bloudlettyng: let them resorte to the sygne of the Sarazens hedde, in the easte lane, and brynge theire waters with them to be sene, and they shall have remedie
> By me Thomas Luffkin[34]

Luffkin must have been able to count on there being enough people who would see his bill and be able to read it to themselves, and perhaps to others. Though such bills do not survive today, we should not forget that they may have been common enough in English towns, if not villages, in the mid sixteenth century. They would have served to advertise medical expertise, and to have taken custom away from those like John Hall, whose own medical works in English were aimed at a readership of practitioners and literate gentlemen and gentlewomen far higher in the social scale than a fuller such as Thomas Luffkin.

34. *STC* 15192, fol. Aaa 3 recto.

III

THE LAY READER

22

Schools and school-books

NICHOLAS ORME

Between the introduction of literacy to England in 597 and the beginning of the fifteenth century, 800 years elapsed. During this period, a rich variety of schools grew up all over the kingdom. Religious houses were the earliest centres of education, and in 1400 there were still many schools in monasteries, friaries, cathedrals, collegiate churches and nunneries. Some were for adult novices, and others for children who lived in the communities as altar-boys, choristers, or wealthy pupils being brought up by an abbot or abbess. By the time of King Alfred, schooling had spread to the royal household, and in 1400 training was still provided there for noble wards and boy choristers, as it was in the great noble households which modelled themselves on the King's. In the tenth century, Church legislators had urged the parish clergy to teach boys and, while this task was never universally observed, some clergy gave instruction to single pupils or small groups in the fifteenth century, to enhance their income or provide themselves with assistants. From a very early date, too, there must have been informal teaching by one literate person of another: parent to child, merchant to apprentice, senior clerk to junior learner.[1]

Schools open to the public may also have originated in Saxon times and certainly existed by the late eleventh century. They were particularly to be found in towns, where a master could gather enough pupils to live off their fees, and from boarding them too if they came from a distance. At first such schools were often personal ventures and easily came to grief, but by 1400 they had frequently gained stability through the emergence of a local patron (bishop, monastery or lord of the manor) who appointed new masters when necessary. They often acquired their own buildings, books and scholarships – resources which also promoted continuity. The

---

1. On medieval schools, see Orme 1973, *passim*, with a longer perspective and further thoughts in Orme 1989.

fifteenth century saw a further development: the endowment of schools by wealthy benefactors, so that the master received a regular salary and education was free. This kind of endowment became popular after Henry VI founded Eton College in 1440, and continued during the rest of the fifteenth and sixteenth centuries. At least eighty endowed schools had been founded in England by the beginning of the Reformation in the 1530s, especially in smaller towns which could less easily support a fee-charging schoolmaster, and others appear in the 1540s and 1550s, but they were still a minority of schools in 1557.[2] In most places, masters continued to be supported by fees.

The number of schools, both public and private, which are mentioned in written sources increases in each century after the Norman Conquest. This gives an impression of continuous expansion, which may be misleading. The population of England, which stood at between about 2.5 and 3 million people in 1377, was only half as large as it had been a century earlier, and probably fell to between 2 and 2.5 million by the middle of the fifteenth century, after which it rose again, but very slowly.[3] The number of schools in small towns and smaller religious houses may have declined proportionately. In about 1439, William Bingham, a London rector, claimed that the national supply of schools had fallen in the previous 50 years, and estimated the loss at 70 in the eastern half of England alone – a salutary warning against assuming that numbers only expanded.[4] It remains virtually impossible to say how many schools and pupils there were in England between 1400 and 1557. References to them occur by chance and, as we cannot check every record to find even those that survive, we have to resort to rough guesswork. In the fifteenth century, an English county of average size probably contained between 5 and 10 public schools, giving a national total of 200–400 schools and schoolmasters. If we assume that each school had 20 pupils (we know that some had as many as 50 or 80), this produces a minimum total of pupils of 4,000–8,000 at one time. We need to add to these the schoolmasters and students in religious houses and great households, and those learning privately with the clergy and other informal teachers. They probably increase the total to 400–600 professional schoolmasters, and may well double the number of pupils to 8,000–16,000 – meaning pupils

2. For a map of free schools in 1530, see Orme 1973, p. 216, to which some additions now need to be made, e.g. Bradford-on-Avon, Wilts., and Cockermouth, Cumb., both existing by the 1520s.　　3. Hatcher 1977, pp. 44, 68–9.
4. The best edition of Bingham's account is in Lloyd 1934, pp. 356–7. His belief in decline resembles the view of falling population in Hatcher 1977, p. 44.

who were doing structured literary study rather than basic and informal learning. This would have been only about 1 in 20 of the nation's boys and youths between the ages of 7 and 18 (who constituted about 10 per cent of the population in the mid sixteenth century, so perhaps the total of pupils ought to be higher).[5] No ingenuity, however, can produce reliable figures at present. All we can do is to gain a sense of the importance of schoolmasters and pupils: there were several thousands of them at least. They made up a significant group of people who used books and wrote them, and for whom books were written and copied – books of a distinct and specialized kind.

Schooling began at an early age – as young as three or four among the aristocracy – and sometimes continued until the early twenties. Even at the universities (which generally recruited boys in their late teens), students often needed 'remedial' instruction in elementary Latin grammar, while advanced Latin grammar formed part of the undergraduate course.[6] There was a similar overlap in the training of novices in religious houses. In terms of gender, some girls partook of schooling (at least informally), as well as some boys. By 1400, most daughters of the nobility and gentry probably learned to read English in their own households or in nunneries: from parents, chaplains or nuns.[7] In a few towns, notably London, there were elementary schools for small boys and girls together, or perhaps girls alone, taught by chaplains or schoolmistresses, and these schools presumably catered for wealthy burgess families.[8] For boys and girls alike, schooling began by learning the alphabet – usually the Latin alphabet – written on a board or in a small book.[9] This was followed by reading practice, starting with basic prayers like the Paternoster, Ave Maria and Apostles' Creed in Latin or English and, especially in formal schools for boys, the sight-reading, pronunciation and chanting of Latin texts from the Psalter and antiphonal which were used in church services. Boys who proceeded with their education went on to study the grammar of Latin, and learnt how to understand the language and to write and speak it. The study of Latin by girls was rare until about 1500, when an increasing perception of its value to the laity caused the daughters of Henry VII to be taught the language, a practice which spread to other aristocratic girls during the sixteenth century.[10]

5. Wrigley and Schofield 1981, p. 528.
6. See the purchases of the Cambridge tutors, William Buckmaster and William Pannell, in Leedham-Green, Rhodes and Stubbings 1992, pp. 158–9, 162.   7. Orme 1984, pp. 156–63.
8. Orme 1973, pp. 54–5.   9. Orme 1973, pp. 60–2; Orme 1993.   10. Orme 1984, pp. 161–2.

Latin was a difficult language for English people, because of its different grammar and syntax. Ever since Saxon times, educationists in the British Isles had been exercised to find ways of teaching it effectively, and had written treatises to do so.[11] They had built on the work of Roman grammarians, particularly Aelius Donatus whose *Ars minor* was a short work aiming to correct and polish the Latin of natural Latin speakers. The medieval grammarians turned the *Ars minor* into an elementary grammar suitable for non-Latinists, which became known as 'Donatus' or 'the *Donet*': a prose exposition of the eight parts of speech and their morphology, cast in the form of a series of questions and answers. The most popular version of this text in fifteenth-century England was written or revised by the famous Oxford schoolmaster, John Leland (d. 1428), and was known as the *Accedence*, later *Accidence*. It was in English, reflecting the victory of English over French for vernacular purposes, though Latin versions of the *Donet* continued to circulate for use at a higher level or by more ambitious schoolmasters. Leland was an influential teacher and text-writer, and other works by him or like his were used widely in fifteenth-century schools. They included the *Comparacio*, a short tract on the comparison of adjectives, and the *Informacio*, an introduction to Latin construction and how the language was composed. The *Formula* was a reworking of the *Informacio*, apparently by one of Leland's pupils, and *Sum es fui*, probably also by someone other than Leland, gave the forms of *esse* and other common irregular verbs. Like the *Accedence*, these works were short, elementary in nature and written in English.[12]

Once pupils had mastered basic Latin, they continued their studies with texts in Latin itself. Several of these more advanced texts dated from the early thirteenth century and were in verse to facilitate memorization. They included the *Synonyma* (a list of synonyms for a number of key words) and the *Equivoca* (a dictionary of homonyms – words of similar spelling but different meanings), both ascribed to the Anglo-French grammarian, John of Garland. The *Grecismus* by Evrard of Béthune gave help with the derivations, meanings and characteristics of words (including a chapter on words of Greek origin), and the *Doctrinale* of Alexander de Villa Dei (Ville-Dieu) provided a systematic survey and analysis of

11. On the teaching of Latin in medieval England, see particularly Law 1982, especially pp. 9–10; T. Hunt 1991, I, *passim*; J. N. T. Miner 1990, pp. 133–92; Orme 1973, pp. 87–98; D. Thomson 1979 and 1984.
12. On Leland and these works, see D. Thomson 1979, pp. 4–12; 1984, *passim*; and Gwosdek 1993.

Latin morphology, syntax, quantity and metre. The *Doctrinale* was especially popular all over western Europe until the early sixteenth century as a standard work which teachers expounded and quoted and which pupils studied and memorized. Dictionaries in prose were also available, listing words and their meanings. These included such works as Papias's *Elementarium*, Hugutio of Pisa's *Derivationes verborum*, and the *Catholicon* of Johannes Balbus ('Januensis'). All were in Latin, but scholars in fifteenth-century England also created the first dictionaries relating English to Latin. The *Medulla grammatice*, a Latin dictionary with English meanings, is first mentioned in 1438 and was widely used until a better version, *Ortus vocabulorum*, was produced towards the end of the century. The more difficult task of compiling an English dictionary with Latin equivalents was accomplished by a Dominican recluse of King's Lynn, who completed the work, called *Promptorium parvulorum*, in 1440. A similar dictionary, the *Catholicon anglicum*, was in existence by 1483.

The other important school texts were Latin poems, which the pupils read and studied for the sake of their literary style and wise moral precepts. Prose literature, in contrast, was not studied, prose style being learnt chiefly through the writing of Latin sentences and letters. In late medieval Europe the *Auctores octo*, an anthology of eight Latin poems, was widely used in schools, but this was not usually the case in England. This judgment is made on the basis of surviving English school manuscripts. However, the *Auctores octo* was printed on the Continent in the late fifteenth century. Copies appear to have made their way to England and may have been used in schools: e.g., one of about 1493–5, which belonged to John Sowthe, yeoman, of Lincolnshire, in the mid sixteenth century, and another of the same date belonging to an early sixteenth-century Dominican friar, William Dakke.[13] In England, masters chose more freely from a group of poems similar to, but not all the same as, those used on the Continent, and they were not gathered into a set anthology. Seven poems were particularly popular in England. One, the *Distichs of Cato*, a collection of wise sayings, originated from classical Rome but the others were all medieval. They included the *Eclogue of Theodulus*, which compared Hebrew history with Greek mythology; the proverbs (*Liber parabolarum*) of Alain de Lille; a poem on penance, *Peniteas cito*, probably by the Englishman, William de Montibus; and the anonymous poem, *Cartula*, which reflected on the vanity of the world and

13. Bodleian, Auct. 2Q.inf.2.75; CUL, ULC 4197.3 (*c.* 1493–5), part iii (*Facetus*).

human life. Finally, there were two poems which taught good behaviour and courtesy: the *Facetus* (also anonymous) and the short poem on etiquette, *Stans puer ad mensam*, usually ascribed to Robert Grosseteste. Schools also gave attention to one further text in verse: the hymnal used in the daily services of the Church. From about the twelfth century, there was an *Expositio hymnorum* which presented the hymns without music but with Latin glosses, suitable for use in schools. This text was particularly appropriate for the classroom, considering how many pupils would become clergy in adult life.[14]

English schools were not without resources of books. Monasteries, friaries and cathedrals usually possessed libraries, where masters and even pupils may have had access to Latin grammars, poems and dictionaries. The choristers of St Paul's Cathedral (London) were bequeathed several dozen books by benefactors in the fourteenth century, ranging from grammar and poetry to logic, law and medicine. Winchester College (founded 1382) and Eton College (founded 1440) both had collections of grammar books.[15] On the other hand, the young monks of Glastonbury Abbey complained in 1538 that they were not allowed to use the large and well-stocked abbey library, so that we should not assume that nearby books were always available.[16] We know very little about the book resources of town schools, though there are occasional mentions of volumes. A priest named John Elwyn left all his grammar books to Hedon School (Yorkshire) in 1465; the parish church of Bridport (Dorset) had Hugutio's dictionary, two Latin grammars and a book of logic in 1476 (probably for the use of the local schoolmaster); and Rotherham School (Yorkshire) owned Isidore's *Liber etymologiarum* and Johannes Balbus's *Catholicon* in 1498.[17] A carefully written fifteenth-century manuscript survives, which was apparently produced for, or belonged to, Battlefield College (Shropshire) or one of its masters.[18] Sometimes the books belonged to the schoolmaster personally; in a unique case, John Bracebridge, master of Lincoln School in 1420, had a collection of about sixty-six works, including the standard Latin dictionaries.[19]

It is probably safe to say, however, that every schoolmaster of grammar had one or more books. Numerous manuscripts survive from the fifteenth century which originated in schools and consist of collections

---

14. On these works, see Bonaventure 1961; Orme 1973, pp. 102–6; T. Hunt 1991, I, *passim*.
15. T. Hunt 1991, I, pp. 124–5.   16. Orme 1991, p. 296.   17. Orme 1973, pp. 125–6.
18. Cambridge, Trinity Coll., ms. o.5.4; D. Thomson 1979, pp. 158–68.
19. On school manuscripts, see D. Thomson 1979, *passim*.

of elementary Latin treatises like those of Leland, school poems such as those mentioned above, vocabularies, and exercises in the form of sentences and passages of Latin – sometimes with English translations indicating work from one language into the other.[20] True, most of the manuscripts appear to have been compiled by pupils rather than masters, but they may have survived through the pupils becoming masters and keeping them, and, in any case, the pupils could not have had access to literary texts unless the masters had too. There are other indications that some pupils had individual copies of texts. Books were bought for grammar boys associated with Merton College, Oxford, in the fourteenth century, and Edmund Stonor, son of a gentleman, possessed a personal copy of a basic Donatus-like grammar at Oxford in the 1390s.[21] Manuscript illustrations of noble boys in school show them with books in their hands, and so do woodcuts of schoolboys by the early sixteenth century.[22] Masters and pupils are likely to have got such books in various ways. There may have been some professional production of school texts by scriveners, chiefly larger works like dictionaries but possibly also smaller ones for royal or noble pupils. Those who worked in schools did copying themselves, and, as the manuscripts show, they could produce a comprehensive miscellany of texts by their own efforts. Finally, texts circulated at second hand. Worn-out psalters and antiphonals sometimes ended their days as reading texts for young children, like the thirteenth-century grammatical manuscript, formerly belonging to the Middleton family which seems to have been consigned to schoolboys by the end of the Middle Ages.[23] Other miscellanies sometimes include leaves of grammatical material which came from somebody other than the compiler,[24] and wills mention grammar books being passed on to younger scholars.[25]

There was another kind of literature for children, or about them, besides that of the grammar schools. In the great lay households, boys and girls of the nobility and gentry were trained for lay careers rather than ecclesiastical ones, with greater emphasis on the vernacular than on Latin.[26] For them, learning the alphabet was probably followed by learning to read prayers from the primer – the prayer-book (sometimes in Latin, sometimes in English) containing the basic prayers and simple offices (or hours) of the Virgin Mary which the laity used for their private

20. Garton 1980.   21. Orme 1973, p. 127.
22. E.g., Orme 1989, p. 152; Hodnett, figs 76–80, 139–40; see also Schreiber and Heitz 1908; Conway 1884.   23. W. H. Stevenson 1911.   24. E.g., D. Thomson 1979, pp. 313–14.
25. For examples, see Moran 1985, pp. 200–1.   26. Orme 1984, pp. 142–63.

devotions. Courtesy-books – poems about good manners – were also used for teaching aristocratic children.[27] They first appeared on the Continent and in England in the twelfth century in Latin, were later produced in French and (from about 1400) in English. One of the best-known was John Lydgate's English version of *Stans puer ad mensam*,[28] with its advice on behaviour for boys in noble households, but several similar texts circulated in the fifteenth century. The most popular Latin school poem, the *Distichs of Cato*, was translated into English in the mid fifteenth century by Benedict Burgh for a young nobleman, and several authors did the same to the *Dicts and Sayings of the Philosophers*, a French anthology of wise sayings: notably Lord Rivers for his pupil, the Prince of Wales (afterwards Edward V), in the 1470s.[29] Noble and gentle children in households were probably also encouraged to read Caxton's translations of the romances (Caxton dedicated his editions of *Jason* and *Eneydos* to young royal princes), and they may have been taught from practical handbooks too. Chaucer's treatise on the astrolabe was written for his young son Lewis, and the well-known hunting poem, *Tristram*, claimed to have been composed by a mother to teach her son.[30] Finally, there were works which set out plans of noble education, notably *De Regimine Principum* by Aegidius Romanus. Versions of this work, in French and English, circulated among the aristocracy in fifteenth-century England.[31]

It followed that when printed books became available in England, from English presses or through importation, large possibilities existed for selling educational books to noble households, and schools in towns and religious houses. From the outset, Caxton preferred to concentrate on the household market. In 1474, even before he came to England, he printed an English translation of *The Game and Play of Chess* by Jacobus de Cessolis in Bruges – a work of moral and social philosophy based on the game of chess, which belongs to the broad category of didactic and educational works for the aristocracy.[32] In 1476, soon after setting up his press at Westminster, he printed two small English texts (the English *Cato* and Lydgate's English *Stans puer ad mensam*) and the longer *Dicts and Sayings of the Philosophers*, all apposite for the training of noble children.[33] A further work of the same period, the translation of *Jason* already men-

---

27. On courtesy literature, Orme 1984, pp. 134–40, and Nicholls 1985.
28. Lydgate 1989–90, *passim*.   29. Bühler 1941, pp. xxxvii–xxxix; Orme 1984, pp. 103, 105.
30. Orme 1984, pp. 104, 195.   31. Orme 1984, pp. 96–7.   32. *STC* 4920.
33. *STC* 4850, 17030, 6826. For the dating, see L. Hellinga 1982, pp. 68, 83.

tioned, was dedicated to the young prince of Wales 'to the intent he may begin to learn [to] read English'.[34] Indeed, of the thirteen texts with educational associations which survive from Caxton's output, all but two were primarily aimed at noble households and one of the exceptions – the French-and-English phrase book (1480) – can be classed as a household work if we extend the term to include the households of merchants, their sons and apprentices.[35] Notable among Caxton's later educational works was his own translation of *The Book of the Knight of the Tower* by Geoffrey de la Tour Landry, printed in 1484 (see fig. 25.2).[36] This provided for the first time in England a widely available text on the education of noble girls, and remained virtually the only work on this topic until Henry Pepwell printed an English translation of Christine de Pisan's *Boke of the Cyte of Ladyes* in 1521.[37]

In contrast, Caxton displayed little interest in printing books for the public and private grammar schools. He published only one, as far as we know: a version of Donatus called *Rudimenta grammatices*, edited by the Italian humanist, Antonio Mancinelli.[38] This was in 1487, late in Caxton's career and after other printers in England had issued Latin grammars, so it was not a pioneer venture. As a work by a foreign scholar unfamiliar to most English schools, it bears the marks of having been commissioned by a schoolmaster or wealthy patron desirous of promoting humanist learning. As such, even this work may belong with Caxton's output aimed at the nobility. There was, perhaps, an economic motive in this choice of household texts rather than texts for schools. *Cato*, the *Dicts* and *The Book of the Knight of the Tower* could be expected to appeal to adults as well as children, for an absolute demarcation had not yet developed between the two readerships. Caxton may also have dealt in school-books by importing them – especially texts like *Cato* and the *Doctrinale*, which were common to England and the Continent. Still, many school-books existed which were not yet in print, and Caxton's avoidance of them seems to have been largely his own decision. Apparently, he preferred translating and publishing works for the nobility and concerned himself with educational works only when they came within that sphere.

Instead, it was other printers who sought to exploit the market in school text-books. The first to do so seems to have been Theodoric Rood, who started to print in Oxford in 1481 after an earlier anonymous printer

34. *STC* 15384. 35. *STC* 24865. 36. *STC* 15296; Offord 1971.
37. *STC* 7271. 38. *STC* 7013.

had begun to do so in 1478. Rood's main preoccupation was to print academic text-books for the university, but he soon extended his activities to schools by issuing (in about 1482) the 'Long' version of the *Parvula*, a widely used text in English dealing with Latin construction and composition, which had evolved from Leland's earlier *Informacio*.[39] Three years later, in 1485, he brought out Alexander de Villa Dei's *Doctrinale*, a university as well as a school text, and one which represented (like the *Parvula*) a sensible conservative choice of text with a wide appeal.[40] The third printer to work in England, the nameless schoolmaster of St Albans who started work in 1479, is not known to have issued a school grammar. He rather resembles Caxton by publishing a work of noble education, *The Book of St Albans* (1486), containing texts teaching heraldry, hunting, and social ranks,[41] but William de Machlinia, who began to operate in London in about 1481, also interested himself in the school market. In about 1483-5, he issued at least two school texts: one a Latin version of Donatus's basic grammar, the other a new work by John Anwykyll, to be discussed presently.[42] None of these other presses, however, lasted for very long. All three came to an end in about 1486, and the number of grammars they are known to have produced is small: four titles by Rood and two by Machlinia. Of course, other works in this genre may well have perished, as the survivors often exist in single copies or fragments, but the brief life of the presses and Caxton's interests elsewhere still encourage the conclusion that relatively few school-books were printed in England before the early 1490s.

Rood and Machlinia at least achieved something original during their short careers. They published two new school texts probably written by John Anwykyll, master of a new and important grammar school attached to Magdalen College, Oxford.[43] Anwykyll was the first English schoolmaster, as far as we know, to be influenced by European humanism and to teach Latin in school according to its principles. The first of these texts was a Latin grammar in Latin entitled *Compendium totius grammatice*, claiming to draw on the work of the Italian humanist grammarians, Niccolò Perotti and Lorenzo Valla. It identifies its author only as John, but links him with William Wayneflete, Bishop of Winchester, founder of the college and school where Anwykyll was then working.

---

39. *STC* 23163.13.   40. *STC* 315.   41. *STC* 3308; Hands 1975.
42. *STC* 7014.5, 23904-5.
43. On Anwykyll, see *BRUO*, I, p. 39; Weiss 1967, pp. 169-72, 175, 200; Brodie 1974; and cf. Jensen above, p. 359.

The second text, usually printed with the *Compendium*, is a collection of *Vulgaria* or sentences for translation from English to Latin, based on Latin phrases in the plays of Terence. Anwykyll, to whom both texts may plausibly be ascribed, was a shrewd innovator. He taught the writing of Latin in accordance with humanist, rather than late medieval, standards, but the form of his works was traditional. The grammar contains mnemonic Latin verses of a long-established kind and the sentences in the *Vulgaria* resemble those which occur in earlier school manuscripts, so that much in his work was familiar. His presentation of new wine in old bottles was successful, for both works had a long life. Rood printed them together in 1483, and Machlinia issued at least the *Vulgaria* at about the same time.[44] The *Compendium* was subsequently brought out, by various English and continental printers, at least six times between 1483 and about 1517, and the *Vulgaria* at least five times, the last occasion being as late as 1529.[45] A manuscript text of the *Compendium* was also written at Chirk (Denbigh) in the 1480s.[46] Anwykyll was thus the first English schoolmaster to produce bestselling grammars – an achievement so precocious in the history of printing that (like Caxton's edition of Mancinelli) it may well have been assisted by an important patron. The fact that Rood and Machlinia printed Anwykyll's work in different places at about the same time together with a dedicatory poem in the grammar by the Italian humanist scholar, Pietro Carmeliano, addressed to William Wayneflete, Bishop of Winchester, points to Wayneflete as having encouraged the publication and even having helped with the costs.

It was not until the 1490s that grammar books became, at last, a regular and important part of English printing output. The credit for this is due to Richard Pynson, who started to print grammars in London in about 1492, followed (apparently a little later) by Wynkyn de Worde, who took over Caxton's press. Pynson's first known school-books were editions of Alexander's *Doctrinale* and 'Donatus's' *Rudimenta grammatices*, previously issued by Rood and Caxton respectively.[47] In 1494, he printed the grammar of the humanist grammarian, Giovanni Sulpizio, for the first time in England (see fig. 22.1),[48] and in the following year he was facing competition from De Worde who produced an edition of the *Long Accidence*, derived from Leland's version, and a grammar called *Introductorium lingue Latine* by a contemporary schoolmaster, William

44. *STC* 695–6, 23904–5.   45. *STC* 696.1–696.7, 23907–8.
46. NLW, ms. NLW 423D; Thomson 1979, p. 106.   47. *STC* 316, 7014.   48. *STC* 23425.

Horman, headmaster of Winchester College.[49] Pynson and De Worde adopted the policy of Rood and Machlinia. They issued popular traditional texts, along with one or two humanist or original works which may have been funded by patrons. The difference was that their businesses had a long existence and the production of grammars became a regular event, with at least one school-book coming out each year after 1495 from one press or the other, and soon more than one. In 1499, Pynson published the first printed English–Latin dictionary, *Promptorium parvulorum*, and, in 1500, De Worde countered this with the first printed Latin–English volume, *Ortus vocabulorum*.[50] By the latter year, in which they each published an edition of the *Synonyma* attributed to John of Garland, we can regard them as outright competitors.[51] Each had discerned the school market, found it profitable and set out to exploit and provide for it. Even so, we should not exaggerate the speed of their achievement. Not until about 1505–10 were English printers able to supply the range of books required in grammar schools: an *Accidence* for learning morphology, a *Parvula* for learning composition, or vocabularies such as *Os facies mentum*, *Synonyma* and *Equivoca*. The printers were also slow to provide the poems read in schools. The *Expositio hymnorum* and the *Eclogue of Theodulus* are not recorded until about 1497 (Pynson), Alain de Lille's proverbs until 1505 (J. Notary), *Cato* in Latin until about 1508 or *Peniteas cito* until about 1514 (both De Worde).[52]

Why was the printing of school-books relatively late to develop in England? There were certainly problems for the printers in exploiting the market. Some texts, particularly the elementary English grammars in the Leland tradition, existed in different versions and it may have seemed doubtful which one would satisfy would-be purchasers. Large texts like the *Doctrinale* were fairly expensive and required capital outlay; small ones were cheap but generated small profits. There may have been resistance from schoolmasters used to copying and selling texts themselves. The sale of school-books from London to schools scattered all over England may have been hard to arrange. However, Pynson and De Worde eventually coped with these problems. They printed cheap texts, expensive texts, and texts in more than one version, and it may be that the greatest obstacles to the early development of school-book printing were adventitious ones: Caxton's different interests and the short lives of the other three early presses. Continental printers seem to have discerned the

49. *STC* 23153.4, 13809.   50. *STC* 13829, 20434.   51. *STC* 11610–11.
52. *STC* 16110–12, 23939.5, 252, 4839.4, 20079.

possibilities for selling school-books in England by the 1480s. In 1486, Aegidius van der Heerstraten produced, from Louvain, an edition of the humanist grammar of Niccolò Perotti containing English material, and Gheraert Leeu brought out Anwykyll's *Vulgaria* in Antwerp (see fig. 22.3).[53] Three years later, Richard Pafraet printed Anwykyll's grammar at Deventer,[54] and Wolfgang Hopyl issued the *Synonyma* in Paris, for the French book-seller Nicolas Lecomte in London, in 1494.[55] These and other printers also issued some of the school poems, equally used on the Continent, but which may also have been sent across to England. Cato, Theodulus and the other works mentioned in the previous paragraph all appeared from European printing houses before they did in England.[56] As late as about 1505–10, Martin Coeffin, a French stationer living in Exeter, considered it worthwhile to have two standard texts printed for him in Rouen: the vocabulary, *Os facies mentum*, and the basic grammar, *Sum es fui*.[57] These works were evidently not easily available from London for the schools of the south-west of England. In about 1506–9, Hugo Goes in York felt that a market existed for printing *Ortus vocabulorum*, although it had already been issued from London.[58] The activities of Coeffin and Goes may lead us to discern either the problems of London printers in reaching provincial schools or their lack of persistence in doing so. School texts, after all, were only one group of titles, and there was more prestige (and perhaps more profit) to be had from producing liturgical books or famous literary works.

The first decades of printing in England coincided with an important change in the English schools. From Anwykyll onwards, schoolmasters began to be influenced by humanism, to substitute classical Latin authors for the medieval poets read in schools, and to revise grammatical usages to accord with classical standards rather than medieval ones. Scholars from Europe were important in driving this process. The earliest influence in England was that of the Italian grammarians, Perotti, Sulpizio and Lorenzo Valla, in the late fifteenth century. Anwykyll used Valla along with Perotti;[59] copies of Valla's *Elegantiae linguae latinae* found their way to England,[60] and they were regularly sold by the Oxford

---

53. *STC* 19767.7, 23907.   54. *STC* 696.1.   55. *STC* 11608a.7.

56. E.g., Bodleian, Auct.10.7.35 contains editions of Alain de Lille, Cato and Theodulus printed at Deventer and Paris, 1494–7; *Peniteas cito* was issued at Antwerp in about 1490 (BL, IA.49904).

57. *STC* 18872; Orme 1988, where the *Tractatus* mentioned should now be identified with *Sum es fui* (cf. *STC* 23155.9–23163.2).   58. *STC* 13829.7.   59. *STC* 695.

60. E.g., CUL, ULC 1697 (belonging to Durham Cathedral); Cambridge, Corpus Christi Coll., Ep.E.14; Oxford, All Souls' Coll., S.R.14.c.1.

book-seller, John Dorne, in 1520. The normal price, between 1s 8d and
2s, suggests that the work was bought by masters and university scholars
rather than schoolboys.[61] Valla's Latin translation of Aesop's *Fables* was
published in England in the same year.[62] A copy of the *Regulae grammaticales* of another Italian grammarian, Guarino Veronese, printed in Paris
in about 1499, subsequently belonged to an English schoolboy.[63] Later,
in the early sixteenth century, the work of humanist scholars from northern Europe reached England too. Joannes de Spouter or Despauterius,
the Flemish humanist (d. 1520) and author of *Ninivitae* on accentuation,
was printed by De Worde in 1525, used for guidance on versifying at Eton
in 1530, and sold at Cambridge at about the same time.[64] Eton also
employed the *Figurae dictionis* of the German scholar, Peter Schede or
Mosellanus (d. 1524), which was published as an appendix to the edition
of Lily's grammar issued at Antwerp in 1536.[65] The most important of
the northern humanists in England was Erasmus. He assisted William
Lily, High Master of St Paul's, London, to produce his popular elementary school text on the eight parts of speech, first published in 1513.[66] His
commentary on the *Distichs of Cato* replaced the medieval commentary in
English editions after 1525;[67] his work on composition, *De copia rerum et
verborum*, was printed in England in 1528 and used at Eton College two
years later;[68] and his work on good behaviour for children, *De civilitate
morum puerilium*, with an English translation by Robert Whittinton, was
printed by De Worde in 1532 and went into six editions.[69] On the whole,
however, it is probably true to say that the influence from the Continent
primarily acted on English grammarians and schoolmasters rather than
directly on their pupils. Not many foreign texts were directly used in
schools, Sulpizio's grammar being the most popular of them. Most students received the work of the European grammarians at second hand,
diffused through grammars written by English authors.

The most influential of these authors in the early sixteenth century was
John Stanbridge (d. 1510), an Oxfordshire man who studied at Winchester
College and New College, Oxford, before graduating as MA and becoming
Anwykyll's assistant, and later his successor as master of Magdalen
College School, Oxford (1488–91). He ended his career as master of
Banbury School (Oxon.), from 1501 to 1510. In about 1505, Pynson printed

61. Madan and Bradshaw 1885–90, p. 174.　62. *STC* 170.3.
63. Leeds UL, Ripon xviii.E.16.　64. *STC* 6780.5; Leach 1911, p. 451; below, note 89.
65. Leach 1911, p. 451; *De octo orationis partium constructione* (Antwerp, Widow of Martin de
Keyser, 1536): NK 2905.　66. *STC* 15601.3–15604.　67. *STC* 4841.5.
68. *STC* 10471.4; Leach 1911, p. 451.　69. *STC* 10467–9.7.

a version of the basic *Accidence*, which he described as 'Maister Stanbridges awne makyng', and this work was frequently published by him and other printers during the next thirty years.[70] It was the first printed school-book to reach large numbers of schools all over the country, from Eton and Winchester downwards. Other versions of the basic English school texts were printed in the following years, with titles claiming that Stanbridge had edited them. They included a *Parvula* on Latin construction in about 1507, *Gradus comparationum* on the comparison of adjectives in about 1509, a collection of *Vulgaria* (Latin and English sentences for translation) in the same year, and a basic verse *Vocabula* and a tract on common irregular verbs (*Sum es fui*) in about 1510. By that year, it was possible at last to teach a class all the main parts of elementary Latin from printed works by Stanbridge – the first time that such a wide range of grammars by a single author had been available through English use of the new technology. Recent studies of the dating of these works suggests that most of them came out in Stanbridge's lifetime and supports the probability that the attributions to his editorship are correct.

Various factors aided his success. He worked at or near Oxford – still (as in Leland's time) a major English centre of school teaching – and he had the patronage of William Smith, Bishop of Lincoln, a prominent educationist. Probably, however, he triumphed most of all because, even more than Anwykyll, he found a formula which satisfied both humanists and traditionalists. The advent of change in the school curriculum caused by humanism was potentially divisive and ruffled some feathers. On the one hand, a writer with conservative sympathies at Magdalen College School could complain, in about 1500, of the diversity of grammars, and ask if new ideas on the subject might not be worse than the old.[71] On the other, the poet and schoolmaster Alexander Barclay could sneer, in 1510, at those who preferred the *Doctrinale* to the grammars of Priscian and Sulpizio.[72] That humanist learning came in with little fuss was very much due to the willingness of English grammarians to compromise, and this was particularly true of Stanbridge. He took the well-known school texts in the Leland genre, familiar to traditionalists, and brought them nearer the standard demanded by humanists. The impact of his writings was immense. The *Vulgaria* are known to have been printed in 18 editions up to 1534; 24 of the *Gradus comparationum* and *Sum es fui* (the two works being usually linked together) were printed up to the same year; 25 of the

---

70. *STC* 23139.5.   71. Nelson 1956, pp. 19–20.   72. Barclay 1874, I, 142–7.

Parvula, up to 1545; and 33 of the *Accidence*, up to 1539. Longest-lived of all was the *Vocabula*, of which 26 editions are known up to 1538, and 14 more from 1560 until 1644.[73] Stanbridge gave the printers their first great victory in the campaign to produce school books, and the wide diffusion of his works raised the possibility, for the first time, that a single course of grammar could be used in every school.

The realization of that possibility was still a generation away when Stanbridge died in 1510. During the following decade in particular, the printers went on producing a wide variety of school texts. Traditional anonymous editions of the *Short* and *Long Accidence* continued to appear, alongside the grammars of Stanbridge, Sulpizio and recent or practising schoolmasters such as John Holt (see fig. 22.2), William Horman, William Lily and Robert Whittinton.[74] Some of these texts were in English, others in Latin alone. The 1510s were also an important decade in the consolidation of humanism in the schools. By the end of the decade, some traditional texts were no longer being printed – presumably because of falling sales. The non-Stanbridgian *Parvula* did not appear after about 1510, the *Short Accidence* after 1515, and its big brother, the *Long Accidence*, after 1519.[75] The old vocabulary, *Os facies mentum*, made its last appearance in 1518.[76] The change is noticeable in the editions of school poems too. Of those texts which the English printers had published, the *Eclogue of Theodulus* appeared for the last time in 1515, *Peniteas cito* in about the following year, and Alain de Lille's proverbs in about 1525, if not earlier. The latter date looks late for such a text and is some twelve years after the previous edition of the work, so the printer's date of 1525 may well be a mistake.[77] The treatises on household education were a little slower to change and two typical late medieval works, the English translations of Christine of Pisan's *Body of Polycye* and *Boke of the Cyte of Ladyes* (including advice on noble education), were published as late as 1521.[78] Here, the change was chiefly signalled by the appearance of Richard Hyrde's translation of *The Instruction of a Christian Woman*, by Joannes Ludovicus Vives, in 1529, and Sir Thomas Elyot's book on the upbringing and behaviour of noble men, *The Governor*, in 1531.[79]

The reading texts of the late Middle Ages disappeared because they were ousted during the early Tudor period by texts from classical Rome.

---

73. *STC*, II, pp. 359–63, and, for the post-1640 editions, Wing 5197B–5200.
74. On Holt's work, see Orme 1996.   75. *STC* 23164.1, 23155.2, 23154.3.   76. *STC* 18875.
77. *STC* 23943, 20081, 254.7.   78. *STC* 7270–1.
79. *STC* 24856, 7635. On these works, see Orme 1984, pp. 224–35.

This may have begun at Magdalen College School, Oxford, in Anwykyll's time, given his apparent use of Terence as a model for school exercises, and by 1500 the school (or at any rate its master) was reading Cicero, Horace, Ovid, Sallust and Virgil.[80] The first surviving scheme of authors to be read in the classroom is that of John Colet, the re-founder of St Paul's School, London, issued in 1512 and 1517, which required the pupils to study late Roman Christian authors of the fourth and fifth centuries, such as Juvencus, Lactantius, Sedulius, Proba Falconia and Prudentius.[81] This plan did not command support; instead, the Magdalen College tradition of studying pagan Latin authors spread to grammar schools as a whole, including St Paul's. The earliest records of precisely which authors were being studied come from Eton and Winchester in 1530.[82] In these schools, only two or three reading texts still survived from the late medieval curriculum. One was *Cato*, though it had been updated, since 1525, with Erasmus's commentary.[83] Another was the hymnal, which was read only at Eton and was about to disappear generally, since the school edition was not printed after 1530.[84] A third, perhaps, was Aesop's *Fables* which had been known in the later Middle Ages and continued in use in the Tudor period.[85] The old poem on table manners, *Stans puer ad mensam*, had been replaced by a similar version in a more humanist kind of Latin, *Quos decet in mensa* by William Lily, printed in Colet's *Aeditio*, of which the earliest surviving copy is dated 1527.[86] Other schools used an analagous new work by Sulpizio, *Carmen de moribus*, *Stans puer ad mensam* or *Carmen juvenile*.[87] Otherwise, the texts for reading were all pagan classical ones, not normally studied in English schools before the 1480s: Cicero's *Epistles*, Horace's poems, Lucian's *Dialogues* in Latin, Ovid's *Metamorphoses*, Sallust's works, the plays of Terence and Virgil's *Eclogues* and *Aeneid*. Only three of these works were printed in England in the first half of the sixteenth century: Lucian, Terence and the *Eclogues*.[88] These were read in the lower forms in grammar schools. The rest were available in print only from the Continent and must have been imported. Being more advanced works, there was at first, perhaps, a smaller market for them, and most were not printed in England until the second half of the century.

The triumph of humanism is also apparent in the earliest large-scale

80. Nelson 1956, *passim*; Orme 1989, pp. 123–51.   81. Orme 1973, p. 113.
82. Leach 1911, pp. 448–51.   83. *STC* 4841.3, 4841.5.   84. *STC* 16128.7.
85. *STC* 168–71.   86. *STC* 5542.   87. *STC* 23428–31.7.
88. *STC* 16891–2, 23885–23885.5, 24813–5.

records of book-sellers which we possess: the accounts of John Dorne in Oxford (1520) and Garrett Godfrey in Cambridge (*c.* 1527–33).[89] Dorne's book, which is a daily list of sales, shows him disposing of large numbers of ABCs on both paper and parchment, the elementary school-books of Stanbridge and Whittinton, and the grammars of Perotti and Sulpizio. He sold one copy of *Peniteas cito* and possibly one of Alain's parables, but these late medieval works no longer attracted significant purchasers.[90] In Godfrey's accounts (which are arranged under the names of customers), the ABC, Stanbridge and Whittinton also figure largely, as do the grammars of William Lily and continental works by Despauterius, Erasmus, Melanchthon and Peter Mosellanus. Dorne's and Godfrey's accounts show that elementary texts were cheap: the ABC a mere 1d (2d on parchment), Stanbridge's *Accidence* 2d, and a set of works by Stanbridge only 7d. Dorne tended to sell texts one by one to individual customers; occasionally he sold multiple copies of Stanbridge or Whittinton – perhaps to schoolmasters – but his sales imply that pupils usually bought their own texts rather than being supplied with them by their masters. Godfrey, on the other hand, frequently sold multiple copies. His customers included Cambridge college tutors who taught their pupils grammar as well as university studies, and presumably took charge of buying the texts. Dorne's large sales of individual copies suggest that pupils might simply have a Stanbridge *Accidence*, or might gradually build up a set of texts. If they did the latter, they did not need to keep to Stanbridge but could mix him with (say) Whittinton; one such surviving set contains five Stanbridge tracts and eight by Whittinton.[91]

We have already noticed the variety of grammars in circulation during the fifteenth and early sixteenth centuries. Not only were there different authors, but many texts did not exist in standard versions. The twelve known manuscript copies of Leland's *Accidence* which survive from the fifteenth century, for example, contain variations of spelling, wording and even material.[92] The early printers prolonged this state of affairs. They issued a *Long* and a *Short Accidence*, a *Long* and a standard *Parvula*, and the works they printed differed as the manuscripts had done. Dr Hedwig Gwosdek, who has made a detailed study of the eight surviving editions of the *Long Accidence* and the four of the *Short*, has

89. Madan and Bradshaw 1885–90, pp. 71–177; Leedham-Green, Rhodes and Stubbings 1992. For a short third source, see Jackson 1936.
90. Madan and Bradshaw 1885–90, pp. 91 (no. 361), 99 (no. 614).
91. Exeter UL, Crediton Deposit 1523/STA.   92. D. Thomson 1984, *passim.*

shown that the printers of the former were working from at least three different texts: editing freely, inserting and deleting material. Their compositors also made changes, especially of spelling.[93] As a result, a class whose pupils had bought (or acquired) their copies of the *Long Accidence* at different times would have exhibited a good deal of variety in its texts, causing difficulties for the master. That this was a problem is shown by the advice of the schoolmaster, Leonard Cox, in 1526, that a teacher should begin the study of a new work by reading the whole text aloud. He should then tell the pupils 'to correct whatever mistakes they notice in their own copies, to fill in gaps and rub out what does not appear in the teacher's text'.[94] There were even larger divergences between schools which used different grammatical authors. Warrington School (Lancashire), for example, adopted Whittinton's grammar, Eton College employed Stanbridge and Lily, while Winchester College preferred Stanbridge and Sulpizio.[95] A decree of the Convocation of Canterbury (the clergy of the south of England), meeting at London in 1530, claimed that a boy who moved from one school to another, because of plague or the master's death, would encounter such different methods that he would be 'almost laughed at by all, and so it happens that those who are still raw in grammar suffer great loss in the progress of their learning'.[96]

These problems of variation between schools, pupils and texts were ancient ones, but in the age of manuscripts there was no means of overcoming the problem, save by the copying of texts within each school or the large-scale use of oral work. Once printing became well established, however, it became technically possible not only to perpetuate textual variations but to abolish them by the production of standard texts for general use. In England, the schools and the printers – the former dispersed and the latter in rivalry – were not capable of establishing uniformity by themselves even through an author like Stanbridge, and when uniformity came it was imposed from outside by the public authorities. Here, the Reformation was the decisive factor. Among both Catholics and Protestants, uniformity was a major preoccupation. Beliefs, forms of worship and patterns of behaviour were all codified and enforced to a greater extent than before. Education, to which the Church and lay authorities had previously given little attention, was now brought under

93. Gwosdek 1991, 1993, 1994.   94. Breeze and Glomski 1991, pp. 142–3.
95. VCH, *Lancaster*, II, 1908, p. 601; Leach 1911, pp. 448–51.
96. Wilkins 1737, III, pp. 722–3, translated in Leach 1911, pp. 446–7; Gwosdek 1993; 1994.

this policy. It mattered more how children were brought up, because their education was crucial to the success of whatever religious settlement was in force. The Reformation in England began with initiatives by Church leaders, and it was they who first conceived the idea of a uniform school grammar. In 1525, the revised statutes of Manchester Grammar School envisaged a grammar 'to be ordained universally throughout the province of Canterbury' (i.e. by the Church authorities).[97] In 1529, Peter Treveris, the Southwark printer, issued a version of Colet's and Lily's grammar with revisions by Cardinal Wolsey, which Treveris alleged had been prescribed for all the schools in England.[98] Wolsey may have planned to authorize this book, but he fell from power in the autumn of 1529 and the project passed to the Convocation of Canterbury, which set up a commission of clergy in March 1530 to choose a grammar for general use.[99] In the event, nothing came of this scheme either – probably because the leaders of the Church became embroiled in difficulties with the King, over his jurisdiction and remarriage – and when Henry VIII became head of the Church in 1534, the responsibility passed to him. Henry too had other things on his mind in the next few years, however, notably the Dissolution of the Monasteries.

During the 1530s, therefore, a variety of grammars continued to circulate. When the decade opened, the works most frequently printed were those of Colet, Lily, Stanbridge and Whittinton. Whittinton's works ceased to appear between 1532 and 1534, partly because of a quarrel he had with his printer, Peter Treveris.[100] Stanbridge's *Gradus comparationum* and *Vulgaria* too were no longer issued after 1534, apparently because they were out of fashion, but his *Accidence*, *Parvula* and *Vocabula* went on being published, so it does not seem that the disappearance of some of his works around 1534 was a matter of public policy connected with the King's new headship of the Church. However, when Henry finally appointed a new commission to choose a uniform grammar in about the late 1530s, its members turned, like Wolsey, to the work of Lily and Colet – high master and re-founder of St Paul's School, London, respectively. Lily's work was an elementary *Libellus de constructione*, to which Colet's *Aeditio* (revised by Lily and Wolsey) formed a more advanced sequel.[101] Unlike the works of Whittinton and some of Stanbridge's texts, Lily's and Colet's grammar had been frequently reis-

97. Orme 1973, p. 255.   98. *STC* 5542.3; Orme 1973, p. 255.
99. Wilkins 1737, III, pp. 722–3.   100. See, for example, *STC* 25477, 25493.3.
101. On the history of this work, see V. J. Flynn 1943, and C. G. Allen 1954.

sued during the 1530s, implying a high and consistent degree of public esteem.[102] Between 1540 and 1542, it was republished by the King's Printer, Thomas Berthelet, in two parts: the elementary *An introduction of the eyght partes of speche* (1542), and an advanced *Institutio compendiaria totius grammatice* (1540).[103] Each was issued by royal authority, and the use of other grammars was prohibited throughout the kingdom. After 1542, the two works were usually printed together.

Judging by the lack of new editions of grammars by other authors, the imposition of an authorized grammar was effective as a measure, though a single edition of Stanbridge's *Parvula* came out in London in about 1545 and one of his *Accidence* at Canterbury in about 1550.[104] Moreover, the principle of uniformity was maintained for the rest of the sixteenth century, despite the religious changes which characterized the years between 1540 and 1559. With the coming of uniformity, schools entered a new age of their history. They were no longer a purely educational interest as they had largely been in 1400. They were now a part of the settlement by which Crown and Church together ruled the country, and they had a common grammar, though freedom remained to choose other school-books and literary works. Printing contributed to this change, and underwent change itself in the process. The early London printers had struggled to serve the schools. They were slow to do so effectively, and printers and publishers elsewhere in England, as well as sellers of imported books found gaps which they filled. By 1510, the Londoners were establishing a monopoly and their provincial rivals were left with little scope. London produced a national best-selling author in Stanbridge, and by the 1530s its printers were dominating all the schools with the texts they produced. They were not, of course, alone in leading these developments. Patrons appear to have played a part early on, as we discerned in the cases of Anwykyll's and Mancinelli's works. At least one schoolmaster, William Horman, seems to have taken the initiative in getting his own works published in 1519.[105] The attitudes of customers were also crucial, though they are now largely unknown. The printers supplied the essential technology, however, and much of the marketing impetus. Their success helped to promote the idea of uniformity, and provided the authorities with the means to enforce it when the wish to do so came.

102. *STC* 5542.4–5543b.9, 15601.7–15610.   103. *STC* 15610.5–15710.6.
104. *STC* 23175.5, 23153.   105. *LP Henry VIII*, III, 1, p. 118.

23
Practical books for the gentleman

GEORGE R. KEISER

In 1486, a little more than a decade after William Caxton introduced printing to England, the Schoolmaster Printer of St Albans produced the first folio edition of *The book of hawking, hunting, and blasing of arms*.[1] Wynkyn de Worde reprinted this compilation of hunting, hawking, and heraldic treatises in folio in 1496, adding to it a treatise on angling (see fig. 23.1).[2] Having so little information about the financial workings of the earliest English presses, we cannot speak, except in qualified terms, about a 'market' for this or other printed editions of practical treatises in late fifteenth-century England. Still, we can reasonably assume that such rapid reprinting of the work attests to an audience eager for access to works of practical writings. Buttressing that conclusion is a colophon in the 1496 edition, in which De Worde explains why he included *The Treatyse of Fysshynge with an Angle* within the larger volume, rather than issuing it in a separate edition.

> And for by cause that this treatyse sholde not come to the hondys of eche ydle persone whyche wolde desire it yf it were enpryntyd allone by itself & put in a lytyll plaunflet therfore I haue compylyd it in a greter volume of dyuerse bokys concernynge to gentyll & noble men, to the entent that the forsayd ydle persons whyche sholde haue but lytyll mesure in the sayd dysporte of fysshynge sholde not by this meane vtterly dystroye it.[3]

Even allowing for a certain overstatement on De Worde's part, we can reasonably assume that the trade in printed books in quarto was by this time sufficient for him to recognize the potential audience for a work of this kind.

While De Worde may not have issued the fishing treatise itself in a separate 'plaunflet' until 1533,[4] he did print the hunting, hawking, and

---

1. *STC* 3308.   2. *STC* 3309.   3. Fol. I4v.   4. *STC* 3313.5.

they bey not good ¶ Whan the hoke is beholde bete the vpuer
ende abrode: ¢ fyle it smothe for fretynge of thy lyne. Thenne
put it in the fyre agayn: and yeue it an easy redde hete. Thenne
sodaynly quenche it in water: and it woll be harde ¢ stronge.
And for to haue knowlege of your Instrumentes: lo them he=
re in fygure portrayd.

¶ Hamour.   Knyfe.   Pynsons.   Clam

Wegge.   Fyle.   Wreste.   ¢ Anuelde.

Whan ye haue made thus your hokis: thenne must ye set
them on your lynes acordynge in gretnesse ¢ strength
in this wyse. ¶ Ye shall take smalle redde silke. ¢ yf it be
for a grete hoke thene double it: not twynyd. And elles for sma
le hokys lete it be syngle: ¢ therwyth frette thycke the lyne the
re as the one ende of your hoke shal sytte a strawe brede. Then

23.1 Instructions for a gentleman: tools used for making fishing tackle, illustrated in
the *Treatyse of fysshynge wyth an angle* added to *The book of hawking, hunting and blasing
of arms* in Wynkyn de Worde's edition of 1496.

fishing treatises in a quarto edition in around 1518,[5] the low cost of which
surely permitted many an 'ydle persone' to purchase it. By 1518 De
Worde had already printed quarto editions of other practical treatises,
among them *The proprytees and medycynes for hors* (1497 and 1502?),[6]
Walter of Henley's *Book of husbandry* (1508?),[7] *The boke of keruynge* (1508,
1513),[8] *The boke of cokery* (1510)[9] and *The crafte of graffynge and plantynge*
(1518).[10] For all of them, as De Worde would have known, an audience
was well established.

That there was an audience, we know from the fact that these treatises,
including the 'dyuerse bokys' in *The book of hawking*, had had a long
history of preservation in manuscript form in the fifteenth century. From
the contents and, where it is possible to discover it, the early ownership
of the manuscript miscellanies into which they were copied, both before
and well after the introduction of printing, we know that these treatises

5. *STC* 3309.5.   6. *STC* 20439.5 and 20439.3; cf. below, p. 489.   7. *STC* 25007.
8. *STC* 3290, 3291.   9. *STC* 3297.5 – a reprint of Pynson's 1500 edition, *STC* 3297.
10. *STC* 5953 – a reprint of a *c.* 1505 Antwerp edition, *STC* 5952.5.

reached the readership to which they were directed, that is, the English landholding classes and those responsible to them.

For a better understanding of the nature of that readership and its common interests, we shall begin by looking at eight manuscript miscellanies into which *The proprytees and medycynes for hors* was copied. Its long history in manuscript and printed form makes this treatise an excellent witness to the continuity from script to print.[11] A work of moderate length, and hence attractive to scribes and ideal for a quarto edition, this treatise is an economical presentation of receipts for equine maladies and other information regarding the care of horses. The intrinsic merit of its remedies, debatable from a modern perspective perhaps, must have been sufficient for contemporary readers, if we are to account for the enduring appeal of the treatise. From at least the middle of the fifteenth century, and through the next two centuries, the treatise was well received by a wide readership.

After considering what these miscellanies tell us about that readership, we shall turn to another group of practical books – military manuals, and the miscellanies into which they were copied. Translated or adapted from a classical source, produced under aristocratic patronage, and preserved in manuscripts far more lavish than any of the modest, serviceable miscellanies containing the equine medicine treatise and its companion-works, these manuals cast additional light on the readership of the late medieval practical book. We shall conclude with an examination of the record of printed editions of such works to see how the press acted as an agent of continuity, and we shall also look at John Fitzherbert's *The book of husbandry*,[12] to illustrate how the printing press expanded the potential of the practical book.

By the middle of the fifteenth century, the landholding classes of England and those responsible to them had a long tradition of literacy and book-owning – and indeed of relying on didactic treatises for guidance. Michael Clanchy has shown that practical or utilitarian literacy among landholders had its origins in the twelfth and thirteenth centuries, when the emergence of a central administrative bureaucracy required the keeping of records and documents and hence led to at least a minimal ability to read and to write among those who held land and, especially, the officers who managed their estates.

Clanchy's argument builds upon the work of Dorothea Oschinsky,

11. See Keiser 1995.   12. *STC* 10994.

whose edition of thirteenth-century treatises of estate management makes clear that officers of seignorial estates, specifically stewards and bailiffs, could keep records and read warrants, both in Anglo-Norman and Latin. Moreover, as Oschinsky demonstrates, from the time of Edward I it was necessary that these officers be trained in the common law. Thus, the *Seneschaucy* (*c.* 1276), a treatise on the responsibilities of the steward and the officers of a manor, and a complementary treatise, the *Husbandry* of Walter of Henley (*c.* 1286), were written, Oschinsky observes, 'for a rising profession of estate administrators who, together with all lawyers practising in common law, received theoretical training outside the university by the study of practical manuals'.[13]

As for the lords of seignorial estates, their need for literacy, including a grasp of the technical language of husbandry and estate management, is attested by Walter of Bibbesworth's *Tretiz de langage*. The Essex knight who composed this treatise *c.* 1240–50, and of whom little is known, was responding to the request of an English noblewoman, Dyonisie de Mounchensi, whose first language was English and who, apparently having only an elementary knowledge of French, felt inadequately prepared to teach that language to her children.

Many of the late thirteenth- and early fourteenth-century manuscripts containing these Anglo-Norman treatises are almost prototypes for the miscellanies that preserve practical books in fifteenth-century England. For example, a legal text-book, compiled *c.* 1300, preserves a text of the *Seneschaucy*, along with copies of treatises on officers of the forest and the office of escheator, the *Magna carta* and numerous statutes.[14] Evidence of the wider interests of the compiler of this manuscript is the presence of two works of different character, a collection of culinary receipts and a text of a French lapidary, *Le livre des pierres*. Similar evidence is to be found in other early legal collections. A Cheshire compilation, from the latter half of the thirteenth century, has a treatise on veterinary medicine, *Practica equorum*.[15] One early fourteenth-century legal miscellany contains a treatise on physiognomy, another on astrological influences, and brief medical texts.[16]

Other miscellanies of this period, which are not legal collections, demonstrate a comparable or wider range of interests. In the Bodleian Library is a text of Walter of Bibbesworth's *Tretiz* with two works from which Walter borrowed material: Nicholas Bozon's *Proverbes de bon*

---

13. Oschinsky 1971, p. 3; see also Clanchy 1991.   14. BL, Add. ms. 32085.
15. BL, Add. ms. 35179.   16. BL, Add. ms. 33969.

enseignement and Walter of Henley's *Husbandry*.[17] Another early four-teenth-century miscellany which preserves Walter's *Tretiz* was compiled by an Oxford scholar: the Franciscan, William Herebert of Hereford.[18] In it, along with Anglo-Norman works by Nicholas Bozon, many of devotional character, and Herebert's own Latin sermons and English versions of Latin hymns, are several practical books: one of the two extant copies of the Anglo-Norman version of Twiti's hunting treatise, *La Venerie*; a unique text of an Anglo-Norman treatise on falconry; an English cookery book; and brief pieces on hawks and hawking, horses and armour.

Though a volume at the Beinecke Library, made up of 193 parchment folios, was compiled well over a century later than these Anglo-Norman miscellanies, it comes directly from the tradition they represent.[19] Among the many works in this volume is a text of the *Modus tenendi parliamentum* (*c.* 1320), which is normally found in legal collections. Its editors describe *Modus* as a legal treatise, best understood against the background of such works as the treatises on estate management, for, like them, it is a technical manual intended for use by members of the new professional classes emerging at the time.[20] By the third quarter of the fif-teenth century, when John Whittocksmead of Wiltshire (1410–82) compiled this collection, these manuals were clearly of interest to members of the English gentry, that class of non-aristocratic landholders who were literate, at least in English, and who had a voracious appetite for writings of education and edification, particularly in the vernacular. A prominent member of the West Country gentry, Whittocksmead was active in the affairs of the region and sat in parliament numerous times between 1442 and 1475. The public record attests to his connections with other members of the gentry from the region and, on several occasions, with Sir John Fortescue, Chief Justice of the King's Bench (1442–60). Whittocksmead frequently served on royal commissions (Yorkist or Lancastrian, depending on who was in power), and his activities, includ-ing service as bailiff of the Bishop of Salisbury, brought him into regular contact with religious houses and the ecclesiastical nobility.

Given this circle of associations, it is not surprising that Whittocksmead had access to the variety of texts preserved in his miscel-lany, and, given the nature of his activities, it is not surprising that many of the works should be technical manuals – practical books for a gentle-man – in both Latin and English. For example, the Beinecke manuscript

17. Bodleian, Selden Supra ms. 74.   18. BL, Add. ms. 46919 (formerly Phillipps 8336).
19. Yale University, Beinecke Library, ms. 163.   20. Pronay and Taylor 1980.

includes both a vernacular astrological treatise, *The wise book of philosophers*, and a Latin work, *Liber destinationum secundum Aristotelem*. It has two treatises on equine medicine – the work printed by De Worde under the title *The proprytees and medycynes for hors* and the *Marescalcia equorum* of Jordanus Rufus de Calabria, a thirteenth-century treatise composed at the imperial court of Frederick II. Among other vernacular works in the Beinecke manuscript are a remedy-book for human ailments, a herbal, a cookery book and the unique text of a poem on falconry. If the latter two texts recall the Herebert manuscript discussed above, so too does Whittocksmead's copy of *The Master of game* (*c.* 1406), a hunting treatise prepared for Henry V prior to his accession to the throne, adapted from *Le livre de chasse* by Gaston III, Count of Foix and Béarn (Gaston Phoebus), by Edward Plantagenet, second Duke of York.

Even the two major spiritual works in the Beinecke manuscript resemble practical books. *De spiritu Guidonis*, a Latin work roughly contemporary with the *Modus tenendi parliamentum*, narrates a Dominican prior's interrogation of the soul of a southern French burgher. This didactic tract, presented in catechetical form, methodically explains hell and purgatory, the benefits of particular suffrages for those in purgatory, the judgment occurring immediately after death, the gravity of sinfulness and of particular sins, and the need for shrift and penance. If this treatise succeeded in encouraging a fear of sin and evoking penitence, the reader could then turn to an English confessional manual that Whittocksmead included in the volume. This prose treatise, like Chaucer's *Parson's Tale*, uses the seven deadly sins to conduct an examination of conscience, thereby preparing the penitent for confession.

For a better understanding of what miscellanies such as Whittocksmead's reveal about their readers, we must consider not only the texts they contain, but also the presentation of them. Of particular importance is the apparatus accompanying these texts, which indicates that the compilers and early owners of these miscellanies were persons who recognized, to a greater or lesser degree, that finding-devices would permit efficient access to material within the treatises. In later medieval England, even scribes without clerical education were regularly incorporating finding-devices developed by scholars and preachers in the twelfth and thirteenth centuries – and were superimposing them in books previously copied without such devices. Especially in a study of the practical book, we can better understand how readers were using these miscellanies by examining the *ordinatio*, that is, the division of a text into parts and the ordering of those parts, as well as the apparatus that facilitated use of *ordinatio*.

The apparatus in the Beinecke manuscript suggests that Whittocksmead was a man who certainly recognized the desirability of locating specific material efficiently, but who provided only limited means for doing so. No table of contents for the volume, if there ever was one, has survived. Preceding the texts of *Marescalcia equorum* and of a book on waters, *Liber de diuersis aquis*, are tables of chapter headings; however, these are merely lists of contents, lacking any numbering systems that would make them genuinely useful finding-devices. The vernacular veterinary treatise which follows the *Marescalcia* lacks a table, though its neat arrangement, with headings set apart from the text and underscored in red, would have had some value for the patient reader. The cookery book in the following leaves begins, like the *Marescalcia*, with a table lacking a numbering system. Whittocksmead's text of *The Master of game* begins with a *tabula* containing chapter numbers for chapters 19–35 only; no chapter numbering occurs in the text itself.

When we look at Whittocksmead's presentation of the well-known *Virtues of herbs*, we see that for the compiler the healing powers of the herbs were of most importance: preceding each recipe is a heading which names the disease to be cured by it, and each heading (not set apart from the text) is underscored in red. (This style of presentation is commonly found in late medieval remedy books.) Whittocksmead has also underscored the name of each herb at the beginning of the section devoted to it, and that name, usually preceded by 'the vertu off', appears in the outer margins. However, these compete for attention with the recipe headings, which are sometimes written in the margins, as well as in the text. This duplication certainly points to Whittocksmead's awareness of the value of finding-devices, if also revealing a certain lack of skill in providing them as successfully as he might have.

Of the seven other miscellanies containing the vernacular treatise on equine medicine, the one with the most learned contents and sophisticated apparatus, a Bodleian codex, makes an interesting contrast to the Beinecke manuscript.[21] While John Whittocksmead was a gentleman amateur, the compiler of this collection was a cleric, Thomas Ponteshyde, rector of Blisland in Cornwall, who assembled the miscellany *c.* 1484–5, according to information he provided in colophons. The difference

21. Bodleian, ms. Wood D.8.

between this miscellany and Whittocksmead's are to an extent a matter of scale and thus easily exaggerated; still, Ponteshyde's education is apparent from the contents. While the Beinecke manuscript has two treatises on astrology, one English and one Latin, Ponteshyde's miscellany consists primarily of learned Latin treatises on astrology, such as Walter Brit's *Theorica planetarum*, and cosmography, including Walter Burley's commentary on Aristotle's *Meteorologica*.

The major English works in the Bodleian manuscript are the equine medicine treatise and the herbal, *Agnus castus*, printed in 1525 by Richard Banckes.[22] These are items 27 and 37 (of 39) in a table devised by Ponteshyde.[23] To facilitate use of the volume, item numbers in the table correspond to arabic numerals centred in the top margin on each leaf. For the English treatises, Ponteshyde provided separate *tabulae* to permit relatively easy access to their contents. Following the *Agnus castus* is an alphabetized (by first letter only) list of the English names of each herb, with a folio number and indication of recto or verso. These correspond to folio numbers (1–48) at the top outer edge of each leaf containing the herbal. Within the work, the herbs are arranged alphabetically (by first letter only) according to their Latin names; as a further aid, Ponteshyde placed the first letter of the Latin names at the top outer edge of each leaf. In the case of the veterinary treatise, a table precedes it, with chapter numbers corresponding to those found in the outer margins next to the recipe(s) for each malady.

The equine medicine treatise circulated far more widely than these West-Country miscellanies would suggest. In another Bodleian manuscript of about 1500, a paper codex of 125 leaves folded in quarto fashion, the treatise ends with 'Explicit per Sothebe'.[24] This scribe, who also copied, a few leaves later, a much larger treatise on equine medicine, the *Boke of marschalsi*, had a name that is common in Yorkshire, particularly in the East Riding; appropriately, northern forms occur throughout the text. Sothebe is probably not responsible for making up the table of numbered chapters that precedes the text of the equine treatise under discussion here and which corresponds to the chapter numbering within the text. We may suppose this from the fact that no other text, neither the *Marchalsi* nor the medical texts copied by another hand in the first 57 folios of the manuscript, has apparatus to help in finding specific material.

22. *STC* 13175.1; cf. Brodin 1950.   23. Fols. 251v–252r.
24. Bodleian, ms. Wood empt. 18, fol. 79v.

477

A far more interesting codex of north-eastern origin, now at Cambridge UL, is a late fifteenth-century collection of writings in 150 paper leaves, including heraldic materials, medical writings and a legal formulary.[25] In it the treatise on equine medicine is part of a booklet comprised of texts on hawking, hunting and cookery. Like the Beinecke manuscript, this text of the equine treatise has headings set apart from and above each remedy to help locate specific material. Fragmentary leaves at the beginning of the treatise make clear that it was not preceded by a table of contents. Several leaves (perhaps an entire quire) are lacking at the end of the text, and they may have contained a table of contents of the veterinary treatise (as well, perhaps, as a table for the hawking treatise that precedes it). If so, it would have been simply an unnumbered table, for no chapter or folio numbers appear in the text.

Other evidence indicates that this scribe (one of several who copied the miscellany) did consider finding-devices important. As noted above, the Beinecke manuscript contains a cookery treatise with a table listing its contents, lacking a numbering system to facilitate its use. The Cambridge miscellany has a variant version of this treatise, here named *The Ordinance of Potage*, which also begins with a *tabula*; in it, the scribe has bracketed groups of recipes and set a folio number to the right of each group (see fig. 23.2). The scribe has also placed a folio number in the top right corner, recto, of each leaf containing the cookery. Whether the scribe simply followed the model of his exemplar or devised the numbering system himself, we cannot know. In either case, its presence certainly indicates an awareness of the value of finding-devices.

Still another point of contact between the Beinecke and Cambridge miscellanies is the formulary found in the latter. As the *Modus tenendi parliamentum* does in the case of the Beinecke manuscript, the formulary relates this volume to the tradition of Anglo-Norman legal collections. Its presence encourages speculation that this miscellany, copied by several hands, was compiled under the direction of a household officer, probably with clerical training, who had responsibility for producing such documents for an ecclesiastical or lay lord. Though it seems unlikely that we shall ever know that lord's identity, the documents in the formulary inform us of the specific milieu in which the miscellany took shape.

Many of these documents record transactions involving William Booth or Bothe (d.1464), who became Chancellor to Queen Margaret

25. CUL, ms. Ll.1.18.

478

soon after her marriage to Henry VI in 1445 and, in turn, Bishop of Coventry and Lichfield in 1447 and Archbishop of York in 1452. At the very end of the manuscript are copies, in Latin and English, of letters from Edward IV to the President and Regents of the University of Cambridge, regarding the appointment of John Booth as Chancellor of the University in October 1463. A nephew of William, John Booth became Bishop of Exeter in 1465. These sons of the Lancashire gentry illustrate very well the social mobility possible for determined and capable members of the provincial gentry in fifteenth-century England. After having trained as a common lawyer, William took clerical orders c. 1420 and then began a steady and deliberate rise to power, on which he was accompanied by members of his family and their circle. That rise was made possible, in part, by his patron, Edward de la Pole, Duke of Suffolk (himself a descendant of a Hull merchant family).[26]

William's half-brother Laurence also enjoyed great power, as Chancellor to Queen Margaret in 1452, Dean of St Paul's, London, in 1456, Chancellor of the University of Cambridge and Bishop of Durham in 1457, and Archbishop of York in 1476. Another brother, John Booth, held several important ecclesiastical posts, including that of Chancellor to the Bishop of Durham in 1479. In the formulary, and elsewhere in the public record, Seth, Robert and William Worsley turn up regularly as close associates of the Booths. These Lancashiremen, apparently three brothers, were cousins, or perhaps merely friends, of the Booths; William Worsley, evidently the youngest, became Dean of St Paul's, London, in 1479.

It is notable that several documents in the Cambridge formulary concern the collegiate church at Southwell, one of four major foundations within the York archdiocese, and that a set of accounts headed 'Suthwell' appears later in the codex. Among the earliest of William Booth's ecclesiastical appointments was a benefice as Canon of this Nottinghamshire church, and the connection continued throughout the remainder of his life. While William was Archbishop of York, he frequently spent time at Southwell, and both he and his brother Laurence were interred there. Very likely, the Cambridge miscellany was assembled at Southwell within the social and political circle that had surrounded the Booths and Worsleys.

These Lancashiremen seem never to have lost sight of their origins. In

26. Reeves 1981, pp. 265–362.

the 1450s William, his brothers and their associates founded two chantries at the church of St Katherine, Eccles, Lancashire, and William provided endowments for it and for Southwell in his will. The Booths and Worsleys are representative of, and must have been sympathetic with, upwardly aspiring gentry, such as John Whittockshead seems to have been. Their common aspirations, apparent in the similarities of the Cambridge and Beinecke miscellanies, are best expressed in a statement at the end of the prologue to *The master of game* regarding the love of hunting: 'ffor sothly þat cometh of hym of ryght grete nobelnesse and also ryght gentylnesse of his goodely kynde and free hert what so euery estate the man be of, othir that he be a gret lorde othir a lytyll, or a pore lorde or a ryche lorde'.[27]

The careful wording of that statement indicates that when Edward Plantagenet prepared *The master of game* for the future Henry V, he anticipated that his work would reach an audience of persons aspiring to 'ryght grete nobelnesse and also ryght gentylnesse'. So too did authors of other works in the miscellanies under discussion here. The Beinecke's hawking treatise is addressed to 'Thu that art a gentilman, / And gentilmanys game wylt lere'.[28] The Cambridge version of the cookery treatise has an opening colophon with the unlikely claim that it was 'compyleit by maysteris off fysyke and mayster cokys off Kyng Rycherd þe fyrst'.[29] Even without such claims, it is clear that the books in these miscellanies addressed both the practical needs and the aspirations of their early owners. They no doubt thought of themselves as the 'gentill men' to whom the Schoolmaster Printer of St Albans directed *The book of hawking*.[30] Appropriately, that compilation, like the Cambridge miscellany, provides 'dyuerse bokys' for a readership interested in heraldry, hunting, and hawking, including one common text, the hawking treatise known elsewhere as *Prince Edward's book*.

In a manuscript now owned by the Duke of Gloucester is an inscription recording that the volume 'has been long in the possession of the Dansey Family of Brinsop Court, Herefordshire, April 15th 1770'.[31] If not the forebears of this gentry family, then perhaps another provincial family of the same social station were the readers for whom this small folio codex, of 285 leaves, was compiled in the second half of the fifteenth century. As the equine treatise is found together with both *Prince*

27. Yale University, Beinecke Library, ms. 163, fol. 138v.
28. Yale University, Beinecke Library, ms. 163, fol. 125r.　　29. Fol. 19r.　　30. Fol. a2r.
31. York House, ms. 45, p. 164.

Edward's book and *The master of game*, it is safe to say this volume serves many of the same interests and aspirations as the miscellanies previously discussed. The presence of texts of *Carte foresta* and *Here is the Charge in Swanymote* recalls the similar documents found in a British Library manuscript,[32] and reminds us again of the relationship between these miscellanies and their Anglo-Norman antecedents. The concern with agricultural matters, often seen in Anglo-Norman miscellanies, is also evident in the Duke of Gloucester's codex, specifically in the texts of treatises on planting and grafting, *Godfridus super palladium* and *þe tretice of Nicholas Bollard*. The former is a vernacular translation of a Latin work compiled from various sources, including the *De re rustica* of Palladius, by an otherwise unknown Geoffrey of Bologna, perhaps originally a German from Franconia, in the mid fourteenth century. The latter is a shorter piece, a translation of a Latin work compiled by a Westminster Abbey monk who flourished in the early or middle years of the fourteenth century.[33]

Agricultural concerns dominate in a smaller miscellany, a collection of 77 paper leaves from the last quarter of the fifteenth century, which brings together an English *Walter of Henley*, the treatises on planting and grafting, the equine treatise and a small group of receipts for human ills.[34] The tables usually incorporated into the texts of the first two works occur here, but the medical treatises lack any finding-devices. At the beginning of the codex, the *Walter* forms a separate unit; another hand, perhaps slightly later, has copied the other works in a booklet with signatures A–F. It is possible that the two parts of the codex were not a single unit in their early history. The only evidence concerning early ownership is a note, in a sixteenth-century hand, at the foot of one of the leaves in the *Walter*: 'God saue my mester Ihon Peyton for euer & euer.'[35] Peyton is a common name in Cambridgeshire and Essex documents. Possibly the volume was owned at an early point by the Peytons – who were then becoming established in Doddington, Isle of Ely, before achieving some prominence late in the sixteenth century.

The two remaining texts of the equine medicine treatise are preserved in volumes that are, like Wood empt. 18 in the Bodleian Library, predominantly medical miscellanies. The first is a paper volume of 119 leaves (with the paper folded in quarto), of which fols. 113r–118v contain the equine medical treatise, imperfect at beginning and end.[36] Most of the

---

32. BL, Add. ms. 32085; see above, p. 473.   33. Braekman 1985, 1989.
34. BL, Sloane ms. 686.   35. Fol. 12r.   36. BL, Sloane ms. 372.

preceding leaves are filled with medical treatises for human maladies; at the front of the codex are *tabulae*, made by an early sixteenth-century owner, for all the treatises. From the numerous inscriptions in the volume, we know that it was in use as late as 1567.[37] 'Harry Pauncefot', written in a bold textura, indicates that among its earliest owners were a West-Country family whose land transactions brought them into contact with John Whittocksmead.[38] Very likely, the inscription is that of the Henry Pauncefoot who was, from around 1492 until his death in 1507, Lord of the Manor of Hasfield, 6 miles north of Gloucester on the Severn, which his family held from at least 1166 until 1598.[39]

In another Bodleian Library manuscript, made up of paper folded in quarto style, the equine treatise comes near the end, following extensive collections of Latin and English medical works, some rather learned in character.[40] With the equine treatise, and comprising a separate section at the end of the volume, are several practical books in the vernacular: *Medicina piscium*, a fishing treatise related to that found in De Worde's edition of *The book of hawking*; *Tractatus Galafridi super palladium*; a few prescriptions for human maladies; *The Boke of Haukyng afftir Prynce Edwarde*; and *þe maner of staynyng & þe vaters perfor*.[41] Nowhere in this early sixteenth-century volume, probably compiled over a period of time, are there any finding-devices. Except for a brief scrap, apparently from a will – 'Ego Humpfridus Harrison capellanus'[42] – the volume contains no information about its original provenance. However, the text of the equine treatise is so close to that of the Cambridge manuscript[43] that it seems safe to assume a common exemplar, or very closely related exemplars, and similarities in dialect permit us to suppose that the two copies were made in the same geographical region.

From this survey of the miscellanies containing the equine medicine treatise we see that its readers were also interested in other practical books, particularly (though not exclusively) those concerned with hawking, hunting, and planting and grafting. As for the nature of that readership, while we cannot identify all of the compilers and early owners of these miscellanies, we have sufficient evidence to conclude that they were, by and large, members of the landholding classes of provincial England, or clerics closely connected with them. Probably, like John Whittocksmead, they were members of the gentry, rather than aristo-

---

37. Fol. 112v.   38. Fol. 113v.   39. VCH, *Gloucester*, VIII, (London, 1968), p. 283.
40. Bodleian, Rawlinson ms. C.506.   41. Fols. 287–332.   42. Fol. 355v.
43. CUL, ms. Ll.1.18.

crats, or, like Thomas Ponteshyde, they were clerics who served the spiritual and practical needs of the gentry. Literacy and books were, as the gentry understood, a means to both security and social advancement, and they were encouraged in that understanding by clerics, often children of the gentry themselves, who shared the interests and aspirations of the laity they served. As with the Booths and the Worsleys, a clerical education or training in the law was the means for gentry sons to attain social advancement for themselves and their families. That was clear to John Whittocksmead, for one of his sons was an attorney and another, apparently, a cleric.

The spread of literacy among the gentry of fifteenth-century England was due in great measure to clerics who conducted provincial grammar schools, and the transmission of practical books was due in part to the movement of those clerics from region to region. Thomas Ponteshyde, the cleric–scribe who compiled ms. Wood D.8, reports having copied the equine treatise at Writtle in Essex, 10 May 1485 (f. 128r), and thus invites comparison with John Reed, who copied a medical miscellany in 1528–9, while he was parson of Nether Broughton in Leicestershire and vicar of Melbourne in southern Derbyshire.44 His principal text, *Liber de diversis medicinis*, was obtained in Yorkshire, from the Pickerings of Oswaldkirk in the East Riding, who had acquired it a century earlier from the rector of Oswaldkirk.45

Clerics were probably responsible for the composition of many of the practical books that were copied into the miscellanies we have been considering. Nicholas Bollard, who compiled a treatise of grafting and planting and probably translated Geoffrey of Bologna's treatise, was a Westminster monk. The Anglo-Norman *Walter* was written by a Dominican prior, and many of the manuscripts in which it is preserved were in monastic libraries. From such a source, it may have come into the hands of a late medieval English cleric who prepared the Middle English version, attributing the original to Robert Grosseteste, Bishop of Lincoln. While the advice on estate management 'became out-of-date', as Dorothea Oschinsky observes, the translator recognized that 'the farming content of the treatise, however, retained its validity' and adapted the treatise on demesne farming to meet the needs of late medieval tenant farmers.46

While it is appropriate to conclude that gentry who hoped to achieve

---

44. Bodleian, Rawlinson ms. A.393.   45. Keiser 1980.   46. Oschinsky 1971, pp. 141–2.

'ryght grete nobelnesse and also ryght gentylnesse' were a substantial part of the readership for these practical books, it would be a serious mistake to exclude Londoners and aristocratic readers from that readership. Of relevance here is E. F. Jacob's rightful caution that it is wrong to describe the 'gentill men and honest persons', to whom *The book of hawking* is directed, as *country* gentlemen.[47] Sick horses and sick hawks were a steady concern for members of the Cely family, the London merchants whose letters survive from the late fifteenth century. Two London merchants who compiled miscellanies for their own use included the grafting treatises in them. As for aristocratic readers, we have the fact that many of the hawking and hunting treatises are associated with noble figures, especially *The master of game*, which was originally made for the future Henry V.

A translation of Palladius's *De re rustica*, in rime royal, was commissioned by Henry V's brother, Humfrey, Duke of Gloucester. Aware, perhaps, of the interest in the treatise by Geoffrey of Bologna and of the value of making all of Palladius available to English readers, including persons on his own estates, Humfrey commissioned this work not simply as a humanistic exercise. That it was intended for practical use is evident from the apparatus in the dedication copy, of around 1440–5: arabic folio numbers and stanza letters in the text correspond to those found with entries alphabetically arranged in a *tabula* at the front of the volume.[48] The other copies, of about 1445 and 1450,[49] preserve the apparatus, which facilitated access to specific information within a somewhat bulky work.[50]

The royal duke may also have commissioned the *Book of nurture* by John Russell, who styled himself a sometime servant with Humfrey, Duke of Gloucester. This rime royal treatise on household service and good conduct uses the same fictional structure as the *Walter*: instructions to a youth from an older man. It is likely that the Anglo-Norman *Walter* and the related *Seneschausy* were models for this book which, like the latter, sets forth the duties and responsibilities of household officers, as well as providing, like *Walter*, detailed practical information – in this instance, about wines, cookery and carving. Its preservation in five manuscripts, of different character, its possible influence on *The Book of courtesy*,[51] and the abbreviated version printed twice by Wynkyn de Worde as *The boke of*

---

47. Jacob 1944, p. 19.   48. Bodleian, ms. Duke Humfrey d.2.
49. Glasgow UL, ms. Hunter 104 (T.5.6), and Bodleian, ms. Add. A.369, respectively.
50. Bodleian, ms. Duke Humfrey d.2; De la Mare 1985a.   51. BL, Sloane ms. 1986.

keruynge, in 1508 and 1513, and repeatedly thereafter, indicate how well Russell's *Book of nurture* was regarded in its time.

Of the five manuscripts in which the *Book of nurture* is found, three have other works produced under aristocratic patronage. One (1475–1500) contains John Lydgate's *Lyf of our lady*, commissioned by Henry V.[52] Another (1450–75) contains, along with the *Canterbury Tales*, Lancastrian and Yorkist writings by Sir John Fortescue, and a poem celebrating Edward IV's return to the throne in 1471.[53] A third (1450–75) contains *Secrees of the old philosoffres* – a rime royal version of *Secretum secretorum*, begun by Lydgate and completed by Benedict Burgh for Henry VI – and the prose translation of Vegetius's *De re militari* made for Thomas IV, tenth Lord Berkeley, in 1408.[54]

Mention of the latter translation brings us to the other form of practical book to be discussed in this chapter – the military manual. The authors of these treatises, drawing heavily on Vegetius and bringing his work up to date, had a common purpose with the Calais parson who turned Vegetius's treatise into rime royal as *Knyghthode and bataile*: 'wele it is, a werreour / To have aswel good crafte as grete vigour'.[55] The 1408 Vegetius and its successors contain detailed information about such matters as the selection and preparation of warriors; officers and their responsibilities; movements and strategies of armies; and engines of war. Though they share an obvious didactic purpose with the treatises discussed previously, the military manuals represent an entirely different kind of practical book for their readers, as is obvious when we consider the circumstances in which they were produced and the forms in which they were preserved.

Thomas, Lord Berkeley, patron of the 1408 Vegetius, was a Lancastrian who had been in the service of Richard II and then served Henry IV in wars with the Welsh. The collocation of this text and another work of Lancastrian patronage, the Lydgate–Burgh *Secrees of the old philosoffres*, occurs in five miscellanies.[56] Other aspects of the miscellanies containing the Vegetius point to a somewhat different readership from that of the manuals on hawking, hunting and horses, and to a readership that saw these works differently. Five miscellanies contain lavish decorations, including coats of arms, which attest to the pride of their

52. BL, Harl. ms. 4011.   53. BL, Royal ms. 17.D.xv.   54. BL, Sloane ms. 2027.
55. Dyboski and Arend, 1935, lines 262–3.
56. BL, Sloane ms. 2027 (noted above), Add. ms. 14408 (1473); Lansdowne ms. 285 (*c.* 1470);
    Bodleian, Laud Misc. ms. 416 (1459); PML, ms. M775 (*c.* 1470).

owners.[57] Obviously, these miscellanies are not meant for use in the stable or mews.

Early owners of three of these manuscripts had their origins in the provincial gentry: Douce 291, owned by the Chalons (or possibly Bamfield) family of Devon; Lansdowne 285, assumed to be the 'Grete Boke' of John Paston II; Morgan M775, owned by John Astley of Leicestershire. The latter two gentlemen, as is well known, spent much of their time in London. The first owners of Douce 291 may have been connected with the John Chalons who killed Louis de Bueuil in a joust held before Charles VII in Tours, 5 February 1446.[58] If so, three of the manuscripts were owned by courtiers of gentry background, one by Richard III and Ann Neville,[59] and another possibly by Thomas Lord Berkeley.[60]

Aristocratic and royal interest in Vegetius is apparent in two other works derived from his treatise. *Knyghthode and bataile* was originally presented to Henry VI; the revised dedication to Edward IV in two copies suggests that it continued to enjoy royal esteem after Henry's passing. *The boke of fayttes of armes and of chyualrye* was Caxton's translation of *Les faits d'armes et de chevalerie*, compiled by Christine de Pisan from Vegetius, and Honoré Bonet's *L'arbre des batailles*, as well as from other classical and medieval sources. In a colophon, Caxton explained that the translation and printing were commissioned by Henry VII on 24 January 1489 and intended for a very wide audience: the King desired its printing 'to thende that euery gentylman born to armes & all manere men of werre captayns / soldiours / vytayllers & all other shold haue knowledge how they ought to behaue them in the fayttes of warre & of bataylles'. Caxton adds, 'in myn oppinyon it is as necessary a boke & as requysite as ony may be for euery estate hye & lowe that entende to the fayttes of werre'.[61]

Whereas *Knyghthode and bataile* was presented to the King by one of his subjects, *Fayttes* was presented to his subjects by the King. Christine's intention, as expressed by Caxton – 'I entende not to treat but to the most playn and entendible langage that I shal mowe / to that ende that the doctryne gyuen by many auctors . . . may be to alle men clere and entendible'[62] – must have suited the purpose of raising national awareness of the nature, necessity and practical workings of war at a crucial

---

57. PML, ms. M775; Oxford, Magdalen Coll., ms. 30 (*c.*1450); Bodleian, Digby ms. 233 (*c.* 1450), Douce ms. 291 (*c.* 1440); BL, Royal ms. 18.A.XII (*c.* 1480).
58. BL, Lansdowne ms. 285, fols. 48r–52r.   59. BL, Royal ms. 18.A.XII.
60. BL, Royal ms. 18.A.XII; Bodleian, ms. Digby 233; see Lester 1988; Hanna 1989.
61. Fol. S5r.   62. Fol. A1v.

moment. The King's meeting with Caxton in January 1489 took place just as a truce with France, negotiated after Henry's accession in 1485, was about to lapse and just a few days after Henry had dispatched emissaries, on 19 January, to negotiate a marital contract between Prince Arthur and Catherine of Aragon, which anticipated a joint campaign against France. Henry's third parliament, convened on 13 January, was considering a request for a grant of £100,000 to permit the King to protect Brittany from a forced union with France. In the printed book, which was completed on 14 July, Caxton referred pointedly to the Anglo-French conflict, praising Henry, 'whom I byseche almyghty god to preserue / kepe / & contynue in his noble & most redoubted enterpryses as wel in bretayn / flaundres & other placis that he may haue victorie honour / & renommee to his perpetual glorye'.[63]

Prior to *Fayttes*, Caxton had published, in 1480, one work that might be described as a practical book – *Frensshe Englissh*, or *The doctrine to learn French and English*[64] – probably at the request of merchants, for whom this pre-Berlitz phrase manual is clearly intended. In 1485, William de Machlinia had printed three editions of a plague treatise, translated from a Latin redaction of a treatise now attributed to Johannes Jacobi (d. 1384), of the University of Montpellier, and formerly attributed to Benedictus Kamisius, Kamintus, Kanutus or Kanuti.[65] In addition, of course, the Schoolmaster Printer had issued *The book of hawking* in 1486.

It is reasonable to suppose that the success of these practical books produced by English printers had some part in Henry's commissioning the printing of *Fayttes*. De Machlinia's press, which regularly produced year-books and books of statutes and, in 1486, had printed the papal bull confirming Henry's marriage to Elizabeth of York, was familiar to the King. The successful reception of De Machlinia's editions of the plague treatise would have received particular notice from Henry if, as is sometimes thought, these editions were a response to an onset of the sweating sickness that occurred after Bosworth. So, too, the publication of *The book of hawking* would not have escaped the notice of a king intensely interested in hunting and hawking. An awareness that these books had been successfully received may account for Henry's expectation that Caxton's *Fayttes* would reach a wide readership from the aristocracy and middle classes – 'euery gentylman born to armes & all manere men of werre captayns / soldiours / vytayllers'.

63. Fol. S5v.   64. *STC* 24865.   65. *STC* 4589–91; Pickett 1994.

Henry VII's interest in hawking and hunting, and in printing, invites speculation as to the possibility of royal or, at least, courtly patronage of the 1496 edition of *The book of hawking* by Wynkyn de Worde. At least two copies of this edition were printed on vellum, probably for wealthy patrons.[66] Production costs for the book must have been high, in part because the fishing treatise with its illustrations – a half-page cut of an angler pulling a fish from a stream and six smaller cuts of tools and tackle – increased the size of the book. Then, too, there would have been the cost of making these cuts and of new cuts of the coats-of-arms in the heraldry treatise, as well as another showing a group of nobles and huntsmen with a falcon and hounds.[67] The presence of the latter, along with a Tudor emblem that appears for the first time in the 1496 volumes of statutes for 11 Henry VII, encourages speculation about a courtly patron.[68] Finally, the red printing and colouring by hand according to the printer's instructions must have added to the cost of each copy.

Not long after this second printing of *The book of hawking*, the quarto edition*s* – such as the 'lytyll plaunflet' to which De Worde alluded in the colophon at the end of the fishing treatise – became a significant part of the output from his press. A quarto edition of two or three quires, in 4s and 6s, was ideal for issuing such works as the treatises on equine medicine and grafting, for these printed tracts could be assembled into miscellanies that addressed all the interests of a reader or a familiar circle. With little effort, a compiler might assemble a miscellany consisting of printed books – not only of such practical books, but also of devotional books and romances – that would rival any of the known manuscript miscellanies that contain the equine medical treatise.[69]

The Schoolmaster Printer of St Albans and Wynkyn de Worde, whose editions of *The book of hawking* were off-the-rack miscellanies, were not alone in recognizing how much their contemporaries desired to have compilations of practical books. Among their continental counterparts who produced such works was Adriaen van Berghen, who printed *Arnold's chronicle* (Antwerp, 1503?) – a miscellany compiled by Richard Arnold, a London haberdasher.[70] Along with the first printed text of the grafting treatise, receipts for making gunpowder and ypocras, and the earliest copy of 'The Ballad of the Nut-Brown Maid',[71] the volume contains lists of names of London officers, oaths of office for civic officials,

---

66. Now in JRUL and BL.   67. Hodnett 982.   68. *STC* 9349, 9353, 9354; Keiser 1986.
69. For information on miscellanies made up of printed books, see Needham 1986a, pp. 69–80.
70. *STC* 782.   71. IMEV 467.

and other documents and information of value for London merchants, especially those engaged in international trade. Scattered throughout the volume are sample documents that, taken together, comprise a formulary.

This printed miscellany is similar in many respects to other metropolitan miscellanies or commonplace books. One, of about 1470, best known for the unique text of *Gregory's chronicle*, contains a medical treatise and several small pieces on hawking and hunting, which also appear in *The book of hawking*.[72] For another, of 1520–36, Richard Hill, a London Grocer, drew upon *Arnold's chronicle* for various texts, including 'The Nut-Brown Maid' and the treatise on grafting.[73] From another source, Hill obtained a portion of the *Boke of marschalsi*. In this compilation, as in other London miscellanies, treatises on such matters as grafting and equine medicine represent a much smaller proportion of the volume than in the miscellanies described above. Nevertheless, it is clear that among Londoners there was an audience for such works.

In view of their wide appeal, it is surprising to find that the record of surviving printed books suggests that early English printers gave very limited attention to practical books. Perhaps the printers overlooked opportunities to bring these works to a well-established audience, but it is as likely that the record is wholly misleading. Survival of only one or two copies of a pamphlet edition, in some cases the survival of only a few leaves from an edition, must make us wary of relying on the bibliographical record of extant copies. So, too, long gaps between printings of a pamphlet invite suspicions that intervening editions have not survived. After all, these pamphlets, even if bound up with other materials, may have been kept in circumstances that ensured a relatively short life.

The record of printed versions of *The proprytees and medycynes for hors* is somewhat problematic, and it is likely that editions have vanished without trace. Wynkyn de Worde's quarto edition first appeared around 1497 and was reprinted a few years later, around 1502. More than six decades separate the latter from the next edition on record, issued around 1565 by William Copland.[74] De Worde's two editions are extant only in unique copies, and the copy of the *c*.1502 edition lacks the third and last quire (which may have contained other material). Three copies of

---

72. BL, Egerton ms. 1995.   73. Oxford, Balliol Coll., ms. 354.
74. Wynkyn de Worde's first edition, although dated '*c*. 1525' in *STC* 20439.5, was shown to be printed in or about 1497 in Christie's catalogue 8.7.1998, lot 7. This edition preceded, therefore, De Worde's second edition, *STC* 20439.3, by about five years. William Copland's edition is *STC* 20439.7.

Copland's edition are extant, but two seem to be imperfect. Unknown until recently was an edition issued by John King in 1560 under the title *A treatyse: contaynynge the orygynall causes, and occasions of the diseases, growynge on horses*,[75] which represents another textual tradition than that found in the De Worde – Copland printed editions. King's edition had gone unnoticed because the unique copy is in a somewhat remote (and unlikely) archive, the Clark Art Institute in Williamstown, Massachusetts. Large portions of the treatise were incorporated into Gervase Markham's equine treatise, *Markham's maister-peece* (1609),[76] and it seems clear that Markham was not drawing upon any of the known printed editions. The evidence of interest in the treatise makes it hard to believe that, from 1525 until 1560, the early printers would have ignored it. Consultation of manuscripts that preserved it, probably including some that are now lost, and compilation of others not now known may have continued during those years. That, however, does not preclude the possibility of lost or still unknown printed editions.

The text of *The craft of grafting and planting of trees* included in the 1530 Antwerp printing of *Arnold's chronicle* was the basis for a quarto edition, probably printed in Antwerp, about 1505.[77] Of this latter edition, only one leaf exists. As noted above, an abbreviated version of the grafting treatise was circulating in manuscript with the English *Walter*, and De Worde printed this combination of texts in a quarto pamphlet (1508?), of which only one copy is known.[78] De Worde issued a separate text of the grafting treatise in a quarto pamphlet in 1518, of which only the first quire is extant,[79] and it appeared again in a reprint, about 1525, of *Arnold's chronicle*, by Peter Treveris.[80] Four decades later, a long hiatus for such a work, William Copland issued quarto editions of the treatise in around 1563 and in 1565.[81] In Copland's editions are included two other brief treatises: *A lyttle treatyse of the iiii seasons of the yeare, and also of the iiii elementes* and *The fourme and the measure to mete land by*. Probably these same treatises appeared in lost portions of the earlier quarto editions, for they were part of *Arnold's chronicle*.

Two other practical books printed in quarto also have problematic publication records. Richard Pynson produced *The boke of cokery* in 1500, and De Worde apparently reprinted it in 1510. Only one copy of Pynson's edition and only one leaf from De Worde's are known. *The boke of keruyng*, a reduced version of John Russell's *Book of nurture*, was printed by De

75. *STC* 24237.5.   76. *STC* 17376.   77. *STC* 5952.5.   78. *STC* 25007.
79. *STC* 5953.   80. *STC* 783.   81. *STC* 5954 and 5954.2.

Worde in 1508 and reprinted in 1513; it was then reprinted *c.* 1560 and *c.* 1570 for Abraham Veale.[82] Again a long gap between the printings of the earlier and later editions defies credulity, as does the idea that the printed cookery book disappeared from sight, when there was little to replace it before the last quarter of the century.

The problematic nature of the printing record is evident in still other instances of excessively long gaps between editions of practical books. The *Governal of health*, which circulated widely in manuscripts,[83] was printed in a quarto by Caxton in 1490,[84] reprinted by De Worde about 1506 and again about 1530.[85] Of the 1506 edition only one copy, and of the last edition only an imperfect copy are extant. In 1497 De Worde printed a quarto edition of *A lytell treatyse for to lerne Englysshe and Frensshe*[86] – a successor to Walter of Bibbesworth's *Tretiz* and Caxton's *Frensshe Englissh*. There is only one known copy of this edition and of a reprint by Richard Pynson (1500?).[87] From a later edition of about 1533, attributed to Robert Wyer, only three leaves are extant. In these instances, the record, with its long gaps between the second and third editions, probably does not reflect the true history of either work.

Perhaps the most telling example is the record of *The book of hawking*, which is not likely to be complete, as Eloise Pafort argued long ago.[88] After the folio editions printed in 1486 and 1496, no other edition is known until about 1518, when Wynkyn issued it in quarto;[89] one complete copy and a fragment of three leaves attest to this edition. No other full edition is known before that printed about 1547, of which two variant copies exist.[90] However, there exist single copies of De Worde's separate editions of the hunting book (1530?)[91] and of the fishing book (1533?).[92] This record is even more difficult to accept when we consider that between about 1550 and about 1565 six editions were printed, one in a variant form.

The publication of at least twenty editions of John Fitzherbert's *Book of husbandry* between 1523 and 1598 points to a substantial, steady, even an avid readership for the practical book throughout the sixteenth century.[93] In many ways a culmination of the tradition of late medieval English farming literature, as well as a departure from it, the *Book of husbandry* is closely related to the late medieval miscellanies described above.

---

82. *STC* 3289–3291.5.   83. CUL, ms. Ll.1.18, for example.   84. *STC* 12138.
85. *STC* 12139–9.5.   86. *STC* 24866.   87. *STC* 24867.   88. Pafort 1952–3.
89. *STC* 3309.5.   90. *STC* 3310, 3310.3.   91. *STC* 3313.3.   92. *STC* 3313.5.
93. *STC* 10994–1004.

As we might expect, Fitzherbert's book has instructions for ploughing and planting, for the care of sheep, cattle and horses, and for trimming and grafting trees. At the same time, the entire work is informed by a moral concern; for example, an early chapter among those devoted to sowing begins, 'There is a sede that is called discressyon and yf a husbande haue of that sede and myngle it amonge his other cornes they wyll growe moche the better.'[94] The last 18 of the 65 leaves in the 1523 edition are devoted to moral and spiritual concerns, with instructions for moderate living, alms-deeds and proper penitence. Concerning the latter, the author writes, 'We can nat do more sharpar sorrowes to the deuyls than whan we wayle or wepe in confession & doinge of penaunce.'[95] John Whittocksmead, whose miscellany contained the *De spiritu Guidonis* and a confessional manual, would have felt comfortable with such a book as this.

Apparently, Fitzherbert, who had been trained in the law, was familiar not only with the English *Walter*, but also with the Anglo-Norman version and other thirteenth-century treatises on estate management. His *Book of surveying*, which treats the valuation and improvement of manors and thus complements the *Book of husbandry*, treats subjects that had been excluded from the English *Walter*. Translating the *Extenta manerii* and using it as the basis for his *Book of surveying*, Fitzherbert was extending and developing the tradition of the earlier treatises.

His close familiarity with the English *Walter*, which had been printed at least once in his lifetime, is certain when Fitzherbert addresses the question, 'wheder is better a plough of horses or a plough of oxen'. His statement, 'And oxen woll plowe in tough clay / and vpon hilly ground wher as horses woll stande styll',[96] echoes the English *Walter*: '& the grounde be tough / oxen shall werke where your hors shall stande styll'.[97] His final conclusion, appropriate to the woodcut on the title-page showing a team of oxen pulling a plough – 'all thynges consydred / the plough of oxen is moche more profytable than the plough of horses'[98] – also echoes that of *Walter*: 'The plough of oxen is better than the plough of hors.'[99]

Fitzherbert, nevertheless, offers a more detailed, methodological and comprehensive survey of agriculture than *Walter* and one which is self-consciously addressed to a national readership. The first chapter, 'Dyuers maners of plowes', illustrates an awareness of the wide readership

94. *STC* 10994, fol. A8r.   95. *STC* 10994, fol. M1r.   96. *STC* 11005, fol. A5v.
97. *STC* 25007, fol. A4r.   98. *STC* 11005, fol. A6r.   99. *STC* 25007, fol. A4r.

Fitzherbert expected his book to reach: 'ther is many maner of groundes and soyle. Some white cley / some reed cley / some grauell or chilturfe some sande / some meane yerth / some medeled with marle / and in many places hygh ground / and one plough wyll nat serue in all places'.[100] A recognition that husbandmen in diverse regions faced diverse problems and would seek solutions for them in his book never falters. Thus, Fitzherbert attempts, and achieves, a remarkable comprehensiveness in his treatment of all aspects of farming. To illustrate, one need only turn to the account of 'dyuers maners of wedes',[101]where the descriptions of weeds are unprecedented in thoroughness and detail. Similarly, the account of maladies that beset sheep and cattle, and the remedies for each, goes far beyond the corresponding portions of *Walter*. Somewhat surprising then is the fact that, after describing the equine maladies and implying that horse leeches are not to be trusted, Fitzherbert wittily remarks,

> It were also conuenyent to shewe medycens and remedyes for all these dyseases and sorances / but it wolde be to long a processe at this tyme: for it wolde be as moche as halfe this boke. And I haue nat the parfet connynge nor the experyence to shewe medycens and remedyes for them all. And also the horse leche wold natte be content therwith: for it myght fortune to hurt or hynder their ocupacyon.[102]

Perhaps his knowledge of printed editions of *The proprytees and medycynes for hors* explains his reluctance. Perhaps too the fact that his careful discussion of grafting does not duplicate information found in *The planting and grafting of trees* indicates that he knew of the ready availability of that work.

Attesting to the value and appeal of Fitzherbert's book are the annotations early readers made in their copies. The owners of an edition printed about 1540 by Thomas Berthelet,[103] and of an edition printed about 1552 by Nicholas Hill for John Walley,[104] both found the list of weeds important enough to mark carefully for future reference. For the owner of the latter volume, this subject was serious enough to lead to a note on the time for weeding corn at the end of the text. The specific conditions of his land evidently explain a marginal note – 'no[ta] when to sowe vpon gravelye and sandye ground' – near a text on sowing barley. Marginal jottings in manuscripts and early printed books indicate that

---

100. *STC* 11005, fol. A2r.   101. *STC* 11005, fols. C1v–2r.   102. *STC* 11005, fol. G1v.
103. *STC* 10996; CUL, Syn 8.54.221.   104. *STC* 11000; BL, 969.a.51.

their readers delighted in proverbs; thus they marked such proverbial expressions as 'It is an old saynge the oxe is neuer wo tyll he to the harowe go.'[105]

Access to the contents of the *Book of husbandry* was facilitated by a *tabula*, placed at the end in the 1523 edition and moved to the beginning in all later editions. Pynson provided folio numbers for the chapters in the *tabula* and, in the text, large and prominent folio numbers in the upper corner of each recto leaf, and subsequent publishers provided comparable apparatus. No doubt John Fitzherbert expected the book to be used for the kind of quick reference that this apparatus supported, but he offered other advice concerning the use of the book to 'a yong gentyl-man that intendeth to thriue', advice that suggests how important practical books had become for an English gentleman:

> I auyse hym to gete a copy of this present boke and to rede it from the beginnyng vnto thendyng / wherby he may percuyue the chapiters and contentes of the same / and by reason of oft redynge he may waxe parfet what shuld be done at all seasons ... Ryght so a man shalbe made wyse / nat all onely by himself but by his oft redyng. And so may this yonge gentylman: acording to the season of the yere / rede to his seruauntes what chapyter he woll.[106]

This scene of idealized domestic harmony is an appropriate place to conclude this chapter. With *The Book of husbandry* in hand, rather than a grammar-book, the young gentleman becomes the schoolmaster before the assembled servants, on whose memory he must depend. Perhaps Fitzherbert was supposing that the servants of a gentleman would be completely unlettered or, at least, not sufficiently lettered to find their way in his book. Perhaps, too, Fitzherbert was supposing that the young gentleman would want to protect from heavy and ill use a book of intrinsic and enduring worth, as well as some cost, of which only a few hundred copies would have been printed in 1523. Even for all his optimism, Fitzherbert could not have foreseen, when those first copies of *The Book of husbandry* issued from the press in 1523, that so many more hundreds, even thousands, of copies would become available in the next seventy-five years. That the success of the work probably exceeded Fitzherbert's hopes or imaginings is testimony to what we have seen: the importance of practical books for gentlemen by the first quarter of the sixteenth century.

<hr />

105. *STC* 10994, fol. B2v.   106. *STC* 10994, fol. H3r-v.

24

Devotional literature

MARY C. ERLER

In examining the books which both manifested popular devotion and guided it, two elements are particularly intriguing. Investigation of the audience for such books, their readers and owners, furnishes some notion of the climate in which the reading took place, and hence gives a sense of what we may call the culture of religious reading. This understanding can be enlarged as well by consideration of how devotional books were employed, since the range of cultural uses which attached themselves to these texts and to their accompanying pictures is remarkably wide.

*

To a substantial extent, devotional reading was everyone's reading. Because this is so, ownership of devotional texts does not correlate so neatly as we might wish with extraordinary piety. Certain texts, in fact, are found very widely and somewhat indiscriminately in male and female, lay and clerical hands. The predominance of religious literature among the books that we know to have been owned by Margaret of York, for instance, may be an indication that she was genuinely very devout, but it may also have caused her piety to be over-emphasized by modern writers. The libraries of many fifteenth-century lay people show a similar preponderance of spiritual books.[1] Possession of these volumes signals membership in a common religious culture, an affirmation which is sometimes more powerful than individual interests. The most important such book, because the most widely owned, is the book of hours or primer, which assumed an extraordinary centrality in popular culture.

The book's core was the hours of the Virgin; these were preceded by a calendar and by set passages from the four Gospels, and were followed (in the book's sparest form) by the seven penitential psalms, the litany of the

1. N. Morgan 1992, p. 71; Cavanaugh 1980, pp. 9–11; Tanner 1984, p. 41.

saints, and the office of the dead.[2] Originating in the middle of the thirteenth century, the book of hours achieved its most extreme popularity over two centuries later,[3] perhaps due to the accelerating effect of printing on a fashion already strongly in place.

While the coming of English printing in the latter part of the fifteenth century placed more books of hours in more hands, manuscript primers continued to be produced simultaneously with printed ones well into the sixteenth century, both appearing in immense quantities. No count of surviving manuscript *horae* according to the Use of Sarum (the rite used in England) has ever been attempted. They form part of a much larger group whose numbers likewise have only been estimated. A very partial tabulation of existing manuscript *horae* from all countries and uses would include the British Library's collection of about 400 examples;[4] the Bibliothèque Nationale de France's holdings of about 350; the Walters Art Gallery's approximately 300; and the more than 300 copies scattered throughout 7 additional American collections.[5] This total of nearly 1,400 manuscript primers represents only a fraction of those which remain, and a still smaller fraction of those which once existed.

Christopher de Hamel has suggested that the number of manuscript survivors may be greater than the number of remaining printed copies, though at least 760 editions of books of hours were published between 1485 and 1530.[6] Were we to guess conservatively that each edition comprised 300 copies, about a quarter of a million printed *horae* would have been published in this half-century. Even at the very end of this period, in the 1530s when religious change was well advanced, the book of hours remained at the heart of most peoples' spiritual lives. In this decade, John Rastell suggested that heterodox ideas might receive the widest possible dissemination if they could be inserted in books of hours since everyone possessed such books. He wrote to Cromwell: 'People are loth to buy any such [reforming] books, and if they be given them they will scantly read them; but when the matter in English is put in primers, which they bring

2. Harthan 1977, pp. 14–19; Calkins 1983, pp. 243ff. Sutton and Visser-Fuchs 1990, pp. 41–66, for a detailed description and explanation of the contents of a particular primer: Richard III's (Lambeth ms. 474, *c.* 1420).
3. Delaissé 1974, p. 203; for a brief overview of ms. *horae* production by country, see Wieck 1988, pp. 28–32; De Hamel 1986, pp. 168–9.   4. De Hamel 1986, p. 150.
5. Wieck 1988, p. 32.
6. De Hamel 1986, p. 164. On the basis of printed library catalogues, Bohatta 1924 lists 1,585 *horae* editions in the fifteenth and sixteenth centuries, mostly French. For the period 1485–1530, the number would be about 1,325 (substantially larger than De Hamel's estimate of 760 editions), according to Winn 1993, p. 337.

with them to church, they shall, in a manner, be compelled to read them.'[7]

If books of hours thus cross the line separating orthodoxy and heterodoxy, their appeal transcends the boundaries of class as well. As accoutrements of wealth, they were familiar objects of connoisseurship. Sixty years after the introduction of printing in England, the 1537 will of Elizabeth, Countess of Oxford, evokes such luxurious manuscript possessions: 'Item I give and bequathe to the Lady Surrey a booke of golde having dyvers leffys of golde with the salutatcion of Our Lady att the begynnyng . . . To the Lady Anne Veer . . . a boke of golde of the valewe of C.s with the picture of the crucifix, and the salutation of our ladye to be newly made . . . Item I give and bequeath to my suster Dame Mary . . . my booke of golde sett with perle'.[8]

Records of such rich books, and the books themselves, have come down to us plentifully. The fainter traces left by humbler books of this kind are scarce, although the desire for them can occasionally be glimpsed. In 1500, Avis Godfrey was charged with stealing a book called a 'premar' from Elizabeth Sekett, servant to William Ward, outside the London church of St Margaret, New Fish Street. The defendant asserted that she had found the book in Pudding Lane. Because she was a pauper, the case was dismissed.[9] This book's unexpected passage between two poor women, whether due to chance or theft, echoes the more controlled transmission of books between friends and relatives which is familiar from wills. In such passages, as in the exchange between Avis Godfrey and Elizabeth Sekett, the book's significance is difficult to interpret. In some exchanges it represents a personal talisman, in others a spiritual guide, while in still other transmissions it is present as an economic counter.

The locale of Avis Godfrey's act might point to a heterodox context in which reading was particularly important. St Margaret's was a lively parish which included some members not entirely orthodox: Joan Baker, who abjured Lollardy in 1511 and Richard Hunne, who defended her and whose copy of the English Bible lay open in the church for all to read.[10] These two books, Richard Hunne's and Avis Godfrey's, raise the question of literacy. Could many St Margaret's parishioners read Hunne's Bible, and could Avis Godfrey read the primer she found or stole?

7. LP Henry VIII, VII, no. 1073, undated, catalogued '1534'.
8. Plomer 1904, pp. 119–20. A gold-initialled book given to the Countess by her husband survives as Bodl. ms. Rawl. liturg. f. 37, reproduced in Doyle 1958, plate II (fols. 105v-106r).
9. Hale 1847, p. 71, Commissary Court of London, f. 270.   10. Brigden 1989, pp. 98, 102.

It seems clear that a wide range of gradations must have existed along a spectrum from 'litteratus' to 'illiteratus'.[11] The non-literate Margery Kempe, for instance, was injured while in church, 'hir boke in hir hand'.[12] Various explanations have been offered for the undoubted ownership of books by persons who, other evidence suggests, could not read: for instance, that the books had symbolic value as sacred objects, and in this way should be considered parallel to sacramentals.[13] Other work has centred on the various forms which reading took. The distinction offered between phonetic and comprehension literacy, for instance, suggests that Margery, and others as well, could decode Latin syllable by syllable and pronounce it, though unable to read and understand silently.[14]

Sarum primers provide an especially suggestive field for such inquiries, since, despite the addition of more vernacular elements in the sixteenth century, primers printed for the English market, until the 1530s, remained mostly in Latin. The 1408 constitutions of Clarendon, formulated in a period of anxiety about Lollardy, had forbidden the translation of scripture into the vernacular. They were thus responsible for an anomalous situation in the sixteenth century when English books of hours, unlike those printed in France, for instance, continued to be heavily Latinate.[15] That this Latin book remained so long at the centre of religious life for most people, even those usually considered non-Latinate, argues some partial, adaptive, complex, accommodation to a language deeply familiar to the ear, moderately familiar to the eye.

The history of the book of hours in England represents only a comparatively small corner of the book's larger history. The great centres of manuscript production were France and later Flanders, and the story of the book of hours in England is at least as much about foreign books' importation and subsequent ownership as it is about the local production of books. In fact, the careers of Englishmen abroad, 'charting the errands of war and peace', can provide a kind of index to their book acquisitions, and the history of several notable books of hours illustrates their owners' peregrinations.[16]

Unlike French or Flemish *horae*, English fifteenth-century books of hours at present suffer from the lack of an overview, which would survey their illumination and consider their methods of production. Nevertheless some notable examples of fifteenth-century *horae* can be

11. Bäuml 1980; D. N. Bell 1995, p. 60; Clanchy 1993, chapter 7; Trapp above, pp. 32–9.
12. Meale 1993a, p. 133.   13. Duffy 1992, pp. 214–17.   14. Saenger 1987.
15. D. M. Rogers 1970, p. 356.   16. K. Harris 1989, pp. 180–1.

mentioned, books either made in England or made by English artists. Like the Countess of Oxford's 'books of gold', they represent the most sophisticated work of their period. The best-known illuminator of the early part of the century, the London-based Herman Scheerre, an artist from Cologne or Bruges, contributed to several remarkable *horae* (see fig. 2.1).[17] In the middle of the century, William Abell or his posited atelier worked on the Warwick Psalter-Hours, made before 1446.[18] A little later, between 1450 and 1460, the anonymous 'Caesar master' decorated a Sarum book of hours with his exuberant borders.[19] At the turn of the century, Simon Bening and the Master of James IV of Scotland, probably Gerard Horenbout, may be added to the listing of *horae* artists (see fig. 2.7).[20] Except for Abell, these artists were foreign, and it has been suggested that this highest level of commissioned work was reserved for non-native illuminators while, as the century progressed, Englishmen worked on manuscripts less spectacular and less prestigious than these devotional ones.[21]

During the last quarter of the fifteenth century and somewhat earlier, increased demand for books of hours elicited two responses, one involving manuscripts, the other printed books. The first of these was the widespread production of Flemish manuscript books of hours for the English market. Created mainly at Ghent and Bruges and characterized by their *trompe l'oeil* borders with realistic birds and flowers, these books have been described as expensive souvenirs of travel abroad. In the last quarter of the fifteenth century, English merchants trading overseas brought home such souvenirs in quantity: over 200 examples survive.[22] They have been thought to be mostly commissioned work, and in this way distinguished from printed *horae* which were made without a particular patron in mind. Recently, however, some standardization in the production of these manuscript books has been suggested: such features include the copying of standard calendars and the assembly of books from uniform units.[23]

Illustrations too were produced singly (and sometimes identically), ready to insert in the book at a late stage of production. One writer sug-

17. BL, Add. ms. 16998; Bodleian, ms. Lat. lit. F.2; and others; Kuhn 1940; Spriggs 1974; Marks and Morgan 1981, pp. 27–8, 30, 103; Scott 1996, nos. 21–2; Alexander, above, pp. 47, 50, 52.
18. PML, ms. M.893; Alexander 1972; Christianson 1989c, pp. 91–2, 96–9; Marks and Morgan 1981, pp. 30, 31–3, 114; Scott 1996, no. 88, who disagrees with the attribution to Abell; Alexander, above, p. 49.   19. BL, Add. ms. 62523; Scott 1996, no. 100.
20. Kren 1983, *passim*; Alexander, above, p. 56.   21. Marks and Morgan 1981, p. 30.
22. De Hamel 1983, p. 33; N. Rogers 1982; Alexander above, p. 52.
23. K. Harris 1989, pp. 181–3.

gests: 'Maybe the patron could go to a bookshop and actually choose from stock the miniatures that he or she would like inserted in a particular manuscript.'[24] From 1426 to 1500, the city of Bruges attempted to regularize the illustration of such books. Legislation was passed in 1457 ruling that those wishing to place images in books must be citizens of Bruges who had paid a 40s fee. A number of single-leaf miniatures survive carrying the artist's stamp, all in books of hours, mostly made for export.[25] These stamps are certificates that the miniatures were legally produced; they are also a sign of the desire to increase production as well as to regulate it. Because of the extreme popularity of books of hours, it is in these books that we might expect techniques for increased production to have been developed, and it is in such books that the evidence can be read.

The second event which focuses our attention on books of hours for the English market is Caxton's decision to print the Sarum hours, a decision made at the very opening of his English printing career. Whether in fact his Sarum primer was printed in Bruges or in Westminster has long been considered an open question. Recent work based on type analysis, however, has shown that the book's compositorial practices are found only in Bruges-printed books, never in Westminster ones. Thus, if the Sarum hours were printed in Bruges, the book might be assigned to 1475.[26]

The 'Englishness' of Caxton's first major project, the Canterbury Tales, has been noted.[27] His decision to print the Sarum hours, a book for an English readership, may partake of similar motives. Significantly, Caxton did not at this point embark on a programme to make other Sarum service books available in English. With the exception of the earliest Sarum breviary, issued in the Southern Netherlands about 1475, no other printed Sarum service books appeared until 1483. Caxton may rightly have seen the individual demand for horae as larger and more attractive than the institutional demand for missals, graduals and hymnals, with their difficult technical requirements. The book of hours did not require music printing, was owned most widely, and, in its English form, represented a national market which Caxton would be the first to broach.

If we compare Caxton's printing of an English-use primer to the efforts of his continental contemporaries, we can perhaps see something

24. Alexander 1989, p. 68.   25. Farquhar 1980; Alexander 1992, p. 174 n.30.
26. L. Hellinga 1982, pp. 59–61; STC 15867 has revised its 1477–8 dating to 1476 (III, p. 285).
27. L. Hellinga 1982, p. 101.

of his strategy. Though his was not the first printed book of hours, it was remarkably early. The first such volume of which *ISTC* has a record was published in Rome around 1473 by a printer usually identified as Theobald Schencbecher. In Venice, regular *horae* production started in 1474 (two editions by Nicholas Jenson, three more by him in 1475). Editions appeared at Ferrara in 1475 and Naples in 1476. These were the predecessor and peer editions surrounding Caxton's: none, of course, offered the Sarum rite. His *c.* 1475 Sarum volume was thus among the earliest printed books of hours; it preceded *horae* of various uses brought out in Deventer (1477–9), and Poitiers (1479), Geneva and Speyer (*c.* 1479).[28] Since this summary is based on surviving editions, it can only represent approximately these early books' appearances, but it can provide a general sense of how to place Caxton's book in relation to parallel continental efforts.

The early decision to print the Sarum book of hours produced at least six editions of the book, two of them known only from offsets in other works. These six *horae* might in fact be thought to constitute English printing's first large market success. Their commercial viability was signalled early: in Caxton's lifetime his six editions had to compete with two editions issued abroad, in Paris and Antwerp, and with one published in London.[29]

The same pattern is visible in the career of Caxton's successor, Wynkyn de Worde, whose *horae* dominated the English market for a time, but were challenged both by foreign printers and by other Englishmen. In 1494, though De Worde printed three books of hours, two competing editions from Rouen appeared, as well as a primer commissioned in Venice for sale in London by the Flemish entrepreneurs, Frederic de Egmont and Gerard Barrevelt.[30]

Early primers such as these must have been important in the development of the English wholesale book-trade, since primers' popularity meant that these were the books which retailers would seek to purchase in quantity. The 1494 Venice book which challenged De Worde's productions, for instance, features in a chancery suit where the complainant, James Ravenell of London, Stationer, asserted that four years earlier he bought 'of one Federyke Egemounde douchman as many bokes called

---

28. For dates of continental *horae*, see *ISTC*.
29. Caxton: *STC* 15867, 15868, 15871, 15872. Offsets: Painter 1976; Paris: *STC* 15870 [1488?]; Antwerp: *STC* 15873 [1491–2]; London: *STC* 15869 [1485].
30. Wynkyn de Worde: *STC* 15875, 15876, 15878; Rouen: *STC* 15877, 15879; Venice: *STC* 15874.

prymers vnboundon as amounted to the value of xv s'. If we were to posit a price of three or four pence for an unbound primer, Ravenell would have bought forty-five to sixty copies for resale. Since Egmont's Venice-printed primer appeared in 1494, the suit was probably initiated in 1498. It illustrates the growth of the wholesale market in books, particularly since Ravenell asserted that he settled with Egmont later that year at Nottingham Fair, a venue for the wholesale book trade.[31]

By the next year, 1495, five new Parisian books of hours provided competition for De Worde's *horae*, while at home Pynson had brought out two.[32] From De Worde's time on, the production of printed Sarum *horae* was divided between English-based printers and Frenchmen from Paris and Rouen. Entrepreneurs on both sides of the channel were involved. In a 1498 colophon, the printer Jehan Jehannot identified himself as a member of the University of Paris, living temporarily in England for the purpose of selling books. The colophon appeared in a book of hours, presumably the book he intended to market in England.[33] In London, the merchant grocer William Bretton underwrote two primer editions printed in Paris in 1506 and 1510, for instance, while, until about 1529, the Cologne native Francis Birckman sold *horae* and service books printed for him abroad from his shop in St Paul's Churchyard.[34] So, although production of this English book of hours for an English market was begun by an English printer, its lucrative possibilities meant that his monopoly was soon challenged.

In the end, French editions overwhelmed the English ones. Although the number of surviving texts cannot be a reliable guide to the number which originally existed, it may be suggestive to note that, from before 1500, representatives of twenty-nine Sarum primer editions remain: twelve are English-printed, fifteen French, with one example each from Venice and Antwerp. Thus, in the period of incunable printing, Sarum *horae* seem to have been produced in roughly equal numbers at home and abroad. As time went on the dominance of foreign editions became more pronounced. From the more than fifty years following Caxton's first Sarum primer (*c.* 1475–1527), books of hours for the Use of Sarum survive in ninety-eight editions. Caxton's, De Worde's and Pynson's books

31. PRO, C 1/221/70; *STC* 15874.
32. Paris: *STC* 15880, 15881, 15881.3, 15881.5, 15883; Pynson: *STC* 15873.5 and 15882.
33. *STC* 15888; Pollard and Ehrman 1965, p. 13; Duff 1905, p. 81.
34. *STC* 15903 and 15909; Duff 1905, pp. 14, 18. In a few cases, colophons specify that they were for sale at an English printer's and presumably underwritten by him (J. Notary, two; R. Fakes, one; R. Bankes, one).

account for about one-third of the total (thirty-one), while the rest were printed abroad.

The abrupt cessation after 1528 of De Worde's *horae* printing – an enterprise which had been initiated by Caxton and enthusiastically continued by his successor – requires some explanation. Caxton and De Worde had from the start relinquished the printing of other Sarum liturgical books to foreign printers. Caxton printed no breviaries, for instance, and De Worde produced only three. (By comparison, Francis Birckman commissioned seven editions.) What made De Worde give up printing the apparently successful book of hours? Certainly he had been pressed very hard by Birckman who, starting in 1511, commissioned a series of Paris-printed Sarum *horae* to be sold at his London shop. In the sixteen years between 1511 and 1527, Birckman offered fourteen surviving editions, almost one a year. By contrast, in these years De Worde produced seven editions, only half as many.

Birckman died about 1529 – his last three primers had appeared in 1527 – and it may be that by the time of his death De Worde had already come to some agreement with another foreign printer, François Regnault. It was in 1526, about half a century after Caxton's first Sarum primer, that Regnault began production of the French-printed Sarum primers which were to dominate the English market for the next dozen years. These books feature a systematic attempt to present more vernacular elements: English verse, an English title-page and more English devotional material. Three Regnault editions in 1526, five in 1527, and massive subsequent efforts towards coverage at several economic levels signalled an attempt to sweep the Sarum primer market – a market whose major figures until 1527 were Birckman and De Worde. Though De Worde published a primer in 1528 which survives as a fragment,[35] this was apparently his last effort. Whether he concluded a business arrangement with Regnault or simply conceded defeat in the face of this powerful competition cannot now be known. The presence in Regnault's primers, starting in 1529, of a devotional piece translated by De Worde's associate, Robert Copland, however, might suggest the former interpretation.[36]

These issues of commercial dominance exist side by side with considerations of linguistic dominance (and, after 1534, of religious dominance as well). Though a gradual growth in English elements can be traced in De Worde's primers from 1494 to 1526, it was the Regnault primers

35. *STC*, III, p. 285 (under *STC* 15936).   36. Erler 1984, p. 229.

which systematized these additions into a successful formula. During the years between 1529 and 1538, when his primer production ceased, Regnault maintained two primer 'lines'. His quarto model, of which only four editions survive, retained a Latin title-page, though it included some English material. His smaller-format books, octavo and sextodecimo, used an English title-page and included considerably more English elements. Twenty-three editions of this model exist. Clearly, two different markets were addressed; yet while the movement towards vernacular texts was more successful commercially, Regnault also thought it worthwhile, in this decade whose conclusion saw the final break with Rome, to maintain a somewhat more conservative primer as well. The coming of English in these popular books is thus partly attributable to market factors, and Regnault's evolution of this successful primer may be seen as a response to readers' demand. Though prohibitions on scriptural translation delayed the coming of English in the primer, we may also wonder whether this evolution towards the vernacular might have happened more rapidly if it had not been a foreign printer who held a virtual monopoly on Sarum *horae*.

Commercial, linguistic and religious uniformity were all disarranged with the appearance of the first reforming primer in English in 1529. No copies survive and its impact was perhaps not felt by many at the time, but five years later in 1534 – a watershed year which saw the death of De Worde as well as the rupture of papal authority in the Act of Supremacy – William Marshall's *A Prymer in Englyshe* appeared.[37]

The cultural centrality of books of hours – perhaps due to what Delaissé called their 'more humanized expression of religious feeling' – accounts for the intensity of the reformers' condemnation of them and the seriousness of the efforts to change them. The 'Admonition to the Reader' in Marshall's 1535 *Goodly Prymer* revises and strengthens the largely translated preface of his first primer. It warns against the primers' 'goodly glorious titles [headings], that promyse innumerable dayes, & yeres of pardon, some more, some lesse, to the sayers of suche blasphemous prayers, yea sometyme to the bearers aboute of them' – a reference to the belief in prayers' physical protection. The prayers themselves, such primer staples as the 'Obsecro te', the 'Fifteen Oes', the prayer of St Bernard, and many others, 'of truthe ben of no more alliaunce, consanguinitie, and kynred vnto true prayer, than was Symon Magus, that

37. *STC* 15986.

false man, vnto Symon Peter, that good man, and true seruaunt of Iesu Christ'.[38]

From 1535, when both the *Goodly Prymer* and the first Sarum primer entirely in English were published, diversity in books of hours was the rule. The Sarum primer lost its dominance, becoming one of many, itself available in both English and Latin forms.[39] John Rastell's assessment of the primer's popularity had been written around 1534, before the break with Rome, but even after this defining event the shower of printed primers continued unabated, protean in their doctrinal variety and produced by a new collection of entrepreneurial printers and publishers, English and foreign, reforming and traditional.

Who owned these books of hours? As we have seen, their popularity antedated printing: for instance a study of York lay wills (1321–1500) which contained 107 book bequests shows that the largest number, 53, were primers – almost all, of course, in manuscript.[40] An examination of the figures for early printed *horae*, however, can allow a more precise answer. During the nearly 60 years in which the printed Sarum primer dominated the English market, 130 editions are recorded by *STC* – about 2¹/₂ editions each year between Caxton's first primer and 1534. In view of the numerous editions which register their existence only through a single fragment, it seems likely that many editions have disappeared entirely. Hence an estimate of 3 Sarum primer editions annually, published both at home and abroad, would be a conservative one. Perhaps the reality might be as high as 4 or 5 editions yearly.

Information on the size of *horae* editions is sparse, but, about 1490, Richard Pynson contracted with the London merchant, John Russhe, to print 600 copies each of various service books – diurnals, festivals, missals and primers.[41] In addition, the London customs accounts for 1502–3 show that, in that year, 6 persons imported over 1800 primers (and more primers may be concealed under the general heading 'printed books'). The increments listed in the accounts – 500 primers, 400 primers – perhaps suggest what the size of whole editions might have been.[42]

A conservative estimate, then, both of number of editions and of edition size – 400 or 500 copies (smaller in the earlier years, larger in the sixteenth century) – suggests that around 1,500 primers were produced

38. *STC* 15988, fols. A3, A4.
39. *STC* 15988, 15988a.Butterworth 1953; H. C. White 1951; Lewis 1995.
40. Goldberg 1994, p. 184.   41. Plomer 1909.
42. Plomer 1923–4, pp. 149–50; Kerling 1955; Needham above, p. 159.

annually from the London presses and imported from the continent. (Recent work on the customs accounts may enlarge this total.) To gain an idea of what this number means, we might juxtapose this projected output of books with the population of the capital. Current research on London's size estimates that, at the opening of the sixteenth century, just past the midpoint of the period under consideration, it was a city of about 50,000 people.[43] Although of course books were purchased nationally, from provincial book-sellers and at fairs for instance, the vast majority were bought initially in London. Consequently, at the turn of the century, we might imagine 1 out of every 35 London merchants, wives, artisans and nuns being supplied with a printed Sarum book of hours.

The survival rate of these books is not high. Of the 29 incunable Sarum primer editions registered by *STC*, half (15 editions) are known only from incomplete fragments of a few pages. To put it another way, from these 29 incunable editions, only 35 more-or-less complete books remain. The number of surviving *copies* recorded by *STC* from between 1475 and 1534 is 312. Since *STC* is not a census of all copies, the total number of survivors is higher than this, perhaps by 10 or 20 per cent, and we might judge that about 350 or 375 printed Sarum books of hours now remain.

It is impossible to identify the owners of the very earliest printed books of hours from these survivals, since the first 9 editions are represented, for the most part, only by fragments of a few leaves. Not until De Worde's first 1494 book, printed at the request of Margaret Beaufort, do multiples from a single *horae* edition survive.[44] These 5 copies from one printing, however, allow us to draw some conclusions about this primer's readership.

That Brigittine nuns owned the Lambeth Palace copy of the 1494 primer seems likely since it contains, loose, an early engraving of St Katherine of Sweden, the daughter of the Brigittine foundress. Its inscription, 'ex teneramunda', shows the engraving was commissioned by Dendermonde, a Brigittine abbey in Flanders. This house, Maria Troon, provided shelter for Syon *émigré* nuns at the Dissolution.[45] Slighter evidence associates the Bodleian copy of this primer also with Syon, since it bears the parchment fore-edge tabs which Neil Ker thought characteristic of Syon's library.[46] The calendar only from this

43. Rappaport 1989, p. 61 n. 1.   44. *STC* 15875.
45. Bradshaw 1889, pp. 274–5; Aungier 1840, pp. 97, 100.
46. E.g., from Ker's slips for Ker 1964–87, now in the Bodleian, his description of Bodl Auct. D.3.1 with such tabs and 'cf. Harley 42, Bodl. 630, Rawl. C.941, etc.'. These fore-edge tabs are more frequent in continental manuscripts than in English ones.

primer survives as the first item in a tract-volume in the British Library, which bears the name of a nun, Dame Margaret Necollson, who may have belonged either to the community of Elstow, Bedfordshire, or to that of Watton, Yorkshire.[47] Finally, one of two copies in the University Library, Cambridge, contains the signatures of the child Catherine Parr, her brother, her sister, and their mother Maud Parr, who wrote gift inscriptions in the primer to the children's uncle Sir William Parr.[48] This first English book of hours to survive in multiple copies thus seems to have been associated particularly with women and suggests a readership where literacy might be expected: nuns and aristocrats.

Syon ownership of one, perhaps two, copies of this early primer is not surprising. Eight Syon manuscript *horae* survive as well, an unusually large number. Since St Bridget evolved the office for her nuns from her own daily recitation of the Hours of the Virgin, Brigittine books of hours thus 'represent a spirituality which is halfway between the secular and the monastic', and such extensive possession of books of hours would not have been characteristic of other orders.[49] Hence, in analysing ownership of popular devotional books, the role of Brigittines will be significant, both as commissioners of manuscript books and as purchasers of printed ones.

Syon signatures, in fact, are found in several surviving printed *horae*. Ownership by community members of two copies of a 1532 primer suggests that this might have been a Syon-commissioned edition, or that Syon purchased a block of books from one edition for distribution to the community.[50] Books of hours from other printed editions too were owned by Syon members: in a 1514 printed book of hours, eight parchment leaves have been inserted beginning 'Of viij Anniuersaryes to be kept in this monastery of Syon'.[51] In a 31 October 1532 primer by Regnault, a presumably Brigittine owner has written next to a woodcut of St Bridget: 'Off your blessyng mother I you pray.'[52] Thus, copies from four editions printed between 1494 and 1532 show Brigittine ownership. Though the two copies from the 1532 edition are most likely to signify

47. BL, C.20.c.20; Birrell 1987b, p. 27; Meale 1990, p. 132n.
48. Oates 1954, 4150. The other Cambridge copy, Oates 1954, 4151, is wanting all of the A gathering, the same portion found in Margaret Necollson's collection. It is possible that her section of the book originally belonged to this CUL copy, particularly since the soiled condition of the latter's fol. B 1 indicates that the A gathering was missing early on, but the two copies have not been examined together.   49. De Hamel 1991, pp. 76–7.
50. Erler 1992, pp. 194–200; *STC* 15978, BL, C.35.a.14, and *STC* 15979, BL, C.35.a.12.
51. F. Birckman; *STC* 15918, CUL Rit.c.351.1.
52. *STC* 15980, Bodl. Douce BB 228.

block purchase, even these single copies testify to Syon's continuing relation with commercial printing. (Further work on the patronage relationship between English religious institutions and early printers is needed, particularly since continental printing shows evidence of commissions from religious houses.)[53]

The physical continuities between manuscript and printed books are most evident in a variety of well-known productions by Antoine Vérard during the 1490s, particularly in his more than eighty editions of books of hours.[54] Here full-page metal-cuts have frequently been overpainted to give the appearance of illumination, producing what has been called a manuscript aesthetic.[55] Such illumination of printed books contrasts with another technique: painting of the cut while leaving its printed outlines visible. This latter treatment may instead represent a step away from the manuscript and towards a 'print' identity for the book in question.

A luxurious Parisian book of hours published around 1495 survives in the British Library, the gift of Prince Arthur to Sir Thomas Poyntz, Knight of the Body to Henry VII. Printed on vellum, the book is professionally decorated: its full-page woodcuts have been coloured and it has been rubricated in red, blue and gold.[56] The elegant prettiness of such French printed books, in illustration, decoration and general presentation, continues a mode established by luxury manuscript primers. They are often printed on vellum, a high proportion are coloured, and their sophisticated cuts contrast with the English primer illustrations' naive liveliness. Gifts of such printed *horae* within court circles like Prince Arthur's indicate that printed volumes were not regarded as less desirable than manuscript ones, particularly in the early years of printing when such books possessed the charm of novelty. Instead, a familiar and widely accessible text was now made available in a freshly intriguing form.

To some extent it is possible to distinguish levels of expense in decoration of these incunable books of hours. Prince Arthur's gift to Sir Thomas Poyntz, with its full-page coloured cuts, contains the most costly kind of embellishment. A more modest alternative is provided by a nearly contemporary Parisian book in which only a tiny printed rectangular cut appearing at the top of each recto calendar leaf has been

53. Chrisman 1982, pp. 81–4.   54. Winn 1993, p. 337; 1997, pp. 207–36.
55. Driver 1989, plates 2 and 3, for juxtaposed print and painting.
56. *STC* 15881.5, BL, IA.40910.

coloured.[57] Surviving identical copies from a single edition are sometimes differently decorated at different levels of cost. For instance, a 1497
book of hours printed by Jean Philippe for Thielman Kerver includes
full-page woodcuts.[58] In two copies printed on vellum, the cuts are
uncoloured, but the initial letter below each illustration has been illuminated with gold, the only colour used in the book except for alternating
red and blue initials throughout.[59] Two humbler paper copies from the
same edition, at Oxford and Cambridge,[60] instead have their majuscules
picked out throughout in off-shades of red and blue, closer to brown and
aqua. The identity of the colours in these two books shows both were
decorated at the same time, presumably in a workshop. All four copies'
decoration appears to be professional work. That two copies from the
edition were produced on vellum and decorated differently, and more
grandly, from the two copies printed on paper indicates that the French
publisher's awareness of several different audiences was shaping his
product. Indeed the use of standardized, different, levels of decoration in
printed books of hours such as these probably follows manuscript workshop practice.

Though they signal a particular level of expense, the primary function
of the coloured initials is to move the reader's eye through the structure
of the text. The use of colour guides the viewer's gaze more effectively
than does mere black and white. The book just discussed, for instance, in
its table of contents, alternates red and blue squares at the beginning of
each line; their colour differentiates the topic sought more clearly than
do the uniform black printed majuscules which they replace. Notably, it
is books of hours, among early printed books, which retain substantial
amounts of colour and thus resist what has been called 'the blackening of
the page' – a change in which the coming of print may represent a decline
in general legibility.[61]

Closely allied to books of hours are the *preces privatae*, books of prayers
collected by an owner for private use and hence individual in their choice
of material. Though these books have not been given much attention,
they offer a rich conspectus of popular devotion. In addition, study of
their hands and their choice of texts might provide additional insights on
literacy, since the conjunction of Latin and English prayers is frequent.
How, for instance, were these two languages employed in private prayer

57. *STC* 15881.3, Bodl. Arch. B.f.42.   58. *STC* 15885.
59. BL, IA.40487, and PML, Ch.L.1497.   60. Bodl. Douce 25 and Oates 1954, 3098.
61. Saenger and Heinlen 1991, p. 251.

by owners who would conventionally be considered unlikely to be fully Latinate?

One of the most interesting of these small books is in Lambeth Palace Library. Its monogram on fol. 56, 'Sister EW', probably indicates it was owned by Elizabeth Woodford, who appears as the most senior nun in the Syon election list of 1518 and who died in March 1523, according to the Syon necrology.[62] Because it is written in a variety of hands the book has something of the character of an *album amicorum*. A piece on the fifteen sorrows of Our Lady, for instance, is signed by 'Master John Warde', who was steward of Syon in 1485.[63] A section containing a text of the golden litany concludes 'Robart Davemport your pore bedeman miserrimo peccatori. Jhesus mercy lady helpe'. A chaplain by this name supplicated for the degree of Bachelor of Canon Law at Oxford in 1515.[64] A longer section has been identified as in the hand of William Darker, a Carthusian of Sheen.[65] Still another hand has written, on fol. 55, below a devotion attributed to Rolle: 'Good Syster of your charyte I you pray remember the scrybeler when that ye may, with an aue maria or els thys swete word Ihesu haue marcy on my wreched syster whose name by the mercy of god I trust shall be wrytyn in the boke of lyfe.' It has recently been pointed out that this contribution to the miscellany is clearly by a female scribe.[66] In its jointly produced, perhaps accumulative, character, this volume seems closer to a household miscellany like the Findern anthology, with its diverse contributions by various hands, than to more conventional books of private prayer with their individual nature and singular audience.

Prayer books, whether *horae* or personal compilations, are located at the intersection of the emotive, the aesthetic, the personal and the religious, and hence must always have sustained an uneasy balance amongst these conflicting elements. In such books, addition and emendation of all sorts abounds: indeed Rose Tresham's late fifteenth-century comment, written in her manuscript psalter, offers a conservative dictum which many bookowners disregarded: 'Lerne to kepe your bookes fayre & ockapy [use] them well & use to clasp them whan you haue done'.[67]

Fortunately, however, many readers did not keep their books pristine. Books of hours, both manuscript and print, were regularly appropriated

62. Lambeth, ms. 546; Aungier 1840, p. 81; Sion necrology: BL, Add. ms. 22285, fol. 29v.
63. Wedgwood 1936, p. 359.   64. Boase 1885, p. 95.   65. Parkes 1969, p. 8.
66. O'Mara 1990, pp. 396–8.
67. Bodl. ms. Auct. D.4.3, Pächt and Alexander 1966–73, I, no. 289. This advice was given as well by Syon's Thomas Betson in his *Ryght Profytable Treatyse* (STC 1978).

to secular uses. Registration of family births and deaths in the books' calendars is of course very frequent. One of the fullest examples is found in a fifteenth-century manuscript book of hours which Elizabeth Hull, abbess of Malling, Kent, gave to her godchild, Margaret Nevill, at the child's baptism. Its calendar subsequently records Margaret's marriage, the birth of her children, her husband's death, her second marriage, her own death, and her widower's remarriage. The dates span the sixteenth century, from 1520 to 1576.[68]

The political world, rather than the personal, is invoked in a Parisian printed primer of 1495, where significant events of Henry VII's reign have been entered in the calendar margins: his 7 August 1485 landing at Milford Haven, his 30 October crowning at Westminster, his 16 June 1487 victory at Stoke 'beside Newark', the births of Prince Arthur and Princess Margaret. Most interesting are the inserted dates in late September and October 1501 when 'my lady princess', i.e., Catherine of Aragon, took ship from Spain and landed, blown off course, at Plymouth, Devon.[69]

Secular passion (or literary allusion) registers as well: in a 1542 primer, 'be my treweth I can not tel but yt I loue you wel'.[70] In a 1495 book of hours: 'I whas & ys & euer schell be yowre awne true bedwoman tyll I dee.'[71] Such adaptive mingling of public and private, secular and religious, illustrates the central place of these books in contemporary life.

The most frequently found additions to devotional books, however, are religious in character. Perhaps the best-known of such annotations are found in Sir Thomas More's prayer book. The volume's two parts, a printed psalter and a book of hours, have each been annotated by More. The psalter notes reflect his anxieties and fears as he read meditatively through the psalms, while in the top and bottom margins of the book of hours More wrote the phrases of his 'Godly Meditation' – each phrase a self-contained injunction to himself (see fig 24.1).[72]

Pictures as well as words were added by owners. These sparse and fascinating visual survivals of popular devotion cluster particularly in books of hours and books of private prayer. Campbell Dodgson's listing of

68. Blackburn Museum and Art Gallery ms. 091.21040, described in Ker 1969–82, I: 109–11. For the annotations, Furnivall 1868. For more examples from manuscript *horae*, Littlehales 1895–7, II, pp. xlv–li.
69. *STC* 15880, Bodl. Douce 24. For similar marginal notes on the events of Henry VII's life, Oxford, Exeter Coll. ms. 47.　70. *STC* 16026, JRUL 19638.
71. *STC* 15880, BL, IA.41332.
72. *STC* 16260 (1522) and *STC* 15963 (1530); Martz and Sylvester 1969.

twenty-three fifteenth-century English single-sheet woodcuts contains nine examples found in books of hours or *preces privatae*. A remarkable manuscript in the British Library, for instance, contains four such coloured woodcuts, two of them dramatically stippled with red drops, suggesting the meditative context for their use.[73] Gazing at images, in fact, may be viewed as another form of spiritual reading which, like the act of following the words on the page, gives rise to meditation and to prayer.[74]

A Parisian printed primer from 1495 in the Bodleian Library[75] originally contained two separate woodcuts, now removed, each showing a shield with the *arma Christi* superimposed on a crucifix. One cut is headed 'Ex domo Ihesu de Betheleem', i.e., from Sheen, the Carthusian house near London, and it bears sewing holes which match those on fol. eij of the primer.[76] The second woodcut has no holes, however, and it perhaps was merely placed loose in the book. Its employment cannot be called either aesthetic or devotional. Below its coloured image of the five wounds is written, 'I haue sent vnto your Lordship a litill englysh boke not to passe ye tyme with whill ye be here & haue leyser but for to kepe tyme wi*th*. which we shulde desire i*n* our wyll & intente. Impute it not to p*re*sum*p*tion but rat*her* to wantyng of wytte. *Amor non timet.* Your pore bedema*n* for eu*er*. d.E.G'. [77] In this case the Sheen-associated woodcut above the jotted note might suggest that the writer was a member of that community and that the woodcut was being used not for meditation but as a kind of social stationery.

More straightforwardly religious in their intention are the four devotional cards sewn into a 1534 Regnault book of hours owned by Dame Elizabeth Atherton (d. 1576), as the inscription before its colophon testifies.[78] The most striking of these cards features three painted gold nails in combination with wounded silver hands and feet and heart. Remaining thread shows that the volume originally contained more such pictures. Similarly, in the Lambeth 1494 book of hours mentioned above, which contains the engraved card picturing St Katherine of Sweden, two additional contemporary pictures are found, loose (there were originally

---

73. BL, Egerton ms. 1821; Dodgson 1936, and see Dodgson 1929.
74. Gillespie 1984, pp. 10–11.   75. Bodl. Douce 24.
76. *STC* 15880. The removed woodcuts are Arch. G.f. 13–14. The first is reproduced by Duffy 1992, plate 99, who calls it 'a devotional card circulated by the Carthusians of Sheen'.
77. The note, in a late-fifteenth or early sixteenth-century hand, may originally not have been associated with Douce 24; see Dodgson 1936, pp. 102–3.
78. *STC* 15984, Bodl. Gough missals 177.

eighteen): one a coloured woodcut Image of Pity and the other a woodcut of the Virgin and child at a window, she giving milk from her breast to a kneeling St Bernard.[79]

These printed devotional cards have manuscript predecessors: for instance a fifteenth-century Lambeth primer owned for three generations by the Lewkenor family of Sussex contains two such inserted illuminations. The first, a miniature of the diamond-shaped wound in Christ's side (fol. 78v) is sewn into the earlier portion of the book (see fig. 24.2). The second part of the primer was written some time after 1471. It contains a pasted-in painted image of the rood of Bromholm (Norfolk), in which Christ is shown on a cross of Lorraine (two horizontal bars) surrounded by the outline of a gold heart. Around three sides is written 'This cros þat here peyntyd is. signe of þe cros of bromholm is.' It has been suggested that a similar picture found in a manuscript now in Cambridge may have been produced at Bromholm Priory, for sale to pilgrims.[80] Belief in this miraculous relic continued, in some quarters after the rood's 1538 removal, since the Lewkenor book passed out of the family's hands around 1544, and at this time its new owner wrote below the picture of the rood of Bromholm: 'thys ys the holy cros that ys or sped. be me mary Euerard.' In this book of hours, religious devotion is reinforced by familial *pietas* (the primer was bequeathed in a Lewkenor will) and by the local, regional, piety of East Anglia.[81]

Similar to these inserted devotional cards in their additional character are the pasted-in printed images found in both manuscript and printed books from the end of the fifteenth century. The owner of a 1532 Sarum primer, for instance, has attempted to reconstruct traditional Brigittine devotional imagery in which St Bridget kneels before the apparition of a half-length Christ, his arms crossed on his breast. In this instance the figure of a kneeling Brigittine nun has been cut from a printed woodcut and pasted into the book's left margin, facing another cut-out printed figure of Christ. This collage prefaces the text of the *Fifteen Oes* attributed to St Bridget. Relying on the unconventional materials of paper collage, the book's owner has re-created an entirely conventional and familiar image.[82]

The most frequent subjects of these devotional images include the

79. Bradshaw 1889, pp. 256–57.   80. Cambridge, Fitzwilliam Museum, ms. 55.
81. Lambeth ms. 545. James and Jenkins 1930–2, I, no. 545, pp. 747–50; Wormald 1937–8;
    Sparrow Simpson 1874b; Gurewich 1957. For Sir Roger Lewkenor (1420–78), see
    Wedgwood 1936, pp. 541–2.   82. Erler 1992, p. 197; Alexander 1992, p. 49.

Man of Sorrows (Image of Pity), the instruments of the Passion (*arma Christi*) and the five wounds. All these, of course, in emphasizing powerfully the physical suffering of Christ, require from the viewer a response of corresponding intensity. The intimate nature of this response perhaps explains the frequent appearance of this exotic and moving iconography in small forms: in tiny books, in cards, in rolls.

Four small books, for instance, each about four by five inches, present the five wounds devotion. Two, now in Oxford and in Princeton, are manuscripts, from the late fifteenth century. Unique copies from two printed editions also exist: around 1523, Richard Fawkes printed *A gloryous medytacyon of Ihesus crystes passyon*, while Robert Copland published a rhymed life of Christ in about 1533.[83] The devotion's iconography includes images of Christ's right and left hand, his heart, and his right and left foot, with a corresponding prayer directed to their wounds as wells of mercy, grace, life, pity and comfort. The first three of these books are particularly close in both text and illustrations, and though the relationship has not been resolved, they show how this devotion's popularity crossed the manuscript/print divide. The portability which their size guarantees, and the incremental nature of the devotion they contain, made it possible to read or to gaze at these small books briefly, frequently, privately. They are likely to have been carried on the person or kept at a bedside. Consequently their interest for us lies in their deeply personal character.

The five wounds are illustrated also, very simply, in a Glazier manuscript in the Pierpont Morgan Library, as are the three nails, here combined with the crown of thorns and the four evangelists' symbols (see fig. 24.3). This late fifteenth-century roll was made by a Premonstratensian canon named Percevall, of the abbey of Coverham, Yorkshire, who identifies himself in a concluding verse.[84] By contrast with books of hours (or even books of private prayer) which exist in the thousands, surviving rolls are few indeed, perhaps not more than fifty in number.[85] Despite arguments for the public nature of rolls, based on their suitability for display and thus for public reading,[86] they must also have been owned and used privately, in the same way as small books and cards were.

83. Bodleian, ms. Douce 1; Princeton University, Scheide Library, Taylor ms. 17 (formerly Amherst ms. 20). Fawkes: *STC* 14550. Copland: *STC* 14552.7. I am grateful to Dr W. Stoneman for a typescript description of Taylor ms. 17. For five wounds devotion, D. Gray 1963 and Duffy 1992, pp. 238–48.

84. PML, ms. G.39; Plummer 1968, no. 50; Legge 1904; Bühler 1964.

85. Krochalis 1983, p. 210.   86. Robbins 1939a.

Glazier ms. 39, for instance, makes its promises to those who 'with deu-ocion worshippis yaim [the picture of the nails] dayly and berith yame a pone thaim' – a practice which recalls the reformers' criticism of the 'bearers aboute' of 'blasphemous prayers'. The private nature of the roll is again stressed when we are told elsewhere in its text that if a pregnant woman lays the pictured cross upon her womb she will be delivered without peril.

Rolls then, like books of hours, collections of private prayers, or image cards, can allow us a glimpse of an intimate, sometimes idiosyncratic, spirituality. It may be particularly in hybrid forms such as these which fuse words and images that popular belief is recorded most fully.

*

Although books of hours perhaps manifest popular religious mentality in its widest distribution (especially from the latter part of the fifteenth century), many devotional texts originated before the surge in popularity of books of hours – and, like the *horae*, continued their popularity in printed versions. In fact, during the last quarter of the fifteenth century when English printing began, printed vernacular religious texts outnum-bered books of hours by almost 3 to 1 (88 of the former, 29 of the latter).[87] It has been suggested, in fact, that the best way for *any* text to continue in popularity later was for it to appear in a fifteenth-century edition.[88]

Not all of the most popular spiritual texts negotiated the transition from manuscript to print. The most widely copied of all religious poems, the *Prick of Conscience*, for instance, did not do so. Its great length, 9,600 lines, survives in 115 manuscripts,[89] but it saw print only in forms which were late and partial. Its first 3 sections (of 7) were published by Robert Wyer around 1542. Earlier, about 1534, Wyer had printed its fourth section (on purgatory).[90] Publication by instalment might have been conceived as a way to deal with the poem's scope, but these two editions, in fact, did not publicize the poem under its familiar title. They pre-sented the text merely in terms of its subject matter: 'Here begynneth a newe treatyse deuyded in thre parties . . . the wretchednes of all man-kynde . . . the vnstedfastnes, of this world . . . bytter death'. There were no succeeding editions.

Similarly comprehensive is the *Speculum Vitae*, a late fourteenth-century verse commentary on the Pater Noster over 16,000 lines long. Written by William Nassington, a secular priest and ecclesiastical lawyer,

87. R. White 1994, appendix 1.   88. *IPMEP*, p. xxv.   89. Lewis and McIntosh 1982, pp. 5, 9. 90. *STC* 24228; *STC* 3360.

it was designed for reading aloud and also was consulted as what has been called 'the nearest thing to a vernacular *summa*'.[91] Though 39 manuscripts survive, it was never printed.

Some widely read prose texts experienced a similar abrupt drop in production. The *Pore Caitif* (*c.* 1400), a common instructional compilation for the laity, contained homilies on the creed, the commandments, the Pater Noster, the counsels of perfection, and various short tracts. Though about 30 manuscripts of the whole manual exist,[92] no editions were published. Indeed it may be misguided to think of widespread manuscript popularity as determining early printers' selections. The large role still played by clientage in selection of texts to be printed should be acknowledged, and this role may be viewed as a carryover from the situation of manuscript production. In English printing, individual or small-group demand, rather than popular response, remained for some time a powerful determinant of what texts were made available.[93]

At least two devotional texts, one written just after 1400, the other just before, sustained their great popularity on both sides of the print divide. Nicholas Love's translation of the *Meditationes Vitae Christi*, *The Myrrour of the Blessed Lyfe of Jesu Criste*, survives in 56 manuscripts and 9 editions from this period,[94] while Walter Hylton's *Scale of Perfection* exists in 47 manuscripts and 7 editions.[95] The narrative and meditative treatment of Christ's life provided by the *Myrrour* eventually reached an audience perhaps almost as widespread as that for books of hours, while the *Scale*, a guide to contemplation, was directed towards a more specialized readership.

The *Myrrour* was translated into English before 1410 by Nicholas Love, Carthusian prior of Mount Grace, Yorkshire, from the ps-Bonaventuran Latin text. About 1410 the work was submitted for approval to Thomas Arundel, Archbishop of Canterbury, though it may have circulated before this date. Written originally for a particular Franciscan nun, this gospel-based account of Christ's life, in Love's hands, was confirmed in its homiletic and meditative character. The *Myrrour* was explicitly aimed, as well, at the Lollard heresy. Doyle attributes the uniformity of its manuscript presentation to the existence of a few archetype manuscripts pre-

91. Doyle 1953, I. pp. 79–81; Gillespie 1989, pp. 332–3.
92. Jolliffe 1974, pp. 65–7 lists 55 manuscripts, but many contain only one text, or a series of extracts.   93. Doyle 1953, I. pp. 205, 289, but see K. Harris 1989, p. 183.
94. Sargent 1992, Introduction p. lxiii, including fragments, plus 'four extracts, and an additional composite version'; *STC* 3259–67.
95. Minnis 1984, pp. 75–6; *STC* 14041–5; *STC* 4602.

pared for that purpose, and he traces its manuscript distribution mostly in the metropolitan area and the Midlands, chiefly by direct contact rather than planned distribution, and, before the middle of the fifteenth century, mostly through religious hands.[96]

Some evidence, both from manuscripts and wills, suggests that, though its earliest readers were religious, lay people too owned this text by mid-century, and even before. One copy, of which the illumination has been dated *c.* 1400–10, was given away by Joan, Countess of Kent, the widow of Mount Grace's founder, before her death in 1442.[97] Another bears the arms of Neville and Beaufort, perhaps indicating ownership by Joan, Countess of Westmoreland (d. 1440), or her brother, Thomas, Duke of Exeter (d. 1426).[98] Another bears the arms of Robert, Lord Willoughby d'Eresby (d. 1452).[99] All these early lay owners are elevated ones.

The earliest will evidence is ambiguous: layman Thomas Dautree's 1437 bequest of 'librum meum Bonaventure' may have been a Latin book, and Agnes Stapilton's 1448 legacy of 'librum meum vocatum Bonaventure' may refer to the *Stimulus Amoris*.[100] In 1468, however, Elizabeth Sywardby, a Yorkshire widow, left 'unum librum de Vita Christi in lingua materna', and Sir Peter Ardern, Chief Baron of the Exchequer, of Yorkshire and Essex, bequeathed to his wife 'my boke of Englissh called Bonaventura de Vita et Passione Christi'.[101]

By the end of the fifteenth century, evidence for lay ownership had become much more visible. Doyle cites, for instance, a 1498 bequest by a London merchant, Thomas Pettit, of a manuscript on parchment, written with gold letters.[102] It may even be that some manuscripts were produced speculatively, since it is in extremely popular texts such as the *Myrrour* that evidence can be sought for the commercial pursuit of a wide audience.[103]

Caxton first printed the work around 1484. There were nine editions before 1535;[104] *STC* gives the whereabouts of thirty-five copies or fragments. Doyle's list of owners, taken mostly though not entirely

---

96. Doyle 1953, I, pp. 147–8.   97. Tokyo, Takamiya ms. 8.
98. Bodleian, ms. e. Mus. 35; Doyle 1983b, pp. 86–7.
99. Glasgow UL, ms. Gen. 1130; Sargent 1992, Introduction p. lxxix.
100. Doyle 1953, I, pp. 151–2; Thrupp 1948, p. 162, for a 1439 London merchant's bequest of an English translation of Bonaventura (no reference given).
101. Doyle 1953, I, pp. 152–3, with many other instances.   102. Doyle 1983b, p. 89.
103. K. Harris 1989, p. 183; Doyle 1983b, p. 88.
104. *STC* 3259 [1484]; *STC* 3260 [1490]; *STC* 3261, 1494; *STC* 3262 [1494]; *STC* 3263 [1506]; *STC* 3263.5 [1507?]; *STC* 3264, 1517; *STC* 3266, 1525; *STC* 3267, 1530. See L. Hellinga 1997a.

from these copies, includes a nun of Syon; a monk of Christ Church, Canterbury; a London hermit (see fig. 9.1); 'certain students of Canterbury College, Oxford'; the Clerk of Works to Margaret Beaufort, and three unidentified men.[105] Two more early inscriptions may be added: 'This Boke is myn Elizabeth Massy' in a copy of Pynson's [1494] edition;[106] and, at the foot of the well-known verses 'O man vnkynde', written marginally in a copy of Pynson's 1506 edition: 'quod Harry Wateʒ'.[107] Only two of these ten names belong to religious, suggesting that printing accelerated the gradual trend towards lay possession of this text, a trend which was illustrated earlier in the pattern of manuscript acquisition.

Walter Hylton's *Scale of Perfection* likewise offers the opportunity to examine its audience through the testimony of manuscripts, prints and wills. Forty-two English manuscripts survive, complete or nearly so. Twenty-one of these contain both books; nineteen have book I only; two, book II only.[108] The more popular first book, addressed to an anchoress and conceived as a guide to contemplation, was perhaps written in the 1380s. The second book, written either to the original recipient or to another, was probably completed soon before Hylton's death in 1396. Since editions of both books of the *Scale* are currently in progress, observations about ownership at this point must be preliminary, but the prominence of the Charterhouses of London and Sheen and the Brigittine house of Syon is clear. It has recently been calculated that eight of the surviving manuscripts are associated with these religious houses.[109]

The connection with Syon, in particular, seems to have been made very early. Doyle noted long ago that one of the earliest *Scale* manuscripts, which the anchorite Margery Pensax gave to Syon perhaps between 1415 and 1420, was only one of a group of *Scale* manuscripts at Syon before mid-century, and suggested that the longer interpolated version of the *Scale* might have been developed at Syon.[110] Certainly that house seems to have adopted a special relation to this text, beginning early in its institutional history and lasting well into the seventeenth century. The manuscript which Margery Pensax gave Syon, a late fourteenth- or early fifteenth-century one written in London and addressed to a 'ghostly brother,'[111] may in fact have been closely connected with Hylton. She had

---

105. Doyle 1953, I. p. 157.   106. *STC* 3262, BL, IB.55527, Pynson [1494], on fol. d1.
107. *STC* 3263, JRUL R 18012, Pynson [1506], on fol. N6.
108. Information from Prof. S. S. Hussey, Lancaster University.
109. Sargent 1983, p. 187.   110. BL, Harl. ms. 2387; Doyle 1953, I, pp. 265–6.
111. Doyle 1953, I, p. 257; De Hamel 1991, pp. 57–8; McIntosh 1986, III, p. 298.

been enclosed at Hawton, Nottinghamshire, about six miles east of Thurgarton, Hylton's priory, for an unspecified period, until March 1399, three years after Hylton's death. At that time Archbishop Scrope's register records permission for her to choose a new cell and a prelate to seclude her. In November 1399, she received a royal pension towards her maintenance at London's Bishopsgate anchorage,[112] where she remained, certainly until 1414,[113] probably until 1417,[114] perhaps even until 1426.[115]

It might have been Syon, indeed, which provided the exemplar for one of the well-known 'common profit' manuscripts, which contains *Scale* I and II. Doyle pointed out the identity of contents between this manuscript and the entry for M 26 in the Syon brothers' catalogue.[116] The five 'common profit' manuscripts, whose texts differ, seem all to have been produced at the instigation of John Colop, a shadowy figure who was in the service of Richard Whittington, Mayor of London, and was an acquaintance of the London Town Clerk, John Carpenter. During a period probably between the late 1420s and the late 1440s, Colop commissioned these five books, using money from the estates of various well-off London cloth-trade men.[117] Each one carried an inscription stipulating that the volume was to pass from owner to owner, using a model of book transmission which may owe something to clerical wills.[118] The possible connection between Syon and this London merchant milieu, in this effort which mixed initiatives of instruction, devotion, and perhaps religious reform, is suggestive. Certainly the *Scale*, like Love's *Myrrour*, found lay readers early, before mid-century.

Another subgroup of this text's owners might be noted: that of religious women. The Syon manuscripts of *Scale* are associated with both male and female members of the house,[119] but in addition at least three other *Scale* manuscripts belonged to women's institutions. Some time between 1455/6 and 1481, Elizabeth Horwode, Abbess of the London minoresses, 'bowȝht' a manuscript of *Scale* II, Hylton's *Mixed Life* and *Bonum est* for the use of her community.[120] Later in the century, John Horder donated a manuscript of *Scale* I and II to the abbess and convent

112. Warren 1985, p. 78n.
113. London, Guildhall ms. 9171/2, f. 315v–316, will of William de Bergh.
114. London, Guildhall ms. 9171/2, f. 384, will of Margery de Nerford.
115. Nichols 1780, p. 250, will of Thomas Beaufort, Duke of Exeter.
116. Lambeth ms. 472; Doyle 1953, II, p. 208.
117. Doyle 1953, II, pp. 208–14; Sargent 1983, p. 206.   118. Scase 1992, pp. 263–5.
119. Sargent 1983, p. 187.   120. BL, Harl. ms. 2397; Doyle 1953, II. p. 213.

of Shaftesbury.[121] In the early sixteenth century, Elizabeth Wylby, a nun of Campsey, gave a book containing *Scale* I and II and Suso's *Treatise of Seven Points* to her fellow religious, Catherine Symonde.[122] In addition, Doyle has suggested that a manuscript made for western religious may have been intended for nuns, and that two manuscripts related to each other were made probably for a male and female religious community, either Syon or another.[123]

The inclusion in several *Scale* manuscripts of what came to be called 'Book III' of the *Scale*, the epistle on the mixed life, is significant. It has been suggested 'that it was specifically the addition of the *Mixed Life* that facilitated the appropriation of the *Scale* to its new audience'.[124] Written, like *Scale* I, in the late 1380s, *Mixed Life* itself (sixteen manuscripts)[125] must, however, have appealed to a lay readership from its first appearance, directed as it was to 'a devout man in temporal estate' whom it advised on ways to combine an ardent spirituality with life in the world.

Much will evidence for *Scale* ownership is ambiguous: in 1414 John Newton, a clerical lawyer, Treasurer of York cathedral and Master of Peterhouse, owned an unspecified work of Hylton's. Lady Eleanor Roos, daughter of Sir Thomas Roos of Igmanthorpe, was willed 'unum librum vocatum primum Mr Walteri Hilton' by William Authorpe, rector of Kirk Deighton, Yorkshire, in 1432/3. Both Roos and Authorpe were buried at Mount Grace, the northern Carthusian house, and Lady Eleanor may have lived a life of seclusion there. At her death in 1438, she bequeathed 'unum librum Anglicum vocatum librum primum Magistri Walteri' to her nephew Robert Roos, knight, of Igmanthorpe, and his wife. In 1467, Robert Est of York bequeathed a work of Hylton's. The widow of a Norwich mayor, Margaret Purdans, willed a copy of Hylton in 1481 to Alice Barley, perhaps the sister of two well-known Norfolk clerics, while in 1495, Cecily, widow of Richard, Duke of York, wrote: 'Also I geve to my doughter Anne priores of Sion, a boke of Bonaventura, and Hilton in the same in Englishe' (probably a manuscript rather than a printed book).[126] These owners include men and women, lay persons and clerics, members of the aristocracy and urban bourgeoisie – a fifteenth-

121. BL, Add. ms. 11748; Doyle 1953, II, p. 251. For other Shaftesbury books, D. N. Bell 1995, pp. 163–8.
122. Cambridge, Corpus Christi Coll. ms. R.5 (268), and see D. N. Bell 1995, pp. 125–6 for another Wylby–Symonde book.
123. Cambridge, Magdalene Coll. ms. F.4.17; Doyle 1953, I, p. 267. Bodl. ms. Rawl. C.894 and BL, Royal ms. 17.C.XVIII; Doyle 1953, note xvii (II, pp. 215–21).
124. Sargent 1992, p. lxii.   125. Ogilvie-Thomson 1986, Introduction, p. iii.
126. J. Hughes 1988, pp. 102, 106, 292; Doyle 1953, II, p. 316; Meale 1997, *pace* Deanesly 1920, p. 355.

century manuscript audience which foreshadows (and at the end of the century overlaps with) the readers of Caxton's books.

The *Scale* was first printed in 1494. Part of the edition included the *Mixed Life* as well, and it appears in five surviving copies of this work. Syon owners' names are found in two copies of which *Mixed Life* is part, while a third copy belonged to a minoress in Louvain, and a fourth was given by Margaret Beaufort and Elizabeth of York to their gentlewoman, Mary Roos.[127] Other copies from this first edition (those containing books I and II only) were owned by John Colman, the last Master of St Mark's hospital in Bristol;[128] by a Thomas Sampson, perhaps the Protestant divine (1517?–89);[129] by 'Thomas Rawlines of dawntre in the County of Buckyngham marchaunt' and by members of the Churche family, otherwise unidentified;[130] by a Lewis Harrold;[131] and by a woman who signed, below the title-page cut, 'Elizabeth Cl' (cf. fig. 9.2).[132] Copies whose edition is unknown are recorded in the inventory of William More, of Loseley, Surrey, in 1556 and in the library of a group of former monks of Monk Bretton, Yorkshire, in 1558.[133]

Four editions followed this first one, in 1507, 1519, 1525 and 1533,[134] and thirty-eight complete copies are listed by *STC*, plus two fragments. (These thirty-eight copies of the *Scale* are roughly comparable to the thirty-three surviving copies recorded by *STC* for Love's *Myrrour*.) Doyle noted that both the British Library copy of the 1525 edition and the Trinity College, Cambridge, copy of the 1533 edition were bound up in composite volumes 'of contemplative interest' and suggested that at least the earlier of these might have been Brigittine.[135] Surely it was Syon too which commissioned the 1516 edition of *Mixed Life*, which was issued along with the *Nova Legenda Angliae* and with a life of St Bridget;[136] *Mixed Life* was printed again around 1530 by Robert Wyer.[137] The interpenetration of lay and religious readership for the *Scale*, despite the work's original designation for an anchoress, thus seems to have taken place from an early date, with London religious houses, perhaps Syon in particular, assuming a central role in its dissemination.

*

If certain books of hours have the status of *objets d'art*, books of spiritual reading may equally be seen as religious objects. In wills they are often

127. *STC* 14042, Sargent 1983, pp. 207–8; Croft 1958b; Jones and Underwood 1992, p. 183.
128. Doyle 1953, II, p. 299.   129. JRUL 15046.   130. Yale, Beinecke Library Zi +9694.
131. Doyle 1953, I. p. 274.   132. Cambridge, St John's Coll.
133. Doyle 1953, I. p. 275; *CBMLC*, IV, p. 275, no. B58.
134. *STC* 14043, 1507; *STC* 14043.5, 1519; *STC* 14044, 1525; *STC* 14045, 1533.
135. Doyle 1953, I, pp. 140–1.   136. *STC* 4602.   137. *STC* 14041.

grouped with treasures like beads or religious pictures, where their transmission testifies to spiritual friendship, and sometimes to the existence of circles within which a shared spirituality is to be understood. Gifts of such books, in particular, imply the existence of a common vision, intellectual and spiritual at once. The best-known example might be James Grenehalgh's decoration of the 1494 *Scale*'s last leaf for Joan Sewell, in which her name and those of 'Sanctus Saluator', 'Birgitta', 'Sanctus Augustinus' and 'Maria' are surrounded by a drawn shape which Sargent suggested might be that of 'an idealized "urbs refugii", with a fountain clearly visible in the centre (of a cloister?)'.[138] Grenehalgh's design situates the book's owner and reader centrally, in the midst of an idealized spiritual community which at the same time is physically delimited by its symbolic enclosing line.

The same consciousness of reading's shared nature is found in the inscriptions of two elderly friends written in the Rylands copy of the 1495 *Vitas patrum*, St Jerome's biographies of the desert saints, which Caxton translated from French (see fig. 24.4).[139] The first note reads: 'mi owne gud ladi pole pray for my your ione regent & dam anes mi doter of sion i prai you for god sake'. Joan Regent was widow of a Bristol mayor, probably living at the Bristol hospital of St Mark, or Gaunts: her will, made 14 December 1509 and proved 13 February 1510, leaves plate and linen to her daughter Agnes, a nun of Syon.[140] Although the will does not mention the book, *Vitas patrum* must have passed to Agnes at her mother's death, since the daughter's name, in a handsome Tudor italic, appears above the colophon: 'Liber do*mine* Agne*tis* Regent qua*m* saluet Ih*esus*'. Joan Regent's friend, Katherine Pole, whom Ian Doyle has identified as the granddaughter of Cecily Neville, Duchess of York,[141] responded to the first message with her own marginal inscription: 'my one gude ladi regent prai for me your frend kateryn pole I do prai for you & for my ladi agnes yor doter eueri day'.

The position of these inscriptions may be significant: Katherine Pole's is found below the story of the city of Exirynque, where lived 10,000 male and 20,000 female religious, and it might be conjectured that this holy congregation constituted a model for the Bristol community, which in these years had a number of retired lay persons living there. The placement of Joan Regent's inscription is even more pointed: it appears next to Jerome's story of Paula, the widow of noble lineage who gave up all

138. Sargent 1984, p. 26n, plate 10; also reproduced in Deanesly 1915.
139. *STC* 14507.   140. PRO, PROB 11/25, fol. 16.   141. Doyle 1953, 11, p. 320.

522

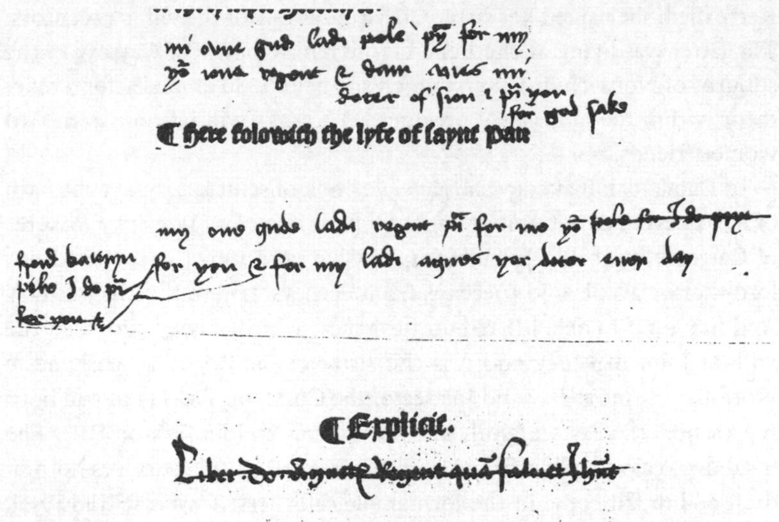
Here folowith the lyfe of saynt Pau
Explicit.

24.4 Reading shared by two elderly friends, Joan Regent and Katherine Pole: early sixteenth-century inscriptions in a copy of ps-Jerome, *Vitas patrum*, translated by William Caxton.

worldly goods for a life of holiness, and who was the mother of the saintly virgin, Eustochium – clearly models for Joan and Agnes Regent.

Another narrative, one which draws on the testimony of several East Anglian wills, can further illuminate the ways in which devotional books were transmitted among friends. In this local Norwich subculture shared by clerical and lay persons, spiritual books, together with painted cloths, alabaster carvings, beads of amber and sacred relics, constitute not only instruments of spiritual progress, but tokens of social connection as well.

In 1498 a Norwich widow named Katherine Kerre died and bequeathed two books.[142] Under the name Katherine Moryell, she herself had been remembered thirty-four years earlier in the 1464 will of the Norwich hermit, Richard Ferneys. A well-known local figure, Ferneys had, for instance, been left a bequest by a former Norwich mayor to go on pilgrimage for him to Rome and to Jerusalem. The hermit's will included bequests to three other male anchorites and to seven laywomen – a kind of devout society within the larger local community. Besides Katherine Moryell he also remembered her sister, Christine Veyl, whom he referred to as 'custodi mee' ('my guardian').[143] When Katherine Moryell

142. NCC Register Multon, fols. 89v–91, made 21 April 1498, proved 16 June.
143. Tanner 1984, pp. 233–4.

Kerre died, she named her sister Christine as one of the will's executors. The latter was living at the Benedictine female house of Carrow in the suburbs of Norwich in 1484/5, when she paid 6s 8d annually for a tenement within the monastery precinct.[144] Kerre's will left books to two women friends.

To Dame Joan Blakeney she gave 'ye book of seint kateryn yt she hath of me, a peyer bedys Aumbyr *with* gylt paternosteres / yt wer ye Ankeres of Carrowe [probably Julian Lampett's], a gold rynge yt towched our lordys grave as it is said [perhaps from Ferneys' trip to the Holy Land]. And iii s iiij d to dele [distribute] for me'. Joan Blakeney had been the wife of John Blakeney and was the sister of Sir Roger Townshend, a Norfolk serjeant-at-law and Justice of the Common Pleas who had both represented the Paston family and lent money to John Paston II.[145] She lived five years after her friend, dying in 1503. Her will survives both in draft and in fair copy: in the former she calls herself 'woesse' [vowess], but in the latter 'wedowe', perhaps reflecting the difference betweeen idiomatic and more formal usage. She commends her soul to God, the Virgin, St John Baptist and St Dominic, asks for burial at the Norwich Blackfriars, and leaves bequests to three friars. Her private chapel's chalice, two vestments, altarcloths and mass book witness to her affluent piety.[146]

The book of St Katherine which Katherine Kerre first lent and then gave to her friend might be John Capgrave's life of St Catherine of Alexandria. One of its surviving manuscripts, like Katherine Kerre and Joan Blakeney, comes from East Anglia: it carries the name of Domina Katerina Babynton, subprioress in 1492 of Campsey, Suffolk.[147] Or the book might have been the version of St Catherine of Alexandria's life from the *Gilte Legende*, of which fourteen manuscripts exist in three different versions.[148] Equally, it might have been St Catherine of Siena's life printed by De Worde in about 1492,[149] or a manuscript version of St Catherine of Siena's *Dialogue*, printed later as *The Orcharde of Syon*.[150]

A second book bequest in this will also represents a loan. To the anchoress of St Julian's Church in Conisford (Norwich), whose identity is not known, Katherine Kerre bequeathed 6s 8d, a fox-furred gown, 'and ye boke yt she hath of me'. This loan to the anchoress suggests the extent to

144. Redstone 1946.   145. For Sir Roger Townshend see *DNB*. His 1492 will is PCC 2 Vox.
146. NCC Register Popy, fols. 315v–317 and 362–5 (draft), made 16 March 1502 (i.e., probably 1503) and proved 20 June 1504.   147. BL, Arundel ms. 396; Ker 1964–87, pp. 28, 238.
148. Lewis *et al.* 1985, no. 28.   149. *STC* 24766.   150. *STC* 4815; Lewis *et al.* 1985, no. 561.

which secular women's freer access to books influenced religious women's reading.

In Kerre's will, the books exist side by side with religious objects – a St John's head of alabaster, for instance, and 'a varnacle yt cam from Rome with the Image peynted theron' – and both sorts of material possessions, books and objects, may be seen as elements in a culture of popular spirituality. The will's beneficiaries include almost ninety named persons, laymen and laywomen as well as four clerical Cambridge graduates, five friars and five parish priests. Indeed the book of St Katherine which Kerre left to her friend Dame Joan Blakeney was itself designated for a later recipient: 'and yf Sir John Walsham preest ouer lefe hyr I desyre yt yan yt book may be conueyed to hym'.

Katherine Kerre's friends who were readers, as she was, comprise only a small portion of her wide East Anglian acquaintanceship. Nevertheless their identity is intriguing: an anchoress and another widowed laywoman like herself – one who had taken formal vows of chastity, however. These three women, none of whom were nuns, represent a new readership emerging during the fifteenth century. Katherine Kerre, Joan Blakeney, and the nameless anchoress are accompanied, however, though at a slight remove, by a more traditional book owner: Sir John Walsham, priest. Hence this group of friends and acquaintances includes both traditional and nontraditional readers. In their variety, these Norfolk men and women may thus be seen as thoroughly representative of a late medieval audience interested in devotional literature.

25

Gentlewomen's reading

CAROL M. MEALE and JULIA BOFFEY

> It syttyt ffwyll wele a woman to be styll, meke, serwy-
> seabyl, dredfwl, chaste, devoute, warre, sobre, softe,
> beynge glade, but nat nyce, newere idyl, but eyþer
> workyng, prayyng, redyng, spynnynge, sewyng or
> wepyng or mornyng for synne for departyng fro her
> spowse þᵗ ys Cryste.

Adding this code of conduct, in 1457, to a blank leaf in a copy of the revised Wycliffite translation of St Paul's Epistles,[1] an otherwise unknown man named Austin Fishmonger firmly set women's reading in the context of a programme of virtuous activities designed to occupy body and mind. His perception of the value of directed reading is commonplace in the late Middle Ages and early Renaissance,[2] reiterated, for example, by Geoffrey de la Tour-Landry and his English translators,[3] and in Richard Hyrd's version of Vives's *Instruction of a Christian Woman*.[4]

Most fifteenth- and early sixteenth-century books which explicitly recommend themselves to women are directed to those who claim or aspire to 'gentility'. They are rarely gentry-exclusive, however, in the sense that they might seek specifically to address those of a precisely definable 'gentry' class: those whose families ranked just below the peerage, according to one definition, or whose annual incomes from land were assessed at between £10 and £40.[5] In terms of cultural interests, distinctions between gentry and nobility are hard to draw, and would assume a fixity of class distribution which is not borne out by the evidence of social mobility. Caxton's preface to his translation of *The Book of the Knight of the Tower* recounts that the French text first came his way through the agency of a 'noble lady' who thought it suitable for the edifi-

---

1. Bodleian, ms. Lyell 27, fol. 150v: De la Mare 1971, p. 58.   2. Hannay 1985.
3. Offord 1971, p. 122.   4. 1529, STC 24856, fol. Eij; facsim. intro. Bornstein 1978.
5. C. Carpenter 1992; D. A. L. Morgan 1986.

526

cation of the young (and who presumably owned a manuscript copy), and he offers his own version 'for al maner peple in generally but in especial for ladyes & gentilwymen douȝters to lordes & gentilmen' (see fig. 25.2).[6] Definition of a precisely targeted audience is similarly hard to find in texts of a less overtly didactic cast. The edition of Thomas Malory's *Morte Darthur* which Caxton undertook is directed comprehensively at lords and ladies, gentlemen and gentlewomen, and even his translation of the romance *Blanchardin and Eglantyne* – which as the preface recalls, was commissioned by no less than Lady Margaret Beaufort – is recommended only to the vague category of 'gentil' readers.[7] A special category of 'books for gentlewomen', clearly distinguishable from the reading matter of aristocratic women treated elsewhere in this volume, is hard to isolate, and its construction is not attempted in this discussion. We have chosen rather to investigate the diverse and often opaque records[8] which suggest the range of texts read and used by women from the ranks of the gentry, and from the growing numbers of families of equivalent status, such as those of professional administrators, merchants and aldermen, and lawyers[9].

One means of documenting and exploring women's reading is through the study of particular texts in relation to the manuscripts in which they survive: copies of devotional works such as *Pore Caitif*, John Lydgate's *Life of Our Lady* and the English translations of *The Myrrour of the Blossod Lyfe of Jesu Criste* and Deguileville's *Pilgrimage of the Soul* are rich sources of information, suggesting circulation amongst a socially diverse female audience.[10]

A Bodleian Library manuscript of Lydgate's poem, for example, dating from the third quarter of the fifteenth century, is revealing for the evidence it offers of a succession of female readers over a period of approximately one hundred years.[11]

This is not one of the earliest copies of the *Life*, neither is it one of the most elaborate: it is a nicely produced parchment book with a modest amount of border decoration, but no illustration. The names of 'Domina margareta more' and 'domina Elyȝabethe Wyndesore' are found on the verso of the first flyleaf (once the pastedown), and at the end of the book

---

6. *STC* 15296; Offord 1971, p. 3.   7. Blake 1973, pp. 106–11, 57–8.
8. Such records include inventories and last testaments, and annotations to manuscripts and printed books. For discussion of their relative value, and for extensive bibliography, see the essays in Meale 1993b, and Hannay 1985.   9. Fleming 1987; Jewell 1982; Storey 1982.
10. Lydgate 1961; E. Salter 1981; Meale 1997; McGerr 1990.
11. Bodleian, ms. Hatton 73; Pächt and Alexander 1966–73, III, no. 1004.

are further inscriptions relating to these women: on fol. 121v, in a neat, late-medieval bookhand, 'Thys is my lady more boke / and sumtym it // was Quene margarete boke'; on fol. 122r, 'Thys ys my lady Dame Eliȝabeth / wyndesore boke the xiiij^th day of december / In the iiij^th yere of the Reygn off kyng herre the viij^th'; and on fol. 123r, 'Thys Boke was late my lady dame Eliȝabeth / Windesore who decessed owte of thys wourlde the / xviij^th day of January in the yere of oure lord / god m^v c^v xxxj^th And the yere of the Reygn. of kyng / henry the viiij^th xxij^th On whose sowll Ihu haue mercy Aamen', and 'quod Clarke'. These inscriptions are the work of different hands. The possible signature of 'Gartrude Powlet' is written in italic on fol. 1v, and the names of 'Gertrude' and 'Marya' appear on fol. 9v. In chronological order, the owners and/or users would therefore seem to have been Queen Margaret, Lady Margaret More, Dame Elizabeth Windsor and Gertrude Powlet.

The identity of the Queen Margaret mentioned is not certain; it is perhaps more likely, given the probable date of the manuscript, that she was Margaret of Anjou, Henry VI's queen, rather than the alternative candidate, Margaret Tudor, daughter of Henry VII, who became Queen of Scotland on her marriage in 1503. The Margaret More of this manu-script was not the eldest daughter of Sir Thomas More, as has recently been suggested;[12] Sir Thomas's daughter was not born until 1505, and the titles of 'lady' and 'domina' applied to her before marriage would be problematic. The title of 'domina' could refer to a woman who was either a secular or a religious, though that of 'lady' might tip the balance in favour of the assumption that she was not professed. The only woman of this name at present known from printed sources is, intriguingly, the Dame Margaret More who was elected abbess of Godstow in Oxfordshire in 1471; a general pardon issued to her by Edward IV in 1480 describes her as 'Margaret More . . . late of Godstowe, co. Oxford, nun, *alias* "gen-tilwoman"', *alias* late abbess of Godstowe'.[13] It would, perhaps, be in order to assume a connection between the Margaret More who was the owner of Hatton 73, and the court; she may even at one time have been a *domicella* of Margaret of Anjou, but the only surviving household records of Margaret's reign, dating from 1452 to 1453, have yielded no-one of that name.[14] The manuscript's next owner, Elizabeth Windsor, may be more securely identified. She was the daughter of William Blount; elder sister and co-heir of Edward, second Baron Mountjoy; and wife of

12. Tarvers 1992, p. 318.   13. *CPR, 1476–1485*, p. 220; see also *CPR, 1467–77*, pp. 239, 241.
14. Myers 1967–8.

Andrew Windsor of Stanwell in Middlesex, Knight of the Bath and Keeper of the Great Wardrobe under Henry VII and Henry VIII, who lived from 1467 to 1543.[15] It has been suggested that the manuscript remained in the possession of the Windsors until its acquisition by Hatton in the seventeenth century,[16] and the occurrence of the name 'Powlet' would support this idea, since Elizabeth's grandson, William, married into the Powlet, or Paulet, family: his second wife was Elizabeth, the widow of Richard Powlet, younger brother of William, first Marquess of Winchester.[17]

This evidence of the book's continued use is itself of note with regard to establishing patterns of devotional reading amongst laywomen. Also of significance, however, is the way in which the manuscript can be seen as fitting into a network in which texts and individuals amongst its women readers were linked during a specific timespan. Of Elizabeth Windsor's other interests not much more is known, although a mid-fifteenth-century Hours of the Use of Sarum carries the name 'Elizabeth wyndesor', in a late medieval hand.[18] There is also a short love epistle to a 'Mystres Anne' copied by one 'AW' on the end flyleaf, but we would hesitate to identify these as Andrew Windsor's initials. Elizabeth's sister-in-law, Margaret Windsor, however, is known to have owned several books. Prioress of Syon in 1518, Margaret was holder of the office at the time of the abbey's dissolution in 1539, when she was awarded a pension of fifty marks.[19] She was still living in 1543, when she received a legacy from her brother, Andrew. The inscription 'Cest Liure apertient a moy / Marguerete Wyndesore' occurs on the first page of a copy of Boccaccio's *De casibus virorum*, in the edition printed in Lyons in 1483, probably by Huss and Schaebling. This book was a gift from a certain Henry Parker.[20] Another printed text in which her name is found is the *Tree and xij frutes of the holy goost*, issued by Michael Fawkes and Robert Copland in two parts, in 1534 and 1535.[21] A third volume was a manuscript, a fifteenth-century psalter, the present whereabouts of which are not known.[22] Margaret was also the recipient of 'A booke of prayers', with a request to pray for the donor, in the 1519 will of Anne Andrew, wife of Sir Thomas Bourchier, of Wetherden in Suffolk.[23] Anne was the aunt of Margaret and

---

15. *Complete Peerage*, XII (2), pp. 792–4.   16. *BSC*, II (2), pp. 850–1, no. 4119.
17. *Complete Peerage*, XII (2), pp. 795–6.
18. Huntington, ms. HM 1087; Dutschke 1989, II, pp. 393–6.
19. Aungier 1840, p. 81n; *LP Henry VIII*, XIV (2) (1539), no. 581.
20. It is now PML, 600.   21. *STC* 13608; CUL, C.7.12.
22. Ker 1964–87, p. 310.   23. Richmond 1987, p. 227.

Andrew Windsor, her sister, Elizabeth, having married Thomas Windsor.

Anne Andrew is an interesting figure in her own right. Other books itemized in her will were her best massbook and second massbook, which she left, respectively, to the altar of St Blaise in Wetherden church, and to her son, Andrew. Her 'litle masbooke' was to go to her daughter Alice Rous and her husband, Sir William, to have for their lifetimes, and thereafter to go to any one of their sons who should become a priest.[24] Other books Anne owned she did not mention in this context. A copy of the Middle English prose *Brut* was in her possession during her two marriages (her first husband was Sir John Sulyard, Justice of the King's Bench);[25] and, like her nephew's wife, Elizabeth Windsor, Anne owned Lydgate's *Life of Our Lady*: Bodleian Library ms. Ashmole 39 contains what are almost certainly the signatures of Anne and Sir Thomas Bourchier on front and rear pastedowns, together with a short prayer – 'Anne Bowrgcher lady *preser*ue hyr in good helthe'. Other evidence can be found to suggest the kind of circles in which she moved. Colin Richmond has pointed out a connection with the household of Cecily Neville, Duchess of York, who was notable for her piety and her interest in books:[26] two of the beneficiaries of Cecily's will were Nicholas Talbot and his wife Jane, and it was this Nicholas who, in his will registered at Bury St Edmunds in 1501, left Anne 'a seynt Gregorius pyte [i. e. 'Image of Pity'] of gold enamelyd and a lytyll boke she gaue me'. This was possibly an image of the Man of Sorrows, as incorporated in visual representations of the Mass of St Gregory, at which the saint was believed to have seen such an image.[27] There is also a link with another owner of Lydgate's *Life of Our Lady*: Anne's first husband, John Sulyard, was nephew to Thomasin Hopton of Blythburgh in Suffolk, who, on her death in 1498, left a copy of the poem to her granddaughter, Thomasin Sidney.[28] Documentary sources indicate that the families of Hopton and Sulyard were close.[29] The coincidence of interest in the Lydgate text amongst this group of women who were connected with one another through ties of kinship, friendship, or service, is marked, and indicates that the poem may have much to tell us about their devotional reading practices.

This charting of the connections of individuals is suggestive of the

24. Richmond 1987, pp. 226, 224, 225.   25. Princeton UL, ms. 150.
26. Richmond 1987, p. 218 n. 77; C. A. J. Armstrong 1973.
27. Rubin 1991, pp. 308–10; Tymms 1850, p. 88.   28. PRO Prob, 11/11, fols. 151r–152r.
29. Richmond 1981, pp. 115, 241–2, 245–7, 252.

multiple and fluid networks to which gentlewomen might have had access, and by which their reading might have been shaped. The operation of such networks in a metropolitan context can be illustrated from what is known of Beatrice Lynne, daughter of William Lynne, a wealthy London woolman and grocer, who died in 1421, and of Alice, who on her husband's death took a vow of chastity, leaving Beatrice to grow up under the guardianship of a London mercer. She married, first, Thomas Oxney, and second Avery Corneburgh, Yeoman of the King's Chamber, Under-treasurer of England, and eventually Keeper of the Great Wardrobe.[30] Family connections brought her into the circle of London readers and book-producers associated with John Shirley: her sister Margaret became Shirley's wife, probably during the 1430s, and the relationship is documented in a copy of Hoccleve's *Regiment of Princes*, apparently owned by Corneburgh, to which Shirley added some shorter poems and an engrossed inscription which links his name with those of his wife and sister-in-law.[31] Whether or not Beatrice actually read this manuscript, it demonstrates her association with a circle which actively promoted a wide range of texts in the vernacular and drew on the services of a number of professionals in the book-trade. Other acquaintances are suggested by the appearance in the Huntington manuscript of the names of Nicholas and Elizabeth Gaynesford, who served in the household of Queen Elizabeth Woodville, and Queen Elizabeth of York,[32] and whose daughter Elizabeth married a gentleman porter to Cardinal Morton. Gaynesford names appear also in a copy of the *Brut*.[33] Alongside the literary interests which might be inferred from the Corneburghs' connections is a marked piety. Before his death in 1487, Avery Corneburgh established a chantry chapel in Romford parish and made provision for a tomb on which was to be inscribed a lengthy poem (adapted from an epitaph which enjoyed a wide circulation) giving details of the foundation, and instructions for the reading of the bederoll which was to include his wife's name with his own.[34]

Beatrice lived until 1502, and at her death was buried at St Dunstan's in the East, in Stepney, with her parents. Her own piety is manifested in concern for a local community of religious, the Minoresses of the house of the Virgin and St Francis without Aldgate, to whom she donated an illuminated psalter: 'M*emorandum* that this sawter was gevyn by Beterice

30. Erler 1993a; see now Boffey 1996.
31. Huntington, ms. EL 26. A. 13; Doyle 1983a, p. 177; Dutschke 1989, I, pp. 35–9.
32. Myers 1967–8.   33. BL, Royal ms. 18.B.III.
34. McIntosh 1986; Gray 1961; Duffy 1992.

Carneburgh' unto Dame Grace Centurio to have it to her for terme of her lyfe and aftir hir discesse to remayne unto what syster of the meneres that is shall plese the seme grace to gyf it never to be gevyn awey solde nor lent but onely to the meneres, they to pray perpetually for the sawles named in this present Sawter.'[35]

Although she had access to various potential sources of books, Beatrice's single personal record is left, entirely typically, in a devotional manuscript which was to be passed by another woman to a community of female religious. From the community of the Minoresses survives further evidence of networks of women readers, both religious and lay, whose spheres of activity overlapped in significant ways. Of the nuns and lay sisters, who numbered thirty-two at the Dissolution, many came from gentry and mercantile families, and the community was further enlarged by the households who inhabited two mansions which had been constructed within the precinct.[36] Although the version of the 'rewle of the sustris menouresses enclosid', translated from Latin via French and copied for the house in a manuscript, makes no specific recommendations about reading,[37] it is clear that books were an important interest of the community.[38] Dame An Frenell was given a book of hours, by another Dame Anne's porter.[39] Dame Margaret Hasley gave to Sister Anne Bassyngburne a copy of *Pore Caitif* (untraced), and Dame Christine Saint Nicolas, at her death in 1455/6, bequeathed to her sisters 'a tretice made to religious wommen which is clepid the doctrine of the hert', a fifteenth-century translation of Gerard of Liège's *De Doctrina Cordis*, which survives in manuscript (see fig. 25.1).[40] The provision of devotional material translated from Latin into the vernacular for female audiences appears an entirely consistent practice for this period; Dame Eleanor Hull's aptitude for Latin may not have been representative of women of her class.[41] Other important devotional books were passed between different members of this community, as is indicated by an inscription in a copy of the works of Walter Hylton: 'Dame Elyzabeth horwode abbas of the menoresse off / london to her gostle comfforthe bow3te thys boke hyt / to remayne to the vse off 3e systerres of 3e sayde / place to pray fore 3e yeuere & ffore 3e sowles off hyre ffader / & here modere Thomas horwode

35. Wellington, Bible Society of New Zealand Library, ms. 135; Manion, Vines and De Hamel 1989, p. 119.
36. *VCH, London*, pp. 516–19; Tomlinson 1907; Bourdillon 1926; Carlin 1987.
37. Bodleian, ms. Bodley 585; Chambers and Seton 1914.   38. Ker 1964–87, p. 123.
39. Reigate Parish Church, Cranston Library, ms. 2322; Ker 1969–92, IV, pp. 201–3.
40. Cambridge, Trinity Coll. ms. B.14.15.   41. Barratt 1993, 1995.

& beatryxe & ʒe sowle / off mayster Robert Alderton.'[42] Elizabeth, who is recorded as abbess in 1469, has a characteristic concern for family, community, and perhaps for one of the priests who ministered to the sisters. Margaret de la Pole, of the Suffolk De la Pole family, a lay resident in one of the houses within the precinct, disposed in her will, proved 15 December 1473, of a mass book and a porteous.[43]

The reading of these associates of a relatively well-endowed religious house close to London may perhaps be thought atypical of gentlewomen in less specialized milieux, but an almost exact parallel to the texts listed here is to be found in the will of a Norwich widow, Margaret Purdans, which was made in 1481.[44] Here an English psalter is left to a priest and a small psalter to Margaret's son, a copy of 'Le Doctrine of the Herte' to the Franciscan nuns of Bruisyard in Suffolk, an English book of Saint Bridget to the Benedictine nuns of Thetford, and 'a book called Hylton' to a certain Alice Barly. Furthermore, it seems likely that manuscripts connected with the Minoresses reached lay readers outside their own immediate circle. A version of the prose *Three Kings of Cologne* was specially adapted, by means of an acrostic, for two women called Margaret Moningtown and Maud Stranslea: the first of these is perhaps to be identified with the Margaret Monynton recorded as abbess at Aldgate in 1433 and 1441.[45] In one of the manuscripts which preserve the acrostic, the text forms part of a carefully produced anthology catering for the spiritual concerns of women readers.[46] Another copy of this version of the text, however, is amalgamated with William Nassington's *Speculum Vitae* and the unique surviving copy of Quixley's translation of Gower's *Traitie pour essampler les amantz mariets*, seemingly made in Yorkshire – a collection which addresses the needs of lay readers, and purveys texts which originated some distance from London.[47] A further copy of the text is accompanied by the romance *Titus and Vespasian* (now fragmentary), and scientific treatises in Latin prose.[48]

Even within the precinct at Aldgate, books on secular subjects seem to have been available. A manuscript copy of Caxton's editions of *The Game of the Chesse*[49] and *The Cordyall*,[50] made in 1484 by 'Dominus Grace', came into the possession of Dame Margaret Woodward.[51] She is possibly to be

---

42. BL, Harl. ms. 2397, f. 94v.   43. PRO, Prob. 11/6, f. 90r.
44. NCC Register A. Caston (16), fols. 163v–165r; Harrod 1855, p. 331.
45. Horstmann 1886.   46. BL, Royal ms.18.A.x.
47. BL, Stowe ms. 951; MacCracken 1908.   48. BL, Cotton ms. Vespasian E. xvi.
49. 1474; *STC* 4920.   50. 1479; *STC* 5758.
51. BL, Sloane ms. 779; A. G. Watson 1979, I, p. 159.

identified as the Margaret Woodward included in the pension list made at the suppression of the abbey in 1539, who was at this time noted to be fifty-two years of age. Several of the lay inhabitants were women whose lives brought them into contact with books and book-owners, just as some of the sisters themselves came from gentry families with literary interests. Recorded as a sister in 1494, for example, is Mary Turell, niece of John Clopton of Long Melford in Suffolk, whose family read the poems of Lydgate and Chaucer,[52] while in the household of the widowed Elizabeth Mowbray (a later tenant of the mansion constructed for Elizabeth de Burgh in the precinct) was Jane Talbot, widow of Sir Humphrey Talbot (d. 1494) whose will disposes of a copy of the 'Seege of Troy'[53] and whose name appears in a copy of the *Anciennes Chroniques de Flandres*.[54] By the early sixteenth century, access to learned humanist circles is suggested by Sir Thomas More's dedication of his translation of *The lyfe of Johan Picus Erle of Mirandula* to 'his right entierly beloved sister in crist Joyeuce Leigh', granddaughter of a mayor of London, whose mother was a resident of the house, and who in turn became a sister;[55] and by Beatrice Corneburgh's acquaintance with the Colet family, mentioned in her will: John Colet was vicar of St Dunstan's, Stepney, where Beatrice and her parents were buried.

Communities associated with spiritual advisers or religious houses clearly played a central role in the provision of women's reading, and the details assembled here confirm evidence such as that generated by studies of the Brigittines of Syon and the Benedictine nuns of Barking.[56] Women's primary interests appear at first sight, from the surviving evidence, to have lain in the areas of didactic and devotional reading, and a glance at the output of the early printers would seem to confirm that books which fell into this category were often specifically targeted at women. Margaret Beaufort and her daughter-in-law, Elizabeth of York, for instance, sponsored Caxton's edition of *The Fifteen Oes*,[57] and Margaret herself, through the medium of the printing press, continued to be actively involved in the promotion of religious materials, such as Hylton's *Scale of Perfection*.[58] Texts such as the *Scale*, *The tretyse ... of loue*[59] and the *Shorte treatyse of contemplacyon taken out of the boke of Margerie kempe*,[60] issued by Wynkyn de Worde respectively in 1494, 1493 and

52. G. M. Gibson 1989, pp. 79–96; Chaucer 1940, I, pp. 288, 616.
53. Perhaps JRUL, ms. Eng. 1; see Ker 1969–92, III, pp. 398–400.
54. BL, Cotton ms. Nero A. iii.   55. Parks 1976; *CWM* I, xxxix–xl.
56. Hutchison 1989; Doyle 1958; D. N. Bell 1992, 1995.   57. 1491; *STC* 20195.
58. *STC* 14042; Edwards and Meale 1993.   59. *STC* 24234.   60. *STC* 14924.

1501, seem designed to foster an awareness of the value of works of spiritual direction amongst a female audience (cf. fig. 9.2).[61] Indeed, the publication of what is in effect a seven-page epitome of Margery's text is eloquent of the desire of someone – whether printer or sponsor, or some prior reader – to disseminate a text in which the potentially subversive elements of Margery's account of her struggle with Church authorities have been excised in favour of producing an unproblematic endorsement of meditative prayer.[62]

The strictures voiced by moralists such as Vives against allowing young women, in particular, access to secular literature are in accord with this aspect of publishing policy, and their protests were reiterated by writers such as Roger Ascham[63] and Thomas Salter, who fulminated against the 'excityng' of young women's memories by 'bookes, ballades, songes, sonettes, and ditties of daliance'.[64] The anxieties evinced by these writers, however, who addressed audiences of gentry status and above, suggest that women routinely took advantage of the available opportunities to read a wide variety of texts in both manuscript and print. It was not necessarily, for example, only in the matter of religion that women may have joined together in associations more or less formal. It would be rewarding to look at the so-called Findern manuscript – an anthology of courtly poetry, including extracts from works by Chaucer and Gower, and the romance of *Sir Degrevant*, the compilation of which began in Derbyshire in the 1440s – from the point of view of the collaborative interests of the women whose names occur on its pages, but whose identities and relationships with one another have not yet been convincingly explained.[65]

To interpret 'reading' in its broadest sense to include the material which women may have listened to as it was read aloud or used for instruction, or books which they occasionally consulted as well as those which they carefully perused, draws into this discussion a number of volumes which may have been generally accessible in family or household contexts. The extensive household responsibilities often exercised by women necessitated competence in many areas for which written record or instruction would have been of use.[66] Service and devotional books

61. Sargent 1983; Fisher 1951; Meech and Allen 1940; Hull 1982.
62. Meech and Allen 1940, pp. xlvi–xlviii; Holbrook 1987.
63. *The Scholemaster* (1570), *STC* 832; Ascham 1904, p. 231.
64. *A mirrhor mete for all mothers* (1579), *STC* 21634; L. B. Wright 1931.
65. CUL, ms. Ff.1.6; Beadle and Owen 1977; K. Harris 1983; McNamer 1991.
66. Archer 1992; Ward 1992, 1995.

(often used for elementary instruction in reading),[67] works of religious instruction, practical manuals, and assorted material for private or social diversion, such as songs or romances and other narratives, might have been communally available. Evidence that women made use of books such as these is of various kinds, and often no more than inferential. In certain cases, as in the Findern manuscript, their names may occur in the volumes, perhaps as signatures, or else copied by some other family or household member. The later 'Devonshire Manuscript', in which are drawn together many of the poems associated with Wyatt and his circle, contains the names of some of the gentlewomen of Anne Boleyn's household, who may themselves have contributed to the copying of the collection.[68] In other cases, books contain texts which make direct reference to female family members, and there would surely have been little point to their preservation if they were not to be read to or by the women concerned. The combined cartulary and miscellany put together by Humphrey Newton in Cheshire in the late fifteenth and early sixteenth centuries includes several apparently autograph copies of poems which seem (albeit cryptically) to address identifiable female members of his family,[69] and the rather later Shropshire 'Welles Anthology' contains references, not always flattering, to local male and female acquaintances of the compilers.[70] Such allusions depend upon an audience or readership of intimates for their effect, and were presumably for delectation in a household context.

In the case of certain anthologies, the assortment of contents implies use among a mixed readership, even though more concrete evidence (in the form of ownership inscriptions, for example) cannot confirm this. Thus the twin collections of romances and devotional material compiled by the Yorkshire gentleman, Robert Thornton, in the fifteenth century,[71] have been categorized as family reading.[72] Practical information on the calendar, medicine and hawking, as well as on household matters such as dyeing fabrics, preparing writing materials and the cultivation of fruit, is amalgamated with material for spiritual instruction and for diversion in a fifteenth-century collection probably put together in some kind of gentry or near-gentry milieu close to the Welsh borders.[73] Several of the medical receipts are devised with specific female ailments in mind, and

---

67. Erler 1984.   68. BL, Add. ms. 17492; Southall 1964; Heale 1995.
69. Bodleian, ms. Lat. misc. c. 66; Robbins 1950.
70. Bodleian, ms. Rawl. c. 813; E. Wilson 1990.
71. BL, Add. ms. 31042, and Lincoln Cathedral Library, ms. 91.   72. Thompson 1987.
73. NLW, ms. Porkington 10; Kurvinen 1953.

the manuscript also includes a text of *The good wyfe wold a pylgremage*,[74] a verse code of conduct for the single girl, directed from a mother to her daughter. The incorporation of the obscene verse *Tale of Ten Wives*,[75] in which gossips discuss the sexual prowess of their husbands, is a reminder of the wealth of inflammatory anti-female texts whose flourishing manuscript circulation quickly recommended them to printers.

Multi-purpose anthologies and miscellanies of these kinds were compiled well into the era of printing, and the geographical range of their various provenances makes clear their widespread appeal, or usefulness, to gentry families. In a metropolitan context, we might look for similar collections in the hands of aldermanic or merchant families, whose households (often including apprentices among the family dependants) could be large, wealthy and well situated in terms of access to books and exemplars for fresh copies. A compendious anthology of religious material was illustrated and rubricated for the mercer Roger Thorney, and its range of contents, which include lives of female saints and certain of Lydgate's poems elsewhere associated with female patrons, may indicate that it was compiled with Thorney's female relatives in mind.[76] The dense concentration of Latin in the commonplace book associated with the Ramston family of Essex in the sixteenth century prompts questions about the Latin literacy of the female members of this family.[77] Here, in a volume copied by many hands over an extended period, are many Latin notes, legal formulae, proverbs, and poems, some of a hallowed clerical anti-feminist slant, which at first sight would appear to constitute a range of reference material for the use of male members of the family. Alongside them, however, are texts less specifically targeted: a prayer in English for the safety of Henry VIII and that of Rowland Ramston and his wife Mary; notes on the nativities of certain family members; an English prayer attributed to Queen Elizabeth of York; hymns, prayers, lyrics and medical receipts in both English and Latin. A volume such as this seems less for 'reading' than for occasional and probably selective consultation by many different members of the household.

That women's reading habits and tastes were in practice more eclectic than is often supposed, and remained so throughout the period under consideration, is evidenced by their continuing use of manuscript copies of works by authors of well-established reputation, and by their acquisi-

---

74. *IMEV* 3363; Riddy 1996, pp. 71, 76–7.   75. *IMEV* 1852.
76. Cambridge, Trinity Coll., ms. R.3.21; Boffey and Thompson 1989, pp. 287–8; Boffey 1995.
77. Cambridge, Trinity Coll., ms. O.2.53; M. R. James 1900–4, III, pp. 169–74.

tion of newly printed texts.[78] Women formed an important part of the
reading constituency of Chaucer, Gower and Lydgate in the sixteenth
century, for example, just as they had in the fifteenth.[79] Owners of the
Confessio amantis later in our period include Anne Russell, associate of
Spenser and John Dee; and Margaret Clifford, wife of Henry Stanley, Earl
of Derby.[80] The copy of Lydgate's *Fall of Princes* known as the Rutland
Manuscript was given in the early part of the sixteenth century to
Margaret Nevill, daughter of Ralph Nevill, 4th Earl of Westmoreland, by
her 'louyng mother Katheryn Westmoreland';[81] Mary Sidney, mother of
Sir Philip, had another.[82] Other manuscripts of the *Fall* containing
inscriptions and annotations made by women survive: the names of 'dam
Anne dacres', 'mastres ellenore suster to lord dacres', 'ellenore goffe',
'Elysabeth lawarr', 'Anne Oxebrygg' and 'Margaret belknapp' occur, in
the manner of a *liber amicorum*, in a codex which a later owner notes was
once in the possession of 'the lady Elizabeth Carewes of Bedyngton';[83]
and what may be the signature of 'Elysabethe Seynt John' occurs in
another.[84] Women also left their mark on copies of texts which fit more
comfortably into the category of instructive works. Trevisa's translation
of Higden's *Polychronicon*, for instance, was owned in Caxton's 1482
edition[85] by 'Ellenor clyfford', daughter of Charles Brandon, Duke of
Suffolk, and first wife of Henry Clifford, 2nd Earl of Cumberland (the
name of 'Margaret Wynnyngetone' also appears). A copy of the second
edition, published by De Worde in 1495,[86] commemorates 'mystres
breget heydon' and 'Elizabeth heydon', along with 'John heydon', probably to be identified as three of the children of Sir Henry Heydon of
Baconsthorp in Norfolk, steward to Cecily, Duchess of York.[87]

The association of women with romance, though expected, is less
easily established. A few manuscripts only of Middle English texts may
be securely assigned to female owners, though evidence is more forth-

78. Significant information on women's ownership of early printed books is incorporated in
the database on 'Books and Readers, 1400–1557' compiled by Margaret Lane Ford, where,
alongside service books and devotional texts, are to be found, *inter alia*, a Latin version of
Plutarch's *Lives*, chronicles of both France and England, and a medical text-book.
79. Meale 1993a.   80. Tuve 1940, pp. 152–3.   81. Belvoir Castle, Duke of Rutland, fol. 1v.
82. As testified by a manuscript sold at Sotheby's, 8 July 1970, lot 98.
83. BL, ms. Sloane 4031.
84. Bodleian, ms. e Mus. 1; for descriptions of these manuscripts, see Bergen 1924–7, IV, pp.
14, 61, 79.
85. *STC* 13438; Bodleian, Douce 206 (information from Margaret Lane Ford's database).
86. *STC* 13439.
87. Durham, UL, Bamburgh Select 13, sigs. cccxliiii^v, clxxxii^v, cccxxxix^v; Blomefield 1805–10,
VI, pp. 505–6.

coming with regard to their possession of works in French.[88] Following the introduction of printed editions of both new works and those with a proven popularity, however, much may be deduced about the earlier circulation of romances amongst a female readership. Caxton invokes the approval of noblewomen such as Margaret of York and Margaret Beaufort, as well as unnamed gentlewomen, in his publication of recent prose translations, while Richard Hyrd's translation of Vives's treatise for Catherine of Aragon[89] is of interest in signalling some of the titles of older romances, many in verse, which would seem to have been likely to appeal to women of all classes.[90] Lord Berners' statement, on the title-page of his translation of the peninsular romance of *The castell of loue*,[91] that he undertook the work 'at the instaunce of the lady / Elizabeth Carew, late wyfe to syr Nicholas Carew knyght' (and the one-time owner, as we have seen, of a Lydgate manuscript), is a more public, and less contentious declaration of women's interests in the genre,[92] but it was not until the publication in 1578 of the first part of the translation from the Spanish of *The mirrour of princely deedes and knighthood*[93] by 'M. T.' – Margaret Tyler, by her own account 'seruant' to the parents of her work's dedicatee, 'the Lord Thomas Haward' – that a woman was able to write an apologia for the genre.[94] Tyler writes in her preface of her 'olde reading' in romance and her 'delight' in the original Spanish text,[95] and her justification for her activity in translating this work of chivalry – that it is for 'profit & delight'[96] – recalls a tradition of commentary on romance which encompasses Caxton, and the late fifteenth-century annotator of the unique copy of the alliterative romance of *William of Palerne*, who commended the English work's patron, Humphrey Bohun, for his 'entent to kepe youythe from ydellnes'.[97] Tyler's detailed comments on the chivalric action of the *Mirrour*, furthermore – as when she writes that 'to report of armes is not so odious / but yt it may be borne withal, not onely in you men which / your selues are fighters, but in vs women, to whom the benefit in equal part apperteineth of your victories'[98] – constitute an early example of reader-response to the genre on the part of a woman.

Most literary genres of any significance in the fifteenth and sixteenth centuries can be associated, in the form of at least one representative sur-

88. Meale 1993a and 1994.   89. Blake 1973, pp. 57–8, 97–101, 103–6, 106–11; *STC* 24856.
90. Facsim. intro. Bornstein 1978, fol. E4r.   91. *STC* 21739.5.   92. Crane 1936.
93. *STC* 18859.   94. Krontiris 1988.   95. Fols. A2r, A3r.   96. Fol. A3r.
97. Cambridge, King's Coll. ms. 13, fol. 86r; Skeat 1897, p. xxiii.   98. Fol. A3v.

viving text, with gentlewomen readers. These survivals suggest that French texts were virtually as accessible to them as those in the vernacular. Latin Bibles and service-books, stray examples of other Latin texts, and certain works of information in both English and Latin were also clearly available to some of these readers, as Margaret Lane Ford's research has made apparent. The surviving evidence suggests that the only categories of book which may have been unfamiliar to women from the ranks of the gentry were professionally oriented ones such as law-books, university teaching texts and some medical compilations. Whatever routine advice about suitable reading matter may have been dispensed throughout the period, the reality, for gentlewomen, involved access to a range of books much wider than has been suspected.[99]

99. We are very grateful to Mary Erler, Margaret Lane Ford, A. S. G. Edwards and Anne Sutton, who generously offered help and information which contributed to the writing of this chapter.

26

Music

JOHN MILSOM

Music is first and foremost a performance art, and it relies only selectively upon written record for its propagation, practice and preservation. For that reason, music books (and the various forms of ephemera that existed alongside them) shed light on only a limited number of the musical activities that existed in late medieval Britain.[1] To take an extreme case, very few notated sources of British instrumental music survive from before the sixteenth century. Almost certainly few ever existed, at least in permanent form.[2] From pictorial and documentary evidence we know that musical instruments were played and appreciated at all levels of late medieval British society, from the most powerful and privileged down to the humblest. In almost all cases, however, the playing was done from memory and by ear. Professional instrumentalists – the trumpeters who performed on ceremonial occasions, the wind-players who accompanied meals or provided music for dance, the minstrels who entertained royalty and nobility, the waits who played at civic events – all appear to have learnt their repertoires largely by rote rather than from the book. It is unlikely that many of them relied upon musical notation; there was no reason why they should do so. Only with the rise of amateur music-making during the second half of the sixteenth century did notated instrumental music become at all common.[3]

The situation was apparently little different among professional players of keyboard instruments. Although at least one organ could be found in every pre-Reformation church of any substance, many organists

---

1. For an introduction to the social context of late medieval British music, see Sandon and Page 1992, Milsom 1992b. Caldwell 1991 provides more detailed coverage of specifically musical issues.
2. Musicians commonly made use of erasable surfaces such as slates and wax-covered tablets, although surviving examples are rare. For a photographic illustration of an erasable slate with permanently inscribed blank staves, used in the Low Countries probably in the sixteenth century, see Schreurs 1995, p. 125, plate 48.
3. Pictorial evidence supports this view; see Salmen 1976.

appear to have played extempore, by memory, or with nothing before them except a book of plainchant – the unaccompanied liturgical melodies that formed the staple of organized worship. Decorated plainchant must have been a common sound in medieval churches, the organist playing the chant melody with one hand, and accompanying it with the other. For the experienced player, however, a notated musical score was superfluous, at least up to the point where the complexity of the accompaniment demanded some degree of pre-planning, or a need arose for his music to be fixed permanently in writing.[4] A conceptual distinction should be drawn between an organist's provision of 'music', and the performance of 'musical works' (or 'compositions'); the extempore embellishment of a plainchant melody falls into the first of those two categories; a more artful working-out of an accompaniment, which might lead both to the notation of music, and to identical repeated performances of it, falls into the latter category. It is probably no coincidence that the rise of notated keyboard music and the emergence of a repertoire of true 'compositions' (by named composers) again dovetails with the rise of non-professional musicianship and a demand for pieces that amateurs could play.

Even for church choirs, the only musical repertoire that regularly called for notation and the presence of a music book on the lectern was plainchant (see fig. 26.1). During the early stages of their training, both novices within the religious orders and boy choristers were expected to read the relatively simple musical notation used to preserve liturgical chant. (Plainchant notation records the pitches of melodies, but not the precise durations or rhythms used to perform it.) Books containing plainchant were also used by church singers to perform primitive forms of polyphony, without the need for any additional notation. For instance, a chant melody might be accompanied by one or more extemporized (or previously memorized) melodic lines that moved in harmony with it, largely in parallel motion. More elaborate conventions also existed, in which the accompaniment assumed greater independence from the chant. None of this primitive polyphony, however, demanded notation other than the plainchant book itself. Only when the singers were particularly inexperienced, or an attempt was made to go beyond convention, might any form of written record be found necessary.[5]

4. For evidence of books used by organists before 1500, see Wathey 1988. For a list (with transcriptions) of the earliest surviving English keyboard sources, see Caldwell 1995.
5. For examples of notated sources of simple polyphony, see Trowell 1978. The practice of improvising polyphony from plainchant is discussed in Harrison 1980, *passim*.

A considerable intellectual gulf existed between the system used to notate plainchant and the more sophisticated mensural notation that was needed to specify the rhythm as well as the pitch of fully composed musical works. Until the sixteenth century, mensural notation was principally the preserve of professional church musicians, the majority of whom learnt to read and sing from it during their years as choirboys.[6] Once acquired, this form of musical literacy was effectively self-perpetuating, since the boy choristers of one generation became the adult singers, choirmasters, composers, music-copyists and teachers of the next, or the clerics and diplomats who employed that next generation of literate performing musicians. During the later Middle Ages, male singers attached to cathedrals, abbey churches, certain parish churches, colleges and private household chapels were the principal makers and users of music books. The English and Scottish royal household chapels, the Lady Chapels of Canterbury and Durham Cathedrals, the chapels of Eton College and Magdalen College, Oxford, the greater parish churches in the City of London, are all typical examples of foundations at which fully literate singers are known to have been present, at which new music was composed using mensural notation, and where music books containing polyphony were used on a daily or regular basis.[7]

For musical works, the concept of the 'book' as an ideal medium for permanent storage was not a standard and invariable one.[8] Individual musical compositions during this period occupied only a small amount of written space – at most, fewer than twenty double-page spreads even for an elaborate setting of the Ordinary of the Mass. For that reason, it is unusual to find any single work occupying a book on its own. A rare exception is the anonymous five-part *Missa O quam suavis*, which takes up virtually the entire written space of an 18–folio choirbook in Cambridge.[9] Composed early in the sixteenth century, the mass is an unusually elaborate showpiece of considerable length, and it is presented as a high-quality manuscript, possibly for submission as a degree requirement at one of the universities, although nothing certain is known about the composer of the music or the makers of the book.[10] This is, however,

6. On the musical education of choristers, see J. Flynn 1995. Between chant notation and mensural notation there existed various forms of *ad hoc* notation that attempted to convey information about duration and rhythm. See Bent 1968, pp. 149–50; Bowers and Wathey 1983, pp. 28–36; and various examples of musical graffiti illustrated in Pritchard 1967.
7. For further information on choral foundations that promoted polyphony in late medieval Britain, see Baillie 1958, R. Bowers 1975, 1981, and Wathey 1989b, all of which expand upon the foundation research of Harrison 1980.
8. This point is developed in Wathey 1989a.   9. CUL, ms. Nn.6.46.
10. See Fenlon 1982, pp. 18–21; Bray 1995, p. 4.

an unrepresentative case. More typically, individual compositions were either preserved and transmitted on loose leaves, rolls and gatherings, or brought together into book-like collections of pieces.

It is also important to note that singers in the fifteenth and sixteenth century conventionally performed from individual voice-parts, not from scores in which all the voice-parts are aligned with one another. When a polyphonic composition was copied into a single book, it was customary for the various voice-parts to be distributed on to different areas of a double-page spread (or 'opening'). To perform from such a 'choirbook', singers would assemble around a lectern and simultaneously read their parts from different areas of the opening. Page-turns were carefully synchronized. In sixteenth-century Britain, choirbook format was supplemented (and eventually replaced) by 'partbook' format, in which individual voice-parts were copied into separate volumes; four-voice music, for example, would require a four-partbook set. Ephemera such as rolls might adapt the layout of the choirbook, or replace the function of the partbook. In all of those formats, however, the physical layout of a polyphonic composition on the written page made it difficult or impossible for a silent reader to construct a fully rounded mental idea of the work's sound by looking at the notation alone. For the same reason, the concept of the conductor with full visual control over the music of his singers did not exist during this period.

Books of polyphony came into being either when a stable repertoire of pieces accumulated within an existing institution, or when a new (or revitalized, or newly expanded) choir imported a repertoire from elsewhere. In the first instance – that of recording an established and often expanding repertoire – book production often fell to the hands of local scribes, above all the singers themselves. Payments made for their labour as copyists are common, and the more crudely executed and utilitarian books are always likely to be their work. For higher-quality productions, copying may have involved dedicated craftsmen or organized groups of penmen that existed within (or had association with) professional singing-men, although relatively little is known about the identity, location, organization and activity of such persons or groups.[11] In principle, the contents of a new music book could be fully worked out in advance. In practice, however, relatively few show signs of having been copied in

11. For further discussion of professional music copying, see especially Wathey 1989a; also Skinner 1994, pp. 397–9, and references to Robert Colson, 'pricker of bookes for the kinges chapell', in Ashbee 1993.

systematic fashion from beginning to end. More commonly they were expanded as new compositions became available, or assembled out of previously discrete fascicles. No example has yet come to light from late medieval Britain of two books of polyphony whose contents are identical and arranged in the same order.

With few exceptions, the life-span of composed polyphony was finite, almost never exceeding fifty years. To take a single example, the music of John Dunstaple (d. 1453) had virtually fallen out of circulation by 1500. A single Magnificat by him was included in the Eton Choirbook of around 1503,[12] surrounded by newer music; one puzzle-canon by him was copied into the 'Henry VIII's ms.' of around 1515,[13] again in the company of more recent compositions; and mention of his music is made in a 1529 inventory of chapel books at King's College, Cambridge.[14] By the end of the sixteenth century, Dunstaple appears to have been of interest only to theorists and collectors; he is cited once, for example, in Thomas Morley's treatise *A plaine and easie introduction to practicall Musicke* (London 1597).[15] Changes in musical fashion were largely responsible for the demise of Dunstaple's works, and those of his contemporaries. In addition, musical notation evolved during the period, to the extent that many musicians of around 1550 would have found it difficult or impossible to sing from a book of polyphony written in around 1400. Changes in the size and ability of choirs could also have a significant impact upon the musical requirements of institutions, leading to a turn-over of repertoire. Since the most famous composer of one generation might be little more than a name to the next, it follows that no canon of polyphonic compositions existed for which there was a perennial demand. Only in the wake of the Reformation did attitudes towards the music of the past change significantly. Many Elizabethan music books contain large amounts of obsolete Catholic church music from the earlier sixteenth century, collected in a spirit of respect and nostalgia, or perhaps even in the hope that those works might some day be useful to a restored Catholic liturgy.[16] Older music still, however, is absent from the Elizabethan collections. The works of Dunstaple, for example, are missing from them.

For all of those reasons, the destruction of obsolete performing materi-

12. Eton Coll., ms. 178.   13. BL, Add. ms. 31922.
14. Harrison 1956–67, I, p. xvi; Stevens 1973, no. 32; Harrison 1980, p. 433.
15. *STC* 18133; Morley 1952, p. 291.
16. These retrospective collections are studied in Milsom 1995.

als must have been commonplace. Once the contents of a music book had fallen out of use, there was little reason to preserve it – or for that matter the rolls and other unbound materials that existed alongside or in place of books. Because performing copies of musical works were made for the eyes of singing-men, they were rarely objects of special visual appeal, and until the reign of Elizabeth there is little evidence of antiquarian interest in old music. Widespread destruction also took place at the Reformation, when many music books and service books used for the celebration of the Latin rite were either burned or sold off to stationers for recycling. Under those circumstances, it will come as no surprise to find that no complete library of music books survives from any pre-Reformation choral foundation. Only from inventories can the repertoires of choirs and the contents of lost libraries be determined; and since choirs regularly discarded their old music, even an inventory usually provides nothing more than a snap-shot of the music and music books that were in use at the time when the list was made.

Taken together, these factors have led to very considerable losses. The majority of performing copies of music used by British choirs in the fifteenth and sixteenth centuries have either disappeared without trace, or survive only in fragmentary form, most commonly as parchment or paper waste used by bookbinders.[17] From odd leaves or strips recovered from the spines, covers or linings of later books, more than a hundred otherwise lost books of polyphony have been identified. Many others are known only from mention of them in inventories, wills, account-books and other archival sources.[18] Even England's premier choir of the period, that of the royal household chapel, is very poorly represented by surviving materials. One of its choirbooks from the early fifteenth century, the Old Hall Manuscript, is still three-quarters intact.[19] Isolated folios and half-folios from its successor have come to light in various locations, but much of the book remains lost.[20] Thereafter, no music book (or fragment of one) is known to survive from the English chapel royal until the seventeenth century. Scotland's chapel royal has also suffered badly, with only the early sixteenth-century Carver Choirbook still extant.[21] From the

17. For details of surviving sources of English liturgical polyphony, see Curtis and Wathey 1994; Hofman and Morehen 1987; *Census-catalogue*.
18. For some examples, see Wathey 1988.
19. BL, Add. ms. 57950. For a summary of current views on this important manuscript, with further bibliography, see Wathey 1989a, pp. 151–5.
20. See Bent 1984, 1996; Wathey 1989a, pp. 151–5.
21. NLS, ms. 5.1.15 (from the Advocates' Library). The fullest study is Woods 1984.

colleges of Cambridge and Oxford we possess nothing except the Forrest–Heather Partbooks, made for Cardinal College (later Christ Church) in the late 1520s,[22] and some strips from choirbooks once used by the choir of New College, which have been recovered from their secondary use as wallpaper.[23] The losses from King's College, Cambridge, and Magdalen College, Oxford, are known to have been very considerable.[24] Eton College is fortunate still to possess approximately two-thirds of the large choirbook that was copied around the year 1500 for use in its chapel.[25] A massive choirbook and a singer's roll survive from Arundel College in the 1520s.[26] Pages from a book used at one of Scotland's greater parish churches, probably Inverness, have recently been identified at Fort Augustus Abbey.[27] In these and a few dozen other cases, it has been possible to match the physical remains of a music book to its former owners and users. Fragments from otherwise lost books, however, are often impossible to link precisely to their places of origin.

Many of the books of polyphony used by church, chapel or collegiate choirs were institutionally owned, and will be found listed as chapel goods alongside the books of plainchant that were also required during church services.[28] Others were privately owned, most frequently by singing-men, members of the clergy or individual members of royal and noble households.[29] Inventories, wills, records of donation and other documentary sources are, however, often vague about the nature of books that contain musical notation, and it may be impossible to tell whether an item listed as 'a book of music' contained polyphony or was a service book with plainchant notation. With the exception of richly decorated items, music books generally had little appeal to non-musicians, and it is virtually unknown for them to have fallen into the hands of bibliophiles, or to have found homes in libraries.

In Britain, the advent of printing had no impact upon the manuscript production of books of sacred polyphony. Because different institutions had different needs, dictated by the number and ability of the singers as well as by local liturgical and ceremonial requirements, they continued to rely upon hand-copied selections of pieces. In any case, the small scale

22. Bodl., mss. Mus. Sch. e. 376–81. Facsimile with discussion in Milsom 1986.
23. Oxford, New Coll., ms. 368; contents listed in Curtis and Wathey 1994, pp. 18–19.
24. Harrison 1980, pp. 431–3; Wathey 1988, pp. 4 and 9.
25. Eton Coll., ms. 178. Edition with commentary in Harrison 1956–67.
26. Lambeth, ms. 1, and CUL, ms. Buxton 96; see Fugler 1983; Skinner 1997.
27. See Allenson 1989.   28. Wathey 1989a, pp. 145–6 and 149–50.
29. For some examples, see Wathey 1988, pp. 14–17; 1989a, pp. 148–9.

of the potential market would probably have made printing commercially unviable. There was no prospect of exporting printed polyphony. Although during the first half of the fifteenth century English music won respect abroad, by 1500 continental demand for it had ceased, and printed copies would have been unsaleable abroad. In England, the only commercial music printing before 1557 was of service books with plainchant notation, and a very small amount of secular music for the nascent amateur market. In Scotland, Wales and Ireland, there was no music printing at all during this period.

To date there has been no systematic study of the plainchant books that were used in medieval British churches, and little is known about the principal centres that produced them – their location, personnel, specialities and individual characteristics.[30] Whether or not the sources of supply for such books changed markedly during the century and a half after 1400 is as yet unknown. Without question, however, plainchant books continued to be in regular demand until the abolition of the Latin rite in 1549. They were needed not only to enlarge or replace the holdings of existing institutions but also to equip the choirs of new foundations, such as collegiate and private household chapels. For institutions that were unable to organize in-house copying, those demands must have been met, at least in part, by organized scriptoria, either through direct negotiation with the manufacturers or through the agency of stationers and other members of the book trade.[31] From the 1480s onwards they were also partly met by printers, both English and (especially) continental.[32] In particular, printing facilitated the bulk purchase of identical items. For example, on 24 April 1511, Henry VIII authorized a payment of 40s to the London printer, Richard Pynson, 'for 8 processioners which he hathe delivered to Doctor William Atwater, dean of our chapel'.[33] From inventories of chapel books at Magdalen College, Oxford, and Winchester College, it is clear that existing collections of large-format manuscript books such as graduals and antiphonals were sometimes augmented with multiple copies of smaller printed books, such as processionals and hymnals.[34] A printer such as Pynson probably worked

---

30. For a survey of the nature, function, contents and organization of service books with music notation, see A. Hughes 1982.
31. See Wathey 1989a, p. 150, for some provisional remarks on the manuscript production of notated service books before 1500.
32. See Steele 1903 and Meyer-Baer 1962, both of which should be read in conjuction with the more up-to-date information in *STC*.   33. Ashbee 1993, p. 34.
34. Harrison 1980, pp. 166–7 (Magdalen) and 434–5 (Winchester).

speculatively, producing categories of book for which a widespread and long-term market was likely to exist. Of those categories, the smaller and more portable books – missals, processionals and hymnals – were the most commonly issued.

During the various stages of Tudor reform, printing played a role in the dissemination of newly authorized liturgical music, although the potential of the press was arguably not fully realized. Only three editions of Cranmer's litany of 1544 included music,[35] and even these probably had limited impact because of problems of distribution. A sample survey of churchwarden accounts shows that many London parish churches acquired copies soon after publication, but that the rate of dispersal to other parts of England was much slower.[36] Performing materials for church choirs were inadequately provided by the early Protestant reformers, possibly because of their own uncertainty about the role music should play in liturgical practice. No musical notation was included in the 1549 Prayer Book, despite the fact that its rubrics gave priests and clerks the choice of singing or speaking the texts. In a few surviving copies of the book, makeshift musical solutions have been added in manuscript.[37] To meet the singers' market, in 1550 John Merbecke issued a miscellany of chant-melodies for the new liturgy, *The booke of Common praier noted*. Whether or not this volume was commissioned by the reformers is unknown.[38] If it was, the book can never have been adopted widely within the English Church, for it passed through a single edition and was never reprinted.[39] Only with the publication of the 1552 Prayer Book was the situation clarified: its rubrics virtually eliminate references to singing.[40]

English choral foundations reaped their richest harvest from the printing press during the years of Catholic restoration. In Mary's reign, printed missals, processionals and hymnals of largely English production were widely available, and a sample of parish church accounts suggests that some of the losses incurred under the Protestant regime were quickly made good.[41] No attempt was made, however, to print the most substantial liturgical music books containing plainchant, the gradual and

---

35. *STC* 10621.5, 10621.7 and 10622.   36. Hutton 1987, p. 118.
37. Milsom 1992a. To the annotated copies listed there should be added Oxford, The Queen's Coll., Sel.d.41.
38. *STC* 16441; facsimile with historical and bibliographical notes in Leaver 1980.
39. For references to the purchase and use of this book, especially by London parish churches, see Leaver 1980, pp. 37–8.
40. For a comparative listing of 1549 and 1552 rubrics for Holy Communion, see Le Huray 1978, p. 27.   41. Hutton 1987, p. 129.

antiphonal. Those institutions whose copies had been destroyed would have had to commission new manuscripts, secure second-hand copies, or do without.

During the years of liturgical change, only one attempt was made to print polyphony for use by church choirs, and even this appears to have been abortive. By 1552 at the latest, John Day had assembled a collection of service music and anthems suitable for the new Protestant rite; but the only known edition is dated variously 1560 and 1565.[42] During the reign of Edward VI, English church choirs that attempted to maintain a polyphonic tradition had to rely upon newly composed repertoires of music transmitted entirely in manuscript.[43] There is no evidence to show that either church choirs or congregations made use of the various printed books of metrical psalmody or devotional songs that were becoming available at the time.[44] More probably, such books were targeted specifically at the newly emerging domestic market and the literate amateur, and were used for secular music-making.

Until the early years of the sixteenth century, books and ephemera containing notated forms of vernacular polyphony – carols, songs and composed art-music for instruments – are relatively uncommon in England, and absent altogether from Scotland. In most if not all cases, such items derive from circles close or identical to those that supported church polyphony. Many books are of reasonably fine quality, and they can be linked either with royal and noble households, or with collegiate or monastic foundations that used carols for devotional recreation.[45] Less formal copies may have been made by singers as their own personal repositories of songs.[46] It was only in the early years of the sixteenth century, when musical literacy began to extend to amateurs, that books for non-professional singers and players began to appear. Notable within that new category of literate amateurs was the King himself. Henry VIII sang, and played a variety of instruments. He was also, most unusually, a composer, and some of his compositions survive.[47] All of Henry's children were given tuition in music; Elizabeth in particular was noted for

42. *STC* 6418–19, discussed in Aplin 1981, Nixon 1984b.
43. For some examples, see Le Huray 1978, pp. 172–82.
44. For a study of congregational music under Edward VI, see Temperley 1979, I, chapter 2.
45. For lists of sources containing songs and carols, see Stevens 1961, esp. appendices B and C; 1970; Fallows 1977.
46. An example is the music section (fols.161–72) of CUL, Add. ms. 5943, described in Fenlon 1982, pp. 84–7; reproduced in *A fifteenth-century song book* 1973.   47. See Fallows 1993.

her proficiency at the keyboard, and is shown playing the lute in a portrait miniature by Nicholas Hilliard. It is possible that the rise of amateur musicianship in sixteenth-century England, led by Italian and French Renaissance trends, was partly stimulated by royal example. By the end of the sixteenth century, musical literacy and the ability to take part in a musical performance were widely regarded as evidence of good breeding in both men and women, and training in music became a regular part of secular education.[48]

Amateur music-making created a new demand for music books; across Europe, commercial music printing attempted to satisfy it. By the mid sixteenth century, firms that specialized in music were well established in Venice, Lyons, Paris, Rome and Antwerp, producing books of general appeal that were intended for sale and for use in places far distant from the point of manufacture.[49] In marked contrast to this, London's music printers showed no interest in the possibilities of export. Instead they set out to serve a local market. During the 1520s, John Rastell issued English-texted songs printed individually on large folio sheets, a format that was taken up in the early 1530s by his son William. Three examples of their work survive, all of them fragments of single copies (see figs. 26.2, 26.3).[50] As well as being bibliographical curiosities – single-sheet publication of polyphonic songs (as opposed to monophonic ballads) is otherwise virtually unknown – the Rastell song-sheets pioneered the use of single-impression printing from movable type, at a time when production elsewhere in Europe was still by the double impression or woodblock processes. Cheap to manufacture, and musically undemanding of the performer, these song-sheets were ideally suited to the amateur market. In 1530, an unidentified London printer associated with John Rastell issued a collection of more difficult songs, this time in partbook format and printed by the double-impression method. Again, only fragments of a single copy survive.[51] This same printer also produced sheets of empty printed staves, a form of musical stationery that would have found a market among both professional and amateur musicians.[52] A few further isolated examples of London music-printing followed over the

48. Amateur musical literacy in late Tudor England is discussed in Price 1981.
49. For summary accounts of early music printing in Europe, see Krummel and Sadie 1990; Fenlon 1995.
50. The Rastell song-sheets are discussed in Milsom 1997. Only one of the song-sheets is listed in STC (as 20700.3).   51. STC 22924, discussed in Milsom 1997.
52. See Milsom 1997.

next two decades, including the earliest metrical psalms and political ballads.[53] On their own, these publications do not create an impression of continuity within the trade; but in view of the low rate of survival of these known examples, it is impossible to calculate what else of their kind has disappeared without trace. Also largely lost are the manuscript materials prepared by or for amateur musicians, which do not survive in quantity until the second half of the sixteenth century.[54]

Although foreign music can be found in some fifteenth-century English and Scottish manuscripts, there is little evidence of music books of continental manufacture being brought or sent to Britain until after 1500. Most of the Tudor monarchs received finely illuminated music manuscripts as diplomatic gifts: workshop-made choirbooks or partbooks that almost always include the recipients' emblems or coats of arms.[55] On rare occasions, English music was sent to foreign book producers for sumptuous copying, again for presentation purposes. An example is a book of English polyphony, including a mass by Robert Fayrfax, that was copied at the court workshop of Pierre Alamire, either in Brussels or Mechlin, probably in the region of 1516.[56] Bearing the pomegranate emblem of Catherine of Aragon and the coat of arms of Henry VIII, it was intended as a gift to them by Maximilian I. Friction between the parties led to the book being modified into a gift for Frederick the Wise, Elector of Saxony. One of the principal Flemish music-copyists active in Brussels and Mechlin at the court of Charles V, Alamire is also known to have acted as a spy for the court of Henry VIII.[57]

During the first quarter of the century, foreign printed music was still sufficiently rare to be of curiosity as well as material value; Wolsey may have received as a gift the 'priksongbooke in printe' listed in the 1523 inventory of chapel goods at Hampton Court.[58] Foreign music-printing is thought to have made no significant impact on the repertoire of England's church and chapel choirs, but, in Scotland, interest in French models may have stimulated more widespread acquisition, both before and after the Reformation. For example, French printed sources of

53. For a reasonably complete list, see Steele 1903. It is unknown what was intended by the licence for music-printing issued to John de Buys and Henry Lewes in 1541/2, noted in Ashbee 1993, p. 85.
54. For a catalogue of mid sixteenth-century sources of English song, see Naylor forthcoming. The earliest known sources of lute music are discussed in Ward 1992. For sources of keyboard music, see n. 4 above.   55. For a summary discussion of these, see Fenlon 1981.
56. Jena, Universitätsbibliothek, ms. 9. For Pierre Alamire (Peter van den Hove), see Sadie 1980, I, pp. 192–3.   57. Census-catalogue, I, p. 292; Picker 1965, pp. 32–5.
58. R. Bowers 1991, p. 184.

motets were available to the copyist of the so-called 'Dunkeld Partbooks'.[59] As for the potential amateur market for foreign printed music, it is not known what opportunities existed for making purchases in Britain. The largest music collection in sixteenth-century England, assembled by Henry Fitzalan, 12th Earl of Arundel, almost certainly benefited from purchases made during foreign travel.[60] A fine set of Venetian partbooks owned by the Hoby family probably reached England under similar circumstances.[61] Foreign musicians resident in Britain may have acted as agents; the accounts for 1552 of Sir Thomas Chaloner include a payment of 10s 'to a Fleming musician who teaches my daughter for song books Italian in four parts'.[62] Nothing is known about the part played by the English and Scottish book-trade in importing foreign music. Possibly the trade was reasonably lucrative, for in 1575 Thomas Tallis and William Byrd were given exclusive rights in England to 'bring or cause to be brought out of any forren Realmes . . . any songe or songes made and printed in any forren countrie'.[63] (The term 'song' covered all forms of composed music, whether vocal or instrumental, sacred or secular.)

Amateur musical literacy and the rise of music-printing emerge as the most significant new themes in the history of music books during the period 1400–1557. From a codicological point of view, however, it will be remembered above all as the age of the great choirbooks. The Old Hall Manuscript, compiled during the first quarter of the fifteenth century, is a volume of considerable size and grandeur, but it is dwarfed by the great choirbook now at Gonville and Caius College, Cambridge, made a hundred years later for St Stephen's, Westminster, which stands 71 cm tall and is 95 cm wide when opened up.[64] As church choirs expanded in numbers, to the point where twenty or more singers might gather around a lectern to read from a single book, it was inevitable that the books themselves should increase in size, sometimes to enormous dimensions. Such books called for robust parchment and stout protective bindings. Being conspicuous upon the lectern, they had to be handsome, the quality of their calligraphy and decoration reflecting the wealth and pres-

59. Edinburgh UL, ms. 64, described in Elliott 1964. The connection between these books and Dunkeld has been challenged.
60. Arundel's collection is described and evaluated in Milsom 1993.
61. Dublin, Trinity College, printed books B.1.27–31; see Milsom 1995, p. 178.
62. Woodfill 1953, p. 256.
63. STC 23666: Thomas Tallis and William Byrd, *Cantiones, quae ab argumento sacrae vocantur* (London 1575), letters patent included at rear of all six partbooks.
64. Gonville and Caius Coll. ms. 667; described in Fenlon 1982, pp. 126–8, and studied in greater depth in Skinner 1997 (with a colour reproduction, much reduced in size).

tige of their owners. A few, such as the Caius Choirbook, verge on the ostentatious, being larger than was strictly necessary for practical use. It is appropriate that these imposing books – or at least, those that we are fortunate enough still to possess – should also be repositories for some of the most elaborate and magnificent music ever to have been created by British composers.[65]

65. I am indebted to Margaret Bent, Bonnie J. Blackburn, John Caldwell, David Fallows, Leofranc Holford-Strevens, David Skinner, Reinhard Strohm and Andrew Wathey for commenting on a preliminary version of this chapter.

27
Literary texts

JULIA BOFFEY and A. S. G. EDWARDS

The period between 1400 and 1557 is of great potential significance to an understanding of the ways in which a taste for literature in English might be both supplied and created, since the period before the career of Geoffrey Chaucer and his late fourteenth-century contemporaries offered little to readers in the way of 'literature' in the vernacular.[1] Various reasons have been advanced for the sudden surge of imaginative writing in English after 1400, amongst which one of the simplest – that Chaucer existed – is also one of the most important. The fifteenth and early sixteenth centuries also saw a great increase in general literacy, which served to stimulate demand for a wide range of texts. At the same time it promoted habits of silent, private reading which permitted rumination on those features of texts which most clearly mark them as 'literary': imaginative appeal, for example, or evidence of formal or stylistic experiment.[2] As the perfection of techniques for printing with movable type made possible the rapid multiplication of texts in large numbers, so with the establishment of printing came changes in the relationship between author and audience and in the essential notion of 'publication'.[3] Other events in the period, of less overtly bibliographical moment, were nonetheless important to the general national enhancement of the significance of the written, or printed, word: among these we might cite Lollard operations and counter-movements, and the political and ecclesiastical agitation which culminated in the reformation of the Church.[4]

Against this background, our sense of the reading and transmission of literary texts needs at the outset to be brought into sharper definition by reference to the extent and nature of the material which has survived for study. 'Literature', even if it is understood in the crudest possible terms

---

1. On this period, see E. Salter 1983 and 1988, Swanton 1987.
2. Parkes 1973, Saenger 1982.   3. Hindman and Farquhar 1977; Hindman 1991.
4. Hudson 1985.

as textual matter conceived or read for purposes not primarily connected with information, or with religious precept or devotion, is still an enormous field, comprehending many things both between and beyond the four lines of the lyric 'Western wind'[5] and Thomas Malory's extensive compilation of tales making up the *Morte Darthur*, which occupies 484 folio-sized leaves in the Winchester manuscript.[6] The 'use' we might suspect of such texts also has to accommodate both the private reading enjoyed by readers of, for example, Thynne's 1532 printed edition of the works of Chaucer,[7] and the much more historically remote activities of the family groups or coteries responsible for creating the kinds of manuscript anthologies in which romances or lyrics, put to communal use in oral performance or circulated among intimates, might be committed to more lasting, 'literary' form. Any reconstruction of the forms of such use, furthermore, is, at best, speculation. The availability or popularity of texts has in general to be deduced from the very fallible evidence of the numbers of surviving copies. Our sense of the nature of audiences depends on prefatory material or internal references which may well be untrustworthy – currying favour with a dedicatee who may then never have read the book, for instance – or on inscrutable ownership inscriptions. Readers' responses have to be deduced from sparse and no doubt often idiosyncratic annotation and commentary. In the light of these factors, which preclude definitive statements about the reading of literature in this period, the most promising course seems to be a consideration of some of the continuities and changes to be observed in the supply of literature to fifteenth- and early sixteenth-century readers.

The period from around 1400 saw the swift emergence of Middle English as a broadly based literary vernacular.[8] Prior to the last quarter of the fourteenth century, the literary potential of the language had been largely expressed in local, provincial forms of verse, such as the metrical romance or the various works of the so-called 'alliterative revival'.[9] In other respects, the evidence of the surviving manuscripts suggests that earlier Middle English verse was primarily a means of vernacular religious instruction, as indicated through the popularity of such works as the *Prick of Conscience*, the *Northern Homily Cycle* and the *South English Legendary*; the use of verse for these ends achieved its apotheosis in the

5. BL, Royal ms. Appendix 58; Davies 1963, p. 291.
6. BL, Add. ms. 59678; Vinaver 1992; Ker 1976.　　7. *STC* 5068.　　8. Blake 1992.
9. Turville-Petre 1977.

massive Vernon manuscript.[10] Prose also was primarily a means of religious instruction, in large part as a result of response to the pressures of the Fourth Lateran Council in 1215, with its emphasis on the vernacular instruction of the laity.[11]

The question of what constitutes vernacular literature during the period after 1400 is an altogether more complex one. The term must identify both various new kinds of fictional, poetic texts and also newer forms of prose narrative of secular kinds, as well as developments of earlier forms of religious writing. These writings, whether original or translations from French or Latin, form the chief constituents of what we now term 'literature'. Of paramount importance here is the example and influence of Chaucer. The acknowledging of a specific debt to Chaucer and his creation of a new poetic vernacular was to become a topos in fifteenth- and early sixteenth-century verse. Such poetry achieved its most distinctive expression in the single-work codex, the form in which were transmitted the major works of Chaucer, Gower, Lydgate and others.[12] Chaucer's *Canterbury Tales* and *Troilus & Criseyde* circulated most commonly as separate works, as did the *Confessio Amantis* of his contemporary, John Gower. It was particularly the influence of the Chaucerian example that led to the imitation of this model of the 'authorial' book (which received its most spectacular – and untypical – representation in the Ellesmere manuscript of *The Canterbury Tales*)[13] in the early years of the fifteenth century by Chaucer's earliest followers: Thomas Hoccleve, in his *Regiment of Princes*, John Walton, in his translation of Boethius's *Consolation of Philosophy*, and various of John Lydgate's works – particularly his *Troy Book*, *Siege of Thebes*, *Fall of Princes*, *Life of Our Lady* and *Lives of SS Edmund & Fremund*. All of these works achieved a wide circulation, and in some instances, notably Lydgate's works, were at times produced in elaborate, de luxe forms.[14]

We also see, however, the emergence of new forms of vernacular compilation, often with a significant poetic component, such as anthologies or miscellanies. Such compilations are adumbrated in the fourteenth century in collections like the famous Auchinleck manuscript (containing now unique copies of many romance texts),[15] and the British Library manuscript which includes, among other things, the 'Harley'

10. Information about the survival of these and other Middle English verse texts can be found in *IMEV*. On Vernon, see Doyle 1987, Pearsall 1990.   11. Boyle 1985.
12. Edwards and Pearsall 1989.   13. See Hanna 1989.
14. On these de luxe forms, see Lawton 1983; Scott 1989.
15. Pearsall and Cunningham 1977.

lyrics.[16] It was, however, a form of compilation that significantly developed in the fifteenth century, largely as a consequence of the new literary vernacular. It is a form that resists very precise taxonomy. At the most professional (that is, commercial) level, it often comprised small booklets that could be collocated according to the interests of individual purchasers. Such booklets seem to have come to provide the basis for larger anthologies, of which the most distinctive are the various collections of the shorter works of Chaucer and his followers, manuscripts such as those of the so-called 'Oxford group'.[17] At the other extreme is the private compilation, reflecting the unsystematic gathering of materials by individuals or families, a famous example of which is the Findern Anthology.[18] In between are various types of collection that resist rigorous classification, drawing together heterogeneous materials, verse and prose, literary and instructional, secular and religious. These include household books (usually of marginal 'literary' significance), various kinds of private anthologies and miscellaneous collections, and other compilations assembled on more discernibly coherent principles.

One kind of coherent collection parallels the vogue for the single-work codex by amalgamating the works of a single author. In the case of Chaucer, who apparently never organized his works with the care exercised by Gower or by some of his French near-contemporaries,[19] this process seems to have been initiated through the energies of those early fifteenth-century readers who were responsible for procuring scattered texts and arranging for their compilation in carefully 'through-copied' collections, such as the first attempt at a collected works of Chaucer, now in Cambridge.[20] Rather differently, and perhaps in response to this formalization of Chaucer's oeuvre, Thomas Hoccleve made some of his writings available in ready-organized anthologies, some of which survive in autograph copies; notably few of his shorter works survive outside the context of such collections.[21] The forms in which the smaller body of English material associated with Charles of Orleans has been preserved are not dissimilar. While Lydgate's output of shorter works, too vast to conceive in the terms of a collected edition, leaks into more varied manuscripts, there nonetheless survive a number of substantial

16. BL, Harl. ms. 2253; Ker 1965.
17. Bodleian, mss. Fairfax 16, Tanner 346, Bodley 638; Brusendorff 1925; Boffey and Thompson 1989; Robinson 1980.   18. CUL, ms. Ff.1.6; Beadle and Owen 1977.
19. See Parkes 1995 and Lucas 1995.
20. CUL, ms. Gg.4.27; Parkes and Beadle 1979–80; on the metropolitan copying of the works of Gower, see Doyle and Parkes 1978.   21. J. M. Bowers 1989.

collections of his shorter poems which take his authorship as an organizing principle.[22]

Further possibilities for anthologies were opened by the circulation of short texts (alone or in small miscellanies) in the form of manuscript booklets. Stationers or readers might make their own choice of units and compose customized anthologies on a variety of principles – thematic, generic, or dependent on individual taste or financial resource. Through these means came into circulation what have been termed 'aureate' collections of the poems of Chaucer and his disciples – golden treasuries in which his shorter poems are brought together with examples of the writings of Sir Thomas Clanvowe, Lydgate, Hoccleve and minor figures such as Richard Roos.[23] It is perhaps worth remarking that, although Hoccleve's works were extremely popular in manuscript, the only one of them that is known to have reached print (outside the lyric incorporated in the translation of Deguileville's *Pilgrimage of the Soul*) is his *Letter of Cupid*, which, although included in his autograph collections, also circulated in the fifteenth century, with Chaucer's minor poems, in an adaptable booklet context; it was printed in editions of Chaucer's works from Thynne's edition of 1532[24] onwards, down to the eighteenth century. Early printers were not slow to see the potential of short, cheap pamphlets which reproduced some of the features of manuscript booklets. Several of the shorter works of Lydgate had been printed before the end of the fifteenth century in this format,[25] and were successively reprinted in it, as far forward as 1529 (Berthelet's *Temple of Glas*),[26] around 1540 (Redman's *Stans puer*),[27] around 1550 (Mychel's *Churl and Bird*, printed at Canterbury)[28] and around 1565 (William Copland's *Churl and Bird*).[29] Such productions may reflect the earlier features of manuscript *compilatio* common to booklet-based Chaucerian collections from the mid fifteenth century. We see, perhaps, more ambitious attempts to replicate forms of manuscript compilation in the efforts of Pynson to assemble the first printed collected Chaucer in three volumes in 1526, where the first two volumes, respectively *Troilus & Criseyde*[30] and *The Canterbury Tales*,[31] stand parallel to single-work codices, and the collection of shorter works in the third printed volume, *The Book of Fame*,[32] can be compared to earlier manuscript anthologies.

22. BL, Harl. mss. 2255 and Lansdowne 699; Bodleian, ms. Laud misc. 683; and Cambridge, Jesus Coll., ms. 56.   23. B. Y. Fletcher 1987.   24. *STC* 5068ff.

25. For example, *STC* 17008–11, 17018–21, 17030.   26. *STC* 17034.   27. *STC* 17030.9.

28. *STC* 17013.   29. *STC* 17014.   30. *STC* 5096.   31. *STC* 5086.   32. *STC* 5088.

Seemingly random compilations representing the whims of individual taste, or determined by unrecoverable peculiarities in the availability of exemplars, might perhaps be regarded as distinctive products of a manuscript culture. Literary texts are preserved in some numbers in such miscellanies, and it occasionally proves possible, through a combination of codicological and archival scholarship, to recover a sense of the milieu in which the compiling presence (or group of presences) was at work. Provincial families anxious about the reading matter of children and household members (evident in the two manuscripts copied in North Yorkshire in the mid fifteenth century by Robert Thornton,[33] the Bodleian manuscript copied by one Rate,[34] and others),[35] Londoners with civic and mercantile as well as literary interests (evident in certain collections),[36] and coteries experimenting with the cultivation of polite social verse (in the so-called Findern Anthology,[37] and the Devonshire Manuscript),[38] have been convincingly associated with certain surviving collections. The disparate sources from which their texts were often acquired are sometimes represented physically in changes of text layout as compilers or scribes switched from exemplar to exemplar (*Sir Degrevaunt* in the Findern Anthology, for example, the only substantial romance text in the collection, shifts from the general single-column layout to double column). These features serve as reminders of the fragile forms – booklets, individual gatherings, bifolia and single leaves – in which so many texts must have circulated. Despite what might be thought of as its inimicality to the informal processes of compilation which brought these manuscripts into being, printing did not do away with possibilities for miscellaneousness. Comparable to continental printed miscellanies, such as the small collections produced in France by Guy Marchant, are fragmentary English survivals – like *The Court of Venus*, a sixteenth-century assortment which includes some poems – that preserve the variety of manuscript compilations; and the printing of texts in the form of single gatherings or small pamphlets offered the option of assembling small libraries, or indeed of incorporating printed material into an otherwise manuscript miscellany. The history of *The Book of St Albans* ([1486] etc.),[39] whose assorted contents occupy the border territo-

---

33. Now Lincoln Cathedral ms. 91, and BL, Add. ms. 31042; J. J. Thompson 1987.
34. Bodleian, ms. Ashmole 61; Blanchfield 1991.
35. E.g., NLW, ms. Porkington 10; Kurvinen 1953.
36. Cambridge, Trinity Coll., ms. R.3.19; B. Y. Fletcher 1987; and BL, Harl. ms. 2252; Meale 1983.   37. CUL ms. Ff.1.6.; Beadle and Owen 1977.
38. BL, Add. ms. 17492; Southall 1964.   39. *STC* 3308ff.

ries between information and literature, and in some cases came to be printed in individual parts (for example, [1530?], [1533?]),[40] further illustrates these possibilities. Similarly, Thomas Alsoppe's modernization of Chaucer's *Man of Law's Tale* [*c.* 1525][41] reflects earlier manuscript excerpting impulses. It remains, however, the only printed evidence we have of the separate printing of any of *The Canterbury Tales*, in contrast to their quite frequent excerpting in manuscript.

The development of secular literature in the vernacular produced both pronounced continuities and equally pronounced disjunctions after the introduction of printing into England. The most pronounced continuity, in quantitative terms – which in this instance may be an accurate reflection of actuality – is perhaps the enduring appeal of Chaucer's works, particularly *The Canterbury Tales*. Over eighty manuscripts of this survive. It was also the earliest major work printed by Caxton at Westminster [1477][42] and it was printed, either separately or in collected editions, some ten times down to 1561.[43] In addition, several of Chaucer's other works, notably *Troilus & Criseyde* and *The Parliament of Fowls*, enjoyed popularity both in manuscript and in separate early printings ([1483], 1517, [1526?]; and [1477?], [1525?], 1530).[44]

There are, however more pronounced discontinuities. Gower's *Confessio Amantis* was evidently very popular in the fifteenth century (over fifty manuscripts survive), was printed by Caxton [1483],[45] but then fell from favour, with only two printed editions in the sixteenth century, in 1532 and 1554.[46] *Piers Plowman* was equally popular in manuscript, but it did not reach print until the editions by Crowley and Rogers in the 1550s and 1560s,[47] and after this it was never reprinted. The *Regiment of Princes* of Thomas Hoccleve, which rivalled these works in the numbers of surviving manuscripts, was never printed at all. Since both Langland and Hoccleve wrote in and about London, and manuscript copies of their writings were clearly accessible to metropolitan readers well into the sixteenth century, their neglect by early printers must be explicable simply in terms of shift in taste. The popular earlier verse religious texts already mentioned were likewise ignored: the *South English Legendary* and the *Northern Homily Cycle* were also never printed (although individual saints' lives were printed in booklet form), and the *Prick of Conscience* – the most popular of all Middle English verse works, as

40. *STC* 3313.3; *STC* 3313.5.   41. *STC* 538.5.   42. *STC* 5082.
43. *STC* 5068–9, 5075, 5077, 5080, 5082–6.   44. *STC* 5094–96, 5091–2, respectively.
45. *STC* 12142.   46. *STC* 12143–4.   47. *STC* 19906–7a; *STC* 19908.

evidenced by the surviving manuscripts – appears to have been only partially printed, twice ([1534?; 1542?]).[48]

The reasons for this state of affairs are complex. One may suspect that it was the very range of the Chaucerian corpus that became an important factor in its continuing appeal. After fifty or so years in which shorter texts such as *The Parliament of Fowls* and *Troilus and Criseyde* enjoyed some independent currency, it is noteworthy that Chaucer survived from the early sixteenth century until the late eighteenth only in collected editions, with no significant editions of separate works. He survives as a compendious Chaucer capable of encompassing a diversity of genres – not just those of *The Canterbury Tales* – within a single volume. One may suspect that length, together with uniformity of subject and style, told against the English writings of Gower (whose French and Latin works never reached print), and against the works of Hoccleve and Langland, and that in the case of the last the increasing inaccessibility of the alliterative form reduced his appeal, except for the religious zealot – like Crowley, his first printer. Apart from Chaucer, only Lydgate, among medieval poets, seems to have sustained any approximation to his manuscript popularity after the advent of printing.

Other genres enjoyed rather different fates after 1400. Short and easily memorable texts such as lyrics, which probably enjoyed wider circulation than is attested by manuscript survivals from the thirteenth and fourteenth centuries, came to be recorded in greater numbers (if still often relegated to the role of fillers). Recorded sales of songs, carols and ballads in book-sellers' accounts suggest that this is an area in which the fragmentary survivals of printed texts can give no real indication of the extent of circulation. Related to these forms are jest collections and comic tales such as *Jack and his Stepdame* which seem to have been popular into the sixteenth century and even beyond.[49] Verse romance continued to circulate in both manuscript and print throughout our period, and, indeed, in degraded forms, far beyond it. Apart from Malory (discussed below), however, prose romance rather lost its impetus in the early sixteenth century, and never regained the popularity it enjoyed in the age of Caxton until it reappeared as virtually a new form in the late sixteenth century.

Non-publication of medieval religious verse was probably due in large measure to the emergence by the early fifteenth century of prose as a

---

48. *STC* 3360; *STC* 24228.   49. *STC* 14522–4.3.

more significant form of religious instruction and expression – a development probably related to the increase in private reading.[50] This is evidenced through the writings of Richard Rolle, Walter Hylton and Nicholas Love and their followers, as well as through the rapid growth in the transmission of Wycliffite writings, notably, but not in any sense exclusively, through the great popularity of the Bible translations.[51] That the vogue for these religious writings was never wholly sustained after the invention of printing can be attributed to discernible historical causes. Religious prose was popular to some degree with Caxton and Pynson and more markedly with De Worde (who seems to have made some effort to develop this market) but it lost much of its appeal after the early 1530s.[52] The Dissolution of the Monasteries and the establishing of the Protestant Church clearly helped to destroy any general interest in the works of medieval vernacular religious writers. Insofar as they were read or printed at all after this time, they were only accessible clandestinely.

Instead, the 1530s saw the emergence of a literature of religious controversy, which, while new in subject and approach, is part of a tradition of such writings going back to Wycliffe and his followers. It is hardly coincidental that this period also saw the first printing of works of a Wycliffite cast.[53] Such a new controversial approach to literature can also be observed in the transformation of such popular medieval forms as hagiography, which retained much of its popularity after the introduction of printing and showed itself capable of renewal by adaptation to a new, politicized form, most notably embodied in John Foxe's very popular *Book of Martyrs* (1563ff.).[54]

Accumulation of evidence, nonetheless, seems to offer more indications of significant disjunctions in literary taste than of continuities, as a consequence of the advent of printing and other factors. Apart from Chaucer, few Middle English works or authors seem to have found an audience after the first half of the sixteenth century.

In part, this may simply indicate a certain casualness on the part of authors who saw no need to ensure a posterity for their writings. Evidence of the transmission of the poems of Robert Henryson and William Dunbar has depended crucially on the energies of sixteenth-century Scottish antiquarians, such as George Bannatyne, John Asloan

---

50. Edwards 1984.   51. Hudson 1988.   52. Edwards and Meale 1993.
53. For example *STC* 5098, 5099.5, 1462.3, 1462.5, 3021–2, 20036, 20036.5, 15225, 24045, 25587.5, 25588, 25590; Hudson 1983 and 1988.   54. *STC* 11222ff.

and Sir Richard Maitland, who preserved, in more substantial volumes, texts which must originally have been transmitted in relatively ephemeral forms.[55] In the case of Henryson, for example, we have only the evidence of some jotted extracts from the *Fables* in a student notebook (the 'Makculloch' manuscript) that his poems circulated at all during his lifetime.[56] The most extensive collections (the Bannatyne manuscript, copied in 1568, and the later sixteenth-century Scottish prints of 1570, 1571, 1621, 1593)[57] date from many years after his death, by which period they sometimes seem to have undergone substantial adaptation for Protestant sensibilities. Yet isolated survivals, such as the printing of *Orpheus and Eurydice* by Chepman and Myllar in Edinburgh around 1508, as one of a series of quarto pamphlets (see fig. 27.1),[58] and Thynne's access in London before 1532 to a copy of *The Testament of Cresseid* (which he printed as an adjunct to *Troilus* in his Chaucer collection),[59] indicate that the works were clearly available in some form. Textual evidence, which suggests that many of the pieces copied into the Bannatyne and the earlier sixteenth-century Asloan manuscripts were derived from prints, has led to suggestions that more of Henryson's poems than *Orpheus* were printed early in the sixteenth century. That these books, if they once existed, have so completely disappeared might lead us to suppose that they were small-scale undertakings (along the lines of the Chepman and Myllar quarto booklets) rather than compendious collected works.

Dunbar seems to have been similarly unassiduous about collecting or arranging his poems, many of which were generated by or for occasions at the court which he served, and which in their brevity and specificity of reference must have run considerable risk of obsolescence; beside them, Henryson's collection of *Fables* and his *Testament* seem positively substantial. Surviving copies again mostly date from the much later sixteenth century, although the incorporation of six of the poems, including *The Golden Targe*, in the Chepman and Myllar quarto series [1508],[60] points to some earlier reputation. This was perhaps given, for the printers, the practical appeal of proximity – or an added selling point – by Dunbar's position at court. One might note here the continuity of native Scottish interest in various poets such as Lyndsay throughout our period and beyond, as testimony to a distinct sense of literary nationalism.[61]

---

55. NLS, mss. Adv. 1.1.6 and Accession 4233, and Cambridge, Magdalene Coll. ms. Pepys 2253; Bawcutt 1991; Fox and Ringler 1980; Craigie 1919–27, 1923–5.

56. Edinburgh UL, ms. 205; Fox 1977, pp. xxxix–xl.   57. *STC* 185, 185.5, 186, 13165.

58. *STC* 13166; Beattie 1950.   59. *STC* 5068.   60. *STC* 7347–9.   61. *STC* 15658–83.

Elsewhere it is possible to discern the emergence of literary figures and forms able to exploit the distinctive potentialities of the print medium. In the early sixteenth century, Stephen Hawes, Alexander Barclay and a number of lesser versifiers all used print as their primary means of publication to present new kinds of verse texts. The case of John Skelton demonstrates the strategic ambivalences of a writer conscious of the differing possibilities of both manuscript and print. Skelton is, in fact, the first major English writer to use print at all. His *Bouge of Court* was printed by De Worde in 1499,[62] and De Worde continued to print various of his works throughout his career. He reprinted the *Bouge* in 1510,[63] and also produced an edition of *The Tunning of Elynour Rumming* [?1521].[64] Few other works, however, seem to have been printed before Skelton's death in 1529: Faques printed his poem celebrating Flodden in 1513[65] and his *Garland of Laurel* a decade later;[66] two collections of lyrics, *Against a Comely Coystron* and *Dyuers Balettys & Dyties Solacious* were printed by Rastell in 1527 and 1528,[67] and *A replycacion agaynst certayne yong scolers* by Pynson in the latter year.[68] His play *Magnificence* only survives in a version printed shortly after his death [1530?].[69]

These works may suggest the parameters of the publicly acceptable Skelton. The *Bouge* and the *Garland* are dream visions produced while he was still at court; the burlesque *Elynour Rumming* and the two late lyric collections printed by Rastell employ relatively innocuous literary forms, while both his Flodden poem and *A Replycacion*, the latter printed by the King's Printer, Pynson, show Skelton in politically correct modes, the celebratory and the recriminatory, respectively.

It is instructive, however, to compare those of Skelton's works which either he chose to print, or a printer was willing to print, with those which circulated by other means. We can contrast the publication of Skelton's *Bouge* with his *Speculum Principis*, written only a couple of years later.[70] Although both works have in common a concern with royal admonition, in every other respect they stand in contrast: one in English, the other in Latin; one in verse, the other in prose; one in print, the other in manuscript;[71] one addressed to a generalized public audience, the other to a particular individual – the future Henry VIII, Skelton's tutorial charge. In a very obvious way, the divergent senses of audience mani-

---

62. *STC* 22597.   63. *STC* 22597.5.   64. *STC* 22611.5.   65. *STC* 22593.
66. *STC* 22610.   67. *STC* 22611, 22604.   68. *STC* 22609.   69. *STC* 22607.
70. See Edwards 1991; for the *Speculum Principis*, see F. M. Salter 1934.
71. BL, Add. ms. 26787.

fested in these two works reveal an awareness of the dichotomies of the alternative cultures of manuscript and print. Elsewhere, we see this awareness demonstrated primarily through subject matter. Those of Skelton's works which survive in manuscript from his lifetime are his overtly satiric, political works – poems directed against Wolsey, like *Speak Parrot* and *Colin Clout*; poems that were unlikely to find a printer because of their subject and which, in any case, gain their force as coterie invective, works best transmitted through private circulation among knowledgeable individuals. A consciousness of the differing potentialities of manuscript and print cultures is evident in the choices Skelton made as to the modes of circulation for his different kinds of works. Clearly, different voices, poetic and hortatory, required different modes of transmission.

We see elsewhere an emergent sense of the new kinds of possibilities that print affords for writers of English verse. Thus we find Stephen Hawes seemingly collaborating with his publisher, De Worde, to ensure a careful integration of text and image in his poems, and De Worde later taking care to illustrate the poems of Christopher Goodwyn and William Walter in an appropriate way.[72] One can also discern, in Pynson's use of the presentation illustration, a desire to focus attention on the figure of the poet and to define aspects of his relation to his work.

De Worde's quarto editions of some of the works of Lydgate (the *Proverbs* and *Stans puer ad mensam*, for example)[73] use standardized formats and the same factotum figures in their illustrations as if to underline the connections of the books with a common author. The routine provision of illustration in printed versions of literary texts such as these is a distinct innovation when compared to their presentation in manuscripts. While substantial, single-work manuscripts of texts such as Lydgate's *Troy Book* contained programmes of illustration, most manuscript anthologies of shorter poetic texts were relatively plain productions. De Worde in particular, however, seems to have pioneered the use of the illustrated title-page in his printed equivalents of the manuscript booklet, and may have seen the standardization of format and type as an invitation to buyers to collect uniform editions, possibly for binding together in larger volumes.

One literary form in which printers evidently saw new potential was drama. The civic drama which flourished in England during the fourteenth and fifteenth centuries made its effects in performance, and not

72. Edwards 1980. For reproductions of some of these illustrations, see Hodnett.
73. *STC* 17026–7, 17030.5, 17030.7.

through the circulation of written copies.[74] Manuscripts of major cycles of plays, such as those from York, served primarily as a register for consultation. The composition of the rather more complex surviving copy of the N-town plays reflects the difficulty of giving permanent written form to material which was essentially constantly in process.[75] Copies of separate plays, such as the Brome *Abraham and Isaac*,[76] occasionally made their way into individual anthologies or commonplace books, but there is little evidence that these texts were ever transmitted in multiple copies.

Printers seem to have sought to give permanence to newer kinds of dramatic material in rather different forms. De Worde's earliest printed drama texts were the interludes, *Hicke Scorner* [?1515],[77] *The Worlde and the Childe* (1522)[78] and *Youth* [c.1530],[79] all of which are reading texts, without stage directions or other reminders of performance. In appearance, they have much in common with verse satires like *Cocke Lorelles Bote* [1518?], [1519?][80] and *The Treatyse of a Galaunt* ([1510?], [1520?], [1521?]).[81] Like De Worde, other printers such as Rastell, Skot and Pynson seized on the potential of interludes because of the apparent clerical and aristocratic interest in the form in the metropolis. Henry Medwall's *Fulgens and Lucrece*, for example, has been connected with the household of Archbishop Morton at Lambeth, and the anonymous *Hicke Scorner* with Suffolk Place, the Southwark manor of Charles Brandon, Duke of Suffolk.[82]

Other literature of an ephemeral kind – carols, riddles and jests – which must have circulated in manuscript, if not in forms likely to ensure any permanence, also made its way into print. De Worde's *Christemasse carolles, demaundes joyous* (1521)[83] and the now lost *Ragman's Roll* were cheap books for social diversion which seem to have sold well.[84] The later collection of *Songs and Sonnets* organized by Richard Tottel (1557) attempted a more formal collection of lyrics, drawn mostly from the writings of Wyatt and his circle.[85]

While print gave a new permanence to forms such as the interlude and the lyric anthology, manuscript circulation often remained, in literary terms, a means of coterie or personal transmission for poetic works. This

---

74. Beadle and Meredith 1983; Meredith and Kahn 1977; Meredith 1991; Beadle 1994.
75. BL, ms. Cotton Vespasian D. viii.
76. New Haven, Beinecke Library, ms. 365, fols. 15–22.   77. *STC* 14039.
78. *STC* 25982.   79. *STC* 14111.   80. *STC* 5456, 5456.3.   81. *STC* 24240–2.3.
82. Nelson 1980; Lancashire 1980.   83. *STC* 5204.
84. Madan and Bradshaw 1885–90; Duff 1907a; Jackson 1936.   85. *STC* 13860; Boffey 1991.

may be seen in, for example, the circulation of the poems of Wyatt and Surrey.[86] Personal transmission of a rather different kind is embodied in the forms of later private manuscript literary anthologies or miscellanies (such as the Bannatyne collection) to be found in this period, some of which may, in part at least, be copied from printed sources. What is notable in all this is the movement, virtually complete after the 1550s, away from the distinctive Middle English manuscript form of the long single poem that was widespread during the fifteenth century to shorter printed works or diversified manuscript collections that reflect personal or coterie interests.

Geographical concerns were also of some importance in determining the appeal and longevity of Middle English texts. Dialectal features in large part suggest the confinement of the appeal of many alliterative poems to areas close to their point of origin, but it is difficult to be sure.[87] *Sir Gawain and the Green Knight*, for example, seems to have circulated within Cheshire (its putative county of origin) since it appears to have been known to one late fifteenth-century reader there, Humfrey Newton; but it also may have circulated more widely, since it seems to have been known in some form in the seventeenth century to the compiler of the Percy folio manuscript, a collection often derived from printed sources. The circulation of the alliterative *Morte Arthur*, however, which was clearly somehow available to Malory, cannot be traced beyond his adaptation of it. The fact that only two alliterative poems, *The Quatrefoil of Love* [1510?][88] and *Pierce the Ploughmans crede* (1553),[89] are known to have been printed (apart from *Piers Plowman* – which had a very short printing history) may not be an accurate reflection of contemporary interest in the form. The provinciality of such verse may, however, have proved an impediment to its longevity. Caxton, De Worde, Pynson, and later printers such as Copland and Tottel seem to have relied primarily on metropolitan or continental networks and gauges of popularity in procuring material for print. The eventual sixteenth-century printing of *Piers Plowman* was no doubt attributable in large part to its perceived potential for Reformation polemics as well as to its unusual appropriation of London as subject. The increasing shaping of literary taste in the sixteenth century by metropolitan printing allowed few opportunities for provincial counter-statements of a more conservative kind. The trans-

86. Harrier 1975; Wyatt 1975. For consideration of the manuscript transmission of texts copied from printed books, see Blake 1989.   87. Doyle 1982.
88. *STC* 15345; Blake 1970.   89. *STC* 19904.

ference into print of Lydgate's *Life of St Alban* (1534),[90] for example, was secured by a St Albans printer, but the text only seems to have been printed once. The history of John Walton's verse translation of Boethius's *Consolation of Philosophy*, which survives in over twenty manuscript copies, may also illustrate this point: it did reach print, but only in Tavistock, in 1525, and not again.[91]

The continuity of interest in the writings of Chaucer and his imitators is obviously connected with the early multiplying of copies in flourishing centres of book production such as London and East Anglia. Healthy circulation of these copies would then have recommended the texts to speculative producers of manuscripts or to prospective printers, whose further efforts to promote the commodity in turn ensured a market. The assortment and afterlife of the contents of one distinctively non-metropolitan Chaucer anthology of the late fifteenth century demonstrates the effects of some of these processes. This collection, which survives in a large folio volume enhanced with historiated initials and demi-vinets, was apparently compiled in Scotland, for Henry, Lord Sinclair.[92] Its primary interest in Chaucer is demonstrated by the inclusion of texts of *Troilus*, *The Legend of Good Women*, *The Parliament of Fowls*, and several of his short poems, as well as of works which commonly circulated with these texts (sometimes apparently in booklet format) such as Clanvowe's *Book of Cupid*, Hoccleve's *Letter of Cupid*, and Lydgate's *Complaint of the Black Knight*. These all reappear, if in textually distinct forms, in sixteenth-century printed editions, and are incorporated in Thynne's 1532 Chaucer collection; the Lydgate was also separately printed (as 'The maying and Disport of Chaucer') around 1508 by Chepman and Myllar in Edinburgh.[93] Some texts may also have leaked, directly or indirectly, into later Scottish anthologies like the Bannatyne and Maitland manuscripts. The remaining literary contents of the manuscript, however – pieces of some distinction which respond to Chaucer's models just as overtly as do the Clanvowe, Hoccleve and Lydgate – are otherwise untraceable outside its confines: *The Kingis Quair*, *The Quare of Jelusy* and two Ovidian verse laments. Their Scottishness, and perhaps their very intimate connections with the originators of this anthology (Sinclair's maternal grandmother was sister to James I of Scotland, presumed author of *The Kingis Quair*), seem to have limited their possibilities for influential circulation. English texts reached Scotland, but fewer seem to have travelled, or at least to

90. *STC* 256. 91. *STC* 3200.
92. Bodleian, ms. Arch. Selden. B. 24; Boffey and Edwards 1997. 93. *STC* 17014.3.

have been promoted, in the other direction. Douglas's *Palace of Honour* was printed in Edinburgh in 1535,[94] but not in London until almost twenty years later [1553?],[95] and his *Aeneid* translation, with its copious reference to Chaucer, although apparently available in some form to Surrey, while he worked on his own version, was not printed in London until 1553.[96]

In the case of prose texts other than religious ones the situation is a little different. Certain individual works found a continuing appeal in both manuscript and print, as with the extraordinarily popular *Mandeville's Travels*.[97] Malory's *Morte Darthur* was, from its initial manuscript copying, closely linked to printing and was regularly reprinted into the seventeenth century.[98] More striking, however, is the emergence in print of forms of informational texts – the outer limits of literature – which seem to have provided, in some instances, very lucrative markets. The most striking of these is possibly the printing, from the late fifteenth century, of large numbers of grammatical texts, particularly those by Stanbridge and Whittinton.[99] Courtesy books, and more sophisticated treatises such as Sir Thomas Elyot's *Governor*, also became staple printed forms. The emergence of various forms of printed, comprehensive chronicle writings, by Robert Fabyan, Richard Grafton, John Stow and others, largely displaced earlier national, universal or local histories such as the *Brut* or the various forms of Higden's *Polychronicon* or town chronicles (except for some London chronicles, none of the last was printed).

Much more difficult to assess is the extent of knowledge of the literature of other European vernaculars or of classical literature. Knowledge of Italian literature was probably to a large degree filtered through English or French intermediaries. The borrowings and translations from Dante in Chaucer's writings demonstrate an acquaintance with his works, but the evidence of any circulation in manuscript in England is scanty and none of Dante's works had been printed in England by the end of our period.[100] The early fifteenth-century commissioning of a Latin translation of *The Divine Comedy* by Nicholas Bubwith, Bishop of Bath and Wells and one-time Chancery Clerk, seems an isolated example of interest.[101] Chaucer, again, provides the best evidence for English knowledge of any of Boccaccio's vernacular works. He manifestly had access to the *Filostrato* and the *Teseida*, but again there is no evidence to

94. STC 7072.8.   95. STC 7073.   96. STC 24797.   97. STC 17246–54.
98. STC 801–6.   99. STC 23139.5–23199; 25443.2–25579; cf. Orme above, pp. 462–9.
100. Dédéyan 1961–6, I, pp. 1–119.   101. Catto 1985.

suggest a manuscript tradition in England. A few of Boccaccio's Latin works clearly found their way to England, and both of his large Latin works, the *De casibus virorum illustrium* and the *De claris mulieribus*, were also translated into English.[102] The former circulated very widely in both manuscript and print in Lydgate's translation, *The Fall of Princes*, but this is not a direct translation from the Latin but from a French prose version. The *De claris mulieribus* survives in translation only in a single manuscript. Nor is there much evidence for the circulation of Boccaccio's most famous work, the *Decameron*. There do not appear to be any manuscripts of English provenance and the only manuscript translation of any part of it, associated with Gilbert Banister, appears to derive from a French intermediary. Only a few other selected translations, by William Walter, had appeared in print by 1557.[103]

Petrarch may have been somewhat better known: prose translations of parts of his *De remediis utriusque fortunae* and of parts of his *Secretum* survive in manuscript from the fifteenth century;[104] and the early sixteenth century saw verse translations of the *Trionfi* (by Henry Morley) in print [1555?].[105] There seem in addition to have been manuscript traditions in England for some of his works. Over forty now survive which were either copied and/or owned in England in the fifteenth and early sixteenth centuries, including the *De remediis*, the *Secretum* and the *Griseldis historia*. This last work, brought to the attention of English readers in the prologue to Chaucer's Clerk's Tale, was presented to Humfrey, Duke of Gloucester, in a manuscript, now lost, from which Robert Shirborne – a Fellow of New College, Oxford, in the 1470s – made a copy.[106] In Humfrey's library were, of course, further manuscripts of various of the writings of Petrarch, Dante and Boccaccio.[107] More general access to Petrarch's lyrics, previously known only through Chaucer's translation of Sonnet 88 (Canzoniere 132) in *Troilus & Criseyde*, can be postulated from the translations and adaptations produced by Wyatt and Surrey;[108] Petrarch's lyrics were printed in Italy from 1470 (the period of the first printed editions of the works of Dante).

Wyatt's documented journeys to Spain, and the Anglo-Spanish negotiations concerning the marriage of Henry VIII, perhaps stimulated some interest in Spanish literature, but the evidence remains sparse, apart from translations made via French, such as some of Berners' works,

---

102. Haveley 1980; H. G. Wright 1957.   103. *STC* 3183.5, 3184.5.   104. Mann 1975b.
105. *STC* 19811.   106. Extant as Bodleian, ms. Lat. misc. d. 34.
107. De la Mare and Hunt 1970.   108. P. Thomson 1964.

and the first English version of *Arnalte and Lucenda*, and the 'chastened' English adaptation of the *Celestina*, *Calisto and Melebea*, which may have contributed to the development of the interlude.[109] Printed Spanish–English vocabularies did not appear until the 1550s.

Knowledge of classical literature in verse or prose during the period has routinely been spoken of dismissively, perhaps in part following the lead of Gavin Douglas, who, in the prologue to his translation of the *Aeneid*, deplored the entrenched taste for debased adaptations of classical texts:

> Thocht Wilyame Caxtoune, of Inglis natioun,
> In proys hes prent ane buke of Inglys gros,
> Clepand it Virgill in Eneados,
> Quhilk that he says of Franch he dyd translait,
> It has na thing ado tharwith, God wait.[110]

Caxton's translation was based not directly on Virgil, but on *Le livre des Eneides translate de latin en francois* of Guillaume le Roy.[111] The availability of this and similar adaptations, in both manuscript and print, may sit oddly alongside what is known of the activities of humanist scholars in the same period, but the vehemence of Douglas's fulminations perhaps suggests widespread casual tolerance about the precise status of such texts. The level of demand for classical literature is in fact peculiarly hard to assess. Many manuscripts copied in the fourteenth century or even earlier presumably remained in libraries, and the frequency with which they were consulted by fifteenth- and sixteenth-century readers cannot be known. (This is true of certain other influential texts, of course, such as *Le Roman de la Rose*.) New manuscripts were acquired (most spectacularly by Humfrey, Duke of Gloucester), and certain favourite Latin works printed, both in the original (parts of Cicero and Ovid, Virgil's *Bucolics*) and in translation (parts of Cicero, again; Terence; and the versions of the *Aeneid* produced by Douglas and Surrey). The extent of the circulation of continental printed texts in England and Scotland merits reassessment.[112] Current research (such as that undertaken by Margaret Lane Ford, elsewhere in this volume) confirms that English printers saw little need to duplicate books which were already efficiently printed in Venice, or in Lyons or Paris, and perhaps also efficiently marketed from these centres. The range of readers able to procure such importations is to be

109. Blake 1971; Axton 1979.   110. Caldwell 1957–64.   111. Culley and Furnivall 1890.
112. L. Hellinga 1991a; Edwards 1995; cf. Ford above, pp. 179–228.

gauged largely from inscriptions on surviving copies. Some of these bear the 'ex libris' inscriptions of noted humanist bibliophiles, but others carry traces of less exalted readers: a Paris edition of the *Georgics* marked 'liber Johannis Nortun' was perhaps in the hands of a late fifteenth-century prior of the Carthusian house of Mountgrace, for example.[113]

The enduring availability of texts from France – whether written in French, in Latin, or translated into French from Latin or one of the other European vernaculars, and whether printed or in manuscript – is perhaps in the end among the most notable continuities of the period. At about the time of Chaucer's death in 1400, Christine de Pisan was apparently sending copies of her writings to England; they circulated both in French, and in translations starting with Hoccleve's *Letter of Cupid* in 1402, continuing through Caxton's printed contributions, and appearing (sometimes in new versions) in mid sixteenth-century editions.[114] A number of the writings of Alain Chartier (royal notary and secretary to the future King Charles VII of France) reached England. His controversial love debate, *La belle dame sans merci*, and some of his political writings were translated and read in both manuscript and print, attracting interest in the fifteenth century in Lancastrian circles which included figures like the political theorist, Sir John Fortescue,[115] who may have seen in Chartier's experience of political exile a reflection of the events of their own time. Some of the most extensive manuscript collections of the works of fourteenth-century French poets so important to Chaucer – Froissart, Machaut, Deschamps – came into English hands during this later period:[116] Jean de Berry's collection of Machaut's poems was given to Thomas, Duke of Clarence, in 1412, and Froissart's personally overseen collection of his lyrics was at some stage in the possession of Richard Beauchamp. The lack of attention which these poems attracted from early French printers, oddly reflective of the neglect in England of Gower and Hoccleve, may have had something to do with the dispersal of manuscripts in England and elsewhere; another important Machaut collection came to England before reaching the Burgundian library of Louis de Gruthuyse, Protector of Edward IV.

Military campaigns and political alliances throughout the period ensured the continuing currency of French among cultivated English readers.[117] Manuscripts were bought, borrowed, exchanged and possibly pillaged, and that these methods of acquisition also extended to printed

113. Now BL, IA.40375.   114. Campbell 1925.   115. Seaton 1961; Blayney 1974–80.
116. Boffey 1994.   117. Stratford 1993.

books is suggested by a sixteenth-century inscription in a 1499 edition of the *Compost et calendrier des bergeres*, which reads: 'Ihon Raimo oweth thys boke / the wyche he stale at mourley in brytayn.'[118] The Parisian printer, Vérard, offering special editions of some of his works to Henry VII, was able to rely on tastes nourished by manuscripts procured from the Louvre library early in the fifteenth century by John of Bedford, and by an English royal library, overseen by a Flemish librarian, with a focus on French and Burgundian books.[119] The production of translations was generated not always to aid the uncomprehending, but sometimes to enhance the status of English and to stress the national significance of particular texts: Caxton's preface to Malory's *Morte Darthur* effectively reclaims the story in this way. Chaucer's activities as 'grant translateur' perhaps prompted later experiments by those concerned to draw English writing into important continental literary controversies. Poems connected with the great debate over *Le Roman de la Rose* and the subsidiary *querelle* about Chartier's *La belle dame sans merci* were translated into English, and the concerns of both disputes were reflected in the composition of certain Chaucerian and post-Chaucerian manuscript anthologies and later printed collections. Chaucer's translation of the *Romaunt de la Rose* was printed in 1532,[120] and at least one manuscript of the French original[121] was annotated by sixteenth-century readers. Undoubtedly, as the market for books widened to include those with less linguistic competence, French material also offered a ready source of new texts. Extending Caxton's own precedent, both De Worde and Pynson seem to have maintained contacts with writers, such as Watson and Copland, who could turn their hands to quick translations of French works which had established some success. French printers themselves organized translations for the English market, such as Vérard's editions of *The Castle of Labour* ([c. 1503]) and *The Kalendayr of Shyppars* (1503).[122]

Such translations are of course only one aspect of the gradual widening of both the scope and the audience of literature during the period from 1400 to the 1550s. The movement from manuscript to print and the manifest continuities and disjunctions we have been sketching cannot be conveniently delineated in chronological terms. The 1550s, however, are an obvious watershed in the history of English poetry, a decade of both retrospection and innovation. These years saw the final reprintings – until the twentieth century – of the major works of Lydgate and of his

---

118. BL, IB.39718.   119. Backhouse 1987; cf. above, pp. 272, 274.   120. *STC* 5068.
121. Bodleian, ms. e Mus. 65.   122. *STC* 12379, 22407; J. Macfarlane 1901.

disciple Stephen Hawes, and of Thynne's first collected Chaucer. They also saw the first printings of *Tottel's Miscellany* and *The Mirror for Magistrates*, as well as the first printing in England of Gavin Douglas's *Eneydos*, the harbinger of several later sixteenth-century translations of Virgil, the manuscript of which is preserved in Trinity College, Cambridge (see fig. 27.2). The decade is not a clear-cut point of transition. It does, however, see a discernible shift, a re-orientation of literary emphases and priorities that adumbrates, in the history of the book, new developments that are more appropriately the subject of a history of the Renaissance book.

28

Press, politics and religion

PAMELA NEVILLE-SINGTON

Politics and organized religion are each branches of the persuasive arts. With the invention of the press, the printed word was immediately seized upon by the Church as the most rapid and effective means of disseminating doctrine and seeking support as well as money. Thus, the first dateable productions from the presses of both Gutenberg in Mainz (1454/5) and Caxton in Westminster (1475/6) were indulgences to raise money for that project dearest to the heart of the papacy, a crusade against the Infidel. Once Caxton had introduced the printing press into England, the highly centralized nature of government meant that the Crown too could be quick to exploit the printed word in order to legitimize the reign, glorify the monarch, justify policy and promulgate the law.[1]

Received opinion associates this exploitation of the press with the Reformation, and in England with Thomas Cromwell in particular, as Henry VIII's agent.[2] There is no doubt that its use by both sides in the Reformation controversy was intensified in the late 1520s and 1530s. It is equally true, however, that English rulers had been using the printed word as a means of persuasion since the reign of Edward IV. An important development came with Henry VII's creation of the office of King's Printer; Henry VIII and his Chancellor, Cardinal Wolsey, turned this post into an efficient government tool. Two ingredients only were needed for an effective printed propaganda campaign: a cause and an imaginative campaign strategist. The Reformation provided one and Cromwell the other. Although Cromwell cannot be said to have discovered the potential of the press for political ends, his campaign certainly broke new ground, for his mission was not simply to persuade but to indoctrinate an entire nation.

1. I am grateful to Dr David Starkey, Dr Katharine F. Pantzer, Mr Peter Blayney, Philip Ward, Tania String and Glenn Richardson, and the editors of this volume.
2. Baumer 1940; Elton 1981; Baskerville 1979.

The first piece of English printed propaganda to survive, *The promisse of matrimonie*, probably dates from early 1483.[3] The text consists of the nuptial agreement concerning England's princess and France's dauphin contained in the Treaty of Picquigny (1475), followed by the Treaty of Arras (23 December 1482), wherein the French King breaks his promise to Edward and betrothes his son to Archduke Maximilian's daughter. Edward IV or one of his councillors probably intended that this pamphlet be distributed to members of the parliament which the King convened on 20 January 1483 to stir up enthusiasm (and money) for a resumption of the war against France. *The promisse of matrimonie* came off the press of William de Machlinia, a Dutchman resident in London who specialized in legal printing for both the Inns of Court and the Crown. In about 1484, Machlinia printed the statutes of Richard III's first and only parliament in the traditional law French.[4]

The first monarch to make regular use of printed propaganda, however, was Henry VII. The papal dispensation allowing his marriage to Elizabeth of York on 18 March 1486 (they were related in the fourth degree of kinship) was printed in an English translation by Machlinia.[5] This broadside, which was declared from the pulpit and probably displayed for the public to see, emphasized Henry VII's right to the throne and also threatened excommunication to any who dared rebel against the King and his heirs.

Several more versions of the bull were printed between 1494 and 1497, possibly in response to the threat posed by Perkin Warbeck's claim to the throne, by Wynkyn de Worde and by Pynson.[6] After Warbeck's surrender to Henry's forces in September 1498, Bernard André tells us, the King commanded that his confession be printed so that its words might strike fear into the hearts of those who would oppose him.[7] No copy of this publication survives, but it is clear that Henry was using the press in a subtle and effective manner to legitimize his reign. The publication of a work by Pynson in about 1496, entitled *The epitaffe of the moste noble & valyaunt Iaspar late duke of Beddeforde*, written by the late Duke's falconer, was probably sanctioned by Henry VII, for in paying homage to his uncle Jasper Tudor, it traced the King's royal lineage from Aeneas of Troy to the saintly Henry VI.[8]

---

3. *STC* 9176.   4. *STC* 9347; see Baker above, pp. 423–4.
5. *STC* 14096. For this and for other information in this chapter, see Neville 1990.
6. *STC* 14097 (reissue); 14098 (abridgement); 14098.5; 14099 (exemplification).
7. Gairdner 1858, p. 73.   8. *STC* 14477.

A policy which the King was eager to promote, especially since it meant extracting a 'benevolence' from a number of his subjects, was the invasion of France to 'vindicate' England's age-old claim to the throne.[9] Henry therefore commissioned Caxton to translate and publish Christine de Pisan's *Fayttes of arms*: the colophon is dated 14 July 1489.[10] According to Caxton's epilogue, Henry, delivering the manuscript to him at Westminster, 'desired & wylled me . . . to put it in enprynte to thende that every gentylman born to armes . . . shold have knowlege how they ought to behave theym in the fayttes of warre & of bataylles'. Caxton then spells out the propaganda message: 'I byseche almyghty god to preserve, kepe, & contynue [Henry] in his noble & most redoubted enterpryses as wel in bretayn, flaundres, & other placis that he may have victorie honour, & renomme to his perpetual glorye.'[11]

In late 1491 and in 1492 Henry prepared a military campaign in France which ended on 3 November 1492 with the Treaty of Etaples. On signing their indentures, early in May 1492, each officer was to be issued with a printed copy of the *Ordenaunces of Warre*, which had been commissioned for this purpose, as its colophon states: 'by [the King's] high Commaundement & by his owne propre handys delyvered to me Richard Pynson prynter of this boke'.[12] This booklet was to serve as an important model for subsequent government publications. It is the first official work from the press to declare in forthright terms that, thanks to printing, the King's subjects will not be able to claim ignorance of the law:

> and to thentent they have no cause to excuse theim of their offences by pretense of ignorance of the saide ordenances, his highnesse hath ovir and above the open proclamacion of the saide statutes commaunded and ordeyned by wey of emprynte diverse and many several bokes conteignyng the same statutes to be made and delivered to the capitaignes of his ost charginge them as they wyl avoyde his greate displeasure to cause the same twyes or ones at the lest in every weke hooly to be redde in the presence of theire retynue.

The *Ordenaunces of warre* is also the first extant printed document to bear the royal arms. Royal and papal arms begin to appear at about this time in statutes and other official publications printed in Germany, Spain and Rome. Coins and seals, as well as medieval records of the Crown courts,

9. *CPR, Henry VII*, 1, p. 353.   10. *STC* 7269.
11. Fol. S5r/v.   12. *STC* 9332; Condon 1986.

which had long used royal arms and other images to convey authority and prestige, were undoubtedly the model.[13] Through this quite elaborate full-page woodcut, Henry VII also announces his claim to France, for it displays the shields of both France and England with an angel above – a detail borrowed from the French royal arms – surrounded by Tudor and Beaufort badges of the rose and portcullis. Many versions of these arms, emblems and badges were to appear on printed editions of statutes, proclamations and treatises over the next thirty years.

In peacetime, Henry VII maintained a high profile among his subjects, courtiers and foreign ambassadors by staging ceremonials and festivals, and it was during Henry's reign that the press first began to play a significant role in the preparation and preservation of these regal occasions.[14] An elaborate programme was drawn up in June 1500, perhaps by Henry's councillor Richard Fox, for the marriage of Prince Arthur and Catherine of Aragon. *The traduction & mariage of the princesse* was then printed by Pynson, presumably so that it could be more quickly and widely distributed among those officials involved in the arrangements.[15] (The marriage was subsequently delayed because of an outbreak of sweating sickness in London.) Fox privately commissioned pious works from the London and Westminster printers,[16] as did another of Henry VII's councillors, John Morton.[17] Their appreciation of the new medium may have influenced the Crown's use of the press.

In 1507, Henry VII negotiated another dynastic alliance, between his daughter Mary and Prince Charles (later Emperor Charles V). The betrothal took place at the palace of Richmond on 17 December 1508 and a permanent record worthy of the occasion – with a poem by Henry VII's Latin secretary, Pietro Carmeliano, and the arms of Henry VII supported by two angels – was printed by Richard Pynson: *Pro sponsalibus et matrimonio inter principem Karolem, & dominam Mariam.*[18] This Latin edition was intended for members of the courts of England, Spain and the rest of Europe. Some time in the next year Pynson produced, still with the royal arms but without Carmeliano's poem, an English translation for domestic consumption: *The solempnities, & triumphes doon at the spousells of the kyngs doughter.*[19]

When the *Pro sponsalibus* was published, Richard Pynson had held the title *impressor regius* for at least two years, beginning in 1506/7. Henry VII had created the post of King's Printer almost certainly in 1504 to coin-

---

13. Challis 1978; Auerbach 1954.   14. Anglo 1969.   15. *STC* 4814.
16. *STC* 1859, 5643, 16232.6.   17. *STC* 16173.   18. *STC* 4659.   19. *STC* 17558.

cide with the last parliament of his reign, 19 Henry VII (25 January–30 March 1504). Possibly, he was looking to the French example: from 1487 the Parisian printer Pierre Le Rouge identified himself as *impressor regius*.[20] In France, the office of King's Printer seems to have died with Le Rouge in 1493, however, not to be resurrected until 1538. In any case, Le Rouge's 'official' publications comprised beautifully executed folio volumes of religious texts and fashionable histories rather than official government documents. The English Crown's first appointee, William Faques, identifies himself in the colophon of the printed statutes for 19 Henry VII as 'ye King [*sic*] Printer'.[21] In this same year 1504, Faques produced the earliest surviving printed proclamation, regarding coinage, in the form of a broadside to be distributed, proclaimed and posted throughout the realm (see fig. 28.1).[22]

The statutes of parliament had appeared in print since the reign of Richard III. From the beginning, their publication was of an official nature; their manuscript source was the Statute Roll until 1489, and thereafter the original Acts. There were as many steps backwards as forwards in the evolution of these early printed statutes which came from the workshops of De Machlinia,[23] Caxton,[24] De Worde[25] and Pynson.[26] However, within just a few decades, the printed statutes, partly by design and partly by chance, had come to be accepted by the Crown and its subjects as the primary means of promulgating parliamentary law, superseding the manuscript record hitherto kept by the Court of the Exchequer. The introduction of printing to the legislative process limited the King's prerogative and strengthened the authority of the law itself.[27] Henry VII contributed to this development by making the language of the statutes English, not the traditional law French, and by creating the office of King's Printer.

The first opportunity which Pynson had to print the original edition of the sessional statutes in his official role came with the opening parliament of Henry VIII's reign (21 January–23 February 1510).[28] It seems that the rights of the King's Printer were not exclusive: another edition also dating from 1510 came off the press of Richard Faques, probably a relative of William and certainly his successor in the business.[29] Wynkyn de

20. See Goff O.16.   21. *STC* 9357.
22. *STC* 7760.4; reprinted by Wynkyn de Worde: *STC* 7760.6, 7761.   23. *STC* 9347.
24. *STC* 9348.   25. *STC* 9349, 9351a.7, 9352, 9353, 9354, 9355.5.   26. *STC* 9355.
27. Elton 1974–83, III, pp. 92–109; Pantzer 1983, pp. 69–114; and Neville 1990, Chapter 2. For printed statutes in relation to other law books, see Baker above, pp. 422–3.
28. *STC* 9357.8.   29. *STC* 9357.9.

Worde and Richard Faques, not Pynson, had printed the first proclamations to be issued under Henry VIII in 1509.[30] It is unclear whether Faques jumped the gun in printing this session of parliament or pirated Pynson's work. In any case, the King's Printer almost certainly made an official complaint to the Crown. In a later edition of 1 Henry VIII, printed by Pynson in about 1513, there duly appears a privilege granting the King's 'trusty & welbelovyd servaunte' the exclusive right to print these statutes for two years.[31] It is evident that, by the end of the parliament of 4 Henry VIII (4 November–20 December 1512), this privilege had been extended: the statutes for the parliaments of 3 and 4 Henry VIII were printed together by Pynson in 1513;[32] and the King's Printer was to be solely responsible for all extant statutes and proclamations printed from 1513 onwards.

In view of the political agenda for 1512–13, it seems likely that Thomas Wolsey had a hand in this decision, which effectively made the press an extremely useful and (generally) controllable mechanism of government. The first major policy which Henry VIII initiated independently of his father's councillors was participation in the Holy League to defend the papacy and prosecute the subsequent war with France – and its architect was Wolsey. Probably at the end of 1512, Pynson printed a charter, or *inspeximus*, drawn up by Wolsey (22 September 1512), of a bull of Julius II which announced the formation of the Holy League, declared Louis XII an enemy of the Church, and absolved his subjects from allegiance to their monarch. The arms of Julius II appear on this broadside to emphasize papal authority and approval.[33] In preparation for the war against France, Pynson also printed a revised edition of the *Ordenaunces of warre* in 1513.[34]

The *inspeximus* and ordinances were part of a general onslaught by Henry and Wolsey against the French. The King, no doubt with Wolsey's advice if not at his instigation, commissioned three more works from the King's Printer in 1512–13. Designed to stir up the indignation of both his English subjects and the international community, they are very different in character but all sport the full regalia of badges, emblems and papal and royal arms (the latter still supported by angels). James Whytstons' *De iusticia & sanctitate belli* is the 'official' justification of the war, composed in Latin, employing a great array of scholastic and legal authorities to

---

30. Henry VII's final pardon and Henry VIII's accession pardon: *STC* 7761.3, 7761.7; *STC* 7762, 7762.3.   31. *STC* 9358; see *STC*, I, p. 421n.   32. *STC* 9361.   33. *STC* 25947.7.   34. *STC* 9333.

justify the Holy League.[35] The second work is a 'popular' account of the Holy League in English, probably by Alexander Barclay, entitled *The gardyners passetaunce touchyng the outrage of fraunce*.[36]

Whereas Whytsons' *De iusticia* and the anonymous *Gardyner's passetaunce* are slim quarto treatises, the third work, John Lydgate's *Troy Book*, is a grand folio edition with illustrations throughout, including a full-page woodcut of the Tudor arms on the title-page.[37] Lydgate had translated the work in 1412–21 for his patron Henry V. Henry VIII saw himself as Henry V *redivivus* and Pynson states in his colophon that he printed *The hystorye, sege and dystruccyon of Troye* at the King's express commandment.

By the middle of 1513 England was drawn into war on another front, against France's ally, James IV of Scotland. Henry and Wolsey were not slow to take advantage of the propaganda value of the Earl of Surrey's victory over the Scots at Flodden in September of that year. They commissioned Pynson to publish no fewer than three works, once again directed at different audiences. One work from Pynson's press today survives only in a Rome reprint.[38] The *Epistola regis Scotorum ad Angliae regem* includes not only James IV's declaration of war but also Henry's reply, which contains yet another justification of his campaign against the French. We know of the existence of the two other works only through a late sixteenth-century manuscript.[39] James IV was killed at Flodden, and Henry thought to prove himself magnanimous even to his enemies in time of war by giving the Scottish King burial in St Paul's Cathedral (though he later changed his mind). Pietro Carmeliano composed the appropriate Latin epitaph and Pynson printed it, either as a separate publication or possibly as an epilogue to the third work, the anonymous *Thordre and behavyoure of the right honourable Erle of Surrey . . . ayonst the kynge of Scottes*. This text was intended to satisfy the public's thirst for news and to make the Earl of Surrey into a hero. There was always a market for 'popular', unofficial accounts of battles and great occasions: in 1513 Richard Faques produced *Hereafter ensue the trew encountre, or batayle lately don betwene Englande and Scotlande*.[40]

In order to raise money for the offensive against France, the parliament of November–December 1512 granted a subsidy.[41] The novel idea of a subsidy was the brain-child of Wolsey, and it was no doubt Wolsey who,

---

35. *STC* 25585. 36. Barclay 1985; *STC* 11562.5. 37. *STC* 5579.
38. [S. Guileretus 1513]; for Pynson's edition, now lost, see Lowndes 1885–1908, III, p. 1186.
39. BL, Add. ms. 29506. 40. *STC* 11088.5. 41. 4 Henry VIII, c. 19.

to maximize its success, ordered that the grant be printed not only as a broadside to be posted, but also as a booklet in the same folio format as the statutes.[42] Although printed copies have not survived in every case, records of payment by the Crown suggest that the King's Printer continued to publish subsidies, revenue acts and certain other single acts, such as pardons, separately from the sessional statutes. These acts had a limited duration and it was vital that they reach the commissioners, King's agents and Justices of the Peace quickly.[43]

Wolsey was almost certainly behind another innovative use of the press connected with the subsidy. To aid in the collection of this tax the London commissioners had forms printed as broadsides, with blank spaces to fill in certain names and details. Three different printed subsidy forms have survived; more may have been issued. The first, connected with the original subsidy of 1512 and summoning the aldermen of London to appear and supply information, was printed by Wynkyn de Worde in 1513.[44] The other two documents, one which defines the information to be given by the commissioners, the other ordering certification of the names in each London ward, came off Pynson's press in 1515.[45] The model for these primitive bureaucratic forms was the indulgence, which provided blank spaces for the name of the buyer and date of purchase.[46] They were also the first official printed documents in England to have leaded (that is, double-spaced) text, a feature common in schoolbooks of the period but which would transform the appearance of proclamations well into the next century. By 1526 their original size, roughly 'A4', had doubled to accommodate the leaded text, ensuring that these proclamations, once posted, could and would be easily read, not simply heard, by as many people as possible.[47] To make more room for the leaded text, Pynson no longer displayed the royal arms across the top of proclamations, as he had before 1526. The royal arms were to reappear sporadically on proclamations after 1530 and more consistently in Elizabeth I's reign. The imprint of the King's Printer invariably appears at the bottom.

Wolsey, understanding Henry's international ambitions, used the printing press, among other means at his disposal, to glorify the King not

---

42. *STC* 7763, 9361.4.   43. Pantzer 1983, pp. 76–7.   44. *STC* 7764.
45. *STC* 7766, 7767.
46. Slavin, who did not know of the existence of these subsidy forms, wrongly attributes the earliest use of printed forms for tax collection to John Longland, Bishop of Lincoln, in 1538, closely followed by Edmund Bonner, Bishop of London (see below): Slavin 1982; 1986, pp. 90–109.   47. *STC* 7769.6ff.

only at home but across Europe. His advice may have strengthened Henry's resolve, in order to celebrate – and make a virtue of – the peace at home, to commission Pynson to print Robert Fabyan's *New cronycles of Englande and of Fraunce*, which appeared in two folio volumes in early 1516.[48] Fabyan, who died in 1513, had written his chronicles to mark the *rapprochement* with France at the end of the Hundred Years' War. In the preface he speaks of 'the fatall warre that hath endured so longe Twene Fraunce & England, to both theyr damage' and bids the English maintain 'that peace that hath been undersong both by great oathes and each by marriage'.[49] The same full-page woodcut of the royal arms which appeared in 1513 in Lydgate's *Troy Book*, urging Henry's subjects to war, is placed on the title-page of Fabyan's *New cronycles* in 1516, glorifying peace.

Propaganda burns most strongly during times of conflict. With the important exception of Fabyan's *New cronycles*, no blatantly propagandist works, such as those which flourished in 1512–13, came off Pynson's press for several years. The number of indulgences, however, judging from what has survived, dramatically increased after 1515. Indulgences were an accurate barometer of relations between Crown and papacy, and they acted to some extent like proclamations, conveying propaganda and providing news.[50] Henry VIII, although non-committal about the crusade which Leo X desired, demonstrated his good faith by sanctioning a relatively large number of ransom indulgences. These were issued by the King and Pope jointly, printed by the King's Printer, and sold to those contributing alms for the redemption of Christians taken hostage by the Turks.[51] Across the top of these broadsides the King's arms appear beside those of the Pontiff, displaying not only the King's devotion to the Pope but also the importance of his own position within Europe. Henry VIII, undoubtedly encouraged by Wolsey, who was made a cardinal in 1515, was especially eager to promote these indulgences, for he coveted the title 'Defender of the Faith' which it was in Leo's power to bestow.

Henry's position – and pride – was threatened, however, in 1515, when a youthful rival, Francis I, ascended the throne in France. To put Henry back at centre stage, Wolsey stole the initiative over the five-year truce among the European states which Leo X had proclaimed on 6 March 1518, and arranged for the treaty to be signed in London on 2 October of that year. Wolsey celebrated his success on the next day with a High Mass

48. *STC* 10659.   49. Fol. a3r.
50. See *STC*, ii, pp. 2–9; for indulgences in England, see Lunt 1962.   51. *STC* 14077c.124–133.

at St Paul's during which Richard Pace, Henry VIII's secretary and ambassador, delivered an oration. On 5 October, the betrothal of Princess Mary to the dauphin took place at Greenwich, accompanied by an oration by Cuthbert Tunstal, Master of the Rolls. On 13 November 1518, Pynson published Tunstal's Latin address, followed several weeks later by that of Pace (5 December).[52] Both works bear the arms of Henry VIII on the title-page, and both were printed, not in the traditional gothic fonts, but in roman type, which Pynson had introduced into England in 1509, the first book printed in roman type being Pietro Griffo's *Oratio*.[53] It was used for Pace's and Tunstal's orations in conscious imitation of the humanist works which were appearing on the Continent. Hereafter, until Elizabeth I's reign, Latin texts would normally appear in roman type and English in gothic or black-letter.

This press campaign seems to have achieved Wolsey's purpose. The two orations, glorifying England's role as the peacemaker of Europe, were reprinted, both in Latin and in translation, on the Continent.[54] The unsteady balance of power among the European nations soon shifted, however. In 1522, Henry allied himself with Charles V and declared war on France. To convince Henry's subjects that Charles was a fitting ally, Pynson printed the Latin verses (together with an English translation) composed by William Lily for the Emperor's reception in London in June 1522, under the title *Of the tryumphe and the verses that Charles thempe-rour, & kyng of England, Henry the viii were saluted with*.[55] The arms of Henry VIII are prominently displayed in the text along with a portrait of Charles V in full armour.

The title-page to Lord Berners's translation of Jean Froissart's chronicles of the Hundred Years' War states that it was made at the command-ment of Henry VIII. Its intention, like Christine de Pisan's *Fayttes of arms* and Lydgate's *Troy Book*, was to remind Englishmen that France was their traditional enemy and to inspire its readers to feats of glory on the battle-field. Pynson published the first volume of Froissart's *Cronycles* on 28 January 1523, when Henry was once more claiming France as his rightful inheritance, like Henry V before him.[56] The Crown almost certainly delayed the publication of the second and final part, describing the close of the Hundred Years' War, to coincide with the signing of the peace treaty between England and France at the More, one of Wolsey's resi-dences, on 30 August 1525. According to the colophon, volume II of

---

52. *STC* 24320, 19081a.   53. *STC* 12413.   54. Shaaber 1975, P1, P2, T162, T163.
55. *STC* 15606.7.   56. *STC* 11396.

Froissart's chronicles was issued the following day, 31 August.[57] Both volumes sport the same full-page woodcut of the Tudor arms which had appeared in Lydgate's *Troy Book*, though the appearance of Pynson's device suggests that he shared the cost of publication with the Crown – an arrangement which may have been advantageous to both parties.

Wolsey's most sophisticated press campaign via the King's Printer centred on religious orthodoxy in the 1520s – and Henry's renewed hope of the title 'Defender of the Faith'. The carefully planned offensive began with the *Assertio septem sacramentorum*, composed by Henry VIII and others, defending the Church against the pernicious assaults of Martin Luther. Wolsey instructed his agent in Rome, John Clerk, to deliver a manuscript copy of the *Assertio* to Leo X in private; if the Pope approved of the work (which he did), he was to present the same manuscript[58] together with the text printed on vellum,[59] in public consistory (2 October 1521). Other printed copies, some on vellum, were then distributed to sovereigns, cardinals and universities.[60]

The first two printed editions are wholly humanistic publications, with a woodcut title-page border originally designed by Hans Holbein the Younger (see fig. 28.2).[61] The copies intended for the dignitaries of Europe have classicizing painted borders, of indifferent quality. The impression aimed at is of a modern and enlightened ruler wholly in tune with the Renaissance. On 11 October 1521, nine days after Clerk delivered the *Assertio*, Leo X issued a bull formally conferring upon Henry VIII the coveted title 'Fidei Defensor'. Pynson subsequently issued a supplement to the original edition of the *Assertio*, containing the oration which Clerk gave at the presentation ceremony and two bulls of Leo X, one granting the title to Henry and the other announcing an indulgence for those who read the book.[62] Many editions of the *Assertio* were printed on the Continent; never before had Henry VIII achieved such prominence in Europe.[63]

Luther published a vigorous reply to Henry in both German and Latin in the autumn of 1522; on 20 January 1523, Henry replied by sending to the Saxon dukes his *Epistola regia*, printed by Pynson as yet another supplement to the *Assertio*.[64] In this letter, Henry VIII warns of the dangers of Lutheranism and also remarks that he considers it unseemly to

---

57. *STC* 11397.   58. BAV, ms. Vat. Lat. 3731.   59. *STC* 13078.
60. Vian 1962; cf. Alexander, above, p. 63.   61. *STC* 13078, 13079.
62. *STC* 13083, pt. 1; pt. 2 is a reissue of *STC* 13078.   63. Shaaber 1975, H140–H150.
64. *STC* 13083, pt. 3.

respond to Luther's attacks. Instead, the King had already rallied the humanists to the defence of the Church. By the end of 1522, several learned men attached to Henry's court had set pen to paper against Luther. However, Henry and Wolsey delayed this propaganda offensive for several reasons. They were hoping to receive the Saxon dukes' reply to the King's letter or even to hear news of Luther's recantation. The dukes' answer in May 1523 was not encouraging. The King also wanted the endorsement of the most celebrated humanist, Erasmus.

At last, in September 1523, Erasmus wrote to Henry with the long-awaited intimation that he was writing against Lutheranism.[65] A month later, Pynson published a work by Catherine of Aragon's confessor, Alphonsus de Villa Sancta, entitled *De libero arbitrio* – undoubtedly written with the Queen's support.[66] Villa Sancta also contributed to the campaign with his *Problema indulgentiarum*:[67] the preface is dated 19 January 1523, suggesting that its author had jumped the gun. This might, however, be old-style dating, thus making the year 1524, or possibly its publication date was delayed.

Although Edward Powell had written in November 1522 to ask Wolsey's approval for a work against Luther which he had begun, the *Propugnaculum adversus Lutherum* did not come off Pynson's press until 3 December 1523. In it Powell criticizes Erasmus's long silence.[68] Henry and Wolsey also delayed the publication of Sir Thomas More's pseudonymous *Responsio ad Lutherum*. The prefatory letter of the first version is signed 'Ferdinandus Baravellus' and dated 11 February 1523: only one copy survives of this edition (once belonging to Bishop Tunstal's chaplain), probably printed in May–June 1523.[69] While Henry and Wolsey were stalling for time, More decided to revise the work, creating a completely new fictional setting under the pen-name Guilielmus Rosseus,[70] and it probably came off Pynson's press after Powell's *Propugnaculum*. As with Henry VIII's *Assertio* two years earlier, Pynson ensured that the books in this English campaign against Luther resembled continental humanist publications by setting the titles within handsome woodcut borders and the text in roman type. No royal arms appear to mar the effect.

For the next two years Pynson's press was silent against Luther. Perhaps Henry thought that his orchestrated publishing campaign of

65. *CE*, x, no. 1385 (4 September 1523); *CWM*, v, pp. 719–23, 791–8.   66. *STC* 24728.
67. *STC* 24729.   68. *STC* 20140; *LPHenry VIII*, III, no. 2652.   69. *STC* 18088.5.
70. *STC* 18089.

1523–4 would be enough to persuade Luther to retreat. English protest, however, was not mute during this period. Bishop John Fisher's *Assertionis Lutheranae confutatio* and *Defensio regie assertionis contra Bablyonicam captivitatem* appeared on the Continent in 1523 and 1525, respectively.[71] Fisher was directing his own, independent campaign and probably underwrote the cost of publication himself.

Eventually Henry returned to the King's Printer to reply to Luther's letter of September 1525, written on the mistaken assumption that Henry was now receptive to his ideas. Henry's printed rebuke did not appear until 2 December 1526 in Latin,[72] and soon afterwards in English.[73] In accordance with Wolsey's urgent request, Luther's own letter was included in the publication so that he could not disclaim it. In order to discourage dissent at home, Pynson also printed *A replycacion agaynst certayne yong scolers*, composed by John Skelton at Wolsey's suggestion.[74] The scholars in question were the Cambridge heretics, Thomas Bilney and Thomas Arthur, who had been forced to recant at Paul's Cross in December 1527.

The Crown soon found it necessary to clamp down on Lutheranism by other means, namely by preventing the importation and circulation of heretical texts, including New Testament translations, printed in Germany and the Low Countries. The 'Proclamation for resysting . . . heresyes' of 1529, one of Pynson's last publications before his death at the end of that year and one of Wolsey's last acts as Lord Chancellor, effectively transferred the power of censorship from the ecclesiastical courts to the Privy Council. It may have contained the first list of prohibited books to appear in England.[75]

Wolsey's appreciation of the press's usefulness had extended to every corner of his jurisdiction, in both royal and ecclesiastical administration. Although none survive, there is evidence that in 1519 Wolsey ordered printed copies of his 'new articles of instruction' for sheriffs and justices of the peace[76] as well as his 'constitutions' for the clergy.[77] Notification of Wolsey's papal visitation as legate *a latere* in 1525[78] and the *inspeximus*

71. Shaaber 1975, F42, F76.   72. *STC* 13084, 13084.5.   73. *STC* 13086.
74. *STC* 22609.
75. *TRP* 122, *STC* 7772; the only surviving copy is imperfect. For the dating, see *CWM*, VI, p. 883; the best account of the heretical books and their fates is now contained in the apparatus to *CWM*, V, VII–XI; see also Greenslade 1963; for Tyndale, see Daniell 1994; for the Church's efforts before 1529, Gleason 1982. For the Wycliffite versions, see Hargreaves 1969; and for Lollard books in general, Hudson 1985, 1989.
76. Huntington, Ellesmere mss. 2652, fol. 7; 2655, fol. 15v.
77. Bannister 1921; Guy 1977, pp. 32–3.   78. *STC* 25947.3.

of 1529 granting privileges to his Cardinal College in Oxford[79] both came off Pynson's press. In about 1527, Wolsey also commissioned Pynson to print an indulgence, in English, to those who said a psalm, Pater Noster and Ave for the prosperity of Henry VIII, the Queen and the Princess – ironically, near the time when Henry was trying to initiate divorce proceedings against Catherine.[80] Henry VIII, like his father, undoubtedly grasped the power of the press and was keen to use it, but the evidence points to Wolsey as the guiding force behind the government's publishing policy from 1512 until his downfall in 1529. The government seems to have been left in some confusion by Pynson's death that same year: John Rastell (brother-in-law of Wolsey's successor as Lord Chancellor, Sir Thomas More) printed the statutes for the parliament which ended on 17 December 1529.[81]

Thomas Cromwell's use of the press in the 1530s has been well documented, particularly by Sir Geoffrey Elton.[82] Every observation which Elton makes for Cromwell's 'pioneering' propaganda campaign via the King's Printer Thomas Berthelet (a printer of humanist sympathies who had taken up the post by 15 February 1530),[83] however, can be applied to the earlier decade under their predecessors, Thomas Wolsey and Richard Pynson.[84] Both ministers mobilized scholars, humanists and churchmen to forward the King's cause, supervised the work of the King's Printer, targeted different audiences at home and abroad with texts printed in Latin and English, and ensured the careful timing of publications. It was more a matter of degree: the Reformation demanded of Cromwell a campaign on a grander scale than anything before.

In the 1530s, as during Henry VII's reign and Wolsey's ministry, the Crown used the press to justify and legitimize (in this case, the King's divorce from Catherine and the Royal Supremacy, respectively), to promulgate the law and to quell rebellion. As in the 1520s, Henry's inclination was to impress continental rulers and scholars alike with learned arguments in Latin, as in the *Gravissimae . . . totius Italiae, et Gallicae academiarum censurae* of 1530, which comprises testimonials from the leading European universities in favour of the divorce.[85] However, Cromwell, who came to prominence after Sir Thomas More resigned the Great Seal in 1532, had the 'common' – and more practical – touch. A lawyer by

---

79. *STC* 24323.5.   80. *STC* 14077c.146.   81. *STC* 9363.6.
82. Baumer 1940; Elton 1972, chapter 4; Scarisbrick 1968, chapter 12.
83. *LP Henry VIII*, IV, no. 6248(22).   84. For Berthelet, see Pantzer 1993, p. 64.
85. *STC* 14286; 1531 English translation, *STC* 14287; Bedouelle and Le Gal 1987; Surtz and Murphy, 1988.

training, he would already have been familiar with those printers specializing in legal texts near the Inns of Court. Cromwell would also, of course, have had ample opportunity to observe the use of the press for propaganda from the time he entered Wolsey's service, in October 1524. His relations with the London presses date back to 1523 when the alderman of the guild of St Mary's in Boston had bid Cromwell to 'tell Pynson to print 4000 letters [of confraternity] and as many briefs'.[86]

Thus, Cromwell supervised the publication of such works as *A glasse of the truthe* (1532), a lively dialogue between a theologian and a canon lawyer on the divorce and papal jurisdiction;[87] the nine *Articles* (1533), written 'not only to exhorte, but also to enfourme his lovynge subiectis of the trouthe' concerning the divorce, remarriage and Royal Supremacy;[88] and *A litel treatise ageynste the mutterynge of some papistis in corners* (1534), intended to silence all opposition.[89] Cromwell marshalled scholars and polemicists to advance the King's cause and counsel obedience among his subjects. Berthelet printed the sermons and treatises, both learned and popular, of Edward Fox, Richard Sampson, Stephen Gardiner, Thomas Starkey and the prolific Richard Morison. When rebellion broke out in the north, the King himself wrote, or at least put his name to, an *Answere to the petitions of the traytours and rebelles in Lyncolneshyre* (and later *Yorkshire*) in 1536.[90]

Cromwell's attempt to convert the nation to the Church of England began in 1536 with Berthelet's publication of the ten *Articles devised by the kynges highnes maiestie, to stablysshe christen quietnes and unitie amonge us.*[91] These Articles were followed the next year by *The institution of a christen man, conteynynge the exposytion of the commune crede, of the seven sacramentes* [etc.], also known as the *Bishops' Book*. Berthelet published this work in both quarto and the more convenient and less expensive octavo formats.[92]

The physical appearance of all these works, from Morison's treatises to the *Bishops' Book*, continued to be very much like the 'continental' style of the 1520s: small, handy octavo or quarto volumes; restrained title-pages with architectural borders, borders filled with putti, or no ornamentation at all; Latin texts in roman type, English texts in black-letter and similar gothic fonts. No doubt this look reflected Berthelet's own prefer-

---

86. *LPHenry VIII*, III, no. 3015.
87. *STC* 11918, 11919; French translation, *STC* 11919.5. For Cromwell's involvement, Ellis 1824-46, II, pp. 196–7; *LPHenry VIII*, v, no. 1320.   88. *STC* 9177, 9178.
89. *STC* 23551.5.   90. *STC* 13077.5, 13077.   91. *STC* 10033–10033.8.   92. *STC* 5163–7.

ences and stock; however, it also seemed to suit both Cromwell's purpose and his taste, as it had Wolsey's. Berthelet (though sparingly) and other printers continued to use royal arms, mainly on legal texts, throughout the sixteenth century as a mark of authority. In about 1538, the King's Printer acquired a title-page border which incorporates Henry VIII's arms at the bottom.[93] This would become a common method of displaying royal arms under Berthelet's successors.[94]

The principal means of enforcing change during the Reformation were the injunction and the visitation; both were anticipated to some extent by Wolsey but only fully implemented by Cromwell. In 1536, Berthelet printed a circular letter from Cromwell to individual deaneries (a blank is left for the name) which begins 'Iniunctions gyuen by the auctoritie of the kynges highnes to the clergie'.[95] Some bishops also had injunctions, visitation articles and similar mandates printed in order to disseminate them more widely and quickly within their dioceses. In 1535, John Longland, Bishop of Lincoln, circulated a form printed by John Byddell commanding that his clergy proclaim the King's new style as head of the Church of England.[96] Nicholas Shaxton, Bishop of Salisbury, commissioned Byddell to print a set of injunctions in 1538 'to sell at the closeyate in Salysbury'.[97] It is possible that other bishops did the same, though no copies survive to bear witness. On 5 August 1538, Roland Lee, Bishop of Lichfield and Coventry, wrote to Cromwell: 'I have set forth certain injunctions for my diocese now in my visitation, as other prelates do, and have sent them to Mr Bartlett [Berthelet], the printer, to have them put in print if you approve of them.'[98] As with indulgences earlier, bishops could commission any printer of their choice. After 1534, when bishops became the chief agents for gathering annates and first fruits and tenths, Bishops Longland, Bonner and others used printed forms to aid in tax collection, as Wolsey had done in 1512.[99]

The Articles and *Bishops' Book*, although they were to be radically revised, were at the time of publication straightforward documents which ultimately emanated from a single authority, the government. The English Bible, however, had a much more chequered history. Printed versions translated by Coverdale or Tyndale[100] had been in circulation in England for five years before Henry and Cromwell settled on an author-

---

93. McK and F 36.   94. Beale 1926, illus. 17, 17a.   95. *STC* 10084.7.
96. *STC* 16794.5 and vol. III, addenda.   97. *STC* 10326.   98. *LPHenry VIII*, XIII:1, no. 1231.
99. Longland: *STC* 16794; Bonner: *STC* 9175b.5, 9175b.15, 9175b.20, 9175b.25, 9175b.30;
    William Jugge, Bishop of Norwich: *STC* 9175b.10.
100. *STC* 2063; DMH 18; *STC* 2063.3, 2063.5; and below.

ized text and a system of monopoly to guarantee that it be read publicly to the exclusion of all others.[101]

In September 1538, Cromwell sent out an injunction to the clergy ordering that 'the hole byble of the largyest volume' be 'set up in sum convenient place wythin the said church that ye have cure of, where as your parishioners may moste commodiously resorte to the same and reade it'.[102] This was the Great Bible, a new revision by Coverdale who was working under Cromwell's direct patronage.[103] It has the well-known title-page woodcut representing Henry VIII, Cranmer and Cromwell distributing Bibles, with the people shouting 'Vivat Rex' and 'God save the King.'[104] The printing was begun by François Regnault in Paris, where better materials and workmanship were easily available.[105] Regnault was no doubt pleased with the commission, for his trade in missals, breviaries and Hours printed exclusively for the English market had been ruined by the Reformation.[106] Owing to trouble with the French authorities, however, the job was completed in London in April 1539 by Richard Grafton and Edward Whitchurch, two of the ever-growing number of Protestant-minded printers.

Except for the very first example printed in England (Coverdale, folio),[107] all the early editions of the English Bible had boasted the phrase 'Set forth with the King's most gracious licence' (Coverdale, quarto;[108] 'Matthew's Bible', Coverdale and Tyndale[109]). Since at least 1518, the phrase 'cum privilegio regali', or something equivalent, had appeared on many publications. Regarding a particular class of book, such as year-books and other law texts, it evidently signified that the printer had obtained from the Crown the exclusive right to publish and sell these. Individual authors or compilers could also secure this same privilege for their own works, such as Thomas Linacre's *Progymnasmata* (1512 or 1515),[110] the orations of Pace and Tunstal (1518)[111] and the works of William Horman (1519),[112] John Palsgrave (1524/30)[113] and the translator Gentian Hervet (1520).[114] However, many readers mistook this privilege, which represented a purely commercial agreement, for royal approbation of a work's contents. Thus, in 1534, the Lutherans of Langham,

---

101. Greenslade 1963.
102. *STC* 10086; also 10085, an edition of the 1536 injunctions to which this requirement was added.   103. *STC* 2068, DMH 46.   104. McK and F 45.
105. *LPHenry VIII*, XIII:1, no. 1249; XIII:2, no. 336.   106. *LPHenry VIII*, XI, no. 1488.
107. *STC* 2064, DMH 32.   108. *STC* 2065, DMH 33.   109. *STC* 2066, DMH 34.
110. *STC* 15635.   111. *STC* 19081a, 24320.   112. *STC* 13811.   113. *STC* 19166.
114. *STC* 699. Furnivall 1867; Neville 1990, app. 3, for a general discussion of 'cum privilegio regali'.

Essex filed an official complaint that, though the King 'puts forthwith Certyne bookes printed and openly sold with his ryght royal privyledge sett unto the same to the intente tryly (as we do take it) that no man shoulde feare but rather be encoragede to accoupye them', a certain questman, named John Vigorous, still troubled them for reading these same works.[115]

Once Henry and Cromwell had decided on Coverdale's revised edition as the approved version of the Bible, it was important to sort out this confusion. The King decreed on 16 November 1538 that

> no person or persons in this realm shall from henceforth print any book in the English tongue, unless upon examination made by some of his grace's Privy Council, or other such as his highness shall appoint, they shall have licence so to do; and yet so having, not to put these words *cum privilegio regali*, without adding *ad imprimendum solum* [for sole, or exclusive, printing], and that the whole copy, or else at the least the effect of his licence and privilege be therewith printed, and plainly declared and expressed in the English tongue underneath them.[116]

Nevertheless, printers were opposed. On 1 December 1538 Richard Grafton complained to Cromwell concerning the phrase 'ad imprimendum solum':

> which wordes we never heard of before neither do we take it that these wordes shoulde be added in the pryntyng of the Scripture (yf yt be truely translated) for then shuld yt be great occasyon to the enemys to say that yt is not the Kynges acte or mynde to set forth, but only lycence the prynters to sell soche as is put forth.

Grafton had clearly used the phrase 'cum privilegio' to imply royal approbation.[117]

Yet neither Henry's decree, Cromwell's injunctions nor the appearance of the Great Bible guaranteed that this approved version would be printed, sold and read exclusively. That there was still great confusion is shown by the publication by John Byddell for Berthelet in 1539 of Richard Taverner's translation of the Bible, with the phrase 'cum privilegio ad imprimendum solum'.[118] On 14 November 1539, the same day that Cromwell was granted a five-year patent to oversee the printing of Bibles,[119] Cranmer wrote to the Minister that both Berthelet and

---

115. Reed 1926, pp. 179–81.   116. *TRP* 186; *STC* 7790.   117. Greg 1966, p. 406n.
118. *STC* 2067, DMH 45.   119. *TRP* 192.

Whitchurch, who had produced separate editions of the Great Bible,[120] could sell the work for 10 shillings, the price Cromwell had requested to make it more affordable, only if they were granted a monopoly.[121] Cranmer favoured Whitchurch and his partner Grafton, and it is their edition alone which states on its title-page: 'This is the Byble apoynted to the use of the churches.'

Just as the Crown, no doubt with Wolsey's advice, had after a period of some confusion finally granted Pynson the monopoly on printed statutes and proclamations in 1512–13, so Henry and Cromwell granted Grafton and Whitchurch the exclusive right to print the Great Bible in 1540. Both grants of monopoly, although they were prompted by the printers' commercial interests, were crucial in further increasing and centralizing power. Commercial interests were to remain a determining factor. Anthony Marler, a member of the Haberdashers' Company, received a licence on 25 April 1541 to sell copies of the Great Bible.[122] He immediately petitioned that he would be ruined unless every church without a Bible was required to purchase one before a certain date. A proclamation to that effect was duly issued on 6 May 1541 – unusually but appropriately printed by Grafton and Whitchurch.[123]

In 1539, Cromwell's enemies at court undermined his position, and Henry planned a religious settlement of his own choosing, which culminated in the Act of Six Articles – a complete reversal of his chief minister's policy. Cromwell was executed in July 1540; no one took his place as 'minister for propaganda'. Rather, the Privy Council returned to its role as advisory body to the King. The religious policy for the rest of Henry VIII's reign, until 1547, 'was less a "conservative reaction" than an attempt at "conservative reform"'.[124] Thus, on 29 May 1543, Berthelet published *A necessary doctrine and erudition for any christen man, sette furthe by the kynges maiestie*, also known as the *King's Book*, a revision of the *Bishops' Book* in line with this new conservatism.[125] It appeared in both quarto and octavo formats and the price was fixed and printed at the back: the quartos 'bounded in paper bourdes or in claspes, not to be solde above .xvi.d.', with the octavos at 12 pence.[126]

'Doctrine was that of the Act of Six Articles, but "reformed" instru-

---

120. Berthelet: *STC* 2069, DMH 52; Whitchurch: *STC* 2070, DMH 53.
121. *LPHenry VIII*, XIV:2, no. 517.   122. *PPC*, VII, pp. 181, 185–6.
123. *TRP* 222, *STC* 7793; Mozley 1953, pp. 270–1; Butterworth 1953, pp. 222–4; Pollard 1911, pp. 260–5.   124. Guy 1988, p. 193.
125. *STC* 5168–77; Latin translation 1544, *STC* 5178.
126. *STC* 5171 is priced 14 pence, a misprint or miscalculation.

ments such as vernacular statements of faith, an English Litany, and an English Primer were used to transmit it' – and the reforming Cranmer still had Henry VIII's confidence.[127] An English Litany would meet an important need, for the various bans on the importation of books since 1530[128] had proved ineffective in the face of an overwhelming demand for service books, such as missals and antiphoners. Between 1541 and 1544, Grafton and Whitchurch had attempted to meet the demand with printed editions of the Latin Breviary, expurgating all references to the authority of Rome over the English Church.[129] Their efforts apparently met with neither success nor approval. On 23 January 1543, the King granted Whitchurch and Grafton a seven-year privilege for the sole printing of 'the Masse booke, the Graill, the Antyphoner, The Himptnall, the Portans and the Prymer, both in Latyne and in Englishe'.[130] There followed in May 1544 at least twelve editions of Cranmer's translation of the English translation of the Litany, *An exhortation unto prayer*, which suppressed all invocations to saints.[131]

As with the English Bible, numerous printed versions of an English Primer (devotional manuals for the laity) had been circulating since 1534,[132] some with the King's privilege, one 'at the commaundemente of Thomas Crumwell'.[133] Two proclamations, on 6 and 28 May 1545, announced that there was now to be 'one uniform order of all such books [that is, primers] throughout all our dominion' and that Grafton and Whitchurch had received the patent for its publication.[134] The colophon of the Primer, 'set foorth by the kynges maiestie and his clergie, to be taught lerned, & read: and none other to be used', is dated 29 May 1545.[135] Grafton produced an edition in English and Latin[136] as well as a Latin translation.[137] That this Primer, which eschews any commemoration of saints in its calendar, was prompted, at least in part, by Henry's interest in Prince Edward's religious training is made clear by the fact that the colophon identifies Richard Grafton as 'Printer to the Prince's grace'. Perhaps to draw attention to his elevated position, Grafton includes a woodcut of the initials 'E.P'. In 1509, Wynkyn de Worde had been 'Printer to the King's Grandame'.

It was once suggested that Cranmer was able to persuade Henry to

---

127. Guy 1988, p. 193.   128. *TRP* 129, 186; 25 Henry VIII, c. 15.   129. *STC* 15833.5–15835.
130. *LPHenry VIII*, XVIII:1, no. 100(31).   131. *STC* 10620–10625.7, some with printed music.
132. *STC* 15986ff.
133. *STC* 16009. For the many versions of English Primers, see *STC*, II, pp. 76–8; Butterworth
    1953, *passim*.   134. *TRP* 248, 251.   135. *STC* 16034; see also *STC* 16035–9.
136. *STC* 16040.   137. *STC* 16042.

authorize the reformed English Litany by including, in the *Exhortation*, prayers for the King's prosperity and victory against the French in 1544.[138] The text declares:

> And here specially let us pray for our most dere and soveraygne Lord
> . . . who at this presente tyme, hath taken upon hym the great and
> daungerous affayres of warre. Let us pray for our brethern, that bende
> them selves to battayle for goddes cause and our defence, that god may
> graunt them prosperous successe, to our comfort and the increase of
> his glory.[139]

Henry's Queen, Catherine Parr, following in the pious tradition of Lady Margaret Beaufort and Catherine of Aragon, contributed to the King's cause in like manner.[140] On 2 June 1545, Berthelet published her *Prayers stirryng the mynd unto heavenlye medytacions*, a slim volume which includes at the end 'A prayer for the king': 'So strengthe hym, that he may vanquyshe and overcome al his and our foes, and be dred and feared of all the enemies of his realme.' This is followed by 'A praier for men to say entring into battayle'.[141]

'First the threat of war and then the actuality' coloured the Crown's policy in the 1540s. As David Starkey remarks, Protestant theology 'opened the way to a conscientious patriotism that could embrace war, and even rejoice in it'.[142] In a sermon preached on Palm Sunday 1539, when a French invasion seemed imminent, and printed that same year by Berthelet, Bishop Tunstal urged the nation: 'Thou hast god on thy syde, who hath gyven this realme to the generation of englyshemen. only take an englyshe hart unto the, and mystruste not god.'[143] Richard Morison contributed to the stiffening of England's resolve against invasion (from both France and Scotland) with *An exhortation to styrre all Englyshe men to the defence of theyr countreye*[144] and his translation of Frontinus, entitled *The strategemes, sleyghtes, and policies of warre*.[145] John Elder wrote to Sir William Paget on 6 October 1545, concerning the Scottish campaign, that three wards marched towards the Abbey of Kelso in such array 'that if Vegicius Frontinus were present, which wrote the "Stratigemes, Ordre and Policies of Civill Warres", he could not have mended our proceedings'.[146]

---

138. Kingdon 1901, p. 21.   139. *STC* 10623, fols. A4v–5.
140. For the devotional texts printed at Lady Margaret's behest, see Neville 1990, pp. 146–51;
     and on Lady Margaret in general, Jones and Underwood 1992, esp. pp. 180–89.
141. *STC* 4818, 4818.5; for later editions, see *STC*, 1, p. 215.   142. Starkey 1992, p. 159.
143. *STC* 24322, fols. E2v.   144. *STC* 18110.   145. *STC* 11402.
146. *LP Henry VIII*, xx:2, no. 533, p. 246.

These works had been conceived and printed under the supervision of Cromwell. The nature of war propaganda was to change once he had been ousted. The only original treatises to appear in the 1540s justifying the war were Thomas Becon's *The new pollecye of warre* of 1542,[147] and Edward Walshe's *The office and duety in fightying for our countrey* of 1545,[148] apparently read out to his comrades in arms at Boulogne. These were not printed by Berthelet and do not appear to have had any official backing – indeed Becon, a Protestant divine who wrote under the pseudonym 'Theodore Basille', was forced to burn *The new pollecye of warre* along with other heretical texts in May 1543.[149]

With no government 'press officer' to commission, oversee and approve propaganda, translations of classical texts were much the easiest – and safest – way to court royal favour in the 1540s. In 1541, the year of the Lincolnshire rebellion, Berthelet published Thomas Paynell's translation of Constantius Felicius's *The conspiracie of Lucius Catiline*.[150] In 1544, Peter Betham translated Jacopo di Porcia's *Precepts of warre*, dedicated to the Lord Chancellor Sir Thomas Audeley and printed by Whitchurch.[151] That same year Berthelet brought out Anthony Cope's compilation of Livy and other classical authors, entitled *The historie of two the moste noble capitaines of the worlde, Anniball and Scipio*, and dedicated to both Henry VIII and Prince Edward.[152] Berthelet was exempted from attending the King in war: rather, he continued as King's Printer to publish official documents such as *A declaration, conteynyng the iust causes of this present warre with the Scottis*[153] and the *Statutes of war*, a reissue of the ordinances printed by Pynson in 1492 and 1513.[154] No doubt Berthelet's age – he was by now about fifty-four – was another factor in keeping him at home.

Age was one reason why, after Henry VIII's death in January 1547, Berthelet stood down as King's Printer, in favour of Richard Grafton. Although the annuity of the King's Printer was 'for life', in practice this meant for the life of the monarch rather than the printer. The fact that Grafton shared the religious convictions of Protector Somerset made Somerset's ambition to create a wholly Protestant state all the easier. To this end, he harnessed the full power of the press: in April 1547, Grafton was granted the privilege to print not only 'all books of statutes, acts, proclamations, injunctions, and other volumes issued by the King', but

147. STC 1735; reprinted under the title *The true defence of peace* in 1542 and 1543: STC 1775, 1776.   148. STC 25000.   149. *LPHenry VIII*, xviii:1, no. 538.   150. STC 10751.
151. STC 20116.   152. STC 5718.   153. STC 9179, 9179.3.
154. STC 9334; see *LPHenry VIII*, xix:2, no. 340(47).

also all books 'concerning divine service or containing any kind of sermons or exhortations that shall be used, suffered or authorized in our churches' – that is, the Book of Common Prayer and the Homilies (see below). Grafton's load was lightened by the appointment of the almost certainly better-qualified Reyner Wolfe as King's Printer in Latin, Greek and Hebrew.[155] In the first parliament of Edward VI's reign (November–December 1547; I Edward VI, c. 12), Somerset secured the repeal of all treason and heresy statutes made since Edward I, including Henry VIII's Act of Six Articles, thus effectively lifting censorship of the press – though the government retained the authority to silence Catholic opposition. Somerset became an active patron of Protestant polemicists and opened the floodgates to reform.[156] However, in propaganda Somerset was not an innovator: he merely used the tried and tested methods of his predecessors.

In order to emphasize the continuity of Edward's and Henry's reigns and the peaceful transition from one to another, Grafton published Edward Halle's *Union of the two noble and illustrate families of Lancastre & York* in 1548.[157] Dedicated to Edward, this chronicle extends to 'the reigne of the high and prudent prince King Henry the eight', who, it is claimed, set religion along the path of righteousness with the creation of the Church of England. A woodcut initial incorporating the appropriate royal arms begins the chronicle of each monarch. A full-page woodcut on the last leaf portrays Henry VIII in Council; across the top of the title-page border is a vignette of Edward VI in Council.[158] (The second edition of Halle's chronicle[159] has a different title-page design, with two rose trees displaying the lineage of Henry VIII.)[160] This same title-page border of Edward VI in Council appears on all the statutes printed during Edward's reign, apart from the first few issues which have woodcuts of Mark, Matthew, Luke and John – perhaps to make the King's joint role as head of both Church and State explicit.[161] In any case, with his extensive use of royal arms and badges in official publications, Grafton went some way to returning to the style of the 1510s and earlier.

As in the first half of the 1540s, the two major preoccupations of the Crown (that is, Somerset) continued to be war – this time, with Scotland – and the English liturgy. Somerset ensured that propaganda relating to Scotland flew off Grafton's press in 1547–8. The Scotsman, James

155. *CPREdward VI*, 1, pp. 100, 187.   156. J. N. King 1976a, b, and above.
157. *STC* 12721–3a.   158. McK and F 67.   159. *STC* 12723.   160. McK and F 75.
161. *STC* 9419–21.1; Beale 1926, illus. 36.

Harrison, who was in Somerset's pay, wrote *An exhortacion to the Scottes to conforme to the union, betwene Englande and Scotlande*.[162] Somerset himself addressed a letter, dated 5 February 1548, to his enemies: *An epistle or exhortacion to unitie & peace*.[163] As with Henry VIII's epistles, this was translated and printed in Latin the same year by Reyner Wolfe.[164] Added ammunition came in the treatise of Nicholas Bodrugan (or Adams), overseen by Sir Thomas Smith and dedicated to Edward VI: *An epitome of the title that the kynges maiestie of Englande, hath to the sovereigntie of Scotlande*. J. N. King believes that this was sponsored by Somerset and Cranmer.[165]

As in 1544, the people of England were urged to join in *A prayer for victorie and peace*, 'set furthe by the Kynges Maiestie, by thadvyse of his moste dere Uncle', 'to bee saied to the people of hym that dooeth preach when he moveth the people to praie'.[166] This prayer came off Grafton's press when marriage between Edward and the young Scottish Queen, Mary – and thus a peaceful union of the two countries – was still a possibility. War was not averted and tales of Somerset's military exploits were glorified in William Patten's *Expedicion into Scotlande of Edward, duke of Soomerset* (30 June 1548).[167] When rebellion at home threatened in the summer of 1549, Edward VI, like his father before him, petitioned his subjects through the press: in July of that year Grafton printed *A message sent by the kynges maiestie, to certain of his people, assembled in Devonshire*.[168] In 1549 John Day and William Seres printed *A copye of a letter contayning certain newes, & the articles or requestes of the Devonshyre & Cornyshe rebelles*, intended to discredit the rebels.[169] This may also have been an officially sponsored work which Grafton did not have the time or resources to print himself.

Just as insistent as this war propaganda was the inducement of religious orthodoxy by Somerset and Cranmer. In the first year of Edward VI's reign, Grafton printed *Certain sermons, or homilies, appoynted by the kynges maiestie, to be declared and redde, by all persones, vicars, or curates, every Sunday in their churches*, written by Cranmer and others.[170] Catherine Parr, now Queen Dowager, continued to encourage piety of the reformed kind, and in 1547–8 Whitchurch printed two exemplary works: her *Lamentacion of a sinner*[171] and an impressive two-volume folio edition of *The paraphrase of Erasmus upon the newe testamente*, which was

162. STC 12857.   163. STC 22268.   164. STC 22269.
165. STC 3196; J. N. King 1976b, p. 328.   166. STC 16503, fols. A2, A5.   167. STC 19476.5.
168. STC 7506.   169. STC 15109.3, 15109.7.   170. STC 13638.5.   171. STC 4827, 4828.

sponsored by and dedicated to Catherine.[172] Her arms are incorporated along with those of Edward in the title-page border.[173] On 31 July 1547, a proclamation setting out new injunctions had required that the Homilies be read during services, that copies of Erasmus's *Paraphrase* in English be placed alongside the English Bible in every church, and that Henry VIII's authorized Primer (1545) be used.[174] A later proclamation repeated the command to preach the Homilies, banning all other sermons (23 September 1548).[175]

Somerset and Cranmer reworked the English liturgy with *The order of the communion*, printed by Grafton on 8 March 1548[176] and, exactly one year later, the Book of Common Prayer, printed by Whitchurch and Grafton (Whitchurch, 7 March 1549;[177] Grafton, 8 March 1549[178]). Later editions include one printed in Worcester on 24 May 1549 'also to sell at Shrewesburye'[179] and another in Dublin in 1551.[180] Like Cromwell with the Great Bible and *King's Book*, Somerset fixed the price: the Book of Common Prayer was to cost 2s 2d unbound (June 1549).[181] Also in March 1549 appeared *The forme and maner of makyng and consecratyng of archbi-shoppes, bishoppes, priestes and deacons*.[182] In 1548, Nicholas Hill printed, for Walter Lynne, Cranmer's *Catechismus*.[183] Other related works from the presses of Grafton and Whitchurch, all aimed at spreading God's word in English, include *Devout psalmes and colletes . . . for dayly meditacions* (5 November 1547),[184] *Devout meditacions, psalmes and praiers to bee used aswell in the morning as eaventyde* (20 May 1548),[185] and John Marbecke's Bible concordance which displays a title-page border with the King in Council at the top.[186] Again, the commercial interests of the printer and the Crown's desire to reach its subjects were in harmony: Marbecke states in his dedication to Edward VI that Grafton had insisted the work be kept to a reasonable length, otherwise copies 'would beare so excessive price, as fewe of your highnes lovyng subiectes should bee able to attain unto theim'.[187]

The appearance of the exact date of publication in most of these works of religious doctrine was intended to reassure the public that they were following the most up-to-date and approved forms of worship. Somerset and his bishops used the same methods of enforcement, in addition to

172. *STC* 2854–4.5; vol. II, edited by Coverdale: *STC* 2854.6, 2854.7.   173. McK and F 68.
174. *TRP* 287.   175. *TRP* 313; *STC* 7818.
176. *STC* 16456.5, 16457, 15458.3 (quarto); *STC* 16458.5 (octavo), printed by Raynalde and Hill.
177. *STC* 16267.   178. *STC* 16268.   179. *STC* 16271.   180. *STC* 16277.
181. *TRP* 335.   182. *STC* 16462, 16462.5.   183 *STC* 5992.5–5994.   184. *STC* 2999.
185. *STC* 2998.5.   186. *STC* 17300.   187. Fol. a3v.

statutes and proclamations, which Cromwell had instituted: Grafton printed injunctions, dated 31 July 1547,[188] and visitation articles, both general and local.[189] On 1 June 1548, Grafton issued *A copie of a lettre sent to preachers* from the Lord Protector and Council, commanding the clergy to avoid controversy.[190] The number of publications, great and small, which came from Grafton and Whitchurch's press during Somerset's protectorship was such that, on 18 December 1547, Whitchurch was authorized, for one year, to take up 'as manye prynters, composytours founders prentyces and jornymen', as well as 'paper, ynke, presses and matrices', as necessary, paying for them at a reasonable rate.[191] The restrictions imposed by Henry VIII in favour of the Great Bible were apparently lifted: between 1549 and 1553 a number of different translations, including those of Coverdale, Taverner, and the 'Matthew' and 'Great' Bibles', were printed in England.[192] However, after the rebellions of 1549, the Privy Council, convinced that more control was needed, reinstituted censorship, appointing William Cecil and two others as censors in August of that year.[193]

Two months later, in October 1549, John Dudley, the Earl of Warwick, staged a coup against Somerset, advanced himself as Duke of Northumberland, and became quasi-king of England. Nevertheless, he continued to forward the cause of Protestantism. A proclamation on Christmas Day 1549 required that all older service books, now super-seded by the Book of Common Prayer, be destroyed.[194] The first Edwardian Primer 'set furth . . . corrected accordynge to the statute' – wholly Protestant in spirit – came off Grafton's press in 1551.[195] In May–June 1553, Grafton printed the *Articles agreed on by the bishoppes, . . . in the synode at London* [1552], *for the avoiding of controversie in opinions*.[196] These were appended to the catechism in Latin and English which the Duke of Northumberland had commissioned the then Bishop of Winchester, John Ponet, to compile in September 1552. Reyner Wolfe, 'always a furtherer of godly things', received the monopoly;[197] John Day was authorized to print the complete English translation (with King Edward's letters patent, 25 March 1553)[198] and also the ABC and brief

188. *STC* 10087.5–10093.5; also a variant dated 31 July 1548, *STC* 10093.7; for an abridged Latin version printed abroad, see *STC* 10094.
189. General: *STC* 10114–6.5; Canterbury: *STC* 10148, 10148.5; Lincoln: *STC* 10228; London: *STC* 10247; Norwich: *STC* 10285.   190. *STC* 9181.5.   191. *CPREdward VI*, II, p. 98.
192. *STC* 2077–92.
193. *APC, 1542–1604*, II, pp. 311–12; J. N. King 1976a, p. 8; above, pp. 166–9.   194. *TRP* 353.
195. *STC* 16053.   196. *STC* 10034, 10034.2.   197. *STC* 4807–10; *SPEdward VI*, no. 713.
198. *STC* 4812.

catechism. In the Second Book of Common Prayer, printed by Grafton in 1552, all traces of the Sarum rite of the Catholic mass had been expurgated.[199] Its publication was delayed by the Privy Council until certain faults had been corrected and the 'Black Rubric', concerning kneeling during Communion, added by an insert, cancel or reprinted leaf.[200]

In the confusion after Edward's death, Grafton, perhaps in an excess of Protestant zeal, printed a proclamation of 10 July 1553 in the name of Lady Jane Grey, 'by the grace of God Quene of England', claiming succession for her. His colophon at the bottom of the third and last sheet reads 'in aedibus Richardi Graftoni, Reginaea typographia excusum'.[201] Nine days later, he used the exact same colophon, but this time it was on Mary's accession proclamation.[202] Grafton gives an account of this episode in his *Chronicle*, printed in 1569.[203] Grafton cannot have lasted as Queen's Printer to Mary for more than a week or two, if that. He chose, for all intents and purposes, to give up his career as a printer and remain in England during Mary's reign.[204] However, many Protestant printers and polemicists fled to the Continent to continue the war of words there.[205]

By the end of July, John Cawood, a printer with Catholic leanings, had effectively become Queen's Printer when on 28 July he received the commission to print and send forth 'into all shyres' a proclamation against seditious rumours.[206] He received the grant for his office on 29 December 1553.[207] One of his first acts was to print the confession of Northumberland, *The saying of John late duke of Northumberlande uppon the scaffolde*: the same tactic employed by Mary's grandfather, Henry VII, to discredit the traitor Perkin Warbeck.[208] Also in 1553, Cawood printed John Gwynneth's *A briefe declaration of the victory of quene Marye*[209] and Wolfe produced John Seton's *Panegyrici in victoriam illustrissimae dominae Mariae reginae*.[210]

With these publications, Mary and her councillors had shown themselves quick to turn to the press to quell their enemies. In the spring of 1554, Sir Thomas Wyatt the Younger had led an uprising to prevent Mary's marriage to Philip of Spain. The rebellion was put down and Wyatt executed on 11 April. Mary and her councillors, no doubt fearing more civil disturbances, ensured that Cawood issued, the day before the

199. STC 16279–90.5.   200. SPEdward VI, no. 725.   201. STC 7846.   202. STC 7847.
203. STC 12147.   204. For his pardon on 8 November 1553, see CPRPhilip and Mary, 1, p. 455.
205. For the cross-Channel press war, see King above; Loades 1964; Baskerville 1979; Loach 1975, 1986.   206. APC, 1542–1604, IV, p. 421; TRP 389; STC 7848.
207. CPRPhilip and Mary, 1, p. 53.   208. STC 7283.   209. STC 12556.7.   210. STC 22258.

wedding, on 24 July 1554, *An exhortation to all menne to take hede and beware of rebellion*, by her chaplain John Christopherson.[211] At the end are prayers for the Queen, 'very conveniente to be sayde daylye of all her faythful and lovyng subiectes', and for 'a quiete and prosperouse estate'.

At about the same time as this warning was issued, works came out which glorified Mary's reign and her marriage while legitimizing Philip as King. Thus, Cawood included in some copies of Christopherson's *Exhortation* a folding genealogical table of Philip and Mary. That same year, Berthelet, perhaps revealing his true sympathies, printed Hadrianus Junius's *Carmen heroicum*, which traces Philip's descent from Edward III,[212] and Cawood produced a Latin oration, possibly by Hugh Weston, touching on the hope that Mary would soon produce an heir.[213] At the end of 1554, Cawood published *A copie of a letter sent from the counsell* ordering public thanksgiving and prayers for Mary's (erroneously diagnosed) pregnancy. This was evidently intended to be posted since the two surviving issues – one addressed to Bonner, Bishop of London,[214] the other to Gardiner,[215] reinstated as Bishop of Winchester – are broadsides. William Riddell published a 'popular' ballad that year to the same effect: 'Now singe, nowe springe, oure care is exild, / Oure vertuous quene, is quickned with child.'[216] In 1555, John Wayland, who had recently been granted a monopoly on primers and prayer books, printed John Elder's *The copie of a letter sent in to Scotlande, of the arivall and marryage of Philippe prynce of Spaine to Marye quene of England*, which includes a 'brefe overture' by Cardinal Pole 'for reconcilement to the catholyke churche'.[217]

Mary was determined to implement a complete reversal in religious doctrine and worship. It was perhaps to this end that, when she granted Cawood the post of Queen's Printer, she also authorized him, as Somerset had Grafton, to take on as many extra workmen as necessary. The liturgy of Edward VI's reign was proscribed (13 June 1555)[218] and no more vernacular Bibles were published in England (although plans to produce a new translation were mooted at Pole's legatine synod in 1555). On 4 June 1555, the first Marian Primer appeared,[219] followed within two months by a book of hours.[220] In November, Bonner published *An honest godlye instruction* to supersede all other such works for children.[221] Wayland's grant for the sole printing of primers and manuals of prayer

211. *STC* 5207. Baskerville 1979, p. 13, wrongly claims that this work appeared too late to be of any use.   212. *STC* 14861.   213. *STC* 19836; Loach 1986, p. 144.   214. *STC* 7753.6.
215. *STC* 7753.8.   216. *STC* 17561.   217. *STC* 7552, with Wayland's grant at the end.
218. *TRP* 422; *STC* 7865.   219. *STC* 16060.   220. *STC* 16061.   221. *STC* 3281.

proved ineffective, perhaps because Mary wanted to encourage the importation and production of as much Catholic literature as possible. From a variety of presses, some abroad, appeared other Hours (Use of Sarum and of York) and primers, mainly in Latin, or Latin and English,[222] as well as Latin breviaries,[223] manuals,[224] missals,[225] processionals[226] and psalters.[227] For the first time in a quarter of a century, the royal printer issued a papal bull, dated 24 December 1554, granting a plenary indulgence to Mary's subjects on England's reconciliation with Rome.[228] At least one more indulgence was printed, again by Cawood, during Mary's reign, connected with the Treaty of Vaucelles, 8 March 1556.[229]

Cawood printed numerous documents relating specifically to Bishop Bonner's diocese of London: a declaration 'to the laye people of his diocesse concerynge theyr reconciliation' (19 February 1554)[230] and a copy of a letter from the Queen restoring the Church as it was at the end of Henry VIII's reign (4 March 1554).[231] No printed copies of general injunctions or visitation articles exist from this period. What has survived, however, reveals that the energetic Bonner, as well as Reginald Pole, Archbishop of Canterbury, continued to issue forms and injunctions to aid in the administration of their dioceses.[232] In 1557, Pole commissioned Cawood to print, as a broadside to be posted, the transcript of his letter to Bonner concerning the use of confessionals.[233]

Tracts and sermons, of course, appeared from Cawood's presses to advance the Catholic cause.[234] Many were in English but, as we have already seen with Seton's *Panegyrici*, Junius's *Carmen heroicum* and Weston's oration, there was also a return to Latin: a collection of Latin orations by John Harpsfield and others given at St Paul's in October 1553,[235] Jodocus Harchius's speech to parliament on the return of Cardinal Pole and the ending of the schism[236] and, in Latin and English, five of Cranmer's 'submissions and recantations' before he was finally executed in 1556.[237] The two most prominent propagandists of Mary's reign, Bonner and Gardiner, clearly resented having to use the English language in religious matters. In his *Profitable and necessarye doctryn, with certayne homelies adioyned therunto*, Bonner's intention was to provide sermons in English to be read 'to thintent [laymen] shall have no cause to

222. *STC* 16062–81.5.   223. *STC* 15836–47, 15860.   224. *STC* 16151–6.
225. *STC* 16215–19, 16224.7.   226. *STC* 16244–50, 16252.   227. *STC* 16264–6.
228. *STC* 14077c.147.   229. *STC* 14077c.147A.   230. *STC* 3280.3.
231. *STC* 9182, 9182.5.   232. Bonner: *STC* 10248, 10249; Pole: *STC* 10149.
233. *STC* 20088.5.   234. Loach 1986, *passim*.   235. *STC* 12794.   236. *STC* 12753.
237. *STC* 5990.

murmure or grudge, for lacke of certayne bokes in the englishe tongue for their instruction . . . trustynge that the people thus ordered and taught, wyll take this my doynge in good parte'.[238]

The emphasis was on instructing the laity not through self-education but through the two pillars of the Catholic Church, the clergy and ritual.[239] Catholic advocates printed works in English to combat the Protestant propaganda coming out of northern Europe, but in their souls many believed that giving lay people direct access to the Bible – and, by implication, inviting them to join in religious debate – would lead to disorder and, in Gardiner's view, 'fleshly liberty'.[240] With this attitude, whether or not the hearts and minds of English subjects remained true to Catholic belief, it is not surprising that the Protestants won the propaganda battle through the printed word.

'Mary saw the future in terms of the past.'[241] Certainly, her attempt via the press to return the country to orthodoxy had all the hallmarks of the Crown's campaign in the 1520s. Since the 1530s, religious reform had been a matter for largely internal debate carried on by Englishmen, for Englishmen, in English. However, from 1553, Mary and her councillors were once again looking to the Continent, as Wolsey and Henry had thirty years earlier, attempting to win over the Pope and other European rulers by producing learned works in Latin, printed neatly in roman type with little or no decoration. (Cawood, like his predecessors, continued to place title-page borders incorporating the royal arms on the printed statutes to denote authority.)[242] As in the 1520s, these treatises were duly reprinted – or printed for the first time – on the Continent.[243]

'God works for His church', wrote John Foxe, 'not with sword and target . . . but with printing, writing and reading . . . How many presses there be in the world, so many black houses there be against the high castle of St Angelo, so that either the pope must abolish knowledge and printing, or printing must at length root him out.'[244] There is no question that the press was at its most effective as an instrument of polemic in the hands of reformers such as Cromwell and Somerset. However, the press, through the office of King's Printer, had already become in England an efficient tool of government, whether that government was

238. *STC* 3281.5, A3v-4; *Doctryn* and *Homelies* printed both separately and together: *STC* 3281.5–3285.10.
239. Loach 1986, p. 139. See also Duffy 1992, pp. 529–37, and *passim* for Catholicism in England and changes in the liturgy.   240. Loach 1986, pp. 137–8.   241. Guy 1988, p. 227.
242. Beale 1926, illus. 37, 38.   243. Shaaber 1975, M167–70.
244. Foxe 1877–9, III, p. 720.

Protestant or Catholic, and in this Wolsey's contribution was crucial. By granting the King's Printer the exclusive right to print all official publications, in 1512, Wolsey had ensured that government legislation, whether it concerned trade, apparel or religion, was made widely available in an accessible and authoritative form. Cromwell's contribution was to apply this same principle of monopoly to the publication of 'authorized' and 'approved' religious texts. Two things must be kept in mind. First, although guided by Wolsey and Cromwell, Henry VIII's significant, if shadowy, role in the government's press campaigns should never be underestimated. Secondly, the Crown granted these monopolies at the behest of the printers themselves who had commercial concerns, as we have seen with Pynson apropos the statutes and Grafton apropos the Great Bible.

By the end of Mary's reign it seems that the Council had decided to allow the printers' own interests to work further to the Crown's advantage. Government's efforts since the 1530s to control the publication and importation of banned books had not proved sufficient. The same grant which appointed Cawood Queen's Printer also gave him the authority to seize all prohibited books, and he acted upon it. In March 1556, the printers Riddell and Copland were ordered to hand over to Cawood all copies of their unauthorized English translation of Cranmer's recantation to be burned.[245] The Crown finally gave over control of the press entirely to the printers when, on 4 May 1557, the Council granted the ancient Stationers' Company a charter of incorporation, making it a self-regulating closed shop. The master and wardens were given the authority to search and seize any books printed 'contrary to the form of any statute, act or proclamation made or to be made'.[246] Words still had to be examined by an authorized agent to receive a licence. Membership of the Company was largely concentrated in London, where it could be more closely watched by the Crown. The government continued to issue regulations concerning the book-trade, but it left 'the tiresome and often difficult job of implementing its commands to the officials of the Company'.[247]

In the eighty years since Caxton had introduced printing to England the number of printers had increased dramatically. This was owing neither to improved technology, nor to greater literacy, but to religious

245. STC 6005.5; APC, 1542–1604, v, pp. 247–8.
246. Arber, I, pp. xxviii–xxxiii; CPRPhilip and Mary, III, p. 480; Blagden 1960, Chapter 1.
247. Bennett 1965, p. 57.

and political controversy. Although the press had served royal interests well since Edward IV, it was only in reaction to the religious heresies of the 1520s – when the printed word was ammunition and printers were partisans – that the Crown first fully exploited this powerful new medium. Henry VIII and Wolsey defended the faith against Lutheran propaganda with the barrage of scholarly texts which flew off the royal press. In the 1530s the King, with Cromwell, went on the offensive, converting an entire nation to a new religious orthodoxy. Although the Crown had been quick to fight fire with fire, the printing press had become – and would forever remain – a dangerous weapon in the hands of the enemy. Nevertheless, the political acumen, and especially the centralized nature, of English government ensured that the printed word continued to advance the Crown's interests both at home and in Europe. Over the following decades the same techniques of propaganda exercised by government would be deployed by new independent bodies, such as the Muscovy, East India and Virginia Companies, as they sought to encourage investment and, eventually, colonization further afield. The outward expansion of England's empire was to be matched by the inward expansion of the book-trade.

Appendix

An Act touching the Marchauntes of Italy:
1 Richard III (1484), cap. 9

Purveu toutz foitz que cest acte ou ascune part dicell, ne ascune autre acte fait ou affaire en le dit parlement, en null maner extende ou soit prejudiciall ascun destourbance damage ou empediment au ascun artificer ou marchaunt estraunge, de quell nacion ou paiis il soit ou soira, de ou pur amesnance en cest Roialme ou vendicion par retaille ou autrement dascuns maners livres escriptez ou enpressez, ou pur lenhabitacion deinz le dit Roialme pur mesme lentent, ou au ascun escrivener alluminour liour ou enpressour autrement dit imprintour de tielx livres, quelx il ad ou avera a vendre par voie de marchandise, ou pur leur demeure en mesme le Roialme pur lexcercicion de les ditz occupacions; cest acte ou ascune part dicell nient contristeant.

Provided alwey that this Acte or any part therof, or any other Acte to be made in this present parliament, in no wise extende or be prejudicall any lette hurte or impediment to any Artificer or merchaunt straungier of what Nacion or Countrey he be or shalbe of, for bryngyng into this Realme, or sellyng by retaill or otherwise, of any maner bokes wrytten or imprynted, or for the inhabitynge within the said Realme for the same intent, or to any writer lympner bynder or imprynter of such bokes, as he hath or shall have to sell by wey of merchaundise, or for their abode in the same Realme for the exercisyng of the said occupacions; this Acte or any parte therof notwithstandyng.

(*SRealm*, ii, p. 493)

An Acte for prynters & bynders of bokes:
25 Henry VIII (1534), cap. 15

Where as by the provysyon of a statute made in the fyrst yere of the reigne of Kynge Richarde the thride it was provyded in the same acte, that all strangers reparyng into this Realme myght lawfully bryng into the saide Realme pryntyt and wrytyn bokes to sell at theire libertie and pleasure; by force of which provysyon there hath commen into this Realme sithen the makyn of the same a marveylous nombre of pryntyd bokes and dayly doth; And the cause of the makyng of the same provysion semeth to be, for that there were but fewe bokes and fewe prynters within this Realme at that tyme which cold well exercise and occupie the seid science and crafte of pryntyng; Never the lesse sithen the makyng of the seid provysion many of this Realme being the Kynges naturall subjectes have geven theyme soo dylygently to lerne and exercyse the seid craft of pryntyng that at this day there be within this Realme a greate nombre connyng and expert in the seid science or craft of pryntyng as abyll to exercyse the seid craft in all poyntes as any Stranger in any other Realme or Countre; And furthermore where there be a great nombre of the Kynges subjects within this Realme which lyve by the crafte and mysterie of byndyng of bokes and that there be a great multytude well expert in the same; yet all this not withstondyng there are dyverse persones that bryng frome beyonde the See great plentie of pryntyd bokes not only in the latyn tonge but also in our maternall englishe tonge, somme bounde in bourdes, somme in lether and somme in perchement and theym sell by retayle, wherby many of the Kynges Subjectes being bynders of bokes and havyng none other facultie wherwith to gett theire lyvyng be destitute of worke and lyke to be undon, except somme reformacion here in be hade; Be it therfore enacted by the Kyng our Soveraigne Lorde the Lordes spirituall and temporall and the Comons in this present parliament assembled and by auctoritie of the same, that the seid provysyon made the furst yere of the seid Kyng Richard the thride frome the feast of the natyvytie of our Lorde God next commyng shalbe voyde and of none effect.

And further be it enacted by the auctoritie aforseid that noo person or persones recyant or inhabytaunt within this Realme, after the seid feast of Cristemas next commyng, shall bye to sell agayn any prynted bokes brought frome any partes out of the Kynges obeysaunce redy bounden in bourdes lether or perchement, uppon payne to lose and forfett for every boke bounde out of the seid Kynges obeisaunce and brought into this Realme and bought by any person or persons within the same to sell agayne contrary to this Acte vj s. viij d.

And be it further enacted by the auctoritie aforseid that no person or persones inhabytaunte or reciaunt within this Realme, after the seid feast of Cristemas, shall by within this Realme of any Stranger borne out of the Kynges obedyence other then of denyzens, any maner of pryntyd bokes brought frome any the parties [behonde] the See, except only by engrose and not by retayle uppon payne of forfayture of vj s. viij d. for every boke soo bought by retayle contrary to the forme and effecte of this estatute: The seid forfaytures to be alwayes levyed of the beyers of any suche bokes contrary to this Acte, the one half of all the seid forfaytures to be to the use of our Soveraigne Lorde the Kynge, and the other moytie to be to the partie that wyll sease or sue for the same in any of the Kynges Courtes, be it by byll playnt or informacion wherin the defendaunt shall not be admytted to wage hys lawe nor noo proteccion ne essoyne shalbe unto hym allowed.

Provided alway and be enacted by the auctoritie aforseid, that yf any of the seid prynters or sellers of prynted bokes, inhabyted within this Realme, at any tyme hereafter happen in suche wyse to enhaunce and encrease the prices of any suche prynted bokes in sale or byndyng at to high and unreasonable pryces, in suche wyse as complaynt be made therof unto the Kynges Highnes or unto the Lorde Chaunceler Lorde Tresourer or any of the chefe Justices of the one benche or of the other, that then the seid Lord Chaunceler Lorde Tresourer and two chefe Justices or two of any of theym, shall have power and auctoritie to enquyre therof as well as by the other of twelf honest and discrett persones as otherwyse by due examynacion by theire discreacions; And after the same enhaunsyng and encresyng of the seyd pryces of the seid bokes and byndyng shalbe soo founde by the seid xij men, or other wayes by examynation of the seid Lord Chaunceler Lord Tresourer and Justices or two of theym, that then the same Lorde Chaunceler Lorde Tresourer and Justices or two of theym at the least frome tyme to tyme shall have power and auctoritie to reforme and redresse suche enhaunsyng of the pryces of prynted bokes from tyme to tyme by theire discreacions and to lymytt pryces aswell of the bokes as for the byndyng of theym; and over that the offender or offenders thereof being convicte by the examynacion of the same Lorde Chaunceler Lorde Tresourer and two Justices or two of theym or otherwyse, shall lose and forfett for every boke by theym solde wherof the pryce shalbe enhaunsed, for the boke or byndyng thereof iij s. iiij d. the one half therof shalbe to the Kynges Highness and the other half unto the parties greved that wyll complayne upon the same in maner and forme before rehersed.

(*SRealm*, III, p. 456)

Abbreviations

Allen   Allen, P. S., Allen, H. M. and Garrod, H. W. (eds.), *Opus*
                 epistolarum Des. Erasmi Roterodami, 12 vols., Oxford 1906–58
Allison and Rogers Allison, A. F. and Rogers, D. M., *The contemporary printed*
                 literature of the English Counter-Reformation between 1558 and 1640,
                 2 vols., Aldershot 1989–94
APC, 1542–1604 *Acts of the Privy Council, 1542–1604*, new series, 32 vols.,
                 London 1890–1907
Arber   Arber, E. (ed.), *A transcript of the registers of the Company of*
                 Stationers of London, 1554–1640, 5 vols., London 1875–94; rpt.
                 Gloucester, MA 1967
ASD   *Opera omnia Desiderii Erasmi Roterodami*, Amsterdam 1969–
BAV   Biblioteca Apostolica Vaticana
BC   *Book Collector*
BJRL   *Bulletin of the John Rylands (University) Library*
BL   British Library, London
BLJ   *British Library Journal*
BLR   *Bodleian Library Record*
BMC   *Catalogue of books printed in the XVth century now in the British*
                 Museum, vols. I–X and Supplement, London 1908–
BNF   Bibliothèque Nationale de France, Paris
Bodleian   Bodleian Library, Oxford
BPPB   Griffiths, J. and Pearsall, D. A., *Book production and publishing in*
                 Britain 1375–1475, Cambridge 1989
BQR   *Bodleian Quarterly Review*
BRUC   Emden, A. B., *A biographical register of the University of Cambridge to*
                 1500, Cambridge 1963
BRUO   Emden, A. B., *A biographical register of the University of Oxford to*
                 1500, 3 vols., Oxford 1957–9
BRUO 1540   Emden, A. B., *A biographical register of the University of Oxford,*
                 1501–1540, Oxford 1974
BSC   Madan, F. *et al.*, *Summary catalogue of western manuscripts in the*
                 Bodleian Library at Oxford, 7 vols. in 8, Oxford 1895–1953
Campbell   Campbell, M. F. A. G., *Annales de la typographie néerlandaise au*
                 XVme s., and *Suppléments*, The Hague 1874–90
CBMLC   *Corpus of British medieval library catalogues*, London: I. Humphreys,
                 K. W. (ed.), *The Friars' libraries*, 1990; II. Mynors, R. A. B., Rouse,

	R. H. and Rouse, M. A. (eds.), *Registrum Anglie de libris doctorum et auctorum veterum*, 1991; III. Bell, D. N. (ed.), *The Libraries of the Cistercians, Gilbertines and Premonstratensians*, 1992; IV. Sharpe, R., et al. (eds.), *English Benedictine libraries: the shorter catalogues*, 1996; V. Webber, T. and Watson, A. G. (eds.), *The Libraries of the Augustinian Canons*, 1998.
CBS	Cambridge Bibliographical Society
CCR	*Calendar of Close Rolls*
CE	Mynors, R. A. B. *et al.* (trans.), *Correspondence of Erasmus*, Toronto, Buffalo, London, 1974–
CHB	*Cambridge History of the Bible*, Cambridge: II. Lampe, G. W. H. (ed.), *The West from the Fathers to the Reformation*, 1969; III. Greenslade, S. L. (ed.), *The West from the Reformation to the present day*, 1963
CIBN	BNF, *Catalogue des incunables*, Paris, 1981–
CLRO	Corporation of London Record Office
Coll.	College
CPR 1467–77	*Calendar of patent rolls, Edward IV and Henry VI*, London 1900
CPR 1471–85	*Calendar of patent rolls, Edward IV and Richard III*, London 1901
CPREdward VI	*Calendar of the patent rolls, Edward VI*, 6 vols., London 1924–9
CPREliz	*Calendar of the patent rolls of Elizabeth*, 14 vols., London 1939–94
CPRHenry VII	*Calendar of patent rolls, Henry VII*, 2 vols., London 1914–16
CPRPhilip and Mary	*Calendar of the patent rolls, Philip and Mary*, 4 vols., London, 1937–9
CUL	Cambridge University Library
CWE	*The collected works of Erasmus in English*, Toronto, Buffalo, London, 1974–
CWM	The Yale edition of the works of St Thomas More, New Haven and London: I. Edwards, A. S. G., Miller, C. H. and Rodgers, K. G. (eds.), *English poems, Four last things, Life of John Picus, earl of Mirandula*, 1997; II. Sylvester, R. S. (ed.), *The History of King Richard III*, 1963; III.i. Thompson, C. R. (ed.), *Translations of Lucian*, 1974; III.ii. Miller, C. H., Bradner, L., Lynch, C. A. and Oliver, R. P. (eds.), *Latin poems*, 1984; V. Headley, J. M. (ed.), *Responsio ad Lutherum*, 1969; VI. Lawler, T. M. C., Marc'hadour, G. and Marius, R. C. (eds.), *A Dialogue concerning heresies*, 1981; VII. Manley, F. M., Marc'hadour, G., Marius, R. C. and Miller, C. H. (eds.), *Letter to Bugenhagen, Supplication of souls, Letter against Frith*, 1990; VIII. Schuster, L. A., Marius, R. C., Lusardi, J. P. and Schoeck, R. J. (eds.), *The Confutation of Tyndale's answer*, 1973; IX. Trapp, J. B. (ed.), *The Apology*, 1979; X. Guy, J. A., Keen, R., Miller, C. H. and McGugan, R. (eds.), *The Debellation of Salem and Bizance*, 1987; XI. Foley, S. M. and Miller, C. H. (eds.), *The Answer to a poisoned Book*, 1985; XV. Kinney, D. (ed.), *In defense of humanism: Letters to Dorp, Oxford, Lee and a Monk; Historia Richardi Tertii*, 1986

DMH	Darlow, T. H. and Moule, H. F., rev. Herbert, A. S., *Historical catalogue of printed editions of the English Bible 1525–1961*, London 1968
DNB	*Dictionary of national biography*; see also *New DNB*
EETS (ES/OS/SS)	Early English Text Society (Extra Series/Original Series/ Supplementary Series)
EHR	*English Historical Review*
ELM	Baker, J. H., *English legal manuscripts*, 2 vols., Zug 1975–8
ELMUSA	Baker, J. H., *English legal manuscripts in the United States of America: Part I: Medieval and Renaissance*, London 1985
ELR	*English Literary Renaissance*
EMS	*English Manuscript Studies*
Goff	Goff, F. R., *Incunabula in American libraries. A third census*, rpt Millwood NY 1973, with compiler's annotations
GW	*Gesamtkatalog der Wiegendrucke*, Leipzig 1925–
HLQ	*Huntington Library Quarterly*
Hodnett	Hodnett, E., *English woodcuts 1480–1535*, Bibliographical Society Illustrated Monographs (Oxford 1935), rev. edn 1973
HPT	Hellinga, W. and Hellinga, L., *The fifteenth-century printing types of the Low Countries*, 2 vols., Amsterdam 1966
Hum.Lov.	*Humanistica Lovaniensia*
Huntington	San Marino CA, Henry E. Huntington Library
HUO I–III	*The History of the University of Oxford*, Oxford: I. Catto, J. I. (ed.), *The early schools*, 1984; II. Catto, J. I. and Evans, T. A. R. (eds.), *Late Medieval Oxford*, 1992; III. McConica, J. K. (ed.), *The collegiate University*, 1986
IMEP	*The Index of Middle English Prose. A handlist of manuscripts*, Cambridge, 1984–
IMEV	Brown, Carleton and Robbins, R. H., *The index of Middle English verse*, New York 1943; *Supplement*, Lexington KY 1965
IMU	*Italia medioevale e umanistica*
IPMEP	Lewis, R. L., Blake, N. F. and Edwards, A. S. G. (eds.), *Index of printed Middle English prose*, New York and London 1985
ISTC	*Incunabula short-title catalogue* (database in progress)
JRUL	John Rylands University Library, Manchester
JWCI	*Journal of the Warburg and Courtauld Institutes*
Lambeth	Lambeth Palace Library, London
Library	*The Library. Transactions of the Bibliographical Society*
LPHenry VIII	Brewer, J. S. *et al.* (eds.), *Letters and papers, foreign and domestic, of the reign of Henry VIII*, 22 vols. in 38, London 1864–1932
LQR	*Law Quarterly Review*
MAE	*Medium Aevum*
McK and F	McKerrow, R. B. and Ferguson, F. S., *Title-page borders used in England and Scotland, 1485–1640*, Bibliographical Society Illustrated Monographs, 21, London 1932
ME	Middle English

Mitchell	Mitchell, W. S., *Catalogue of the incunabula in Aberdeen University library*, Edinburgh 1968
MLN	*Modern Language Notes*
MLQ	*Modern Language Quarterly*
MLR	*Modern Language Review*
MSML	Parkes, M. B. and Watson, A. G. (eds.), *Medieval scribes, manuscripts and libraries: essays presented to N. R. Ker*, London 1978
NCC	Norwich Consistory Court
NeuphilMitt	*Neuphilologische Mitteilungen*
New DNB	*The New Dictionary of National Biography*, Oxford forthcoming
NK	Nijhoff, W. and Kronenberg, M. E., *Nederlandsche bibliographie van 1500 tot 1540*, 3 vols. and Supplements, The Hague 1923–
NLS	National Library of Scotland, Edinburgh
NLW	National Library of Wales, Aberystwyth
N&Q	*Notes and Queries*
OBS	Oxford Bibliographical Society
OHS	Oxford Historical Society
ÖNB	Österreichische Nationalbibliothek, Vienna
PBSA	*Papers of the Bibliographical Society of America*
PCC	Prerogative Court of Canterbury [Wills at Public Record Office, London]
Pell.	Pellechet, M. and Polain, M. L., *Catalogue général des incunables des bibliothèques publiques de France*, 3 vols., rpt Nendeln 1970
PLRE	Fehrenbach, R. J. and Leedham-Green, E. S. (eds.), *Private libraries in Renaissance England. A collection and catalogue of Tudor and early Stuart book-lists*, 4 vols. to date, Binghamton NY and Marlborough, 1992–5
PML	Pierpont Morgan Library, New York
PMLA	*Publications of the Modern Language Association of America*
PPC	Nicolas, Sir H. N. (ed.), *Proceedings and ordinances of the Privy Council of England*, 7 vols., London 1834–7
Pr.	Proctor, R., *An index to the early printed books in the British Museum from the invention of printing to the year MD, with notes of those in the Bodleian Library*, 2 vols. and 4 supplements, London 1898–1902
PRO	Public Record Office, London
RenQ	*Renaissance Quarterly*
RES	*Review of English Studies*
RHS	Royal Historical Society
SB	*Studies in Bibliography*
SP	*Studies in Philology*
SPEdward VI	Knighton, C. S. (ed.), *Calendar of State Papers, Domestic Series of the Reign of Edward VI*, rev. edn, London 1992
SR	*Studies in the Renaissance*
SRealm	Luders, A. *et al.* (eds.), *Statutes of the Realm*, 11 vols., London 1810–28
STC	*A short-title catalogue of books printed in England, Scotland and*

Bibliography

Abrams, L. and Carley, J. P. (eds.) 1991 *The archaeology and history of Glastonbury abbey. Essays in honour of the 90th birthday of C. A. Ralegh Radford*, Woodbridge.

Adamson, J. W. 1946 'The extent of literacy in England in the fifteenth and sixteenth centuries: notes and conjectures', *Library*, 4th ser., 10, 1929–30, 163–93; rpt in Adamson, *The illiterate Anglo-Saxon and other essays*, Cambridge, 38–61.

Aeschbach, M. (ed.) 1989 *Raoul Lefèvre, le recueil des histoires de Troyes*, Publications universitaires Européennes, ser. 13: Langue et littérature française 120, Berne.

Alexander, J. J. G. 1971 'A lost leaf from a Bodleian book of hours', *BLR*, 8, 248–51.

1972 'William Abell "lymnour" and English fifteenth-century illumination', in A. Rosenauer and G. Weber (eds.), *Kunsthistorische Forschungen Otto Pächt zu ehren*, Vienna, 166–72.

1980 'An English illuminator's work in some fourteenth-century Italian law books at Durham', *Medieval Art and Architecture at Durham Cathedral. British Archaeological Assoc. Conference Trans. for 1977*, 149–53.

1983 'Painting and manuscript illumination for royal patrons in the later Middle Ages', in Scattergood and Sherborne, 1983, 141–62.

1989a 'Copies and variations: the relationship to the model in Medieval and Renaissance European illuminated manuscripts', in K. Preciado (ed.), *Retaining the original: multiple originals, copies and reproductions*, Washington DC, 61–72.

1989b 'Katherine Bray's Flemish book of hours', *Ricardian* 8, 107, 308–17.

1992 *Medieval illuminators and their methods of work*, New Haven and London.

Alexander, J. J. G. and Binski, P. (eds.) 1987 *Age of chivalry. Art in Plantagenet England 1200–1400*, London.

Alexander, J. J. G. and Temple, E. 1985 *Illuminated manuscripts in Oxford College libraries, the University Archives and the Taylor Institution*, Oxford.

Allen, C. G. 1954 'The sources of Lily's Latin grammar', *Library*, 5th ser., 9, 85–100.

Allen, P. S. 1910 'Bishop Shirwood of Durham and his library', *EHR*, 25, 445–56.

1924 'Early documents connected with the library of Merton College', *Library*, 4th ser., 4, 249–76.

Allenson, S. 1989 'The Inverness fragments: music from a pre-Reformation Scottish parish church and school', *Music and Letters*, 70, 1–45.

Allmand, C.T. 1982 'The civil lawyers', in C. H. Clough (ed.), *Profession, vocation, and culture in later medieval England: essays dedicated to the memory of A. R. Myers*, Liverpool, 155–80.

Alston, R. C. 1994 *Books with manuscript. A short-title catalogue of books with manuscript notes in the British Library*, London.

1996 *Books printed on vellum in the collections of the British Library. With a catalogue of Hebrew books printed on vellum compiled by B. S. Hill*, London.

Anglo, S. 1969 *Spectacle, pageantry and early Tudor policy*, Oxford (2nd edn 1996).

Anstey, H. (ed.) 1898 *Epistolae Academiae Oxoniensis*, 2 vols., OHS 35–6, Oxford.

Aplin, J. 1981 'The origins of John Day's "Certaine notes"', *Music and Letters*, 62, 295–9.

Aquilon, P. and Martin, H.-J. (eds.) 1988 *Le livre dans l'Europe de la Renaissance. Actes du 28ᵐᵉ colloque internationale d'études humanistes de Tours*, Paris.

Archer, R. 1992 ' "How ladies . . . who live on their manors ought to manage their households and states": women as landholders and administrators in the later Middle Ages', in P. J. P. Goldberg (ed.), *Woman is a worthy wight: women in English society, c.1200–1500*, Gloucester, 149–81.

Armstrong, C. A. J. 1973 'The piety of Cicely, Duchess of York' (1942), in D. Woodruff (ed.), *For Hilaire Belloc: essays in honour of his 72nd birthday*; rpt in C. A. J. Armstrong, *England, France and Burgundy in the fifteenth century*, 1973, 135–56.

Armstrong, E. 1979 'English purchases of printed books from the Continent 1465–1526', *EHR*, 94, 268–90.

1990 'Origins and development of book-privileges in Europe', in E. Armstrong, *Before copyright. The French book-privilege system 1498–1526*, Cambridge.

Arnould, A. 1992 'The art historical context of the library of Raphael de Mercatellis,' unpub. Ph.D. thesis, Ghent University.

1993 Contribution to *Splendours of Flanders: late medieval art in Cambridge collections*, Fitzwilliam Museum, Cambridge, 66–220.

Ascham, R. 1864–5 *The whole works of Roger Ascham . . . collected and revised by J. A. Giles*, London.

1904 *English works*, ed. W. A. Wright, Cambridge (rpt 1970)

Ashbee, A. (ed.) 1993 *Records of English court music*. Vol. VII: *1485–1558*, Aldershot.

Ashworth, E. J. 1978 'A note on Paul of Venice and the Oxford logica of 1483', *Medioevo*, 4, 93–9.

1979a 'The "Libelli sophistarum" and the use of medieval logic texts at Oxford and Cambridge in the early sixteenth century', *Vivarium*, 17, 134–58.

1979b 'A note on an early printed logic text in Edinburgh University Library', *Innes Rev.*, 30, 77–9.

1985a 'English *Obligationes* texts after Roger Swyneshed: the tracts beginning "Obligatio est quaedam ars"', in P. P. Lewry (ed.), *The rise of British logic*, Toronto, 309–33.

1985b Introduction to R. Sanderson, *Logicae artis compendium*, ed. Ashworth, Bologna.

1991 'Logic in late sixteenth-century England: humanist dialectic and the new Aristotelianism', *SP*, 88, 224–36.

1992 'The *Obligationes* of John Tarteys: edition and introduction', *Documenti e studi sulla tradizione filosofica medievale* 3, 653–753.

Ashworth, E. J. and Spade, P. V. 1992 'Logic in late medieval Oxford', in *HUO*, II, 35–64.

Aston, M. 1984 *Lollards and reformers: images and literacy in late medieval religion*, London.

Auerbach, E. 1954 *Tudor artists: a study of painters in the royal service and of portraiture on illuminated documents from the accession of Henry VII to the death of Elizabeth I*, London.

Aungier, G. J. 1840 *The history and antiquities of Syon Monastery*, London.

Avis, F. C. 1973 'England's use of Antwerp printers 1500-1540', *Gutenberg-Jahrbuch 1973*, 234-40.

Avril, F. and Reynaud, N. 1993 *Les manuscrits à peintures en France 1440-1520*, catalogue of the exhibition in the Bibliothèque nationale de France, Paris.

Axton, R. (ed.) 1979 *Three Rastell plays*, Cambridge.

Backhouse, J. M. 1973 'Bourdichon's "Hours of Henry VII"', *British Museum Quarterly*, 37, 95-102.

1985 *Books of hours*, London.

1987 'Founders of the Royal Library: Edward IV and Henry VII as collectors of illuminated manuscripts', in D. Williams (ed.), *England in the fifteenth century: proceedings of the Harlaxton Symposium for 1986*, Woodbridge, 23-41.

1989 'Illuminated manuscripts and the early development of the portrait miniature', in D. Williams (ed.), *Early Tudor England: proceedings of the 1987 Harlaxton Symposium*, Woodbridge, 1-17, pls. 1-13.

1993 *The Isabella breviary*, London.

1994 'Sir John Donne's Flemish manuscripts', in Monks and Owen 1994, 48-53.

1995 'Illuminated manuscripts associated with Henry VII and members of his immediate family', in B. Thompson (ed.), *The reign of Henry VII: proceedings of the 1993 Harlaxton Symposium*, Harlaxton Medieval Studies 5, Woodbridge and Stamford CT, 175-87, pls. 43-51.

1996 *The Hastings Hours*, London.

Baillie, H. 1958 'London churches, their music and musicians, 1485-1560', unpub. Ph.D. thesis, University of Cambridge.

Baker, J. H. 1988 Introduction to C. St German, *Doctor and student* (rpt of 1787 edn), Birmingham AL.

1989a 'John Bryt's reports (1410-1411) and the year books of Henry IV', *Cambridge Law Jnl*, 48, 98-114.

1989b 'Records, reports and the origins of case-law in England', in J. H. Baker (ed.), *Judicial records, law reports and the growth of case law*, Berlin, 15-46.

1990a *The third university of England: the Inns of Court and the common-law tradition*, Selden Society, London.

1990b *Manual of law French*, 2nd edn, Aldershot.

1990c intro. to *Readings and moots at the Inns of Court*, II, Selden Society 105, London.

Baker, J. H. (ed.) 1977-8 *The reports of Sir John Spelman*, Selden Society 93-4, London.

1986 *The Notebook of Sir John Port*, Selden Society 102, London.

1994 *Reports from the lost notebooks of Sir James Dyer*, Selden Society 109-10, London.

Baker-Smith, D. 1984 'Florens Wilson and his circle: emigrés in Lyons, 1539-1543', in G. Castor and T. C. Cave (eds.), *Neo-Latin and the vernacular in Renaissance France*, Oxford, 83-97.

Bale, J. 1990 *The Vocacyon of Johan Bale to the bishoprick of Ossorie in Irelande*, ed. P.

Happé and J. N. King, Renaissance English Text Society, 7th ser. 14, Binghamton NY.

Balogh, J. 1975 *Die Anfänge der Renaissance in Ungarn. Matthias Corvinus und die Kunst*, Graz.

Banks, C., Searle, A. and Turner, M. (eds.) 1993 *Sundry sorts of music books: essays on the British Library collections presented to O. W. Neighbour on his 70th birthday*, London.

Bannister, A. J. (ed.) 1921 *Registrum Caroli Bothe episcopi Herefordensis A. D. 1516-1535*, Canterbury and York Society, 28, London.

Barber, G. 1977 'Thomas Linacre: a bibliographical survey of his works', in F. Maddison, M. Pelling and C. Webster (eds.), *Linacre studies: essays on the life and work of Thomas Linacre c. 1460-1524*, Oxford, 291-336.

Barclay, A. 1874 *The Ship of fools*, ed. T. H. Jamieson, 2 vols., Edinburgh and London.

[Barclay, A.] 1985 *The gardyners passetaunce touchying the outrage of Fraunce*, ed. F. B. Williams Jr and H. M. Nixon, Roxburghe Club, London.

Barker, N. J. 1972 'A register of writs and the Scales binder', *BC*, 21, 227-44, 356-79.

1976 'Caxton's typography', *Jnl of the Printing Historical Soc.* 11 (Papers presented to the Caxton International Congress 1976), 114-33, and plates.

1978 *The Oxford University Press and the spread of learning, an illustrated history, 1478-1978*, Oxford.

1979 'The St Albans press: the first punch-cutter in England and the first native typefounder?' *TCBS*, 8, 257-78.

1985 'The importation of books into England 1460-1526', in H. G. Göpfert *et al.* (eds.), *Beiträge zur Geschichte des Buchwesens im konfessionellen Zeitalter*, Wolfenbütteler Schriften zur Geschichte des Buchwesens, Wiesbaden, 251-66.

Barker, N. J. (ed.) 1993 *A potencie of life: books in society*, Clark Lectures 1986-7, Cambridge.

Baron, H. 1989 'The "Blage" manuscript: the original compiler identified', *EMS*, 1, 85-119.

Barratt, A. (ed.) 1993 *Women's writing in Middle English*, Harlow.

1995 *The seven Psalms. A commentary on the penitential Psalms translated from French into English by Dame Eleanor Hull*, EETS OS 307, Oxford.

Barry, John C. (ed.) 1967 *William Hay's lectures on marriage*, Stair Society 24, Edinburgh.

Bartlett, K. 1977 'The decline and abolition of the master of grammar: an early victory of humanism at the university of Cambridge', *History of Education*, 6, 1-8.

Barton, J. L. 1971 'Roman law in England', in *Ius romanum Medii AEvi*, pars v, Milan, 13a.

1984 'The study of civil law before 1380', in *HUO*, I, 519-30.

1986 'The faculty of law', in *HUO*, III, 257-93.

1992 'The legal faculties of late medieval Oxford', in *HUO*, II, 281-314.

Baskerville, E. J. 1979 *A chronological bibliography of propaganda and polemic published in English between 1553 and 1558 from the death of Edward VI to the death of Mary I*, Memoirs of the American Philosophical Soc. 136, Philadelphia PA.

Bataillon, L. J. *et al.* 1988 (eds.), *La production du livre universitaire au moyen âge: exemplar et pecia. Actes du symposium tenu au Collegio San Bonaventura de Grottaferrata en mai 1983*, Paris.

Bateson, M. 1898 *Catalogue of the library of Syon Monastery, Isleworth*, Cambridge.

Baumer, Franklin Le Van 1940 *The early Tudor theory of kingship*, New Haven (rpt 1961).

Bäuml, F. H. 1980 'Varieties and consequences of medieval literacy and illiteracy', *Speculum*, 55, 237–65.

Baurmeister, U. and Laffitte, M.- P. 1992 *Des livres et des rois: la bibliothèque royale de Blois*, Paris.

Bawcutt, P. 1991 'The earliest texts of Dunbar', in Riddy 1991, 183–98.

Bazire, J. and Colledge, E. (eds.) 1957 *The Chastising of God's children and the Treatise of perfection of the sons of God*, Oxford.

Beadle, H. R. L. (ed.) 1994 *The Cambridge companion to medieval theatre*, Cambridge.

Beadle, H. R. L. and Owen, A. E. B. (eds.) 1977 *The Findern anthology*, London.

Beadle, H. R. L. and Meredith, P. (eds.) 1983 *The York play*, Leeds Texts and Monographs. Medieval Drama Facsimiles, Leeds.

Beadle, H. R. L. and Piper, A. J. (eds.) 1995 *New science out of old books. Studies in manuscripts and early printed books in honour of A. I. Doyle*, Aldershot.

Beal, P. G. 1980 *Index of English literary manuscripts*. Vol. I: *1450–1625*, London and New York.

Beale, J. H. 1926 *A bibliography of early English law books*, Cambridge MA.

Beattie, W. (ed.) 1950 *The Chepman and Millar prints: a facsimile*, Edinburgh.

Bedouelle, G. and Le Gal, P. 1987 *Le 'Divorce' du roi Henry VIII: études et documents*, Geneva.

Bell, D. N. 1984 'The books of Meaux Abbey', *Analecta Cisterciensia*, 40, 25–83.

    1989a 'A Cistercian at Oxford: Richard Dove of Buckfast and London, BL, Sloane 513', *Studia Monastica*, 31, 69–87.

    1989b 'The English Cistercians and the practice of medicine', *Cîteaux*, 40, 139–74.

    1992 *An index of authors and works in Cistercian libraries in Great Britain*, Kalamazoo MI.

    1995 *What nuns read: books and libraries in medieval English nunneries*, Cistercian Studies Series 158, Kalamazoo MI.

Bell, H. E. 1937 'The price of books in medieval England', *Library*, 4th ser., 17, 312–32.

Bell, M. and Barnard, J. 1992 'Provisional count of *STC* titles 1475–1640', *Publishing History*, 31, 49–55.

Bennett, H. S. 1946–7 'The production and dissemination of vernacular manuscripts in the fifteenth century', *Library*, 5th ser., 1, 167–78.

    1950 'Notes on English retail book-prices, 1480–1560', *Library*, 5th ser., 5, 172–8.

    1952 *English books and readers 1475 to 1557*, Cambridge (rpt 1969).

    1965 *English books and readers 1558–1603*, Cambridge.

Bent, M. 1968 'New and little-known fragments of English medieval polyphony', *Jnl of the American Musicological Soc.*, 21, 137–56.

    1984 'The progeny of Old Hall: more leaves from a royal English choirbook', in L. Dittmer (ed.), *Gordon Athol Anderson (1929–1981): in memoriam*, 2 vols., Wissenschaftliche Abhandlungen 39, Henryville, Ottawa and Binningen, 1–54.

    1996 'A new canonic gloria and the changing profile of Dunstaple', *Plainsong and Medieval Music*, 5, 45–67.

Bergen, H. (ed.) 1924–7 *Lydgate's Fall of princes*, 4 vols., EETS ES 121–4, London.

Berty, A. 1885 *Topographie historique du vieux Paris*, Vol. 1: *Région du Louvre et des Tuileries*, Paris, 181–99.

La Biblioteca Medicea Laurenziana, cenni storici, 1981, Florence.

Bibliotheca Erasmiana Bruxellensis, 1993, Brussels.

Bietenholz, Peter G. 1971 *Basle and France in the sixteenth century*, Toronto.

Bietenholz, Peter. G. (ed.) 1985–7 *Contemporaries of Erasmus: a biographical register of the Renaissance and Reformation*, 3 vols., Toronto.

Biller, P. and Hudson, A. (eds.) 1994 *Heresy and literacy, 1000–1530*, Cambridge.

Birley, R. 1956 'The history of Eton College library', *Library*, 5th ser., 11, 231–61.

Birrell, T. A. 1987a *English monarchs and their books from Henry VII to Charles II*, Panizzi Lectures 1986, London.

    1987b 'The printed books of Dame Margaret Nicollson: a pre-Reformation collection', in J. Bakker, J. A. Verleun and J. Van der Vriesenaerde (eds.), *Essays on English and American literature . . . offered to D. Wilkinson*, Costerus, n.s. 63, Amsterdam, 27–33.

Blades, W. 1861–63 *The life and typography of William Caxton, England's first printer, with evidence of his typographical connection with Colard Mansion*, 2 vols., London.

Blagden, C. 1960 *The Stationers' Company: a history, 1403–1959*, London.

Blake, N. F. 1968 *Caxton and his world*, London.

    1970 'Wynkyn de Worde and "The Quatrefoil of Love"', *Archiv*, 206, 189–200.

    1971 'Lord Berners, a survey', *Mediaevalia et humanistica*, n.s. 2, 119–32.

    1973 *Caxton's own prose*, London.

    1985 *William Caxton: a bibliographical guide*, New York.

    1989 'Manuscript to print', in *BPPB*, 403–32.

    1996 *William Caxton* (*Authors of the Middle Ages*, vol. 3, nos. 7–11: 'English Writers of the late Middle Ages', gen. ed. M. C. Seymour), Gateshead.

Blake, N. F. (ed.) 1992 *The Cambridge history of the English language*. Vol. 11: *1066–1476*, Cambridge.

Blanchfield, L. S. 1991 'The romances in MS Ashmole 61: an idiosyncratic scribe', in M. Mills, J. Fellows and C. M. Meale (eds.), *Romance in medieval England*, Cambridge, 65–87.

Blayney, M. S. (ed.) 1974–80 *English translations of Alain Chartier's 'Le traité de l'esperence' and 'Le quadrilogue invectif'*, EETS OS 270, 281, Oxford.

Blodgett, J. E. 1979 'Some printer's copy for William Thynne's 1532 edition of Chaucer', *Library*, 6th ser., 1, 97–113.

Blomefield, F. 1805–10 *An essay towards a topographical history of the county of Norfolk*, 11 vols., London.

Bloy, C. H. 1967 *A history of printing ink, ball and rollers, 1440–1850*, London.

Blunt, J. H. (ed.) 1873 *The Myroure of oure Ladye*, EETS ES 19, London (rpt 1983).

Boase, C. W. (ed.) 1885 *Register of the University of Oxford*. Vol. 1: *1449–63, 1505–71*, OHS 1, Oxford.

Bödeker, H. E. (ed.) 1995 *Histoires du livre, nouvelles orientations. Actes du colloque du 6 et 7 septembre 1990 à Göttingen*, Collection 'In Octavo', Paris.

Boersma, F. L. 1981 *An introduction to Fitzherbert's Abridgement*, Abingdon.

Boffey, J. 1991 'Early printers and English lyrics: sources, selection, and presentation of texts', *PBSA*, 85, 11–26.

1994 'English dream poems of the fifteenth century and their French connections', in D. Maddox and S. Sturm-Maddox (eds.), *Literary aspects of courtly culture: selected papers from the seventh triennial congress of the International Courtly Lit. Soc.*, Cambridge, 113–21.

1995 'Lydgate's lyrics and women readers', in L. J. Smith and J. H. M. Taylor (eds.), *Woman, the book and the worldly: selected proceedings of the St Hilda's Conference*, Cambridge, 139–49.

1996 'Some London women readers and a text of The three kings of Cologne', *Ricardian*, 10, no. 132, 387–96.

Boffey, J. and Edwards, A. S. G. (eds.) 1997 *Bodleian Library ms. Arch. Selden B. 24: The works of Chaucer and the 'Kingis Quair'*, with appendix by B. C. Barker-Benfield, Cambridge.

Boffey, J. and Thompson, J. J. 1989 'Anthologies and miscellanies: selection and presentation of texts', in *BPPB*, 279–315.

Bohatta, H. 1924 *Bibliographie der livres d'heures des 15. und 16. Jahrhunderts*, 2nd edn, Vienna.

Bonaventure, Brother 1961 'The teaching of Latin in later medieval England', *Medieval Stud.*, 23, 1–30.

Bond, E. A. (ed.) 1853 *Statutes of the colleges of Oxford, with royal patents of foundation . . .* 3 vols., Oxford.

Bond, W. H. 1948 'Casting off copy by Elizabethan printers: a theory', *PBSA*, 42, 281–91.

Bone, G. 1932 'Extant manuscripts of books printed from by Wynkyn de Worde, with notes on the owner, Roger Thorney', *Library*, 4th ser., 12, 284–306.

Bornstein, D. (ed.) 1978 *Distaves and dames: Renaissance treatises for and about women*, New York.

Bosanquet, E. F. 1917 *English printed almanacks and prognostications. A bibliographical history to the year 1600*, Bibliographical Soc. Illustrated Monographs 17, London.

Bourdillon, A. F. C. 1926 *The order of Minoresses in England*, Manchester.

Bowers, J. M. 1989 'Hoccleve's Huntington holographs: the first "collected poems" in English', *Fifteenth-Century Stud.*, 15, 27–51.

Bowers, R. 1975 'Choral institutions within the English church, 1340–1500', unpub. Ph.D. thesis, University of East Anglia.

1981 'Obligation, agency, and *laissez-faire*: the promotion of polyphonic composition for the church in fifteenth-century England', in I. Fenlon (ed.), *Music in medieval and early modern Europe: patronage, sources and texts*, Cambridge, 1–19.

1991 'The cultivation and promotion of music in the household and orbit of Thomas Wolsey', in S. J. Gunn and P. G. Lindley (eds.), *Cardinal Wolsey. Church, state and art*, Cambridge, 178–218.

Bowers, R. and Wathey, A. (comps.) 1983 'New sources of English fourteenth- and fifteenth-century polyphony', *Early Music History*, 3, 123–73.

Bowker, M. 1968 *The secular clergy in the diocese of Lincoln*, Cambridge.

Boyle, L. E. 1955 'The *Oculus sacerdotis* and some other works of William of Pagula', *TRHS*, 5th ser., 5, 81–110.

1965 'The *Summa summarum* and some other English works of canon law', in S. Kuttner and J. J. Ryan (eds.), *Proceedings of the second international congress of medieval canon law*, Vatican City, 415–56.

1985 'The fourth Lateran Council and manuals of popular theology', in T. J. Heffernan (ed.), *The popular literature of medieval England*, Knoxville TN, 30–43.

Bradshaw, H. 1860 'Two lists of books in the University Library', *Communications made to the Cambridge Antiquarian Soc.*, Oct. ser., 10, 2, 239–78 (rpt Bradshaw 1889, 16–53).

1887 *A half-century of notes on the Day Book of John Dorne*, Cambridge (rpt Bradshaw 1889, 421–50).

1889 *Collected papers*, Cambridge.

Braekman, W. L. 1985 'Bollard's Middle English Book of planting and grafting and its background', *Studia neophilologica*, 57, 19–39.

Braekman, W. L. (ed.) 1989 *Geoffrey of Franconia's Book of trees and wine*, Scripta 24, Brussels.

Bray, R. 1995 'Music and the quadrivium in early Tudor England', *Music and Letters*, 76, 1–18.

Breeze, A. and Glomski, J. 1991 'An early British treatise upon education: Leonard Cox's *De erudienda iuventute* (1526)', *Hum. Lov.*, 40, 112–67.

Brévart, F. B. 1988 'The German *Volkskalender* of the fifteenth century', *Speculum*, 63, 312–42.

Brewer, D. S. and Owen, A. E. B. (eds. and intro.) 1978 *The Thornton manuscript: Lincoln Cathedral Library MS 91*, 2nd edn, London.

Brigden, S. 1989 *London and the Reformation*, Oxford.

Brodie, A. R. 1974 'Anwykyll's *Vulgaria*', *NeuphilMitt*, 75, 416–27.

Brodin, G. (ed.) 1950 *Agnus castus: a Middle English herbal reconstructed from various manuscripts*, Uppsala.

Brooke, C. N. L. 1985 *A history of Gonville and Caius College*, Woodbridge and Dover NH.

Brotherton-Ratcliffe, Chantal J. 1994 'Illustrations of the four last things in English pre-Reformation printed books of devotion', unpub. Ph.D. thesis, University of London, Warburg Institute.

Brown, A. J. 1984 'The date of Erasmus' Latin translation of the New Testament', *TCBS*, 8, 4, 351–80.

Brown, R. A. and Colvin, H. M. 1963 'The king's houses 1066–1485', in R. A. Brown, H. M. Colvin and A. J. Taylor, *The history of the King's works: the Middle Ages*, 2 vols., London.

Browne, M. P. (ed.) 1826 *Decisions of the Court of Session . . . 1766–1791, collected by Sir David Dalrymple of Hailes . . . sel. by M. P. Browne*, 2 vols., Edinburgh.

Brownrigg, L. L. (ed.) 1990 *Medieval book production: assessing the evidence*, Los Altos Hills CA.

Brusendorff, A. 1925 *The Chaucer tradition*, London.

Buettner, B. 1988 'Jacques Raponde "marchand de manuscrits enluminés"', *Langue, texte, histoire médiévales (La culture sur le marché)*, 14, 23–32.

Bühler, C. F. 1940 'Caxton studies', *Gutenberg-Jahrbuch*, 169–76 (rpt Bühler 1973, 43–52).

1950–1 'Observations on two Caxton variants', *SB*, 3, 97–104 (rpt Bühler 1973, 154–61).

1953 'The first edition of the *Abbey of the Holy Ghost*', *SB*, 5, 101–6 (rpt Bühler 1973, 205–11).

1960 *The fifteenth-century book: the scribes, the printers, the decorators*, Philadelphia.

1964 'Prayers and charms in certain Middle English scrolls', *Speculum*, 39, 270–8, (rpt Bühler 1973, 564–75).

1973 *Early books and manuscripts: forty years of research*, New York.

Bühler, C. F. (ed.) 1941 *The Dicts and sayings of the philosophers. The translations made by Stephen Scrope, William Worcester and an anonymous translator*, EETS OS 211, London.

Von Bülow, G. (ed.) 1892, assisted by Powell, W., 'Diary of the journey of Philip Julius, duke of Stettin-Pomerania, through England in the year 1602', *TRHS*, n.s., 6, 1–67.

Bush, M. L. 1975 *The government policy of Protector Somerset*, London.

Butterworth, C. C. 1953 *The English primers, 1529–1545, their publication and connection with the English Bible and the Reformation in England*, Philadelphia.

Byrom, H. J. 1927 'Richard Tottell: his life and work', *Library*, 4th ser., 8, 195–232.

Caldwell, D. F. C. (ed.) 1954–67 *Virgil's 'Aeneid' translated into Scottish verse by Gavin Douglas*, 4 vols., STS, 3rd ser., 25, 27, 28, 30, Edinburgh.

Caldwell, J. 1991 *The Oxford history of English music*. Vol. 1: *From the beginnings to c. 1715*, Oxford.

1995 *Tudor keyboard music c. 1520–1580*, Musica Britannica 66, London.

Calkins, R. G. 1983 *Illuminated books of the Middle Ages*, London.

Campbell, L. and Foister, S. 1986 'Gerard, Lucas and Susanna Horenbout', *Burlington Mag.*, 128, 719–27.

Campbell, P. G. C. 1925 'Christine de Pisan en Angleterre', *Rev. de littérature comparée*, 5, 659–71.

Capp, B. 1979 *Astrology and the popular press: English almanacs 1500–1800*, London.

Cargill-Thompson, W. D. J. 1954 'Notes on King's College library, 1500–1570', *TCBS*, 2, 1, 38–54.

Carley, J. P. 1986 'John Leland and the contents of English pre-Dissolution libraries: the Cambridge friars', *TCBS* 9, 1, 90–100.

1989a 'John Leland and the foundation of the royal library: the Westminster inventory of 1542', *Bull. of the Soc. for Renaissance Stud.*, 7, 13–22.

1989b 'John Leland and the contents of English pre-Dissolution libraries: Lincolnshire', *TCBS*, 9, 3, 330–57.

1997a 'Sir Thomas Bodley's library and its acquisitions: an edition of the Nottingham benefactions of 1604', in J. P. Carley and C. C. G. Tite (eds.), *Books and collectors 1200–1700. Essays presented to Andrew G. Watson*, London, 357–86.

1997b 'Marks in books and the libraries of Henry VIII', *PBSA*, 91, 583–606.

1998 '"Her moost lovyng and fryndely brother sendeth gretyng": Anne Boleyn's manuscripts and their sources', in M. P. Brown and S. McKendrick (eds.), *Illuminating the book: makers and interpreters. Essays in honour of Janet Backhouse*, London and Toronto, 261–80.

Carlin, M. 1987 'Historical gazetteer of London before the Great Fire: St Botolph, Aldgate', University of London, Institute of Historical Research, Social and Economic Study of Medieval London, typescript in IHR.

Carlson, D. R. 1993 *English humanist books: writers and patrons, manuscript and print, 1475–1525*, Toronto, Buffalo, London.

  1997 'Woodcut illustrations of the *Canterbury Tales*, 1483–1602', *Library*, 6th ser., 19, 25–67.

Carpenter, C. 1992 *Locality and polity: a study of Warwickshire landed society, 1401–1499*, Cambridge.

Carpenter, K. E. (ed.) 1983 *Books and society in history: papers of the Association of College and Research Libraries, Rare Books and Manuscripts Preconference . . . 1980*, New York.

Carroll, C. 1996 'Humanism and English literature in the fifteenth and sixteenth centuries', in J. Kraye (ed.), *The Cambridge companion to Renaissance humanism*, Cambridge, 246–68.

Carter, H. 1969 *A view of early typography up to about 1600*, Oxford.

Catto, J. I. 1985 'Religious change under Henry V', in G. L. Harriss (ed.), *Henry V: the practice of kingship*, Oxford, 97–115.

  1992 'Scholars and studies in Renaissance Oxford', in *HUO*, II, 769–83.

Cavanaugh, S. H. 1980 'A study of books privately owned in England, 1300–1450', 2 vols., unpub. Ph.D. thesis, University of Pennsylvania.

Census-catalogue of manuscript sources of polyphonic music 1400–1550, 1979–88, 5 vols., Neuhausen and Stuttgart.

Challis, C. E. 1978 *The Tudor coinage*, Manchester.

Chambers, R. W. and Seton, W. W. (eds.) 1914 *A fifteenth-century courtesy book* (ed. Chambers) and *Two fifteenth-century Franciscan rules* (ed. Seton) EETS OS 148, London.

Charles, B. G. and Emanuel, H. D. 1949–50 'Notes on old libraries and books', *Cylchgrawn Llyfrgell Genedlaethol Cymru*, 6, 353–72.

Chartier, R. (ed.) 1989 *The culture of print: power and the uses of print in early modern Europe*, Princeton NJ and London.

Chatsworth House 1991 *Treasures of Chatsworth. A private view*, London.

Chaucer, G. 1940 *The Text of the Canterbury Tales*, ed. J. M. Manly and E. Rickert, 8 vols., Chicago.

Chaytor, H. J. 1945 *From script to print: an introduction to medieval literature*, Cambridge.

Cheney, C. R. 1961 'William Lyndwood's *Provinciale*', *Jurist*, 21, 405–34 (rpt Cheney, *Medieval texts and studies*, Oxford, 1973, 158–84).

  1973 'The records of medieval England' (Cambridge University inaugural lecture 1955), in Cheney, *Medieval texts and studies*, Oxford, 1–15.

  1987 'A register of manuscripts borrowed from a college library, 1440–1517: Corpus Christi College, Cambridge, MS 232', *TCBS*, 9, 2, 103–29.

  1988 'A register of *electiones* of manuscripts of Corpus Christi College, Cambridge, 1440–1517', in S. Kramer and M. Bernhard (eds.), *Scire litteras: Forschungen zum mittelalterlichen Geistesleben*, Bayerische Akademie der Wissenschaften, Phil.-Hist. Klasse, Abh., N. F. 99, 95–101.

Cherry, T. A. F. 1963 'The library of Henry Sinclair, Bishop of Ross, 1560–1565', *Bibliotheck*, 4, 1, 13–24.

Chobham, T. 1968 *Thomae de Chobham Summa confessorum*, ed. F. Broomfield, Louvain and Paris.

Chomarat, J. 1981 *Grammaire et rhétorique chez Erasme*, 2 vols., Paris.

Chrisman, M. Usher 1982 *Lay culture, learned culture: books and social change in Strasbourg, 1480–1559*, New Haven CT.

Christ, K., Kern, A. and Otto, T. M. 1984 *The handbook of medieval library history*, Metuchen NY.

Christianson, C. Paul 1985 'Early London bookbinders and parchmeners', *BC*, 41–54.

1987a 'An early Tudor stationer and the "prynters of bokes"', *Library*, 6th ser., 9, 259–62.

1987b *Memorials of the book trade in medieval London: the archives of Old London Bridge*, Woodbridge.

1989a 'A community of book artisans in Chaucer's London', *Viator*, 20, 209–18.

1989b 'Chancery standard and the records of Old London Bridge', in J. B. Trahern, Jr (ed.), *Standardizing English: essays in the history of language change*, Knoxville TN, 82–112.

1989c 'Evidence for the study of London's late medieval manuscript-book trade', in *BPPB*, 87–108.

1989d 'Paternoster Row and the Tudor book-trade community', *Library*, 6th ser., 11, 352–6.

1990 *A directory of London stationers and book artisans 1300–1500*, New York.

1993 'The stationers of Paternoster Row, 1534–1557', *PBSA*, 87, 81–91.

Church of England, Central Council for the Care of Churches, 1959 *The parochial libraries of the church of England*, London.

Clanchy, M. T. 1993 *From memory to written record: England 1066–1307*, 2nd edn, Oxford.

Clapperton, R. H. 1934 *Paper: an historical account of its making by hand*, Oxford.

Clark, J. W. 1975 *The care of books* (1902), Cambridge.

Clough, C. H. 1977 'Thomas Linacre, Cornelio Vitelli, and humanistic studies at Oxford', in F. Maddison, M. Pelling and C. Webster (eds.), *Linacre studies. Essays on the life and work of Thomas Linacre, c.1460–1524*, Oxford, 1–23.

Coates, A. 1991 'The old library at Trinity College, Oxford', *BLR*, 13, 466–79.

Cobb, Henry S. 1959 'Local port customs accounts prior to 1550', *Jnl of the Soc. of Archivists*, 1, 213–24.

1971 'Books of rates and the London customs, 1507–1558', *Guildhall Misc.*, 4, 1, 2–13.

1990 *The overseas trade of London: Exchequer customs accounts 1480–1*, London Record Soc. Pubs. 27, London.

Cobban, A. B. 1969 *The King's Hall within the university of Cambridge in the later Middle Ages*, Studies in medieval life and thought, 3rd ser., 1, Cambridge.

1988 *The medieval English universities: Oxford and Cambridge to c. 1500*, Aldershot.

1991 'Pembroke College: its educational significance in late medieval Cambridge', *TCBS*, 10, 1, 1–16.

Coing, H. (ed.) 1973–7 *Handbuch der Quellen und Literatur der neueren europäischen Privatrechtsgeschichte*. Vol. I: *Mittelalter 1100–1500. Die gelehrten Rechte und die Gesetzgebung*, 1973; Vol. II: *Neuere Zeit 1500–1800. Das Zeitalter des gemeinen Rechts*. 1. *Wissenschaft*, 1977; 2. *Gesetzgebung und Rechtsprechung*, 1976.

1975 'Das Schrifttum der englischen Civilians und die kontinentale Rechtsliteratur in der Zeit zwischen 1550 und 1800', *Ius commune*, 5, 1–55.

Coleman, D. C. 1958 *The British paper industry 1495–1860*, Oxford.

Colledge, E. 1978 'South Netherlandish books of hours made for England', *Scriptorium*, 32, 55–7.

Collins, A. J. 1955 *Jewels and plate of Queen Elizabeth I: the inventory of 1574*, London.

Collinson, P. 1996 'William Tyndale and the course of the English Reformation', *Reformation*, 1, 72–97.

Collinson, P., McKitterick, D. and Leedham-Green, E. 1991 *Andrew Perne. Quatercentenary studies*, CBS Monographs 11, Cambridge.

The Complete Peerage by G.E.C., 13 vols. in 14, London.

Condon, M. M. 1986 'An anachronism with intent? Henry VII's Council Ordinance of 1491/2', in R. A. Griffiths and J. Sherborne (eds.), *Kings and nobles in the later Middle Ages: a tribute to Charles Ross*, Gloucester, New York, 228–53.

Conway, W. M. 1884 *The woodcutters of the Netherlands in the fifteenth century*, Cambridge.

Copland, R. 1993 *Poems*, ed. M. C. Erler, Toronto.

Coppens, C. 1992 'Sixteenth-century octavo publishers' catalogues, mainly from the Omont collection', *De Gulden Passer*, 70, 5–61.

1993 *Reading in exile: the libraries of John Ramridge (d. 1568), Thomas Harding (d. 1572) and Henry Joliffe (d. 1573), recusants in Louvain*, Cambridge.

Coquillette, D. R. 1988 *The civilian writers of Doctors' Commons, London. Three centuries of juristic innovation in comparative, commercial and international law*, Berlin.

Corrie, G. E. 1840 'A late fifteenth-century St Catharine's booklist', *Cambridge Antiquarian Soc. Quarto Pub.*, 1, 1–5.

1860a 'A catalogue of the books given to Trinity Hall, by the founder', *Communications made to the Cambridge Antiquarian Soc.*, Oct. ser., 10, 2, 73–8.

1860b 'A list of books presented to Pembroke College, Cambridge, by different donors, during the fourteenth and fifteenth centuries', *Cambridge Antiquarian Soc. Report*, 10, 11–23.

Corsten, S. 1999 'Johann Veldener in Köln: Geschichte eines Problems', *E codicibus impressisque: Opstellen voor Elly Cockx-Indestege*, Louvain.

Corsten, S. and Fuchs, R. W. (eds.) 1988–93 *Der Buchdruck im 15. Jahrhundert: eine Bibliographie*, 2 vols., Stuttgart.

Courtenay, W. J. 1987 *Schools and scholars in fourteenth-century England*, Princeton NJ.

Cowley, J. D. 1932 *A bibliography of abridgments, digests, dictionaries, and indexes of English law to the year 1800*, London.

Craigie, W. A. (ed.) 1919–27 *The Maitland folio manuscript*, 2 vols., STS 7, 20, Edinburgh.

1923–5 *The Asloan manuscript*, 2 vols., STS, 2nd ser., 14, 16, Edinburgh.

Crane, W. G. 1936 'Lord Berners' translation of Diego de San Pedro's *Carcel de amor*', *PMLA*, 49, 1032–5.

Craster, E. 1914–16 'Index to Duke Humphrey's gifts to the Old Library', *BQR*, 1, 131–5.

1971 *The history of All Souls College library*, ed. E. F. Jacob, London.

Crawley, C. 1992 *Trinity Hall, the history of a Cambridge college 1350–1992*, Cambridge.

Cressy, D. 1977 'Levels of illiteracy in England, 1530–1730', *Historical Jnl*, 20, 1–23.

1980 *Literacy and the social order. Readers and writers in Tudor and Stuart England*, Cambridge.

Croft, P. J. 1958a 'A copy of Walter Hylton's *Scala perfectionis*', sale catalogue, B. Quaritch, London.

1958b *Lady Margaret Beaufort, Countess of Richmond, Elizabeth of York and Wynkyn de Worde*, London.

1973 *Autograph poetry in the English language*, 2 vols., London and New York.

Cross, M. C. 1989 'A medieval Yorkshire library', *Northern History*, 25, 288.

Crotch, W. J. B. (ed.) 1928 *The prologues and epilogues of William Caxton*, EETS OS 176, London.

Culley, W. T. and Furnivall, F. J. (eds.) 1890 *Caxton's Eneydos, 1490*, EETS ES 67, London.

Curtis, G. and Wathey, A. 1994 'Fifteenth-century English liturgical music: a list of the surviving repertory', *Royal Musical Assoc. Research Chron.*, 27, 1–69.

Curtis, M. H. 1958 'Library catalogues at Tudor Oxford and Cambridge', *SR*, 5, 111–20.

Daiches, D. and Thorlby, A. K. (eds.) 1973 *Literature and western civilisation: the material world*, London.

Dale, A. W. W. 1911 *Warren's books*, Cambridge.

Daniell, D. 1994 *William Tyndale, a biography*, London and New Haven.

Darlington, I. (ed.) 1967 *London Consistory Court wills 1492–1574*, London Record Soc. 3, London.

Darnton, R. 1980 'What is the history of books', in K. E. Carpenter 1983, 3–26.

1986 'First steps towards a history of reading', *Australian Journal of French Studies*, 23, 5–30 (rpt Darnton, *The kiss of Lamourette: reflections in cultural history*, New York 1989).

Davenport, C. 1896 *Royal English bookbindings*, London.

1899 *English embroidered bookbindings*, London.

1901 *Thomas Berthelet, royal printer and bookbinder to Henry VIII*, Chicago.

Davies, R. T. (ed.) 1963 *Medieval English lyrics*, London.

Davis, H. W. C. 1914 'The canon law in England', *Zeitschrift der Savigny-Stiftung für Rechtsgeschichte*, 34, 349–50.

Davis, N. (ed.) 1971–6 *The Paston letters*, 2 vols., Oxford.

1979 *Non-Cycle plays and the Winchester dialogues*, Leeds Texts and Monographs, Medieval Drama Facsimiles, Leeds.

Davison, P. (ed.), 1992 *The book encompassed: studies in twentieth-century bibliography*, Cambridge.

Deanesly, M. 1920 'Vernacular books in England in the fourteenth and fifteenth centuries', *MLR*, 15, 349–58.

Deanesly, M. (ed.) 1915 *The Incendium amoris of Richard Rolle of Hampole*, Manchester.

Dédéyan, C. 1961–6 *Dante en Angleterre*, 2 vols., Paris.

Delaissé, L. M. J. 1974 'The importance of books of hours for the history of the medieval book', in U. McCracken, L. M. C. Randall and R. H. Randall, Jr (eds.), *Gatherings in honor of Dorothy E. Miner*, Baltimore MD, 203–26.

De la Mare, A. C. 1971 *Catalogue of the collection of medieval manuscripts bequeathed to the Bodleian Library, Oxford, by James P. R. Lyell*, Oxford.

    1973 *The handwriting of Italian humanists*, vol. I, fasc. 1, Oxford.

    1977 'Humanistic script: the first ten years', in F. Krafft and D. Wuttke (eds.), *Das Verhältnis der Humanisten zum Buch*, Deutsche Forschungsgemeinschaft: Kommission für Humanismusforschung, Mitteilung 4, Bonn and Bad Godesberg, 89–110.

    1980 'Humanistic hands in England', in De la Mare and Barker-Benfield 1980, 93–101.

    1985a 'Duke Humfrey's English Palladius (MS. Duke Humfrey d.2)', *BLR*, 12, 39–51.

    1985b 'New research on humanistic scribes in Florence', in A. Garzelli (ed.), *Miniatura fiorentina del Rinascimento 1440–1525*, Florence.

De la Mare, A. C. and Barker-Benfield, B. C. (eds.) 1980 *Bodleian Library, Oxford: manuscripts at Oxford: R. W. Hunt memorial exhibition*, Oxford.

De la Mare, A. C. and Gillam, S. 1988 *Duke Humfrey's library and the Divinity School 1488–1988. An exhibition at the Bodleian Library*. Vol. I: De la Mare, A. C., *The history of the library*; Vol. II: Gillam, S., *The history of the building*, Oxford.

De la Mare, A. C. and Hellinga, L. 1978 'The first book printed in Oxford: the *Expositio symboli* of Rufinus', *TCBS*, 7, 2, 184–244.

De la Mare, A. C. and Hunt, R. W. (eds.) 1970 *Duke Humfrey and English humanism in the fifteenth century. Catalogue of an exhibition held in the Bodleian Library, Oxford*, Oxford.

Delisle, L. 1868–81 *Le Cabinet des manuscrits de la Bibliothèque impériale [nationale]*, 3 vols., Paris.

    1896 'L'imprimeur parisien Josse Bade et le professeur écossais Jean Vaus', *Bibliothèque de l'Ecole des Chartes*, 57, 1–12.

    1907 *Recherches sur la librairie de Charles V*, 2 vols., Paris.

Denholm-Young, N. 1952 *Handwriting in England and Wales*, Oxford.

Derolez, A. 1979 *The library of Raphael de Mercatellis, abbot of St Bavon's, Ghent, 1437–1508*, Ghent.

Descriptive list of wardrobe books, Edward I – Edward IV, 1980, List and Index Society 168, London.

Destrez, J. 1935 *La pecia dans les manuscrits universitaires du XIIIe et du XIVe siècle*, Paris.

Devereux, E. J. 1968 *A check-list of English translations of Erasmus to 1700*, OBS Occasional Publications 3, Oxford.

    1969 'The publication of the English *Paraphrases* of Erasmus', *BJRL*, 51, 348–67.

Dionisotti, A. C. 1995 'Claude de Seyssel', in M. H. Crawford and C. R. Ligota (eds.), *Ancient history and the antiquarian. Essays in memory of Arnaldo Momigliano*, Warburg Institute Colloquia 2, London, 73–103.

Dodgson, C. 1929 'English devotional woodcuts of the late fifteenth century, with special reference to those in the Bodleian Library', *Walpole Society*, 17, 95–108.

    1936 *English woodcuts of the fifteenth century*, Strasbourg.

Dogaer, G. 1975 'Margaretha van York, bibliofiele', *Handelingen van de Koninklijke kring voor oudheidkunde, letteren en kunst van Mechelen*, 79, 99–111.

Dowling, M. 1986 *Humanism in the age of Henry VIII*, London.

1991 'Anne Boleyn as patron', in Starkey 1991, 107–11.

Doyle, A. I. 1952 'Further monastic books', *Durham Philobiblon* 1, 7, 45–8.

1953 'A survey of the origins and circulation of theological writings in English in the fourteenth, fifteenth and early sixteenth centuries, with special consideration to the part of the clergy therein', unpub. Ph.D. thesis, University of Cambridge.

1957 'The work of a late fifteenth-century scribe, William Ebesham', *BJRL*, 39, 298–325.

1958 'Books connected with the Vere family and Barking Abbey', *Trans. of the Essex Archaeological Soc.*, n.s., 25, 222–43.

1982 'The manuscripts', in D. Lawton (ed.), *Middle English alliterative poetry and its literary background*, Cambridge, 88–100.

1983a 'English books in and out of court from Edward III to Henry VII', in Scattergood and Sherborne 1983, 163–81.

1983b'Reflexions on some manuscripts of Nicholas Love's *Myrrour of the blessed lyf of Jesu Christ*', *Leeds Studies in English*, n.s., 14, 82–93.

1988 'The printed books of the last monks of Durham', *Library*, 6th ser., 10, 203–19.

1989 'Publication by members of the religious orders', in *BPPB*, 109–23.

1990 'Book production by the monastic orders in England (c. 1375–1530): assessing the evidence', in L. L. Brownrigg (ed.), *Medieval book production: assessing the evidence*, Los Altos Hills CA, 1–29.

Doyle, A. I. (ed.) 1987 *The Vernon manuscript: a facsimile of Bodleian Library, Oxford, MS Eng. Poet. a.1*, Cambridge.

Doyle, A. I. and Parkes, M. B. 1978 'The production of copies of the *Canterbury Tales* and the *Confessio Amantis* in the early fifteenth century', in *MSML*, 163–210.

Dreyfus, J. 1988 'The invention of spectacles and the advent of printing', *Library*, 6th ser., 10, 93–106.

Driver, M. W. 1987 'Illustrations in early English books: methods and problems', *Books at Brown*, 33, 1–57.

1989 'Pictures in print: late fifteenth- and early sixteenth-century English religious books for lay readers', in M. G. Sargent (ed.), *De cella in seculum: religious and secular life and devotion in late medieval England*, Woodbridge, 229–44.

1995 'Nuns as patrons, artists, readers: Bridgettine woodcuts in printed books produced for the English market', in C. G. Fisher and K. L. Scott (eds.), *Art into life: collected papers from the Kresge Art Museum medieval symposia*, East Lansing MI, 237–67.

1996 'The illustrated De Worde: an overview', in R. K. Emmerson and P. Sheingorn (eds.), *Studies in Iconography*, 17, 349–403.

1997 'Ideas of order: Wynkyn de Worde and the title page', in J. Boffey and V. J. Scattergood (eds.), *Texts in context*, Dublin, 1–28.

Drummond, H. J. H. 1979 *A short-title catalogue of books printed on the continent of Europe, 1501–1600, in Aberdeen University Library*, Oxford and New York.

Duck, Sir A. 1668 *De usu et authoritate juris civilis Romanorum in dominiis principum Christianorum*, Leipzig (rpt Vienna and Cologne 1990).

Duff, E. G. 1902 *English printing on vellum to the end of the year 1600*, Publications of the Bibliographical Society of Lancashire 1, Aberdeen.

1905 *A century of the English book trade. Short notices of all printers, stationers, book-binders, and others connected with it from the issue of the first dated book in 1457 to the incorporation of the Company of Stationers in 1557*, London (rpt 1948).

1906 *The printers, stationers and booksellers of Westminster and London from 1476 to 1535*, Cambridge.

1907a 'A bookseller's accounts, c.1510', *Library*, 2nd ser., 8, 255–66.

1907b 'Early Chancery proceedings concerning members of the book trade', *Library*, 2nd ser., 8, 408–20.

1907c 'Some early Scottish book-bindings and collectors', *Scottish Historical Rev*, 4, 430–42.

1908 'Notes on stationers from the Lay Subsidy Rolls of 1523–4', *Library*, 2nd ser., 9, 251–66.

1917 *Fifteenth century English books*, Oxford.

Duffy, E. 1992 *The stripping of the altars: traditional religion in England, 1400–1580*, New Haven and London.

Duggan, C. 1963 *Twelfth-century decretal collections and their importance in English history*, London.

Duncan, G. D. 1986 'Public lectures and professorial chairs', in *HUO*, III, 335–61.

Dunlop, A. I. (ed.) 1964 *Acta facultatis artium universitatis Sanctiandree 1413–1588*, Edinburgh and London.

Durham 1838 *Catalogues of the Library of Durham Cathedral, at various periods, from the Conquest to the Dissolution, including catalogues of the library of the abbey of Hulne, and of the mss. preserved in the library of Bishop Cosin, at Durham*, Surtees Society 7, London.

Durkan, J. 1953 'The beginnings of humanism in Scotland', *Innes Rev.*, 4, 5–24.

1959 'The cultural background in sixteenth-century Scotland', *Innes Rev.*, 10, 382–439.

1961a 'An Arbroath book inventory of 1473', *Bibliotheck*, 3, 144–6.

1961b 'The library of St Salvator's College, St Andrews', *Bibliotheck*, 3, 97–100.

1976 'The early history of Glasgow University Library: 1470–1710', *Bibliotheck*, 8, 102–26.

1980 'Early humanism and King's College', *Aberdeen University Rev.*, 48, 259–79.

1981 'Giovanni Ferrerio, humanist: his influence in sixteenth-century Scotland', in K. Robbins (ed.), *Religion and humanism: papers read at the meeting of the Ecclesiastical History Society*, Studies in church history 17, 181–94.

Durkan, J. and Kirk, J. 1977 *Glasgow University, 1451–1577*, Glasgow.

Durkan, J. and Ross, A. 1961 *Early Scottish libraries*, Glasgow. (Supplements: Durkan, J., *Bibliothek*, 4 (1963), 22–3; 9 (1978), 13–20; 10 (1981), 87–98; 11 (1982), 57–8; 12 (1985), 85–90.)

Durling, R. J. 1977 'Linacre and medical humanism', in F. R. Maddison, M. Pelling and C. Webster (eds.), *Linacre studies. Essays on the life and work of Thomas Linacre*, Oxford, 76–106.

Dutschke, C. 1989 *Guide to medieval and Renaissance manuscripts in the Huntington Library*, 2 vols., San Marino CA.

Dyboski, R. and Arend, Z. M. (eds.) 1935 *Knyghthode and bataile*, EETS OS 201, London.

Eccles, M. (ed.) 1969 *The Macro plays*, EETS OS 262, London.

Edmunds, S. 1991 'From Schoeffer to Vérard: concerning the scribes who became printers', in Hindman 1991, 21–40.

Edwards, A. S. G. 1980 'Poet and printer in sixteenth-century England: Stephen Hawes and Wynkyn de Worde', *Gutenberg-Jahrbuch*, 82–8.

1984 *Middle English prose: a critical guide to major authors and genres*, New Brunswick NJ.

1991 'From manuscript to print: Wynkyn de Worde and the printing of contemporary poetry', *Gutenberg-Jahrbuch*, 143–8.

1995 'Continental influences on London printing and reading in the fifteenth and early sixteenth centuries', in J. Boffey and P. King (eds.), *London and Europe in the later Middle Ages*, 229–56.

Edwards, A. S. G. (ed.) 1985 *MS Pepys 2006*, Norman OK.

Edwards, A. S. G. and Meale, C. M. 1993 'The marketing of printed books in late medieval England', *Library*, 6th ser., 15, 95–124.

Edwards, A. S. G. and Pearsall, D. 1989 'The manuscripts of the major English poetic texts', in *BPPB*, 257–78.

Eisner, S. (ed.) 1980 *The Kalendarium of Nicholas of Lynn*, London.

Elliott, K. 1964 'Church musick at Dunkell', *Music and Letters*, 45, 228–32.

Ellis, Sir H. (ed.) 1824–46 *Original letters illustrative of English history*, 1st–3rd ser., 11 vols., London.

Elrington, C. R. (ed.) 1968 *VCH, Gloucester*, vol. VIII, London.

Elton, G. R. 1974–83 *Studies in Tudor and Stuart politics and government*, 3 vols., Cambridge.

1978 'The sessional printing of statutes, 1484 –1547', in Ives 1978, 68–86 (rpt in Elton 1974–83, III, pp. 92–109).

1981 *Policy and police: the enforcement of the Reformation in the age of Thomas Cromwell*, Cambridge (rpt).

Elvey, E. M. (ed.) 1975 *Courts of the Archdeaconry of Buckingham, 1483–1528*, Buckinghamshire Record Soc. 19, London.

Emden, A. B. 1968 *Donors of books to S. Augustine's Abbey Canterbury*, OBS, Occasional Pub. 4, Oxford.

Epistolae Tigurinae de rebus potissimum ad ecclesiae Anglicanae reformationem conscriptae A. D. 1531–1558, 1848, Parker Soc., Cambridge .

Erler, G. (ed.) 1895–1902 *Der Matrikel der Universität Leipzig*, 3 vols., Codex diplomaticus Saxoniae Regiae, 2. 17, Leipzig.

Erler, M. C. 1984 'The *Maner to lyue well* and the coming of English in François Regnault's primers of the 1520s and 1530s', *Library*, 6th ser., 6, 229–43.

1988 'Wynkyn de Worde's will', *Library*, 6th ser., 10, 107–21.

1992 'Pasted-in embellishments in English manuscripts and printed books c. 1480–1533', *Library*, 6th ser., 14, 185–206.

1993 'The books and lives of three Tudor women', in Jean R. Brink (ed.), *Privileging gender in early modern England*, Sixteenth-century essays and studies 23,

Kirksville MO, 5–17.

1994 'Three fifteenth-century vowesses', in C. Barron and A. Sutton (eds.), *Medieval London widows, 1300–1500*, London, 165–81.

Evans, T. A. R. 1992 'The number, origins and careers of scholars', in *HUO*, II, 485–538.

Fairfield, L. P. 1972 'The mysterious press of "Michael Wood" (1553–1554)', *Library*, 5th ser., 27, 220–32.

Fallows, D. 1977 'English song repertories of the mid-fifteenth century', *Proc. of the Royal Musical Assoc.*, 103, 61–79.

1993 'Henry VIII as a composer', in Banks, Searle and Turner 1993, 27–39.

Farquhar, J. D. 1976 *Creation and imitation: the work of a fifteenth-century manuscript illuminator*, Fort Lauderdale FL.

1980 'Identity in an anonymous age: Bruges manuscript illuminators and their signs', *Viator*, 2, 371–83.

Farrer, W. and Brownbull, J. (eds.) 1908 VCH, *Lancaster*, II, London.

Farris, G. 1972 *Umanesimo e religione in Lorenzo Guglielmo Traversagni, 1425–1505*, Milan.

Fava, D. and Salmi, M. 1950–73 *I manoscritti miniati della Biblioteca Estense di Modena*, 2 vols., Florence.

Febvre, L. and Martin, H.-J. 1958–76 *L'apparition du livre*, Paris. Transl. *The coming of the book*, London, 1976.

Fenlon, I. 1981 'La diffusion de la chanson continentale dans les manuscrits anglais entre 1509–70', in J.-M. Vaccaro (ed.), *La chanson à la Renaissance. Actes du XXe colloque d'etudes humanistes du Centre d'Etudes Supérieures de la Renaissance de l'Université de Tours, juillet 1977*, Tours, 172–89.

1995 *Print and culture in early sixteenth-century Italy* (The Panizzi Lectures, 1994), London.

Fenlon, I. (ed.) 1982 *Cambridge music manuscripts 900–1700*, Cambridge.

Ferdinand, C. Y. 1997 'Magdalen College and the book-trade: the provision of books in Oxford 1450–1550', in A. Hunt, G. Mandelbrote and A. Shell (eds.), *The book trade and its customers, 1450–1900: historical essays for Robin Myers*, Winchester and New Castle DE, 175–87.

Ferme, B. 1989 'The testamentary executor in Lyndwood's *Provinciale*', *Jurist*, 49, 632–78.

A fifteenth-century song book, 1973, Early music in facsimile 1, Leeds.

Fisher, J. H. (ed.) 1951 *The Tretyse of loue*, EETS OS 223, London.

Fitzherbert, Sir A. 1516 *La graunde abridgement de le ley*, London.

1534 *La nouel natura brevium*, London.

Fleming, P. W. 1987 'The Hautes and their "circle": culture and the English gentry', in D. Williams (ed.), *England in the fifteenth century: proceedings of the 1986 Harlaxton Symposium*, Woodbridge.

Fletcher, B. Y. (ed.) 1987 *Manuscript Trinity College R.3.19*, Norman OK.

Fletcher, J. M. 1961 'Addendum to "Provost Argentine of King's and his books"', *TCBS*, 3, 3, 263.

1962 'The teaching and study of arts at Oxford *c.* 1400–*c.* 1520', unpub. D.Phil. thesis, University of Oxford.

1967 'The teaching of arts at Oxford', *Paedagogica historica*, 7, 417–54.

1974 'A fifteenth-century benefaction to Magdalen College library', *BLR*, 9, 3, 169–72.

1981 'Change and resistance to change: a consideration of the development of English and German universities during the sixteenth century', *History of Universities*, 1, 1–36.

1986 'The faculty of arts', in *HUO*, III, 157–99.

1992 'Developments in the faculty of arts 1370–1530', in *HUO*, II, 315–45.

Fletcher, J. M. (ed.) 1974 *Registrum annalium Collegii Mertonensis 1521–1567*, OHS n.s. 24, Oxford.

Fletcher, J. M. and McConica, J. K. 1961 'A sixteenth-century inventory of the library of Corpus Christi College, Cambridge', *TCBS*, 3, 3, 187–99.

Flynn, J. 1995 'The education of choristers in England during the sixteenth century', in Morehen 1995, 180–99.

Flynn, V. J. 1943 'The grammatical writings of William Lily, ?1468–?1523', *PBSA*, 37, 85–113.

Fogelmark, S. 1990 *Flemish and related panel-stamped bindings*, New York.

Foot, M. M. 1978 *The Henry Davis Gift*, 1, London.

1992 'The future of bookbinding research', in Davison 1992, 99–106.

1993 *Studies in the history of bookbinding*, Aldershot.

Fortescue, Sir J. 1942 *De laudibus legum Anglie*, ed. S. B. Chrimes, Cambridge.

Fowler, T. 1893 *The history of Corpus Christi College*, OHS 25, Oxford.

Fox, D. 1977 'Manuscripts and prints of Scots poetry in the sixteenth century', in A. J. Aitken *et al.* (eds.), *Bards and makars*, Glasgow, 156–71.

Fox, D. and Ringler, W. A. (eds.) 1980 *The Bannatyne manuscript*, Edinburgh.

Foxe, J. 1877–9 *Acts and monuments of John Foxe*, ed. S. R. Cattley and J. Pratt, 8 vols., London.

Francis, F. C. (ed.) 1945 *The Bibliographical Society 1892–1942: studies in retrospect*, London.

Fryde, E. B. 1983 'The library of Lorenzo de' Medici', in Fryde, *Humanism and Renaissance historiography*, London, 159–227.

Fugler, P. 1983 'The Lambeth and Caius choirbooks', *Jnl of the Plainsong and Mediaeval Music Soc.*, 6, 15–25.

Fuller, T. 1840 *History of the University of Cambridge*, ed. M. Prickett and T. Wright, Cambridge.

Furnivall, F. J. 1867 'Pynson's contracts with Horman for his *Vulgaria*, and Palsgrave for the *Lesclairissement*, with Pynson's letter of denization', *Trans. of the Philological Soc.*, 362–74.

1868 'The Neville and Southwell families of Mereworth in Kent', *N&Q*, 4th ser., 2, 577–8.

Gabel, L. C. 1928–9 *Benefit of clergy in England in the later Middle Ages*, Smith College Studies in History 14, Northampton, MA (rpt 1969).

Gairdner, J. (ed.) 1858 *Historia Regis Henrici Septimi*, Rolls Series 10, London.

Gameson, R. and Coates, A. 1988 *The Old Library, Trinity College, Oxford*, Oxford.

Gardiner, S. 1933 *The letters of Stephen Gardiner*, ed. J. A. Muller, Cambridge.

Garrod, H. W. 1928 'The library regulations of a medieval college', *Library*, 4th ser., 8, 312–35.

Garton, C. 1980 'A fifteenth-century headmaster's library', *Lincolnshire History and Archaeology*, 15, 29–38.

Gaskell, P. 1972 *A new introduction to bibliography*, Oxford.

1980 *Trinity College Library: the first 150 years. The Sandars Lectures, 1978–9*, Cambridge.

1983 'An early inventory of Trinity College books', *TCBS*, 8, 3, 334–41.

Geoghegan, D. 1957 'A license of Henry VI to practise alchemy', *Ambix* 6, 10–17.

Geritz, A. J. and Laine, A. L. 1983 *John Rastell*, Boston, MA.

Getz, F. M., 1992 'The faculty of medicine before 1500', in *HUO*, 11, 373–405.

Getz, F. M. (ed.)1991 *Healing and society in medieval England: a Middle English translation of the pharmaceutical writings of Gilbertus Anglicus*, Madison WI.

Giard, L. 1985 'La production logique de l'Angleterre au 16ᵉ siècle', *Les études philosophiques*, 3, 303–24.

Gibson, G. M. 1989 *The theater of devotion: East Anglian drama and society in the late Middle Ages*, Chicago and London.

Gibson, R. W. 1961 *St Thomas More: a preliminary bibliography of his works and of Moreana to the year 1750*, New Haven and London.

Gibson, S. 1903 *Early Oxford bindings*, OBS Illustrated Monographs 10, Oxford.

Gibson, S. (ed.) 1931 *Statuta antiqua Universitatis Oxoniensis*, Oxford.

Gillespie, V. 1984 'Lukynge in haly bukes: *lectio* in some late medieval spiritual miscellanies', *Analecta Cartusiana*, 106, 1–27.

1989 'Vernacular books of religion', in *BPPB*, 317–44.

Given-Wilson, C. J. 1986 *The Royal household and the king's affinity: service, politics and finance in England, 1360–1413*, New Haven and London.

Glazebrook, P. R. 1972 Introduction to Sir A. Fitzherbert, *The newe boke of justices of the peas (1538)*, London.

Gleason, J. B. 1982 'The earliest evidence for ecclesiastical censorship of printed books in England', *Library*, 6th ser., 4, 135–41.

Goldberg, P. J. P. 1994 'Lay book ownership in late medieval York: the evidence of wills', *Library*, 6th ser., 16, 181–9.

Goldschmidt, E. P. 1943 *Medieval texts and their first appearance in print*, London (rpt 1965).

1955 *The first Cambridge press in its European setting*, Cambridge.

Goody, J. (ed.) 1968 *Literacy in traditional societies*, Cambridge.

Goulet, R. 1965 *Compendium recenter editum de multiplici Parisiensis Universitatis magnificentia, 1517*, in L. Lukács (ed.), *Monumenta paedogogica Soc. Iesu 1, 1540–56*, Rome, 618–31.

Grafton, A. 1981 'Teacher, text and pupil in the Renaissance class-room: a case study from a Parisian college', *History of Universities*, 1, 37–70.

1985 'Renaissance readers and ancient texts: comments on some commentaries', *Renaissance Quarterly* 38, 615–49; rpt Grafton, *Defenders of the text: the traditions of scholarship in an age of science, 1450–1800*, Cambridge MA and London 1991, 23–46.

1997a 'Is the history of reading a marginal enterprise? Guillaume Budé and his books', *PBSA*, 91, 139–57.

1997b 'How Guillaume Budé read his Homer', in A. Grafton, *Commerce with the classics: ancient books and Renaissance readers* (Thomas Spencer Jerome Lectures 20), Ann Arbor MI, 135–83.

Grafton, A. (ed.) 1993 *Rome reborn: the Vatican Library and Renaissance culture*, Washington DC and New Haven.

Grafton, A. and Jardine, L. A. 1986 *From humanism to the humanities: education and the liberal arts in fifteenth- and sixteenth-century Europe*, London.

1990 '"Studied for action": how Gabriel Harvey read his Livy', *Past and Present*, 129, 30–78.

Graham, H. J. 1954 'The Rastells and the printed English law book of the Renaissance', *Law Lib. Jnl*, 47, 6–25.

1965 'The first Englishing and printing of the medieval statutes at large', *UCLA Law Rev*, 13, 58–98.

Graham, H. J. and Heckel, J. W. 1958 'The Book that "made" the common law', *Law Lib. Jnl*, 51, 100–16.

Gras, N. S. B. 1918 *The early English customs system*, Harvard Economic Stud. 18, Cambridge MA.

Gray, D. 1961 'A Middle English epitaph', *N&Q*, 206, pp. 132–5.

1963 'The five wounds of our Lord', *N&Q*, 208, 50–1, 82–9, 127–34, 163–8.

Gray, G. J. 1904 *The earlier Cambridge stationers and bookbinders and the first Cambridge printer*, Bibliographical Soc. Illust. Monographs 13, London.

Gray, G. J. and Palmer, W. M. 1915 *Abstracts from the wills and testamentary documents of printers, binders and stationers of Cambridge, from 1504 to 1699*, London.

Green, R. F. 1976 'King Richard II's books revisited', *Library*, 5th ser., 31, 235–9.

1980 *Poets and princepleasers: literature and the English court in the late Middle Ages*, Toronto.

Greenslade, S. L. 1963 'English versions of the Bible 1525–1611', in S. L. Greenslade (ed.), *The Cambridge history of the Bible*. Vol. III: *The West from the Reformation to the present day*, Cambridge, 141–74.

Greg, W. W. 1945 'Bibliography – a retrospect', *Studies in Retrospect*, 23–31.

1956 *Some aspects and problems of London publishing between 1550 and 1650*, Oxford.

1966 'Ad imprimendum solum', *Library*, 5th ser., 9, 242–7 (rpt in Greg, *Collected papers*, ed. J. C. Maxwell, Oxford 1966, 406–12).

Griffiths, A. 1996 *Prints and printmaking: an introduction to the history and techniques*, London.

Groag Bell, S. 1992 'Medieval women book owners: arbiters of lay piety and ambassadors of culture', *Signs*, 7, 742–68.

Guiges I. 1984 *Coutumes de Chartreuse*, ed. Un Chartreux, Sources chrétiennes 313, Paris.

Gunner, W. H. 1858 'Catalogue of books belonging to the College of St Mary, Winchester, in the reign of Henry VI', *Archaeological Jnl*, 15, 59–74.

Gurewich, V. 1957 'Observations on the iconography of the wound in Christ's side', *JWCI*, 20, 358–62.

Guy, J. A. 1977 *The Cardinal's court: the impact of Thomas Wolsey on the Star Chamber*, Hassocks.

1988 *Tudor England*, Oxford (rpt 1990).

Gwosdek, H. 1991 *Early printed editions of the Long Accidence and Short Accidence grammars*, Heidelberg.

1993 'Subject matter and its arrangement in the *Accedence* manuscripts and in the early printed *Long Accidence* and *Short Accidence* Grammars', *Leeds Stud. in English*, n.s., 24, 133–53.

1994 'A new fragment of the early printed *Long Accidence* grammar', *BJRL*, 76, 187–93.

Gwynne, P. G. 1990 'The life and works of Johannes Michael Nagonius, "poeta laureatus", c. 1450–c. 1510', unpub. Ph.D. thesis, University of London, Warburg Institute.

Haines, C. R. 1928 'The library of Dover Priory: its catalogue and extant volumes', *Library*, 4th ser., 8, 73–118.

Hale, W. H. (ed.) 1847 *A series of precedents and proceedings . . . 1475 to 1640*, London.

Halkin, L.-E., Bierlaire, F. and Hoven, R. 1972 Introduction to *ASD*, I, 3, Amsterdam, 3–23.

Hallam, E. M. and Roper, M. 1978 'The capital and the records of the nation: seven centuries of housing the public records of London', *London Jnl*, 4, 73–94.

Halyburton, A. 1867 *The Ledger of Andrew Halyburton. Conservator of the privileges of the Scottish nation in the Netherlands, 1492–1503*, Edinburgh.

Hamburger, J. 1991 'The Casanatense and the Carmelite missals: continental sources for English manuscript illumination of the early 15th century', in K. van der Horst and J.-C. Clamt (eds.), *Masters and miniatures. Proceedings of the congress on medieval manuscript illumination in the northern Netherlands (Utrecht, 10–13 December 1989)*, Doornspijk, 161–73.

De Hamel, C. F. R. 1983 'Reflexions on the trade in books of hours at Ghent and Bruges', in Trapp 1983, 29–33.

1986 *A history of illuminated manuscripts*, Oxford; 2nd edn 1990.

1991 *Syon Abbey: the library of the Bridgettine nuns and their peregrinations after the Reformation*, Roxburghe Club, London.

[De Hamel, C. F. R.] 1988 *The Astor Collection of illuminated manuscripts*, Sotheby's book auction, 21 June, London.

Hamesse, J. (ed.) 1974. *Les Auctoritates Aristotelis. Un florilège médiéval. Etude historique et édition critique*, Philosophes médiévaux 17, Louvain, Paris.

Hammond, E. P. 1904 'MS Longleat 258: a Chaucerian codex', *MLN*, 19, 96–8.

Hammond, E. P. (ed.) 1927 *English verse between Chaucer and Surrey*, Durham NC.

Hands, Rachel (ed.) 1975 *English hunting and hawking in the Boke of St Albans*, facsim., London.

Hanham, A. (ed.) 1975 *The Cely letters, 1472–1488*, EETS 273, London.

Hanna, R., III, 1989a 'Sir Thomas Berkeley and his patronage', *Speculum*, 64, 878–916.

Hanna, R., III (ed.), 1989b *The Ellesmere manuscript. A working facsimile*, Cambridge.

Hannay, M. P. (ed.). 1985 *Silent but for the word: Tudor women as patrons, translators, and writers of religious works*, Kent OH.

Hargreaves, H. 1969 'The Wycliffite versions', in G. W. H. Lampe (ed.), *The Cambridge history of the Bible. Vol. II: The West from the Fathers to the Reformation*, Cambridge, 387–414.

Harper-Bill, C. (ed.) 1987–91 *The Register of John Morton, Archbishop of Canterbury 1486–1500*, 2 vols., Canterbury and York Society, London.

Harrier, R. 1975 *The canon of Sir Thomas Wyatt's poetry*, Cambridge MA.

Harris, J. 1995 *Greek emigrés in the West 1400–1520*, Camberley.

Harris, K. 1983 'The origins and make-up of Cambridge University Library MS Ff. 1. 6', *TCBS*, 8, 3, 299–333.

1989 'Patrons, buyers and owners: the evidence for ownership, and the role of book owners in book production and the book trade', in *BPPB*, 163–99.

Harrison, F. L. 1980 *Music in medieval Britain*, 4th edn, Buren.

Harrison, F. L. (ed.) 1956–67 *The Eton choirbook*, Musica Britannica 10–12, London: 2nd edn, 10 only.

Harriss, G. L. 1972 'Henry V's books', in K. B. McFarlane (ed.), *Lancastrian kings and Lollard knights*, Oxford, 233–8.

Harrod, H. 1855 'Extracts from early Norfolk wills', *Norfolk Archaeology*, 4, 317–39.

Härtel, H. and Hellinga, L. (eds.) 1981 *Buch und Text im 15. Jahrhundert. Book and text in the 15th century. Arbeitsgespräch in der Herzog August Bibliothek Wolfenbüttel ... proceedings of a conference held in the Herzog August Bibliothek ... 1978*, Hamburg.

Harthan, J. 1977 *The book of hours*, London and New York.

Hatcher, J. 1977 *Plague, population and the English economy 1348–1530*, London.

Haveley, N. R. 1980 *Chaucer's Boccaccio*, Cambridge.

Heale, E. 1995 'Women and the courtly love lyric: the Devonshire ms. (BL Add. 17492)', *MLR*, 90, 296–313.

Heath, Terrence 1971 'Logical grammar, grammatical logic and humanism in three German universities', *SR*, 18, 9–64.

Hector, L. C. 1966 *The handwriting of English documents*, 2nd edn, London.

Hellinga, L. 1981a 'The Book of St Albans 1486', in C. F. R. de Hamel and R. A. Linenthal (eds.), *Fine books and book collecting: books and manuscripts acquired from Alan G. Thomas ...*, Leamington Spa, 31–4.

1981b 'The Malory manuscript and Caxton', in T. Takamiya and D. Brewer (eds.), *Aspects of Malory*, Cambridge, 127–41.

1982 *Caxton in focus: the beginning of printing in England*, London.

1983 'Manuscripts in the hands of printers', in Trapp 1983, 3–11.

1987 'Three notes on printers' copy: Strassburg, Oxford, Subiaco', *TCBS*, 9, 2, 194–204.

1988 ' "Aesopus moralisatus", Antwerp 1488 in the hands of English owners: some thoughts on the study of the trade in Latin books', in W. Milde and W. Schuder (eds.), *De captu lectoris. Wirkungen des Buchs im 15. und 16. Jt. dargestellt an ausgewählten Handschriften und Drucken*, Berlin and New York, 135–43.

1991a 'Importation of books printed on the Continent into England and Scotland before c. 1520', in Hindman 1991, 205–24.

1991b 'Reading an engraving: William Caxton's dedication to Margaret of York, Duchess of Burgundy', in S. Roach (ed.), *Across the narrow seas: studies in the history and bibliography of Britain and the Low Countries presented to Anna C. Simoni*, London, 1–15.

1994 'Peter Schoeffer and the book-trade in Mainz: evidence for the organization', in D. E. Rhodes (ed.), *Bookbindings & other bibliophily: essays in honour of Anthony Hobson*, Verona, 131–83.

1995 'Wynkyn de Worde's native land', in R. Beadle and A. J. Piper (eds.), *New science out of old books: studies in manuscripts and early printed books in honour of A. I. Doyle*, Aldershot, 342–59.

1997a 'Nicholas Love in print', in S. Oguro, R. Beadle and M. G. Sargent (eds.), *Nicholas Love at Waseda: proceedings of the international conference 20–22 July 1995*, Woodbridge, 144–62.

1997b 'Text and press in the first decades of printing', in *Libri, tipografi, biblioteche: ricerche storiche dedicate a Luigi Balsamo*, Biblioteca di bibliografia Italiana 148, Florence, 1–23.

Hellinga, L. and Goldfinch, J. (eds.) 1987 *Bibliography and the study of fifteenth-century civilization*, BL Occasional Papers 5, London.

Hellinga, L. and Hellinga, W. 1974 'Regulations relating to the planning and organization of work by the master printer in the Ordinances of Christopher Plantin', *Library*, 5th ser., 29, 52–60.

Hellinga, W. Gs 1962 *Copy and print in the Netherlands: an atlas of historical bibliography*, with introductory essays by H. de la Fontaine Verwey and G. W. Ovink, Amsterdam.

Helmholz, R. H. 1974 *Marriage litigation in medieval England*, Cambridge.

1987 *Canon law and the law of England*, London and Ronceverte WV.

1990 *Roman canon law in Reformation England*, Cambridge.

1992 'Canon law in post-Reformation England', in *Canon law in Protestant lands*, Berlin, 218–21.

Henderson, E. G. 1975 'Legal literature and the impact of printing on the English legal profession', *Law Lib. Jnl*, 68, 288–93.

Henkel, N. 1988 *Deutsche Übersetzungen lateinischer Schultexte: Ihre Verbreitung und Funktion in der frühen Neuzeit, mit einem Verzeichnis der Texte*, Munich, 242–3.

Herendeen, W. M. and Bartlett, K. R. 1991 'The library of Cuthbert Tunstall, bishop of Durham: BL, Add. MS 40676', *PBSA*, 85, 235–96.

Hill, G. 1964 'The sermons of John Watson, canon of Aberdeen', *Innes Rev.*, 15, 3–34.

Hills, R. 1992 'John Tate and his paper: England's first paper mill', in H. Morris (ed.), *Three lions and the Cross of Lorraine: Bartholomaeus Anglicus, John of Trevisa, John Tate, Wynkyn de Worde, and 'De proprietatibus rerum'*, Newtown PA, 23–33.

Hillyard, B. 1994 'Durkan and Ross revisited', in MacDonald, Lynch and Cowan 1994, 367–84.

Hilton, W. 1991 *The Scale of Perfection*, trans. J. P. H. Clark and R. Dorward, New York.

Hind, A. M. 1935 *An introduction to a history of woodcut, with a detailed survey of work done in the fifteenth century*, London.

1952 *Engraving in England in the sixteenth and seventeenth centuries*, pt 1: *The Tudor period*, Cambridge.

Hindman, S. (ed). 1991 *Printing the written word: the social history of books, circa 1450–1520*, Ithaca NY and London.

Hindman, S. and Farquhar, J. D. (eds.) 1977 *Pen to press: illustrated manuscripts and printed books in the first century of printing*, Baltimore MD.

Hinman, C. 1963 *The printing and proof-reading of the First Folio of Shakespeare*, Oxford.

Hirsch, R. 1967 *Printing, selling and reading 1450–1550*, Wiesbaden.

Hobson, G. D. 1929 *Bindings in Cambridge libraries*, Cambridge.

Hofman, M. and Morehen, J. (eds.) 1987 *Latin music in British sources c. 1485 – c. 1610* (*Early English church music*, supplementary vol. II), London.

Holbrook, S. E. 1987 'Margery Kempe and Wynkyn de Worde', in M. Glasscoe (ed.), *The Medieval mystical tradition in England: Exeter symposium IV, Dartington 1987*, Cambridge, 27–46.

Holman, P. 1991 'Music at the court of Henry VII', in Starkey 1991, 104–6.

Holmes, R. R. 1893 *Specimens of royal fine and historical bookbinding selected from the Royal Library, Windsor Castle*, London.

Holthöfer, E. 1977 'Die Literatur zum gemeinen und partikularen Recht in Italien, Frankreich, Spanien und Portugal', in Coing 1973–7, II, 1, pp. 103–500.

Horn, N. 1973 'Die legistische Literatur der Kommentatoren und der Ausbreitung des gelehrten Rechts', in Coing 1973–7, I, pp. 261–354.

Horstmann, C. (ed.) 1886 *The Three kings of Cologne. An early English translation of the 'Historia trium regum' by John of Hildesheim*, EETS OS 85, London.

Hoskins, E. 1901 *Horae Beatae Mariae Virginis, or Sarum and York primers, with kindred books and primers of the reformed Roman rite*, London.

Howell, W. S. 1956 *Logic and rhetoric in England, 1500–1700*, Princeton.

Howlett, D. 1975 'Studies in the works of John Whethamstede', unpub. D.Phil. thesis, University of Oxford.

Hubay, I. 1979 'Die bekannten Exemplare der zweiundvierzigzeilen Bible und ihre Besitzer', in W. Schmitt and F. A. Schmidt-Künsenmüller (eds.), *Johannes Gutenbergs zweiundvierzigzeilige Bibel . . . Kommentarband*, Munich, 127–55.

Hudson, A. 1983 ' "No newe thyng": the printing of medieval texts in the early Reformation period', in D. Gray and E. G. Stanley (eds.), *Middle English studies presented to Norman Davis*, Oxford, 153–74.

1985 *Lollards and their books*, London.

1988 *The premature Reformation: Wycliffite texts and Lollard history*, Oxford.

1989 'Lollard book-production', in *BPPB*, 125–42.

1994 'Laicus literatus', in Biller and Hudson 1994, 222–36.

Hughes, A. 1982 *Medieval manuscripts for mass and office: a guide to their organization and terminology*, Toronto.

Hughes, J. 1988 *Pastors and visionaries: religion and secular life in late medieval Yorkshire*, Woodbridge.

Hughes, M. J. 1984 'Margaret of York, Duchess of Burgundy: diplomat, patroness, bibliophile, and benefactress', *Private Library*, 3rd. ser., 7, 2–17, 53–78.

Hull, S. 1982 *Chaste, silent and obedient: English books for women 1475–1640*, San Marino CA.

Hume, A. 1973 'English Protestant books printed abroad, 1525–1535; an annotated bibliography', *CWM*, VIII, 1063–92.

Hunt, R. W. 1950 'Medieval inventories of Clare College Library', *TCBS*, 1, 2, 105–25.

1950–1 'The manuscript collection of University College, Oxford', *BLR*, 3, 13–34.

1978 'The library of the abbey of St Albans', in *MSML*, 251–77.

Hunt, T. 1987 'The "Novel Cirurgerie" in MS London, British Library, Harley 2558', *Zeitschrift für romanische Philologie*, 103, 271–99.

1991 *Teaching and learning Latin in thirteenth-century England*, 3 vols., Woodbridge.

Hunter, D. 1978 *Papermaking: the history and technique of an ancient craft*, rev. edn, New York, London.

Hunter, G. K. 1951 'The marking of "sententiae" in Elizabethan printed plays, poems and romances', *Library*, 5th ser., 6, 171–88.

Hunter, J. 1831 *English monastic libraries*, London.

Hutchinson, A. M. 1989 'Devotional reading in the monastery and in the late medieval household', in Sargent 1989, 215–27.

Hutton, R. 1987 'The local impact of the Tudor Reformations', in C. Haigh (ed.), *The English Reformation revised*, Cambridge, 114–38.

Inderwick, F. A. 1896–1919 *A calendar of the Inner Temple records, 1505–1714*, 3 vols., London.

Iniunccions geven by the kynges maiestie . . . M.D.XLVII, 1547, London.

Isaac, F. 1930–2 *English & Scottish printing types 1501–35, 1508–41; 1535–58, 1552–58*, Bibliographical Soc. Illustrated Monographs 2, Oxford.

    1931 'Egidius van der Erve and his English printed books', *Library*, 4th ser., 12, 336–52.

    1936 *English printers' types of the sixteenth century*, Oxford.

Ives, E. W. 1969 'A lawyer's library in 1500', *LQR*, 85, 104–16.

    1973 'The purpose and making of the later Year Books', *LQR*, 89, 64–86.

    1983 *The Common lawyers of pre-Reformation England*, Cambridge.

    1986 *Anne Boleyn*, Oxford.

Ives, E. W., Knecht, R.J. and Scarisbrick, J. J. (eds.) 1978 *Wealth and power in Tudor England: essays presented to S. T. Bindoff*, London.

Jackson, W. A. 1936 'A London bookseller's ledger of 1535', *Colophon* n.s., 1, 498–509.

Jacob, E. F. 1944 'The Book of St Albans', *BJRL*, 28, 99–118.

    1971 'Panormitanus and the council of Basel', in S. Kuttner (ed.), *Proceedings of the third international Congress of medieval canon law*, Vatican City, 205–15.

Jacob, E. F. and Johnson, H. C. (eds.) 1938–47 *The Register of Henry Chichele, Archbishop of Canterbury 1414–1443*, 4 vols., Oxford.

James, M. R. 1895 *A descriptive catalogue of the manuscripts other than oriental in the library of King's College, Cambridge*, Cambridge.

    1899 'A catalogue of Thomas Markaunt's library from ms Corpus Christi College, Cambridge, 232', *Cambridge Antiquarian Soc. Octavo series*, 32, 76–82.

    1900–4 *The Western manuscripts in the library of Trinity College, Cambridge*, 4 vols., Cambridge.

    1903 *The ancient libraries of Canterbury and Dover*, Cambridge.

    1909 'The catalogue of the library of the Augustinian friars at York', *Fasciculus Ioanni Willis Clark dicatus*, Cambridge, 2–96.

    1912 *A descriptive catalogue of the manuscripts of Corpus Christi College*, Cambridge.

    1933 'The manuscripts of St George's Chapel, Windsor', *Library*, 4th ser., 13, 55–76.

    1980 'Collections of manuscripts at Cambridge: their history, sources and contents', *TCBS*, 7, 4, 395–410.

James, M.R. (ed.) 1936–41 'Catalogue of the library of Leicester abbey', *Trans. of the Leicestershire Archaeological Soc.*, 19 (1936–7), 111–61, 377–440; 21 (1939–41), 1–88.

James, M. R. and Jenkins, C. 1930–2 *A descriptive catalogue of the manuscripts in the library of Lambeth Palace*, 4 vols., Cambridge.

James, T. 1605 *Catalogus librorum bibliothecæ publicæ quam vir ornatissimus Thomas Bodleius eques auratus in Academia Oxoniensi nuper instituit*, Oxford.

Jannetta, M. J. 1997 'Good news from Stuttgart. A previously unrecorded copy of the 1525 Worms edition of William Tyndale's New Testament translation', *Reformation*, 2, 1–5.

Jardine, L. A. 1974 'The place of dialectic teaching in sixteenth-century Cambridge', *SR*, 21, 31–62.

1975 'Humanism and the sixteenth-century Cambridge arts course', *History of Education* 4, 16–31.

1988 'Humanistic logic', in *Cambridge history of Renaissance philosophy*, Cambridge, 173–98.

Jarvis, R. C. 1959 'The archival history of the customs records', *Jnl of the Soc. of Archivists*, 1, 239–45.

1977 'Books of rates', *Jnl of the Soc. of Archivists*, 5, 515–26.

Jayne, S. R. 1963 *John Colet and Marsilio Ficino*, London.

1983 *Library catalogues of the English Renaissance*, Berkeley and Los Angeles (1956); rev. rpt Godalming.

Jensen, K. 1986 '*De emendata structura Latini sermonis*: the Latin grammar of Thomas Linacre', *JWCI*, 49, 106–25.

1993 'Notable accessions', *BLR*, 14, 321–31.

Jeudwine, W. 1979 *Art and style in printed books: six centuries of typography, decoration and illustration*. Vol. 1: *The fifteenth and sixteenth centuries*, privately printed for the author, London.

Jewell, H. M. 1982 'The cultural interests and achievements of the secular personnel of the local administration', in C. H. Clough (ed.), *Profession, vocation and culture in later medieval England: essays dedicated to the memory of A. R. Myers*, Liverpool, 130–54.

Johnson, J. and Gibson, S. 1946 *Print and privilege at Oxford to the year 1700*, London.

Jolliffe, P. S. 1974 *A check-list of Middle English prose writings of spiritual guidance*, Toronto.

Jones, M. K. and Underwood, M. G. 1992 *The King's mother, Lady Margaret Beaufort, Countess of Richmond and Derby*, Cambridge.

Jones, P. H. and Rees, E. (eds.) 1998 *A nation and its books: a history of the book in Wales*, Aberystwyth.

Jones, P. M. 1984 *Medieval medical miniatures*, London.

1989 'Four Middle English translations of John of Arderne', in A. J. Minnis (ed.), *Latin and vernacular: studies in late medieval manuscripts*, Woodbridge, 61–89.

1990 'British Library ms Sloane 76: a translator's holograph', in L. L. Brownrigg (ed.), *Medieval book production: assessing the evidence*, Los Altos Hills CA, 21–39.

1994 'Information and science', in R. Horrox (ed.), *Fifteenth-century attitudes*, London, 97–111.

1995a 'Harley ms 2558: a fifteenth-century medical commonplace book', in M. R. Schleisner (ed.), *Manuscript sources of medieval medicine*, New York, 35–54.

1995b 'Reading medicine in Tudor Cambridge', in V. E. Nutton and R. Porter (eds.), *The history of medical education in Britain*, Amsterdam, 153–83.

Jones, R. F. 1953 *The triumph of the English language: a survey of opinions concerning the vernacular from the introduction of printing to the Restoration*, Stanford CA.

Juchhoff, R. 1954 'Johannes de Westfalia als Buchhändler', *Gutenberg-Jahrbuch 1954*, 133–56.

Keen, M. H. 1986 'The influence of Wyclif', in A. J. P. Kenny (ed.), *Wyclif and his times*, Oxford, 126–45.

Keiser, G. R. 1980 'MS Rawlinson A. 393: another Findern manuscript', *TCBS*, 7, 3, 445–8.

1986 'The Middle English *Treatyse of fysshynge wyth an angle* and the gentle reader', *YULG*, 61, 22–48.

1995 'Medicines for horses: the continuity from script to print', *YULG*, 70, 111–28.

Ker, N. R. 1949 'Medieval manuscripts from Norwich Cathedral priory', *TCBS*, 1, 8–9.

1954 *Fragments of medieval manuscripts used as pastedowns in Oxford bindings with a survey of Oxford binding, c. 1515–1620*, OBS Publications, n.s., 5, Oxford.

1956 *Oxford college libraries in 1556. Guide to an exhibition held* [at the Bodleian Library] *in 1956*, Oxford.

1969–92 *Medieval manuscripts in British libraries*, 4 vols. (vol. IV with A. J. Piper), Oxford.

1971 *Records of All Souls College Library 1437–1600*, OBS Publications, n.s., 16, Oxford.

1978 'Oxford college libraries before 1500', in J. IJsewijn and J. Paquet (eds.), *The universities in the late Middle Ages*, Louvain, 293–311.

1981 'The books of philosophy distributed at Merton College in 1372 and 1375', in P. L. Heyworth (ed.), *Medieval studies for J. A. W. Bennett aetatis suae LXX*, Oxford (rpt Ker 1985, 331–78).

1985 *Books, collectors and libraries: collected studies*, ed. A. G. Watson, London and Ronceverte WV.

1986 'The provision of books', in *HUO*, III, 441–519.

Ker, N. R. (ed.) 1965 *A facsimile of British Museum, ms Harley 2253*, EETS OS 255, Oxford.

1976 *The Winchester Malory. A facsimile* with an introduction, EETS SS 4, London.

Ker, N. R. and Watson, A. G. 1964–87 *Medieval libraries of Great Britain: a list of surviving books*, 2nd edn, RHS, London 1964 (Ker); *Supplement to the second edn*, RHS, London 1987 (ed. Watson).

Kerling, N. J. M. 1955 'Caxton and the trade in printed books', *BC*, 4, 190–9.

1958 'Relations of English merchants with Bergen op Zoom, 1480–1481', *Bull. of the Institute of Historical Research*, 31, 130–40.

De Kescl, L. 1992 'Cambridge University Library ms. Add. 4100: a book of hours illuminated by the Master of the Prayer book of circa 1500?' *TCBS*, 10, 2, 182–97.

Kindrick, R. L. 1997 'Introduction: Caxton, Malory, and an authentic Arthurian text', *Arthuriana*, 7, 6–26.

King, H. W. 1869 'Ancient wills (No. 5)', *Trans. Essex Archaeological Soc.*, 4, 1–24.

King, J. N. 1976a 'Freedom of the press, Protestant propaganda, and Protector Somerset', *HLQ*, 40, 1–9.

1976b 'Protector Somerset, patron of the English Renaissance', *PBSA*, 70, 307–31.

1982 *English Reformation literature: the Tudor origins of the Protestant tradition*, Princeton NJ.

1987 'The account book of a Marian bookseller, 1553–4', *BLJ*, 13, 33–57.

Kingdon, J. A. 1901 *Richard Grafton, printer to Edward prince and king*, London.

Kingsford, C. L. 1918–20 'Two forfeitures in the year of Agincourt', *Archaeologia*, 70, 71–100.

1925 *Prejudice and promise in fifteenth-century England*, Oxford (rpt London 1962).

Kink, R. 1854 *Geschichte der kaiserlichen Universität zu Wien*, 2 vols., Vienna.

Kintgen, E. R. 1996 *Reading in Tudor England*, Pittsburgh PA.

Knighton 1995 *Knighton's chronicle 1337–1396*, ed. and trans. G. H. Martin, Oxford.

Knott, B. I. 1988 Introduction to *ASD*, I, 6, Amsterdam, 1–20.

Knowles, D. 1948–55 *The religious orders in England*, 3 vols., Cambridge.

König, E. 1979 'Die Illuminierung der Gutenbergbibel', in W. Schmidt and F. A. Schmidt-Künsemüller (eds.), *Johannes Gutenbergs zweiundvierzigzeilige Bibel . . . Kommentarband*, Munich, 69–125.

1983 'A leaf from a Gutenberg Bible illuminated in England', *BLJ*, 9, 32–50.

1991 'New perspectives on the history of Mainz printing: a fresh look at illuminated imprints', in Hindman 1991, 143–73.

Kren, T. (ed.) 1983 *Renaissance painting in manuscripts: treasures from the British Library. Catalogue and essays by J. M. Backhouse, M. Evans, T. Kren and M. D. Orth*, London and New York.

Kristeller, P. O. 1986 'Bartolomeo, Musandino, Mauro di Salerno e altri antichi commentatori dell' "Articella", con un elenco di testi e di manoscritti', in *Studi sulla scuola medica salernitana*, Naples, 97–151.

Krochalis, J. E. 1983 'God and Mammon: prayers and rents in Princeton ms 126', *Princeton Univ. Lib. Chron.*, 44, 209–21.

Kronenberg, M. E. 1929 'Notes on English printing in the Low Countries (early sixteenth century)', *Library*, 4th ser., 9, 139–63.

1947 'Forged addresses in Low Countries books in the period of the Reformation', *Library*, 5th ser., 2, 81–94.

Krontiris, T. 1988 'Breaking barriers of genre and gender: Margaret Tyler's translation of *The mirrour of knighthood*', *ELR*, 18, 19–39.

Krummel, D. W. and Sadie, S. (eds.) 1990 *Music publishing and printing*, The New Grove Handbooks in Music, London.

Kuhn, C. L. 1940 'Herman Scheerre and English illumination of the early sixteenth century', *Art Bull.*, 22, 138–56.

Kurvinen, A. 1953 'MS Porkington 10: description with extracts', *Neuphil Mitt*, 54, 33–67.

Kuttner, S. and Rathbone, E. 1951 'Anglo-Norman canonists of the twelfth century', *Traditio*, 7, 279–358.

Labarte, J. 1879 *Inventaire du mobilier de Charles V, roi de France*, Collection de documents inédits sur l'histoire de France, Paris.

Lancashire, I. (ed.) 1980 *Two Tudor interludes: the interludes of Youth and Hickscorner*, Manchester.

Lanfrancus 1565 *A most excellent and learned woorke of chirurgerie . . . now first published in the Englyshe prynte by John Halle . . .*, London.

Law, V. 1982 *The insular Latin grammarians*, Woodbridge.

Lawton, L. 1983 'The illustration of late medieval secular texts with special reference to Lydgate's *Troy Book*', in Pearsall 1983, 41–69.

Leach, A.F. 1896 'Wyckham's books at New College', in M. Burrows (ed.), *Collectanea*, 3rd ser., OHS 32, 213–44.

1903 *Early Yorkshire schools*, 2 vols., Yorkshire Archaeological Society Record Series 33, Leeds.

1911 *Educational charters and documents, 598–1909*, Cambridge.

Leader, D. R. 1983a 'Grammar in late medieval Oxford and Cambridge', *History of Education*, 12, 9–14.

1983b 'Professorships and academic reform at Cambridge, 1488–1520', *Sixteenth Century Jnl*, 14, 215–27.

1984a 'John Argentein and learning in medieval Cambridge', *Hum.Lov.*, 33, 71–85.

1984b 'Philosophy at Oxford and Cambridge in the fifteenth century', *History of Universities*, 4, 25–40.

1988 *A history of the University of Cambridge*. Vol. I: *The University to 1546*, Cambridge.

Leaver, R. A. (ed.) 1980 *The booke of Common praier noted*, Courtenay Facsimiles 3, Oxford.

Leedham-Green, E. S. 1986 *Books in Cambridge inventories: book-lists from Vice-Chancellor's Court probate inventories in the Tudor and Stuart periods*, 2 vols., Cambridge.

Leedham-Green, E. S., Rhodes, D. E. and Stubbings, F. H. (eds.) 1992 *Garrett Godfrey's accounts, c. 1527–1533*, CBS Monograph 12, Cambridge.

Legge, W. H. 1904 'A decorated mediaeval roll of prayers', *Reliquary*, n.s., 10, 99–112.

Lehmann, P. 1924 'Bücherliebe und Bücherpflege bei den Kartäusern', *Miscellanea Francesco Ehrle* (Rome), 5, 364–89 (rpt Lehmann, *Erforschung des Mittelalters* (Stuttgart), 3, 1960, 121–42).

Le Huray, P. 1978 *Music and the Reformation in England 1549–1660*, 2nd edn, Cambridge.

Leinsle, U. G.1984 *Das Ding und die Methode: Methodische Konstitution und Gegenstand der frühen protestantischen Metaphysik*, 2 vols., Augsburg.

Leland, J. 1549 *The laboryouse journey & serche of Johan Leyland, for Englandes antiquitees . . .*, London (rpt Amsterdam 1975).

1774 *De rebus Britannicis collectanea*, ed. T. Hearne, 2nd edn, 6 vols., Oxford (rpt 1970).

Lenhart, J. M. 1935 *Pre-Reformation printed books*, New York.

Lester, G. A. 1987 'The books of a fifteenth-century English gentleman: Sir John Paston', *NeuphilMitt*, 88, 200–17.

Lester, G. A. (ed.) 1988 *The earliest English translation of Vegetius'* De re militari, Heidelberg.

Lewis, F. 1995 '"Garnished with gloryous tytles": indulgences in printed books of hours in England', *TCBS*, 10, 577–90.

Lewis, R. E. and McIntosh, A. (eds.) 1982 *A descriptive guide to the manuscripts of the Prick of Conscience*, MAE Monographs n.s., 12, Oxford.

Liber quotidianus contrarotulatoris garderobae, 28 Edward I, A.D. 1299–1300, London, 1787.

Liddell, J. R. 1935 'Some notes on the library of Reading Abbey', *BQR*, 8, 47–54.

1937–8 'The library of Corpus Christi College, Oxford, in the sixteenth century', *Library*, 4th ser., 18, 385–416.

1939 'Leland's lists of manuscripts in Lincolnshire monasteries', *EHR*, 54, 88–95.

Limentani Virdis, C. 1989 'La produzione miniata fiamminga e il mercato inglese. Due esemplari alla Biblioteca del Seminario', *Miniatura*, 2, 107–20.

Littlehales, H. (ed.) 1895–7 *The Prymer or lay folk's prayer book*, 2 vols., EETS OS 105, 109, London.

Lloyd, A. H. 1934 *The early history of Christ's College Cambridge*, Cambridge.

Lloyd Jones, G. 1983 *The discovery of Hebrew in Tudor England: a third language*, Manchester.

Loach, J. 1975 'Pamphlets and politics, 1553–8', *Bull. of the Institute of Historical Research*, 47, 31–44.

    1986 'The Marian establishment and the printing press', *EHR*, 101, 135–48.

Loades, D. M. 1964 'The press under the early Tudors', *TCBS*, 4, 1, 29–50.

    1991 *Politics, censorship, and the English Reformation*, London.

Lovatt, R. 1992 'The library of John Blacman and contemporary Carthusian spirituality', *Jnl of Ecclesiastical History*, 43, 195–230.

    1993 'Two collegiate loan chests in late medieval Cambridge', in P. N. R. Zutshi (ed.), *Medieval Cambridge: essays on the pre-Reformation university*, Cambridge and Woodbridge, 129–65.

Lowndes, W.T. 1869 *The bibliographer's manual of English literature*, London.

    1885–1908 *The bibliographer's manual of English literature*, 2nd edn, 6 vols., London.

Lowry, M. 1987 'Diplomacy and the spread of printing', in Hellinga and Goldfinch 1987, 124–37.

    1988 'The arrival and use of Continental printed books in Yorkist England', in Aquilon and Martin 1988, 449–59.

Luborsky, R. S. and Ingram, E. M. 1998 *A guide to English illustrated books 1536–1603*, 2 vols., Tempe AZ.

Lucas, P. J. 1995 'The author as copyist of his own work: John Capgrave OSA (1393–1464)', in Beadle and Piper 1995, 227–48.

Lucet, B. 1977 *Les codifications cisterciennes de 1237 et de 1257*, Paris.

Lunt, W. E. 1962 *Financial relations of the Papacy with England 1327–1534*, Medieval Academy of America 74, Cambridge MA.

Luxton, I. 1977 'The Reformation and popular culture', in F. Heal and R. O'Day (eds.), *Church and society in England: Henry VIII to James I*, London, 57–77.

Lyall, R. J. 1989 'Materials: the paper revolution', in *BPPB*, 11–29.

Lydgate, J. 1961 *A critical edition of Lydgate's Life of our Lady*, ed. J. A. Lauritis, R. A. Klinefelter and V. F. Gallagher, Duquesne Studies, Philological Series 2, Pittsburg.

    1989–90 *Table manners for children*, ed. and trans. N. Orme, Salisbury and London.

Lyell, L. (ed.) 1936 *Acts of Court of the Mercers' Company, 1453–1527*, Cambridge.

Lyndewood, W. 1679 *Provinciale seu constitutiones Anglie*, Oxford (rpt 1968).

McConica, J. K. 1965 *English humanists and Reformation politics under Henry VIII and Edward VI*, Oxford.

    1979 'Humanism and Aristotle in Tudor Oxford', *EHR*, 94, 291–317.

    1986 'The rise of the undergraduate college', in *HUO*, III, 1–68.

MacCracken, H. N. 1908 'Quixley's Ballades royal (?1402)', *Yorkshire Archaeological Jnl*, 20, 33–50.

MacCulloch, D. 1996 *Thomas Cranmer: a life*, New Haven and London.

MacDonald, A. A., Lynch, M. and Cowan, I. B. (eds.) 1994 *The Renaissance in Scotland. Studies in literature, religion, history and culture offered to John Durkan*, Leiden, New York, Cologne.

Macfarlane, J. 1901 *Antoine Vérard*, Bibliographical Society Monographs 7, London.

McFarlane, K. B. 1957 'The investment of Sir John Fastolf's profits of war', *TRHS*, 5th ser., 7, 91–116.

Macfarlane, L. J. 1957–8 'William Elphinstone's library', *Aberdeen Uni. Rev.*, 37, 253–71.

    1960 'The book of hours of James IV and Margaret Tudor', *Innes Rev.*, 11, 3–21.

    1985 *William Elphinstone and the kingdom of Scotland, 1431–1514: the struggle for order*, Aberdeen.

    1994 'William Elphinstone's library revisited', in MacDonald, Lynch and Cowan 1994, 66–81.

McGerr, R. P. (ed.) 1990 *The Pilgrimage of the soul. A critical edition of the Middle English dream vision*, New York and London.

McIntosh, A., Samuels, M. L. and Benskin, M. 1986 *A linguistic atlas of late mediaeval English*, Aberdeen.

McIntosh, M. K. 1986 *Autonomy and community: the royal manor of Havering, 1200–1500*, 4 vols., Cambridge.

McKendrick, S. 1990 '*La grande histoire César* and the manuscripts of Edward IV', *EMS*, 2, 109–38.

    1992 'Lodewijk van Gruuthuse en de librije van Edward IV', in Martens 1992, 153–9.

    1994 'The *Romuléon* and the manuscripts of Edward IV', in N. Rogers (ed.), *England in the fifteenth century*, Harlaxton Medieval Studies 4, Woodbridge, 149–69.

McKerrow, R. B. 1927 *An introduction to bibliography for literary students*, Oxford (rev. rpt 1928).

McKitterick, D. J. 1978 'Two sixteenth-century catalogues of St John's College library', *TCBS*, 7, 2, 135–55.

    1992 *A history of Cambridge University Press*, 1, Cambridge.

McNamer, S. 1991 'Female authors, provincial setting. The re-versing of courtly love in the Findern manuscript', *Viator*, 22, 279–310.

Macray, W. D. 1890 *Annals of the Bodleian Library*, 2nd edn, Oxford.

McRoberts, D. 1952 'Some sixteenth-century Scottish breviaries and their place in the history of the Scottish liturgy', *Innes Rev.*, 3, 33–48.

    1959 'Notes on Scoto-Flemish artistic contacts', *Innes Rev.*, 10, 91–6.

    1968 'Dean Brown's book of hours', *Innes Rev.*, 19, 144–67.

Madan, F. and Bradshaw, H. (eds.) 1885–90 'The Day-Book of John Dorne, bookseller in Oxford A. D. 1520', OHS 5 (=*Collectanea*, 1st ser.), 1885, 68–177, and 'Corrections and additions . . .' (Madan); and 'Notes on the former edition', OHS 16 (=*Collectanea*, 2nd ser.), 1890, 453–78 (Bradshaw).

Mahoney, E. P. (ed.) 1976 *Philosophy and humanism: Renaissance essays in honor of P. O. Kristeller*, New York.

Maitland, F. W. 1901 *English law and the Renaissance*, Cambridge.

Maitland, F. W. (ed.) 1903 *Yearbooks of Edward II*, 1, Surtees Society 17, London.

Malden, H. F. 1902 *Trinity Hall*, London.

Mancini 1969 *The usurpation of Richard III. Dominicus Mancinus ad Angelum Catonem de occupatione regni Anglie per Riccardum Tercium libellus*, trans. and with intro. by C. A. J. Armstrong, 2nd edn, London (rpts 1984, 1989).

Manion, M. M. and Vines, V. F. 1984 *Medieval and Renaissance illuminated manuscripts in Australian collections*, London.

Manion, M. M, Vines, V. F. and De Hamel, C. F. R. 1989 *Medieval and Renaissance manuscripts in New Zealand collections*, Melbourne, London and New York.

Mann, N. 1971 'The manuscripts of Petrarch's *De remediis*. A check-list', *IMU*, 14, 57–90.

    1975a *Petrarch manuscripts in the British Isles*, Censimento dei codici Petrarcheschi 6, Padua.

    1975b 'La prima fortuna in Inghilterra di Francesco Petrarca', in G. Billanovich and G. Frasso (eds.), *Il Petrarca ad Arquà. Atti del Convegno internazionale di studi nel VI centenario (1370–1374), Arquà Petrarca*, Studi sul Petrarca 5, Padua, 279–89.

Margolin, J.-C. 1971a Introduction to *De ratione studii, ASD*, I, 2, Amsterdam, 83–109.

    1971b Introduction to *De conscribendis epistolis, ASD*, I, 2, 157–203.

De Marinis, T. 1947–69 *La Biblioteca napoletana dei re d'Aragona*, 4 vols., Milan 1947–52, and supplement, 2 vols., Verona, 1969.

Marks, R. 1993 *Stained glass in England during the Middle Ages*, London.

Marks, R. and Morgan, N. 1981 *The golden age of English manuscript painting, 1200–1500*, New York.

Marotti, Arthur F. 1995 *Manuscript, print and the English Renaissance lyric*, Ithaca and London.

Marrow, J. (ed.) 1990 *The golden age of Dutch manuscript illumination*, exhibition catalogue, New York.

Martens, M. P. J. (ed.) 1992 *Lodewijk van Gruuthuse, Mecenas en Europees diplomaat ca. 1427–1492*, Bruges.

Martin, H.-J. 1982 'Classements et conjectures', in H.-J. Martin, R. Chartier and J. P. Vivet (eds.), 1982, 429–57.

    1987 *Le livre dans l'ancien régime*, Paris.

Martin, H.-J., Chartier, R. and Vivet, J. P. 1982 *Histoire de l'édition française*. Vol. I: *Le livre conquérant. Des origines au milieu du XVIIme siècle*, Paris.

Martin, J. W. 1981a 'The Marian regime's failure to understand the importance of printing', *HLQ*, 44, 231–47.

    1981b 'Miles Hogarde: artisan and aspiring author in sixteenth-century England', *RenQ*, 34, 359–83.

Martz, L. L. and Sylvester, R. S. (eds.) 1969 *Thomas More's prayer book. A facsimile reproduction of the annotated pages, transcription and translation, with an introduction*, New Haven and London.

Maskell, W. (ed.) 1846 *Monumenta ritualia ecclesiae anglicanae*, 2 vols., London.

Matheson, L. M. (ed.) 1994 *Popular and practical science of medieval England*, East Lansing MI.

Meale, C.M. 1982 'Wynkyn de Worde's setting-copy for *Ipomydon*', *SB*, 35, 156–72.

    1983 'The compiler at work: John Colyns and BL Harley 2252', in Pearsall 1983, 82–103.

1989 'Patrons, buyers and owners: book production and social status', in *BPPB*, 201–38.

1990 'The miracles of our lady', in D. Pearsall (ed.), *Studies in the Vernon manuscript*, Woodbridge, 115–36.

1992 'The publication of romance in late Medieval England', *Library*, 6th ser., 14, 283–98.

1993a '". . . alle the bokes that I haue of latyn, englische, and frensche": laywomen and their books in late medieval England', in Meale 1993b, 128–58.

1994 '"gode men / Wiues maydnes and alle men": romance and its audiences', in Meale (ed.), *Readings in medieval English romance*, Cambridge, 209–25.

1996 '"The Hoole Book": editing and the creation of meaning in Malory's text', in E. Archibald and A. S. G. Edwards (eds.), *A companion to Malory*, Cambridge, 3–17.

1997 '"Oft sithis with grete deuotion I thought what I might do plesyng to God": the early ownership and readership of Love's *Mirror*, with special reference to its female audience', in S. Oguro, H. R. L. Beadle and M. G. Sargent (eds.), *Nicholas Love at Waseda. Proceedings of the international conference, 20–22 July 1995*, Woodbridge, 19–46.

Meale, C. M. (ed.) 1993b *Women and literature in Britain, 1150–1500*, 2nd edn 1996, Cambridge.

Means, L. B. 1984 'Scientific and utilitarian prose', in Edwards 1984, 231–88.

1993 *Medieval lunar astrology. A collection of representative Middle English texts*, Lewiston MI.

Meech, S. B. and Allen, H. E. (eds.) 1940 *The Book of Margery Kempe*, EETS OS 212.

Meredith, P. 1991 'Manuscript, scribe and performance: further looks at the N-Town manuscript', in Riddy 1991, 109–28.

Meredith, P. and Kahrl, S. J. (eds.) 1977 *The N-Town Plays: a facsimile of British Library ms Cotton Vespasian D. VIII*, Leeds texts and monographs, Medieval drama facsimiles, Leeds.

Meyer-Baer, K. 1962 *Liturgical music incunabula: a descriptive catalogue*, Bibliographical Society Monographs, London.

Mézières, Philippe de 1975 *Letter to King Richard II*, ed. G. W. Coopland, Liverpool.

Midmer, R. 1979 *English medieval monasteries 1066–1540: a summary*, Athens GA.

Milanesi, G. 1885 *Nuovi documenti per la storia dell'arte Toscana dal XII al XV secolo*, Florence (rpt 1973).

Milsom, J. 1992a 'English-texted chant before Merbecke', *Plainsong and Medieval Music*, 1, 77–92.

1992b 'Music', in B. Ford (ed.), *The Cambridge cultural history of Britain*. Vol. III: *16th-century Britain*, Cambridge, 169–207.

1993 'The Nonsuch music library', in Banks, Searle and Turner 1993, 146–82.

1995 'Sacred songs in the chamber', in Morehen 1995, 161–79.

1997 'Songs and society in early Tudor London', *Early Music History*, 16, 235–93.

Milsom, J. (ed.) 1986 *Oxford, Bodleian Library, MSS Mus. Sch. e. 376–81; facsimile with an introduction*, Renaissance Music in Facsimile 15, New York and London.

Miner, D. E. (ed.) 1957 *The history of bookbinding 525–1950 AD*, exhibition at the Walters Art Gallery, Baltimore MD.

Miner, J. N. T. 1990 *The grammar schools of medieval England*, Montreal and Kingston.

Minnis, A. J. 1984 'The *Cloud of Unknowing* and Walter Hilton's *Scale of Perfection*', in Edwards 1984, 61–81.

Mitchell, W. S. 1955 *A history of Scottish bookbinding*, Edinburgh and London.

1961 'Some German bindings in Aberdeen University Library', *Festschrift Ernst Kyriss*, Stuttgart, 175–90.

Mitchner, R. W. 1951 'Wynkyn de Worde's use of the Plimpton manuscript of *De proprietatibus rerum*', *Library*, 5th ser., 6, 7–18.

Monks, P. R. and Owen, D. D. R. (eds.) 1994 *Medieval codicology, iconography, literature, and translation. Studies for K. V. Sinclair*, Leiden, New York and Cologne.

Mooney, L. R. 1997 'Almanacks from script to print', in J. Scattergood and J. Boffey (eds.), *Texts and their contents: papers of the Early Book Society*, Dublin, 11–25.

Mooney, L. R. (ed.) 1998 *The Kalendarium of John Somer*, Athens GA.

Moore, J. K. 1992 *Primary materials relating to copy and print in English books of the sixteenth and seventeenth centuries*, OBS Occasional Publications 24, Oxford.

Moran, J. A. Hoeppner 1985 *The growth of English schooling 1340–1548*, Princeton NJ.

Morehen, J. (ed.) 1995 *English choral practice, c. 1450–c. 1625*, Cambridge.

Morello, G. 1985–6 *Raffaello e la Roma dei papi*, exhibition catalogue, Salone Sistino, Città del Vaticano.

Moreton, C. E. 1991 'The "library" of a late-fifteenth-century lawyer', *Library*, 6th ser., 13, 338–46.

Morgan, D. A. L. 1986 'The individual style of the English gentleman', in M. Jones (ed.), *Gentry and lesser nobility in late medieval Europe*, Gloucester, 15–35.

Morgan, N. 1992 'Texts of devotion and religious instruction associated with Margaret of York', in T. Kren (ed.), *Margaret of York, Simon Marmion, and the Visions of Tondal*, Malibu CA, 63–76.

Morgan, P. and Painter, G. D. 1957 'The Caxton *Legenda* at St Mary's, Warwick', *Library*, 5th ser., 12, 225–39.

Morley, T. 1952 *A plain & easy introduction to practical music*, ed. R. A. Harman, London.

Moss, A. 1996 *Printed commonplace books and the structuring of Renaissance thought*, Oxford.

Moxon, J. 1962 *Mechanical exercises on the whole art of printing (1683–4) by Joseph Moxon*, ed. H. Davis and H. Carter, 2nd edn, Oxford.

Mozley, J. F. 1953 *Coverdale and his Bibles*, London.

Mukai, T. 1996 'Textual editing in early printed editions of Chaucer's *Parliament*', *Medieval English Studies Newsletter*, 35, 7–9.

1997 'The prologue, text and epilogue of de Worde – Copland's edition of *The Parliament of fowls*', in *Essays on English language and literature in honour of Shunichi Noguchi*, Tokyo, 65–74.

Müller, J. 1882 *Quellenschriften und Geschichte des deutschsprachlichen Unterrichtes bis zur Mitte des 16. Jahrhunderts*, Gotha.

Mullinger, J. B. 1873 *The University of Cambridge from the earliest times to the royal injunctions of 1535*, Cambridge.

1884 *The University of Cambridge from the royal injunctions of 1535 to the accession of Charles the First*, Cambridge.

Munby, A. N. L. 1951 'Notes on King's College Library in the fifteenth century', *TCBS*, 1, 3, 280–6.

Myers, A. R. 1967–8 'The household of Queen Elizabeth Woodville, 1466–7', *BJRL*, 50, 207–35.

Mynors, R. A. B. 1950 'A fifteenth-century scribe: T. Werken', *TCBS*, 1, 2, 97–104.

1957 'The Latin classics known to Boston of Bury', in D. J. Gordon (ed.), *Fritz Saxl, 1890–1948. A volume of memorial essays from his friends in England*, London, Edinburgh, Paris, Melbourne, Toronto and New York, 199–217.

1963 *Catalogue of the manuscripts of Balliol College Oxford*, Oxford.

Mynors, R. A. B. and Thomson, R. M. 1993 *Catalogue of the manuscripts of Hereford Cathedral Library*, Cambridge.

Naylor, C. forthcoming 'English partsong c. 1520–1570: an edition with commentary', D.Phil. thesis in progress, University of Oxford.

Needham, P. 1986a *The printer and the pardoner*, Washington DC.

1986b 'William Caxton and his Cologne partners: an enquiry based on Veldener's Cologne type', in H. Limburg, H. Lohse and H. Schmitz (eds.), *Ars impressoria: Entstehung und Entwicklung des Buchdrucks. Eine internationale Festgabe fur Severin Corsten zum 65. Geburtstag*, Munich, New York, London, Paris, 103–31.

Nelson, A. H. (ed.) 1980 *The Plays of Henry Medwall*, Cambridge.

Nelson, W. (ed.) 1956 *A fifteenth-century school book from a ms. in the British Museum (ms. Arundel 249)*, Oxford.

Neville, P. 1990 'Richard Pynson, king's printer (1506–1529): printing and propaganda in early Tudor England', unpub. Ph.D. thesis, University of London, Warburg Institute.

Nicholls, J. W. 1985 *The matter of courtesy*, Woodbridge.

Nichols, J. 1780 *A collection of the wills . . . of the kings and queens of England*, London.

Nicolas, Sir N. H. (ed.) 1830 *Privy purse expenses of Elizabeth of York: Wardrobe accounts of Edward the Fourth*, London.

1834–7 *Proceedings and ordinances of the Privy Council of England*, 6 vols., London.

Nielsen, H. C., Borch, M. and Sørensen, B. A. 1986 *From script to book, a symposium. Proceedings of the 7th International Symposium organized by the Centre for the study of vernacular literature in the Middle Ages, held at Odense University . . . 1982*, Odense.

Nieuwstraten, R. 1994 'Overlevering en verandering: de pentekeningen van de Jasonmeester en de houtsneden van de Meester van Bellaert in de *Historie van Jason*', in J. M. M. Hermans and K. van der Hoek (eds.), *Boeken in de late middeleeuwen: verslag van de Groningse codicologendagen 1992*, Groningen, 111–24.

Nixon, H. M. 1956 *The Broxbourne Library*, London.

1964 'Early English gold-tooled bookbindings', *Studi di bibliografia e di storia in onore di Tammaro de Marinis*, Verona, 283–308.

1971 *Sixteenth-century gold-tooled bookbindings in the Pierpont Morgan Library*, New York.

1976 'Caxton, his contemporaries and successors in the book trade from Westminster documents', *Library*, 5th ser., 31, 305–26.

1978 *Five centuries of English bookbinding*, London.

1984a *Catalogue of the Pepys library at Magdalene College Cambridge*. Vol. vi: *Bindings*, Cambridge.

1984b 'Day's *Service book*', *BLJ*, 10, 1–31.

Nixon, H. M. and Foot, M. M. 1992 *The history of decorated bookbinding in England*, Oxford.

North, J. D. 1969 '"Kalenderes enlumyned ben they." Some astronomical themes in
  Chaucer', *RES*, n.s., 20, 129–54, 257–83, 418–44.
  1988 *Chaucer's universe*, Oxford.
  1992 'Astronomy and mathematics', in *HUO*, II, 103–74.
Norton, F. J. 1958 'The library of Bryan Rowe, Vice-Provost of King's College (1521)',
  TCBS, 2, 5, 339–51.
Norton-Smith, J. (ed.), 1979 *Bodleian MS Fairfax 16*, London.
Oates, J. C. T. 1954 *A catalogue of the fifteenth-century printed books in the University
  Library Cambridge*, Cambridge.
  1986 *Cambridge University Library: a history*. Vol. I: *From the beginnings to the
  Copyright Act of Queen Anne*, Cambridge.
Oates, J. C. T. and Pink, H. L. 1952 'Three sixteenth-century catalogues of the
  University Library', *TCBS*, 1, 4, 310–40.
Offord, M. Y. (ed.) 1971 *The book of the Knight of the Tower*, translated by William
  Caxton, EETS SS 2, London.
Ogilvie-Thompson, S. J. (ed.) 1986 *Walter Hilton's Mixed life, edited from Lambeth Palace
  ms. 472*, Salzburg.
Oldham, J. B. 1952 *English blind stamped bindings*, Cambridge.
  1958 *Blind panels of English binders*, Cambridge.
Olin, J. C. (ed.) 1987 *Christian humanism and the Reformation*, New York.
O'Mara, V. M. 1990 'A Middle English text written by a female scribe', *N&Q*, 235,
  396–8.
Omont, H. 1891 'Les manuscrits français des rois d'Angleterre au château de
  Richmond', in *Etudes romanes dédiées à Gaston Paris*, Paris, 1–13.
Orme, N. 1973 *English schools in the Middle Ages*, London.
  1984 *From childhood to chivalry: the education of the English kings and aristocracy
  1066–1530*, London.
  1988 'Martin Coeffin, the first Exeter publisher', *Library*, 6th ser., 10, 220–30.
  1989 *Education and society in medieval and Renaissance England*, London and
  Ronceverte WV.
  1991 'Glastonbury Abbey and education', in Abrams and Carley 1991, 285–99.
  1993 'Education in the Cornish play *Beunans meriasek*', *Cambridge Med. Celtic Stud.*,
  20, 1–13.
  1996 'John Holt (d. 1504), Tudor grammarian', *Library*, 6th ser., 18, 283–305.
Oschinsky, D. (ed.) 1971 *Walter of Henley and other treatises on estate management and
  accounting*, Oxford.
Osler, D. 1988 'Towards a legal-historical bibliography: a census of 16th-century legal
  imprints', *Ius commune*, 15, 231–42.
Otway-Ruthven, J. 1939 *The King's secretary and the Signet Office in the fifteenth century*,
  Cambridge.
Ovid 1968 *The Metamorphoses of Ovid translated by William Caxton 1480*, 2 vols., New
  York.
Owen, D. M. 1985 'Two medieval parish books from the diocese of Ely: New College
  MS. 98 and Wisbech Museum MS. 1', in M. Barber *et al.* (eds.), *East Anglian and
  other studies presented to Barbara Dodwell: Reading Medieval Stud.*, 11, 121–32.
  1990 *The medieval canon law: teaching, literature and transmission*, Cambridge.
Owen, G. 1892 *The Description of Pembrokeshire, 1603*, ed. H. Owen, London.

Pächt, O. 1948 *The Master of Mary of Burgundy*, London.

1953–4 'Manuscripts', in the exhibition catalogue *Flemish Art*, London, Royal Academy of Arts, pp. 150–67, nos. 555–626.

Pächt, O. and Alexander, J. J. G. 1966–73 *Illuminated manuscripts in the Bodleian Library, Oxford*, 3 vols., Oxford.

Pächt, O. and Thoss, D. 1977 *Die illuminierten Handschriften und Inkunabeln der Öster- reichischen Nationalbibliothek: Französische Schule 2*, Österreichische Akademie der Wissenschaften, Phil.-hist. Kl., Denkschriften 128, Vienna.

Pafort, E. 1952–3 'Notes on the Wynkyn de Worde editions of the *Boke of St Albans* and its separates', *SB*, 5, 43–52.

Paget, H. 1959 'Gerard and Lucas Hornebolt in England', *Burlington Mag.*, 101, 396–402.

Painter, G. D. 1963 'Caxton through the looking-glass', *Gutenberg-Jahrbuch 1963*, 73–80.

1976 *William Caxton: a quincentenary biography of England's first printer*, London.

Palgrave, F. (ed.) 1836 *Kalendars and inventories of the Exchequer*, 3 vols., London.

Palmer, J. J. N. 1972 *England, France and Christendom*, Oxford.

Pantin, W. A. 1947–50 *Canterbury College Oxford*, 3 vols., OHS, n.s., 6–8, Oxford.

Pantzer, K. 1983 'Printing the English statutes, 1484–1640: some historical implica- tions', in K. E. Carpenter 1983, 69–114.

1993 'Thomas Berthelet', in C. S. Nicholls (ed.), *DNB: missing persons*, Oxford, 64.

Paris 1981 *Les fastes du Gothique: le siècle de Charles V*, exhibition catalogue, Paris.

Parker, M. 1974 'Early typefounders' moulds at the Plantin-Moretus Museum', *Library*, 5th ser., 29, 93–102.

Parkes, M. B. 1961 'A fifteenth-century scribe: Henry Mere', *BLR*, 6, 654–9.

1969 *English cursive book hands 1250–1500*, Oxford (rpt London 1980).

1973 'The literacy of the laity', in Daiches and Thorlby 1973, 555–78.

1991 *Scribes, scripts and readers: studies in the communication, presentation and dissemi- nation of medieval texts*, London.

1992a 'The provision of books', in *HUO*, 11, 407–83.

1992b *Pause and effect: an introduction to the history of punctuation in the West*, Aldershot.

1995 'Patterns of scribal activity and revisions of the text in early copies of works by John Gower', in Beadle and Piper 1995, 81–121.

Parkes, M. B. and Beadle, H. R. L. (eds.) 1979–80 *Geoffrey Chaucer. Poetical works. A fac- simile of Cambridge University Library MS Gg. iv. 27*, 3 vols., Cambridge.

Parks, G.B. 1976 'Pico della Mirandola in Tudor translation', in Mahoney 1976, 352–69.

Partridge, W. E. 1983 'The use of William Caxton's type 3 by John Lettou and William de Machlinia in the printing of their *Yearbook 35 Henry VI*, c. 1481–1482', *BLJ*, 9, 56–65.

Pearsall, D. (ed.), 1983 *Manuscripts and readers in fifteenth-century England: the literary implications of manuscript study*, Cambridge.

1990 *Studies in the Vernon manuscript*, Cambridge.

Pearsall, D. A. and Cunningham, I. C. (eds.) 1977 *The Auchinleck manuscript: National Library of Scotland, Advocates' MS 19. 2. 1*, London.

Pearson, D. 1992 'The libraries of English bishops, 1600–40', *Library*, 6th ser., 14, 221–57.

Peartree, S. M. 1905 'A portrait of William Caxton', *Burlington Mag.* 7, 383–7.

Peckham, J. 1504 *Perspectiva communis*, Venice.

Pellegrin, E. 1955 *La bibliothèque des Visconti et des Sforza ducs de Milan, au XVe siècle*, Paris.

    1966 *Manuscrits de Pétrarque dans les bibliothèques de France*, rpt from *IMU*, 4, 6–7, Padua.

Phaer, T. 1543 *A new boke of presidentes*, London.

Phelps, W. H. 1979 'Some sixteenth-century stationers' wills', *SB*, 32, 48–59.

Philip, I. G. 1951 *Gold-tooled bookbindings*, Oxford.

Piccolomini, E. S. (Pope Pius II) 1984 *I commentarii*, ed. L. Totaro, Milan.

Piccope, G. J. (ed.) 1857 *Lancashire and Cheshire wills and inventories from the ecclesiastical court*, Chetham Society 33, Manchester.

Picker, M. 1965 *The chanson albums of Marguerite of Austria*, Berkeley and Los Angeles.

Pickett, J. P. 1994 'A translation of the "Cantus" plague treatise', in L. M. Matheson (ed.), *Popular and practical science of medieval England*, East Lansing MI, 263–82.

Piepho, L. 1993 'Mantuan's religious poetry in early Tudor England: humanism and Christian latin verse', *Medievalia et humanistica*, 20, 65–83.

Pinborg, J. 1967 *Die Entwicklung der Sprachtheorie im Mittelalter*, Beiträge zur Geschichte der Philosophie im Mittelalter 42, Münster i.W.

Pinkernell, G. 1971 *Raoul Lefèvre, l'Histoire de Jason*, Frankfurt am Main.

Piper, A. J. 1978 'The libraries of the monks of Durham', in *MSML*, 213–49.

Plant, M. 1965 *The English book trade. An economic history of the making and sale of books*, 2nd edn, London.

Plomer, H. R. 1904 'Books mentioned in wills', *Trans. of the Bibliographical Soc.*, 7, 99–121.

    1905 'Westminster Hall and its booksellers', *Library*, 2nd ser., 6, 380–90.

    1909 'Two lawsuits of Richard Pynson', *Library*, 2nd ser., 10, 115–33.

    1913 'Bibliographical notes from the Privy Purse Expenses of King Henry the Seventh', *Library*, 3rd ser., 4, 291–305.

    1915 'An inventory of Wynkyn de Worde's house "The Sun in Fleet Street" in 1553', *Library*, 3rd ser., 6, 228–34.

    1923 'Richard Pynson, glover and printer', *Library*, 4th ser., 3, 49–51.

    1923–4 'The importation of books into England in the fifteenth and sixteenth centuries: an examination of some customs rolls', *Library*, 4th ser., 4, 146–50.

    1925 *Wynkyn de Worde & his contemporaries from the death of Caxton to 1535*, London.

    1928–9 'The importation of Low Country and French books into England, 1480 and 1502–3', *Library*, 4th ser., 9, 164–8.

Plummer, J. H. 1968 *The Glazier collection of illuminated manuscripts*, New York.

Plummer, J. H. and Clark, G. 1982 *The last flowering: French painting in manuscripts 1420–1530*, Pierpont Morgan Library, New York.

Pollard, A. W. 1905 'Recent Caxtoniana', *Library*, 2nd ser., 6, 337–45.

    1937 'The regulation of the book-trade in the sixteenth century', in Pollard, *Shakespeare's fight with the pirates and the problems of the transmission of his text*, 2nd edn, Cambridge, 1–25.

Pollard, A. W. (ed.) 1911 *Records of the English Bible. The documents relating to the transla-*
tion and publication of the Bible in English, 1525–1611, London.

Pollard, G. 1937a 'The Company of Stationers before 1557', *Library*, 4th ser., 18,
1–38.

1937b 'The early constitution of the Stationers' Company', *Library*, 4th ser., 18,
235–60.

1941 'Notes on the size of the sheet', *Library*, 4th ser., 22, 105–37.

1964 'The university and the book trade in medieval Oxford', in P. Wilpert (ed.),
Beiträge zum Berufsbewusstsein des mittelalterlichen Menschen, Miscellanea mediae-
valia 3, Berlin, 336–45.

1970 'The names of some English fifteenth-century binders', *Library*, 5th ser., 25,
193–218.

1978a 'The English market for printed books: the Sandars Lectures 1959',
Publishing History, 4, 7–48.

1978b 'The *pecia* system in the medieval universities', in *MSML*, 145–61.

Pollard, G. and Ehrman, A. 1965 *The distribution of books by catalogue from the invention*
of printing to A. D. 1800, Roxburghe Club, London.

Porter, R. and Teich, M. (eds.) 1992 *The Renaissance in national context*, Cambridge.

Postan, M. M. 1933 'The economic and political relations of England and the Hanse
from 1400 to 1475', in E. Power and M. M. Postan (eds.), *Studies in English trade*
in the fifteenth century, London, 91–153.

Powell, S. 1996 'Syon, Caxton, and the *Festial*', *Birgittiana*, 2, 189–207.

1998 'Lady Margaret Beaufort and her books', *Library*, 6th scr., 20, 197–240.

Powicke, F. M. 1931 *The medieval books of Merton College*, Oxford.

Van Praet, J. B. B. 1822 *Catalogue des livres imprimés sur vélin de la Bibliothèque du Roi*,
Paris.

1824–8 *Catalogue des livres imprimés sur vélin qui se trouvent dans les bibliothèques tant*
publiques que particulières, pour servir de suite au catalogue des livres imprimés sur
vélin de la Bibliothèque du Roi, 4 vols., Paris.

Von Prantl, C. 1872 *Geschichte der Ludwig-Maximilians-Universität Ingolstadt, Landshut,*
München, 2 vols., Munich.

Prestwich, M. 1988 *Edward I*, London.

Price, D. C. 1981 *Patrons and musicians of the English Renaissance*, Cambridge.

Pritchard, V. 1967 *English medieval graffiti*, Cambridge.

Pronay, N. and Taylor, J. (eds.) 1980 *Parliamentary texts of the later Middle Ages*,
Oxford.

Pronger, W. A. 1938–9 'Thomas Gascoigne', *EHR*, 53, 606–26; 54, 20–37.

Putnam, B. H. 1924 *Early treatises on the practices of the Justices of the Peace in the fifteenth*
and sixteenth centuries, Oxford.

Raine, J. (ed.) 1838 *Catalogi veteres librorum ecclesiae cathedralis Dunelm*, Surtees Society
7, London.

Randall, L. M. C. 1993 *Medieval and Renaissance manuscripts in the Walters Art Gallery*
Vol. II: *France, 1420–1540*, Baltimore MD.

Rappaport, S. 1989 *Worlds within worlds: structures of life in sixteenth-century London*,
Cambridge.

Redstone, L. J. 1946 'Three Carrow account rolls', *Norfolk Archaeology*, 29, 41–88.

Reed, A. W. 1920 'The regulation of the book trade before the proclamation of 1538',
  Trans. of the Bibliog. Soc., 15, 157–84.
  1926 *Early Tudor drama*, London (rpt New York, 1969).
Reeves, A. C. 1981 *Lancastrian Englishman*, Washington.
Rex, R. 1990 'The earliest use of Hebrew in books printed in England: dating some
  books by Richard Pace and Robert Wakefield', *TCBS*, 9, 6, 517–25.
  1991 *The theology of John Fisher*, Cambridge.
Reynolds, C. 1993 'The Shrewsbury Book; London, British Library Royal ms. 15 E.
  VI', in J. Stratford (ed.), *Medieval art, architecture and archaeology at Rouen*, British
  Archaeological Assoc. Conference Trans. 12 (for 1987), Leeds, 109–16.
  1994 'English patrons and French artists in fifteenth-century Normandy', in D.
  Bates and A. Curry (eds.), *England and Normandy in the Middle Ages*, London,
  299–313.
Rhodes, D. E. 1956a 'Provost Argentine of King's and his books', *TCBS*, 2, 3, 205–12.
  1956b 'Variants in the 1479 Oxford edition of Aristotle's Ethics', *SB*, 8, 209–12.
  1958 'Don Fernando Colon and his London book purchases, June 1522', *PBSA*, 52,
  231–48.
  1967 *John Argentine, Provost of King's: his life and his library*, Amsterdam.
  1982 *A catalogue of incunabula in all the libraries of Oxford outside the Bodleian*,
  Oxford.
De Ricci, S. 1937 *Census of medieval and Renaissance manuscripts in the United States and
  Canada*, 2 vols., New York.
Rice, E. F., Jr 1964 review of S. Jayne, *John Colet and Marsilio Ficino*, *Ren. News*, 17,
  108–9.
Richmond, C. 1981 *John Hopton: a fifteenth-century Suffolk gentleman*, Cambridge.
  1987 'The Sulyard papers: the rewards of a small family archive', in D. Williams
  (ed.), *England in the fifteenth century: proceedings of the 1986 Harlaxton Symposium*,
  Woodbridge, 199–228.
Rickert, M. 1952 *The reconstructed Carmelite missal*, London.
  1965 *Painting in Britain: the Middle Ages*, 2nd edn, Harmondsworth.
Riddy, F. 1993 ' "Women talking about the things of God": a late medieval subculture', in Meale 1993b, 104–27.
  1996 'Mother knows best: reading social change in a courtesy text', *Speculum*, 71,
  66–86.
Riddy, F. (ed.) 1991 *Regionalism in late medieval manuscripts and texts: essays celebrating
  the publication of 'A linguistic atlas of late medieval English'*, Cambridge.
De Rijk, L. M. 1975 'Logica cantabrigiensis – a fifteenth-century Cambridge manual
  of logic', *Rev. internationale de philosophie*, 29, fasc. 113, 'In memory of M.
  Grabmann', 297–315.
  1976 'Richard Billingham's works on logic', *Vivarium*, 14, 121–38.
  1977 'Logica oxoniensis: an attempt to reconstruct a fifteenth-century Oxford
  manual of logic', *Medioevo*, 3, 121–64.
Rizzo, S. 1986 'Il latino nell'umanesimo', in *Letteratura italiana*. Vol. v: *Le questioni*,
  Turin.
Ro: Ba: 1950 *The Life of Syr Thomas More, somtymes Lord Chancellour of England*, ed. E. V.
  Hitchcock and P. E. Hallett, London (rpt 1957, EETS OS 222).

Robbins, R. H. 1939a 'The arma Christi rolls', *MLR*, 34, 415–21.

1939b 'English almanacks of the fifteenth century', *Philological Quarterly*, 18, 321–31.

1950 'The poems of Humphrey Newton esq., 1466–1536', *PMLA*, 65, 249–81.

Roberts, R. J. 1979 'John Rastell's inventory of 1538', *Library*, 6th ser., 1, 34–42.

1988 'The Bibliographical Society as a band of pioneers', in R. Myers and M. Harris (eds.), *Pioneers in bibliography*, Winchester, 86–99.

1989 'The import of books into England in the sixteenth century', unpub. lecture to the Bibliographical Soc.

1997 'Importing books for Oxford, 1500–1640', in J. P. Carley and C. G. C. Tite (eds.), *Books and collectors 1200–1700*, London, 317–33.

Robin, F. 1989 'Le luxe des collections aux xivme et xvme siècles', in A. Vernet (ed.), *Histoire des bibliothèques françaises. Les bibliothèques médiévales du vime siècle à 1530*, Paris, 193–213.

Robinson, H. (ed. and trans.) 1842–5 *The Zurich letters, comprising the correspondence of several English bishops and others with some of the Helvetian reformers, during the early part of the reign of Queen Elizabeth* and *The Zurich Letters, Second Series*, 2 vols., Parker Society, Cambridge.

Robinson, P. R. (ed.) 1980 *MS Tanner 346*, Norman OK.

1981 *MS Bodley 638*, Norman OK.

Rogers, D. M. 1970 'Johann Hamman at Venice: a survey of his career, with a note on the Sarum horae of 1494', in D. E. Rhodes (ed.), *Essays in honour of Victor Scholderer*, Mainz, 349–68.

Rogers, E. F. (ed.) 1947 *The Correspondence of Sir Thomas More*, Princeton.

Rogers, N. 1982 'Books of hours produced in the Low Countries for the English market in the fifteenth century', unpub. M.Phil. thesis, University of Cambridge.

1992 'The miniatures of St John the Baptist in Gonville and Caius MS 241/127 and its context', *TCBS*, 10, 2, 125–38.

Rosenberg, A., Boghardt, M., Dittmann, H., Heinermann, D., Hein, A., Mommsen, H. 1998 'Röntgenfluoreszenzanalyse der Druckerschwärzen des Mainzer *Catholicon* und anderer Frühdrucke mit Synchrotronstrahlung', *Gutenberg-Jahrbuch 1998*, 231–55.

Rosenthal, B. M. 1997 *The Rosenthal collection of printed books with manuscript annotations: a catalogue of 242 editions mostly before 1600, annotated by contemporary readers*, New Haven.

Ross, A. 1962 'Some notes on the religious orders in pre-Reformation Scotland', in D. McRoberts (ed.), *Essays on the Scottish Reformation, 1513–1625*, Glasgow, 185–244.

1969 'Libraries of the Scottish Blackfriars 1481–1560', *Innes Rev.*, 20, 3–36.

Rouse, R. H. and Rouse, M. A. 1982 '*Statim invenire*: schools, preachers, and new attitudes to the page', in R. L. Benson and G. Constable (eds.), *Renaissance and renewal in the twelfth century*, Cambridge MA, 201–25.

Rubin, M. 1991 *Corpus Christi: the eucharist in late medieval culture*, Cambridge.

Ruddock, A. A. 1941 *Italian merchants and shipping in Southampton 1270–1600*, Southampton.

Rüegg, W. 1992 'The rise of humanism', in H. de Ridder-Symoens (ed.), *A history of the university in Europe*, Cambridge, 42–68.

Rundle, D. 1996 'On the difference between virtue and Weiss: humanist texts in England during the fifteenth century', in D. E. S. Dunn (ed.), *Court, counties and the capital in the later Middle Ages*, Stroud and New York, 181–203.

Ruysschaert, J. 1953a 'Lorenzo Guglielmo Traversagni (1452–1503): un humaniste franciscain oublié', *Archivum Franciscanum historicum*, 46, 193–210.

　　1953b 'Les manuscrits autographes de deux oeuvres de Lorenzo Guglielmo Traversagni imprimées chez Caxton', *BJRL*, 36, 191–7.

Rymer, T. (ed.) 1739–45 *Foedera, conventiones, literae e cuiusque generis acta publica*, 20 vols. in 10, 3rd edn, The Hague.

Sabbe, M. 1935 *De Plantijnsche Werkstede: Arbeidsregeling, tucht en maatschappelijke voorzorg in de oude Antwerpsche drukkerij*, Antwerp.

Sadie, S. (ed.) 1980 *The new Grove dictionary of music and musicians*, 20 vols., London.

Saenger, P. 1982 'Silent reading: its impact on late medieval script and society', *Viator*, 13, 367–414.

　　1987 'Books of hours and the reading habits of the later Middle Ages', in R. Chartier 1989, 141–73.

Saenger, P. and Heinlen, M. 1991 'Incunable description and its implications for the analysis of fifteenth-century reading habits', in Hindman 1991, 225–58.

Salmen, W. 1976 *Musikleben im 16. Jahrhundert*, Musikgeschichte in Bildern, 3, 9, Leipzig.

Salter, E. 1981 'The manuscripts of Nicholas Love's *Myrrour of the Blessed Lyf of Jesu Christ* and related texts', in A. S. G. Edwards and D. Pearsall (eds.), *Middle English prose: essays on bibliographical problems*, New York and London, 115–27.

　　1983 *Fourteenth-century English poetry: contexts and readings*, Oxford.

　　1988 *English and international: studies in the literature, art and patronage of medieval England*, Cambridge.

Salter, F. M. 1934 'Skelton's *Speculum principis*', *Speculum*, 9, 25–37.

Salter, H. E. (ed.) 1932 *Registrum Cancellarii Oxoniensis 1434–1469*, 2 vols., OHS 93, 94, Oxford.

Salzman, L. F. 1929–30 'Medieval glazing accounts (continued)', *Jnl of the British Soc. of Master Glass-Painters*, 3, 25–30.

Sammut, A. 1980 *Unfredo duca di Gloucester et gli umanisti italiani*, Medioevo e Umanesimo 41, Padua.

Sandler, L. F. 1986 *A survey of manuscripts illuminated in the British Isles*, Vol. v: *Gothic manuscripts 1285–1385*, ed. J. J. G. Alexander, London.

Sandon, N. and Page, C. 1992 'Music', in B. Ford (ed.), *The Cambridge cultural history of Britain*, Vol. II: *Medieval Britain*, 2nd edn, Cambridge.

Sargent, M. G. 1983 'Walter Hilton's *Scale of perfection*: the London manuscript group reconsidered', *MAE*, 52, 189–216.

　　1984 'James Grenehalgh: the biographical record', *Analecta Cartusiana*, 4, 20–54.

Sargent, M. G. (ed.) 1989 *De cella in seculum: religious and secular life and devotion in late medieval England*, Cambridge.

　　1992 *Nicholas Love's Mirror of the blessed life of Jesus Christ. A critical edition based on Cambridge University Library Additional mss. 6578 and 6686*, New York.

Savage, E. A. 1911 *Old English libraries. The making, collection, and use of books during the Middle Ages*, New York and London (rpt 1970).

Sayle, C. E. 1916 *Cambridge University Library annals*, Cambridge.

1923 'King's Hall library', *Proc. of the Cambridge Antiquarian Soc.*, 24, 54–76.

Scarisbrick, J. J. 1968 *Henry VIII*, London.

Scase, W. 1992 'Reginald Pecock, John Carpenter and John Colop's "common profit" books', *MAE*, 61, 261–74.

Scattergood, V. J. 1968 'Two medieval book-lists', *Library*, 5th ser., 23, 236–9.

1983 'Literary culture at the court of Richard II', in Scattergood and Sherborne 1983, 29–43.

Scattergood, V. J. and Sherborne, J. W. (eds.) 1983 *English court culture in the later Middle Ages*, London.

[Schäfer, O.] 1987 *Fünf Jahrhunderte Buchillustration: Meisterwerke der Buchgraphik aus der Bibliothek Otto Schäfer*, Nuremberg.

Schirmer, W. F. 1963 *Der englische Frühhumanismus*, 2nd edn, Tübingen.

Schmitt, C. B. 1983a *Aristotle in the Renaissance*, Martin Classical Lectures 27, Cambridge MA and London.

1983b *John Case and Aristotelianism in Renaissance England*, Kingston and Montreal.

1988 'The rise of the philosophical text-book', in *Cambridge history of Renaissance philosophy*, Cambridge, 792–804.

Schoeck, R. J. 1962 'The libraries of common lawyers in the Renaissance', *Manuscripta* 6, 155–67.

Schofield, R. W. 1968 'The measure of literacy', in Goody 1968, 311–25.

Scholderer, V. 1940 *Hand-list of incunabula in the National Library of Wales*, Aberystwyth.

1966 'Printing at Venice to the end of 1481', in D. F. Rhodes (ed.), *Fifty essays in fifteenth- and sixteenth-century bibliography*, Amsterdam, 74–89.

Schrage, E. J. H. 1992 *Utrumque ius: eine Einführung in das Studium der Quellen des mittelalterlichen gelehrten Rechts*, Berlin.

Schramm, W. L. 1933 'The cost of books in Chaucer's time', *MLN*, 48, 139–45.

Schreiber, W. L. and Heitz, P. 1908 *Die deutschen 'Accipies' und Magister cum discipulis – Holzschnitte als Hilfsmittel zur Inkunabel-Bestimmung*, Studien zur deutschen Kunstgeschichte 100, Strasbourg.

Schreurs, E. 1995 *An anthology of music fragments from the Low Countries (Middle Ages–Renaissance)*, Louvain and Peer.

Von Schulte, J. F. 1875–80 *Die Geschichte der Quellen und Literatur des canonischen Rechts*, 3 vols., Stuttgart (rpt Graz 1956).

Schulz, E. 1924 *Aufgaben und Ziele der Inkunabelforschung*, Munich.

Schwab, R. N., Cahill, T. A., Kusko, H. K. and Wick, D. L. 1983 'Cyclotron analysis of the ink in the 42-line Bible', *PBSA*, 77, 285–315.

[Schwenke, P.] 1923 *Johannes Gutenbergs zweiundvierzigzeilige Bibel: Ergänzungsband zur Faksimile-Ausgabe*, Leipzig.

Scott, K. L. 1968 'A mid-fifteenth-century English illuminating shop and its customers', *JWCI*, 31, 170–96.

1976 *The Caxton Master and his patrons*, Cambridge Bibliographical Society Monograph 8, Cambridge.

1980a 'Additions to the oeuvre of the English border artist: the *Nova statuta*', in *The Mirrour of the Worlde: MS Bodley 283*, Roxburghe Club, London, 1–68.

1980b 'A late fifteenth-century group of *Nova Statuta* Manuscripts', in De la Mare and Barker-Benfield 1980, 103–5.

1989 'Design, decoration and illustration', in *BPPB*, 31–64.

1996 *A survey of manuscripts illuminated in the British Isles*, Vol. VI: *Later Gothic manuscripts c. 1390–1490*, ed. J. J. G. Alexander, London.

1997 'The illustration and decoration of manuscripts of Nicholas Love's *Mirror of the Blessed Life of Jesus Christ*', in S. Oguro, H. L. R. Beadle and M. G. Sargent, *Nicholas Love at Waseda*, Woodbridge, 61–86.

Scribner, R. W. 1981 *For the sake of simple folk. Popular propaganda for the German Reformation*, Cambridge.

Searle, W. G. 1864 'Catalogue of the library of Queens' College, 1472', *Antiquarian Communications: Being Papers Presented at the Meetings of the Cambridge Antiquarian Soc.*, 2, 165–93.

Seaton, E. 1961 *Sir Richard Roos, Lancastrian poet*, London.

Seifert, A. 1984 'Der Humanismus an den Artistenfakultäten des katholischen Deutschland', in W. Reinhard (ed.), *Humanismus im Bildungswesen des 15. und 16. Jahrhunderts*, Mitteilungen der Kommission für Humanismusforschung 12, Weinheim, 135–54.

Selwyn, D. G. 1996 *The library of Thomas Cranmer*, Oxford.

Senior, W. 1931 'Roman Law manuscripts, in England', *LQR*, 47, 337–44.

Shaaber, M. A. 1975 *Check-list of works of British authors printed abroad, in languages other than English, to 1641*, New York.

Shadwell, C. L. 1885 'The catalogue of the library of Oriel College in the year 1375 A.D.', *OHS*, 5, 57–70.

Sharpe, J. 1990 *Quaestio super universalia*, ed. A. D. Conti, Florence.

Sharpe, R. 1997 *A handlist of the Latin writers of Great Britain and Ireland before 1540*, Publications of the *Jnl of Medieval Latin*, 1, Louvain.

Sharpe, R. R. (ed.) 1889–1912 *Calendar of letter-books of the City of London*, 11 vols., London.

Sheehan, M. W. 1984 'The religious orders 1220–1370', in *HUO*, I, 193–221.

Sherman, W. L. 1995 *John Dee: the politics of reading and writing in the English Renaissance*, Amherst MA.

Shorter, A. H. 1957 *Paper mills and paper makers in England 1495–1800*, Hilversum.

Sider, S. 1990 '"Interwoven with poems and pictures". A protoemblematic Latin translation of the *Tabula Cebetis*', in B. F. Scholz, M. Bath, and D. Weston, (eds.), *The European emblem: selected papers from the Glasgow conference 1987*, Leiden, New York, Cologne, 1–18.

Simon, E. 1988 *The Türkenkalender (1454) attributed to Gutenberg and the Strasbourg lunation tracts*, Speculum Anniversary Monographs 14, Cambridge MA.

Simpson, A. W. B. 1957 'The circulation of year books in the fifteenth century', *LQR*, 73, 492–505.

1971 'The source and function of the later year books', *LQR*, 87, 94–118.

Simpson, P. 1935 *Proof-reading in the sixteenth, seventeenth and eighteenth centuries*, London (rpt 1970).

Singer, D. W. 1919 'Hand-list of scientific manuscripts in the British Isles dating from before the sixteenth century', *Library*, 2nd ser., 15, 1–7.

Skeat, W. W. (ed.) 1897 *The Romance of William of Palerne*, EETS ES 1, London.

Skelton, J. (trans.) 1956–7 *The Bibliotheca historica of Diodorus Siculus*, 2 vols., ed. F. M. Salter and H. L. R. Edwards, EETS OS 233, 239, London.

    1983 *The complete English poems*, ed. J. Scattergood, Harmondsworth and New York.

Skinner, D. 1994 'At the mynde of Nycholas Ludford', *Early Music*, 22, 393–413.

    1997 'Discovering the provenance and history of the Caius and Lambeth choir-books', *Early Music*, 25, 245–66.

Slack, P. 1979 'Mirrors of health and treasures of poor men: the uses of the vernacular medical literature of Tudor England', in C. Webster (ed.), *Health, medicine and mortality in the sixteenth century*, Cambridge, 237–73.

Slavin, A. J. 1982 'The Tudor revolution and the devil's art: Bishop Bonner's printed forms', in D. J. Guth and J. W. McKenna (eds.), *Tudor rule and revolution*, Cambridge, 3–23.

    1986 'The Gutenberg galaxy and the Tudor revolution', in G. P. Tyson and S. S. Wagonheim (eds.), *Print and culture in the Renaissance*, Newark, London and Toronto, 90–109.

Smalley, B. 1960 *English friars and antiquity in the early fourteenth century*, Oxford.

Smith, D. B. 1936 *Sources and literature of Scots law*, Stair Society 1, Edinburgh.

Smith, J. J. 1997 'Dialect and standardisation in the Waseda manuscript of Nicholas Love's *Mirror of the Blessed Life of Jesus Christ*', in S. Oguro, H. R. L. Beadle and M. G. Sargent (eds.), *Nicholas Love at Waseda*, Woodbridge, 129–41.

Smout, T. C. (ed.) 1986 *Scotland and Europe, 1200–1850*, Edinburgh.

Söllner, A. 1977 'Die Literatur zum gemeinen und partikularen Recht in Deutschland, Österreich, den Niederlanden und der Schweiz', in Coing 1973–7, II.1, 501–614.

Somerville, R. 1936 'The Cowcher books of the Duchy of Lancaster', *EHR*, 51, 598–615.

Sommer, H. O. (ed.) 1892 *The Kalender of Shepherdes. The edition of Paris 1503 in photographic facsimile; a faithful reprint of R. Pynson's ed. of London 1506*, London.

Southall, R. 1964 'The Devonshire manuscript collection of early Tudor poetry, 1532–41', *RES*, n.s., 15, 142–50.

Sparrow Simpson, W. 1874a 'On the measure of the wound in the side of the redeemer', *Jnl of the British Archaeological Assoc.*, 30, 357–74.

    1874b 'On the pilgrimage to Bromholm in Norfolk', *Jnl of the British Archaeological Assoc.* 30, 52–61.

Spriggs, G. 1974 'The Nevill Hours and the school of Herman Scheerre', *JWCI*, 37, 104–30.

Squibb, G. D. 1977 *Doctors' Commons*, Oxford.

Stamp, A. E. 1924 *Notes on the history of Michaelhouse published on the 600th anniversary of the foundation of the Society by Hervey de Stanton*, Cambridge.

Stapleton, T. 1928 *The life and illustrious martyrdom of Sir Thomas More*, trans. P. E. Hallett, London (rpt 1966).

Starkey, D. 1992 'England', in Porter and Teich 1992, 146–63.

Starkey, D. (ed.) 1991 *Henry VIII: a European court in England, catalogue of the exhibition in the National Maritime Museum, Greenwich*, London.

1998 *The inventory of Henry VIII*, Vol. 1: *The transcript*, London.

Statuta Academiae Cantabrigiensis, Cambridge 1785.

Steele, R. 1903 *The earliest English music printing*, London.

Stein, P. G. 1988 *The character and influence of the Roman civil law: historical essays*, London and Ronceverte, WV.

Stevens, J. 1961 *Music and poetry in the early Tudor court*, London.

Stevens, J. (ed.) 1970 *Mediaeval carols*, Musica Britannica 4, 2nd edn, London.

1973 *Music at the court of Henry VIII*, Musica Britannica 18, 2nd edn, London.

Stevenson, A. 1967 'Tudor roses from John Tate', *SB*, 20, 15–34.

1968 Introduction to rpt of C. M. Briquet, *Les filigranes: dictionnaire historique des marques du papier dès leur apparition vers 1282 jusqu'en 1600* (1923), Amsterdam, *15–*53.

Stevenson, W. H. 1911 'Nottingham University Library, Middleton MS Mi LM2', in W. H. Stevenson (ed.), *HMC, Report on the mss of Lord Middleton*, London, 212–20.

Storey, R. L. 1982 'Gentlemen-bureaucrats', in C. H. Clough (ed.), *Profession, vocation and culture in later medieval England: essays dedicated to the memory of A. R. Myers*, Liverpool, 90–129.

Stratford, J. 1987 'The manuscripts of John, Duke of Bedford: library and chapel', in D. Williams (ed.), *England in the fifteenth century: proceedings of the 1986 Harlaxton Symposium*, Woodbridge, 329–50.

1993 *The Bedford inventories: the worldly goods of John, Duke of Bedford, Regent of France (1389–1435)*, London.

Straub, R. E. F. 1995 *David Aubert, escripvain et clerc*, Amsterdam.

String, T. C. 1996 'Henry VIII's illuminated "Great Bible"', *JWCI*, 30, 315–24.

Strode, R. forthcoming *Logica*, ed. E. J. Ashworth and A. Maierù.

Strong, P. and Strong, F. 1981 'The last will and codicils of Henry V', *EHR*, 96, 79–102.

Strype, J. 1820 *The life of the learned Thomas Smith*, Oxford.

1822 *Ecclesiastical memorials*, Oxford.

Stuart, J. 1872 *Records of the monastery of Kinross*, Edinburgh.

Sturge, C. 1938 *Cuthbert Tunstall: churchman, scholar, statesman, administrator*, London.

Suggett, H. 1946 'The use of French in England in the later Middle Ages', *TRHS*, 4th ser., 28, 61–83.

Surtz, E. and Murphy, V. (eds.) 1988 *The divorce tracts of Henry VIII*, Angers.

Sutton, A. F. 1992 'Caxton was a mercer: his social milieu and friends', in N. Rogers (ed.), *England in the fifteenth century: proceedings of the 1992 Harlaxton Symposium*, Harlaxton Medieval Studies 4, Stamford, 118–48.

Sutton, A. F. and Hammond, P. W. 1978 'The problems of dating and the dangers of redating: the Acts of Court of the Mercers' Company 1453–1527', *Jnl of the Soc. of Archivists*, 6, 87–91.

Sutton, A. F. and Visser-Fuchs, L. 1990 *The Hours of Richard III*, Stroud.

1997 *Richard III's books*, Stroud.

Swanton, M. 1987 *English literature before Chaucer*, Harlow.

Sylla, E. 1982 'The Oxford calculators', in N. Kretzmann, A. J. P. Kenny and J.

Pinborg (eds.), *The Cambridge history of later medieval philosophy*, Cambridge, 540–63.

Taavitsainen, I. 1987 'The identification of Middle English lunary manuscripts', *NeuphilMitt*, 88, 1–26.

1988 *Middle English lunaries: a study of the genre*, Helsinki.

Tait, H. 1985 'The girdle prayerbook or "tablett": an important class of Renaissance jewellery at the court of Henry VII', *Jewellery Stud.*, 2, 29–58.

Takamiya, T. 1996 'Chapter divisions and page breaks in Caxton's *Morte Darthur*', *Poetica*, 45, 63–78.

Talbot, C. H. 1958 'The universities and the mediaeval library', in Wormald and Wright 1958, 66–84.

1961 'A medieval physician's vade mecum', *Jnl of the History of Medicine and Allied Sciences*, 16, 212–33.

1962 'The English Cistercians and the universities', *Studia Monastica*, 4, 197–220.

Tanner, N. P. 1984 *The Church in late medieval Norwich 1370-1532*, Toronto.

Tarvers, J. K. 1992 '"Thys ys mystrys boke": English women as readers and writers in late medieval England', in C. M. Cook, P. Reed Doob and M. C. Woods (eds.), *The uses of manuscripts in literary studies: essays in memory of Judson Boyce Allen*, Studies in Medieval Culture 31, Kalamazoo MI, 305–27.

Temperley, N. 1979 *The music of the English parish church*, 2 vols., Cambridge.

Testamenta Eboracensia I–VI, 1836–1902, Surtees Society 2, 4, 30, 45, 79, 106, London.

Thielemanns, M.-R. 1966 *Bourgogne et Angleterre: relations politiques et économiques entre les Pays-Bas bourguignons et l'Angleterre 1435–1467*, Brussels.

Thompson, A. H. (ed.) 1969 *Visitations of religious houses in the Diocese of Lincoln (1519–27)*, Canterbury and York Society, Oxford.

Thompson, E. M. 1930 *The Carthusian order in England*, London and New York.

Thompson, J. J. 1987 *Robert Thornton and the London Thornton manuscript*, Cambridge.

Thomson, D. 1979 *A descriptive catalogue of Middle English grammatical texts*, New York and London.

1984 *An edition of the Middle English grammatical texts*, New York and London.

Thomson, D. F. S. and Porter, H. C. (eds.) 1963 *Erasmus in Cambridge: the Cambridge letters of Erasmus*, Cambridge.

Thomson, J. A. F. 1965 *The later Lollards, 1414–1520*, Oxford.

Thomson, P. 1964 *Sir Thomas Wyatt and his background*, London.

Thrupp, S. L. 1948 *The merchant class of medieval London, 1300–1500*, Chicago (rpt 1989).

Tieken-Boon van Ostade, I. 1995 *The two versions of Malory's* Morte Darthur: *multiple negations and the editing of the text*, Cambridge.

Tierney, B. 1982 *Religion, law, and the growth of constitutional thought 1150–1650*, Cambridge.

Tomlinson, E. M. 1907 *A history of the Minorites, London*, London.

Took, P. 1977 'Government and the printing trade, 1540-1560', unpub. Ph.D. thesis, University of London.

Toulmin Smith, L. (ed.), 1906–10 *The itinerary of John Leland in or about the years 1535–1543*, 5 vols., London.

Tout, T. F. 1920–33 *Chapters in the administrative history of medieval England*, 6 vols., Manchester.

Trapp, J. B. 1975 'Notes on manuscripts written by Peter Meghen', *BC*, 24, 80–96.

1981 *CWM*, vi, 883.

1981–2 'Peter Meghen 1466/7 – 1540, scribe and courier', *Erasmus in English*, 11, 28–35.

1982 'John Colet and the *Hierarchies* of the ps-Dionysius', *Stud. in Church History*, 18, 127–48.

1990 'Christopher Urswick and his books. The reading of Henry VII's almoner', in Trapp, *Essays on the Renaissance and the classical tradition*, Aldershot 1990, item 15.

1991 *Erasmus, Colet and More: the early Tudor Humanists and their books* (Panizzi Lectures 1990), London.

1996 'Erasmus on William Grocyn and Ps-Dionysius: a reconsideration', *JWCI*, 59, 294–303.

Trapp, J. B. (ed.) 1983 *Manuscripts in the fifty years after the invention of printing. Some papers read at a colloquium at the Warburg Institute . . . 1982*, London.

Trapp, J. B. and Schulte Herbrüggen, H. 1997 *The King's good servant. Sir Thomas More 1477/8 – 1535*, exhibition catalogue, National Portrait Gallery, London.

Traversagni, L. G. 1971–86 'The *Epitome margaritae eloquentiae* . . .', ed. and trans., with intro., by R. H. Martin, *Proc. Leeds Philosophical and Literary Soc., Lit. and Hist. Section*, 14, 4, 99–187; 20, 2, 131–269.

1978 *Margarita eloquentiae castigatae*, ed. G. Farris, Savona.

Treptow, O. 1970 *John Siberch; Johann Lair von Siegburg*, CBS Monograph 6, Cambridge.

Trio, P. 1984 'Financing of university students in the Middle Ages – a new orientation', *History of Universities*, 4, 1–24.

Troje, H. E. 1977 'Die Literatur des gemeinen Rechts unter dem Einfluss des Humanismus', in Coing 1973–7, ii, 1, Munich, 615–796.

Trovato, P. 1991 *Con ogni diligenza corretto: la stampa e le revisioni editoriali dei testi letterari italiani (1470–1570)*, Bologna.

Trowell, B. 1978 'Faburden – new sources, new evidence: a preliminary survey', in E. Olleson (ed.), *Modern musical scholarship*, Stocksfield, 28–78.

Tudor-Craig, P. 1987 'The Hours of Edward V and William, Lord Hastings: British Library Manuscript Additional 54782', in D. Williams (ed.), *England in the fifteenth century: proceedings of the 1986 Harlaxton Symposium*, Woodbridge, 351–69.

Turner, D. H. 1983 *The Hastings Hours. A fifteenth-century Flemish book of hours made for William, Lord Hastings, now in the British Library, London*, London.

Turner, T. H. 1845 'The will of Humphrey de Bohun . . .', *Archaeological Jnl*, 2, 339–49.

Turville-Petre, T. 1977 *The alliterative revival*, Cambridge.

Turville-Petre, T. (ed.) 1989 *Alliterative poetry of the later Middle Ages: an anthology*, London.

Tuve, R. 1940 'Spenser and some pictorial conventions, with particular reference to illuminated manuscripts', *SP*, 37, 149–76.

Twigge, J. 1987 *A History of Queens' College, Cambridge, 1448–1986*, Woodbridge.

Tymms, S. (ed.) 1850 *Wills and inventories from the registers of the Commissary of Bury St Edmunds and the Archdeacon of Sudbury*, Camden Society 49, London.

Tyson, G. P. and Wagonheim, S. S. 1986 *Print and culture in the Renaissance*, Newark, London and Toronto.

Ullman, B. L. 1955 'Manuscripts of Duke Humphrey of Gloucester', in Ullman, *Studies in the Italian Renaissance*, Rome, 345–55.

    1960 *The origin and development of humanistic script*, Storia e letteratura 79, Rome.

Underwood, M. G. 1987 'Politics and piety in the household of Lady Margaret Beaufort', *Jnl of Ecclesiastical History*, 38, 39–52.

    1989 'John Fisher and the promotion of learning', in B. Bradshaw and E. Duffy (eds.), *Humanism, reform and the Reformation: the career of Bishop John Fisher*, Cambridge, 25–46.

Unterkircher, F. and Wilkie, J. (eds.) 1987 *Das Gebetbuch Jakobs von Schottland und seiner Gemahlin Margaret Tudor*, Codices Selecti 85, Graz.

Vale, J. 1982 *Edward III and chivalry: chivalric society and its context, 1270–1350*, Woodbridge.

Vale, M. G. A. 1976 *Piety, charity and literacy among the Yorkshire gentry 1370–1480*, Borthwick papers 50, York.

Venn, J. A. (ed.) 1910 *Grace book [Greek] D, containing the records of the University of Cambridge for the years 1542–1589*, Cambridge.

Vezin, J. 1990 'Manuscrits "imposés"', in H.-J. Martin and J. Vezin (eds.), *Mise en page et mise en texte du livre manuscrit*, Paris, 423–5.

Vian, N. 1962 'La presentazione e gli esemplari Vaticani della *Assertio septem sacramentorum* di Enrico VIII', in *Collectanea Vaticana in honorem Anselmi M. Card. Albareda*, Vatican City, 2, 355–75.

Vinaver, E. (ed.) 1992 *The Works of Sir Thomas Malory*, rev. P. J. C. Field, 3 vols., Oxford.

Visitations and memorials of Southwell Minster, 1891, Camden Society, n.s. 48, London.

De Vocht, H. 1951 *History of the foundation and the rise of the Collegium trilingue lovaniense (1517–50)*, Louvain.

Voelkle, W. M. and Wieck, R. S., 1992, with the assistance of Saffiotti, M. F. P., *The Bernard Breslauer collection of manuscript illuminations*, exhibition catalogue, Pierpont Morgan Library, New York.

Voigts, L. E. 1989 'Scientific and medical books', in *BPPB*, 345–402.

    1995 'A doctor and his books: the manuscripts of Roger Marchall (d. 1477)', in Beadle and Piper 1995, 249–314.

Voigts, L. E. and McVaugh, M. L. 1984 'A Latin technical phlebotomy and its Middle English translation', *Trans. of the American Philosophical Soc.*, 74, 2, Philadelphia PA.

Wakefield, R. 1989 *On the three languages, 1524*, ed. and trans. with an intro. by G. Lloyd Jones, Manchester.

Waldstein 1981 *The Diary of Baron Waldstein, a traveller in Elizabethan England*, ed. and trans. G. W. Groos, 1981.

Ward, J. 1992 *Music for Elizabethan lutes*, 2 vols., Oxford.

Ward, J. (ed. and trans.) 1995 *Women of the English nobility and gentry 1066–1500*, Manchester Medieval Sources Series, Manchester.

Warner, Sir G. F. and Gilson, J. P. 1921 *Catalogue of Western manuscripts in the old Royal and Kings' collections, in the British Museum*, 4 vols., London.

Warner, L. 1996 'Fellows, students and their gifts to Jesus College [Cambridge] library, 1496–1610', *TCBS*, 11, 1–48.

Warren, A. K. 1985 *Anchorites and their patrons in medieval England*, Berkeley CA.

Wathey, A. 1988 'Lost books of polyphony in England: a list to 1500', *Royal Musical Assoc. Research Chron.*, 21, 1–19.

   1989a 'The production of books of liturgical polyphony', in *BPPB*, 143–61.

   1989b *Music in the royal and noble households in late medieval England: studies of sources and patronage*, New York and London.

   1992 'The marriage of Edward III and the transmission of French motets to England', *Jnl of the American Musicological Soc.*, 45, 11–12.

Watson, A. G. 1979 *Catalogue of dated and datable manuscripts in the Department of Manuscripts in the British Library, c. 700–1600*, 2 vols., London.

Watson, R. 1984 *The Playfair hours: a late fifteenth-century illuminated manuscript from Rouen*, London.

Weaver, F. W. (ed.) 1901–5 *Somerset medieval wills (1383–1500; 1501–1530; 1531–1558)*, 3 vols., Somerset Record Society 16, 19, 21, London.

Webb, C. A. 1970 'Caxton's "Quattuor Sermones": a newly discovered edition', in D. E. Rhodes (ed.), *Essays in honour of Victor Scholderer*, Mainz, 407–25.

Wedgwood, J. C. 1936 *History of Parliament: biographies of the members of the Commons House 1439–1509*, London.

Weisheipl, J. A. 1964 'Curriculum of the faculty of arts at Oxford in the early fourteenth century', *Med. Stud.*, 26, 143–85.

   1966 'Developments in the arts curriculum at Oxford in the early fourteenth century', *Med. Stud.*, 28, 151–75.

   1969 'Repertorium Mertonense', *Med. Stud.*, 31, 174–224.

Weiss, R. 1938 'The earliest catalogue of the library of Lincoln College', *BQR*, 8, 343–59.

   1942 'Henry VI and the library of All Souls College', *EHR*, 57, 102–5.

   1947 'Notes on Thomas Linacre', *Miscellanea Giovanni Mercati*, Vatican City, IV, pp. 378–9.

   1967 *Humanism in England during the fifteenth century*, 3rd edn, *MAE* Monographs 4, Oxford.

Wenzel, S. (ed. and trans.) 1989 *Fasciculus morum. A fourteenth-century preachers' handbook*, University Park PA.

Wernham, R. B. 1956 'The public records in the sixteenth and seventeenth centuries', in L. Fox (ed.), *English historical scholarship in the sixteenth and seventeenth centuries*, London, 11–30.

White, H. C. 1951 *The Tudor books of private devotion*, Madison WI.

White, R. 1994 'Early print and purgatory: the shaping of a Henrician ideology', unpub. Ph.D. thesis, Australian National University, Canberra.

Whitworth Art Gallery 1976 *Medieval and early Renaissance treasures in the North West*, cat. of the exhibition at the Whitworth Art Gallery, University of Manchester.

Wieck, R. 1988 *Time sanctified: the book of hours in medieval art and life*, New York and Baltimore MD.

Wijffels, A. 1992a *Late sixteenth-century lists of law books at Merton College*, Cambridge.
    1992b 'Sir Edward Stanhope's bequest of books to Trinity College, 1608', *PLRE*, I,
    47–78.
    1993a 'Law books at Cambridge 1500–1640', in P. Birks (ed.), *The life of the law: pro-
    ceedings of the tenth British legal history conference*, London, 59–88.
    1993b 'Law books in Cambridge libraries 1500–1640', *TCBS*, 10, 3, 359–412.
Wilkins, D. (ed.) 1737 *Concilia Magnae Britanniae et Hiberniae, 446–1717*, 4 vols.,
    London.
Willan, T. S. (ed.) 1962 *A Tudor book of rates*, Manchester.
*William Caxton: an exhibition to commemorate the quincentenary of the introduction of print-
    ing into England*, 1976, British Library Reference Division, London.
Williams, T. W. 1908 'Gloucestershire medieval libraries', *Trans. of the Bristol and
    Gloucestershire Archaeological Soc.*, 31, 112–15.
Willis, R. and Clark, J. W. 1886 *The architectural history of the University of Cambridge
    and of the colleges of Cambridge and Eton*, 4 vols., Cambridge (vols. I–II rpt 1988).
Willoughby, H. R. 1942 *The first authorized English Bible and the Cranmer preface*,
    Philadelphia PA.
Wilson, E. 1990 'Local habitations and names in MS Rawlinson c.813 in the Bodleian
    Library, Oxford', *RES*, n.s., 41, 12–44.
Wilson, F. P. 1945 'Shakespeare and the "New Bibliography"', *Studies in Retrospect*,
    76–135 (rev. rpt 1970, ed. H. Gardner, Oxford).
Wilson, R. M. 1940 'The medieval library of Titchfield Abbey', *Proc. of the Leeds
    Philosophical and Literary Soc. (Literary and Historical Section)*, 5, 150–77, 252–76.
    1958 'The contents of the medieval library', in Wormald and Wright 1958,
    85–111.
Winfield, P. 1923 'Abridgments of the year books', *Harvard Law Rev.*, 37, 214–44.
Winger, H. R. 1956 'Regulations relating to the book trade in London from 1357 to
    1586', *Lib. Q.*, 26, 157–95.
Winn, M. B. 1983 'Antoine Vérard's presentation manuscripts and printed books', in
    Trapp 1983, 66–74.
    1993 'Verard's Hours of 8 February 1489/90', *PBSA*, 87, 337–62.
    1997 *Anthoine Vérard, Parisian publisher, 1485–1512: prologues, poems and presenta-
    tions*, Travaux d'humanisme et Renaissance 313, Geneva.
De Winter, P. 1981 'A book of hours of Queen Isabel la Catolica', *Bull. of the Cleveland
    Museum of Art*, 342–427.
Woodcock, B. L. 1952 *Medieval ecclesiastical courts in the diocese of Canterbury*, Oxford.
Woodfill, W. L. 1953 *Musicians in English society from Elizabeth to Charles I*, Princeton
    NJ.
Woods, I. 1984 'The Carvor choirbook', unpub. Ph.D. thesis, Princeton University.
Woolfson, J. 1997 'John Claymond, Pliny the Elder and the history of Corpus Christi
    College, Oxford', *EHR*, 112, 882–903.
Wormald, F. 1937–8 'The rood of Bromholm', *JWCI*, 1, 31–45.
    1958 'The monastic library', in Wormald and Wright 1958, 15–31.
Wormald, F. and Wright, C. E. (eds.) 1958 *The English library before 1700: studies in its
    history*, London.
Worman, E. J. 1906 *Alien members of the book-trade during the Tudor period*, London.

Woudhuysen, H. R. 1996 *Sir Philip Sidney and the circulation of manuscripts 1558–1640*, Oxford.

Wright, C. E. 1958 'The dispersal of the libraries in the sixteenth century', in Wormald and Wright 1958, 148–75.

  1960 *English vernacular hands from the twelfth to the fifteenth centuries*, Oxford palaeographical handbooks, Oxford.

Wright, H. G. 1957 *Boccaccio in England*, London.

Wright, L. B. 1931 'The reading of Renaissance English women', *SP*, 28, 671–88.

Wright, S. A. 1986 'The Big Bible: Royal MS. 1 E. ix and manuscript illumination in London in the early fifteenth century', unpub. Ph.D. thesis, University of London.

  1992 'The author portraits in the Bedford psalter-hours: Gower, Chaucer and Hoccleve', *BLJ*, 18, 190–201.

Wrigley, E. A. and Schofield, R. S. 1981 *The population history of England 1541–1871*, London.

Wyatt, Sir T. 1975 *Collected poems*, ed. J. Daalder, Oxford.

Zulueta, F. de and Stein, P. G. 1990 *The teaching of Roman law in England around 1200*, Selden Society, London.

Photo credits

Biblioteca Apostolica Vaticana 3.7
Bodleian Library 2.6, 9.5
The British Library, Reprographic Service 2.1, 2.3, 3.5, 3.8(b), 4.1, 4.2, 4.4. 12.1, 12.2,
    13.1, 14.5, 22.2, 26.2, 26.3
The British Museum, Photographic Service 4.3
Cambridge University Library 2.10, 3.1, 3.2, 3.4, 3.8a, c–d, 3.9, 3.10, 9.1, 9.2, 9.3, 9.4,
    13.2, 14.4, 20.1, 20.2, 21.1, 21.2, 21.3, 22.1, 22.3, 23.1, 23.2, 25.1, 25.2, 27.2,
    28.2
Chatsworth Settlement Trustees, 2.8
Courtauld Institute of Art, Conway Library 2.4
Fitzwilliam Museum 2.5
Mr John Gibbons, Oxford 14.2
John Rylands University Library 24.4a–c
National Library of Scotland 27.1
Österreichische Nationalbibliothek 2.7, 3.3
Pierpont Morgan Library 2.9, 24.3a–b
Public Record Office, London 6.1
Society of Antiquaries, London 28.1
The Warburg Institute, University of London 1, 3.6, 14.3
Yale University, the Beinecke Library 24.1

Contributing institutions

Cambridge, Emmanuel College, 2.10.
    By permission of the Master, Fellows and Scholars of Emmanuel College.
Cambridge, Fitzwilliam Museum, 2.5.
Cambridge, Gonville and Caius College, 9.4.
    With permission of the Librarian of Gonville and Caius College, Cambridge.
Cambridge, King's College, 21.1.
Cambridge, Magdalene College, Pepys Library, 9.1, 22.1, 23.1.
    By permission of the Librarian, Magdalene College, Cambridge.
Cambridge, Trinity College, 13.2, 25.1, 27.2.
    By permission of the Master and Fellows of Trinity College.
Cambridge University Archives, 21.4.
Cambridge University Library, 3.1, 3.2, 3.4, 3.8a, 3.8c–d, 3.9, 3.10, 9.2, 9.3, 14.4,
    20.1, 20.2, 21.2, 22.3, 23.2, 25.2, 28.2.

By permission of the Syndics of Cambridge University Library.
Chatsworth, 2.8.
    Reproduced by permission of the Chatsworth Settlement Trustees.
Città del Vaticano, Biblioteca Apostolica Vaticana, 3.7.
Edinburgh, National Library of Scotland, 27.1.
    By permission of the Trustees of the National Library of Scotland.
London, British Library, 2.1, 2.3, 3.5, 3.8b, 4.1, 4.2, 4.4, 12.1, 12.2, 12.3, 12.4, 13.1, 14.5, 22.2, 26.1, 26.2, 26.3.
    With permission from the British Library Board.
London, British Museum, 4.3a–b.
London, Lambeth Palace Library, 24.2.
London, Public Record Office, 6.1.
    Crown copyright material in the Public Record Office is reproduced by permission of the Controller of Her Majesty's Stationery Office.
London, Society of Antiquaries, 28.1.
New York, Pierpont Morgan Library, 2.9, 24.3.
    By permission of the Pierpont Morgan Library, New York.
Manchester, John Rylands University Library, 24.4.
    By permission of the Director and University Librarian, the John Rylands University Library of Manchester.
New Haven, Yale University, Beinecke Rare Book and Manuscript Library, 24.1.
    By permission of the Beinecke Rare Book and Manuscript Library, Yale University Library.
Oxford, Bodleian Library, 2.6, 9.5.
Oxford, Christ Church, 2.2.
    With permission of The Governing Body of Christ Church, Oxford.
Oxford, Corpus Christi College, 14.1.
    With permission of the Librarian of Corpus Christi College, Oxford.
Oxford, Magdalen College, 14.2.
Swaffham Parish Church, Norfolk, 2.4.
Vienna, Österreichische Nationalbibliothek, 2.7, 3.3
Wooster (Ohio), College of Wooster, Andrews Library, 5.1–2.

General index

As well as names, this index lists topics selected for their particular relevance to the production, importation, distribution, ownership, use and survival of books in Britain. Subject entries are sometimes presented in hierarchical rather than alphabetical order for clarity. Compiled by the editors.

Newbold, William (Mercers' Clerk) 162
Newdosk 395
Newland, Glos. 34
Newton, Humphrey, Cheshire 536, 568
Newton, John, Treasurer of York Minster
 520
Niccoli, Niccolò (humanist, scribe) 288
Nicholas de Birckendalia, *Deponentale* 246
Nicholas of Lynn, *Kalendarium* 439
Nicholas of Lyra 60, 247, 332, 334
Nicholson, Segar (stationer), Cambridge
 339
Niclaes, Hendric 348–9
Nicolaus de Tudeschis *see* Panormitanus
Nicolson, James (printer), London 25–6, 27
Nider, Johannes 249
Nifo, Agostino 209
Niger, Franciscus 372
 Grammatica 364n45, 369
 Modus epistolandi 369n81, 372, 375
Nix, Thomas (bishop of Norwich) 38
Nizard, Adam, *Neutrale* 246
Nonius Marcellus 292, 295
Normandy, paper making 96
North, Elizabeth (widow of John Lettou,
 printer) 139
Northern Homily Cycle 557, 561
Northumberland, 1st Duke of 124, 165, 170,
 174, 176, 601–2
 The saying of . . . uppon the scaffolde 602
Nortun, Johannes (prior of Mount Grace)
 573
Norwich 33, 140, 144, 395n52, 460, 502n34,
 523–5
 archdeaconry 213
 Blackfriars 524
 Consistory Court 523n142, 524n146,
 533n44
 devout society at 523
 St Julian's Church, Conisford 524
 see also LIBRARIES
Notary, Julian (printer), Westminster 91, 94,
 362n33
Novae Narrationes, see LAW, common law
Nova Legenda Angliae, see Capgrave, John
Nuremberg (centre of printing) 9, 10, 65,
 76, 148
 place of printing 226
 book-trade in 225
 city school 356

Obligationes 380–6
Obsecro te 504

Ockham, William 321, 382
Odofredus de Denariis (civilian) 403, 404
Odo of Morimond, ps.-, on *Genesis*, etc. 280
Odorico da Pordenone 324
Office of Sheryffes 421
 see also *Loffice et Auctoryte des Justyces de
 Peas*
Oldcastle, Sir John (heretic) 37
Olde, John 172
Oldendorp, Johan 405
Old Tenures 412, 423n93, 425–7, 429
Old Termes 415
oral instruction in teaching 354
oral tradition in court 411
Orcharde of Syon 524
Ordenaunces of Warre 578–9, 581, 597
Order of Communion, The 600
Ordinale Sarum 75
Ordinance of potage 478, fig. 23.2
Origen (in Latin) 220, 234, 237
Orkney 223
Ortus vocabulorum 453, 460–1
Osborne, Henry 332
Os facies mentum 460–1, 464
Osnabrück 152
Osney Abbey, Oxon 116, 355
Oswaldkirk, Yorks. 483
Oswen, John (printer), Ipswich 167, 169
Ouseflete, Thomas (Controller of the King's
 Chamber) 258
Overton, John 168–9
Ovid 238, 240, 295, 464
 Ovidian verse laments 569
 'parts of Ovid' 572
 Opera (1515) 124n35
Ovide moralisé (ms.) 99
Owen, William, editor
 Le Bregement de toutes les Estatutes 430
Owl and the nightingale 239
OWNERSHIP
 see also LIBRARIES
 Owners (substantial collections)
 inventories of private libraries 287
 Abingdon, Henry 328
 Arderne, Sir Peter 416
 Argentine, John 299, 323
 Bale, John 281
 Bancroft, Richard, Archbishop of
 Canterbury 281
 Bekynton, Thomas, bishop of Bath and
 Wells 296
 Bodley, Sir Thomas 281
 Boteler, Sir John 414

Printers and publishers, see:

Index of manuscripts

Eponymous manuscripts

Bibliographic index of printed books

I · STC

Corrigenda in STC Vol. III are indicated as
'+III' followed by page reference.

II · References to books printed before 1501, not in STC

Since there is not a single bibliographical reference system including all books printed after 1500 and thus placing individual works in a larger context, no attempt is made here to index the references given in the text to a variety of catalogues and bibliographies. For incunabula, only the *Gesamtkatalog der Wiegendrucke* and F. R. Goff's *Census* are indexed. Both are a convenient entry point to the ISTC database, and lead to further bibliographical information. In a few rare cases, by default, L. Hain's *Repertorium Bibliographicum* and M. F. A. G. Campbell's *Annales*, both with supplements, are quoted.

One of the first printed books published by an Englishman: Bartholomaeus Anglicus, *De proprietatibus rerum*, the largest of three Latin books published by William Caxton in Cologne, *c.*1472.

2.1 Miniature in a prayer book, 'St John the Evangelist', signed by Herman Scheerre, a book-painter from Cologne, active in London *c*.1400–10.

2.2 Miniature, dated 1528 and attributed to the Netherlandish painter Lucas or Susanna Horenbout, 'The Feast of the Relics', in the Epistolary of Cardinal Wolsey, written by Pieter Meghen. In the text a reference to the Feast of the Translation of Thomas Becket was erased at a later date.

2.3 Opening with miniature 'The Agony in the Garden' (above), and the beginning of the
Hours of the Virgin with borders and painted initials (right), in a book of hours of Sarum Use,
mid-fifteenth century. The space for a coat of arms was left blank to be filled in by the first buyer.

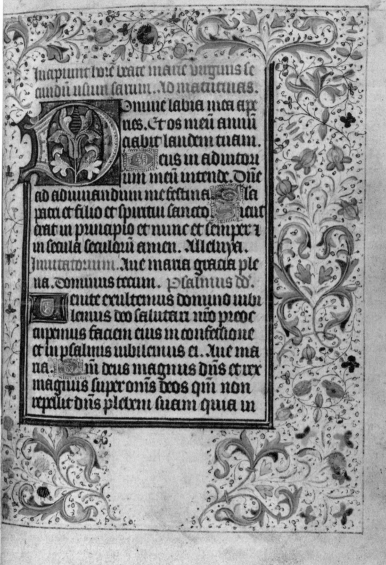

Incipiunt hore beate marie virginis se
cundii usum sarum. Ad matutinas.

Domine labia mea ape
ries. Et os meü annii
tiabit laudem tuam.
Deus in adiutori
um meü intende. Dñe
ad adiuuandum me festina. Gla
patri et filio et spiritui sancto. Sicut
erat in principio et nunc et semper et
in secula seculorum amen. Alleluya.
Inuitatorium. Aue maria gracia ple
na. Dominus tecum. Psalmus xciiii.

Venite exultemus domino iubi
lemus deo salutari nostro preoc
cupemus faciem eius in confessione
et in psalmis iubilemus ei. Aue ma
ria. Quoniam deus magnus dñs et rex
magnus super oñis deos quia non
repellet dñs plebem suam quia in

De sancto georgio martir.
Gorgi martir inclite te decet laus
et gloria predicaui miliaa per
quem puella regia existens in

2.4 Import at the lower end of the market, early in the fifteenth century. Miniature 'St George and the dragon' in a book of hours of Sarum Use.

2.5 Miniature of 'The Last Judgment' in a more luxurious, imported book of hours of Sarum Use, mid-fifteenth century.

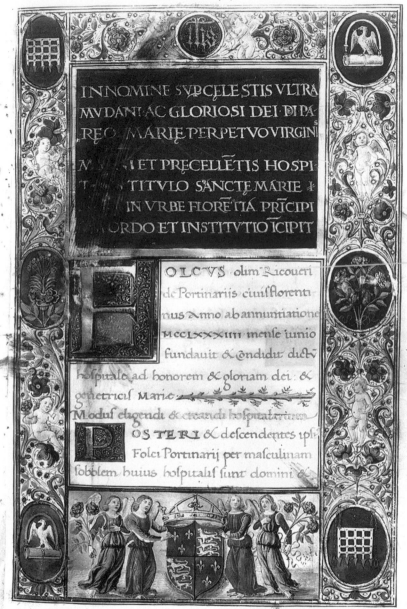

2.6 Border attributed to the Florentine book-painter Attavante degli Attavanti,
in the Statutes of the Hospital of Sta Maria Nuova in Florence, presented to Henry VII
by the merchant and diplomat, Francesco Portinari, *c.*1500

2.7 Miniature by Gerard Horenbout, working in Ghent, c.1502–3, 'The donor,
King James IV of Scotland, in prayer'. This book of hours was commissioned for the
wedding of the King to Margaret Tudor, daughter of Henry VII.

2.8 Flemish miniature 'St Anne teaching the Virgin to read', in a book of hours given by Henry VII to his daughter, Margaret Tudor, possibly commissioned in Flanders, late fifteenth century. Border with *trompe l'oeil* effect.

2.9 Miniature attributed to the 'Associate of Maître François', 'King Henry VII kneeling before King David', in a book of hours of Sarum Use, probably commissioned in France after 1480.

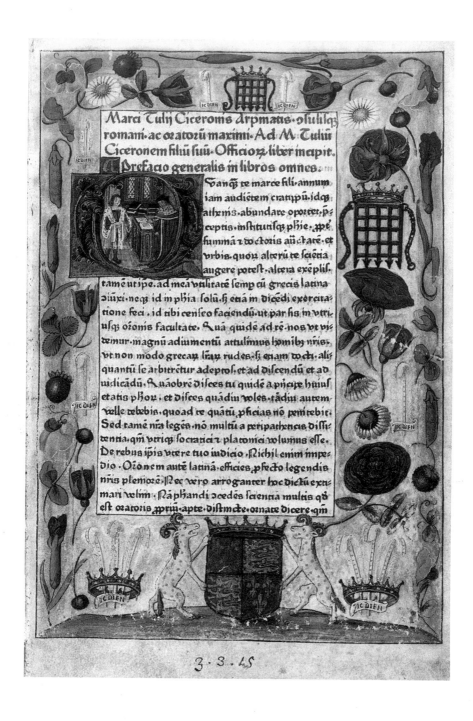

2.10 The education of a prince: historiated initial 'Q' in a Cicero *De officiis*, printed in Mainz in 1465. The border with the motto 'Ic dien' and insignia makes it clear that the pupil is a Prince of Wales (Prince Arthur?), early sixteenth century.

3.1 Bartholomaeus Anglicus, *De proprietatibus rerum*, published by William Caxton in Cologne, c.1472 (detail of fol. 55r). The aspect of the page is that of the Cologne region.

¶Hiere begynneth the seconde booke of the recueill of
the historyes of Troye/that speketh of the prowesses
of the stronge Hercules and of his deth &c::.

¶Howe hercules foughte ayenst thre lyons in the fo‑
reste of nemee.and how he slewe them and tooke their
skynnys or hides &c::.

IN the fyrste booke is begonnen the faytes & pro wesse
of the stronge and puyssaut geant hercules.And how
he destroyed fyrste the cyte of Troye vpon kynge Lao
medon after whiche feet and conqueste he retorned into
Grece.where he helde hym a certayn space of time with
out doyng of ony thynge that is founde by writyng/
But than as the olde Juno by her euyll & cursid enuye
gaf her to ymagyne and thynke how she myght make
hercules to be destroied & dye/Tidynges cam ito Crete
that in the foreste of nemee were comen many lyons
And amonge all other ther was oon that was syxteen
palme of heyght that destroyed and wasted alle the
contree.And this Juno had warre agaynst cristens.and
than for to haue aqueyntance of hercules & vnder fay
ned colour of good loue for to sende hym into the clawes
es of this lyon.She maad pees with cristens.and sende
for hym to come into Crete for to conferme the pees
Cristens that thought no thynge but well wente into
Crete and brought with hym hercules/the pees was
made . Juno acqueyntid her with hercules/ they cam to
speke of the lyons in the forest of nemee &c:.And so
moche spake Juno and accountid of hem.that she said
to hercules that hit were wel his faite for to gete hym
honour and worship/as for to go vnto the foreste of

3.2 The first book printed in English: Raoul Lefèvre, *The recuyell of the historyes of Troye*,
Translated from the French by William Caxton and published by him in Bruges [*c*.1473].
The style of the typeface is modelled on the script of Flemish manuscripts.

FOr asmoche as late by the comaudement of the right
hye & noble pryncesse my right redoubted lady / My
lady Margarete by the grace of god Duchesse of Bourgoyne Brabant &c. I translated a boke out of frensshe in
to Englissh named Recuyel of the historie of Troye in
Whiche is comprehended how Troye was thries destroyed
And also the labours & historie of Saturnus . Tytan .
Jubpter Perseus and Hercules / & other moo then in Rehersed . But as to the historie of Jason / towchyng the conqueste of the golden flese / myn auctor hath not sett it in his
boke . But breuely and the cause is for asmoche as he hadde
made before a boke of the hoole lyf of Jason . Whyche he presented vnto the noble prynce in his dayes Phillip Duc
of bourgoyne / And also the sayd boke shulde haue ben to
grete . if he hady sett the said historie in his boke . for it con-
teyneth thre bokes beside thistorie of Jason . These for as
moche as this sayd boke is late newe made aparte of alle
thistories of the sayd Jason & the historie of him Whiche
that Dares Frigius & Guido de columpnys Wrote in the
begynnyng of their bokes / touchyng the conqueste of the
sayd golden flese . by occasion Wherof greue the cause of the
seconde destruccion of the sayd cite of Troye . is not sett in
the sayd boke of Recuyel of thistories of Troye . Therfore
vnder the proteccion & suffraunce of the most hyghe puis-
sant & ypen kyng . my most dradde naturel liege Lord
Edward by the grace of god kyng of englond and of
fraunce and lord of Irland . I entende to translate the
sayd boke of thistories of Jason . folowyng myn auctor
as nygh as I can or may not chaungyng the sentence ne

3.3 Raoul Lefèvre, *The history of Jason*. Translated from the French by William Caxton and printed by him in Westminster in *c*.1477. In a prologue Caxton dedicated the book to Edward, Prince of Wales, then six years old. The border decoration was probably executed in England.

Ichardi par la grace de dieu Roy
Dengleterre ⁊ de Fraunce ⁊ seignour Dir-
loundr al viscounte de Northampton Sa-
lutz Sachez que al honour de dieu ⁊ reuerēce
de Seint Esglise pur nurrer peas vnite ⁊ con-
cordr en toutes parties dinz nostre roialme
Dengleterre le quele nous desirons moult entierment del assent des Prelates Dukes Con-
tes ⁊ Barouns de mesme nostre roialme al
instaunce ⁊ especial requeste dez cões de nostre roialme auaunt assem-
bles a nostre perlement tenuz a westm̄ a la quinzisme de seint hiller lan
de nostre reigne premer a nous fait ordigner ⁊ establier certeins estatutes en amendement ⁊ releuement de mesme nostre roialme en mesme
la fourme que ensuit ꝃ Ca · i · ꝃ Premirment est assentuz et
establiz que la seint Esglise eit ⁊ enioise toutes ses droitures libertees
⁊ fraunchises entierment ⁊ sauns emblemissement ⁊ qe le grandr chīe
quele a la requeste de la dit cōe estoit lieu en le dit perlement Et auxi
la chartre de la foreste ⁊ toutes les autres bones ordignaunces et esta-
tuttez faites en le temps des pgenitours nostre seignour le Rop qui
ore est ⁊ nient repellez soient tenus ⁊ fermement gardez en toutes pointes ꝃ Ca ii ꝃ Item nostre seignour le rop desiraunt soueragne-
ment la transquilise ⁊ quiete de mesme soun people soet ⁊ commaundr
estreitement que la peas dinz soun roialme Dengleterre soit fermemēt
tenuz ⁊ gardr, issīnt que toutes ses loialx subgites purroient desore sau-
uement ⁊ peisiblement aler seignir ⁊ demurrer solonqz les lepes et vsa-
ges de la roialme ⁊ que bone Iustice ⁊ owell droit soit fait a chescunp
ꝃ· Ca iii · ꝃ Item que les estatuites nadgairs faites en tempz
le noble rop Edwardr aiel nostre seignour le rop qui ore est des purueours ⁊ achatours soient fermement tenus ⁊ gardez en toutes pointes
adioustau nt a icell que pur ceo q Prelates ⁊ Clerks ne purroient ent
faire lour suites enuers nullup per soye de crime come lez ditz estatui
tez demandent q toutz Prelatz ⁊ Clercs ent eient desore lour accions enuers toutes tieux purueours ⁊ achatours per soie de trespas ⁊ p recoue-
rent lour damages au treble ꝃ Ca iiii Item est ordigne ⁊ esta-
blie ⁊ le rop nfe ꝓ defendr estreitement q nul asseiler officer ou huaunt
nautre ouesqz lup nascume autre persone du roial dengl de quel estat ou
condicion qils soient nempreignent desore ou sustepnent ascune querele
per maynteraunce en pays naillours sur greuouse peyne cestassauoi lez
ditz counseilours ⁊ grandz officers le Rop sur peyne que fra ordigne
                                                          li vii

---

3.4 Printing for the Inns of Court: *Statuta Nova*. In about 1485 William de Machlinia printed in his workshop near Fleet Street, a collection of statutes (from Edward I to Edward IV). The main typeface conforms to the style familiar to lawyers, but a larger type obtained from Caxton served to indicate the structural division of the text. The printer commissioned a local limner to provide every copy with coloured initials to signal the beginnings of reigns. (Opening page of 1 Richard II.)

ssionem non solum diuine uoces.
sed et ipius domini et saluatoris ex
emplum et consequentia naturalis
· rationis assignet. Si inquam hec secū
dum traditionis supra exposite re
gulam consequamur aduertimus
deprecemur ut nobis et omnibus
qui hoc audiunt concedat dominus
fide quam suscepimus custodia cursu
consumato expectare iustitie reposi
tam coronam · et inueniri inter eos
qui resurgunt in uitam eternam
Liberari uero a confusione · et obpro
brio eterno · per xpm dominum no
strum per quem est deo patri omni
potenti cum spu sancto gloria et im
perium in secula seculorum amen ·

finis laus deo

3.5 Printer's copy: manuscript of Rufinus, *Expositio Symboli Apostolorum*, written in Florence
for Vespasiano da Bisticci and acquired by Bishop John Goldwell, used in 1478 as exemplar for
the first book printed in Oxford. Four dots before l.4 indicate where the compositor was to
begin the last page of the printed book.

supereminēs via/id est caritas: q̄
merito oleo significatur. lectō vj.
Omnibus humorib9 oleū su-
pereminet. Mitte aquam ⁊
supinfunde oleū: supeminet. Mitte oleū supinfunde aquā:oleū su-
pereminet. Si ordinē seruaueris
vincit.Si ordinē mutaueris: vin-
cit. Caritas nuq̄ cadit. Quid ergo fr̄es iam disceptemus de quiq̄
virginibus prudētibus,et quinq̄
fatuis?Voluerūt ire obuiā spōso
Quid est ire obuiaz spōso: Corde
ire.expectare eius aduentū:sed ille tardauit Dū tardat ille:dormie
rūt oēs Quid est oēs:Et sapiētes
et fatue/obdormitauerūt et dormi
erūt.putamus bonū est somnus
iste:Quid est somn9 iste: Ne for-
te tardāte sponso. qm̄ abūdat ini
quitas:refrigescat caritas multo
rum.Sic intellecturi sum9 istum
somnum. Non mihi placet dico.
Quare:Quia sunt ibi prudētes.
Et vtiq̄ qm̄ dixit dñs. qm̄ abūda-
uit iniqtas,refrigescet caritas m̄
torum:subiecit et ait. Qui autē p
seuerauerit vsq̄ in finez:hic salu9
erit.Dbi vultis esse istas prudētes
Nōne in his qui pseuerauerūt vl
q̄ in finez: Non ob aliud fr̄es.nō
ob aliud prorsus admittent̄ intro
nisi quia pseuerauerūt vsq̄ in fi-
nē Euangel.scōm matheū lc. vij.
In illo tp̄e: Dixit iesus discipulis suis parabolā hāc. Si
mile est reguū celorū decē virgini-

Et reliqua.
Spe vo[...]
neo praua o[...]
ius inquina[...]
dierna sci eu[...]
dicere.vt et [...]
magna cau[...]
hoc qd a vol[...]
aut gr̄a hun[...]
petit9 laudis[...]
ris ostendit[...]
Ecce eni red[...]
gines et oēs[...]
intra beat[...]
recepte.quia[...]
ginitate sua[...]
in vasis suie[...]
Riue[...]
bis e[...]
aut cur dece[...]
etiā prudēte[...]
tur.Dū eni[...]
reproborū n[...]
tuis vginib[...]
Sed sciend[...]
cro eloquio:[...]
tp̄is eccl̄a di[...]
co dñs dicit[...]
gelos suos:[...]
oīa scādala.[...]
beatitudini[...]
inueniri scā[...]
ligant.Et v[...]
ergo solueri[...]
minimis ⁊ d[...]
mus vocabi[...]
aute fecerit[...]

3.6 Proof correction: a marked-up page in the unique copy of the *Legenda ad usum Sarum* printed for Caxton in Paris in 1488. The instructions for correction (punctuation, capitals, replacing single letters) are as clear now as they were at the time. The type is in the Parisian style which was soon to prevail in printing in England.

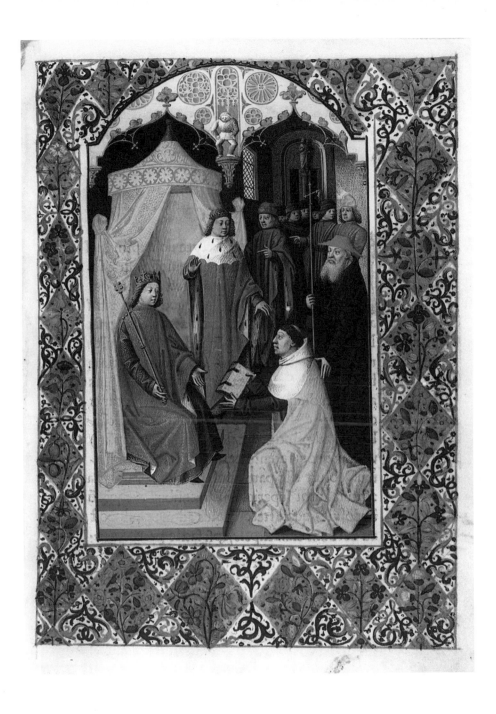

3.7 Dedication to Edward IV: the *Epistole et orationes* of Cardinal Bessarion were a plea to rulers to take up arms against the progress of the Turks. The text was printed in 1471 by the first printers at the Sorbonne and almost fifty copies were presented to those thought to have influence, including a copy illuminated in Paris for Edward IV.

¶ Incipit liber · xvi. de lapi-
dibus & metallis.

Of the proprytees of þe
erthe and of the partyes
þerof it generall by þel
pe of god is now to our
purpose to treate here
somwhat of þe dyuerse
ornament thereof. in specyall of thynges

þer conteyned therin / some ben clene with
out soule & without kynge. And al the
þat groweth vnder grounde· is get-
tred to þownes of therth. as quatrepedes
nes. colours & metall. we shall rehete a
now. And some with þof a soule· as stones
herbes & trees. & some with soule & felin-
ge. as men & other bestes/ of whom we
shall last speke And we shall speke fyrste to speke of the· a.b.c. of thynges· & by
ginneȝ in þ erthe· & to begynne therof.

it falleth of. for the thyne is to thyne· or
for larȝsse of humours/ There falleth
nat behynde þ poile· & that is for sadnes
& thienne of þ thyne & is there. wherby the
beth & falyeth· so layth Arystotle. ye
There hee of þ ben hepyth· & defeni-
oyth· & þrenth· þ hee· And þ a may be
to our hee or þ hee. be tenifyȝ more
bohonesse/ This defence falleth in yon
the· but most in agȝ · for the foulaype
causes & reasons/

¶ Incipit liber septus de etate
hois in generali et speciali.

¶ Des pierres et des metaulx

comment a chasser et a posseder commu nement de leur nature .

¶ce .clxv.

Angle est une pouince ou est la grant cartaige et la partie aufrir que entre bisance et romme est so longuant a la mer de sicile vers aquilo ne et estant iusques a la region de genu lie par de aure mdi si ome dit iy so ge le ca

¶ Cy commence le tresiesme liure du propice a ire lequel traicte des pierres et des me taux, et commence le premier chapitre de la sync que nous appellons sablon.

plus proucbaines parties de cesse pouir ce et par de aure; nous poir ou bis ouffisa ment, mais les parties qui sont plus loig de nous sont plaines de bestes et de ser pens, et la sont troues les asnes sauuai ges et moult sauure bestes mostrucuses et contrefaictes si comme dit yisdore en cestuy liure. Et a uant si ce le .ry. liure des propietes des pouinces et des pays.

¶ Cy quelte proprie tes de la terre et de les parties sont des crip tes en general si reste a dire culaur ne chose a laybe de nostre seigneur de

son nom en et en especial des choses qui appartienent a la ourmenonde la terre aucunes sont simples inscribles et sans ame si comme sont les choses q sont egē bres et ame focture si one sont les pi erres es a uaine si les metaux et de cele cbe seent iroirons premier par ordre. Zes c.i.

3.8 Wynkyn de Worde's English translation of Bartholomaeus Anglicus is illustrated with woodcuts (above) modelled on the Dutch 'Ages of Man' (below left), and the French 'Mining' (below right).

CALENI PERGAMEN-
SIS DE TEMPERA-
MENTIS, ET DE IN-
AEQVALI INTEMPE
RIE LIBRI TRES
THOMA LINACRO
ANGLO INTER-
PRETE ∴

Opus non medicis modo, sed et
philosophis oppido cp̃ necessariũ
nunc primum prodit in lucem
CVM GRATIA
& Priuilegio.

3.9 Johann Siberch, from Cologne, working in 1520–3 in Cambridge, decorated the title-page of Thomas Linacre's translation of Galen, *De temperamentis*, with a woodcut border.

3.10 An elaborate woodcut title-page was given to Hector Boece, *The hystory and croniklis of Scotland*, printed by T. Davidson in Edinburgh, *c*.1540.

4.1 Doublure of blind-tooled brown calf, probably taken from another binding, on a copy of Quintus Curtius Rufus, *De rebus gestis Alexandri Magni … opus*, Antwerp, 1546.

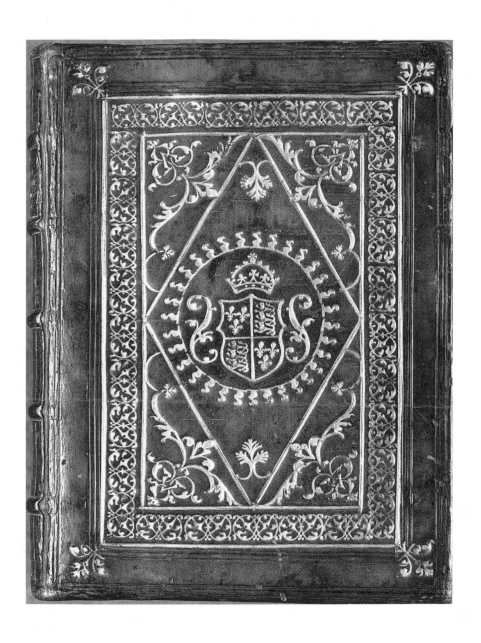

4.2 A binding by the King Edward and Queen Mary binder, in gold-tooled brown calf decorated with black paint, on Queen Mary I's copy of Edmund Bonner, *A profitable and necessarye Doctryne*, London, 1555.

4.3 Gold binding with enamelled scenes bossed in relief, 'The brazen serpent' (left, upper cover) and 'Judgment of Solomon' (below, lower cover). Made *c.*1540–5 by Hans van Antwerpen. Now on Lady Elizabeth Tyrwhit, *Morning and evening prayers*, London, 1574 (*remboîtage*).

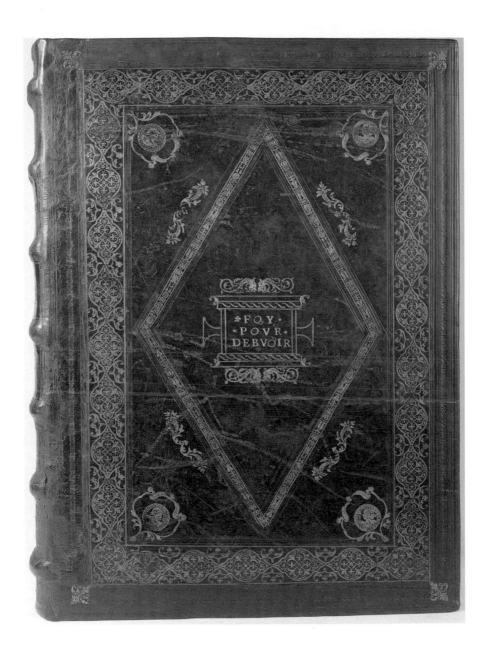

4.4 A binding by the Medallion binder, in gold-tooled brown calf, for the Lord Protector Somerset, on a late fifteenth-century manuscript on vellum of the French translation of Giovanni Boccaccio, *Decameron*.

5.1–5.2 A London shop-work book of devotion, c. 1450–60. Two pages from a manuscript book of hours of Sarum Use, first owned by William Gurney.

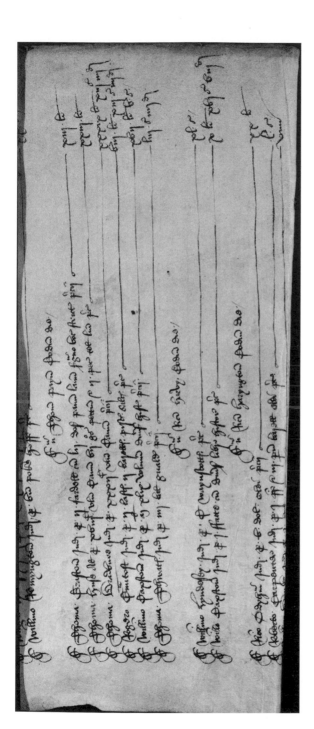

6.1 Among cargoes of ships entering the Port of London on 25 April 1488, duty incurred on books destined for William Caxton was recorded in the Controlment of Subsidy of tunnage and poundage: 'Wilmo Caxston *pro* m xlix volum*inibus* diversa*rum* historiarum … xvij li v s' and on the same day in another ship: 'willo Caxston … *pro* l ffatto cu*m* diversis libris histor*iarum* x li xvj s viijd'.

9.1 Above and below Richard Pynson's printer's device is written: 'Richard Spencer Lederseller of London / Aremit of the chappell of sant katheryn / At charyng crosse', in a copy of Pynson's second edition of ps-Bonaventura, *Myrrour of the Life of Christ*, London, *c.* 1506.

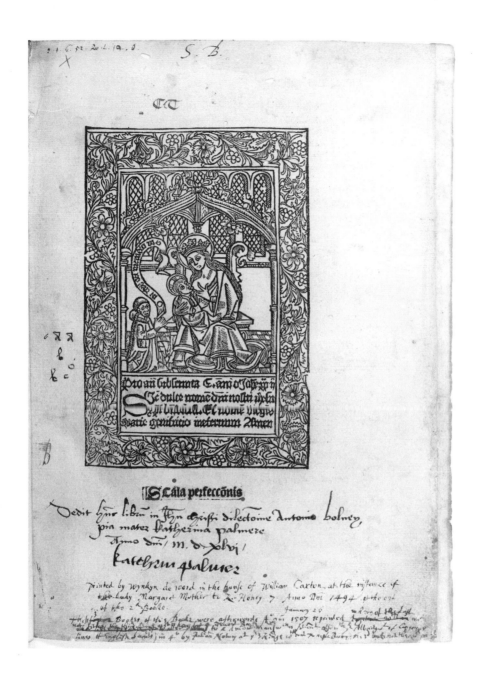

9.2 The title-page of Walter Hylton, *Scala Perfectionis*, Wynkyn de Worde, 1494, with woodcut, has ownership inscriptions of Katherine Palmer and Antonia Bolney.

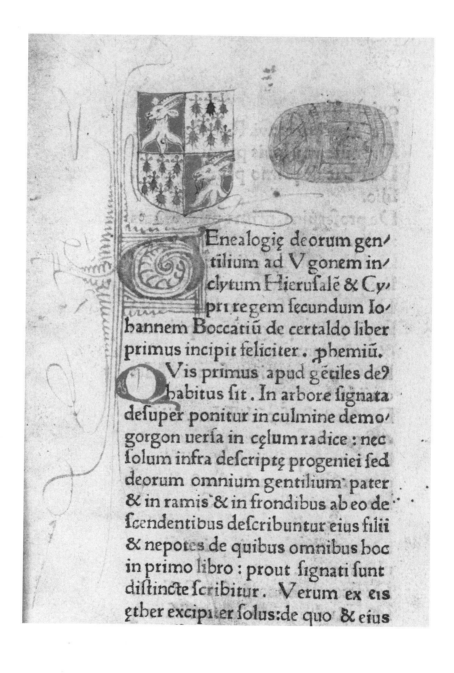

Enealogie deorum gen‐
tilium ad Vgonem in‐
clytum Hierufalē & Cy‐
pri regem fecundum Io‐
bannem Boccatiū de certaldo liber
primus incipit feliciter. ꝓbemiū.
Vis primus apud gētiles de9
babitus fit. In arbore fignata
defuper ponitur in culmine demo‐
gorgon uerfa in cęlum radice : nec
folum infra defcriptę progeniei fed
deorum omnium gentilium pater
& in ramis & in frondibus ab eo de‐
fcendentibus defcribuntur eius filii
& nepotes de quibus omnibus boc
in primo libro : prout fignati funt
diftincte fcribitur. Verum ex eis
ęther excipiter folus:de quo & eius

9.3 The coat of arms and ownership notes of Cardinal John Morton appear in this copy of Giovanni Boccaccio, *De genealogiis deorum*, printed in Venice in 1472 by Vindelinus de Spira, and probably decorated in England.

pro domibus. ⁊ ceteris ligneis ope/
ribus faciendis. Item cedunt silue ac
rami superflui arborum. ⁊ sepes uiri
des pro igne. Item cedunt partice et
canne pro vineis ⁊ parantur ⁊ fiunt
pali· ⁊ iunci similiter pro vineis cedi
possunt. Et ex uiminibus fieri possunt
corbes· ⁊ ciste ⁊ cauee multaque alia v
tensilia oportuna· ⁊ sepes sicce. Item
hoc mense diuersis ingeniis capiuntur
bestie fere· ⁊ precipue canibus tempo
re niuium· Item aues auibus dome/
sticis ⁊ retibus diuersis ac uisco.

Et sic est finis libri ruralium commo
dorum. Laus sit altissimo qui uiuit p
seculorum secula sine fine benedictus
Amen·

Presens opus ruralium commodo
rum Petri de crescentiis hoc industri
oso caracterisandi stilo ad cunctor
utilitatem omnipotentis dei suffra/
gio nouissime impressum e. in domo
Johannis de Westfalia. Alma ac flo
rentissima in uniuersitate Louaniensi·

9.5 Ownership and other inscriptions of Ricardus Kynman, written in Louvain in 1492 while
in the service of the Archbishop William Schevez, 'when I was 27 years old', in the presence of
several Scottish friends, followed by his monogram and motto. Below the colophon of a copy
of Petrus de Crescentiis, *Ruralia commoda*, printed by Johannes de Westfalia in Louvain, *c.* 1480.

12.1 Opening page of a manuscript written in 1480 in Ghent for King Edward IV by the scribe David Aubert: Roberto della Porta, *Romuléon*, the history of Rome from its foundation, in a French translation by Jean Miélot.

The manuscript text within the illustration reads:

*ar la grace de mreigneur ihe
sucrist / dont tous biens proce
dent me vient deuocion ; vou
lente daler visiter la glorieu
se vierge marie en son eglise
de hals en la conte de hayn
nau Et pour ceste chose accomplir me party de*

12.2 First text page of a manuscript written in 1496 at Sheen for King Henry VII by Quentin Poulet, his librarian, who was also a professional scribe. A French version of Ramon Lull, *Imaginacion de la vraie noblesse.*

12,3 The signature of Quentin Poulet beneath the colophon of a book printed in Paris by Antoine Vérard, purchased for the royal collection: Guillaume Deguilleville, *Le pèlerinage de l'âme*, 1499.

12.4 Enguerrand de Monstrelet, *Chroniques*, printed c.1500 in Paris by Antoine Vérard, with miniatures painted for the Royal Library. Printed text covered by the miniatures was copied by hand in the margins.

13.1 King Henry VIII reading and making notes in his book. From Henry VIII's Psalter, written by Jean Mallard, c.1540.

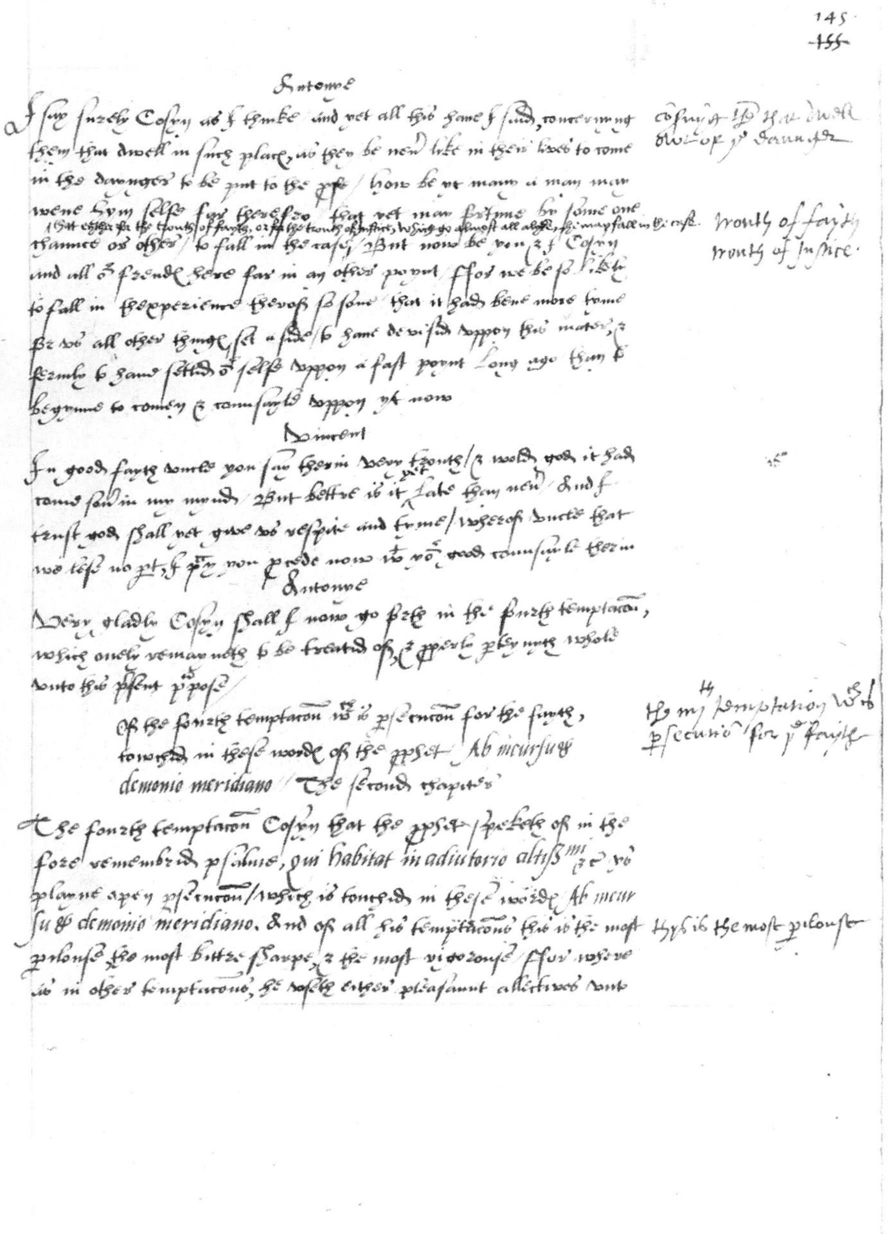

14.1 A page transcribed *c.*1540–5 from a manuscript of Thomas More's *Dialogue of Comfort*, showing English text in secretary hand and Latin quotations in italic.

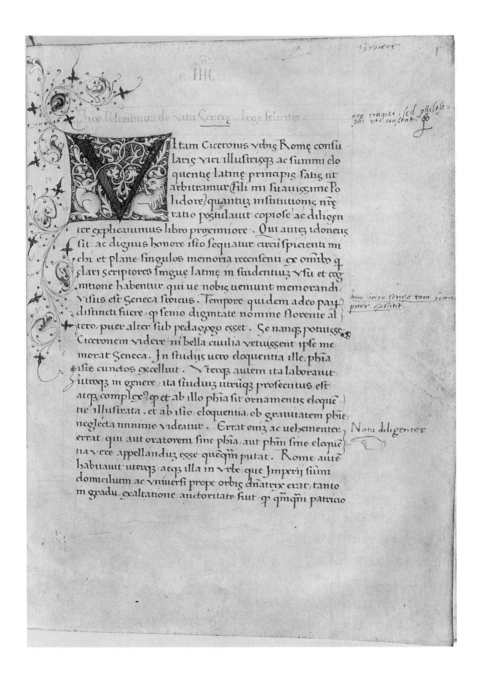

14.2 Thomas Candour, an English scribe, writing, in England in the third quarter of the fifteenth century, an upright humanist script. A page in a manuscript with miscellaneous texts.

ſtitiæ. Sic illi. Plutarchus Ariſtide. τοῖσ μὲρ πολεμιοισ συγ=
γνώμκρ ἔχἐρ φάσκοντισ, ἐι πάντα πλόυτου καὶ χϱκμάτωρ
ὤνεκ νομίζοιερ. Xenoph. pædia Cyri. ἐγὼ τοίνυρ ἔφκ ὁ τῖγϱά
νκσ, ἐι μὲρ ἄγασαι ᾽τ πατϱόσ, κ̈ ὅσα εισόυλευται, κ̈ ὅσα πέπϱα=
χϗ᾽τ Αϱκεῖρ πάντα κμασ τκκέναι, παυῦ σοι συμσουλέυω τοῦτο
μιμεῖϑαι.   Huc ſpectat et illud Saluſt. ın Iugurth. Quæ
poſtquam glorioſa modo neᶊ belli patrandi cognouit.
Vbi Priſcianus (cauſa) ſubaudit.

   GRAECA non minus conſtructio eſt, et quam Latini
poſt uerba, quæ in infinıtum non ferũtur per delectum (ut)
finalis, per infinitum tamen eloquunt̃, ſed quod per (ut) eſt
interpretandum. ut illa eſt Perſij. Et pectore læuo Excutias
guttas, lætari prætrepidum cor. Similiter poſt adiectiua. ut
Vergıl. Peſtis acerba boum, pecorıᶊ aſpergere uirus. In ta=
libus enim auditur (ut) pro ὥsε, quod apud Græcos infi=
nito ſæpiſſime iũgitur. Iſocrat. πϱόσ Νικοκλία. καὶ γάϱτοι
κύϱιοι γενόμενοι καὶ χϱκμάτωρ πλεῖσωρ καὶ πϱχγμάτωρ μεγί=
σωρ Διὰ τὸ μἠκαλῶς χϱῆϑαι ταύταισ τῶσ ἀφοϱμῶσ πεποιή
κασι, ὥsε πολλοὺσ ἀμφισσκτεῖρ πό τεϱορ ἐsὶρ ἄξιορ ἐλῖσϑαι
τῶρ σίωρ τὸρ τῶρ ἰλιωτῶρ μετϱίωσ δὲ πϱατ]όρτωρ, κ̈ τὸρ τῶρ
τυϱαννευόντωρ. Latinum enim potius ſit. Vt lætetur. Vt aſper
gat. Huc ıpſe cum Seruio et illa Vergilıj referenda putem.
Dederatᶒ comas diffundere uentis. Et ille ſuo moriens dat
habere nepoti. Et magnum dat ferre talentum. Niſi Quintil.
et poſt eum Donatus in poſtremo Enallagen facerent uer=
bi pro participio, ut ſit. Dat ferendum. Seruıus tamen no=
biſcum græcam ait figuram. pro ut diffunderentur, uel̃ po=
tius ut ipſe interprétor, ut diſiunderent ſe. Αϱιsοφάνκσ. Ἐι μοι
ποϱίσασ ἄϱτον τίρ ἐῦ πεπεμμένορ, Λόικσ καταφαγεῖρ. Theo=
crit.

14.3 A page printed by Richard Pynson in the roman type first used in England in 1509, here
combined with Greek, in Thomas Linacre, *De emendata structura Latini sermonis liori sex*, 1524.

ignominiam irrogantes. Iam uo laboribus plurimis animi remissio/
nes indulgemus/sacra certamina/anniuersariaq̅ sacrificia/cum de
centi priuatorum apparatu interponentes/quorum quotidiana
delectatio tristitiam discutit. Importantur huc propter magnitu/
dinem ciuitatis ex omnibus terris omnia/euentuq̅ nobis ut non
magis hinc natiuis bonis fruamur/q̅s quae sunt apud alios ho
mines. In studiis autem rei bellicae/hinc q̅ differimus ab hostibus q̅
hanc urbem omnibus exhibemus/nullisq̅ explosionibus hospitu̅
quempiam uel discere uel spectare prohibemus/quasi hec non oc/
cultata sint profutura hosti se uiderit. Ne/magis aut apparatui
bellorum aut fraudibus confidimus q̅ id qd̅ ipsi prestare possum

14.4 Upright humanist script from a volume written before 1453 in Italy for William Gray, Bishop of Ely, containing a Latin translation of Thucydides, *Historia belli Peloponneciaci*. (Detail of a page.)

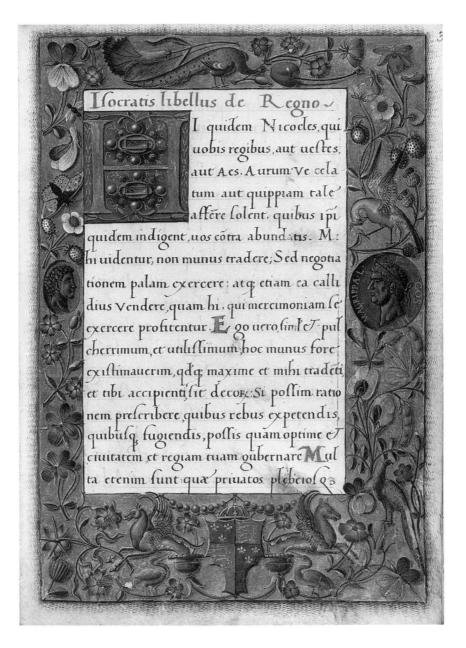

Isocratis libellus de Regno

I quidem Nicocles, qui uobis regibus, aut ueftes, aut Aes. Aurum ve cela tum aut quippiam tale affere folent, quibus ipi quidem indigent, uos cotra abundatis. Mihi uidentur, non munus tradere; Sed negotiationem palam exercere: atq etiam ea callidius uendere, quam hi, qui mercimoniam fe exercere profitentur. Ego uero, fimul et pul cherrimum, et utiliffimum hoc munus fore exiftimauerim, qdq maxime et mihi tradenti et tibi accipienti, fit decor. Si poffim rationem prefcribere, quibus rebus expetendis, quibufq fugiendis, poffis quam optime et ciuitatem et regiam tuam gubernare Multa etenim funt quæ priuatos plebeiof q3

14.5 A translation by Giovanni Boerio from texts by Isocrates and Lucian, written, probably in Bologna, by Pierantonio Sallando of Reggio Emilia, and presented by Boerio to Henry VIII when Prince of Wales, *c.*1507.

Countreple de Garrantie

¶ En bré delchete le b̃. vouche a gary vne J q̃ vient ꝑ dde de lup q̃il au de lup liey a gary q̃ mra̅ ꝑ fait demesne ꝑ b̃ vouche dit q̃ b̃ b̃.q̃ lup voncha nau rien; en le bỹ iouꝛ de bre purchace ꝑ ꝑ̃. Et ꝑ̃ ꝑ̃ q̃il au dde de lup q̃il au de lup liey l'oppion q̃il naila b̃ ple nie̅t pl꜖ q̃ lou home dde q̃ auez del refꝭ il ne aniendỹ en apꝛe; de pleder chose en abate̅t de bre̅. Et ꝺ̃ m̃ b̃ ple q̃ en gary de chre̅ il eſt bon̄ ple a dire q̃ il nau rien; en b̃ bỹ iouꝛ ꝑ ꝑ̃ tn̅ quere ꝑ ꝑ̃. Hillarii.xl b̃. E̅. iii.

¶ Bon̄ countreple de gary q̃ long temps puis le feoffe̅ nre̅ pe q̃ vous mre̅; q̃ nre̅ pe mutuſt ſſi ꝑ vous abat꜖ ꝑ ꝑ̃ en donner. Michaelis. b̃. E̅. iii.

¶ Il neſt contreple de gary a dire q̃ ꝑ̃ pe nau rien; en b̃ bỹ ſinon en b̃ tail b̃ qͤ terre il ad vne bre penoiñt ꝑ ꝑ̃ en donner. Trinitatis .viii. E̅. ii

Countreple de Apde

¶ Aide en Scire fac deuꝛ conb̃ plee; de Aide ꝑ ꝑ̃ mab̃ia bona en aide.

¶ En fourmdon̄ le b̃. mra̅ co̅t le terre deſcend a lup ꝑ a vne ꝼꝼ q̃ꝛ fuỹ purptie de cto acỹ en dde et vne antỹ acỹ ꝑ pꝛia aide ꝑ ꝑ̃ Hamon Vous m̃ eſte; ſſi dambadeuꝛ acre; iugeꝛſi leiẟ Belknaꝝ ꝑ entu̅t q̃ vous dedit; b̃ purptie ꝑ ne mre̅; coment bre̅ ſee no꜖ enfeoffẜ inge̅t ꝑ ꝑ̃ qͬ meſq; no꜖ ne poio꜖ recee pꝛo rata porcẟe no꜖ an̄o꜖ le gary ꝑ amonnt Thoꝛp il enten q̃ vous ne poie; au b̃ gary ſonk pͬ bre̅ ꝑte Et en plufieuꝛ caſe; le lep eſt iſſint . Qͬꝛ ſi accion ſoit pͬ par ii . copceñ; a l'un conuſt l'accio̅ b̃ do̅rnt lautỹ pͬ voucher ꝼꝼyne Verum eſt m̃ b̃ lep eſt dun lien fait a eny m̃ cɛme en le cas de iopntermit; ꝑ ꝑ̃ . Thoꝛp iſſint icy quar en ambadeuꝛ caſe; q̃ñt il mra̅ ꝑ lien il lup ayder̅a par eſpecialb̃ mab̃ ꝑ mra̅ coment ꝑ compaignon̄ ne voilb̃ ꝑ voucheỹ cu q̃il au fait feoffement ꝑ ſincñ q̃il mre̅ tiel eſpecialb̃ mab̃ le vouche lup extoñtra del lien ꝑ ꝑ̃ ꝑ q̃ ma entent le; caſe; ſonnt tout vne mez vncoꝛe le dema̅diñt naila amitage de cto ꝑ ꝑ̃. Michls.xxvi. E̅. iii.
Michls. xl vi. E̅. iii.

Countreplee; de Receipte

Vide de contreplee; de Receipte en le title de Receipte

g ii

20.1 Law French printed in appropriate style. Richard Pynson commissioned *c*. 1490 an edition of the *Abridgment of cases* (known as 'Statham') from G. le Talleur in Rouen, and later obtained similar type himself which conformed to the script traditionally used for Law French.

ENRICVS OCTAVVS DEI Gratia
Angliæ & Fráciæ rex, fidei defenſor & dominus Hy-
bernie, balliuis ſuis de J.ſalutem. Præcipimus vobis, ꝑ
ſine dilatione plenũ rectum teneatis W.B, de vno meſ-
ſuagio cum pertinentijs in M, quod clamat tenere de
nobis per liberum ſeruitium vnius denarij per ánum pro
omni ſeruitio, quod R.K.ei deforciat. Et niſi feceritis,
vicecomes Eborum faciat,ne ãplius inde clamorem au-
diamus pro defectu recti. Teſte me ipſo apud weſtmonaſteriũ xx.die Auguſti , anno
regni noſtri viceſimo tertio.

Bꝛene de Recto patens.

❧ Iſtud bꝛene de Recto ſemper ſit patens: et noꞃ dirigitur Balliuis alicuius/ſed ip
ſi domino : niſi Balliuis regis vel regine aut alicuius electi/niſi dominus curie fuerit
eꞩtra regnum de licentia regis : ꝗ opoꝛtet quod cancellarius inde certioꝛetur.

Regula.

❧ Rex balliuis ſuis, vel balliuis Katerinæ regine Angliæ conſortis noſtræ chari
ßimæ honoris Penerellæ in comitatu Lincoln ſalutem , vel balliuis de Soka de I ,
vel cuſtodi honoris de I. in comitatu Eſſex ſalutem. Præcipimus vobis vel tibi , ꝗ
ſine dilatione plenum rectum teneatis vel teneas A.de B , de decem acris terræ cũ
pertinẽtijs in C , quas clamat tenere de nobis, vel de predicta regina, vel de pdicta
Soka, vel de prædicto honore, ꝑ liberũ ſeruitium faciendi ſectam ad curiam noſtra
vel prædictæ reginæ honoris prædicti in comitatu pdicto de menſe in meſem, vel ꝑ
liberũ ſeruitium táti per annũ pro omni ſeruitio: quas R.de K.ei deforciat. Et niſi
feceritis .vicecomes E.E.faciat : ne amplius E.E.

Aliter Balliuis honoꝛis.

❧ Thus endyth thys boke callyd the Register of the wryttys
orygynall and iudiciall, prentyd at London by Wyllyam
Raſtell, and it is to ſell in Fleteſtrete at the
houſe of the ſayde Wyllyam,or in Poulys
chyrch yarde,or els at temple barre
at the houſe of Robert
Redman.

⁂

❧ CVM PRIVILEGIO.

20.2 A tradition of lively presentation in legal manuscripts continued occasionally in printing.
Details of two pages of William Rastell, *Registrum Omnium Brevium*, London 1531, show,
respectively, a woodcut initial portraying Henry VIII and an hour-glass colophon.

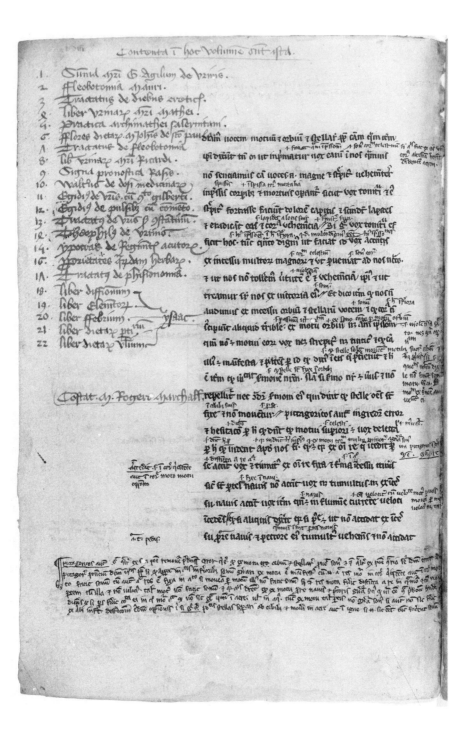

21.1 Roger Marchall (MD Cambridge 1453) thoroughly annotated medical texts and provided many tract volumes of manuscripts with lists of their contents. Here he added a note of ownership.

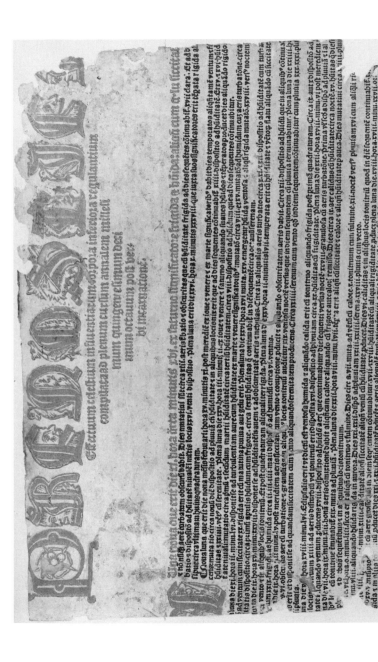

21.2 Fragment of a broadside almanac, printed in Oxford, 1517/18. Gaspar Laet the Elder's advice on health was based on experience and guided by the lunar calendar and astrology.

21.3 An inventory, drawn up in 1552, of the medical books of John Seward, surgeon and scholar at Clare Hall, Cambridge.

Sulpitii Verulani oratoris prestantissi
mi, opus grammatices insigne, feliciter
incipit.

22.1 The grammar of Giovanni Sulpizio da Veroli was favoured at Winchester College for
drilling young pupils in the elements of Latin grammar. The title-page with woodcut of
Richard Pynson's edition, 1498.

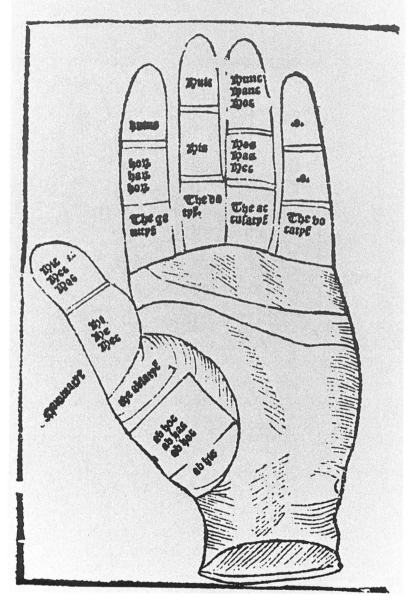

22.2 John Holt's *Lac puerorum*, or 'milk for children' was used for elementary instruction in Latin. The woodcut shows the use of the hand, an instrument available to every child, as a help for remembering declensions.

⸿Vulgaria quedã abs Therentio in anglicam
linguam traducta.

Hunc ſtudioſe puer menti committe libellum
Anglica qui cupis verba latina loqui
Nãqz docet noſtre vulgaria plurima lingue
Quo pacto latius dicere ſermo ſolet
Suntqz fere comici que ſunt hic ſcripta Therenti
Ad cuius ſenſuz commoda multa dabunt.

God ſpede you. ſaue iou/or reſt mery
Aluete   Salue.   Salu? ſis chriſto
Jubeo te ſaluere
Thow art welcome or ʒe ʒce.
Bñ veniſti Saluũ te adueniſſe gratuloꝛ
Adueniſſe gaudeo
Gramercy or J thanke ʒou or the
Gratiam ago vel habeo tibi: vobis
How haue ʒe faryd many a day
Qua valitudine fuiſt? iã diu. q̃lit valuiſti lõgo nũc tpe
I thanke god oꝛ thankyd be god J haue faryd wele.
Eſt deo vel dÿs gratia bene me habui
And the bettꝛ that ʒe fare wele
Et melius multo me habeo ſi vales
⸿iij.oꝛ iiij. days ʒit J was euyll at cſe in my bede
Triduo t̃ſaut quatriduo male me habui in capite
Ge of gode chere thou ſhalt amende and fare right wele
Bono aio es ſis vel eſto :conualeſces:optime qz h̃ebis
I thanke ʒou foꝛ the grete chere ʒe made me at london
Gratias vobis habeo de ingẽti huãnitate lõdonÿs f̃ca
What ſoeuyꝛ it was thou were welcome therto J wolde it
bad̃ be miche mooꝛe

22.3 The *Vulgaria*, compiled by the Oxford schoolmaster John Anwykyll, was a collection of
scraps of dialogue from the Latin plays of Terence, with English translations. The book was
reprinted several times, here by the Antwerp printer, Gheraert Leeu, in 1486, adapting his
text type to English scribal conventions.

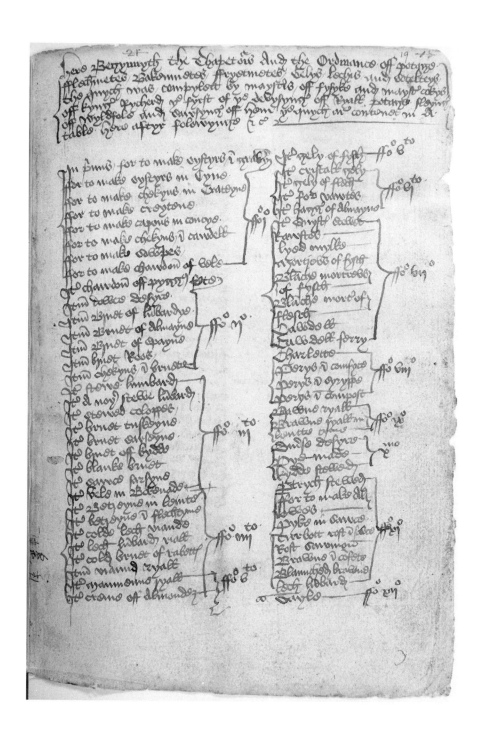

23.2 Finding-devices in a treatise on cookery: *The Ordinance of Potage* was foliated and the contents listed correspondingly for the convenience of the user.

24.1 Part of a prayer written by Thomas More in his book of hours, Paris, François Regnault, 1530.

24.2 Devotional cards: a miniature showing the wound in Christ's side was sewn into a book of hours.

24.3 Prayer roll: a late 15th-century prayer roll made by Percevall, a Premonstratensian canon of the abbey of Coversham in Yorkshire. (Below) A detail shows the five wounds of Christ, with an accompanying prayer beginning 'Agyos. O theos Sancte deus Agyos Iskiros...' and ending 'And yow moste say this same thre tymes with gude deuocione'. (Opposite) A detail shows the three nails securing Christ to the Cross, the crown of thorns and the symbols of the Evangelists.

Theis er the verap treis leinth of the thre Nalis of our
Lorde Ihu criste to whame pape Innocent sent this
same leinth vn to kyng charls. and gruntid to hym and all
so to euy man and womán y' with denocóñ wor shippis þai
daplÿ and berith payne a pone thai. with .v. Pater noſt.
v. Aue mar. and a Crede ꝛꝛ. that shall haue vij. petitions
grūtede þ ame. ꝏ he first is þat þai shal not dy no sodly.
ne evil dede. The. ii. is þai shall not be slayn with no man of
weppin with owtÿn ye sacriments of ye kirk. The. iii. is þ
þ enimys shal not our come þai. The iiii.y' no poison ne fals
wittnes shall not greve þai. The. v. is. þat þai shall haue
sufficient gudis. The. vi. is he shal se our lady Thure ꝛ cóforth
to hys saluacóñ. The. vij. is he shalbe defendid fro all ma
ñ of wickid spritis. pestilens. fevers with many other.

25.1 Notes written by successive owners from 1455 onwards in a fifteenth century manuscript of *De Doctrina Cordis*.

The vertuouse doctryne & techynge had & lerned of suche
as haue endeuoured them to leue for a remembraunce
after theyr dethe to us/ By whiche we ben enfourmed
in scyence/ wysedom and vnderstandyng of knowleche/ hou we
ougzt to rewle our self in this present lyf haue caused vs to
know many good reules/ & vertuouse maners to be gouerned
by/ Emonge al other this book is a special doctryne & techyng
by whiche al yong gentyl wymen specially may lerne to bihaue
ue them self vertuously/as wel in their vyrgynyte as in their
wedloke & wedolwhede/as al a long shal be more playnly said in
the same/ whiche booke is comen to my handes by the request & de
syre of a noble lady whiche hath brouzt forth many noble & fay
r douzters whiche ben vertuously nourisshed & lerned/ And for
very ziele & loue that she hath alway had to her fayr childryn
& yet hath for to haue more knowleche in vertue to thende y they
may alwey perseuer in y same hath desired & required me to tras
late & reduce this said book out of frensshe in to our bulgar en
glisshe/to thende that it may the better be vnderstode of al suche as
shal rede or here it/ Wherfor atte contemplacion of her good grace
after the lytel connyng that god hath sent me/ I haue endeuoy
red me to obeye her noble desyre/ & in whiche werke I
fynd many vertuous good enseygnementis & lernynges by euy
dent historyes of auctorite & good ensamples for al maner peple
in generally/but in especial for ladyes & gentilwymen douzters
to lordes & gentilmen / For whiche book al the gentilwymen
now lyuyng & herafter to come or shal be arn bounde to gyue
laude praysyng & thankynges to the auctor of this book & also
to the lady that caused me to traslate it & to pray for her long
lyf & welfare/& whan god wil calle her fro this transitory lyf
that she may regne in heuen sempiternally where as is Joye &
blysse without ende/ Thenne for as moche as this book is neces
sary to euery gentilwoman of what estate she be I aduyse eue
ry gentilman or woman hauyng suche childryn/desyryng them
to be vertuously brouzt forth to gete & haue this book to thende
that they may lerne/ hou they ouzt to gouerne them vertuously
in this present lyf/by whiche they may the better & hastelyer co
me to worship and good renommee/ And I desyre al them
that shal lerne or see ony thynge in this sayd book/by whiche
they shal bey the wyser & better/that they gyue laude & thankyng

26.1 Monks singing plainchant from a choir-book.
Historiated initial 'C' in a psalter from the
Old Royal Library, printed in Cologne *c.*1485
and probably illuminated in Bruges.

26.2 The first polyphonic music printed in England. Fragment of a single-sheet song, *As power and wytt*, printed in London by John Rastell, *c*.1523.

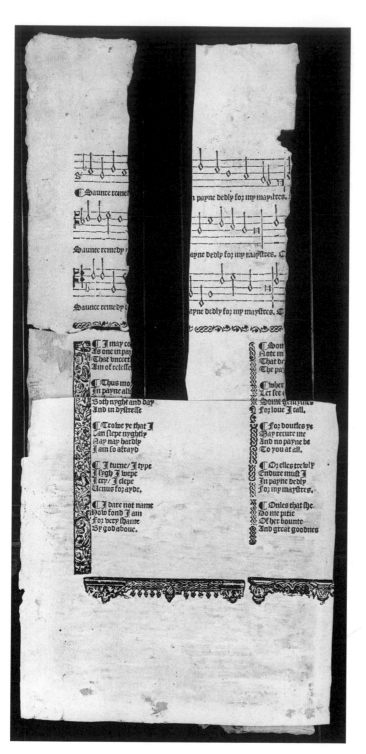

26.3 Music printing by William Rastell. Fragment of a single-sheet song *Saunce remedy*, printed *c.*1532–4. The woodcut decorations are characteristic of English printing of the period.

27.1 Isolated evidence for the circulation of a literary text in Scotland: Robert Henryson, *Traitie of Orpheus*, printed in Edinburgh by W. Chepman and A. Myllar, *c.*1508. Title-page of the imperfect but unique surviving copy.

27.2 Gavin Douglas's translation of Virgil's *Aeneid*. The opening page of the manuscript of *Eneydos* made about 1515 by Douglas's amanuensis and annotated, perhaps by Douglas himself.

28.1 The printing press used for a public document. A proclamation of Henry VII's regarding the issue of silver coin, printed by the 'Regius Impressor' Guillam Faques in 1504. The ornate woodcut initial 'H' is in the tradition of chancery script. The coins are clearly described and illustrated by small woodcuts.

ASSERTIO SEPTEM SA=
cramentorum aduersus Martin.
Lutherũ, ædita ab inuictis=
simo Angliæ et Fran=
ciæ rege, et do. Hy=
berniæ Henri=
co eius no
minis
o=
ctauo.

28.2 Henry VIII's tract against Luther: *Assertio septem sacramentorum adversus Martin. Lutherum*, printed by Richard Pynson in 1521. The woodcut border of the title-page by Hans Holbein the Younger shows Mutius Scaevola and the encampment of Porsenna.